Universidad de Chicago

DICCIONARIO
Español-Inglés
Inglés-Español

Edición Revisada

*Un Nuevo y Conciso Diccionario Que Contiene las
Voces y Locuciones Básicas de Ambos Idiomas*

Recopilación de
Carlos Castillo y Otto F. Bond

Con la ayuda de
Barbara M. García

Revisado por
D. Lincoln Canfield

PUBLISHED BY POCKET BOOKS NEW YORK

The University of Chicago

SPANISH DICTIONARY
Spanish-English
English-Spanish

Revised Edition

*A New Concise Spanish-English and English-Spanish
Dictionary of Words and Phrases Basic to the Written
and Spoken Languages of Today*

Compiled by
Carlos Castillo & Otto F. Bond

With the Assistance of
Barbara M. Garcia

Revised by
D. Lincoln Canfield

PUBLISHED BY POCKET BOOKS NEW YORK

**POCKET BOOKS, a Simon & Schuster division of
GULF & WESTERN CORPORATION
1230 Avenue of the Americas, New York, N.Y. 10020**

Copyright 1948, © 1972 by The University of Chicago

Published by arrangement with The University of Chicago
Library of Congress Catalog Card Number: 78-177425

ISBN: 0-671-80559-2

First Pocket Books printing August, 1975

20   19   18   17   16   15   14

Trademarks registered in the United States and other countries.

Printed in the U.S.A.

Foreword

The University of Chicago Spanish Dictionary has been compiled for the general use of the American learner of Spanish and the Spanish-speaking learner of English, with special reference in either case to New World usages as found in the United States and in Spanish America.

With this purpose in mind, the editors and the author of the revisions of the new (1972) edition have selected the words to be defined, first according to the relative frequence of their occurrence, secondly in keeping with dialectal variations of the New World, both Anglo and Hispanic, and thirdly in accordance with the growth in the technological lexicon during the past two decades.

The Spanish-English section of this revised edition contains all the items listed in Juilland and Chang Rodríguez's *Frequency Dictionary of Spanish Words* (The Hague: Mouton & Co., 1964) which in turn follows Buchanan's *Graded Spanish Word Book* (Toronto: University of Toronto Press, 1929), L. Rodríguez Bou's *Recuento de Vocabulario Español* (Puerto Rico, 1952), and V. García Hoz's *Vocabulario Usual, Vocabulario Común y Vocabulario Fundamental* (Madrid, 1953). Furthermore, the original edition of the dictionary had listed all the items of Keniston's *Standard List of Spanish Words and Idioms* (Boston: D. C. Heath & Co., 1941), supplemented by many words occurring in textbooks and literary masterpieces of Spanish-speaking countries used in the United States and Canada in the instruction of Spanish at several levels. Hundreds of dialectal variants of Spanish America have been indicated in the Spanish-English section of the revised edition, and have been labeled according to the region or regions in which they are used. In the first edition these were all marked *Am.* New regionalisms have been added. In addition, many items related to developments in the fields of aviation, atomic energy, linguistics, and other areas of technological advancement have been added.

The words selected originally for definition in the English-Spanish section of the *Dictionary* were taken from the first nine thousand entries in Thorndike and Lorge's *Teacher's Word Book of 30,000 Words* (New York: Bureau of Publications, Teachers College, Columbia University, 1944), supplemented by residual words in the combined-words lists of Eaton, Buckingham-Dolch, and the *Interim Report on Vocabulary Selection* (London: P. S. King & Co., 1936). Additions to these in the revised edition include hundreds of terms related to technological developments of recent years as well as Spanish-American dialectal variants, with indications of regional usage wherever possible.

In order to coordinate the two parts and not leave undefined words used in definitions, it was necessary to introduce into each section a number of secondary entries which are a by-product of the primary definitions. This brought the total number of entries for the first edition to approximately 30,000 words and brings the total for the revised edition to about 32,000. Besides the approximately 500 new words in the Spanish-English section, more than 1500 items have been added to the English-Spanish section, and relatively few have been deleted.

No pretense is made to equalize the two parts in terms of the number of items for the simple reason that in the past three decades many more new terms of universal usage have been coined in English than in Spanish. Many of these have been taken bodily into Spanish.

The New World application of the *Dictionary* is further emphasized by its acceptance of American standards of speech in indicating the pronunciation of English entries and by the inclusion of American and Spanish-American equivalents and usages throughout. To enhance the usefulness and accuracy of the *Dictionary*, as has been stated, Spanish-American usages have been identified by words or abbreviations for specific countries or regions rather than by the general abbreviation *Am*. This latter abbreviation has been retained, however, to indicate general Spanish-American usage, usually with the implication of obsolescence in Spain. The abbreviation is also employed to identify words that are currently little used but which may occur in literary masterpieces of bygone days.

Certain auxiliary data have been provided at the beginning of each part, such as a list of abbreviations, an explanation of speech sounds; a summary of the use and value of suffixes; a list of numerals; a brief treatment of nouns, adjectives, and adverbs; and a table of irregular verb forms. In the Spanish-English section a superior number following a verb entry refers to a similarly numbered verb listed in the table preceding the section. Additional features of the Spanish-English part in the revised edition are a list of monetary units and values, a list of adjectives of nationality, and a rather extensive discussion of the Spanish of America and its regional dialects, with maps that indicate the occurrence of distinctive phonological and syntactic features.

One of the principal additions to the revised edition is the introduction of parenthetical identifying expressions to help the speaker of the first language distinguish among the several possible definitions that are traditionally given for a particular word. Hundreds of entries of this type have been added to both parts of the dictionary.

A dictionary should be an instrument for better understanding between peoples. It is the earnest wish of the editors of this one that it may serve that end.

Part One Spanish-English

List of Abbreviations

adj.	adjective	*math.*	mathematics
adv.	adverb	*neut.*	neuter
arith.	arithmetic	*num.*	numeral
conj.	conjunction	*p.p.*	past participle
contr.	contraction	*pers.*	personal
def.	definite	*pers. pron.*	personal pronoun
def. art.	definite article	*pl.*	plural
dem.	demonstrative	*poss.*	possessive
dem. adj.	demonstrative adjective	*prep.*	preposition
dem. pron.	demonstrative pronoun	*pron.*	pronoun
etc.	et cetera	*refl.*	reflexive
f.	feminine noun	*refl. pron.*	reflexive pronoun
fam.	familiar	*rel.*	relative
indef.	indefinite	*rel. adv.*	relative adverb
indef. art.	indefinite article	*rel. pron.*	relative pronoun
inf.	infinitive	*sing.*	singular
interj.	interjection	*subj.*	subjunctive
interr.	interrogative	*v.*	verb
irr.	irregular	*v. irr.*	irregular verb
m.	masculine noun		

Special Words and Abbreviations Used to Indicate Regional Occurrence

Am.[1]	Spanish-American
Andalusia	
Andes	(Ecuador, Peru, Bolivia)
Arg.	Argentina

[1] This abbreviation is employed to indicate general Spanish-American usage, usually with the implication of obsolescence in Spain. It is also used to identify words that are currently little used but which may occur in literary works of bygone days.

Bol.	Bolivia
Carib.	(Cuba, Puerto Rico, Dominican Republic)
C.A.	Central America (Guatemala, El Salvador, Honduras, Nicaragua, Costa Rica)
Ch.	Chile
Col.	Colombia
C.R.	Costa Rica
Cuba	
Ec.	Ecuador
Guat.	Guatemala
Hond.	Honduras
Mex.	Mexico
Nic.	Nicaragua
N.Sp.	Northern Spain
Pan.	Panama
Par.	Paraguay
Peru	
P.R.	Puerto Rico
Riopl.	Río de la Plata region (Eastern Argentina, Uruguay)
S.A.	South America
Sal.	El Salvador
Spain	
Ur.	Uruguay
Ven.	Venezuela

Spanish Pronunciation

The Spanish of Spain (except the southwest) has 24 phonemes, or minimum units of sound-meaning distinction. The Spanish of southwest Spain and most of Spanish America has 22 phonemes. These minimum units of sound are indicated in the following charts and descriptions by slashes, /b/, /e/, /č/, and stand for an abstract representation of a group or class of sounds, the individual members of which are variants or allophones. The latter are indicated by brackets: [b̦], [e], [ŷ]. Some of the phonemes of Spanish have two or three variants, depending on position within the phrase.

The two principal characteristics of Spanish pronunciation as contrasted with English are tenseness of articulation and continuity in transition from word to word within the breath group. Thus all the vowels have a clear nondiphthongal character and sound "clipped" to the English-speaking person. The consonants, especially /p/, /t/, /k/, /l/, /r/, /rr/, have much less vocalic interference than in English, and the first three have no aspiration. The glottal stop, so common in the Germanic languages, including English, is very rare in Spanish. The transition between vowels of contiguous words is smooth. **El hado, helado, el lado** sound very much alike. **Para hacerlo** is [paraasérlo] or in rapid speech [parasérlo]. So marked is the continuity that following sounds influence the preceding ones: **los dos niños** [lozdózniños]; **un peso** [umpéso] **en que** [éŋke].

The Consonantal Phonemes of the Spanish of Northern Spain

/p/	/b/	/t/	/d/	/k/	/g/
	/f/	/θ/	/S/	/y/	/x/
				/č/	
/m/			/n/	/ñ/	
			/l/	/ʎ/	
		/r/	/rr/		

24

Phonetic Manifestations of the Phonemes of Spanish

Voice	Bilabial		Labiodental		Interdental		Dental		Alveolar		Palatal		Velar		Glottal	
	vs	vd	vs	vd	vs	vd	vs	vd	vs	vd	vs	vd	vs	vd	vs	vd
Occlusive	p	b			t	d	t	d					k	g		
Fricative	φ	β	f		θ	đ		ð				y	x	ǥ	h	
Sibilant							s	z	S	Z	(ŝ)	(ẑ)				
Affricate											č	ŷ				
Nasal										n		ñ		ŋ		
Lateral										l		ļ				
Vibrant										r rr						
Semiconsonant		w										j				

The Vocalic Phonemes of Spanish

i   u

e   o

a

The Consonantal Phonemes of Andalusian and Latin American Spanish

/p/	/b/	/t/	/d/	/k/	/g/
	/f/		/s/	/y/	/x/
				/č/	
/m/			/n/	/ñ/	22 or 23
			/l/	(/ḷ/) [Bolivia, Paraguay, Peru]
			/r/	/rr/	

The Spanish Spelling System and the Sounds Represented

I. The Vowels

1. **i** as a single vowel always represents [i], similar to the second vowel of *police*. Examples: **hilo, camino, piso.** As a part of a diphthong, it represents [j], much like English /y/ in *yes, year*. Examples: **bien** [bjen], **diablo** [djaβlo], **ciudad, baile, reina, boina.** The first syllable of **baile** is much like *by* in English.

2. **e** represents [e], which has no exact equivalent in most English dialects. It is higher than the /e/ of *get* but without the diphthong of *they*. It is much more tense in articulation than either English sound. It varies slightly according to adjacent sounds. The vowel of **perro** is more open than that of **pero.** Generally it is more open in a closed syllable. Examples: **mesa, del, hablé, en, tres.**

3. **a** represents [a], which is similar to the first vowel of *mama*, stressed on the first syllable. Examples: **caso, cano, ¡ah!, América.** Even when not stressed, it has the same clear sound. English *America* has at least two neutral or *schwa* sounds [ə].

4. **o** represents [o], which is more like the Scotch-English sound of *auld* than the British or American *old*. It has no off-glide or diphthongal character such as is heard in the latter. It varies slightly according to adjacent sounds: the first syllable of **corro** is slightly more open than the first of **coro.** **Sol** is slightly more open than **no.** Examples: **boto, modo, señor, oso, amó.**

5. **u** represents [u], which always has the value of the sound indicated by English *oo* in *boot, fool*, never that of *book*, nor that of the *u* in *union*. Examples: **cura, agudo, uno.**
   a. Note that the spelling combinations **qui, que, gui, gue** represent [ki], [ke], [gi], [ge].
   b. **u** is used to represent the semiconsonant [w] in a diphthong: **cuida, cuento, cuadro, cuota** [kwíḍa], [kwénto], [kwáḍro], [kwóta].
   c. Likewise **u** is used to represent the semivocalic element of a diphthong: **bou, deuda, causa** [bow], [déwḍa], [káwsa].

II. The Consonants

1. **p** represents [p], which never has the aspiration of English /p/ (*pill, papa*), but is like that of *spot*. Examples: **padre, capa, apuro, punto.**

2. **b** and **v** represent /b/, which has two variants, according to position in the phrase: [b], [b̸]. These do not depend on spelling, which goes back centuries. Either letter represents [b] at the beginning of a breath group or when preceded by [m] (spelled either **m** or **n**), and is much like English /b/. Examples: **bomba, burro, en vez de, vine, invierno.** In spite of spelling, the last three examples are [embézđe], [bíne], [imbjérno]. Either letter represents [b̸] in all other situations. English has no equivalent. It is a /b/ with the lips slightly open. Examples: **haba, uva, Cuba, la vaca, habla, la barba.**

3. **m** represents [m], which is essentially the same as English /m/ (*much*). Examples: **madre, mano, cama.** [m] does not occur syllable final in Spanish. **Álbum** is pronounced [álb̸un].

4. **f** represents [f], which is similar to the /f/ of English. In some areas and among certain strata of Hispanic society the articulation is bilabial rather than labiodental.

5. **t** represents [t], which never has the aspiration of English /t/ in prevocalic stressed position (*tea, two, ten*). It is more similar to the English /t/ of the cluster [st] (*stop, step*). Examples in Spanish: **tela, tino, tinta.** The point of articulation is dental.

6. **d** represents /d/, which has three variants according to position in the phrase: [d], [đ], [Ø]. At the beginning of the breath group or after /n/ and /l/, **d** represents [d], which is similar to the English /d/ of *dame, did, darn.* Examples: **donde, falda, conde.** In all other situations the letter represents [đ], or even [Ø]. There is a tendency in modern Spanish to move from the fricative [đ] (similar to the sound represented by the *th* in *mother, this, then*) to zero articulation [Ø]. Examples: **hado, cuerda, es de, dos dados, cuadro, padre, abad, usted, Madrid.** The last two words are usually pronounced without final consonant, and the consonant tends to be very weak in the ending /-ado/: **hablado, estado, mercado.**

7. **s** In Spain, except the southwest, this letter represents [S], an apico-alveolar sibilant, similar to the /s/ of southern Scotland and that of older speakers of the Midland dialect of the United States. Examples: **solo, casa, es.** Before a voiced consonant within the phrase it usually represents [Z]. Examples: **desde, mismo, es verde, los labios, las manos.**

   In southwestern Spain and in all of Spanish America except a small area of Colombia, this letter represents [s], a dental sibilant of high resonance similar to the usual "feminine" sibilant of much of the United States. In some areas it is actually lisped. Before a voiced consonant within the phrase it usually represents [z], a voiced sibilant similar to the /z/ of English *razor, ooze,* Examples: **desde, mismo, es verde, los labios, las manos.** In the Caribbean and in coastal Spanish generally, there is a strong tendency to aspirate the /s/ syllable final, and the above voicing does not occur.

8. **z,** and **c** before **e** and **i** represent in Spain, except the southwest, [θ], an interdental fricative of tenser and more prolonged articulation than that represented by English *th* in *thin, cloth, ether.* Examples: **zagal, zorro, luz** [θagál], [θórro], [luθ]; or **luces, ciento, cerro** [lúθes], [θjento], [θerro].

In southwestern Spain and in Spanish America, these letters represent [s] (see paragraph 7). Examples: **zagal, zorro, luz, luces, ciento, cerro** [saǵál], [sórro], [lus], [lúses], [sjénto], [sérro]. Before a voiced consonant in the phrase, the **z** represents [z] (see paragraph 7). Examples: **en vez de, mayorazgo, la luz de.**

9. **l** always represents [l], a clear alveolar lateral that is rarely heard in English, except in Irish and Scotch dialects. It is never velar as in English *bell, full.* Examples: **lado, ala, el, al, sol.**

10. **n** represents /n/, which has variants according to the following consonants. It stands for [n] in all cases except before /b/, /p/, /m/, where it represents [m], and before /k/, /g/, /x/, where it represents [ŋ] (similar to the final consonant of *sing*). Examples of [n]: **no, nada, mano, aman**; of [m]: **en vez de, en Barcelona, un peso**; of [ŋ]: **anca, banco, en que, tengo, naranja.**

11. **ll** represents [l] (a palatal lateral) in northern Spain and in Bolivia, Paraguay, and most of Peru, as well as in the Bogotá area of Colombia. This sound is similar to that heard in English *million.* In other parts of the Spanish-speaking world, *ll* represents [y]. Examples: **calle, llano, olla.**

12. **ñ** represents [ñ] among all speakers of Spanish. It is similar to the sound heard in English *canyon,* but is more one articulation than the English. Examples: **cañón, año, ñato.**

13. **ch** represents [č], which is similar to English /č/ (*church, cheek, reach*). Examples: **chato, chaleco, mucho.**

14. **y** represents [y], which varies regionally from [y] to [ž] (as in *azure*), and in most regions it represents [ŷ] (similar to *just* of English) in initial position in the phrase and after /l/ and /n/. Examples: **ayer, mayo** [ayér], [máyo]; **¡yo! un yugo, el yerno** [ŷo], [unŷúgo], [elŷérno]. In nearly all areas, Spanish /y/ has more palatal friction than English /y/.

15. a. **x** represents between vowels [ǵs] or simply [S] in Spain (see paragraph 7) and [ks] in Spanish America. Examples: **examen, próximo.**

    b. Before a consonant **x** represents [S] in Spain and [s] in Spanish America, except in affected speech, when one hears [ks]. Examples: **extranjero, experiencia.**

    c. In several Indian words of Mexico and Central America **x** represents [x] (see paragraph 20). **México** is one of these and is spelled **Méjico** in most of the Spanish-speaking world.

16. a. **c** represents [k] before **a, o, u, l**, or **r**. The [k] of Spanish does not have the aspiration of English /k/ in the unprotected prevocalic position (*can, quill, coal*) but is more like the sound in *scan.* Examples: **casa, cosa cuna, quinto, queso, crudo, aclamar.** Note that **quinto** and **queso** are [kínto] and [késo]. The syllable final [k] in Spanish occurs only in "learned" terms and is dealt with in various ways by the people. In Spain generally it tends to voice to [ǵ]: **técnico, acto, doctor** [téǵnico], [áǵto], [doǵtór], but today in Madrid and farther north, the latter becomes [doθtór]. In Central America, Cuba, Venezuela, and Colombia [kt] often becomes [pt] and vice versa; [ps] is [ks]: **Pepsi Cola** [péksi kóla].

b. **c** before **e** and **i** represents [θ] in Spain, except the southwest, and [s] in Spanish America (see paragraph 8).

17. **k** represents [k] in certain words of foreign origin, mainly Greek, German, and English: **kilo, kilómetro, kermesse, kiosko.**

18. **q** combined with **u** represents [k]. Examples: **queso, aquí, quien** [késo], [akí], [kjen]. **qu** occurs only before **e** and **i**.

19. a. **g** represents [g] before **a, o, u** when initial in the breath group or after /n/. Examples: **ganga, goma, guarda, tengo. gue, gui** represents [ge], [gi]; **güe, güi** represent [gwe], [gwi].
    Before **a, o, u** under other circumstances, **g** represents [g], a voiced velar fricative. Examples: **la guerra** [laġérra], **lago** [láġo], **la goma** [laġóma], **agrado** [aġráḍo].

    b. **g** before **e, i,** represents [x], a palatal or velar fricative, which is also represented by **j.** Examples: **gente, giro** [xénte], [xíro]. In the Caribbean and Central America, as well as in southern Spain, the /x/ is simply [h].

20. **j** always represents /x/. The usual manifestation of this phoneme is [x], but in some areas (see paragraph 19) it is [h]. Examples: **jamás, jugo, jota** [xamás], [xúġo], [xóta].

21. **h** represents a former aspiration that is no longer present except in some rural areas of southern Spain and Spanish America. Examples: **hoja** [óxa], **humo** [úmo], **harto** [árto].

22. **r** represents [r], an alveolar single flap, similar to the sound represented by *tt* in American English *kitty* in rapid speech. However, at the beginning of a word or after **n, l, s,** it represents [rr], a multiple vibrant (trill). Examples of [r]: **caro, farol, mero, tren, comer.** Examples of [rr] written **r: rosa, rana, Enrique, Israel, alrededor.**
    rr represents [rr] under all circumstances. Examples: **carro, correr, guerrero.**

The Noun

I. Gender[2]

A. *Masculine Gender*

1. Names of male beings are naturally masculine: **el hombre** the man; **el muchacho** the boy; **el tío** the uncle; **el rey** the king; **el buey** the ox.

2. Nouns ending in **-o** are masculine: **el libro** the book; **el banco** the bank. *Exception*: **la mano** the hand.

3. Days of the week, months, rivers, oceans, and mountains are masculine: **el martes** Tuesday; **enero** January; **el Pacífico** the Pacific; **el Rin** the Rhine; **los Andes** the Andes.

4. Many nouns in **-l** or **-r,** and nouns of Greek origin ending in **-ma** are masculine: **el papel** the paper; **el azúcar** the sugar; **el favor**

---

[2] There is no general rule for the gender of nouns that are not treated in this section.

the favor; **el drama** the drama. *Common exceptions*: **la miel** the honey; **la sal** the salt; **la catedral** the cathedral; **la flor** the flower. Note that **mar** is both masculine and feminine.

B. *Feminine Gender*

1. Names of female persons or animals are naturally feminine: **la mujer** the woman; **la muchacha** the girl; **la tía** the aunt; **la vaca** the cow.

2. Nouns ending in **-a** are feminine: **la pluma** the pen; **la carta** the letter; **la casa** the house. *Common exceptions*: **el día** the day; **el mapa** the map; nouns of Greek origin ending in **-ma**: **el dogma** the dogma; **el programa** the program.

3. Letters of the alphabet are feminine: **la *e*, la *s*, la *t*.**

4. Nouns ending in **-ión, -tad, -dad, -tud, -umbre** are feminine: **la canción** the song; **la facultad** the faculty; **la ciudad** the city; **la virtud** the virtue; **la muchedumbre** the crowd. *Exceptions*: **el gorrión** the sparrow; **el sarampión** the measles.

C. *Formation of the Feminine*

1. Nouns ending in **-o** change **-o** to **-a**: **tío** uncle, **tía** aunt; **niño** boy, **niña** girl.

2. Nouns ending in **-ón, -or,** and **-án** add **-a**: **patrón** patron, **patrona** patroness; **pastor** shepherd, **pastora** shepherdess; **holgazán** lazy man, **holgazana** lazy woman.

3. Certain nouns have a special form for the feminine: **el poeta, la poetisa; el cantante, la cantatriz; el sacerdote, la sacerdotisa; el emperador, la emperatriz; el abad, la abadesa; el conde, la condesa; el duque, la duquesa.**

   Note that (*a*) some nouns have different genders according to their meanings: **el corte** the cut or the cutting edge; **la corte** the court; **el guía** the guide; **la guía** the guidebook; **el capital** the capital (money); **la capital** the capital (city); (*b*) some nouns have invariable endings which are used for both the masculine and the feminine: **artista** (and all nouns ending in **-ista**), **amante, mártir, testigo, reo, demócrata, aristócrata, intérprete, consorte, comensal, homicida, suicida, indígena, cómplice, cliente.**

II. Plural of Nouns[3]

1. Nouns ending in an unaccented vowel add **-s** to form the plural: **el libro, los libros; la casa, las casas.**

2. Nouns ending in a consonant, in **-y,** or in an accented vowel add **-es**: **el papel, los papeles; la canción, las canciones: la ley, las leyes; el rubí, los rubíes.** The accepted plural, however, of **papá** is **papás,** and of **mamá** is **mamás.**

3. Nouns ending in unaccented **-es** and **-is** do not change in the plural: **el lunes** Monday, **los lunes** Mondays; **la tesis** the thesis, **las tesis** the theses.

   Note that (*a*) nouns ending in **-z** change **z** to **c** before **-es**: **lápiz, lápices;** (*b*) nouns ending in **-ión** lose the written accent in the plural: **canción, canciones.**

---

[3] The plurals of certain masculine nouns may include the masculine and feminine genders: **los padres** the father(s) and mother(s), the parents; **los tíos** the uncle(s) and aunt(s); **los reyes** the king(s) and queen(s).

The Adjective and the Adverb

I. The Adjective

A. *Agreement.* The adjective in Spanish agrees in gender and number with the noun it modifies: **el lápiz rojo** the red pencil; **la casa blanca** the white house; **los libros interesantes** the interesting books; **las muchachas hermosas** the beautiful girls.

B. *Formation of the plural.* Adjectives follow the same rules as nouns for the formation of the plural: **pálido, pálidos** pale; **fácil, fáciles** easy; **cortés, corteses** courteous; **capaz, capaces** capable.

C. *Formation of the feminine.*

1. Adjectives ending in -o change -o to -a: **blanco, blanca.**

2. Adjectives ending in other vowels are invariable: **verde** green; **fuerte** strong; **indígena** indigenous, native; **pesimista** pessimistic; **baladí** trivial.

3. Adjectives ending in a consonant are invariable: **fácil** easy; **cortés** courteous. *Exceptions:* (*a*) adjectives ending in -ón, -án, -or (except comparatives) add -a to form the feminine: **holgazán, holgazana** lazy; **preguntón, preguntona** inquisitive; **hablador, habladora** talkative (Note that **mayor, mejor, menor, peor, superior, inferior, exterior, interior, anterior,** and **posterior** are invariable). **Superior** adds an -a when it is used as a noun meaning ("mother superior"). (*b*) adjectives of nationality ending in a consonant add -a to form the feminine: **francés, francesa** French; **español, española** Spanish; **alemán, alemana** German; **inglés, inglesa** English.

II. The Adverb

Many adverbs are formed by adding -**mente** to the feminine form of the adjective: **claro, claramente; lento, lentamente; fácil, fácilmente.**

III. Comparison of Adjectives and Adverbs

A. *Comparative of inequality.* The comparative of inequality is formed by placing **más** or **menos** before the positive form of the adjective or adverb: **más rico que** richer than; **menos rico que** less rich than; **más tarde** later; **menos tarde** less late. The superlative is formed by placing the definite article **el** before the comparative: **el más rico** the richest; **el menos rico** the least rich. Note the position of the article in the following examples: **la niña más linda** or **la más linda niña** the prettiest girl.

The following adjectives and adverbs have in addition irregular forms of comparison:

Positive	Comparative	Superlative
bueno	mejor	el (la) mejor
malo	peor	el (la) peor
grande	mayor	el (la) mayor
pequeño	menor	el (la) menor
alto	superior	supremo
bajo	inferior	ínfimo
mucho	más	
poco	menos	

B. *Comparative of equality.* With adjectives and adverbs the comparative of equality is formed with **tan . . . como: tan fácil como** as easy as; **tan bien como** as well as; with nouns the comparative of equality is formed with **tanto (tanta, tantos, tantas) . . . como: tanto dinero como** as much money as; **tantas personas como** as many people as.

C. *Absolute superlative of adjectives.* The absolute superlative of adjectives is formed by placing **muy** (very) before the adjective or by adding the suffix **-ísimo:**

Positive	Absolute Superlative
feliz	**muy feliz, felicísimo**
fácil	**muy fácil, facilísimo**
importante	**muy importante, importantísimo**
limpio	**muy limpio, limpísimo**
feo	**muy feo, feísimo**
rico	**muy rico, riquísimo**
largo	**muy largo, larguísimo**
notable	**muy notable, notabilísimo**

A few adjectives have, in addition, other forms derived from the Latin superlatives:

bueno	**muy bueno, bonísimo[4], óptimo**
malo	**muy malo, malísimo, pésimo**
grande	**muy grande, grandísimo, máximo**
pequeño	**muy pequeño, pequeñísimo, mínimo**

Some adjectives ending in **-ro** or **-re** revert to the corresponding Latin superlative:

acre	**muy acre, acérrimo**
célebre	**muy célebre, celebérrimo**
mísero	**muy mísero, misérrimo**
salubre	**muy salubre, salubérrimo**

D. *Absolute superlative of adverbs.* The absolute superlative of adverbs not ending in **-mente** is formed in the same manner as that of adjectives:

tarde	**muy tarde, tardísimo**
pronto	**muy pronto, prontísimo**
mucho	**muchísimo**
poco	**poquísimo**
cerca	**muy cerca, cerquísima**
lejos	**muy lejos, lejísimos**

Superlative adverbs ending in **-mente** are formed by adding the suffix **-ísima** to the corresponding feminine adjective:

claramente	**muy claramente, clarísimamente**
noblemente	**muy noblemente, nobilísimamente**

Common Spanish Suffixes

I. Diminutives

The most common diminutive endings in Spanish are:

-ito, -ita (**-cito, -cita, -ecito, -ecita**). Examples: **librito** (from **libro**), **casita** (from **casa**), **corazoncito** (from **corazón**), **mujercita** (from **mujer**), **cochecito** (from **coche**), **florecita** (from **flor**).

---

[4] Also **buenísimo.**

-illo, -illa	(**-cillo, -cilla, -ecillo, -ecilla**). Examples: **corderillo** (from **cordero**), **dolorcillo** (from **dolor**), **viejecillo** (from **viejo**), **piedrecilla** (from **piedra**).
-ico, -ica	(**-cico, -cica, -ecico, -ecica**). Examples: **niñico** (from **niño**), **hermanica** (from **hermana**), **corazoncico** (from **corazón**), **mujercica** (from **mujer**), **pobrecico** (from **pobre**).
-uelo, -uela	(**-zuelo, -zuela, -ezuelo, -ezuela**). Examples: **arroyuelo** (from **arroyo**), **mozuela** (from **moza**), **mujerzuela** (from **mujer**), **reyezuelo** (from **rey**), **piedrezuela** (from **piedra**).
-ete, -eta	Examples: **vejete** (from **viejo**), **vejeta** (from **vieja**).
-uco, -uca	Example: **casuca** (from **casa**).
-ucho, -ucha	Examples: **serrucho** (from **sierra**), **casucha** (from **casa**).

II. Augmentatives

The most common augmentative endings in Spanish are:

-acho, -acha	Example: **ricacho** (from **rico**).
-azo, -aza	Examples: **gigantazo** (from **gigante**), **bribonazo** (from **bribón**), **manaza** (from **mano**), **bocaza** (from **boca**).
-on, -ona	Examples: **hombrón** (from **hombre**), **mujerona** (from **mujer**), **almohadón** (from **almohada**), **borrachón** (from **borracho**).
-ote, -ota	Examples: **grandote** (from **grande**), **muchachote** (from **muchacho**), **muchachota** (from **muchacha**).

III. Depreciatives

The most common depreciative endings in Spanish are:

-aco, -aca	Example: **pajarraco** ugly bird.
-ejo, -eja	Example: **librejo** old, worthless book.

Note that a depreciative or ironic connotation is often conveyed by many of the augmentatives and by the diminutive endings **-uelo, -ete, -uco, -ucho, -illo.**

IV. Other Suffixes

-ada	*a*. is sometimes equal to the English suffix *-ful*: **cucharada** spoonful; **palada** shovelful;
	b. often indicates a blow: **puñada** blow with the fist; **puñalada** stab or blow with a dagger; **topetada** butt, blow with the head;
	c. indicates a group or a crowd of: **peonada** a group or crowd of peons; **indiada** a group or crowd of Indians.

-al, -ar	denote a grove, field, plantation or orchard: **naranjal** orange grove; **cauchal** rubber plantation; **pinar** pine grove.
-azo	indicates a blow or explosion: **puñetazo** blow with the fist; **topetazo** butt, blow with the head; **escobazo** blow with a broom; **cañonazo** cannon shot.
-dad, -tad	are suffixes forming many abstract nouns and are usually equivalent to the English suffix *-ty*: **fraternidad** fraternity; **facultad** faculty; **cantidad** quantity; **calidad** quality.
-dizo	is an adjective-forming suffix which means sometimes *tending to*, or *in the habit of*: **resbaladizo** slippery; **olvidadizo** forgetful; **enojadizo** irritable, easily angered; **asustadizo** easily frightened, scary, timid; **movedizo** movable.
-ería	*a.* denotes a place where something is made or sold: **panadería** bakery; **librería** bookstore; **zapatería** shoestore; **pastelería** pastry shop; *b.* indicates a profession, business or occupation: **carpintería** carpentry; **ingeniería** engineering; *c.* means sometimes a collection: **pastelería** pastry, pastries; *d.* is sometimes equivalent to English suffix *-ness*; it also suggests a single act or action: **tontería** foolishness; foolish act; **niñería** childishness; childish act.
-ero	*a.* indicates a person who makes, sells, or is in charge of: **panadero** baker; **librero** bookseller; **zapatero** shoemaker, **carcelero** jailer; **cajaro** cashier; *b.* is an adjective-forming suffix; **parlero** talkative; **guerrero** warlike.
-ez, -eza	are used to make abstract nouns: **vejez** old age; **niñez** childhood; **viudez** widowhood; **grandeza** greatness.
-ia	*a.* is the ending of the names of many arts and sciences: **geología** geology; **geometría** geometry; **biología** biology; *b.* see **-ería**.
-iento	indicates a *resemblance*, or a *tendency to*: **ceniciento** ashlike; **soñoliento** sleepy, drowsy.
-isimo	is the ending of the absolute superlative: **hermosísimo** very beautiful.
-izo	is a suffix meaning *tending to* or *somewhat*: **rojizo** reddish. See **-dizo**.
-mente	is the adverbial ending attached to the feminine form of the adjective: **generosamente** generously; **claramente** clearly.

-ón	*a.* is an augmentative suffix; *b.* is also a suffix without an augmentative force, meaning *in the habit of*, or *full of*: **juguetón** playful; **preguntón** full of questions, inquisitive; **llorón** tearful; crybaby; *c.* indicates suddenness or violence of an action: **estirón** pull, tug, jerk; **apretón** squeeze.
-or, -dor	*a.* are equivalent to the English suffixes *-or*, *-er*, and indicate the agent or doer: **hablador** talker; **regulador** regulator; *b.* may also be used as adjectives: **hablador** talkative; **regulador** regulating.
-oso	is an adjective-forming suffix which usually means *having*, *full of*, or *characterized by*: **rocoso** rocky; **tormentoso** stormy; **fangoso** muddy; **herboso** grassy; **lluvioso** rainy; **maravilloso** marvelous; **famoso** famous.
-udo	is an adjective-forming suffix meaning *having* or *characterized by*: **zancudo** long-legged; **peludo** hairy; **panzudo** big-bellied; **caprichudo** stubborn.
-ura	is a suffix forming many abstract nouns: **negrura** blackness; **blancura** whiteness; **altura** height; **lisura** smoothness.
-uzco	indicates *resemblance* or *a tendency to*; it is akin to the English suffix *-ish*: **blancuzco** whitish; **negruzco** blackish.

Spanish Irregular and Orthographic Changing Verbs

The superior number, or numbers, after a verb entry indicate that it is conjugated like the model verb in this section which has the corresponding number. Only the tenses which have irregular forms or spelling changes are given. The irregular forms and spelling changes are shown in bold-face type.

1. pensar (if stressed, the stem vowel **e** becomes **ie**)
   Pres. Indic.   **pienso, piensas, piensa,** pensamos, penséis, **piensan.**
   Pres. Subj.   **piense, pienses, piense,** pensemos, penséis, **piensen.**
   Imper.   **piensa** tú, **piense** Vd., pensemos nosotros, pensad vosotros, **piensen** Vds.

2. contar (if stressed, the stem vowel **o** becomes **ue**)
   Pres. Indic.   **cuento, cuentas, cuenta,** contamos, contáis, **cuentan.**
   Pres. Subj.   **cuente, cuentes, cuente,** centemos, contéis, **cuenten.**
   Imper.   **cuenta** tú, **cuente** Vd. contemos nosotros, contad vosotros, **cuenten** Vds.

3.*a.* sentir (if stressed, the stem vowel **e** becomes **ie**; if unstressed, the stem vowel **e** becomes **i** when the following syllable contains stressed **a, ie,** or **ió**)
   Pres. Indic.   **siento, sientes, siente,** sentimos, sentís, **sienten.**
   Pres. Subj.   **sienta, sientas, sienta, sintamos, sintáis, sientan.**

Pret. Indic. **sentí, sentiste, sintió,** sentimos, sentisteis, **sintieron.**

Imp. Subj. **sintiera** or **sintiese, sintieras** or **sintieses, sintiera** or **sintiese, sintiéramos** or **sintiésemos, sintierais** or **sintieseis, sintieran** or **sintiesen.**

Imper. **siente** tú, **sienta** Vd., **sintamos** nosotros, sentid vosotros, **sientan** Vds.

Pres. Part. **sintiendo.**

 b. erguir (this verb has same vowel changes as *sentir*, but the initial i of the diphthong **ie** is changed to **y**. For regular spelling changes see No. 12,*a*)

Pres. Indic. **yergo, yergues, yergue,** erguimos, erguís, **yerguen.**

Pres. Subj. **yerga, yergas, yerga,** irgamos, irgáis, **yergan.**

Pret. Indic. erguí, erguiste, **irguió,** erguimos, erguisteis, **irguieron.**

Imp. Subj. **irguiera** or **irguiese, irguieras** or **irguieses, irguiera** or **irguiese, irguiéramos** or **irguiésemos, irguierais** or **irguieseis, irguieran** or **irguiesen.**

Imper. **yergue** tú, **yerga** Vd., **irgamos** nosotros, erguid vosotros, **yergan** Vds.

Pres. Part. **irguiendo.**

4. dormir (if stressed, the stem vowel **o** becomes **ue**; if unstressed, the stem vowel **o** becomes **u** when the following syllable contains stressed **a, ie,** or **ió**)

Pres. Indic. **duermo, duermes, duerme,** dormimos, dormís, **duermen.**

Pres. Subj. **duerma, duermas, duerma, durmamos, durmáis, duerman.**

Pret. Indic. dormí, dormiste, **durmió,** dormimos, dormisteis, **durmieron.**

Imp. Subj. **durmiera** or **durmiese, durmieras** or **durmieses, durmiera** or **durmiese, durmiéramos** or **durmiésemos, durmierais** or **durmieseis, durmieran** or **durmiesen.**

Imper. **duerme** tú, **duerma** Vd., **durmanos** nosotros, dormid vosotros, **duerman** Vds.

Pres. Part. **durmiendo.**

5. pedir (if stressed, the stem vowel **e** becomes **i**; if unstressed, the stem vowel **e** becomes **i** when the following syllable contains stressed **a, ie,** or **ió**)

Pres. Indic. **pido, pides, pide,** pedimos, pedís, **piden.**

Pres. Subj. **pida, pidas, pida, pidamos, pidáis, pidan.**

Pret. Indic. **pedí,** pediste, **pidió,** pedimos, pedisteis, **pidieron.**

Imp. Subj. **pidiera** or **pidiese, pidieras** or **pidieses, pidiera** or **pidiese, pidiéramos** or **pidiésemos, pidierais** or **pidieseis, pidieran** or **pidiesen.**

Imper. **pide** tú, **pida** Vd., **pidamos** nosotros, pedid vosotros, **pidan** Vds.

Pres. Part. **pidiendo.**

6. buscar (verbs ending in **car** change **c** to **qu** before **e**)

Pres. Subj. **busque, busques, busque, busquemos, busquéis, busquen.**

Pret. Indic.	**busqué,** buscaste, buscó, buscamos, buscasteis, buscaron.
Imper.	busca tú, **busque** Vd., **busquemos** nosotros, buscad vosotros, **busquen** Vds.

7. llegar (verbs ending in **gar** change the g to **gu** before **e**)

Pres. Subj.	**llegue, llegues, llegue, lleguemos, lleguéis, lleguen.**
Pres. Indic.	**llegué,** llegaste, llegó, llegamos, llegasteis, llegaron.
Imper.	llega tú, **llegue** Vd., lleguemos nosotros, llegad vosotros, **lleguen** Vds.

8. averiguar (verbs ending in **guar** change the **gu** to **gü** before **e**)

Pres. Subj.	**averigüe, averigües, averigüe, averigüemos, averigüéis, averigüen.**
Pret. Indic.	**averigüé,** averiguaste, averiguó, averiguamos, averiguasteis, averiguaron.
Imper.	averigua tú, **averigüe** Vd., **averigüemos** nosotros, averiguad vosotros, **averigüen** Vds.

9. abrazar (verbs ending in **zar** change **z** to **c** before **e**)

Pres. Subj.	**abrace, abraces, abrace, abracemos, abracéis, abracen.**
Pret. Indic.	**abracé,** abrazaste, abrazó, abrazamos, abrazasteis, abrazaron.
Imper.	abraza tú, **abrace** Vd., **abracemos** nosotros, abrazad vosotros, **abracen** Vds.

10.*a.* convencer (verbs ending in **cer** preceded by a consonant change **c** to **z** before **a** and **o**)

Pres. Indic.	**convenzo,** convences, convence, convencemos, convencéis, convencen.
Pres. Subj.	**convenza, convenzas, convenza, convenzamos, convenzáis, convenzan.**
Imper.	convence tú, **convenza** Vd., **convenzamos** nosotros, convenced vosotros, **convenzan** Vds.

b. esparcir (verbs ending in **cir** preceded by a consonant change **c** to **z** before **a** and **o**)

Pres. Indic.	**esparzo,** esparces, esparce, esparcimos, esparcís, esparcen.
Pres. Subj.	**esparza, esparzas, esparza, esparzamos, esparzáis, esparzan.**
Imper.	esparce tú, **esparza** Vd., **esparzamos** nosotros, esparcid vosotros, **esparzan** Vds.

c. mecer (some verbs ending in **cer** preceded by a vowel change **c** to **z** before **a** and **o**; see No. 13.*a*)

Pres. Indic.	**mezo,** meces, mece, mecemos, mecéis, mecen.
Pres. Subj.	**meza, mezas, meza, mezamos, mezáis, mezan.**
Imper.	mece tú, **meza** Vd., **mezamos** nosotros, meced vosotros, **mezan** Vds.

11.*a.* dirigir (verbs ending in **gir** change **g** to **j** before **a** and **o**)

Pres. Indic.	**dirijo,** diriges, dirige, dirigimos, dirigís, dirigen.
Pres. Subj.	**dirija, dirijas, dirija, dirijamos, dirijáis, dirijan.**

Imper.   dirige tú, **dirija** Vd., **dirijamos** nosotros, dirigid vosotros, **dirijan** Vds.

   b. coger (verbs ending in **ger** change **g** to **j** before **o** and **a**)
     Pres. Indic.   **cojo**, coges, coge, cogemos, cogéis, cogen.
     Pres. Subj.   **coja, cojas, coja, cojamos, cojáis, cojan.**
     Imper.   coge tú, **coja** Vd., **cojamos** nosotros, coged vosotros, **cojan** Vds.

12. *a.* distinguir (verbs ending in **guir** drop the **u** before **o** and **a**)
     Pres. Indic.   **distingo,** distingues, distingue, distinguimos, distinguís, distinguen.
     Pres. Subj.   **distinga, distingas, distinga, distingamos, distingáis, distingan.**
     Imper.   distingue tú, **distinga** Vd., **distingamos** nosotros, distinguid vosotros, **distingan** Vds.

   b. delinquir (verbs ending in **quir** change **qu** to **c** before **o** and **a**)
     Pres. Indic.   **delinco**, delinques, delinque, delinquimos, delinquís, delinquen.
     Pres. Subj.   **delinca, delincas, delinca, delincamos, delincáis, delincan.**

13. *a.* conocer (verbs ending in **cer** when preceded by a vowel insert **z** before **c** when **c** is followed by **o** or **a**; see No. 10.*c*)
     Pres. Indic.   **conozco**, conoces, conoce, conocemos, conocéis, conocen.
     Pres. Subj.   **conozca, conozcas, conozca, conozcamos, conozcáis, conozcan.**
     Imper.   conoce tú, **conozca** Vd., **conozcamos** nosotros, conoced vosotros, **conozcan** Vds.

   b. lucir (verbs ending in **cir** when preceded by a vowel insert **z** before **c** when **c** is followed by **o** or **a**; see No. 25)
     Pres. Indic.   **luzco,** luces, luce, lucimos, lucís, lucen.
     Pres. Subj.   **luzca, luzcas, luzca, luzcamos, luzcáis, luzcan.**
     Imper.   luce tú, **luzca** Vd., **luzcamos** nosotros, lucid vosotros, **luzcan** Vds.

14. creer (unstressed **i** between vowels is regularly changed to **y**)
     Pret. Indic.   creí, creíste, **creyó**, creímos, creísteis, **creyeron.**
     Imp. Subj.   **creyera** or **creyese, creyeras** or **creyeses, creyera** or **creyese, creyéramos** or **creyésemos, creyerais** or **creyeseis, creyeran** or **creyesen.**
     Pret. Part.   **creyendo.**

15. reír (like No. 5, except that when the **i** of the stem would be followed by **ie** or **ió** the two **i**'s are reduced to one)
     Pres. Indic.   **río, ríes, ríe**, reímos, reís, **ríen.**
     Pres. Subj.   **ría, rías, ría, riamos, riáis, rían.**
     Pret. Indic.   reí, reíste, **rió**, reímos, reísteis, **rieron.**
     Imp. Subj.   **riera**, or **riese, rieras** or **rieses, riera**, or **riese, riéramos** or **riésemos, rierais** or **rieseis, rieran** or **riesen.**
     Imper.   rie tú, **ría** Vd., **riamos** nosotros, reíd vosotros, **rían** Vds.
     Pres. Part.   **riendo**

16. podrir or pudrir
    Pres. Indic.   **pudro, pudres, pudre**, podrimos or pudrimos, podrís or pudrís, **pudren.**
    Pres. Subj.   **pudra, pudras, pudra, pudramos, pudráis, pudran.**
    Imp. Indic.   pudría or podría, etc. (Seldom *podría* because of confusion with *poder*)
    Pret. Indic.   podrí or pudrí, podriste or pudriste, **pudrió**, podrimos or pudrimos, podristeis or pudristeis, **pudrieron.**
    Imp. Subj.   **pudriera** or **pudriese, pudrieras** or **pudrieses, pudriera** or **pudriese, pudriéramos** or **pudriésemos, pudrierais** or **pudrieseis, pudrieran** or **pudriesen.**
    Fut. Indic.   pudriré or podriré, etc.
    Cond.   pudriría or podriría, etc.
    Pres. Part.   **pudriendo.**
    Past Part.   podrido or pudrido.

17. enviar
    Pres. Indic.   envío, envías, envía, enviamos, enviáis, envían.
    Pres. Subj.   envíe, envíes, enviemos, enviéis, envíen.
    Imper.   envía tú, envíe Vd., enviemos nosotros, enviad vosotros, envíen Vds.

18. continuar
    Pres. Indic.   continúo, continúas, continúa, continuamos, continuáis, continúan.
    Pres. Subj.   continúe, continúes, continúe, continuemos, continuéis, continúen.
    Imper.   continúa tú, continúe Vd., continuemos nosotros, continuad vosotros, continúen Vds.

19. gruñir (i of the diphthong ie or ió is lost after ñ)
    Pret. Indic.   gruñí, gruñiste, **gruñó**, gruñimos, gruñisteis, **gruñeron.**
    Imp. Subj.   **gruñera** or **gruñese, gruñeras** or **gruñeses, gruñera** or **gruñese, gruñéramos**, or **gruñésemos, gruñerais** or **gruñeseis, gruñeran** or **gruñesen.**
    Pres. Part.   **gruñendo.**

20. bullir (i of the diphthong ie or ió is lost after ll)
    Pret. Indic.   bullí, bulliste, **bulló**, bullimos, bullisteis, **bulleron.**
    Imp. Subj.   **bullera** or **bullese, bulleras** or **bulleses, bullera** or **bullese, bulléramos** or **bullésemos, bullerais** or **bulleseis, bulleran** or **bullesen**
    Pres. Part.   **bullendo.**

21. andar
    Pret. Indic.   **anduve, anduviste, anduvo, anduvimos, anduvisteis, anduvieron.**
    Imp. Subj.   **anduviera** or **anduviese, anduvieras** or **anduvieses, anduviera** or **anduviese, anduviéramos anduviésemos, anduvierais** or **anduvieseis, anduvieran** or **anduviesen.**

22. asir
    Pres. Indic.   **asgo,** ases, ase, asimos, asís, asen.
    Pres. Subj.   **asga, asgas, asga, asgamos, asgáis, asgan.**
    Imper.   ase tú, **asga** Vd., **asgamos** nosotros, asid vosotros, **asgan** Vds.

23. **caber**
    - *Pres. Indic.* **quepo,** cabes, cabe, cabemos, cabéis, caben.
    - *Pres. Subj.* **quepa, quepas, quepa, quepamos, quepáis, quepan.**
    - *Pret. Indic.* **cupe, cupiste, cupo, cupimos, cupisteis, cupieron.**
    - *Imp. Subj.* **cupiera** or **cupiese, cupieras** or **cupieses, cupiera** or **cupiese, cupiéramos** or **cupiésemos, cupierais** or **cupieseis, cupieran** or **cupiesen.**
    - *Fut. Indic.* **cabré, cabrás, cabrá, cabremos, cabréis, cabrán.**
    - *Cond.* **cabría, cabrías, cabría, cabríamos, cabríais, cabrían.**
    - *Imper.* cabe tú, **quepa** Vd., **quepamos** nosotros, cabed vosotros, **quepan** Vds.

24. **caer**
    - *Pres. Indic.* **caigo,** caes, cae, caemos, caéis, caen.
    - *Pres. Subj.* **caiga, caigas, caiga, caigamos, caigáis, caigan.**
    - *Pret. Indic.* caí, caiste, **cayó,** caímos, caísteis, **cayeron.**
    - *Imp. Subj.* **cayera** or **cayese, cayeras** or **cayases, cayera** or **cayese, cayéramos** or **cayésemos, cayerais** or **cayeseis, cayeran** or **cayesen.**
    - *Imper.* cae tú, **caiga** Vd., **caigamos** nosotros, caed vosotros, **caigan** Vds.
    - *Pres. Part.* **cayendo.**

25. **conducir** (all verbs ending in **ducir** have the irregularities of conducir)
    - *Pres. Indic.* **conduzco,** conduces, conduce, conducimos, conducís, conducen.
    - *Pres. Subj.* **conduzca, conduzcas, conduzca, conduzcamos, conduzcáis, conduzcan.**
    - *Pret. Indic.* **conduje, condujiste, condujo, condujimos, condujisteis, condujeron.**
    - *Imp. Subj.* **condujera** or **condujese, condujeras** or **condujeses, condujera** or **condujese, condujéramos** or **condujésemos, condujerais** or **condujeseis, condujeran** or **condujesen.**
    - *Imp.* conduce tú, **conduzca** Vd., **conduzcamos** nosotros, conducid vosotros, **conduzcan** Vds.

26. **dar**
    - *Pres. Indic.* **doy,** das, da, damos, dais, dan.
    - *Pres. Subj.* dé, des, dé, demos, deis, den.
    - *Pret. Indic.* **dí, diste, dió, dimos, disteis, dieron.**
    - *Imp. Subj.* **diera** or **diese, dieras** or **dieses, deira** or **diese, diéramos** or **diésemos, dierais** or **dieseis, dieran** or **diesen.**

27. **decir**
    - *Pres. Indic.* **digo, dices, dice,** decimos, decís, **dicen.**
    - *Pres. Subj.* **diga, digas, diga, digamos, digáis, digan.**
    - *Pret. Indic.* **dije, dijiste, dijo, dijimos, dijisteis, dijeron.**
    - *Imp. Subj.* **dijera** or **dijese, dijeras** or **dijeses, dijera** or **dijese, dijéramos** or **dijésemos, dijerais** or **dijeseis, dijeran** or **dijesen.**
    - *Fut. Indic.* **diré, dirás, dirá, diremos, deréis, dirán.**
    - *Cond.* **diría, dirías, diría, diríamos, diríais, dirían.**

Imper. **di** tú, **diga** Vd., **digamos** nosotros, decid vosotros, **digan** Vds.

Pres. Part. **diciendo.**

Past Part. **dicho.**

NOTE. The compound verbs of *decir* have the same irregularities with the exception of the following:
- *a.* The future and conditional of the compound verbs *bendecir* and *maldecir* are regular: *bendeciré, maldeciré,* etc.; *bendeciría, maldeciría,* etc.
- *b.* The familiar imperative is regular: *bendice tu, maldice tu, contradice tu,* etc.
- *c.* The past participles of *bendecir* and *maldecir* are regular when used with *haber : bendecido, maldecido;* when used as an adjective with *estar,* the forms are: *bendito, maldito.*

28. errar (like No. 1, except that the initial ie is spelled ye)

Pres. Indic. **yerro, yerras, yerra,** erramos, erráis, **yerran.**

Pres. Subj. **yerre, yerres, yerre,** erremos, erréis, **yerren.**

Imper. **yerra** tú, **yerre** Vd., erremos nosotros, errad vosotros, **yerren** Vds.

29. estar

Pres. Indic. **estoy, estás, está,** estamos, estáis, **están.**

Pres. Subj. **esté, estés, esté,** estemos, estéis, **estén.**

Pret. Indic. **estuve, estuviste, estuvo, estuvimos, estuvisteis, estuvieron.**

Imp. Subj. **estuviera** or **estuviese, estuvieras** or **estuvieses, estuviera** or **estuviese, estuviéramos** or **estuviésemos, estuvierais** or **estuvieseis, estuvieran** or **estuviesen.**

Imper. **está** tú, **esté** Vd., estemos nosotros, estad vosotros, **estén** Vds.

30. haber

Pres. Indic. **he, has, ha, hemos,** habéis, **han.**

Pres. Subj. **haya, hayas, haya, hayamos, hayáis, hayan.**

Pret. Indic. **hube, hubiste, hubo, hubimos, hubisteis, hubieron.**

Imp. Subj. **hubiera** or **hubiese, hubieras** or **hubieses, hubiera** or **hubiese, hubiéramos** or **hubiésemos, hubierais** or **hubieseis, hubieran** or **hubiesen.**

Fut. Indic. **habré, habrás, habrá, habremos, habréis, habrán.**

Cond. **habría, habrías, habría, habríamos, habríais, habrían.**

31. hacer

Pres. Indic. **hago,** haces, hace, hacemos, hacéis, hacen.

Pres. Subj. **haga, hagas, haga, hagamos, hagáis, hagan.**

Pret. Indic. **hice, hiciste, hizo, hicimos, hicisteis, hicieron.**

Imp. Subj. **hiciera** or **hiciese, hicieras** or **hicieses, hiciera** or **hiciese, hiciéramos,** or **hiciésemos, hicierais** or **hicieseis, hicieran** or **hiciesem.**

Fut. Indic. **haré, harás, hará, haremos, haréis, harán.**

Cond. **haría, harías, haría, haríamos, haríais, harían.**

Imper. **haz** tú, **haga** Vd., **hagamos** nosotros, haced vosotros, **hagan** Vds.

Past Part. **hecho.**

32.*a.* huir

Pres. Indic.	**huyo, huyes, huye,** huimos, huís, **huyen.**
Pres. Subj.	**huya, huyas, huya, huyamos, huyáis, huyan.**
Pret. Indic.	huí, huiste, **huyó,** huimos, huisteis, **huyeron.**
Imp. Subj.	**huyera** or **huyese, huyeras** or **huyeses, huyera** or **huyese, huyéramos** or **huyésemos, huyerais** or **huyeseis, huyeran** or **huyesen.**
Imper.	**huye** tú, **huya** Vd., **huyamos** nosotros, huid vosotros, **huyan** Vds.
Pres. Part.	**huyendo.**

b. argüir

Pres. Indic.	**arguyo, arguyes, arguye,** argüimos, argüís, **arguyen.**
Pres. Subj.	**arguya, arguyas, arguya, arguyamos, arguyáis, arguyan.**
Pret. Indic.	argüí, argüiste, **arguyó,** argüimos, argüisteis, **arguyeron.**
Imp. Subj.	**arguyera** or **arguyese, arguyeras** or **arguyeses, arguyera** or **arguyese, arguyéramos** or **arguyésemos, arguyerais** or **arguyeseis, arguyeran** or **arguyesen.**
Imper.	**arguye** tú, **arguya** Vd., **arguyamos** nosotros, argüid vosotros, **arguyan** Vds.
Pres. Part.	**arguyendo.**

33. ir

Pres. Indic.	**voy, vas, va, vamos, vais, van.**
Pres. Subj.	**vaya, vayas, vaya, vayamos, vayáis, vayan.**
Imp. Indic.	**iba, ibas, iba, íbamos, ibais, iban.**
Pret. Indic.	**fui, fuiste, fué, fuimos, fuisteis, fueron.**
Imp. Subj.	**fuera** or **fuese, fueras** or **fueses, fuera** or **fuese, fuéramos** or **fuésemos, fuerais** or **fueseis, fueran** or **fuesen.**
Imper.	**ve** tú, **vaya** Vd., **vayamos (vamos)** nosotros, id vosotros, **vayan** Vds.
Pres. Part.	**yendo.**

34. jugar (cf. Nos. 2 and 7)

Pres. Indic.	**juego, juegas, juega,** jugamos, jugáis, **juegan.**
Pres. Subj.	**juegue, juegues, juegue,** juguemos, juguéis, **jueguen.**
Pret. Indic.	**jugué,** jugaste, jugó, jugamos, jugasteis, jugaron.
Imper.	**juega** tú, **juegue** Vd., **jueguemos** nosotros, jugad vosotros, **jueguen** Vds.

35. adquirir

Pres. Indic.	**adquiero, adquieres, adquiere,** adquirimos, adquirís, **adquieren.**
Pres. Subj.	**adquiera, adquieras, adquiera,** adquiramos, adquiráis, **adquieran.**
Imper.	**adquiere** tú, **adquiera** Vd., adquiramos nosotros, adquirid vosotros, **adquieran** Vds.

36. oír

Pres. Indic.	**oigo, oyes, oye,** oímos, oís, **oyen.**
Pres. Subj.	**oiga, oigas, oiga, oigamos, oigáis, oigan.**

Pret. Indic.   oí, oíste, **oyó**, oímos, oísteis, **oyeron**.

Imp. Subj.   **oyera** or **oyese, oyeras** or **oyeses, oyera** or **oyese, oyéramos** or **oyésemos, oyerais** or **oyeseis, oyeran** or **oyesen**.

Imper.   **oye** tú, **oiga** Vd., **oigamos** nosotros, oíd vosotros, **oigan** Vds.

Pres. Part.   **oyendo**.

37. **oler** (like No. 2, except that initial **ue** is spelled **hue**)

Pres. Indic.   **huelo, hueles, huele**, olemos, oléis, **huelen**.

Pres. Subj.   **huela, huelas, huela**, olamos, oláis, **huelan**.

Imper.   **huele** tú, **huela** Vd., olamos nosotros, oled vosotros, **huelan** Vds.

38. **placer**

Pres. Indic.   **plazco**, places, place, placemos, placéis, placen.

Pres. Subj.   **plazca, plazcas, plazca, plazcamos, plazcáis, plazcan**. (There are also the antiquated forms, **plegue** and **plega**, used now only in the third person in poetic language.)

Pret. Indic.   In addition to the regular forms, there is the antiquated form **plugo**, used now only in poetic language.

Imp. Subj.   In addition to the regular forms, there are the antiquated forms, **pluguiera** and **pluguiese**, used now only in poetic language.

39. **poder**

Pres. Indic.   **puedo, puedes, puede**, podemos, podéis, **pueden**.

Pres. Subj.   **pueda, puedas, pueda**, podamos, podáis, **puedan**.

Pret. Indic.   **pude, pudiste, pudo, pudimos, pudisteis, pudieron**.

Imp. Subj.   **pudiera** or **pudiese, pudieras** or **pudieses, pudiera** or **pudiese, pudiéramos** or **pudiésemos, pudierais** or **pudieseis, pudieran** or **pudiesen**.

Fut. Indic.   **podré, podrás, podrá, podremos, podréis, podrán**

Cond.   **podría, podrías, podría, podríamos, podríais, podrían**.

Pres. Part.   **pudiendo**.

40. **poner**

Pres. Indic.   **pongo**, pones, pone, ponemos, ponéis, ponen.

Pres. Subj.   **ponga, pongas, ponga, pongamos, pongáis, pongan**.

Pret. Indic.   **puse, pusiste, puso, pusimos, pusisteis, pusieron**.

Imp. Subj.   **pusiera** or **pusiese, pusieras** or **pusieses, pusiera** or **pusiese, pusiéramos** or **pusiésemos, pusierais** or **pusieseis, pusieran** or **pusiesen**.

Fut. Indic.   **pondré, pondrás, pondrá, pondremos, pondréis, pondrán**.

Cond.   **pondría, pondrías, pondría, pondríamos, pondríais, pondrían**.

Imper.   **pon** tú, **ponga** Vd., **pongamos** nosotros, poned vosotros, **pongan** Vds.

Past Part.   **puesto**.

41. **querer**

Pres. Indic.   **quiero, quieres, quiere**, queremos, queréis, **quieren**.

Pres. Subj.   **quiera, quieras, quiera**, queramos, queráis, **quieran**.

Pret. Indic.	**quise, quisiste, quiso, quisimos, quisisteis, quisieron.**
Imp. Subj.	**quisiera,** or **quisiese, quisieras** or **quisieses, quisiera** or **quisiese, quisiéramos** or **quisiémos, quisierais** or **quisieseis, quisieran** or **quisiesen.**
Fut. Indic.	**querré, querrás, querrá, querremos, querréis, querrán.**
Cond.	**querría, querrías, querría, querríamos, querríais, querrían.**
Imper.	**quiere** tú, **quiera** Vd., queramos nosotros, quered vosotros, **quieran** Vds.

42. saber

Pres. Indic.	**sé,** sabes, sabe, sabemos, sabéis, saben.
Pres. Subj.	**sepa, sepas, sepa, sepamos, sepáis, sepan.**
Pret. Indic.	**supe, supiste, supo, supimos, supisteis, supieron.**
Imp. Subj.	**supiera** or **supiese, supieras** or **supieses, supiera** or **supiese, supiéramos** or **supiésemos, supierais** or **supieseis, supieran** or **supiesen.**
Fut. Indic.	**sabré, sabrás, sabrá, sabremos, sabréis, sabrán.**
Cond.	**sabría, sabrías, sabría, sabríamos, sabríais, sabrían.**
Imper.	sabe tú, **sepa** Vd., **sepamos** nosotros, sabed vosotros, **sepan** Vds.

43. salir

Pres. Indic.	**salgo,** sales, sale, salimos, salís, salen.
Pres. Subj.	**salga, salgas, salga, salgamos, salgáis, salgan.**
Fut. Indic.	**saldré, saldrás, saldrá, saldremos, saldréis, saldrán.**
Cond.	**saldría, saldrías, saldría, saldríamos, saldríais, saldrían.**
Imper.	**sal** tú, **salga** Vd., **salgamos** nosotros, salid vosotros, **salgan** Vds.

NOTE. The compound *sobresalir* is regular in the familiar imperative: sobresale tú.

44. ser

Pres. Indic.	**soy, eres, es, somos, sois, son.**
Pres. Subj.	**sea, seas, sea, seamos, seáis, sean.**
Imp. Indic.	**era, eras, era, éramos, erais, eran.**
Pret. Indic.	**fuí, fuiste, fué, fuimos, fuisteis, fueron.**
Imp. Subj.	**fuera** or **fuese, fueras** or **fueses, fuera** or **fuese, fuéramos** or **fuésemos, fuerais** or **fueseis, fueran** or **fuesen.**
Imper.	**sé** tú, **sea** Vd., **seamos** nosotros, sed vosotros, **sean** Vds.

45. tener

Pres. Indic.	**tengo, tienes, tiene,** tenemos, tenéis, **tienen.**
Pres. Subj.	**tenga, tengas, tenga, tengamos, tengáis, tengan.**
Pret. Indic.	**tuve, tuviste, tuvo, tuvimos, tuvisteis, tuvieron.**
Imp. Subj.	**tuviera** or **tuviese, tuvieras** or **tuvieses, tuviera** or **tuviese, tuviéramos** or **tuviésemos, tuvierais** or **tuvieseis, tuvieran** or **tuviesen.**

| | Fut. Indic. | tendré, tendrás, tendrá, tendremos, tendréis, tendrán. |

Cond.

tendría, tendrías, tendría, tendríamos, tendríais, tendrían.

Imper.

ten tú, tenga Vd., tengamos nosotros, tened vosotros, tengan Vds.

46. traer

Pres. Indic.

traigo, traes, trae, traemos, traéis, traen.

Pres. Subj.

traiga, traigas, traiga, traigamos, traigáis, traigan.

Pret. Indic.

traje, trajiste, trajo, trajimos, trajisteis, trajeron.

Imp. Subj.

trajera or trajese, trajeras or trajeses, trajera or trajese, trajéramos or trajésemos, trajerais or trajeseis, trajeran or trajesen.

Imper.

trae tú, traiga Vd., traigamos nosotros, traed vosotros, traigan Vds.

Pres. Part.

trayendo.

47. valer

Pres. Indic.

valgo, vales, vale, valemos, valéis, valen.

Pres. Subj.

valga, valgas, valga, valgamos, valgáis, valgan.

Fut. Indic.

valdré, valdrás, valdrá, valdremos, valdréis, valdrán.

Cond.

valdría, valdrías, valdría, valdríamos, valdríais, valdrían.

Imper.

val or vale tú, valga Vd., valgamos nosotros, valed vosotros, valgan Vds.

48. venir

Pres. Indic.

vengo, vienes, viene, venimos, venís, vienen.

Pres. Subj.

venga, vengas, venga, vengamos, vengáis, vengan.

Pret. Indic.

vine, viniste, vino, vinimos, vinisteis, vinieron.

Imp. Subj.

viniera or viniese, vinieras or vinieses, viniera or viniese, viniéramos or viniésemos, vinierais or vinieseis, vinieran or viniesen.

Fut. Indic.

vendré, vendrás, vendrá, vendremos, vendréis, vendrán.

Cond.

vendría, vendrías, vendría, vendríamos, vendríais, vendrían.

Imper.

ven tú, venga Vd., vengamos nosotros, venid vosotros, vengan Vds.

Pres. Part.

viniendo.

49. ver

Pres. Indic.

veo, ves, ve, vemos, veis, ven.

Pres. Subj.

vea, veas, vea, veamos, veáis, vean.

Imp. Indic.

veía, veías, veía, veíamos, veíais, veían.

Imper.

ve tú, vea Vd., veamos nosotros, ved vosotros, vean Vds.

Past Part.

visto.

50. yacer

Pres. Indic.

yazco, or yazgo, yaces, yace, yacemos, yacéis, yacen.

Pres. Subj.

yazca or yazga, yazcas or yazgas, yazca or yazga, yazcamos, or yazgamos, yazcáis or yazgáis, yazcan or yazgan.

Imper.   yace tú, **yazca** or **yazga** Vd., **yazcamos** or **yazgamos** nosotros, yaced vosotros, **yazcan** or **yazgan** Vds.

51. Defective Verbs

   a. The following verbs are used only in the forms that have an **i** in the ending: abolir, agredir, aterirse, empedernir, transgredir.

   b. atañer

   This verb is used only in the third person. It is most frequently used in the present indicative: atañe, atañen.

   c. concernir

   This verb is used only in the third person of the following tenses:

   Pres. Indic.   **concierne, conciernen.**
   Pres. Subj.   **concierna, conciernan.**
   Imp. Indic.   concernía, concernían.
   Imp. Subj.   concerniera or concerniese, concernieran or concerniesen.
   Pres. Part.   concerniendo.

   d. soler

   This verb is used most frequently in the present and imperfect indicative. It is less frequently used in the present subjunctive.

   Pres. Indic.   **suelo, sueles, suele,** solemos, soléis, **suelen.**
   Pres. Subj.   **suela, suelas, suela,** solamos, soláis, **suelan.**
   Imp. Indic.   solía, solías, solía, solíamos, solíais, solían.

   The preterit is seldom used. Of the compound tenses, only the present perfect is commonly used: he solido, etc. The other tenses are very rare.

   e. roer

   This verb has three forms in the first person of the present indicative: **roo, royo, roigo,** all of which are infrequently used. In the present subjunctive the perferable form is **roa, roas, roa,** etc., although the forms **roya** and **roiga** are found.

52. *Irregular Past Participles*

abrir—**abierto**	escribir—**escrito**
absorber—absorbido, **absorto**	freir—**frito**, freído
bendecir—bendecido, **bendito**	hacer—**hecho**
componer—**compuesto**	imprimir—**impreso**
cubrir—**cubierto**	inscribir—**inscrito, inscripto**
decir—**dicho**	maldecir—maldecido, **maldito**
deponer—**depuesto**	morir—**muerto**
descomponer—**descompuesto**	poner—**puesto**
describir—**descrito**	prescribir—**prescrito, prescripto**
descubrir—**descubierto**	proscribir—**proscrito, proscripto**
desenvolver—**desenvuelto**	proveer—proveído, **provisto**
deshacer—**deshecho**	resolver—**resuelto**
devolver—**devuelto**	revolver—**revuelto**
disolver—**disuelto**	romper—rompido, **roto**
encubrir—**encubierto**	satisfacer—**satisfecho**
entreabrir—**entreabierto**	subscribir—**subscrito**
entrever—**entrevisto**	ver—**visto**
envolver—**envuelto**	volver—**vuelto**

The Spanish Language in America

Introduction

In a sense Latin is not dead. The speech of Roman soldiers, merchants, and colonists, the Latin of another day, was taken bodily to Iberia, to Gaul, to Dacia, and to many other regions. As it developed under some influence from the languages previously spoken in these areas, it became known eventually by several other names—Spanish, Portuguese, French, Italian, Romanian, etc.

The Latin of northern Spain came to be called Castilian since its speakers were from the province of Castilla (Latin *Castella*, "castles"), and although later it was often called Spanish (**español**), to this day the people of many regions of Spanish speech refer to their language as **castellano,** and the children of Argentina and Chile, for instance, study **composición castellana.**

Castilian, among other Latin dialects, became prominent in the Iberian peninsula because of the hegemony of north central Spain in the reconquest of the peninsula from the Moors during the Middle Ages and subsequently in the discovery and settlement of America. Thus its predominance over other manifestations of Latin is not due to its own nature but rather to non-linguistic factors: political and military power and organization, church-state relations, and finally literary ascendance.

The Spanish of Latin America, like most "colonial" speech, tends to be conservative in its structural changes compared with that of the mother country. In addition, it reflects regional traits of the southwestern part of Spain, notably Andalusia and adjacent areas, from where a large part of the sailors, conquistadores, and colonists came. In other words, the Spanish of America would seem to be Andalusian Castilian of the sixteenth and seventeenth centuries, as far as pronunciation and grammar are concerned. But in vocabulary hundreds of Indian words have entered the language, especially in Mexico, Guatemala, the Andes (Ecuador, Peru, and Bolivia), and in the Río de la Plata region. The Indian words of the Caribbean islands were taken to other parts of Latin America by the original Spanish settlers and often form a part of the general Spanish lexicon. It should be noted that these Indian languages belong to distinct, unrelated families, so that an **ahuacate** (avocado) in Mexico and Central America becomes a **palta** in the Andes. Although Spanish Americans generally have little difficulty understanding each other, the following variants represent rather extreme divergences:

	Little boy	*bus*	*blond*
Mexico	**chamaco**	**camión**	**güero**
Guatemala	**patojo**	**camioneta**	**canche**
El Salvador	**cipote**	**camioneta**	**chele**
Panamá	**chico**	**chiva**	**fulo**
Colombia	**pelado**	**autobús**	**mono**
Argentina	**pibe**	**colectivo**	**rubio**
Chile	**cabro**	**micro**	**rubio**
Cuba	**chico**	**guagua**	**rubio**

Although most of these words are actually Spanish (of Latin origin), several are from the Indian languages of the respective areas. The fact that there are differences of this sort is to be expected in a general culture that contains so many national boundaries.

Today Spanish (**castellano**) is the most extensive manifestation of the former spoken Latin. Those who think and express themselves in this language number about 200,000,000, and they live in some twenty countries, most of which have rapidly growing populations. It is estimated as of 1970 that by A.D. 2000 Spanish will be the language of nearly 500,000,000 people, most of whom will be **hispanoamericanos.** It is one of the principal languages of the world.

The Pronunciation of Latin-American Spanish

The fundamental phonological traits of American Spanish are to be found in Castilla, but only changes that have taken place in the Andalusian dialect of Castilian have become established in America. Furthermore, these changes apparently took place between the fifteenth and the eighteenth centuries, during the settlement of Latin America. Evidence indicates that inaccessible areas of Spanish America (the mountainous regions of Mexico, Guatemala, Colombia, Ecuador, Peru, Bolivia, as well as Paraguay, inland Venezuela, and northern Argentina) received only the early changes of Andalusian Castilian, while the accessible coastal areas and port cities tend to reflect both early changes and those of the late colonial period. Thus it is that Cuban and Panamanian Spanish resemble that of present-day Sevilla more than does Mexican Spanish or that of Bogotá. In the meantime Madrid Spanish (called Castilian by many North Americans) developed one or two features that never reached America.

The outstanding common feature of American-Spanish pronunciation that goes back to the early colonial period is the so-called **seseo.** About the time of Columbus the people of southwestern Spain began to confuse the two sibilant sounds of **casa** [KáSa] ("house") and **caza** [kása] ("hunt") (the capital [S] representing a "thick" alveolar sound and the [s] representing a "normal" dental sound), with the result that only the dental sound survived. Since most settlers of America were from the south, this became the general Spanish-American tendency. **Coser** and **cocer** are alike in southern Spain and in Latin America. The sibilant is a delicate dental one. In northern and central Spain a distinction between these two sounds is still maintained, and the second or dental one has become interdental [θ], similar to the voiceless *th* of English. The former [S] is still apicoalveolar, and to the foreigner approaches the sound represented by English *sh.*

In the seventeenth and eighteenth centuries other changes occurred in the pronunciation of southern Spanish. As has been indicated, these became part of the Spanish of the accessible areas of America, but most did not reach the high mountains and plateaus. The first of these was the aspiration or even the loss of /s/ syllable final. **Estos** becomes [éhtoh] or even [éto], the result of what might be termed a "relaxed" articulation. About the same time the /l/ (written **ll**) tended to be "relaxed" to the extent that it coincided with the /y/ (written **y**), so that **valla** and **vaya** were levelled to [báya] in Andalusia and parts of America. Today Bolivia, Paraguay, and much of Peru and Ecuador still maintain a distinction. One of the latest levelings of Andalusia was the confusion of /l/ and /r/ syllable final. This is heard today in Puerto Rico, Panama, and Venezuela, and to a certain extent in Cuba, the Dominican Republic, and central Chile. **Puerta** sounds like [pwelta], **mar** like [mal] and the infinitives seem to end in /l/. A final Andalusian trait is the velar /n/ [ŋ] as a sign of open transition. **Enamora**

Map 1

 Vos used instead of tú in informal address.

 In Chile the distinction is one of class: vos is used in the lower economic levels.

Map 2

 Aspiration or loss of /s/ syllable final.

Map 3

Distinction between /ʎ/ and /y/.

Assibilation of /rr/ and /tr/.

is [enamóra], but **en amor** is [eŋamór]. English-speakers think of *ng* when they hear **son** and **pan** pronounced [soŋ] and [paŋ].

Perhaps the only outstanding feature of American Spanish that is not traceable to Andalusia is the assibilation of /rr/ [řř] and /r/ [ř] final and postconsonantal. This occurs in vast areas of America: Guatemala, Costa Rica, in the eastern cordillera of Colombia, highland Ecuador, Bolivia, Chile, western and northern Argentina, and Paraguay.

The maps show the distribution of the distinguishing features of Spanish-American pronunciation.

Syntactic Features

The familiar form of address in Spanish, **tú**, is a direct descendant of the Latin *tu*. The Latin plural form *vos* also came down to Spanish, but by the late Middle Ages it had assumed the function of polite singular as well as familiar plural. To make the distinction, people began to say **vosotros** (you others) for the plural. In the sixteenth century there came into being a very polite form of address: **vuestra merced** (your mercy), used with the third person of the verb, as one might say, "Does his majesty wish to enter?" It has been shortened to **usted.** With this new polite form, **vos,** the former polite singular, lost prestige and became a familiar form. This was the state of affairs when the colonists came to America. As a result, vast sections of Latin America use **vos** instead of **tú** as the singular familiar form of address. All of Spanish America uses **ustedes** for the familiar plural as well as the polite plural. It will be noted in the map on page xxxiii that the **vos** areas are generally far from the old Viceroyalties of Mexico and Lima. Only in Chile is there a social distinction.

The verb used with **vos** is the modified plural of Old Spanish: **hablás, comés, vivís**; the imperative is **hablá, comé, viví.** The object pronoun and the possessive are from the singular, the object of the preposition, **vos: LLevate tu perro con vos.** Since the imperative of **ir** would be simply **i,** the verb **andar** is used instead: **¡andate!** Another interesting syntactic trait is the general tendency to differentiate gender of nouns of occupation and status of people and to create feminine forms where they may not have existed in so-called standard Spanish. **Presidenta, ministra, dependienta, liberala, abogada,** and **arquitecta** have been heard. Equally general are the tendencies to use adjectives as adverbs (**corre ligero, toca el piano lindo**) and to make certain adverbs "agree" with adjectives they modify (**media muerta; medias locas**) as well as to use the impersonal **haber** in the plural (**habían dos; ¿cuántos habrán?**).

The Vocabulary of Spanish America

There are three main tendencies in the development of Hispanic-American lexical elements: (1) to use words that were popular at the time of the settlement of America, especially maritime terms or rural expressions, often out of popular etymology; (2) to adopt Indian words, especially those related to the domestic scene; and (3) to borrow directly from English and to develop cases of correlative analogy due to English influence.

Of the first category are such terms as **flota** for a bus line, **amarrar** for **atar; botar** for **echar; virar** for **volverse.** In the tropical zone of America (from Guatemala south through Peru), where there are no seasons of heat and cold, since these depend on altitude, the Spaniards began to call the wet periods **invierno** (winter) and the dry, **verano** (summer). The custom continues to this day in Guatemala, El Salvador, Honduras, Nicaragua, Costa Rica, Panama, Colombia, Venezuela, Ecuador, and Peru. One may ask, **¿qué tal el invierno?** ("How was the winter?") and receive the answer **¡copioso!** ("copious").

Indian words entered the Spanish of America by the hundreds. In the Caribbean the Spaniards learned **tabaco, canoa, huracán, maíz, ají**; in Mexico, from Náhuatl, **chocolate, tomate, coyote, chicle, cacao**; in the Andes, from Quechua, **pampa, quinina, cóndor, puma, poncho**; and in the Río de la Plata region, from Guaraní, **ananás, ñandú, ombú, yajá, tapioca**.

During the twentieth century the influence of English has been strong in Latin America, and the direct borrowings in some areas could be counted in the hundreds: **control, lonche, lonchería, sandwich, jaibol** ("high-ball"), **cóctel, ponche, bar, twist, chance, fútbol, béisbol, fildear** ("to field"), **jonrón** ("home run"), **noquear** ("to knock out"), **lobista**, and even such verbs as **taipear** ("to type") and **blofear** ("to bluff"). In the realm of correlative analogy or sense loans, English has tremendous influence, and **educación** ("upbringing") takes the place of **pedagogía, instrucción,** and **enseñanza; argumento** ("plot of a story") moves into the slot of **discusión; atender** ("to wait on") into that of **asistir; audiencia** into that of **concurrencia; acta** ("minutes") takes the place of **ley; complexión** ("physical constitution") takes the place of **tez.**

Regional Features: Mexico

Among speakers of Spanish, a Mexican is recognized by his intonation and by his tendency to lengthen the articulation of his /s/ and by his general preference for the consonant over the vowel. If intonation of Spanish is represented in a pattern of four levels, Mexicans, especially males in a "man-about-town" mood, tend to strike a terminal point between standard statement and emphatic statement, giving the utterance a "minor-key" effect. The tensely-grooved /s/ of Mexican Spanish leads to the virtual elimination of unstressed vowels, especially /e/, in rapid speech: **accidentes de coches** may tend to be [aksidénts de kočs].

Typical adjectives of Mexico are **mero** and **puro**. The first of these is so popular that it means not only "mere" but "very," "real," "just," "same," and many other things, and is even used adverbially: **ya merito** ("It won't be long now").

As has been noted, Mexico is the center of Aztec vocabulary that has entered Spanish and eventually many languages of the world: **tomate, chocolate, cacao, coyote, chicle,** and hundreds of less common terms.

Guatemala

The Spanish of Guatemala is characterized by a strong assibilated /rr/ [r̃r̃] and by [r̃] for /r/ except in intervocalic position. The **jota** tends to be [h] rather than [x], and velar /n/ marks open transition. Along with those of other Central-American areas, Guatemalan speakers tend to weaken inter-vocalic /y/ to the extent that **silla** sounds like [sía] and **bella** like [bea]. Through a process of ultracorrection, **vea** may become [béya]. Guate-malans generally pronounce their /s/ syllable final with clarity and tension.

A fairly universal feature of the Spanish of Guatemala is the **voseo**, or use of **vos** as the subject form of familiar address in the singular. The verb used with this is the plural familiar, but the pronoun objects and possessives are always singular. **Cuando te vayas, llévate tu perro contigo**, as one might say in Spain or in Mexico, would be **Cuando te vayás, llevate tu perro con vos** in Guatemala.

Little boys are **patojos** in Guatemala, and blonds are **canches.**

El Salvador, Honduras, Nicaragua

Perhaps more than any other group of independent countries, these three form a linguistic unity in most respects. They represent in phonology a middle point between the highland conservatism (Mexico and the Andes, for instance) and the later trends of the lowlands (Cuba and Panamá, for example). The inhabitants of these countries call each other **guanacos, catrachos,** and **nicas** respectively, and are always talking of Central-American union.

The phonological phenomenon of recent discovery—although it is probably an "archaic" trait—is the occlusive pronunciation of /b/, /d/, /g/ after another consonant, a situation in which they would be fricative in "standard" Spanish.

It is in this region of Central America that one hears a lisped /s/ that approaches [θ] among many residents, and especially among the working classes. As in northern Mexico, the intervocalic /y/ (representing orthographic **y** and **ll**) tends to be a semivowel or even disappears. The **jota** /x/ is [h] in all speakers, and there is a strong tendency to aspirate syllable final /s/.

The Salvador-Honduras-Nicaragua region is rich in forms of combinative analogy, especially noun formation on the basis of other nouns. The suffixes **-ada** and **-ón** are of extensive application: **babosada, pendejada, lambida, atolada, paisanada, perrada, barbón, narizón, pistón, quemazón**; and the longer diminutive form **-ecito** that might be used in Spain and in Mexico is simply **-ito: llavita, lucita, crucita, piedrita.** The place where things grow or are to be found is indicated by the suffix **-al: cañal, guacal, platanal, cafetal, piñal, pinal.**

Along with Guatemala and the other Central-American countries, except Panama, this region uses the **vos** form of familiar address, and in the way described for Guatemala: **Vení y decime, ¿ son vos y tu padre ladrones?**

Many indigenous words are used in everyday conversation, most of them from the Pipil, a sublanguage of the Náhuatl. A blond is a **chele,** a boy is a **cipote, pushco** is dirty, **peche** is slender, and there is the usual stock of Aztec terms that were imported after the conquest of Mexico.

Costa Rica

Like Guatemala, Costa Rica is noted for its assibilated /rr/, along with assibilated /r/ syllable final. It also shares with Guatemala a fairly conservative articulation of /s/ syllable final. As in all Central-American and Caribbean countries, the /n/ is velar when final, as a sign of open juncture: [eŋ amor] but [enamorár], and intervocalic /y/ weakens to the point of elimination through vocalization.

As a part of the syntactic structure of the dialect, **vos** and related forms operate where **tú** would prevail in Spain or Mexico today, and lexically, Costa Rica shows less Aztec influence than Guatemala, El Salvador, or Honduras.

Panama

The Spanish of Panama might be termed "trade route Spanish," in that it has the phonological character of parts of America that were in constant communication with Spain at the grass-roots level and yet were removed from the courtly influences of the viceregal centers (Mexico and Lima). It resembles strongly the Spanish of Cuba, Puerto Rico, and Venezuela and the northern coast of Colombia.

Along with other Caribbean residents, the Panamanians tend to aspirate their /s/ at the end of a syllable, or to eliminate it entirely.

Colombia

The development of the language in Colombia, which has three high mountain ranges and several important ports, might serve as an example of how American Spanish grew in disparate ways from Peninsular models. The relative inaccessibility of the high sierras and valleys makes it possible to find at least five distinct linguistic zones in the former Nueva Granada. The "dialects" therefore represent stages in the historical development of southern Peninsular Spanish, the most inaccessible regions generally representing the earliest and the most accessible in general representing the latest in Andalusian vogues, before independence.

Strange as it may seem, Colombian Spanish has two general traits in common with that of El Salvador, Honduras, and Nicaragua: the /x/ is [h] in all regions, and the /b/, /d/, /g/ are occlusive after any consonant. Thus **pardo, barba, algo, desde, las vacas,** all have occlusives where a Spaniard or a Mexican would use fricatives.

The Spanish of Bogotá has the conservative distinction of /l/ and /y/ and, like that of Costa Rica and Guatemala, tends to assibilate the /rr/, the /tr/, and the /r/ final.

Pastuso Spanish (of Nariño) is in many ways Ecuadorean, and like the Spanish of highland Mexico, slights the vowel in favor of the consonant, tends to pronounce the /d/ of **-ado,** and uses an apicodental /s/, strong and well defined.

Antioquia's Spanish is unique in America in one way. The /s/ is apico-alveolar [S], like that of Spain, and although no distinction is made between **casa** and **caza,** the Colombian ambassador to Spain, an **antioqueño,** gave the impression of "talking like a Spaniard." The second distinguishing feature of this region's Spanish is the /y/ of such tenseness that it even becomes affricate intervocalically [maẏo, kabaẏo].

Colombia is unusually formal in most sections as far as direct address is concerned. Many speakers use **usted** almost exclusively—even to cats and dogs. Not only is this the case within the family, but some relatives speak to each other as **su merced.** The **voseo** prevails in Antioquia and in Santander and in the **Valle,** while Bogotá and the Coast always employ the **tuteo.**

Typical of Colombia are the idiomatic expressions ¡**siga!** and ¡**a la orden!** The first is said to invite one to enter, and the other to ask, "What can I do for you?" Black coffee, especially the demitasse, is a **tinto,** and to invite one to partake, one says: ¿**Le provoca un tinto?** This same sentence to a Spaniard might mean, "Does red wine make you fight?" Instead of sending regards with **saludos,** Colombians use **saludes** ("healths").

Venezuela

The speech pattern of Venezuela is for the most part that of the Caribbean, and therefore late Andalusian. One "eats" his final /s/; /l/ and /r/ are confused at syllable end; /n/ is velar as a sign of finality; and as in El Salvador, Honduras, and Nicaragua, many people pronounce the /s/ as [θ].

As far as address is concerned, most of Venezuela is **tuteo** country, but sections near the Colombian frontier are **vos** areas.

Ecuador

In a country where thousands speak Quechua (the language of the Incas) in preference to Spanish and where many are bilingual, the Spanish language of the upper inter-Andean region is very conservative in its phonological evolution. Ecuadoreans (except those of the coast) still distinguish /l/ and /y/ as [ž] and [y], still pronounce /s/ with deliberate tenseness and, like many Mexicans, slight the vowel in favor of the consonant. Because Quechua is so widely spoken, and because this language has a simple three-vowel system, the Spanish of the highlands tends to heighten /o/ to /u/ and /e/ to /i/. Unique in Latin America is the final /s/ as [z] before a vowel in the following word: [laz agwas].

Peru

About 11,000,000 **peruanos,** or as their neighbors may say, **peruleros** or **cholos,** occupy the territory of the central Inca Empire of preconquest days. Their money is counted in **soles** and their babies are **guaguas.** Along with Ecuador and Bolivia, Peru belongs to heavily populated Andean Spanish America, and besides having many Quechua-speaking inhabitants, the region boasts a clear Spanish that gives evidence of sixteenth-century origin and viceregal nurture.

Except in Lima and along the northern coast, Peruvians still distinguish the /l/ and /y/, and the general impression of Peruvian Spanish is similar to that of Mexico, Bolivia, and Ecuador.

Nearly all of Peru uses the **tú** form of familiar address, and as one might expect, hundreds of Quechua words have entered the Spanish of everyday life. In fact, several **quechismos** have become universal terms: **pampa, cóndor, puma, puna, quinina, llama, alpaca, gaucho, china** ("sweetheart"), **poncho,** and many others.

Chile

Linguistically, Chile can be divided into three sections, north, middle, and south. The north and the south resemble each other more than they do the middle. The heavily populated central valley partakes of many of the traits of late Andalusian, through the port of Valparaíso and the city of Santiago. Final /s/ is aspirated, /l/ and /r/ are confused in the syllable final situation, and /l/ and /y/ are not distinguished. Chiloé still distinguishes these latter two, and in the north there are vowel-heightening influences of Quechua. Two features that seem to characterize all Chilean Spanish are the /č/ of alveolar articulation rather than palatal and the /x/ with a palatal element of semiconsonantal nature before /e/. One seems to hear **la gente de Chile** as [la xjénte de tSíle].

Argentina, Uruguay, Paraguay

The Spanish of this vast territory is of two main types, according to the direction from which the settlers came. The western and northwestern sections were settled from Peru and Chile from about 1590. Although Buenos Aires and the humid Pampa were first settled about 1535, it was not until 1580 that a permanent settlement was established. The important factor producing the differences of today was the accessibility of Buenos Aires and surrounding country to constant influences from the ports of southern Spain in the colonial period. Thus the interior shows more conservative features: an /s/ of more tense articulation, a distinction between /l/ and /y/ in some areas, and the assibilated /rr/ of Costa Rica, Bogotá, and Guatemala.

The **porteño** of the Río de la Plata region is noted for his /y/ with strong [ž] articulation: **bayo, calle** [bážo], [káže].

Both Argentina and Uruguay are **voseo** territories, and the style has been recorded extensively in gaucho poetry. As a cattle region, the pampas have a lexicon that is rich in the terminology of the ranch and of horses. English and French are contributors to the vocabulary of the area, and one hears of **five o'clock tea a todas horas,** and the frequency of **chau** for "good-by" attests the influence of Italian, the original language of more than half of the inhabitants of Argentina. **Argentinos** are often called **che,** since they use this term to attract attention.

Paraguay, being more inaccessible, has two conservative features in its phonology: the distinction of /l/ and /y/, and the assibilation of /rr/. It is unique in that nearly all its inhabitants are bilingual. They speak the original Indian language, Guaraní, and Spanish. The occasion usually dictates which will be used, and speakers will often shift from one to the other in the same utterance.

Cuba, The Dominican Republic, and Puerto Rico

The Spanish of the Caribbean, like that of Panama, could be termed "trade route" Spanish, since it shows rather typically the American evolution of Andalusian trends of the seventeenth and eighteenth centuries, trends that do not seem to be present in the more inaccessible hinterland. Add to this the Afro-Cuban influences of slave days and the many American English loans of the twentieth century, and we have perhaps the least "conservative" Castilian.

Cubans tend to aspirate their syllable final /s/ or drop it altogether, and the tendency is as marked or more so in Puerto Rico and Santo Domingo. In all three, syllable final /l/ and /r/ are confused, most of all in Puerto Rico, where the /l/ is favored: **puerta, izquierdo** [pwélta], [ihkjéldo]. In contrast to Mexico, Ecuador, Peru, and Bolivia, where the vowel may be slighted, those of the Caribbean tend to slight the consonant in favor of the vowel. In Puerto Rico /rr/ is now velar in about half of the population. It resembles the **jota** of Spain: [x].

Cuba, Puerto Rico, and the Dominican Republic are **tuteo** countries.

This brief description of some of the features of the Castilian of America may help to show that distinctive features do not correspond to geographical or political entities to the extent that has been believed, and one might indicate as many as a hundred dialects—and yet it is all Spanish.

Numerals—Números

Cardinal Numbers	Números Cardinales	Ordinal Numbers	Números Ordinales[5]
1........ one	uno, una	first	primero
2........ two	dos	second	segundo
3........ three	tres	third	tercero
4........ four	cuatro	fourth	cuarto
5........ five	cinco	fifth	quinto
6........ six	seis	sixth	sexto
7........ seven	siete	seventh	séptimo
8........ eight	ocho	eighth	octavo
9........ nine	nueve	ninth	noveno, nono
10...... ten	diez	tenth	décimo
11...... eleven	once	eleventh	undécimo
12...... twelve	doce	twelfth	duodécimo
13...... thirteen	trece	thirteenth	décimotercio
14...... fourteen	catorce	fourteenth	décimocuarto
15...... fifteen	quince	fifteenth	décimoquinto
16...... sixteen	dieciseis, diez y seis	sixteenth	décimosexto
17...... seventeen	diecisiete, diez y siete	seventeenth	décimoséptimo
18...... eighteen	dieciocho, diez y ocho	eighteenth	décimoctavo
19...... nineteen	diecinueve, diez y nueve	nineteenth	décimonono
20...... twenty	veinte	twentieth	vigésimo
21...... twenty-one	veintiuno, veinte y uno	twenty-first	vigésimo primero
30...... thirty	treinta	thirtieth	trigésimo
40...... forty	cuarenta	fortieth	cuadragésimo
50...... fifty	cincuenta	fiftieth	quincuagésimo
60...... sixty	sesenta	sixtieth	sexagésimo
70...... seventy	setenta	seventieth	septuagésimo
80...... eighty	ochenta	eightieth	octogésimo
90...... ninety	noventa	ninetieth	nonagésimo
100...... one hundred	ciento	(one) hundredth	centésimo
101...... one hundred and one	ciento (y) uno	(one) hundred and first	centésimo primo
200...... two hundred	doscientos	two-hundredth	ducentésimo
300...... three hundred	trescientos	three-hundredth	tricentésimo
400...... four hundred	cuatrocientos	four-hundredth	cuadringentésimo
500...... five hundred	quinientos	five-hundredth	quingentésimo
600...... six hundred	seiscientos	six-hundredth	sexagésimo
700...... seven hundred	setecientos	seven-hundredth	septingentésimo
800...... eight hundred	ochocientos	eight-hundredth	octingentésimo
900...... nine hundred	novecientos	nine-hundredth	noningentésimo
1000 .... one thousand	mil	(one) thousandth	milésimo
100,000 .. one hundred thousand	cien mil	(one) hundred thousandth	cienmilésimo
1,000,000 one million	un millón	(one) millionth	millonésimo

Nations, Cities, and Adjectives of Nationality

Afganistán	afgano
Albania	albanés
Alto Volta	voltaico
Arabia Saudita	árabe saudita

[5] The ordinals beyond the "tenth" are less used in Spanish than in English. They are often replaced by the cardinals: *Alfonso the Thirteenth* **Alfonso trece.**

Argelia	argelino
Argentina	argentino
Asunción	asunceño
Basutolandia	basutolandés
Bechuanalandia	bechuanalandés
Bélgica	belga
Birmania	birmano
Bogotá	bogotano
Bolivia	boliviano
Brasil	brasileño
Bruselas	bruselense
Buenos Aires	bonaerense or porteño
Bulgaria	búlgaro
Burundi	burundi
Camboya	camboyano
Camerún	camerunés
Canadá	canadiense
Caracas	caraqueño
Ceilán	ceilanés
Colombia	colombiano
Congo (both)	congoleño
Costa de Marfil	marfileño
Costa Rica	costarricense
Cuba	cubano
Chad	chadiano
Checoslovaquia	checoslovaco
Chile	chileno
China	chino
Chipre	chipriota
Dahomey	dahomeyano
Dinamarca	dinamarqués or danés
Ecuador	ecuatoriano
El Salvador	salvadoreño
España	español
Estados Unidos de América	estadounidense
Etiopía	etíope
Filipinas	filipino
Finlandia	finlandés or finés
Francia	francés
Gabón	gabonés
Gambia	gambio
Ghana	ghanés
Ginebra	ginebrino
Grecia	griego
Guatemala	guatemalteco
Guayaquil	guayaquileño
Guinea	guineo
Haití	haitiano
Honduras	hondureño
Hungría	húngaro

Ifni	ifneño
India	indio
Indonesia	indonesio
Irak	iraqués
Irán	iranio
Irlanda	irlandés
Islandia	islandés
Israel	israelí
Italia	italiano
Jamaica	jamaicano
Japón	japonés
Jordania	jordanio
Jerusalém	jerosolimitano
Kenia	kenio
Kuwait	kuwaiteño
Laos	laosiano
La Paz	paceño
Líbano	libanés
Liberia	liberiano
Libia	libio
Lima	limeño
Lisboa	lisboeta or lisbonense
Londres	londinense
Luxemburgo	luxemburgués
Madagascar	malache
Madrid	madrileño
Malasia	malayo
Malavi	malavio
Malí	maliense
Managua	managüense
Marruecos	marroquí
Mauritania	mauritano
México (Mejico)	mejicano (mexicano)
Mongolia	mongol
Montevideo	montevideño or montevideano
Nepal	nepalés
Nicaragua	nicaragüense
Níger	nigerino
Nigeria	nigeriano
Noruega	noruego
Nueva York	neoyorquino
Nueva Zelandia	neozelandés
Paises Bajos	holandés
Pakistán	pakistano
Panamá	panameño
Paraguay	paraguayo
París	parisiense
Perú	peruano
Polonia	polaco

Portugal	portugués
Puerto Rico	puertorriqueño or portorriqueño
Reino Unido de Gran Bretaña e Irlanda del Norte	británico
República Árabe Unida	egipcio
República Centroafricana	centroafricano
República Dominicana	dominicano
República Socialista Soviética de Bielorrusia	bieloruso
República Socialista Soviética de Ucrania	ucranio
Río de Janeiro	carioca
Río Muni	ríomuniense
Rodesia	rodesio
Rumania	rumano
Rwanda	rwandés
San José	josefino
São Paulo	paulistano
Santa Cruz	cruceño
Santiago	santiagueño or santiaguino
Senegal	senegalés
Sierra Leona	leonense
Siria	sirio
Somalia	somalí
Suazilandia	suazilandés
Sudáfrica	sudafricano
Sudán	sudanés
Suecia	sueco
Tailandia	tailandés
Tanganyica	tanganyikano
Tanzania	tanzanio
Tegucigalpa	tegucigalpense
Tenerife	tinerfeño
Tetuán	tetuaní
Togo	togolés
Trinidad y Tobago	trinitario
Túnez	tunecí
Turquía	turco
Uganda	ugandés
Unión de Repúblicas Socialistas Soviéticas	ruso
Uruguay	uruguayo
Venecia	veneciano or véneto
Venezuela	venezolano
Viena	vienés
Yemen	yemenita
Yugoslavia	yugoslavo
Washington	washingtoniano
Zambia	zambio
Zanzíbar	zanzibareño

Monetary Units and Exchange Rates

Country	Basic Unit	Standard Subdivision	Exchange Rate*	
Argentina	peso	100 centavos	M$N	0.003
Bolivia	peso	100 centavos	$b	0.084
Brazil	cruzeiro	100 centavos	Cr$	0.260
Chile	escudo	100 centésimos	E°	0.112
Costa Rica	colon	100 céntimos	¢	0.128
Cuba	peso	100 centavos	$	1.000
Dominican Republic	peso	100 centavos	RD$	1.000
Ecuador	sucre	100 centavos	S/	0.045
El Salvador	colon	100 centavos	¢	0.400
Guatemala	quetzal	100 centavos	Q	1.000
Haiti	gourde	100 centimes	G	0.200
Honduras	lempira	100 centavos	L	0.500
Mexico	peso	100 centavos	Mex$	0.080
Nicaragua	cordoba	100 centavos	C$	0.142
Panama	balboa	100 centésimos	B	0.800
Paraguay	guarani	100 céntimos	₲	0.010
Peru	sol	100 centavos	S/	0.024
Spain	peseta	100 céntimos	Pts	0.014
Uruguay	peso	100 centésimos	UR$	0.004
Venezuela	bolívar	100 céntimos	Bs	0.220

* U.S. dollar = 1.000.

A

a *prep.* to; in, into; on; by.

abacería *f.* grocery; grocery store; **abacero** *m.* grocer.

abad *m.* abbot; **abadía** *f.* abbey.

abadejo *m. N.Sp.* codfish.

abadesa *f.* abbess.

abajarse *v.* to lower oneself, humiliate oneself.

abajeño *adj. Mex., C.A.* lowland; *n.* lowlander.

abajo *adv.* down, below; downstairs.

abalanzar[9] *v.* to balance; to hurl, impel; **-se** to hurl oneself; to rush (upon), swoop down (upon); *Am.* to rear, balk.

abalear *v.* to "shoot up."

abanderado *adj.* standard-bearing; *n.* standard-bearer.

abandonamiento *m.* = **abandono.**

abandonar *v.* to abandon, desert; to give up.

abandono *m.* abandon; desertion; neglect.

abanicar[6] *v.* to fan.

abanico *m.* fan.

abaratar *v.* to cheapen, lower the price of.

abarcar[6] *v.* to embrace, contain, include; *Carib., Ríopl.* to buy up, monopolize.

abarrancarse[6] *v.* to fall into an opening; to get into a difficult situation.

abarrotería *f. Mex., C.A., Andes* grocery, grocery store; **abarrotero** *m. Mex., C.A., Andes* grocer.

abarrotes *m. pl.* small packages (*in hold of a ship*); *Mex., C.A., Andes* groceries; **tienda de —** *Mex., C.A., Andes* grocery store.

abastecer[13] *v. irr.* to supply.

abastecimiento *m.* supply; provisions.

abasto *m.* supply; **no dar — a** to be unable to cope with.

abatido *adj.* dejected, depressed, crestfallen, humbled; fallen; lowered.

abatimiento *m.* discouragement, dejection, depression; descent, swoop, drop.

abatir *v.* to lower; to knock down; to depress; to humble; **-se** to become discouraged; to swoop down.

abdicar[6] *v.* to abdicate.

abdomen *m.* abdomen.

abecedario *m.* alphabet; primer.

abedul *m.* birch.

abeja *f.* bee; **abejera** *f.* beehive; **abejón** *m.* drone; bumblebee; **abejorro** *m.* bumblebee.

aberración *f.* aberration, mental or moral deviation.

abertura *f.* aperture, opening, hole, slit.

abeto *m.* fir (*tree and wood*).

abierto *p.p. of* **abrir** opened; *adj.* open; frank; *Am.* proud, self-satisfied; *Am.* generous.

abigarrado *adj.* motley; multicolored; variegated.

abigeato *m.* cattle stealing.

abismado *p.p.* absorbed, buried in thought; overwhelmed.

abismal *adj.* abysmal.

abismar *v.* to overwhelm; to depress; **-se** to be plunged (into); to bury oneself (*in thought, grief, etc.*).

abismo *m.* abyss, precipice, chasm.

abjurar *v.* to abjure; to renounce solemnly.

ablandar *v.* to soften.

abnegación *f.* abnegation, self-denial, self-sacrifice.

abnegado *adj.* self-sacrificing.

abnegarse[7] *v.* to deny oneself, sacrifice oneself.

abobado *adj.* stupid, silly.

abocar[6] *v.* to bite; to bring near; to flow into.

abocinar *v.* to flare; to fall on one's face.

abochornar *v.* to overheat; to embarrass; **-se** to get overheated; to blush; to be embarrassed.

abofetear *v.* to slap.

abogacía *f.* the legal profession; a law career.

abogado *m.* lawyer.

abogar[7] *v.* to advocate, plead in favor of; to intercede.

abolengo *m.* lineage, ancestry; inheritance, patrimony.

abolición *f.* abolition.

abolir[51] *v.* to abolish; to repeal.

abolsarse *v.* to bag (*said of trousers, skirts, etc.*).

abollado *p.p. & adj.* dented; bumped; bruised.

abolladura *f.* dent, bump.

abollar *v.* to dent; to bump; to crush, crumple; to bruise.

abombar *v.* to make bulge; **-se** *Ríopl.* to get drunk.

abominable *adj.* abominable, detestable.

abominar *v.* to abominate, abhor, detest.

abonado *m.* subscriber; *p.p. of* **abonar.**

abonar *v.* to credit with; to make a payment; to endorse, back (*a person*); to fertilize (*soil*); **-se** to subscribe.

abonaré *m.* promissory note; I.O.U.

abono *m.* (*monetario*) payment; installment; endorsement; guarantee; (*del suelo*) fertilizer; (*suscripción*) subscription.

abordar *v.* to board (*a ship*); to dock, put into port; to approach; to undertake, take up (*a matter, problem, etc.*).

aborigen *adj.* aboriginal, indigenous, native; **aborígenes** *m. pl.* aborigines, primitive inhabitants.

aborrascarse[6] *v.* to become stormy.

aborrecer[13] *v. irr.* to abhor, hate, detest.

aborrecible *adj.* abominable, hateful.

aborrecimiento *m.* abhorrence; hatred.

abortar *v.* to miscarry, have a miscarriage; to give birth prematurely; to fail.

aborto *m.* abortion, miscarriage; monster.

abotagarse[7] *v.* to bloat; to swell.

abotonador *m.* buttonhook.

abotonar *v.* to button, button up; to bud; **-se** to button up.

abovedar v. to vault, cover with a vault; to arch.

abozalar v. to muzzle.

abra f. cove; mountain gap or pass; dale; *Am.* breach (*in the jungle*); *Am.* leaf (*of a door*).

abrasador adj. burning, very hot.

abrasar v. to burn; to parch; **-se** to burn up, be consumed.

abrazar[9] v. to hug, embrace; to include.

abrazo m. hug, embrace.

abrebotellas m. bottle opener.

abrelatas m. can opener.

abrevadero m. drinking trough; watering place for cattle.

abrevar v. to water (*livestock*).

abreviación f. abbreviation.

abreviar v. to abbreviate, shorten, condense.

abreviatura f. abbreviation.

abrigar[7] v. to shelter, cover, protect; to wrap up; to harbor (*fear*), cherish (*hope*); **-se** to find shelter; to wrap oneself up.

abrigo m. shelter, cover, protection; wrap; overcoat.

abril m. April.

abrillantar v. to polish, shine; to glaze.

abrir[52] v. to open; to unlock.

abrochar v. to button; to clasp; to fasten.

abrogación f. repeal.

abrogar[7] v. to abrogate, repeal, annul.

abrojo m. thistle, thorn; **-s** reef.

abrumador adj. crushing, overwhelming; oppressive; fatiguing.

abrumar v. to crush, overwhelm; to trouble, annoy; **-se** to become foggy.

abrupto adj. abrupt, steep.

absceso m. abscess.

absolución f. absolution; acquittal.

absoluto adj. absolute; unconditional.

absolver[2,52] v. irr. to absolve, free from guilt; to pardon, acquit.

absorbente adj. & m. absorbent.

absorber[52] v. to absorb.

absorción f. absorption.

absorto p.p. irr. of **absorber** & adj. absorbed, engrossed; amazed.

abstenerse[45] v. irr. to abstain, refrain.

abstinencia f. abstinence; fasting.

abstracción f. abstraction, reverie.

abstracto adj. abstract.

abstraer[46] v. irr. to abstract; to withdraw, remove; **-se** to be lost in thought.

abstraído adj. lost in thought, absent-minded; aloof.

absuelto p.p. of **absolver** absolved, acquitted.

absurdo adj. absurd, ridiculous, senseless; m. absurdity.

abuela f. grandmother.

abuelo m. grandfather; **-s** grandparents; ancestors.

abulia f. abulia, loss of will power.

abultado adj. bulky, bulgy.

abultar v. to bulge; to be bulky; to enlarge.

abundancia f. abundance, plenty.

abundante adj. abundant, plentiful.

abundar v. to abound, be plentiful.

aburrido p.p. & adj. bored; boring, tiresome; weary.

aburrimiento m. weariness, dullness, boredom.

aburrir v. to bore, vex; **-se** to become bored or vexed.

abusar v. to abuse, mistreat; to misuse; **— de** to take unfair advantage of; to impose upon.

abuso m. abuse; misuse.

acá adv. here, over here; this way, hither.

acabado m. a finishing material: paint, varnish.

acabamiento m. finish, completion, end; death; *Am.* exhaustion, physical decline.

acabar v. to end, finish, complete; **— de** (+ *inf.*) to have just; **— por** (+ *inf.*) to end by; **— con** to put an end to, make short work of; to destroy; **-se** to be over, finished; to be consumed; *Am.* to wear oneself out; *Riopl., Mex., C.A.* to age or decline in health.

academia f. academy; a special school; a scientific, literary, or artistic society.

académico adj. academic; m. academician, member of an academy.

acaecer[13] v. irr. to happen, occur.

acaecimiento m. event, happening.

acalorado adj. heated, excited, angry.

acaloramiento m. heat, ardor, excitement.

acalorar v. (*calentar*) to heat, warm; (*emocionar*) to excite.

acallar v. to silence; to calm, quiet.

acampar v. to encamp; to camp.

acanalar v. to groove; to flute (*as a column*); to form a channel in.

acantilado adj. sheer, steep (*cliff*); m. bluff, cliff.

acantonar v. to quarter (*troops*).

acaparar v. to corner (*the market*); to monopolize; to gather in (*for one's gain or profit*).

acarear v. to bring face to face; to confront.

acariciar v. to caress, pet; to cherish (*a hope or illusion*).

acarreador m. carter; carrier.

acarrear v. to cart, transport; to bring about (*harm, disaster*).

acarreo m. cartage, carriage, transport, haul.

acaso adv. perhaps; by chance; **por si —** just in case; m. chance, accident.

acatamiento m. homage, reverence, respect.

acatar v. to revere, respect; to pay homage to; *Mex., C.A., Ven.* to realize; *Mex., C.A., Ven.* to notice, pay attention.

acatarrar v. to chill; *Mex., Ven.* to bother, annoy; **-se** to get chilled, catch cold; *Riopl.* to get tipsy.

acaudillar v. to lead, command.

acceso m. access; entrance, admittance; attack; fit (*of madness, anger, etc.*).

accesorio adj. & m. accessory.

accidentado *adj.* seized with a fit; in a swoon; rough, uneven (*ground*).

accidental *adj.* accidental, casual.

accidentarse *v.* to have a seizure or fit; to swoon, faint.

accidente *m.* accident, mishap; chance; sudden fit, swoon.

acción *f.* (*física*) action; act; gesture; (*militar*) battle; (*de bolsa*) share of stock; — **de gracias** thanksgiving.

accionar *v.* to gesticulate, make gestures; *Am.* to act, be active.

accionista *m. & f.* shareholder, stockholder.

acecinar *v.* to dry-cure; to salt down.

acechanza *f.* snare; ambush.

acechar *v.* to lurk; to spy.

acecho *m.* ambush; spying; **al** (*or* **en**) — waiting in ambush, lying in wait.

acedo *adj.* rancid; acid; sour; harsh, disagreeable.

aceitar *v.* to oil, grease.

aceite *m.* oil; — **alcanforado** camphorated oil; — **de hígado de bacalao** cod-liver oil; — **de oliva** olive oil; — **de ricino** castor oil.

aceitera *f.* oil can; oil cruet (*bottle for the table*).

aceitoso *adj.* oily.

aceituna *f.* olive; **aceitunado** *adj.* olive green.

aceituno *m.* olive tree.

aceleración *f.* acceleration.

acelerador *m.* accelerator.

acelerar *v.* to accelerate, speed up; to quicken; to hurry, hasten.

acémila *f.* pack mule.

acendrado *adj.* pure, without blemish; purified.

acendrar *v.* to refine (*metals*); to purify, cleanse.

acento *m.* accent; emphasis.

acentuar[18] *v.* to accentuate, emphasize; to accent; **-se** to become worse (*as an illness*).

acepción *f.* acceptation, usual meaning.

acepillar *v.* to brush; to plane.

aceptación *f.* acceptance; approval.

aceptar *v.* to accept; to approve; to admit.

acequia *f.* irrigation canal or ditch; *Peru, Ch.* small stream; *Ven., Mex., Andes* sewer.

acera *f.* sidewalk.

acerado *adj.* steely, made of steel; steel-like; sharp.

acerar *v.* to steel.

acerbo *adj.* bitter; harsh, cruel.

acerca de *prep.* about, concerning.

acercamiento *m.* approach; approaching; rapprochement (*coming together*).

acercar[6] *v.* to bring near, draw up; **-se** to get near, approach.

acero *m.* steel.

acérrimo *adj.* very sour, very tart; very harsh; very strong, stanch, stalwart, steadfast.

acertado *adj.* accurate; right; sure.

acertar[1] *v. irr.* to hit (*the mark*); to hit upon; find by chance; to guess right; — **a** (+ *inf.*) to happen to.

acertijo *m.* riddle.

aciago *adj.* ill-fated, unlucky.

acicalado *p.p. & adj.* polished; dressed up; adorned; trim, neat.

acicalar *v.* to polish; to adorn; **-se** to dress up, doll up.

acicate *m.* spur; incentive.

acidez *f.* acidity, sourness.

ácido *m.* acid; *adj.* acid, sour.

acierto *m.* right guess; lucky hit; good aim; good judgment; **con** — effectively, successfully.

aclamación *f.* acclamation, applause.

aclamar *v.* to acclaim, cheer, hail, applaud.

aclaración *f.* explanation.

aclarar *v.* to clarify, explain; to clear up; to rinse; to dawn.

aclimatar *v.* to acclimatize, accustom to a climate or new environment.

acobardar *v.* to frighten, intimidate.

acogedor *adj.* friendly; hospitable.

acoger[11] *v.* to receive; to give shelter; **-se** to take refuge.

acogida *f.* reception, welcome; refuge.

acogimiento *m.* reception, welcome.

acojinar *v.* to cushion; to quilt.

acolchar *v.* to quilt.

acólito *m.* acolyte, altar boy.

acometer *v.* to attack; to undertake.

acometida *f.* **acometimiento** *m.* attack, assault.

acomodadizo *adj.* obliging; accommodating.

acomodado *adj.* well-off, wealthy; suitable, convenient; *p.p. of* **acomodar.**

acomodador *m.* usher (*in a theater*).

acomodar *v.* (*cosa*) to arrange, adjust; (*a una persona*) to lodge; to give employment to; **-se** to make oneself comfortable; to adapt oneself.

acomodo *m.* occupation, employment; arrangement.

acompañador *m.* companion; accompanist.

acompañamiento *m.* accompaniment; retinue, company.

acompañante *m.* companion; escort; attendant; accompanist.

acompañar *v.* to accompany; to escort; to be with; to enclose (*in a letter*).

acompasado *adj.* rhythmical; measured; slow, deliberate.

acondicionado *adj.* conditioned; comfortable; air-conditioned; *Am.* adequate, suitable.

acondicionar *v.* to condition; to prepare; to arrange; **-se** to become conditioned or prepared.

acongojar *v.* to grieve; **-se** to grieve; to be distressed.

aconsejar *v.* to advise, counsel.

acontecer[13] *v. irr.* to happen, occur.

acontecimiento *m.* event, happening.

acopiar *v.* to gather, accumulate, store up.

acopio *m.* storing; accumulation; stock, store, supply.

acoplamiento *m.* coupling; joint, connection.

acoplar v. to couple, connect; to fit or join together; to yoke; to pair, mate.

acorazado m. armored ship, battleship.

acorazar⁹ v. to armor.

acordar v. irr. (estar conforme) to arrange, to decide; (instrumento) to tune, put in harmony (stringed instrument) Peru, Ch., Riopl., Mex., Cuba to grant; **-se** to remember.

acorde adj. in harmony; in tune; m. chord.

acordelar v. to measure with a cord; to rope off, put a cord around.

acordeón m. accordion.

acordonar v. to tie with a cord, string, or rope; to rope off, tie a rope around (a place); to mill (a coin).

acornear v. to gore, wound with a horn; to butt.

acorralar v. to corral; to surround.

acortamiento m. shortening.

acortar v. to shorten, diminish; **-se** to shrink; to be shy, bashful.

acosar v. to pursue, harass.

acostado adj. reclining, lying down, in bed; tilted.

acostar² v. irr. to put to bed; to lay down; **-se** to lie down, go to bed; to tilt.

acostumbrado adj. accustomed, used, usual, habitual.

acostumbrar v. to accustom, train; to be used to, be accustomed to; **-se** to get accustomed.

acotación f. marginal note; stage directions (for a play); boundary mark; mark on a map showing altitude.

acotar v. to mark off (with boundary marks); to make marginal notes or citations; to put the elevation marks on (maps).

acre adj. sour, tart, sharp; rude, harsh; m. acre.

acrecentamiento m. growth, increase.

acrecentar¹ v. irr. to increase; to advance, promote.

acreditar v. to credit; to bring fame or credit to; to accredit, authorize; **-se** to win credit or fame.

acreedor adj. worthy, deserving; m. creditor.

acribillar v. to riddle; to perforate; to pierce.

acriollar v. to make Spanish American; **-se** to become Spanish American like; to take on Spanish-American customs.

acróbata m. & f. acrobat.

acta f. minutes (of a meeting); document; **levantar —** to write the minutes.

actitud f. attitude; posture, pose.

activar v. to activate, make active; to speed up, hasten.

actividad f. activity, energy.

activista m. & f. activist.

activo adj. active, lively; m. assets.

acto m. act; action, deed; ceremony; **— continuo** (or **seguido**) immediately after; **en el —** immediately.

actor m. actor; **actriz** f. actress.

actuación f. action; intervention, participation, performance; **-es** legal proceedings.

actual adj. present (time); of the present month; **-mente** adv. at present, nowadays.

actualidad f. present time; **-es** latest news, fashions, or events; **de —** current, up-to-date.

actuar¹⁸ v. to act, perform a function or act; to set in motion, cause to act.

acuarela f. water color.

acuario m. aquarium.

acuartelar v. to quarter (troops).

acuático adj. aquatic; **deportes -s** water sports.

acuchillar v. to knife; to stab; to slash.

acudir v. to go or come (to aid, or in response to a call); to attend, be present; to resort or turn to for help.

acueducto m. aqueduct, water channel or pipe.

acuerdo m. agreement; decision, resolution; opinion; remembrance; **estar de —** to be in agreement; **ponerse de —** to come to an agreement; **tomar un —** to take a decision.

acullá adv. yonder, over there.

acumulación f. accumulation.

acumulador m. storage battery.

acumular v. to accumulate, gather, pile up.

acuñación f. coinage, minting; wedging.

acuñar v. to mint, coin; to wedge.

acuoso adj. watery.

acurrucarse⁶ v. to cuddle, nestle; to huddle.

acusación f. accusation, charge.

acusado p.p. & adj. accused; m. defendant.

acusar v. to accuse, denounce; to acknowledge (receipt).

acuse m. acknowledgment (of receipt).

acústica f. acoustics (science of sound).

achacar⁶ v. to impute, attribute.

achacoso adj. sickly.

achaparrado adj. shrub, of shrub size; squat, squatty.

achaque m. slight chronic illness; excuse; pretext; infirmity.

achicar⁶ v. to shorten; to make small; to bail (water); to humiliate; Col. to kill; Riopl. to tie, fasten; **-se** to get smaller; to shrink.

adagio m. adage, proverb, wise saying; adagio (musical Spanish America).

adaptar v. to adapt, fit, adjust.

adecuado adj. adequate, fit, suitable.

adecuar v. to fit, adapt.

adefesio m. absurdity, nonsense; ridiculous sight, dress, or person.

adelantado p.p. & adj. anticipated; advanced; ahead; forward, bold; **por —** in advance; m. governor of a province (in colonial Spanish America).

adelantamiento m. advancement, progress, betterment.

adelantar v. to advance; to move forward; to progress; to better; **-se** to get ahead.

adelante adv. forward, ahead; **en —** from now on.

adelanto *m.* advance; advancement; progress; betterment.

adelgazar² *v.* to thin out, taper; **-se** to get thin, slender.

ademán *m.* gesture, gesticulation; attitude.

además *adv.* moreover, besides; **— de** *prep.* in addition to, besides.

adentro *adv.* within, inside; **tierra —** inland; **mar —** out to sea; **hablar para sus -s** to talk to oneself.

aderezamiento *m.* dressing; adornment, decoration.

aderezar *v.* (*embellecer*) to fix up, adorn, beautify, garnish; (*condimentar*) to season, prepare; (*almidonar*) to starch, stiffen.

aderezo *m.* (*adorno*) adornment, garnish, trappings, finery, set of jewels; (*alimento*) seasoning; (*almidón*) starch, stiffener, filler (*used in cloth*).

adestrado *adj.* trained, skilled.

adestrar¹ *v. irr.* to train; to guide.

adeudado *adj.* indebted; in debt; *p.p.* of **adeudar**.

adeudar *v.* to owe; to debit, charge; **-se** to run into debt.

adeudo *m.* debt, indebtedness; duty (*on imports*); debit, charge.

adherencia *f.* adherence; attachment.

adherir³ *v. irr.* to adhere, stick.

adhesión *f.* adhesion; attachment.

adicto *adj.* addicted; devoted; *m.* addict; follower.

adiestrado = **adestrado**.

adiestramiento *m.* training; drill.

adiestrar = **adestrar**.

adinerado *adj.* wealthy.

¡adiós! *interj.* good-bye!; farewell!; hello!; *Am.* you don't say!

aditamento *m.* addition; annex.

adivinación *f.* divination, prediction; guess.

adivinanza *f.* conundrum, riddle.

adivinar *v.* to guess.

adivino *m.* fortuneteller; soothsayer.

adjetivo *m. & adj.* adjective.

adjudicar⁶ *v.* to adjudge, award, assign; **-se** to appropriate.

adjuntar *v.* to put with; to bring together; to enclose (*in a letter*).

adjunto *adj.* adjoining; attached, enclosed.

adminículo *m.* accessory; gadget.

administración *f.* administration, management; headquarters; *Ven., Mex., Cuba* extreme unction, last sacrament.

administrador *m.* administrator, manager.

administrar *v.* to administer; to manage; **-se** *Ven., Mex., Cuba* to receive the extreme unction or last sacrament.

administrativo *adj.* administrative.

admirable *adj.* admirable, wonderful.

admiración *f.* admiration, wonder; **punto de —** exclamation point.

admirador *m.* admirer.

admirar *v.* to admire; **-se** to be astonished or amazed; to wonder.

admisible *adj.* admissible, allowable.

admisión *f.* admission; acceptance; acknowledgment.

admitir *v.* to admit; to let in; to accept; to allow, permit.

adobar *v.* to fix, cook, prepare (*food*); to tan (*hides*); to pickle (*meats, fish*).

adobe *m.* adobe, sun-dried mud brick.

adobo *m.* mending; sauce for seasoning or pickling; mixture for dressing skins or cloth; rouge.

adoctrinamiento *m.* indoctrination, teaching, instruction.

adoctrinar *v.* to indoctrinate, teach, instruct.

adolecer¹³ *v. irr.* to suffer (*from an illness, defect, etc.*).

adolescencia *f.* adolescence.

adolescente *adj.* adolescent.

adonde *rel. adv.* where; **¿adónde?** *interr. adv.* where to?; where?

adoptar *v.* to adopt; to accept (*an opinion*).

adoptivo *adj.* adoptive, related by adoption; adopted.

adoración *f.* adoration, worship.

adorar *v.* to adore, worship.

adormecer¹³ *v. irr.* to make sleepy or drowsy; to lull; **-se** to get sleepy; to get numb; to fall asleep.

adormilado *adj.* drowsy.

adornar *v.* to adorn, decorate, ornament.

adorno *m.* adornment, ornament, decoration.

adquirir³⁵ *v. irr.* to acquire, gain, win, obtain.

adquisición *f.* acquisition; attainment.

adrede *adv.* on purpose, intentionally.

aduana *f.* customhouse.

aduanero *m.* customhouse officer; *adj.* customhouse.

aduar *m.* gypsy camp; *Ríopl.* Indian camp or ranch.

aducir²⁵ *v. irr.* to cite, allege, offer as proof.

adueñarse *v.* to take possession.

adulación *f.* flattery.

adulador *m.* flatterer.

adular *v.* to flatter.

adulterar *v.* to adulterate, corrupt, make impure.

adulterio *m.* adultery.

adúltero *m.* adulterer.

adulto *m. & adj.* adult.

adusto *adj.* stern, severe, austere.

advenedizo *m.* newcomer, stranger; upstart; *Mex., Carib., Andes* novice, beginner; *adj.* newly arrived; upstart; *Mex., Carib., Andes* inexperienced.

advenimiento *m.* advent, arrival, coming.

adverbio *m.* adverb.

adversario *m.* adversary, opponent; foe.

adversidad *f.* adversity; calamity.

adverso *adj.* adverse; contrary; unfavorable.

advertencia *f.* notice; warning; advice.

advertir³ *v. irr.* to notice; to warn; to advise.

adyacente *adj.* adjacent.

aéreo *adj.* aerial; airy; **correo — air mail.**

aerodinámico *adj.* aerodynamic; *f.* aerodynamics.

aeródromo *m.* airport.

aerofluyente *adj.* streamlined.

aeronave *f.* airship.

aeropista *f.* landing strip; runway.

aeroplano *m.* airplane.

aeropuerto *m.* airport.

afabilidad *f.* friendliness, pleasantness, courtesy; **afable** *adj.* affable, pleasant, courteous.

afamado *adj.* famous.

afán *m.* eagerness, anxiety, ardor.

afanar *v.* to urge, press; **-se** to hurry; to worry; to work eagerly; to toil.

afanoso *adj.* laborious; hardworking.

afasia *f.* aphasia.

afear *v.* to make ugly; to disfigure; to blame, censure, condemn.

afección *f.* affection, fondness; disease.

afectado *p.p.* & *adj.* affected; *Am.* hurt, harmed; *Am.* **estar — del corazón** to have heart trouble.

afectar *v.* (*promover*) to affect, move; (*fingir*) to pretend to have or feel; *Am.* to hurt, to harm, to injure.

afecto *m.* affection; *adj.* fond; **— a** fond of; given to; prone to.

afectuoso *adj.* affectionate, tender.

afeitada *f. Am.* shave, shaving.

afeitar *v.* to shave; **-se** to shave oneself; to put on make-up.

afeite *m.* make-up, cosmetics.

afeminado *adj.* effeminate.

aferrado *adj.* stubborn, obstinate; *p.p.* of **aferrar.**

aferramiento *m.* grasping, seizing; attachment; stubbornness; tenacity.

aferrar *v.* to seize, grasp, grapple; **-se** to take or seize hold of; to cling; **-se a una opinión** to cling to an opinion.

afianzar[8] *v.* to fasten, secure; to steady; to give bail or bond.

afición *f.* taste, inclination; fondness, affection.

aficionado *adj.* fond; *m.* amateur, fan.

aficionar *v.* to inspire a liking or fondness; **-se a** to become fond of.

afiche *m. Riopl.,* poster.

afilador *m.* grinder, sharpener.

afilar *v.* to sharpen; to grind; *Am.* to make love to, woo; *Am.* to flatter; *Am.* **— con** to flirt with.

afín *adj.* kindred, related; **ideas afines** related ideas.

afinador *m.* piano tuner.

afinar *v.* to refine, polish; to tune.

afinidad *f.* affinity; similarity; relationship.

afirmación *f.* affirmation, assertion.

afirmar *v.* to affirm, assert; to make firm; *Am.* **— un golpe** to deal a blow.

afirmativa *f.* affirmative.

afirmativo *adj.* affirmative.

aflicción *f.* affliction, trouble, pain, grief.

afligir[11] *v.* to afflict, trouble, grieve;

Riopl., Ven. to mistreat, harm, beat, strike; **-se** to worry, grieve.

aflojar *v.* to slacken; to loosen, unfasten; to let go; *Mex., Riopl., Carib.* to let go of money, spend easily; *Mex., Riopl., Carib.* **— un golpe** to give a blow.

afluente *m.* tributary; *adj.* abundant.

afluir[32] *v. irr.* to flow (into).

afortunado *adj.* fortunate; lucky.

afrenta *f.* affront, offense, insult.

afrentar *v.* to insult, offend, dishonor.

afrentoso *adj.* outrageous, shameful, disgraceful.

africano *adj.* & *m.* African.

afrontar *v.* to face; to confront.

afuera *adv.* out, outside; **-s** *f. pl.* outskirts.

agachar *v.* to lower; to bend down; **-se** to stoop, bend down, duck; to crouch; *Am.* to give in, yield; *Col.* **-se con algo** to make away with or steal something.

agalla *f.* gill; tonsil; *Col., Ven.* greed; **tener -s** to have guts, have courage; *Riopl., Ch., Carib.* to be unscrupulous and bold in business deals; *Riopl., Ch., Carib.* to be greedy or stingy; *C.A.* to be smart, astute, cunning.

agarrar *v.* to seize, grasp, grab; **-se** to cling, hold on.

agarro *m.* clench, clutch, grasp, grip, grab; **agarrón** *m.* tight clench, sudden grasp, grab; *Mex., Col., Ven., C.A.* pull, tug.

agasajar *v.* to entertain; to flatter.

agasajo *m.* entertainment, kind reception; friendliness; flattery.

agazapar *v.* to nab, seize (*a person*); **-se** to crouch; to squat.

agencia *f.* agency; *Ch.* pawnshop.

agenciar *v.* to negotiate; to procure by negotiation; to promote.

agente *m.* agent; *Am.* officer, official.

ágil *adj.* agile, nimble, limber.

agilidad *f.* agility, nimbleness.

agitación *f.* agitation; excitement.

agitador *m.* agitator; *adj.* agitating; stirring.

agitar *v.* to agitate, excite; to stir; to wave; to shake.

aglomeración *f.* conglomeration, heap, pile, mass.

aglomerar *v.* to mass together; to cluster; **-se** to crowd together, pile up.

agobiar *v.* to oppress, weigh down; to overwhelm.

agolparse *v.* to crowd together, jam.

agonía *f.* agony.

agonizante *adj.* dying; *m.* dying person.

agonizar[9] *v.* to be dying.

agorero *adj.* ominous, of bad omen; prophetic; *m.* augur, prophet, fortune-teller.

agostar *v.* to parch, dry up; to pasture; to plow (*in August*).

agosto *m.* August; harvest; **hacer su — to** make hay while the sun shines.

agotado *adj.* & *p.p.* exhausted; out-of-print.

agotamiento *m.* exhaustion; draining.

agotar v. to exhaust, use up; to drain off; **-se** (*acabarse*) to be exhausted, used up; (*terminarse la edición*) to go out of print.

agraciado adj. graceful; m. winner (*of a favor, prize, etc.*).

agraciar v. to grace; to adorn.

agradable adj. agreeable, pleasant.

agradar v. to please, be agreeable (to).

agradecer[13] v. irr. to thank for; to be grateful for.

agradecido adj. thankful, grateful.

agradecimiento m. gratitude, thankfulness.

agrado m. agreeableness; liking, pleasure; **de su —** to his liking.

agrandar v. to enlarge; to aggrandize, make greater.

agravar v. to aggravate, make worse; to make heavier; to oppress; **-se** to get worse.

agraviar v. to offend, insult, affront.

agravio m. offense, insult, affront.

agredir[51] v. to assail, assault, attack.

agregado m. attaché, person attached to a staff; aggregate, collection.

agregar[7] v. to add; to join; to attach.

agresivo adj. aggressive, offensive.

agresor m. agressor; assailant.

agreste adj. rustic; wild (*fruit, flower, etc.*).

agriar[17] v. to sour, make sour; **-se** to sour, turn sour, become sour.

agrícola adj. agricultural.

agricultor m. agriculturist, farmer.

agricultura f. agriculture.

agridulce adj. bittersweet, tart.

agrietarse v. to crack; to chap (*said of the skin*).

agrimensura f. survey, surveying (*of land*).

agrio adj. sour; disagreeable.

agropecuario adj. farming (*crops and cattle*).

agrupación f. group; bunch; grouping; gathering.

agrupar v. to group, bunch up.

agrura f. sourness.

agua f. water; rain; **— abajo** downstream; **— arriba** upstream; **aguas inmundas** f. sewage.

aguacate m. Am. avocado, alligator pear; Am. avocado tree; Am. phlegmatic person.

aguacero m. shower.

aguada f. watering place; supply of drinking water; flood in a mine; wall wash; water color.

aguadero m. watering place.

aguado adj. watery; watered; Am. soft, unstarched; Am. weak, limp; Andes insipid, uninteresting, dull; **sopa aguada** thin soup; p.p. of **aguar.**

aguaitar v. Col., Ven., Andes, Ch. to spy; to watch; to wait for.

aguantar v. to endure, bear; to resist; **-se** to be silent, restrain oneself.

aguante m. endurance, fortitude, resistance.

aguar[9] v. to water, dilute with water; to spoil (*pleasure*); Riopl., Ven., C.A.

to water (*livestock*); **-se** to become diluted; to get watery; to fill up with water; **se aguó la fiesta** the party was spoiled.

aguardar v. to wait; to wait for.

aguardentoso adj. alcoholic; hoarse, raucous.

aguardiente m. brandy, hard liquor; **— de caña** rum.

aguarrás m. turpentine, oil of turpentine.

aguazal m. marsh, swamp.

agudeza f. sharpness; keenness; wit; witty remark or saying.

agudo adj. sharp; sharp-pointed; keen, witty; acute; shrill.

agüero m. augury, prediction; sign, omen; Riopl., Mex., Carib. fortune-teller.

aguijar v. (*picar*) to prick, goad, spur; (*animar*) to encourage, excite.

aguijón m. prick; sting; spur, goad.

aguijonear v. to goad; to prick.

águila f. eagle; **es un —** he is a shark.

aguileño adj. aquiline; eaglelike.

aguinaldo m. Christmas or New Year's gift; bonus.

aguja f. needle; crochet hook; watch hand; church spire; railroad switch.

agujerear v. to pierce, perforate; to riddle.

agujero m. hole; needle peddler; needle box; pincushion.

aguzar[9] v. to sharpen; to goad, stimulate; **— las orejas** to prick up one's ears.

ahí adv. there; **por —** over there.

ahijado m. godchild.

ahinco m. effort, eagerness, zeal.

ahogar[7] v. to drown; to choke, strangle; to smother; to quench, extinguish.

ahogo m. suffocation; breathlessness; anguish, grief.

ahondar v. to deepen; to dig; to penetrate, go deep into.

ahora adv. now; **— mismo** right now; **por —** for the present; **— que** Am. as soon as; **ahorita** instantly, this very minute; **ahoritica, ahoritita** Am. this very second, in a jiffy.

ahorcar[6] v. to hang, kill by hanging.

ahorrar v. to save; to spare; to avoid.

ahorro m. saving, economy; **caja de -s** savings bank.

ahuecar[6] v. to make hollow; to hollow out; **— la voz** to speak in a hollow voice; Am. **¡ahueca!** get out of here!; **-se** to become puffed up, get conceited.

ahuehuete m. Am. a Mexican cypress.

ahumado adj. smoked; smoky.

ahumar v. to smoke; to fume.

ahuyentar v. to drive away; to scare away;**-se** to go away, flee; Ven., Carib., Mex. to stop frequenting a place.

aindiado adj. Indian-like.

airar v. to annoy, irritate; **-se** to get angry.

aire m. air; wind; tune; appearance; conceit; **-cito** m. breeze; a little tune; a certain air or appearance.

airear v. to air, ventilate.

airoso adj. windy; airy; graceful, elegant; lively, spirited.

aislador m. insulator; isolator; adj. insulating; isolating.

aislamiento m. isolation; insulation.

aislar v. to isolate, place apart; to insulate.

ajar v. to crumple, wither.

ajedrez m. chess.

ajeno adj. (de otro) another's; (inconciente) unaware; (extranjero) alien; **— a mi voluntad** beyond my control; **— de cuidados** free from cares.

ajetrearse v. to hustle and bustle; to get tired out.

ajetreo m. bustle, hustle; hubbub; fuss; fatigue.

ají m. S.A., Carib. chili pepper, chili sauce.

ajo m. garlic; garlic clove; garlic sauce; swear word.

ajuar m. furniture set; trousseau, bride's outfit; bride's portion or dowry.

ajustado adj. tight, fitting tight; agreed upon (as a price); **— a la ley** in accordance with the law; p.p. of ajustar.

ajustamiento m. adjustment.

ajustar v. to adjust; to fit tight; to regulate; to tighten; to settle (accounts); to hire (a person); Col. to stint, scrimp, save; C.A. **— una bofetada** to give a good slap; C.A., Mex. **hoy ajusta quince años** he is just fifteen years old today; **-se** to come to an agreement.

ajuste m. adjustment, fit; agreement; settlement (of accounts).

ajusticiar v. to execute, put to death.

al = a + el to the.

ala f. wing; hat brim.

alabanza f. praise.

alabar v. to praise.

alacena f. cupboard; closet; Am. booth, stall, market stand.

alacrán m. scorpion.

alado adj. winged.

alambicado p.p. & adj. distilled; over-refined, over-subtle (applied to style).

alambique m. still.

alambrada f. wire entanglement.

alambrado m. wire fence; wire screening; wiring.

alambre m. wire.

alameda f. poplar grove; park.

álamo m. poplar.

alancear v. to lance, spear.

alano m. mastiff.

alarde m. boast, bluff, brag.

alardear v. to boast, brag.

alargar[7] v. to lengthen; to prolong; to stretch out, extend.

alarido m. shout, scream, howl.

alarma f. alarm.

alarmar v. to alarm.

alazán adj. chestnut-colored; sorrel.

alba f. dawn; alb (white robe worn by priest).

albacea m. executor.

albañal m. sewer.

albañil m. mason, brickmason; **albañilería** f. masonry.

albaricoque m. apricot; **albaricoquero** m. apricot tree.

albayalde m. white lead.

albazo m. Mex. early morning serenade; Mex. bad surprise, surprise attack at dawn.

albear v. to show white (in the distance); Am. to rise at dawn.

albedrío m. free will.

albéitar m. veterinary.

alberca f. water reservoir, tank; pool.

albergar[7] v. to house, shelter, lodge; **-se** to take shelter; to lodge.

albo adj. white; Am. white-footed (horse).

albóndiga f. meat ball; fish ball.

albor f. dawn; whiteness.

alborada f. dawn; reveille (morning bugle call).

alborear v. to dawn.

alborotador m. agitator, troublemaker.

alborotar v. to disturb, upset; Am. to excite, arouse enthusiasm; **-se** to get upset; to mutiny; to riot; Am. to get excited; Am. to rear, balk (said of a horse).

alboroto m. uproar, disturbance; riot; Am. excitement, enthusiasm; Col., C.A. popcorn, candied popcorn ball.

alborozado adj. elated, excited.

alborozar[9] v. to gladden; **-se** to rejoice.

alborozo m. joy, delight.

albricias f. pl. good news; reward (for good news).

alcachofa f. artichoke; Ch. sock, blow.

alcahuete m. procurer, pander; go-between; **alcahueta** f. bawd, procuress, go-between.

alcaide m. warden (of a fortress, prison, etc.).

alcalde m. mayor; justice of the peace; **— mayor** mayor.

alcance m. (extensión) reach, scope; (capacidad) talent, capacity; (noticias) last minute news, newspaper extra; **cortos -s** meagre intellect; **dar — a** to catch up with.

alcancía f. money box (with slit for coin); savings bank.

alcanfor m. camphor.

alcantarillado m. sewage system.

alcanzado adj. needy; broke, short of funds.

alcanzar[9] v. to reach; to overtake; to obtain; to befall; to be enough; Am. to hand, pass, put within reach.

alcayata f. wall hook; meat hook.

alcázar m. castle, fortress.

alcoba f. alcove, bedroom.

alcohol m. alcohol; **alcohólico** adj. alcoholic.

alcor m. hill.

alcornoque m. cork tree; cork wood; blockhead, dunce.

alcuza f. oil can; cruet, oil bottle.

aldaba f. knocker (of a door); crossbar, bolt, latch; handle (of a door, chest, *etc.*); **tener buenas -s** to have "pull", influential connections.

aldabón *m.* large iron knocker; large handle; **aldabonazo** *m.* knock, knocking.

aldea *f.* village; **aldehuela** *f.* little village, hamlet.

aldeano *adj.* rustic, countrified; *m.* villager; peasant.

aleación *f.* alloy; alloying.

alear *v.* to alloy, mix (*metals*); to flutter; to flap (*wings, arms, etc.*).

aleccionar *v.* to coach; to teach, instruct; to train; to drill.

aledaños *m. pl.* borders, frontiers.

alegar[7] *v.* to allege, assert; *Am.* to argue, dispute.

alegato *m.* allegation; assertion.

alegrar *v.* to cheer up, gladden; to brighten; **-se** to be glad, rejoice; to get tipsy.

alegre *adj.* merry, gay, joyful, cheerful, bright; tipsy.

alegría *f.* joy, mirth, gaiety, merriment.

alejamiento *m.* withdrawal; retirement, aloofness.

alejar *v.* to remove, move away from; **-se** to move away; to withdraw, be aloof.

alelado *adj.* stupefied, open-mouthed; silly.

alemán *adj. & m.* German.

alentar[1] *v. irr.* to breathe; to encourage, cheer, cheer up; **-se** to take heart; *Am.* to recover (*from illness*).

alergia *f.* allergy.

alero *m.* eaves; projecting edge.

alerón *m.* aileron; flap.

alerto *adj.* alert, watchful; **¡alerta!** attention! look out!; **estar alerta** to be on the alert.

aleta *f.* small wing; flap; fin (*of a fish*).

aletargado *adj.* drowsy, sluggish.

aletargarse[7] *v.* to fall into a state of lethargy; to become drowsy.

aletazo *m.* flap, blow with a wing.

aletear *v.* to flap, flutter.

aleteo *m.* flapping, flutter (*of wings*).

aleve *adj.* treacherous.

alevosía *f.* treachery.

alevoso *adj.* treacherous.

alfabeto *m.* alphabet.

alfalfa *f.* alfalfa; **alfalfar** *m.* alfalfa field.

alfarería *f.* pottery; **alfarero** *m.* potter.

alfeñicar[6] *v.* to frost with sugar (*a cake, cookie, etc.*); **-se** to get frail, delicate; to act affectedly.

alfeñique *m.* sugar paste; delicate person.

alférez *m.* ensign; second lieutenant.

alfil *m.* bishop (*in chess*).

alfiler *m.* pin; brooch; **-es** pin money; **ponerse de veinticinco -es** to doll up, dress up.

alfombra *f.* carpet; **alfombrilla** *f.* (*para el suelo*) carpet, rug; (*enfermedad*) measles; *Mex.* plant of the vervain family; *Carib.* black smallpox; *Carib.* skin eruption.

alforja *f.* saddlebag; knapsack; food provisions for a trip; *Am.* **pasarse a la otra —** to take undue liberties.

alforza *f.* tuck, fold, pleat; scar.

algarabía *f.* jargon; chatter; uproar.

algarrobo *m.* locust tree; carob tree.

algazara *f.* clamor; shouting; uproar.

álgebra *f.* algebra.

algo *pron.* something; *adv.* somewhat.

algodón *m.* cotton; **algodonal** *m.* cotton plantation.

alguacil *m.* policeman, constable.

alguien *pron.* somebody, someone.

algún(o) *adj.* some; any; *pron.* someone.

alhaja *f.* jewel.

alharaca *f.* rumpus, clamor, racket.

aliado *adj.* allied; *m.* ally.

alianza *f.* alliance, union; *Andes* wedding ring; *Am.* mixture of liquors.

aliar[17] *v.* to ally; to unite; **-se** to form an alliance; to unite.

alicaído *adj.* crestfallen, downcast, discouraged; drooping.

alicates *m. pl.* pliers, small pincers.

aliciente *m.* inducement, incentive, attraction.

alienista *m.* alienist (*doctor who treats mental diseases*).

aliento *m.* (*de los pulmones*) breath; (*ánimo*) encouragement.

aligerar *v.* to lighten; to hasten.

alimentación *f.* nourishment, food, nutrition; feeding.

alimentar *v.* to feed, nourish.

alimenticio *adj.* nutritious, nourishing.

alimento *m.* food.

alinear *v.* to line up, put into line; to range; **-se** to fall in line, form into a line.

aliño *m.* ornament, decoration; neatness; condiment, dressing, seasoning.

alisar *v.* to smooth; to polish; to plane.

alistamiento *m.* enlistment; enrollment.

alistar *v.* to enlist; to enroll; to make ready; **-se** to enlist; to get ready; *Am.* to dress up.

aliviar *v.* to lighten; to alleviate, relieve, remedy, soothe; **-se** to get better, recover.

alivio *m.* relief, remedy; aid, help; improvement.

aljibe *m.* cistern, reservoir, tank; water tanker; *Ríopl.* well, artesian well, spring.

alma *f.* soul, spirit; inhabitant.

almacén *m.* warehouse; department store; store.

almacenaje *m.* storage.

almacenar *v.* to store, store up; to put in storage.

almacenista *m. & f.* department store owner; warehouse owner or manager; wholesale merchant.

almanaque *m.* almanac, calendar.

almeja *f.* clam.

almendra *f.* almond; **almendrado** *m.* almond paste; **almendro** *m.* almond tree.

almíbar *m.* syrup.

almidón *m.* starch; *Col., Ven.* paste (*for gluing*).

almidonar v. to starch.

alminar m. turret.

almirante m. admiral.

almirez m. metal mortar.

almohada f. pillow; **almohadón** m. large cushion or pillow.

almohaza f. currycomb (for grooming horses).

almoneda f. auction.

almorzar[2,9] v. irr. to lunch, eat lunch.

almuerzo m. lunch.

alojamiento m. lodging.

alojar v. to lodge; to house; to quarter (troops); **-se** to lodge, room.

alondra f. lark.

alpaca f. alpaca (sheeplike animal of South America); alpaca wool; alpaca cloth.

alpargata f. sandal (usually of canvas and with hemp sole).

alquería f. farmhouse.

alquilar v. to rent; to hire; **-se** to hire out.

alquiler m. rent, rental; **de —** for rent, for hire.

alquitrán m. tar.

alrededor adv. about, around; **— de** prep. around; **-es** m. pl. environs, outskirts.

altanería f. haughtiness.

altanero adj. haughty, proud.

altar m. altar; **— mayor** high altar.

altavoz m. loud-speaker.

alteración f. alteration, change; disturbance.

alterar v. to alter, change; to disturb.

altercar[6] v. to argue, dispute; to quarrel.

alternar v. to alternate; to take turns; **— con** to rub elbows with, be friendly with.

alternativa f. alternative, choice, option.

alternativo adj. alternating, alternative.

alterno adj. alternate.

alteza f. highness (title); lofty height.

altibajo m. downward thrust (in fencing); **-s** ups and downs; uneven ground.

altiplanicie f. upland; high plateau.

altiplano m. Am. high plateau.

altisonante adj. high-sounding.

altitud f. altitude.

altivez f. haughtiness, arrogance.

altivo adj. haughty, proud, arrogant.

alto adj. (tamaño) high; m. height; upper story (of a building); Am. heap, pile; **-s** Am. upper floors; v. **hacer —** to halt, stop; **pasar por —** to omit, overlook; **¡ — !** halt!

altoparlante m. loud-speaker.

altura f. height, altitude.

alud m. avalanche.

aludir v. to allude, refer indirectly.

alumbrado m. lighting; adj. lit, lighted; tipsy.

alumbramiento m. childbirth; lighting.

alumbrar v. to light, give light; to enlighten; to give birth; **-se** to get tipsy.

aluminio m. aluminum.

alumnado m. student body.

alumno m. student.

alusión f. allusion.

alza f. rise; lift (for shoes).

alzada f. height (of a horse).

alzamiento m. raising, lifting; uprising, insurrection.

alzar[9] v. to lift, raise; to cut (cards); **-se** to rebel, rise up in arms; Col., Ven., C.A., Mex., Andes to puff up with pride; **-se con algo** to run off with something, steal something.

allá adv. there, over there; **más —** farther.

allanar v. to level, even off; to invade, break into (a house); to raid; **— una dificultad** to smooth out a difficulty.

allegado adj. near; related; allied; m. relative; partisan, follower.

allegar[7] v. to accumulate, heap up, gather.

allende adv. on the other side; beyond; **— el mar** across the sea, overseas.

allí adv. there; **por —** through that place, around there.

ama f. mistress, owner; **— de leche** wet nurse; **— de llaves** housekeeper.

amabilidad f. kindness, courtesy.

amable adj. kind, amiable.

amador m. lover.

amaestrar v. to teach, coach, train.

amagar[7] v. to threaten; to feint, make a threatening motion; to strike at.

amago m. threat; indication.

amalgamar v. to amalgamate, combine, mix, blend.

amamantar v. to nurse, suckle.

amanecer[13] v. irr. to dawn; **— malo** to wake up ill; m. dawn, sunrise.

amanecida f. dawn, sunrise.

amansar v. to tame; to subdue; to pacify.

amante m. lover; **— de** fond of.

amañarse v. Ec., Col., Ven. to be accustomed; to acclimate oneself.

amapola f. poppy.

amar v. to love.

amargar[7] v. to embitter, make bitter.

amargo adj. bitter; m. bitters; Am. mate (Paraguayan tea) without sugar.

amargor m. bitterness.

amargura f. bitterness; grief.

amarillear v. to show or have a yellowish tinge; to turn yellow.

amarillento adj. yellowish.

amarillo adj. yellow.

amarra f. cable; rope; strap.

amarrar v. to tie, fasten, rope; to moor (a ship); Am. **amarrárselas** to get "tight," drunk.

amasar v. to knead, mix; to mash; Am. to amass, accumulate (a fortune).

amatista f. amethyst.

ambages m. pl. circumlocutions; **hablar sin —** to go straight to the point, speak plainly, not to beat about the bush.

ámbar m. amber; **ambarino** adj. amber; like amber.

ambición f. ambition; aspiration.

ambicionar *v.* to seek, aspire after; to covet.

ambicioso *adj.* ambitious, eager; greedy, grasping.

ambiente *m.* atmosphere, environment.

ambigüedad *f.* ambiguity.

ambiguo *adj.* ambiguous; uncertain, doubtful.

ámbito *m.* precinct, enclosure.

ambos *adj.* & *pron.* both.

ambulancia *f.* ambulance; field hospital.

ambulante *adj.* walking; itinerant; moving; wandering.

amedrentar *v.* to scare, frighten.

amenaza *f.* menace, threat.

amenazador, amenazante *adj.* threatening.

amenazar⁹ *v.* to menace, threaten.

amenguar⁸ *v.* to lessen, diminish; to defame, dishonor.

amenidad *f.* pleasantness.

amenizar⁹ *v.* to make pleasant, cheer, brighten.

ameno *adj.* pleasant, agreeable.

americana *f.* suit coat.

americano *adj.* & *m.* American.

ametrallador *m.* gunner; **ametralladora** *f.* machine gun.

amigable *adj.* friendly; affable, pleasant.

amígdala *f.* tonsil; **amigdalitis** *f.* tonsilitis.

amigo *m.* friend; — **de** fond of.

aminorar *v.* to lessen.

amistad *f.* friendship; friendliness.

amistoso *adj.* friendly.

amo *m.* master, owner, boss.

amodorrado *adj.* drowsy.

amodorrar *v.* to make drowsy; **-se** to become drowsy.

amolador *m.* grinder, sharpener; *adj.* grinding, sharpening.

amolar *v. irr.* to grind, hone, sharpen; to annoy; *Col., Mex., C.A.* to ruin, harm; **-se** *Mex., C.A., Col.* to go to rack and ruin.

amoldar *v.* to mold; to shape; to adjust; to adapt.

amonestación *f.* admonition, advice, warning; **-es** marriage bans (or banns).

amonestar *v.* to admonish, advise, warn.

amoníaco *m.* ammonia.

amontonamiento *m.* accumulation, pile, heap.

amontonar *v.* to heap up, pile up, crowd up.

amor *m.* love; — **propio** self-esteem.

amoratado *adj.* livid, bluish, purplish.

amordazar⁹ *v.* to gag; to muzzle.

amorío *m.* love affair; love-making.

amoroso *adj.* loving, tender, affectionate.

amortajar *v.* to shroud.

amortiguador *m.* shock absorber; silencer, muffler.

amortiguar⁸ *v.* to muffle; to deafen (*a sound*); to deaden (*a blow or sound*); to soften, tone down (*a color or sound*).

amortizar⁹ *v.* to pay on account; to liquidate, pay (*a debt*); to provide a sinking fund.

amoscarse⁶ *v.* to get peeved, annoyed; *Am.* to blush, be inhibited or embarrassed.

amostazar⁹ *v.* to anger, irritate; **-se** to get angry or irritated.

amotinar *v.* to incite to rebellion; **-se** to mutiny; to riot.

amparar *v.* to protect; to defend; *Am.* to grant mining rights; **-se** to seek protection or refuge; to protect oneself.

amparo *m.* protection; habeas corpus (*protection against imprisonment*); *Am.* mining rights.

ampliación *f.* enlargement, widening.

ampliar¹⁷ *v.* to enlarge, widen.

amplificador *m.* amplifier.

amplificar⁶ *v.* to amplify, expand, extend, enlarge; to magnify.

amplio *adj.* ample; wide, large, roomy.

amplitud *f.* breadth, extent, width.

ampolla *f.* (*condición*) blister, water bubble; (*vasija*) narrow-necked bottle or vase, cruet.

ampollar *v.* to blister; **-se** to blister.

ampuloso *adj.* inflated, wordy, bombastic, pompous.

amputar *v.* to amputate, cut off.

amueblar *v.* to furnish (*with furniture*).

ánade *m.* & *f.* duck; **anadeja** *f.* duckling.

anadear *v.* to waddle.

anales *m. pl.* annals, historical records.

analfabeto *adj.* & *m.* illiterate; **analfabetismo** *m.* illiteracy.

análisis *m.* analysis.

analizar⁹ *v.* to analyze, examine.

analogía *f.* analogy, similarity.

análogo *adj.* analogous, similar, comparable.

ananá, ananás *f.* pineapple. *See* piña.

anaquel *m.* shelf; bookshelf; **anaquelería** *f.* shelves, bookshelves, library stacks.

anaranjado *adj.* orange-colored; *m.* orange color.

anarquía *f.* anarchy.

anatomía *f.* anatomy.

anca *f.* haunch, hind quarter, rump; *Andes* popcorn.

ancianidad *f.* old age.

anciano *adj.* old, aged; *m.* old man.

ancla *f.* anchor.

anclar *v.* to anchor.

ancho *adj.* wide, broad; loose; roomy; *Col., Ven.* self-satisfied, conceited; **a sus anchas** at one's ease; comfortable; leisurely; *m.* width.

anchoa, anchova *f.* anchovy.

anchura *f.* width, breadth; comfort, ease.

anchuroso *adj.* vast, extensive; spacious.

andada *f. Mex., Ven.* walk, stroll; **-s** track, footprints; **volver a las -s** to fall back into one's old ways or habits.

andadura *f.* gait, pace.

andaluz *adj.* Andalusian, of or pertaining to Andalusia, Spain; *m.* Andalusian, native of Andalusia.

andamiada *f.*, **andamiaje** *m.* scaffolding; framework.

andamio *m.* scaffold, scaffolding.

andanada *f.* (*localidad*) grandstand; (*descarga*) broadside; **soltar una —** to discharge a broadside; to reprimand.

andante *adj.* walking; errant, wandering; moderately slow (*music*); **caballero — knight-errant.

andanzas *f. pl.* rambles, wanderings.

andar[21] *v. irr.* to walk; to go, go about; to run (*as a watch or machinery*); — **con cuidado** to be careful; **anda en quince años** he is about fifteen; **a todo —** at full (walking) speed; **a más —** walking briskly; **¡anda!** move on!; **¿qué andas haciendo?** what are you doing?; *Am.* — **andando** to be walking around; *Am.* **¡ándale!** hurry!

andariego *adj.* fond of walking; roving; *m.* walker.

andas *f. pl.* portable platform; litter.

andén *m.* railway station platform; *C.A., Col.. Ven.,* sidewalk.

andino *adj.* Andean, of or from the Andes.

andrajo *m.* rag.

andrajoso *adj.* ragged, in rags.

anécdota *f.* anecdote, story.

anegar[7] *v.* to drown; to flood.

anejo *adj.* annexed, attached.

anestésico *m. & adj.* anesthetic.

anexar *v.* to annex.

anexo *m.* annex; *adj.* annexed, joined.

anfiteatro *m.* amphitheater.

anfitrión *m.* generous host.

ángel *m.* angel.

angélico *adj.* angelic.

angina *f.* angina, inflammation of the throat; *Mex., Ven.* tonsil; **— del pecho** angina pectoris.

anglosajón *adj. & m.* Anglo-Saxon.

angostar *v.* to narrow; **-se** to narrow, become narrow; to contract.

angosto *adj.* narrow.

angostura *f.* narrowness; narrows (*narrow part of a river, valley, strait, etc.*).

anguila *f.* eel.

angular *adj.* angular; **piedra — corner-stone.

ángulo *m.* angle, corner.

anguloso *adj.* angular, sharp-cornered.

angustia *f.* anguish, sorrow, grief, worry.

angustiar *v.* to distress, grieve, worry.

angustioso *adj.* anguished, worried, grievous; distressing.

anhelante *adj.* anxious, desirous, longing; panting.

anhelar *v.* to long for; to breathe hard; to pant.

anhelo *m.* longing.

anheloso *adj.* anxious; eager.

anidar *v.* to nest; to nestle; to dwell; to shelter.

anillo *m.* ring.

ánima *f.* soul, spirit.

animación *f.* animation, liveliness, life.

animal *m.* animal; *adj.* animal; stupid; beastly; **animalejo** *m.* little animal; **animalucho** *m.* insignificant animal; hideous little beast.

animar *v.* to animate, give life to; to inspire, encourage.

ánimo *f.* spirit, mind; courage, valor; intention.

animosidad *f.* animosity, ill will; courage, energy.

animoso *adj.* spirited; courageous.

aniñado *adj.* boyish; childish; **aniñada** girlish.

aniquilar *v.* to annihilate, wipe out, destroy completely.

aniversario *m.* anniversary.

anoche *adv.* last night.

anochecer[13] *v. irr.* to grow dark; to be or arrive at nightfall; *m.* nightfall.

anochecida *f.* nightfall.

anonadar *v.* to annihilate; to humiliate.

anónimo *adj.* anonymous; nameless; *m.* anonymous letter or note.

anormal *adj.* abnormal.

anotación *f.* annotation; note.

anotar *v.* to annotate, provide with notes; to write down.

anquilosado *adj.* stiff-jointed; gnarled.

anquilosarse *v.* to become stiff in the joints; to become mentally stagnant.

ansia *f.* anxiety, anguish; longing, eagerness; **-s** anguish; *Col., Ven., P.R.* nausea.

ansiar[17] *v.* to long for, desire eagerly.

ansiedad *f.* anxiety; worry.

ansioso *adj.* anxious, troubled; eager.

antagonismo *m.* antagonism.

antagonista *m. & f.* antagonist, adversary, opponent.

antaño *adv.* yesteryear, formerly; **días de —** days of old.

ante *prep.* before, in the presence of; **— todo** above all; *m.* elk; buckskin.

anteanoche *adv.* night before last.

anteayer *adv.* day before yesterday.

antebrazo *m.* forearm.

antecámara *f.* antechamber, waiting room.

antecedente *m.* antecedent; *adj.* antecedent, preceding.

antecesor *m.* ancestor; predecessor.

antedicho *adj.* aforesaid.

antelación *f.* precedence, priority (*in time*).

antemano: de — beforehand.

antena *f.* antenna (*of a radio or wireless*); lateen yard (*of a ship*); **-s** antennae, feelers; **— emisora** *f.* broadcasting antenna; **— receptora** *f.* receiving antenna; **— parabólica** *f.* parabolic (*TV*) antenna.

antenoche = anteanoche.

anteojera *f.* blinder.

anteojo *m.* spyglass; small telescope; eyeglass; **-s** spectacles; **-s de larga vista** field glasses.

antepasado *adj.* passed; **año —** year before last; *m.* ancestor.

antepecho *m.* sill, railing.
anteponer[40] *v. irr.* to place before; to prefer.
antepuesto *p.p.* of **anteponer.**
anterior *adj.* front, toward the front; earlier, previous; **el día —** the day before.
antes *adv.* before, formerly; **— de** *prep.* before; **— (de) que** *conj.* before.
antesala *f.* anteroom, waiting room.
antiaéreo *adj.* antiaircraft.
anticipación *f.* anticipation, advance consideration; **con —** in advance.
anticipado *adj.* early, ahead of time; advanced (*payment*); **por —** in advance; *p.p.* of **anticipar** anticipated.
anticipar *v.* to anticipate; to advance, pay in advance; **-se** to get ahead (of).
anticipo *m.* advance, advance payment.
anticlericalismo *m.* anticlericalism (*opposition or antagonism to the clergy*).
anticuado *adj.* antiquated, out-of-date.
antídoto *m.* antidote.
antigualla *f.* antique; anything old.
antigüedad *f.* antiquity, ancient times; **-es** antique objects, antiques.
antiguo *adj.* ancient, old; antique.
antílope *m.* antelope.
antiparras *f. pl.* goggles; spectacles.
antipatía *f.* antipathy, dislike; mutual antagonism.
antipático *adj.* disagreeable; unlikeable, unpleasant.
antipoliomielítico *adj.* antipolio.
antiséptico *adj.* & *m.* antiseptic.
antojadizo *adj.* fanciful, whimsical.
antojarse *v.* : **antojársele a uno** to take a notion or fancy to; to strike one's fancy; to want, desire.
antojo *m.* whim, notion, fancy.
antorcha *f.* torch.
antracita *f.* anthracite, hard coal.
anual *adj.* annual, yearly.
anuario *m.* annual, yearbook.
anublar *v.* to cloud; to dim, obscure; **-se** to become cloudy.
anudar *v.* to knot; **anudársele a uno la garganta** to choke up with emotion.
anulación *f.* voiding, cancellation.
anular *v.* to annul, void, cancel, abolish.
anunciador *m.* announcer; advertiser; *adj.* announcing; advertising.
anunciante *m.* & *f.* announcer, advertiser.
anunciar *v.* to announce; to advertise.
anuncio *m.* announcement; advertisement.
anzuelo *m.* fishhook; lure, attraction.
añadidura *f.* addition.
añadir *v.* to add.
añejado *adj.* aged (*wine, cheese, etc.*).
añejo *adj.* old; of old vintage; stale.
añicos *m. pl.* bits, shatters, fragments; **hacer(se) —** to shatter, break into a thousand pieces.
añil *m.* indigo (*plant*); indigo blue.
año *m.* year; **— bisiesto** leap year; **¿cuántos -s tiene Vd?** how old are you?
añoranza *f.* nostalgia, longing.

añorar *v.* to long for, yearn for, be homesick for; to make reminiscences.
añoso *adj.* old, aged.
aojar *v.* to bewitch; to cast the evil eye.
apabullar *v.* to crush, crumple.
apacentar[1] *v. irr.* to graze, pasture; to feed (*the spirit, desires, passions, etc.*); **-se** to graze, pasture.
apacibilidad *f.* gentleness, mildness, pleasantness; **apacible** *adj.* pleasant, quiet, gentle.
apaciguamiento *m.* appeasement.
apaciguar[8] *v.* to pacify, calm, appease; **-se** to calm down.
apachurrar *v. Mex., C.A., Carib., Andes* to crush. See **despachurrar.**
apadrinar *v.* to sponsor; to act as a godfather; to act as a second in a duel.
apagar[7] *v.* to put out, extinguish; to deafen (*a sound*).
apagón *m.* blackout.
apalabrar *v.* to speak for, engage, reserve; **-se con** to make a verbal agreement with.
apalear *v.* to beat up, thrash; to thresh.
aparador *m.* sideboard; cupboard; showcase; show window; workshop.
aparato *m.* apparatus; pomp.
aparatoso *adj.* pompous, ostentatious.
aparcero *m.* co-owner of land; *Am.* pal, comrade.
aparear *v.* to mate; to match; to pair; **-se** to mate; to match; to pair.
aparecer[13] *v. irr.* to appear, show up.
aparecido *m.* ghost, specter, phantom.
aparejar *v.* to prepare; to harness; to rig; to equip.
aparejo *m.* harness; packsaddle; rigging (*of a boat*); preparation; fishing tackle; **-s** equipment, tools.
aparentar *v.* to appear, seem; to pretend, feign, affect.
aparente *adj.* apparent.
aparición *f.* apparition, ghost; appearance.
apariencia *f.* appearance.
apartado *m.* compartment; **— postal** post office letter box; *p.p.* of **apartar.**
apartamento *m.* apartment.
apartamiento *m.* separation; retirement; aloofness; retreat, refuge; *Am.* apartment, flat.
apartar *v.* to set apart, separate; to remove; *Am.* **— las reses** to sort out cattle; **-se** to withdraw; to step aside; to go away.
aparte *adv.* apart; aside; *m.* aside (*in a play*); new paragraph; *Am.* sorting out of cattle.
apasionado *adj.* passionate; very fond (of); impassioned, emotional.
apasionar *v.* to arouse passion; to fill with passion; **-se** to become impassioned; to fall ardently in love.
apatía *f.* apathy, indolence, indifference.
apático *adj.* apathetic, indifferent, indolent.
apear *v.* (*de caballo*) dismount; (*bajar*) to lower, take down; to shackle (*a horse*); to fell (*a tree*); *Ríopl.* to fire, dismiss from a position; **— el**

tratamiento to omit the title (*in addressing a person*); **-se** to get off, alight; *Am.* **-se por la cola** (*or por las orejas*) to go off at a tangent, make an irrelevant remark.

apechugar[7] *v.* to push with the chest; to push ahead; — **con** to accept reluctantly; to go through with (*something*) courageously; *P.R.* to snatch, take possession of.

apedrear *v.* to stone, hit with stones.

apegado *adj.* devoted, attached; *p.p.* of **apegarse.**

apegarse[7] *v.* to become attached (to); to become fond (of).

apego *m.* attachment, fondness.

apelación *f.* appeal.

apelar *v.* to appeal.

apelotonar *v.* to form or roll into a ball; to pile up, bunch together.

apellidar *v.* to call, name; **-se** to be named; to have the surname of.

apellido *m.* surname.

apenar *v.* to grieve, afflict; **-se** to be grieved; *Col., Ven., C.A., Carib.* to feel embarrassed, feel ashamed.

apenas *adv.* hardly, scarcely; *conj.* as soon as.

apéndice *m.* appendix.

apercibir *v.* to prepare beforehand; to supply; to warn, advise; to perceive; **-se a la pelea** to get ready to fight; *Am.* **-se de** to notice.

apergaminado *adj.* parchment-like; dried up.

aperitivo *m.* aperitif, appetizer; cocktail.

aperlado *adj.* pearly, pearl-colored.

apero *m.* farm equipment; **-s** tools, implements; *Ríopl., Ch., Mex., Ven., Andes* saddle and trappings.

apertura *f.* opening (*act of opening or beginning*).

apestar *v.* to infect; to corrupt; to sicken; to stink; **-se** to turn putrid, become corrupted; *Am.* to catch cold.

apestoso *adj.* putrid, foul-smelling.

apetecer[13] *v. irr.* to desire, crave.

apetecible *adj.* desirable; appetizing.

apetencia *f.* hunger, appetite; desire.

apetito *m.* appetite; hunger.

apetitoso *adj.* appetizing; gluttonous.

apiadarse *v.* to pity; — **de** to pity, take pity on.

ápice *m.* apex, top, summit.

apilar *v.* to pile up, stack, heap.

apiñado *p.p.* of **apiñar** & *adj.* crowded, jammed; cone-shaped, shaped like a pine cone.

apiñamiento *m.* crowd, jam (*of people or animals*); crowding together.

apiñar *v.* to cram together; to crowd; **-se** to pile up, crowd together.

apio *m.* celery.

apisonar *v.* to pack down, flatten by pounding.

aplacar[6] *v.* to appease, pacify, soothe.

aplanamiento *m.* flattening, leveling; dejection, depression.

aplanar *v.* to level; to flatten; to astonish; *Am.* — **las calles** to tramp the streets; **-se** to be flattened out; to be

leveled to the ground; to lose one's strength; *Col.* to give in, yield.

aplastar *v.* to squash, crush, flatten; *Am.* to tire out, break (*a horse*); **-se** *Am.* to plump oneself down; *Col., Andes* to overstay a call (*remaining seated*).

aplaudir *v.* to applaud, clap; to approve, praise.

aplauso *m.* applause; praise, approval.

aplazamiento *m.* postponement; adjournment.

aplazar[9] *v.* to postpone; to adjourn.

aplicable *adj.* applicable, suitable, fitting.

aplicación *f.* application; effort, diligence; **-es** appliqué (*trimming laid on a dress*).

aplicado *adj.* industrious, diligent.

aplicar[6] *v.* to apply; to put on, lay on; **-se** to apply oneself, work hard.

aplomado *adj.* gray, lead-colored; *p.p.* of **aplomar.**

aplomar *v.* to plumb (*a wall*); to make vertical; to make heavier; **-se** *Am.* to become ashamed or embarrassed; *Am.* to be slow.

aplomo *m.* assurance, confidence, self-possession, serenity; **estar** — to be plumb, vertical.

apocado *adj.* cowardly; timid; *p.p.* of **apocar.**

apocamiento *m.* timidity; bashfulness; belittling.

apocar[6] *v.* to lessen; to belittle, give little importance to; **-se** to humble oneself.

apodar *v.* to nickname.

apoderado *m.* attorney; proxy, substitute.

apoderar *v.* to empower, give power of attorney; **-se de** to take possession of, seize.

apodo *m.* nickname.

apogeo *m.* apogee (*point at which a planet, satellite, or rocket is at the greatest distance from the earth*); highest point, height (*of glory, fame, etc.*).

apolillado *adj.* moth-eaten; worm-eaten.

apología *f.* apology.

apoplejía *f.* apoplexy, stroke.

aporrear *v.* to beat; to maul; *Am.* to beat (*in a game*), defeat.

aportación *f.* contribution.

aportar *v.* to bring; to contribute; to arrive in port; to reach an unexpected place (*after having gone astray*); **-se** *Am.* to appear, approach.

aporte *m.* contribution.

aposento *m.* room; lodging.

apostar[2] *v. irr.* to bet; to post, station.

apóstol *m.* apostle; religious leader.

apostólico *adj.* apostolic (*pertaining to the apostles, or to the Pope and his authority*).

apostura *f.* elegant bearing, graceful carriage.

apoyar *v.* to lean, rest; to back, support; to aid, favor; to confirm; **-se** to lean (on).

apoyo *m.* support; favor, protection.

apreciable *adj.* estimable, esteemed; valuable; appraisable; noticeable.

apreciación *f.* appreciation; valuation; estimation.

apreciar *v.* to appreciate, value, esteem; to price, fix the price of; to appraise.

aprecio *m.* esteem, high regard; appraisal, valuation, estimate; *Mex.*, *Ven.*, *Cuba* hacer — to notice, pay attention.

aprehender *v.* to apprehend, seize, arrest.

aprehensión, aprensión *f.* apprehension; fear, dread; seizure, arrest; *Am.* prejudice.

aprehensor, aprensor *m.* captor.

apremiante *adj.* pressing, urgent.

apremiar *v.* to press, urge onward, hurry.

apremio *m.* pressure; urgency.

aprender *v.* to learn.

aprendiz *m.* apprentice.

aprendizaje *m.* apprenticeship; learning (*act of learning*).

apresar *v.* to seize, grab; to capture; to imprison.

aprestar *v.* to prepare, make ready; **-se** to get ready.

apresto *m.* preparation; readiness.

apresurado *adj.* hasty.

apresurar *v.* to hurry, hasten; **-se** to hurry, hasten.

apretado *adj.* tight; compact; stingy, miserly; difficult, dangerous; *p.p. of* **apretar**.

apretar[1] *v. irr.* to press, squeeze, tighten; to urge on; *Am.* to increase in strength or intensity (*as rain, wind, etc.*); *Am.* to redouble one's effort; — a correr to start to run; **-se** *Col.* to gorge, overeat.

apretón *m.* sudden pressure; squeeze; dash, short run; — de manos handshake.

apretura *f.* jam, crush; tight squeeze, narrow place; difficulty, predicament; dire poverty.

aprieto *m.* tight spot, difficulty.

aprisa *adv.* quickly, fast, speedily.

aprisco *m.* sheepfold.

aprisionar *v.* to imprison; to tie, fasten.

aprobación *f.* approbation, approval; consent; pass, passing grade.

aprobar[2] *v. irr.* to approve; to pass (*in an examination*).

aprontar *v.* to make ready; to expedite; to hand over without delay; *Am.* to pay in advance.

apropiación *f.* appropriation; confiscation.

apropiado *adj.* appropriate, proper, fitting, suitable; *p.p. of* **apropiar**.

apropiar *v.* to fit; to adapt; **-se** to take possession (of); to confiscate.

aprovechable *adj.* available; usable, fit to use.

aprovechado *adj.* diligent, industrious; *p.p. of* **aprovechar**.

aprovechamiento *m.* use, utilization; exploitation; profit, benefit; progress.

aprovechar *v.* to profit, be profitable; to progress, get ahead; to utilize; **-se de** to take advantage of; ¡que aproveche! may you enjoy it!

aproximado *adj.* approximate; near; nearly correct.

aproximar *v.* to place or bring near; to approximate; **-se** to get near, approach.

aproximativo *adj.* approximate.

aptitud *f.* aptitude, capacity, ability.

apto *adj.* apt; competent.

apuesta *f.* bet, wager.

apuesto *adj.* smart, stylish; good-looking.

apuntación *f.* note; memorandum; musical notation, set of musical symbols or signs.

apuntalar *v.* to prop; to shore up.

apuntar *v.* (*señalar*) to point; (*arma*) to aim; (*escribir*) to write down; (*a un actor*) to prompt; (*remendar*) to mend, to stitch; to sharpen; (*brotar*) to begin to show; — el día to begin to dawn; **-se** to sprout.

apunte *m.* note, memorandum.

apuñalar *v.* to stab.

apuración *f.* worry; trouble.

apurado *adj.* worried; needy; difficult; dangerous; in a hurry.

apurar *v.* (*acabar*) to exhaust, to drain to the last drop; (*preocupar*) to worry, annoy; (*acelerar*) to hurry, press; **-se** to be or get worried; to hurry up.

apuro *m.* worry; predicament; *Am.* rush, hurry.

aquejar *v.* to grieve, afflict.

aquel, aquella *dem. adj.* that (*at a distance*); **aquellos, aquellas** those; **aquél, aquélla** *m.*, *f. dem. pron.* that one; the former; **aquello** that, that thing; **aquéllos, aquéllas** *m.*, *f. pl.* those; the former.

aquí *adv.* here; **por** — this way; through here; around here.

aquietar *v.* to quiet, calm; to hush; **-se** to calm down, become calm.

aquilón *m.* north wind.

ara *f.* altar.

árabe *adj. & m.* Arab; Arabic.

arado *m.* plow; *Am.* plowed land, piece of cultivated land.

aragonés *adj.* Aragonese, of or from Aragón, Spain; *m.* Aragonese.

arancel *m.* tariff; — de aduanas customs, duties; **arancelario** *adj.* pertaining to tariff.

araña *f.* spider; chandelier.

arañar *v.* to scratch; to claw.

araño *m.* scratch; **arañazo** *m.* big scratch.

arar *v.* to plow.

arbitración *f.* arbitration.

arbitrador *m.* arbitrator; referee, umpire.

arbitraje *m.* arbitration.

arbitrar *v.* to arbitrate; to umpire.

arbitrario *adj.* arbitrary.

arbitrio *m.* free will; scheme, means; compromise, arbitration; sentence (*of a judge*); judgment.

árbitro *m.* arbitrator, sole judge, umpire.

árbol *m.* tree; mast; **arbolado** *adj.* wooded; *m.* grove of trees.

arboleda *f.* grove.

arbusto *m.* shrub.

arca *f.* ark; chest, coffer; **arcón** *m.* large coffer or chest; bin.

arcada *f.* arcade; archway.

arcaico *adj.* archaic.

arcano *adj.* hidden, secret; *m.* secret, mystery.

arce *m.* maple, maple tree.

arcilla *f.* clay.

arco *m.* arc; arch; bow; violin bow; — **iris** rainbow.

archipiélago *m.* archipelago (*group of many islands*).

archisabido *adj.* very well-known.

archivo *m.* archives; file; public records; *Am.* office, business office; **archivero** *m.* keeper of archives; city clerk.

arder *v.* to burn; to be consumed (*with fever or passion*); *Col., Carib.* to smart, sting.

ardid *m.* trick, scheme.

ardiente *adj.* ardent, burning, fervent; passionate; fiery.

ardilla *f.* squirrel.

ardite *m.* ancient coin of small value; bit, trifle; **no valer un** — not to be worth a penny.

ardor *m.* ardor; heat; fervor, eagerness.

ardoroso *adj.* ardent, fiery.

arduo *adj.* arduous, hard, difficult.

área *f.* area.

arena *f.* sand; arena; -s kidney stones; **arenal** *m.* sand pit.

arenga *f.* address, speech.

arenisco *adj.* sandy; gritty; **piedra arenisca** sandstone.

arenoso *adj.* sandy; gritty.

arenque *m.* herring.

arepa *f. Col., Ven., Carib.* a fried (*griddle*) cake made of corn meal that corresponds to the Mexican tortilla.

arete *m.* earring.

argamasa *f.* mortar.

argentar *v.* to plate (*with silver*); to polish.

argentino *adj.* silvery; Argentine; *m.* Argentine; Argentine gold coin worth 5 pesos.

argolla *f.* large iron ring; *Am.* plain finger ring, engagement ring; *Am.* **tener** — to be lucky.

argucia *f.* cunning, astuteness; scheme; subtlety.

argüir[32] *v. irr.* to argue; to deduce, infer.

argumentación *f.* argumentation, argument, reasoning.

argumento *m.* reasoning; substance, subject matter, resumé (*of a play or story*)

aridez *f.* barrenness; dryness; drought.

árido *adj.* arid, dry, barren; -s *m. pl.* grains and dry vegetables; **medida para -s** dry measure.

ariete *m.* ram, battering ram; —**hidráulico** hydraulic ram.

arisco *adj.* gruff, harsh, unsociable; *Am.* shy, distrustful.

arista *f.* sharp edge; ridge; beard (*of wheat or corn*).

aristocracia *f.* aristocracy.

aristócrata *m. & f.* aristocrat.

aristocrático *adj.* aristocratic.

aritmética *f.* arithmetic.

arma *f.* arm, weapon; branch (*of the army*); -s armed forces; —**arrojadiza** missile weapon; — **blanca** sword or knife; **de -s tomar** ready for any emergency; ready to fight.

armada *f.* armada, fleet.

armador *m.* shipbuilder; assembler.

armadura *f.* armor; armature (*of a generator or dynamo*); framework; mounting.

armamento *m.* armament; equipment.

armar *v.* to arm; to set up, assemble, rig up; — **una pendencia** to start a quarrel; *Col.* — **un trique** to lay a snare, set a trap; *Am.* -**se** to balk, to be stubborn; *Ven., Mex.* -**se con alguna cosa** to refuse to return something.

armario *m.* wardrobe, clothes closet; cabinet.

armatoste *m.* unwieldy object or machine; clumsy thing; heavy, clumsy fellow.

armazón *f.* framework, skeleton; *m.* skeleton (*of an animal*); *Am.* shelf, set of shelves.

armella *f.* staple; screw eye.

armiño *m.* ermine.

armisticio *m.* armistice.

armonía *f.* harmony.

armónico *adj.* harmonic; harmonious.

armonioso *adj.* harmonious, musical.

armonizar[9] *v.* to harmonize.

arnés *m.* harness; coat of mail; -es harness and trappings; equipment, outfit.

aro *m.* hoop; rim (*of a wheel*); *Am.* finger ring; *Ch., Riopl.* earring.

aroma *f.* aroma, scent, perfume.

aromático *adj.* aromatic, fragrant, spicy; **sales aromáticas** smelling salts.

arpa *f.* harp.

arpía *f.* shrew.

arpón *m.* harpoon, spear.

arqueado *adj.* arched.

arquear *v.* to arch.

arquitecto *m.* architect.

arquitectónico *adj.* architectural.

arquitectura *f.* architecture.

arrabal *m.* outlying district; -es outskirts, suburbs.

arracada *f.* earring.

arraigar[7] *v.* to root, take root; -**se** to become rooted, attached.

arrancado *adj. Mex., Carib., C.A., Andes* without money, broke.

arrancar[6] *v.* to uproot; to pull out; to start, start out; *Ch., Mex.* to flee, run away.

arranque m. start; pull; uprooting; automobile starter; **— de ira** fit or outburst of anger; **punto de —** starting point.

arrasar v. to level; to tear down, raze; to fill to the brim; **-se** to clear up (said of the sky); **-se de lágrimas** to fill up with tears.

arrastrado adj. poor, destitute; mean, vile; wretched; rascally; **llevar una vida arrastrada** to lead a dog's life.

arrastrar v. to drag, haul; Ven. to harrow (land); **-se** to drag along, crawl.

arrayán m. mýrtle.

¡arre! interj. gee! get up there!

arrear v. to drive (mules, cattle); Guat. to rustle, steal cattle; Am. **-le a uno una bofetada** to give a person a slap.

arrebatamiento m. snatch; ecstasy; rage.

arrebatar v. to snatch away; **-se de cólera** to have a fit of anger.

arrebatiña f. grab, snatch; scramble; **arrebatón** m. quick or violent grab.

arrebato m. rage; rapture, ecstasy; fit.

arrebol m. red color of the sky; rouge; **-es** red clouds.

arreciar v. to increase in intensity, get stronger.

arrecife m. reef.

arredrar v. to frighten, intimidate; **-se** to be or get scared.

arreglar v. to arrange, put in order; to regulate; to fix; to adjust, settle; Am. to pay (a debt); Am. to correct, punish; **-se** to doll up, fix oneself up; to settle differences, come to an agreement.

arreglo m. arrangement; adjustment; settlement; conformity, agreement; **con — a** according to.

arrellanarse v. to sprawl, lounge; to be self-satisfied.

arremangado adj. & p.p. turned up; **nariz arremangada** turned up nose.

arremangar[7] v. to tuck up, turn up, roll up (the sleeves, trousers, etc.); **-se** to roll up one's sleeves; **-se los pantalones** to roll up one's trousers.

arremeter v. to attack, assail, assault.

arremetida f. thrust, push, attack.

arremolinarse v. to whirl, swirl; to eddy; to mill around.

arrendamiento m. renting; lease; rental, rent.

arrendar[1] v. irr. to rent, lease, let; to hire; to tie (a horse); to bridle; Am. to head for.

arrendatario m. renter, tenant.

arreo m. raiment; ornament; Am. driving of horses or mules; Ríopl., Ch., Mex., Ven. drove of horses or mules; **-s** trappings; equipment; finery; adv. uninterruptedly, without interruption.

arrepentido adj. repentant; p.p. of **arrepentirse.**

arrepentimiento m. repentance, regret.

arrepentirse[3] v. irr. to repent, regret.

arrestado adj. daring, rash; p.p. of **arrestar.**

arrestar v. to arrest; Am. to return, strike back (a ball); Peru to reprimand; **-se** to dare, venture.

arresto m. arrest, imprisonment; detention; daring, rashness; rash act.

arriar[17] v. to haul down, lower (the flag); to lower (the sails); to slacken (a rope).

arriba adv. above; upstairs; **de — abajo** from top to bottom; up and down; **río —** upstream; **¡ — !** hurrah!

arribada f. arrival; Am. back talk, impudent answer.

arribar v. to arrive; to put into port; Am. to prosper, better one's lot.

arribo m. arrival.

arriendo = **arrendamiento.**

arriero m. muleteer.

arriesgado adj. risky, daring.

arriesgar[7] v. to risk; **-se** to dare, run a risk.

arrimar v. to bring or place near; to lay aside; to strike (a blow); **-se** to lean (on); to get near; to seek shelter.

arrinconar v. to corner; to put in a corner; to lay aside; to slight, neglect; **-se** to retire; to live a secluded life.

arriscado adj. bold; daring; brisk; spirited (horse); craggy, rugged.

arriscar[6] v. to risk, venture; Mex. to roll up, curl up, tuck up, fold back; Col. to have vim and vigor; Am. **— a** to reach, amount to; **-se** to get angry; Peru., C.A. to dress up, doll up.

arroba f. weight of 25 pounds.

arrobamiento m. trance, rapture.

arrobarse v. to be entranced; to be in a trance; to be enraptured.

arrodillarse v. to kneel.

arrogancia f. arrogance, pride.

arrogante adj. arrogant, haughty, proud.

arrogarse[7] v. to appropriate, usurp, assume (power or rights).

arrojadizo adj. missile; **arma arrojadiza** missile weapon.

arrojado adj. daring, rash, fearless; p.p. of **arrojar.**

arrojar v. to throw, hurl, cast; to expel; Am. to throw up, vomit; **— un saldo de** to show a balance of; **-se a** to hurl oneself upon or at; to dare to.

arrojo m. boldness, daring.

arrollador adj. sweeping, overwhelming, violent; winding (that serves to wind or roll up).

arrollar v. to roll up; to sweep away; to trample upon; to destroy.

arropar v. to wrap, cover; Col. to snap up, accept on the spot (a deal); **-se** to wrap up, cover up.

arrostrar v. to face, defy; **-se** to dare, dare to fight face to face.

arroyada f. gully, valley of a stream; bed (formed by a stream); river flood.

arroyo m. brook, small stream, rivulet; gutter; **arroyuelo** m. rivulet.

arroz m. rice; **arrozal** m. rice field.

arruga f. wrinkle.

arrugar[7] v. to wrinkle; Carib. to bother, annoy; **-se** to get wrinkled; Mex., Col. to crouch with fear, be afraid.

arruinar v. to ruin, destroy; **-se** to become ruined; Am. to go "broke", lose all one's fortune.

arrullar v. to lull; to coo.

arrullo m. lullaby; cooing.

arrumbar v. to lay aside (as useless), put away in a corner, discard; to dismiss, remove (from office or a position of trust); to take bearings; **— a su adversario** to corner one's opponent, overpower him.

arsenal m. arsenal; navy yard.

arsénico m. arsenic.

arte m. & f. art; skill, ability; cunning; craft; **por — de** by way or means of; **bellas -s** fine arts.

artefacto m. piece of workmanship, manufactured object; handiwork; contrivance.

arteria f. artery.

artero adj. crafty, astute.

artesa f. trough.

artesano m. artisan, craftsman; **artesanía** f. arts and crafts; workmanship, craftsmanship.

artesonado m. ceiling decorated with carved panels.

ártico adj. arctic.

articulación f. articulation; pronunciation; joint.

articular v. to articulate; to join, unite.

artículo m. article; **— de fondo** editorial.

artífice m. artisan, craftsman.

artificial adj. artificial.

artificio m. artifice, clever device; craft, skill; cunning, deceit.

artificioso adj. cunning, astute, deceitful; skillful.

artillería f. artillery, gunnery; **— de plaza** (or **de sitio**) heavy artillery; **— de montaña** light mountain artillery.

artillero m. artilleryman, gunner.

artimaña f. trick.

artista m. & f. artist.

artístico adj. artistic.

arveja f. C.A., Col., Ven. pea. Also referred to as **alverja**.

arzobispo m. archbishop.

arzón m. saddletree.

as m. ace.

asa f. handle.

asado m. roast; p.p. & adj. roasted.

asador m. spit (for roasting).

asaltante m. assailant; highway robber.

asaltar v. to assault, attack; **-le a uno una idea** to be struck by an idea; Riopl., Carib. **— la casa de un amigo** to give a surprise party.

asalto m. assault, attack; Am. surprise party.

asamblea f. assembly, legislature; meeting.

asar v. to roast; **-se** to roast; to feel hot.

asaz adv. enough, very.

ascendencia f. ancestry; origin.

ascendente adj. ascendant, ascending, upward, rising.

ascender[1] v. irr. to ascend, climb; to promote; to amount (to).

ascendiente m. ancestor; influence.

ascensión f. ascension; ascent.

ascenso m. ascent, rise; promotion.

ascensor m. elevator.

asco m. disgust, loathing; nausea; **me da —** it makes me sick; it disgusts me; Mex., Ven. **poner a uno del —** to call a person all kinds of bad names; to soil.

ascua f. ember.

aseado adj. clean, neat; p.p. of asear.

asear v. to adorn; to make neat and clean; **-se** to clean oneself up.

asechanza = **acechanza**.

asediar v. to besiege, attack.

asedio m. siege.

asegurar v. to assure; to secure; to affirm; to insure; **-se** to make sure; to hold on; to get insured.

asemejar v. to liken, compare; **-se a** to resemble.

asentaderas f. pl. buttocks.

asentador m. razor strop.

asentar v. (poner) to set; to put down in writing; (afirmar) to assert; to iron out; to establish; (afilar) to hone, strop; **-se** to settle.

asentimiento m. assent, acquiescence, agreement.

asentir[3] v. irr. to assent, agree.

aseo m. neatness, cleanliness.

asequible adj. obtainable, available.

aserción f. assertion, affirmation.

aserradero m. sawmill.

aserrar[1] v. irr. to saw.

aserrín m. sawdust.

aserto m. assertion.

asesinar v. to assassinate, murder.

asesinato m. assassination, murder.

asesino m. assassin, murderer; adj. murderous.

asestar v. to point, aim, direct; **— un golpe** to deal a blow; **— un tiro** to fire a shot.

aseveración f. assertion, affirmation, contention.

aseverar v. to assert, affirm.

asfalto m. asphalt.

asfixia f. suffocation.

asfixiar v. to suffocate, smother.

así adv. so, thus, like this; therefore; **— — so-so; — que** so that; **— (or como)** conj. as soon as; Riopl., Ch., Ven., Mex., Andes **— no más** so-so; just so.

asiático adj. & m. Asiatic.

asidero m. handle; hold.

asiduo adj. assiduous, diligent, persevering.

asiento m. seat; site, location; bottom; entry (in bookkeeping); **-s** dregs, sediment.

asignación f. assignment; allowance.

asignar v. to assign; to allot; to attribute; to appoint.

asilado m. inmate (of an asylum).

asilar v. to house, shelter; to put in an asylum.

asilo m. asylum, refuge, shelter.

asimilar v. to assimilate, digest, absorb; to liken, compare.

asimismo adv. likewise, also.

asir²² v. irr. to seize, take hold of.

asistencia f. presence; attendance; assistance, help; Mex. sitting room; **-s** allowance; Col., Ven., Mex. **casa de —** boarding house.

asistente m. assistant; helper; military orderly; Col., Ven., P.R. servant; **los -s** those present.

asistir v. to attend, be present; to help; Am. to board, serve meals.

asno m. ass, donkey.

asociación f. association.

asociado m. associate.

asociar v. to associate; **-se** to join; to associate.

asolamiento m. devastation, ravage, havoc, destruction.

asolar² v. irr. to raze; to lay waste; to parch; **-se** to dry up, become parched; to settle (as liquids).

asoleado adj. sunny; p.p. of **asolear**.

asolear v. to sun; **-se** to bask in the sun; to get sunburnt.

asomar v. to show, appear; **— la cabeza** to stick one's head out; **-se** to look out (of a window); to peep out (or into); Peru to draw near, approach.

asombrar v. (hacer sombra) to cast a shadow, darken; (asustar) to astonish, amaze, frighten; **-se** to be astonished, amazed.

asombro m. astonishment, amazement; fright.

asombroso adj. astonishing, amazing.

asomo m. sign, indication; conjecture, suspicion; **ni por —** by no means.

aspa f. wing of a windmill; blade (of a propeller); reel (for winding yarn).

aspecto m. aspect, look, appearance.

aspereza f. roughness, ruggedness; harshness; severity.

áspero adj. rough, uneven, harsh; gruff.

aspiración f. aspiration, ambition, -longing; inhalation, breathing in.

aspiradora f. vacuum cleaner.

aspirante m. & f. applicant; candidate.

aspirar v. (anhelar) to aspire; long for, seek; (inspirar) to breathe in, to inhale; to aspirate (a sound).

asquear v. to disgust, nauseate, sicken.

asqueroso adj. loathsome, disgusting, sickening, filthy.

asta f. horn; antler; mast, pole, staff, flagstaff; lance; **a media —** at half mast.

asterisco m. asterisk, star (used in printing).

astilla f. chip; splinter; splint.

astillar v. to chip; to splinter; **-se** to splinter, break into splinters.

astillero m. dry dock; shipyard; lumber yard; rack (for lances or spears).

astro m. star; planet.

astronauta m. & f. astronaut.

astronomía f. astronomy; **astrónomo**

m. astronomer.

astucia f. shrewdness, cunning; trick.

asturiano adj. Asturian, of or from Asturias, Spain; m. Asturian.

astuto adj. astute, shrewd, wily, crafty.

asueto m. recess, vacation; **día de —** holiday.

asumir v. to assume.

asunto m. topic, subject matter; business; affair.

asustadizo adj. shy, scary, easily frightened, jumpy.

asustar v. to frighten, scare.

atacante m. attacker; adj. attacking.

atacar⁶ v. to attack; to tighten, fasten; to ram; to plug, wad (a gun).

atadura f. tie, knot; fastening.

atajar v. to intercept; to interrupt, cut off; to take a short cut; to cross out.

atajo m. short cut; interception; Am. drove. See **hatajo**.

atalaya f. lookout, watchtower; m. lookout, watchman, guard.

atañer¹⁹,⁵¹ v. to concern.

ataque m. attack; fit.

atar v. to tie, fasten; **-se** to get tied up; to be puzzled or perplexed.

atareado adj. busy, over-worked.

atarear v. to overwork, load with work; **-se** to toil, work hard; to be very busy.

atascadero m. muddy place; obstruction.

atascar⁶ v. to stop up; to jam, obstruct; **-se** to get stuck; to stick; to jam, get obstructed; to stall.

ataúd m. coffin.

ataviar¹⁷ v. to attire, deck, adorn; **-se** to dress up, doll up.

atavío m. attire, costume; ornaments, finery.

atemorizar⁹ v. to frighten, scare.

atención f. attention, care, thought; courtesy; **-es** business, affairs; **en — a** having in mind, considering.

atender¹ v. irr. to heed, pay attention; to attend to, take care of; to take into account or consideration.

atendido adj. Am. attentive, courteous.

atenerse⁴⁵ v. irr. to rely (on); to accept, abide (by).

atenido adj. Mex., Carib., C.A., Andes habitually dependent on another; p.p. of **atenerse**.

atentado m. offense, violation; crime, violence.

atentar¹ v. irr. to attempt, try; **— contra la vida de alguien** to attempt the life of someone.

atento adj. attentive; courteous, polite.

atenuar¹⁸ v. to attenuate, lessen; to tone down; to dim; to make thin or slender.

ateo m. atheist; adj. atheistic.

aterciopelado adj. velvety.

aterido adj. stiff, numb from cold.

aterirse³,⁵¹ v. irr. to become numb with cold.

aterrador adj. terrifying, appalling.

aterrar v. to terrify, frighten.

aterrizaje m. landing (of a plane); **pista de —** landing strip.

aterrizar[9] *v.* to land (*said of a plane*).

aterronar *v.* to make lumpy, form into lumps; **-se** to lump, form into lumps, become lumpy.

aterrorizar[9] *v.* to terrify, frighten, appal.

atesorar *v.* to treasure; to hoard, lay up, accumulate.

atestado *adj.* crowded, jammed, stuffed; witnessed; *p.p.* of **atestar.**

atestar *v.* (*legal*) to attest, testify, witness; (*llenar*) to fill up, cram, stuff, crowd; **-se de** to stuff oneself with, to get stuffed with.

atestiguar[8] *v.* to testify, witness; to attest.

atiborrar *v.* to stuff; **-se** to stuff oneself.

atiesar *v.* to stiffen.

atildado *adj.* spruce, trim; painstaking in dress or style.

atinar *v.* to hit the mark; to guess right.

atisbar *v.* to spy, look cautiously; to watch, pry; to catch a glimpse of; to peek.

atisbo *m.* glimpse; insight; peek; spying.

atizar[9] *v.* to poke, stir (*the fire*); to kindle, rouse; to trim (*a wick*); **— un bofetón** to give a wallop.

atlántico *adj.* Atlantic; **el Atlántico** the Atlantic.

atlas *m.* atlas.

atleta *m.* & *f.* athlete.

atlético *adj.* athletic.

atletismo *m.* athletics.

atmósfera *f.* atmosphere, air.

atmosférico *adj.* atmospheric.

atole *m.* *Am.* Mexican drink made of corn meal.

atolondrado *p.p.* & *adj.* confused, muddled; stunned; heedless, harebrained, thoughtless.

atolondramiento *m.* thoughtlessness, recklessness; confusion, perplexity.

atolondrar *v.* to confuse, muddle, perplex; to stun; **-se** to get muddled, confused; to get stunned.

átomo *m.* atom; small particle, tiny bit.

atónito *adj.* astonished, amazed.

atontado *adj.* stupefied, stupid, stunned.

atontar *v.* to stupefy, stun; to confuse.

atorar *v.* to jam; to stop up, clog; *Am.* to hold up, stop; **-se** to get stuck (*in the mud*); to get clogged; to get jammed; to choke (*with food*).

atormentar *v.* to torment; to worry, afflict; to tease, bother, vex.

atornasolado = **tornasolado.**

atornillar *v.* to screw; *Am.* to bother, torment.

atorrante *m.* & *f.* *Col.*, *Ch.*, *Riopl.*, *Bol.* vagabond, tramp.

atrabancar[6] *v.* to rush awkwardly; to run over; **-se** *Riopl.* to get involved in difficulties; *Riopl.* to rush into things.

atrabiliario *adj.* melancholy; bad-tempered.

atracar *v.* (*llenar*) to cram, stuff; (*amarrar*) to moor, to approach land; (*atacar*) to hold up, assault; *Am.* to seize; *Col.* to pursue, harass; *Am.* to treat severely; *Mex.*, *C.A.* to thrash, beat; **— al muelle** to dock, moor to the wharf; **-se** to stuff oneself, overeat; *Ch.* to have a fist fight; *Riopl.* to falter, stutter; **-se a** to come alongside of (*a ship*).

atracción *f.* attraction.

atraco *m.* holdup, assault; *Am.* **darse un — de comida** to stuff oneself, gorge.

atracón *m.* stuffing, gorging; *C.A.* violent quarrel; **darse un —de comida** to stuff oneself, gorge.

atractivo *adj.* attractive; *m.* attractiveness, charm.

atraer[46] *v. irr.* to attract.

atragantarse *v.* to gobble up; to choke (*with food*).

atrancar[6] *v.* to bolt, fasten with a bolt; *Am.* **-le a una cosa** to face something, stand up against something; **-se** to get crammed, obstructed; *Am.* to be stubborn, stick to one's opinion; *Col.* to stuff oneself, choke (*with food*).

atrapar *v.* to trap, ensnare; to seize, grab; to overtake.

atrás *adv.* back; behind; backward; *Am.* **echarse —** (*or* **para —**) to back out, go back on one's word.

atrasado *adj.* late; behind time; backward; behind (*in one's work, payments, etc.*); slow (*said of a clock*); *p.p.* of **atrasar.**

atrasar *v.* to delay; to be slow or behind time; **-se** to get behind, lose time; *Am.* to suffer a setback (*in one's health or fortune*).

atraso *m.* backwardness; delay; setback; **-s** arrears.

atravesar[1] *v. irr.* to cross; to walk across; to go through; to pierce; *Am.* to buy wholesale.

atreverse *v.* to dare, risk; to be insolent, saucy.

atrevido *adj.* bold, daring; insolent.

atrevimiento *m.* boldness, daring; insolence.

atribuir[32] *v. irr.* to attribute, ascribe, impute.

atribular *v.* to grieve, distress; **-se** to grieve; to be distressed.

atributo *m.* attribute, quality.

atril *m.* lectern, reading desk; book stand; music stand.

atrincherar *v.* to entrench, fortify with trenches; **-se** to entrench oneself.

atrio *m.* court, patio in front of a church; entrance hall.

atrocidad *f.* atrocity.

atronador *adj.* thunderous, deafening.

atronar[2] *v. irr.* to deafen; to stun.

atropellar *v.* to run over, run down, knock down; to trample upon; to insult; **— por** to knock down, overcome with violence; **-se** to rush.

atropello *m.* violent act; insult; outrage; trampling.

atroz *adj.* atrocious, awful; inhuman.

atún *m.* tunny fish, tuna fish.

aturdido *adj.* & *p.p.* stupid, awkward; stunned, bewildered.

aturdimiento *m.* daze, bewilderment, confusion.

aturdir *v.* to stun; to deafen; to bewilder.

audacia *f.* daring, boldness.

audaz *adj.* daring, bold.

audiencia *f.* audience, hearing; court of justice.

auditor *m.* judge advocate.

auditorio *m.* audience.

auge *f.* boom (*in the market*); boost (*in prices*); topmost height (*of fortune, fame, dignity, etc.*); **estar** (*or* **ir**) **en —** to be on the increase.

augurar *v.* to foretell, predict.

augusto *adj.* venerable; majestic.

aula *f.* schoolroom, classroom; lecture hall.

aullar *v.* to howl; to shriek; to bawl.

aullido *m.* howl.

aumentar *v.* to augment, increase.

aumento *m.* increase, advance, rise.

aun (aún) *adv.* even, still, yet.

aunque *conj.* though, although.

aura *f.* breeze; favor, applause; *Am.* bird of prey, buzzard, vulture.

áureo *adj.* golden.

aureola *f.* aureole, halo.

aureomicina *f.* Aureomycin (*trademark for chlortetracycline*).

aurora *f.* dawn; beginning; **— boreal** aurora borealis, northern lights.

auscultar *v.* to sound, examine by listening to (*the chest, lungs, heart, etc.*).

ausencia *f.* absence.

ausentarse *v.* to absent oneself; to be absent; to leave.

ausente *adj.* absent.

auspicios *m. pl.* auspices, patronage; omens.

austeridad *f.* austerity, severity, sternness, harshness.

austero *adj.* austere, stern, strict; harsh.

austral *adj.* southern.

austríaco *adj.* & *m.* Austrian.

austro *m.* south wind.

auténtico *adj.* authentic, true, genuine.

auto *m.* auto, automobile; one-act play; writ, order; **— sacramental** one-act religious play; **-s** proceedings.

autobús *m.* bus, autobus.

autóctono *adj.* indigenous, native.

automático *adj.* automatic.

automotriz *adj.* automotive, self-moving.

automóvil *m.* automobile, auto.

automovilista *m.* & *f.* motorist.

autonomía *f.* autonomy.

autopista *f.* expressway, superhighway, freeway, throughway, turnpike.

autor *m.* author.

autoridad *f.* authority.

autoritario *adj.* authoritative; authoritarian, domineering; bossy.

autorización *f.* authorization, sanction.

autorizar[9] *v.* to authorize, give power (to).

auxiliar *v.* to aid, help; *adj.* auxiliary, helping, assisting; *m.* assistant.

auxilio *m.* aid, help.

avaluación *f.* valuation, appraisal, assessment.

avaluar[18] *v.* to value, appraise.

avalúo *m.* valuation, appraisal.

avance *m.* advance, progress, headway; advanced payment; attack.

avanzada *f.* advance guard; outpost; advanced unit, spearhead.

avanzar[9] *v.* to advance.

avaricia *f.* avarice, greed.

avariento *adj.* avaricious, miserly; *m.* miser.

avaro *adj.* miserly, greedy; *m.* miser.

avasallar *v.* to subject, dominate, subdue.

ave *f.* bird; fowl; **— de corral** domestic fowl; **— de rapiña** bird of prey.

avecindarse *v.* to settle, locate, establish oneself, take up residence (*in a community*).

avellana *f.* hazelnut; **avellano** *m.* hazel; hazelnut tree; **avellanado** *adj.* hazel, light brown.

avena *f.* oats.

avenencia *f.* harmony, agreement; conformity.

avenida *f.* avenue; flood.

avenir[48] *v. irr.* to adjust; to reconcile; **-se a** to adapt oneself to; **-se con alguien** to get along with someone.

aventador *m.* fan (*for fanning a fire*); ventilator; winnower (*machine for separating wheat from chaff*).

aventajar *v.* to excel; to be ahead (of); **-se a** to get ahead of.

aventar[1] *v. irr.* to fan; to winnow, blow chaff from grain; to throw out, expel; *Am.* to pitch, throw; *Am.* to dry sugar (*in the open*); *Am.* to rouse (*game*); **-se** to be full of wind; to flee, run away; *Am.* to attack, hurl oneself (*on someone*).

aventura *f.* adventure; risk, danger; chance.

aventurado *adj.* adventurous, risky; bold, daring.

aventurar *v.* to venture, risk; **-se a** to risk, run the risk of; to dare.

aventurero *adj.* adventurous; *m.* adventurer.

avergonzar[2,9] *v. irr.* to shame; **-se** to feel ashamed.

avería *f.* damage; aviary, birdhouse; *Am.* misfortune; *Mex.*, *Cuba* mischief.

averiar[17] *v.* to damage, spoil, hurt; **-se** to become damaged; to spoil.

averiguar[8] *v.* to find out; to investigate.

aversión *f.* aversion, dislike; reluctance.

avestruz *m.* ostrich.

avezado *p.p.* & *adj.* accustomed; trained, practiced.

aviación *f.* aviation.

aviador *m.* aviator, flyer; purveyor, provider; *Am.* moneylender (*to miners or laborers*), promoter.

aviar[17] *v.* to equip; to supply; to prepare, make ready; *Am.* to lend money or equipment; **estar aviado** to be surrounded by difficulties; to be in a fix.

ávido adj. eager; greedy.

avinagrado adj. sour; acid; cross.

avinagrar v. to sour, make sour or acid; **-se** to sour, become sour.

avío m. provision, supply; preparation; *Cuba, Mex.* loan of money or equipment; **-s** equipment; **-s de pescar** fishing tackle.

avión m. airplane; martin (*a bird similar to a swallow*).

avisar v. to inform, give notice, advise; to announce; to warn.

aviso m. notice, advice, announcement; warning.

avispa f. wasp; **avispero** m. wasp's nest; **avispón** m. hornet.

avispado adj. lively, keen, clever, wide-awake; *Am.* frightened, scared.

avispar v. to spur, incite; **-se** to be on the alert; to be uneasy; *Am.* to become frightened, scared.

avistar v. to glimpse, catch sight of; **-se** to see each other, meet.

avivar v. to enliven, give life to; to revive; to brighten; to quicken.

avizor adj. alert, watchful.

avizorar v. to spy, watch closely.

aya f. child's nurse, governess; **ayo** m. tutor, guardian.

ayer adv. yesterday.

ayuda f. aid, help.

ayudante m. assistant.

ayudar v. to aid, help.

ayunar v. to fast.

ayunas: en — fasting; **en — de** totally ignorant of.

ayuno m. fast; **— de** wholly ignorant of.

ayuntamiento m. municipal government; town hall.

azabache m. jet; **-s** jet ornaments.

azada f. spade; hoe; **azadón** m. hoe.

azafrán m. saffron.

azahar m. orange or lemon blossom.

azar m. hazard; chance; accident; disaster.

azogue m. quicksilver.

azolvar v. to clog, obstruct; **-se** to clog, get clogged.

azorar v. to disturb, startle; to bewilder; **-se** to be startled, astonished; to be bewildered, perplexed; to be uneasy.

azotaina f. flogging, lashing, beating.

azotar v. to whip, lash, beat; *Am.* to thresh (*rice*); **— las calles** to "beat the pavement", walk the streets.

azote m. whip; lash with a whip; scourge; affliction, calamity.

azotea f. flat roof.

azteca adj., m. & f. Aztec.

azúcar m. sugar.

azucarar v. to sugar; to sweeten; **-se** to become sweet; *Am.* to crystallize, turn to sugar.

azucarera f. sugar bowl; sugar mill.

azucarero adj. sugar (*used as adj.*); m. sugar manufacturer, producer or dealer; sugar bowl.

azucena f. white lily.

azufre m. sulphur.

azul adj. blue; **— celeste** sky-blue; **— marino** navy blue; **— turquí** indigo; *Am.* **tiempos -es** hard times.

azulado adj. bluish.

azular v. to dye or color blue.

azulejo m. glazed tile; *Am.* bluebird; adj. bluish.

azuzar[9] v. to urge, egg on; to incite.

B

baba f. drivel, slaver, saliva; slime, slimy secretion; *Am.* small alligator.

babear v. to drivel; to slobber.

babero m. baby's bib.

babor m. port, port side (*of a ship*).

babosear v. to slaver, drivel; to keep one's mouth open; to act like a fool.

baboso adj. driveling, slobbering; slimy; foolishly sentimental; *Am.* silly, idiotic, foolish; **babosa** f. slug (*creature like a snail, but without a shell*).

babucha f. slipper; *Riopl.* **a —** pickaback, on the back or shoulders.

bacalao, bacallao m. *Andalusia, Am.* codfish.

bacilo m. bacillus.

bacín m. pot, chamber pot; **bacinica** f. chamber pot.

bacteria f. bacterium; **-s** bacteria.

bacteriología f. bacteriology.

bacteriológico adj. bacteriological, pertaining to bacteriology.

báculo m. staff, cane; aid, support.

bache m. rut, hole in the road.

bachiller m. bachelor (*one who holds degree*); talkative person; **bachillerato** m. bachelor's degree; studies for the bachelor's degree.

badajo m. clapper of a bell; foolish talker.

badana f. sheepskin.

bagaje m. baggage; army pack mule.

bagatela f. trifle.

bagazo m. waste pulp (*of sugarcane, olives, grapes, etc.*).

bagual adj. *Riopl.* wild, untamed, unruly; *Riopl.* rude, discourteous; *Riopl.* lanky, awkward; m. *Riopl.* wild horse.

bahía f. bay, harbor.

bailador m. dancer; adj. dancing.

bailar v. to dance; to spin around.

bailarín m. dancer; **bailarina** f. dancer.

baile m. dance; ball; ballet.

bailotear v. to jig, jiggle; to dance poorly; to dance around.

baja f. fall (*of prices*); war casualty; **dar de —** to discharge, muster out.

bajada f. descent; slope, dip (*on a road*); **de —** on the way down; **subidas y -s** ups and downs.

bajar v. to go down; to drop (*as price or value*); to lower; to take or carry down; to humble; **-se** to get down or off; to alight; *Am.* to stop at a hotel.

bajel m. boat, ship.

bajeza f. vile act or remark; meanness; baseness; degradation.

bajío m. shoal, sand bank; *Am.* lowland.

bajo adj. low; short; soft, bass (*tone or voice*); shallow (*water*); subdued (color); humble; base; **piso —** first floor, ground floor; *prep.* under, underneath; *m.* bass.

bala *f.* bullet, shot, ball; bale (*of cotton*).

balada *f.* ballad.

baladí *adj.* trivial; flimsy.

balance *m.* balance; equilibrium; balance sheet; rocking, rolling.

balancear *v.* to balance; to rock, roll; to swing, sway; to waver.

balanceo *m.* rocking, rolling; swinging; balancing; wavering; wobbling.

balanza *f.* balance, scale.

balar *v.* to bleat.

balaustrada *f.* balustrade, banister, railing.

balaustre *m.* banister.

balazo *m.* shot; bullet wound; *adj. Ch.* clever, cunning.

balbucear *v.* to stammer, stutter; to babble.

balbuceo *m.* babble.

balcón *m.* balcony.

baldado *m.* cripple; *adj. & p.p.* crippled.

baldar *v.* to cripple; to trump (*a card*).

balde *m.* pail; bucket; **de —** free of charge; **en —** in vain.

baldío *adj.* barren; fallow, uncultivated; *m.* fallow land; wasteland.

baldón *m.* infamy, insult.

baldosa *f.* floor tile; paving stone.

balido *m.* bleat, bleating.

balneario *m.* bathing resort; *adj.* pertaining to bathing resorts or medicinal springs.

balompié *m.* football.

balota *f.* ballot.

balotar *v.* to ballot, vote.

balsa *f.* (*de agua*) pond, pool; (*embarcación*) raft; *Am.* marsh; *Am.* a species of ceiba (*a tropical tree*).

bálsamo *m.* balsam, balm.

baluarte *m.* bulwark.

ballena *f.* whale; whalebone.

bambolear *v.* to sway, swing, rock; **-se** to stagger; to sway.

bambú *m.* bamboo.

banana *f.* banana; **banano** *m.* banana tree.

banasta *f.* large basket.

banca *f.* bench; card game; banking; banking house.

bancario *adj.* bank, pertaining to a bank.

bancarrota *f.* bankruptcy; failure, collapse.

banco *m.* bank; bench, stool; school (*of fish*); *Mex.* pile of grain; *Am.* small hill on a plain.

banda *f.* (*musical*) band; (*cinta*) ribbon, sash; (*grupo*) gang, group, party; flock; (*lindero*) side, edge, border.

bandada *f.* flock of birds; *Am.* gang.

bandeja *f.* tray; *Mex., Ven., Col.* bowl.

bandera *f.* banner, flag; *Riopl., Cuba., Mex.* **parar uno —** to take the lead, be a gangleader.

banderilla *f.* dart with a small flag or streamers (*used in bullfights*); **clavar a uno una —** tog oad or taunt someone; **tercio de — the banderilla**

phase of the bullfight; *Am.* **pegar una — to** touch for a loan.

banderillero *m.* bullfighter who sticks the **banderillas** into the bull.

banderín *m.* small flag; signal flag; pennant; recruiting office.

banderola *f.* streamer, small banner or flag; pennant.

bandidaje *m.* banditry, highway robbery; bandits.

bandido *m.* bandit, gangster.

bando *m.* (*decreto*) decree, proclamation; (*partido*) party, faction.

bandolero *m.* bandit.

bandurria *f.* bandore (*stringed instrument*); *Am.* a species of wading bird.

banquero *m.* banker.

banqueta *f.* bench (*without a back*); stool; footstool; *Mex.* sidewalk.

banquete *m.* banquet.

banquetear *v.* to banquet, feast.

banquillo *m.* bench, stool.

bañada *f.* shower, spray; dip, bath.

bañar *v.* to bathe, wash; to dip; **-se** to take a bath.

bañera *f.* bathtub.

bañista *m. & f.* bather.

baño *m.* (*aseo*) bath; bathtub; (*acabado*) cover, coating; **— de María** double boiler; *Am.* **—ruso** steam bath.

baqueta *f.* rod; whip; **-s** drumsticks; **tratar a la —** to treat scornfully, despotically.

baquiano, baqueano *m. Riopl., Ven., Andes* native guide (*through the wilderness, pampas, etc.*); *adj. Riopl., Andes* having an instinctive sense of direction.

bar *m.* bar, taproom, tavern.

baraja *f.* pack of cards.

barajar *v.* to shuffle; to mix, jumble together; to scuffle, wrangle; *Am.* to hinder, obstruct.

baranda *f.* railing; **barandal** *m.* banister, railing.

barandilla *f.* balustrade, rail, railing.

barata *f.* barter, exchange; *Am.* bargain sale; *Peru, Ch.* cockroach.

baratear *v.* to sell cheap; to cheapen; to cut the price of.

baratija *f.* trinket, trifle.

barato *adj.* cheap; *m.* bargain sale; money given by the winning gambler.

baratura *f.* cheapness.

baraúnda *f.* clamor, uproar, clatter.

barba *f.* chin; beard; **-s** whiskers.

barbacoa *f. Am.* barbecue; barbecued meat.

barbado *adj.* bearded.

barbaridad *f.* cruelty, brutality; rudeness; **una — de** a lot of; **¡que —** ! what nonsense!; what an atrocity!

barbarie *f.* barbarousness; savagery; lack of culture, ignorance; cruelty, brutality.

bárbaro *adj.* barbarous, cruel, savage; crude, coarse; *m.* barbarian.

barbechar *v.* to plow; to fallow.

barbecho *m.* first plowing; plowed land; fallow, fallow land.

barbería *f.* barbershop.

barbero m. barber; *Am.* flatterer.
barbilla f. point of the chin.
barbón, barbudo adj. bearded.
barca f. boat, launch, barge.
barco m. boat, ship.
bardo m. bard, minstrel, poet.
baritono m. baritone.
barniz m. varnish; glaze; printer's ink.
barnizar⁹ v. to varnish; to glaze.
barómetro m. barometer.
barquero m. boatman; bargeman.
barquillo m. rolled wafer; ice-cream cone.
barquinazo m. tumble, bad fall, hard bump, somersault; *Am.* lurch (*of a vehicle or boat*).
barra f. bar; rod; railing; sand bar; claque, audience; **— de jabón** bar of soap.
barrabasada f. mischief, mean prank; rash, hasty act.
barraca f. hut, cabin; *Andes* large shed, warehouse.
barranca f., **barranco** m. ravine, gorge; *Am.* cliff.
barreminas m. mine-sweeper.
barrena f. auger, drill; gimlet (*small tool for boring holes*); spinning dive (*of a plane*).
barrenar v. to drill, bore; to scuttle (*a ship*); to blast (*a rock*).
barrendero m. sweeper.
barrer v. to sweep; to sweep away; *Am.* to defeat; *Am.* **al —** altogether, as a whole.
barrera f. barrier; obstacle.
barreta f. small iron bar; *Mex., Cuba, Col.* pick, pickaxe.
barrica f. cask, keg.
barrida f. *Am.* sweep, sweeping.
barrido m. sweep, sweeping; sweepings; *p.p.* of **barrer.**
barriga f. belly; bulge.
barrigón, barrigudo adj. big-bellied.
barril m. barrel, keg.
barrio m. district, neighborhood, quarter; **-s bajos** slums.
barro m. (*tierra*) mud, clay; (*granillo*) pimple; *Am.* **hacer** (*or* **cometer**) **un —** to commit a blunder.
barroso adj. muddy; pimply; reddish.
barrote m. short, thick bar; brace; rung (*of a ladder or chair*).
barruntar v. to foresee; to have a presentiment; to conjecture.
barrunto m. foreboding, presentiment; guess; hint, indication, sign.
bártulos m. pl. household goods; implements, tools.
barullo m. hubbub, racket, disorder.
basa f. base, pedestal; basis, foundation.
basar v. to base; to put on a base.
basca f. nausea, sickness to one's stomach; **tener -s** to be nauseated, sick to one's stomach.
báscula f. scale (*for weighing*), platform scale.
base f. base, basis, foundation.
básico adj. basic.
basquear v. to heave, try to vomit; to be nauseated, sick to one's stomach.

basquetbol m. basketball.
bastante adj. enough, sufficient; adv. enough.
bastar v. to be enough; to suffice.
bastardilla f. italic type, italics.
bastardo adj. bastard.
bastidor m. wing (*of a stage*); frame; embroidery frame; window sash; easel (*support for a picture, blackboard, etc.*); **entre -es** behind the scenes, off stage.
bastilla f. hem.
bastimento m. supply, provisions; vessel, ship.
basto adj. coarse; m. club (*in cards*); *Am.* saddle pad.
bastón m. cane, walking stick.
basura f. rubbish, scraps; garbage; refuse.
basurero m. garbage or rubbish dump; manure pile; garbage man, rubbish man; street cleaner.
bata f. lounging robe; housecoat, wrapper, dressing gown; smock; **batín** m. smock.
batahola f. hubbub, racket, uproar.
batalla f. battle; struggle.
batallar v. to battle, fight, struggle.
batallón m. battalion.
batata f. sweet potato.
bate m. *Am.* baseball bat.
batea f. tray; trough; bowl; barge; *Am.* washtub.
bateador m. *Am.* batter (*in baseball*).
batear v. *Am.* to bat.
batería f. battery (*military, naval, or electric*); **— de cocina** set of kitchen utensils; **— de jazz** a jazz combo; *Mex.* **dar —** to raise a rumpus; to plod, work hard.
batidor m. beater; scout.
batintín m. gong.
batir v. (*combatir*) to beat, whip, defeat; (*reconocer*) reconnoiter, explore; (*mover*) to flap; *Ch.* to rinse (*clothes*); *Riopl.* to denounce; **-se** to fight; **— palmas** to clap, applaud.
batisfera f. bathysphere.
baturrillo m. medley, mixture; hodgepodge.
batuta f. orchestra conductor's baton or wand; **llevar la —** to lead; to be the leader.
baúl m. trunk, chest; **— mundo** large trunk.
bautismo m. baptism, christening; **nombre de —** Christian name.
bautista m. & f. Baptist; baptizer.
bautizar⁹ v. to baptize, christen.
bautizo m. christening, baptism.
baya f. berry.
bayeta f. flannel; flannelette; **bayetón** m. thick wool cloth; *Col.* long poncho lined with flannel.
bayo adj. bay, reddish-brown.
baza f. trick (*cards played in one round*); **meter —** to meddle; to butt into a conversation; **no dejar meter —** not to let a person put a word in edgewise.
bazar m. bazaar; department store.

bazo *m.* spleen.

bazofia *f.* scraps, refuse, garbage; dregs.

beatitud *f.* bliss, blessedness.

beato *adj.* blessed; beatified; devout; overpious; hypocritical.

bebé *m.* baby.

bebedero *m.* drinking trough; watering place; spout.

bebedor *m.* drinker; drunkard.

beber *v.* to drink; to drink in, absorb.

bebida *f.* drink, beverage; **dado a la** — given to drink.

beca *f.* scholarship, fellowship; sash worn over the academic gown.

becario *m.* scholar, fellow, holder of a scholarship.

becerro *m.* young bull (*less than a year old*); calf; calfskin.

becuadro *m.* natural sign (*in music*).

bedel *m.* beadle.

befa *f.* scoff, jeer.

befar *v.* to scoff, jeer at, mock.

bejuco *m.* cane; **silla de** — cane chair.

beldad *f.* beauty.

belga *adj.*, *m.* & *f.* Belgian.

bélico *adj.* warlike.

beligerante *adj.*, *m.* & *f.* belligerent.

bellaco *adj.* sly, deceitful; *m.* villain; rascal.

bellaquear *v.* to cheat; to play tricks; *Am.* to rear, stand up on the hind legs; *Am.* to balk; *Am.* to be touchy, oversensitive.

bellaquería *f.* cunning, trickery; sly act or remark.

belleza *f.* beauty.

bello *adj.* beautiful.

bellota *f.* acorn.

bemol *adj.* flat (*in music*); **tener** - to have difficulties.

bendecir[27,52] *v. irr.* to bless.

bendición *f.* benediction, blessing; *Mex.*, *C.A.*, *Col.*, *Ven.* **echarle la — a una cosa** to give something up for lost.

bendito *adj.* blessed; saintly; **es un —** he is a saint, he is a simple soul; *p.p.* of **bendecir.**

benefactor *m.* benefactor; patron.

beneficencia *f.* beneficence, kindness, charity.

beneficiar *v.* to benefit, do good; to cultivate (*land*); to exploit (*a mine*); to treat (*metals*); *Col.*, *Ven.* to slaughter (*cattle*) for marketing.

beneficio *m.* (*provecho*) benefit, profit; exploitation of a mine; (*cultivo*) cultivation of land; *Am.* fertilizer; *Am.* slaughtering (*of cattle*).

benéfico *adj.* beneficent, good, kind.

benemérito *m.* worthy, notable; *adj.* worthy.

benevolencia *f.* benevolence, kindness.

benévolo *adj.* benevolent, good, kindly.

benigno *adj.* benign, gentle, mild, kind.

beodo *adj.* drunk; *m.* drunkard.

berenjena *f.* eggplant; *Mex.*, *C.A.* kind of squash; **berenjenal** *m.* eggplant patch; **meterse uno en un —** to get into a mess.

bergantín *m.* brigantine, brig (*square-rigged ship with two masts*).

bermejo *adj.* crimson, bright red.

bermellón *adj.* vermilion (*bright red*).

berrear *v.* to bellow; to scream; to sing off key.

berrido *m.* bellow, bellowing; scream.

berrinche *m.* fit of anger; tantrum.

berza *f.* cabbage.

besar *v.* to kiss.

beso *m.* kiss.

bestia *f.* beast.

bestialidad *f.* bestiality, brutality.

besugo *m.* sea bream (*a fish*).

besuquear *v.* to kiss repeatedly.

betabel *f.* *Mex.* beet.

betún *m.* bitumen (*combustible mineral*); black pitch; shoeblacking.

Biblia *f.* Bible.

bíblico *adj.* Biblical.

biblioteca *f.* library; set of volumes; bookcase.

bibliotecario *m.* librarian.

bicicleta *f.* bicycle; **biciclista, bici-cletista** *m.* & *f.* bicyclist, bicycle rider.

bicho *m.* insect, bug; any small animal; an insignificant person.

biela *f.* connecting rod (*of an engine*).

bien *adv.* well; **— que** although; **ahora — now then; más — rather; si — although; m. good, benefit; -es property; -es inmuebles** real estate; **-es raíces** real estate.

bienaventurado *adj.* blessed, happy.

bienaventuranza *f.* blessedness; beatitude; bliss.

bienestar *m.* well-being, comfort, welfare.

bienhechor *m.* benefactor.

bienvenida *f.* welcome.

bienvenido *adj.* welcome.

biftec, bistec, bisté *m.* beefsteak.

bifurcación *f.* fork, forking, branching out; railway junction; branch railroad.

bifurcarse[6] *v.* to fork, branch off, divide into two branches.

bigamía *f.* bigamy.

bigote *m.* mustache.

bikini *m.* bikini bathing suit.

bilis *f.* bile.

billar *m.* billiards; billiard room.

billete *m.* ticket; note; bill, banknote.

billón *m.* billion.

bimestre *m.* two-month period; bimonthly salary, rent, etc.; *adj.* bimonthly; **bimestral** *adj.* bimonthly.

biografía *f.* biography.

biología *f.* biology.

biombo *m.* folding screen.

birlar *v.* to snatch away; to steal; to kill or knock down with one blow.

bisabuelo *m.* great-grandfather; **bisa-buela** *f.* great-grandmother.

bisagra *f.* hinge.

bisiesto *adj.* leap (*year*).

bisojo *adj.* squint-eyed.

bisonte *m.* bison; the American buffalo.

bisturí *m.* bistoury, surgical knife.

bitoque *m.* barrel plug, stopper; *Am.* faucet; *Col.*, *Cuba*, *Mex.* injection point (*of a syringe*).

BA

bizarría *f.* gallantry, bravery; generosity.

bizarro *adj.* gallant, brave; generous.

bizco *adj.* cross-eyed.

bizcocho *m.* hardtack, hard biscuit; cake; cookie; — **borracho** cake dipped in wine.

biznieto *m.* great-grandson; **biznieta** *f.* great-granddaughter.

blanco *adj.* (*color*) white; *m.* white man; (*nada escrito*) blank, blank sheet; (*objeto de tiro*) target, goal.

blancura *f.* whiteness.

blancuzco, blanquecino, blanquizco *adj.* whitish.

blandir *v.* to brandish, flourish, swing.

blando *adj.* bland, smooth; soft; **blanducho** *adj.* flabby; soft.

blandura *f.* softness; mildness, gentleness.

blanquear *v.* to whiten, bleach; to whitewash; to show white; to begin to turn white.

blanqueo *m.* whitening, bleach, bleaching.

blanquillo *adj.* whitish; white (*flour*); *m. Mex., C.A.* egg; *Peru, Ch., Andes* white peach.

blasfemar *v.* to blaspheme, curse, swear.

blasfemia *f.* blasphemy.

blasón *m.* coat of arms; honor, glory.

blasonar *v.* to boast.

blindaje *m.* armor, armor plating.

blindar *v.* to armor.

bloc *m. Am.* tablet, pad of paper.

blocaje *m.* action of blocking.

blondo *adj.* blond.

bloque *m.* block (*of stone, wood, etc.*); *Am.* tablet, pad of paper; *Cuba, Mex., Riopl.* political bloc.

bloquear *v.* to blockade.

bloqueo *m.* blockade.

blusa *f.* blouse.

boato *m.* pomp, ostentation.

bobada *f.* foolishness, folly.

bobalicón *adj.* foolish, silly; *m.* simpleton, blockhead, dunce.

bobear *v.* to act like a fool; to fool around; to gawk, stare foolishly.

bobería *f.* foolishness, folly; nonsense; foolish remark.

bobina *f.* bobbin, reel; electric coil; — **distribuidora** feeding reel; — **receptora** rewind reel (*on a tape recorder*).

bobo *adj.* simple, foolish, stupid; *m.* booby, fool, dunce.

boca *f.* mouth; opening; — **abajo** face downward; — **arriba** face upward; **a** — **de jarro** at close range; **bocaza** *f.* large mouth.

bocacalle *f.* street intersection.

bocado *m.* mouthful, morsel, bite; bit (*of a bridle*); **bocadillo, bocadito** *m.* snack; sandwich; tidbit; *Am.* piece of candy.

bocanada *f.* mouthful; puff (*of smoke*).

boceto *m.* sketch; outline; skit.

bocina *f.* horn; trumpet; automobile horn; speaking tube; megaphone.

bochorno *m.* sultry weather; suffocating heat; blush, flush; embarrassment.

bochornoso *adj.* sultry; embarrassing.

boda *f.* marriage, wedding; — **de negros** a noisy party; **-s de Camacho** lavish feast, banquet.

bodega *f.* cellar; wine cellar; storeroom; warehouse; *Cuba, Ven., Col.* grocery store; **bodeguero** *m.* keeper of a wine cellar; liquor dealer; *Cuba, Ven., Col.* grocer.

bodoque *m.* wad; lump; dunce; *Am.* bump, swelling.

bofe *m.* lung; *P.R.* snap, easy job; **echar uno los -s** to throw oneself into a job; to work hard; *Am.* **ser un** — to be a bore; to be repulsive.

bofetada *f.* slap; **bofetón** *m.* big slap, blow, hard sock, wallop.

boga *f.* vogue, fashion; rowing; *m.* rower.

bogar[7] *v.* to row.

bohemio *adj. & m.* Bohemian.

bohío *m. Carib., Ven.* cabin, shack, hut.

boina *f.* cap.

bola *f.* (*esfera*) ball, bowling; (*mentira*) fib, lie; (*betún*) shoe polish; *Am.* disturbance, riot, false rumor; **no dar pie con** — not to do things right; not to hit the mark; to make mistakes; *Am.* **darle a la** — to hit the mark.

boleada *f. Riopl.* lassoing with **boleadoras**; *Riopl.* hunting expedition (*with* **boleadoras**); *Mex.* shoeshine; *Col.* affront, insult.

boleadoras *f. pl. Am.* lasso with balls at the ends.

bolear *v.* to play billiards; to bowl; to lie, fib; *Am.* to lasso with **boleadoras**; *Am.* to entangle; *Am.* to polish (*shoes*); *Am.* to dismiss; *Am.* to blackball, vote against; *Am.* to flunk; **-se** *Am.* to rear, balk (*said of a horse*); *Am.* to blush, be ashamed.

boleta *f.* certificate; pass; pay order; *Mex., C.A.* ballot; *Ch.* first draft of a deed.

boletín *m.* bulletin.

boleto *m. Am.* ticket; **boletería** *f. Am.* ticket office.

boliche *m.* bowl (*wooden ball for bowling*); bowling alley; *Riopl.* cheap tavern; *Ch.* gambling joint; *Riopl.* cheap store or shop, notions store, variety store.

bolita *f.* small ball; *Am.* ballot (*small ball used in voting*); *Col., Ven.* marble; *Am.* armadillo.

bolo *m.* one of the ninepins (*used in bowling*); dunce, stupid fellow; **-s** bowls, bowling; **jugar a los -s** to bowl.

bolsa *f.* bag, purse; stock exchange; *Riopl.* pocket.

bolsillo *m.* pocket; pocketbook.

bolsista *m.* stockbroker, market operator.

bollo *m.* bun, muffin; bump, lump; puff (*in a dress*); tuft (*on upholstery*); *Andes* loaf of bread; *Am.* a kind of tamale; **-s** *Am.* difficulties, troubles.

bomba *f.* pump; lamp globe; bomb; **— atómica** atomic bomb; **— de hidrógeno** hydrogen bomb; *Carib.* false news; *Am.* stanza improvised by a dancer; *Ríopl.* firecracker, sky-rocket; *Mex.*, *Col.* satirical remark; *Am.* large drum; **— para incendios** fire engine; *Am.* **estar con una —** to be drunk; **bombita** *f.* soap bubble; *Col.* shame, embarrassment.

bombachas *f. pl. Am.* loose-fitting breeches.

bombacho *adj.* loose-fitting (*trousers or breeches*)

bombardear *v.* to bomb.

bombardeo *m.* bombardment, bombing; **avión de —** bomber, bombing plane.

bombardero *m.* bombardier; bomber.

bombear *v.* (*echar bombas*) to bomb; (*alabar*) to praise, extol; *Am.* to pump; *Col.* to fire, dismiss; *Am.* to puff hard on a cigar or cigarette.

bombero *m.* fireman; pumper.

bombilla *f.* electric-light bulb; *Am.* kerosene lamp tube; *Am.* small tube for drinking **mate.**

bombo *m.* large drum; bass drum; player on a bass drum; *Mex.*, *Col.*, *Ch.* pomp, ostentation; *Ríopl.* buttocks, rump; **dar —** to praise, extol (*in the press or newspapers*); *Col.*, *Ríopl.* **darse —** to put on airs; *Am.* **irse uno al —** to fail; *adj.* stunned; *Am.* luke-warm; *Am.* slightly rotten; *Am.* stupid, silly, simple; *Cuba* **fruta bomba** papaya (*tropical fruit*).

bombón *m.* bonbon, candy; **— de altea** marshmallow.

bonachón *adj.* good-natured; naïve, simple.

bonanza *f.* fair weather; prosperity; rich vein of ore.

bondad *f.* goodness.

bondadoso *adj.* good, kind.

boniato *m. Am.* sweet potato.

bonito *adj.* pretty; *m.* striped tunny (a fish).

bono *m.* certificate; bond.

boñiga *f.* dung, manure.

boqueada *f.* gape, gasp.

boquear *v.* to open one's mouth; to gape, gasp; to be dying.

boquete *m.* breach, gap, hole, opening.

boquiabierto *adj.* openmouthed.

boquilla *f.* (*abertura*) little mouth; small opening; (*de cigarro*) holder; (*de instrumento*) mouthpiece.

borbollón, borbotón *m.* spurt; spurting; big bubble; bubbling up; **a -es** in spurts.

borbotar *v.* to bubble up; to spurt, gush forth; to boil over.

bordado *m.* embroidery.

bordadura *f.* embroidery.

bordar *v.* to embroider.

borde *m.* border, edge.

bordear *v.* to skirt, go along the edge of; *Am.* to trim with a border; *Am.* to make a **bordo** (*small, temporary dam*); **-se** *Ch.*, *Mex.*, *Ven.* to approach, get near.

bordo *m.* board, side of a ship; tack (*of a ship*); *Mex.* small dam; **a —** on board.

borla *f.* (*indumentaria*) tassel; doctor's cap; (*título*) doctor's degree; (*cosmético*) powder puff; tuft; **tomar uno la —** to get a doctor's degree.

borlarse *v. Am.* to get a doctor's degree.

borrachera *f.* drunkenness; drunken spree.

borrachín *m.* toper.

borracho *adj.* drunk; *m.* drunkard; **borrachón** *m.* drunkard, heavy drinker.

borrador *m.* rough draft; *Am.* rubber eraser.

borrar *v.* to blot out; to erase.

borrasca *f.* storm, tempest.

borrascoso *adj.* stormy.

borrego *m.* lamb; fool, simpleton; *Mex.*, *C.A.* false news.

borrico *m.* donkey, ass; fool; sawhorse.

borrón *m.* blotch (*of ink*), blot.

borronear *v.* to blot, blotch; to scribble; to blur; to make a rough sketch.

boruca *f.* racket, noise.

boscaje *m.* grove, thicket, woods; landscape (*picture of natural scenery*).

bosque *m.* forest, woods; **bosquecillo** *m.* small forest, grove.

bosquejar *v.* to sketch; to outline.

bosquejo *m.* sketch, plan, outline, rough draft.

bostezar[6] *v.* to yawn.

bostezo *m.* yawn.

bota *f.* (*calzado*) boot; (*bolsa*) leather wine bag; *adj. Am.* stupid, clumsy; *Mex.* drunk.

botar *v.* (*echar*) to launch; to fling; to throw away; (*rebotar*) to bounce; *Ven.* to waste, squander; *Am.* to fire, dismiss; **-se** *Am.* to lie down.

botarate *m.* fool; braggart; *Mex.*, *Carib.* spendthrift.

bote *m.* (*jarro*) small jar; (*embarcación*) boat; (*rebote*) bounce; (*golpe*) blow; jump; *Ríopl.* liquor bottle; *Mex.*, *C.A.* jail; **estar de — en —** to be crowded, completely filled up.

botella *f.* bottle.

botica *f.* drugstore.

boticario *m.* druggist.

botija *f.* earthen jug; fat person; *Am.* buried treasure; *Am.* belly; *Col.* **poner a uno como — verde** to dress down, scold, insult a person.

botín *m.* booty, plunder; high shoe; *Am.* sock.

botiquín *m.* medicine cabinet; medicine kit; *Am.* liquor store, wine shop.

botón *m.* bud; button; knob; handle; **-es** bellboy.

bóveda *f.* arched roof; vault, underground cellar; burial place.

boxeador *m.* boxer.

boxear *v.* to box, fight with the fists.

boxeo *m.* boxing.

boya *f.* buoy; float net; *Am.* crease, dent; *Am.* rich mineral vein; *Am.* **estar en la buena —** to be in good humor.

B1

bozal _m._ (_de animal_) nuzzle; (_cascabel_) bells on a harness; (_novicio_) novice; (_negro_) Negro native of Africa; _Am._ headstall (_of a halter_); _Spain_ person (_especially a Negro_) who speaks broken Spanish; _Am._ coarse, crude individual; _adj._ green, inexperienced; wild, untamed; stupid.

bozo _m._ down (_on the upper lip_); mustache; outside part of the mouth; headstall (_of a halter_).

bracear _v._ to swing one's arms; to struggle; to crawl, swim with a crawl.

bracero _m._ laborer; **de — arm** in arm; **servir de — a una señora** to serve as an escort, give a lady one's arm.

bracete: de — arm in arm.

bramante _m._ hemp cord, hemp string; Brabant linen; _adj._ roaring, bellowing.

bramar _v._ to bellow, roar, howl; to rage.

bramido _m._ roar; howl; bellow.

brasa _f._ red-hot coal.

brasero _m._ brazier (_pan for burning coal_), grate; hearth; _Riopl._ brick cooking stove.

bravata _f._ bravado, boastfulness, defiance.

bravear _v._ to bluster; to bully.

bravío _adj._ savage, wild; rustic.

bravo _adj._ (_agresivo_) wild, ferocious, harsh; ill-tempered; (_valiente_) brave; _Carib._, _C.A._, _Andes_ angry; _Am._ hot, highly seasoned.

bravura _f._ fierceness; courage; bravado, show of boldness.

braza _f._ fathom; stroke.

brazada _f._ armful; movement of the arms (_swimming stroke_); **a una —** at arm's length.

brazalete _m._ bracelet.

brazo _m._ arm; branch; **-s** day laborers; _Riopl._, _Cuba_ **de —** arm in arm; **luchar a — partido** to wrestle; to fight hand to hand.

brea _f._ pitch; tar; canvas.

brecha _f._ breach, gap.

bregar[7] _v._ to struggle; to fight.

breña _f._ rough, craggy ground covered with brambles; bramble; **breñal** _m._ brambles; bush country.

breve _adj._ brief, short; **en —** shortly.

brevedad _f._ brevity, shortness.

bribón _adj._ idle, indolent; _m._ rascal, rogue; **bribonazo** _m._ scoundrel, cheat.

brida _f._ bridle; rein.

brigada _f._ brigade.

brillante _adj._ brilliant, bright; _m._ diamond.

brillantez _f._ brilliance, dazzle.

brillar _v._ to shine.

brillo _m._ luster, sparkle, shine.

brincar[6] _v._ to hop, skip, jump, bounce.

brinco _m._ hop, skip, bounce, leap.

brindar _v._ to toast, drink to the health of; to offer.

brindis _m._ toast (_to a person's health_).

brío _m._ vigor, liveliness; valor, courage.

brioso _adj._ lively; brave.

brisa _f._ breeze.

británico _adj._ British.

brizna _f._ particle, chip, fragment; blade of grass.

brocal _m._ curb, curbstone (_of a well_).

brocha _f._ painter's brush; loaded dice; **cuadro de — gorda** badly done painting; **pintor de — gorda** house painter; **brochada** _f._ stroke of the brush, brush stroke; **brochazo** _m._ blow with a brush; brush stroke.

broche _m._ brooch; clasp, clip, fastener; hook and eye.

broma _f._ jest, joke; fun, merriment; _Am._ disappointment, irritation; **de —** in jest; **fuera de —** all joking aside.

bromear _v._ to joke, jest.

bronca _f._ quarrel, dispute, wrangle; **armar una —** to cause a disturbance, raise a rumpus.

bronce _m._ bronze.

bronceado _adj._ bronzed; bronze-colored; _m._ bronze finish.

bronco _adj._ hoarse; raspy, harsh; coarse, rough; uncouth; wild, untamed (_horse_).

bronquio _m._ bronchus, bronchial tube.

broquel _m._ buckler, shield (_worn on the arm_).

brotar _v._ to shoot forth; to bud; to break out (_on the skin_); to gush, flow; to spring forth.

broza _f._ brushwood, underbrush; rubbish, refuse, trash; coarse, hard brush.

bruces: de — face downward.

bruja _f._ witch; hag; owl; _adj._ _Mex._ broke, poor; **brujo** _m._ sorcerer, magician, wizard.

brújula _f._ (_compds_) compass; magnetic needle; (_mira_) peephole; gunsight.

bruma _f._ mist, fog; **brumoso** _adj._ foggy, misty, hazy.

bruñir[19] _v. irr._ to burnish, polish; to put on make-up.

brusco _adj._ blunt, rude, abrupt.

brutal _adj._ brutal, beastly, savage.

brutalidad _f._ brutality.

bruto _adj._ (_tonto_) stupid, brutal; (_burdo_) coarse, rough; **peso —** gross weight; **diamante en —** diamond in the rough, unpolished diamond; _m._ brute, beast.

bucal _adj._ oral, pertaining to the mouth.

bucear _v._ to dive; to dive into, plunge into; to explore thoroughly a subject.

bucle _m._ curl, ringlet.

buche _m._ crop (_of a bird_); mouthful (_of water_); wrinkle, bag (_in clothes_); _Riopl._, _Mex._, _Ven._ goiter.

budín _m._ pudding.

buen(o) _adj._ good; kind; useful; well, in good health; **de buenas a primeras** all of a sudden, unexpectedly, on the spur of the moment; **por la(s) buena(s) o por la(s) mala(s)** willingly or unwillingly, by hook or crook.

buey _m._ ox.

búfalo _m._ buffalo.

bufanda _f._ muffler, scarf.

bufar v. to snort; to puff with anger; **-se** Mex. to swell, bulge (as a wall).

bufete m. desk, writing table; lawyer's office.

bufido m. snort.

bufón m. buffoon, jester, clown; adj. comical, funny; **bufonada** f. wise-crack; jest.

bufonear v. to clown; to jest.

buhardilla f. garret, attic; skylight.

buho m. owl.

buhonero m. peddler.

buitre m. vulture.

buje m. bushing; axle box.

bujía f. candle; candle power; candle-stick; spark plug.

bula f. bull (papal document); papal seal.

buldozer m. bulldozer.

bulevar m. boulevard.

bulto m. (cuerpo) body, bundle, shadow, lump, swelling; (tamaño) bulk, volume; **a —** haphazardly, by guess; **escurrir el —** to dodge; **imagen de —** statue, sculpture; **una verdad de —** an evident truth.

bulla f. shouting, uproar; noisy crowd.

bullicio m. noise, uproar.

bullicioso adj. boisterous, noisy; gay, lively; turbulent, stormy.

bullir[20] v. irr. to boil; to buzz about; to bustle, to stir, move; Am. to deride.

buñuelo m. fritter; botch, poor piece of work.

buque m. ship, boat.

burbuja f. bubble.

burdo adj. coarse.

burgués adj. bourgeois, middle-class.

burla f. jest, mockery; **de —** in jest.

burlador m. practical joker; jester; scoffer; seducer.

burlar v. to mock, ridicule, deceive; **-se de** to scoff at; to make fun of.

burlón m. jester, teaser.

burro m. ass, donkey; Mex., Cuba, Ríopl. stepladder; adj. stupid; **burrito** m. small donkey; Am. saddle rack.

busca f. search; hunting party; Am. **-s** profit on the side; graft.

buscar[6] v. to seek, search, look for; Andes to provoke.

búsqueda f. search.

busto m. bust (upper part of body).

butaca f. armchair; orchestra seat; **butacón** m. large armchair.

buzo m. diver.

buzón m. mailbox; letter drop.

C

cabal adj. complete, entire; exact; **estar uno en sus -es** to be in one's right mind.

cabalgar[7] v. to ride, mount (a horse); to ride horseback.

caballa f. horse mackerel.

caballada f. herd of horses; Am. non-sense, stupidity, blunder.

caballejo m. nag; poor horse.

caballeresco adj. gentlemanly; knight-ly; chivalrous, gallant.

caballería f. cavalry; horsemanship; mount, horse; knighthood; chivalry.

caballeriza f. stable; horses of a stable.

caballerizo m. groom, stableman.

caballero m. gentleman; knight, horse-man; adj. gentlemanly.

caballerosidad f. chivalry, gentlemanly conduct.

caballeroso adj. chivalrous, gentle-manly.

caballete m. (de casa) ridge of a roof; (madero) sawhorse; (de la cara) bridge of the nose.

caballo m. horse; knight (in chess); Am. stupid or brutal person; **a —** on horseback; **caballuco** m. nag.

cabaña f. hut, cabin; Am. cattle ranch.

cabecear v. to nod; to shake the head; to pitch (as a boat); Am. to begin to rise or fall (said of a river).

cabeceo m. nodding; pitching (of a boat).

cabecera f. head (of bed or table); seat, chief city (of a district).

cabecilla f. small head; m. ringleader.

cabellera fe head of hair, long hair; wig; tail of a comet.

cabello m. hair; **traer algo por los -s** to bring in a far-fetched fact or quota-tion; **-s de ángel** cotton candy.

cabelludo adj. hairy; **cuero —** scalp.

caber[23] v. irr. to fit into, go into; to have enough room for; to befall; **no cabe duda** there is no doubt; **no cabe más** there is no room for more; **no — uno en sí** to be puffed up with pride; **no cabe en lo posible** it is absolute-ly impossible.

cabestro m. halter; leading ox; Carib., Mex. rope, cord; Am. advance pay-ment; **cabestrillo** m. sling (for an arm).

cabeza f. (parte superior) head; upper part; (director) chief, leader; capital (of a district); Carib. source (of a river); **— de playa** beachhead; **— de puente** bridgehead; **— sonora** re-cording head.

cabezada f. butt (with the head); bump on the head; nod; shake of the head; pitching (of a ship); headgear (of a harness).

cabezazo m. butt (with the head); bump on the head.

cabezudo adj. big-headed; hard-head-ed, pig-headed, stubborn, headstrong.

cabezón adj. big-headed; pig-headed, stubborn; Ch. strong (liquor); m. large head; cavesson (iron noseband used in breaking a horse); Col. rapids or whirlpool in a river.

cabida f. space, room, capacity; **tener — con alguien** to have influence with someone.

cabildo m. cathedral chapter; munici-pal council; council room; town hall.

cabina f. cabin (of an airplane).

cabizbajo adj. crestfallen, downcast; pensive.

cable m. cable.

cablegrafiar[17] v. to cable.

cablegrama m. cablegram.

cabo *m.* (*cosa*) end, tip, handle; piece of rope; (*geográfico*) cape, headland; (*persona*) foreman, corporal; **al —** finally; **al fin y al —** anyway, in the long run; **de — a rabo** from beginning to end; **estar al — de** to be well informed about; **llevar a —** to carry out, finish.

cabra *f.* goat; *Col.* fraud, trick; *Am.* loaded dice; *Am.* light two-wheeled carriage; **cabrillas** *f. pl.* whitecaps (*small waves with white crests*); Pleiades (*constellation*); game of skipping stones on the water.

cabrío *adj.* goatish; **macho —** he-goat; *m.* herd of goats.

cabriola *f.* caper, leap, hop, skip; somersault; **hacer -s** to cut capers; to prance.

cabriolar *v.* to prance; to caper; to romp, frolic, frisk.

cabrito *m.* kid; **cabritilla** *f.* kid, kid-skin.

cabrón *m.* he-goat; cuckold (*man whose wife is unfaithful*).

cacahuate *m. Mex., C.A.* peanut; *Spain* **cacahuete, cacahuey.**

cacao *m.* cocoa.

cacarear *v.* to cackle; to boast; *Am.* to run away from a fight.

cacareo *m.* cackle.

cacería *f.* hunt, hunting.

cacerola *f.* saucepan.

cacha *f.* handle (*of a knife or pistol*); *Am.* the horns of a bull; *C.A.* **hacer la —** to complete a task, to get.

cacharro *m.* earthen pot or vase; broken piece of a pot; crude utensil; *Am.* cheap trinket.

cachaza *f.* slowness; calm; rum.

cachazudo *adj.* slow, easy going.

cachetada *f. Am.* slap on the face.

cachete *m.* cheek; slap on the cheek.

cachimbo *m. Am.* pipe (*for smoking*); *Cuba* small sugar mill; also **cachimba.**

cachivache *m.* piece of junk; worthless fellow; *Mex., Carib., Ven.* trinket.

cachorro *m.* cub; small pistol; *Am.* rude, ill-bred person.

cachucha *f.* cap; rowboat; popular Andalusian dance, song and music; *Am.* slap.

cacique *m.* chief; political boss; *Mex.* tyrant; *Ch., Ven.* one who leads an easy life.

caciquismo *m.* political bossism (*rule by political bosses*).

cacto *m.* cactus.

cacumen *m.* acumen, keen insight.

cada *adj.* each, every; **— uno** each one; **— y cuando que** whenever; *Am.* **a — nada** every second.

cadalso *m.* gallows; scaffold, platform.

cadáver *m.* corpse; **cadavérico** *adj.* deadly, ghastly, pale, like a corpse.

cadena *f.* chain.

cadencia *f.* cadence.

cadencioso *adj.* rhythmical.

cadera *f.* hip.

cadete *m.* cadet.

caducar[6] *v.* to dote, be in one's dotage; to lapse, expire; to become extinct, fall into disuse.

caduco *adj.* decrepit, very old, feeble; perishable.

caer[24] *v. irr.* to fall; to fall down; to fall off; **-se** to fall down, tumble; **— a** to face, overlook; **— bien** to fit, be becoming; **— en cama** to fall ill; **— en la cuenta** to catch on, get the point; **— en gracia** to please; **al — de la noche** at nightfall; **dejar —** to drop.

café *m.* coffee; café; *Am.* annoyance, bad time.

cafeína *f.* caffein.

cafetal *m.* coffee plantation.

cafetera *f.* coffeepot; woman café owner, coffee vendor or merchant; coffee-bean picker.

cafetería *f.* café, bar, lunchroom.

cafetero *adj.* pertaining to coffee; *m.* coffee grower; coffee merchant; owner of a café or coffee-house; *Am.* coffee drinker.

cafeto *m.* coffee bush.

caída *f.* fall, drop; descent; **a la — del sol** (*or* **de la tarde**) at sunset.

caimán *m.* cayman, alligator.

caja *f.* case, box; **— de ahorros** savings bank; **— de cambios** transmission (*automobile*); **— de píldora** pillbox; **— fuerte** safe; **echar a uno con -s destempladas** to give someone the gate.

cajero *m.* cashier; box maker.

cajetilla *f.* small box; package of cigarettes.

cajón *m.* large box, chest; drawer; vendor's booth or stand; *Ch., Mex.* narrow canyon; **— de muerto** coffin; *Mex.* **— de ropa** dry-goods and clothing store.

cal *f.* lime (*mineral*).

calabaza *f.* pumpkin, squash; gourd; an ignorant person; **dar -s** to jilt, turn down (*a suitor*); to flunk, fail.

calabozo *m.* dungeon; prison cell.

calado *m.* drawn work; openwork (*in wood, metal, linen, etc.*), fretwork; draft (*of a ship*).

calamar *m.* squid, cuttlefish.

calambre *m.* cramp.

calamidad *f.* calamity, misfortune.

calandria *f.* lark, skylark.

calar *v.* (*penetrar*) to pierce, penetrate; to soak through; to make openwork (*in cloth, metal*); (*probar*) to probe, search into; **-se el sombrero** to put on one's hat; to pull down one's hat.

calavera *f.* skull; *m.* madcap, rounder, reckless fellow; *Mex.* taillight.

calcar[6] *v.* to trace; to copy, imitate.

calceta *f.* hose, stocking; **hacer —** to knit; **calcetería** *f.* hosiery shop; hosiery (*business of making hose*).

calcetín *m.* sock.

calcinar *v.* to burn, char, heat.

calcio *m.* calcium.

calco *m.* tracing, traced copy; exact copy; imitation.

calculadora f. calculator (*machine for performing mathematical operations*); **— electrónica** computer.

calcular v. to calculate, figure, estimate.

cálculo m. calculation, estimate; calculus; gravel (*in the gall bladder, kidney, etc.*).

caldear v. to heat; to weld; **-se** *Am.* to become overheated, excited; *Am.* to get "lit up", get drunk.

caldera f. boiler; caldron, kettle; **calderilla** f. copper coin.

caldo m. broth; gravy.

calefacción f. heat, heating.

calendario m. calendar; almanac.

caléndula f. marigold.

calentador m. heater.

calentar¹ v. *irr.* to warm, heat; to spank; *Am.* to annoy, bother; **-se** to warm oneself; to become heated, excited; to be in heat; *Am.* to become angry.

calentura f. fever; *Col.* fit of temper; **— de pollo** feigned illness; **calenturón** m. high fever.

calenturiento adj. feverish; *Ch.* tubercular.

caletre m. judgment, acumen, keen insight.

calibrar v. to gauge, measure; to measure the caliber of.

calibre m. caliber; bore, gauge (*of a gun*); diameter (*of a pipe, tube, wire*).

calicanto m. stone masonry.

calicó m. calico, cotton cloth.

calidad f. quality.

cálido adj. warm, hot.

caliente adj. warm, hot; heated; fiery; *Am.* angry; *Col.* bold, brave; m. *Am.* brandy in hot water; **calientito** adj. nice and warm.

calificación f. qualification; grade, mark (*in a course or examination*); judgment.

calificar⁶ v. to qualify; to rate, consider, judge; to grade; *Am.* to compute (*election returns*); **-se** *Ch.* to qualify or register (*as a voter*).

caligrafía f. penmanship.

calina f. haze, mist.

cáliz m. chalice, communion cup; cup, goblet; calyx (*of a flower*).

calma f. calm, quiet.

calmante adj. soothing; m. sedative.

calmar v. to calm, quiet, soothe.

calmo adj. calm, quiet.

calmoso adj. calm; soothing; phlegmatic, slow.

calor m. heat, warmth; ardor.

calorífero m. heater, radiator; furnace.

calosfrío, calofrío m. chill.

calumnia f. slander.

calumniar v. to slander.

caluroso adj. (*literal*) hot, warm; (*figurado*) heated, excited; cordial, enthusiastic.

calva f. bald head; bald spot; barren spot.

calvario m. Calvary, place of the Cross; suffering, tribulation.

calvo adj. bald; barren.

calza f. wedge; shoehorn; *Col., Ven.* gold inlay, tooth filling; **-s** breeches.

calzada f. paved road; highway; *Mex., Carib.* wide avenue.

calzado m. footwear.

calzador m. shoehorn.

calzar⁹ v. to put on (*shoes, gloves, spurs*); to put a wedge under a wheel; *Am.* to fill (*a tooth*).

calzón m. (or **calzones**) breeches, short trousers; *Mex., Ven.* drawers; *Mex.* white cotton trousers; **calzoncillos** m. pl. drawers, men's shorts; **calzoneras** f. pl. *Mex.* trousers open down the sides.

callado adj. silent, quiet.

callar v. to be silent; to hush; **-se** to be or keep silent.

calle f. street.

calleja f. small street, alley, lane; **callejuela** f. small, narrow street; lane.

callejear v. to walk the streets, ramble.

callejero m. street-rambler, street-stroller; street-loiterer; adj. fond of walking the streets; rambling.

callejón m. alley; lane; narrow pass; **— sin salida** blind alley.

callo m. callus, corn; **-s** tripe (*food*).

calloso adj. callous, hard.

cama f. bed, couch, cot; litter; **caer en — to fall ill; guardar —** to be confined to bed; *Am.* **tenderle uno la — a otro** to help one in his love affairs; to set a trap for someone; **camastro** m. poor, uncomfortable bed.

camada f. litter; brood.

cámara f. chamber, hall, parlor; house (*of a legislative body*); cabin, stateroom; chamber (*of a gun*); **— de aire** inner tube; **— fotográfica** camera.

camarada m. comrade; **camaradería** f. comradeship, companionship.

camarera f. waitress; chambermaid; stewardess.

camarero m. waiter; chamberlain; steward; valet.

camarilla f. political lobby; small group of politicians; "kitchen cabinet", group of unofficial advisers; small room.

camarón m. shrimp.

camarote m. cabin, stateroom.

cambalache m. swap, barter, exchange.

cambalachear v. to swap, barter, exchange.

cambiador m. barterer; money changer; *Am.* switchman.

cambiante adj. changing; exchanging; **-s** m. pl. iridescent colors.

cambiar v. to change; to exchange; to shift; **— de marcha** to shift gears.

cambiavía m. *Carib., Mex., Andes* railway switchman. *See* **guardaagujas** *and* **cambiador**.

cambio m. change; exchange; railway switch; **libre —** free trade; **en —** on the other hand; in exchange.

cambista m. exchange broker, banker; *Am.* railway switchman.

camello m. camel.

camilla *f.* stretcher; cot; **camillero** *m.* stretcher bearer.

caminante *m.* & *f.* walker, traveler.

caminar *v.* to travel; to walk; *Am.* to progress, prosper.

caminata *f.* long walk; hike; jaunt.

camino *m.* road; course; *Riopl.* table runner; *Am.* hall runner; **— de hierro** railroad; *Am.* **— real** highway; **de — on** the way.

camión *m.* truck; wagon; *Mex.* bus; **camionero** *m.* truck driver; **camioneta** *f.* small truck; *C.A.* bus.

camisa *f.* shirt; **— de fuerza** straitjacket; **meterse en — de once varas** to attempt more than one can manage, bite off more than one can chew; **camiseta** *f.* undershirt.

camisón *m.* long shirt; *Am.* nightgown; *Am.* gown, dress.

camote *m. Am.* a kind of sweet potato.

campamento *m.* encampment; camp.

campana *f.* bell; *Riopl., Andes* spy, lookout (*for thieves*); **campanada** *f.* stroke of a bell; *Am.* **por — de vacante** once in a blue moon, very seldom.

campanario *m.* bell tower.

campanilla *f.* small bell; bubble; uvula; tassel; bell-flower.

campanillazo *m.* loud ring of a bell.

campanilleo *m.* ringing; tinkling.

campaña *f.* level, open country; campaign; period of active service.

campear *v.* to pasture; to grow green (*said of the fields*); to excel; to be prominent, stand out; to be in the field; *Riopl.* to search the plains for lost cattle; *Col., Ven.* to act the bully.

campechano *adj.* frank, open.

campéon *m.* champion; defender

campeonato *m.* championship.

campesino *adj.* rural, rustic; *m.* peasant, countryman; farmer.

campestre *adj.* rural, rustic.

campiña *f.* large field; open country.

campo *m.* country; field; camp; **a — raso** in the open; **a — traviesa** (*or* **travieso**) cross-country.

camposanto *m.* churchyard, cemetery.

camuesa *f.* pippin (*a variety of apple*).

camuflaje *m.* camouflage.

can *m.* dog; trigger (*of a gun*).

cana *f.* white hair, grey hair; *Carib.* a kind of palm; **echar una — al aire** to go out for a good time; to go out on a fling.

canadiense *adj., m.* & *f.* Canadian.

canal *m.* canal, channel; *f.* eaves trough.

canalla *f.* rabble, mob; *m.* mean fellow.

canana *f.* cartridge belt; **-s** *Col., Ven.* handcuffs.

canapé *m.* couch, lounge, sofa; settee.

canario *m.* canary; native of the Canary Islands; *interj.* great Scott!

canasta *f.* basket; crate.

cancelación *f.* cancellation.

cancelar *v.* to cancel.

canciller *m.* chancellor.

canción *f.* song; a kind of lyric poem; **volver a la misma —** to repeat, harp on the same thing.

cancha *f.* court (*for tennis, etc.*); sports ground or field; cockpit, enclosure for cockfights; *Peru* roasted corn or beans; *Am.* **¡abran —!** gangway!; make room!

candado *m.* padlock; *Col.* goatee.

candela *f.* candle; fire, forest fire; light.

candelero *m.* candlestick.

candente *adj.* incandescent, white-hot, red-hot.

candidato *m.* candidate.

candidatura *f.* candidacy.

candidez *f.* candor, simplicity.

cándido *adj.* candid, simple, innocent; white.

candil *m.* lamp; *Riopl., Mex.* chandelier; **candileja** *f.* small oil lamp; oil receptacle (*of a lamp*); **-s** footlights (*of a stage*).

candor *m.* candor, simplicity, innocence; frankness, sincerity.

canela *f.* cinnamon; an exquisite thing.

cangrejo *m.* crab.

canguro *m.* kangaroo.

caníbal *m.* cannibal.

canica *f.* marble (*small glass or marble ball*).

canilla *f.* long bone (*of the arm or leg*); cock (*of a barrel*), faucet; spool (*for a sewing machine*); *C.A.* slender leg; *Ch., Col., Riopl.* calf (*of the leg*); *Mex., Ven.* **tener —** to have physical strength; **canillita** *m. Riopl., Ch., C.A., Andes* newspaper boy.

canino *adj.* canine; **tener un hambre canina** to be ravenous; to be hungry as a dog.

canje *m.* interchange, exchange.

canjear *v.* to exchange, interchange.

cano *adj.* grey-headed, grey-haired.

canoa *f.* canoe.

canon *m.* canon; precept, rule, principle.

canónigo *m.* canon (*churchman*).

canonizar[9] *v.* to canonize, saint.

canoso *adj.* grey, grey-haired.

cansado *adj.* tired; tiresome, boring.

cansancio *m.* fatigue, weariness.

cansar *v.* to tire, fatigue; **-se** to get tired.

cantar *v.* to sing; to squeal, confess; *Am.* **— alto** to ask a high price; **— claro** (*or* **-las claras**) to speak with brutal frankness; *m.* song, epic poem.

cántaro *m.* pitcher, jug.

cantatriz *f.* singer.

cantera *f.* quarry; *Riopl., Mex., Carib.* stone block.

cántico *m.* canticle, religious song.

cantidad *f.* quantity.

cantilena *f.* song, ballad; monotonous repetition.

cantimplora *f.* canteen; metal vessel for cooling water; *Col.* flask for carrying gunpowder.

cantina *f.* mess hall; wine cellar; wine shop; canteen; *Carib., Mex., Riopl.* barroom, tavern; *Col.* saddlebag.

cantinela = **cantilena**.

cantinero *m.* bartender; tavern keeper.

canto *m.* song; singing; canto (*division of a long poem*); stone; edge; *Col.* lap; *Am.* piece.

cantón *m.* canton, region; corner; *Am.* cotton cloth.

cantor *m.* singer; song bird.

canturrear, canturriar *v.* to hum, sing softly.

canturreo *m.* hum, humming.

caña *f.* cane, reed; tall, thin glass; stem; *Riopl., Col., Ven.* sugar-cane brandy; *Am.* a kind of dance; *Am.* bluff, boast.

cañada *f.* narrow canyon, dale, dell, gully, ravine; *Am.* brook.

cáñamo *m.* hemp; hemp cloth; *Am.* hemp cord, rope; **cañamazo** *m.* canvas.

cañaveral *m.* cane field; reed patch; sugar-cane plantation.

cañería *f.* conduit, pipe line; tubing, piping; gas or water main.

caño *m.* pipe, tube; spout; sewer; narrow channel; *Ven.* branch of a river, stream.

cañón *m.* (*arma*) cannon, gun; barrel (*of a gun*); (*topográfico*) ravine, gorge, canyon; (*tubo*) pipe, tube; (*figurado*) beard stubble; pinfeather; quill (*of a feather*); chimney shaft; **cañonazo** *m.* cannon shot.

cañonear *v.* to cannonade, bombard.

cañoneo *m.* cannonade; bombardment.

cañonero *m.* gunboat; gunner; **lancha cañonera** gunboat.

caoba *f.* mahogany.

caos *m.* chaos, confusion.

capa *f.* (*ropa*) cape, cloak; (*cubierta*) covering, coating; layer; scum; **so — de** under the guise of, under pretense of.

capacidad *f.* capacity; ability.

capacitar *v.* to enable, prepare, fit, qualify; *Col.* to empower, authorize.

capataz *m.* boss, foreman, overseer.

capaz *adj.* capable, able, competent; spacious, roomy.

capellán *m.* chaplain, priest, clergyman.

caperuza *f.* pointed hood.

capilla *f.* chapel; hood.

capirote *m.* hood; **tonto de —** dunce, plain fool.

capital *m.* capital, funds; *f.* capital, capital city; *adj.* capital; **capitalismo** *m.* capitalism; **capitalista** *m. & f.* capitalist; *adj.* capitalistic.

capitalizar⁹ *v.* to capitalize.

capitán *m.* captain.

capitanear *v.* to command, lead.

capitolio *m.* capitol.

capitular *v.* to surrender; to come to an agreement.

capítulo *m.* chapter.

caporal *m.* boss, leader; *Am.* foreman in a cattle ranch.

capote *m.* cloak (*with sleeves*); bull-fighter's cloak; *Ch.* thrashing, beating; **decir para su —** to say to oneself; *Am.* **de —** in an under-handed way; *Ven., Carib.* **dar —** to get ahead; to deceive.

capricho *m.* caprice, whim, notion.

caprichoso *adj.* capricious, whimsical; changeable, fickle.

caprichudo *adj.* whimsical; stubborn, willful.

cápsula *f.* capsule; percussion cap, cartridge shell; metal cap (*on bottles*).

captar *v.* to win, attract; to captivate; *Am.* to get, tune in on (*a radio station*).

captura *f.* capture.

capturar *v.* to capture, arrest.

capucha *f.* hood.

capullo *m.* cocoon; bud; acorn cup.

cara *f.* face; expression, countenance; front; **de —** opposite; **echar** (*or* **dar**) **en —** to reproach, blame; **sacar la — por alguien** to take someone's part, defend him.

carabina *f.* carbine, rifle.

caracol *m.* snail; winding stairs; *Am.* embroidered blouse; *Am.* curl.

caracolear *v.* to caper, prance around (*said of horses*); *Col., Ven.* to muddle, entangle; *Am.* to sidestep an obligation.

caracoleo *m.* prancing around; winding, turn.

carácter *m.* character; temper.

característico *adj.* characteristic; **característica** *f.* characteristic, trait.

caracterizar⁹ *v.* to characterize.

¡caramba! *interj.* great guns! great Scott!

carámbano *m.* icicle.

caramelo *m.* caramel.

caramillo *m.* reed pipe, small flute; **armar un —** to raise a rumpus, create a disturbance.

carancho *m.* *Riopl.* hawk, buzzard.

carátula *f.* mask; *Col., Ven., Riopl., Carib., Andes* title page of a book; *C.A., Mex., Andes* dial, face of a watch.

caravana *f.* caravan.

carbólico *adj.* carbolic.

carbón *m.* carbon; coal; **— de leña** charcoal; **carbono** *m.* carbon.

carbonera *f.* coal bin; coal cellar; woman coal or charcoal vendor; *Am.* coal mine; **carbonero** *m.* coal dealer; charcoal vendor; *adj.* coal, relating to coal or charcoal.

carburador *m.* carburetor.

carcajada *f.* loud laughter, peal of laughter.

cárcel *f.* jail, prison.

carcelero *m.* jailer; *adj.* relating to a jail.

carcomido *adj.* worm-eaten; decayed.

cardar *v.* to card, comb (*wool*).

cardenal *m.* cardinal; cardinal bird; bruise.

cárdeno *adj.* dark-purple.

cardo *m.* thistle; a kind of cactus.

carear *v.* to confront, bring face to face; to compare; **-se** to meet face to face.

carecer¹³ *v. irr.* to lack, be in need of.

carencia *f.* lack, want.

carente *adj.* lacking.

carero *adj.* overcharging; profiteering; *m.* profiteer.

carestía *f.* dearth, scarcity; high price.

careta *f.* mask.

carga *f.* load, burden; freight; cargo; charge of gunpowder; **volver a la —** to insist again and again.

cargado *p.p.* & *adj.* loaded; strong (*as tea or coffee*); cloudy, sultry; **— de espaldas** round-shouldered, stoop-shouldered.

cargador *m.* loader; stevedore; *Am.* carrier, errand boy, mover.

cargamento *m.* cargo.

cargar[6] *v.* (*poner carga*) to load; to charge; (*atacar*) to charge; (*molestar*) to bother, annoy; *Am.* to carry, lug; *Am.* to punish; **— con** to carry away; to assume (*responsibility*); **— con el muerto** to get the blame (*unjustly*).

cargo *m.* charge, position, duty, burden; loading; accusation; **hacerse — de** to take charge of; to realize.

carguero *adj.* load-carrying; freight-carrying; *m.* *Am.* beast of burden; *Am.* skilled loader of pack animals; *Am.* patient, long-suffering person.

caribe *adj.* Caribbean; *m.* Carib, Caribbean Indian; cannibal; savage.

caricatura *f.* caricature; cartoon.

caricia *f.* caress.

caridad *f.* charity; alms.

caries *f.* decay (*of a bone*); tooth cavity.

cariño *m.* affection, love; *Am.* gift.

cariñoso *adj.* affectionate, loving.

caritativo *adj.* charitable.

carmesí *adj.* & *m.* crimson.

carmín *m.* crimson.

carnal *adj.* carnal, sensual.

carnaval *m.* carnival.

carne *f.* meat; flesh; **— de gallina** "goose flesh", "goose pimples"; **echar -s** to put on weight, get fat; *Am.* **— de res** beef.

carneada *f.* *Riopl.* butchering, slaughtering.

carnear *v.* *Riopl.* to butcher; *Riopl.* to kill.

carnero *m.* (*animal*) ram, male sheep; (*carne*) mutton; *Am.* a weak-willed person; *Am.* waste basket; *Am.* **— de la tierra** llama (*or any fleece-bearing animal*); *Am.* **cantar uno el — to** die.

carnicería *f.* (*tienda*) meat market; (*matanza*) butchery, slaughter; *C.A., Ec.* slaughterhouse.

carnicero *m.* butcher; *adj.* carnivorous, flesh-eating; cruel.

carnívoro *adj.* carnivorous.

carnosidad *f.* fleshiness, fatness; abnormal growth (*on animal or plant tissues*).

carnoso *adj.* fleshy; meaty; pulpy.

caro *adj.* expensive; dear; *adv.* at a high price.

carona *f.* saddle pad.

carozo *m.* cob, corncob.

carpa *f.* carp (*fresh-water fish*); *Am.* canvas tent, circus tent; **— dorada** goldfish.

carpeta *f.* (*cubierta*) table cover; desk pad; (*cartera*) portfolio, letter case or file; *Andes* office desk; *Am.* book-keeping department; **carpetazo: dar — to** table (*a motion*); to set aside, pigeonhole or dismiss.

carpintería *f.* carpentry; carpenter's workshop.

carpintero *m.* carpenter; **pájaro —** woodpecker.

carraspear *v.* to cough up; to clear one's throat; to be hoarse.

carraspera *f.* hoarseness.

carrera *f.* career; race, run; course; stocking run.

carreta *f.* long, narrow wagon; cart; *Col., Ven.* wheelbarrow.

carretaje *m.* cartage (*transporting by cart, truck, etc.*); price paid for cartage.

carrete *m.* spool; reel; **— distribuidor** feeding reel; **— receptor** take-up reel (*tape recorder*).

carretel *m.* reel, spool, bobbin; fishing reel; log reel (*of a boat*).

carretera *f.* highway.

carretero *m.* carter, teamster; cart maker; **camino —** highway.

carretilla *f.* wheelbarrow; small cart; baggage truck; *Ríopl.* wagon; *Am.* jaw; *Col.* string, series (*of lies, blunders, etc.*); *Am.* firecracker; **repetir de — to** rattle off, repeat mechanically.

carretón *m.* truck; wagon, cart.

carril *m.* rail; rut; furrow.

carrillo *m.* (*de la cara*) cheek; (*mecánico*) pulley; cart.

carrizo *m.* reed; reed grass.

carro *m.* cart; cartload; *Am.* car, auto, streetcar, coach; *Am.* **pararle a uno el — to** restrain someone; *Am.* **pasarle a uno el — to** suffer an injury or misfortune; **carroza** *f.* large and luxurious carriage; chariot; *Am.* hearse.

carrocería *f.* chassis; frame for a parade float.

carroña *f.* dead and decaying flesh; putrid, decaying carcass.

carruaje *m.* carriage, vehicle.

carta *f.* (*misiva*) letter; (*naipe*) card; (*documento*) charter; map; **— blanca** full authority, freedom to act; **— de naturaleza** naturalization papers; **— de venta** bill of sale; *Ch.* **retirar — to** repent, back down; *Am.* **ser la última — de la baraja** to be the worst or most insignificant person or thing.

cartearse *v.* to correspond, write to each other.

cartel *m.* poster, handbill; cartel, written agreement; **cartela** *f.* tag, slip of paper, small card, piece of cardboard; **cartelera** *f.* billboard; **cartelón** *m.* large poster.

cartera *f.* (*objeto*) wallet; briefcase; desk pad; (*puesto*) portfolio, cabinet post; **carterista** *m.* & *f.* pickpocket.

cartero *m.* mailman, letter carrier, postman.

cartilla f. primer; note, short letter; **leerle a uno la —** to scold, lecture someone concerning his duties.

cartografiar[17] v. to chart; to make charts.

cartón m. cardboard; pasteboard; **cartulina** f. fine cardboard.

cartuchera f. cartridge belt.

cartucho m. cartridge; roll of coins; paper cone or bag.

casa f. (doméstica) house, home; household; (negocio) business firm; square (of a chessboard); Am. bet, wager; **— de empeños** pawnshop; **— de huéspedes** boardinghouse; **echar la — por la ventana** to spend recklessly, squander everything; **poner —** to set up housekeeping.

casabe, cazabe m. Am. cassava; Am. cassava bread.

casaca f. long military coat; **volver —** to be a turncoat, change sides or parties.

casamiento m. wedding; marriage.

casar v. to marry; to match; Am. to graft (trees); **-se** to get married.

cascabel m. jingle bell, tinkle bell; snake's rattle; Am. rattlesnake; **cascabela** f. C.R. rattlesnake.

cascada f. cascade, waterfall.

cascajo m. coarse gravel; crushed stone; pebble; fragment; rubbish.

cascanueces m. nutcracker.

cascar[6] v. to crack, break; **-se** to crack or break open.

cáscara f. shell, husk, hull, rind; bark of a tree; Riopl. **dar a uno — de novillo** to give someone a whipping; **cascarudo** adj. having a thick husk; having a thick rind.

cascarrabias m. & f. crab, grouch, ill-tempered person; adj. grouchy, cranky, irritable.

casco m. helmet; hoof; skull; broken piece of earthenware; cask; empty bottle; hull of a ship; Mex., Riopl. compound, main building of a farm; **caliente de -s** hot-headed; **ligero de -s** light-headed, frivolous; **romperse los -s** to rack one's brain.

caserío m. hamlet, small settlement.

casero adj. domestic; homemade; m. landlord; janitor, caretaker; Ch. customer; Col., Peru, Ven. delivery boy; **casera** f. landlady; housekeeper.

caseta f. small house, cottage; booth, stall.

casi adv. almost.

casilla f. (puesto) stall, booth; (apartado) post office box; pigeonhole; **sacarle a uno de sus -s** to change someone's way of life or habits; to irritate, annoy, try someone's patience; **salirse de sus -s** to lose one's temper; to do something out of the way.

casino m. club, society; clubhouse; recreation hall.

caso m. case; point; matter; event; **— que** (or **en — de que**) in case that; **dado —** supposing; **hacer — de** to pay attention to; **hacer — omiso de**

to omit; **no viene al —** that is not to the point.

casorio m. wedding, marriage.

caspa f. dandruff.

casta f. race, breed; caste, distinct class; quality, kind.

castaña f. chestnut; jug; knot or roll of hair; Am. small barrel; Mex. trunk, large suitcase.

castañetear v. to rattle the castanets; to chatter (said of the teeth); to crackle (said of the knees or joints); **— con los dedos** to snap one's fingers.

castañeteo m. rattle or sound of castanets; chatter, chattering (of the teeth).

castaño m. chestnut (tree and wood); adj. chestnut-colored.

castañuela f. castanet.

castellano adj. & m. Castilian.

castidad f. chastity.

castigar[7] v. to chastise, punish.

castigo m. punishment; correction.

castillo m. castle.

castizo adj. pure, correct (language); pure-blooded.

casto adj. chaste, pure.

castor m. beaver; beaver cloth.

casual adj. casual, accidental.

casualidad f. chance, accident.

casuca f. little house; hut, shanty.

casucha f. hut, hovel, shack.

catadura f. aspect, appearance.

catalán adj. Catalan, Catalonian, of or from Catalonia, Spain; m. Catalan.

catalejo m. telescope.

catalogar[7] v. to catalogue.

catálogo m. catalogue.

catar v. to look at, examine; to taste, sample.

catarata f. cataract; waterfall.

catarro m. catarrh, cold.

catástrofe f. catastrophe, mishap.

catear v. to explore, look around; Ch., C.A., Mex. to search or raid (a home); Am. to explore for ore; Col., Riopl. to test, try.

catecismo m. catechism.

cátedra f. class; subject; chair, professorship.

catedral f. cathedral.

catedrático m. professor.

categoría f. category, rank; kind, class.

categórico adj. categorical, positive.

catequizar[9] v. to catechize, give religious instruction (to); to induce, persuade.

católico adj. Catholic; universal; m. Catholic; **catolicismo** m. Catholicism.

catre m. cot, small bed; Am. raft, float; C.A., camp stool, folding stool; **— de tijera** folding cot.

catrín m. Am. dandy; adj. Mex., C.A. over-elegant, dressy.

cauce m. river bed.

caución f. precaution; security, guarantee; bail.

cauchero m. Am. rubber gatherer; Am. rubber producer; adj. Am. rubber, pertaining to rubber.

caucho m. rubber; **— sintético** synthetic rubber; *Am.* rubber tree; *Col.* rubber raincoat or cloak; **cauchal** m. rubber grove or plantation.

caudal m. *(monetario)* wealth; *(torrente)* river current; volume of water.

caudaloso adj. wealthy; abundant.

caudillaje m. military leadership; *Am.* political bossism; *Am.* tyranny.

caudillo m. leader, chief; *Am.* political boss.

causa f. cause; case, lawsuit; *Am.* light lunch, snack.

causar v. to cause.

cautela f. caution; cunning, craftiness; trick, deception.

cauteloso adj. cautious; crafty.

cautivar v. to capture; to charm, fascinate.

cautiverio m. captivity.

cautivo m. captive, war prisoner.

cauto adj. cautious.

cavar v. to dig, spade; to excavate.

caverna f. cavern, cave.

cavernoso adj. cavernous, like a cavern; hollow; **voz cavernosa** deep, hollow voice.

cavidad f. cavity.

cayado m. shepherd's crook, staff.

cayo m. key, island reef. -

caza f. hunt, hunting; wild game; m. attack plane; **dar —** to pursue, track down.

cazador adj. hunting; m. hunter.

cazar v. to chase, hunt; to track down.

cazatorpedero m. destroyer, torpedo-boat.

cazo m. dipper; pot, pan.

cazuela f. stewing pan; earthenware cooking pan; topmost theatre gallery; *Ven.* stewed hen; *P.R.* candied sweet potatoes with spices.

cebada f. barley; *Am.* brewing of **mate**; **cebadal** m. barley field.

cebar v. to feed, fatten *(animals)*; to encourage, nourish *(a passion)*; to prime *(a gun, pump, etc.)*; to bait *(a fishhook)*; *Ríopl.* to brew and serve **mate** or tea; **-se** to vent one's fury.

cebo m. feed *(for animals)*; bait; incentive.

cebolla f. onion.

cecear v. to lisp.

ceceo m. lisp, lisping.

cecina f. dried beef, jerked beef.

cedazo m. sieve.

ceder v. to cede, transfer; to yield, surrender, submit; to diminish, abate.

cedro m. cedar.

cédula f. slip of paper; certificate; **— de vecindad** *(or* **— personal)** official identification card.

céfiro m. zephyr, soft breeze; *Am.* fine muslin.

cegar[1,7] v. irr. to blind; to become blind; to confuse; to fill up, stop up *(a hole)*.

ceguedad, ceguera f. blindness.

ceiba f. *Am.* ceiba, silk-cotton tree.

ceja f. eyebrow; brow of a hill.

cejar v. to go backward; to back; to

back down, give in, yield; to slacken.

cejijunto adj. frowning; with knitted eyebrows.

celada f. ambush, snare, trap.

celaje m. colored clouds; skylight; presage, portent; *P.R.* shadow, ghost; *Am.* **como un —** like lightning.

celar v. to guard, watch; to watch over jealously; to conceal.

celda f. cell.

celebración f. celebration.

celebrar v. to celebrate; to praise, honor; to be glad.

célebre adj. famous; funny, witty; *Col.* graceful, pretty *(woman)*.

celebridad f. fame, renown; celebrity, famous person; celebration.

celeridad f. swiftness, speed.

celeste adj. celestial, heavenly.

celestial adj. celestial, heavenly, divine.

célibe adj. unmarried; m. & f. unmarried person.

celo m. *(humano)* zeal, ardor; envy; *(animal)* heat *(sexual excitement in animals)*; **-s** jealousy, suspicion; **tener -s** to be jealous.

celosía f. window lattice; Venetian blind.

celoso adj. jealous; zealous, eager; suspicious.

célula f. cell.

celuloide m. celluloid.

cellisca f. sleet; rain and snow.

cementar v. to cement.

cementerio m. cemetery.

cemento m. cement; **— armado** reinforced concrete.

cena f. supper.

cenagal m. quagmire, muddy ground, swamp.

cenagoso adj. muddy, miry.

cenar v. to eat supper.

cencerrada f. racket, noise *(with cowbells, tin cans, etc.)*; tin pan serenade.

cencerrear v. to make a racket *(with cowbells, tin cans, etc.)*.

cencerro m. cowbell.

cendal m. gauze; thin veil.

cenicero m. ash tray; ash pit; ash pan.

cenicienta f. a Cinderella.

ceniciento adj. ashen, ash-colored.

cenit m. zenith.

ceniza f. ashes, cinders.

cenizo adj. ash-colored.

censo m. census.

censor m. censor.

censura f. censure, criticism, disapproval; censorship.

censurador m. censor, critic; critical person; adj. critical.

censurar v. to censure, critcize, reprove; to censor.

centavo m. cent.

centella f. lightning, flash; spark.

centelleante adj. sparkling, flashing.

centellear v. to twinkle; to sparkle, glitter; to flash.

centelleo m. glitter, sparkle.

centenar m. one hundred; field of rye.

centenario m. centennial, one hundredth anniversary; adj. centennial; old, ancient.

centeno *m.* rye.
centésimo *adj. & m.* hundredth.
centímetro *m.* centimeter *(one hundredth part of a meter)*.
céntimo *m.* one hundredth part of a **peseta**.
centinela *m.* sentry, sentinel.
central *adj.* central; *f.* main office; headquarters; *Am.* main sugar mill or refinery.
centrar *v.* to center.
céntrico *adj.* central.
centro *m.* center, middle.
ceñidor *m.* girdle, belt, sash.
ceñir [5,19] *v. irr. (rodear)* to gird, girdle; to tighten; to encircle; *(abreviar)* to diminish; to limit; **-se a** to limit oneself to.
ceño *m.* frown; scowl; **fruncir el —** to frown; to scowl.
cepa *f.* stump, stub *(of a tree or plant)*; vinestock; origin, stock *(of a family)*; *Am.* mass of plants growing from a common root; *Am.* excavation *(for a building)*, hole, pit *(for planting trees)*; **de buena —** of good stock.
cepillo *m.* brush; alms box; carpenter's plane; *Am.* flatterer; **— de dientes** toothbrush.
cepo *m.* branch, stock.
cera *f.* wax.
cerámica *f.* ceramics, pottery.
cerca *adv.* near, near by; **— de** *prep.* near, nearly; *f.* fence, low wall.
cercado *m.* enclosure; fenced-in garden; fence; *Am.* Peruvian political division; *p.p. of* **cercar**.
cercanía *f.* proximity, **-s** surroundings, vicinity.
cercano *adj.* near; neighboring.
cercar [6] *v.* to fence, enclose; to surround; to besiege.
cercenar *v.* to clip off; to curtail, diminish, reduce.
cerciorar *v.* to assure, affirm; **-se** to ascertain, find out.
cerco *m.* fence, enclosure; siege; circle; *Ch.* small farm or orchard.
cerda *f.* bristle; *Am.* **ir en -s** to go halves or share in a deal.
cerdo *m.* hog, pig; pork.
cerdoso *adj.* bristly.
cereal *m.* cereal, grain.
cerebro *m.* brain.
ceremonia *f.* ceremony.
ceremonial *adj. & m.* ceremonial.
ceremonioso *adj.* ceremonious.
cereza *f.* cherry; **cerezo** *m.* cherry tree; cherry wood.
cerilla *f.* wax taper; wax match; earwax.
cerillo *m. Mex., C.A., Ven., Andes* match.
cerner [1] *v. irr.* to sift; to drizzle; *Am.* to strain through a sieve; **-se** to hover *(as a bird or plane)*.
cero *m.* zero; nothing.
cerquita *adv.* quite near, nice and near.
cerrado *adj.* closed, cloudy; thick *(beard)*; reserved *(person)*; dull; *Am.* stubborn.

cerradura *f.* locking, closing; lock; **— de golpe** spring lock.
cerrajería *f.* locksmith's shop; locksmith's trade.
cerrajero *m.* locksmith.
cerrar [1] *v. irr.* to close, shut, lock; **-se** to close; **-se el cielo** to become overcast or cloudy.
cerrazón *f.* cloudiness, darkness.
cerro *m.* hill.
cerrojo *m.* latch, bolt.
certamen *m.* contest, literary contest; debate; competition.
certero *adj.* accurate, exact; well-aimed; **tirador —** good shot.
certeza *f.* certainty.
certidumbre *f.* certainty.
certificado *adj.* certified, registered; *m.* certificate.
certificar [6] *v.* to certify; to register *(a letter)*.
cervato *m.* fawn, young deer.
cerveza *f.* beer; **cervecería** *f.* beer tavern; brewery.
cesante *adj.* unemployed.
cesar *v.* to cease, stop; to quit.
cesta *f.* basket; a kind of racket for playing jai alai *(Basque ball game)*.
cesto *m.* large basket, hamper.
cetrino *adj.* greenish-yellow, lemon-colored; citronlike; melancholy, gloomy.
cetro *m.* scepter, staff.
cibernética *f.* cybernetics, computer science.
cicatero *adj.* miserly, stingy.
cicatriz *f.* scar.
cicatrizar [9] *v.* to heal, close *(a wound)*.
ciclo *m.* cycle; period of time; school term.
ciclón *m.* cyclone.
ciclotrón *m.* cyclotron.
ciego *adj.* blind; **a ciegas** blindly; *m.* blindman.
cielo *m.* sky; heaven; **— de la boca** palate; **poner en el —** to praise, extol; **poner el grito en el —** to "hit the ceiling"; **cielito** *m. Am.* gaucho group dance and tune.
ciempiés, cientopiés *m.* centipede.
ciénaga *f.* swamp, bog, quagmire, marsh.
ciencia *f.* science; learning; skill; **a** *(or* **de) — cierta** with certainty.
cieno *m.* mud, mire.
científico *adj.* scientific; *m.* scientist.
cierre *m.* clasp, fastener; zipper; closing, fastening, locking; method of closing.
cierto *adj.* certain, true, sure; **por —** certainly; *Col., C.A.* **ciertas hierbas** so-and-so *(person not named)*.
ciervo *m.* deer; **cierva** *f.* doe, hind, female deer.
cierzo *m.* north wind.
cifra *f.* cipher, number; figure; abridgment, summary; code; monogram; emblem.
cifrar *v.* to write in code; to summarize; **— la esperanza en** to place one's hope in.
cigarra *f.* cicada, locust.

cigarrera f. cigar or cigarette case; woman cigar maker or vendor.

cigarrillo m. cigarette.

cigarro m. cigar; cigarette.

cigüeña f. stork; crank, handle (for turning).

cigüeñal m. crankshaft.

cilíndrico adj. cylindrical.

cilindro m. cylinder; Mex. hand organ.

cima f. peak, summit, top; **dar —** to complete, carry out.

cimarrón adj. Ríopl., Mex., Carib., Ven., Andes wild, untamed; Am. **mate —** black, bitter mate.

cimarronear v. Ríopl. to drink mate without sugar.

cimbrar, cimbrear v. to brandish, flourish, swing; to shake; to bend; Am. to swing around, change suddenly one's direction; **— a uno de un golpe** to knock a person down with a blow; **-se** to swing, sway; to vibrate, shake.

cimiento m. foundation, base; source, root; **abrir los -s** to break ground for a building.

cinc m. zinc.

cincel m. chisel.

cincelar v. to chisel; to engrave.

cincha f. cinch, girth; Am. blows with the flat of a sword; Col., Ríopl. **a revienta** unwillingly; hurriedly; at breakneck speed.

cinchar v. to cinch, tighten the saddle girth; Am. to hit with the flat of a sword.

cine, cínema m. cinema, motion picture, movie; **cinematógrafo** m. motion picture.

cinematografía f. cinematography, the science of motion picture photography.

cíngulo m. girdle, cord, belt.

cínico adj. cynical, sarcastic, sneering; m. cynic.

cinta f. ribbon, band; tape; strip; movie film; coarse fishing net; Am. tin can.

cintarada f. beating, flogging; **cintarazo** m. blow with the flat of a sword.

cintilar v. to sparkle, twinkle; to glimmer.

cinto m. belt; girdle.

cintura f. waist; **meter en —** to subdue, subject.

cinturón m. belt; **— de seguridad** safety belt.

ciprés m. cypress.

circo m. circus.

circuito m. circuit.

circulación f. circulation; traffic.

circular v. to circulate; to circle; adj. circular; f. circular letter, notice.

círculo m. circle; group; club; clubhouse.

circundante adj. surrounding.

circundar v. to surround.

circunferencia f. circumference.

circunlocución f. circumlocution, roundabout expression.

circunspección f. circumspection, decorum, prudence, restraint.

circunspecto adj. circumspect, prudent.

circunstancia f. circumstance.

circunstante adj. surrounding; present; **-s** m. pl. bystanders, onlookers, audience.

circunvecino adj. neighboring, surrounding.

cirio m. wax candle; saguaro cactus.

ciruela f. plum; prune; **— pasa** prune, dried prune; **ciruelo** m. plum tree.

cirugía f. surgery.

cirujano m. surgeon.

cisne m. swan; Ríopl. powder puff.

cisterna f. cistern.

cita f. date, appointment; citation, summons; quotation.

citación f. citation, quotation; summons.

citar v. (convocar) to make a date or appointment with; (referir) to cite, quote; (incitar) incite, provoke; to summon.

ciudad f. city.

ciudadano m. citizen; resident of a city; adj. of or pertaining to a city; **ciudadanía** f. citizenship.

ciudadela f. citadel.

cívico adj. civic.

civil adj. civil; polite, courteous.

civilidad f. civility, courtesy.

civilización f. civilization.

civilizador adj. civilizing; m. civilizer.

civilizar⁹ v. to civilize.

cizaña f. weed; vice; discord; **sembrar —** to sow discord.

clamar v. to clamor, shout; to whine.

clamor m. clamor, shout; whine; knell.

clamoreo m. clamoring; shouting.

clamorear v. to clamor, shout; to toll, knell.

clandestino adj. clandestine, underhanded, secret.

clara f. white of egg; bald spot; thin spot (in a fabric); **a las -s** clearly, openly, frankly.

claraboya f. skylight.

clarear v. (poner claro), to clarify, make clear; (haber más luz) to grow light, begin to dawn; to clear up; Am. to pierce through and through; **-se** to become transparent; to reveal oneself.

claridad f. clarity, clearness; blunt remark, slam; fame.

claridoso adj. Mex., Ven., C.A. blunt, outspoken, plainspoken.

clarificar⁶ v. to clarify, make clear.

clarín m. bugle; bugler; organ stop; Am. song bird.

clarinete m. clarinet; clarinet player.

clarito adj. & adv. quite clear, nice and clear.

clarividencia f. clairvoyance; keen insight.

claro adj. clear; light (color); illustrious; adv. clearly; m. skylight; space, gap; clearing (in a forest); **pasar la noche de — en —** not to sleep a wink; Mex., Carib. **en —** without eating or sleeping; Am. **poner en —** to copy (a rough draft).

clase f. class; classroom; kind, sort.

clásico adj. classic, classical.

clasificación f. classification.

clasificar[6] v. to classify.

claustro m. cloister; meeting of a university faculty; **— de profesores** university faculty.

cláusula f. clause.

clausura f. closing; seclusion, monastic life.

clavado m. Mex. a dive.

clavar v. to nail; to fix; to deceive, cheat; **-se** to be deceived; Mex. to fall into a trap; Mex. to dive.

clave f. key, code; keystone; clef.

clavel m. carnation, pink.

clavetear v. to nail; to stud with nails.

clavícula f. collarbone.

clavija f. peg; electric plug; peg (of a stringed instrument).

clavijero m. hat or clothes rack.

clavo m. nail; clove (spice); sharp pain or grief; sick headache; Mex. rich mineral vein; Am. bother, worry; Col. surprise, disappointment; Ríopl. drug on the market (unsaleable article); **dar en el —** to hit the nail on the head; Am. **meter a uno en un —** to put a person in a predicament; Am. **ser un —** to be punctual, exact.

clemencia f. mercy; **clemente** adj. merciful.

clerical adj. clerical, of a clergyman or the clergy.

clérigo m. clergyman.

clero m. clergy.

cliché m. photographic plate; also **clisé.**

cliente m. & f. client; customer; **clientela** f. cleintele, clients; customers.

clima m. climate.

clímax m. climax.

clínica f. clinic.

clíper m. clipper.

cloaca f. sewer.

cloquear v. to cluck.

cloqueo m. cluck, clucking.

cloro m. chlorine.

club m. club, society.

clueca f. brooding hen.

coacción f. compulsion, force; enforcement.

coagular v. to coagulate, thicken, clot; to curd, curdle; **-se** to coagulate, clot; to curd, curdle.

coágulo m. coagulation, clot.

coartar v. to restrain, limit.

coba f. flattery; fib; **dar —** to flatter; to tease.

cobarde adj. cowardly; timid; weak; m. coward.

cobardía f. cowardice.

cobertizo m. shed; shanty.

cobertor m. bedcover, quilt.

cobertura f. cover, covering.

cobija f. cover; shelter; roof; Am. blanket; Am. shawl, serape, poncho; **-s** Am. bedclothes.

cobijar v. to cover; to shelter.

cobrador m. collector; ticket collector.

cobranza f. collection (of a sum of money); cashing.

cobrar v. to collect (bills, debts); to charge; to cash (a draft, check, etc.); to recover, regain; to gain, acquire; Am. to demand payment; **— cariño a** to take a liking to.

cobre m. copper; copper kitchen utensils; Am. copper coin; **-s** brass musical instruments; **batir el —** to hustle, work with energy; Am. **mostrar el —** to show one's worse side.

cobrizo adj. coppery, copper-colored.

cobro m. collection (of bills); **poner en —** to put in a safe place; **ponerse en —** to take refuge, get to a safe place.

coca f. Am. coca (South American shrub and its leaves); Am. cocaine; Am. coca tea; Am. eggshell; Am. fruit skin or rind; Am. **de —** free of charge; in vain.

cocaína f. cocaine.

cocear v. to kick.

cocer[2,10] v. irr. to cook; to boil; to bake.

cocido m. Spanish stew; p.p. of **cocer.**

cociente m. quotient.

cocimiento m. cooking; baking; liquid concoction (generally made of medicinal herbs).

cocina f. kitchen; cuisine, cooking; **— económica** stove, range.

cocinar v. to cook.

cocinero m. cook.

coco m. coconut; coconut palm; bogeyman, goblin; Am. derby hat; Mex., Carib., Ríopl. head; Am. blow on the head; **hacer -s a** to make eyes at, flirt with; Col., Ven., Andes **pelar a —** to crop the hair; **cocotal** m. grove of coconut palms; coconut plantation.

cocotero m. coconut palm.

cocodrilo m. crocodile.

coche m. coach; car; taxi.

cochero m. coachman; cabman; taxi driver.

cochinada f. filth, filthiness; filthy act or remark; dirty trick; herd of swine.

cochinilla f. cochineal (insect).

cochino m. hog, pig; dirty person; Ch. stingy person; Am. **— de monte** wild boar; adj. filthy, dirty; Ch. miserly, stingy.

codazo m. nudge; poke (with the elbow).

codear v. to elbow; to nudge; **-se con alguien** to rub elbows with someone.

codicia f. greed; greediness.

codiciar v. to covet.

codicioso adj. covetous, greedy.

código m. code of laws.

codo m. elbow; bend; **alzar** (or **empinar**) **el —** to drink too much; **hablar por los -s** to talk too much; **meterse** (or **estar metido**) **hasta los -s** to be up to the elbows, be very busy.

codorniz f. partridge.

coetáneo adj. contemporary.

cofrade m. & f. fellow member (of a brotherhood, club, society, etc.).

cofradía f. brotherhood; sisterhood; guild; trade union.

cofre m. coffer, jewel box; chest, trunk.

coger[11] *v.* to seize; to catch; to grasp; to gather; *Am.* **-se una cosa** to steal something.

cogote *m.* nape, back of the neck.

cohechar *v.* to bribe.

coheredero *m.* joint heir.

coherente *adj.* coherent; connected.

cohete *m.* skyrocket; rocket; *Ríopl.* **al — en vain**, uselessly.

cohetería *f.* rocketry; rocket weaponry; shop for making fireworks.

cohibición *f.* repression, inhibition, restraint.

cohibido *p.p.* & *adj.* inhibited; embarrassed, uneasy.

cohibir *v.* to restrain, repress; to inhibit.

coincidencia *f.* coincidence.

coincidir *v.* to coincide.

cojear *v.* to limp; **cojeamos del mismo pie** we both have the same weakness.

cojera *f.* limp, lameness.

cojín *m.* cushion; pad; **cojincillo** *m.* pad.

cojinete *m.* small pillow or cushion, pad; bearing, ball bearing.

cojo *adj.* lame, crippled; one-legged.

col *f.* cabbage; **— de Bruselas** Brussels sprouts.

cola *f.* (*rabo*) tail; train of a dress; (*hilera de gente*) line of people; **piano de —** grand piano; **piano de media — baby grand; hacer —** to stand in line; *Am.* **comer —** to be the last one in a contest.

colaboración *f.* collaboration, mutual help.

colaborar *v.* to collaborate, work together.

coladera *f.* colander, strainer, sieve; *Mex., Ven.* drain.

colar[2] *v. irr.* to strain, filter; to bleach with lye; **-se** to slip in or out, sneak in.

colcha *f.* quilt; bedspread; **-s** *Ríopl.* saddle and trappings; *Ríopl.* gaucho clothing.

colchón *m.* mattress.

colear *v.* to wag the tail; to grab a bull by the tail and throw him over; *Am.* to flunk (*a student*); *Am.* to trail, tag behind (*a person*); *Col.* to bother, nag, harass; *Am.* to smoke one cigarette after another.

colección *f.* collection; set; gathering.

coleccionar *v.* to collect, make a collection.

coleccionista *m.* & *f.* collector (*of stamps, curios, etc.*).

colecta *f.* collection of voluntary gifts; assessment; collect (*a short prayer of the mass*).

colectivo *adj.* collective; *m. Am.* small bus.

colector *m.* collector; water pipe, drain.

colega *m.* & *f.* colleague, fellow worker.

colegiatura *f.* college fellowship or scholarship; *C.A.* tuition in a college.

colegio *m.* boarding school; school, academy; college, body of professional men.

colegir[5,11] *v.* to gather; to conclude, infer.

cólera *f.* anger, rage; *m.* cholera (*disease*).

colérico *adj.* irritable; angry.

coleto *m.* leather jacket; one's inner self; *Am.* impudence, shamelessness; **decir para su —** to say to oneself; **echarse al —** to drink down; to devour.

colgadero *m.* hanger; hook, peg; hat or clothes rack.

colgadura *f.* drape, hanging; drapery; tapestry.

colgante *adj.* hanging; dangling; **puente —** suspension bridge.

colgar[2,7] *v. irr.* (*suspender*) to hang, suspend; to dangle; to drape (*walls*); (*achacar*) to impute, attribute; *Cuba* to flunk, fail (*a student*); *Col.* **-se** to fall behind.

colibrí *m.* hummingbird.

coliflor *f.* cauliflower.

coligarse[7] *v.* to league together, band together.

colilla *f.* small tail; butt (*of a cigarette*), stub (*of a cigar*).

colina *f.* hill.

colindante *adj.* contiguous, neighboring, adjacent.

colindar *v.* to border (on); to be adjoining.

colisión *f.* collision, clash.

colmar *v.* to fill to the brim; **— de** to fill with; to shower with (*gifts, favors, etc.*); **-le a uno el plato** to exhaust one's patience.

colmena *f.* beehive; *Mex.* bee.

colmillo *m.* eyetooth, canine tooth; tusk; fang.

colmo *m.* overfullness; limit; **— de la locura** height of folly; **¡eso es el —!** that's the limit! *adj.* overfull, filled to the brim.

colocación *f.* placing, arrangement; position, job.

colocar[6] *v.* to place; to put in place, arrange; to give employment to.

colocho *m. C.A.* curly hair; wood shavings.

colombiano *adj.* Colombian, of or pertaining to Colombia, South America.

colon *m.* colon (*of the large intestine*).

colonia *f.* colony; silk ribbon; *Mex., Carib.* city district; *Am.* sugar plantation.

coloniaje *m. Am.* colonial period.

colonial *adj.* colonial.

colonización *f.* colonization.

colonizador *m.* colonizer, colonist; *adj.* colonizing.

colonizar[9] *v.* to colonize.

colono *m.* colonist, settler; tenant farmer; *Carib.* owner of a sugar plantation; *Am.* bootlicker, flatterer.

coloquio *m.* conversation, talk; literary dialogue; *Col.* street comedy, farce.

color *m.* color; coloring; paint; rouge; **so — de** under the pretext of.

coloración *f.* coloring.

colorado *adj.* red, reddish; colored; **ponerse —** to blush.

colorante *adj. & m.* coloring.

colorar *v.* to color; to stain; to dye.

colorear *v.* to color; to redden; to give color to.

colorete *m.* rouge.

colorido *m.* coloring; color; *adj.* colored; colorful.

colosal *adj.* colossal, huge.

columbrar *v.* to see faintly; to glimpse.

columna *f.* column.

columpiar *v.* to swing; **-se** to swing; to sway.

columpio *m.* swing.

collado *m.* hillock, knoll.

collar *m.* necklace; dog collar; *Am.* collar (*of a draft horse*); **collera** *f.* collar (*for draft animals*).

coma *f.* comma; *m.* coma, stupor, prolonged unconsciousness.

comadre *f.* (*amiga*) woman friend; (*chismosa*) gossip; (*partera*) midwife; (*alcahueta*) go-between; *name used to express kinship between mother and godmother;* **comadrona** *f.* midwife.

comadreja *f.* weasel.

comandancia *f.* command; position and headquarters of a commander.

comandante *m.* major; commander.

comandar *v.* to command (*troops*).

comandita *f.* silent partnership; **sociedad en —** limited company.

comando *m.* military command.

comarca *f.* district, region.

comba *f.* bulge, warp.

combar *v.* to warp, bend, twist; **-se** to warp; to sag; to bulge.

combate *m.* combat, battle, fight.

combatiente *m.* combatant, fighter.

combatir *v.* to combat; to fight.

combinación *f.* combination.

combinar *v.* to combine, unite.

comburente *m.* the chemical agent that causes combustion, e.g., oxygen; *adj.* causing combustion.

combustible *adj.* combustible; *m.* fuel.

combustión *f.* combustion.

comedero *m.* trough (*for feeding animals*); *adj.* edible, eatable.

comedia *f.* comedy; farce.

comediante *m.* actor, comedian.

comedido *adj.* courteous, polite; obliging; *p.p.* of **comedirse.**

comedirse[5] *v. irr.* to be civil, polite, obliging; *Ec.* to meddle; *Am.* **— a hacer algo** to volunteer to do something.

comedor *m.* dining room; great eater.

comején *m.* termite.

comelón *m. Am.* big eater. *See* **comilón.**

comendador *m.* commander (*of certain military orders*).

comensal *m. & f.* table companion; dinner guest.

comentador *m.* commentator.

comentar *v.* to comment.

comentario *m.* commentary, explanation.

comentarista *m. & f.* commentator.

comenzar[1,9] *v. irr.* to begin.

comer *v.* to eat; to dine; to take (*in chess or checkers*); **dar de —** to feed; **ganar de —** to earn a living; **-se** to eat; to eat up; to skip (*a letter, syllable, word, etc.*); *Ríopl., Col.* **-se uno a otro** to deceive each other.

comercial *adj.* commercial.

comerciante *m.* merchant; storekeeper.

comerciar *v.* to trade; to have dealings (with).

comercio *m.* commerce, trade.

comestible *adj.* edible, eatable; **-s** *m. pl.* food, groceries.

cometa *m.* comet; *C.A.* person seldom seen; *f.* kite.

cometer *v.* to commit; to entrust; to use (*a figure of speech*).

cometido *m.* commission, assignment, charge; task, duty.

comezón *f.* itch.

comicios *m. pl.* primaries, elections.

cómico *adj.* comic, of comedy; comical, funny, amusing; *m.* comedian, actor.

comida *f.* meal; dinner; good; **comidilla** *f.* small meal; gossip; **la comidilla de la vecindad** the talk of the town.

comienzo *m.* beginning; origin.

comilitona *f.* spread, big feast.

comilón *m.* big eater.

comillas *f. pl.* quotation marks.

comisario *m.* commissary, deputy, delegate; manager; *Am.* police inspector.

comisión *f.* commission; committee.

comisionado *adj.* commissioned, charged, delegated; *m.* commissioner; *Am.* constable.

comisionar *v.* to commission.

comistrajo *m.* mess, strange food concoction, mixture.

comité *m.* committee, commission.

comitiva *f.* retinue, group of attendants or followers.

como *adv. & conj.* as, like, such as; if, provided that, since, when; *Mex., Ven.* about, approximately; **¿cómo?** *interr. adv.* how?; what (did you say)?; *Am.* **¡cómo no!** yes, of course!

cómoda *f.* bureau, chest of drawers.

comodidad *f.* comfort; convenience.

cómodo *adj.* comfortable; convenient; *m. Am.* bedpan.

compacto *adj.* compact.

conpadecer[13] *v. irr.* to pity, sympathize with; **-se con** to be in harmony with; **-se de** to take pity on.

compadrazgo *m.* compaternity (*spiritual affinity between the godfather and the parents of a child*); friendship; relationship; clique, group of friends.

compadre *m.* (*amigo*) pal, crony, comrade; (*padrino*) cosponsor; *name used to express kinship between father and godfather.*

compañero *m.* companion; partner; mate; **compañerismo** *m.* companionship.

compañía *f.* company; *Am.* **— del ahorcado** silent companion, poor company.

comparación f. comparison.

comparar v. to compare.

comparativo adj. comparative.

comparecer[13] v. irr. to appear (before a judge or tribunal).

compartimiento m. compartment.

compartir v. to share; to divide into shares.

compás m. compass; measure; beat; **llevar el —** to beat time.

compasión f. compassion, pity.

compasivo adj. compassionate, sympathetic.

compatible adj. compatible, in harmony.

compatriota m. & f. compatriot, fellow countryman.

compeler v. to compel, force.

compendiar v. to abstract, summarize, condense.

compendio m. summary, condensation.

compensación f. compensation; recompense.

compensar v. to balance; to make equal; to compensate, recompense.

competencia f. competition, rivalry; competence, ability.

competente adj. competent; capable; adequate.

competidor m. competitor; rival; adj. competing.

competir[5] v. irr. to compete, vie.

compilar v. to compile.

compinche m. chum, pal, comrade.

complacencia f. complacency, satisfaction, contentment.

complacer[38] v. irr. to please, humor; to comply, **-se** to take pleasure or satisfaction (in).

complaciente adj. obliging, agreeable, willing to please.

complejidad f. complexity.

complejo adj. & m. complex.

complemento m. complement; object (of a verb).

completamiento m. completion.

completar v. to complete; to finish.

completo adj. complete, full, perfect.

complicar[6] v. to complicate.

cómplice m. & f. accomplice, companion in crime.

complot m. plot, conspiracy; intrigue.

componenda f. adjustment; compromise.

componente adj. component, constituent; m. component, essential part.

componer[40] v. irr. to fix, repair; to fix up; to adorn, trim; to compose; to set up (type); to settle (a dispute); Col. to set (bones).

comportamiento m. conduct, behavior.

composición f. composition; settlement.

compositor m. composer.

compostura f. (arreglo) repair; settlement, adjustment; (aseo) neatness, composition; (dignidad) composure, dignity.

compota f. fruit preserves; **— de manzana** applesauce.

compra f. purchase; buying; **ir de -s** to go shopping.

comprador m. buyer, purchaser.

comprar v. to buy, purchase.

comprender v. to understand, grasp, comprehend; to comprise, embrace.

comprensible adj. comprehensible, understandable.

comprensión f. understanding; comprehension; keenness.

comprensivo adj. comprehensive; understanding.

compresión f. compression.

compresor m. compressor.

comprimir v. to compress; to repress.

comprobación f. confirmation, check, proof, test.

comprobante adj. proving, verifying; m. proof; evidence; certificate; voucher; warrant.

comprobar[2] v. irr. to verify; to check; to prove.

comprometer v. (exponer) to compromise; to endanger; to bind; to force; (concordar) to come to an agreement; **-se** to promise, bind oneself; to become engaged; to compromise oneself.

compromiso m. (convenio) compromise; (obligación) engagement; appointment; (dificultad) predicament, trouble.

compuerta f. sluice (gate to control the flow of water), floodgate.

compuesto p.p. of **componer** & adj. repaired; fixed, adorned; composed; composite; compound; m. composite; compound.

compungirse[11] v. to feel regret or remorse.

computadora electrónica f. electronic computer.

computar v. to compute, calculate.

cómputo m. computation, calculation.

comulgar[7] v. to commune, take communion.

común adj. common; **por lo —** generally; m. toilet; **el — de las gentes** the majority of the people; the average person.

comunero adj. common, popular; Am. pertaining to a community; m. commoner (one of the common people); Col., Ven., Andes member of an Indian community.

comunicación f. communication.

comunicar[6] v. to communicate; to notify; **-se** to communicate; to correspond; to be in touch (with); to connect.

comunicativo adj. communicative, talkative.

comunidad f. community; commonwealth; the common people; commonness; guild.

comunión f. communion; political party.

comunismo m. communism; **comunista** m. & f. communist; adj. communistic, communist.

con *prep.* with; — **ser** in spite of being; — **tal que** provided that; — **todo** however.

concavidad *f.* hollow, cavity; hollowness.

cóncavo *adj.* concave, hollow.

concebible *adj.* conceivable.

concebir[5] *v. irr.* to conceive; to imagine; to understand, grasp.

conceder *v.* to concede, grant; to admit.

concejal *m.* councilman, alderman.

concentración *f.* concentration.

concentrar *v.* to concentrate.

concepción *f.* conception.

concepto *m.* concept, idea, thought.

concernir[51] *v. irr.* to concern.

concertar[1] *v. irr.* (*arreglar*) to arrange, plan, settle; to conclude (*a treaty or business deal*); (*concordar*) to harmonize; to agree.

concesión *f.* concession, grant; granting; acknowledgment.

conciencia *f.* conscience.

concienzudo *adj.* conscientious.

concierto *m.* concert; harmony; agreement; **de —** by common agreement.

conciliar *v.* to conciliate, win over; to reconcile, bring into harmony; — **el sueño** to get to sleep.

concilio *m.* council.

concisión *f.* conciseness, brevity.

conciso *adj.* concise, brief.

conciudadano *m.* fellow citizen, fellow countryman.

concluir[32] *v. irr.* to conclude, finish; to infer.

conclusión *f.* conclusion.

concordancia *f.* concord, agreement, harmony.

concordar[2] *v. irr.* to agree; to be in harmony; to put in harmony.

concordia *f.* concord, harmony, agreement.

concretar *v.* to summarize, condense; to limit; **-se a** to limit oneself to.

concreto *adj.* concrete, real, specific; **en —** concretely; to sum up; *m. Am.* concrete.

concupiscente *adj.* sensual.

concurrencia *f.* gathering, audience; concurrence, simultaneous meeting or happening; competition.

concurrido *adj.* well-patronized, well-attended, much frequented.

concurrir *v.* to concur, meet together; to happen at the same time or place; to attend; to agree.

concurso *m.* gathering; contest; competitive examination; assistance.

concha *f.* shell; shellfish; prompter's box; *Mex.* **tener —** to be indifferent, unruffled, tough.

conchabar *v.* to unite, join; *Mex., S.A.* to hire (*labor*); **-se** to join, gang together; to conspire; *Ríopl.* to hire oneself out, get a job.

conchabo *m. Am.* hiring of a laborer or servant; *Ríopl.* job, menial job.

conde *m.* count; **condesa** *f.* countess.

condecoración *f.* decoration; badge, medal.

condecorar *v.* to decorate (*with a badge or medal*).

condena *f.* term in prison, sentence, penalty.

condenación *f.* condemnation; conviction (*of a prisoner or criminal*); damnation.

condenar *v.* to condemn; to sentence; *Am.* to annoy, irritate; **-se** to be damned, go to hell.

condensar *v.* to condense.

condescendencia *f.* condescension, patronizing attitude.

condescender[1] *v. irr.* to condescend; to comply, yield.

condición *f.* condition.

condimentar *v.* to season.

condimento *m.* condiment, seasoning.

condiscípulo *m.* schoolmate, classmate.

condolerse[2] *v. irr.* to condole (with), sympathize (with), be sorry (for).

cóndor *m. Am.* condor, vulture; *Am.* gold coin of Ecuador, Chile and Colombia.

conducir[25] *v. irr.* to conduct, lead; to drive (*an auto*); **-se** to behave, act.

conducta *f.* conduct; behavior; convoy, escort; management.

conducto *m.* conduit, pipe, channel; **por —** through.

conductor *adj.* conducting; *m.* leader; chauffeur; guide; conductor (*electrical*); *Am.* conductor, ticket collector (*on trains, buses, streetcars*); *Am.* teamster, driver.

conectar *v.* to connect.

conejera *f.* burrow; rabbit warren (*piece of land for breeding rabbits*); den, joint, dive (*of ill repute*).

conejo *m.* rabbit; *Am.* guinea pig; **conejillo de Indias** guinea pig.

conexión *f.* connection.

conexo *adj.* connected; coherent.

confección *f.* making; confection; manufactured article; workmanship; concoction, compound.

confeccionar *v.* to make; to manufacture; to mix, put up (*a prescription*).

confederación *f.* confederation, alliance, league.

confederar *v.* to confederate; **-se** to confederate, form into a confederacy.

conferencia *f.* lecture; conference, meeting.

conferenciante *m. & f.* lecturer.

conferencista *m. & f.* lecturer.

conferir[3] *v. irr.* to confer, to give, bestow.

confesar[1] *v. irr.* to confess.

confesión *f.* confession.

confesionario *m.* confessional, confessional box.

confesor *m.* confessor.

confiado *adj.* confident, trusting, credulous; presumptuous, self-confident.

confianza *f.* confidence, trust; familiarity; informality; **reunión de —** informal gathering or party.

confianzudo *adj.* over-friendly, over-familiar; *Am.* meddlesome.

confiar[17] *v.* to confide, entrust; to trust, hope firmly.

confidencia *f.* confidence, trust; secret, confidential remark; **confidencial** *adj.* confidential.

confidente *m.* confidant; spy, secret agent; settee or sofa for two people, love seat; *adj.* faithful, trustworthy.

confín *m.* limit, border, boundary; *adj.* bordering, limiting.

confinar *v.* to border (upon); to confine, exile to a specific place.

confirmación *f.* confirmation.

confirmar *v.* to confirm.

confiscar[6] *v.* to confiscate.

confitar *v.* to candy (*with sugar syrup*); to make into candy or preserves; to sweeten.

confite *m.* candy, bonbon; **confitería** *f.* confectionery; candy shop; **confitura** *f.* confection.

conflicto *m.* conflict.

confluencia *f.* junction (*of two rivers*).

conformar *v.* to adapt, adjust; **-se** to conform, comply; to agree; to be resigned (to); to be satisfied.

conforme *adj.* in agreement; resigned, satisfied; alike, similar; **— a** in accordance with.

conformidad *f.* conformity; agreement, harmony; compliance; **— con la voluntad de Dios** resignation to the will of God; **en — con** in compliance with; **estar de — con** to be in accordance or agreement with.

confortar *v.* to comfort, console.

confraternidad *f.* brotherhood.

confrontar *v.* to confront; to face; to compare, check.

confundir *v.* to confound, confuse, mix up; to bewilder; to shame.

confusión *f.* confusion.

confuso *adj.* confused, bewildered; blurred; vague.

congelado *p.p. & adj.* frozen; icy.

congelar *v.* to congeal, freeze.

congenial *adj.* congenial.

congeniar *v.* to be congenial (with); to harmonize, be in harmony (with).

congoja *f.* anguish, grief, anxiety.

congratular *v.* to congratulate.

congregación *f.* congregation, assembly; religious fraternity.

congregar[7] *v.* to congregate, call together; to assemble; **-se** to congregate, assemble.

congresista *m.* congressman; *f.* congresswoman.

congreso *m.* congress, assembly; **— de los Diputados** House of Representatives.

conjetura *f.* conjecture, guess, surmise.

conjeturar *v.* to conjecture, guess, surmise.

conjugación *f.* conjugation; coupling, joining together.

conjugar[7] *v.* to conjugate.

conjunción *f.* conjunction; union, combination.

conjunto *m.* total, whole, entirety; **en — as** a whole; *adj.* joined; related, allied.

conjuración *f.* conspiracy, plot.

conjurado *m.* conspirator.

conjurar *v.* to conspire, plot; to join a conspiracy; to entreat; to conjure; to ward off.

conmemorar *v.* to commemorate.

conmemorativo *adj.* memorial, serving to commemorate.

conmigo with me.

conminación *f.* threat.

conminatorio *adj.* threatening.

conmoción *f.* commotion.

conmovedor *adj.* moving, touching; stirring.

conmover[2] *v. irr.* to move, touch, affect (*with emotion*); to stir (*emotions*).

conmutador *m.* electric switch; **cuadro —** switchboard.

connatural *adj.* inborn.

cono *m.* cone; pine cone.

conocedor *adj.* knowing, aware, expert; *m.* connoisseur, judge, expert; **ser — de** to be judge of.

conocer[13] *v. irr.* (*tener idea de*) to know, be acquainted with; to recognize; (*llegar a conocer*) to meet; **se conoce que** it is clear or evident that.

conocido *p.p. & adj.* known; well-known; *m.* acquaintance.

conocimiento *m.* (*inteligencia*) knowledge, understanding; acquaintance; (*documento*) bill of lading; **-s** knowledge, learning; **poner en — to** inform.

conque *conj.* so then, well then, and so.

conquista *f.* conquest.

conquistador *m.* conqueror; *adj.* conquering, victorious.

conquistar *v.* to conquer, defeat; to win.

consabido *adj.* aforementioned, aforesaid.

consagración *f.* consecration.

consagrar *v.* to consecrate.

consciencia *f.* consciousness.

consciente *adj.* conscious.

consecución *f.* attainment.

consecuencia *f.* consequence; result; **a — de** as a result of; **por** (*or* **en**) **—** therefore; consequently.

consecuente *adj.* consequent, logical; consistent; *m.* consequence, result.

consecutivo *adj.* consecutive, successive.

conseguir[5,12] *v. irr.* to get, obtain; to reach, attain.

conseja *f.* old wives' tale, fable.

consejero *m.* adviser, counselor.

consejo *m.* counsel, advice; council; council hall.

consentimiento *m.* consent.

consentir[3] *v. irr.* to consent, permit; to pamper, spoil.

conserje *m.* janitor, caretaker.

conserva *f.* preserve; pickled fruit or vegetables; *Ch.* filling (*for tarts or candy*).

conservación *f.* conservation.

conservador *m.* conservative; preserver; guardian; *adj.* conservative.

conservar *v.* to conserve, keep; to preserve.

considerable *adj.* considerable.

consideración *f.* consideration.

considerado *adj.* considerate, thoughtful; respected; prudent.

considerar *v.* to consider; to treat with consideration.

consigna *f.* watchword, password; *Am.* checkroom.

consignar *v.* to consign; to deliver; to deposit; to assign; to check (*baggage*).

consigo with oneself; with himself (herself, themselves).

consiguiente *adj.* consequent; *m.* consequence; **por —** consequently.

consistente *adj.* firm, substantial.

consistir *v.* to consist; to be based on; **¿en qué consiste?** why?; what is the explanation for it?

consocio *m.* associate, partner.

consolación *f.* consolation.

consolar² *v. irr.* to console, cheer.

consolidar *v.* to consolidate, make solid; to unite, combine.

consonante *m.* perfect rhyme; *f.* consonant; *adj.* in harmony.

consorte *m.* & *f.* consort; mate; companion.

conspicuo *adj.* conspicuous.

conspiración *f.* conspiracy, plot.

conspirador *m.* conspirator, plotter.

conspirar *v.* to conspire, plot.

constancia *f.* (*firmeza*) constancy; perseverance; (*certeza*) evidence, certainty; *Am.* documentary proof, record.

constante *adj.* constant; continual; firm, faithful.

constar *v.* to be evident, clear; to consist (of), be composed (of); to be on record.

constatación *f. Am.* proof, check, evidence.

constelación *f.* constellation.

constipado *adj.* suffering from a cold; *m.* cold in the head.

constipar *v.* to stop up (*the nasal passages*); to cause a cold; **-se** to catch cold.

constitución *f.* constitution.

constitucional *adj.* constitutional.

constituir³² *v. irr.* to constitute, form; to set up, establish; **-se en** to set oneself up as.

constitutivo = **constituyente.**

constituyente *adj.* constituent.

constreñir⁵,¹⁹ *v. irr.* to constrain; to compel, oblige.

construcción *f.* construction; structure; building.

construir³² *v. irr.* to construct, build.

consuelo *m.* consolation, comfort; relief; cheer.

consuetudinario *adj.* habitual, customary; **derecho —** common law.

cónsul *m.* consul.

consulado *m.* consulate.

consulta *f.* consultation; opinion.

consultar *v.* to consult.

consultorio *m.* office for consultation; doctor's office or clinic.

consumado *p.p. of* **consumar;** *adj.* consummate, perfect, complete; accomplished.

consumar *v.* to consummate, complete.

consumidor *m.* consumer; *adj.* consuming.

consumir *v.* to consume; to waste; **-se** to be consumed; to burn out; to be exhausted; to waste away.

consumo *m.* consumption (*of food, provisions, etc.*).

consunción *f.* consumption (*illness*).

contabilidad *f.* accounting; bookkeeping.

contacto *m.* contact.

contado : al — in cash; **de —** immediately; **por de —** of course; **contados** *adj.* few, scarce, rare.

contador *m.* accountant; purser, cashier; counter; meter (*for water, gas, or electricity*); **— geiger** Geiger counter; Geiger-Müller counter.

contaduría *f.* accountant's or auditor's office; box office; cashier's office; accounting.

contagiar *v.* to infect; to corrupt; to contaminate.

contagio *m.* contagion; infection.

contagioso *adj.* contagious; infectious.

contaminar *v.* to contaminate, defile; to corrupt.

contar² *v. irr.* to count; to tell, relate; **— con** to count on, rely on; **a — desde** starting from, beginning with.

contemplación *f.* contemplation; gazing; meditation.

contemplar *v.* to contemplate, gaze at; to examine; to meditate.

contemporáneo *adj.* contemporary.

contender¹ *v. irr.* to contend, fight; to compete.

contener⁴⁵ *v. irr.* to contain; to restrain, check; **-se** to refrain; to restrain oneself.

contenido *m.* contents; *adj.* restrained, moderate.

contentamiento *m.* contentment, joy.

contentar *v.* to give pleasure, make happy; **-se** to be satisfied, pleased; *Am.* to make up, renew friendship.

contento *adj.* content, contented, satisfied, glad; *m.* gladness, contentment.

contera *f.* metal tip (*of a cane, umbrella, etc.*); tip, end; refrain of a song; **por —** as a finishing touch.

contertulio *m.* fellow-member.

contestación *f.* answer, reply; argument.

contestar *v.* to answer, reply.

contextura *f.* texture, composition; structure (*of animal or vegetable tissues*).

contienda *f.* fight; dispute; contest.

contigo with you (with thee).

contiguo *adj.* contiguous, next, neighboring.

continental *adj.* continental.

continente *m.* continent; countenance; *adj.* continent, moderate, sober.

contingencia *f.* contingency, possibility; risk.

contingente *adj.* contingent, accidental; *m.* quota; military contingent.

continuación *f.* continuation; continuance; **a —** below, as follows.

continuar[18] *v.* to continue; to last.

continuidad *f.* continuity.

continuo *adj.* continuous, connected; continual; steady, constant.

contonearse *v.* to strut, swagger; to waddle.

contoneo *m.* strut; waddle.

contorno *m.* (*circuito*) environs, surrounding country (*usually used in plural*); (*línea*) contour, outline.

contra *prep.* against; **el pro y el —** the pro and con; *f.* opposition; *Am.* antidote, remedy; **-s** *Am.* play-off, final game (*to determine the winner*); **llevar a uno la —** to contradict a person, take the opposite view.

contraalmirante *m.* rear admiral.

contrabajo *m.* bass fiddle, string bass.

contrabandear *v.* to smuggle.

contrabandista *m.* smuggler.

contrabando *m.* contraband; smuggled goods; smuggling.

contracción *f.* contraction; *Ch., Peru* diligence, application, devotion.

contradecir[27] *v. irr.* to contradict.

contradicción *f.* contradiction.

contradictorio *adj.* contradictory, contrary, opposing.

contradicho *p.p.* of **contradecir.**

contraer[46] *v. irr.* to contract; **— matrimonio** to get married; **-se** to shrink; to contract.

contrafuerte *m.* buttress; spur (*of a mountain*); **-s** secondary chain of mountains.

contrahacer[31] *v. irr.* to counterfeit; to forge; to copy, imitate; to mimic.

contrahecho *p.p.* of **contrahacer** & *adj.* counterfeit; forged; deformed.

contralor *m. Am.* controller or comptroller (*of accounts or expenditures*). *See* **controlador.**

contraorden *f.* countermand; cancellation of an order.

contrapelo : a — against the grain.

contrapesar *v.* to counterbalance, balance; to offset.

contrapeso *m.* counterpoise, counterweight, counterbalance; *Am.* fear, uneasiness.

contrariar[17] *v.* to oppose; to contradict; to irritate, vex.

contrariedad *f.* opposition; contradiction; bother, irritation; disappointment.

contrario *adj.* contrary, opposite; *m.* opponent.

contrarrestar *v.* to counteract; to resist, oppose; to strike back (*a ball*).

contraseña *f.* password, watchword; mark; check (*for baggage*); **— de salida** theatre check (*to re-enter during the performance*).

contrastar *v.* (*contrapesar*) to contrast; to test (*scales, weights, measures, etc.*); to assay (*metals*); (*resistir*) to resist, oppose.

contraste *m.* contrast; assay, test; assayer, tester; assayer's office.

contrata *f.* contract, bargain, agreement.

contratar *v.* to contract for; to trade; to engage, hire (*men*); **-se** to come to, or make, an agreement.

contratiempo *m.* accident, mishap.

contratista *m.* & *f.* contractor.

contrato *m.* contract.

contraventana *f.* shutter.

contribución *f.* contribution; tax.

contribuir[32] *v. irr.* to contribute.

contribuyente *m.* contributor; taxpayer; *adj.* contributing.

control *m. Am.* control.

controlador *m. Am.* controller.

controlar *v. Am.* to control.

controversia *f.* controversy.

contumacia *f.* stubbornness, obstinacy; contempt of court, failure to appear in court; rebelliousness.

contumaz *adj.* stubborn, rebellious.

contusión *f.* bruise.

convalecer[13] *v. irr.* to convalesce, recover from an illness.

convecino *adj.* near, neighboring; *m.* neighbor.

convencedor *adj.* convincing.

convencer[10] *v.* to convince.

convencimiento *m.* conviction, belief; convincing.

convención *f.* convention, assembly; pact, agreement; *Ríopl., Col., Ven., Mex., Carib.* political convention; **convencional** *adj.* conventional.

convenido *adj.* agreed; O.K., all right; *p.p.* of **convenir.**

conveniencia *f.* convenience; comfort; utility, profit.

conveniente *adj.* convenient, useful, profitable; fit, proper, suitable; opportune.

convenio *m.* pact, agreement.

convenir[48] *v. irr.* to agree; to convene, assemble; to be suitable, proper, advisable; to suit, fit; **-se** to agree.

conventillo *m. Ríopl., Ch.* tenement house.

convento *m.* convent.

convergente *adj.* convergent, coming together.

converger,[11] **convergir**[11] *v.* to converge.

conversación *f.* conversation.

conversar *v.* to converse.

conversión *f.* conversion.

convertir[3] *v. irr.* to convert.

convicción *f.* conviction.

convicto *p.p. irr.* of **convencer;** convicted, guilty.

convidado *m.* guest; *Am.* **— y con ollita** guest who abuses hospitality.

convidar *v.* to invite; **-se** to volunteer one's services; to invite oneself.

convincente *adj.* convincing.

convite *m.* invitation; banquet.

convocación f. convocation.

convocar[6] v. to convoke, call together.

convoyar v. to convoy, escort.

convulsión f. convulsion.

convulsivo adj. convulsive; **tos convulsiva** whooping cough.

conyugal adj. conjugal, pertaining to marriage or a married couple; **vida —** married life.

cónyuge m. husband; f. wife.

cooperación f. cooperation.

cooperador adj. cooperating, cooperative; m. cooperator, co-worker.

cooperar v. to cooperate.

cooperativo adj. cooperative; **cooperativa** f. cooperative, cooperative society.

coordinación f. coordination.

coordinar v. to coordinate.

copa f. (vaso) goblet; (de árbol) treetop; (de sombrero) crown; (palo de la baraja) card in the suit of copas (Spanish deck of cards); Am. **empinar la —** to drink, get drunk.

copartícipe adj. participant; m. & f. joint partner.

copete m. tuft; crest; top, summit; ornamental top on furniture; **de —** of high rank, important; proud; **estar uno hasta el —** to be stuffed; to be fed up; **tener mucho —** to be arrogant, haughty.

copia f. copy; imitation; abundance.

copiar v. to copy.

copioso adj. copious, abundant.

copita f. little glass; little drink.

copla f. couplet; stanza (of variable length and meter); popular song.

copo m. (de nieve) snowflake; (mechón) wad, tuft (of wool or cotton).

coqueta f. coquette, flirt.

coquetear v. to flirt.

coquetería f. coquetry, flirting.

coraje m. courage, valor; anger.

coral m. coral; Am. red poisonous snake; **-es** coral beads; adj. choral, pertaining to a choir; **coralino** adj. coral, like coral.

coraza f. cuirass, armor; armor plate or plating; shell (of a turtle).

corazón m. heart; core, center.

corazonada f. presentiment, foreboding; hunch.

corbata f. necktie; cravat; Am. colorful kerchief, scarf.

corcel m. charger, steed.

corcova f. hump, hunch; **corcovado** adj. hunchbacked; m. hunchback.

corcovear v. to prance about, leap; Am. to kick, protest against.

corchete m. hook and eye.

corcho m. cork; beehive; adj. Am. cork-like, spongy.

cordel m. cord, rope.

cordero m. lamb; lambskin.

cordial adj. cordial, friendly; **dedo —** middle finger.

cordialidad f. cordiality, friendliness, warmth.

cordillera f. mountain range.

cordobés adj. Cordovan, of or pertaining to Cordova; m. native of Cordova.

cordón m. cord; braid; cordon, line of soldiers; Ríopl. **— de la acera** curb, curbstone of the sidewalk; **cordonería** f. lace or cord maker's shop; collection of cords and laces; cordmaker's work; braiding.

cordoncillo m. small cord, drawstring, lace, lacing; braid; mill (ridged edge of a coin); ridge, rib (of certain fabrics).

cordura f. good judgment, wisdom; sanity.

cornada f. goring; butt with the horns; **dar -s** to gore, horn, butt with the horns.

corneta f. cornet; bugle; horn; m. bugler.

cornisa f. cornice.

coro m. choir; chorus.

corona f. crown; wreath.

coronar v. to crown; to top.

coronel m. colonel.

coronilla f. small crown; crown of the head; **estar uno hasta la —** to be fed up, be satiated.

corpanchón m. large body; carcass.

corpiño m. bodice.

corporación f. corporation.

corporal adj. corporal, of the body; m. corporal (small piece of linen used at Mass).

corpóreo adj. corporeal, bodily; tangible, material.

corpulento adj. corpulent, fat, stout.

corral m. yard; corral, cattle yard; **corralón** m. large corral; Am. lumber warehouse.

correa f. leather strap; resistance; Ch. **-s** leather blanket carrier; Am. **tener muchas -s** to be phlegmatic, calm.

corrección f. correction; correctness.

correcto adj. correct, proper.

corredizo adj. sliding, slipping; **nudo —** slip knot.

corredor m. (que corre) runner, racer; (pasillo) corridor; gallery around a patio; (revendedor) broker; Carib., Andes covered porch; Am. beater of wild game; adj. running; speedy.

corregidor m. corrector; Spanish magistrate.

corregir[5,11] v. irr. to correct; to reprove; to punish; **-se** to mend one's ways.

correligionario adj. of the same religion; of the same political party or sympathies; m. coreligionist.

correntada f. Ch., Ríopl., C.A., Carib. strong river current.

correo m. mail; mail service; postman; post office; **— aéreo** air mail.

correón m. large strap.

correoso adj. flexible; leathery, tough; **correosidad** f. toughness; flexibility.

correr v. (caminar) to run; to blow (said of the wind); (encarrera) to race; to chase; (pasar) to pass, elapse (time); to draw (a curtain); Am. to dismiss, throw out; **-se** to slip through; to slide; to be embarrassed.

correría *f.* foray, raid for plunder; excursion, short trip; **-s** wanderings, travels; raids.

correspondencia *f.* correspondence; letters, mail; agreement; interchange.

corresponder *v.* to reciprocate, return (*love, favors*); to belong; to concern; to correspond (*one thing with another*).

correspondiente *adj.* corresponding, agreeing; respective; *m.* correspondent.

corresponsal *m.* correspondent; agent; newspaper reporter.

corretear *v.* to run around; to roam, rove; *Am.* to pursue, chase.

corrida *f.* race; *Ch.* row, file; *P.R.* night spree; *Am.* beating up of game; **— del tiempo** swiftness of time; **— de toros** bullfight; **de —** without stopping.

corrido *adj.* embarrassed, ashamed; worldly-wise; flowing, fluent; **de —** without stopping; *m. Mex., Col., Ven., Ríopl., Andes* popular ballad.

corriente *adj.* (*que corre*) running; flowing, fluent; (*común*) usual, common, ordinary; *Am.* frank, open; **¡ — !** all right! O.K.!; **el ocho del —** the eighth of the current month; **estar al —** to be up-to-date; to be well-informed (*about current news*); **poner a uno al —** to keep someone posted or well informed; *f.* current; flow; course; *Am.* **hay que llevarle la —** one must humor him.

corrillo *m.* circle or group of gossipers.

corro *m.* group of talkers or spectators.

corroer[51] *v. irr.* to corrode.

corromper *v.* to corrupt; to seduce; to bribe; **-se** to rot; to become corrupted.

corrompido *adj.* corrupt; rotten, spoiled; degenerate; *p.p. of* **corromper**.

corrupción *f.* corruption.

corrupto *adj.* corrupt, rotten.

corsé *m.* corset.

cortada *f. Col., Ven., Carib.* cut, slash.

cortador *m.* cutter.

cortadura *m.* cut; gash; slash.

cortante *adj.* cutting; sharp.

cortaplumas *m.* penknife.

cortar *v.* to cut; to cut off; to cut out; to cut down; to interrupt; *Ven.* to harvest, pick (*fruit*); to gossip, speak ill of someone; **-se** to be embarrassed, ashamed; to sour, curdle (*said of milk*); *Am.* to become separated, cut off; *Mex., Cuba* to leave in a hurry; *Am.* to die.

corte *m.* cut; cutting; cutting edge; fit, style; *Carib., Mex., Ríopl.* cut (*in cards*); *Am.* harvest; *Am.* weeding; *Am.* gracefulness in dancing; *f.* royal court; retinue; *P.R., Ven.* court of justice; **-s** Spanish parliament; **hacer la —** to court, woo; *Am.* **darse uno — ** to put on airs.

cortedad *f.* smallness; timidity; bashfulness, shyness.

cortejar *v.* to court, woo.

cortejo *m.* cortege, procession; retinue; courtship; suitor.

cortés *adj.* courteous, polite.

cortesana *f.* courtesan, prostitute.

cortesano *m.* courtier; *adj.* courtlike; courteous.

cortesía *f.* courtesy, politeness.

corteza *f.* bark; crust; peel.

cortijo *m.* farmhouse.

cortina *m.* curtain.

corto *adj.* short; scanty; bashful.

corveta *f.* buck, leap, bound (*of a horse*); **hacer -s** to prance.

corvo *adj. see* **curvo.**

cosa *f.* thing; **— de** approximately, about; **no es —** it is not worth anything; **otra —** something else; **como si tal —** serene, as if nothing had happened; *Am.* **ni por una de estas nueve -s** absolutely not, not for anything in the world.

cosecha *f.* crop; harvest.

cosechar *v.* to reap; to harvest.

coser *v.* to sew; to stitch.

cosmético *m. & adj.* cosmetic.

cosquillas *f. pl.* ticklishness; tickling; **hacer —** to tickle; to excite (*one's desire or curiosity*); **tener —** to be ticklish.

cosquillear *v.* to tickle; to excite (*one's curiosity or desire*).

cosquilleo *m.* tickle, tickling sensation.

cosquilloso *adj.* ticklish; touchy.

costa *f.* coast; cost, expense, price; **a toda —** at all costs, by all means.

costado *m.* side; flank.

costal *m.* sack; **estar hecho un — de huesos** to be nothing but skin and bones; to be very thin.

costanero *adj.* coastal, relating to a coast; sloping.

costar[2] *v. irr.* to cost; **— trabajo** to be difficult.

costarricense *adj., m. & f.* Costa Rican.

coste, costo *m.* cost; expense.

costear *v.* (*pagar*) to defray or pay costs; to pay, be profitable; (*pasar junto a*) to navigate along the coast; to go along the edge of; **no costea** it does not pay.

costero *adj.* coastal; **navegación costera** coastal navigation.

costilla *f.* rib; chop, cutlet.

costoso *adj.* costly, expensive.

costra *f.* crust; scab.

costroso *adj.* crusty, scabby.

costumbre *f.* custom, habit.

costura *f.* sewing; stitching; seam.

costurera *f.* seamstress.

costurero *m.* sewing table or cabinet; sewing box; sewing room.

costurón *m.* coarse stitching; large seam; patch, mend; big scar.

cotejar *v.* to confront, compare.

cotejo *m.* comparison.

cotense *m. Ch., Mex.* burlap.

cotidiano *adj.* daily.

cotizable *adj.* quotable (*price*).

cotización *f.* quotation of prices; current price.

cotizar[9] *v.* to quote (*prices*); *Ch.* to

contribute one's share or quota; *Am.* to prorate, distribute proportionally.

coto *m.* enclosure; landmark; limitation; limit, boundary; **poner — a** to set a limit to; to put an end to.

cotorra *f.* small parrot; magpie; talkative person, chatterbox.

cotorrear *v.* to chatter; to gossip.

covacha *f.* small cave; grotto; *Mex., Cuba, Andes* hut, shanty; *Col.* cubbyhole, small dark room.

coyote *m. Am.* coyote, prairie wolf; *Mex.* shyster, tricky, lawyer; *C.A.* agent, broker (*often illegal*).

coyuntura *f.* joint; articulation; occasion; precise moment.

coz *f.* kick; recoil of a gun; butt of a firearm; **dar** (*or* **tirar**) **coces** to kick.

cráneo *m.* cranium, skull.

craso *adj.* fat; thick, coarse, gross; **ignorancia crasa** gross ignorance.

cráter *m.* crater of a volcano.

creación *f.* creation.

creador *m.* creator; *adj.* creating, creative.

crear *v.* to create.

crecer[13] *v. irr.* to grow; to increase; **-se** to swell (*as a river*); to become or feel important.

crecida *f.* river flood.

crecido *adj.* grown, increased; large; swollen.

creciente *adj.* growing, increasing; crescent (*moon*); *f.* river flood; *m.* crescent.

crecimiento *m.* growth, increase.

credenciales *f. pl.* credentials.

crédito *m.* credit; credence, belief; fame, reputation; letter of credit; **dar a —** to loan on credit.

credo *m.* creed; **en un —** in a jiffy, in a minute.

crédulo *adj.* credulous, too ready to believe.

creencia *f.* belief, faith.

creer[14] *v.* to believe; to think, suppose; **¡ya lo creo!** I should say so!; yes, of course!

creíble *adj.* credible, believable.

crema *f.* cream; custard; cold cream.

crepitar *v.* to crackle, snap; to creak; to rattle.

crepuscular *adj.* twilight.

crepúsculo *m.* twilight.

crespo *adj.* curly; artificial (*style*); angry; crisp.

crespón *m.* crepe.

cresta *f.* crest; top, summit; tuft, comb (*of a bird*).

cretona *f.* cretonne.

creyente *m. & f.* believer; *adj.* believing.

creyón *m. Am.* crayon.

cría *f.* brood; suckling; breeding.

criadero *m.* tree nursery; breeding place; hotbed; rich mine.

criado *m.* servant; *adj.* bred; **mal —** ill-bred; **criada** *f.* maid, servant.

criador *m.* breeder, raiser, rearer; creator; *adj.* creating, creative; breeding; nourishing.

crianza *f.* breeding; nursing; manners.

criar[17] *v.* to breed; to bring up, rear, educate; to nurse.

criatura *f.* creature; baby, child.

criba *f.* sieve.

cribar *v.* to sift.

crimen *m.* crime.

criminal *adj., m. & f.* criminal.

crin *f.* mane.

crinudo *adj. Am.* with a long or thick mane.

criollo *m. Am.* Creole; native of America (*especially Spanish America*); *adj. Am.* national, domestic (*not foreign to Spanish America*).

crisantema *f.,* **crisantemo** *m.* chrysanthemum.

crisis *f.* crisis.

crisol *m.* crucible, melting pot; hearth of a blast furnace.

crispar *v.* to contract (*muscles*); to clench (*fists*); to put (*nerves*) on edge.

cristal *m.* crystal; glass; mirror; lens.

cristalería *f.* glassware shop or factory; glassware.

cristalino *adj.* crystalline, transparent, clear; *m.* lens of the eye.

cristalizar[9] *v.* to crystallize.

cristiandad *f.* Christianity; Christendom.

cristianismo *m.* Christianity.

cristiano *m.* Christian; person; **hablar en —** to speak clearly; *adj.* Christian.

criterio *m.* criterion, rule, standard; judgment.

crítica *f.* criticism; censure; gossip.

criticador *adj.* critical; *m.* critic, faultfinder.

criticar[6] *v.* to criticize; to censure; to find fault with.

crítico *adj.* critical; *m.* critic, judge; *Am.* faultfinder, slanderer; **criticón** *m.* critic, knocker, faultfinder; *adj.* critical, over-critical, faultfinding.

croar *v.* to croak.

cromo *m.* chromium.

cromosoma *m.* chromosome.

crónica *f.* chronicle, history; **cronista** *m. & f.* chronicler.

crónico *adj.* chronic.

cronómetro *m.* chronometer, timepiece.

croquis *m.* rough sketch.

cruce *m.* crossing; crossroads; crossbreeding.

crucero *m.* (*cruciforme*) crossing; crossbearer; crossroads; transept (*of a church*); crossbeam; cross (*a constellation*); (*buque*) cruiser.

cruceta *f.* crosspiece; crosstree; universal joint (*automobile*).

crucificar[6] *v.* to crucify.

crucifijo *m.* crucifix.

crucigrama *m.* crossword puzzle.

crudo *adj.* raw; uncooked; unripe; harsh; **agua cruda** hard water; **petróleo —** crude oil; *Mex.* **estar —** to have a hang-over; **cruda** *f. Mex.* hang-over.

cruel *adj.* cruel.

crueldad *f.* cruelty.

crujido *m.* creak, crack, creaking; rustle.

crujir *v.* to creak, crackle; to grate (*one's teeth*); to rustle; to crunch.

cruz *f.* cross.

cruzada *f.* crusade; holy war; campaign.

cruzado *m.* crusader; *adj.* crossed; cross, crosswise, transverse.

cruzamiento *m.* crossing; crossroads.

cruzar[9] *v.* to cross; *Am.* to fight, dispute; **-se con** to meet.

cuaco *m. Mex.* horse; *Am.* cassava flour.

cuaderno *m.* notebook; memorandum book; booklet; *Mex.*, *Ven.* pamphlet.

cuadra *f.* hall, large room; stable; hospital or prison ward; *Am.* city block; *Am.* reception room.

cuadrado *adj.* square; *m.* square; square ruler; die, metal block or plate.

cuadrante *m.* dial, face of a clock or watch; sundial; quadrant (*fourth part of circle*; *instrument used in astronomy*).

cuadrar *v.* (*cuadriforme*) to square; to form into a square; (*agradar*) to please; to conform; to harmonize; to set well; *Am.* to be becoming (*said of clothes*); *Am.* to be ready; *Am.* to contribute a large sum; *Am.* to come out well, succeed; **-se** to stand at attention.

cuadricular *v.* to square off, divide into squares.

cuadrilla *f.* group, troupe, gang; armed band; quadrille, square dance.

cuadro *m.* square; picture; scene; frame; flower bed; *Am.* blackboard; *Ch.* slaughterhouse.

cuajada *f.* curd.

cuajado *p.p.* & *adj.* coagulated, curdled; filled, covered; **— de** full or covered with (*flowers, dew, etc.*).

cuajar *v.* to coagulate, thicken, curd, curdle; to turn out well; to jell; to please; *Am.* to chatter, prattle; **-se** to coagulate, curd; to become crowded, be filled; **la cosa no cuajó** the thing did not work, did not jell.

cuajarón *m.* clot.

cual *rel. pron.* which; **cada —** each one; **— más, — menos** some people more, others less; **el —, la —, los -es, las -es** which; who; **lo —** which; *adv.* as, like; **¿cuál?** *interr. pron.* which one? what?

cualidad *f.* quality; trait.

cualquier(a) *indef. adj.* & *pron.* any, anyone, whichever; **un hombre cualquiera** any man whatever.

cuando *rel. adv.* & *conj.* when; **aun —** even though; **¿cuándo?** *interr. adv.* when?

cuantía *f.* quantity; rank, importance.

cuantioso *adj.* plentiful, abundant; numerous.

cuanto *rel. adj.* & *pron.* as much as, as many as; all that; **— antes** as soon as possible, immediately; **en —** *conj.* as soon as; **en — a** as for, with regard to; **unos -s** a few; **¿cuánto?** *interr. adj.* & *pron.* how much?; **¿cuántos?** how many?

cuaquerismo *m.* the Quaker sect, or doctrine.

cuáquero *m.* Quaker.

cuarentena *f.* quarantine; forty units of anything; period of forty days, months, or years.

cuarentón *m.* man in his forties; **cuarentona** *f.* woman in her forties.

cuaresma *f.* Lent.

cuarta *f.* fourth, fourth part; span of a hand; *Am.* horse whip; *P.R.* **echar — a** to beat, flog.

cuartear *v.* to quarter, divide into quarters; *P.R.* to whip; **-se** to crack, split (*said of walls or ceilings*); *Mex.* to back down, go back on one's word.

cuartel *m.* quarter, one fourth; quarters, barracks; district; quarter, mercy; **no dar —** to give no quarter.

cuartelada *f.* military coup d'état, uprising, insurrection.

cuartelazo *m. Am.* military coup d'état, insurrection.

cuarterón *m.* quarter, fourth part; fourth of a pound; panel (*of a door or window*); *adj.* & *m.* quarter-breed (*one fourth Indian and three fourths Spanish*); quadroon (*person of quarter negro blood*).

cuarteto *m.* quartet; quatrain (*stanza of four lines*).

cuartilla *f.* (*hoja*) sheet of paper; (*medida*) about 4 quarts; about 1½ pecks; fourth of an **arroba** (about 6 pounds); *Am.* three cents' worth; *Am.* **no valer uno —** not to be worth a penny.

cuartillo *m.* fourth of a peck; about a pint; fourth of a **real**.

cuarto *m.* room; quarter, one fourth; **tener -s** to have money; *adj.* fourth.

cuarzo *m.* quartz.

cuate *adj.*, *m.* & *f. Mex.* twin; pal, buddy.

cuatrero *m.* horse thief, cattle thief; *Am.* Indian who speaks "broken" Spanish.

cuba *f.* cask, barrel; tub, vat; bigbellied person; drunkard.

cubano *adj.* & *m.* Cuban.

cubeta *f.* small barrel or keg; bucket, pail.

cúbico *adj.* cubic.

cubierta *f.* cover; covering; envelope; deck (*of a ship*); *Am.* sheath.

cubierto *p.p.* of **cubrir**; *m.* cover; place setting for one person at a table.

cubo *m.* cube; bucket, pail; hub of a wheel; mill pond; *Am.* finger bowl.

cubremesa *f.* table cover.

cubrir[52] *v.* to cover; to hide; to coat; to settle, pay (*a bill*); **-se** to cover oneself; to put on one's hat.

cucaracha *f.* cockroach.

cuclillas : en — in a squatting position; **sentarse en —** to squat.

cuclillo *m.* cuckoo.

cuco *adj.* dainty, cute; sly, shrewd; *m.* cuckoo; a kind of caterpillar; card game; *Riopl.* peach, peach tree; *Am.* **hacer — a** to make fun of; to fool.

cucurucho m. paper cone; *Am.* peak, summit; *Peru, C.A., Mex.* cowl, cloak with a hood (*worn by penitents in Holy Week processions*).

cuchara f. spoon; scoop; *Am.* mason's trowel; **media** — mediocre person; *Am.* mason's helper; *Am.* **hacer** — to pout; *Am.* **meter uno su** — to butt into a conversation; to meddle; **cucharada** f. spoonful; scoop; **cucharón** f. large spoon; ladle; dipper; scoop.

cuchichear v. to whisper.

cuchicheo m. whispering, whisper.

cuchilla f. large knife, cleaver; blade (*of any cutting instrument*); *Peru* penknife; *Riopl., Mex., P.R.* mountain ridge; *Am.* gore (*in a garment*); *Am.* narrow tract of land.

cuchillada f. thrust with a knife, stab, slash; cut, gash.

cuchillo m. knife; gore (*in a garment*); **— de monte** hunting knife; **cuchillería** f. cutlery; cutlery shop.

cueca f. *Am.* a Chilean dance.

cuello m. neck; collar.

cuenca f. river basin; narrow valley; wooden bowl; socket of the eye.

cuenco m. earthen bowl.

cuenta f. (*cálculo*) count, calculation; bill; account; (*bolita*) bead (*of a rosary or necklace*); **a fin de -s** in the final analysis; **caer en la** — to see, get the point; **darse** — to realize; *Col.* **de toda** — anyway; **eso corre de mi** — that is my responsibility; I'll have charge of that; **eso no me tiene** — that does not pay me; it is of no profit to me; **en resumidas -s** in short; *P.R.* **hacerle** — **una cosa a uno** to be useful or profitable for one; **tomar en** — to take into account; **tomar una cosa por su** — to take charge of something, take the responsibility for it; **vamos a -s** let's understand or settle this.

cuentagotas m. dropper (*for counting drops*).

cuento m. story, tale; **— de nunca acabar** never-ending tale; **déjese de -s** come to the point; **no viene a** — it is not opportune or to the point.

cuerda f. cord, string, rope; chord; watch spring; **dar** — **a** to wind (*a watch*).

cuerdo adj. sane; wise.

cuereada f. *Mex., C.A., Col., Ven.* flogging, whipping; *Am.* skinning of an animal.

cuerear v. *Am.* to flog, whip; *Am.* to harm, dishonor; *Am.* to beat (*in a game*); *Am.* to skin (*an animal*).

cuerno m. horn; antenna, feeler; **poner -s a** to be unfaithful to, deceive (*a husband*); *Am.* **mandar al** — to send to the devil.

cuero m. hide, skin; leather; wineskin; *Col., Ven.* whip; **en -s** naked.

cuerpeada f. *Riopl.* dodge; evasion.

cuerpo m. body; bulk; corps; **en** — without hat or coat; **luchar** — **a —**

to fight in single combat; *Am.* **sacar el** — to dodge; to escape, avoid doing something.

cuervo m. crow; raven; *Ven.* buzzard; *Am.* dishonest priest; *Riopl., Ch.* **hacer uno la del** — to leave abruptly and not return.

cuesta f. hill, slope; **a -s** on one's shoulders or back; in one's care; **— abajo** downhill; **— arriba** uphill.

cuestión f. question; controversy, dispute; problem, matter.

cuestionario m. questionnaire, list of questions.

cueva f. cave, cavern; cellar.

cuico m. *Mex.* cop, policeman; *Am.* gossiper, tattletale, "squealer"; *Ch., Bol., Peru* half-breed; *Riopl.* short, chubby person.

cuidado m. care, attention; worry, misgiving; **al — de** in care of; **tener** — to be careful; **¡** — **!** look out!; be careful! **¡cuidadito!** be very careful!

cuidadoso adj. careful; attentive; anxious.

cuidar v. to take care of, look after, keep; to make or do carefully.

cuita f. grief, care, anxiety; misfortune; *C.A.* bird dung.

cuitado adj. unfortunate; timid, shy.

culata f. haunch, buttock; rear; butt (*of a firearm*).

culatazo f. blow with the butt of a rifle; recoil, kick of a firearm.

culebra f. snake; coil; *Mex.* money belt.

culebrear v. to zigzag; to twist, wriggle.

culminación f. culmination, climax.

culminar v. to culminate; to come to a climax.

culpa f. fault; guilt; blame; **echar la — a** to blame; **tener la** — to be to blame.

culpabilidad f. guilt; **culpable** adj. guilty.

culpar v. to blame; to declare guilty.

cultivación f. cultivation.

cultivador m. cultivator; **máquina cultivadora** cultivator.

cultivar v. to cultivate.

cultivo m. cultivation, culture.

culto adj. cultured; *m.* cult, worship; religious sect; **rendir — a** to pay homage to; to worship.

cultura f. culture; cultivation.

cumbre f. summit; top.

cumpleaños m. birthday.

cumplido adj. (*completo*) complete, full; perfect; (*cortés*) courteous; *p.p.* fulfilled; due, fallen due; **tiene tres años -s** he is just over three years old; *m.* courtesy, attention; compliment.

cumplimentar v. to compliment; to congratulate; to pay a courtesy visit.

cumplimiento m. fulfilment; courtesy; completion; compliment; **de** — formal, ceremonious.

cumplir v. to fulfill; to comply; to carry out; to fall due; **— años** to have a birthday; to be (*so many*) years old.

cúmulo m. pile, heap; accumulation; cumulus (*mass of clouds*).

cuna f. cradle; origin; *Am.* coffin for the poor; *Am.* dive, den (*for gambling and dancing*).

cundir v. to spread (*as news, disease, liquids*); to propagate, extend, multiply.

cuña f. wedge; splinter; *Ch., Ríopl.* influential person.

cuñado m. brother-in-law; **cuñada** f. sister-in-law.

cuota f. quota; dues, fee; — **de entrada** admission fee.

cuotidiano adj. everyday, daily.

cupé m. coupé.

cupón m. coupon.

cúpula f. dome.

cura f. cure; m. curate, priest.

curación f. cure.

curandero m. healer (*not a doctor*); quack; medicine man (*among Indians*).

curar v. to cure, heal; to treat; to cure (*meats, tobacco*); to tan (*skins*); *Am.* to load (*dice*), fix (*cards*); — **de** to take care of; **-se** to cure oneself; to get well; *Ríopl.* to get drunk.

curiosear v. to snoop, peek, peer, pry; to observe with curiosity.

curiosidad f. curiosity; neatness, daintiness.

curioso adj. curious; neat, dainty; **libros raros y -s** rare books.

curro adj. showy, gaudy, flashy; m. dandy.

currutaco m. fop, dandy; adj. affected (*in one's dress*).

cursi adj. common, in bad taste; cheap, ridiculous; **cursilería** f. bad taste, cheapness, false elegance; group of cheap, ridiculous people.

curso m. course, direction; scholastic year; course of study.

curtidor m. tanner.

curtiduría f. tannery.

curtir v. to tan; to harden, accustom to hardships; *Col., Ven.* to dirty, soil; **-se** to get tanned or sunburned; to become accustomed to hardships.

curva f. curve.

curvo adj. curved; bent, crooked; arched.

cúspide f. summit, peak, top; spire, steeple.

custodia f. custody; guard, guardian; monstrance (*vessel in which the consecrated Host is exposed*).

custodiar v. to guard, watch; to keep in custody.

custodio m. guardian, keeper.

cutícula f. cuticle.

cutis m. skin; complexion.

cuyo rel. poss. adj. whose, of whom, of which.

CH

chabacano adj. crude, unpolished; inartistic; cheap, in bad taste; m. *Mex.* a variety of apricot.

chacota f. fun; jest; **echar a —** to take as a joke; **hacer — de** to make fun of.

chacotear v. to frolic, joke, make merry; to be boisterous; to show off.

chacra f. *Ec., Peru, Ch.* small farm; *Col.; Ec.* cultivated field.

chagra f. *Col., Ec.* farm, piece of farm land; m. & f. *Ec.* peasant; adj. uncivilized, unrefined.

chal m. shawl.

chalán m. horse trader; *Am.* broncobuster, horse breaker.

chaleco m. waistcoat, vest.

chalupa f. sloop, sailboat; launch; *Mex., Col., Ven., Ríopl.* canoe; *P.R.* raft; *Mex.* Mexican tortilla with sauce.

chamaco m. *Mex., C.A.* boy; **chamaquito** m. *Mex., C.A.* little boy.

chamarra f. coarse wool jacket or sweater; *Mex.* sheepskin jacket, leather jacket; *Am.* heavy wool blanket.

chamarreta f. short loose jacket; *Am.* square poncho.

chambergo m. gaucho sombrero.

chambón adj. clumsy, awkward, unskillful; m. bungler, clumsy performer, awkward workman; clumsy player.

champaña f. champagne.

champú m. shampoo.

champurrado m. *Mex.* a mixed drink of chocolate and **atole**; *Col.* a mixed alcoholic beverage.

champurrar, *Am.* **champurrear** v. to mix (*drinks*).

chamuscada, chamuscadura f. *Am.* singe, scorch.

chamuscar v. to scorch; to singe; to sear; *Am.* to sell at a low cost; **-se** to get scorched, singed, or seared; *Am.* to get peeved, offended.

chamusquina f. singe, scorch.

chancear v. to fool, joke, jest.

chancero m. jester, joker; adj. jolly.

chancla f. slipper; old shoe; **chancleta** f. slipper; m. *Am.* good-for-nothing.

chanclo m. galosh, overshoe; clog; rubber overshoe; **-s** rubbers.

chancho m. *S.A.* pig, pork.

changador m. *Ríopl.* carrier, porter; *Am.* handy man, person who does odd jobs.

chango m. *Mex.* monkey; **ponerse —** to be alert, wary.

chantaje m. blackmail, blackmailing.

chanza f. joke, jest.

chapa f. metal plate; veneer (*thin leaf of wood*); rosy spot on the cheeks; *Mex., C.A., Andes* lock; *Am.* Indian spy; **-s** game of tossing coins; **hombre de —** serious, reliable man.

chapado adj. veneered (*covered with a thin layer of wood or other material*); — **a la antigua** old-fashioned.

chapalear = chapotear.

chaparro m. scrub oak; short, chubby person; *Am.* a kind of tropical shrub with rough leaves; *Am.* short whip; adj. *Mex., C.A.* short, squatty.

chaparrón m. downpour, heavy shower.

chapitel *m.* spire, steeple; capital (*of a column*).

chapotear *v.* to splash, paddle in the water.

chapoteo *m.* splash.

chapucear *v.* to fumble; to botch, bungle, do or make clumsily; *Am.* to deceive, trick.

chapulín *m.* *Mex.*, *C.A.* grasshopper.

chapurrar *v.* to speak (*a language*) brokenly; to mix (*drinks*).

chapuz *m.* dive, duck, ducking.

chapuza *f.* botch, clumsy piece of work; *Am.* foul trick, fraud.

chapuzar⁹ *v.* to duck; to dive.

chaqueta *f.* jacket; **chaquetón** *m.* long jacket, coat.

charamusca *f.* *Mex.* twisted candy stick or cane; *Col.*, *Ven.* brushwood, firewood; *C.A.* hubbub, uproar.

charamusquero *m.* *Am.* candy-stick maker or vendor.

charca *f.* pond.

charco *m.* puddle, pool; **pasar el —** to cross the pond, cross the ocean.

charla *f.* chat, chatter, prattle.

charladuría *f.* chatter, gossip.

charlar *v.* to chat, chatter, prate.

charlatán *m.* chatterer, prater; gossiper; charlatan, quack.

charol *m.* varnish; patent leather; *Col.* tray; **charola** *f.* *Mex.* tray.

charolar *v.* to varnish, polish.

charqui *m.* jerky, jerked beef.

charro *m.* *Spain* a villager of Salamanca province; *Mex.* Mexican horseman of special costume and cultural status.

charrúa *m. & f.* *Am.* Charruan Indian (*Indian of Uruguay*).

chascarrillo *m.* joke, funny story.

chasco *m.* joke, prank; surprise; disillusionment, disappointment; **llevarse —** to be disappointed, surprised or fooled; *adj.* *Am.* thick, curly (*hair*); *Am.* ruffled (*plumage*).

chasquear *v.* to play a trick on; to disappoint; to crack (*a whip*); to smack (*the lips*); to click (*the tongue*); to crack, snap; *Col.*, *Ven.* to chatter (*said of the teeth*); *Am.* to munch (*food*); **-se** to be disappointed or disillusioned; to be tricked or fooled.

chasqui *m.* *Andes*, *Ríopl.* courier, messenger.

chasquido *m.* crack of a whip; crackle; smack (*of the lips*); click (*of the tongue*).

chata *f.* bedpan; scow, barge, flat-bottomed boat; *Am.* platform wagon, platform car, flatcar; **chatita** *f.* *Mex.* "honey", "cutie", "funny face".

chato *adj.* snub-nosed, flat-nosed; flat; flattened; squatty; *Mex.* **quedarse uno —** to be left flat or in the lurch; to be disappointed. —

chaval *m.* lad; young man.

chayote *m.* *Am.* vegetable pear (*a tropical fruit growing on a vine*); *Am.* dunce, silly fool.

che *interj.* *Ríopl.* word used to attract attention among intimates; say! listen! hey!; nickname for citizens of Argentina.

cheque *m.* check, bank check.

chica *f.* little girl; girl; maid, servant.

chicle *m.* *Am.* chicle; *Am.* chewing gum.

chico *adj.* small, little; *m.* child, boy; *Col.* each game of billiards; *Am.* = **chicozapote** (*tropical fruit and tree from which chicle is extracted*)

chicote *m.* cigar; piece of rope; *Am.* whip; *Col.*, *Ven.* cigar butt.

chicotear *v.* *Ríopl.*, *Col.*, *Peru* to lash, whip, flog; *Am.* to fight, quarrel; *Am.* to kill.

chicoteo *m.* *Ríopl.* whipping; *Am.* shooting, killing; *Am.* crackling, rattling (*as of machine guns*); *Am.* quarreling.

chicha *f.* *Peru*, *Col.*, *Ch.*, *Ríopl.*, *C.A.* chicha (*a popular alcoholic beverage*); *Peru* thick-soled shoe; **no ser ni — ni limonada** to be worth nothing, be neither fish nor fowl.

chícharo *m.* pea; *Col.* bad cigar; *Am.* apprentice.

chicharra *f.* cicada, locust; talkative person; *Mex.* person with a shrill voice; *Am.* rickety, squeaky car; *Ch.* harsh-sounding musical instrument or bell; *C.A.*, *Mex.*, *Cuba* piece of fried pork skin.

chicharrón *m.* crackling, crisp piece of fried pork skin; burned piece of meat; sunburnt person; *Am.* dried-up, wrinkled person; *Am.* bootlicker, flatterer.

chiche *m.* *Mex.*, *C.A.* breast, teat; wet nurse.

chichón *m.* bump, lump; *Am.* joker, jester; **chichona** *adj.* *Mex.*, *C.A.* large-breasted.

chiflado *adj.* "cracked", "touched", crazy; *p.p.* of **chiflar.**

chifladura *f.* craziness, mania; mockery, jest.

chiflar *v.* to whistle; to hiss; *Am.* to sing (*said of birds*); **-se** to lose one's head; to become unbalanced, crazy.

chiflido *m.* whistle; hiss; *Am.* **en un —** in a jiffy, in a second.

chile *m.* chili, red pepper.

chileno *adj. & m.* Chilean.

chillante *adj.* flashy, bright, showy, loud; shrieking.

chillar *v.* to shriek, scream; to hiss; *Am.* to shout, protest, moan; *Am.* to "squeal", turn informer; *Ríopl.*, *Ven.*, *C.A.*, *P.R.* **no** — not to say a word; *Mex.* **-se** to be piqued, offended.

chillido *m.* shriek, scream.

chillón *adj.* shrieking, screaming; shrill; loud, gaudy; *Col.*, *Andes* whining, discontented; *Ríopl.* touchy.

chimenea *f.* chimney; fireplace, hearth.

china *f.* (*de la China*) Chinese woman; China silk or cotton; porcelain; (*piedra*) pebble; marble; *Andes*, *Ch.*,

Ríopl., *Col.* girl, young woman (*usually half-breed or Indian*); *Am.* servant girl; *P.R.* sweet orange; *Col.* spinning top; **chinita** *f. Am.* little Indian girl; darling.

chinche *f.* bedbug; thumbtack; tiresome person, bore; *Col.*, *Ven.*, *Ríopl.* touchy or irritable person; *Am.* plump, squatty person.

chinchorro *m. Ven.*, *Col.* hammock.

chino *adj.* Chinese; *Mex.* curly; *m. Ríopl.* Chinese; Chinaman; *Am.* pig; *Am.* half-breed (*Negro and Indian, white and Indian*); *Am.* Indian; *Col.* house servant; *Am.* coarse, rough, ugly person; *Col.* straight, coarse hair.

chiquero *m.* pigsty, pigpen; pen for bulls; goat shelter.

chiquilín *m. Am.* tot, little boy; **chiquilina** *f. Am.* little girl.

chiquito *adj.* tiny, very small; *m.* tiny tot, tiny child; **chiquitico** *adj.* tiny.

chiripa *f.* stroke of good luck.

chiripá *m. Ríopl.* loose riding trousers (*square of cloth draped from the waist and between the legs*).

chirola *f. Mex.*, *Ven.*, *Ríopl.* "jug", jail; *Am.* coin of low value.

chirona *f.* "jug", jail.

chirriado *adj. Col.* attractive; lively.

chirriar[17] *v.* to squeak, creak; to sizzle; to chirp; to sing out of tune; *Col.* to go on a spree.

chirrido *m.* creak, squeak; chirp; squeaking, creaking; chirping.

chisguete *m.* squirt.

chisme *m.* gossip, piece of gossip; trifle, trinket, knickknack, gadget.

chismear *v.* to gossip; to tattle.

chismería *f.* gossiping, talebearing.

chismero *adj.* gossiping; *m.* gossip.

chismoso *adj.* gossiping; *m.* gossip, talebearer, tattletale.

chispa *f.* spark; small diamond; wit; *Col.* false rumor, lie; *Am.* two-wheeled cart; *Mex.* brazen, shameless woman; *Am.* **da —** it clicks, works, functions; *Am.* **ponerse —** to get drunk.

chispeante *adj.* sparkling.

chispear *v.* to spark; to sparkle; to twinkle; to drizzle.

chisporrotear *v.* to sputter, throw off sparks.

chiste *m.* joke, jest; **dar en el —** to guess right, hit the nail on the head.

chistera *f.* top hat; fish basket.

chistoso *adj.* funny, amusing, humorous.

¡chito! ¡chitón! *interj.* hush!

chiva *f.* female goat; *Am.* goatee; *Pan.*, *Col.* flivver, small bus; **chivo** *m.* he-goat; *Am.* fit of anger; *Am.* insulting remark; *Am.* **estar hecho un —** to be very angry; *adj. Am.* angry; **chivato** *m. Cuba* informer, squealer.

chocante *adj.* striking, surprising; shocking; disgusting; *Col.*, *Andes* tiresome, annoying, impertinent.

chocar[6] *v.* to bump, collide, clash; to fight; to shock, surprise, disgust; **me**

choca ese hombre I loathe that man.

chocarrear *v.* to tell coarse jokes; to clown.

chocarrería *f.* coarse joke; **chocarrero** *adj.* coarse, vulgar; clownish.

choclo *m.* overshoe; clog; *Mex.* low shoe or slipper; *Andes*, *Col.*, *Ch.*, *Ríopl.* ear of corn; *Am.* corn stew; *Am.* spike, ear of wheat.

chocolate *m.* chocolate.

chochear *v.* to be in one's dotage, act senile.

chochera, chochez *f.* senility, dotage; **chocheras, chocheces** senile actions or habits.

chocho *adj.* doting; *m.* childish old man.

chófer *m.* chauffeur.

cholo *m. Andes*, *Ríopl.*, *Ch.* half-breed; *Am.* half-civilized Indian; *adj. Am.* coarse, rude; *C.R.* dark-skinned; *Ch.* black (*dog*).

chopo *m.* black poplar; *adj. Am.* stupid.

choque *m.* collision, bump; shock; clash, conflict; dispute.

chorizo *m.* sausage; *Am.* string of things; *Am.* fool.

chorrazo *m.* spurt, large stream or jet.

chorrear *v.* to drip; to spout.

chorro *m.* spurt, jet; stream, flow; *Am.* strand of a whip; *Am.* river rapids.

choteador *m. Am.* joker, jester.

chotear *v. Cuba* to make fun of, jeer, jest, mock, kid; *Mex.*, *C.A.* to idle, fool around; *Am.* to pamper.

choteo *m. Cuba* joking, jeering, kidding.

choza *f.* hut, cabin.

chubasco *m.* squall, sudden shower; **aguantar el —** to weather the storm.

chuchería *f.* trifle, trinket; knickknack; tidbit.

chueco *adj. Am.* crooked, bent; *Col.* crook-legged, bow-legged, knock-kneed; *Am.* worn-out, dejected; *Mex.* disgusted, annoyed; *Am.* **comerciar en —** to trade in stolen goods.

chuleta *f.* cutlet, chop; blow, slap.

chulo *m.* dandy; effeminate man; clownish fellow; bullfighter's assistant; *Col.* buzzard; *Am.* coarse, thick brush; *adj. C.A.*, *Col.*, *Mex.* good-looking, pretty.

chumpipe *m. C.A.* turkey; also **chompipe**.

chupada *f.* sucking; suction; suck, sip; *Mex.*, *C.A.*, *Ven.*, *Andes* puff from a cigarette; *Ríopl.* big swallow of liquor.

chupador *m.* sucker; teething ring; *Am.* toper, heavy drinker; *Am.* smoker.

chupaflor, chuparrosa *m. Am.* hummingbird.

chupar *v.* to suck; to sip; to absorb, take in; *Am.* to smoke; *C.A.*, *Ríopl.*, *Andes* to drink, get drunk; **-se** to shrivel up.

churrasco *m. Ríopl.*, *Andes* roasted meat; *Ríopl.*, *Andes* barbecued meat; *Ríopl.*, *Andes* large piece of meat for barbecuing.

churrasquear v. *Ríopl.*, *Andes* to barbecue, roast over coals; *Ríopl.*, *Andes* to prepare (*meat*) for barbecuing; *Ríopl.*, *Andes* to eat barbecued meat.

churrasquito m. small piece of roast.

churrigueresco adj. baroque, ornate (*architecture*).

chuscada f. jest, joke.

chusco adj. funny, witty; ridiculous; *Peru* **perro** — mongrel dog.

chusma f. rabble, mob.

D

dable adj. feasible, possible.

daca = **da acá.**

dádiva f. gift.

dadivoso adj. liberal, generous.

dado m. die; **-s** dice.

dador m. giver.

daga f. dagger.

dama f. lady; **jugar a las -s** to play checkers.

damisela f. damsel, girl.

danza f. dance.

danzante m. & f. dancer.

danzar[9] v. to dance.

danzarina f. dancer.

dañar v. to harm, hurt, damage; **-se** to spoil, rot; to get hurt; to get damaged.

dañino adj. harmful; destructive.

daño m. damage, harm, loss.

dañoso adj. harmful.

dar[26] v. irr. (*hacer don*) to give, confer; (*golpear*) to strike, hit; (*emitir*) give off, emit; **— a luz** to give birth to; to publish; **— con** to encounter, find; **— de comer** to feed; **— de sí** to give, stretch; **— en** to hit upon; to persist in; **— largas a un asunto** to prolong or postpone a matter; *C.A.*, *Ven.*, *Col.* **— cuero (guasca, puños)** to beat, thrash, lash; **lo misma da** it makes no difference; **-se** to give up; **dárselas de** to boast of.

dardo m. dart, arrow.

dares y tomares m. pl. give-and-take, dispute; dealings.

dársena f. dock, wharf.

datar v. to date; **— de** to date from.

dátil m. date (*fruit of the date palm*).

dato m. datum, fact; **-s** data.

de prep. of, from; about, concerning; in (*after a superlative*); if (*before inf.*); **— no llegar** if he does not arrive; **el — la gorra azul** the one with the blue cap; **el mejor — América** the best in America; **más — lo que dice** more than he says.

debajo adv. under, underneath; **— de** prep. under.

debate m. debate; dispute, quarrel.

debatir v. to debate, argue, discuss; to fight; **-se** to struggle.

debe m. debit.

debelar v. to subdue, defeat.

deber v. to owe; to have to (must, should, ought); **debe de ser** it must be, probably is; **¡me la debes!** I have an account to settle with you!

deber m. duty, obligation; debt; debit, debit side (*in bookkeeping*).

debido adj. due, owing; just, appropriate.

débil adj. weak, feeble.

debilidad f. debility, weakness.

debilitación f., **debilitamiento** m. weakening; weakness.

debilitar v. to weaken.

débito m. debt; debit.

debutar v. to make a debut, make a first public appearance.

década f. decade, ten years; series of ten.

decadencia f. decadence, decline, falling off.

decaer[24] v. irr. to decay, decline, wither, fade; to fall to leeward.

decaimiento m. decline, decay; dejection; weakness.

decano m. dean; senior member of a group.

decantado p.p. & adj. much talked about; overrated.

decapitar v. to behead.

decencia f. decency; **decente** adj. decent; respectable; fair.

decenio m. decade.

decepción f. disillusion, disappointment.

decepcionante adj. disappointing.

decepcionar v. to disillusion, disappoint.

decibel m. decibel (*unit for the measurement of the intensity of sound*).

decidir v. to decide, resolve; **-se a** to make up one's mind to; to decide to.

décima f. tenth; tithe; stanza of ten octosyllabic lines.

décimo adj. tenth.

decir[27] v. irr. to say; to tell; to speak; **es —** that is; **querer —** to mean, signify.

decisión f. decision.

decisivo adj. decisive, final.

declamar v. to declaim, recite.

declaración f. declaration; statement; deposition, testimony.

declarar v. to declare, state, affirm; to testify; **-se** to propose, declare one's love; to give one's views or opinion.

declinar v. to decline; to go down; to lose vigor, decay; to bend down.

declive m. declivity, slope.

decoración f. decoration, ornament; stage setting.

decorar v. to decorate, adorn.

decorativo adj. decorative, ornamental.

decoro m. decorum, propriety, dignity; honor.

decoroso adj. decorous, becoming, proper, decent.

decrépito adj. decrepit, old, feeble.

decretar v. to decree.

decreto m. decree; decision, order.

dechado m. model, pattern, example.

dedal m. thimble.

dedicar[6] v. to dedicate; to devote; **-se** to apply oneself.

dedicatoria f. dedication, inscription.

dedo m. (*de la mano*) finger; (*del pie*)

toe; — **del corazón** middle finger; — **meñique** little finger; — **pulgar** thumb; **no mamarse el** — not to be easily fooled; **dedillo** *m.* small finger; **saber al dedillo** to know perfectly, know by heart.

deducción *f.* deduction; inference.

deducir[25] *v. irr.* to deduce, conclude; to deduct.

defecto *m.* defect, fault.

defectuoso *adj.* defective, faulty.

defender[1] *v. irr.* to defend.

defensa *f.* defense; *Am.* automobile bumper.

defensivo *adj.* defensive; *m.* defense, safeguard; **defensiva** *f.* defensive.

defensor *m.* defender.

deficiencia *f.* deficiency; **deficiente** *adj.* deficient.

déficit *m.* deficit, shortage.

definición *f.* definition.

definido *adj.* definite; *p.p. of* **definir**.

definir *v.* to define, explain; to determine.

definitivo *adj.* definitive, conclusive, final; **en definitiva** in short, in conclusion; definitely.

deformación *f.* deformation, deformity.

deformar *v.* to deform; **-se** to become deformed; to lose its shape or form.

deforme *adj.* deformed; ugly.

deformidad *f.* deformity.

defraudar *v.* to defraud, cheat, rob of.

defunción *f.* death, decease.

degenerado *adj.* & *m.* degenerate.

degenerar *v.* to degenerate.

deglución *f.* swallowing.

deglutir *v.* to swallow.

degollar[1] *v. irr.* to behead; to slash the throat; to cut (*a dress*) low in the neck.

degradar *v.* to degrade; to debase.

degüello *m.* beheading; throat-slashing.

dehesa *f.* pasture, grazing ground.

deidad *f.* deity.

dejadez *f.* lassitude, languor, listlessness; self-neglect, slovenliness.

dejado *adj.* indolent, listless; slovenly.

dejar *v.* (*abandonar*) to leave; to quit; to abandon; to omit; (*permitir*) to permit, let; (*soltar*) to let go; — **de** to stop, cease; — **caer** to drop; *Am.* **no -se** not to be an easy mark, not to let others pick on one.

dejo *m.* (*sabor*) aftertaste; slight taste; (*acento*) slight accent, peculiar inflection.

del = de + el of the.

delantal *m.* apron.

delante *adv.* before, in front; — **de** *prep.* in front of.

delantera *f.* lead, forepart, front.

delantero *adj.* front, foremost, first.

delatar *v.* to denounce, accuse, inform against.

delator *m.* accuser, informer.

delegación *f.* delegation.

delegado *m.* delegate.

delegar[7] *v.* to delegate.

deleitable *adj.* delightful, enjoyable.

deleitar *v.* to delight, please.

deleite *m.* delight, joy, pleasure.

deleitoso *adj.* delightful.

deletrear *v.* to spell.

deleznable *adj.* perishable; brittle.

delfín *m.* dolphin; dauphin.

delgadez *f.* thinness; slimness; fineness.

delgado *adj.* thin, slender, slim.

deliberado *adj.* deliberate; *p.p. of* **deliberar**.

deliberar *v.* to deliberate, consider, ponder.

delicadeza *f.* fineness; delicacy; softness, exquisiteness.

delicado *adj.* delicate; weak, frail; exquisite, dainty; tender.

delicia *f.* delight.

delicioso *adj.* delicious, delightful.

delincuente *adj.*, *m.* & *f.* delinquent.

delineación *f.*, **delineamiento** *m.* delineation, design, outline, drawing; portrayal.

delinear *v.* to delineate, sketch, outline.

delirante *adj.* delirious, raving.

delirar *v.* to be delirious; to rave, talk wildly or foolishly.

delirio *m.* delirium, temporary madness; wild excitement; foolishness.

delito *m.* crime; misdemeanor.

demacrado *adj.* scrawny, emaciated, thin.

demanda *f.* demand; petition; question; claim; complaint; lawsuit.

demandado *m.* defendant; *p.p. of* **demandar**.

demandante *m.* & *f.* plaintiff.

demandar *v.* to demand; to petition; to sue, file a suit; to indict.

demás *indef. adj.* & *pron.*: **los** — the rest; the others; **las** — **personas** the other people; **lo** — the rest; **por** — useless; uselessly; **por lo** — as to the rest; moreover.

demasía *f.* excess; boldness, insolence; offense, outrage; **en** — excessively.

demasiado *adv.* too much, excessively; too; *adj.* too much, excessive.

demente *adj.* demented, insane, crazy.

democracia *f.* democracy; **demócrata** *m.* & *f.* democrat; **democrático** *adj.* democratic.

demoler[2] *v. irr.* to demolish, tear down.

demonio *m.* demon, devil; evil spirit.

demontre *m.* devil; ¡ — ! the deuce!

demora *f.* delay.

demorar *v.* to delay; to retard; **-se** to linger; to be delayed.

demostración *f.* demonstration; proof, explanation.

demostrar[2] *v. irr.* to demonstrate, show, prove, explain.

demostrativo *adj.* demonstrative.

demovilizar[9] *v.* to demobilize.

demudar *v.* to change, alter; to disguise; **-se** to change color or one's facial expression; to turn pale.

dengoso, denguero *adj.* affected; finicky.

dengue *m.* primness; coyness, affectation; dengue, breakbone fever; *Am.*

marigold; *Col.* zigzag; *Am.* swagger;
hacer -s to act coy, make grimaces.

denigrar *v.* to blacken, defame, revile,
insult.

denodado *adj.* dauntless, daring.

denominación *f.* denomination; name,
title, designation.

denominar *v.* to name, call, entitle.

denostar[2] *v. irr.* to insult, outrage,
revile.

denotar *v.* to denote, indicate, mean.

densidad *f.* density.

denso *adj.* dense, compact; thick.

dentado *adj.* toothed, notched.

dentadura *f.* set of teeth.

dentar[1] *v. irr.* to tooth, furnish (*a saw*)
with teeth; to indent; to cut teeth,
grow teeth (*referring to a child*).

dentellada *f.* bite; tooth mark; **a -s**
with big bites.

dentición *f.* teething.

dentífrico *m.* dentrifice, tooth cleanser;
pasta dentífrica toothpaste; **polvos
dentífricos** toothpowder.

dentista *m.* dentist.

dentro *adv.* inside, within; **— de** *prep.*
inside of; **por —** on the inside.

denuedo *m.* spirit, courage, daring.

denuesto *m.* affront, insult.

denuncia *f.* denunciation; condemnation, accusation; miner's claim.

denunciar *v.* to denounce, accuse; to
proclaim, advise, give notice; to claim
(*a mine*).

deparar *v.* to furnish, offer, supply.

departamento *m.* department; compartment; apartment.

departir *v.* to talk, converse.

dependencia *f.* dependence; dependency; branch office.

depender *v.* to depend, rely (on).

dependiente *m.* clerk; dependent, subordinate; *adj.* dependent.

deplorar *v.* to deplore, lament, regret.

deponer[40] *v. irr.* to set aside; to depose,
remove (*an official*); to testify, declare;
to have a bowel movement; *Am.* to
vomit.

deportar *v.* to deport, banish.

deporte *m.* sport; pastime, recreation.

deportista *m.* sportsman; *f.* sports-
woman.

deportivo *adj.* sport, sports (*used
as an adj.*); **copa deportiva** loving
cup.

deposición *f.* declaration, assertion;
testimony; dismissal, removal (*from
office or power*); bowel movement.

depositar *v.* to deposit; to deliver, intrust.

depositario *m.* receiver, trustee.

depósito *m.* deposit; storage; warehouse; **— de agua** reservoir.

depravado *adj.* depraved, corrupt, degenerate.

depravar *v.* to corrupt, pervert, contaminate.

depreciar *v.* to depreciate, lessen the
value of.

depresión *f.* depression; dip, sag.

deprimente *adj.* depressing.

deprimir *v.* to depress; to press down;
to humiliate, belittle.

depuesto *p.p.* of **deponer.**

depurar *v.* to purify.

derecha *f.* right hand; right side; right
wing (*in politics*); **a la —** to the right;
derechazo *m.* a blow with the right
hand, a right (*boxing*).

derecho *adj.* right; straight; *m.* law;
duty, tax; fee.

derechura *f.* straightness.

deriva *f.* drift (*of a boat or plane*); **irse**
(*or* **andar**) **a la —** to drift, be drifting.

derivar *v.* to derive; to come (from).

derogar[7] *v.* to revoke, repeal, abolish.

derramamiento *m.* spill, spilling,
shedding; overflow; scattering; **— de
sangre** bloodshed.

derramar *v.* to spill; to spread, scatter;
to shed.

derrame *m.* spill, spilling, shedding;
overflow; discharge (*of secretion, blood,
etc.*); slope.

derredor *m.* circuit; contour; **al —**
around; **en —** around.

derrengado *p.p. & adj.* lame, crippled;
dislocated (*said of hip or spine*).

derrengar[1,7] *v. irr.* to dislocate or
sprain (*hip or spine*); to cripple; to
bend.

derretimiento *m.* thaw, thawing, melting.

derretir[5] *v. irr.* to melt, dissolve; **-se** to
be consumed; to melt.

derribar *v.* to demolish, knock down,
fell; to overthrow; **-se** to lie down,
throw oneself down.

derrocamiento *m.* overthrow.

derrocar[6] *v.* to fling down; to fell; to
overthrow.

derrochador *m.* squanderer, spendthrift; *adj.* wasteful, extravagant.

derrochar *v.* to waste; to squander.

derroche *m.* waste; dissipation, lavish
spending.

derrota *f.* rout, defeat; ship's route or
course.

derrotar *v.* to defeat; to squander; to
destroy, ruin; to lose or shift its
course (*said of a ship*).

derrotero *m.* course, direction; ship's
course; book of marine charts.

derrumbadero *m.* precipice.

derrumbamiento *m.* landslide; collapse.

derrumbar *v.* to fling down; *Am.* to
knock down; *Am.* to go down in a
hurry; **-se** to crumble away; to topple
over; *Col., Ven.* to dwindle (*as a
business*).

derrumbe *m.* landslide; collapse.

desabotonar *v.* to unbutton.

desabrido *adj.* tasteless, insipid; harsh;
sour.

desabrigar[7] *v.* to uncover; **-se** to uncover oneself.

desabrimiento *m.* tastelessness; harshness; sourness.

desabrochar *v.* to unfasten, unbutton,
unclasp; **-se** to unbutton oneself, unfasten one's clothes.

desacato m. irreverence, disrespect; profanation.

desacierto m. mistake, error.

desacostumbrado adj. unaccustomed; unusual; p.p. of **desacostumbrar**.

desacostumbrar v. to disaccustom, rid of a habit; **-se** to become unaccustomed; to lose a custom.

desacreditar v. to discredit; to disgrace.

desacuerdo m. disagreement; discord; blunder; forgetfulness.

desafiar[17] v. to challenge; to compete; to defy.

desafinado adj. out of tune.

desafinar v. to be discordant; to be out of tune; **-se** to get out of tune.

desafío m. challenge, defiance; duel; contest.

desafortunado adj. unfortunate, unlucky.

desafuero m. violation; outrage, abuse.

desagradable adj. disagreeable, unpleasant.

desagradar v. to displease.

desagradecido adj. ungrateful.

desagrado m. displeasure; discontent.

desagraviar v. to make amends; to compensate for a damage or injury; to right a wrong; to apologize; to vindicate.

desagravio m. reparation; compensation for a wrong or injury; vindication; apology.

desaguadero m. drain, drain pipe, water outlet.

desaguar[8] v. to drain, draw off; to flow (into); Ch. to wash (something) two or more times; Am. to extract the juice from; Col., Ven., Mex. to urinate; **-se** to drain.

desagüe m. drainage; drain.

desaguisado m. outrage, violence, wrong.

desahogado p.p. & adj. (aliviado) relieved; (espacioso) roomy, spacious; **estar —** to be in easy or comfortable circumstances; to be well-off.

desahogar[7] v. to relieve from pain or trouble; **-se** to find relief or release; to unbosom oneself, disclose one's feelings.

desahogo m. relief from pain or trouble; release; ease, comfort, relaxation; freedom, unrestraint.

desairar v. to slight, snub, disdain; to rebuff; to disappoint; to neglect.

desaire m. rebuff, snub, slight, disdain.

desalentar[1] v. irr. to put out of breath; to discourage; **-se** to get discouraged.

desaliento m. discouragement, dejection.

desaliñado adj. disheveled, slovenly, unkempt, untidy; disorderly.

desaliño m. slovenliness, untidiness; neglect, carelessness; disorder.

desalmado adj. soulless, cruel, inhuman.

desalojar v. to dislodge; to evict, expel from a lodging; to vacate.

desamarrar v. to untie, unfasten; to unmoor (a ship).

desamparar v. to abandon, forsake.

desamparo m. desertion, abandonment.

desamueblado adj. unfurnished.

desangrar v. to bleed, draw blood from; to drain; **-se** to bleed, lose blood.

desanimado adj. discouraged; lifeless; dull (said of a party, meeting, etc.).

desanimar v. to dishearten, discourage.

desaparecer[13] v. irr. to disappear; to hide; **-se** to disappear, vanish.

desaparición f. disappearance.

desapasionado adj. dispassionate; free from passion; calm; impartial.

desapego m. aloofness, indifference, detachment.

desapercibido adj. unprepared; unprovided; unnoticed.

desaprobación f. disapproval.

desaprobar[2] v. irr. to disapprove.

desarmar v. to disarm; to dismount, take apart.

desarme m. disarmament.

desarraigar[7] v. to root-out, uproot.

desarreglado p.p. & adj. disordered; disorderly; slovenly.

desarreglar v. to disarrange, disorder, disturb, upset.

desarreglo m. disorder, confusion.

desarrollar v. to unroll, unfold; to develop, explain; **-se** to develop; to unfold.

desarrollo m. development.

desaseado adj. unkempt, untidy.

desaseo m. slovenliness, untidiness.

desasir[22] v. irr. to loosen, unfasten; **-se** to get loose (from); to let go (of).

desasosiego m. unrest, uneasiness, restlessness.

desastrado adj. unfortunate, unhappy; ragged, dirty, untidy.

desastre m. disaster.

desastroso adj. disastrous, unfortunate.

desatar v. to untie, loosen; to dissolve; to unravel, clear up; **-se** to let loose, let go; to break loose; **-se en improperios** to let out a string of insults.

desatención f. inattention, lack of attention; discourtesy.

desatender[1] v. irr. to disregard, pay no attention (to); to slight, neglect.

desatento adj. inattentive; discourteous.

desatinado adj. senseless; reckless.

desatinar v. to act foolishly; to talk nonsense; to blunder; to rave; to lose one's bearings.

desatino m. blunder, error; folly, nonsense.

desatracar[6] v. to push off (from shore or from another ship); to cast off, unmoor.

desavenencia f. disagreement, discord; dispute, misunderstanding.

desayunarse v. to eat breakfast; **— con la noticia** to hear a piece of news for the first time.

desayuno m. breakfast.

desazón f. uneasiness, anxiety; insipidity, flatness, tastelessness; displeasure.

desbandarse v. to disband, scatter, disperse; to desert the army or a party.

desbaratar v. to destroy, ruin; to upset, disturb; to disperse, put to flight; to talk nonsense; **-se** to be upset, be in disorder; to fall to pieces.

desbocado adj. runaway (horse), dashing headlong; foul-mouthed, abusive; broken-mouthed (jar, pitcher, etc.).

desbordamiento m. overflow, flood.

desbordante adj. overflowing; Am. frantic.

desbordar v. to overflow, flood; **-se** to spill over; to get overexcited.

descabalar v. to break (a given amount, making it thereby incomplete).

descabello m. the act of killing the bull by piercing the brain with the sword.

descabezado p.p. beheaded; adj. headless; harebrained, thoughtless.

descabezar[9] v. to behead; to chop off the head or tip of; **— el sueño** to take a nap; **-se** to break one's head; to rack one's brains.

descaecido adj. feeble, weak; **— de ánimo** depressed, dejected, despondent.

descaecimiento m. languor, weakness; depression, dejection.

descalabradura f. blow or wound on the head; scar on the head.

descalabrar v. to wound on the head; to hurt, injure; to damage; **-se** to suffer a head wound or skull fracture.

descalabro m. loss, misfortune.

descalzar[9] v. to take off (someone's) shoes or (and) stockings; **-se** to take off one's shoes or (and) stockings; to lose a shoe (said of horses).

descalzo adj. barefoot; shoeless.

descaminar v. to mislead, lead astray; **-se** to go astray.

descamisado adj. shirtless; in rags; m. ragamuffin, ragged fellow.

descansar v. to rest.

descanso m. rest; staircase landing.

descarado adj. shameless, impudent, brazen.

descarga f. discharge; unloading.

descargar[7] v. to discharge; to unload.

descargo m. discharge (of a duty or obligation); unloading; relief.

descargue m. unloading; discharge.

descarnado adj. fleshless, scrawny.

descarnar v. to pull the flesh from the bone; to corrode, eat away; **-se** to become thin, emaciated.

descaro m. effrontery, shamelessness, impudence, audacity.

descarriar[17] v. to mislead, lead astray; to separate (cattle) from the herd; **-se** to stray; to go astray.

descarrilar v. to derail (cause a train to run off the track); to wreck (a train); **-se** to get or run off the track; to go astray.

descartar v. to discard; to put aside.

descascarado p.p. & adj. peeled off; chipped off.

descascarar v. to shell, hull, husk; to peel; to chip off (plaster); Am. to defame, discredit; Col. to flay; **-se** to chip off, peel off.

descendencia f. descent, lineage; descendants, offspring.

descendente adj. descending, downward.

descender[1] v. irr. to descend, go down; to get down; to come (from), originate.

descendiente m. & f. descendant; adj. descending.

descendimiento m. descent.

descenso m. descent; fall.

descifrar v. to decipher, puzzle out, figure out.

descolgar[2,7] v. irr. to unhang, take down; to let down; **-se** to climb down (a rope, tree, etc.); to drop in, appear unexpectedly.

descolorar v. to discolor; to fade; **-se** to fade, lose its color; to discolor.

descolorido adj. pale.

descollar[2] v. irr. to excel; to stand out, tower (above).

descomedido adj. rude, discourteous, impolite; unobliging.

descompletar v. to make incomplete, break (a unit, sum, set, etc.).

descomponer[40] v. irr. (estorbar) to upset, disturb; (echar a perder) to put out of order; to decompose; **-se** to decompose, rot; to become upset, ill; to get out of order; Col., Ven., C.A., Carib., Mex. **se me descompuso el brazo** I dislocated my arm, my arm got out of joint.

descomposición f. decomposition; decay, corruption; disorder, confusion.

descompuesto p.p. of **descomponer**; adj. out of order; insolent; brazen; immodest.

descomunal adj. colossal, enormous, monstrous.

desconcertante adj. disconcerting, disturbing, confusing, baffling, embarrassing.

desconcertar[1] v. irr. to disconcert, bewilder, confuse; to disturb; **-se** to be confused, perplexed.

desconcierto m. disorder; confusion; disagreement; feeling of discomfort.

desconchadura f. chip (chipped off place); chipping off, peeling off (of plaster, varnish, etc.).

desconchar v. to scrape off (plaster or stucco); **-se** to peel off, chip off (as plaster).

desconectar v. to disconnect.

desconfiado adj. distrustful, suspicious.

desconfianza f. mistrust, distrust.

desconfiar[17] v. to distrust; to lose confidence.

desconocer[13] v. irr. to fail to recognize or remember; to disown; to disregard, slight; not to know.

desconocido adj. unknown; unrecognizable; m. stranger.

desconocimiento *m.* disregard; ignorance.

desconsolado *p.p.* & *adj.* disconsolate, forlorn; disheartened, grieved.

desconsolador *adj.* disheartening, saddening.

desconsolar² *v. irr.* to sadden, grieve; to discourage; **-se** to become disheartened, grieved.

desconsuelo *m.* dejection, sadness, distress.

descontar² *v. irr.* to discount, deduct; to allow for.

descontentadizo *adj.* discontented, fretful, hard to please.

descontentar *v.* to displease.

descontento *adj.* discontent, displeased; *m.* discontent, displeasure.

descorazonado *adj.* disheartened, discouraged, depressed.

descorchar *v.* to uncork; to remove the bark from (*a cork tree*); to force or break open.

descortés *adj.* discourteous, rude, impolite.

descortesía *f.* discourtesy, rudeness, impoliteness.

descortezar⁹ *v.* to bark, strip the bark from (*trees*); to remove the crust or shell from; to peel; to civilize, remove the rough manners from.

descoser *v.* to rip, unsew, unstitch; **-se** to rip, come unstitched; to talk too much or indiscreetly.

descosido *m.* rip; *adj.* too talkative, indiscreet; disorderly; *p.p. of* **descoser**.

descostrar *v.* to flake; to scale off; to remove the crust from; **-se** to flake, scale off.

descoyuntado *p.p.* & *adj.* dislocated, out of joint.

descoyuntar *v.* to dislocate, put out of joint; **-se** to get out of joint.

descrédito *m.* discredit.

descreído *adj.* incredulous, unbelieving; *m.* unbeliever.

descreimiento *m.* unbelief, lack of faith.

describir⁵² *v.* to describe.

descripción *f.* description.

descriptivo *adj.* descriptive.

descrito *p.p. irr. of* **describir**.

descuartizar⁹ *v.* to quarter (*an animal*); to tear or cut into parts.

descubierto *p.p. of* **descubrir** & *adj.* (*sin cubierta*) uncovered; hatless, bareheaded; (*hallado*) discovered; *m.* deficit, shortage; **al —** openly, in the open; **en —** uncovered, unpaid.

descubridor *m.* discoverer.

descubrimiento *m.* discovery; find; invention.

descubrir⁵² *v.* to discover; to uncover; **-se** to uncover; to take off one's hat.

descuento *m.* discount; deduction.

descuidado *adj.* careless, negligent; untidy, slovenly; unaware; thoughtless.

descuidar *v.* to neglect; to overlook; to be careless or negligent; **-se** to be careless or negligent.

descuido *m.* carelessness; neglect; oversight; disregard; inattention; slip, error.

desde *prep.* from; since; **— luego** of course; **— que** *conj.* since, ever since.

desdecir²⁷ *v. irr.* to be out of harmony (with); to detract (from); **-se** to retract; to contradict oneself.

desdén *m.* disdain, scorn.

desdentado *adj.* toothless.

desdeñar *v.* to disdain, scorn.

desdeñoso *adj.* disdainful, scornful.

desdicha *f.* misfortune; misery; poverty.

desdichado *adj.* unfortunate; unhappy, wretched; miserable; *m.* wretch.

desdoblamiento *m.* unfolding.

desdoblar *v.* to unfold; to spread out.

desdorar *v.* to remove the gilt from; to tarnish; to dishonor.

desdoro *m.* tarnish, blemish; dishonor.

deseable *adj.* desirable.

desear *v.* to desire, want.

desecación *f.*, **desecamiento** *m.* drying; drainage.

desecar⁶ *v.* to dry; to dry up; to drain (*land*).

desechar *v.* to discard; to reject; to refuse, decline; *Col.* to cut across, take a short cut.

desecho *m.* remainder, residue; waste material; piece of junk; discard; **-s** refuse, scraps, junk; **hierro de —** scrap iron; **papel de —** wastepaper, scraps of paper.

desembalar *v.* to unpack.

desembarazar⁹ *v.* to rid, free, clear; *Ch.* to give birth; **-se** to get rid of.

desembarazo *m.* freedom, ease, naturalness; *Ch.* childbirth.

desembarcadero *m.* dock, wharf, pier.

desembarcar⁶ *v.* to disembark, land; to unload; to go ashore.

desembarco, desembarque *m.* landing; unloading.

desembocadura *f.* mouth (*of a river, canal, etc.*); outlet.

desembocar⁶ *v.* to flow (into); to lead (to).

desembolsar *v.* to disburse, pay out.

desembolso *m.* disbursement, outlay, expenditure.

desembragar⁷ *v.* to throw out the clutch; to disconnect.

desemejante *adj.* unlike.

desempacar⁶ *v.* to unpack.

desempeñar *v.* to recover, redeem, take out of pawn; **— un cargo** to perform the duties of a position; **— un papel** to play a part; **-se** to get out of debt.

desempeño *m.* fulfillment, carrying out, discharge; performance (*of a duty*); acting (*of a role*); redeeming (*of a thing pawned*).

desempleado *adj.* unemployed.

desempleo *m.* unemployment.

desempolvar *v.* to dust, remove the dust from.

desencadenar *v.* to unchain, free from chains; to loosen, set free; **-se**

DE

to free oneself; to break loose.

desencajado *p.p.* & *adj.* disjointed; disfigured; sunken (*eyes*); emaciated.

desencantar *v.* to disillusion, disappoint.

desencanto *m.* disillusion, disappointment.

desenfado *m.* ease, freedom; calmness.

desenfrenado *p.p.* & *adj.* unbridled; wanton, reckless; loose, immoral.

desenganchar *v.* to unhitch; to unhook; to unfasten.

desengañador *adj.* disappointing, disillusioning.

desengañar *v.* to undeceive, disillusion, disappoint.

desengaño *m.* disillusion, disappointment, blighted hope.

desengranar *v.* to throw out of gear.

desenmarañar *v.* to untangle; to unravel.

desenmascarar *v.* to unmask.

desenredar *v.* to disentangle, unravel.

desenrollar *v.* to unroll.

desensartar *v.* to unstring; to unthread; to unfasten from a ring.

desensillar *v.* to unsaddle.

desentenderse[1] *v.* *irr.* to neglect, ignore, pay no attention to; to pretend not to see, hear or understand.

desentendido *adj.* unmindful, heedless; *p.p.* of **desentenderse; hacerse el —** to pretend not to notice.

desenterrar[1] *v.* *irr.* to unearth, dig up.

desentonado *adj.* inharmonious, out of tune.

desentonar *v.* to be out of tune; to be out of harmony; to sing off key, play out of tune.

desenvoltura *f.* freedom, ease, abandon; boldness, impudence.

desenvolver[2,52] *v.* *irr.* to unroll, unfold; to unwrap; to develop.

desenvolvimiento *m.* development, unfolding.

desenvuelto *adj.* free, easy; forward, bold; shameless, brazen; *p.p.* of **desenvolver.**

deseo *m.* desire, wish.

deseoso *adj.* desirous, eager.

desequilibrado *adj.* unbalanced; *p.p.* of **desequilibrar.**

desequilibrar *v.* to unbalance; to derange.

desequilibrio *m.* lack of balance; derangement, mental disorder.

deserción *f.* desertion.

desertar *v.* to desert; to abandon; **-se de** to desert.

desertor *m.* deserter; quitter.

desesperación *f.* despair; desperation; fury.

desesperado *adj.* desperate; despairing; hopeless; *p.p.* of **desesperar.**

desesperanzado *p.p.* & *adj.* discouraged; hopeless; desperate, in despair.

desesperanzar[9] *v.* to discourage, deprive of hope; **-se** to be discouraged; to despair, lose one's hope.

desesperar *v.* to despair, lose hope; to

make (*someone*) despair; **-se** to despair, be desperate; to be furious.

desfachatez *f.* shamelessness, effrontery, impudence.

desfalcar[6] *v.* to embezzle; to remove a ~~part of.~~

desfalco *m.* embezzlement; diminution, decrease.

desfallecer[13] *v.* *irr.* to grow weak; to faint.

desfallecimiento *m.* faintness; weakness; languor; swoon, faint.

desfavorable *adj.* unfavorable.

desfigurar *v.* to disfigure; to deface; to distort.

desfiladero *m.* narrow passage, narrow gorge; road on the edge of a precipice.

desfilar *v.* to march, parade, pass by.

desfile *m.* parade.

desgana *f.* lack of appetite; reluctance.

desgarrado *p.p.* torn; *adj.* shameless; impudent.

desgarradura *f.* tear.

desgarrar *v.* to tear, rend; to expectorate, cough up; **-se** to tear; to separate oneself (from).

desgastar *v.* to waste, consume, wear away; **-se** to waste away, lose one's strength or vigor; to wear off.

desgaste *m.* waste; wear and tear.

desgracia *f.* misfortune, mishap; disgrace.

desgraciado *adj.* unfortunate, wretched.

desgranar *v.* to thrash, thresh (*grain*); to remove the grain from; to shell (*peas, beans, etc.*).

desgreñado *adj.* disheveled.

deshabitado *adj.* uninhabited, deserted; empty, vacant.

deshacer[31] *v.* *irr.* to undo; to dissolve; to destroy; to untie; **-se** to dissolve; to melt; to waste away; **-se de** to get rid of.

desharrapado, desarrapado *adj.* ragged, shabby, tattered.

deshecha *f.* simulation, pretense; **hacer la —** to feign, pretend.

deshecho *p.p.* of **deshacer** & *adj.* undone; ruined, destroyed, in pieces; violent (*said of rainstorms*); worn-out, fatigued; *Am.* disorderly, untidy.

deshelar[1] *v.* *irr.* to melt; to thaw; **-se** to melt; to thaw.

desherbar[1] *v.* *irr.* to weed.

deshielo *m.* thaw.

deshierbe *m.* weeding.

deshilachar *v.* to ravel, fray.

deshilar *v.* to unravel; **-se** to unravel; to fray.

deshojar *v.* to strip off the leaves, petals, or pages; **-se** to lose its leaves (*said of a plant or book*); to lose petals.

deshollejar *v.* to husk, hull; to peel, pare, skin; to shell (*beans*).

deshonesto *adj.* immodest; unchaste, lewd.

deshonra *f.* dishonor; disgrace.

deshonrar v. to dishonor, disgrace; to insult, offend; to seduce.

deshonroso adj. dishonorable; shameful.

deshora f. inopportune time; **a —** (or **a -s**) unexpectedly; **comer a —** to piece, eat between meals.

deshuesar v. to stone, remove the pits or stones from (fruits); to bone, remove the bones from (an animal).

desidia f. indolence, laziness.

desidioso adj. indolent, negligent, lazy; listless.

desierto adj. deserted, uninhabited; alone, lonely; m. desert, wilderness.

designación f. designation; appointment.

designar v. to designate, appoint, select; to design, plan, intend.

designio m. design, plan, purpose.

desigual adj. unequal; uneven; variable, changeable.

desigualdad f. inequality; unevenness; roughness (of the ground).

desilusión f. disillusion, disappointment.

desilusionar v. to disillusion, disappoint; **-se** to become disillusioned; to lose one's illusions.

desinencia f. termination, ending (of a word).

desinfectante adj. disinfecting; m. disinfectant.

desinfectar v. to disinfect.

desinflado adj. deflated, not inflated, flat.

desinterés m. disinterestedness, unselfishness, impartiality.

desinteresado adj. disinterested, unselfish, fair, impartial.

desistir v. to desist, stop, cease.

deslavado p.p. & adj. half-washed; weakened; faded; pale; saucy.

deslavar v. to wash away; to fade; to wash superficially.

desleal adj. disloyal, faithless.

desleír[15] v. irr. to dissolve; to dilute, make thin or weak; **-se** to become diluted.

deslindar v. to mark off, mark the boundaries of.

desliz m. slip, slide; error.

deslizador m. glider.

deslizamiento m. slip, slipping; glide; sliding, skidding.

deslizar[9] v. to slip, slide; **-se** to slip; to skid; to glide; to slip out.

deslucido p.p. & adj. tarnished; dull; discredited; dingy, shabby; awkward, ungraceful; inelegant.

deslucir[13] v. irr. to tarnish, dull the luster of; to discredit.

deslumbrador adj. dazzling, glaring.

deslumbramiento m. dazzle, glare, daze, confusion.

deslumbrar v. to dazzle.

deslustrado adj. & p.p. tarnished; dim, dull; opaque.

deslustrar v. to tarnish; to soil, stain (one's honor or reputation).

deslustre m. tarnish; disgrace.

desmadejado p.p. & adj. enervated, exhausted; depressed.

desmadejar v. to enervate, weaken.

desmán m. misconduct, abuse, insult; calamity, disaster.

desmantelar v. to dismantle, strip of furniture, equipment, etc.

desmañado adj. unskillful, awkward, clumsy.

desmayar v. to dismay; to lose strength, courage; **-se** to faint.

desmayo m. faint, swoon; dismay, discouragement.

desmazalado adj. dejected, depressed.

desmejorar v. to impair; to make worse; **-se** to grow worse; to waste away, lose one's health.

desmentir[3] v. irr. to contradict; to give the lie; **-se** to contradict oneself; to retract, take back one's word.

desmenuzar[9] v. to crumble, break into bits; to mince; to shred; **-se** to crumble, fall to pieces.

desmerecer[13] v. irr. to become unworthy of; to deteriorate, lose merit or value; to be inferior to.

desmigajar v. to crumb (bread); to crumble; **-se** to crumble.

desmochar v. to cut off, chop off (the top or tip).

desmolado adj. toothless, without molars.

desmontar v. to dismount; to cut down (a forest); to clear or level off (ground); to dismantle, take apart; to tear down; **-se** to dismount, alight, get off.

desmoronar v. to crumble; **-se** to crumble down, fall gradually to pieces.

desnatar v. to skim, take the cream from (milk).

desnaturalizado adj. unnatural, cruel; **alcohol —** denatured alcohol (made unfit for drinking); **madre desnaturalizada** unnatural mother (one without motherly instincts).

desnudar v. to undress, uncover; **-se** to undress.

desnudez f. nudity, nakedness.

desnudo adj. nude, naked, bare.

desobedecer[13] v. irr. to disobey.

desobediencia f. disobedience; **desobediente** adj. disobedient.

desocupación f. unemployment; idleness; vacationing.

desocupado adj. unoccupied; unemployed, idle; empty, vacant.

desocupar v. to empty, vacate; **-se de un negocio** to get rid of, or not pay attention to, a business.

desoír[36] v. irr. to turn a deaf ear to, not to heed; to refuse (a petition).

desolación f. desolation; ruin; loneliness; anguish, affliction, grief.

desolado adj. desolate; p.p. of **desolar**.

desolar[2] v. irr. to lay waste, ruin; **-se** to be in anguish; to grieve.

desollar[2] v. irr. to skin, flay; to fleece, extort money from.

desorbitado adj. out of its orbit; out of

place or proportion; decentered; *Ch.*, *Andes* popeyed, with bulging eyes; *Am.* crazy, eccentric.

desorden *m.* disorder, confusion.

desordenado *adj.* disorderly; lawless; unsettled; *p.p. of* **desordenar.**

desordenar *v.* to disturb, confuse, upset.

desorientar *v.* to throw off one's bearings; to lead astray; to misdirect, mislead; to confuse; **-se** to lose one's bearings; to go astray, get lost.

despabilado *adj.* wakeful; wide-awake; bright, lively.

despabilar *v.* to snuff, trim the wick of (*a candle*); to enliven, awaken (*the mind*), sharpen (*the wits*); **-se** to wake up, rouse oneself, shake off drowsiness.

despacio *adv.* slowly.

despacioso *adj.* slow.

despachar *v.* to dispatch; to send; to facilitate; to ship.

despacho *m.* (*oficina*) office, bureau; salesroom; (*comunicación*) dispatch; (*envío*) sending; shipment; (*sin demora*) promptness; *Ch.* country store, farm store.

despachurrar *v.* to crush, squash.

desparejo *adj.* unequal, uneven.

desparpajar *v.* to upset, disarrange; to rant, talk too much; *Mex.* to disperse, scatter.

desparpajo *m.* ease, freedom of manner; freshness, pertness; *Col.* dispersion, scattering; *Am.* disorder, jumble.

desparramar *v.* to scatter, spread; to spill; to squander; **-se** to "spread" oneself, spend lavishly; to scatter; to spill.

desparramo *m. Ch., C.A.* scattering, spreading, spilling; *Ríopl., Carib.* disorder, commotion.

despatarrarse *v.* to sprawl; to fall sprawling to the ground.

despecho *m.* spite; grudge; despair; weaning; **a — de** in spite of.

despedazar⁹ *v.* to break, cut, tear into pieces.

despedida *f.* farewell; departure; dismissal.

despedir⁵ *v. irr.* (*cesar*) to discharge, dismiss; (*emitir*) emit, throw off, give off; to see (*a person*) off (*at a station, airport, etc.*); **-se** to take leave, say good-bye.

despegar⁷ *v.* to detach; to unfasten; to take off (*said of a plane*); *Am.* to unhitch; **no — los labios** not to say a word, not to open one's mouth; **-se** to grow apart; to come loose or become detached.

despego = **desapego.**

despegue *m.* takeoff (*of an airplane*).

despejado *adj.* clear, cloudless; smart, bright; *p.p.* of **despejar.**

despejar *v.* to clear; to remove obstacles from; **-se** to clear up (*as the sky*); to clear one's mind.

despellejar *v.* to skin, flay.

despensa *f.* pantry; storeroom (*for food*); food provisions.

despensero *m.* butler; steward.

despeñadero *m.* steep cliff, precipice.

despeñar *v.* to fling down a precipice; **-se** to fall down a precipice; to throw oneself down a cliff.

despepitar *v.* to seed, remove the seeds from; **-se** to talk or shout vehemently; to rave, talk wildly; **-se por una cosa** to long for something; to be crazy about something.

desperdiciado *adj.* wasteful; *p.p.* of **desperdiciar.**

desperdiciar *v.* to squander; to waste.

desperdicio *m.* waste; extravagance; **-s** leftovers, garbage; residue.

desperdigar⁷ *v.* to disperse; to scatter; to strew.

desperezarse⁹ *v.* to stretch oneself.

desperfecto *m.* damage; flaw, defect.

despertador *m.* alarm clock.

despertar¹ *v. irr.* to awaken; to wake up; **-se** to wake up.

despiadado *adj.* pitiless, heartless, cruel.

despierto *adj.* awake; wide-awake.

despilfarrado *adj.* wasteful, extravagant; ragged; *p.p.* of **despilfarrar.**

despilfarrar *v.* to squander; to waste.

despilfarro *m.* extravagance, squandering; waste.

despistar *v.* to throw off the track.

desplante *m.* arrogance; impudent remark or act.

desplazar⁹ *v.* to displace.

desplegar¹,⁷ *v. irr.* to unfold; to unfurl; to show, manifest.

desplomar *v.* to cause (*a wall*) to lean; **-se** to slump; to topple over, tumble down, collapse.

desplome *m.* collapse; toppling over; landslide.

desplumar *v.* to pick, pluck (*a fowl*); to fleece, skin, rob, strip; **-se** to molt, shed the feathers.

despoblado *adj.* uninhabited, desolate; **— de árboles** treeless; *m.* open country; uninhabited place; wilderness.

despojar *v.* to despoil, rob; to strip (of), deprive (of); **-se** to undress; to deprive oneself.

despojo *m.* plundering, robbery; spoil, booty; leftover, scrap; **-s** remains.

desportilladura *f.* chip; nick.

desportillar *v.* to chip; to nick.

desposar *v.* to marry; **-se** to become formally engaged; to get married.

déspota *m. & f.* despot, tyrant.

despótico *adj.* despotic, tyrannical.

despotismo *m.* despotism, tyranny.

despreciable *adj.* contemptible; worthless; insignificant, negligible.

despreciar *v.* to despise, scorn.

desprecio *m.* scorn, contempt.

desprender *v.* to unfasten, loosen; to detach; **-se** to get loose, come unfastened; to climb down; to get rid (of); to be inferred, be deduced.

desprendimiento *m.* detachment; generosity; unfastening; landslide.

despreocupado *p.p.* & *adj.* unbiased; liberal, broadminded; unconventional, carefree; *Am.* careless, slovenly; *Am.* indifferent to criticism.

desprestigiar *v.* to discredit, harm the reputation of; **-se** to lose one's prestige.

desprestigio *m.* discredit, loss of prestige.

desprevenido *adj.* unprepared; unaware.

despropósito *m.* absurdity, nonsense.

desprovisto *adj.* destitute; lacking; devoid.

después *adv.* after, afterward; then, later; **— de** *prep.* after; **— (de) que** *conj.* after.

despuntado *adj.* blunt, dull; *p.p.* of **despuntar.**

despuntar *v.* (*quitar la punta*) to blunt; to cut off (*a point*); nip; (*brotar*) to bud or sprout; (*sobresalir*) to excel; to be clever, witty; **— el alba** to begin to dawn.

desquitar *v.* to retrieve, restore (*a loss*); **-se** to get even, take revenge; to win back one's money; to make up (for).

desquite *m.* retaliation, revenge; getting even; recovery of a loss; return game or match.

desrazonable *adj.* unreasonable.

destacado *adj.* outstanding; *p.p.* of **destacar.**

destacamento *m.* military detachment.

destacar⁶ *v.* to detach (*troops*); to make stand out; to stand out; **hacer —** to emphasize; to make stand out; **-se** to stand out.

destapar *v.* to uncover; to uncork; *Am.* to start running; **-se** to uncover, get uncovered; to get uncorked; *Am.* to burst out talking.

destartalado *adj.* in disorder; in rack and ruin; dismantled, stripped of furniture.

destechado *adj.* roofless.

destellar *v.* to flash; to sparkle, twinkle; to gleam.

destello *m.* flash, sparkle, gleam.

destemplado *adj.* out of tune, out of harmony; immoderate; **sentirse —** not to feel well; to feel feverish.

desteñir⁵,¹⁹ *v. irr.* to discolor; to fade; to bleach; **-se** to become discolored; to fade.

desternillarse *v.* **— de risa** to split one's sides with laughter.

desterrado *m.* exile; outcast; *p.p.* & *adj.* exiled, banished.

desterrar¹ *v. irr.* to exile, banish; to remove earth (from).

destetar *v.* to wean.

destierro *m.* exile.

destilación *f.* distillation.

destiladera *f.* still; *Am.* filter.

destilar *v.* to distill; to drip, trickle; to filter.

destilería *f.* distillery.

destinación *f.* destination.

destinar *v.* to destine; to employ.

destinatario *m.* addressee.

destino *m.* destiny, fate; destination; employment, job.

destituido *adj.* destitute; *p.p.* of **destituir.**

destituir³² *v. irr.* to deprive.

destornillador *m.* screwdriver.

destornillar *v.* to unscrew.

destrabar *v.* to unlock, unfasten; to untie; to separate; to unfetter.

destreza *f.* dexterity, skill, ability.

destronar *v.* to dethrone, depose, overthrow.

destrozar⁹ *v.* to shatter, cut to pieces; to destroy; to squander.

destrozo *m.* destruction; ruin.

destrucción *f.* destruction.

destructivo *adj.* destructive.

destructor *adj.* destructive; *m.* destroyer.

destruir³² *v. irr.* to destroy; to ruin.

desunir *v.* to divide, separate.

desusado *adj.* unusual, unaccustomed; obsolete, out of use.

desuso *m.* disuse; obsoleteness.

desvaído *adj.* lanky, tall and awkward; gaunt; dull, faded.

desvainar *v.* to shell (*peas, beans, etc.*).

desvalido *adj.* abandoned; destitute; helpless.

desvalijar *v.* to ransack the contents of a valise; to rob.

desván *m.* garret, attic.

desvanecer¹³ *v. irr.* to fade, dissolve; to make vain; to make dizzy; **-se** to evaporate; to vanish; to fade out, disappear; to get dizzy.

desvanecido *adj.* (*desmayado*) dizzy, faint; (*orgulloso*) proud, haughty; *p.p.* of **desvanecer.**

desvanecimiento *m.* dizziness, faintness; vanity.

desvariar¹⁷ *v.* to rave, be delirious; to rant, talk excitedly; to talk nonsense.

desvarío *m.* raving; delirium; madness; inconstancy.

desvelado *adj.* sleepless, awake; watchful; *p.p.* of **desvelar.**

desvelar *v.* to keep (*another*) awake; **-se** to keep awake; to have insomnia, lose sleep; to be worried, anxious.

desvelo *m.* lack of sleep; restlessness; vigilance, watchfulness; worry, anxiety.

desvencijado *adj.* tottering, rickety, shaky, falling apart.

desventaja *f.* disadvantage.

desventura *f.* misfortune, unhappiness.

desventurado *adj.* unfortunate, unhappy, miserable, wretched.

desvergonzado *adj.* shameless, brazen.

desvergüenza *f.* shamelessness; disgrace; shame; insolence; impudent word.

desvestir⁵ *v. irr.* to undress; **-se** to undress.

desviación *f.* deviation, turning aside, shift; detour.

desviar¹⁷ *v.* to deviate, turn aside; to swerve; **-se** to shift direction; to branch off, turn off the main road; to swerve.

desvío *m.* deviation, turning aside; indifference, coldness; side track, railroad siding; detour.

desvirtuar[18] *v.* to impair, diminish the value or quality of.

desvivirse *v.* **— por** to long for; to be excessively fond of, be crazy about, make a fuss over; to do one's best for; **ella se desvive por complacerme** she does her utmost to please me.

desyerbar = desherbar.

detallar *v.* to detail, report in detail; to retail.

detalle *m.* detail; retail; **¡ahí está el —!** that's the point.

detallista *m. & f.* retailer; detailer, person fond of detail.

detective, detectivo *m.* detective.

detención *f.* detention, arrest; stop, halt; delay.

detener[45] *v. irr.* to detain, stop; to arrest; **-se** to halt; to delay oneself, stay.

detenimiento *m.* detention; delay; care, deliberation.

deteriorar *v.* to deteriorate, damage; **-se** to deteriorate, become impaired or damaged; to wear out.

deterioro *m.* deterioration, impairment.

determinación *f.* determination; firmness.

determinar *v.* to determine; to decide; **-se** to resolve, decide.

detestable *adj.* detestable; hateful.

detestar *v.* to detest.

detonación *f.* detonation, report (*of a gun*), loud explosion; pop.

detonar *v.* to detonate, explode with a loud noise; to pop.

detrás *adv.* behind; **— de** *prep.* behind; **por —** from the rear, by the rear, from behind.

deuda *f.* debt; indebtedness.

deudo *m.* relative, kinsman.

deudor *m.* debtor; *adj.* indebted, obligated.

devanar *v.* to spool, wind on a spool; **-se los sesos** to rack one's brain.

devaneo *m.* frenzy; dissipation; wandering; idle pursuit; giddiness.

devastar *v.* to devastate, lay waste, destroy.

devenir[48] *v. irr.* to befall; to become, be transformed into.

devoción *f.* devotion; piety; attachment.

devocionario *m.* prayer book.

devolución *f.* return, giving back; replacement.

devolver[2, 52] *v. irr.* to return, give back, pay back.

devorador *adj.* devouring; absorbing; ravenous; *m.* devourer.

devorar *v.* to devour, gobble up.

devoto *adj.* devout, religious, pious; very fond (of).

devuelto *p.p. of* **devolver.**

día *m.* day; **al otro —** on the next day; **hoy —** nowadays; **un — sí y otro no** every other day.

diablo *m.* devil, demon.

diablura *f.* deviltry, mischief, devilish prank.

diabólico *adj.* diabolic, devilish, fiendish.

diácono *m.* deacon.

diadema *f.* diadem, crown.

diáfano *adj.* transparent, clear; sheer.

diagnosticar[6] *v.* to diagnose.

diagrama *m.* diagram; graph.

dialecto *m.* dialect.

dialogar[7] *v.* to dialogue.

diálogo *m.* dialogue.

diamante *m.* diamond.

diámetro *m.* diameter.

diantre *m.* devil.

diapasón *m.* pitch (*of a sound*); tuning fork.

diapositiva *f. Spain* slide, lantern slide.

diario *adj.* daily; *m.* newspaper; daily expense; journal, diary.

diarrea *f.* diarrhea.

dibujante *m. & f.* draftsman; designer.

dibujar *v.* (*diseñar*) to draw, make a drawing of; (*describir*) depict, portray; describe; **-se** to appear, show.

dibujo *m.* drawing; delineation, portrayal, picture; **— natural** drawing of the human figure, drawing from life.

dicción *f.* diction; word; choice of words, style.

diciembre *m.* December.

dictado *m.* dictation; title; dictate; **escribir al —** to take dictation.

dictador *m.* dictator.

dictadura *f.* dictatorship.

dictamen *m.* opinion, judgment.

dictaminar *v.* to give an opinion or judgment.

dictar *v.* to dictate.

dicha *f.* happiness; good luck.

dicharachero *adj.* fond of making wisecracks; witty.

dicharacho *m.* wisecrack, smart remark; malicious remark.

dicho *p.p. of* **decir** said; **— y hecho** no sooner said than done; *m.* saying, popular proverb.

dichoso *adj.* happy, lucky.

diente *m.* tooth; tusk; **— de león** dandelion; **de -s afuera** insincerely; *Am.* **pelar el —** to smile affectedly.

diéresis *f.* diaeresis (*as in* **vergüenza**).

diesel *m.* diesel; diesel motor.

diestra *f.* right hand.

diestro *adj.* skillful; right; *m.* matador; skillful swordsman; halter.

dieta *f.* diet; assembly; salary, fee.

diezmo *m.* tithe.

difamación *f.* libel, slander.

difamador *m.* slanderer.

difamar *v.* to defame, libel, malign, slander.

difamatorio *adj.* scandalous, slandering.

diferencia *f.* difference.

diferenciar *v.* to differentiate, distinguish; to differ, disagree; **-se** to distinguish oneself; to become different.

diferente *adj.* different.

diferir[3] v. irr. to defer, put off, delay; to differ, disagree; to be different.

difícil adj. difficult.

dificultad f. difficulty.

dificultar v. to make difficult; **— el paso** to impede or obstruct the passage; **-se** to become difficult.

dificultoso adj. difficult, hard.

difteria f. diphtheria.

difundir v. to diffuse, spread out, scatter; to broadcast by radio.

difunto adj. deceased, dead; m. corpse.

difusión f. diffusion, spreading, scattering; wordiness; broadcasting.

difuso adj. diffuse; diffused, widespread.

digerible adj. digestible.

digerir[3] v. irr. to digest.

dignarse v. to deign, condescend.

dignatario m. dignitary (person in a high office).

dignidad f. dignity.

digno adj. worthy; dignified.

digresión f. digression.

dije m. trinket, small piece of jewelry; locket; woman of fine qualities, a "jewel"; Am. locket or charm.

dilación f. delay.

dilatado adj. vast, spacious; extensive; p.p. of **dilatar**.

dilatar v. to dilate, widen, enlarge; to expand; to lengthen, extend; to spread out; to defer, put off, retard; **-se** to expand; to be diffuse, wordy; Am. to delay oneself, take long.

diligencia f. diligence, care, industry; speed; stagecoach; business, errand.

diligente adj. diligent; quick, speedy.

diluir[32] v. irr. to dilute.

diluvio m. flood.

dimensión f. dimension.

dimes: — y diretes quibbling, arguing; **andar en — y diretes** to quibble, argue.

diminución f. diminution, decrease.

diminutivo adj. diminutive, tiny; diminishing; m. diminutive.

diminuto adj. tiny, little.

dimisión f. resignation (from an office).

dimitir v. to resign, give up (a position, office, etc.).

dinámica f. dynamics; **dinámico** adj. dynamic.

dinamismo m. vigor, forcefulness; dynamic force or energy.

dinamita f. dynamite.

dínamo m. dynamo.

dinastía f. dynasty.

dineral m. a lot of money.

dinero m. money; currency; Peru Peruvian silver coin equivalent to about ten cents; **— contante y sonante** ready cash, hard cash.

dios m. god; **Dios** God; **a la buena de —** without malice; without plan, haphazard, at random.

diosa f. goddess.

diplomacia f. diplomacy; tact.

diplomático adj. diplomatic; tactful; m. diplomat.

diputación f. deputation; committee.

diputado m. deputy; representative.

diputar v. to depute, delegate, commission.

dique m. dike; barrier; **— de carena** dry dock.

dirección f. direction, course; advice, guidance; management; board of directors; office of the board of directors; address.

directivo adj. directive, directing, guiding; **mesa directiva** board of directors.

directo adj. direct, straight.

director m. director, manager; adj. directing.

directorio adj. directory, directive, directing; m. directory, book of instructions; directorate, board of directors.

dirigente adj. directing, leading; m. leader, director.

dirigir[11] v. to direct, manage, govern; to guide; to address (letters, packages); to dedicate; **-se a** to address (a person); to go to or toward.

discernimiento m. discernment, keen judgment, insight, discrimination.

discernir[3] v. irr. to discern; to distinguish; to discriminate.

disciplina f. discipline, training; rule of conduct; order; any art or science; scourge, whip.

disciplinar v. to discipline, train; to drill; **-se** to discipline oneself; to scourge oneself.

discípulo m. pupil; disciple.

disco m. disk; discus; phonograph record.

díscolo adj. unruly, disobedient; unfriendly.

discordancia f. discord, disagreement.

discordia f. discord.

discreción f. discretion; keenness; wit; **darse (or rendirse) a —** to surrender unconditionally; **discrecional** adj. optional.

discrepancia f. discrepancy.

discreto adj. discreet, prudent; clever.

disculpa f. excuse; apology.

disculpable adj. excusable.

disculpar v. to excuse, free from blame; **-se** to excuse oneself, apologize.

discurrir v. (charlar) to discuss; (recorrer) to ramble about; (imaginar) to invent, think out.

discursear v. to make speeches.

discurso m. discourse; speech; reasoning; lapse of time.

discusión f. discussion.

discutible adj. debatable, questionable.

discutir v. to discuss.

disecar[6] v. to dissect; to stuff and mount (the skins of animals).

diseminación f. dissemination, spread, scattering.

diseminar v. to disseminate, scatter, spread.

disensión f. dissension, dissent, disagreement.

disentería f. dysentery.

disentir[3] *v. irr.* to dissent, differ, disagree.

diseñador *m.* designer.

diseñar *v.* to design; to sketch, outline.

diseño *m.* design; sketch, outline.

disertar *v.* to discourse, discuss.

disforme *adj.* deformed; ugly, hideous; out of proportion.

disfraz *m.* disguise, mask; masquerade costume.

disfrazar[9] *v.* to disguise, conceal; **-se** to disguise oneself; to masquerade.

disfrutar *v.* to enjoy; to reap benefit or advantage; to make use of.

disfrute *m.* enjoyment, benefit, use.

disgustar *v.* to disgust, displease; **-se** to get angry; to get bored.

disgusto *m.* displeasure; unpleasantness; annoyance; quarrel; grief; disgust.

disidente *m. & f.* dissident; protester.

disimulado *adj.* underhanded, sly, cunning; *p.p. of* **disimular.**

disimular *v.* to feign, hide, mask; to overlook, excuse.

disimulo *m.* dissimulation, feigning, pretense; slyness; reserve.

disipación *f.* dissipation; waste, extravagance.

disipar *v.* to dissipate, scatter; to squander; **-se** to vanish.

dislocar[6] *v.* to dislocate, put out of joint; **-se** to become dislocated, get out of joint.

disminución = **diminución.**

disminuir[32] *v. irr.* to diminish, decrease, lessen.

disociación *f.* dissociation, separation.

disociar *v.* to dissociate, separate.

disolución *f.* dissolution, breaking up; dissoluteness, lewdness.

disoluto *adj.* dissolute, loose, immoral, dissipated.

disolver[2,52] *v. irr.* to dissolve; to melt.

disonancia *f.* discord.

disparada *f. C.A., Mex., Carib., Riopl.* rush, run.

disparar *v.* to shoot, fire, discharge; to throw; **-se** to run away, dart out.

disparatado *adj.* absurd, foolish, senseless.

disparatar *v.* to talk nonsense; to blunder; to act foolishly.

disparate *m.* nonsense, blunder.

disparidad *f.* inequality.

disparo *m.* shooting, discharge, explosion; shot; sudden dash, run.

dispensa *f.* dispensation; exemption.

dispensar *v.* to excuse, absolve, pardon; to grant, give.

dispensario *m.* dispensary; pharmaceutical laboratory; pharmacopoeia (*book containing list and description of drugs*).

dispersar *v.* to disperse, scatter.

dispersión *f.* dispersion, dispersal.

displicencia *f.* displeasure, discontent, dislike.

displicente *adj.* unpleasant, disagreeable, cross.

disponer[40] *v. irr.* (*arreglar*) to dispose;

to arrange, put in order; to prepare; (*mandar*) to order, command; **-se** to get ready; to make one's will and testament.

disponible *adj.* spare, available; on hand.

disposición *f.* disposition; arrangement; order, command; aptitude; disposal.

dispuesto *p.p. of* **disponer** & *adj.* disposed; ready; fit; smart, clever.

disputa *f.* dispute.

disputar *v.* to dispute.

distancia *f.* distance.

distante *adj.* distant.

distar *v.* to be distant, far (from).

distender[1] *v. irr.* to distend, stretch; to inflate; **-se** to distend, expand.

distinción *f.* distinction.

distinguido *adj. & p.p.* distinguished.

distinguir[12] *v.* to distinguish; **-se** to distinguish oneself, excel; to differ, be different.

distintivo *adj.* distinctive, distinguishing; *m.* distinguishing characteristic; mark, sign; badge.

distinto *adj.* distinct, plain, clear; different.

distracción *f.* distraction; diversion, amusement; lack of attention.

distraer[46] *v. irr.* to distract; to divert, amuse; to lead astray; to divert (*funds*); **-se** to have a good time; to be absentminded; to be inattentive.

distraído *adj.* distracted; inattentive; absentminded; *Am.* slovenly, untidy.

distribución *f.* distribution, apportionment.

distribuidor *m.* distributor; *adj.* distributing.

distribuir[32] *v. irr.* to distribute; to sort, classify.

distrito *m.* district; region.

disturbio *m.* disturbance.

disuelto *p.p. of* **disolver.**

divagación *f.* rambling, digression.

divagar[7] *v.* to ramble; to digress.

diván *m.* divan, sofa.

divergencia *f.* divergence; difference (*of opinion*).

divergir[11] *v.* to diverge; to differ.

diversidad *f.* diversity; variety.

diversión *f.* amusement.

diverso *adj.* diverse; different; **-s** several, various.

divertido *adj.* amusing, funny.

divertir[3] *v. irr.* to amuse, entertain; to divert, turn aside; **-se** to have a good time, amuse oneself.

dividendo *m.* dividend.

dividir *v.* to divide, split.

divinidad *f.* divinity, deity; ¡qué —! what a beauty!

divino *adj.* divine.

divisa *f.* device, emblem.

divisar *v.* to sight; to make out, distinguish.

división *f.* division.

divorciar *v.* to divorce; to separate.

divorcio *m.* divorce.

DI

divulgar[7] *v.* to divulge, spread, make public, give out.

diz = **dice; dizque** they say that . . .

dobladillar *v.* to hem.

dobladillo *m.* hem; **— de ojo** hemstitch.

doblar *v.* to bend, fold; to double; to toll, knell; *Riopl.* to knock down; **— la esquina** to turn the corner; **-se** to stoop; to bend down; to give in.

doble *adj.* double, twofold; double-faced, hypocritical; *Am.* broke, poor; *m.* fold; toll, tolling of bells, knell.

doblegar[7] *v.* to bend; to fold; **-se** to bend over; to stoop; to submit, yield.

doblez *m.* fold, crease; duplicity, hypocrisy.

docena *f.* dozen.

docente *adj.* teaching; educational; **cuerpo —** faculty (*of a school*).

dócil *adj.* docile, obedient, manageable, meek; flexible; **docilidad** *f.* obedience, meekness, gentleness; flexibility.

docto *adj.* learned; expert.

doctor *m.* doctor.

doctorar *v.* to grant a doctor's degree to; **-se** to get a doctor's degree.

doctrina *f.* doctrine.

documentar *v.* to document.

documento *m.* document.

dogal *m.* halter; noose.

dogma *m.* dogma; **dogmático** *adj.* dogmatic, pertaining to dogma; positive.

dolencia *f.* ailment; ache, aching.

doler[2] *v. irr.* to ache, hurt, cause pain; to cause grief; **-se de** to feel pity for, feel sorry for; to repent from.

doliente *adj.* sorrowful; suffering; aching; *m.* sick person, patient; mourner.

dolor *m.* pain, ache; sorrow, grief.

dolorido *adj.* aching, sore; afflicted; repentant; doleful.

doloroso *adj.* painful; sorrowful.

doma *f.* breaking of horses.

domador *m.* horsebreaker, bronco-buster.

domar *v.* to tame, subdue.

domeñar *v.* to tame; to subdue; to dominate.

domesticar[6] *v.* to domesticate, tame.

doméstico *adj.* domestic; *m.* house servant.

domiciliar *v.* to house, lodge; *Riopl.* to address (*a letter*); **-se** to take up residence; to settle down; to dwell, reside.

domicilio *m.* home, dwelling.

dominación *f.* domination, rule, authority.

dominador *adj.* dominant, dominating; domineering, bossy; *m.* ruler, boss.

dominante *adj.* dominant; domineering; tyrannical; prevailing, predominant.

dominar *v.* to dominate, rule, lead; to stand out, tower above; to master.

dómine *m.* teacher; pedagogue; pedant.

domingo *m.* Sunday; **— de ramos** Palm Sunday.

dominio *m.* domain; dominion; authority; mastery (*of a science, art, language, etc.*).

dominó *m.* domino.

don *m.* gift; ability, knack; Don (*title used only before Christian names of men*).

donación *f.* donation; grant.

donador *m.* donor, giver.

donaire *m.* grace, elegance; wit; humor; witty remark.

donairoso *adj.* elegant, graceful; witty.

donar *v.* to donate.

doncella *f.* virgin, maiden; maidservant; *Col.* felon (*sore or inflammation near a finger or toenail*).

donde *rel. adv.* where, in which; **a —** (**adonde**) where, to which; *C.A.*, *Riopl.* to the house of; **de —** from where, from which; **en —** where, in which; **por —** where, through which; wherefore; **— no** otherwise; if not; **¿dónde?** *interr. adv.* where?; **¿por —?** which way?

dondequiera *adv.* wherever; anywhere.

donjuanismo *m.* Don Juanism, conduct reminiscent of Don Juan Tenorio.

donoso *adj.* witty, gay; graceful.

doña *f.* Doña (*title used only before Christian names of women*).

dorado *p.p.* & *adj.* gilded, gilt; golden; *m.* gilding; *Am.* a kind of hummingbird; **doradillo** *adj. Am.* honey-colored, golden (*applied to horses*).

dorar *v.* to gild.

dormir[4] *v. irr.* to sleep; **-se** to go to sleep, fall asleep; to become numb.

dormitar *v.* to doze.

dormitorio *m.* dormitory; bedroom.

dorso *m.* back, reverse.

dosel *m.* canopy.

dosis *f.* dose.

dotación *f.* endowment, endowing; donation, foundation; dowry; complement (*personnel of a warship*); office force.

dotar *v.* to endow; to provide with a dowry.

dote *m.* & *f.* dowry; *f.* natural gift, talent, or quality.

draga *f.* dredge, dredging machine.

dragado *m.* dredging.

dragaminas *m.* mine sweeper.

dragar[7] *v.* to dredge.

dragón *m.* dragon.

drama *m.* drama.

dramático *adj.* dramatic; *m.* dramatic actor; playwright, dramatist.

dramatizar[9] *v.* to dramatize.

dramaturgo *m.* playwright, dramatist.

drenaje *m. Am.* drainage.

drenar *v. Am.* to drain.

dril *m.* drill (*strong cotton or linen cloth*).

droga *f.* (*medicina*) drug, medicine; (*mentira*) lie, fib; trick; (*molestia*) bother, nuisance; *Peru, Carib.* bad debt; *Riopl.* drug on the market, unsalable article.

droguería *f.* drugstore; drug business.

droguero *m.* druggist; *Am.* cheat, debt evader.

droguista *m. & f.* druggist; cheat, crook.

ducha *f.* shower bath; douche.

ducho *adj.* expert, skillful.

duda *f.* doubt.

dudable *adj.* doubtful.

dudar *v.* to doubt; to hesitate.

dudoso *adj.* doubtful; uncertain.

duela *f.* stave (*of a barrel*); *Mex., Andes* long, narrow floor board.

duelo *m.* (*luto*) grief, sorrow; mourning; mourners; (*pleito*) duel; **estar de —** to be in mourning; to mourn.

duende *m.* goblin.

dueña *f.* owner, landlady; duenna, chaperon or governess.

dueño *m.* owner; master.

dueto, duo *m.* duet.

dulce *adj.* sweet; pleasant, agreeable; fresh (*water*); soft (*metal*); *m.* sweet-meat; candy; preserves; *Am.* sugar, honey; **dulcería** *f.* candy shop.

dulcificar[6] *v.* to sweeten; to soften.

dulzón *adj.* over-sweet, sickeningly sweet.

dulzura *f.* sweetness; meekness.

duna *f.* dune, sand dune.

duplicado *adj. & m.* duplicate; **por —** in duplicate; *p.p. of* **duplicar.**

duplicar[6] *v.* to duplicate, double; to repeat. •

duplicidad *f.* duplicity, deceit, deceitfulness, treachery.

duque *m.* duke.

duquesa *f.* duchess.

durabilidad *f.* durability, durable quality, wear.

durable *adj.* durable.

duración *f.* duration.

duradero *adj.* durable, lasting.

durante *prep.* during, for.

durar *v.* to last, endure; to wear well.

durazno *m.* peach; peach tree; **duraznero** *m.* peach tree.

dureza *f.* hardness; harshness.

durmiente *adj.* sleeping; *m.* sleeper; crossbeam; *Col., Ven., Mex., Ch.* railroad tie.

duro *adj.* (*sólido*) hard; firm, solid; untiring; (*cruel*) cruel; harsh; rigid; (*tacaño*) stubborn; stingy; **a duras penas** with difficulty; *Am.* **— y parejo** eagerly, tenaciously; *Am.* **hacer —** to resist stubbornly; *m.* **duro** (*Spanish dollar*).

E

e *conj.* and (*before words beginning with i or* **hi**).

ébano *m.* ebony.

ebrio *adj.* drunk.

ebullición *f.* boiling, bubbling up.

eclesiástico *adj.* ecclesiastic, belonging to the church; *m.* clergyman.

eclipsar *v.* to eclipse; to outshine, surpass.

égloga *f.* eclogue, pastoral poem, idyll.

eco *m.* echo.

economía *f.* economy; **— política** economics, political economy.

económico *adj.* economic; economical, saving; **economista** *m.* economist.

economizar[9] *v.* to economize, save.

ecuación *f.* equation.

ecuador *m.* equator.

echar *v.* (*tirar*) to throw, cast; to expel; to throw out; (*emitir*) to give off; to sprout; **— a correr** to run away; **-(se) a perder** to spoil; **— a pique** to sink; **-(se) a reír** to burst out laughing; **— carnes** to get fat; **— de menos** to miss; **— de ver** to notice; to make out; **— mano** to seize; **— papas** to fib; **— raíces** to take root; **—suertes** to draw lots; **-se** to lie down; *Am.* **echársela** to boast.

edad *f.* age.

edén *m.* Eden; paradise.

edición *f.* edition; publication.

edificación *f.* edification (*moral or spiritual uplift*); construction.

edificar[6] *v.* to construct, build; to edify, uplift.

edificio *m.* edifice, building.

editar *v.* to publish.

editor *m.* publisher; *adj.* publishing.

editorial *adj.* publishing, editorial; *m.* editorial; *f.* publishing house.

edredón *m.* down quilt, comforter, quilted blanket.

educación *f.* education, training; breeding, manners.

educador *m.* educator; *adj.* educating.

educando *m.* pupil; inmate (*of an orphanage, boarding school, etc.*).

educar[6] *v.* to educate, teach, train, raise, bring up.

educativo *adj.* educational.

efectivo *adj.* effective; real; in operation, active; *m.* cash.

efecto *m.* (*resultado*) effect, result; (*fin*) end, purpose; **-s** goods, personal property; **en —** in fact, actually; **llevar a —** to carry out; **surtir —** to come out as expected; to give good results.

efectuar[18] *v.* to effect, bring about.

eficacia *f.* efficacy; efficiency; effectiveness.

eficaz *adj.* effective; active; efficient.

eficiencia *f.* efficiency; **eficiente** *adj.* efficient.

efímero *adj.* ephemeral, short-lived, brief.

efluvio *m.* emanation, exhalation, vapors.

efusión *f.* effusion, unrestrained expression of feeling, gushy manner; **— de sangre** bloodshed.

efusivo *adj.* effusive, too demonstrative, over-emotional.

egipcio *adj. & m.* Egyptian.

egocéntrico *adj.* egocentric, self-centered.

egoísmo *m.* selfishness.

egoísta *adj.* selfish; *m. & f.* selfish person.

egolatría *f.* self-worship.

eje *m.* axis; axle.

ejecución f. execution; carrying out.

ejecutar v. to execute; to carry out; to perform, do.

ejecutivo adj. executive; active; m. executive.

ejecutor m. executor; — **de la justicia** executioner.

ejemplar adj. exemplary, model; m. copy; specimen.

ejemplo m. example; model, pattern.

ejercer[10] v. to practice (a profession); to exert.

ejercicio m. exercise; practice; military drill; exercise (of authority); **hacer** — to take exercise.

ejercitar v. to practice, exercise; to drill, train; **-se** to train oneself; to practice.

ejército m. army.

ejido m. public land, common.

ejote m. Mex., Guat. string bean.

el def. art. m. the; — **de** the one with, that one with; — **que** rel. pron. he who, the one that; **él** pers. pron. he; him, it (after a prep.).

elaboración f. manufacture, making; development.

elaborar v. to elaborate.

elasticidad f. elasticity.

elástico adj. elastic; flexible; m. elastic; elastic tape; wire spring; **-s** Am. suspenders.

elección f. election; choice.

electo adj. elect, chosen; m. elect, person chosen.

elector m. elector, voter; adj. electoral, electing.

electoral adj. electoral.

electricidad f. electricity.

electricista m. electrician; electrical engineer.

eléctrico adj. electric, electrical.

electrizar[9] v. to electrify; to thrill, excite; Am. to anger, irritate.

electrocardiógrafo m. electrocardiograph.

electroimán m. electromagnet.

electrónico adj. electronic; **electrónica** f. electronics.

elefante m. elephant.

elegancia f. elegance, grace, distinguished manner.

elegante adj. elegant, graceful, polished; stylish.

elegir[5,11] v. irr. to elect, choose.

elemental adj. elementary; elemental, fundamental.

elemento m. element; **-s** elements, fundamentals; personnel; — **químicos** chemical elements, simple substances; Am. **ser** (or **estar**) **hecho un** — to be an idiot, a fool.

elevación f. elevation; height; rise; rapture.

elevador m. Am. elevator, hoist.

elevar v. to elevate, raise, lift; **-se** to go up; to soar.

eliminación f. elimination, removal.

eliminar v. to eliminate.

elocuencia f. eloquence.

elocuente adj. eloquent.

elogiar v. to praise.

elogio m. praise.

elote m. Mex., C.A. ear of corn, corn on the cob.

elucidación f. elucidation, explanation.

elucidar v. to elucidate, illustrate, explain.

eludir v. to elude, avoid, dodge.

ella pers. pron. she; her, it (after a prep.).

ello pron. it; — **es que** the fact is that.

emanación f. emanation, flow; fumes, vapor, odor; manifestation.

emanar v. to emanate, spring, issue.

emancipación f. emancipation.

emancipar v. to emancipate, set free; **-se** to become free.

embajada f. embassy; errand, mission.

embajador m. ambassador.

embalador m. packer.

embalaje m. packing.

embalar v. to pack; to bale, crate.

embaldosar v. to pave with flagstones or tiles.

embalsamar v. to embalm; to scent, perfume.

embarazar[9] v. (impedir) to hinder, to obstruct; (preñar) to make pregnant; **-se** to become pregnant; to become embarrassed.

embarazo m. (obstáculo) impediment, obstacle; (preñez) pregnancy; (timidez) bashfulness, awkwardness.

embarazoso adj. embarrassing; cumbersome, unwieldly.

embarcación f. ship, boat; embarkation.

embarcadero m. wharf, pier.

embarcador m. shipper.

embarcar[6] v. to embark; to ship; Am. to ship by train or any vehicle; **-se** to embark, sail; to engage (in); Am. to board, get on a train.

embarco m. embarkation.

embargar[7] v. to impede; to restrain; to attach, confiscate; to lay an embargo on; **estar embargado de emoción** to be overcome with emotion.

embargo m. embargo, restriction on commerce; attachment, confiscation; **sin** — nevertheless.

embarque m. shipment.

embarrado p.p. & adj. smeared; plastered; muddy.

embarrar v. to smear, daub.

embaucador m. cheat, impostor.

embaucar[6] v. to fool, trick, swindle, deceive.

embebecido p.p. & adj. absorbed; amazed.

embebecimiento m. absorption; rapture.

embeber v. to imbibe, absorb; to soak; to shrink; **-se** to be fascinated; to be absorbed.

embelesar v. to enrapture, delight, charm.

embeleso m. delight, ecstasy.

embellecer[13] v. irr. to embellish, beautify, adorn.

embestida f. sudden attack, onset, assault.

embestir[5] v. irr. to attack, assail.

embetunar v. to cover with pitch; to black.

emblanquecer[13] v. irr. to whiten; to bleach; to become white; **-se** to whiten, become white.

emblema m. emblem.

embobar v. to fool; to amuse; to fascinate; to amaze; **-se** to be amazed; to be fascinated.

embobinado m. reel assembly (of a tape recorder or computer).

embocadura f. mouth (of a river); entrance (through a narrow passage); mouthpiece (of a wind instrument); bit (of a bridle); taste, flavor (said of wines).

embolado m. bull whose horns have been tipped with balls; impotent, ineffectual person; p.p. of **embolar**.

embolar v. (al toro) to tip a bull's horns with balls; (dar lustre) to polish, to black; **-se** C.A. to get drunk.

émbolo m. piston; plunger (of a pump); embolus (clot in a blood vessel).

embolsar v. to put into a pocket or purse; **-se** to pocket, put into one's pocket.

emborrachar v. to intoxicate; **-se** to get drunk.

emborronar v. to blot; to scribble.

emboscada f. ambush.

emboscar[6] v. to ambush; **-se** to lie in ambush; to go into a forest.

embotado adj. dull, blunt; p.p. of **embotar**.

embotamiento m. dullness, bluntness; dulling, blunting.

embotar v. to dull, blunt; to enervate, weaken.

embotellador m. bottling machine; **embotelladora** bottling works.

embotellar v. to bottle; to bottle up; Am. to jail.

embozado adj. cloaked; muffled, covered up to the face.

embozar[7] v. to muffle; to cloak, conceal, disguise; to muzzle; **-se** to muffle oneself, wrap oneself.

embragar[7] v. to engage or throw in the clutch.

embrague m. clutch (of a machine); coupling.

embriagar[7] v. to intoxicate; **-se** to get drunk, intoxicated.

embriaguez f. intoxication; drunkenness.

embrollar v. to involve, ensnare, entangle; to confuse.

embrollo m. confusion, tangle; trickery, lie, deception.

embromar v. to chaff, make fun of, "kid"; Am. to bother, molest; Am. to delay unnecessarily; Col., Ven. to ruin, harm; **-se** Am. to be bothered, disgusted; Mex. to get delayed.

embrujar v. to bewitch, enchant.

embrujo m. charm, enchantment; glamour.

embrutecer[13] v. irr. to stupefy, render brutish; to dull the mind, make insensible.

embudo m. funnel; trick.

embuste m. lie, fraud; trinket.

embustero m. liar; adj. deceitful, tricky.

embutido m. sausage; inlaid work; Am. insertion of embroidery or lace; p.p. of **embutir**.

embutir v. to insert, inlay; to stuff.

emerger[11] v. to emerge, come out.

emigración f. emigration.

emigrante m. & f. emigrant.

emigrar v. to emigrate; to migrate.

eminencia f. eminence; height.

eminente adj. eminent, high, lofty.

emisión f. issue (of bonds, money, etc.); radio broadcast.

emisor adj. emitting; broadcasting; m. radio transmitter; **emisora** f. broadcasting station.

emitir v. to emit, give off; to utter; to send forth; to issue; to broadcast.

emoción f. emotion.

emocional adj. emotional.

emocionante adj. moving, touching, thrilling.

emocionar v. to cause emotion, touch, move; **-se** to be touched, moved, stirred.

emotivo adj. emotional.

empacador m. packer.

empacar[6] v. to pack up, wrap up, bale, crate; Riopl. to goad, irritate (an animal); **-se** to be stubborn; to get angry; Riopl. to balk; Riopl. to put on airs.

empachado p.p. & adj. (relleno) clogged; stuffed; upset from indigestion; (tímido) embarrassed; bashful.

empachar v. to stuff, cram; to cause indigestion; **-se** to get upset; to get clogged; to be stuffed; to suffer indigestion; to get embarrassed.

empacho m. indigestion; bashfulness; **no tener — en** to have no objection to; to feel free to.

empalagar[7] v. to cloy; to pall on, become distasteful; to disgust.

empalagoso adj. cloying; sickeningly sweet; boring, wearisome.

empalizada f. stockade, palisade.

empalmar v. to splice; to join; **— con** to join (as railroads or highways).

empalme m. junction; joint, connection; splice.

empanada f. pie, meat pie; swindle, fraud.

empanizar[9] v. Carib., C.A., Mex. to bread.

empañado adj. & p.p. tarnished; dim, blurred.

empañar v. to blur, dim, tarnish.

empapada f. Am. drenching, soaking.

empapar v. to soak, drench, saturate.

empapelador m. paper hanger.

empapelar v. to paper; to wrap in paper.

empaque m. (bulto) packing; (parecer) looks, appearance, air; airs, importance; Am., Peru impudence.

empaquetar v. to pack; to pack in; to make a package; **-se** to dress up, doll up.

EJ

emparedado *adj.* shut up, confined between walls; *m.* sandwich; prisoner confined in a narrow cell.

emparejar *v.* to even up, level off; to match; to pair off; to overtake, catch up with.

emparentado *adj.* & *p.p.* related by marriage.

emparentar *v.* to become related by marriage.

emparrado *m.* vine arbor.

empastar *v.* to paste; to fill (*a tooth*); to bind (*books*); **-se** *Ch.* to get lost in the pasture; *Mex.* to become overgrown with grass.

empaste *m.* tooth filling; binding (*of a book*).

empatar *v.* (*igualar*) to tie (*in a game*), have an equal score; to have an equal number of votes; (*impedir*) to hinder, obstruct; *Col., Ven., Carib.* to tie, join.

empate *m.* tie, draw, equal score, equal number of votes; hindrance, obstruction; *Am.* joint, junction.

empecinado *adj. Am.* stubborn.

empedernido *adj.* hardened, hardhearted.

empedernir[61] *v.* to harden, toughen; **-se** to become hardened.

empedrado *m.* cobblestone pavement; *p.p.* & *adj.* paved with stones.

empedrar[1] *v. irr.* to pave with stones.

empeine *m.* instep; groin (*hollow between lower part of abdomen and thigh*).

empellón *m.* push, shove; **a -es** by pushing.

empeñar *v.* (*dar en prenda*) to pawn; (*obligar*) to oblige, compel; **-se** to persist, insist; to apply oneself; to go into debt; **-se por** to plead for, intercede for; **se empeñaron en una lucha** they engaged in a fight.

empeño *m.* (*fianza*) pledge, pawn; (*deseo*) persistence, insistence; eagerness; perseverance; *Am.* pawnshop; **tener — en** to be eager to.

empeorar *v.* to impair; to make worse; to grow worse; **-se** to grow worse.

empequeñecer[13] *v. irr.* to diminish, make smaller; to belittle.

emperador *m.* emperor; **emperatriz** *f.* empress.

emperifollar *v.* to decorate, adorn; **-se** to dress up, deck out, doll up.

empero *conj.* however, nevertheless.

empezar[1, 9] *v. irr.* to begin.

empiezo *m. Càrib., Mex., C.A.* beginning.

empinado *adj.* steep; lofty.

empinar *v.* to raise, lift; to incline, bend; **— el codo** to drink; **-se** to stand on tiptoes; to rear (*said of horses*); to rise high; *Am.* to overeat.

empiojado *adj.* lousy, full of lice.

emplasto *m.* plaster, poultice.

empleado *m.* employee; *p.p.* of **emplear**.

emplear *v.* to employ; to invest, spend; **-se en** to be employed in.

empleo *m.* employment, position, job; employ; occupation; aim; investment.

emplumar *v.* to feather; to adorn with feathers; to tar and feather; *C.A.* to deceive; *Ec.* to send away to a house of correction or prison; *Am.* **— con algo** to run away with something, steal it; *Ch., Col., Ven.* **-las** (*or* **emplumárselas**) to take to one's heels, flee, escape.

empobrecer[13] *v. irr.* to impoverish; **-se** to become poor.

empobrecimiento *m.* impoverishment.

empolvado *adj.* dusty, covered with dust or powder.

empolvar *v.* to sprinkle powder; to cover with dust; **-se** to get dusty; to powder one's face.

empollar *v.* to hatch, brood.

emponzoñar *v.* to poison.

emprendedor *adj.* enterprising.

emprender *v.* to undertake.

empreñar *v.* to impregnate, make pregnant.

empresa *f.* enterprise, undertaking; symbol; company, management.

empresario *m.* manager; impresario, promoter.

empréstito *m.* loan.

empujar *v.* to push, shove.

empuje *m.* push; shove; impulse; energy.

empujón *m.* shove, push.

empuñar *v.* to grasp, grab, clutch, seize.

émulo *m.* rival, competitor.

en *prep.* in, on, upon.

enaguas *f. pl.* underskirt, petticoat; short skirt.

enajenamiento *m.* trance; abstraction, absence of mind; transfer (*of property*); **— mental** mental disorder; **— de los sentidos** loss of consciousness.

enajenar *v.* (*distraer*) to enrapture, charm; to deprive (*of one's sense*); (*trasladar*) to transfer property; to dispossess; **— el afecto de** to alienate the affection of; **-se** to be enraptured, be in a trance.

enaltecer[13] *v.* to extol, exalt.

enamorado *adj.* in love; *m.* lover.

enamorar *v.* to make love, woo, court; to enamor; **-se** to fall in love.

enano *m.* dwarf; *adj.* dwarfish, tiny, little.

enarbolar *v.* to hoist, lift, raise on high; to brandish (*a sword, cane, etc.*); **-se** to rear, balk.

enarcado *p.p.* arched.

enarcar[6] *v.* to arch; to hoop (*barrels, kegs, etc.*); **— las cejas** to arch one's eyebrows.

enardecer[13] *v. irr.* to excite, kindle, fire with passion; **-se** to become excited; to become passionate; to get angry.

enardecimiento *m.* ardor, passion, unbridled enthusiasm; inflaming.

encabezado *m.* headline; heading.

encabezamiento *m.* heading; headline; list or roll of taxpayers; registration of taxpayers.

encabezar⁹ v. to give a heading or title to; to head; to lead; to make up (a list or tax roll); to strengthen (wine).

encabritarse v. to rear, rise up on the hind legs.

encadenar v. to chain; to link together.

encajar v. to thrust in, fit into, insert; **-se** to squeeze into; to intrude, meddle.

encaje m. lace; adjustment; fitting together; socket, groove, hole; inlaid work.

encajonar v. to box (put or pack in a box).

encallar v. to strand, run aground; to get stuck.

encamado p.p. confined in bed.

encaminar v. to direct, guide; **-se** to betake oneself, go (toward); to start out on a road.

encanecer¹³ v. irr. to get grey, get grey-haired.

encanijado adj. emaciated, thin, sickly.

encanijarse v. to get thin, emaciated.

encantado p.p. & adj. delighted, charmed; enchanted.

encantador adj. charming; m. charmer, enchanter.

encantamiento m. enchantment.

encantar v. to charm, enchant.

encanto m. charm, enchantment, delight.

encapillar v. P.R. to confine in the death cell.

encapotado p.p. & adj. cloaked; overcast, cloudy; in a bad humor.

encapotarse v. to become overcast, cloudy; to cover up, put on a cloak or raincoat; to frown.

encapricharse v. to persist in one's whims; to get stubborn.

encaramar v. to raise; to elevate; to extol; **-se** to climb; to climb upon, get upon, perch upon; Ch. to be ashamed; Carib. to go to one's head (said of liquor).

encarar v. to face; to aim; **-se con** to face; to confront.

encarcelación f. imprisonment.

encarcelamiento = **encarcelación**.

encarcelar v. to imprison, jail.

encarecer¹³ v. irr. (alzar precio) to go up in value; to make dear, raise the price of; (ponderar) to exaggerate; to extol; to recommend highly, to enhance.

encarecidamente adv. earnestly.

encargar⁷ v. (dar cargo) to put in charge; to entrust; to commission; (aconsejar) to recommend, advise; (pedir) to order; to beg; **-se de** to take charge of.

encargo m. recommendation, advice; charge; order; commission; errand.

encariñado adj. & p.p. attached, fond, enamored.

encariñamiento m. affection, fondness, attachment.

encariñar v. to awaken love or affection; **-se** to become fond (of), attached (to).

encarnado adj. flesh-colored; red; p.p of encarnar.

encarnar v. to incarnate, embody; to bait (a fishhook).

encarnizado adj. bloody; hard-fought, fierce.

encarnizar⁹ v. to infuriate, enrage; **-se** to get furious, enraged; to fight with fury.

encasillar v. to pigeonhole, put in a pigeonhole or compartment; to put in a stall; to classify, sort out.

encender¹ v. irr. to light, kindle; to set on fire; **-se** to take fire, be on fire; to get red.

encendido adj. red; p.p. of encender; m. ignition (of a motor).

encerado m. blackboard; oilcloth; wax coating; p.p. & adj. waxed; wax-colored; **papel —** wax paper.

encerar v. to wax; to thicken (lime).

encerramiento m. enclosure, confinement; locking up; retreat; prison.

encerrar¹ v. irr. to enclose; to lock up; to contain; **-se** to lock oneself up, go into seclusion.

encía f. gum (of the teeth).

enciclopedia f. encyclopedia.

encierro m. confinement; retreat; prison.

encima adv. above, overhead, over, on top; besides, in addition; **— de** on top of; **por — de** over; Am. **de —** besides, in addition; (Col., C.A., Riopl., Carib. **echárselo todo —** to spend everything on clothes.

encina f. live oak.

encinta adj. pregnant.

encintado m. curb (of a sidewalk).

enclaustrar v. to cloister.

enclavar v. to nail, fix, fasten.

enclenque adj. sickly, wan; weak, feeble.

encoger¹¹ v. to shrink, shrivel, shorten, contract; **-se** to shrink; to shrivel; **-se de hombros** to shrug one's shoulders.

encogido p.p. & adj. shrunk, shrivelled; timid, shy.

encogimiento m. shrinking; timidity; **— de hombros** shrug.

encolerizar⁹ v. to anger; **-se** to get angry.

encomendar¹ v. irr. (encargar) to charge, advise; to entrust; (recomendar) to recommend, commend; **-se** to put oneself in the hands (of); to send regards; to pray (to).

encomiar v. to extol, praise.

encomienda f. charge, commission; recommendation; royal land grant (including Indian inhabitants); Am. warehouse (for agricultural products); Am. parcel-post package.

encomio m. encomium, high praise.

enconado p.p. & adj. inflamed; infected; sore; angry.

enconar v. to inflame; to infect; to irritate; **-se** to become inflamed, infected; to get irritated.

encono m. rancor, animosity, ill will; Cuba, Mex. inflammation, swelling.

encontrado *adj.* opposite; opposing; contrary; *p.p.* of **encontrar**.

encontrar² *v. irr.* to encounter, meet; to find; **-se** to meet; to coincide; to be; to be found, be situated; to collide; to conflict; **-se con** to come across, meet up with.

encontrón, encontronazo *m.* bump, collision; **darse un —** to collide (with) bump (into); to bump into each other.

encordelar *v.* to string; to tie with strings.

encorvar *v.* to curve, bend; **-se** to bend down; to stoop.

encrespar *v.* (*rizar*) to curl; to ruffle; (*agitar*) to irritate; **-se** to curl; to get ruffled; to become involved or entangled (*a matter or affair*); to become rough (*said of the sea*).

encrucijada *f.* crossroads, street intersection; ambush.

encuadernación *f.* binding (*of books*).

encuadernar *v.* to bind (*books*).

encuadrar *v.* to enclose in a frame; to encompass; to fit (into); *Am.* to suit; *Ven.* to summarize briefly, give a synthesis of.

encubierto *p.p.* of **encubrir**.

encubrir⁵² *v.* to cover, hide.

encuentro *m.* (*hallazgo*) encounter, meeting; find, finding; (*conflicto*) conflict, clash; collision; **salir al — de** to go out to meet; to make a stand against, oppose; *Am.* **llevarse de —** to run over, knock down; to drag along.

encuerado *adj. Am.* naked.

encuerar *v. Am.* to strip of clothes; *Am.* to skin, fleece, strip of money; **-se** *Am.* to strip, get undressed.

encuesta *f.* search, inquiry, investigation; survey.

encumbrado *p.p.* & *adj.* elevated; exalted; high, lofty.

encumbramiento *m.* elevation; exaltation; height; eminence.

encumbrar *v.* to elevate; to exalt, extol; **-se** to climb to the top; to rise up; to hold oneself high; to soar.

encurtido *m.* pickle; *p.p.* of **encurtir**.

encurtir *v.* to pickle.

enchilada *f. Mex., C.A.* rolled **tortilla** served with chili.

enchuecar⁶ *v.* to bend, twist; **-se** *Col., Ven., Mex., Ríopl.* to get bent or twisted.

enchufar *v.* to plug in; to telescope; to fit (*a tube or pipe*) into another.

enchufe *m.* socket; plug; electric outlet; *Spain* influence; position obtained through influence.

ende : por — hence, therefore.

endeble *adj.* weak, feeble; flimsy.

endemoniado *adj.* possessed by the devil; devilish, fiendish; mischievous.

endentar¹ *v. irr.* to indent, form notches in; to furnish (*a saw, wheel, etc.*) with teeth; to mesh.

enderezar⁹ *v.* to straighten; to set upright; to right, correct; to direct; to

address; **-se** to go straight (to); to straighten up.

endeudado *p.p.* & *adj.* indebted; in debt.

endeudarse *v.* to get into debt, become indebted.

endiablado *adj.* devilish; possessed by the devil; ugly; mean, wicked; *Col., Ven., Mex., Ríopl.* dangerous, risky.

endomingado *p.p.* & *adj.* dressed up in one's Sunday, or best, clothes.

endosante *m.* endorser.

endosar *v.* to endorse (*a check, draft, etc.*).

endose, endoso *m.* endorsement.

endulzar⁹ *v.* to sweeten; to soften.

endurecer¹³ *v. irr.* to harden; **-se** to get hardened; to get cruel.

enemigo *m.* enemy; devil; *adj.* hostile; unfriendly; **ser — de una cosa** to dislike a thing.

enemistad *f.* enmity, hatred.

enemistar *v.* to cause enmity between; **-se con** to become an enemy of.

energía *f.* energy; **— nuclear** nuclear energy.

enérgico *adj.* energetic.

enero *m.* January.

enervar *v.* to enervate, weaken.

enfadar *v.* to anger; **-se** to get angry.

enfado *m.* anger, disgust.

enfadoso *adj.* annoying.

enfardar *v.* to bale, pack.

énfasis *m.* emphasis; **enfático** *adj.* emphatic.

enfermar *v.* to become ill; to make ill; to weaken; **-se** to become ill.

enfermedad *f.* sickness, illness.

enfermería *f.* infirmary.

enfermero *m.* male nurse; **enfermera** *f.* nurse (*for the sick*).

enfermizo *adj.* sickly; unhealthy.

enfermo *adj.* sick, ill; feeble; *m.* patient.

enflaquecer¹³ *v. irr.* to become thin; to make thin; to weaken.

enfocar⁶ *v.* to focus.

enfrenar *v.* to bridle; to brake, put the brake on; to check, curb.

enfrentar *v.* to put face to face; **-se con** to confront, face, meet face to face.

enfrente *adv.* in front, opposite; **— de** in front of, opposite.

enfriamiento *m.* cooling; chill; refrigeration.

enfriar¹⁷ *v.* to cool, chill; *Carib.* to kill; **-se** to cool, cool off; to get chilled.

enfurecer¹³ *v. irr.* to infuriate, enrage; **-se** to rage; to get furious; to get rough, stormy (*said of the sea*).

enfurruñarse *v.* to get angry; to grumble.

engalanar *v.* to adorn, decorate; **-se** to dress up, primp.

enganchamiento = enganche.

enganchar *v.* to hitch; to hook; to ensnare; to draft; to attract into the army; *Col., Ven., Mex., Ríopl.* to hire (*labor with false promises*); **-se** to engage, interlock; to get hooked; to enlist in the army.

enganche *m.* hooking; coupling; draft

(*into the army*); *Col., Ven., Mex., Riopl.* enrolling of laborers (*for a rubber plantation or other risky business under false promises*); *Mex.* down payment.

engañador *adj.* deceitful, deceiving; *m.* deceiver.

engañar *v.* to deceive; to while away (*time*); to ward off (*hunger or sleep*); **-se** to deceive oneself; to be mistaken.

engaño *m.* deceit, trick, fraud; mistake, misunderstanding; *Ch., C.A.* bribe.

engañoso *adj.* deceitful; tricky; misleading.

engastar *v.* to mount, set (*jewels*).

engaste *m.* setting (*for a gem or stone*).

engatusar *v.* to coax, entice; to fool.

engendrar *v.* to engender, beget, produce; to cause.

engolfarse *v.* to get deep (into); to go deeply (into); to become absorbed, lost in thought.

engomar *v.* to gum; to glue.

engordar *v.* to fatten; to get fat; to get rich.

engorroso *adj.* cumbersome; bothersome.

engranaje *m.* gear, gears, gearing.

engranar *v.* to gear, throw in gear; to mesh gears.

engrandecer[13] *v. irr.* to aggrandize, make greater; to magnify; to exalt.

engrane *m.* engagement (*of gears*); gear.

engrasar *v.* to lubricate, grease; to stain with grease; to fertilize, manure; to dress (*cloth*).

engreído *adj. & p.p.* conceited, vain; *Col.* attached, fond.

engreír[15] *v. irr.* to make vain, conceited; **-se** to puff up, get conceited; *Col.* to become fond (of), become attached (to).

engrosar[2] *v. irr.* to enlarge; to thicken; to fatten; to get fat.

engrudo *m.* paste (*for gluing*).

engullir[20] *v.* to gobble, devour; to gorge.

enhebrar *v.* to thread (*a needle*); to string (*beads*).

enhiesto *adj.* straight, upright, erect.

enhorabuena *f.* congratulation; *adv.* safely; well and good; all right; with much pleasure.

enigma *m.* enigma, riddle, puzzle.

enjabonar *v.* to soap; to soft-soap, flatter.

enjaezar[9] *v.* to harness.

enjalbegar[7] *v.* to whitewash; **-se** to paint (*one's face*).

enjambre *m.* swarm of bees; crowd.

enjaular *v.* to cage; to confine; to jail.

enjuagar[7] *v.* to rinse, rinse out.

enjuague *m.* mouth wash; rinse; rinsing; scheme, plot.

enjugar[7] *v.* to dry; to wipe; **-se** to dry oneself.

enjuiciar *v.* to indict; to prosecute, bring suit against; to try (*a case*); to judge.

enjundia *f.* substance, essence; fat; force, strength.

enjuto *adj.* dried; thin, skinny; **-s** *m. pl.* dry kindling.

enlace *m.* link; tie, bond; marriage.

enladrillado *m.* brick pavement or floor.

enladrillar *v.* to pave with bricks.

enlatar *v.* to can; *Col.* to roof with tin.

enlazar[9] *v.* to join, bind, tie; to rope; *Ven., Mex.* to lasso; **-se** to join; to marry; to become related through marriage.

enlodar *v.* to cover with mud; to smear, sully, soil, dirty; **-se** to get in the mud; to get muddy.

enloquecer[13] *v. irr.* to make crazy; to drive mad; to lose one's mind; **-se** to go crazy.

enlosado *m.* flagstone pavement; *p.p.* of **enlosar**.

enlosar *v.* to pave with flagstones.

enmantecado *m. Am.* ice cream. See **mantecado**.

enmantecar[6] *v.* to butter; to grease (*with lard or butter*).

enmarañar *v.* to entangle; to snarl; to confuse, mix up.

enmascarar *v.* to mask; **-se** to put on a mask; to masquerade.

enmendar[1] *v. irr.* to amend, correct; to indemnify, compensate; **-se** to reform, mend one's ways.

enmienda *f.* correction; amendment; reform, indemnity, compensation.

enmohecer[13] *v.* to rust; to mold; **-se** to rust, become rusty; to mold.

enmudecer[13] *v. irr.* to silence; to remain silent; to lose one's voice; to become dumb.

ennegrecer[13] *v. irr.* to blacken; to darken; **-se** to become dark; to get cloudy.

ennoblecer[13] *v. irr.* to ennoble, dignify.

enojadizo *adj.* irritable, ill-tempered.

enojado *adj.* angry.

enojar *v.* to make angry, vex, annoy; **-se** to get angry.

enojo *m.* anger; annoyance.

enojoso *adj.* annoying, bothersome.

enorgullecer[13] *v. irr.* to fill with pride; **-se** to swell up with pride; to be proud.

enorme *adj.* enormous.

enramada *f.* arbor, bower; shady grove.

enrarecer[13] *v. irr.* to rarefy, thin, make less dense (*as air*); **-se** to become rarefied; to become scarce.

enrarecimiento *m.* rarity, thinness (*of the air*); rarefaction (*act of making thin, rare or less dense*).

enredadera *f.* climbing vine.

enredar *v.* (*enmarañar*) to entangle, snare; to snarl; to mix up; to wind (*on a spool*); (*enemistar*) to raise a rumpus; **-se** to get tangled up, mixed up; to get trapped; **-se con** to have an affair with.

enredista *m. Am.* liar; *Am.* talebearer.

enredo *m.* tangle; confusion; lie; plot.

enredoso *adj.* tangled up; *Am.* tattler.

enrejado *m.* trellis; grating.

enrevesado *adj.* turned around; intricate, complicated; unruly.

enriquecer[13] *v. irr.* to enrich; to become rich; **-se** to become rich.

enrojecer[13] *v. irr.* to redden; **-se** to get red, blush.

enrollar *v.* to roll, roll up; to coil.

enronquecer[13] *v. irr.* to make hoarse; to become hoarse; **-se** to become hoarse.

enroscar[6] *v.* to coil; to twist, twine; **-se** to coil; to curl up.

ensacar[6] *v.* to sack, bag, put in a bag or sack.

ensalada *f.* salad; hodgepodge, mixture.

ensalzar[9] *v.* to exalt, praise.

ensanchar *v.* to widen, enlarge; **-se** to expand; to puff up.

ensanche *m.* widening, expansion, extension.

ensangrentado *adj.* gory, bloody; *p.p. of* ensangrentar.

ensangrentar *v.* to stain with blood; **-se** to be covered with blood; to get red with anger.

ensartar *v.* to string; to thread; to link; to rattle off (*tales, stories, etc.*); *Ch.* to tie to a ring; *Am.* to swindle, trick; **-se** *Andes* to fall into a trap.

ensayar *v.* to try; to attempt; to test; to rehearse; **-se** to practice, train oneself.

ensayo *m.* trial, attempt; rehearsal; test; experiment; essay.

ensenada *f.* small bay, cove.

enseñanza *f.* teaching; education, training.

enseñar *v.* to show; to teach; to train; to point out.

enseres *m. pl.* household goods; utensils; implements; equipment.

ensillar *v.* to saddle; *Ch.* to abuse, mistreat, domineer; *Riopl.* **— el picazo** to get angry.

ensimismarse *v.* to become absorbed in thought; *Col., Ven., Ch.* to become conceited or vain.

ensoberbecer[13] *v. irr.* to make proud or haughty; **-se** to puff up with pride; to become haughty; to get rough, choppy (*said of the sea*).

ensordecer[13] *v. irr.* to deafen; to become deaf.

ensortijar *v.* to curl; to ring the nose of (*an animal*); **-se** to curl.

ensuciar *v.* to dirty, soil; to stain; **-se** to get dirty; to soil oneself.

ensueño *m.* illusion, dream.

entablar *v.* to board up; to plank; to splint; **— una conversación** to start a conversation; **— un pleito** to bring a lawsuit.

entablillar *v.* to splint; *Mex.* to cut (*chocolate*) into tablets or squares.

entallar *v.* to fit closely (*a dress*); to carve.

entapizar[9] *v.* to cover with tapestry; to drape with tapestries; to upholster.

entarimar *v.* to floor (*with boards*).

ente *m.* entity, being; queer fellow.

enteco *adj.* sickly, skinny.

entender[1] *v. irr.* to understand; **— de** to know, be an expert in; **— en** to take care of; to deal with; **-se con** to have dealings or relations with; to have an understanding with.

entendido *p.p.* understood; *adj.* wise, prudent; well-informed; able, skilful; **no darse por —** to pretend not to hear or understand; not to take the hint.

entendimiento *m.* understanding, intellect; mind.

enterado *p.p. & adj.* informed; aware.

enterar *v.* to inform, acquaint; **-se** to know, learn, find out; to understand, get the idea.

entereza *f.* entirety; integrity; fortitude; serenity; firmness; perfection.

enternecedor *adj.* touching, moving, pitiful.

enternecer[13] *v. irr.* to soften, touch, stir, move; **-se** to become tender; to be touched, stirred.

entero *adj.* (*completo*) entire, whole; (*justo*) just, right; firm; *m.* integer, whole number; *Col.* payment, reimbursement; *Ch.* balance of an account; **caballo —** stallion.

enterramiento *m.* burial.

enterrar[1] *v. irr.* to bury; *Am.* to sink, stick into.

entibiar *v.* to make lukewarm; **-se** to become lukewarm.

entidad *f.* entity; unit, group, organization; **de —** of value or importance.

entierro *m.* burial; funeral; grave; *Am.* hidden treasure.

entintar *v.* to ink; to stain with ink; to dye.

entoldar *v.* to cover with an awning; **-se** to puff up with pride; to become overcast, cloudy.

entonación *f.* intonation.

entonar *v.* to sing in tune; to start a song (*for others to follow*); to be in tune; to harmonize; **-se** to put on airs.

entonces *adv.* then, at that time; **pues — well** then.

entornado *adj.* half-open; half-closed; ajar.

entornar *v.* to half-open.

entorpecer[13] *v. irr.* to stupefy; to benumb, make numb; to delay, obstruct; to thwart, frustrate.

entorpecimiento *m.* numbness; dullness; delay, obstruction.

entrada *f.* (*apertura*) entrance; entry; gate; opening; (*acción o privilegio*) entering, admission; entrée (*dish or dinner course*); *Am.* attack, assault, goring; *Mex.* beating; **-s** cash receipts.

entrambos *adj. & pron.* both.

entrampar *v.* to trap, ensnare; to trick; to burden with debts; **-se** to get trapped or entangled; to run into debt.

entrante *adj.* entering; incoming; **el año —** next year.

entraña *f.* entrail; innermost recess; heart; disposition, temper; **-s** entrails, "innards", insides; **hijo de mis -s**

child of my heart; **no tener -s** to be cruel.

entrar v. to enter, go in, come in; to attack; **me entró miedo** I became afraid; **-se** to slip in, get in, sneak in; to enter.

entre prep. between; among; **dijo — sí** he said to himself; **— tanto** meanwhile; Am. — **más habla menos dice** the more he talks the less he says.

entreabierto p.p. of **entreabrir;** adj. ajar, half-open, partly open.

entreabrir[55] v. to half-open.

entreacto m. intermission; intermezzo (entertainment between the acts); small cigar.

entrecano adj. greyish.

entrecejo m. space between the eyebrows; **fruncir el —** to wrinkle one's brow.

entrecortado adj. hesitating, faltering (speech); breathless, choking; p.p. interrupted.

entrecortar v. to cut halfway through or in between; to interrupt at intervals.

entrecruzar[9] v. to intercross, cross; to interlace; **-se** to cross.

entredicho m. prohibition, injunction.

entrega f. (acto de ceder) delivery; surrender; (parte suelta) installment (of a book); **novela por -s** serial novel.

entregar[7] v. to deliver, hand over; **-se** to surrender, submit, give up; to devote oneself (to); to abandon oneself (to).

entrelazar[9] v. to interlace; to weave together.

entremés m. relish, side dish (of olives, pickles, etc.); one-act farce (formerly presented between the acts of a play.)

entremeter v. to insert; to place between; **-se** to meddle; to intrude.

entremetido adj. meddlesome; m. meddler; intruder.

entremetimiento m. intrusion, meddling.

entremezclar v. to intermix, intermingle.

entrenador m. Am. trainer.

entrenamiento m. Am. training, drill.

entrenar v. Am. to train, drill; **-se** Am. to train.

entresacar[6] v. to pick out, select.

entresuelo m. mezzanine; second floor.

entretanto adv. meanwhile.

entretejer v. to weave together; to intertwine.

entretener[45] v. irr. to delay, detain; to amuse, entertain; **-se** to amuse oneself; to delay oneself; **— el tiempo** to while away the time.

entretenido adj. entertaining, amusing; p.p. of **entretener.**

entretenimiento m. entertainment; pastime; delay.

entrever[49] v. to glimpse, catch a glimpse of; to half-see, see vaguely.

entreverar v. to intermingle, intermix.

entrevista f. interview; date, appointment.

entrevistar v. to interview; **-se con** to have an interview with.

entrevisto p.p. of **entrever.**

entristecer[13] v. irr. to sadden, make sad; **-se** to become sad.

entrometer = **entremeter.**

entrometido = **entremetido.**

entumecer[13] v. irr. to make numb; **-se** to get numb; to surge; to swell.

entumido adj. numb, stiff; Am. timid, shy, awkward.

entumirse v. to get numb.

enturbiar v. to make muddy; to muddle; to disturb; to obscure; **-se** to get muddy; to get muddled.

entusiasmar v. to excite, fill with enthusiasm; **-se** to get enthusiastic, excited.

entusiasmo m. enthusiasm.

entusiasta m. & f. enthusiast; **entusiástico** adj. enthusiastic.

enumeración f. enumeration, counting.

enumerar v. to enumerate.

enunciar v. to express, state, declare.

envainar v. to sheathe.

envalentonar v. to make bold or haughty; **-se** to get bold; to brag, swagger.

envanecer[13] v. irr. to make vain; **-se** to become vain.

envasar v. to pack, put up in any container; to bottle; to can.

envase m. packing; container, jar, bottle, can (for packing).

envejecer[13] v. irr. to make old; to grow old, get old; **-se** to grow old, get old.

envenenamiento m. poisoning.

envenenar v. to poison; to infect.

envergadura f. span (of an airplane); spread (of a bird's wings); breadth (of sails).

envés m. back or wrong side.

enviado m. envoy.

enviar[17] v. to send; **— a uno a paseo** to give someone his walking papers.

enviciar v. to vitiate, corrupt; **-se** to become addicted (to), overly fond (of)

envidar v. to bid (in cards); to bet.

envidia f. envy.

envidiable adj. enviable, desirable.

envidiar v. to envy.

envidioso adj. envious.

envilecer[13] v. irr. to revile, malign, degrade; **-se** to degrade or lower oneself.

envilecimiento m. degradation, humiliation, shame.

envío m. remittance, sending; shipment.

envite m. bid; stake (in cards); offer; push.

envoltorio m. bundle, package.

envoltura f. wrapping, cover; wrapper.

envolver[2,52] v. irr. to involve, entangle; to wrap; to wind (a thread, rope, etc.); to surround; **-se** to become involved, entangled; to cover up, wrap up.

envuelto p.p. of **envolver.**

enyesar v. to plaster; to chalk.

enzolvar v. Am. to clog, obstruct; Am. **-se** to clog, get clogged. See **azolvar.**

¡**epa!** *interj.* *Ríopl.*, *Ven.*, *Col.*, *Mex.* hey! listen! stop! look out!

épico *adj.* epic.

epidemia *f.* epidemic.

episodio *m.* episode.

epístola *f.* epistle; letter.

epitafio *m.* epitaph.

época *f.* epoch.

epopeya *f.* epic poem.

equidad *f.* equity, justice, fairness.

equidistante *adj.* equidistant, equally distant, halfway, midway.

equilibrar *v.* to balance, poise.

equilibrio *m.* equilibrium, balance; poise.

equipaje *m.* baggage, luggage; equipment, outfit; crew.

equipar *v.* to equip, fit out; to man, equip and provision (*a ship*).

equipo *m.* (*materiales*) equipment, equipping; outfit; (*grupo*) work crew; sport team; — **de novia** trousseau.

equitación *f.* horsemanship; horseback riding.

equitativo *adj.* fair, just.

equivalente *adj.* equivalent.

equivaler[47] *v. irr.* to be equivalent.

equivocación *f.* error, mistake.

equivocado *p.p. & adj.* mistaken.

equivocar[6] *v.* to mistake; **-se** to be mistaken; to make a mistake.

equívoco *adj.* equivocal, ambiguous, vague; *Am.* mistaken; *m.* pun, play on words; *Am.* mistake, error.

era *f.* era, age; threshing floor.

erario *m.* public treasury.

erguido *adj.* erect; *p.p.* of **erguir**.

erguir[9] *v. irr.* to erect, set upright; to lift (*the head*); **-se** to sit up or stand erect; to become proud and haughty.

erial *m.* uncultivated land; *adj.* unplowed, untilled.

erigir[11] *v.* to erect, build; to found.

erizado *adj.* bristly, prickly; — **de** bristling with.

erizar[9] *v.* to set on end, make bristle; **-se** to bristle; to stand on end (*hair*).

erizo *m.* hedgehog, porcupine; thistle; — **de mar** sea urchin; **ser un —** to be irritable, harsh.[6]

ermitaño *m.* hermit.

erosión *f.* erosion.

errabundo *adj.* wandering.

errado *adj.* mistaken, wrong, in error; *p.p.* of **errar**.

errante *adj.* errant, roving, wandering.

errar[28] *v. irr.* to err, make mistakes; to miss (*target, road*); to rove, wander.

errata *f.* misprint, printer's error.

erróneo *adj.* erroneous, mistaken, wrong, incorrect.

error *m.* error, fault, mistake.

eructar *v.* to belch.

eructo *m.* belch.

erudición *f.* erudition, learning.

erudito *adj.* erudite, scholarly, learned; *m.* scholar.

erupción *f.* eruption; outburst; rash.

esbelto *adj.* slender.

esbozar[9] *v.* to sketch, outline.

esbozo *m.* sketch, outline.

escabechar *v.* to pickle.

escabeche *m.* pickled fish; pickle (*solution for pickling*).

escabel *m.* stool; footstool.

escabrosidad *f.* roughness, unevenness; harshness; improper word or phrase.

escabroso *adj.* rough; rugged; scabrous, rather indecent.

escabullirse[20] *v. irr.* to slip away; to slip through; to scoot, scamper, scurry.

escala *f.* ladder; scale; port of call; stopover; **hacer — en** to stop over at; **escalafón** *m.* army register.

escalar *v.* to scale; to climb.

escaldar *v.* to scald; to make red-hot; **-se** to get scalded.

escalera *f.* stairs, staircase; ladder; — **mecánica** escalator.

escalfar *v.* to poach (*eggs*).

escalinata *f.* flight of stairs (*usually on the outside*).

escalofriarse[17] *v.* to become chilled.

escalofrío *m.* chill; **-s** chills and fever.

escalón *m.* step (*of a ladder or staircase*); stepping stone; *Am.* **-es** tribe of **quichua** Indians.

escalonar *v.* to echelon (*arrange in step-like formation*); to terrace; **-se** to rise in terraces.

escama *f.* scale, fish scale; flake.

escamoso *adj.* scaly.

escamotear *v.* to whisk out of sight; to steal or snatch away with cunning; to conceal by a trick or sleight of hand.

escandalizar[9] *v.* to scandalize, shock; **-se** to be shocked.

escándalo *m.* scandal; bad example.

escandaloso *adj.* scandalous, shocking; *Mex.*, *C.A.*, *Col.*, *Andes* showy, loud (*color*).

escapada *f.* escape, flight.

escapar *v.* to escape, flee, avoid; **-se** to run away, escape.

escaparate *m.* show window; glass case, glass cabinet or cupboard.

escapatoria *f.* escape, loophole, excuse.

escape *m.* escape; vent, outlet; exhaust; **a —** rapidly, at full speed.

escarabajo *m.* black beetle.

escaramuza *f.* skirmish; quarrel.

escarbar *v.* to scrape, scratch; to dig out; to pry into, investigate.

escarcear *v.* *Ch.*, *Ríopl.* to prance.

escarcha *f.* frost; frosting.

escarchar *v.* to frost; to freeze.

escardar *v.* to weed; to weed out.

escarlata *f.* scarlet; scarlet fever; scarlet cloth; **escarlatina** *f.* scarlet fever.

escarmentar[1] *v. irr.* to punish (*as an example or warning*); to profit by one's misfortunes, punishment, etc.; — **en cabeza ajena** to profit by another's mistake or misfortune.

escarmiento *m.* lesson, example, warning; punishment.

escarnecer[13] *v. irr.* to jeer, insult, mock.

escarnio *m.* scoff, jeer.

escarpa f. steep slope, bluff, cliff; scarp (of a fortification).

escarpado adj. steep; rugged.

escarpia f. hook (for hanging something).

escasear v. to be scarce; to grow less, become scarce; to stint.

escasez f. scarcity, lack, scantiness.

escaso adj. scarce, limited; scant; scanty; stingy.

escatimar v. to stint, skimp; to curtail.

escena f. scene; scenery; theatre, stage.

escenario m. stage.

escenificación f. dramatization, stage adaptation.

escepticismo m. scepticism; doubt, unbelief.

escéptico m. & adj. sceptic.

esclarecer[13] v. irr. to lighten, illuminate; to elucidate, make clear, explain.

esclarecimiento m. clarification, illumination, illustration; worth, nobility.

esclavitud f. slavery.

esclavizar[9] v. to enslave.

esclavo m. slave.

esclusa f. lock (of a canal); sluice, floodgate.

escoba f. broom.

escobazo m. blow with a broom.

escobilla f. whisk broom; small broom.

escocer[2,10] v. irr. to sting, smart.

escocés adj. Scotch; m. Scotch; Scotchman.

escoger[11] v. to choose, select, pick out.

escolar adj. scholastic, academic; m. scholar, student.

escolástico adj. & m. scholastic.

escolta f. escort; convoy.

escoltar v. to escort; to convoy.

escollo m. reef; danger; obstacle.

escombro m. debris, rubbish; mackerel.

esconder v. to hide, conceal; -se to hide, go into hiding.

escondidas: a — on the sly, under cover; Am. jugar a las — to play hide-and-seek.

escondite m. hiding place; Spain jugar al — to play hide-and-seek.

escondrijo m. hiding place.

escopeta f. shotgun.

escopetazo m. gunshot; gunshot wound; sudden bad news; Am. offensive or ironic remark.

escoplo m. chisel.

escoria f. slag; scum; **escorial** m. dump, dumping place; pile of slag.

escorpión m. scorpion.

escote m. low neck; **convite a —** Dutch treat (where everyone pays his share).

escotilla f. hatchway; **escotillón** m. hatch, hatchway; trap door.

escozor m. smarting sensation, sting.

escribano m. court clerk; lawyer's clerk; notary.

escribiente m. clerk, office clerk.

escribir[52] v. to write.

escrito p.p. of **escribir** written; m. writing, manuscript.

escritor m. writer.

escritorio m. desk; office.

escritura f. writing, handwriting; deed, document; **Sagrada Escritura** Holy Scripture.

escrúpulo m. scruple, doubt.

escrupuloso adj. scrupulous; particular, exact.

escrutador adj. scrutinizing, examining; peering; penetrating; m. scrutinizer, examiner; inspector of election returns.

escrutar v. to scrutinize.

escrutinio m. scrutiny, careful inspection.

escuadra f. squadron; fleet; square (instrument for drawing or testing right angles).

escuadrón m. squadron.

escualidez f. squalor.

escuálido adj. squalid, filthy; thin, emaciated.

escuchar v. to listen; to heed.

escudar v. to shield.

escudero m. squire.

escudo m. shield; escutcheon, coat of arms; gold crown (ancient coin); Am. Chilean gold coin.

escudriñar v. to scrutinize, search, pry into.

escuela f. school.

escuelante m. & f. Col. schoolboy; schoolgirl.

escueto adj. plain, unadorned, bare.

esculcar[6] v. Am. to search; Carib., Col., Ven. to frisk (a person's pockets).

esculpir v. to sculpture; to engrave.

escultor m. sculptor.

escultura f. sculpture.

escupidera f. cuspidor.

escupir v. to spit.

escurrir v. to drip; to drain; to trickle; -se to ooze out, trickle; to slip out, sneak out.

ese, esa dem. adj. that; **esos, esas** those; **ése, ésa** m., f. dem. pron. that one; **ésos, ésas** m., f. pl. those.

esencia f. essence.

esencial adj. essential.

esfera f. sphere; clock dial.

esférico adj. spherical.

esforzado adj. strong; valiant; courageous.

esforzar[2,9] v. irr. to give or inspire strength; to encourage; -se to make an effort; to strive, try hard.

esfuerzo m. effort; spirit, courage, vigor; stress.

esfumar v. to shade, tone down; -se to vanish, disappear.

esgrima f. fencing.

esgrimir v. to fence; to brandish; to wield (the sword or pen).

eslabón m. link of a chain; steel knife sharpener; black scorpion.

eslabonar v. to link; to join; to connect.

esmaltar v. to enamel; to beautify, adorn.

esmalte m. enamel; enamel work; smalt (a blue pigment).

esmerado adj. painstaking, careful, conscientious; p.p. of **esmerar.**

esmeralda *f.* emerald; *Am.* an eel-like fish; *Col.* hummingbird; *Mex.* variety of pineapple.

esmerar *v.* to polish, clean; **-se** to strive, take special pains, use great care.

esmero *m.* care, precision.

esmoquin *m.* tuxedo, dinner coat.

eso *dem. pron.* that, that thing, that fact; **— es** that is it; **a — de** at about (*referring to time*); *Am.* **¡eso!** that's right!

espaciar[17] *v.* to space; to spread; to expand; **-se** to enlarge (*upon a subject*); to relax, amuse oneself.

espacio *m.* space; interval; slowness, delay; *adv. Mex.* slowly.

espacioso *adj.* spacious; slow.

espada *f.* sword; skilled swordsman; matador (*bull-fighter who kills the bull*); **-s** swords (*Spanish card suit*).

espalda *f.* back, shoulders; **-s** back, back part; **a -s** behind one's back; **de -s** on one's back; **dar la — a** to turn one's back on; **espaldilla** *f.* shoulder blade.

espaldar *m.* back (*of a chair*); trellis (*for plants*); backplate of a cuirass (*armor*).

espantadizo *adj.* scary, shy, timid.

espantajo *m.* scarecrow.

espantapájaros *m.* scarecrow.

espantar *v.* to frighten, scare; to scare away; *Col.* to haunt; **-se** to be scared; to be astonished; *Mex.* **espantárselas** to be wide-awake, catch on quickly.

espanto *m.* fright, terror; astonishment; *Col., Ven., Mex.* ghost.

espantoso *adj.* frightful, terrifying; wonderful.

español *adj.* Spanish; *m.* Spaniard; Spanish language.

esparadrapo *m.* court plaster, adhesive tape. *See* **tela adhesiva.**

esparcir[10] *v.* to scatter, spread; **-se** to relax, amuse oneself.

espárrago *m.* asparagus.

esparto *m.* esparto grass (*used for making ropes, mats, etc.*).

espasmo *m.* spasm; horror.

espátula *f.* spatula.

especia *f.* spice.

especial *adj.* special; **en —** in particular, specially.

especialidad *f.* specialty.

especialista *m.* & *f.* specialist.

especializar[9] *v.* to specialize; **-se en** to specialize in.

especie *f.* species; kind, sort; pretext; idea.

especificar[6] *v.* to specify; to name.

específico *adj.* specific; *m.* specific (*medicine*).

espécimen *m.* specimen, sample.

espectacular *adj.* spectacular.

espectáculo *m.* spectacle.

espectador *m.* spectator.

espectro *m.* spectre, ghost; spectrum.

especulación *f.* speculation.

especulador *m.* speculator.

especular *v.* to speculate.

especulativo *adj.* speculative.

espejismo *m.* mirage; illusion.

espejo *m.* mirror; model; **— de cuerpo entero** full-length mirror.

espeluznante *adj.* hair-raising, terrifying.

espeluznarse *v.* to be terrified; to bristle with fear.

espera *f.* wait; stay (*granted by judge*), delay; extension of time (*for payment*); **sala de —** waiting room; **estar en — de** to be waiting for; to be expecting.

esperanza *f.* hope; expectation.

esperanzado *adj.* hopeful.

esperanzar[9] to give hope to.

esperar *v.* (*tener esperanza*) to hope; to expect; to trust; (*permanecer*) to wait, wait for; **— en alguien** to place hope or confidence in someone.

esperezarse = **desperezarse.**

esperpento *m.* ugly thing; nonsense.

espesar *v.* to thicken; to make dense; **-se** to thicken; to become thick or dense.

espeso *adj.* thick, dense; compact; slovenly; *Ríopl.* bothersome, boring.

espesor *m.* thickness.

espesura *f.* density, thickness; thicket; thickest part (*of a forest*).

espetar *v.* to spring (*a joke, story, etc.*) on (*a person*), surprise with (*a joke, speech, story, etc.*); to pop (*a question*); to run a spit through (*meat, fish, etc. for roasting*); to pierce; **-se** to be stiff, pompous.

espía *m.* & *f.* spy.

espiar[17] *v.* to spy; *Col., Mex.* **-se** to bruise the hoofs, get lame (*said of horses*).

espiga *f.* ear of wheat; peg; spike.

espigar[7] *v.* to glean; to grow spikes (*said of corn or grain*); **-se** to grow tall and slender.

espina *f.* thorn; sharp splinter; fish bone; spine; fear, suspicion; **darle a uno mala —** to arouse one's suspicion.

espinaca *f.* spinach.

espinazo *m.* spine, backbone.

espinilla *f.* shin (*front part of leg*); blackhead (*on the skin*).

espino *m.* hawthorn; thorny shrub; thorny branch.

espinoso *adj.* thorny; difficult, dangerous.

espionaje *m.* espionage, spying.

espiral *adj.* & *f.* spiral.

espirar *v.* to exhale; to emit, give off; to die. *See* **expirar.**

espíritu *m.* spirit; soul; courage; vigor; essence; ghost.

espiritual *adj.* spiritual.

espita *f.* spigot, faucet, tap; toper, drunkard.

esplendidez *f.* splendor.

espléndido *adj.* splendid.

esplendor *m.* splendor.

esplendoroso *adj.* resplendent, shining.

espliego *m.* lavender (*plant*).

espolear *v.* to spur; to incite.

espoleta *f.* bomb fuse.
espolón *m.* spur (*on a cock's leg*); ram (*of a boat*); spur; buttress.
espolvorear *v.* to powder, sprinkle with powder.
esponja *f.* sponge; sponger, parasite; Col., Peru, Ch., Riopl. souse, habitual drunkard.
esponjado *adj.* fluffy; spongy; puffed up; *p.p.* of **esponjar**.
esponjar *v.* to fluff; to make spongy or porous; **-se** to fluff up; to become spongy or porous; to swell, puff up; to puff up with pride.
esponjoso *adj.* spongy.
esponsales *m. pl.* betrothal.
espontaneidad *f.* spontaneity, ease, naturalness.
espontáneo *adj.* spontaneous.
esposa *f.* wife; **-s** handcuffs.
esposo *m.* husband.
espuela *f.* spur.
espulgar[7] *v.* to delouse, remove lice or fleas from; to scrutinize.
espuma *f.* foam, froth; scum; **— de jabón** suds.
espumar *v.* to skim; to froth, foam.
espumarajo *m.* froth, foam (*from the mouth*); **echar -s** to froth at the mouth; to be very angry.
espumoso *adj.* foamy.
esputo *m.* sputum, spit, saliva.
esquela *f.* note, letter; announcement.
esqueleto *m.* skeleton; carcass; framework; Mex., C.A., Col., Ven. blank (*to fill out*); Am. outline.
esquema *f.* scheme, outline.
esquí *m.* ski, skiing; **— náutico, — acuático** water ski.
esquiar[17] *v.* to ski.
esquila *f.* small bell; cow bell; sheep-shearing.
esquilar *v.* to shear; to clip; to crop.
esquina *f.* corner, angle; **esquinazo** *m.* corner; Am. serenade; **dar esquinazo** to avoid meeting someone; to "ditch" someone.
esquivar *v.* to avoid, dodge; to shun; **-se** to withdraw, shy away.
esquivez *f.* shyness; aloofness; disdain.
esquivo *adv.* reserved, unsociable; shy; disdainful, aloof.
estabilidad *f.* stability.
estable *adj.* stable, firm, steady.
establecer[13] *v. irr.* to establish; to found; to decree, ordain.
establecimiento *m.* establishment; foundation; statute, law.
establo *m.* stable; **establero** *m.* groom.
estaca *f.* stake, club; stick; picket.
estacada *f.* stockade; picket fence; Am. predicament.
estacar[6] *v.* to stake; to tie to a stake; to stake off, mark with stakes; Am. to fasten down with stakes; **-se** to remain stiff or rigid.
estación *f.* station; season; railway station.
estacionar *v.* to station; to place; to park (*a car*); **-se** to remain stationary; to park.

estacionario *adj.* stationary; motionless.
estada *f.* sojourn, stay.
estadía *f.* detention, stay; stay in port (*beyond time allowed for loading and unloading*); C.A., Carib. sojourn, stay (*in any sense*).
estadio *m.* stadium.
estadista *m.* statesman.
estadística *f.* statistics.
estado *m.* state, condition; station, rank; estate; **— mayor** army staff; **hombre de —** statesman; Am. **en — interesante** pregnant.
estadounidense *adj.* from the United States, American.
estafa *f.* swindle, fraud, trick.
estafador *m.* swindler, crook.
estafar *v.* to swindle, defraud, cheat.
estallar *v.* to explode, burst; to creak, crackle.
estallido *m.* explosion, outburst; crash; creaking; crack (*of a gun*), report (*of a gun or cannon*).
estambre *m.* woolen yarn; stamen (*of a flower*).
estampa *f.* image; print; stamp; cut, picture; footprint; figure, appearance.
estampado *m.* print, printed fabric; printing.
estampar *v.* to stamp, print.
estampida *f.* crack, sharp sound; Col., Ven., C.A. stampede (*sudden scattering of a herd of cattle or horses*).
estampido *m.* crack, sharp sound; report of a gun.
estampilla *f.* stamp, seal; Mex., C.A., Andes postage stamp.
estancar[6] *v.* to stem; to stanch; to stop the flow of; to corner (*a market*); **-se** to stagnate, become stagnant.
estancia *f.* (*permanencia*) stay (*lugar*) hall, room; mansion; Riopl. farm, cattle ranch; Carib. main building of a farm or ranch,
estanciero *m.* Riopl. rancher, ranchowner, cattle raiser; *adj.* pertaining to an **estancia**.
estanco *m.* monopoly; government store (*for sale of monopolized goods such as tobacco, stamps and matches*); tank, reservoir; Ec., C.A. liquor store.
estándar *m.* Am. standard, norm.
estandardizar, estandarizar[9] *v.* Am. to standardize.
estandarte *m.* standard, flag, banner.
estanque *m.* pond, pool, reservoir.
estanquillo *m.* tobacco store; Am. small store; C.A., Mex. small liquor store, tavern.
estante *m.* shelf; bookshelf; Am. prop, support; **estantería** *f.* shelves; bookcases.
estaño *m.* tin.
estaquilla *f.* peg; spike.
estar[29] *v. irr.* to be; **-le bien a uno** to be becoming to one; **— de prisa** to be in a hurry; **¿a cuántos estamos?** what day of the month is it today?; **-se** to keep, remain.

estático *adj.* static; **estática** *f.* statics; radio static.

estatua *f.* statue.

estatura *f.* stature, height.

estatuto *m.* statute.

este, esta *dem. adj.* this; **estos, estas** these; **éste, ésta** *m., f. dem. pron.* this one, this thing; the latter; **esto** this, this thing; **éstos, éstas** *m., f. pl.* these; the latter.

este *m.* east; east wind.

estela *f.* wake of a ship.

estenógrafo *m.* stenographer.

estentóreo *adj.* loud, thundering (*voice*).

estepa *f.* steppe, treeless plain.

estera *f.* matting; mat.

estercolar *v.* to manure, fertilize with manure.

estercolero *m.* manure pile, manure dump; manure collector.

estereoscopio *m.* stereoscope.

estereotipo *m.* stereotype.

estéril *adj.* sterile, barren.

esterilidad *f.* sterility, barrenness.

esterilizar⁹ *v.* to sterilize.

esterlina *adj.* sterling; **libra —** pound sterling.

estero *m.* estuary.

estertor *m.* death-rattle; snort.

estético *adj.* aesthetic; **estética** *f.* aesthetics.

estetoscopio *m.* stethoscope.

estibador *m.* stevedore, longshoreman.

estibar *v.* to stow (*in a boat*); to pack down, compress.

estiércol *m.* manure; fertilizer.

estigma *m.* stigma; brand, mark of disgrace; birthmark.

estilar *v.* to use, be accustomed to using; **-se** to be in style (*said of clothes*).

estilete *m.* stiletto, narrow-bladed dagger; stylet (*instrument for probing wounds*); long, narrow sword.

estilo *m.* style; fashion.

estima *f.* esteem.

estimación *f.* esteem, regard; valuation.

estimar *v.* to esteem, regard highly; to estimate, appraise; to judge, think.

estimulante *adj.* stimulant, stimulating; *m.* stimulant.

estimular *v.* to stimulate, excite, goad.

estímulo *m.* stimulation, incitement; stimulus.

estío *m.* summer.

estipulación *f.* stipulation, specification, provision, proviso.

estipular *v.* to stipulate, specify.

estirado *p.p. & adj.* stretched; extended, drawn out; stuck-up, conceited.

estirar *v.* to stretch, extend; **— la pata** to die; **-se** to stretch out; *Am.* to die.

estirón *m.* hard pull, tug; stretch; **dar un —** to grow suddenly (*said of a child*).

estirpe *f.* lineage, family, race.

estival *adj.* summer, relating to the summer.

estocada *f.* thrust, stab; stab wound.

estofa *f.* stuff, cloth; class, quality; **gente de baja —** low class people, rabble.

estofado *m.* stew, stewed meat; *p.p. of* **estofar.**

estofar *v.* to quilt; to stew.

estoico *adj. & m.* stoic.

estola *f.* stole; **— de visón** mink wrap.

estómago *m.* stomach.

estopa *f.* burlap; oakum (*loose fiber of old ropes*).

estoque *m.* long, narrow sword.

estorbar *v.* to hinder; to obstruct.

estorbo *m.* hindrance; nuisance, bother.

estornudar *v.* to sneeze.

estornudo *m.* sneeze.

estrado *m.* dais (*platform for a throne, seats of honor, etc.*); main part of a parlor or drawing room.

estragado *p.p. & adj.* corrupted; spoiled; ruined; tired, worn out.

estragar⁷ *v.* to corrupt, contaminate; to spoil; to ruin.

estrago *m.* havoc, ruin; massacre.

estrangulador *m.* strangler, choke (*of an automobile*); *adj.* strangling.

estrangular *v.* to strangle; to choke, throttle.

estratagema *f.* stratagem, scheme.

estrategia *f.* strategy.

estratégico *adj.* strategic; *m.* strategist, person trained or skilled in strategy.

estrato *m.* stratum, layer (*of mineral*).

estratorreactor *m.* supersonic jet plane.

estratosfera *f.* stratosphere.

estrechar *v.* to tighten; to narrow down; to embrace, hug; **— la mano** to squeeze, grasp another's hand; to shake hands.

estrechez, estrechura *f.* narrowness, tightness; austerity; dire straits; poverty; closeness.

estrecho *adj.* narrow; tight; *m.* strait, narrow passage.

estrella *f.* star; **— de mar** starfish.

estrellado *adj.* starry; spangled with stars; **huevos -s** fried eggs.

estrellar *v.* to shatter; to dash to pieces; to star, spangle with stars; **-se** to shatter, break into pieces; to fail.

estremecer¹³ *v. irr.* to shake; **-se** to shiver, shudder; to vibrate.

estremecimiento *m.* shiver, shudder; vibration; shaking.

estrenar *v.* to wear for the first time; to perform (*a play*) for the first time; to inaugurate; to begin.

estreno *m.* début, first appearance or performance.

estreñimiento *m.* constipation.

estreñir⁵,¹⁹ *v. irr.* to constipate; **-se** to become constipated.

estrépito *m.* racket, noise, crash.

estrepitoso *adj.* noisy; boisterous.

estriado *p.p. & adj.* fluted, grooved; streaked.

estriar¹⁷ *v.* to groove; to flute (*as a column*).

estribación *f.* spur (*of a mountain or mountain range*).

estribar *v.* to rest (upon); **eso estriba en que ...** the basis or reason for it is that ...

estribillo *m.* refrain.

estribo *m.* (*de caballo o vehículo*) stirrup; footboard, running board; (*apoyo*) support; brace; spur (*of a mountain*); **perder los -s** to lose one's balance; to lose control of oneself.

estribor *m.* starboard.

estricto *adj.* strict.

estrofa *f.* strophe, stanza.

estropajo *m.* fibrous mass (*for scrubbing*); **tratar a uno como un —** to treat someone scornfully.

estropear *v.* to spoil, ruin, damage; to cripple.

estructura *f.* structure.

estructural *adj.* structural.

estruendo *m.* clatter; clamor, din, racket.

estruendoso *adj.* thunderous, uproarious, deafening.

estrujamiento *m.* crushing, squeezing.

estrujar *v.* to squeeze, press, crush.

estrujón *m.* squeeze, crush; smashing.

estuario *m.* estuary.

estuco *m.* stucco.

estuche *m.* jewel box; instrument case, kit; small casket; sheath.

estudiantado *m.* the student body (*of a school or college*).

estudiante *m.* & *f.* student.

estudiar *v.* to study.

estudio *m.* study; studio.

estudioso *adj.* studious; *m.* learner.

estufa *f.* heater; stove; hothouse; steam room; steam cabinet.

estupefacto *adj.* stunned; speechless.

estupendo *adj.* stupendous, marvelous.

estupidez *f.* stupidity.

estúpido *adj.* stupid.

etapa *f.* stage, lap (*of a journey or race*); army food rations; epoch, period.

éter *m.* ether.

etéreo *adj.* ethereal; heavenly.

eternidad *f.* eternity.

eternizar[9] *v.* to prolong excessively; to perpetuate, make eternal.

eterno *adj.* eternal, everlasting.

ética *f.* ethics; **ético** *adj.* ethical, moral.

etiqueta *f.* etiquette; formality; tag; **de —** formal (*dress, function, etc.*).

eucalipto *m.* eucalyptus.

europeo *adj.* & *m.* European.

evacuación *f.* evacuation; bowel movement.

evacuar[18] *v.* to evacuate, empty; to vacate.

evadir *v.* to evade, elude; **-se** to slip away, escape.

evaluar[18] *v.* to evaluate, appraise.

evangelio *m.* gospel.

evaporar *v.* to evaporate; **-se** to evaporate; to vanish, disappear.

evasión *f.* evasion, dodge, escape.

evasiva *f.* evasion, dodge, escape.

evasivo *adj.* evasive.

evasor *m.* evader, dodger.

evento *m.* event.

evidencia *f.* evidence.

evidenciar *v.* to prove, show, make evident.

evidente *adj.* evident.

evitable *adj.* avoidable.

evitar *v.* to avoid, shun.

evocar[6] *v.* to evoke, call forth.

evolución *f.* evolution.

evolucionar *v.* to evolve; to perform maneuvers; to go through changes.

exacerbar *v.* to exasperate, irritate; to aggravate, make worse.

exactitud *f.* exactness, precision; punctuality.

exacto *adj.* exact, precise; punctual.

exagerar *v.* to exaggerate.

exaltación *f.* exaltation; excitement.

exaltado *adj.* elated; excited; hotheaded.

exaltar *v.* to exalt, elevate, glorify; to praise; **-se** to get excited; to become upset emotionally.

examen *m.* examination; inspection.

examinar *v.* to examine; to inspect.

exangüe *adj.* lacking blood; anemic; exhausted.

exánime *adj.* lifeless, motionless; weak, faint.

exasperar *v.* to exasperate, irritate, annoy.

excavar *v.* to excavate, dig, dig out.

excedente *m.* surplus; *adj.* exceeding, extra.

exceder *v.* to exceed, surpass; to overdo; **-se** to go beyond the proper limit; to misbehave.

excelencia *f.* excellence, superiority; excellency (*title*).

excelente *adj.* excellent.

excelso *adj.* lofty, elevated; sublime; **El Excelso** the Most High.

excéntrico *adj.* eccentric; queer, odd.

excepción *f.* exception.

excepcional *adj.* exceptional, unusual.

excepto *adv.* except, with the exception of.

exceptuar[18] *v.* to except.

excesivo *adj.* excessive.

exceso *m.* excess; crime; **— de equipaje** excess baggage; **en —** in excess, excessively.

excitación *f.* excitement.

excitante *adj.* exciting; stimulating.

excitar *v.* to excite, stir; **-se** to get excited.

exclamación *f.* exclamation.

exclamar *v.* to exclaim.

excluir[32] *v. irr.* to exclude.

exclusivo *adj.* exclusive.

excomunicar[6] *v.* to excommunicate.

excomunión *f.* excommunication.

excrecencia, excrescencia *f.* excrescence (*abnormal growth or tumor*).

excremento *m.* excrement.

excursión *f.* excursion, tour, outing.

excusa *f.* excuse.

excusado *p.p.* & *adj.* excused; exempt; superfluous; unnecessary; reserved; private; *m.* toilet.

ES

excusar v. (disculpar) to excuse; to exempt; (evitar) to avoid, shun; **-se** to excuse oneself, apologize; to decline.

exención f. exemption.

exentar v. to exempt. See **eximir**.

exento adj. exempt, freed; free, unobstructed.

exequias f. pl. obsequies, funeral rites.

exhalar v. to exhale; to emit, give off; to breathe forth; **-se** to evaporate; to run away.

exhibición f. exhibition; exposition; Mex. payment of an installment.

exhibir v. to exhibit; Mex. to pay for in installments (stocks, policies, etc.); **-se** to exhibit oneself, show off.

exhortar v. to exhort, admonish.

exigencia f. demand; urgent want; emergency.

exigente adj. demanding, exacting; urgent.

exigir[11] v. to require; to demand; to exact.

exiguo adj. scanty, meager.

eximio adj. very distinguished.

eximir v. to exempt, except, excuse; **-se de** to avoid, shun.

existencia f. existence; **-s** stock on hand, goods; **en —** in stock, on hand.

existente adj. existent, existing; in stock.

existir v. to exist.

éxito m. outcome, result; success; **tener buen (mal) —** to be successful (unsuccessful).

éxodo m. exodus, emigration.

exonerar v. to exonerate, free from blame; to relieve of a burden or position; to dismiss.

exorbitante adj. exorbitant, excessive, extravagant.

exótico adj. exotic, foreign, strange; quaint.

expansión f. expansion; relaxation; recreation.

expansivo adj. expansive; demonstrative, effusive.

expatriar v. to expatriate, exile; **-se** to expatriate oneself, renounce one's citizenship; to emigrate.

expectación f. expectation.

expectativa f. expectation; hope, prospect; **estar en — de algo** to be expecting, or on the lookout for, something.

expectorar v. to expectorate, cough up.

expedición f. expedition; dispatch, promptness; papal dispatch or bull.

expedicionario adj. expeditionary; m. member of an expedition; explorer.

expediente m. certificate; papers pertaining to a business matter; expedient, means; dispatch, promptness.

expedir[5] v. irr. to dispatch; to issue officially; to remit, send.

expeler v. to expel, eject.

experiencia f. experience; experiment.

experimentado adj. & p.p. experienced.

experimental adj. experimental.

experimentar v. to experiment, try, test; to experience, feel.

experimento m. experiment, trial.

experto adj. expert, skillful; m. expert.

expiación f. expiation, atonement.

expiar[17] v. to atone for; to make amends for; to purify.

expirar v. to die; to expire, come to an end.

explayar v. to extend; **-se** to become extended; to relax in the open air; to enlarge upon a subject; **-se con un amigo** to unbosom oneself, speak with utmost frankness with a friend.

explicable adj. explainable.

explicación f. explanation.

explicar[6] v. to explain; **— una cátedra** to teach a course; **-se** to explain oneself; to account for one's conduct.

explicativo adj. explanatory, explaining.

explícito adj. explicit, express, clear, definite.

exploración f. exploration.

explorador m. explorer, scout; adj. exploring.

explorar v. to explore.

explosión f. explosion.

explosivo adj. & m. explosive.

explotación f. exploitation; operation of a mine; development of a business; plant.

explotar v. to exploit, operate, develop; to utilize, profit by; to make unfair use of; Am. to explode.

exponer[40] v. irr. (dejar ver) to expose, reveal; to show, exhibit; to display; (sin protección) to leave unprotected, to expose (film); (explicar) to expound; to explain; **-se a** to expose oneself to; to run the risk of.

exportación f. exportation; export.

exportar v. to export.

exposición f. exposition; exhibition; explanation; exposure.

exprés m. Am. express; Am. express company.

expresar v. to express; **-se** to express oneself, speak.

expresión f. expression; utterance; **-es** regards.

expresivo adj. expressive; affectionate.

expreso adj. expressed; express, clear, exact; fast; m. express train.

exprimir v. to squeeze, extract (juice); to wring out; to express, utter.

expuesto p.p. of **exponer** & adj. exposed; expressed; displayed; risky, dangerous; **lo —** what has been said.

expulsar v. to expel, eject.

expulsión f. expulsion, expelling.

exquisitez f. exquisiteness.

exquisito adj. exquisite.

extasiado adj. rapt, in ecstasy; p.p. of **extasiar**.

extasiar[17] v. to delight; **-se** to be in ecstasy; to be entranced.

éxtasis m. ecstasy.

extender[1] v. irr. to extend; to spread; to unfold; to draw up (a document); **-se** to extend, spread; to expatiate, be too wordy.

extensión f. extension; extent; expanse; expansion.

extensivo adj. extensive.

extenso p.p. irr. of **extender** extended; adj. extensive, vast, spacious; **por —** extensively, in detail.

extenuado adj. wasted, weak, emaciated.

exterior adj. exterior, outer; m. exterior; outside; outward appearance.

exterminar v. to exterminate.

exterminio m. extermination, destruction.

externo adj. external, outward.

extinguir[12] v. to extinguish, put out; to destroy.

extinto adj. extinct.

extintor m. extinguisher; **— de espuma** fire extinguisher.

extirpar v. to eradicate, pull out by the roots, root out; remove completely; to destroy completely.

extorsión f. extortion.

extorsionar v. Am. to extort, extract money, blackmail.

extorsionista m. Am. extortioner, profiteer, racketeer.

extracto m. extract; abstract, summary.

extraer[46] v. irr. to extract.

extranjero adj. foreign; m. foreigner.

extrañamiento m. wonder, surprise, amazement.

extrañar v. to wonder at; to banish; Am. to miss (a person or thing); **-se** to marvel, be astonished.

extrañeza f. strangeness; surprise, astonishment; oddity, odd thing.

extraño adj. strange; rare; odd; m. stranger.

extraordinario adj. extraordinary.

extravagancia f. extravagance; folly.

extravagante adj. extravagant, fantastic; queer, odd.

extraviar[17] v. to lead astray; to strand; to misplace; **-se** to lose one's way; to get stranded; to get lost; to miss the road.

extravío m. deviation, straying; error; misconduct; damage.

extremado adj. extreme; extremely good or extremely bad; p.p. of **extremar.**

extremar v. to carry to an extreme; **-se** to take great pains, exert great effort.

extremidad f. extremity; extreme degree; remotest part; **-es** extremities, hands and feet.

extremo adj. extreme; last; farthest; excessive; utmost; m. extreme, highest degree or point; end, extremity; extreme care; **con (en** or **por) —** very much, extremely.

exuberante adj. exuberant; luxuriant.

F

a m. fourth note of the musical scale (solfa syllables).

ábrica f. manufacture; factory, mill; structure.

abricación f. manufacture.

fabricante m. manufacturer, maker.

fabricar[6] v. to manufacture, make; to construct, build; to fabricate, make up, invent.

fabril adj. manufacturing.

fábula f. fable, tale; falsehood.

fabuloso adj. fabulous; false, imaginary.

facción f. faction, band, party; battle; **-es** features; **estar de —** to be on duty.

faceto adj. Am. cute, funny; Am. affected.

fácil adj. easy; docile, yielding, manageable; likely; probable.

facilidad f. facility, ease; opportunity.

facilitar v. to facilitate, make easy; to furnish, give; **— todos los datos** to furnish all the data.

facón- m. Ríopl., Bol. dagger, large knife; **faconazo** m. Ríopl., Bol. stab.

factible adj. feasible.

factor m. factor; element, joint cause; commercial agent; baggage man.

factoría f. trading post; Am. factory.

factura f. (cuenta) invoice, itemized bill; (hechura) make; workmanship, form; Am. roll, biscuit, muffin; **—simulada** temporary invoice, memorandum.

facturar v. to invoice, bill; to check (baggage).

facultad f. faculty; ability, aptitude; power, right; permission; branch of learning; school or college of a university.

facultativo m. doctor, physician.

facundia f. eloquence, fluency, facility in speaking; gift of expression.

facha f. appearance, figure, aspect, looks.

fachada f. façade, front (of a building); title page.

fachenda f. ostentation, vanity.

fachendoso adj. vain, boastful, ostentatious.

faena f. task, job, duty; Carib., Mex., C.A. extra job; Ch. work crew, labor gang.

faja f. sash; girdle; band; Am. belt, waist band.

fajar v. to girdle; to bind, wrap, or bandage with a strip of cloth; Am. to beat, strike, thrash; Am. **— un latigazo a uno** to whip, thrash someone; **-se** to put on a sash or belt; to tighten one's sash or belt; Am. **-se con** to have a fight with, come to blows with.

fajo m. bundle; sheaf.

falaz adj. illusive, illusory; deceitful, deceiving.

falda f. skirt; lap; hat brim; foothill, slope; **faldón** m. coattail; shirttail.

faldear v. to skirt (a hill).

falsario m. crook, forger; liar.

falsear v. to falsify, misrepresent; to counterfeit; to forge; to pick (a lock); to flag, grow weak; to hit a wrong note.

falsedad f. falsehood, lie; deceit.

falsificación f. falsification, forgery; counterfeit.

falsificar[6] *v.* to falsify, make false; to counterfeit; to forge.

falso *adj.* false; untrue, unreal; deceitful; counterfeit; sham; *C.A.* cowardly; *m.* inside facing of a dress; lining; *Mex.* false testimony, slander; **en —** upon a false foundation; without proper security; *Am.* **coger a uno en —** to catch one lying.

falta *f.* (*defecto*) lack, want; fault, mistake; defect; absence; (*infracción*) misdemeanor, offense; **a — de** for want of; **hacer —** to be necessary; to be missing; **me hace —** I need it; **sin —** without fail.

faltar *v.* to be lacking, wanting; to be absent or missing; to fail, be of no use or help; to fail to fulfill (*a promise or duty*); to die; *Mex.*, *C.A.* to insult; **— poco para las cinco** to be almost five o'clock; **¡no faltaba más!** that's the last straw!; why, the very idea!

falto *adj.* lacking; deficient, short; *Am.* foolish, stupid.

faltriquera *f.* pocket.

falla *f.* fault, defect; failure; fault (*fracture in the earth's crust*); *Riopl.* baby's bonnet.

fallar *v.* (*juzgar*) to render a verdict; (*fracasar*) to fail, be deficient; to default; to miss; to fail to hit; to give way, break; to trump.

fallecer[13] *v. irr.* to die.

fallecimiento *m.* decease, death.

fallido *adj.* frustrated; bankrupt.

fallo *m.* verdict, judgment; decision; *adj.* lacking (*a card, or suit, in card games*); *Ch.* silly, foolish.

fama *f.* fame, reputation; rumor, report; *Ch.* bull's-eye, center of a target.

famélico *adj.* ravenous, hungry, starved.

familia *f.* family.

familiar *adj.* domestic, homelike; familiar, well-known; friendly, informal; colloquial (*phrase or expression*); *m.* intimate friend; member of a household; domestic servant; familiar spirit, demon; *Am.* relative.

familiaridad *f.* familiarity, informality.

familiarizar[9] *v.* to familiarize, acquaint; **-se** to acquaint oneself, become familiar (with).

famoso *adj.* famous; excellent.

fanal *m.* beacon, lighthouse; lantern; headlight; bell jar, glass cover.

fanático *adj.* & *m.* fanatic.

fanatismo *m.* fanaticism.

fanega *f.* Spanish bushel; **— de tierra** land measure (*variable according to region*).

fanfarrón *m.* braggart, boaster; bluffer.

fanfarronada *f.* boast, brag, swagger, bluff.

fanfarronear *v.* to bluff, brag; to swagger.

fango *m.* mud, mire.

fangoso *adj.* muddy, miry.

fantasear *v.* to fancy; to imagine.

fantasía *f.* fantasy, imagination, fancy, whim; **-s** string of pearls; *Ven.* **tocar por —** to play by ear.

fantasma *m.* phantom, image; vision, ghost; *f.* scarecrow.

fantasmagórico *adj.* fantastic, unreal, illusory.

fantástico *adj.* fantastic.

fardel *m.* knapsack, bag; bundle.

fardo *m.* bundle; bale; *Riopl.*, *Andes* **pasar el —** to "pass the buck", shift the responsibility to someone else.

faringe *f.* pharynx.

faríngeo *adj.* pharyngeal.

farmacéutico *m.* pharmacist, druggist; *adj.* pharmaceutical (*pertaining to a pharmacy or pharmacists*).

farmacia *f.* pharmacy; drugstore.

faro *m.* lighthouse; beacon; *Am.* headlight.

farol *m.* (*linterna*) lantern; street lamp; (*fachendoso*) conceit, self-importance; *Riopl.* balcony; *Am.* presumptuous man; *Am.* bluff; **darse —** to show off; to put on airs.

farola *f.* street light; lamppost.

farolero *adj.* vain, ostentatious; *m.* lamp maker or vendor; lamplighter (*person*).

farra *f.* *Riopl.*, *Ch.*, *Col.*, *Ven.*, *Andes* spree, revelry, wild party, noisy merrymaking; *Riopl.*, *Ch.*, *Col.*, *Ven.*, *Andes* **ir de —** to go on a spree.

farsa *f.* farce; company of actors; sham, fraud.

farsante *m.* charlatan, bluffer; quack comedian; wag.

fascinación *f.* fascination; glamour.

fascinador *adj.* fascinating, glamorous, charming.

fascinar *v.* to fascinate, bewitch, charm; to allure.

fase *f.* phase, aspect.

fastidiar *v.* to annoy, bother; to bore; *Col.*, *P.R.* to hurt, harm, ruin.

fastidio *m.* boredom; disgust; nuisance; annoyance.

fastidioso *adj.* annoying, bothersome, boring, tiresome.

fatal *adj.* fatal; mortal, deadly; unfortunate.

fatalidad *f.* fatality, destiny; calamity, misfortune.

fatiga *f.* fatigue, weariness; toil; **-s** hardships.

fatigar[7] *v.* to fatigue, weary; to bother.

fatigoso *adj.* fatiguing, tiring.

fatuo *adj.* foolish, stupid; vain; **fuego —** will-o'-the-wisp.

favor *m.* favor; kindness; help, aid; protection; *Am.* ribbon bow; **a — de** in favor of; **hágame el —** please.

favorable *adj.* favorable.

favorecer[13] *v. irr.* to favor, help, protect.

favoritismo *m.* favoritism.

favorito *adj.* & *m.* favorite.

faz *f.* face.

fe *f.* faith; **— de bautismo** baptismal certificate.

fealdad *f.* ugliness, homeliness; foulness, foul or immoral action.

febrero *m.* February.

febril *adj.* feverish.
fécula *f.* starch.
fecundar *v.* to fertilize.
fecundo *adj.* fruitful, fertile, productive.
fecha *f.* date.
fechar *v.* to date.
fechoría *f.* misdeed, misdemeanor.
federación *f.* federation, union.
federal *adj.* federal.
felicidad *f.* happiness; ¡-es! congratulations!
felicitación *f.* congratulation.
felicitar *v.* to congratulate.
feligrés *m.* parishioner.
feliz *adj.* happy; lucky.
felpudo *adj.* plushy, like plush; *m.* small plushlike mat; door mat.
femenil *adj.* womanly, feminine.
femenino *adj.* feminine.
fementido *adj.* false; treacherous.
fenecer[13] *v. irr.* to die; to finish, end.
fénico *adj.* carbolic; **acido —** carbolic acid.
fénix *m.* phoenix (*mythical bird*).
fenómeno *m.* phenomenon.
feo *adj.* ugly, homely; *Am.* bad (*referring to taste or odor*); **feote** *adj.* hideous, very ugly.
féretro *m.* bier; coffin.
feria *f.* fair; market; *Mex.* change (*money*); *Am.* tip; **-s** *Am.* present given to servants or the poor during holidays.
feriante *m. & f.* trader at fairs; trader; peddler.
fermentar *v.* to ferment.
fermento *m.* ferment; yeast, leaven.
ferocidad *f.* ferocity, fierceness.
feroz *adj.* ferocious, wild, fierce.
férreo *adj.* ferrous (*pertaining to or derived from iron*); ironlike; harsh; **vía férrea** railroad.
ferretería *f.* hardware shop; hardware.
ferrocarril *m.* railroad.
ferroviario *adj.* railway, railroad (*used as adj.*); *m.* railroad man; railroad employee.
fértil *adj.* fertile, productive; **fertilidad** *f.* fertility.
fertilizar[9] *v.* to fertilize.
ferviente *adj.* fervent, ardent.
fervor *m.* fervor, zeal, devotion.
fervoroso *adj.* fervent, ardent; pious, devout; zealous.
festejar *v.* to feast, entertain; to celebrate; to woo; *Mex.* to thrash, beat.
festejo *m.* entertainment, festival, celebration; courtship; *Am.* revelry.
festín *m.* feast; banquet.
festividad *f.* festival; holiday; holy day; festivity, gaiety, rejoicing.
festivo *adj.* festive, gay; **día —** holiday.
fétido *adj.* foul, foul-smelling.
fiado *p.p.* of **fiar; al —** on credit.
fiador *m.* guarantor, backer, bondsman; *Ec.,* *Ch.* chin strap, hat guard.
fiambre *m.* cold meat; cold or late news; *Ríopl., Mex., Col., Ven.* cold meat salad; *Am.* flop, failure (*referring to a party*).

fianza *f.* bond, security, surety, guarantee; bail.
fiar[17] *v.* to trust; to guarantee, back; *Am.* to borrow on credit; **-se de** to place confidence in.
fibra *f.* fiber; **fibroso** *adj.* fibrous.
ficción *f.* fiction.
ficticio *adj.* fictitious.
ficha *f.* (*pieza*) chip; token; domino; (*tarjeta*) file card; *Am.* check (*used in barbershops and stores*); *Am.* rascal, scamp; **fichero** *m.* file, card index, filing cabinet.
fidedigno *adj.* trustworthy, reliable.
fidelidad *f.* fidelity, faithfulness.
fideo *m.* vermicelli, thin noodle; thin person.
fiebre *f.* fever; excitement, agitation; *Ch.* astute person.
fiel *adj.* faithful; true, accurate; *m.* public inspector; pointer of a balance or scale; pin of the scissors; **los -es** the worshipers, the congregation.
fieltro *m.* felt; felt hat; felt rug.
fiera *f.* wild beast; *Am.* go-getter, hustler; **ser una — para el trabajo** to be a demon for work.
fiereza *f.* ferocity, fierceness; cruelty; ugliness.
fiero *adj.* fierce, ferocious, wild; cruel; ugly, horrible; huge; *m.* threat; **echar** (*or* **hacer**) **-s** to threaten; to boast.
fierro *m.* *Am.* iron; *Am.* iron bar; *Am.* cattle brand; **-s** *Am.* tools, implements. *See* **hierro.**
fiesta *f.* festivity, celebration, entertainment; holiday; **estar de —** to be in a holiday mood; **hacer -s a uno** to fawn on a person.
fiestero *adj.* fond of parties, fond of entertaining; gay, festive; playful; *m.* merrymaker.
figón *m.* cheap eating house, "joint."
figura *f.* figure; shape, form; countenance; face card.
figurado *adj.* figurative.
figurar *v.* to figure; to form; to represent, symbolize; **-se** to imagine; **se me figura** I think, guess, or imagine.
figurín *m.* fashion plate; dandy.
fijar *v.* to fix, fasten; to establish; **-se** to settle; **-se en** to notice, pay attention to.
fijeza *f.* firmness, solidity, steadiness.
fijo *adj.* fixed; firm; secure.
fila *f.* row, tier; rank.
filamento *m.* filament.
filete *m.* (*moldura*) edge, rim; (*carne*) fillet, tenderloin; (*freno*) snaffle bit (*for horses*); hem; screw thread.
filial *adj.* filial.
filmar *v.* to film, screen (*a play or novel*).
filo *m.* cutting edge; *Andes* hunger; **por — exactly;** *Am.* **de —** resolutely.
filón *m.* seam, layer (*of metallic ore*).
filoso *adj.* *Am.* sharp, sharp-edged.
filosofía *f.* philosophy.
filosófico *adj.* philosophic, philosophical.
filósofo *m.* philosopher.

filtrar v. to filter; **-se** to leak through, leak out; to filter.

filtro m. filter.

filudo adj. Am. sharp, sharp-edged.

fin m. end, ending; purpose; **al — at** last; **al — y al cabo** at last; anyway; in the end; **a — de que** so that; **a -es del mes** toward the end of the month; **en —** in conclusion; well; in short.

finado m. the deceased.

final adj. final.

finalizar[9] v. to finish; to end.

financiamiento m. Am. financing.

financiar v. Am. to finance.

financiero adj. financial; m. financier.

financista m. Am. financier.

finanza f. Am. finance; **-s** Am. public treasury, government funds.

finca f. real estate; property; country house; Am. ranch, farm.

fincar v. to buy real estate; Am. to rest (on), be based (on); Am. to build a farmhouse or country house.

fineza f. fineness; nicety; courtesy; favor, kindness; present.

fingimiento m. pretense, sham.

fingir[11] v. to feign, pretend, fake; to imagine.

finiquito m. settlement (of an account); quittance, final receipt; **dar —** to finish up.

fino adj. fine; nice; delicate; sharp; subtle; refined.

finura f. fineness; nicety; subtlety; courtesy, good manners.

fiordo m. fjord.

firma f. signature; firm, firm name.

firmamento m. firmament, sky.

firmante m. & f. signer.

firmar v. to sign.

firme adj. firm; solid; hard; **de —** without stopping, hard, steadily.

firmeza f. firmness.

fiscal m. public prosecutor, district attorney; adj. fiscal.

fisgar[7] v. to pry; to snoop; to spy on.

fisgón m. snoop, snooper; adj. snooping; curious.

fisgonear v. to pry about; to snoop.

física f. physics.

físico adj. physical; Am. vain, prudish, affected; Am. real; m. physicist.

fisiología f. physiology.

fisiológico adj. physiological.

fisionomía f. face, features.

flaco adj. lean, skinny; frail, weak; **su lado —** his weak side, his weakness.

flacura f. thinness.

flama f. flame.

flamante adj. bright, shiny; brand-new.

flameante adj. flaming, flashing.

flamear v. to flame; to flap, flutter (in the wind).

flamenco adj. Flemish; C.A., P.R. skinny; m. Flemish, Flemish language; flamingo; Andalusian dance.

flan m. custard.

flanco m. flank, side.

flanquear v. to flank.

flaps m. pl. flaps (of an airplane).

flaquear v. to weaken, flag.

flaqueza f. thinness, leanness; weakness, frailty.

flauta f. flute; **flautista** m. & f. flute player.

fleco m. fringe; bangs, fringe of hair.

flecha f. arrow, dart.

flechar v. to dart, shoot (an arrow); to strike, wound or kill with an arrow; to cast an amorous or ardent glance; Ven. to prick, sting; Am. to burn (said of the sun).

fletamento m. charter, charter party (of a ship).

fletar v. to charter (a ship); to freight; Ch. to hire (pack animals); Peru to let loose (strong words); Am. to scatter (false rumors); **-se** Col., Mex., Carib., Ch. to run away, slip away; Am. to slip in uninvited; Am. **salir fletado** to leave on the run.

flete m. freight, freightage; cargo; load; Am. fine horse, race horse; Am. bother, nuisance; Col., Ven. **salir sin -s** to leave in a hurry.

flexibilidad f. flexibility; **flexible** adj. flexible.

flexión f. bending, bend; sag.

flojear v. to slacken; to weaken; to idle, to be lazy.

flojedad f. laxity, looseness; slackness; laziness; slack.

flojera = **flojedad**.

flojo adj. (mal atado) lax; loose, slack; (sin fuerza) lazy; weak.

flor f. flower, blossom; compliment; **— de la edad** prime; **— de lis** iris (flower); **— y nata** the best, the cream, the chosen few; **a — de** flush with; **echar -es** to throw a bouquet; to compliment, flatter.

floreado p.p. & adj. flowered; made of the finest wheat.

florear v. to decorate with flowers; to brandish, flourish; to make a flourish on the guitar; to flatter, compliment; to bolt, sift out (the finest flour); Am. to flower, bloom; Am. to choose the best; **-se** C.A. to shine, excel; Am. to burst open like a flower.

florecer[13] v. irr. to flower, bloom; to flourish, thrive.

floreciente adj. flourishing, thriving; prosperous.

florecimiento m. flourishing, flowering, bloom.

floreo m. flourish; idle talk; flattery, compliment.

florería f. florist's shop.

florero m. florist; flower vase; flatterer; adj. flattering.

floresta f. wooded place, grove; arbor.

florete m. fencing foil.

florido adj. flowery.

flota f. fleet; Col., **echar -s** to brag, boast.

flotador m. floater; float; pontoon (of a hydroplane); adj. floating.

flotante adj. floating; m. Col., Ven. bluffer, braggart.

flotar v. to float.
flote: a — afloat.
fluctuación f. fluctuation; wavering, hesitation.
fluctuar[18] v. to fluctuate; to waver; to hesitate.
fluente adj. fluent, flowing.
fluidez f. fluidity, easy flow, fluency.
flúido adj. fluid, flowing, fluent; m. fluid.
fluir[32] v. irr. to flow.
flujo m. flux; flow; flood tide.
fluorescente adj. fluorescent.
flux m. flush (in cards); P.R., Col., Ven. suit of clothes; **hacer —** to use up one's funds, lose everything; Am. **tener uno —** to be lucky.
foca f. seal, sea lion.
foco m. focus, center; Am. electric-light bulb.
fofo adj. spongy, porous; light (in weight); soft.
fogata f. fire, blaze, bonfire.
fogón m. hearth, fireplace; grill (for cooking); vent of a gun; C.A., Mex. fire, bonfire; **fogonazo** m. flash (of gunpowder).
fogoso adj. fiery, ardent; lively, spirited.
follaje m. foliage.
folletín m. small pamphlet; serial story.
folleto m. pamphlet.
fomentar v. to foment, encourage, promote, foster.
fomento m. promotion, encouragement; development; aid.
fonda f. inn; restaurant.
fondear v. to cast anchor; to sound, make soundings; to search (a ship); to sound out; **-se** Cuba to save up for the future.
fondero m. Am. innkeeper.
fondillos m. pl. seat of trousers.
fondista m. & f. innkeeper.
fondo m. (hondura) bottom; depth; background; back, rear end; (esencia) mature, heart, inner self; fund; Cuba, Ven. underskirt; **-s** funds; **a —** thoroughly; **echar a —** to sink.
fonducho m. cheap eating place.
fonema m. phoneme.
fonética f. phonetics, study of pronunciation.
fonógrafo m. phonograph.
fonología f. phonology.
forajido m. outlaw, fugitive; highwayman, bandit.
foráneo adj. foreign; m. outsider, stranger.
forastero m. stranger; foreigner; outsider; adj. foreign.
forcejear, forcejar v. to struggle; to strive; to oppose, resist.
forja f. forge; forging; blacksmith's shop.
forjador m. forger (of metals); smith, blacksmith; inventor (of lies, stories, tricks, etc.).
forjar v. to forge; to form, shape; to invent, feign, fake.
forma f. form, shape, figure; manner; format (size and shape of a book);

host (unleavened bread for communion).
formación f. formation.
formal adj. formal; serious, trustworthy, punctual; reliable.
formalidad f. formality; seriousness, reliability; gravity, dignity; punctuality; red tape.
formalismo m. formality, red tape (excess of formalities); **formalista** adj. fond of excessive formalities, fond of red tape.
formalizar[9] v. to give proper form to; to legalize; to make official; **-se** to settle down, become serious.
formar v. to form; to shape, mold; **-se** to get into line; to be molded, educated; to take form.
formidable adj. formidable; fearful.
formón m. wide chisel.
fórmula f. formula.
formular v. to formulate, word.
fornido adj. stout, strong, sturdy.
foro m. stage; back, rear (of a stage); forum, court; bar (profession of law).
forraje m. forage, green grass, fodder, feed.
forrajear v. to forage, gather forage.
forrar v. to line; to cover, put a sheath, case, or covering on; **-se** Ríopl., C.A. to eat well; Am. to supply oneself with provisions; Ríopl., Mex., Cuba to save money.
forro m. lining, sheathing, casing; covering; book cover.
fortalecer[13] v. irr. to fortify; to strengthen.
fortaleza f. fortress; fortitude; strength, vigor; Ch. stench, stink.
fortificación f. fortification; fort.
fortificar[6] v. to fortify.
fortuito adj. fortuitous, accidental, unexpected.
fortuna f. fortune; fate, chance; wealth; **por —** fortunately.
forzar[9] v. irr. to force; to compel; to take (a fort); to rape; **— la entrada en** to break into.
forzozo adj. compulsory; necessary.
fosa f. grave; cavity.
fosco adj. dark; cross, irritable, frowning.
fosfato m. phosphate.
fosforecer[13], **fosforescer** v. to glow.
fósforo m. phosphorus; match.
fósil adj. & m. fossil.
foso m. hole, pit; stage pit; ditch.
fotograbado m. photoengraving.
fotografía f. photograph; photography.
fotografiar[17] v. to photograph.
fotógrafo m. photographer.
fracasado adj. failed; m. failure.
fracasar v. to fail; to come to ruin; to crumble to pieces.
fracaso m. failure, ruin; calamity; crash.
fracción f. fraction.
fractura f. fracture; break, crack.
fracturar v. to fracture, break.
fragancia f. fragrance, scent, perfume.
fragante adj. fragrant; **en —** in the act.

FI

fragata *f.* frigate.

frágil *adj.* fragile, breakable; frail, weak.

fragmento *m.* fragment.

fragor *m.* clang, din; crash.

fragoroso *adj.* deafening, thunderous.

fragoso *adj.* rugged, craggy, rough, uneven; noisy.

fragua *f.* forge; blacksmith's shop.

fraguar *v.* to forge; to scheme, hatch (*a plot*).

fraile *m.* friar; priest; **frailuco** *m.* little old friar.

frambuesa *f.* raspberry; **frambueso** *m.* raspberry bush.

francés *adj.* French; *m.* Frenchman; French language.

franco *adj.* (*sincero*) frank, open, candid, sincere; (*exento*) free; *m.* franc; **francote** *adj.* very frank, blunt, outspoken.

franela *f.* flannel.

franja *f.* fringe, border; stripe; braid.

franquear *v.* to exempt; to free; to frank (*a letter*); to dispatch, send; to make grants; **— el paso** to permit the passage (of); to unbosom oneself, disclose one's innermost thoughts and feelings.

franqueo *m.* postage; franking (*of a letter*); freeing (*of slaves or prisoners*).

franqueza *f.* frankness; freedom.

franquicia *f.* franchise, grant, privilege; freedom or exemption (*from fees*).

frasco *m.* flask, vial, small bottle.

frase *f.* phrase; sentence.

fraternal *adj.* fraternal, brotherly.

fraternidad *f.* fraternity; brotherhood.

fraude *m.* fraud.

fraudulento *adj.* fraudulent, tricky, deceitful, dishonest.

fray *m.* (*contr. of* **fraile**, *used before Christian name*) friar.

frazada *f.* blanket.

frecuencia *f.* frequency; **con —** frequently.

frecuentar *v.* to frequent.

frecuente *adj.* frequent.

fregadero *m.* sink.

fregado *m.* scrub, scrubbing; *p.p. of* **fregar**; *adj. Ch.*, *Andes* bothersome, annoying; *Col.* stubborn; *Mex.*, *C.A.* brazen.

fregar[7] *v. irr.* to scour; to scrub; to rub; to wash (*dishes*); *Am.* to molest, annoy.

fregona *f.* scrub woman; dishwasher, kitchen maid.

freir[15] *v. irr.* to fry; to tease, bother.

frenesí *m.* frenzy, madness.

frenético *adj.* frantic; furious; in a frenzy.

freno *m.* bridle; brake; control; bit (*for horses*).

frente *f.* forehead; countenance; *m.* front; **en — de** in front of; **— a** in front of, facing; **hacer —** to face.

fresa *f.* strawberry.

fresca *f.* fresh air; fresh remark.

fresco *adj.* (*bastante frío*) fresh; cool, (*sereno*) calm, serene; (*descarado*) forward, bold; *m.* coolness; cool air;

fresco (*painting*); *C.A.*, *Col.* refreshment; **al —** in the open air; **pintura al —** painting in fresco.

frescor *m.* freshness, coolness.

frescura *f.* (*temperatura baja*) freshness; coolness; (*serenidad*) calm; freedom; ease; (*insolencia*) boldness, impudence; impudent remark.

fresno *m.* ash, ash tree.

fresquecillo *adj.* nice and cool; *m.* cool air, fresh breeze; **fresquecito, fresquito** *adj.* nice and cool.

frialdad *f.* coldness; coolness, indifference.

fricción *f.* friction, rub, rubbing.

friccionar *v.* to rub; to massage.

friega *f.* rub, rubbing; *Am.* bother, nuisance, irritation; *Am.* flogging, beating.

frigorífico *adj.* freezing; *m. Spain* refrigerator, icebox; *Riopl.* meatpacking house.

frijol *m.* bean; kidney bean, navy bean.

frío *adj.* cold; frigid; cool, indifferent; *m.* cold; **-s** *Mex.* chills and fever; *Col.*, *C.A.*, *Ven.* malaria.

friolento *adj.* cold-blooded, sensitive to cold; chilly.

friolera *f.* trifle.

fritada *f.* dish of fried food.

frito *p.p. irr. of* **freír** fried; *m.* fry, dish of fried food.

fritura *f.* fry, dish of fried food; fritter.

frivolidad *f.* frivolity; **frívolo** *adj.* frivolous.

fronda *f.* leaf; fern leaf; foliage.

frondoso *adj.* leafy.

frontera *f.* frontier, border; **fronterizo** *adj.* frontier (*used as an adj.*); opposite, facing.

frontero *adj.* facing, opposite.

frontis *m.* façade, front (*of a building*).

frontispicio *m.* front, façade (*front of a building*); title page.

frontón *m.* main wall of a handball court; handball court; jai alai court; game of *pelota*.

frotación *f.* friction, rubbing.

frotar *v.* to rub; to scour.

frote *m.* rubbing; friction.

fructificar[6] *v.* to fruit, bear or produce fruit; to yield profit.

fructuoso *adj.* fruitful.

frugal *adj.* frugal, economical, saving, thrifty; **frugalidad** *f.* frugality, thrift.

fruncir[10] *v.* to wrinkle; to gather in pleats; to contract, shrivel; **— las cejas** to frown; to knit the eyebrows; **— los labios** to purse or curl the lips.

fruslería *f.* trifle, trinket.

frustración *f.* frustration; failure.

frustrar *v.* to frustrate, thwart, foil; **-se** to fail, be thwarted.

fruta *f.* fruit (*not a vegetable*); **frutería** *f.* fruit store.

frutero *m.* fruit vendor; fruit dish; *adj.* fruit (*used as adj.*); **buque —** fruit boat; **plato —** fruit dish.

fruto *m.* fruit (*any organic product of the earth*); result; benefit, profit.

¡fuche! *interj. Mex.* phew! ugh! pew!

phooey!

fuego m. (*incendio*) fire; (*pasión*) passion; (*erupción*) skin eruption; *Am.* cold sore; **-s artificiales** fireworks; **hacer —** to fire, shoot; **estar hecho un —** to be very angry; **romper —** to begin to fire, start shooting.

fuelle m. (*instrumento*) bellows; (*arruga*) pucker, wrinkle, fold; (*hablador*) tattletale, windbag, gossiper.

fuente f. fountain; source, origin; spring; platter, serving dish.

fuera adv. outside, out; **— de** prep. outside of; in addition to.

fuereño m. Mex., Ven., Andes outsider, stranger.

fuero m. law, statute; power, jurisdiction; code of laws; exemption, privilege.

fuerte adj. (*robusto*) strong; loud; secure, fortified; (*grave*) grave, serious; (*áspero*) excessive; Ch. stinking; m. fort; forte, strong point; forte (*music*); Mex. alcohol, liquor; adv. strongly; excessively; loud; hard.

fuerza f. force; power, strength; violence, compulsion; **a — de** by dint of; **a la — (por —, por la —, de por —,** Am. **de —)** by force, forcibly; necessarily; **ser —** to be necessary.

fuete m. Col., Cuba, Riopl., Mex., Ven., Andes whip; **fuetazo** m. Am. lash.

fuga f. flight, escape; leak, leakage; fugue (*musical composition*).

fugarse[7] v. to flee, escape.

fugaz adj. fleeing; fleeting, brief, passing.

fugitivo adj. fugitive; fleeting, passing; perishable; m. fugitive.

fulano m. so-and-so (*referring to person*).

fulgor m. radiance, brilliance.

fulgurar v. to gleam, flash, shine.

fulminar v. to thunder, thunder forth; to utter (*threats*).

fulo m. Pan. blond.

fullero m. cardsharp; crooked gambler; cheat.

fumada f. puff, whiff (*of smoke*).

fumadero m. smoking room.

fumador m. smoker, habitual smoker.

fumar v. to smoke (*tobacco*); Am. **-se a uno** to swindle or cheat someone.

fumigar[7] v. to fumigate.

función f. (*actividad*) function; functioning; (*empleo*) office; occupation; (*espectáculo*) show, performance; religious festival.

funcionamiento m. functioning, action, working, operation.

funcionar v. to function; to work, run (*said of machines*).

funcionario m. public employee, officer or official.

funda f. cover, case; Col. skirt; **— de almohada** pillowcase.

fundación f. foundation.

fundador m. founder.

fundamental adj. fundamental.

fundamento m. foundation, groundwork; basis; Col. skirt.

fundar v. to found, establish; to erect; to base, ground.

fundir v. to smelt, fuse, melt; to cast, mold; Am. to ruin; **-se** to fuse, melt together; to unite; Riopl., Mex. to be ruined.

fundo m. farm, country estate; property, land.

fúnebre adj. funeral; funereal, gloomy, dismal.

funeral adj. & m. funeral.

funeraria f. undertaking establishment, funeral parlor.

funesto adj. ill-fated, unlucky; sad, unfortunate.

fungosidad f. fungus, fungous growth.

furgón m. freight car, boxcar; **furgonada** f. carload.

furia f. fury, rage; speed.

furibundo adj. furious.

furioso adj. furious.

furor m. fury, rage, anger; frenzy.

furtivo adj. furtive, sly, secret.

fuselaje m. fuselage (*of an airplane*).

fusible adj. fusible; m. electric fuse.

fusil m. gun, rifle.

fusilar v. to shoot, execute.

fusión f. fusion; melting; **— nuclear** nuclear fusion.

fustigar[7] v. to lash, whip; to censure severely, scold sharply.

fútil adj. futile, useless; trivial; **futilidad** f. futility, uselessness.

futuro adj. future; m. fiancé, future husband; future.

G

gabacho adj. from or of the Pyrenees; Frenchlike; Am. **me salió —** it turned out wrong; m. Frenchman (*used depreciatively*).

gabán m. overcoat.

gabeta = **gaveta.**

gabinete m. cabinet (*of a government*); studio; study, library room; dressing room; sitting room; private room; dentist's office; laboratory; Am. glassed-in **mirador.**

gaceta f. gazette, official newspaper; professional periodical; Am. any newspaper.

gacetilla f. short newspaper article; column of short news items; gossip column; m. & f. newsmonger, tattletale; **gacetillero** m. newspaper reporter; newsmonger.

gacha f. watery mass or mush; Col. china or earthenware bowl; **-s** porridge, mush; caresses; **-s de avena** oatmeal.

gacho adj. drooping; bent downward; turned down; stooping; slouching; with horns curved downward; **sombrero —** slouch hat; **a gachas** on all fours; **con las orejas gachas** with drooping ears; crestfallen, discouraged.

gafas f. pl. spectacles; grappling hooks.

gaita f. flageolet, a kind of flute; Am. good-for-nothing, lazy bum; **— gallega** bagpipe; **sacar la —** to stick out one's neck; **gaitero** *m.* piper, bagpipe player.

gaje *m.* fee; **-s** wages, salary; fees.

gala *f.* elegance; full dress or uniform; ostentation; *Am.* award, prize, tip; **-s** finery, regalia, best clothes; **-s de novia** trousseau; **hacer — de** to boast of.

galán *m.* gallant, lover; leading man (*in a play*).

galante *adj.* gallant, attentive to ladies; polite.

galanteador *m.* gallant, lady's man; flatterer.

galantear *v.* to court, woo; to make love.

galanteo *m.* wooing, courtship.

galantería *f.* gallantry, compliment, attention to ladies; courtesy; gracefulness; generosity.

galardón *m.* recompense, reward.

galeote *m.* galley slave.

galera *f.* galley; large wagon; women's jail; printer's galley; *Mex.* jail; *Ch., Riopl.* tall hat.

galerada *f.* galley, galley proof; wagon load, van load.

galería *f.* gallery; corridor.

galgo *m.* greyhound; *adj. Col.* gluttonous, always hungry.

galicismo *m.* gallicism.

galillo *m.* uvula.

galón *m.* galloon, braid, trimming; gallon.

galoneado *adj.* gallooned, trimmed with braid.

galopada *f.* gallop; **pegar una —** to break into a gallop.

galopar *v.* to gallop.

galope *m.* gallop; **a (al or de) —** at a gallop; speedily.

galopear = galopar.

galpón *m. Riopl., Andes* large open shed.

gallardete *m.* streamer.

gallardía *f.* elegance; gracefulness; bravery.

gallardo *adj.* elegant, graceful; brave.

gallego *adj.* Galician, from or of Galicia, Spain; *m.* Galician; *Carib., Riopl.* Spaniard (*used as a nickname*).

galleta *f.* cracker; hardtack, hard biscuit; hard cookie; blow, slap; small pot; *Riopl.* bread of coarse meal or bran; *Ch.* reproof; *Am.* **colgarle la — a uno** to fire, dismiss someone; *Am.* **tener —** to have strength, muscle.

gallina *f.* hen; *m. & f.* chickenhearted person.

gallinero *m.* chicken coop, house, or yard; flock of chickens; basket for carrying chickens; poultryman; noisy gathering; top gallery of a theater.

gallo *m.* cock, rooster; aggressive, bossy person; cork float; false note (*in singing*); frog (*in one's throat*); *Am.* secondhand clothing; *Am.* fire wagon; *Mex., Riopl.* serenade.

gamo *m.* buck, male deer.

gamuza *f.* chamois, chamois skin (*soft leather made from the skin of sheep,* goats, deer, etc).

gana *f.* desire, appetite; **de buena (mala) —** willingly (unwillingly); **tener —** (*or* **-s**) to feel like, want to; **no me da la —** I don't want to.

ganadero *m.* cattleman; cattle dealer; *adj.* cattle, pertaining to cattle.

ganado *m.* cattle; herd; livestock; **— mayor** cattle; horses; mules; **— menor** sheep; **— de cerda** swine.

ganador *m.* winner; *adj.* winning.

ganancia *f.* profit, gain; *Am.* something to boot, something extra.

ganancioso *adj.* winning; profitable; *m.* winner.

ganar *v.* to win; to profit, gain; to earn; to get ahead of.

gancho *m.* hook; hooked staff; *Mex., Cuba, Riopl., Col., C.A.* hairpin; *Am.* bait, lure, trick; **aguja de —** crochet hook; **echar a uno el —** to hook someone; **tener —** to be attractive, alluring.

gandul *m.* bum, loafer.

ganga *f.* bargain; snap, easy job; kind of prairie hen.

gangoso *adj.* twangy, nasal (*voice*).

gangrena *f.* gangrene.

gangrenar *v.* to gangrene, cause gangrene; **-se** to gangrene.

ganoso *adj.* desirous; *Am.* lively, spirited (*horse*).

ganso *m.* goose, gander; lazy, slovenly person; dunce.

ganzúa *f.* hook; picklock (*tool for picking locks*); *m. & f.* burglar.

garabato *m.* hook; scrawl, scribble; **hacer -s** to scribble, write poorly.

garaje *m.* garage.

garantía *f.* to guaranty; security; bail, bond.

garantizar⁹ *v.* to guarantee, vouch for.

garañón *m.* jackass, male ass; male camel (*for breeding*); *Riopl., Mex., C.A.* stallion.

garapiñar *v.* to candy (*almonds, fruits, etc.*).

garbanzo *m.* chickpea.

garbo *m.* elegance, graceful air, good carriage.

garboso *adj.* graceful; elegant; sprightly.

garduña *f.* marten.

garfio *m.* hook.

garganta *f.* throat, neck; gorge, ravine; **gargantilla** *f.* necklace.

gárgara *f.* gargling; **-s** *Am.* gargle, gargling solution; **hacer -s** to gargle.

gargarear *v. Am.* to gargle.

gargarismo *m.* gargling; gargle, gargling solution.

gargarizar⁹ *v.* to gargle.

garita *f.* sentry box; watchman's booth; *Col.* vendor's booth.

garito *m.* gambling house, gambling joint; gambler's winnings.

garra *f.* claw, paw; hook; *Am.* strength; *Col.* leather or cloth remnant; *Am.* skinny person or animal; *Am.* margin of profit in a business deal; **echar la — a** to arrest; to grab; *Mex., C.A.,*

Ven., Andes **hacer -s** to tear to pieces.

garrafa *f.* decanter; **garrafón** *m.* large decanter; demijohn.

garrapata *f.* tick (*an insect*).

garrapatear *v.* to scribble, scrawl, write poorly.

garrocha *f.* pole; iron-pointed staff; *Am.* goad (*for goading oxen*).

garrote *m.* club, cudgel, heavy stick; *Mex., Ur.* brake; **dar —** to strangle; *Am.* to brake, set the brakes; **garrotazo** *m.* blow with a club; huge stick.

garrotero *m. Mex., Ven.* brakeman; *Am.* beater (*one who beats with a club*); *adj. Am.* stingy.

garrucha *f.* pulley.

garúa *f. C.A., Ríopl., Ven., Andes* drizzle.

garza *f.* heron.

garzo *adj.* blue, bluish; blue-eyed.

gas *m.* gas, vapor; *Col., Ríopl., Ven.* gasoline.

gasa *f.* gauze.

gaseosa *f.* soda water; soda pop.

gaseoso *adj.* gaseous.

gasolina *f.* gasoline.

gastador *adj.* lavish, extravagant, wasteful; *m.* spendthrift, lavish spender.

gastar *v.* to spend; to wear; to use; to waste; **-se** to wear out; to get old.

gasto *m.* expense, expenditure; wear.

gatas : a — on all fours; **andar a —** to creep, crawl; **salir a —** to crawl out of a difficulty.

gateado *adj.* catlike; veined, streaked; *m. Am.* light-colored horse with black streaks.

gatear *v.* to creep, crawl; to walk on all fours; to claw, scratch; to steal.

gatillo *m.* kitten; trigger; forceps (*for extracting teeth*); petty thief.

gato *m.* cat; moneybag; jack (*for lifting weights*); sneak thief; sly fellow; *Am.* trigger; *Am.* outdoor market; *Am.* hot-water bottle; *Am.* a gaucho song and tap dance (*by extension*, the dancer); *Am.* blunder.

gatuperio *m.* fraud, intrigue.

gauchada *f. Ríopl.* gaucho deed or exploit.

gauchaje *m. Ríopl.* band of Gauchos, Gaucho folk.

gauchesco *adj. Am.* relating to Gauchos.

gaucho *m. Am.* Gaucho, Argentine and Uruguayan cowboy; *Ríopl., Ven.* good horseman; *adj. Am.* relating to Gauchos, Gaucho-like; *Am.* sly, crafty.

gaveta *f.* drawer.

gavilla *f.* sheaf; gang, band (*of rogues, thieves, etc.*).

gaviota *f.* sea gull.

gaza *f.* loop; *Carib.* noose of a lasso.

gazmoñería *f.* prudery, affected modesty; **gazmoño** *adj.* prudish, affected, coy.

gaznate *m.* windpipe; a kind of fritter; *Andes* a sweetmeat made of pineapple or coconut.

gelatina *f.* gelatin; jelly.

gema *f.* gem, jewel; bud.

gemelo *m.* twin; **-s** twins; binoculars, opera glasses, field glasses; cuff links.

gemido *m.* moan; wail, cry.

gemir[1] *v. irr.* to moan; to wail, cry.

gendarme *m. Mex., Ven., Ríopl., C.A.* policeman.

generación *f.* generation.

generador *m.* generator; **— molecular** atom smasher.

general *adj. & m.* general; **por lo —** generally.

generalidad *f.* generality; majority.

generalizar[9] *v.* to generalize; **-se** to spread, become general.

género *m.* (*clase*) kind, sort, class; gender; (*tela*) goods, material, cloth; **— humano** human race.

generosidad *f.* generosity.

generoso *adj.* generous; best (*wine*).

genial *adj.* genial, jovial, pleasant.

genio *m.* genius; temperament, disposition; spirit.

gente *f.* (*personas*) people; crowd; (*pueblo*) race, nation; clan; *Am.* **— bien** upper-class or important person; *Am.* **ser —** to be a somebody; to be cultured; to be socially important.

gentil *adj.* graceful; genteel; courteous; gentile; *m.* pagan; gentile.

gentileza *f.* grace, courtesy; nobility; favor.

gentío *m.* crowd, throng.

gentuza *f.* rabble.

genuino *adj.* genuine.

geofísica *f.* geophysics.

geografía *f.* geography; **geográfico** *adj.* geographical.

geología *f.* geology; **geológico** *adj.* geological.

geometría *f.* geometry; **geométrico** *adj.* geometric.

geranio *m.* geranium.

gerencia *f.* management, administration.

gerente *m.* manager.

germen *m.* germ; origin, source.

germinar *v.* to germinate.

gerundio *m.* gerund; present participle.

gesticular *v.* to gesticulate.

gestión *f.* action, step, maneuver; intervention; **-es** negotiations.

gestionar *v.* to manage; to take steps; to negotiate or carry out (*a deal, transaction, etc.*).

gesto *m.* face, expression; grimace; gesture; **estar de buen** (*or* **mal**) **—** to be in a good (*or* bad) humor; **hacer -s a** to make faces at.

giba *f.* hump, hunch.

gigante *adj.* gigantic; *m.* giant.

gigantesco *adj.* gigantic.

gimnasia *f.* gymnastics; **gimnasio** *m.* gymnasium; German institute (*for secondary instruction*).

gimotear *v.* to whimper, whine.

gimoteo *m.* whimper, whining.

ginebra *f.* gin (*liquor*).

gira *f.* excursion, tour; outing, picnic.

girador *m.* drawer (*of a check or draft*).

girar *v.* to revolve, rotate, whirl; to

GA

send, issue, or draw (*checks, drafts, etc.*); to manage (*a business*).

girasol m. sunflower.

giratorio adj. rotary, revolving.

giro m. (*movimiento circular*) rotation; bend, turn; (*dirección*) direction, trend; (*estructura*) turn of phrase; (*monetario*) draft; **— postal** money order; aaj. yellowish (*rooster*); Am. black and white (*rooster*); Am. cocky.

gitano adj. gypsy; gypsylike; sly, clever; m. gypsy.

gitomate Am. = **jitomate.**

glacial adj. glacial, icy, very cold.

glaciar m. glacier.

glándula f. gland.

glasear v. to glaze (*paper, fruits, etc.*), make glossy.

globo m. globe, sphere; world; balloon.

gloria f. glory; gloria (*song of praise to God*).

gloriarse[17] v. to glory (in), delight (in), be proud (of); to boast (of).

glorieta f. arbor, bower; secluded nook in a park (*with benches*).

glorificar[6] v. to glorify; **-se** to glory (in), take great pride (in).

glorioso adj. glorious.

glosar v. to gloss, comment upon, explain (*a text*).

glosario m. glossary.

glotal adj. glottal.

glotis f. glottis.

glotón m. gluttonous; m. glutton.

glotonería f. gluttony.

gobernador adj. governing; m. governor, ruler.

gobernante adj. governing, ruling; m. governor, ruler.

gobernar[1] v. irr. to govern, rule; to lead, direct; to steer (*a boat*).

gobierno m. government; management; control; helm, rudder.

goce m. enjoyment; joy.

goleta f. schooner, sailing vessel.

golfo m. gulf; open sea; faro (*gambling game*); vagabond, bum; ragamuffin.

golondrina f. swallow; swallow fish.

golosina f. sweet, dainty, tidbit; trifle; appetite, desire.

goloso adj. sweet-toothed, fond of sweets; gluttonous.

golpazo m. bang, whack; heavy blow, hard knock.

golpe m. blow, hit, stroke; knock; beat; Col. facing (*of a garment*); Am. sledge hammer; **— de fortuna** stroke of good luck; **— de gente** crowd, throng; **— de gracia** death blow; finishing stroke; **de —** suddenly; **de un —** all at once; **pestillo de —** spring latch; Am. **al —** instantly, at once; Am. **al — de vista** at one glance.

golpear v. to strike, hit; to knock; to beat; Am. to knock at a door.

golpetear v. to tap, knock or pound continuously; to flap; to rattle.

golpeteo m. tapping, pounding, knocking; flapping; rattling.

gollería f. dainty, delicacy; superfluous thing.

goma f. gum; rubber; elastic; eraser; tire; **— de repuesto** spare tire; Am. **estar de —** to have a hang-over (*after excessive drinking*).

gomero adj. rubber, pertaining to rubber; m. Riopl. gum or rubber tree; Am. rubber producer; Am. rubber-plantation worker; Ven. glue container or bottle.

gomífero adj. rubber-bearing, rubber-producing.

gomoso adj. gummy, sticky; m. dandy.

gordiflón adj. fat; chubby.

gordo adj. fat; plump; m. suet; fat; **gorda** f. Mex. thick tortilla or corn-meal cake; **se armó la gorda** all hell broke loose; there was a big rumpus.

gordura f. fatness; stoutness; fat.

gorgojo m. weevil; puny person; Am. wood borer, wood louse; **gorgojoso** adj. infested with weevils.

gorila m. gorilla.

gorjeador m. warbler; adj. warbling; **pájaro —** warbler.

gorjear v. to warble; to chirp.

gorjeo m. warble; warbling.

gorra f. cap; bonnet; **de —** at another's expense; **vivir de —** to sponge, live at another's expense.

gorrión m. sparrow.

gorro m. cap; bonnet.

gorrón m. sponge, parasite; bum; rake (*dissolute fellow*).

gota f. (*líquido*) drop; (*enfermedad*) gout; **sudar la — gorda** to sweat profusely, toil, work hard.

gotear v. to drip; to leak; to dribble, trickle; to sprinkle, begin to rain; **-se** to leak.

goteo m. trickle, drip.

gotera f. leak, hole (*in the roof*); eaves, trough; **-s** Mex. surroundings, outskirts.

gotero m. Carib., Mex. dropper (*for counting drops*).

gótico adj. Gothic; m. Goth; Gothic language.

gozar[9] v. to enjoy; to possess, have; **-se** to rejoice.

gozne m. hinge.

gozo m. pleasure, joy.

gozoso adj. joyful, glad, merry.

gozque, gozquejo, gozquecillo m. a small dog.

grabación f. recording (*tape*).

grabado adj. engraved; recorded; m. engraving; woodcut, print; **— al agua fuerte** etching.

grabadora f. tape recorder.

grabar v. to engrave; to carve; to fix, impress; to record on tape; **— al agua fuerte** to etch.

gracejada f. C.A. clownish act or expression.

gracejo m. grace; cuteness; humor, wit.

gracia f. (*humorismo*) witty remark; joke; humor; (*garbo*) grace; gracious act; (*favor*) favor; pardon; **caer en —** to please; **hacer —** to amuse, make (*someone*) laugh; **¡ -s!** thanks!

dar -s to thank.

gracioso adj. (chistoso) amusing; funny; witty; (con garbo) graceful, attractive; m. comedian, clown.

grada f. step of a staircase; harrow; **-s** steps; seats of an amphitheater; bleachers.

gradación f. gradation.

gradería f. series of steps; rows of seats (in an amphitheater or stadium); **— cubierta** grandstand; **-s** bleachers.

grado m. (medida) degree; step; (título) degree; **de (buen)** — willingly, with pleasure; **de mal** — unwillingly; **de — en —** by degrees, gradually.

graduación f. graduation; military rank.

gradual adj. gradual; m. response sung at mass.

graduar[18] v. to graduate, give a diploma, rank or degree to; to gauge; to classify, grade; **-se** to graduate, take a degree.

gráfico adj. graphic; vivid, lifelike; **gráfica** f. graph, diagram, chart.

grafito m. graphite.

grajo m. jay.

grama f. grama grass.

gramática f. grammar; **gramatical** adj. grammatical; **gramático** adj. grammatical; m. grammarian.

gramo m. gram.

gran contr. of **grande.**

grana f. cochineal, kermes (insects used for producing a red dye); scarlet color; scarlet cloth; any small seed.

granada f. pomegranate; grenade, shell, small bomb; **— de mano** hand grenade.

granado m. pomegranate tree; adj. notable; illustrious; select.

grande adj. large, big; great; grand; Mex., C.A., Ven., Andes **mamá (papá)** — grandmother (grandfather); m. grandee (Spanish or Portuguese nobleman); **en —** on a large scale.

grandeza f. greatness; grandeur, splendor; bigness; size; grandeeship; body of grandees.

grandiosidad f. grandeur, grandness; greatness; **grandioso** adj. grandiose, great, grand, magnificent.

granero m. granary; grain bin; country or region rich in grain.

granito m. granite; small grain; small pimple.

granizada f. hailstorm; shower, volley.

granizar[9] v. to hail.

granizo m. hail; hailstorm; web or film in the eye; adj. Mex. spotted (horse).

granja f. grange, farm; country house.

granjear v. to earn, gain; to acquire, obtain; Ch., C.A. to steal; **-se** to win for oneself (favor, goodwill, esteem, etc.).

granjería f. farming; business profit.

granjero m. farmer.

grano m. (cereal) grain; seed; grain (unit of measure); **ir al —** to come to the point.

granuja m. ragamuffin, urchin; scamp.

granular v. to granulate; **-se** to become granulated; to break out with pimples.

grapa f. clamp; staple; (carbunclo) pimple.

grasa f. grease; fat; tallow; Mex., Riopl., Ven. shoe polish; Am. **dar —** to polish (shoes).

grasiento adj. greasy, oily.

grasoso adj. greasy, oily.

gratificación f. gratuity, bonus, tip; recompense, reward.

gratis adv. gratis, for nothing, free of charge.

gratitud f. gratitude.

grato adj. pleasing, pleasant; gratuitous; **su grata** your favor, your letter.

gratuito adj. gratuitous, free, free of charge.

grava f. gravel.

gravamen m. burden; mortgage.

grave adj. grave; serious; weighty, heavy; grievous; deep, low (in pitch).

gravedad f. (fuerza) gravity; (seriedad) seriousness, gravity; (tono) depth (of a sound).

gravoso adj. burdensome; **serle a uno — to** be burdensome; to weigh on one's conscience.

graznar v. to caw, croak, squawk, cackle, quack.

graznido m. caw, croak, squawk, cackle, quack.

greca f. fret; ornamental design.

greda f. clay, chalk; chalk cleaner.

gremio m. guild, society, brotherhood; trade union; fold (referring to the Church).

greña f. shock of hair, tangled mop of hair (usually **greñas**); **greñudo** adj. shaggy, with long, unkempt hair.

grey f. flock; congregation (of a church).

griego adj. Greek, Grecian; m. Greek.

grieta f. crevice; crack; fissure.

grifo m. faucet; Am. cheap tavern (where **chicha** is sold); Peru gas station; Am. colored person; Col. drug addict; Am. drunkard; adj. curly, kinky, woolly (hair); Col. vain, conceited; **letra grifa** script; **ponerse —** to bristle, stand on end (said of hair).

grillo m. cricket; sprout, shoot; **-s** fetters; obstacle, hindrance.

grima f. uneasiness; displeasure, disgust; Riopl., Carib. sadness, compassion, pity; Am. bit, small particle; **dar —** to disgust; to make uneasy; Am. to make sad, inspire pity.

gringo adj. Ch., Riopl. (Italian) foreign (not Spanish); m. Ch., Riopl. (Italian) foreigner (not Spanish); Mex., C.A., Andes, Col., Ven. Yankee or English-speaking person.

gripe f. grippe, flu, influenza.

gris adj. grey; **grisáceo** adj. greyish.

grita f. shouting, hooting; clamor, uproar.

gritar v. to shout, cry.

gritería f. shouting, clamor, uproar.

grito m. shout, cry; **poner el — en el**

cielo to complain loudly, "hit the ceiling".

grosella f. currant; **— blanca** gooseberry; **grosellero** m. currant bush.

grosería f. rudeness; coarseness; crudeness; insult.

grosero adj. rough, coarse; rude, impolite.

grosor m. thickness.

grotesco adj. grotesque, fantastic; absurd.

grúa f. crane, derrick.

gruesa f. gross, twelve dozen.

grueso adj. (voluminoso) fat, stout; thick; bulky, big, heavy; (burdo) dense; coarse; m. thickness; bulk; density; main part; **en —** in gross, in bulk, by wholesale.

grulla f. crane (bird).

gruñido m. growl, grumble; grunt.

gruñir[19] v. irr. to grunt; to growl; to snarl; to grumble.

gruñón adj. growling; grunting; grumbly; m. growler; grumbler.

grupa f. rump; **volver -s** to turn around (usually on horseback).

grupo m. group; set.

gruta f. grotto, cavern.

guacal m. Col., Mex., C.A. crate (for transporting fruit, vegetables, etc.). Also **huacal**.

guacamayo m. Am. macaw (large parrot); Am. flashily dressed person.

guacamole m. Mex., C.A., Cuba avocado salad; also **guacamol**.

guacho m. birdling, chick; young animal; Andes, Ríopl. orphan; Andes, Ríopl. foundling, abandoned child; adj. Am. odd, not paired; Andes, Ríopl. forlorn, alone, abandoned.

guadal m. Am. small dune, sand hill; Ven. quagmire, bog, swamp; Am. growth of bamboo grass.

guadaña f. scythe.

guagua f. Carib., Ven. bus; trifle, insignificant thing; m. & f. Andes, Ch., Ríopl. baby; **de —** for nothing, gratis, free.

guaje m. Am. a species of gourd; Am. vessel or bowl made of a gourd; Am. simpleton, fool; Am. trifle, trinket, piece of junk; adj. Am. foolish; Am. **hacerse uno —** to play the fool; Am. **hacer a uno —** to fool, deceive someone.

guajiro m. Indian of the Guajira peninsula (in Venezuela and Colombia); Cuba rustic, peasant.

guajolote m. Mex. turkey; Am. fool.

guanaco m. Andes, Ch., Ríopl. guanaco (a kind of llama); Am. tall, lanky, gawky person; Am. fool, simpleton; nickname for Salvadoreans.

guanajo m. Am. turkey; Am. fool, dunce.

guano m. Carib. palm tree; Carib. palm leaves (used for thatching); Am. guano, bird dung, fertilizer.

guantada f. wallop, blow, slap.

guante m. glove; Andes whip, scourge; **echar el — a uno** to seize or grab a person; **guanteleté** m. gauntlet.

guapo adj. handsome, good-looking; ostentatious, showy; daring, brave; Ch., Andes harsh, severe; Carib., Mex. angry; m. brawler, quarreler, bully.

guarache m. Mex. Mexican leather sandal; Mex. tire patch. Also **huarache**.

guaraní adj. pertaining to the Guarani Indians of Paraguay; m. & f. Guarani Indian.

guarapo m. Col., C.A., Andes juice of the sugar cane; Col., C.A., Andes sugar-cane liquor; Col., C.A., Andes low-grade brandy.

guarda m. & f. guard; keeper; Ríopl. ticket collector on a streetcar; f. custody, care, keeping; observance of a law; **-s** outside ribs of a fan; flyleaves.

guardabarros, guardafango m. fender.

guardabosques m. forest ranger, forester, forest keeper.

guardabrisa f. windshield.

guardafrenos m. brakeman.

guardagujas m. switchman.

guardapapeles m. file, filing cabinet or box.

guardapelo m. locket.

guardar v. to guard, watch over; to keep; to store; to observe (laws, customs); **-se de** to guard against, keep from, avoid.

guardarropa m. wardrobe; cloakroom; keeper of a cloakroom.

guardia f. guard, body of guards; defense, protection; m. guard, guardsman.

guardiamarina f. midshipman.

guardián m. guardian, keeper; guardian, superior of a Franciscan monastery.

guarecer[13] v. irr. to protect, shelter; **-se** to take shelter.

guarida f. den, cave, lair.

guarismo m. number.

guarnecer[13] v. irr. to garnish, decorate; to adorn; to trim; to harness; to garrison; to set (jewels).

guarnición f. adornment; trimming; setting of a jewel; guard of a sword; garrison; **-es** trappings, harness.

guaro m. C.A. rum.

guasca f. Andes, Ch., Ríopl. leather thong; Andes, Ch., Ríopl. rope, cord; Andes, Ch. whip; Andes, Ch., Ríopl. **dar —** to whip, beat, thrash.

guaso m. Am. stag, male deer; Ch., Andes, Ríopl. peasant; Cuba half-breed; Am. lasso; adj. rustic, peasant-like.

guasón adj. funny, comical; m. joker, jester.

guata f. Am. padding; Ven. fib; Col. a species of potato; Ch., Andes paunch, belly; Am. **echar —** to get fat.

guatemalteco m. & adj. Guatemalan.

guayaba f. guava (pear-shaped tropical fruit); **guayabo** m. guava tree; Am. lie, fraud, trick.

gubernativo *adj.* governmental, administrative.

guedeja *f.* forelock; lock of hair; lion's mane.

güero *adj. Mex.* blond; *m. Ven.* cassava liquor. *See* **huero.**

guerra *f.* war; — **a muerte** war to the finish; **dar —** to bother, trouble

guerrear *v.* to war; *Am.* to do mischief or to bother (*said of children*).

guerrero *adj.* warlike, martial; *m.* warrior, soldier.

guerrilla *f.* small war; skirmish; body of soldiers; band of fighters.

guerrillero *m.* guerrilla fighter.

guía *m. & f.* guide, leader; *f.* guidebook, directory; signpost; shoot, sprout; *Riopl.* garland of flowers.

guiar[17] *v.* to guide; to drive (*a car*).

guija *f.* pebble; **guijarro** *m.* pebble.

guijo *m.* gravel.

guinda *f.* a kind of cherry.

guindilla *f. Spain* small hot pepper.

guiñada *f.* wink.

guiñapo *m.* tag, tatter, rag; ragamuffin, ragged person.

guiñar *v.* to wink.

guiño *m.* wink.

guión *m.* hyphen; repeat sign (*in music*); cross (*carried before a prelate in a procession*); guide, leader (*among birds and animals*); leader in a dance.

guirnalda *f.* garland, wreath.

guisa *f.* way, manner; **a — de** like, in the manner of.

guisado *m.* stew.

guisante *m.* pea; **— de olor** sweet pea.

guisar *v.* to cook; to prepare, arrange.

guiso *m.* dish, dish of food.

guisquil *m. C.A.* chayote (*a pear-shape fruit*).

guitarra *f.* guitar.

gula *f.* gluttony.

gusano *m.* worm; caterpillar; **— de la conciencia** remorse; **— de luz** glowworm; *Col., Mex.* **matar el —** to satisfy a need or desire (*particularly hunger or thirst*).

gustar *v.* (*agradar*) to please, be pleasing; (*saborear*) to taste; to experience; **-le a uno una cosa** to like something; **— de** to have a liking for, be fond of.

gusto *m.* (*agrado*) pleasure; whim, fancy; (*sabor*) taste; flavor; **dar —** to please; **estar a —** to be comfortable, contented; **tener — en** to be glad to; **tomar el — a una cosa** to become fond of something.

gustoso *adj.* (*con agrado*) glad; pleasant; willing; merry; (*sabroso*) tasty; *adv.* willingly.

H

haba *f.* large bean; Lima bean.

haber[30] *v. irr.* to have (*auxiliary verb*); **habérselas con** to have it out with; **ha de llegar mañana** he is to arrive tomorrow; **ha de ser verdad** it must be true; **hay** (**había, hubo,** *etc.*) there is, there are (there was, there were, *etc.*); **hay que** (+ *inf.*)

it is necessary; **no hay de qué** you are welcome; **¿qué hay?** what's the matter?

haber *m.* credit, credit side (*in bookkeeping*); **-es** property, goods, cash, assets.

habichuela *f.* bean; **— verde** string bean.

hábil *adj.* skilful, capable, able.

habilidad *f.* ability, skill.

habilitar *v.* to enable; to equip; to qualify.

habitación *f.* apartment; room; lodging.

habitante *m.* inhabitant; resident.

habitar *v.* to inhabit; to live, reside.

hábito *m.* habit; custom.

habitual *adj.* habitual, customary.

habituar[18] *v.* to accustom; **-se** to get used, accustomed.

habla *f.* speech; language, dialect; **al —** within speaking distance; in communication (with).

hablador *m.* talker; gossip; *adj.* talkative.

habladuría *f.* gossip, rumor; empty talk; impertinent remark.

hablar *v.* to speak; to talk; **— alto** (*or* **en voz alta**) to speak loudly; **— bajo** (**quedo** *or* **en voz baja**) to speak softly; **— por los codos** to chatter constantly.

hablilla *f.* gossip, rumor, malicious tale.

hacedero *adj.* feasible.

hacedor *m.* maker; **el Supremo Hacedor** the Maker.

hacendado *m.* landholder; *Riopl., Ch., Ven.* owner of a farm, plantation, or ranch.

hacendoso *adj.* industrious, diligent.

hacer[31] *v. irr.* (*crear*) to do; to make; (*formar*) to form; to accustom; (*causar*) to cause, order (*followed by inf.*); **— caso** to mind, pay attention; **— frío** (**calor**) to be cold (warm); **— la maleta** to pack one's suitcase; **— un papel** to play a part; *Am.* **— aprecio** to pay attention; *Riopl., Mex.* **— caras** (*or* **caritas**) to flirt; **no le hace** it makes no difference; **-se** to become, grow, get to be; **-se a** to get used to; **-se de rogar** to want to be coaxed.

hacia *prep.* toward; about; **— adelante** forward; **— atrás** backward.

hacienda *f.* estate; property; finance; large farm; *Riopl.* cattle, livestock.

hacina *f.* shock (*of grain*), stack, pile.

hacinar *v.* to shock (*grain*); to stack, pile up; to accumulate.

hacha *f.* ax; hatchet; torch.

hachero *m.* axman, woodcutter.

hada *f.* fairy.

hado *m.* fate, fortune, destiny.

halagar[7] *v.* to coax; to flatter; to allure, attract.

halago *m.* flattery; caress; allurement.

halagüeño *adj.* alluring, attractive; flattering; promising.

halar = **jalar.**

halcón m. falcon.

hálito m. breath; vapor.

hallar v. to find; to discover, find out; **-se** to be; to fare, get along.

hallazgo m. find; discovery; reward (*for finding something*).

hamaca f. hammock.

hambre f. hunger; famine; appetite; **tener —** to be hungry; **hambruna** f. Am. great hunger, starvation.

hambrear v. to starve; to be hungry.

hambriento adj. hungry; greedy; C.A., Mex., Andes stingy.

hampa f. underworld.

hangar m. hangar.

haragán adj. lazy, indolent; m. loafer, idler.

haraganear v. to lounge, loaf, be lazy.

haraganería f. laziness.

harapiento adj. tattered, ragged.

harapo m. rag, tatter; **andar hecho un —** to be in tatters.

haraposo adj. tattered, ragged.

harina f. flour; **eso es — de otro costal** that is something entirely different; **harinoso** adj. floury; flour-like.

harmonía f. harmony.

hartar v. to fill up, gorge; to sate, satiate; **-se** to have one's fill; to over-eat, eat too much.

harto adj. full; sated, satiated; fed up; too much; adv. too much; Mex., C.A., Col., Ven., Riopl., Andes much, very much.

hasta prep. till, until; up to; **— luego** good-bye, see you later; conj. even; **— que** until.

hastiar[17] v. to surfeit; to cloy; to disgust.

hastío m. surfeit, excess; boredom; loathing, disgust.

hato m. herd; flock; sheepfold; shepherd's hut; gang, crowd; pile; Col., Ven. cattle ranch.

haya f. beech; **hayuco** m. beechnut.

haz f. face; surface; m. fagot, bundle, bunch.

hazaña f. deed, exploit, feat.

he (*used with* **aquí** *or* **allí**) behold, here is, here you have; **heme aquí** here I am; **helo aquí** here it is.

hebilla f. buckle.

hebra f. thread; fiber; fine string; Am. **de una —** all at once, at one stroke, Am. **ni —** absolutely nothing; **hebroso** adj. fibrous, stringy.

hecatombe m. massacre, great slaughter; hecatomb (*sacrifice of 100 oxen*).

hechicera f. witch, enchantress; hag.

hechicería f. witchcraft; magic; charm; enchantment.

hechicero adj. bewitching, charming; m. magician; charmer; sorcerer.

hechizar[9] v. to bewitch; to charm.

hechizo m. charm; enchantment.

hecho m. fact; act, deed; **de —** in fact; p.p. of **hacer** done, made.

hechura f. make; shape, cut; workmanship.

heder[1] v. irr. to stink; to reek.

hediondez f. stink, stench.

hediondo adj. foul-smelling, stinking; filthy; m. Riopl. skunk.

hedor m. stink, stench.

helada f. frost.

helado adj. frozen; freezing; frosty; icy; m. ice cream; ice, sherbet; **heladería** f. Am. ice-cream parlor.

heladora f. freezer.

helar[1] v. irr. to freeze.

helecho m. fern.

hélice f. screw propeller; helix, spiral.

helicóptero m. helicopter.

helio m. helium.

helipuerto m. heliport.

hembra f. female; staple; nut (*of a screw*); **macho y —** hook and eye.

hemisferio m. hemisphere.

henchir[5] v. irr. to swell, stuff, fill.

hendedura, hendidura f. crack, crevice, fissure.

hender[1] v. irr. to split, crack, cleave.

henequén m. Mex., Ven., C.A., Col. sisal, sisal hemp.

heno m. hay; **henil** m. hayloft.

heraldo m. herald.

herbazal m. field of grass.

herboso adj. grassy; weedy.

heredad f. parcel of land; rural property; estate.

heredar v. to inherit; to bequeath, leave in a will.

heredero m. heir; successor; **heredera** f. heiress.

hereditario adj. hereditary.

hereje m. heretic; **cara de —** hideous face.

herejía f. heresy; offensive remark.

herencia f. inheritance; heritage; heredity.

herida f. wound; injury.

herido adj. wounded; m. wounded man; Am. small drainage channel.

herir[3] v. irr. to wound; to hurt; to strike; to offend.

hermana f. sister.

hermanastro m. stepbrother; stepbrother; **hermanastra** f. stepsister, half sister.

hermandad f. brotherhood, fraternity.

hermano m. brother.

hermético adj. hermetic; airtight; tight-lipped; close-mouthed; **hermetismo** m. complete silence.

hermosear v. to beautify, adorn.

hermoso adj. beautiful, handsome.

hermosura f. beauty.

héroe m. hero; **heroína** f. heroine.

heroico adj. heroic.

heroísmo m. heroism.

herradura f. horseshoe.

herraje m. ironwork; iron trimmings; horseshoes and nails; Am. silver saddle trimmings; Am. horseshoe.

herramienta f. set of tools; iron tool.

herrar[1] v. irr. to shoe (*a horse*); to brand; to trim with iron.

herrería f. blacksmith's shop or trade; forge; ironworks.

herrero m. blacksmith.

herrete m. metal tip (*for a shoelace, for*

instance); *Am.* branding iron.

hervidero *m.* bubbling sound (*of boiling water*); bubbling spring; swarm, crowd; **un — de gente** a swarm of people.

hervir[3] *v. irr.* to boil; **— de gente** to swarm with people.

hervor *m.* boiling; boiling point; **soltar el —** to come to a boil.

hez *f.* scum; **la — del pueblo** the scum of society; **heces** dregs, sediment.

hidalgo *m.* hidalgo (*Spanish nobleman*); *adj.* noble, courteous.

hidalguía *f.* nobility; generosity; courtesy.

hidráulico *adj.* hydraulic; **fuerza hidráulica** water power; **ingeniero —** hydraulic engineer.

hidroavión *m.* hydroplane, seaplane.

hidrógeno *m.* hydrogen.

hidroplano *m.* hydroplane.

hiedra *f.* ivy.

hiel *f.* gall, bile; bitterness.

hielo *m.* ice; frost.

hierba *f.* grass; herb; weed; *Ríopl.*, *Andes* mate (*Paraguayan tea*); *Mex.*, *Ven.*, *Cuba* marihuana (*a narcotic*); *C.A.* **ciertas -s** so-and-so (*person not named*).

hierbabuena *f.* mint. *Also* **yerbabuena**.

hierro *m.* iron; brand; iron tool, instrument, or weapon; **-s** irons, chains, handcuffs.

hígado *m.* (*órgano*) liver; (*valentía*) courage; valor; **malos -s** ill will.

higiene *f.* hygiene; **higiénico** *adj.* hygienic, sanitary.

higo *m.* fig; **higuera** *f.* fig tree; **higuerilla** *f. Am.* castor-oil plant.

hija *f.* daughter; native daughter.

hijo *m.* son; native son; offspring; fruit, result.

hilachas *f. pl.* lint; **mostrar uno la hilacha** to show one's worst side or nature; **hilachos** *m. pl. Am.* rags, tatters.

hilado *m.* yarn; *p.p. of* **hilar**.

hilandera *f.* spinner.

hilandería *f.* spinning mill; art of spinning; spinning.

hilandero *m.* spinner; spinning room.

hilar *v.* to spin, make into thread; **— muy delgado** to be very subtle.

hilas *f. pl.* lint, fine ravelings (*for dressing wounds*).

hilaza *f.* coarse thread; yarn.

hilera *f.* file, row, line; **— de perlas** strand or string of pearls.

hilo *m.* (*hebra*) thread; fine yarn; string; (*alambre*) filament; thin wire; (*tela*) linen; **a —** without interruption; **al —** along the thread; *Am.* very well, all right; **de — —** straight, without stopping; *Am.* **de un —** constantly, without stopping; **tener el alma en un —** to be frightened to death; to be in great anxiety or suspense.

hilván *m.* basting stitch; basting; *Am.* hem.

hilvanar *v.* to baste; to put together,

connect; to do hastily; *Am.* to hem.

himno *m.* hymn.

hincapié : hacer — to emphasize, stress; to insist (upon).

hincar[6] *v.* to drive, thrust (into); **-se** (*or* **-se de rodillas**) to kneel down.

hinchado *adj. & p.p.* swollen; inflated; presumptuous.

hinchar *v.* to swell; **-se** to swell; to swell up, puff up.

hinchazón *f.* swelling; inflation; conceit; bombast, inflated style.

hinojos : de — on one's knees.

hipérbole *f.* hyperbole.

hiperbólico *adj.* hyperbolic.

hipo *m.* hiccough; sob; longing; grudge, ill will.

hipocresía *f.* hypocrisy.

hipócrita *adj.* hypocritical, insincere; *m. & f.* hypocrite.

hipódromo *m.* race track.

hipoteca *f.* mortgage.

hipotecar[6] *v.* to mortgage.

hipótesis *f.* hypothesis, theory.

hirviente *adj.* boiling.

hispanista *m. & f.* Hispanist; one who is interested in Hispanic studies.

hispano *adj.* Hispanic, Spanish; *m.* Spaniard.

hispanoamericano *adj.* Spanish-American.

histérico *adj.* hysterical.

historia *f.* history; story; tale, fable; **dejarse de -s** to stop fooling and come to the point; **historieta** *f.* story, anecdote.

historiador *m.* historian.

historial *m.* record, data (*concerning a person or firm*); *adj.* historic.

histórico *adj.* historic, historical.

hocico *m.* snout; **caer de -s** to fall on one's face; **meter el — en todo** to meddle, stick one's nose in everything.

hogaño *adv.* nowadays.

hogar *m.* hearth, fireplace; home.

hogareño *adj.* home-loving, domestic; homelike.

hoguera *f.* bonfire.

hoja *f.* leaf; petal; sheet of paper or metal; blade; **— de lata** tin plate.

hojalata *f.* tin plate.

hojaldre *m. & f.* puff pastry.

hojarasca *f.* fallen leaves; dry foliage; superfluous ornament; trash; useless words.

hojear *v.* to leaf, turn the pages of; to browse.

hojuela *f.* leaflet, small leaf; thin leaf (*of metal*); flake; thin pancake; **— de estaño** tin foil.

¡hola! *interj.* hello!; ho!; ah!

holandés *adj.* Dutch; *m.* Dutchman; Dutch language.

holgado *adj.* (*libre*) free, at leisure; comfortable; (*ancho*) wide, loose; roomy, spacious; *p.p. of* **holgar**.

holgar *v. irr.* to rest; to loaf; **-se** to be glad; to relax, have a good time; **huelga decir** needless to say.

holgazán *m.* idler, loafer; *adj.* lazy,

HA

idle.

holgazanear *v.* to loiter, lounge, idle, bum around.

holgazanería *f.* idleness, laziness.

holgorio *m.* spree.

holgura *f.* (*descanso*) ease; rest, comfort; (*lugar*) roominess, plenty of room.

holocausto *m.* holocaust, burnt offering, sacrifice.

hollar *v.* to tread, trample upon.

hollejo *m.* skin, peel; husk.

hollín *m.* soot.

hombrada *f.* manly act; show of bravery.

hombre *m.* man; **hombría** *f.* manliness, manly strength; **— de bien** honesty.

hombro *m.* shoulder; **arrimar (or meter) el —** to help.

hombruno *adj.* mannish, masculine.

homenaje *m.* homage, honor.

homicida *m.* murderer; *f.* murderess; *adj.* homicidal, murderous.

homicidio *m.* homicide, murder.

homogéneo *adj.* homogeneous, of the same kind or nature.

honda *f.* sling, slingshot.

hondo *adj.* deep; low; *m.* bottom, depth.

hondonada *f.* hollow, gully, ravine.

hondura *f.* depth; **meterse en -s** to go beyond one's depth; to get into trouble.

honestidad *f.* chastity, modesty, decency; decorum, propriety.

honesto *adj.* chaste, modest, decent; just; honest.

hongo *m.* mushroom; fungus; derby hat.

honor *m.* honor; glory; dignity.

honorario *m.* fee (*for professional services*); *adj.* honorary.

honorífico *adj.* honorary; **mención honorífica** honorable mention.

honra *f.* honor; reputation; **-s** obsequies, funeral rites.

honradez *f.* honesty, honor, integrity.

honrado *adj.* honest, honorable; honored.

honrar *v.* to honor; **-se** to be honored; to consider it an honor.

honroso *adj.* honorable; honoring.

hora *f.* hour; time; **-s** canonical hours, office (*required daily prayers for priests and nuns*); **es — de** it is time to; **no ver la — de** (+ *inf.*) to be anxious to; **¿qué — es?** what time is it?

horadar *v.* to pierce, bore, perforate.

horario *m.* schedule, timetable; hour hand.

horca *f.* (*cadalso*) gallows; (*horcón*) pitchfork; *P.R.* birthday present; **— de ajos** string of garlic.

horcajadas: a — astride (*with one leg on each side*); **ponerse a —** to straddle.

horcón *m.* forked pole, forked prop; *Mex., Cuba, Ven.* post, roof support; *Am.* roof.

horda *f.* horde.

horizontal *adj.* horizontal.

horizonte *m.* horizon.

horma *f.* form, mold; block (*for shaping a hat*); shoe last; shoe tree.

hormiga *f.* ant.

hormigón *m.* concrete.

hormiguear *v.* to swarm; to be crawling with ants; **me hormiguea el cuerpo** I itch all over.

hormigueo *m.* itching, creeping sensation; tingle, tingling sensation.

hormiguero *m.* ant hill; ant nest; swarm; **oso —** anteater.

hornada *f.* batch of bread, baking.

hornear *v.* to bake (*in an oven*).

hornilla *f.* burner; grate (*of a stove*).

hornillo *m.* kitchen stove; hot plate.

horno *m.* furnace; oven; kiln (*for baking bricks*).

horquilla *f.* hairpin; forked pole; small pitchfork.

horrendo *adj.* horrible, hideous.

horrible *adj.* horrible.

horripilante *adj.* horrifying.

horror *m.* horror; atrocity; **dar —** to cause fright; to horrify; **tenerle — a uno** to feel a strong dislike for one.

horrorizar [9] *v.* to horrify, shock, terrify.

horroroso *adj.* horrid; frightful, hideous.

hortaliza *f.* vegetables; vegetable garden.

hortelano *m.* gardener.

hosco = fosco.

hospedaje *m.* board and lodging; lodging.

hospedar *v.* to lodge, give lodging; **-se** to take lodging; to room; to stop (*at a hotel*).

hospedero *m.* innkeeper.

hospicio *m.* asylum; orphanage, orphan asylum; poorhouse; **hospiciano** *m.* inmate of a poorhouse or asylum.

hospital *m.* hospital; **— de primera sangre** first-aid station.

hospitalidad *f.* hospitality.

hostia *f.* host (*consecrated wafer*).

hostigar [7] *v.* to harass, vex; to beat, lash; *C.A., Col.* to cloy.

hostil *adj.* hostile; **hostilidad** *f.* hostility.

hotel *m.* hotel; villa; **hotelero** *m.* hotel-keeper; *adj.* pertaining to hotels.

hoy *adv.* today; **— día** nowadays; **de — en adelante** from now on; **— por —** at present; **de — más** henceforth.

hoya *f.* pit, hole; grave; valley; *Am.* river basin.

hoyo *m.* hole; pit; grave; *Ríopl., Carib.* dimple.

hoyuelo *m.* dimple; tiny hole.

hoz *f.* sickle; narrow ravine.

hozar [9] *v.* to root, turn up the earth with the snout (*as hogs*).

huacal = guacal.

huarache = guarache.

huaso = guaso.

hueco *adj.* (*vacío*) hollow, empty; (*vano*) vain, affected; puffed up; high-sounding; *m.* gap, space, hole.

huelga *f.* labor strike; rest; leisure;

declararse en — to strike.
huelguista *m.* striker.
huella *f.* trace; footprint.
huérfano *adj. & m.* orphan.
huero *adj.* empty; rotten, spoiled (*egg*). *See* **güero.**
huerta *f.* orchard and vegetable garden; irrigated land.
huerto *m.* small orchard and vegetable garden; garden patch.
hueso *m.* bone; stone, pit; big seed; **la sin —** the tongue; **soltar la sin —** to talk too much; **no dejarle un — sano** to pick him to pieces.
huésped *m.* (*convidado*) guest; (*anfitrión*) host; **ser — en su casa** to be seldom at home.
hueste *f.* host, army, multitude.
huesudo *adj.* bony.
huevo *m.* egg; **— duro** hard-boiled egg; **— estrellado** fried egg; **— pasado por agua** soft-boiled egg; **-s revueltos** scrambled eggs; *Mex., C.A., Col., Ven.* **-s tibios** soft-boiled eggs; *Col., Ven.* **-s pericos** scrambled eggs; *Ven., Andes* **costar un —** to be very expensive.
huída *f.* flight; escape.
huir[32] *v. irr.* to flee, escape; to avoid, shun.
huizache *m. Mex., C.A.* huisache (*a species of acacia*).
hule *m.* rubber; oilcloth; *Col., Ven.* rubber tree.
hulla *f.* soft coal.
humanidad *f.* humanity, mankind; humaneness; **-es** humanities, letters.
humanitario *adj.* humanitarian, humane, kind, charitable.
humano *adj.* human; humane; *m.* man, human being.
humareda *f.* cloud of smoke.
humeante *adj.* smoking, smoky; steaming.
humear *v.* to smoke, give off smoke; to steam; *Am.* to fumigate.
humedad *f.* humidity, moisture, dampness.
humedecer[13] *v. irr.* to moisten, wet, dampen.
húmedo *adj.* humid, moist, wet, damp.
humildad *f.* humility; humbleness; meekness.
humilde *adj.* humble, lowly, meek.
humillación *f.* humiliation; submission.
humillar *v.* to humiliate, humble, lower, crush; **-se** to humiliate oneself; to bow humbly.
humillos *m. pl.* airs, conceit, vanity.
humo *m.* smoke, fume, vapor; **-s** conceit, vanity.
humor *m.* humor; mood, disposition.
humorada *f.* pleasantry, witty remark; caprice, notion.
humorismo *m.* humor, humorous style.
humorístico *adj.* humorous.
humoso *adj.* smoky.
hundimiento *m.* sinking, collapse, cave-in.

hundir *v.* (*sumir*) to sink, submerge; (*batir*) to crush, oppress; to destroy; **-se** to sink; to collapse, cave in.
huracán *m.* hurricane.
huraño *adj.* diffident, shy, bashful; unsociable.
¡hurra! *interj.* hurrah!
hurtadillas : a — on the sly, secretly, stealthily.
hurtar *v.* to steal, rob; **-se** to withdraw, slip away; to hide; **— el cuerpo** to dodge; to flee.
hurto *m.* robbery, theft; stolen article; **a —** stealthily, on the sly.
husmear *v.* to scent, smell, follow the track of; to nose, pry (into).
husmeo *m.* sniff, sniffing, smelling; prying.
huso *m.* spindle.

I

ibérico, ibero *adj.* Iberian; **ibero-americano** *adj.* Ibero-American (*Spanish or Portuguese American*).
ida *f.* departure; sally; **billete de — y vuelta** round-trip ticket; **-s y venidas** goings and comings.
idea *f.* idea; notion.
ideal *m. & adj.* ideal.
idealismo *m.* idealism.
idealista *adj.* idealistic; *m. & f.* idealist; dreamer.
idear *v.* to form an idea of; to devise, think out, plan.
idem idem (*abbreviation*: id.), ditto, the same.
idéntico *adj.* identical.
identidad *f.* identity.
identificar[6] *v.* to identify.
idilio *m.* idyl.
idioma *m.* language, tongue.
idiota *m. & f.* idiot; *adj.* idiotic, foolish.
idiotismo *m.* idiom; idiocy.
idolatrar *v.* to idolize, worship.
ídolo *m.* idol.
idóneo *adj.* fit, suitable; qualified.
iglesia *f.* church.
ignición *f.* ignition.
ignominia *f.* infamy, shame, disgrace.
ignominioso *adj.* ignominious; infamous, shameful, disgraceful.
ignorancia *f.* ignorance.
ignorante *adj.* ignorant.
ignorar *v.* to be ignorant of, not to know.
ignoto *adj.* unknown, undiscovered.
igual *adj.* (*semejante*) equal; (*liso*) even, smooth; uniform; (*siempre*) constant; **serle — a uno** to be all the same to one, make no difference to one; *m.* equal; **al —** equally.
igualar *v.* to equal; to equalize; to match; to level, smooth; to adjust; to be equal.
igualdad *f.* equality.
igualitario *adj.* equalitarian (*promoting the doctrine of equality*).
iguana *f.* iguana.
ijada *f.* loin; flank (*of an animal*); pain in the side; **ijar** *m.* flank (*of an animal*).

ilegal *adj.* illegal, unlawful.
ilegítimo *adj.* illegitimate; illegal.
ileso *adj.* unharmed, uninjured, unhurt, safe and sound.
ilícito *adj.* illicit, unlawful.
ilimitado *adj.* unlimited.
iluminación *f.* illumination.
iluminar *v.* to illuminate; to light; to enlighten.
ilusión *f.* illusion.
ilusivo *adj.* illusive.
iluso *adj.* deluded; *m.* visionary, dreamer.
ilusorio *adj.* illusive; deceptive; worthless.
ilustración *f.* illustration; elucidation, explanation.
ilustrador *m.* illustrator.
ilustrar *v.* to illustrate.
ilustre *adj.* illustrious, distinguished.
imagen *f.* image.
imaginable *adj.* imaginable, conceivable.
imaginación *f.* imagination.
imaginar *v.* to imagine.
imaginario *adj.* imaginary.
imaginativo *adj.* imaginative; **imaginativa** *f.* imagination.
imán *m.* magnet; attraction.
imbécil *adj.* imbecile, stupid.
imborrable *adj.* indelible, not erasable; unforgettable.
imbuir[32] *v. irr.* to imbue; to instill, infuse, inspire (with).
imitación *f.* imitation.
imitador *m.* imitator; follower; *adj.* imitative, imitating.
imitar *v.* to imitate.
impaciencia *f.* impatience.
impaciente *adj.* impatient.
impar *adj.* odd; **número —** odd number.
imparcial *adj.* impartial; **imparcialidad** *f.* impartiality, fairness, justice.
impasible *adj.* impassive, insensitive, insensible, unfeeling, unmoved.
impávido *adj.* fearless; calm; *Am.* impudent, brazen.
impedimento *m.* impediment, hindrance, obstacle.
impedir[5] *v. irr.* to impede, prevent, hinder.
impeler *v.* to impel, push; to incite, spur.
impenetrable *adj.* impenetrable; impervious; incomprehensible.
impensado *adj.* unforeseen, unexpected; offhand, done without thinking; **impensadamente** *adv.* offhand, without thinking; unexpectedly.
imperar *v.* to rule, command, dominate.
imperativo *adj.* imperative; urgent, compelling; *m.* imperative mood.
imperceptible *adj.* imperceptible.
imperdible *m.* safety pin; *adj.* safe, that cannot be lost.
imperecedero *adj.* imperishable, enduring, everlasting.
imperfecto *adj.* imperfect; *m.* imperfect tense.

imperial *adj.* imperial; *f.* coach top; top seats on a coach or bus.
impericia *f.* inexperience.
imperio *m.* empire; command, rule; sway, influence.
imperioso *adj.* imperious, arrogant, domineering; urgent.
impermeable *adj.* waterproof, impervious, rainproof; *m.* raincoat.
impersonal *adj.* impersonal.
impertinencia *f.* impertinence; impudence; insolent remark or act; **decir -s** to talk nonsense; to make insolent remarks.
impertinente *adj.* impertinent, impudent; meddlesome; irrelevant, not to the point; **-s** *m. pl.* lorgnette (*eyeglasses mounted on a handle*).
ímpetu *m.* impetus; violent force; impulse; *C.A.*, *Riopl.* vehement desire; **— de ira** fit of anger.
impetuoso *adj.* impetuous, violent.
impío *adj.* impious, irreligious; profane.
implacable *adj.* implacable, relentless.
implantación *f.* implantation, establishment, introduction (*of a system*).
implantar *v.* to implant, establish, introduce.
implicar[6] *v.* to imply; to implicate, involve.
implorar *v.* to implore, entreat, beg.
imponente *adj.* imposing.
imponer[40] *v. irr.* to impose; to invest (*money*); **— miedo** to inspire fear; **— respeto** to inspire or command respect; **-se** to inspire fear or respect; to dominate; *Am.* **-se a** to get accustomed or used to.
importancia *f.* importance.
importante *adj.* important.
importar *v.* to be important; to matter; to amount to; to be necessary; to concern; to import.
importe *m.* amount, price, value.
importunar *v.* to importune, nag, tease, pester.
importuno *adj.* annoying, persistent.
imposibilidad *f.* impossibility.
imposibilitado *p.p.* & *adj.* disabled, unfit; helpless.
imposibilitar *v.* to make impossible; to disable.
imposible *adj.* impossible; intolerable, unbearable; *Col.*, *Ven.* disabled (*because of illness*); *Am.* slovenly, untidy.
imposición *f.* imposition; burden; tax.
impostor *m.* impostor, cheat; **impostura** *f.* imposture, fraud, deceit.
impotencia *f.* impotence.
impotente *adj.* impotent, powerless.
impreciso *adj.* vague, indefinite; inaccurate.
impregnar *v.* to impregnate, saturate.
imprenta *f.* press; printing shop; printing.
imprescindible *adj.* essential, indispensable.
impresión *f.* impression; printing; mark; footprint.

impresionante *adj.* impressive.

impresionar *v.* to impress; to move, affect, stir; **-se** to be stirred, moved.

impreso *p.p. irr. of* **imprimir** printed; impressed, imprinted; *m.* printed matter.

impresor *m.* printer.

imprevisión *f.* carelessness, lack of foresight.

imprevisto *adj.* unforeseen, unexpected.

imprimir *v.* to print; to imprint, impress.

improbable *adj.* improbable, unlikely.

improperio *m.* affront, insult.

impropio *adj.* improper; unsuitable.

improvisar *v.* to improvise.

improviso *adj.* unforeseen; **de —** suddenly; *Col., Ven., Mex.* **en un —** in a moment, in the twinkling of an eye.

imprudencia *f.* imprudence, indiscretion, rash act.

imprudente *adj.* imprudent; unwise; indiscreet.

impuesto *p.p. of* **imponer** imposed; informed; *Am.* **estar —** to be used or accustomed to; *m.* tax, duty.

impulsar *v.* to impel, push, move; to force.

impulso *m.* impulse; push.

impureza *f.* impurity.

impuro *adj.* impure.

imputar *v.* to impute, attribute.

inacabable *adj.* unending, endless.

inacabado *adj.* unfinished.

inaccesible *adj.* inaccessible, unobtainable.

inacción *f.* inaction, inactivity, idleness.

inaceptable *adj.* unacceptable, unsatisfactory.

inactividad *f.* inactivity.

inactivo *adj.* inactive.

inadecuado *adj.* inadequate.

inadvertencia *f.* oversight; inattention, heedlessness.

inadvertido *adj.* careless, heedless; unnoticed.

inafectado *adj.* unaffected.

inagotable *adj.* inexhaustible.

inaguantable *adj.* insufferable, unbearable.

inalámbrico *adj.* wireless.

inalterable *adj.* unalterable, unchangeable.

inalterado *adj.* unchanged.

inamovible = inmovible.

inanición *f.* starvation.

inanimado *adj.* inanimate, lifeless.

inapetencia *f.* lack of appetite.

inaplicable *adj.* inapplicable, unsuitable; **— al caso** irrelevant.

inapreciable *adj.* invaluable; inappreciable, too small to be perceived, very slight.

inasequible *adj.* inaccessible, not obtainable; hard to attain or obtain.

inaudito *adj.* unheard-of; unprecedented.

inauguración *f.* inauguration.

inaugurar *v.* to inaugurate, begin, open.

incaico, incásico *adj.* Incan (*of or pertaining to the Incas*).

incalculable *adj.* incalculable; innumerable, untold.

incandescente *adj.* incandescent.

incansable *adj.* untiring, tireless.

incapacidad *f.* incompetence, inability, unfitness.

incapacitar *v.* to cripple, disable, handicap, unfit, make unfit.

incapaz *adj.* incapable, unable.

incauto *adj.* unwary, heedless, reckless.

incendiar *v.* to set fire to; **-se** to catch fire.

incendio *m.* conflagration, fire.

incentivo *m.* incentive, inducement.

incertidumbre *f.* uncertainty, doubt.

incesante *adj.* incessant.

incidental *adj.* incidental.

incidente *adj.* incidental; *m.* incident.

incienso *m.* incense.

incierto *adj.* uncertain, doubtful; unstable; unknown; untrue.

incisión *f.* incision, cut, slit, gash.

incitamiento *m.* incitement, inducement, incentive.

incitar *v.* to incite, rouse, stir up.

incivil *adj.* uncivil, rude, impolite.

inclemencia *f.* inclemency, severity, harshness; **inclemente** *adj.* unmerciful, merciless.

inclinación *f.* inclination, affection; tendency, bent; bow; incline, slope.

inclinar *v.* (*bajar*) to incline; (*persuadir*) to persuade; **-se** to bow; to stoop; to incline, slope, slant; to lean, bend.

incluir [32] *v. irr.* to include; to inclose.

inclusive *adv.* inclusive, including; even; **inclusivo** *adj.* inclusive; comprehensive.

incluso *adj.* inclosed; included; including; even.

incógnito *adj.* unknown; **de —** incognito (*with one's name or rank unknown*); **incógnita** *f.* unknown quantity (*in mathematics*).

incoherente *adj.* incoherent, disconnected, rambling.

incoloro *adj.* colorless.

incombustible *adj.* incombustible; fireproof.

incomodar *v.* to inconvenience, disturb, trouble, annoy.

incomodidad *f.* inconvenience, discomfort; bother, annoyance.

incómodo *adj.* inconvenient, bothersome; uncomfortable.

incomparable *adj.* incomparable.

incompasivo *adj.* merciless, pitiless.

incompatible *adj.* incompatible; unsuitable, uncongenial.

incompetencia *f.* incompetence, inability, unfitness; **incompetente** *adj.* incompetent, unfit.

incompleto *adj.* incomplete.

incomprensible *adj.* incomprehensible.

incondicional *adj.* unconditional.

inconexo *adj.* unconnected; incoherent, disconnected.

inconfundible *adj.* unmistakable.

incongruente *adj.* unsuitable, not appropriate; not harmonious.

inconquistable *adj.* unconquerable.

inconsciencia *f.* unconsciousness; unawareness.

inconsciente *adj.* unconscious; unaware.

inconsecuente *adj.* inconsistent; illogical.

inconsiderado *adj.* inconsiderate, thoughtless.

inconstancia *f.* inconstancy, changeableness, fickleness.

inconstante *adj.* inconstant, fickle, changeable, variable.

incontable *adj.* countless, innumerable.

inconveniencia *f.* inconvenience; trouble.

inconveniente *adj.* inconvenient; improper; *m.* obstacle; objection.

incorporar *v.* to incorporate, unite; to embody; to include; **-se** to sit up; **-se a** to join.

incorrecto *adj.* incorrect.

incredulidad *f.* incredulity, unbelief.

incrédulo *adj.* incredulous, unbelieving; *m.* unbeliever.

increíble *adj.* incredible, unbelievable.

incremento *m.* increment, increase.

incrustar *v.* to inlay; to encrust (*cover with a crust or hard coating*); **-se en** to penetrate, impress itself deeply into.

incubadora *f.* incubator.

inculcar[6] *v.* to inculcate, instill, impress.

inculto *adj.* uncultured; uncultivated; unrefined.

incumbencia *f.* concern, duty, obligation; **no es de mi —** it does not concern me, it is not in my province.

incurable *adj.* incurable.

incurrir *v.* to incur, fall (into); **— en un error** to fall into or commit an error; **— en el odio de** to incur the hatred of.

incursión *f.* raid, invasion.

indagación *f.* investigation, inquiry.

indagador *m.* investigator; inquirer; *adj.* investigating; inquiring.

indagar[7] *v.* to find out, investigate; to inquire.

indebido *adj.* undue, improper; illegal; **indebidamente** *adv.* unduly; illegally.

indecencia *f.* indecency, obscenity, indecent act or remark.

indecente *adj.* indecent, improper.

indecible *adj.* inexpressible, untold.

indeciso *adj.* undecided; doubtful, uncertain.

indefectible *adj.* unfailing; **-mente** unfailingly.

indefenso *adj.* defenseless, unprotected.

indefinible *adj.* indefinable.

indefinido *adj.* indefinite.

indeleble *adj.* indelible.

indemnización *f.* indemnity, compensation.

indemnizar[9] *v.* to indemnify, compensate.

independencia *f.* independence.

independiente *adj.* independent.

indescriptible *adj.* indescribable.

indeseable *adj.* undesirable, unwelcome.

indiada *f. Ríopl., C.A., Col.* community, group, or crowd of Indians; *Col.; Ven., Carib., Andes* an Indianlike remark or act; *Am.* an uncontrollable fit of anger.

indianista *m. & f.* student of Indian culture; *adj.* pertaining to Indian culture.

indiano *adj.* of or pertaining to the West or East Indies; *m.* Spaniard who goes back to settle in his country after having lived for some time in Spanish America.

indicación *f.* indication.

indicar[6] *v.* to indicate, show, point out.

indicativo *adj.* indicative; *m.* indicative, indicative mood.

índice *m.* index; catalogue; sign; pointer; forefinger.

indicio *m.* indication, sign.

indiferencia *f.* indifference.

indiferente *adj.* indifferent.

indígena *adj.* indigenous, native; *m. & f.* native inhabitant; *Am.* Indian.

indignación *f.* indignation.

indignado *p.p. & adj.* indignant, irritated, angry.

indignar *v.* to irritate, anger; **-se** to become indignant, angry.

indignidad *f.* indignity, affront, insult; unworthy or disgraceful act.

indigno *adj.* unworthy; low, contemptible.

indio *adj. & m.* Indian; Hindu.

indirecta *f.* hint, indirect remark, innuendo, insinuation.

indirecto *adj.* indirect.

indisciplinado *adj.* undisciplined, untrained.

indiscreto *adj.* indiscreet, imprudent, unwise, rash.

indiscutible *adj.* indisputable, unquestionable.

indispensable *adj.* indispensable.

indisponer[40] *v. irr.* to indispose; to make ill; **— a uno con otro** to prejudice someone against another; **-se** to become ill; **-se con** to fall out with, quarrel with.

indisposición *f.* indisposition, upset, slight illness; reluctance, unwillingness.

indispuesto *p.p. of* **indisponer** & *adj.* indisposed, unwilling; ill.

indisputable *adj.* unquestionable.

indistinto *adj.* indistinct, dim, vague, not clear.

individual *adj.* individual.

individualidad *f.* individuality.

individuo *adj.* individual; indivisible; *m.* individual; person; member.

indócil *adj.* unruly, disobedient, headstrong.

indocto *adj.* uneducated, ignorant.

índole *f.* disposition, temper; kind, class.

indolencia *f.* indolence, laziness; insensitiveness, indifference.

indolente *adj.* indolent, lazy; insensitive, indifferent.

indomable *adj.* indomitable, unconquerable; unmanageable; untamable.

indómito *adj.* untamed; uncontrollable, unruly.

inducir[25] *v. irr.* to induce; to persuade.

indudable *adj.* unquestionable, certain.

indulgencia *f.* indulgence, tolerance, forgiveness; remission of sins.

indulgente *adj.* indulgent, lenient.

indultar *v.* to pardon, set free; to exempt.

indulto *m.* pardon, forgiveness; exemption; privilege.

indumentaria *f.* costume, dress; manner of dressing.

industria *f.* industry; cleverness, skill; **de —** intentionally, on purpose.

industrial *adj.* industrial; *m.* industrialist; manufacturer.

industrioso *adj.* industrious.

inédito *adj.* unpublished.

inefable *adj.* ineffable, inexpressible.

ineficaz *adj.* ineffective; inefficient.

inepto *adj.* incompetent; unsuitable.

inequívoco *adj.* unmistakable.

inercia *f.* inertia, lifelessness; inactivity.

inerme *adj.* unarmed, defenseless.

inerte *adj.* inert; inactive, sluggish, slow.

inesperado *adj.* unexpected.

inestable *adj.* unstable; unsettled; unsteady.

inestimable *adj.* inestimable, invaluable.

inevitable *adj.* inevitable, unavoidable.

inexacto *adj.* inexact, inaccurate.

inexperiencia *f.* inexperience.

inexperto *adj.* unskilful, unskilled, inexperienced.

inexplicable *adj.* inexplicable.

inextinguible *adj.* inextinguishable, unquenchable.

infalible *adj.* infallible.

infame *adj.* infamous; *m.* scoundrel.

infamia *f.* infamy, dishonor; wickedness.

infancia *f.* infancy.

infante *m.* infant; infante (*royal prince of Spain, esp. the heir to the throne*); infantryman.

infantería *f.* infantry.

infantil *adj.* infantile, childlike, childish.

infatigable *adj.* tireless, untiring.

infausto *adj.* unfortunate; unhappy.

infección *f.* infection; **infeccioso** *adj.* infectious.

infectar *v.* to infect; to corrupt; **-se** to become infected.

infeliz *adj.* unhappy, unfortunate; *m.* poor wretch.

inferior *adj.* inferior; lower; *m.* inferior.

inferioridad *f.* inferiority.

inferir[3] *v. irr.* (*concluir*) to infer; to imply; (*causar*) to inflict.

infernal *adj.* infernal.

infestar *v.* to infest, invade, overrun, plague; to corrupt, infect.

inficionar *v.* to infect; to contaminate.

infiel *adj.* unfaithful, faithless; infidel; inaccurate.

infiernillo *m.* chafing dish.

infierno *m.* hell; **en el quinto —** very far away.

infiltrar *v.* to filter through; **-se** to leak (into), filter (through), infiltrate.

infinidad *f.* infinity; **una — de** a large number of.

infinito *adj.* infinite; *adv.* infinitely; *m.* infinity.

inflamación *f.* inflammation.

inflamado *p.p.* & *adj.* inflamed; sore.

inflamar *v.* to inflame, excite; to kindle, set on fire; **-se** to become inflamed.

inflar *v.* to inflate; to exaggerate; **-se** to become inflated; to swell up with pride.

inflexible *adj.* inflexible, stiff, rigid; unbending.

inflexión *f.* inflection.

infligir[11] *v.* to inflict.

influencia *f.* influence.

influenza *f.* influenza, grippe, flu.

influir[32] *v. irr.* to influence.

influjo *m.* influence; influx, inward flow.

influyente *adj.* influential.

información *f.* information.

informal *adj.* informal; unconventional; unreliable, not dependable, not punctual.

informar *v.* to inform; to give form to; to give a report; to present a case; **-se** to become informed.

informe *m.* report, account; information; brief; *adj.* formless, shapeless.

infortunio *m.* misfortune, mishap; misery.

infracción *f.* infraction, breach, violation (*of a law, treaty, etc.*).

infractor *m.* transgressor, lawbreaker, violator (*of a law*).

infrascrito *m.* undersigned, subscriber, signer (*of a letter, document, etc.*); **el — secretario** the secretary whose signature appears below.

infringir[11] *v.* to infringe, break, violate.

infructuoso *adj.* fruitless.

ínfulas *f. pl.* airs, false importance; **darse —** to put on airs.

infundado *adj.* groundless, without foundation.

infundir *v.* to infuse, inspire; to instill.

infusión *f.* infusion (*liquid extract obtained by steeping*); infusion, inspiration; **poner en —** to steep (*as tea leaves*).

ingeniería *f.* engineering.

ingeniero *m.* engineer.

ingenio *m.* genius; talent; ingenuity; mentality, mental power, mind; wit; **— de azúcar** sugar refinery; sugar plantation.

ingeniosidad *f.* ingenuity, cleverness.

ingenioso *adj.* ingenious, clever.

ingenuidad *f.* candor, frankness; unaffected simplicity.

ingenuo *adj.* frank, sincere; simple, un-affected; naive.

ingerir = injerir.

ingestión *f.* ingestion.

ingle *f.* groin.

inglés *adj.* English; **a la inglesa** in the English fashion; *Am.* **ir a la inglesa** to go Dutch treat; *m.* English-man; the English language.

ingobernable *adj.* ungovernable, un-ruly, uncontrollable.

ingratitud *f.* ingratitude.

ingrato *adj.* ungrateful, thankless; harsh; cruel; disdainful.

ingrediente *m.* ingredient.

ingresar *v.* to enter; **— en** to join (*a society, club, etc.*).

ingreso *m.* entrance; entry; **-s** receipts, profits; revenue.

inhábil *adj.* unskilled; unskilful; unfit.

inhabilidad *f.* inability; unfitness.

inhabilitar *v.* to disqualify; to unfit, disable.

inherente *adj.* inherent.

inhospitalario *adj.* inhospitable.

inhumano *adj.* inhuman, cruel.

iniciador *m.* initiator; pioneer; *adj.* initiating.

inicial *adj. & f.* initial.

iniciar *v.* to initiate; to begin.

iniciativa *f.* initiative.

inicuo *adj.* wicked.

iniquidad *f.* iniquity, wickedness; sin.

injerir[3] *v. irr.* to inject, insert; **-se** to interfere, meddle.

injertar *v.* to graft.

injerto *m.* graft.

injuria *f.* affront, insult; harm, damage.

injuriar *v.* to insult, offend; to harm, damage.

injurioso *adj.* insulting, offensive; harmful.

injusticia *f.* injustice.

injustificado *adj.* unjustified; unjusti-fiable.

injusto *adj.* unjust, unfair.

inmaculado *adj.* immaculate, clean; pure.

inmediación *f.* vicinity; nearness; **-es** environs, outskirts.

inmediato *adj.* near, close; *Am.* **de —** immediately; suddenly; **inmediatamente** *adv.* immediately, at once.

inmensidad *f.* immensity, vastness; vast number.

inmenso *adj.* immense, vast, huge; boundless.

inmersión *f.* immersion, dip.

inmigración *f.* immigration.

inmigrante *adj., m. & f.* immigrant.

inmigrar *v.* to immigrate.

inminente *adj.* imminent.

inmiscuir[32] *v. irr.* to mix; **-se** to med-dle, interfere.

inmoble *adj.* motionless; unshaken.

inmoral *adj.* immoral; **inmoralidad** *f.* immorality.

inmortal *adj.* immortal; **inmortalidad** *f.* immortality.

inmovible *adj.* immovable, fixed; steadfast.

inmóvil *adj.* motionless, still; immov-able.

inmundicia *f.* filth, dirt; nastiness.

inmundo *adj.* filthy, dirty; impure; nasty.

inmune *adj.* immune; exempt.

inmunidad *f.* immunity.

inmutable *adj.* unchangeable, invari-able.

inmutar *v.* to alter, change; **-se** to show emotion (*either by turning pale or blushing*).

innato *adj.* innate, natural, inborn.

innecesario *adj.* unnecessary.

innegable *adj.* undeniable, not to be denied.

innocuo *adj.* innocuous, harmless; **innocuidad** *f.* harmlessness.

innovación *f.* innovation; novelty.

innumerable *adj.* innumerable.

inobservancia *f.* nonobservance, viola-tion (*of a law*), lack of observance (*of a law, rule, or custom*).

inocencia *f.* innocence.

inocente *adj.* innocent; *m.* innocent person; **inocentón** *adj.* quite foolish or simple; easily fooled; *m.* dupe, un-suspecting victim.

inocular *v.* to inoculate.

inodoro *adj.* odorless; *m. C.A., Ven., Col.* toilet, water closet.

inofensivo *adj.* inoffensive; harmless.

inolvidable *adj.* unforgettable.

inopinado *adj.* unexpected.

inoportuno *adj.* inopportune, untimely, unsuitable.

inquietar *v.* to worry, disturb, make uneasy; **-se** to become disturbed, un-easy.

inquieto *adj.* restless; uneasy, anxious.

inquietud *f.* restlessness; anxiety, un-easiness; fear.

inquilino *m.* tenant, renter; lodger.

inquina *f.* aversion, grudge, dislike.

inquirir[35] *v. irr.* to inquire, investigate; to find out.

inquisición *f.* inquisition; inquiry, in-vestigation.

insaciable *adj.* insatiable, never satis-fied, greedy.

insalubre *adj.* unhealthy, unhealthful, unwholesome.

insano *adj.* insane, crazy; unhealthy.

inscribir[52] *v.* to inscribe; to register, en-roll; to record; **-se** to register.

inscripción *f.* inscription; registration.

inscripto, inscrito *p.p.* of **inscribir.**

insecto *m.* insect.

inseguro *adj.* insecure; unsafe; doubt-ful, uncertain.

insensato *adj.* senseless; foolish.

insensibilidad *f.* insensibility, uncon-sciousness; lack of feeling.

insensible *adj.* insensible; unfeeling; imperceptible.

inseparable *adj.* inseparable.

inserción *f.* insertion; insert.

insertar *v.* to insert.

inserto *adj.* inserted.

inservible *adj.* useless.

insidioso *adj.* insidious; sly, crafty.

insigne *adj.* famous.

insignia *f.* badge, medal, decoration; flag, pennant; **-s** insignia.

insignificante *adj.* insignificant.

insinuación *f.* insinuation; intimation, hint.

insinuar[18] *v.* to insinuate, hint; **-se** to insinuate oneself (*into another's friendship*); **a** to creep (into) gradually.

insipidez *f.* flatness, tastelessness, dullness; **insípido** *adj.* insipid; tasteless.

insistencia *f.* insistence, persistence, obstinacy; **insistente** *adj.* insistent, persistent.

insistir *v.* to insist; to persist.

insociable *adj.* unsociable.

insolación *f.* sunstroke.

insolencia *f.* insolence.

insolentarse *v.* to sauce, become insolent, act with insolence.

insolente *adj.* insolent.

insólito *adj.* unusual; uncommon.

insolvente *adj.* insolvent, bankrupt.

insomne *adj.* sleepless.

insondable *adj.* fathomless, deep; impenetrable.

insoportable *adj.* unbearable.

insospechado *adj.* unsuspected.

inspección *f.* inspection.

inspeccionar *v.* to inspect.

inspector *m.* inspector; overseer.

inspiración *f.* inspiration; inhalation, breathing in.

inspirar *v.* to inspire; to inhale.

instalación *f.* installation.

instalar *v.* to install.

instancia *f.* instance, urgent request; petition; **a -s de** at the request of.

instantánea *f.* snapshot.

instantáneo *adj.* instantaneous; sudden.

instante *m.* instant, moment; **al —** at once, immediately; **por -s** continually; from one moment to another; *adj.* instant, urgent.

instar *v.* to urge, press; to be urgent.

instigar[7] *v.* to instigate, urge on, incite.

instintivo *adj.* instinctive.

instinto *m.* instinct.

institución *f.* institution; establishment, foundation; **-es** institutes, collection of precepts and principles.

instituir[32] *v. irr.* to institute; **— por heredero** to appoint as heir.

instituto *m.* institute; established principle, law, or custom; **— de segunda enseñanza** high school.

institutriz *f.* governess.

instrucción *f.* instruction; education.

instructivo *adj.* instructive.

instruir[32] *v. irr.* to instruct, teach; to inform.

instrumento *m.* instrument.

insuficiencia *f.* insufficiency, deficiency; incompetence; dearth, scarcity, lack.

insuficiente *adj.* insufficient.

insufrible *adj.* insufferable, unbearable.

ínsula *f.* island.

insultante *adj.* insulting, abusive.

insultar *v.* to insult; **-se** to be seized with a fit.

insulto *m.* insult; sudden fit or attack.

insuperable *adj.* insuperable; insurmountable.

insurgente *adj.*, *m.* & *f.* insurgent.

insurrección *f.* insurrection, uprising, revolt.

insurrecto *m.* insurgent, rebel; *adj.* rebellious.

intacto *adj.* intact.

intachable *adj.* faultless, irreproachable.

integral *adj.* integral; *f.* integral (*math*).

integrante *adj.* integral; integrating.

integridad *f.* integrity; wholeness; honesty; purity.

íntegro *adj.* whole, complete; honest, upright.

intelecto *m.* intellect.

intelectual *adj.* intellectual.

inteligencia *f.* intelligence.

inteligente *adj.* intelligent.

intemperancia *f.* intemperance, excess.

intemperie *f.* open air; bad weather; **a la —** unsheltered, outdoors, in the open air; exposed to the weather.

intención *f.* intention; **intencional** *adj.* intentional.

intendente *m.* manager, superintendent, supervisor; *Ríopl.* governor of a province; *Am.* police commissioner.

intensidad *f.* intensity; stress.

intenso *adj.* intense; intensive; ardent, vehement.

intentar *v.* to attempt, try; to intend.

intento *m.* intent, purpose, intention; **de —** on purpose.

intercalar *v.* to insert, place between.

intercambio *m.* interchange; exchange.

interceder *v.* to intercede.

interceptar *v.* to intercept.

intercesión *f.* intercession, mediation.

interdicción *f.* interdiction; prevention.

interés *m.* interest.

interesante *adj.* interesting.

interesar *v.* to interest; to give an interest or share; **-se** to be or become interested.

interferencia *f.* interference.

ínterin *m.* interim, meantime; **en al —** in the meantime.

interino *adj.* acting, temporary.

interior *adj.* interior; inner; internal; *m.* interior, inside.

interjección *f.* interjection, exclamation.

interlocutor *m.* participant in a dialogue.

intermedio *adj.* intermediate; intervening; *m.* intermission; interval; **por — de** by means of, through the intervention of.

interminable *adj.* interminable, unending, endless.

intermisión *f.* intermission, interruption, pause, interval.

intermitente *adj.* intermittent, occurring at intervals; **calentura** (*or* **fiebre**) **—** intermittent fever.

internacional *adj.* international.

internado *m.* a boarding student.

internar *v.* to intern, confine; **-se** to penetrate, go into the interior.

interno *adj.* internal; interior; *m.* boarding-school student.

interoceánico *adj.* interoceanic; transcontinental.

interpelar *v.* to interrogate, question, demand explanations; to ask the aid of.

interponer[40] *v. irr.* to interpose, put between, insert; to place as a mediator; **-se** to intervene, mediate.

interpretación *f.* interpretation.

interpretar *v.* to interpret.

intérprete *m.* & *f.* interpreter.

interpuesto *p.p. of* interponer.

interrogación *f.* interrogation, question; **signo de —** question mark.

interrogador *m.* questioner; *adj.* questioning.

interrogar[7] *v.* to interrogate, question.

interrogativo *adj.* interrogative.

interrogatorio *m.* interrogation, questioning.

interrumpir *v.* to interrupt.

interrupción *f.* interruption.

interruptor *m.* interrupter; electric switch.

intersección *f.* intersection.

intervalo *m.* interval.

intervención *f.* intervention; mediation; participation; auditing of accounts.

intervenir[48] *v. irr.* to intervene; to mediate; to audit (*accounts*).

interventor *m.* inspector; controller, comptroller; auditor.

intestino *m.* intestine; *adj.* intestine, internal.

intimación *f.* intimation; hint, insinuation, suggestion.

intimar *v.* to announce, notify; to intimate, hint; to become intimate, become friendly.

intimidad *f.* intimacy.

intimidar *v.* to intimidate.

íntimo *adj.* intimate.

intitular *v.* to entitle; to give a title to (*a person or a thing*); **-se** to be entitled, be called; to call oneself (*by a certain name*).

intolerable *adj.* intolerable.

intolerancia *f.* intolerance; **intolerante** *adj.* intolerant, narrow-minded.

intoxicante *m.* poison.

intoxicar[6] *v.* to poison.

intranquilo *adj.* disturbed, uneasy.

intranquilidad *f.* uneasiness, restlessness.

intransigencia *f.* uncompromising act or attitude; intolerance.

intransigente *adj.* uncompromising, unwilling to compromise or yield; intolerant.

intratable *adj.* unsociable; rude; unruly.

intravenoso *adj.* intravenous (*within a vein or the veins; into a vein*).

intrepidez *f.* fearlessness, courage.

intrépido *adj.* intrepid, fearless.

intriga *f.* intrigue; scheme; plot.

intrigante *m.* & *f.* intriguer, plotter; *adj.* intriguing.

intrigar[7] *v.* to intrigue.

intrincado *adj.* intricate, complicated, entangled.

introducción *f.* introduction.

introducir[25] *v. irr.* to introduce; **-se** to introduce oneself; to get in; to penetrate.

intromisión *f.* meddling; insertion.

intruso *adj.* intrusive, intruding; *m.* intruder.

intuición *f.* intuition.

intuir[32] *v. irr.* to sense, feel by intuition.

inundación *f.* inundation, flood.

inundar *v.* to inundate, flood.

inusitado *adj.* unusual, rare.

inútil *adj.* useless.

inutilidad *f.* uselessness.

inutilizar[9] *v.* to make useless, put out of commission; to disable; to ruin, spoil.

invadir *v.* to invade.

invalidar *v.* to render invalid; to void, annul.

inválido *adj.* invalid; void, null; sickly, weak; *m.* invalid.

invariable *adj.* invariable.

invasión *f.* invasion.

invasor *m.* invader; *adj.* invading; **ejército —** invading army.

invencible *adj.* invincible, unconquerable.

invención *f.* invention.

invendible *adj.* unsaleable.

inventar *v.* to invent.

inventariar[17] *v.* to inventory, take an inventory of.

inventario *m.* inventory.

inventiva *f.* inventiveness, power of inventing, ingenuity.

inventivo *adj.* inventive.

invento *m.* invention.

inventor *m.* inventor; storyteller, fibber.

invernáculo *m.* greenhouse, hothouse.

invernadero *m.* winter quarters; winter resort; winter pasture; greenhouse, hothouse.

invernal *adj.* wintry, winter.

invernar[1] *v. irr.* to winter, spend the winter.

inverosímil, inverisímil *adj.* unlikely, improbable.

inversión *f.* inversion; investment.

inverso *adj.* inverse, inverted; reverse; **a** (*or* **por**) **la inversa** on the contrary.

invertir[3] *v. irr.* to invert; to reverse; to invest; to employ, spend (*time*).

investigación *f.* investigation.

investigador *m.* investigator; *adj.* investigating.

investigar[7] *v.* to investigate.

invicto *adj.* unconquered; always victorious.

invierno *m.* winter; *C.A., Col., Ven., Ec., Peru* the rainy season.

invisible *adj.* invisible.

invitación *f.* invitation.

invitar *v.* to invite.

invocar[6] *v.* to invoke.

involuntario *adj.* involuntary.

inyección *f.* injection.

inyectado *p.p.* injected; *adj.* blood-shot, inflamed.

inyectar *v.* to inject.

ir[33] *v. irr.* to go; to walk; **— corriendo** to be running; **— entendiendo** to understand gradually; to begin to understand; **— a caballo** to ride horseback; **— a pie** to walk; **— en automóvil** to drive, ride in an automobile; **no irle ni venirle a uno** to make no difference to one; **¿cómo le va?** how are you?; **no me va nada en eso** that doesn't concern me; **¡vamos!** let's go! come on!; **¡vaya!** well now!; **¡vaya un hombre!** what a man!; **-se** to go, go away; to escape; **-se abajo** to fall down, topple over; to collapse; **-se a pique** to founder, sink.

ira *f.* ire, anger.

iracundo *adj.* irritable; angry.

iris *m.* iris (*of the eye*); **arco —** rainbow.

irisado *adj.* iridescent, rainbow-hued.

ironía *f.* irony.

irónico *adj.* ironic, ironical.

irracional *adj.* irrational, unreasonable.

irradiar *v.* to radiate.

irreal *adj.* unreal.

irreflexión *f.* thoughtlessness.

irreflexivo *adj.* thoughtless.

irrefrenable *adj.* uncontrollable.

irregular *adj.* irregular.

irreligioso *adj.* irreligious.

irremediable *adj.* irremediable; hopeless, incurable.

irreprochable *adj.* irreproachable, flawless.

irresistible *adj.* irresistible.

irresoluto *adj.* irresolute, undecided, hesitating.

irrespetuoso *adj.* disrespectful.

irreverencia *f.* irreverence.

irreverente *adj.* irreverent.

irrigación *f.* irrigation.

irrigar[7] *v.* to irrigate.

irrisión *f.* mockery, ridicule, derision.

irritación *f.* irritation.

irritante *adj.* irritating.

irritar *v.* to irritate.

irrumpir *v.* to enter violently; to invade.

irrupción *f.* sudden attack, raid, invasion.

isla *f.* island.

isleño *m.* islander.

islote *m.* islet, small rocky island.

istmo *m.* isthmus.

italiano *adj. & m.* Italian.

itinerario *m.* itinerary; timetable, schedule; railroad guide.

izar[9] *v.* to hoist; to heave.

izquierda *f.* left hand; left side; left wing (*in politics*); **a la —** to the left; **izquierdista** *m. & f.* leftist, radical.

izquierdo *adj.* left; left-handed.

J

jabalí *m.* wild boar.

jabalina *f.* javelin; wild sow.

jabón *m.* soap; *Ríopl.* fright, fear; **dar** — to soft-soap, flatter; **dar un —** to give a good scolding; to beat, thrash.

jabonadura *f.* washing, soaping; **-s** suds, lather; **dar a uno una —** to reprimand or scold someone.

jabonar *v.* (*lavar*) to lather, soap; (*reprender*) to scold; reprimand.

jabonera *f.* soap dish; woman soap vendor or maker.

jaca *f.* pony; small horse; **jaco** *m.* small nag; poor horse.

jacal *m. Mex.* shack, adobe hut; **jacalucho** *m. Am.* poor, ugly shack.

jacinto *m.* hyacinth.

jactancia *f.* boast, brag; boasting.

jactancioso *adj.* braggart, boastful.

jactarse *v.* to brag, boast.

jaculatoria *f.* short, fervent prayer.

jadeante *adj.* breathless, panting, out of breath.

jadear *v.* to pant.

jadeo *m.* pant, panting.

jaez *m.* harness; kind, sort; **jaeces** trappings.

jalar *v.* to pull; to haul; to jerk; *C.A.* to court, make love; *Ven., Andes* to flunk (*a student*); *Mex.* **¡jala!** (or **¡jálale!**) get going! get a move on there!; **-se** *Am.* to get drunk; *Mex.* to go away, move away.

jalea *f.* jelly.

jalear *v.* to shout (*to hunting dogs*); to rouse, beat up (*game*); to shout and clap (*to encourage dancers*).

jaleo *m.* shouting and clapping (*to encourage dancers*); an Andalusian dance; revelry, merrymaking; jesting; gracefulness.

jaletina *f.* gelatin.

jalón *m.* marker (*for boundaries*); *Am.* pull, jerk, tug; *Mex., C.A.* swallow of liquor; *Bol., C.A.* stretch, distance.

jalonear *v. C.A., Mex.* to pull, jerk.

jamás *adv.* never.

jamón *m.* ham; *P.R.* fix, difficulty.

japonés *adj. & m.* Japanese.

jaque *m.* check (*in chess*); braggart, bully; **— mate** checkmate (*in chess*); **tener a uno en —** to hold someone under a threat.

jaqueca *f.* headache; sick headache.

jara *f.* rockrose (*shrub*); *Ven., Col.* reed; **jaral** *m.* bramble of rockroses; *Am.* reeds, clump of reeds.

jarabe *m.* syrup; sweet beverage; *Mex., C.A.* a kind of tap dance; *Mex.* song and musical accompaniment of the **jarabe**.

jarana *f.* merrymaking, revelry; trick; fib; jest; *Col., Ec., Carib.* a dance; *Mex.* small guitar; **ir de —** to go on a spree.

jarcia *f.* rigging (*ropes, chains, etc. for the masts, yards and sails of a ship*); fishing tackle; pile, heap; jumble of things.

jardín *m.* flower garden.

jardinero *m.* gardener.

jarra *f.* jar, vase, pitcher; **de** (*or* **en**) **-s** akimbo (*with hands on the hips*).

jarro *m.* jar, jug, pitcher.

jarrón m. large vase or jar.

jaspe m. jasper; veined marble; **jaspeado** adj. veined, streaked, mottled.

jaula f. cage; cagelike cell or prison; Am. roofless cattle car or freight car.

jauría f. pack of hounds.

jazmín m. jasmine.

jefatura f. position of chief; headquarters of a chief.

jefe m. chief, leader, head.

jengibre m. ginger.

jerez m. sherry wine.

jerga f. (tela) thick coarse cloth; straw mattress; (dialecto) jargon; slang; Am. saddle pad; Col. poncho made of coarse cloth.

jergón m. (material) straw mattress; ill-fitting suit or dress; (persona) big clumsy fellow; Ríopl., Mex., Ven. cheap coarse rug.

jerigonza f. jargon; slang.

jeringa f. syringe; **jeringazo** m. injection; squirt.

jeringar[7] v. to inject; to squirt; to bother, molest, vex, annoy.

jesuita m. Jesuit.

jeta f. snout; thick lips.

jiba = **giba**.

jíbaro adj. P.R. rustic, rural, rude, uncultured; m. P.R. bumpkin, peasant.

jícara f. chocolate cup; Am. small bowl made out of a gourd; Am. any small bowl; Am. bald head.

jilguero m. linnet.

jinete m. horseman, rider.

jineteada f. Ríopl., C.A. roughriding, horse-breaking.

jinetear v. to ride horseback; to perform on horseback; Am. to break in (a horse); Am. to ride a bronco or bull.

jira f. excursion, tour; outing, picnic; strip of cloth.

jirafa f. giraffe; boom mike (broadcasting).

jitomate m. Mex. tomato. Also **gitomate**.

jofaina f. basin, washbowl.

jolgorio = **holgorio**.

jornada f. day's journey; military expedition; working day; act (of a Spanish play).

jornal m. day's wages; bookkeeping journal; **a — by the day.

jornalero m. day laborer.

joroba f. hump; nuisance, annoyance.

jorobado adj. hunchbacked; annoyed, bothered, in a bad fix; m. hunchback.

jorobar v. to bother, pester, annoy.

jorongo m. Mex. Mexican poncho.

jota f. name of the letter j; iota (anything insignificant); Aragonese and Valencian dance and music; Am. (= ojota) leather sandal; **no saber una — not to know anything.

joven adj. young; m. & f. youth; young man; young woman.

jovial adj. jovial, jolly, merry; **jovialidad** f. gaiety, merriment, fun.

joya f. jewel; piece of jewelry; **-s** jewels, trousseau.

joyería f. jeweler's shop.

joyero m. jeweler; jewel box.

juanete m. bunion.

jubilación f. retirement (from a position or office); pension.

jubilar v. to pension; to retire; **-se** to be pensioned or retired; to rejoice; Col. to decline, fall into decline; Ven., Guat. to play hooky or truant.

jubileo m. jubilee; time of rejoicing; concession by the Pope of plenary (complete) indulgence.

júbilo m. joy, glee.

jubiloso adj. jubilant, joyful.

jubón m. jacket; bodice.

judía f. bean; string bean; Jewess; **-s tiernas** (or **verdes**) string beans.

judicial adj. judicial; **-mente** adv. judicially.

judío adj. Jewish; m. Jew.

judo m. judo.

juego m. game; play; sport; gambling; pack of cards; set; **— de palabras** pun, play on words; **— de te** tea set; **hacer —** to match; **poner en —** to coordinate; to set in motion.

juerga f. spree, revelry, wild festivity; **irse de —** to go out on a spree; **juerguista** m. & f. merrymaker.

jueves m. Thursday.

juez m. judge; juror, member of a jury; **— arbitrador** (or **árbitro**) arbitrator, umpire.

jugada f. play, move; stroke; trick.

jugador m. player; gambler; **— de manos** juggler.

jugar[34] v. irr. to play; to gamble; to toy; **— a la pelota** to play ball; Am. **— a dos cartas** to be double-faced.

jugarreta f. bad play, wrong play; mean trick; tricky deal; Am. noisy game.

jugo m. juice; sap.

jugosidad f. juiciness; **jugoso** adj. juicy.

juguete m. plaything, toy; jest, joke; **— cómico** skit; **por** (or **de**) **—** jokingly.

juguetear v. to play around, romp, frolic; to toy; to tamper (with), fool (with).

juguetón adj. playful.

juicio m. judgment; sense, wisdom; opinion; trial; **perder el —** to lose one's mind, go crazy.

juicioso adj. judicious, wise; sensible.

julio m. July.

jumento m. ass, donkey.

junco m. rush, reed; junk (Chinese sailboat).

jungla f. Am. jungle.

junio m. June.

junquillo m. reed; jonquil (yellow flower similar to the daffodil), species of narcissus.

junta f. (reunión) meeting, conference; (funcionarios) board, council.

juntar v. to join, unite; to connect; to assemble; to collect; **-se** to assemble, gather; to be closely united; to associate (with).

junto adj. joined, united; **-s** together; adv. near; **— a** near to, close to; **en —**

all together, in all; **por —** all together, in a lump; wholesale.

juntura f. juncture; junction; joint, seam.

jurado m. jury; juror, juryman; adj. & p.p. sworn.

juramentar v. to swear in; **-se** to take an oath, be sworn in.

juramento m. oath; vow; curse.

jurar v. to swear, vow; to take oath; to curse.

jurisconsulto m. jurist, expert in law; lawyer.

jurisdicción f. jurisdiction.

jurisprudencia f. jurisprudence, law.

juro: de — adv. certainly, of course.

justa f. joust, tournament, combat (between horsemen with lances); contest.

justicia f. justice; court of justice; judge; police.

justiciero adj. strictly just, austere (in matters of justice).

justificación f. justification.

justificante adj. justifying; m. voucher; written excuse; proof.

justificar[6] v. to justify; to vindicate, clear of blame.

justo adj. just; pious; exact, correct; tight; adv. duly; exactly; tightly; m. just man; **los -s** the just.

juvenil adj. juvenile, young, youthful.

juventud f. youth; young people.

juzgado m. court, tribunal.

juzgar[7] v. to judge.

K

kermesse f. country fair; bazaar for charity.

kerosena f. kerosene, coal oil.

kilo m. kilo, kilogram.

kilogramo m. kilogram.

kilometraje m. number of kilometers.

kilómetro m. kilometer.

L

la def. art. f. the; **— de** the one with, that one with; obj. pron. her; it; **— que** rel. pron. she who, the one that; which.

la m. sixth note on the musical scale.

laberinto m. labyrinth, maze; labyrinth, internal ear.

labia f. fluency, talkativeness, gift of gab; **tener mucha —** to be a good talker.

labial adj. labial.

labio m. lip.

labiodental adj. labiodental.

labor f. (trabajo) labor, work; (cosido) embroidery; needlework; (agrícola) tillage; **— de punto** knitting; **laborable** adj. workable; tillable; **día laborable** work day; **laboral** adj. pertaining to labor.

laboratorio m. laboratory.

laboriosidad f. laboriousness, industry.

laborioso adj. laborious; industrious.

labrado p.p. & adj. (agrícola) tilled, cultivated; (hecho) wrought; manufactured; carved; m. carving; **— en madera** woodwork, carving; **-s** cultivated lands.

labrador m. farmer; peasant.

labranza f. farming, tillage, plowing; cultivated land, farm.

labrar v. (la tierra) to till, cultivate, farm; to plow; (crear) to carve; to embroider; to work (metals); to build (a monument).

labriego m. peasant.

laca f. lacquer; shellac.

lacayo m. lackey, footman, flunky.

lacio adj. withered; languid; limp; straight (hair).

lacra f. trace of an illness; blemish, defect; Am. sore, ulcer, scab, scar.

lacre m. red sealing wax; adj. Am. red.

lactar v. to nurse, suckle; to feed with milk.

lácteo adj. milky; **fiebre láctea** milk fever; **régimen —** milk diet; **Vía Láctea** Milky Way.

ladear v. to tilt, tip; to go along the slope or side of; to turn aside (from a way or course); **-se** to tilt; to sway; to incline or lean (towards); to move to one side; Am. to fall in love.

ladeo m. inclination, tilt.

ladera f. slope.

ladino adj. crafty, sly, shrewd; conversant with two or three languages; m. Sephardic Jew (Spanish-speaking); Romansch (a Romance language of Switzerland); Guat. Spanish-speaking person (as opposed to one who speaks an Indian language); Am. mestizo, half-breed; Mex., Ven. talker, talkative person.

lado m. side; **al —** near, at hand, at one's side; **de —** tilted, obliquely; sideways; **— a** side by side; **¡a un —!** gangway! **hacerse a un —** to move over, step aside, move to one side; Mex., Ven. **echársela de —** to boast.

ladrar v. to bark.

ladrido m. bark, barking.

ladrillo m. brick.

ladrón m. thief, robber; **ladronzuelo** m. petty thief.

lagartija f. small lizard.

lagarto m. lizard; rascal, sly fellow.

lago m. lake.

lágrima f. tear; **llorar a — viva** to weep abundantly.

lagrimear v. to weep, shed tears.

laguna f. lagoon; gap, blank space.

laico adj. lay; m. layman.

laja f. slab; flat stone.

lamedero m. salt lick (for cattle).

lamentable adj. lamentable, pitiful.

lamentación f. lamentation.

lamentar v. to lament, deplore; **-se** to moan, complain, wail.

lamento m. lament, moan, cry.

lamer v. to lick; to lap.

lamida f. Mex., C.A. lick; also **lambida**.

lámina f. metal plate; sheet of metal; engraving; book illustration.

lámpara f. lamp.

lampiño adj. hairless; beardless.

lana f. wool; Am. tramp, vagabond.

JA

lanar adj. wool-bearing; of wool.
lance m. occurrence, event; cast, throw, move, turn; accident; quarrel; predicament.
lancear v. to lance, spear.
lancha f. launch; boat; slab; **lanchón** m. barge.
langosta f. lobster; locust.
languidecer[13] v. irr. to languish.
languidez f. languor, faintness, weakness.
lánguido adj. languid.
lanilla f. nap (of cloth).
lanudo adj. woolly; Ven. coarse, crude, ill-bred; Am. dull, slow, weak-willed; Ch., C.A., Col. wealthy.
lanza f. lance, spear; Col. swindler, cheat; m. **lanzabombas** bomb launcher; m. **lanzacohetes** rocket launcher; m. **lanzallamas** flame thrower.
lanzada f. thrust (with a spear).
lanzadera f. shuttle.
lanzamiento m. launching (boat or rocket).
lanzar[9] v. to fling, throw; to eject; to launch; **-se** to rush, fling oneself; to dart out.
lanzazo m. thrust with a lance.
lapicero m. pencil (a mechanical pencil, one with an adjustable lead).
lápida f. slab, tombstone; stone tablet.
lapidar v. to stone; Col., Ch. to cut precious stones.
lápiz f. pencil; crayon; **— para los labios** lipstick.
lapso m. lapse.
lardo m. lard.
largar[7] v. to loosen; to let go; to set free; to unfold (a flag or sails); Am. to hurl, throw; Col. to strike (a blow); Ríopl. to give, hand over; **-se** to go away, slip away; to leave.
largo adj. long; generous; m. length; largo (music); **a la larga** in the long run; slowly; **a lo —** along; lengthwise; **¡ — de aquí!** get out of here!
largor m. length.
largucho adj. lanky.
largueza f. generosity, liberality; length.
larguísimo adj. very long.
largura f. length.
laringe f. larynx.
laríngeo adj. laryngeal.
larva f. larva.
las def. art. f. pl. the; obj. pron. them; **— que** rel. pron. those which; which.
lascivia f. lewdness.
lascivo adj. lascivious, lewd.
lástima f. pity; compassion, grief.
lastimadura f. sore, hurt.
lastimar v. to hurt; to offend; **-se** to get hurt; **-se de** to feel pity for.
lastimero adj. pitiful; mournful.
lastimoso adj. pitiful.
lastre m. ballast, weight.
lata f. (metal) tin plate; tin can, can; (madero) small log; thin board; (pesadez) annoyance; embarrassment; boring speech; Am. gaucho saber; Am. prop.

latente adj. latent.
lateral adj. lateral, side; [l] (phonetically).
latido m. palpitation, throb, beat; bark, howl.
latifundio m. large landed estate.
latigazo m. lash, stroke with a whip; crack of a whip; harsh reprimand; unexpected blow or offense.
látigo m. whip; Am. whipping, beating; Ch. end or goal of a horse race.
latín m. Latin language.
latino adj. Latin; m. Latinist, Latin scholar; Latin.
latir v. to throb, beat, palpitate; to bark.
latitud f. latitude; extent, breadth.
latón m. brass.
latrocinio m. larceny, theft, robbery.
laúd m. lute; catboat (long, narrow boat with a lateen sail).
laudable adj. laudable, praiseworthy.
laurel m. laurel; laurel wreath.
lauro m. laurel; glory, fame.
lava f. lava; washing of minerals.
lavable adj. washable.
lavabo m. lavatory, washroom; washstand; washbowl.
lavadero m. washing place.
lavado m. wash, washing; laundry, laundry work.
lavador m. washer; cleaner; adj. washing; cleaning; **lavadora** f. washer, washing machine.
lavadura f. washing; slops, dirty water.
lavamanos m. lavatory, washbowl, washstand.
lavandera f. laundress, washerwoman.
lavandería f. laundry.
lavar v. to wash; to launder; to whitewash.
lavativa f. enema; syringe; bother, nuisance.
lavatorio m. washing (act of washing); wash (liquid or solution for washing); lavatory (ceremonial act of washing); washbowl, washstand; Am. washroom.
lavazas f. pl. slops, dirty water.
lazada f. bow, bowknot; Am. throwing of the lasso, lassoing.
lazar[9] v. to rope, lasso; to noose.
lazarillo m. blindman's guide.
lazo m. (nudo) bow, knot; slipknot; lasso, lariat; (vínculo) tie, bond; (trampa) snare, trap; trick.
le obj. pron. him; you (formal); to him; to her; to you (formal).
leal adj. loyal.
lealtad f. loyalty.
lebrel m. greyhound.
lebrillo m. earthenware basin or tub.
lección f. lesson; reading; **dar la —** to recite the lesson; **dar —** to teach; **tomarle a uno la —** to have someone recite his lesson.
lector m. reader; lecturer.
lectura f. reading; **libro de —** reader.
lechada f. whitewash; Am. milking.
leche f. milk; Col., Ven., C.A., Andes, Ríopl. luck (in games).

lechería f. dairy, creamery; **lechero** adj. milk; milch, giving milk (applied to animals); Am. lucky (in games of chance); m. milkman; **lechera** f. milkmaid; milk can; milk pitcher.

lecho m. bed; river bed.

lechón m. suckling pig; pig.

lechoso adj. milky; m. papaya tree; **lechosa** f. papaya (tropical fruit).

lechuga f. lettuce.

lechuza f. screech owl, barn owl.

leer[14] v. to read.

legación f. legation.

legado m. (donación) legacy; legato; (representante) representative, ambassador.

legal adj. legal, lawful; truthful; reliable; Col., Ven., Andes excellent, best; Am. just, honest.

legalizar[9] v. to legalize.

legar[7] v. to will, bequeath; to send as a delegate.

legendario adj. legendary.

legión f. legion.

legislación f. legislation.

legislador m. legislator; adj. legislating, legislative.

legislar v. to legislate.

legislativo adj. legislative.

legislatura f. legislature, legislative assembly.

legítimo adj. legitimate; real, genuine.

lego adj. lay; ignorant; m. layman.

legua f. league (about 3 miles).

leguleyo m. shyster.

legumbre f. vegetable.

leída f. Am. reading. See **lectura**.

leísta m. & f. one who uses the pronoun le for masculine direct object (le conozco).

lejanía f. distance; distant place.

lejano adj. distant; remote.

lejía f. lye; harsh reprimand.

lejos adv. far, far away; **a lo** — in the distance; Am. **a un** — in the distance; **de** (or **desde**) — from afar; m. view, perspective; background.

lelo adj. silly, stupid, foolish.

lema m. motto; theme; slogan.

lencería f. dry goods; dry-goods store; linen room or closet.

lengua f. tongue; language; interpreter; — **de tierra** point, neck of land.

lenguado m. flounder, sole (a fish).

lenguaje m. language (manner of expression).

lenguaraz adj. talkative, loose-tongued.

lengüeta f. small tongue; **lengüetada** f. lick.

lente m. & f. lens; **-s** m. pl. eyeglasses.

lenteja f. lentil; lentil seed; **lentejuela** f. spangle.

lentitud f. slowness.

lento adj. slow; dull.

leña f. firewood; kindling; beating; **leñera** f. woodshed; woodbox.

leñador m. woodcutter, woodman.

leño m. log; timber; piece of firewood.

león m. lion; **leona** f. lioness; **leonera** f. lion's den or cage; dive, gambling joint; disorderly room.

leontina f. Mex., Carib., Col. watch chain.

leopardo m. leopard.

leopoldina f. Mex., Ven. watch chain.

lerdo adj. dull, heavy, stupid, slow.

les obj. pron. to them; to you (formal).

lesión f. wound, injury.

lesionar v. to injure; to wound; to hurt; to damage.

lesna = **lezna**.

letargo m. lethargy, stupor, drowsiness.

letra f. letter (of the alphabet); printing type; hand, handwriting; letter (exact wording or meaning); words of a song; — **abierta** letter of credit; — **de cambio** draft, bill of exchange; — **mayúscula** capital letter; — **minúscula** small letter; **al pie de la** — literally; **-s** letters, learning.

letrado adj. learned; m. lawyer.

letrero m. notice, poster, sign; legend (under an illustration).

leva f. levy, draft; weighing anchor, setting sail; **echar** — to draft, conscript; Col. **echar -s** to boast.

levadura f. leaven, yeast.

levantamiento m. (revuelta) uprising, revolt, insurrection; (altura) elevation; lifting, raising; adjournment (of a meeting); — **de un plano** surveying.

levantar v. to raise, lift; to set up; to erect; to rouse, stir up; to recruit; Ch. to break land, plow; — **el campo** to break camp; — **la mesa** to clear the table; — **la sesión** to adjourn the meeting; — **un plano** to survey, map out; — **falso testimonio** to bear false witness; **-se** to stand up, get up, rise; to rebel.

levante m. east; east wind.

levantisco adj. turbulent; rebellious.

levar v. to weigh (anchor); — **el ancla** to weigh anchor; **-se** to weigh anchor, set sail.

leve adj. light; slight, unimportant.

levita f. frock coat; m. Levite, member of the tribe of Levi.

léxico m. lexicon, dictionary; vocabulary; glossary.

ley f. law; rule; loyalty; standard quality; **de buena** — of good quality; **plata de** — sterling silver; **-es** jurisprudence, law; system of laws.

leyenda f. legend; reading; inscription.

lezna f. awl.

liar[17] v. to tie, bind; to roll up; to deceive; **-se** to bind oneself; to get tangled up.

libelo m. libel.

libélula f. dragon fly.

liberación f. liberation; deliverance.

liberal adj. liberal; generous; **liberalidad** f. liberality; generosity.

libertad f. liberty.

libertador m. liberator, deliverer.

libertar v. to liberate, free, set free; **-se** to get free; to escape.

libertinaje m. license, licentiousness, lack of moral restraint.

libertino m. libertine (person without

moral restraint).

libra *f.* pound; **Libra** (*sign of the Zodiac*).

librador *m.* drawer (*of a bill, draft, etc.*); deliverer, liberator; measuring scoop.

libranza *f.* bill of exchange, draft.

librar *v.* to free, set free; to issue; to draw (*a draft*); **— guerra** to wage war; **-se** to save oneself; to escape; **-se de** to get rid of, escape from.

libre *adj.* free; unmarried; loose; vacant.

librea *f.* livery (*uniform*).

librería *f.* bookstore.

librero *m.* bookseller; *Am.* bookcase, bookshelves.

libreta *f.* notebook, memorandum book.

libro *m.* book; **— de caja** cashbook; **— mayor** ledger.

licencia *f.* license; permission; furlough, leave; looseness; license to practice.

licenciado *m.* licenciate (*person having a degree approximately equivalent to a master's degree*); *Ríopl., Mex., C.A.* lawyer.

licenciar *v.* to license; to give a license or permit; to dismiss, discharge (*from the army*); to confer the degree of **licenciado**; **-se** to get the degree of **licenciado**.

licenciatura *f.* degree of **licenciado**.

licencioso *adj.* licentious, lewd.

liceo *m.* lyceum; high school; *Col.* primary school or high school.

lícito *adj.* lawful; permissible, allowable.

licor *m.* liquid; liquor.

lid *f.* fight; contest.

líder *m. Am.* leader.

lidiar *v.* to fight; to combat; to contend.

liebre *f.* hare; coward.

lienzo *m.* cotton or linen cloth; canvas; painting.

liga *f.* (*alianza*) league; alliance; (*cinta*) garter; alloy; birdlime.

ligadura *f.* binding; tie, bond.

ligar *v.* to bind, tie, unite; to alloy (*combine metals*); **-se** to unite, combine, form an alliance.

ligereza *f.* lightness; swiftness; flippancy; frivolity.

ligero *adj.* (*leve*) light; (*rápido*) swift; nimble; flippant; *adv. Am.* quickly; **a la ligera** quickly, superficially.

lija *f.* sandpaper.

lijar *v.* to sandpaper.

lila *f.* lilac; pinkish-purple.

lima *f.* file; lime (*fruit*); finishing, polishing.

limar *v.* to file; to file down; to smooth, polish.

limeño *adj.* of or from Lima, Peru.

limitación *f.* limitation; district.

limitar *v.* to limit; to restrict; to bound.

límite *m.* limit; boundary.

limo *m.* slime.

limón *m.* lemon; lemon tree; **limonada** *f.* lemonade; **limonero** *m.* lemon tree; lemon dealer or vendor.

limosna *f.* alms, charity.

limosnero *m.* beggar.

limpiabotas *m.* bootblack; *Ch.* bootlicker, flatterer.

limpiadientes *m.* toothpick.

limpiar *v.* to clean; to wipe; to cleanse, purify; *Am.* to beat up, whip, lash.

límpido *adj.* limpid, clear.

limpieza *f.* cleanliness, neatness; purity; honesty.

limpio *adj.* clean; neat; pure; **poner en —** to make a clean copy; *Am.* **— y soplado** absolutely broke, wiped out.

linaje *m.* lineage, family, race.

linaza *f.* linseed.

lince *m.* lynx; sharp-sighted person.

linchar *v.* to lynch.

lindar *v.* to border, adjoin.

linde *m. & f.* limit, border, boundary; landmark.

lindero *adj.* bordering upon; *m. Carib., C.A.* landmark; boundary.

lindeza *f.* prettiness; exquisiteness; neatness; witty act or remark.

lindo *adj.* pretty; **de lo —** wonderfully; very much; to the utmost.

línea *f.* line; limit.

lineal *adj.* lineal, linear.

lino *m.* linen; flax; **linón** *m.* lawn, thin linen or cotton.

linotipia *f.* linotype.

linterna *f.* lantern.

lío *m.* (*bulto*) bundle; (*enredo*) fib; mess, confusion; **armar un —** to raise a rumpus; to cause confusion; **hacerse un —** to be confused; to get tangled up; **meterse en un —** to get oneself into a mess.

liquidación *f.* liquidation; settlement (*of an account*).

liquidar *v.* to liquidate; to settle (*an account*).

líquido *m.* liquid.

lira *f.* lyre, small harp; a type of metrical composition; lira (*Italian coin*).

lírico *adj.* lyric, lyrical; *Am.* fantastic; *m. Ríopl.* visionary, dreamer.

lirio *m.* lily.

lirismo *m.* lyricism (*lyric quality*); *Am.* idle dream, fantasy.

lisiado *adj.* lame, hurt, injured.

liso *adj.* smooth, even; flat; evident, clear; *Am.* crafty, sly; *Col., Ven., C.A., Andes* fresh, impudent.

lisonja *f.* flattery.

lisonjear *v.* to flatter; to fawn on; to please.

lisonjero *adj.* flattering, pleasing; *m.* flatterer.

lista *f.* list; strip; stripe; **pasar —** to call the roll.

listado *adj.* striped.

listar *v.* to register, enter in a list; *Ríopl., Mex., Ven.* to stripe, streak.

listo *adj.* ready, prompt; clever; *Ríopl., Ch.* mischievous.

listón *m.* ribbon, tape; strip.

lisura *f.* smoothness; sincerity, frankness; *Am.* freshness, impudence; *Andes* insulting or filthy remark.

litera *f.* berth (*on a boat or train*);

litter (*for carrying a person*).
literario *adj.* literary.
literato *adj.* literary, learned; *m.* literary man, writer.
literatura *f.* literature.
litigio *m.* litigation, lawsuit.
litoral *adj.* seaboard, coastal; *m.* coast, shore.
litro *m.* liter (*about 1.05 quarts*).
liviandad *f.* lightness; frivolity; lewdness.
liviano *adj.* (*leve*) light; slight, unimportant; (*lascivo*) frivolous, fickle; lewd; unchaste.
lívido *adj.* livid, having a dull-bluish color; pale.
lo *obj. pron.* him; you (*formal*); it; so; *dem. pron.* — **de** that of, that affair of, that matter of; — **bueno** the good, what is good; **sé** — **bueno que Vd. es** I know how good you are; — **que** that which, what.
loable *adj.* laudable, worthy of praise.
loar *v.* to praise.
lobanillo *m.* growth, tumor.
lobo *m.* wolf.
lóbrego *adj.* dark, gloomy.
lobreguez *f.* darkness, gloominess.
lóbulo *m.* lobe.
local *adj.* local; *m.* place, quarters; site; premises.
localidad *f.* location; locality, town; place; seat (*in a theater*).
localización *f.* localization, localizing.
localizar[9] *v.* to localize.
loco *adj.* insane, mad, crazy; — **de remate** stark mad; *m.* lunatic, insane person.
locomotor *adj.* locomotive.
locomotora *f.* locomotive; — **diesel** diesel locomotive.
locuaz *adj.* loquacious, talkative.
locución *f.* phrase; diction.
locura *f.* madness, insanity.
locutor *m.* radio announcer.
lodazal *m.* muddy place; mire.
lodo *m.* mud; **lodoso** *adj.* muddy, miry.
logaritmo *m.* logarithm.
logia *f.* lodge (*secret society*).
lógica *f.* logic; reasoning.
lógico *adj.* logical.
lograr *v.* to gain, obtain, accomplish; — (+ *inf.*) to succeed in; **-se** to succeed; to turn out well.
logrero *m.* usurer; profiteer.
logro *m.* profit, gain; usury; attainment; realization.
loísta *m.* & *f.* one who uses the pronoun **lo** for the masculine direct object (*lo conozco*).
loma *f.* small hill; **lomerío** *m.* *Am.* group of hills.
lombriz *f.* earthworm.
lomo *m.* back (*of an animal, book, knife, etc.*); loin; ridge between two furrows; *Mex., Ven.* **hacer** — to bear with patience, resign oneself.
lona *f.* canvas.
lonche *m.* *Col., Ven., Mex.* lunch; **lonchería** *f.* *Col., Ven., Mex.* lunchroom.

longaniza *f.* pork sausage.
longevidad *f.* longevity, long life; span of life, length of life.
longitud *f.* longitude; length.
longitudinal *adj.* longitudinal, lengthwise; **-mente** *adv.* longitudinally, lengthwise.
lonja *f.* (*mercado*) exchange; market; (*carne*) slice of meat; (*correa*) leather strap; *Riopl.* raw hide.
lontananza *f.* background; **en** — in the distance, in the background.
loro *m.* parrot.
los *def. art. m. pl.* the; *obj. pron.* them; — **que** *rel. pron.* those which; which.
losa *f.* flagstone; slab; gravestone.
lote *m.* lot, share, part; *Am.* remnant lot; *Col.* swallow of liquor; *Am.* blockhead, dunce.
lotear *v.* *Am.* to subdivide into lots; *Am.* to divide into portions.
lotería *f.* lottery; raffle.
loza *f.* fine earthenware; crockery; — **fina** chinaware.
lozanía *f.* luxuriance (*rich foliage or growth*); vigor.
lozano *adj.* luxuriant; exuberant, vigorous, lusty.
lubricar[6] *v.* to lubricate, or grease.
lucero *m.* morning star; any bright star; star on the forehead of certain animals; splendor, brightness.
lúcido *adj.* lucid, clear; shining, bright.
luciente *adj.* shining, bright.
luciérnaga *f.* firefly; glowworm.
lucimiento *m.* splendor; brilliance; success.
lucir[13] *v. irr.* (*brillar*) to shine; to illuminate; to brighten; (*superar*) to excel; (*alardear*) to show off; **-se** to shine, be brilliant; to show off; to be successful.
lucrativo *adj.* lucrative, profitable.
lucro *m.* profit, gain.
luctuoso *adj.* sad, mournful, dismal.
lucha *f.* fight, struggle; dispute; wrestling match.
luchador *m.* fighter; wrestler.
luchar *v.* to fight; to wrestle; to struggle; to dispute.
luego *adv.* soon, presently; afterwards, then, next; **desde** — immediately, at once; naturally; — **de** after; — **que** as soon as; **hasta** — good-bye, so long; — — right away.
luengo *adj.* long; **-s años** many years.
lugar *m.* (*sitio*) place; site; town; space; (*empleo*) position, employment; (*ocasión*) time, occasion, opportunity; **dar** — **a** to give cause or occasion for; **hacer** (*or* **dar**) — to make room; **en** — **de** instead of.
lúgubre *adj.* mournful, gloomy.
lujo *m.* luxury, extravagance.
lujoso *adj.* luxurious; elegant; showy.
lujuria *f.* lust, lewdness, sensuality.
lujurioso *adj.* lustful, lewd, sensual.
lumbre *f.* fire; brightness.
luminoso *adj.* luminous, bright, shining.
luna *f.* moon; mirror, glass for mirrors.

Ll

lunar adj. lunar; m. mole; blemish, spot.

lunático adj. & m. lunatic.

lunes m. Monday; Ch. **hacer San Lunes** to lay off on Monday.

lunfardo m. social dialect of the Buenos Aires underworld.

lustre m. luster, shine; glory.

lustroso adj. lustrous, glossy, shining.

luto m. mourning; sorrow, grief.

luz f. light; clarity; hint, guidance; **dar a —** to give birth; to publish; **entre dos luces** at twilight.

LL

llaga f. wound; ulcer, sore.

llama f. flame; llama (a South American beast of burden).

llamada f. call; beckon, sign; knock; reference mark (as an asterisk).

llamador m. knocker (of a door); caller.

llamamiento m. call, calling; calling together; appeal.

llamar v. to call; to summon; to name; to invoke; **— a la puerta** to knock at the door; **-se** to be called, named; Am. to break one's word or promise.

llamarada f. flash; sudden flame or blaze; sudden flush, blush.

llamativo adj. showy, loud, gaudy, flashy; thirst-exciting.

llameante adj. flaming.

llana f. mason's trowel.

llanero m. Ven., Col. plainsman.

llaneza f. simplicity; frankness; sincerity; plainness.

llano adj. plain, simple; even, smooth, level; frank; m. plain, flat ground.

llanta f. Spain rim of a wheel; Am. tire, tire casing; Peru large sunshade (used in Peruvian markets).

llanto m. crying, weeping; tears.

llanura f. extensive plain; prairie; evenness, flatness.

llapa f. Andes, Ríopl. a small gift from the vendor to the purchaser; also **yapa, ñapa.**

llave f. key; faucet; clef; **— de tuercas** wrench; **— inglesa** monkey wrench; **— maestra** master key.

llavera f. Am. housekeeper.

llavero m. key ring; key maker; keeper of the keys.

llavín m. small key.

llegada f. arrival.

llegar [7] v. to arrive; to reach; to amount; **— a ser** to get or come to be; **— a las manos** to come to blows; **-se** to approach, get near.

llenar v. to fill; to stuff; **-se** to fill up; to overeat; **-se de** to get filled with; to get covered with, spattered with.

lleno adj. full; m. fullness, completeness; **de —** totally, completely; **un — completo** a full house (said of a theater).

llenura f. fullness; abundance.

llevadero adj. bearable, tolerable.

llevar v. (transportar) to carry; to bear; to transport; to wear; (conducir) to take; to lead; (cobrar) to charge; to

ask a certain price; to keep (accounts); **— ventaja** to be ahead, have the advantage; **— un año a** to be one year older than; **— un mes aquí** to have been here one month; **— un castigo** to suffer punishment; **-se** to carry away; **-se bien con** to get along with.

llorar v. to cry, weep.

lloriquear v. to whimper, whine, weep.

lloriqueo m. whimper, whining.

lloro m. weeping.

llorón adj. weeping; **sauce —** weeping willow; m. weeper, crybaby, whiner.

llorona f. weeping woman; **-s** Am. large spurs.

lloroso adj. tearful; weeping.

llovedizo adj. rain (used as adj.); **agua llovediza** rain water.

llover [2] v. irr. to rain, shower.

llovizna f. drizzle.

lloviznar v. to drizzle, sprinkle.

lluvia f. rain; shower.

lluvioso adj. rainy.

M

macana f. Am. club, cudgel, stick; Am. lie, absurdity, nonsense.

macanudo adj. Ríopl. tremendous! great!

macarrón m. macaroon; **-es** macaroni.

maceta f. (tiesto) flowerpot; (martillo) small mallet; stonecutter's hammer; handle of tools; Am. head; adj. Am. slow.

macilento adj. thin, emaciated; pale.

macizo adj. solid, firm; massive; m. massiveness; firmness; thicket; clump.

machacar [6] v. to pound, crush; to insist, harp on.

machacón adj. persistent; tenacious.

machete m. machete, large heavy knife; **machetazo** m. large machete; blow with a machete.

machismo m. the quality of being a male; proven daring.

macho m. male; he-mule; hook (of a hook and eye); abutment; pillar; stupid fellow; sledgehammer; C.R. a blond; North American; Am. **pararle a uno el —** to halt or repress a person; adj. masculine, male; strong.

machucar [6] v. to pound, beat, bruise; Am. to crush; Am. to break (a horse).

machucón m. smash; bruise.

madeja f. skein; mass of hair; limp, listless person.

madera f. wood; timber; lumber; **maderero** m. lumberman, lumber dealer.

maderaje m. timber, lumber; timber work; woodwork.

maderamen m. timber; timber work; woodwork.

madero m. beam; plank; timber, piece of lumber; blockhead, dunce.

madrastra f. stepmother.

madre f. mother; womb; root, origin; river bed; **salirse de —** to overflow (said of rivers).

madrepeña f. Am. moss.

madreperla f. mother-of-pearl.
madreselva f. honeysuckle.
madriguera f. burrow; den, lair.
madrileño adj. Madrilenian, from or pertaining to Madrid; m. Madrilenian.
madrina f. (patrocinadora) godmother; bridesmaid; sponsor; (correa) strap for yoking two horses; (ganado) leading mare; prop; Am. small herd of tame cattle (used for leading wild cattle).
madrugada f. dawn; early morning; **de —** at daybreak.
madrugador m. early riser.
madrugar[7] v. to rise early; to be ahead of others; to "get the jump" on someone.
madurar v. to mature; to ripen.
madurez f. maturity; ripeness.
maduro adj. ripe; mature; prudent, wise; Am. bruised, sore.
maestría f. mastery; great skill.
maestro m. master, teacher; chief craftsman; adj. master; masterly, skillful; **llave maestra** master key; **obra maestra** masterpiece.
magia f. magic; charm.
mágico adj. magic; m. magician.
magín m. imagination, fancy.
magisterio m. teaching profession.
magistrado m. magistrate, judge.
magistral adj. masterly; masterful; authoritative.
magnánimo adj. magnanimous, noble, generous.
magnético adj. magnetic; attractive.
magnetofónico adj. recording (tape or wire).
magnetófono m. tape recorder.
magnificencia f. magnificence, splendor.
magnífico adj. magnificent, splendid.
magnitud f. magnitude, greatness.
mago m. magician, wizard; **los tres Reyes Magos** the Three Wise Men.
magra f. slice of ham.
magro adj. lean.
maguey m. maguey, century plant.
magullar v. to bruise; to maul; to mangle; Riopl., Ch., Col., Andes, P.R. to crumple.
mahometano adj. & m. Mohammedan.
maíz m. corn; **maizal** m. cornfield.
majada f. sheepfold; dung, manure; Riopl., Ch. flock of sheep or goats.
majadería f. foolishness, nonsense.
majadero adj. foolish; bothersome.
majar v. to pound; to crush; to bruise; to crumple; to mash; to annoy, bother.
majestad f. majesty; dignity.
majestuoso adj. majestic, stately.
majo adj. gaudy, showy; gaily attired; pretty; m. dandy; **maja** f. belle.
mal m. evil; illness; harm; wrong. See **malo**.
malabarista m. & f. juggler; Ch. sly thief.
malacate m. hoist, hoisting machine; winch; Am. spindle (for cotton); Am. **parecer uno un —** to be constantly

on the go, be in constant motion.
malagueña adj. song and dance of Málaga.
malandanza f. misfortune.
malaventura f. misfortune, disaster.
malazo adj. perverse, evil, wicked; vicious.
malbaratar v. to undersell, sell at a loss; to squander.
malcontento adj. discontented; m. malcontent, troublemaker.
malcriado adj. ill-bred, rude.
maldad f. badness, evil, wickedness.
maldecir[27,52] v. irr. to curse; to damn.
maldición f. curse.
maldispuesto adj. unwilling, not inclined.
maldito p.p. of **maldecir** & adj. cursed; wicked; damned; Am. tricky; Am. bold, boastful.
maleante m. crook, rogue, rascal, villain.
malecón m. mole; dike.
maledicencia f. slander.
maleficio m. spell, charm, witchery.
maléfico adj. evil, harmful.
malestar m. indisposition; slight illness; discomfort.
maleta f. travelling bag; suitcase; Col., Ven., C.A. bundle of clothes; Col. hump (on the back); Am. saddlebag; C.A. rogue, rascal; Am. lazy fellow.
maletín m. small valise, satchel.
malevo adj. Bol., Riopl. bad, wicked.
malévolo adj. bad, evil, wicked.
maleza f. underbrush; thicket; weeds.
malgastar v. to squander, waste.
malhechor m. malefactor, evildoer, criminal.
malhora f. Riopl., C.A., Ven. trouble, misfortune.
malhumorado adj. ill-humored.
malicia f. malice; wickedness; shrewdness; suspicion; Ch. bit of brandy or cognac added to another drink.
maliciar v. to suspect.
malicioso adj. malicious; wicked; shrewd; suspicious.
maligno adj. malign, malignant; pernicious, harmful.
malmandado adj. disobedient; stubborn.
mal(o) adj. bad, evil; wicked; ill; difficult; Am. **a la mala** treacherously; Riopl. **de malas** by force; **estar de malas** to be out of luck; **por la mala** unwillingly, by force; **venir de malas** to come with evil intentions; **mal** adv. badly; poorly; wrongly.
malograr v. to waste, lose; **-se** to turn out badly; to fail.
malón m. mean trick; Riopl. surprise Indian raid; Ven. tin-pan serenade, boisterous surprise party.
malpagar[7] v. to underpay, pay poorly.
malparto m. miscarriage, abortion.
malquerencia f. aversion, dislike, ill will.
malsano adj. unhealthy; sickly.
malta f. malt.

LU

maltratar v. to treat badly; to misuse, abuse.

maltrato m. mistreatment, abuse.

maltrecho adj., battered, bruised, injured.

malvado adj. wicked; malicious.

malversación f. graft, corruption, misuse of public funds.

malversar v. to misuse (funds in one's trust); to embezzle.

malla f. mesh; coat of mail; Ch. species of potato; **hacer —** to knit.

mamá f. mamma.

mamada f. suck, sucking.

mamar v. to suckle; to suck; to gorge; **-se** Riopl., C.A. to get drunk; Col. to go back on one's promise; Am. to fold up, crack up; **-se a uno** Col., C.A. to kill someone.

mamífero m. mammal; adj. mammalian, of mammals.

mamón adj. suckling; m. suckling (very young animal or child); shoot, sucker (of a tree); Riopl. cherimoya (tree and fruit); Am. papaya (tree and fruit); Mex. a kind of cake; C.A. public employee.

mampara f. screen.

mampostería f. masonry, stone masonry.

manada f. herd; drove; pack; flock.

manantial m. spring; source, origin.

manar v. to spring, flow (from); to abound.

manaza f. large hand.

manazo m. Riopl. slap. See **manotazo**.

mancarrón m. one-armed or one-handed man; cripple; old nag; Riopl., Andes crude, clumsy fellow; Am. disabled workman; Am. dike, small dam.

mancebo m. youth, young man; bachelor.

mancera f. handle of a plough.

mancilla f. stain, spot; dishonor.

manco adj. one-armed; one-handed; maimed; lame (referring to an arm or the front leg of an animal); faulty, defective; m. Ch. nag.

mancuerna f. pair of animals tied together; Mex., C.A. f. pl. cuff links.

mancha f. spot, stain, blemish; Am. cloud, swarm; Ven., Cuba, Col. roving herd of cattle.

manchar v. to stain, soil, spot; to tarnish.

manchego adj. of or belonging to La Mancha (region of Spain); m. inhabitant of La Mancha.

manchón m. large stain; large patch.

mandadero m. messenger, errand boy.

mandado m. (orden) command, order; (recado) errand; p.p. of **mandar**; **bien —** well-behaved; **mal —** ill-behaved.

mandamiento m. command, order; writ; commandment.

mandar v. (pedir) to command, order; rule; (enviar) to send; to bequeath, will; Col., Ven. to throw, hurl; **—**

hacer to have made; order; Col., Ven., Mex., Carib., Andes **— una bofetada** to give a slap; Col., Ven., Mex., Carib., Andes **— una pedrada** to throw a stone; **-se** Am. to be impudent; **-se mudar** Riopl., Carib. to go away.

mandatario m. attorney, representative; Am. magistrate, chief.

mandato m. mandate; order, command; term of office.

mandíbula f. jaw, jawbone.

mando m. command, authority, power.

mandón adj. bossy, domineering; m. bossy person; Am. boss or foreman of a mine; Am. race starter.

maneador m. Riopl., Ven., Col. hobble, leather lasso (for the legs of an animal); Am. whip; Ven., Andes halter.

manear v. to hobble, lasso, tie the legs of (an animal); **-se** Col., Ven. to get tangled up.

manecilla f. small hand; hand of a watch or clock.

manejable adj. manageable.

manejar v. to manage, handle; to drive (a car); **-se** to move about, get around (after an illness or accident); Carib., Ven. to behave oneself.

manejo m. handling; management; trick, intrigue.

manera f. manner, way, mode; side opening in a skirt; front opening in breeches; **-s** customs; manners, behavior; **a — de** (or **a la — de**) like, in the style of; **de — que** so that; **sobre —** exceedingly; extremely.

manga f. sleeve; bag; hose (for watering); body of troops; Am. multitude, herd, swarm; Am. cattle chute (narrow passageway); Am. corral; **— de agua** waterspout, whirlwind over the ocean; Am. **— de hule** raincape; **por angas o por -s** by hook or crook, in one way or another.

mangana f. lariat, lasso.

manganeso m. manganese.

mango m. handle; Am. mango (tropical tree and its fruit).

manguera f. hose (for water); waterspout; Riopl. large corral (for livestock).

manguito m. muff; knitted half-sleeve (worn on the forearm); oversleeve.

maní m. Carib., C.A., Ch., Andes, Ven., Col. peanut; **manicero** m. Carib., C.A., Ch., Andes, Ven., Col. peanut vendor.

manía f. mania, frenzy; craze, whim.

maniatar v. to tie the hands; to handcuff; to hobble (an animal).

maniático m. crank, queer fellow; adj. cranky, queer, odd.

manicomio m. insane asylum.

manicura f. manicure; manicurist.

manicurar v. to manicure.

manido adj. rotting; Riopl., Carib., Col., Andes trite, commonplace.

manifestación f. manifestation; demonstration.

manifestar[1] v. irr. to manifest; to show.

manifiesto *adj.* manifest, clear, plain; *m.* manifesto, public declaration; customhouse manifest.

manigua *f. Col., Riopl., Cuba, P.R.* Cuban jungle or thicket; *Carib.* **coger — to get feverish;** *Riopl., Carib.* **irse a la — to rise up in rebellion.**

manija *f.* handle; crank; fetter.

manilla *f.* small hand; bracelet; **-s de hierro** handcuffs.

maniobra *f.* maneuver; operation.

maniobrar *v.* to maneuver.

manipulación *f.* manipulation.

manipular *v.* to manipulate, handle.

maniquí *m.* manikin, model, dummy, figure of a person; puppet.

manivela *f.* crank.

manjar *m.* dish, food; choice bit of food.

mano *f.* (*del cuerpo*) hand; forefoot; (*reloj*) clock hand; (*acabado*) coat of paint or varnish; quire (*25 sheets*) of paper; *Am.* adventure, mishap; *Am.* handful; **— de obra** workmanship; labor; **a —** at hand; by hand; *Am.* **estamos a —** we are even, we are quits; *Am.* **doblar las -s** to give up; **ser —** to be first (*in a game*); to lead (*in a game*); **venir a las -s** to come to blows.

manojo *m.* handful; bunch.

manopla *f.* gauntlet; heavy glove; huge hand.

manosear *v.* to handle, touch, feel with the hand; *Am.* to fondle, pet, caress.

manotada *f.* slap, blow; sweep of the hand; *Col.* handful, fistful; **manotazo** *m.* slap.

manotear *v.* to gesticulate; to strike with the hands; *Riopl.* to embezzle, steal; *Am.* to snatch away (*what is given*).

mansalva: a — without danger or risk; treacherously; **matar a —** to kill without warning or without giving a person a chance to defend himself.

mansedumbre *f.* meekness; gentleness.

mansión *f.* sojourn, stay; abode, dwelling.

manso *adj.* meek; mild, gentle; tame; *Riopl., Ch.* cultivated (*plant*), civilized (*Indian*); *m.* leading sheep, goat, or ox.

manta *f.* blanket; large shawl; tossing in a blanket; *Mex., C.A., Ven., Riopl.* coarse cotton cloth; *Am.* poncho; *Am.* **— mojada** dull person, dunce; **darle a uno una — to** toss someone in a blanket.

mantear *v.* to toss (*someone*) in a blanket.

manteca *f.* fat; lard; butter; *Am.* **— de cacao** cocoa butter; *Am.* **— de coco** coconut oil; **mantequera** *f.* churn; butter dish; woman who makes or sells butter.

mantecado *m.* ice cream.

mantel *m.* tablecloth; altar cloth; *C.A., Mex.* **estar de -es largos** to dine in style.

mantener[45] *v. irr.* to maintain; to support; to sustain; to defend; **-se** to continue, remain; to support oneself; **-se firme** to remain firm; **-se quieto** to stay or keep quiet.

mantenimiento *m.* maintenance, support; sustenance; livelihood.

mantequilla *f.* butter; **mantequillería** *f. Am.* creamery, dairy (*for making butter*).

mantilla *f.* mantilla (*Spanish veil or scarf for the head*); saddlecloth.

manto *m.* mantle, cloak; cape; large mantilla; mantel, mantelpiece.

mantón *m.* large shawl; **— de Manila** embroidered silk shawl.

manuable *adj.* handy, easy to handle.

manual *adj.* manual; handy; *m.* manual, handbook.

manubrio *m.* crank; handle.

manufacturar *v.* to manufacture.

manufacturero *adj.* manufacturing; *m.* manufacturer.

manuscrito *adj.* written by hand; *m.* manuscript.

manutención *f.* maintenance; support; conservation.

manzana *f.* apple; block of houses; *Riopl., Ch., Col., Ven., C.A.* Adam's apple; **manzano** *m.* apple tree.

maña *f.* skill, knack; cunning; **malas -s** bad tricks or habits.

mañana *f.* morning; *Riopl.* **media —** mid-morning snack; *adv.* tomorrow, in the near future; **pasado —** day after tomorrow; **muy de —** very early in the morning; *m.* morrow; **mañanitas** *f. pl. Mex., C.A.* popular song sung early in the morning to celebrate a birthday, saint's day, etc.

mañanero *m.* early riser; *adj.* early rising; **mañanista** *m. & f. Am.* procrastinator, one who puts things off until tomorrow.

mañero *adj.* astute, artful, clever; *Am.* tricky; *Ch.* shy (*animal*); *Riopl.* indolent, lazy (*child*).

mañoso *adj.* skillful; clever; sly; tricky; deceitful; *Am.* slow, lazy; *Am.* greedy, gluttonous (*child*).

mapa *m.* map, chart.

mapache *m. Ch.* raccoon.

mapurite, mapurito *m. Col., Ven.* skunk. *See* **zorrino, zorrillo.**

máquina *f.* machine; engine; **— de coser** sewing machine; **—de escribir** typewriter.

maquinación *f.* machination, scheming, plotting; plot, scheme.

maquinador *m.* schemer, plotter.

maquinal *adj.* mechanical, automatic; **-mente** *adv.* mechanically, automatically, in a mechanical manner.

maquinar *v.* to plot, scheme.

maquinaria *f.* machinery; mechanism; mechanics.

maquinista *m.* engineer, locomotive engineer; machinist; mechanic.

mar *m. & f.* sea; **alta** rough sea; **— llena** high tide (*see* **pleamar**); **— de fondo** swell; **a -es** abundantly; **baja**

MA

— low tide; **en alta** — on the high seas; **la** — **de cosas** a lot of things.

maraca *f.* Carib., Col., Ven. maraca *(rhythm instrument made of a dried gourd filled with seeds or pebbles).*

maraña *f.* tangle; snarl; thicket; maze; plot, intrigue.

maravedí *m.* maravedi *(an old Spanish coin).*

maravilla *f.* wonder, marvel; marigold; **a las mil -s** wonderfully, perfectly.

maravillar *v.* to astonish, dazzle; **-se** to wonder, marvel.

maravilloso *adj.* marvellous, wonderful.

marbete *m.* label, stamp; baggage tag or check.

marca *f.* mark, stamp; sign; brand, make; gauge, rule; march, frontier province; — **de fábrica** trademark; **de** — of excellent quality.

marcar[6] *v.* to mark, stamp, brand; to note, observe.

marcial *adj.* martial, warlike; frank, abrupt.

marco *m.* frame; mark *(German coin)*; mark *(unit of weight, equal to 8 ounces).*

marcha *f.* march; course, progress; speed; gait; running, functioning; movement of a watch.

marchamo *m.* customhouse mark; *Am.* tax on each slaughtered animal.

marchante *m. (vendedor)* merchant, dealer; *(cliente)* customer, regular client.

marchar *v.* to march, mark step; to walk; to parade; to run *(said of machinery)*; **-se** to go away.

marchitar *v.* to wither; **-se** to wither; to fade; to shrivel up.

marchito *adj.* withered; faded; shriveled up.

marea *f.* tide; *Riopl., Ch.* sea fog.

mareado *adj.* seasick; dizzy.

marear *v. (navegar)* to navigate, sail; *(fastidiar)* to annoy, upset *(a person)*; to make dizzy; **-se** to get seasick, nauseated; dizzy.

mareo *m.* seasickness; nausea; vexation, annoyance.

marfil *m.* ivory; *Ven.* fine-toothed comb.

margarita *f.* marguerite, daisy; pearl.

margen *m. & f.* margin, border; river bank; **dar** — **a** to give an occasion to.

maricón *m.* sissy, effeminate; *m.* sissy.

marido *m.* husband.

marimba *f.* marimba.

marina *f. (costa)* seacoast, shore; *(fuerza naval)* fleet; navy; *(arte u oficio)* seascape; seamanship; — **de guerra** navy; — **mercante** merchant marine.

marinero *m.* mariner, seaman, sailor.

marino *adj.* marine; *m.* mariner, seaman, sailor.

mariposa *f.* butterfly; moth; *Am.* blindman's buff *(a game).*

mariscal *m.* marshal; blacksmith; — **de campo** field marshal.

marisco *m.* shellfish.

marítimo *adj.* maritime, marine.

marmita *f.* kettle, boiler, teakettle.

mármol *m.* marble.

marmóreo *adj.* marble, of marble, like marble.

maroma *f.* rope; *Am.* somersault; *Am.* acrobatic performance; *Col.* sudden change of political views; **andar en la** — to walk the tightrope; **maromero** *m. Carib.* acrobat.

marqués *m.* marquis.

marquesa *f.* marquise; *Ch.* couch.

marrano *m.* pig, hog; filthy person.

marrazo *m. Am.* bayonet, dagger.

marrón *adj.* maroon.

marroquí *adj.* from Morocco; *pl.* **marroquíes.**

marrullero *adj.* sly, wily.

martes *m.* Tuesday; — **de carnestolendas** Shrove Tuesday *(Tuesday before Lent).*

martillar *v.* to hammer, pound.

martillo *m.* hammer.

martinete *m.* pile driver; drop hammer; hammer of a piano.

mártir *m. & f.* martyr.

martirio *m.* martyrdom; torture, torment.

martirizar[9] *v.* to martyr; to torture, torment.

marzo *m.* March.

mas *conj.* but.

más *adj.* more; most; *adv.* more; most; plus; — **bien** rather; — **de** more than, over; — **que** more than; **no . . . — que** only; **a** — **de** in addition to; **a lo** — at the most; **está de** — it is superfluous, unnecessary; *Am.* **no** — only; *Am.* **no quiero** — **nada** *(instead of* **no quiero nada** —) I don't want anything more.

masa *f. (volumen)* mass; volume; *(pueblo)* crowd, the masses; *(pasta)* dough, paste; mortar; — **coral** glee club, choral society; **agarrarle a uno con las manos en la** — to catch someone in the act; **masilla** *f.* putty.

masaje *m.* massage.

mascada *f.* chewing; *Am.* mouthful; *Riopl.* chew or quid of tobacco; *Am.* reprimand, scolding; *Mex.* silk handkerchief, scarf.

mascar[6] *v.* to chew.

máscara *f.* mask; **-s** masquerade; *m. & f.* masquerader; **mascarada** *f.* masquerade.

masculino *adj.* masculine.

mascullar *v.* to mumble; to munch.

mason *m.* mason, freemason; **masonería** *f.* masonry, freemasonry.

masticar[6] *v.* to chew.

mástil *m.* mast; post.

mastín *m.* mastiff.

mastuerzo *m. (flor)* nasturtium; *(tonto)* simpleton, fool.

mata *f.* shrub, plant, bush; grove; clump of trees; *Ven., Col.* thicket, jungle; — **de pelo** head of hair.

matadero *m.* slaughterhouse; hard

work.

matador *m.* killer, murderer; bull-fighter who kills the bull.

matanza *f.* massacre, butchery; slaughter of livestock; *Mex.* slaughterhouse.

matar *v.* to kill; to murder; **-se** to commit suicide; to overwork; **-se con alguien** to fight with somebody.

'matasanos *m.* quack, quack doctor.

mate *m.* checkmate (*winning move in chess*); *Riopl., Ch.* Paraguayan tea (*used also in Argentina and Uruguay*); *Andes, Col.* teapot (*for* **mate**), any small pot; *Am.* bald head; *adj.* unpolished, dull (*surface*).

matear *v.* to plant seeds or shoots; to hunt among the bushes; *Riopl., Ch.* to drink **mate**; *Am.* to checkmate (*make the winning move in chess*).

matemáticas *f. pl.* mathematics.

matemático *adj.* mathematical; *m.* mathematician.

materia *f.* matter; material; subject; pus; **— prima** (*or* **primera —**) raw material.

material *adj.* material; rude, coarse; *m.* ingredient; material; equipment; *Ven.* **de —** made of adobe.

maternal *adj.* maternal.

maternidad *f.* maternity, motherhood.

materno *adj.* maternal.

matinal *adj.* morning, of the morning.

matiné *m. Am.* matinée.

matiz *m.* tint, shade, color, hue; shading.

matizar⁹ *v.* to blend (*colors*); to tint; to shade, tone down.

matón *m.* bully.

matorral *m.* thicket.

matoso *adj.* bushy; weedy, full of weeds.

matrero *adj.* astute, shrewd; cunning, sly; *m. Col.* trickster, swindler; *Riopl.* bandit, outlaw, cattle thief.

matrícula *f.* register, list; matriculation, registration; certificate of registration.

matricular *v.* to matriculate, enroll, register.

matrimonio *m.* matrimony, marriage; married couple.

matriz *f.* matrix, mold, form; womb; screw nut; *adj.* main, principal, first; **casa —** main office (*of a company*).

matungo *m. Riopl.* nag, old worn-out horse.

matutino *adj.* morning, of the morning.

maullar *v.* to mew.

maullido *adj. m.* mew.

máxima *f.* maxim, rule; proverb.

máxime *adj.* principally, especially.

máximo *adj.* & *m.* maximum.

maya *f.* daisy; May queen; *m.* & *f.* Maya, Mayan Indian; *m.* Mayan language.

mayo *m.* May; Maypole; *Am.* Mayo Indian (*from Sonora, Mexico*); *Am.* language of the Mayo Indian.

mayonesa *f.* mayonnaise; dish served with mayonnaise.

mayor *adj.* greater; larger; older; great-est; largest; oldest; main; major; high (*altar, mass*); *m.* major; chief; **-es** elders; ancestors; **— de edad** of age; **por —** (*or* **al por —**) wholesale; *f.* major premise (*of a syllogism*).

mayoral *m.* head shepherd; stagecoach driver; foreman; overseer, boss.

mayorazgo *m.* primogeniture (*right of inheritance by the first-born*); first-born son and heir; family estate left to the eldest son.

mayordomo *m.* majordomo, steward, butler; manager of an estate.

mayorear *v. Am.* to wholesale, sell at wholesale.

mayoreo *m. Am.* wholesale.

mayoría *f.* majority.

mayorista *m. Am.* wholesale dealer.

maza *f.* mace (*weapon, staff*); **— química** chemical mace.

mazmorra *f.* dungeon.

mazo *m.* mallet; sledgehammer; bunch, handful.

mazorca *f.* ear of corn; *Riopl.* tyrannical government; *Am.* cruel torture (*imposed by tyrants*).

me *obj. pron.* me; to me; for me; myself.

mecánico *adj.* mechanical; *m.* mechanic, machinist, repairman; driver, chauffeur.

mecanismo *m.* mechanism.

mecanografía *f.* stenography, typewriting.

mecanógrafo *m.* stenographer, typist.

mecate *m. Mex., C.A., Col., Ven.* rope, cord.

mecedor *m.* swing; *adj.* swinging, rocking.

mecedora *f.* rocking chair.

mecer¹⁰ *v.* to swing, rock, sway; to shake.

mecha *f.* wick; lock of hair; fuse; strip of salt pork or bacon (*for larding meat*); *Ven.* tip of a whip; *Am.* scare, fright; *Andes, Col.* fib; *Andes, Col.* jest, joke; *Col.* trifle, worthless thing.

mechar *v.* to lard (*meat or fowl*).

mechero *m.* (*canutillo*) lamp burner; gas jet; candlestick socket; (*encendedor*) pocket lighter; large wick; *Col.* disheveled hair; *Am.* joker, jester.

mechón *m.* large wick; large lock of hair.

medalla *f.* medal.

médano *m.* dune, sand hill, sand bank; *Riopl., Carib.* sandy marshland.

media *f.* stocking; *Col., Riopl., Ven.* **— corta** (*or* **—**) sock.

mediación *f.* mediation.

mediador *m.* mediator.

mediados: a — de about the middle of.

medianero *m.* mediator; go-between; *adj.* mediating; intermediate; **pared medianera** partition wall.

medianía *f.* mediocrity; average; middle ground; moderate circumstances; moderation; *Col.* partition wall.

mediano *adj.* medium; moderate; middle-sized; average; mediocre.

medianoche *f.* midnight.

mediante *adj.* intervening; **Dios —** God willing; *prep.* by means of, through, with the help of.

mediar *v.* to mediate, intervene; to intercede; to arrive at, or be in, the middle.

medible *adj.* measurable.

medicamento *m.* medicament, medicine.

medicastro *m.* quack, quack doctor.

medicina *f.* medicine.

medicinar *v.* to doctor, treat, prescribe medicine for; **-se** to take medicine.

medición *f.* measurement; measuring.

médico *m.* doctor, physician; *adj.* medical.

medida *f.* measure; measurement; gauge, rule; **— para áridos** dry measure; **a — del deseo** according to one's desire; **a — que** as, in proportion as; at the same time as.

medio *adj.* half; middle; intermediate; medium, average; **media noche** midnight; **hacer una cosa a medias** to do something halfway; **ir a medias** to go halves; *adv.* half, not completely; *m.* middle; means, way; medium; environment; **-s** means, resources; **meterse de por —** to intervene, meddle in a dispute.

mediocre *adj.* mediocre; **mediocridad** *f.* mediocrity.

mediodía *m.* midday, noon; south.

medioeval, medieval *adj.* medieval.

medir *v. irr.* to measure; to scan (*verses*); *Col., Ven., Mex.* **— las calles** to walk the streets, be out of a job; **-se** to measure one's words or actions; *Mex., C.A., Ven., Col., Riopl.* **-se con otro** to try one's strength or ability against another; to fight with another.

meditación *f.* meditation.

meditar *v.* to meditate; to muse.

medrar *v.* to flourish, thrive; to prosper.

medroso *adj.* timid, faint-hearted; fearful, dreadful.

médula *f.* marrow; pith; **— oblongada** medulla oblongata (*the posterior part of the brain tapering off into the spinal cord*).

megáfono *m.* megaphone.

mejicano *adj.* Mexican; *m.* Mexican; the Aztec language; inhabitant of Mexico City. *Also* **mexicano.**

mejilla *f.* cheek.

mejor *adj.* better; **el —** the best; *adv.* better; **a lo —** suddenly, unexpectedly; **tanto —** so much the better.

mejora *f.* betterment; improvement.

mejoramiento *m.* improvement.

mejorar *v.* to better, improve; to get better, recover; **-se** to get better, recover.

mejoría *f.* betterment, improvement; superiority.

melado *adj.* honey-colored; *m.* sugarcane syrup; honey cake.

melancolía *f.* melancholy, gloom.

melancólico *adj.* melancholy, gloomy.

melaza *f.* molasses.

melena *f.* mane.

melindre *m.* (*acto*) affectation; affected act or gesture; whim; (*comestible*) fritter, marzipan (*sweetmeat made of almond paste*).

melindroso *adj.* affected; too particular, finicky, fussy.

melocotón *m.* peach; **melocotonero** *m.* peach tree.

melodía *f.* melody; **melodioso** *adj.* melodious.

melón *m.* melon; cantaloupe; muskmelon; melon vine.

melosidad *f.* sweetness; softness, gentleness.

meloso *adj.* honeyed; soft, sweet; *m. Am.* honey-voiced person; *Am.* overaffectionate person.

mella *f.* nick; dent; **hacer —** to make a dent or impression; to cause pain, worry, or suffering.

mellar *v.* to notch; to nick; to dent; to impair, damage.

mellizo *adj. & m.* twin.

membrete *m.* heading; letterhead; memorandum.

membrillo *m.* quince (*tree and its fruit*).

membrudo *adj.* sinewy, robust, strong, muscular.

memorable *adj.* memorable, notable.

memorándum *m.* memorandum, note; memorandum book, notebook.

memoria *f.* memory; remembrance; reminiscence; memoir, note, account; memorandum; **de —** by heart; **hacer — to** remember, recollect; **— de gallo** poor memory; **-s** regards; memoirs.

memorial *m.* memorandum book; memorial, brief, petition.

mención *f.* mention.

mencionar *v.* to mention.

mendigar *v.* to beg; to ask alms.

mendigo *m.* beggar.

mendrugo *m.* crumb of bread.

menear *v.* to move, shake, stir; to wiggle; to wag; **-se** to hustle about; to wag; to wiggle.

meneo *m.* shaking; swaying; wagging; wiggle; wiggling.

menester *m.* need; job, occupation; **-es** bodily needs; implements, tools; tasks, chores; **ser —** to be necessary.

menesteroso *adj.* needy, in want.

mengua *f.* diminution, decrease; waning; poverty, want; discredit.

menguante *adj.* waning, diminishing, declining.

menguar *v.* to diminish, decrease; to wane.

menjurje *m.* stuff, mixture.

menor *adj.* smaller, lesser, younger; smallest, least, youngest; minor; *m. & f.* **— de edad** minor; *m.* minor (*music*); Minorite, Franciscan; *f.* minor premise (*of a syllogism*); **por — (al por —)** at retail; in small quantities.

menoría = minoría.

menos *adv.* less; least; except; *adj.* & *pron.* less, least; *m.* minus; **— de** (or **— que**) less than; **a lo — (al —**, or **por lo —)** at least; **a — que** unless; **echar de —** to miss, feel or notice the absence of; **no puede — de hacerlo** he cannot help doing it; **venir a —** to decline; to become weak or poor.

menoscabar *v.* to diminish, lessen; to impair, damage; **— la honra de** to undermine the reputation of.

menoscabo *m.* impairment; damage; diminution, lessening.

menospreciar *v.* to despise, scorn; to underestimate.

menosprecio *m.* scorn, contempt; underestimation.

mensaje *m.* message.

mensajero *m.* messenger.

menstruo *m.* menstruation.

mensual *adj.* monthly.

mensualidad *f.* monthly allowance; monthly payment.

mensurable *adj.* measurable.

menta *f.* mint; peppermint; *Riopl.* rumor, hearsay; *Riopl., Andes* **por -s** by hearsay; *Riopl.* **persona de —** famous person.

mentado *adj.* famous; *p.p.* mentioned.

mental *adj.* mental.

mentalidad *f.* mentality.

mentar¹ *v. irr.* to mention; to call, name.

mente *f.* mind; intellect.

mentecato *adj.* foolish, simple; *m.* fool.

mentir³ *v. irr.* to lie, tell lies.

mentira *f.* lie, falsehood, fib; white spot on the fingernails.

mentiroso *adj.* lying, deceptive, false; *m.* liar, fibber; **mentirosillo** *m.* little fibber.

mentís: dar un — to give the lie (to).

mentón *m.* chin.

menú *m.* menu.

menudear *v.* to occur frequently; to repeat over and over; to fall incessantly (*as rain, stones, projectiles, etc.*); to tell in detail; *Am.* to retail, sell at retail; *Am.* to meet together often.

menudeo *m.* retail; **vender al —** to retail, sell at retail.

menudo *adj.* minute, small; insignificant; exact, detailed; **dinero —** change; **a —** often; **por —** in detail; retail; *m.* entrails, "innards"; change, small coins.

meñique *adj.* tiny, wee; **dedo —** little finger.

meollo *m.* marrow; pith; kernel; substance; brain; brains.

meple *m. Riopl.* maple.

merca *f.* purchase.

mercachifle *m.* peddler, vendor; cheap merchant; cheap fellow.

mercader *m.* trader, merchant.

mercadería *f.* merchandise; trade.

mercado *m.* market; mart.

mercancía *f.* merchandise; goods.

mercantil *adj.* mercantile, commercial.

mercar⁶ *v.* to purchase, buy.

merced *f.* favor; present, gift; mercy; **Vuestra Merced** Your Honor; **a — de** at the mercy of; at the expense of.

mercería *f.* notions (*pins, buttons, etc.*); notions store; *Riopl., P.R.* drygoods store.

mercurio *m.* mercury; quicksilver.

merecedor *adj.* worthy, deserving.

merecer¹³ *v. irr.* to deserve.

merecido *adj.* & *p.p.* deserved; *m.* deserved punishment.

merecimiento *m.* merit.

merendar¹ *v. irr.* to have an afternoon snack or refreshment; *Carib., Ven.* **-se uno a alguien** to fleece or skin someone (*in a game or business deal*); to kill someone.

merendero *m.* lunchroom.

meridiano *adj.* & *m.* meridian.

meridional *adj.* southern; *m.* southerner.

merienda *f.* light afternoon meal; afternoon refreshments.

mérito *m.* merit; **de —** notable.

merito *dim.* of **mero**.

meritorio *adj.* meritorious, worthy, deserving; *m.* employee without salary (*learning trade or profession*).

merluza *f.* hake (*species of codfish*); drunken state.

merma *f.* reduction, decrease.

mermar *v.* to dwindle; to decrease, reduce.

mermelada *f.* marmalade.

mero *adj.* mere, pure; *Mex., C.A.* exact, real; **la mera verdad** the real truth; *adv. Mex., C.A.* very, very same, exactly; *Mex., C.A.* soon; *Col.* only; *Mex., C.A.* **una mera de las tres** only one of the three; *Mex., C.A.* **ya —** (or **merito**) very soon; *Mex., C.A.* **allí —** (or **merito**) right there; *m.* species of perch; *Ch.* species of thrush.

merodear *v.* to rove in search of plunder.

mes *m.* month.

mesa *f.* table; executive board; staircase landing; mesa, plateau; **levantar la —** to clear the table; **poner la —** to set the table; *Col., Carib., C.A., Mex.* **quitar la —** to clear the table.

mesada *f.* monthly salary or allowance.

mesarse *v.* to tear (*one's hair or beard*).

mesero *m. Mex., C.A., Ven., Col.* waiter.

meseta *f.* plateau; staircase landing.

mesón *m.* inn (*usually a large one-story shelter for men and pack animals*).

mesonero *m.* innkeeper.

mestizo *adj.* half-breed; hybrid; **perro —** mongrel dog; *m.* mestizo, half-breed.

mesura *f.* moderation; composure; dignity; politeness.

mesurado *adj.* moderate, temperate; dignified.

meta *f.* goal; objective.

metáfora *f.* metaphor.

ME

metal *m.* metal.

metálico *adj.* metallic, metal; *m.* specie, coined money; cash in coin.

metalurgia *f.* metallurgy.

metate *m. Mex.* flat stone (*used for grinding corn, etc.*).

metátesis *f.* metathesis.

meteorito *m.* meteorite.

meteoro *m.* meteor.

meteorología *f.* meteorology; **meteorológico** *adj.* meteorological; **oficina meteorológica** weather bureau.

meter *v.* to put (in); to get (in); to insert; to smuggle; to make (*noise, trouble, etc.*); to cause (*fear*); *Carib.* to strike (*a blow*); *Ríopl., Carib.* **-le** to hurry up; **-se** to meddle, interfere; to plunge (into); **-se monja** (*Am.* **-se de monja**) to become a nun; also **-se a monja**; **-se con** to pick a quarrel with.

metódico *adj.* methodical.

método *m.* method.

métrico *adj.* metric.

metro *m.* meter; subway.

metrópoli *f.* metropolis.

metropolitano *adj.* metropolitan; *m.* archbishop.

mexicano = **mejicano** (*pronounced identically*).

mezcal *m. Mex.* mescal (*a species of maguey and an alcoholic beverage made from it*).

mezcla *f.* mixture; mortar; mixed cloth; **mezclilla** *f.* mixed cloth (*generally black and white*); tweed.

mezclar *v.* to mix, blend; **-se** to mix, mingle; to meddle.

mezcolanza *f.* jumble, mess, mixture.

mezquindad *f.* meanness; stinginess; dire poverty.

mezquino *adj.* poor, needy; mean, stingy; meager; small, tiny; *m. Col., Mex.* wart (*usually on a finger*).

mi *adj.* my.

mí *pers. pron.* (*used after prep.*) me, myself.

miaja = **migaja**.

miau *m.* mew.

mico *m.* long-tailed monkey; *C.A.* jack (*for lifting heavy objects*).

microbio *m.* microbe.

micrófono *m.* microphone.

microscopio *m.* microscope; **— electrónico** electron microscope; **microscópico** *adj.* microscopic.

miedo *m.* fear; dread; **tener —** to be afraid.

miedoso *adj.* afraid, fearful, timid.

miel *m.* honey; molasses.

miembro *m.* member; limb.

mientes *f. pl.* thought, mind; **parar — en** to consider, reflect on; **traer a las — to recall; venírsele a uno a las —** to occur to one, come to one's mind.

mientras *conj.* while; **— que** while; **— tanto** in the meantime, meanwhile; **— más . . . — menos . . .** the more . . . the less . . .

miércoles *m.* Wednesday.

mies *f.* ripe grain; harvest; **-es** fields of grain.

miga *f.* crumb; soft part of bread; substance; **-s** crumbs; fried crumbs of bread; **hacer buenas -s** (*or* **malas -s**) **con** to get along well (*or badly*) with.

migaja *f.* crumb; bit, fragment, small particle.

migración *f.* migration.

milagro *m.* miracle; wonder.

milagroso *adj.* miraculous.

milicia *f.* militia; military science; military profession.

militar *adj.* military; *m.* soldier, military man; *v.* to serve in the army; to militate, fight (against).

milpa *f. Mex., C.A.* cornfield.

milla *f.* mile.

millar *m.* thousand; **-es** thousands, a great number.

millón *m.* million; **millonario** *adj.* & *m.* millionaire; **millonésimo** *adj.* & *m.* millionth.

mimar *v.* to pamper, spoil, humor; to pet.

mimbre *m.* wicker; **mimbrera** *f.* willow.

mímico *adj.* mimic.

mimo *m.* pampering; caress; coaxing.

mimoso *adj.* tender, sensitive; delicate; finicky, fussy.

mina *f.* mine; source; fortune.

minar *v.* to mine; to undermine; to sow with explosive mines.

mineral *m.* mineral; mine; ore; wealth, fortune; *adj.* mineral.

minería *f.* mining; miners.

minero *m.* miner; wealth, fortune; source; *adj.* mining; **compañía minera** mining company.

miniatura *f.* miniature.

mínimo *adj.* least, smallest; *m.* minimum.

minino *m.* kitten, kitty, pussy.

ministerio *m.* ministry; administration, ministering; portfolio (*office of a cabinet member*); minister's office.

ministrar *v.* to minister; to give (*money, aid, etc.*).

ministro *m.* minister; cabinet member; office of justice.

minoría *f.* minority.

minoridad *f.* minority (*in age*).

minucioso *adj.* minute, detailed; scrupulous.

minúsculo *adj.* small; **letra minúscula** small letter.

minuta *f.* minutes; memorandum; first draft (*of a contract, deed, etc.*); memorandum list; lawyer's bill; *Am.* **a la — breaded and fried** (*said of meat or fish*).

minuto *m.* minute; **minutero** *m.* minute hand.

mío *poss. adj.* my, of mine; *poss. pron.* mine; *Ríopl., Ch.* **detrás —** behind me.

miope *adj.* shortsighted, nearsighted; *m. & f.* nearsighted person.

mira *f.* (*de puntería*) gun sight; guiding point; (*intención*) intention, design; outlook; **estar a la — de** to be on the lookout for; to be on the alert for; **poner la — en** to fix one's eyes on; to aim at.

mirada f. glance, gaze, look.

mirador m. mirador, enclosed balcony (*commanding an extensive view*); watchtower; lookout site; onlooker, spectator; *Ríopl.* penthouse (*small house built on a roof for recreation*).

miramiento m. consideration, respect, regard; reverence; circumspection, prudence.

mirar v. to look; to glance; to behold; to see; **— por alguien** to take care of someone; **¡mira (tú)!** look!

miríada f. myriad, multitude, great number.

mirlo m. blackbird.

mirón m. bystander, onlooker, spectator; *adj.* curious.

mirto m. myrtle.

misa f. mass; **— del gallo** midnight mass.

misceláneo adj. miscellaneous.

miserable adj. miserable, unhappy; forlorn; miserly, stingy; mean.

miseria f. misery; poverty; stinginess; bit, trifle.

misericordia f. mercy, compassion, pity.

misericordioso adj. merciful, compassionate.

misero adj, miserable, unhappy; forlorn; stingy.

misión f. mission.

misionero m. missionary.

mismo adj. same; self; very; **ahora —** right away.

misterio m. mystery; secret.

misterioso adj. mysterious.

místico adj. mystical, mystic; m. mystic.

mitad f. half; middle.

mitigar[7] v. to mitigate, soften, soothe.

mitin m. meeting.

mito m. myth; **mitología** f. mythology.

mitra f. bishop's miter.

mixto adj. mixed; half-breed; m. composite; match; explosive compound.

mobiliario m. furniture.

moblaje = mueblaje.

mocedad f. youth; youthfulness; youthful prank.

mocetón m. tall, robust lad.

moción f. motion.

mocoso adj. sniffling; m. brat, scamp; sniffling boy.

mochar v. *Am.* to cut off, chop off, cut, trim (*see* **desmochar**); *Am.* to snitch, pilfer; *Col.* to depose, dismiss, put out of a job.

mochila f. knapsack; soldier's kit.

mocho adj. cut off; cropped, shorn; *Am.* maimed, mutilated; *Mex.* reactionary, conservative; m. butt of a firearm; *Col., Ven.* nag; *Carib.* cigar butt.

moda f. mode, custom, style, fashion; **de —** fashionable.

modelar v. to model.

modelo m. model, copy, pattern; m. & f. life model.

moderación f. moderation.

moderado adj. moderate; conservative.

moderar v. to moderate, temper; to regulate; to restrain.

moderno adj. modern.

modestia f. modesty.

modesto adj. modest.

módico adj. moderate, reasonable (*price*).

modificación f. modification.

modificar[6] v. to modify.

modismo m. idiom.

modista f. dressmaker; milliner.

modo m. mode, manner, way; mood (*grammar*); **a** (*or* **al**) **— de** like, in the manner of; **de — que** so that; and so; **de todos -s** at any rate, anyway.

modorra f. drowsiness; gid (*a disease of sheep*).

modular v. to modulate, tone down.

mofa f. scoff, jeer, taunt; mockery.

mofar v. to mock, scoff, jeer; **-se de** to make fun of, scoff at.

moflete m. fat cheek; **mofletudo** adj. fat-cheeked.

mohín m. grimace; wry face.

mohino adj. moody, discontented, sad, melancholy; black (*referring to a horse, cow, or bull*).

moho m. rust; mold.

mohoso adj. musty, moldy; rusty.

mojada f. drench, drenching, wetting.

mojado adj. wet, damp, moist; *p.p. of* **mojar**.

mojadura f. wetting, dampening, drenching.

mojar v. to dampen, wet, moisten; *Ríopl., Ch.* to accompany (*a song*); *Am.* to bribe; *Ríopl., Carib., Mex.* to celebrate by drinking; *Am.* **mojársele a uno los papeles** to get things mixed up.

mojicón m. punch, blow; muffin, bun.

mojigatería f. prudery; false humility; affected piety.

mojigato adj. prudish; affectedly pious, overzealous (*in matters of religion*); hypocritical; m. prude; hypocrite.

mojón m. landmark; milestone; heap, pile.

molde m. mold, cast; form; pattern, model; **venir de —** to come pat, be to the point; **letras de —** printed letters; print.

moldear v. to mold; to cast; to decorate with moldings.

moldura f. molding.

mole f. mass, bulk; adj. soft, mild; m. *Mex.* **— de guajolote** a Mexican dish of turkey served with a chili gravy.

molécula f. molecule.

moler[2] v. irr. to mill; to grind; to tire, fatigue; to wear out, destroy; to bother; **— a palos** to give a thorough beating.

molestar v. to molest, disturb; to bother, annoy.

molestia f. bother, annoyance; discomfort.

molesto *adj.* bothersome, annoying; uncomfortable.

molicie *f.* softness; fondness for luxury.

molienda *f.* grind, grinding, milling; portion to be, or that has been, ground; grinding season (*for sugar cane or olives*); fatigue, weariness; bother.

molinero *m.* miller.

molinete *m.* small mill; ventilating fan; pin wheel; twirl, whirl, flourish.

molinillo *m.* small mill or grinder; chocolate beater; restless person.

molino *m.* mill; restless person; **— de viento** windmill.

mollera *f.* crown of the head; judgment, good sense; **ser duro de —** to be stubborn; **no tener sal en la —** to be dull, stupid.

momentáneo *adj.* momentary; sudden, quick.

momento *m.* moment; importance; momentum; **al —** immediately, without delay; **a cada —** continually; frequently.

mona *f.* female monkey; mimic; drunkenness; **dormir la —** to sleep it off; **pillar una —** to get drunk.

monada *f.* (*típico de mono*) monkeyshine; monkey face; (*cosa graciosa*) cute little thing; cute gesture; nonsense; flattery.

monarca *m.* monarch.

monarquía *f.* monarchy.

monasterio *m.* monastery.

mondadientes *m.* toothpick.

mondar *v.* to pare; to peel; to prune; to clean out; *Am.* to beat, thrash; *Am.* to beat, defeat; **-se los dientes** to pick one's teeth.

moneda *f.* coin; money; **— corriente** currency; **— menuda** (*or* **suelta**) change, small coins; **casa de —** mint.

monería *f.* monkeyshine, antic; trifle, trinket; cute little thing.

monetario *adj.* monetary, pertaining to money; financial.

monigote *m.* puppet, ridiculous figure; dunce.

monitorear *v.* to monitor (*a radio or TV program*).

monja *f.* nun.

monje *m.* monk.

mono *m.* monkey; silly fool; mimic; coveralls; *Ch.* pile of fruit or vegetables (*in a market*); **-s** *Ch.* worthless household utensils and furniture; *Am.* **meterle a uno los -s en el cuerpo** to frighten, terrify someone; *adj.* pretty, neat, cute; *Am.* sorrel, reddish-brown; *Col.* blond.

monologar[7] *v.* to soliloquize, talk to oneself; to recite monologues; to monopolize the conversation.

monólogo *m.* monologue.

monopolio *m.* monopoly.

monopolizar[9] *v.* to monopolize; to corner (*a market*).

monosílabo *adj.* monosyllabic, of one syllable; *m.* monosyllable.

monotonía *f.* monotony; **monótono** *adj.* monotonous,

monserga *f.* gabble.

monstruo *m.* monster.

monstruosidad *f.* monstrosity; monster, freak.

monstruoso *adj.* monstrous.

monta *f.* amount, sum; value, importance; **de poca —** of little value or importance.

montaje *m.* assembly, assembling (*of machinery*); mount, support for a cannon.

montante *m.* broadsword; transom; upright; post; *Carib., Ven.* sum, amount, cost; *f.* high tide.

montaña *f.* mountain; **— rusa** roller coaster.

montañés *adj.* mountain (*used as adj.*) of, from or pertaining to the mountains; *m.* mountaineer; native of the province of Santander, Spain.

montañoso *adj.* mountainous.

montar *v.* to mount; to ride horseback; to amount (to); to set (*jewels*); to cock (*a gun*); to assemble, set up (*machinery*); *Carib., C.A.* to organize, establish.

montaraz *adj.* wild, primitive, uncivilized; *m.* forester.

monte *m.* mount, mountain; forest; thicket; monte (*a card game*); *C.A., Mex.* grass, pasture; *Am.* country, outskirts; **montecillo** *m.* mound, small hill; **montepío** *m.* pawnshop.

montera *f.* cap; *Andes* Bolivian cone-shaped hat (*worn by Indians*).

montés *adj.* wild, mountain (*used as adj.*); **cabra —** mountain goat; **gato —** wildcat.

montículo *m.* mound.

montón *m.* pile, heap; mass, great number; **a -es** in abundance, in heaps, by heaps.

montonera *f.* *Col., Ven., Riopl.* band of mounted rebels or guerrilla fighters; *Col.* pile of wheat, hay, straw, etc.; *Am.* pile, heap (*of anything*).

montuoso *adj.* hilly; mountainous.

montura *f.* mount, horse; saddle and trappings.

monumento *m.* monument; **monumental** *adj.* monumental.

moño *m.* knot or roll of hair; bow of ribbon; crest, tuft of feathers; *Mex.* forelock (*lock of hair on the fore part of the head*); *Am.* crest, peak (*of anything*); *Col.* whim; *Am.* a Colombian popular dance; **-s** frippery, gaudy ornaments; *Col.* **estar con el — torcido** to be in an ugly humor.

mora *f.* blackberry; mulberry; brambleberry; *Ch.* blood pudding, sausage.

morada *f.* dwelling, residence; stay.

morado *adj.* purple.

morador *m.* dweller, resident.

moral *adj.* moral; *f.* ethics, moral philosophy; morale; *m.* mulberry tree; blackberry bush.

moraleja *f.* moral, lesson, maxim.

moralidad *f.* morality.

moralista *m. & f.* moralist.

morar *v.* to live, dwell, reside.

morbidez *f.* softness; mellowness.

mórbido *adj.* morbid; soft.

morboso *adj.* morbid, unhealthy, diseased.

morcilla *f.* blood pudding, blood sausage; gag (*an amusing remark by a comedian*).

mordacidad *f.* sharpness (*of tongue*).

mordaz *adj.* biting, cutting, sarcastic.

mordaza *f.* gag (*for the mouth*).

mordedor *adj.* biting; snappy; *m.* biter; slanderer.

mordedura *f.* bite; sting.

mordelón *adj. Col., Ven.* biting, snappy; *m. Am.* biter; *Mex.* public official who accepts a bribe.

morder[2] *v. irr.* to bite; to nip; to gnaw; to corrode; to backbite, slander; *Ven.* to swindle; *Mex., C.A.* to "shake down", exact a bribe.

mordida *f. Am.* bite; *Mex., C.A., Carib., Ven.* graft, money obtained by graft.

mordiscar[6], **mordisquear** *v.* to nibble; to gnaw.

mordisco *m.* bite; nibble.

moreno *adj.* brown; dark, brunette; *m. Riopl., Carib., Mex., Ven., Andes* colored person.

moretón *m.* bruise, black-and-blue mark.

morfema *m.* morpheme.

morfina *f.* morphine; **morfinómano** *m.* morphine addict, drug fiend.

moribundo *adj.* dying.

morir[4,52] *v. irr.* to die; **-se** to die; to die out, be extinguished.

morisco *adj.* Moorish; Moresque, in the Moorish style; *m.* Morisco (*Christianized Moor*); language of the Moriscos.

moro *adj.* Moorish; *Mex., Ven., Riopl., Cuba* dappled, spotted (*horse*); *Col., Ch., Andes* unbaptized; *m.* Moor; *Am.* frosted cookie.

morocho *adj. Am.* robust, strong; *Riopl.* of dark complexion; *Ch.* rough, tough; *Andes* of low social condition.

morral *m.* nose bag; knapsack; hunter's bag.

morriña *f.* melancholy, blues, sadness.

morsa *f.* walrus.

mortaja *f.* shroud; *Am.* cigarette paper.

mortal *adj.* mortal; fatal; deadly; *m.* mortal; **mortalidad** *f.* mortality; death rate.

mortandad *f.* mortality, death rate; massacre, slaughter.

mortecino *adj.* deathly pale; dying; **hacer la mortecina** to pretend to be dead.

morterete *m.* small mortar, small cannon.

mortero *m.* mortar (*for grinding*).

mortífero *adj.* deadly, fatal.

mortificar[6] *v.* to mortify; to torment; to vex, annoy; **-se** to do penance; to be grieved; *Mex., C.A., Ven.* to be embarrassed.

mortuorio *adj.* funeral, funereal, mournful; *m.* funeral, burial.

mosaico *adj. & m.* mosaic.

mosca *f.* fly; bore; bother; *Am.* sponger, parasite; *Mex., C.A., Ven.* bull's-eye, center of a target; **moscón** *m.* large fly; *Am.* **ir de moscón** to go along as a chaperone.

mosquear *v.* to brush off or drive away flies; to whip, beat; *Riopl.* to rage, be furious; **-se** to show pique or resentment; *Ch.* to go away.

mosquito *m.* mosquito; gnat; *Am.* Mosquito Indian of Nicaragua; **mosquitero** *m.* mosquito net.

mostacho *m.* mustache.

mostaza *f.* mustard; mustard seed; bird shot.

mostrador *m.* demonstrator; store counter; clock dial.

mostrar[2] *v. irr.* to show; to demonstrate; to exhibit.

mostrenco *adj.* (*sin dueño*) ownerless; homeless; stray (*animal*); (*torpe*) slow, dull; fat, heavy; *m.* dunce; *C.A.* worthless animal.

mota *f.* mote, speck; knot in cloth; slight defect; mound, knoll; *Col., Ven., Carib.* powder puff; *Am.* tuft.

mote *m.* motto; slogan; nickname; *Andes, Ch., Col.* stewed corn; *Andes* grammatical error (*made by illiterate people and children*); *Am.* **— pelado** hominy.

motear *v.* to speck, speckle; to spot; *Am.* to mispronounce, enunciate badly.

motejar *v.* to jeer at; to call bad names; to insult; to censure; **— de** to brand as.

motín *m.* mutiny; riot.

motivar *v.* to cause; to give a cause for.

motivo *m.* motive, reason; motif, theme; *m.* **con — de** because of; on the occasion of; *adj.* motive.

motocicleta *f.* motorcycle; **motociclista** *m. & f.* motorcyclist, motorcycle rider.

motor *m.* motor; **— de reacción** jet engine; *adj.* motor, causing motion.

motorista *m. & f.* motorist; motorman, motorwoman.

motriz *adj.* motive, impelling, driving; **fuerza —** power, driving force.

movedizo *adj.* movable; shaky; shifting; **arena movediza** quicksand.

mover[2] *v. irr.* (*físicamente*) to move; (*persuadir*) to persuade; to stir, excite; to touch, affect; **-se** to move.

movible *adj.* movable; mobile; fickle.

móvil *m.* motive, inducement, incentive; *adj.* mobile, movable; unstable.

movilización *f.* mobilization.

movilizar[9] *v.* to mobilize.

movimiento *m.* movement; motion; commotion, disturbance.

moza *f.* maid; girl; last hand of a game; *Ch.* last song or dance of a fiesta.

mozalbete *m.* youth, lad.

mozárabe *adj.* Mozarabic (*Christian in*

MO

Moslem Spain).

mozo *adj*. young; unmarried; *m*. youth; manservant; waiter; porter; errand boy; **buen —** handsome man.

mozuela *f*. lass, young girl.

mozuelo *m*. lad, young boy.

mucama *f*. *Andes, Riopl*. servant girl; **mucamo** *m*. *Andes, Riopl*. servant.

mucoso *adj*. mucous; slimy; **membrana mucosa** mucous membrane.

muchacha *f*. child; girl; servant, maid.

muchacho *m*. child; boy, lad.

muchedumbre *f*. multitude; crowd.

mucho *adj*. much, a lot of; long (*referring to time*); **-s** many; *adv*. much; a great deal; **ni con —** not by far, not by a long shot; **ni — menos** not by any means, nor anything like it; **por — que** no matter how much; **no es — que** it is no wonder that.

muda *f*. change; change of clothes; molt (*act or time of shedding feathers*); *Riopl*. relay of draft animals.

mudable *adj*. changeable; fickle.

mudanza *f*. change; removal; inconstancy.

mudar *v*. to change; to remove; to molt; **— de casa** to move; **— de traje** to change one's suit or costume; **-se** to change one's clothes; to change one's habits; to move, change one's abode.

mudez *f*. muteness, dumbness.

mudo *adj*. mute, dumb; silent; *m*. dumb person.

mueblaje *m*. furniture.

mueble *m*. piece of furniture; **-s** furniture, household goods; *adj*. movable; **bienes -s** chattels, movable possessions.

mueca *f*. grimace; wry face.

muela *f*. (*diente*) molar tooth; (*piedra*) millstone; grindstone; **— cordal** (*or* **— del juicio**) wisdom tooth.

muelle *adj*. soft; voluptuous; *m*. spring; wharf; loading platform; **— real** main spring of a watch.

muerte *f*. death.

muerto *p.p. of* **morir** & *adj*. dead; withered; faded; **naturaleza muerta** still life; *m*. corpse.

muesca *f*. notch; groove.

muestra *f*. sample; pattern, model; shop sign; sign, indication; presence, bearing; face, dial (*of a clock or watch*); **muestrario** *m*. book or collection of samples.

mugido *m*. moo; mooing, lowing of cattle.

mugir[11] *v*. to moo, low.

mugre *f*. dirt, grime.

mugriento *adj*. grimy, dirty.

mujer *f*. woman; wife.

mujeril *adj*. womanly, feminine; womanish, like a woman.

mula *f*. mule; *Am*. cushion for carrying loads; *Am*. worthless merchandise; *Riopl*. cruel, treacherous person; *Am*. **echar a uno la —** to give someone the dickens, scold someone.

muladar *m*. rubbish pile or dump;

dunghill, pile of manure.

mulato *adj*. & *m*. mulatto.

muleta *f*. crutch; red cloth draped over a rod (*used by bullfighters*).

muletilla *f*. cane with a crutchlike handle; red cloth draped over a rod (*used by bullfighters*); cliché (*hackneyed or trite phrase*); refrain; repetitious word or phrase; braid frog (*fastener for a coat*).

mulo *m*. mule.

multa *f*. fine.

multicolor *adj*. many-colored, motley.

múltiple *adj*. multiple.

multiplicación *f*. multiplication.

multiplicar[6] *v*. to multiply.

multiplicidad *f*. multiplicity, manifold variety.

múltiplo *m*. multiple number.

multitud *f*. multitude; crowd.

mullido *adj*. soft; fluffy; *m*. stuffing for mattresses or pillows; soft cushion or mattress.

mullir[20] *v*. to fluff; to soften.

mundanal *adj*. worldly.

mundano *adj*. mundane, worldly.

mundial *adj*. universal; **la guerra —** the World War.

mundo *m*. world; trunk; **todo el —** everybody.

munición *f*. ammunition; buckshot; **-es de guerra** war supplies.

municipal *adj*. municipal; **municipalidad** *f*. municipality; town hall; city government.

municipio *m*. municipality.

muñeca *f*. doll; wrist; manikin (*figure for displaying clothes*); **muñeco** *m*. boy doll; dummy, puppet.

muñón *m*. stump (*of an arm or leg*).

muralla *f*. surrounding wall; rampart.

murciano *adj*. of or from Murcia, Spain; *m*. native of Murcia.

murciélago *m*. bat.

murga *f*. brass band.

murmullo *m*. murmur, rumor; whisper; muttering.

murmuración *f*. slander, gossip; grumbling.

murmurar *v*. to murmur; to slander, gossip; to whisper; to grumble.

muro *m*. wall.

murria *f*. sulkiness, sullenness, melancholy, blues; **tener —** to be sulky; to have the blues.

musa *f*. Muse; muse, poetic inspiration; poetry; **-s** fine arts.

muscular *adj*. muscular.

musculatura *f*. muscles; muscular system.

músculo *m*. muscle.

musculoso *adj*. muscular; sinewy.

muselina *f*. muslin.

museo *m*. museum.

musgo *m*. moss.

musgoso *adj*. mossy.

música *f*. music.

musical *adj*. musical.

músico *adj*. musical; *m*. musician.

musitar *v*. to mutter, mumble; to whisper.

muslo *m.* thigh.
mustio *adj.* sad; withered; humble.
mutilar *v.* to mutilate; to butcher; to mar.
mutismo *m.* muteness, silence.
mutuo *adj.* mutual; reciprocal.
muy *adv.* very; greatly; most.

N

nabo *m.* turnip.
nácar *m.* mother-of-pearl; pearl color.
nacarado *adj.* pearly.
nacer[13] *v. irr.* (*salir del vientre*) to be born; (*brotar*) to spring, originate; to bud; to sprout, grow (*said of plants*); **— de pie** (*or* **— de pies**) to be born lucky.
naciente *adj.* rising (*sun*); *m.* orient, east.
nacimiento *m.* birth; origin; beginning; descent; source; crèche (*representation of the Nativity*).
nación *f.* nation.
nacional *adj.* national; *m.* national, citizen.
nacionalidad *f.* nationality.
nada *f.* nothingness; *indef. pron.* nothing, not . . . anything; *adv.* not at all; **de —** you are welcome, don't mention it (*as a reply to* «**gracias**»); *Am.* **a cada —** constantly; **una nadita** a trifle, just a little.
nadada *f.* swim.
nadador *m.* swimmer; *Ven.* fish-net float.
nadar *v.* to swim; to float.
nadería *f.* a mere nothing, trifle, worthless thing.
nadie *indef. pron.* nobody, no one, not . . . anyone.
nafta *f.* naphtha.
naguas = **enaguas**.
náhuatl *adj.* the language of the Aztec Indians.
naipe *m.* playing card.
nalgas *f. pl.* buttocks; rump; **nalgada** *f.* spank; **-s** spanking.
nana *f.* grandma; lullaby; *Mex.*, *Ríopl.*, *Ven.* child's nurse; *Spain* nice old lady.
naranja *f.* orange; **— tangerina** tangerine; **naranjada** *f.* orangeade; orange juice; orange marmalade; **naranjal** *m.* orange grove; **naranjo** *m.* orange tree.
narciso *m.* narcissus; daffodil; fop, dandy.
narcótico *adj.* & *m.* narcotic.
narcotizar[9] *v.* to dope, drug with narcotics.
nariz *f.* nose; nostril; **narices** nostrils.
narración *f.* narration, account, story.
narrar *v.* to narrate, tell, relate.
narrativo *adj.* narrative; **narrativa** *f.* narrative.
nata *f.* cream; best part; scum; **-s** whipped cream with sugar; custard; **natoso** *adj.* creamy.
natación *f.* swimming.
natal *adj.* natal; native; **natalicio** *m.* birthday; **natalidad** *f.* birth rate.

natillas *f. pl.* custard.
nativo *adj.* native.
natural *adj.* natural; native; simple, unaffected; *m.* & *f.* native; *m.* nature, disposition; **al —** without affectation; **del —** from nature, from life.
naturaleza *f.* nature; disposition; nationality; naturalization; **— muerta** still life.
naturalidad *f.* naturalness; simplicity; birthright.
naturalista *adj.* naturalistic; *m.* & *f.* naturalist.
naturalización *f.* naturalization.
naturalizar[9] *v.* to naturalize; to acclimatize, accustom to a new climate; **-se** to become naturalized.
naufragar[7] *v.* to be shipwrecked; to fail.
naufragio *m.* shipwreck; failure, ruin.
náufrago *m.* shipwrecked person.
náusea *f.* nausea; **dar -s** to nauseate, sicken; to disgust; **tener -s** to be nauseated, be sick to one's stomach.
nauseabundo *adj.* nauseating, sickening.
nauseado *adj.* nauseated, sick to one's stomach.
náutica *f.* navigation (*science of navigation*).
navaja *f.* jackknife, pocketknife; penknife; razor.
navajazo *m.* stab with a jackknife or razor; stab wound.
naval *adj.* naval.
navarro *adj.* Navarrese, of or pertaining to Navarre, Spain; *m.* Navarrese.
nave *f.* ship, boat; nave; **— cósmica** spaceship; **— cósmica pilotada** manned space vehicle.
navegable *adj.* navigable.
navegación *f.* navigation; sea voyage; **— aérea** aviation.
navegador navegante *m.* navigator; *adj.* navigating.
navegar[7] *v.* to navigate; to sail.
navidad *f.* Nativity; Christmas; **-es** Christmas season.
navío *m.* vessel, ship; **— de guerra** warship.
neblina *f.* fog, mist.
necedad *f.* foolishness, nonsense.
necesario *adj.* necessary.
neceser *m.* toilet case; sewing kit.
necesidad *f.* necessity, need, want.
necesitado *adj.* needy; in need, destitute, poor; *p.p. of* **necesitar**; *m.* needy person.
necesitar *v.* to need; to necessitate.
necio *adj.* stupid, ignorant; foolish; stubborn; *Col.* touchy.
nefando *adj.* abominable; wicked.
negación *f.* negation, denial; negative (*negative particle*).
negar[1,7] *v. irr.* to deny; to refuse; to prohibit; to disown; **-se** to refuse, decline.
negativa *f.* negative; denial, refusal.
negativo *adj.* negative.
negligencia *f.* negligence, neglect, carelessness.
negligente *adj.* negligent, neglectful,

careless.

negociación f. negotiation; business; business house; management; transaction, deal.

negociante m. merchant, trader, dealer; businessman; adj. negotiating.

negociar v. to negotiate; to trade; to transact.

negocio m. business; business deal; negotiation, transaction; Ríopl., Carib., C.A., Ven., Andes store; **hombre de -s** businessman.

negrear v. to become black; to appear black, look black (in the distance).

negro adj. black; dark; sad, gloomy; unfortunate; m. black color; negro; Ríopl., C.A., Ven., Col. dear, darling; **negra** f. negress; Ríopl., C.A., Ven., Col. dear, darling.

negrura f. blackness.

negruzco adj. blackish.

nena f. baby girl; **nene** m. baby boy.

nepotismo m. nepotism.

nervio m. nerve.

nervioso, nervoso adj. nervous; sinewy, strong.

nerviosidad, nervosidad f. nervousness; flexibility; vigor.

nervudo adj. sinewy, tough, powerful.

neto adj. clear, pure; net (profit, price, etc.); **netamente** adv. clearly, distinctly.

neumático m. tire; adj. pneumatic.

neutralidad f. neutrality.

neutralizar⁹ v. to neutralize, counteract.

neutro adj. neutral; neuter; sexless.

nevada f. snowfall.

nevado adj. snowy, white as snow; covered with snow.

nevar¹ v. irr. to snow.

nevasca f. snowstorm.

nevera f. icebox; refrigerator; ice storehouse; ice or ice-cream vendor (woman).

ni conj. & adv. nor; not even; neither; **— siquiera** not even.

nicho m. niche; recess, hollow in a wall.

nidada f. nestful of eggs; brood of chicks; hatch, brood.

nido m. nest; abode; Am. **patearle el — a alguien** to "upset the apple-cart", upset someone's plans.

niebla f. fog, mist; confusion.

nieto m. grandson, grandchild; **nieta** f. granddaughter.

nieve f. snow; Mex., Ríopl., Ven. sherbet, ice cream; **tiempo de -s** snowy season.

nimio adj. miserly, stingy; Am. very small, insignificant.

ninfa f. nymph.

ningun(o) indef. adj. & pron. no one, none, not . . . any; nobody.

niña f. girl; baby girl; Andes, Ríopl., Mex., Carib. lady, mistress (title of respect and endearment given to adults); **— del ojo** pupil of the eye.

niñada f. childishness, childish act or remark.

niñera f. child's nurse.

niñería f. childish act; child's play; trifle; foolishness.

niñez f. infancy; childhood.

niño m. child, boy; infant; Am. master (title of respect given to a young man by his servants); adj. childlike, childish; very young, immature.

níquel m. nickel.

niquelado adj. nickel-plated; m. nickel plating; nickel plate.

nitidez f. clarity, clearness.

nítido adj. clear.

nitrato m. nitrate; saltpeter.

nitro m. niter, saltpeter.

nitrógeno m. nitrogen.

nivel m. level.

nivelar v. to level; to grade; to equalize.

no adv. no; not; nay; **— bien** as soon as; **un — sé qué** something indefinable; **por sí o por** — just in case, anyway.

noble adj. noble; m. nobleman.

nobleza f. nobility; nobleness.

noción f. notion, idea.

nocivo adj. noxious, harmful, injurious.

nocturno adj. nocturnal, night, nightly; m. nocturne (musical or lyrical composition).

noche f. night; darkness; **a la —** tonight; **de —** by (at) night; **por (en) la —** at night, in the evening; **dejar a uno a buenas -s** to leave a person in the lurch.

Nochebuena f. Christmas Eve.

nocherniego m. night owl (person).

nodriza f. child's nurse; wet nurse.

nogal m. walnut (tree and wood).

nomás Am. **= no más** just; only.

nombradía f. renown, fame.

nombramiento m. nomination; appointment; naming.

nombrar v. to nominate; to name; to appoint.

nombre m. name; fame; noun; watchword; **— de pila** (or **— de bautismo**) Christian name.

nomeolvides f. forget-me-not.

nómina f. list (of names); pay roll.

nominación f. nomination; appointment.

nominal adj. nominal; **valor —** small, insignificant value.

nominar v. to nominate.

non adj. odd, uneven; m. odd number, uneven number; **estar** (or **quedar**) **de —** to be left alone, be left without a partner or companion.

nonada f. trifle, mere nothing.

nopal m. nopal, prickly pear tree (species of cactus).

nordeste adj. & m. northeast.

noria f. draw well; chain pump.

norma f. norm, standard, model.

normal adj. normal; standard; f. perpendicular line.

normalizar⁹ v. to normalize, make normal; to standardize.

noroeste adj. & m. northwest.

nortada f. strong north wind.

nortazo m. Mex., Ven. sudden gust of wind, strong north wind.

norte m. north; north wind; guide;

North Star; direction.

norteamericano *adj.* North American; American (*from or of the United States*).

norteño *adj.* northern; *m.* northerner.

noruego *adj. & m.* Norwegian.

nostalgia *f.* nostalgia, longing, homesickness.

nostálgico *adj.* homesick; lonesome; longing.

nota *f.* note; mark; fame.

notable *adj.* notable; noticeable.

notar *v.* to note, observe; to mark; to write down.

notario *m.* notary.

noticia *f.* notice, information; news; **recibir -s** to receive word, hear (from).

noticiario *m.* news sheet, news column, news bulletin; **noticiero** *m.* = **noticiario;** *adj.* news (*used as adj.*); newsy, full of news.

noticioso *adj.* newsy, full of news; well-informed.

notificación *f.* notification, notifying; notice; summons.

notificar[6] *v.* to notify.

notorio *adj.* well-known; obvious, evident.

novato *m.* novice, beginner.

novedad *f.* novelty; latest news, event, or fashion; change; newness; **hacerle a uno —** to seem strange or new to one; to excite one's curiosity or interest; **sin —** as usual; well.

novel *adj.* new, inexperienced.

novela *f.* novel; fiction.

novelesco *adj.* novelistic, fictional; fantastic.

novelista *m. & f.* novelist.

novia *f.* fiancée; sweetheart; bride.

noviazgo *m.* betrothal, engagement; courtship.

novicio *m.* novice; beginner; apprentice; *adj.* inexperienced.

noviembre *m.* November.

novilla *f.* heifer, young cow.

novillada *f.* herd of young bulls; bull-fight (*using young bulls*).

novillero *m.* a novice bullfighter; a fighter of 3-year-old bulls.

novillo *m.* young bull; steer; **-s** bull-fight (*using young bulls*); **hacer -s** to play hooky, cut classes; to play truant.

novio *m.* fiancé; sweetheart; bridegroom.

nubarrón *m.* large storm cloud.

nube *f.* cloud; film on the eyeball; **poner por las -s** to praise to the skies.

nublado *m.* storm cloud; imminent danger; *adj.* cloudy.

nublar *v.* to cloud; to darken, obscure; **-se** to grow cloudy.

nubloso *adj.* cloudy; gloomy.

nuca *f.* nape.

nuclear *adj.* nuclear.

núcleo *m.* nucleus; kernel.

nudillo *m.* small knot; knuckle; loop, knitted stitch.

nudo *m.* (*vínculo*) knot; joint; union,

bond, tie; (*crisis*) crisis, turning point (*of a play*); knot, nautical mile; **— ciego** hard knot.

nudoso *adj.* knotty, gnarled, knotted.

nuera *f.* daughter-in-law.

nueva *f.* news.

nuevecito *adj.* nice and new, brand-new.

nuevo *adj.* new; newly arrived; **de —** again; **¿qué hay de —?** what's new? what's the news?

nuez *f.* walnut; nut; **—** (*or* **— de Adán**) Adam's apple; **— moscada** (*or* **— de especia**) nutmeg.

nulidad *f.* nullity (*state or quality of being null*); incompetence; nonentity, a nobody.

nulo *adj.* null, void; useless.

numeral *adj. & m.* numeral.

numerar *v.* to number; to calculate; to enumerate.

numérico *adj.* numerical.

numero *m.* number; numeral.

numeroso *adj.* numerous.

nunca *adv.* never; **no . . . —** not . . . ever; **mas que —** more than ever.

nuncio *m.* herald, messenger; nuncio, Papal envoy.

nupcial *adj.* nuptial, relating to marriage or weddings.

nupcias *f. pl.* nuptials, wedding.

nutria *f.* otter.

nutrición *f.* nutrition; nourishment.

nutrido *adj.* full, abundant; substantial; *p.p. of* **nutrir.**

nutrimento, nutrimiento *m.* nutrition; nourishment, food.

nutrir *v.* nourish, feed.

nutritivo *adj.* nutritious, nourishing.

nylon *m.* nylon.

Ñ

ñandu *m.* nandu; American ostrich.

ñapa *f. Andes, Riopl., Cuba, Ven., Col.* additional amount, something extra; *Am.* **de —** to boot, in addition, besides.

ñato *adj. C.A., Col., Ven., Andes* flat-nosed, pug-nosed, snub-nosed; *Am.* ugly, deformed; *Am.* insignificant.

ñoñería *f.* silly remark or action; *Am.* dotage.

ñoño *adj.* feeble-minded; silly; *Am.* old, decrepit, feeble; *Col., Ec.* old-fashioned, out of style.

O

o *conj.* or, either.

oasis *m.* oasis.

obedecer[13] *v. irr.* to obey; **— a cierta causa** to arise from, be due to, a certain cause; **esto obedece a que . . .** this is due to the fact that . . .

obediencia *f.* obedience.

obediente *adj.* obedient.

obertura *f.* musical overture.

obispo *m.* bishop; *Cuba, Andes* **a cada muerte de** (*or* **por la muerte de un**) **—** once in a blue moon.

objeción *f.* objection.

objetar *v.* to object.

NE

objetivo *adj.* objective; *m.* objective (*lens of any optical instrument*); objective.

objeto *m.* object, purpose, aim; thing.

oblea *f.* wafer.

oblicuo *adj.* oblique, slanting, bias.

obligación *f.* obligation; duty; bond, security; engagement.

obligar⁷ *v.* to oblige; to obligate, bind, compel, put under obligation; **-se** to bind oneself, obligate oneself.

obligatorio *adj.* obligatory; compulsory; binding.

oboe *m.* oboe.

óbolo *m.* mite, small contribution.

obra *f.* (*resultado de acción*) work; act; labor, toil; (*creación artística*) book; building (*under construction*); masterpiece of art; repair; **— de** approximately; **por — de** through, by virtue or power of; **hacer mala —** to interfere, hinder; **poner por —** to undertake, begin; to put into practice.

obrar *v.* to work; to act; to operate; to function; to perform; to make; to do; **obra en nuestro poder** we are in receipt of; **la carta que obra en su poder** the letter that is in his possession.

obrero *m.* workman, laborer.

obscenidad *f.* obscenity.

obsceno *adj.* obscene.

obscurecer¹³ *v. irr.* to obscure, darken; to tarnish; to grow dark; **-se** to get dark or cloudy.

obscuridad *f.* obscurity; darkness; dimness.

obscuro *adj.* obscure; dark; dim; **a obscuras** (= **a oscuras**) in the dark; *m.* shade (*in painting*).

obsequiar *v.* to regale, entertain; to court; *Am.* to give, make a present of.

obsequio *m.* attention, courtesy; gift; **en — de** for the sake of, in honor of.

obsequioso *adj.* attentive, courteous, obliging; obsequious, servile.

observación *f.* observation; remark.

observador *m.* observer; *adj.* observing.

observancia *f.* observance (*of a law, rule, custom, etc.*).

observante *adj.* observant (*of a law, custom, or rule*).

observar *v.* to observe; to watch; to remark.

observatorio *m.* observatory.

obsesión *f.* obsession.

obsesionar *v.* to obsess.

obstáculo *m.* obstacle.

**obstante: no — notwithstanding; nevertheless.

obstar *v.* to hinder, impede, obstruct.

obstinación *f.* obstinacy, stubbornness.

obstinado *adj.* obstinate, stubborn.

obstinarse *v.* to persist (in); to be obstinate, stubborn (about).

obstrucción *f.* obstruction.

obstruir³² *v. irr.* to obstruct, block.

obtener⁴⁵ *v. irr.* to obtain, get; to attain.

obtenible *adj.* obtainable, available.

obturador *m.* choke (*of an automobile*); throttle; plug, stopper; shutter (*of a camera*).

obviar *v.* to obviate, clear away, remove.

obvio *adj.* obvious.

ocasión *f.* occasion, opportunity; cause; danger, risk; **de —** reduced, bargain; **avisos de —** want "ads" (*advertisements*); *Am.* **esta —** this time.

ocasional *adj.* occasional.

ocasionar *v.* to occasion, cause.

ocaso *m.* sunset; setting (*of any star or planet*); west; decadence, decline, end.

occidental *adj.* occidental, western.

occidente *m.* occident, west.

océano *m.* ocean.

ocelote *m.* ocelot.

ocio *m.* leisure, idleness; recreation, pastime.

ociosidad *f.* idleness, leisure.

ocioso *adj.* idle; useless.

octubre *m.* October.

ocular *adj.* ocular; **testigo —** eye witness; *m.* eyepiece, lens (*for the eye in a microscope or telescope*).

oculista *m. & f.* oculist; *Am.* flatterer.

ocultar *v.* to hide, conceal.

oculto *adj.* hidden, concealed; *m. Am.* species of mole (*small animal*).

ocupación *f.* occupation; employment.

ocupante *m. & f.* occupant.

ocupar *v.* to occupy; to employ; **-se en** (*Am.* **-se de**) to be engaged in; to pay attention to, be interested in.

ocurrencia *f.* occurrence, event; witticism, joke; bright or funny idea.

ocurrente *adj.* witty, funny, humorous; occurring.

ocurrir *v.* to occur.

ocurso *m. Ríopl.* petition, application.

oda *f.* ode.

odiar *v.* to hate.

odio *m.* hatred.

odioso *adj.* odious, hateful.

odre *m.* wine bag; drunk.

oeste *m.* west; west wind.

ofender *v.* to offend; to displease; **-se** to get offended; to become angry, take offense.

ofensa *f.* offense.

ofensivo *adj.* offensive; obnoxious; attacking; **ofensiva** *f.* offensive.

ofensor *m.* offender; *adj.* offending.

oferta *f.* offer; promise.

oficial *m.* official, officer; skilled workman; *adj.* official.

oficiar *v.* to officiate, serve, minister, perform the duties of a priest or minister; to communicate officially; **— de** to serve as, act as.

oficina *f.* office; shop; **oficinesco** *adj.* clerical, pertaining to an office.

oficio *m.* office, position; trade; function; official communication; religious office (*prayers*).

oficioso *adj.* officious, meddlesome.

ofrecer¹³ *v. irr.* to offer; to promise; **-se** to offer, occur, present itself; to offer oneself, volunteer; **¿qué se le ofrece a Vd.?** what do you wish?

ofrecimiento *m.* offer; offering.

ofrenda *f.* offering, gift.

ofuscamiento *m.* clouded vision, blindness; cloudiness of the mind, bewilderment, mental confusion.

ofuscar⁶ v. to darken, cast a shadow on; to blind; to cloud; to bewilder, confuse.

ogro m. ogre.

oído m. hearing; ear; **al —** confidentially; **de** (or **al**) **—** by ear; **de -s** (or **de oídas**) by hearsay or rumor.

oidor m. hearer, listener; judge.

oír³⁶ v. irr. to hear; to listen; to understand; **— misa** to attend mass; **— decir que** to hear that; **— hablar de** to hear about.

ojal m. buttonhole; hole.

¡ojalá! interj. God grant!; I hope so!; **— que** would that. I hope that.

ojazo m. large eye.

ojeada f. glimpse, quick glance.

ojear v. to stare, eye; to bewitch; to beat up, rouse (wild game).

ojera f. dark circle under the eye; eye-cup.

ojeriza f. grudge, spite.

ojeroso adj. with dark circles under the eyes.

ojiva f. pointed arch; **ojival** adj. pointed (arch); **ventana ojival** window with a pointed arch.

ojo m. (órgano) eye; (agujero) keyhole; hole; **¡—!** careful! look out!; **a —** by sight, by guess; **a -s vistas** visibly, clearly; **— de agua** spring (of water); **— de buey** porthole; **mal** (or **mal de**) **—** evil eye; Am. **hacer —** to cast the evil eye; Am. **pelar el —** to be alert, keep one's eye peeled; Mex., Ven. **poner a uno los -s verdes** to deceive someone; **tener entre -s a** to have ill will toward, have a grudge against.

ojota f. Andes, Ch., Ríopl. leather sandal.

ola f. wave.

oleada f. big wave; swell; surge; abundant yield of oil.

oleaje, olaje m. swell, surge, succession of waves.

oleo m. oil, holy oil; **pintura al —** oil painting.

oleoso adj. oily.

oler³⁷ v. irr. to smell; to scent; **— a** to smack of; to smell like; Am. **olérselas** to suspect it, "smell a rat".

olfatear v. to scent, sniff, smell.

olfateo m. sniff, sniffing.

olfato m. sense of smell.

oligarquía f. oligarchy.

oliva f. olive; olive tree; **olivar** m. olive grove; **olivo** m. olive tree.

olmo m. elm.

olor m. (en el olfato) smell, odor, fragrance; (fama) smack, trace, suspicion; Am. spice; **olorcillo** m. faint odor.

oloroso adj. fragrant.

olote m. Mex., C.A. cob, corncob.

olvidadizo adj. forgetful.

olvidar v. to forget; to neglect; **-se de** to forget; **olvidársele a uno algo** to forget something.

olvido m. forgetfulness; oblivion; neglect; **echar al —** to cast into oblivion; to forget on purpose.

olla f. pot, kettle; olla (vegetable and meat stew); **— podrida** Spanish stew of mixed vegetables and meat.

ombligo m. navel; middle, center.

ombú m. umbra tree.

omisión f. omission; oversight, neglect.

omiso adj. careless, neglectful; N. Arg. guilty; **hacer caso —** to omit.

omitir v. to omit; to overlook.

ómnibus m. omnibus, bus.

omnipotente adj. omnipotent, almighty.

onda f. wave; ripple; sound wave; scallop.

ondear v. to wave; to waver; to ripple; to sway, swing.

ondulación f. undulation, waving motion; wave; **— permanente** permanent wave.

ondulado p.p. & adj. wavy; scalloped (edge); **— permanente** permanent wave.

ondulante adj. wavy, waving.

ondular v. to undulate, wave.

onza f. ounce; ounce, wildcat; Ríopl., Bol. small tiger.

opacidad f. opacity; sadness.

opaco adj. opaque, dim, dull.

ópalo m. opal.

ópera f. opera.

operación f. operation; business transaction.

operador m. operator, surgeon.

operar v. to operate; to take effect, work; to speculate (in business); to manipulate, handle.

operario m. operator, workman, worker.

opereta f. operetta.

opinar v. to express an opinion; to think; to judge; to argue.

opinión f. opinion; reputation.

opio m. opium.

oponer⁴⁰ v. irr. to oppose; **-se** to disapprove; **-se a** to oppose, be against.

oporto m. port wine.

oportunidad f. opportunity.

oportuno adj. opportune, convenient, timely.

oposición f. opposition; competition; **-es** competitive examinations.

opositor m. opponent; competitor.

opresión f. oppression.

opresivo adj. oppressive.

opresor m. oppressor.

oprimir v. to oppress; to crush; to press down.

oprobio m. infamy; insult; shame; dishonor.

optar v. to choose, select; **— por** to decide upon; to choose.

óptica f. optics.

óptico adj. optical, optic; m. optician.

optimismo m. optimism; **optimista** m. & f. optimist; adj. optimistic.

óptimo adj. very good, very best.

opuesto p.p. of **oponer** opposed; adj. opposite; contrary.

opulencia f. opulence, abundance,

OB

wealth.

opulento *adj.* opulent, wealthy.

oquedad *f.* cavity, hollow; chasm.

ora *conj.* now, then; whether; either.

oración *f.* oration; prayer; sentence.

oráculo *m.* oracle.

orador *m.* orator, speaker.

oral *adj.* oral.

orar *v.* to pray.

oratorio *f.* oratory, eloquence.

oratorio *m.* oratory, private chapel; oratorio (*a religious musical composition*); *adj.* oratorical, pertaining to oratory.

orbe *m.* orb, sphere, globe; the earth; world, universe.

órbita *f.* orbit; eye socket.

orden *m.* (*colocación*) order; succession, series; class, group; relation; proportion; *f.* (*mando*) order, command; (*sociedad*) honorary or religious order; *m.* & *f.* sacrament of ordination; **a sus órdenes** at your service.

ordenado *p.p.* & *adj.* ordered; ordained; orderly; neat.

ordenanza *f.* ordinance, decree, law; command, order; *m.* orderly (*military*).

ordenar *v.* to arrange, put in order; to order, command; to ordain; **-se** to become ordained.

ordeña *f.* milking.

ordeñar *v.* to milk.

ordinariez *f.* commonness, lack of manners.

ordinario *adj.* ordinary; usual; common, coarse; *m.* ordinary (*a bishop or judge*); ordinary mail; daily household expense; **de —** usually, ordinarily.

orear *v.* to air; **-se** to be exposed to the air; to dry in the air.

oreja *f.* ear; hearing; loop; small flap; *Am.* handle (*shaped like an ear*); **orejano** *adj.* unbranded (*cattle*); *Ven.*, *Col.* cautious; *m.* *Cuba* aloof, unsociable person; **orejera** *f.* ear muff, ear flap; **orejón** *m.* pull by the ear; *Col.* rancher or inhabitant of the *sabana*; *adj.* *Col.* long-eared, long-horned; *Col.* unbranded (*cattle*); *Col.* coarse, crude, uncouth.

orfandad *f.* orphanage (*state of being an orphan*).

orfanato *m.* orphanage, orphan asylum.

orfanatorio *Am.* = **orfanato.**

orfebre *m.* goldsmith; silversmith.

orfeón *m.* glee club, choir.

orgánico *adj.* organic.

organillo *m.* hand organ, hurdy-gurdy.

organismo *m.* organism.

organización *f.* organization.

organizador *m.* organizer.

organizar⁹ *v.* to organize; to arrange.

órgano *m.* organ; **organillo** *m.* hand organ.

orgía *f.* orgy, wild revel.

orgullo *m.* pride; haughtiness, arrogance.

orgulloso *adj.* proud; haughty, arrogant.

oriental *adj.* oriental, eastern.

orientar *v.* to orientate, orient; **-se** to orient oneself, find one's bearings.

oriente *m.* orient, east; east wind; source, origin.

orificación *f.* gold filling.

orificio *m.* orifice, small hole, aperture, outlet.

origen *m.* origin; source.

original *adj.* original; strange, quaint; *m.* original; manuscript, copy; queer person; **originalidad** *f.* originality.

originar *v.* to originate, cause to be; **-se** originate, arise.

orilla *f.* shore, bank; beach; edge, border; **-s** *Am.* outskirts, environs.

orillar *v.* to border, trim the edge of; to skirt, go along the edge of; to reach the edge or shore.

orín *m.* rust; **orines** *m. pl.* urine.

orina *f.* urine.

orinar *v.* to urinate.

oriol *m.* oriole.

oriundo *adj.* native; **ser — de** to hail from, come from.

orla *f.* border; trimming, fringe.

orlar *v.* to border, edge, trim with a border or fringe.

ornado *adj.* ornate; *p.p.* adorned, ornamented.

ornamentar *v.* to ornament, adorn.

ornamento *m.* ornament; decoration; **-s** sacred vestments.

ornar *v.* to adorn.

oro *m.* gold; gold ornament; **-s** "gold coins" (*Spanish card suit*).

orondo *adj.* self-satisfied, puffed up, vain; *Am.* serene, calm.

oropel *m.* tinsel.

orquesta *f.* orchestra.

orquídea *f.* orchid.

ortiga *f.* nettle.

ortografía *f.* orthography, spelling.

ortográfico *adj.* orthographic (*pertaining to orthography or spelling*).

oruga *f.* caterpillar.

orzuelo *m.* sty (*on the eyelid*).

osadía *f.* boldness, daring.

osado *adj.* bold, daring.

osar *v.* to dare, venture.

oscilación *f.* oscillation, sway; fluctuation, wavering.

oscilar *v.* to oscillate, swing, sway; to waver.

oscurecer = obscurecer.

oscuridad = obscuridad.

oscuro = obscuro.

oso *m.* bear; **— blanco** polar bear; **— hormiguero** anteater; **— marino** seal.

ostentación *f.* ostentation, show, display.

ostentar *v.* to display, show; to show off; to boast.

ostentoso *adj.* ostentatious, showy.

ostión *m.* large oyster.

ostra *f.* oyster.

otate *m.* *Mex.*, *C.A.* species of bamboo; *Mex.*, *C.A.* bamboo stick or cane.

otero *m.* hillock, small hill, knoll.

otoñal *adj.* autumnal, of autumn.

otoño *m.* autumn, fall.

otorgar[7] v. to grant; to promise; to consent to.

otro adj. another; **otra vez** again; Am. **como dijo el** — as someone said.

otrora adv. formerly, in other times.

ovación f. ovation, enthusiastic applause.

oval, ovalado adj. oval; **óvalo** m. oval.

oveja f. sheep.

ovejero m. shepherd; sheep dog.

ovejuno adj. sheep, pertaining or relating to sheep.

overo adj. peach-colored (applied to horses and cattle); Riopl. mottled, spotted; Riopl. multicolored; Riopl. **ponerle a uno** — to insult someone.

overol, overoles m. Ch., Col. overalls.

ovillar v. to ball, wind or form into a ball; **-se** to curl up into a ball.

ovillo m. ball of yarn or thread; tangle; **hacerse uno un** — to curl up into a ball; to become entangled, confused.

oxidado p.p. rusted; adj. rusty.

oxidar v. to oxidize; to rust; **-se** to become oxidized; to rust.

oxígeno m. oxygen.

oyente m. & f. listener, auditor, hearer; adj. listening.

P

pabellón m. pavilion; canopy; banner, flag; shelter, covering; external ear.

pabilo m. wick; snuff (of a candle).

pacer[13] v. irr. to pasture; to graze.

paciencia f. patience.

paciente adj. patient; m. & f. patient.

pacienzudo adj. patient, long-suffering.

pacificar[6] v. to pacify; to appease.

pacífico adj. pacific, peaceful, calm.

pacto m. pact, agreement.

padecer[13] v. irr. to suffer.

padecimiento m. suffering.

padrastro m. stepfather; hangnail.

padre m. father; **-s** parents; ancestors; adj. very great, stupendous.

padrenuestro m. paternoster, the Lord's Prayer.

padrino m. godfather; sponsor, patron; second in a duel; best man (at a wedding).

paella f. a popular rice dish with chicken, vegetables, etc.

paga f. payment; pay, salary.

pagadero adj. payable.

pagado p.p. & adj. paid; self-satisfied, conceited; **— de sí mismo** pleased with oneself.

pagador m. payer; paymaster; paying teller (in a bank).

paganismo m. paganism, heathenism.

pagano adj. pagan; m. pagan; payer; dupe, sucker.

pagar[7] v. to pay; to pay for; to requite, return (love); **-se de** to be proud of; to boast of; to be pleased with; Riopl. **-se de palabras** to let oneself be tricked; Am. **— a nueve** to pay in excess.

pagaré m. promissory note; I.O.U.

página f. page.

paginar v. to page.

pago m. (premio) payment; prize, reward; (distrito) country district; Riopl. one's native farm land or district; adj. paid; Am. **estar -s** to be quits.

paila f. large pan; C.A. saucer.

país m. nation, country; region.

paisaje m. landscape.

paisanaje m. peasantry, country people; civilians; Andes gang of farm laborers.

paisano m. countryman; peasant; fellow countryman; civilian.

paja f. straw; chaff; rubbish; Andes grass for pasture; **echar -s** to draw lots; **por quítame allá esas -s** for an insignificant reason or pretext; **en un quítame allá esas -s** in a jiffy, in a second; **a humo de -s** thoughtlessly; lightly; **no lo hizo a humo de -s** he did not do it without a special reason or intention.

pajar m. straw loft, barn.

pájaro m. bird; shrewd, cautious person; Ch. absent-minded person; Ch., Riopl. person of suspicious conduct; **— carpintero** woodpecker; **— mosca** humming bird.

paje m. page, valet, attendant.

pajizo adj. made of straw; covered with straw; straw colored.

pajonal m. plain or field of tall coarse grass.

pala f. shovel; trowel; scoop; paddle; blade of an oar; racket; upper (of a shoe); cunning, craftiness; **meter la** — to deceive with cunning; Am. **hacer la** — to deceive with cunning; to stall, pretend to work; to flatter; **palada** f. scoop, shovelful; stroke of an oar.

palabra f. word; promise; **de** — by word of mouth; **cuatro-s** a few words; **empeñar la** — to promise, pledge; **tener la** — to have the floor; Am. **¡—!** I mean it, it is true!

palabrero adj. wordy, talkative.

palabrita f. a little word, a few words; a word of advice.

palacio m. palace; **palaciego** m. courtier; adj. relating to a palace or court; court (used as an adj.).

paladar m. palate; taste; relish.

paladear v. to relish, taste with relish.

paladín m. knight; champion, defender.

palanca f. lever; crowbar; bar used for carrying a load.

palangana f. washbowl, basin; S.A. platter; Ch. large wooden bowl; m. Andes bluffer, charlatan.

palatal adj. palatal.

palco m. theater box; **— escénico** stage.

palenque m. palisade, fence; enclosure; Riopl. hitching post or plank.

paleta f. small flat shovel; mason's trowel; shoulder blade; blade (of a rudder, of a ventilating fan); paddle (of a paddle wheel); painter's palette; Am. candy, sweetmeat or ice cream attached to a stick; Am. a wooden paddle to stir with, or for beating clothes; **en dos -s** in a jiffy, in a second; **paletilla** *f.* shoulder blade.

palidecer [13] *v. irr.* to turn pale.

palidez *f.* pallor, paleness.

pálido *adj.* pallid, pale.

palillo *m.* small stick; toothpick; **tocar todos los -s** (*Ch.* **menear uno los -s**) to try every possible means.

paliza *f.* beating (*with a stick*), thrashing.

palizada *f.* palisade; stockade.

palma *f.* palm tree; palm leaf; palm of the hand; **batir -s** to clap, applaud; **llevarse la —** to triumph, win, carry off the honors; to be the best.

palmada *f.* slap; clap.

palmario *adj.* clear, evident.

palmatoria *f.* small candlestick with handle.

palmear *v.* to clap, applaud; *Am.* to pat, clap on the back; *Ríopl.* to flatter.

palmera *f.* palm tree.

palmo *m.* span (*about 9 inches*); **— a —** slowly, foot by foot.

palmotear *v.* to clap, applaud.

palo *m.* stick; pole; log; mast; wood; blow with a stick; suit (*in a deck of cards*); *Am.* tree; *Ríopl.* reprimand, reproof; *P.R., Ven.* large swallow of liquor; **— del Brasil** Brazil wood; *Ven.* **— a pique** rail fence, barbed wire fence; *Mex., C.A.* **a medio —** half-done; half-drunk; *Am.* **a — entero** drunk.

paloma *f.* dove, pigeon; pleasant, mild person; **-s** whitecaps.

palomar *m.* dovecot (*shelter for doves or pigeons*).

palomilla *f.* little dove; moth; small butterfly; **-s** small whitecaps.

palomita *f.* little dove; **-s** *Am.* popcorn.

palpable *adj.* palpable (*that can be felt or touched*); clear, obvious, evident.

palpar *v.* to feel; to touch; to grope.

palpitación *f.* palpitation; beat, throb.

palpitante *adj.* palpitating, throbbing, trembling; exciting; **la cuestión — the burning question.**

palpitar *v.* to palpitate; to throb, beat.

palta *f. Col., Ven., Andes, Ríopl., Ch.* avocado, alligator pear; **palto** *m. Col., Ven., Andes, Ríopl., Ch.* avocado tree. *See* **aguacate.**

palúdico *adj.* marshy; **fiebre palúdica** malarial, or marsh fever; malaria; **paludismo** *m.* malaria.

pampa *f. Am.* pampa (*vast treeless plain of South America*); *Am.* prairie; *Ch.* drill field (*military*); *m. & f.* pampa Indian of Argentina; *m. Am.* language of the pampa Indian; *adj. Am.* pertaining to the pampa Indian *Ríopl.* **caballo —** horse with head and body of different colors; *Ríopl.* **trato —** dubious or dishonest deal; *Am.* **estar a la —** to be in the open; *Ríopl.* **tener todo a la —** to be ragged or to be indecently exposed; *Ch.* **quedar en —** to be left without

clothes; to be left in the lurch.

pampeano *adj. Ríopl.* of, or pertaining to, the pampa.

pampero *adj. Ríopl.* of, or pertaining to, the pampas; *m. Ríopl.* inhabitant of the pampas; *Ríopl.* violent wind of the pampa.

pan *m.* bread; loaf of bread; wheat; **-es** fields of grain; breadstuffs; *Am.* **echar -es** to brag, boast.

pana *f.* corduroy.

panadería *f.* bakery.

panadero *m.* baker; *Ch.* flatterer.

panal *m.* honeycomb; sweetmeat (*made of sugar, egg white, and lemon*).

panamericano *adj.* Pan-American.

pandearse *v.* to bulge, warp; to sag.

pandeo *m.* sag; bulge.

pandilla *f.* gang, band.

panela *f. Col., C.A.* unrefined sugar.

panfleto *m. Am.* pamphlet.

pánico *m.* panic; *adj.* panic, panicky.

panne *f.* accident, car trouble.

panocha *f.* ear of corn; *Mex.* Mexican raw sugar; *Col., C.R.* a kind of tamale.

panqué *m. Col., C.A., Mex.* small cake, cup cake; *Am.* pancake.

pantalón *m.* trousers; pants; **un par de -es** a pair of trousers.

pantalla *f.* light shade; screen; fireplace screen; motion-picture screen; *C.R.* fan, palm leaf fan; *P.R.* earring.

pantano *m.* swamp; dam; difficulty.

pantanoso *adj.* swampy, marshy; muddy.

panteón *m.* cemetery.

pantera *f.* panther.

pantorrilla *f.* calf (*of the leg*).

pantufla *f.* bedroom slipper.

panza *f.* paunch, belly.

panzón, panzudo *adj.* big-bellied.

pañal *m.* diaper; **estar en -es** to be in one's infancy; to have little or no knowledge of a thing.

paño *m.* cloth (*any cloth, especially woolen*); blotch or spot on the skin; film on the eyeball; *Mex., Cuba* parcel of tillable land; *Mex.* kerchief, shawl; **— de manos** towel; **— de mesa** tablecloth; **al —** off-stage; **-s** clothes, garments; **-s menores** underwear; **pañero** *m.* clothier.

pañolón *m.* scarf, large kerchief; shawl.

pañuelo *m.* handkerchief.

papa *m.* Pope; *f.* potato; fib, lie; *Am.* snap, easy job; **-s** pap (*soft food for babies*); soup; *Ríopl., Ch.* **cosa —** something good to eat; excellent thing; **echar -s** to fib, lie; *Am.* **importarle a uno una —** not to matter to one a bit; *Am.* **no saber ni —** not to a know a thing; to be completely ignorant.

papá *m.* papa; *Mex., C.A., Andes* — **grande** grandfather.

papagayo *m.* parrot; talker, chatterer.

papal *adj.* papal.

papalote, papelote *m. Carib., Mex.* kite.

papamoscas *m.* flycatcher (*a bird*); simpleton, half-wit, dunce.

papanatas *m.* simpleton, fool, dunce.
paparrucha *f.* fib, lie; **paparruchero** *m.* fibber.
papaya *f.* papaya.
papel *m.* (**hoja**) paper; sheet of paper; document; (*parte dramática*) role; — **de estraza** brown wrapping paper — **de lija** sandpaper; — **de seda** tissue paper; — **moneda** paper money; — **secante** blotting paper; **hacer el — de** to play the role of; **hacer buen** (*or* **mal**) — to cut a good (*or* bad) figure.
papelera *f.* folder, file, case or device for keeping papers; *Am.* wastepaper basket; **papelero** *m.* paper manufacturer; *adj.* pertaining to paper; vain, ostentatious.
papelería *f.* stationery store; stationery; lot of papers.
papeleta *f.* card, file card, slip of paper.
papelucho *m.* worthless piece of paper.
papera *f.* goiter; **-s** mumps.
paquete *m.* package; bundle; dandy; packet boat (*mail boat*); *adj. Am.* dolled up, dressed up; *Riopl., Col.* important, pompous; *Riopl., Col.* insincere.
par *adj.* even; *m.* pair, couple; peer; **a la —** at par; jointly; at the same time; **al — de** on a par with; **bajo —** below par; **sin —** peerless, without an equal, having no equal; **sobre —** above par; **de — en —** wide-open.
para *prep.* for; to; toward; in order to; **¿— qué?** what for; — **que** so that; — **siempre** forever; — **mis adentros** to myself; **sin qué ni — qué** without rhyme or reason; *m. Riopl.* Paraguayan tobacco; *Riopl.* Paraguayan (*used as nickname*).
parabién *m.* congratulations; **dar el —** to congratulate.
parabrisa *m.* windshield.
paracaídas *m.* parachute; **paracaidista** *m. & f.* parachutist.
parachoques *m.* bumper.
parada *f.* stop; stopping place; bet, stake; military review; *P.R.* parade; *Riopl.* boastfulness; *Riopl.* **tener mucha —** to dress very well.
paradero *m.* stopping place; whereabouts; end.
parado *p.p. & adj.* stopped; unoccupied, unemployed; fixed, motionless; *Ch., P.R.* standing, erect, straight up; *Ch., P.R.* stiff, proud; *Riopl.* cold, unenthusiastic; *P.R., Ch., Andes* **caer uno — o** to land on one's feet; to be lucky; *Am.* **estar bien —** to be well-fixed, well-established; to be lucky; *m. Am.* air, appearance.
paradoja *f.* paradox.
parafina *f.* paraffin.
paraguas *m.* umbrella; **paragüero** *m.* umbrella stand; umbrella maker or seller.
paraguayo *adj. & m.* Paraguayan.
paraíso *m.* paradise, heaven; upper gallery (*in a theater*).
paraje *m.* place; spot; situation.

paralelo *adj.* parallel; similar; *m.* parallel; similarity; **paralela** *f.* parallel line; **paralelismo** *m.* parallelism.
parálisis *f.* paralysis.
paralizar[9] *v.* to paralyze; to stop.
páramo *m.* high, bleak plain; cold region; *Andes* blizzard or a cold drizzle.
parangón *m.* comparison.
parangonar *v.* to compare.
paraninfo *m.* assembly hall, lecture hall, auditorium.
parapeto *m.* parapet.
parar *v.* to stop; to end, end up, come to an end; to parry (*in fencing*); to set up (*type*); *Am.* to stand, place in upright position; — **atención** to notice; — **mientes en** to observe, notice; *Riopl.* — **las orejas** to prick up one's ears; to pay close attention; **-se** to stop; *Am.* to stand up, get up.
pararrayos *m.* lightning rod.
parásito *m.* parasite; *adj.* parasitic.
parasol *m.* parasol.
parcela *f.* parcel of land; particle, small piece.
parcial *adj.* partial; *m.* follower, partisan; **parcialidad** *f.* partiality; faction, party.
parche *m.* mending patch; sticking plaster; medicated plaster; drum.
pardal *m.* sparrow; linnet; sly fellow.
pardear *v.* to grow dusky; to appear brownish-grey.
pardo *adj.* dark-grey; brown; dark; cloudy; *m.* leopard; *Carib., Riopl.* mulatto; **pardusco** *adj.* greyish; brownish.
parear *v.* to pair, couple, match, mate.
parecer[13] *v. irr.* to seem; to appear, show up; **-se** to resemble each other, look alike; *m.* opinion; appearance, looks; **al —** apparently, seemingly.
parecido *adj.* alike, similar; **bien —** good-looking; *p.p.* of **parecer**; *m.* similarity, likeness, resemblance.
pared *f.* wall; — **maestra** main wall; — **medianera** partition wall.
pareja *f.* pair; couple; match; partner; *Am.* team of two horses; *Riopl.* horse race.
parejero *m. Riopl.* race horse; *Riopl.* over-familar person, backslapper, hail-fellow-well-met.
parejo *adj.* even; smooth; equal; *adv. Riopl.* hard.
parentela *f.* relatives, kin.
parentesco *m.* kinship, relationship.
paréntesis *m.* parenthesis; digression; **entre —** by the way.
paria *m. & f.* outcast.
paridad *f.* par, equality.
pariente *m. & f.* relative, relation.
parir *v.* to give birth; to bear (*children*).
parlamentar *v.* to converse; to parley, discuss terms with an enemy.
parlamentario *adj.* parliamentary; *m.* member of parliament; envoy to a parley.
parlamento *m.* speech (*of a character in a play*); parley; parliament, legislative assembly.

PA

parlanchín *adj.* talkative; *m.* talker, chatterer.

parlero *adj.* talkative; gossipy; chattering, chirping.

parlotear *v.* to prate, prattle, chatter, chat.

parloteo *m.* chatter, prattle, idle talk.

paro *m.* work stoppage; lockout; *Am.* throw (*in the game of dice*); *Am.* — **y pinta** game of dice.

parodia *f.* parody, take-off, humorous imitation.

parodiar *v.* to parody, take off, imitate.

parótidas *f. pl.* mumps.

parpadear *v.* to wink; to blink; to flutter the eyelids; to twinkle.

parpadeo *m.* winking; blinking; fluttering of the eyelids; twinkling.

párpado *m.* eyelid.

parque *m.* park; *Am.* ammunition.

parra *f.* grapevine; earthenware jug.

parrafada *f.* chat.

párrafo *m.* paragraph; **echar un — con** to have a chat with.

parranda *f.* revel, orgy, spree; *Col.* gang, band; **andar** (*or* **ir**) **de —** to go on a spree.

parrandear *v.* to revel, make merry, go on a spree.

parrilla *f.* grill, gridiron, broiler; grate.

párroco *m.* parish priest.

parroquia *f.* parish; parish church; clientele, customers.

parroquiano *m.* client, customer; parishioner; *adj.* parochial, of a parish.

parsimonia *f.* thrift, economy; moderation; prudence.

parsimonioso *adj.* thrifty; stingy; cautious; slow.

parte *f.* part; share; place; party (*legal term*); **-s** qualities; **parte** *m.* notice, announcement; *Am.* unnecessary excuses or explanations; **de algún tiempo a esta —** for some time past; **de — de** on behalf of; in favor of; **de — a —** through, from one side to the other; **dar —** to inform; **echar a mala —** to take amiss; **en —** partly; **por todas -s** everywhere; *m.* telegram; message.

partera *f.* midwife.

partición *f.* partition, division.

participación *f.* participation, share; notice.

participante *m. & f.* participant; *adj.* participating, sharing.

participar *v.* to participate, share; to inform, notify.

partícipe *m. & f.* participant; *adj.* participating.

participio *m.* participle.

partícula *f.* particle.

particular *adj.* particular, special; peculiar; private, personal; odd, strange; **en —** specially; **lecciones -es** private lessons; *m.* private citizen; individual; point, detail; matter.

partida *f.* (*salida*) departure, leave; (*entidad*) item, entry; record; band, group; squad; shipment; game; set (*in tennis*); *Am.* part in the hair; **—**

de bautismo (**de matrimonio** *or* **de defunción**) birth (marriage, *or* death) certificate; **— de campo** picnic; **— de caza** hunting party; **— doble** double-entry bookkeeping; *Mex.*, *Ríopl.* **confesar la —** to tell the truth, speak plainly; **jugar una mala —** to play a mean trick.

partidario *m.* partisan, follower, supporter.

partido *m.* party, faction, group; contest, game; profit; district; *Bol.* **a** (*or* **al**) **—** in equal shares; *Am.* **dar —** to give a handicap or advantage (*in certain games*); **darse a —** to yield, give up; **sacar — de** to derive advantage from, make the best of; **tomar un —** to decide, make a decision.

partir *v.* (*dividir*) to split, divide; to crack, break; (*salir*) to depart, leave; **a — de hoy** starting today; from this day on; *Am.* **a** (*or* **al**) **—** in equal parts; *Am.* **— a uno por el eje** to ruin someone.

partitura *f.* musical score.

parto *m.* childbirth, delivery; product, offspring; **estar de —** to be in labor.

parvada *f.* pile of unthreshed grain; brood; *Andes* flock (*of birds or children*).

parvedad *f.* smallness; trifle; snack, bit of food.

párvulo *m.* child; *adj.* small; innocent.

pasa *f.* raisin; woolly hair of negros.

pasada *f.* passing, passage; *Am.* stay *Am.* embarrassment, shame; **una mala —** a mean trick; **de —** on the way; incidentally, by the way; **dar una — por** to pass by, walk by.

pasadizo *m.* aisle; narrow hall; narrow passageway.

pasado *m.* past; *p.p.* past, gone; *adj.* overripe, spoiled *Mex.* dried (*fruits*). *Col.* thin, bony (*animal*); **— mañana** day after tomorrow; **el año —** last year; **en días -s** in days gone by.

pasaje *m.* passage; fare, ticket; total number of passengers; *Carib.*, *Mex. Col.* private alley; *Col.*, *Ven.* anecdote.

pasajero *adj.* passing, temporary, fleeting, transitory; *m.* passenger; guest (*of a hotel*).

pasamano *m.* railing, hand rail; gangplank; gangway (*of a ship*).

pasaporte *m.* passport.

pasar *v.* to pass; to cross; to surpass, exceed; to pierce; to go forward; to go over (*in, by, to*); to enter; to carry over, take across; to happen; to get along; to swallow; to overlook; to tolerate; to suffer; **— las de Caín** to have a hard time; **— por alto** to omit, overlook; **— por las armas** to execute; **-se** to transfer, change over; to get overripe, spoiled; to exceed, go beyond; **se me pasó decirte** I forgot to tell you; *Ch.* **pasársela a uno** to deceive someone, break someone's confidence; **un buen —**

enough to live on.

pasarela f. gangplank.

pasatiempo m. pastime; Am. cookie.

pascua f. Easter; Jewish Passover; — **florida** (or **de resurrección**) Easter Sunday; — **de Navidad** Christmas.

pase m. pass, permit; thrust (in fencing); pass (with the cape in bullfighting).

pasear v. to walk; to take a walk; to ride; **-se** to take a walk; to parade; **-se en automóvil** to take an automobile ride; **-se a caballo** to go horseback riding.

paseo m. walk, ride; parade; public park; boulevard; — **en automóvil** automobile ride; **dar un** — to take a walk.

pasillo m. aisle; hallway, corridor; short step; short skit; Col., Ec. a type of dance music; Mex. runner, hall carpet.

pasión f. passion; suffering.

pasivo adj. passive; inactive; m. liabilities, debts; debit, debit side (in bookkeeping).

pasmar v. to astound, stun; **-se** to be amazed, stunned; to marvel; to get a sudden chill; to get frostbitten; P.R. to become dried up, shriveled up; P.R., Mex. to get bruised by the saddle or pack (said of horses and mules).

pasmo m. amazement, astonishment; wonder, awe.

pasmoso adj. astonishing, astounding; marvellous.

paso m. pass; step; pace; gait; passage; passing; skit; incident; P.R., Ch., Andes ford; Mex. ferry, ferryboat wharf; adv. slowly; **de** — by the way, in passing; **al** — **que** while; **salir del** — to get out of a difficulty; Am. **marcar el** — to mark step, obey humbly; adj. dried (figs, grapes, prunes, etc.); **paso a nivel** grade crossing.

pasta f. paste; dough; noodles; book cover, binding; Am. cookie, cracker; **de buena** — of good temper or disposition.

pastal m. Am. range, grazing land, large pasture.

pastar v. to pasture, graze.

pastear v. Mex., Ríopl. to graze, pasture.

pastel m. pie; pastry roll; filled pastry; trick, fraud; secret pact, plot; pastel crayon; **pintura al** — pastel painting.

pastelería f. pastry shop, bakery; pastry.

pastelero m. pastry cook; Cuba turncoat (person who changes easily from one political party to another); Ríopl. political intriguer.

pasterizar⁹, pasteurizar⁹ v. to pasteurize.

pastilla f. tablet (of medicine, candy, etc.); bar (of chocolate); cake (of soap).

pastizal m. pasture, grassland.

pasto m. pasture; grassland; grazing; nourishment; Am. grass; **a todo** —

without restraint.

pastor m. shepherd; pastor.

pastoral adj. pastoral; f. pastoral play; idyll; pastoral letter; **pastorela** f. pastoral, pastoral play; **pastoril** adj. pastoral.

pastoso adj. pasty, soft; mellow (said of the voice); Am. grassy.

pastura f. pasture; fodder, feed.

pata f. foot, leg (of an animal, table, chair, etc.); female duck; — **de gallo** crow's-foot (wrinkle at the corner of the eye); Ch., Andes — **de perro** wanderer; Ríopl. **hacer** — **ancha** to stand firm, face a danger; **meter la** — to put one's foot in it, make an embarrassing blunder; **-s arriba** upside down, head over heels.

patacón m. Ríopl. silver coin worth about one peso.

patada f. kick; stamp (with the foot); footprint; "kick", intoxicating effect; **a -s** with kicks; in great abundance; Andes **en dos -s** in a jiffy, in a second.

patalear v. to kick around; to stamp.

pataleo m. kicking; stamping.

pataleta f. convulsion; fainting fit.

patán m. boor, ill-mannered person; rustic; adj. rude, boorish, ill-mannered.

patata f. potato.

patear v. to kick; to stamp the foot; to tramp about; to trample on; to humiliate; Am. to kick, spring back (as a gun); Ch. to have a kick or intoxicating effect.

patentar v. to patent.

patente adj. patent, evident, clear; f. patent; grant; privilege; Carib. **de** — excellent, of best quality.

patentizar⁹ v. to evidence, reveal, show.

paternal adj. paternal; fatherly.

paternidad f. paternity, fatherhood; authorship.

paterno adj. paternal, fatherly.

patético adj. pathetic.

patibulario adj. harrowing, frightful, hair-raising; criminal.

patíbulo m. scaffold, gallows.

patilla f. small foot or paw; Col., Ven. watermelon; Ríopl. stone or brick bench (near a wall); Ríopl. railing of a balcony; Ch. slip from a plant; **-s** side whiskers; **Patillas** the Devil.

patín m. skate; a small patio; goosander (a kind of duck); — **de ruedas** roller skate; **patinadero** m. skating rink.

patinar v. to skate; to skid.

patio m. patio, open court, courtyard; Am. railway switchyard; Am. **pasarse uno al** — to take undue liberties.

patituerto adj. crook-legged; knock-kneed; bow-legged.

patizambo adj. knock-kneed.

pato m. duck; **pagar el** — to be the goat; to get the blame; Ríopl. **andar** — to be flat broke, penniless; Am. **hacerse** — to play the fool; Mex., Ríopl. **pasarse de** — **a ganso** to take undue liberties; *Am.* **ser el — de la boda** to be the life of the party; **patito** *m.* duckling.

patochada *f.* stupidity, blunder, nonsense.

patojo *adj.* crooked-legged; bowlegged; *m. & f. Guat.* child; young person.

patraña *f.* fabulous tale; lie, falsehood.

patria *f.* fatherland, native country.

patriarca *m.* patriarch; **patriarcal** *adj.* patriarchal.

patrimonio *m.* patrimony; inheritance.

patrio *adj.* native, of one's native country; paternal, belonging to the father.

patriota *m. & f.* patriot.

patriótico *adj.* patriotic.

patriotismo *m.* patriotism.

patrocinar *v.* to patronize, favor, sponsor.

patrocinio *m.* patronage, protection.

patrón *m.* (*protector*) patron; patron saint; sponsor; (*amo*) master, boss; proprietor, landlord; host; skipper; (*dechado*) pattern, standard, model; **patrona** *f.* landlady; patroness; hostess.

patronato *m.* board of trustees; foundation (*for educational, cultural, or charitable purposes*).

patrono *m.* patron, protector; trustee; patron saint.

patrulla *f.* patrol; squad, gang.

patrullar *v.* to patrol.

pausa *f.* pause, stop, rest.

pausar *v.* to pause.

pauta *f.* norm, rule, standard; guide lines (*for writing*).

pava *f.* turkey hen; *Ríopl.* kettle, teapot, teakettle; *Andes, Ch.* jest, coarse joke; **pelar la —** to talk by night at the window (*said of lovers*).

pavesa *f.* cinder; small firebrand; burnt wick or snuff of a candle; **-s** cinders.

pavimentar *v.* to pave.

pavimento *m.* pavement.

pavo *m.* turkey; *Ch.* sponger, parasite; **— real** peacock; **comer —** to be a wallflower at a dance; *adj.* silly, foolish; vain.

pavón *m.* peacock.

pavonearse *v.* to strut, swagger.

pavoneo *m.* strut, swagger.

pavor *m.* awe, dread, terror.

pavoroso *adj.* frightful, dreadful.

payador *m. Ríopl.* one who sings an improvised song accompanied on the guitar.

payasada *f.* clownish act or remark.

payasear *v.* to clown, play the fool.

payaso *m.* clown.

paz *f.* peace.

pazguato *adj.* simple, dumb, stupid; *m.* simpleton.

peaje *m.* toll (*for crossing a bridge or ferry*).

peal = pial.

pealar = pialar.

peatón *m.* pedestrian.

peca *f.* freckle.

pecado *m.* sin.

pecador *m.* sinner; *adj.* sinful.

pecaminoso *adj.* sinful.

pecar[6] *v.* to sin; **— de bueno** to be too good; **— de oscuro** to be exceedingly unclear, too complicated.

pecera *f.* fish bowl.

pecoso *adj.* freckly, freckled.

peculado *m.* embezzlement.

peculiar *adj.* peculiar; **peculiaridad** *f.* peculiarity.

pechada *f. Ríopl.* bump, push, shove with the chest; *Am.* bumping contest between two riders; *Ríopl., Ch.* overthrowing an animal (*by bumping it with the chest of a horse*).

pechar *v. Ríopl., Ch., Bol.* to bump, push, shove with the chest; *Ríopl., Ch., Bol.* to drive ones' horse against; *Ch., Ríopl.* to borrow, strike (*someone*) for a loan.

pechera *f.* shirtfront; chest protector; bib (*of an apron*).

pecho *m.* chest; breast; bosom; heart; courage; **dar el —** to nurse; **tomar a -s** to take to heart; *P.R., Col.* **a todo —** shouting; *Am.* **en -s de camisa** in shirt sleeves.

pechuga *f.* breast, breast meat of a fowl; bosom; *C.A., Col., Ch., Andes* courage, nerve, audacity, impudence.

pedagogía *f.* pedagogy, science of education.

pedagógica *adj.* pedagogic, relating to education or teaching.

pedagogo *m.* pedagogue, teacher, educator.

pedal *m.* pedal.

pedalear *v.* to pedal.

pedante *adj.* pedantic, affected, vain, superficial; *m.* pedant; **pedantesco** *adj.* pedantic.

pedazo *m.* piece, portion, bit; **hacer -s** to tear or break into pieces; **caerse a -s** fall into pieces.

pedernal *m.* flint.

pedestal *m.* pedestal, base.

pedestre *adj.* pedestrian, walking, going on foot; commonplace, vulgar, low.

pedido *m.* commercial order; request, petition; *p.p. of* **pedir.**

pedigüeño *adj.* begging, demanding.

pedir[5] *v. irr.* to ask, beg, petition; to ask for; to demand; to require; to order (*merchandise*); **a — de boca** exactly as desired.

pedo *m.* wind, flatulence; *Mex.* **andar — to be drunk.**

pedrada *f.* hit or blow with a stone; throw with a stone; mark or bruise made by a stone (*thrown*); **a -s** by stoning; with stones; **dar una —** to hit with a stone; **echar a alguien a -s** to stone someone out; **matar a -s** to stone to death.

pedregal *m.* rocky ground, ground strewn with rocks.

pedregoso *adj.* rocky, stony, pebbly.

pedrería *f.* precious stones; precious stone ornament; jewelry.

pedrusco *m.* boulder.

pedúnculo *m.* stem (*of a leaf, flower or fruit*), stalk.

pegajoso *adj.* sticky; contagious.

pegar[7] *v.* (*golpear*) to hit, strike, slap, beat; (*adherir*) to stick, paste, glue; to sew on (*a button*); to infect; to be becoming; to be fitting, opportune, to the point; *Am.* to tie, fasten; *Am.* to yoke; — **fuego** to set on fire; — **un chasco** to play a trick; to surprise, disappoint; — **un susto** to give a scare; — **un salto** (**una carrera**) to take a jump (a run); **-se** to stick, cling; **pegársela a uno** to fool somebody.

pegote *m.* sticky thing; sticking plaster; clumsy patch; sponger; thick, sticky concoction; clumsy addition or insertion (*in a literary or artistic work*).

peinado *m.* coiffure, hairdo; hairdressing; *p.p.* combed; groomed; *adj.* effeminate; **bien** — spruce, trim.

peinador *m.* hairdresser; short wrapper or dressing gown; **peinadora** *f.* woman hairdresser.

peinar *v.* to comb; *Ríopl.* to flatter.

peine *m.* comb.

peineta *f.* large ornamental comb.

peladilla *f.* small pebble.

pelado *p.p.* & *adj.* peeled; plucked; skinned; hairless; featherless; barren, treeless, bare; penniless, broke; *m. Mex.* ragged fellow (*generally a peon*); *Mex.* ill-bred person; *Col.* child.

pelafustán *m.* tramp, vagabond.

pelagatos *m.* ragged fellow, tramp.

pelaje *m.* animal's coat, fur; external appearance.

pelar *v.* to cut the hair of; to pluck the feathers or hair from; to peel, shell, skin, husk; to fleece, rob; *Am.* to beat, thrash; *Am.* to slander; *C.R.* — **los dientes** to show one's teeth; to smile affectedly; *C.A., Mex., Carib., Col., Andes* — **los ojos** to keep one's eyes peeled; to open one's eyes wide; **-se** to peel off; to lose one's hair; *Col., Ven.* to be confused; *Col., Ven.* to be careless, unaware; *Col., Ven.* to slip away; *Col., Ven.* to die; **pelárselas por algo** to be dying for something, want something very much.

peldaño *m.* step (*of a staircase*).

pelea *f.* fight, quarrel.

pelear *v.* to fight; to quarrel.

peletería *f.* fur store; fur trade; furs; *Am.* leather goods, leather shop; *Cuba* shoe store.

película *f.* thin skin; membrane; film; motion-picture film.

peligrar *v.* to be in danger.

peligro *m.* danger.

peligroso *adj.* dangerous.

pelillo *m.* short, fine hair; **-s** trouble, nuisance; **echar -s a la mar** to "bury the hatchet", become reconciled; **no pararse en -s** not to stop at small details, not to bother about trifles; **no tener -s en la lengua** to speak frankly.

pelirrojo *adj.* redheaded, red-haired.

pelo *m.* (*cabello*) hair; (*haz*) nap (*of cloth*); (*fibra*) grain (*in wood*); **al** — perfectly; agreed; apropos, to the point; along the grain; **eso me viene al** — that suits me perfectly; **con todos sus -s y señales** with every possible detail; *Am.* **por** (*or* **en**) **un** — on the point of, almost, by a hair's breadth; **montar en** — to ride bareback; **tomar el** — **a to** kid, make fun of; *Ríopl., Carib., Mex., Andes* **no aflojar un** — not to yield an inch.

pelota *f.* ball; ball game; *Am.* boat made of cowhide; **en** — (*or* **en -s**) naked; *Am.* **darle a la** — to hit upon by chance; **pelotilla** *f.* pellet, little ball.

pelotari *m.* pelota (*jai-alai*) player.

pelotera *f.* brawl, row, riot; *C.A., Ven.* crowd.

pelotón *m.* large ball; crowd, gang; heap, pile; platoon of soldiers; firing squad.

peluca *f.* wig.

peludo *adj.* hairy; shaggy; *m.* plush carpet with shaggy pile; *Am.* a species of armadillo; *Ríopl.* **agarrar un** — to get drunk.

peluquería *f.* barbershop, hairdresser's shop.

peluquero *m.* hairdresser, barber.

pelusa *f.* down; fuzz; nap (*of cloth*).

pellejo *m.* hide; skin; peel; **salvar el** — to save one's skin, escape punishment; *Am.* **jugarse el** — to gamble one's life.

pellizcar[6] *v.* to pinch, nip.

pellizco *m.* pinching; nipping; pinch, nip.

pena *f.* penalty; grief, worry; hardship; toil; *Mex., Carib., C.A., Col., Ven.* embarrassment; **a duras -s** with great difficulty; hardly; **me da** — it grieves me; *C.A., Mex., Col., Carib.* it embarrasses me; **valer la** — to be worthwhile; **tener** (*or* **estar con**) **mucha** — to be terribly sorry; *Am.* to be greatly embarrassed.

penacho *m.* tuft, crest; plume.

penal *adj.* penal; **código** — penal code.

penalidad *f.* hardship; trouble; penalty.

penar *v.* to suffer; to worry, fret; to impose a penalty; — **por** to long for; to suffer because of.

penca *f.* leaf of a cactus plant; *Am.* sweetheart; *Ven.* **coger una** — to get drunk.

penco *m.* nag, horse; *Am.* boor.

pendencia *f.* quarrel; scuffle, fight.

pendenciero *adj.* quarrelsome.

pender *v.* to hang; to dangle; to depend.

pendiente *f.* slope; *m.* earring; pendant; *Am.* watch chain; *adj.* hanging, dangling; pending.

pendón *m.* banner.

péndulo *m.* pendulum.

penetración *f.* penetration; acuteness; keen judgment.

penetrante adj. penetrating; acute; keen.

penetrar v. to penetrate; to pierce; to fathom, comprehend.

penicilina f. penicillin.

península f. peninsula.

peninsular adj. peninsular.

penitencia f. penance.

penitenciaría f. penitentiary.

penitente adj. repentant, penitent; m. & f. penitent.

penoso adj. painful; hard, difficult; embarrassing; fatiguing; Mex., Carib., C.A., Ven., Col. timid, shy.

pensador m. thinker; adj. thinking.

pensamiento m. thought; mind; pansy.

pensar[1] v. irr. to think; to think over; to intend.

pensativo adj. pensive.

pensión f. pension; board; scholarship for studying; boardinghouse; Col. apprehension, anxiety; — completa room and board.

pensionado m. pensioner (person receiving a pension); adj. & p.p. pensioned.

pensionar v. to pension.

pensionista m. & f. boarder; pensioner (person receiving a pension).

pentagrama m. musical staff.

penúltimo adj. next to the last.

penumbra f. partial shadow, dimness.

penumbroso adj. dim.

peña f. rock, large stone.

peñasco m. large rock; crag.

peñascoso adj. rocky.

peón m. unskilled laborer; foot soldier; spinning top; pawn (in chess); Ch., Riopl., C.A., Carib., Mex. farm hand; Am. apprentice; Mex. — de albañil mason's helper.

peonada f. gang of laborers or peons.

peor adj. & adv. worse; worst; — que worse than; — que — that is even worse; tanto — so much the worse.

pepa f. Andes, Col., Ven., Ch., Mex., Riopl. seed (of an apple, melon, etc.); Am. marble (to play with); Pepa nickname for Josefa.

penenar v. Mex. to pick up; Am. to seize, grab.

pepino m. cucumber.

pepita f. seed (of an apple, melon, etc.); pip (a disease of birds); nugget (lump of gold or other minerals); Am. fruit stone, pit; Pepita = Josefita dim. of Josefa.

pequeñez f. smallness; childhood; trifle; meanness.

pequeño adj. small, little; young; low, humble; m. child.

pera f. pear; goatee; sinecure, easy job; Am. Peruvian alligator pear (see aguacate); Am. hacerle a uno la — to play a trick on someone; peral m. pear tree; pear orchard.

percal m. percale (fine cotton cloth).

percance m. misfortune, accident; occurrence.

percepción f. perception; idea.

perceptible adj. perceptible, noticeable.

percibir v. to perceive; to collect, receive.

percudido adj. dirty, grimy.

percudir v. to soil, make dirty or grimy; -se to get grimy.

percha f. clothes or hat rack; pole; perch, roost; perch (a fish); perchero m. clothes or hat rack.

perder[1] v. irr. to lose; to squander; to ruin, harm; to miss (a train); — de vista to lose sight of; -se to lose one's way; to get lost; to go astray; to get spoiled; to become ruined.

perdición f. perdition, damnation, hell, ruin.

pérdida f. loss; damage.

perdidamente adv. excessively.

perdido p.p. & adj. lost; strayed; mislaid; ruined; estar — por alguien to be crazy about, or very fond of, someone; m. rake, dissolute fellow; bum, vagabond.

perdigón m. young partridge; bird shot, buckshot; losing gambler.

perdiz f. partridge.

perdón m. pardon; forgiveness; remission.

perdonar v. to pardon; to forgive.

perdulario m. rake, dissolute person; reckless fellow; good-for-nothing; tramp.

perdurable adj. lasting, everlasting.

perdurar v. to last, endure.

perecedero adj. perishable.

perecer[13] v. irr. to perish; to die; -se to long (for), pine (for).

peregrinación f. pilgrimage; long journey.

peregrino m. pilgrim; adj. foreign, strange, rare; beautiful, perfect; travelling, wandering; ave peregrina migratory bird, bird of passage.

perejil m. parsley; -es frippery, showy clothes or ornaments.

perenne adj. perennial, enduring, perpetual.

pereza f. laziness; idleness.

perezoso adj. lazy; m. Am. sloth (an animal); Am. safety pin; Am. bed cushion.

perfección f. perfection; a la — to perfection, perfectly.

perfeccionamiento m. perfecting, perfection; completion.

perfeccionar v. to perfect, finish, complete.

perfecto adj. perfect.

perfidia f. perfidy, treachery.

pérfido adj. perfidious, treacherous, faithless.

perfil m. profile; outline; Am. pen or pen point.

perfilar v. to silhouette; to outline; -se to show one's profile; to be silhouetted.

perforación f. perforation, hole; puncture; perforating, boring, drilling.

perforar v. to perforate, pierce; to drill, bore.

perfumar v. to perfume, scent.

perfume m. perfume; fragrance.
perfumería f. perfumery; perfume shop.
pergamino m. parchment.
pericia f. expertness, skill.
perico m. parakeet, small parrot; *Col.* **huevos -s** scrambled eggs.
perifollos m. pl. frippery, finery, showy ornaments.
perifrasear v. to paraphrase.
perigeo m. perigee.
perilla f. small pear; pear-shaped ornament; knob; pommel of a saddle; goatee; **de —** apropos, to the point.
perímetro m. perimeter.
periódico m. newspaper; periodical; adj. periodic, periodical.
periodismo m. journalism; **periodista** m. & f. journalist; newspaper editor or publisher; **periodístico** adj. journalistic.
período m. period; cycle; sentence.
peripecia f. vicissitude, change in fortune; unforeseen incident.
peripuesto adj. dressed up, dolled up, decked out.
perito adj. learned; experienced; skillful; skilled; m. expert.
perjudicar[6] v. to damage, impair, harm.
perjudicial adj. harmful, injurious.
perjuicio m. damage, ruin, mischief; harm.
perjurar v. to perjure oneself; to commit perjury; to curse, swear.
perjurio m. perjury.
perla f. pearl; **de -s** perfectly, just right, to the point.
perlino adj. pearly, pearl-colored.
permanecer[13] v. irr. to-remain, stay.
permanencia f. permanence, duration; stability; stay, sojourn.
permanente adj. permanent.
permiso m. permission; permit.
permitir v. to permit, let; to grant.
permuta f. exchange, barter.
permutar v. to exchange; to barter; to change around.
pernetas : en — barelegged, with bare legs.
pernicioso adj. pernicious, harmful.
perno m. bolt; spike; **-s** *Am.* tricks, frauds.
pero conj. but, except, yet; m. objection, exception; defect; a variety of apple tree; a variety of apple; **perón** m. *Am.* a variety of apple.
perogrullada f. platitude, trite or commonplace remark.
peroración f. peroration, speech, harangue.
perorar v. to make an impassioned speech; to declaim, harangue; to plea, make a plea.
perorata f. harangue, speech.
perpendicular adj., m. & f. perpendicular.
perpetuar[18] v. to perpetuate.
perpetuo adj. perpetual; **perpetua** f. everlasting.
perplejidad f. perplexity.
perplejo adj. perplexed, bewildered.

perra f. bitch, female dog; drunkenness; **— chica** five-centime copper coin; **— grande** (*or* **gorda**) ten-centime copper coin.
perrada f. pack of dogs; **hacer una —** to play a mean trick.
perrera f. kennel; toil, hard work, hard job; tantrum; *Carib., Mex., Ven.* brawl, dispute.
perrilla f. *Am.* sty (*on the eyelid*). See orzuelo.
perro m. dog; **— de busca** hunting dog; **— dogo** bulldog; **— de lanas** poodle; adj. dogged, tenacious; *Mex., C.A.* hard, selfish, mean, stingy; *Ven.,* vagabond.
perruno adj. canine, doglike.
persecución f. persecution; pursuit.
perseguidor m. pursuer; persecutor.
perseguimiento m. pursuit; persecution.
perseguir[5,12] v. irr. to pursue; to persecute; to harass, annoy.
perseverancia f. perseverance.
perseverar v. to persevere.
persiana f. Venetian blind; window shade.
persistencia f. persistence; **persistente** adj. persistent.
persistir v. to persist.
persona f. person; personage.
personaje m. personage; character (*in a book or play*).
personal adj. personal; m. personnel.
personalidad f. personality; individuality; person, personage.
perspectiva f. perspective; view; appearance; outlook; prospect.
perspicacia f. keenness of mind, penetration, keen insight.
perspicaz adj. keen, shrewd.
persuadir v. to persuade.
persuasión f. persuasion.
persuasivo adj. persuasive.
pertenecer[13] v. irr. to belong; to pertain; to concern.
perteneciente adj. pertaining, belonging, concerning.
pértiga f. pole, bar, rod; **salto con —** pole vault.
pertinente adj. pertinent, to the point, apt, fitting.
pertrechos m. pl. military supplies; tools, implements.
perturbación f. uneasiness, agitation, disturbance.
perturbar v. to perturb, disturb.
peruano adj. & m. Peruvian.
perulero adj. m. & f. Peruvian (*slang expression*).
perversidad f. perversity, wickedness.
perverso adj. perverse, wicked; m. pervert.
pervertir[3] v. irr. to pervert; to; corrupt to distort; **-se** to become perverted; to go wrong.
pesa f. weight (*for scales*); **— de reloj** clock weight; **-s y medidas** weights and measures.
pesadez f. heaviness; dullness, drowsiness; slowness; bother; stubbornness.

PE

pesadilla f. nightmare.

pesado adj. heavy; sound (sleep); tiresome, boring; annoying; slow; dull.

pesadumbre f. grief, sorrow; weight, heavinesss.

pésame m. condolence, expression of sympathy.

pesantez f. gravity; heaviness.

pesar v. (penar) to cause grief, sorrow, or regret; (tener gravedad) to weigh; to consider, to have weight, value, or importance; m. grief, sorrow; **a — de** in spite of.

pesaroso adj. grieved, sad; repentant.

pesca f. fishing; catch, fish caught.

pescadería f. fish market; **pescadero** m. fishmonger, dealer in fish.

pescado m. fish (especially after being caught); salted codfish.

pescador m. fisherman.

pescar[6] v. to fish; to catch; to catch unaware, catch in the act.

pescozón m. blow on the back of the head or neck.

pescuezo m. neck.

pesebre m. manger.

peseta f. peseta (monetary unit of Spain).

pesimismo m. pessimism; **pesimista** m. & f. pessimist; adj. pessimistic.

pésimo adj. very bad.

peso m. weight; weighing; burden; importance; Am. peso (monetary unit of several Spanish American countries).

pesquera f. fishery (place for catching fish); **pesquería** f. fishery; fishing.

pesquero adj. fishing; **buque —** fishing boat; **industria pesquera** fishing industry.

pesquisa f. investigation, inquiry; m. Am. police investigator.

pestaña f. eyelash; edging, fringe; **quemarse las -s** to burn the midnight oil, study hard at night.

pestañear v. to blink; to wink; to flicker.

peste f. pest, pestilence, plague; epidemic; stench, stink, foul odor; overabundance, excess; Am. smallpox; Col. head cold; **echar -s** to utter insults.

pestillo m. bolt; latch; lock.

petaca f. tobacco pouch; cigar case; leather covered hamper (used as a pack); Mex., Ven. leather covered trunk, suitcase; adj. Andes heavy, clumsy.

pétalo m. petal.

petate m. bundle; impostor; Mex., C.A., Ven., Col. mat (of straw or palm leaves); Am. dunce; Andes coward; **liar el —** to pack up and go; Mex. to die; Col., Ven. **dejar a uno en un —** to ruin a person, leave him penniless.

petición f. petition, request.

petirrojo m. robin, robin redbreast.

petiso adj. Riopl., Ch., Andes small, short, dwarfish; m. Am. small horse, pony.

pétreo adj. stone, stony.

petróleo m. petroleum.

petrolero m. oil man; dealer in petroleum; **compañía petrolera** oil company.

petulancia f. flippancy; insolence; **petulante** adj. pert, impertinent, flippant.

pez m. fish; f. pitch, tar.

pezón m. nipple; stem, stalk (of a fruit, leaf or flower); small point of land.

pezuña f. hoof.

piadoso adj. pious; kind, merciful.

pial m. Mex. lasso, lariat (thrown in order to trip an animal); Riopl. snare, trap.

pialar v. to lasso by tripping with a **pial.**

piano m. piano; **— de cola** grand piano; **— vertical** upright piano.

piar[17] v. to peep, chirp; to cry, whine.

pica f. pike, spear; picador's goad or lance; stonecutter's hammer; Ven. tapping of rubber trees; Col. trail; Col., Ch. pique, resentment; Am. cockfight.

picada f. prick; bite (as of an insect or fish); puncture; sharp pain; dive (of a plane); Cuba, Riopl. path, trail (cut through a forest); Am. narrow ford; Col., Ven., Mex. peck.

picadillo m. meat and vegetable hash; minced meat, mincemeat.

picador m. picador (mounted bullfighter armed with a goad); horse-breaker; chopping block; Ven. tree tapper.

picadura f. biting; pricking; bite; prick; sting; puncture; cut tobacco.

picante adj. (acerbo) pricking, biting, stinging; (con chile o ají) spicy; highly seasoned; m. strong seasoning; Am. highly seasoned sauce (usually containing chili pepper).

picapleitos m. quarrelsome person (one who likes to pick a fight); shyster.

picaporte m. latch; latchkey; door knocker.

picar[6] v. to prick; to pierce; to bite (said of fish or insects); to sting; to peck; to nibble; to mince, chop up; to goad; to stick, poke; to hew, chisel; to pique, vex; to itch, smart, burn; Am. to chop (wood); Am. to open a trail; Am. to tap (a tree); Am. to slaughter (cattle); **— muy alto** to aim very high; **— en** to border on, be somewhat of; Mex., Ven. **¡picale!** hurry! **-se** to be piqued, angry; to be moth-eaten; to begin to sour; to begin to rot; C.A., Ven. to get tipsy; **-se de** to boast of.

picardía f. roguishness; offensive act or remark; roguish trick; mischief.

picaresco adj. picaresque, roguish.

pícaro m. rogue, rascal; adj. roguish; mischievous; crafty, sly; low, vile; **picarón** m. big rascal.

picazón f. itch, itching.

pico m. beak, bill; sharp point; peak; pickaxe, pick, spout; mouth; additional amount, a little over; C.A., Carib., Riopl., Ven. a small balance; Mex. a goodly sum; **tener el — de**

oro to be very eloquent; **tener mucho — ** to be very talkative.

picotada *f.,* **picotazo** *m.* peck.

picotear *v.* to peck; to chatter; *Am.* to mince, cut into small pieces.

pichel *m.* pitcher; mug.

pichón *m.* pigeon; *C.A.* any male bird *(except a rooster); Am.* dupe, easy mark; *Am.* novice, inexperienced person, apprentice; *adj. Am.* timid, shy.

pie *m.* foot; leg; stand; stem; base; *Am.* down payment; *Mex.* strophe, stanza; *Am.* **— de amigo** wedge; prop; **— de banco** silly remark; **a — juntillas** steadfastly, firmly; **al — de la letra** to the letter, literally, exactly; **de — (or en —)** standing; **a cuatro -s** on all fours; **dar —** to give an opportunity or occasion; *Am.* **estar a — en** to be ignorant of; **ir a —** to walk.

piececito, piecito *m.* little foot.

piedad *f.* piety; pity; mercy; **monte de — ** pawnshop.

piedra *f.* stone; gravel; hailstone; *Ven.* piece of a domino set; **— angular** (or **fundamental**) cornerstone; **— caliza** limestone; **— pómez** pumice, pumice-stone; **a — y lodo** shut tight; **ser — de escándalo** to be an object of scandal.

piel *f.* skin; hide; leather; fur.

piélago *m.* high sea; sea; great abundance, great plenty.

pienso *m.* feed; thought; **ni por — ** not even in thought.

pierna *f.* leg; **dormir a — suelta** to sleep like a log, sleep soundly; *Am.* **ser una buena —** to be a good fellow, be always in a good mood.

pieza *f.* (*pedazo*) piece; part; (*cuarto*) room; (*comedia*) play; **de una —** solid, in one piece; *Am.* **ser de una —** to be an honest, upright man.

pigmento *m.* pigment.

pijama *m.* pajamas.

pila *f.* (*pieza cóncava*) basin; baptismal font; trough; (*cúmulo*) pile; heap; electric battery; **— atómica** atomic pile; *Am.* fountain; *Andes* hairless dog; *Am.* bald head; **nombre de —** Christian name; *Andes* **andar —** to go naked; *Mex.* **tener las -s** (or **tener por -s**) to have a lot, have heaps.

pilar *m.* pillar, column; basin of a fountain.

pilcha *f. Riopl.* any article of clothing; *Am.* mistress; **-s** *Riopl.* belongings.

píldora *f.* pill.

pilmama *f. Mex.* child's nurse, wet nurse.

pilón *m.* basin (*of a fountain*); watering trough; sugar loaf; large wooden or metal mortar (*for grinding grain*); counterpoise; *Mex.* an additional amount, premium (*given to a buyer*); *Mex.* **de —** to boot, in addition, besides; **piloncillo** *m. Am.* unrefined sugar loaf.

pilotar, pilotear *v.* to pilot.

pilote *m.* pile (*for building*).

piloto *m.* pilot; *Mex.* generous entertainer or host.

pillaje *m.* pillage, plunder.

pillar *v.* to pillage, plunder; to pilfer; to seize, snatch, grasp; to catch; *Am.* to surprise, catch in the act.

pillo *adj.* roguish; sly, crafty; *m.* rogue, rascal; *Am.* a species of heron; *Am.* long-legged person; **pilluelo** *m.* little rascal, scamp.

pimentero *m.* pepper plant; pepperbox, pepper shaker.

pimentón *m.* large pepper; cayenne, red pepper; paprika.

pimienta *f.* black pepper.

pimiento *m.* green pepper; red pepper.

pimpollo *m.* rosebud; bud; shoot, sprout; attractive youth.

pináculo *m.* pinnacle, top, summit.

pinar *m.* pine grove.

pincel *m.* artist's brush; **pincelada** *f.* stroke of the brush.

pinchar *v.* to prick; to puncture.

pinchazo *m.* prick; puncture; stab.

pingajo *m.* tag, tatter, rag.

pingo *m. Riopl., Andes* saddle horse; *Mex.* devil.

pingüe *adj.* abundant, copious; fat, greasy.

pino *m.* pine; *Am.* filling for a meat pie; **hacer -s** (or **hacer pinitos**) to begin to walk (*said of a baby*); to begin to do things (*said of a novice*).

pinta *f.* spot, mark; outward sign, aspect; pint; *Mex.* **hacer —** to play hooky, cut class.

pintar *v.* to paint; to describe, depict; to feign; to begin to turn red, begin to ripen (*said of fruit*); to fancy, imagine; *Mex.* to play hooky, play truant; *Am.* to fawn, flatter; **no — nada** to be worth nothing, count for nothing; **las cosas no pintaban bien** things did not look well; *Mex.* **— venados** to play hooky; **-se** to put on make-up; *Am.* to excel (in); to praise oneself; *Ven.* to go away.

pintarrajear *v.* to daub; to smear with paint or rouge.

pinto *adj. Am.* spotted, speckled.

pintor *m.* painter, artist; **— de brocha gorda** house painter; poor artist; *adj. Am.* boastful, conceited.

pintoresco *adj.* picturesque.

pintura *f.* painting; picture; paint, color; description.

pinzas *f. pl.* pincers; tweezers; claws (*of lobsters, crabs, etc.*); *Riopl., Mex., Carib.* pliers, tongs.

piña *f.* pineapple; pine cone; piña cloth; cluster; *Cuba* pool (*a billiard game*).

piñata *f.* pot; hanging pot or other container (*filled with candies, fruit, etc.*).

piñón *m.* pine nut; nut pine; pinion.

pío *adj.* pious, devout; kind; merciful; dappled, spotted (*horse*); **obras pías** pious works, charitable deeds.

piojo *m.* louse.

piojoso *adj.* lousy; mean, stingy.

pipa *f.* tobacco pipe; keg, barrel; reed

PE

pipe (*musical instrument*); fruit seed (*of a lemon, orange, melon*); *Col.* green coconut; *Am.* potato; *Ven.* **estar — de** to be drunk; *m. Am.* species of green frog.

pipiar[17] *v.* to peep, chirp.

pipiolo *m.* novice, beginner; *Am.* child, youngster.

pique *m.* pique, resentment; chigger (*insect*); flea; *Am.* small chili pepper; *Am.* trail; **a — de** in danger of, on the point of; **echar a —** to sink (*a ship*); to destroy; **irse a —** to capsize; to sink.

piquete *m.* prick; bite, sting (*of insects*); small hole; picket, stake; picket (*military*); *Am.* small band of musicians; *Am.* small corral; *Am.* cutting edge of scissors.

piragua *f. Ríopl., Carib., Ven., Col., Andes* Indian canoe.

pirámide *f.* pyramid.

pirata *m.* pirate.

piratear *v.* to pirate.

piropo *m.* flattery, compliment; a variety of garnet (*a semiprecious stone*); **echar un —** to "throw a bouquet"; to compliment.

pirueta *f.* whirl; somersault; caper; **hacer -s** to cut capers; to turn somersaults; to do stunts.

pisada *f.* footstep; footprint; **dar una — to** step on, stamp on; **seguir las -s de** to follow in the footsteps of; to imitate.

pisapapeles *m.* paperweight.

pisar *v.* to step on, tread upon; to trample under foot; to pound; to cover (*said of a male bird*).

piscina *f.* swimming pool, swimming tank; fish pond.

pise *m. Ven.* rut; *Am.* tread (*of a wheel*). *See* **rodadura.**

piso *m.* floor; story; pavement; apartment, flat; tread; *Ríopl., Mex., Carib., Ven.* fee for pasturage rights; *Am.* table scarf; *Am.* stool, footstool; *Am.* small rug.

pisón *m.* heavy mallet (*for pounding, flattening, crushing*).

pisotear *v.* to tramp, tramp on, trample; to tread.

pisotón *m.* hard step, stamp (*of the foot*); **dar un —** to step hard, stamp (upon).

pista *f.* track, trace, trail; clew; race track; **— de aterrizaje** landing field.

pistola *f.* pistol; **pistolera** *f.* holster.

pistón *m.* piston; *Col.* cornet.

pita *f. Am.* agave or century plant; *Am.* fiber, or thread made from the fiber, of the agave or maguey.

pitar *v.* to toot; to whistle; *Ríopl., Andes* to smoke; *Ven.* to hiss; *Carib., Mex.* to slip away, escape; *Am.* **-se una cosa** to steal something; *Ch., Col., Ven., C.A.* (*pitado*) **salir pitando** to leave on the run.

pitazo *m.* toot, whistle, blast.

pitillo *m.* cigarette; **pitillera** *f.* cigarette case.

pito *m.* whistle; cigarette; *Am.* tick (*an insect*); **no vale un —** it is not worth a straw; *Am.* **no saber ni — de una cosa** not to know anything about a subject.

pizarra *f.* slate; blackboard; **pizarrín** *m.* slate pencil; **pizarrón** *m.* blackboard.

pizca *f.* pinch, small bit; *Mex.* harvest.

placa *f.* badge, insignia; plaque, tablet; metal plate; photographic plate; license plate; *Ven.* scab or skin blemish.

placentero *adj.* pleasant, agreeable.

placer[38] *v. irr.* to please, content; *m.* pleasure; sand bank, shoal; placer (*place where gold is obtained by washing*); *Am.* pearl fishing.

placero *m.*, **placera** *f.* market vendor.

plácido *adj.* placid, calm.

plaga *f.* plague; calamity.

plagar[7] *v.* to plague, infest; **-se de** to become plagued or infested with.

plagiar *v.* to plagiarize, steal and use as one's own (*the writings, ideas, etc. of another*); to kidnap, abduct.

plan *m.* plan; design; project; drawing; mine floor; *Am.* clearing; *Am.* building grounds of a ranch.

plana *f.* page; plain, flat country; mason's trowel; tally sheet; **enmendar la — a uno** to correct a person's mistakes.

plancha *f.* flatiron; metal plate; gangplank; blunder; *Cuba* railway flatcar; *Ven., Col.* dental plate; **— de blindaje** armor plate; **hacer una —** to make a ridiculous blunder; **tirarse una —** to place oneself in a ridiculous situation.

planchado *m.* ironing; clothes ironed or to be ironed; *adj. Am.* smart, clever; *Am.* brave; *Ven.* dolled up, dressed up; *Am.* broke, penniless.

planchar *v.* to iron; to smooth out; *Mex.* to leave (*someone*) waiting; *Am.* to strike with the flat of a blade; *Am.* to flatter; *Mex., Ven.* **— el asiento** to be a wallflower at a dance.

planeador *m.* glider airplane.

planear *v.* to plan; to glide (*said of an airplane or bird*).

planeo *m.* planning; glide, gliding (*of an airplane*).

planeta *m.* planet.

plano *adj.* plane, flat, level; *m.* plane; plan; map; **de —** flatly, clearly, openly; **dar de —** to hit with the flat of anything.

planta *f.* (*ser orgánico*) plant; plantation; (*proyecto*) plan; ground plan, ground floor; (*del pie*) sole of the foot; **— baja** ground floor; **buena — good looks; echar -s** to brag.

plantación *f.* plantation; planting.

plantar *v.* to plant; to strike (*a blow*); **-se** to stand firm; to balk; *Am.* to doll up, dress up; **dejar a uno plantado** to "stand someone up", keep someone waiting indefinitely.

plantear *v.* to plan; to establish; to carry out; to state, present (*a prob-*

lem); to try.

plantel *m.* establishment; firm; plant; nursery.

plantío *m.* planting; plantation; recently planted garden; tree nursery.

plasma *m.* plasma.

plástico *adj.* plastic.

plata *f.* silver; silver money; **hablar en — ** to speak in plain language; *Carib., C.A., Ven., Col.* money.

plataforma *f.* platform; **— de lanzamiento** launching pad.

platanal, platanar *m.* grove of banana trees; banana plantation.

plátano *m.* banana; banana tree; plane tree.

platea *f.* main floor of a theatre; a lower box seat.

plateado *adj.* silver-plated; silvery.

platear *v.* to silver, plate, cover with silver.

platel *m.* platter; tray.

platero *m.* silversmith; jeweler.

plática *f.* conversation, talk, chat; informal lecture.

platicador *m.* talker; *adj.* talkative.

platicar[6] *v.* to converse, talk, chat.

platillo *m.* saucer; pan (*of a pair of scales*); cymbal; stew.

platino *m.* platinum.

plato *m.* plate; dish; dinner course; **— de tocadiscos** turntable.

platón *m.* large plate; platter.

platudo *adj. Am.* wealthy, rich.

playa *f.* beach, shore; *Ven.* wide, open space in front of a ranch house; *Riopl., Andes* **— de estacionamiento** parking lot.

plaza *f.* (*pública*) plaza, public square; public market; (*empleo*) job; employment; *Riopl., Ch., Cuba, Ven.* park, promenade; **— de armas** parade ground; public square; fortress; **— fuerte** fortress; **— de gallos** cockpit (*for cockfights*); **— de toros** bull ring; **sacar a —** to bring out into the open, make public; **sentar —** to enlist; **plazoleta, plazuela** *f.* small square, court.

plazo *m.* term, time; **a —** on credit; in installments.

pleamar *m.* flood tide, high tide.

plebe *f.* rabble; masses.

plebeyo *adj.* plebeian.

plebiscito *m.* plebiscite, direct vote.

plegadizo *adj.* folding; pliable, easily bent.

plegar[1,7] *v.* to fold; to pleat; to crease; **-se** to bend, yield, submit.

plegaria *f.* supplication, prayer; prayer hour.

pleito *m.* litigation, lawsuit; dispute; debate; duel; **— de acreedores** bankruptcy proceedings; **pleitista** *m.* & *f.* quarrelsome person.

plenipotenciario *m.* plenipotentiary (*diplomatic agent having full power or authority*); *adj.* plenipotentiary, having full power.

plenitud *f.* plenitude, fullness, completeness; abundance.

pleno *adj.* full, complete; **sesión plena** joint session; **en — día** in broad daylight, openly; **en — rostro** (*or* **en plena cara**) right on the face; *m.* joint session (*of a legislative body*).

pliego *m.* sheet of paper; sealed letter or document.

pliegue *m.* fold, crease, pleat.

plomada *f.* plumb, lead weight, plumb bob.

plomazo *m. Col., Ven., Mex.* shot, bullet.

plomería *f.* plumbing; plumber's shop; lead roof.

plomero *m.* plumber.

plomizo *adj.* leaden, lead-colored.

plomo *m.* lead; plumb, lead weight; bullet; boring person; **a —** vertical; vertically; *adj. Carib., Mex.* lead-colored.

pluma *f.* (*de ave*) feather; plume; (*instrumento*) pen; quill; **— estilográfica** (*or* **— fuente**) fountain pen; **plumada** *f.* dash, stroke of the pen, flourish; **plumaje** *m.* plumage; plume, **plumero** *m.* feather duster; box for feathers; feather ornament (*on hats, helmets, etc.*); **plumón** *m.* down; feather mattress; **plumoso** *adj.* downy, feathery.

plural *adj.* plural.

pluvial *adj.* rain (*used as adj.*); **capa —** cope (*long cape used by priests during certain religious ceremonies*).

pluviómetro *m.* rain gauge.

población *f.* (*acto*) populating; settlement; (*numero*) population; (*lugar*) town, city.

poblado *m.* inhabited place; village; *p.p.* populated; covered with growth.

poblador *m.* settler (*of a colony*).

poblar[2] *v. irr.* to populate, people; to to colonize, settle; to stock (*a farm*); to breed; **-se** to become covered (*with leaves or buds*).

pobre *adj.* poor; *m.* poor man; beggar; **pobrete** *m.* poor devil, poor wretch; **pobretón** *m.* poor old fellow, poor wretch.

pobreza *f.* poverty; need; lack, scarcity; barrenness.

pocilga *f.* pigsty, pigpen.

pocillo *m.* cup.

poco *adj.* little, scanty; small; short (*time*); **-s** few, some; *m.* a little, a bit; *adv.* little; **a —** presently, after a short time; **a — rato** (*or* **al — rato**) after a short while; **a —** slowly, little by little; **a los -s meses** after a few months; **por — me caigo** I almost fell; **tener en — a** to hold in low esteem.

podadera *f.* pruning hook or knife.

podar *v.* to prune, trim, cut off.

podenco *m.* hound.

poder[39] *v. irr.* to be able; can; may; **él puede mucho** (*or* **poco**) he has much (*or* little) power; **puede que** it is possible that, it may be that, perhaps; **hasta más no —** to the utmost, to the limit; **no — más** not to be able to do more; to be exhausted; **no puede menos de hacerlo** he cannot help doing it; **no — con la carga** not to be equal to the burden, not to be able to lift the load; *Col., Ven.* **-le a uno algo** to be worried or affected by something, *m.* power, authority.

poderío *m.* power, dominion; might; wealth.

poderoso *adj.* powerful; wealthy.

podre *f.* pus; decayed matter; **podredumbre** *f.* corruption, decay; pus; rotten matter.

podrido *adj.* rotten; *p.p. of* podrir.

podrir[16] = **pudrir**[16].

poema *m.* poem.

poesía *f.* poetry; poem.

poeta *m.* poet; **poetastro** *m.* bad poet.

poético *asj.* poetic; **poética** *f.* poetics.

poetisa *f.* poetess.

polaco *adj.* Polish; *m.* Polish, Polish language; Pole.

polaina *f.* legging.

polar *adj.* polar.

polea *f.* pulley.

polen *m.* pollen.

policía *f.* police; *m.* policeman.

policial *m. Col., Ven.* policeman.

polilla *f.* moth; larva of the moth.

política *f.* politics; policy; *Am.* **— de campanario** politics of a clique.

politicastro *m.* bad or incapable politician.

político *adj.* political; politic; polite; **madre política** mother-in-law; *m.* politician.

póliza *f.* policy, written contract; draft; customhouse certificate; **— de seguros** insurance policy.

polizonte *m.* policeman.

polo *m.* pole (*of a magnet or or of an axis*); polo (*a game*); **— acuático** water polo.

poltrón *adj.* lazy, idle; **silla poltrona** easy chair.

polvareda *f.* cloud of dust; **armar (or levantar) una —** to kick up the dust; to raise a rumpus.

polvera *f.* powder box; compact; powder puff.

polvo *m.* dust; powder; pinch of snuff or powder; **— férrico** iron oxide filings (*coating for recording tape*); **-s** toilet powder; **-s para dientes** tooth powder; **limpio de — y paja** entirely free; net; *Am.* cleaned out, without a penny; *Am.* innocent, ignorant, unaware; *Mex., Col., Ven.* **tomar el —** to escape, "beat it".

pólvora *f.* gunpowder; fireworks.

polvorear *v.* to powder, sprinkle with powder.

polvoriento *adj.* dusty.

polvorín *m.* powder magazine; priming powder; powder flask; *Am.* tick (*parasitic insect*); *Ríopl.* spitfire, quick-tempered person.

polla *f.* pullet (*young hen*); young lass; pool (*in cards*).

pollada *f.* hatch, brood; flock of chicks.

pollera *f.* woman who raises and sells chickens; chicken coop; a bell-shaped basket for chickens; petticoat; *Ríopl., Ch., Col., Andes* skirt.

pollino *m.* young donkey, ass.

pollo *m.* young chicken; nestling, young bird; *Spain* young man; **polluelo** *m.* chick.

pompa *f.* pomp; pageant, procession; bubble; pump.

pomposo *adj.* pompous.

pómulo *m.* cheek bone.

ponche *m.* punch (*a beverage*); **ponchera** *f.* punch bowl.

poncho *m. Andes, Ch., Ríopl.* poncho; cape.

ponderación *f.* pondering, careful consideration, weighing; exaggeration.

ponderar *v.* (*pensar*) to ponder, consider, weigh; (*exagerar*) to exaggerate; to extol.

ponderativo *adj.* exaggerating.

ponderoso *adj.* ponderous, heavy.

poner[40] *v. irr.* to put; to place; to set; to lay; to suppose; **— como nuevo a alguien** to cover someone with insults; **— en claro** to clarify; **— en limpio** to copy, make a clean copy; **— todo de su parte** to do one's best; **pongamos que...** let us suppose that...; **-se** to place oneself; to become; **-se a** to begin to; **-se al corriente** to become informed; **-se de pie** to stand up; *Carib., Mex., Ch., Andes* **-se bien con alguien** to ingratiate oneself with someone, get on his good side; *Am.* **ponérsela** to get drunk.

poniente *m.* west; west wind; **el sol —** the setting sun.

pontón *m.* pontoon; scow, flat-bottomed boat; log bridge; pontoon bridge.

ponzoña *f.* venom, poison.

ponzoñoso *adj.* venomous, poisonous.

popa *f.* poop, stern; **viento en —** speedily; going well.

popote *m. Mex.* straw for brooms; *Mex.* drinking straw or tube.

populacho *m.* populace, rabble.

popular *adj.* popular.

popularidad *f.* popularity.

populoso *adj.* populous, densely populated.

poquito *adj.* very little; *Cuba, Ven., Col.* timid, shy; *m.* a small bit; **a -s** in small quantities.

por *prep.* by; for; for the sake of, on account of, on behalf of; because of; through; along; on exchange for; in the place of; during; about, around; to, with the idea of; **— ciento** percent; **— consiguiente** consequently; **— entre** among, between; **— escrito** in writing; **— poco se muere** he almost died; **está — hacer** it is yet to be done; **él está — hacerlo** he is in favor of doing it; **recibir — esposa** to receive as a wife; **tener —** to consider, think of as; **¿ — qué?** *interr. adv.* why? for what reason?

porcelana *f.* porcelain, china; enamel.

porcentaje *m.* percentage.

porción f. portion; part, share; **una — de gente** a lot of people.

porche m. porch.

pordiosear v. to beg.

pordiosero m. beggar.

porfía f. stubbornness, obstinacy; persistence, insistence; **a —** in competition; with great insistence.

porfiado adj. stubborn, obstinate, persistent.

porfiar[17] v. to persist; to insist; to dispute obstinately; to argue.

pormenor m. detail.

pormenorizar[9] v. to detail, tell in detail; to itemize.

poro m. pore.

poroso adj. porous.

poroto m. Ch., Ríopl., Andes bean; Ch., Ríopl., Andes runt.

porque conj. because; so that.

porqué m. cause, reason, motive.

porquería f. filth; filthy act or word; nasty piece of food; trifle, worthless object.

porra f. club, stick; Am. **mandar a uno a la —** to send someone to the devil; **porrazo** m. blow; knock; bump; **porrón** m. wine vessel with long snout.

porta f. porthole; cover for a porthole; goal (in football).

portaaviones m. airplane carrier.

portada f. façade, front (of a building); title page.

portador m. carrier; bearer; tray.

portal m. portal; entrance, vestibule; portico, porch; Am. Christmas crèche; **-es** arcades, galleries; **portalón** m. large portal; gangway (of a ship).

portamonedas m. pocketbook, coin purse.

portapapeles m. briefcase.

portaplumas m. penholder.

portar v. Am. to carry; **-se** to behave.

portátil adj. portable.

portaviones m. aircraft carrier; also **portaaviones.**

portavoz m. megaphone; mouthpiece; spokesman.

portazgo m. toll.

portazo m. bang or slam of a door; **dar un —** to bang or slam the door.

porte m. portage, cost of carriage; freight; postage; manner, bearing; size, capacity; Am. birthday present; C.A. size.

portear v. to carry on one's back; Am. to get out in a hurry.

portento m. portent; wonder, marvel.

portentoso adj. marvelous, extraordinary, amazing, terrifying.

porteño adj. from a port; Ríopl. from Buenos Aires.

portería f. porter's quarters; main door of a building.

portero m. doorkeeper, doorman; janitor.

pórtico m. portico, porch.

portilla f. porthole; small gate or passageway.

portón m. gate.

portugués adj. Portuguese; m. Portu-

guese; Portuguese language.

porvenir m. future.

pos : en — de after; in pursuit of.

posada f. lodging; inn; boardinghouse; dwelling, home; Mex. **las -s** a Christmas festivity lasting nine days; **posadero** m. innkeeper.

posaderas f. pl. posterior, buttocks, rump.

posar v. to lodge; to rest; to sit down; to pose (as a model); to perch (said of birds); **-se** to settle (said of sediment); to perch (said of birds).

posdata f. postscript.

poseedor m. possessor, owner.

poseer[14] v. to possess, own; to master, know well; **-se** to have control of oneself.

posesión f. possession.

posesivo adj. & m. possessive.

posesor m. possessor, owner.

posibilidad f. possibility.

posible adj. possible; **hacer lo —** to do one's best; **-s** m. pl. goods, property, means.

posición f. position; posture; status, rank, standing; placing.

positivo adj. positive; effective; true; practical.

posponer[40] v. irr. to postpone, put off; to put after; to subordinate.

pospuesto p.p. of **posponer.**

posta f. (bala) small bullet; (apuesta) bet, wager; (relevo) relay (of post horses); post station; **-s** buckshot; **por la —** posthaste; fast, speedily; m. postboy, courier, messenger.

postal adj. postal; **tarjeta —** postcard.

postdata = **posdata.**

poste m. post, pillar.

postergar[7] v. to delay; to postpone; to disregard someone's right.

posteridad f. posterity.

posterior adj. posterior, back, rear; later.

postigo m. wicket, small door or gate; shutter; peep window.

postizo adj. false, artificial; m. switch, false hair.

postración f. prostration, collapse, exhaustion; dejection, lowness of spirits.

postrar v. to prostrate; to humiliate; to throw down; to weaken, exhaust; **-se** to kneel to the ground; to be weakened, exhausted; to collapse.

postre m. dessert; **a la —** at last.

postrer(o) adj. last; hindmost, nearest the rear.

postulante m. & f. petitioner; applicant, candidate.

póstumo adj. posthumous, after one's death.

postura f. posture, position; bid; wager; pact, agreement; egg-laying.

potable adj. drinkable; **agua —** drinking water.

potaje m. pottage, thick soup; porridge; mixed drink.

pote m. pot; jar; jug; Carib., Ven., Mex., Ríopl. flask; Am. buzzard.

potencia f. potency; power; faculty,

PO

ability; powerful nation.

potente *adj.* potent, powerful, strong.

potestad *f.* power; dominion, authority.

potranca *f.* filly, young mare.

potrero *m.* herdsman of colts; fence d-in pasture land; *Carib., Mex., C.A., Ven., Col., Ch.* cattle ranch, stock farm.

potro *m.* colt; rack, torture; *Col., Ven., Mex., Ch., Riopl.* wild horse.

poyo *m.* stone or brick bench (*usually built against a wall*).

pozo *m.* well; hole, pit; mine shaft; hold of a ship; *Am.* pool, puddle; *Riopl., Ch., Ven., Col., Mex.* spring, fountain.

práctica *f.* practice; exercise; custom, habit; method.

practicante *m.* & *f.* doctor's assistant; hospital intern.

practicar⁶ *v.* to practice; to put into practice.

práctico *adj.* practical; experienced, skilful; *m.* — **de puerto** harbor pilot.

pradera *f.* prairie; meadow.

prado *m.* meadow, field; lawn.

preámbulo *m.* preamble, introduction, prologue.

precario *adj.* precarious.

precaución *f.* precaution.

precaver *v.* to guard (against), keep (from); to warn, caution; **-se** to guard oneself (against); to take precautions.

precavido *adj.* cautious, on guard.

precedencia *f.* precedence; priority.

precedente *adj.* preceding; *m.* precedent.

preceder *v.* to precede; to have precedence.

precepto *m.* precept; rule; order.

preceptor *m.* teacher, tutor.

preciado *adj.* prized, esteemed; precious, valuable.

preciar *v.* to appraise; to value; **-se de** to boast of, be proud of.

precio *m.* price; value, worth; esteem.

precioso *adj.* precious, valuable; fine, exquisite; beautiful.

precipicio *m.* precipice; ruin.

precipitación *f.* precipitation; rush, haste, hurry.

precipitado *adj.* precipitate, hasty, rash; *m.* precipitate (*chemical term*).

precipitar *v.* to precipitate; to hasten, rush; to hurl, throw headlong; **-se** to throw oneself headlong; to rush (into).

precipitoso *adj.* precipitous, steep; rash.

precisar *v.* to determine precisely; to force, compel, make necessary; *Riopl., Col., Ven., Mex., Andes.* to be necessary or urgent; *Am.* to need.

precisión *f.* precision, exactness; accuracy; compulsion, force, necessity; *Am.* haste.

preciso *adj.* necessary; precise, exact; clear; *m. Am.* small travelling bag.

precoz *adj.* precocious.

precursor *m.* precursor, forerunner.

predecir⁸⁷ *v. irr.* to predict, prophesy, forecast, foretell.

predestinar *v.* to predestine.

predicación *f.* preaching.

predicado *adj.* & *m.* predicate; *p.p. o* **predicar.**

predicador *m.* preacher.

predicar⁶ *v.* to preach.

predicción *f.* prediction.

predilección *f.* predilection, preference, liking.

predilecto *adj.* favorite, preferred.

predisponer⁴⁰ *v. irr.* to predispose, bias prejudice.

predispuesto *p.p.* of **predisponer** & *adj.* predisposed, prejudiced, biased

predominante *adj.* predominant; prevailing, ruling.

predominar *v.* to predominate, prevail.

predominio *m.* predominance; sway influence.

prefacio *m.* preface.

prefecto *m.* prefect (*military or civ* *chief; sometimes a mayor, sometime* *governor of a province, as in Peru*)

preferencia *f.* preference; **de** — with preference; preferably.

preferente *adj.* preferable; preferred preferential; **acciones -s** preferred shares.

preferible *adj.* preferable.

preferir³ *v. irr.* to prefer.

prefijar *v.* to prefix; to set beforehand (*as a date*).

prefijo *m.* prefix.

pregonar *v.* to proclaim, cry out; to make known.

pregunta *f.* question; **hacer una** — to ask a question.

preguntar *v.* to ask, inquire.

preguntón *adj.* inquisitive.

prejuicio *m.* prejudice.

prelado *m.* prelate.

preliminar *adj.* & *m.* preliminary.

preludiar *v.* to be the prelude or beginning of; to initiate, introduce; to try out (*a musical instrument*).

preludio *m.* prelude; introduction.

prematuro *adj.* premature, untimely.

premeditado *adj.* premeditated, deliberate.

premiar *v.* to reward.

premio *m.* prize; reward; recompense premium; **a** — with interest, at interest.

premisa *f.* premise (*either of the firs* *two propositions of a syllogism*).

premura *f.* pressure, urgency, haste.

prenda *f.* (*fianza*) pawn, pledge, security; token; (*partes del vestido*) article of clothing; anything vauable; love person; jewel; **-s** good qualities gifts, talents; — **de vestir** garment **juego de -s** game of forfeits; **en** — **d** as a proof of, as a pledge of.

prendar *v.* to pawn, pledge; to charm please; **-se de** to get attached to; to fall in love with.

prendedor *m.* clasp; stickpin; tie pin brooch; *Am.* lighter.

prender *v.* (*asir*) to seize, catch, grab to bite (*said of an insect*); to fasten clasp; to arrest, imprison; (*empezar*) to take root; to begin to burn; catch fire; *Riopl.*, *Carib.*, *C.A.*, *Mex.* to light (*a lamp*); *Am.* to start, begin, undertake; — **el fuego** to start the fire; *Col.* **-las** to take to one's heels; **-se** to dress up.

prendero *m.* pawnbroker; second-hand dealer.

prensa *f.* press; printing press.

prensar *v.* to press.

preñado *adj.* pregnant; full.

preñez *f.* pregnancy.

preocupación *f.* preoccupation; worry; bias, prejudice.

preocupar *v.* to preoccupy; to worry; to prejudice; **-se** to be preoccupied; to worry; to be prejudiced.

preparación *f.* preparation.

preparar *v.* to prepare; **-se** to get ready; to be prepared.

preparativo *adj.* preparatory; *m.* preparation.

preparatorio *adj.* preparatory.

preposición *f.* preposition.

prerrogativa *f.* prerogative, right, privilege.

presa *f.* prey; dam; fang, tusk; claw; **hacer** — to seize.

presagiar *v.* to foretell.

presagio *m.* presage, omen, sign.

presbítero *m.* priest.

prescindir *v.* to disregard, set aside, leave aside; to omit; to dispense (with).

prescribir[52] *v.* to prescribe.

prescrito *p.p.* of **prescribir**.

presencia *f.* presence; figure, bearing; — **de ánimo** presence of mind, serenity.

presenciar *v.* to see, witness; to be present at.

presentación *f.* presentation; personal introduction; *Ven.* petition.

presentar *v.* to present; to introduce; **-se** to appear, present oneself; to introduce oneself; to offer one's services; *Am.* to have recourse to justice, file suit.

presente *adj.* present; *m.* present, gift; **al** — now, at the present time; **por el (la,** *or* **lo)** — for the present; **mejorando lo** — present company excepted; **tener** — to bear in mind.

presentimiento *m.* presentiment, foreboding.

presentir[3] *v. irr.* to have a presentiment, foreboding or hunch.

preservación *f.* preservation.

preservar *v.* to preserve, guard, protect, keep.

presidencia *f.* presidency; office of president; presidential term; chairmanship.

presidencial *adj.* presidential.

presidente *m.* president; chairman; presiding judge.

presidiario *m.* prisoner, convict.

presidio *m.* garrison; fortress; penitentiary, prison; **diez años de** — ten years at hard labor (*in a prison*).

presidir *v.* to preside; to direct.

presilla *f.* loop, fastener; clip.

presión *f.* pressure.

preso *m.* prisoner; *p.p. irr.* of **prender** imprisoned.

prestado *adj.* & *p.p.* loaned, lent; **dar** — to lend; **pedir** — to borrow.

prestamista *m.* & *f.* moneylender.

préstamo *m.* loan.

prestar *v.* to loan, lend; *Col.*, *Ven.*, *C.A.*, *Andes* to borrow; — **ayuda** to give help; — **atención** to pay attention; *Andes* **presta acá** give it here, give it to me; **-se** to lend oneself or itself.

presteza *f.* promptness, speed.

prestidigitación *f.* juggling, sleight of hand.

prestidigitador *m.* juggler.

prestigio *m.* prestige; influence, authority; good reputation.

presto *adj.* quick; nimble; prompt; ready; *adv.* soon, at once; **de** — quickly, promptly.

presumido *adj.* conceited, presumptuous; *p.p.* of **presumir**.

presumir *v.* to presume; to boast; to show off; *Am.* to court, woo; — **de valiente** to boast of one's valor.

presunción *f.* presumption, assumption; conceit, arrogance.

presunto *adj.* presumed; supposed; prospective; **heredero** — heir apparent.

presuntuoso *adj.* presumptuous, conceited.

presuponer[40] *v. irr.* to presuppose, take for granted, imply; to estimate.

presupuesto *p.p.* of **presuponer** presupposed; estimated; *m.* budget, estimate.

presuroso *adj.* quick, prompt; hasty.

pretencioso *adj.* presumptuous; conceited.

pretender *v.* to pretend; to solicit, seek; to claim; to try; to court.

pretendiente *m.* pretender, claimant; suitor; office seeker.

pretensión *f.* pretension; claim; presumption; pretense.

pretérito *adj.* preterite, past; *m.* preterite, the past tense.

pretexto *m.* pretext, pretense, excuse.

pretil *m.* stone or brick railing; *Am.* ledge; *Mex.*, *Ven.* stone or brick bench (*built against a wall*).

pretina *f.* belt, girdle; waistband.

prevalecer[13] *v. irr.* to prevail.

prevaleciente *adj.* prevalent, current.

prevención *f.* prevention; foresight, preparedness; bias, prejudice; provision, supply; admonition, warning; police station; guardhouse.

prevenido *adj.* & *p.p.* prepared, ready; forewarned; cautious; supplied.

prevenir[48] *v. irr.* to prevent, avoid; to prepare beforehand; to foresee; to warn; to predispose; **-se** to get prepared, get ready.

prever[49] *v. irr.* to foresee.

previo *adj.* previous; *m. Am.* preliminary examination.

previsión *f.* foresight.

previsto *p.p. of* **prever.**

prieto *adj.* dark, black; tight; compact; *Riopl., Ven., Col., Mex., C.A., Andes* dark-complexioned, swarthy.

prima *f.* female cousin; premium; prime (*first of the canonical hours*).

primacía *f.* priority, precedence; superiority.

primario *adj.* primary, principal.

primavera *f.* spring; primrose; print, flowered silk cloth.

primaveral *adj.* spring, pertaining to spring.

primer(o) *adj.* first; former; leading, principal; **primera enseñanza** primary education; **primera materia** raw material; **de buenas a primeras** all of a sudden, unexpectedly; **a primera luz** at dawn; *adv.* first; rather.

primicia *f.* first fruit; first profit; **-s** first fruits.

primitivo *adj.* primitive; primary; original.

primo *m.* cousin; simpleton, sucker, dupe; — **hermano** (*or* — **carnal**) first cousin; *Carib.* **coger a uno de** — to deceive someone easily; *adj.* first; **número** — prime number.

primogénito *adj. & m.* first-born.

primogenitura *f.* birthright; rights of the first-born.

primor *m.* beauty; excellence; exquisiteness; skill, ability.

primoroso *adj.* excellent, fine, exquisite; skillful.

prímula *f.* primrose.

princesa *f.* princess.

principal *adj.* principal; renowned, famous; **piso** — main floor (*usually, the second floor*); *m.* principal, capital sum; chief, head.

príncipe *m.* prince; *adj.* princeps, first (*edition*).

principiante *m.* beginner.

principiar *v.* to begin.

principio *m.* principle; beginning; origin, source; entrée (*main dinner course*); **a -s de** towards the beginning of.

pringue *m. & f.* grease drippings (*from bacon, ham, etc.*).

prioridad *f.* priority; precedence.

prisa *f.* speed, haste; **de** (*or* **a**) — quickly, speedily; **a todo** — with the greatest speed; **eso corre** — that is urgent; **dar** — **a** to hurry; **darse** — to hurry; **tener** (*or* **estar de**) — to be in a hurry.

prisión *f.* prison; imprisonment; seizure; shackle; **-es** shackles, fetters, chains.

prisionero *m.* prisoner.

prisma *f.* prism.

pristino *adj.* first, early, former, primitive.

privación *f.* privation; want, lack; loss.

privado *adj.* private; personal; unconscious; *p.p.* deprived; *m.* favorite.

privar *v.* (*destituir*) to deprive; to prohibit; (*tener aceptación*) to enjoy the favor of someone; to be in vogue; **-le a uno del sentido** to stun, daze; **ya no privan esas costumbres** those customs are no longer in vogue or in existence; **-se de** to deprive oneself of.

privativo *adj.* exclusive; particular, distinctive.

privilegiado *adj.* privileged.

privilegiar *v.* to favor; to give a privilege to.

privilegio *m.* privilege; exemption; patent; copyright; — **de invención** patent on an invention.

pro *m. & f.* profit, advantage; **en** — **de** on behalf of; **en** — **y en contra** pro and con, for and against; **hombre de** — man of worth.

proa *f.* prow.

probabilidad *f.* probability.

probable *adj.* probable.

probar² *v. irr.* (*examinar*) to test; to taste; to prove; to try; to try on; (*gustar*) to suit, agree with; **no me prueba el clima** the climate does not agree with me.

probeta *f.* test tube; pressure gauge.

probidad *f.* integrity, uprightness, honesty.

problema *m.* problem.

procedente *adj.* proceeding (from), originating; according to law.

proceder *v.* to proceed; to originate; to behave; to take action (against); *m.* behavior, conduct.

procedimiento *m.* procedure; method; process; conduct.

prócer *m.* distinguished person; hero; great statesman.

procesado *p.p. & adj.* relating to, or included in, a lawsuit; accused, prosecuted; *m.* defendant.

procesar *v.* to prosecute; to accuse; to indict; to sue.

procesión *f.* procession; parade.

proceso *m.* process; lawsuit, legal proceedings; lapse of time; — **verbal** minutes, record.

proclama *f.* proclamation, ban; marriage banns.

proclamación *f.* proclamation.

proclamar *v.* to proclaim.

procurador *m.* attorney.

procurar *v.* (*pretender*) to try, endeavor; (*obtener*) to procure, obtain, get.

prodigar⁷ *v.* to lavish; to bestow upon; to squander, waste.

prodigio *m.* prodigy, wonder, marvel; miracle.

prodigioso *adj.* prodigious, marvelous; fine, exquisite.

pródigo *adj.* prodigal, wasteful; lavish; generous; *m.* spendthrift.

producción *f.* production; produce.

producir²⁵ *v. irr.* to produce; to bring about; to yield; **-se** to express oneself, explain oneself; *Col., Ven.* to occur, happen.

productivo *adj.* productive; fruitful; profitable.

producto m. product; yield; result.

productor m. producer; adj. producing, productive.

proeza f. prowess; Col. boast, exaggeration.

profanación f. profanation.

profanar v. to profane; to defile.

profano adj. profane, not sacred; irreverent; lay, uninformed (about a branch of learning).

profecía f. prophecy; prediction.

proferir[3] v. irr. to utter, express, speak.

profesar v. to profess; to avow, confess.

profesión f. profession; avowal, declaration.

profesional adj., m. & f. professional.

profesionista m. & f. Am. professional.

profesor m. professor, teacher; **profesorado** m. faculty; body of teachers; teaching profession; professorship.

profeta m. prophet.

profético adj. prophetic.

profetizar[9] v. to prophesy.

proficiente adj. proficient, skilled.

profilaxis f. prophylaxis (disease prevention).

prófugo adj. & m. fugitive.

profundidad f. profundity, depth.

profundizar[9] v. to deepen; to go deep into.

profundo adj. profound; deep; low.

profuso adj. profuse; lavish.

programa m. program; plan.

progresar v. to progress.

progresista m., f. & adj. progressive.

progresivo adj. progressive.

progreso m. progress.

prohibición f. prohibition; ban.

prohibir v. to prohibit, forbid.

prójimo m. neighbor, fellow being; Ríopl., Carib., C.A. ese — that fellow.

prole f. progeny, offspring.

proletariado m. proletariat, working class.

proletario adj. proletarian, belonging to the working class; plebeian; m. proletarian.

prolijo adj. prolix, too long, drawn out, too detailed; boring, tedious.

prologar[7] v. to preface, write a preface for.

prólogo m. prologue.

prolongación f. prolongation, extension; lengthening.

prolongar[7] v. to prolong, lengthen, extend.

promediar v. to average; to divide or distribute into two equal parts; to mediate; **antes de — el mes** before the middle of the month.

promedio m. middle; average.

promesa f. promise.

prometedor adj. promising, hopeful.

prometer v. to promise; to show promise; Ríopl., C.A. to affirm, assure; **-se** to become engaged, betrothed.

prometido adj. & p.p. betrothed; m. fiancé, betrothed; promise.

prominente adj. prominent.

promisorio adj. promissory.

promoción f. promotion, advancement.

promontorio m. promontory, headland, cape; anything bulky; bulge.

promotor m. promoter.

promovedor m. promoter.

promover[2] v. irr. to promote; to advance.

promulgación f. promulgation, publication, proclamation (of a law).

promulgar[7] v. to promulgate, proclaim, announce publicly.

pronombre m. pronoun.

pronosticar[6] v. to prophesy, predict.

pronóstico m. forecast; prediction; omen.

prontitud f. promptness; quickness.

pronto adj. quick, speedy; ready; prompt; adv. soon; quickly; **de —** suddenly; **al —** at first; **por de** (or **por lo**) — for the present; m. sudden impulse.

pronunciación f. pronunciation.

pronunciar v. to pronounce; to utter; **-se** to rise up in rebellion.

propagación f. propagation, spread, spreading.

propaganda f. propaganda.

propagar[7] v. to propagate, reproduce; to spread.

propalar v. to spread (news).

proparse v. to overstep one's bounds; to exceed one's authority, go too far.

propensión f. tendency, inclination; bent, natural tendency or ability.

propenso adj. prone, susceptible, inclined.

propicio adj. propitious, favorable.

propiedad f. property; ownership; attribute, quality; propriety, appropriateness.

propietario m. proprietor, owner.

propina f. tip (voluntary gift of money for service).

propinar v. to give (something to drink); to give (a beating, kick, slap); Am. to tip, give a tip to; — **una paliza** to give a beating.

propio adj. proper; suitable; own; same; **amor —** vanity, pride, self-esteem; m. messenger.

proponer[40] v. irr. to propose; to resolve; to present; **-se** to resolve, make a resolution.

proporción f. proportion; dimension; ratio; opportunity, chance.

proporcionar v. to proportion; to adapt, adjust; to furnish, supply; give.

proposición f. proposition; proposal; assertion.

propósito m. purpose, aim, design; **a —** apropos, suitable, fitting; by the way; **de —** on purpose; **fuera de —** irrelevant, beside the point.

propuesto f. proposal, offer; proposition.

propuesto p.p. of **proponer.**

propulsar v. to propel.

propulsión f. propulsion; **— a chorro** (por reacción) jet propulsion; **— a cohete** rocket propulsion.

propulsor m. propeller; adj. propelling.

prorratear v. to prorate, distribute or assess proportionally; to average.

prorrateo m. apportionment, proportional distribution.

prórroga f. renewal, extension of time.

prorrogar[7] v. to put off, postpone; to adjourn; to extend (*time limit*).

prorrumpir v. to break forth; **— en llanto** to burst into tears; **—en una carcajada** to let out a big laugh.

prosa f. prose.

prosaico adj. prosaic; dull; tedious.

proscribir[52] v. to proscribe, banish; to outlaw.

proscripción f. banishment.

proscripto, proscrito p.p. of **proscribir**; m. exile, outlaw.

proseguir[5,12] v. irr. to continue; to follow.

prosperar v. to prosper.

prosperidad f. prosperity; success.

próspero adj. prosperous; successful.

próstata f. prostate.

prostituir[32] v. to prostitute, corrupt.

prostituta f. prostitute.

protagonista m. & f. protagonist (*main character or actor*).

protección f. protection; support.

proteccionista adj. protective; **tarifa — ** protective tariff; m. & f. protectionist (*follower of the economic principles of protection*).

protector m. protector, guardian; adj. protecting, protective.

protectorado m. protectorate.

proteger[11] v. to protect; to shelter; to defend.

proteína f. protein.

proteínico adj. related to the proteins.

protesta f. protest; protestation.

protestación f. protestation, solemn declaration; protest.

protestante m. Protestant; one who protests.

protestar v. (*confesar*) to assert, assure; to avow publicly; (*negar*) to protest; **— una letra** to protest a draft.

protón m. proton.

protoplasma m. protoplasm.

protuberancia f. protuberance, bulge.

protuberante adj. protuberant, prominent, bulging.

provecho m. profit; benefit; utility; advantage; **hombre de —** worthy, useful man.

provechoso adj. profitable; useful; beneficial; advantageous.

proveedor m. provisioner, provider; supply man.

proveer[14, 52] v. irr. to provide; to supply; to confer, bestow; to decide; **-se de** to supply oneself with.

provenir[48] v. irr. to originate, arise, come (from).

proverbio m. proverb.

providencia f. providence; foresight; Providence, God; legal decision, sentence; provision, measure; **tomar una —** to take a step or measure.

providencial adj. providential.

provincia f. province.

provincial adj. provincial.

provinciano adj. & m. provincial.

provisión f. provision; supply, stock.

provisorio adj. provisional, temporary.

provisto p.p. of **proveer**.

provocación f. provocation; dare, defiance.

provocador adj. provoking; — provoker.

provocar[6] v. to provoke; to excite, rouse; to stimulate.

proximidad f. proximity, nearness.

próximo adj. next; neighboring; near; **del — pasado** of last month.

proyección f. projection; jut.

proyectar v. to project; to plan; to throw; to cast; **-se** to be cast (*as a shadow*).

proyectil m. projectile.

proyectista m. & f. designer; schemer; planner.

proyecto m. project; plan; **— de ley** bill (*in a legislature*).

prudencia f. prudence, practical wisdom, discretion.

prudente adj. prudent, wise, discreet.

prueba f. proof; trial; test; fitting; sample; evidence; *Andes, Ríopl., Col., C.A.* acrobatic performance, stunt, trick, sleight of hand; **a — de incendio** fireproof.

prurito m. itch; keen desire.

púa f. prick; barb; prong; thorn; quill (*of a porcupine, etc.*); sharp, cunning person; *Riopl.* cock's spur; **alambre de -s** barbed wire.

publicación f. publication.

publicar[6] v. to publish; to reveal; to announce.

publicidad f. publicity.

público adj. & m. public.

puchero m. pot, kettle; meat and vegetable stew; pout; **hacer -s** to pout.

pucho m. cigar or cigarette butt; *C.A.* something of little value.

pudiente adj. powerful; rich, wealthy; m. man of means.

pudín m. pudding.

pudor m. modesty; shyness.

pudrir[16] v. to rot; to vex, annoy; **-se** to rot.

pueblero m. *Riopl.* townsman (*as opposed to countryman*).

pueblo m. town, village; people, race, nation; populace; common people.

puente m. bridge; *Carib., Mex., Riopl.* dental bridge; *Am.* knife and fork rest; **— colgante** suspension bridge; **— levadizo** drawbridge.

puerca f. sow.

puerco m. pig, hog; **—espín** porcupine; **— jabalí** wild boar; adj. filthy, dirty; coarse, ill-bred.

pueril adj. puerile, childish.

puerta f. door; gate; entrance; **— accesoria** (**excusada,** or **falsa**) side door; **— de golpe** spring door; trap door; **— franca** open door; free entrance or entry; **— trasera** back door;

a — **cerrada** secretly, behind closed doors; *Am.* **en —** in view, in sight, very near.

puerto *m.* port; harbor; refuge; mountain pass; — **franco** free port.

pues *conj.* since, because, for, inasmuch as; then; *adv.* then; well; — **bien** well then, well; — **que** since.

puesta *f.* set, setting (*of a star or planet*); stake at cards; — **de sol** sunset.

puestero *m. Carib., Mex., Ríopl.* vendor, seller (*at a stand or stall*); *Ríopl.* man in charge of livestock on Argentine ranches.

puesto *p.p. of* **poner** placed, put, set; **mal** (*or* **bien**) — badly (*or* well) dressed; *m.* place; vendor's booth or stand; post, position, office; military post; *Andes, Ríopl.* station for watching and taking care of cattle on a ranch; — **de socorros** first-aid station; — **que** *conj.* since.

pugilato *m.* boxing.

pugilista *m.* boxer, prize fighter.

pugna *f.* struggle; conflict; **estar en — con** to be in conflict with; to be opposed to.

pugnar *v.* to fight; to struggle; to strive; to persist.

pujanza *f.* push, force, power.

pujar *v.* to make a strenuous effort; to grope for words; to falter; to outbid (*offer a higher bid than*); *C.A.* to grunt; *Am.* to reject; *Ven.* to dismiss; *Am.* — **para adentro** to forbear, keep silent; *Am.* **andar pujado** to go around crestfallen; to be in disgrace.

pujido *m. Am.* grunt (*due to strenuous effort*).

pulcritud *f.* neatness, trimness; excellence, perfection.

pulcro *adj.* neat, trim; beautiful.

pulga *f.* flea; *Ríopl.* small and insignificant person; **tener malas -s** to be ill-tempered; *Col., Andes* **ser de pocas -s** to be touchy, oversensitive; **pulgón** *m.* blight, plant louse.

pulgada *f.* inch.

pulgar *m.* thumb.

pulido *adj.* polished, refined; polite; neat; exquisite.

pulimentar *v.* to polish.

pulimento *m.* polish; gloss.

pulir *v.* to polish.

pulmón *m.* lung.

pulmonar *adj.* pulmonary, pertaining to the lungs.

pulmonía *f.* pneumonia.

pulpa *f.* pulp.

pulpería *f. Ríopl., C.A., Ch., Ven., Andes* country general store; *Am.* tavern.

pulpero *m. Ríopl., C.A., Ch., Ven., Andes* owner of a country store or tavern.

púlpito *m.* pulpit.

pulpo *m.* octopus.

pulque *m. Mex.* pulque (*fermented juice of the maguey*).

pulsación *f.* pulsation, beat, throb; pulse, beating.

pulsar *v.* to pulsate, throb, beat; to feel the pulse of; to sound out; examine; to play (*the harp*); *Mex., C.A.* to judge or try the weight of (*by lifting*).

pulsera *f.* bracelet; wrist bandage; **reloj de —** wrist watch.

pulso *m.* pulse; steadiness; tact; *Ríopl., Carib., Col.* bracelet, wrist watch; **un hombre de —** a prudent, steady man; *Cuba, Mex.* **beber a —** to drink straight down, gulp down; **levantar a —** to lift with the strength of the wrist or hand; **sacar a — un negocio** to carry out a deal by sheer perseverance.

pulular *v.* to swarm; to multiply rapidly; to sprout, bud.

pulverizar[9] *v.* to pulverize.

pulla *f.* taunt; mean dig, quip, cutting remark; filthy word or remark.

puma *f.* puma, mountain lion.

puna *f. Andes* cold, arid tableland of the Andes; *Ríopl.* desert; *Andes* sickness caused by high altitude.

pundonor *m.* point of honor.

punta *f.* point, tip; bull's horn; cigar or cigarette butt; *Ven.*, gang, band, herd, a lot (*of things, people, etc.*); *Am.* small leaf of fine tobacco; *Am.* jeer, cutting remark; **-s** point lace; scallops; **de —** on end; **de -s** (*or* **de puntillas**) on tiptoe; *Am.* **a —** by dint of, by means of; **estar de — con** to be on bad terms with; **sacar — a un lápiz** to sharpen a pencil; **tener sus -s de poeta** to be something of a poet.

puntada *f.* stitch; hint; *Andes* prick, pricking, sting, sharp pain; **no he dado — en este asunto** I have left this matter completely untouched.

puntal *m.* prop; support; basis; bull's horn; *Col.* snack (*between meals*).

puntapié *m.* kick (*with the toe of the shoe.*

puntazo *m. Col., Ven., Mex., Cuba* stab, jab.

puntear *v.* to pluck (*the strings of a guitar*); to play (*a guitar*); to make dots; to engrave, draw or paint by means of dots; to stitch; to tack (*said of a boat*).

puntería *f.* aim.

puntero *m.* pointer; chisel; blacksmith's punch; *C.A., Col., Ch.* clock or watch hand; *Am.* leader of a parade: *Cuba, Mex., Ven., Col.* leading ox (*or other animal*); *Am.* guide.

puntiagudo *adj.* sharp, sharp-pointed.

puntilla *f.* small point; tip; small dagger; tracing point; point lace; *Ven.* penknife; *Am.* toe rubber; *Am.* ridge (*of a hill*); **de -s** on tiptoe; **puntillazo** *m.* stab (*with a dagger*).

punto *m.* (*parada*) period; stop; point; dot; (*puntada*) stitch; mesh; (*sitio*) place; moment; (*mira*) gun sight; — **de admiración** exclamation mark; — **de interrogación** question mark; — **y coma** semicolon; **dos -s** colon; **al —** at once, immediately; **a — de** on the point of; **de —** knitted, porous knit, stockinet or jersey weave; **en —** exactly, on the dot; **a — fijo** with certainty; **subir de —** to increase or get worse.

puntuación *f.* punctuation.

puntual *adj.* punctual, prompt; exact.

puntualidad *f.* punctuality, promptness; certainty.

puntuar[18] *v.* to punctuate.

punzada *f.* puncture; prick; sharp pain.

punzante *adj.* sharp; pricking; piercing, penetrating.

punzar[9] *v.* to puncture; to sting; to prick; to punch, perforate.

punzón *m.* punch, puncher; pick; awl.

puñada *f.* punch, box, blow with the fist.

puñado *m.* fistful, handful; **a -s** abundantly; by handfuls.

puñal *m.* dagger.

puñalada *f.* stab; sharp pain; **coser a -s** to stab to death.

puñetazo *m.* punch, blow with the fist.

puño *m.* fist; fistful, handful; cuff; hilt, handle; *Ven., Col.* blow with the fist; **a — cerrado** firmly; **ser como un — to** be stingy; **tener -s** to be strong, courageous.

pupila *f.* pupil (*of the eye*).

pupilo *m.* ward; boarding-school pupil; boarder.

pupitre *m.* desk, school desk.

puré *m.* purée, thick soup.

pureza *f.* purity; chastity.

purga *f.* purge, laxative, physic.

purgante *adj.* purgative, laxative; *m.* purgative, physic, laxative.

purgar[7] *v.* to purge; to purify; to atone for; **-se** to purge oneself; to take a laxative.

purgatorio *m.* purgatory.

purificar[6] *v.* to purify.

puro *adj.* (*limpio*) pure; clean; chaste; (*sólo*) mere, only, sheer; **a pura fuerza** by sheer force; **a puros gritos** by just shouting; *m.* cigar.

púrpura *f.* purple; purple cloth.

purpúreo *adj.* purple.

pus *m.* pus.

puta *f.* whore, prostitute.

putativo *adj.* reputed, supposed; **padre — foster** father.

putrefacción *f.* putrefaction, decay, rotting.

putrefacto *adj.* putrid, rotten, decayed.

Q

que *rel. pron.* that; which; who; whom; **el — who**; which; the one who; the one which; *conj.* that; for, because; **más (menos) — more** (less) than; **el mismo — the** same as; **— (=** *subj.*) let, may you, I hope that; **por mucho — no** matter how much; **quieras — no** whether you wish or not.

qué *interr. adj. & pron.* what?; what a!; *interr. adv.* how; **¡ — bonito!** how beautiful!; **¿a —?** what for?; **¿para —?** what for?; **¿por —?** why?; **¿—**

tal? how?; hello!; **¡ — más da!** what's the difference!; **¡a mí —!** so what! and what's that to me!

quebracho *m.* quebracho, breakax wood.

quebrada *f.* ravine; gorge; failure, bankruptcy; *Ríopl., Col., Ven., C.A., Mex.* brook.

quebradizo *adj.* breakable; brittle; fragile; delicate.

quebrado *adj.* broken; weakened; ruptured; bankrupt; rough or rugged (*ground*); *m.* common fraction; *Ven.* navigable waters between reefs.

quebrantar *v.* to break; to break open; to pound, crush; to violate (*a law*); to weaken; to vex; *Mex., Col.* to tame, break in (*a colt*); **— el agua** to take the chill off the water.

quebranto *m.* breaking; grief, affliction; discouragement; damage, loss.

quebrar[1] *v. irr.* to break; to crush; to interrupt; to wither (*said of the complexion*); to become bankrupt; **-se** to break; to get broken; to be ruptured; **-se uno la cabeza** to rack one's brain.

quebrazón *m. Ven., Col.* breakage, breaking.

quechua *adj. Am.* Quichuan; *m. & f.* Quichua, Quichuan Indian; *m.* Quichuan language.

quedar to stay; to remain; to be left over; to be left (*in a state or condition*); **— en** to agree to; *Am.* **— de** to agree to; **— bien** to acquit oneself well; to come out well; *Am.* to suit, become (*said of a dress, hat, etc.*); *Am.* **— bien con alguien** to please someone; **-se** to remain; **-se con una cosa** to keep something; to take something (*buy it*); *Am.* **-se como si tal cosa** to act as if nothing had happened.

quedo *adj.* quiet, still; gentle; *adv.* softly; in a low voice; **quedito** *adj.* nice and quiet; *adv.* very softly.

quehacer *m.* work, occupation; task, duty, chore.

queja *f.* complaint; groan, moan; grudge.

quejarse *v.* to complain; to grumble; to moan; to lament.

quejido *m.* moan; groan.

quejoso *adj.* complaining, whining.

quejumbre *f.* whine, moan; murmur, complaint; **-s** *m. Cuba, Ven.* grumbler, whiner; **quejumbroso** *adj.* whining, complaining.

quemada *f.* burned forest; *Am.* burn.

quemado *m.* burned portion of a forest; *Col.* burned field; *Am.* hot alcoholic drink; *adj.* dark, tan; *Am.* peeved, piqued; *Col., Ven., Cuba, Mex.* ruined; *p.p. of* **quemar.**

quemadura *f.* burn; scald; smut (*plant disease*).

quemar *v.* to burn; to scald; to scorch; to sell at a loss; to annoy; *Am.* to deceive, swindle; **-se** to burn; to be hot.

quemazón *f.* (*calor*) burn, burning;

great heat; fire, conflagration; (*desazón*) pique, anger; bargain sale; *Am.* mirage on the pampas.

querella *f.* quarrel; complaint; controversy.

querellarse *v.* to complain.

querencia *f.* affection; longing; favorite spot; haunt; stable.

querer[41] *v. irr.* to want, wish, desire; to will; to be willing; to love; — **decir** to mean; **sin** — unwillingly; **no quiso hacerlo** he refused to do it; **quiere llover** it is trying to rain, it is about to rain; **como quiera** in any way; **como quiera que** since; no matter how; **cuando quiera** whenever; **donde quiera** wherever; anywhere; **-se** to love each other; *Ríopl., Ven., Col.* to be on the point of, be about to; **se quiere caer esa pared** that wall is about to fall.

querido *p.p.* wanted, desired; *adj.* beloved, dear; *m.* lover; **querida** *f.* darling; mistress.

quesería *f.* dairy, creamery, cheese factory; **quesera** *f.* dairy, cheese factory; cheese dish; dairymaid, woman cheese vendor or cheesemaker; **quesero** *adj.* pertaining to cheese; *m.* cheesemaker.

queso *m.* cheese; *Ven.* — **de higos** fig paste.

quicio *m.* hinge of a door; **sacar a uno de** — to exasperate someone.

quichua = **quechua**.

quiebra *f.* (*rotura*) break; crack; fissure; fracture; (*pérdida*) loss, damage; bankruptcy.

quien *rel. pron.* who, whom; he who, she who; **quién** *interr. pron.* who? whom?

quienquiera *pron.* whoever, whosoever, whomsoever.

quieto *adj.* quiet, still; calm.

quietud *f.* quiet, stillness, calmness.

quijada *f.* jaw; jawbone.

quilate *m.* carat (*twenty-fourth part in weight and value of gold*); unit of weight for precious stones and pearls; **-s** qualities; degree of perfection or purity.

quilla *f.* keel.

quimera *f.* absurd idea, wild fancy.

química *f.* chemistry.

químico *adj.* chemical; *m.* chemist.

quina, quinina *f.* quinine.

quincalla *f.* hardware.

quincallería *f.* hardware; hardware store; hardware trade.

quincena *f.* fortnight; semimonthly pay.

quinta *f.* (*casa*) villa, country house; (*militar*) draft. military conscription; (*cartas*) sequence of five cards.

quintaesencia *f.* quintessence, pure essence, purest form.

quiosco *m.* kiosk, small pavilion.

quirúrgico *adj.* surgical.

quisquilloso *adj.* touchy, oversensitive.

quisto: bien — well-liked, well received, welcome; **mal** — disliked;

unwelcome.

quitamanchas *m.* cleaner, stain remover.

quitar *v.* to remove; to take away (off, or from); to rob of; to deprive of; to subtract; to parry (*in fencing*); **-se** to take off (*clothing*); to remove oneself, withdraw; **-se de una cosa** to give up something, get rid of something; **-se a alguien de encima** to get rid of someone; **¡quita allá!** don't tell me that!; **¡quítese de aquí!** get out of here!

quitasol *m.* large sunshade, parasol.

quite *m.* parry (*in fencing*); dodge, dodging; *Ven., Col., Mex.* **andar a los -s** to be on the defensive; to take offense easily; to be afraid of one's own shadow; **eso no tiene** — that can't be helped.

quizá, quizás *adv.* perhaps, maybe.

R

rabadilla *f.* end of the spinal column; tail of a fowl; rump.

rábano *m.* radish; **tomar el — por las hojas** to take one thing for another; to misinterpret something.

rabia *f.* rabies; rage; **tener — a alguien** to hate someone; *Ríopl., Carib., Mex.* **volarse de** — to get furious, angry.

rabiar *v.* to have rabies; to rage; to rave; to suffer a severe pain; — **por** to be dying to or for, be very eager to; **quema que rabia** it burns terribly.

rabieta *f.* tantrum, fit of temper.

rabino *m.* rabbi.

rabioso *adj.* rabid (*having rabies*), mad; furious, angry, violent.

rabo *m.* tail; **de cabo a** — from beginning to end; **mirar con el — del ojo** to look out of the corner of one's eye.

racimo *m.* bunch; cluster.

raciocinio *m.* reasoning.

ración *f.* ration; allowance; supply.

racional *adj.* rational; reasonable.

racionamiento *m.* rationing.

racionar *v.* to ration.

radar *m.* radar.

radaroscopio *m.* radarscope.

radiación *f.* radiation; — **cósmica** cosmic radiation.

radiactividad *f.* radioactivity.

radiactivo *adj.* radioactive.

radiador *m.* radiator.

radiante *adj.* radiant; shining; beaming.

radiar *v.* to radiate; to radio; to broadcast.

radical *adj.* (*básico*) fundamental, basic; radical; (*extremista*) extreme; *m.* radical; root of a word.

radicar[6] *v.* to take root; to be, be found (*in a certain place*); **-se** to take root; to locate, settle.

radio *m.* radius; radium; *m. & f.* radio.

radiodifundir *v.* to broadcast by radio. *See* **difundir**.

radiodifusión *f.* broadcasting. *See* **difusión**.

radiodifusora, radioemisora *f.*

PU

broadcasting station.

radioescucha *m.* & *f.* radio listener.

radiofónico *adj.* radio (*used as adj.*); **estación radiofónica** radio station.

radiografía *f.* radiography, X-ray photography; X-ray picture.

radiografiar[17] *v.* to take X-ray pictures.

radiolocutor *m.* radio announcer. *See* **locutor.**

radiotelefonía *f.* radiotelephony, radio, wireless.

radiotelegrafía *f.* radiotelegraphy, radio, wireless telegraphy.

radioyente = radioescucha.

raer[24] *v. irr.* to scrape off; to rub off; to scratch off; to fray; to erase.

ráfaga *f.* gust of wind; flash of light.

raído *p.p.* & *adj.* scraped off; rubbed off; frayed; worn, threadbare.

raigón *m.* large root; root of a tooth.

raíz *f.* root; origin; foundation; — **cuadrada** square root; **a — de** close to, right after; **de —** by the roots, completely; **echar raíces** to take root, become firmly fixed.

raja *f.* slice; splinter; crack; split, crevice; **hacer -s** to slice; to tear into strips; to cut into splinters; **hacerse uno -s** to wear oneself out (*by dancing, jumping or any violent exercise*).

rajadura *f.* crack, crevice.

rajar *v.* to split; to crack; to cleave; to slice; to chatter; to brag; *Col., Cuba, Mex., Andes* to defame, insult; *Col.* to flunk, fail (*a student*); **-se** to split open; to crack; *Mex.* to get afraid, back down.

rajatablas *m. Col.* reprimand, scolding; **a —** in great haste.

ralea *f.* breed, race, stock; species, kind.

ralear *v.* to thin out, make less dense; to become less dense.

ralo *adj.* sparse, thin, thinly scattered.

rallador *m.* grater.

rallar *v.* to grate; to grate on, annoy; *Am.* to goad, spur.

rama *f.* branch, limb; **en —** crude, raw; **andarse por las -s** to beat about the bush, not to stick to the point.

ramada *f.* branches, foliage; arbor; *Am.* shed, tent.

ramaje *m.* foliage; branches.

ramal *m.* strand (*of a rope, etc.*); branch; branch railway line; halter.

ramera *f.* harlot, prostitute.

ramificarse[6] *v.* to branch off, divide into branches.

ramillete *m.* bouquet; flower cluster.

ramo *m.* bunch (*of flowers*), bouquet; line, branch (*of art, science, industry, etc.*); branch, bough; **domingo de -s** Palm Sunday.

ramonear *v.* to cut off twigs or tips of branches; to nibble grass, twigs, or leaves; *Am.* to eat scraps or leftovers.

rampa *f.* ramp; apron (*airport*); **— de cohetes, — de lanzamiento** launching ramp.

ramplón *adj.* coarse; crude, uncouth; slovenly.

ramplonería *f.* coarse act or remark; crudeness, coarseness; slovenliness.

rana *f.* frog.

rancio *adj.* rancid, stale; old (*wine*); **linaje —** old, noble lineage.

ranchero *m. Mex.* rancher, farmer; **ranchería** *f.* group of huts; *Col.* inn (*for* **arrieros**).

rancho *m.* camp; hamlet; mess (*meal for a group and the group itself*); *Carib., Ven., Col., Andes, Riopl.* hut; *Carib., Ven., Col., Andes, Riopl.* country house; *Mex.* ranch, small farm (*usually for cattle raising*).

rango *m.* rank, position.

ranura *f.* groove; slot.

rapar *v.* to shave off; to crop (*hair*); to strip bare, rob of everything.

rapaz *adj.* rapacious, grasping, greedy; *m.* lad; **rapaza** *f.* lass, young girl.

rapé *m.* snuff (*pulverized tobacco*).

rapidez *f.* rapidity, speed.

rápido *adj.* rapid, swift; *m.* rapids.

rapiña *f.* plunder; **ave de —** bird of prey.

rapiñar *v.* to plunder; to steal.

raposa *f.* fox,

raptar *v.* to kidnap, abduct.

rapto *m.* (*delito*) abduction, kidnapping; (*sentimiento*) ecstasy, rapture; outburst.

raqueta *f.* racket (*used in games*); tennis.

raquítico *adj.* rickety, feeble, weak, skinny, sickly.

rareza *f.* rarity; oddity; strangeness; freak; curiosity; queer act or remark; peculiarity; **por —** seldom.

raro *adj.* rare; thin, not dense; scarce; strange, odd; ridiculous; **rara vez** (*or* **raras veces**) rarely, seldom.

ras : a — de flush with, even with; **al — con** flush with; **estar — con —** to be flush, perfectly even.

rascacielos *m.* skyscraper.

rascar[6] *v.* to scratch; to scrape; *Andes* to dig up potatoes; *Am.* **— uno para adentro** to seek one's own advantage, look out for oneself.

rasete *m.* sateen.

rasgado *adj.* torn; open; *Col.* generous; *Am.* outspoken; **ojos -s** large, wide-open eyes.

rasgadura *f.* tear, rip, rent.

rasgar[7] *v.* to tear; to rip.

rasgo *m.* (*propiedad*) trait, characteristic; (*rúbrica*) stroke of the pen, flourish; (*hazaña*) feat; *Am.* irrigation ditch; *Ven.* **un — de terreno** a parcel of land; **-s** features; traits.

rasgón *m.* large tear, rent, rip.

rasguñar *v.* to scratch; to claw.

rasguño *m.* scratch.

raso *adj.* (*llano*) plain; flat, smooth; (*despejado*) clear, cloudless; *Riopl., Mex.* even, level (*when measuring wheat, corn, etc.*); *Am.* scarce, scanty; **soldado —** private; **al —** in the open air; *m.* satin.

raspadura *f.* scrape; scraping; erasure;

shaving (*of wood or metal*).

raspar *v.* to scrape, scrape off; to steal; *Andes* to scold, upbraid; *Col.* to leave.

rastra *f.* drag; sled; large rake; harrow; **a -s** dragging; unwillingly.

rastreador *m.* trailer, tracker, tracer.

rastrear *v.* to trail, track, trace; to rake, harrow; to drag (*a dragnet*); to skim, scrape the ground.

rastrero *adj.* low, vile.

rastrillar *v.* to rake; to comb (*flax or hemp*); *Ven.* to scrape; *Am.* to shoot; *Am.* to barter, exchange; *Am.* to pilfer, steal (*in stores*).

rastrillo *m.* rake; *Am.* barter, exchange; *Am.* business deal.

rastro *m.* track, trail, scent; trace, sign; rake, harrow; slaughterhouse.

rastrojo *m.* stubble.

rasura *f.* shave, shaving.

rasurar *v.* to shave.

rata *f.* rat; *m.* pickpocket.

ratear *v.* to pilfer; to pick pockets; to creep, crawl.

ratería *f.* petty larceny; meanness.

ratero *m.* pickpocket; *adj.* contemptible, mean.

ratificar[6] *v.* to ratify.

rato *m.* short time, little while; **buen —** pleasant time; long time; **-s perdidos** leisure hours; **a -s** at intervals, from time to time; **pasar el —** to while away the time, kill time; *Am.* **¡hasta cada —!** so long!; see you later!

ratón *m.* mouse; *Am.* **tener un —** to have a hangover; **ratonera** *f.* mouse-trap.

raudal *m.* torrent, downpour, flood; *Ríopl., Ch., Col., Ven., Andes* rapids.

raudo *adj.* rapid, swift.

raya *f.* line; dash; stripe; boundary line; part in the hair; *Mex.* pay, wage; *Mex.* **día de —** payday; **tener a —** to keep within bounds; to hold in check; **pasar de la —** to overstep one's bounds, take undue liberties; *m.* sting ray (*a species of fish*).

rayador *m. Mex.* paymaster; *Am.* umpire in a game.

rayar *v.* to line, make lines on; to streak; to scratch, mark; to cross out; *Mex.* to pay or collect wages; *Am.* to stop a horse all of a sudden; *Am.* to spur a horse to run at top speed; **— el alba** to dawn; **— en** to border on; *Am.* **-se uno** to help oneself; to get rich.

rayo *m.* ray, beam; lightning, thunder-bolt; spoke; **-s X** X-rays; **-s infra-rrojos** infrared rays.

raza *f.* race; clan; breed; fissure, crevice; **caballo de —** thorough-bred horse.

razón *f.* (*facultad*) reason; (*justicia*) right, justice; (*cuenta*) ratio; account, information, word, message; **— social** firm, firm name; **a — de** at the rate of; **¡con —!** no wonder!; **dar —** to inform; **dar la — a una persona** to admit that a person is right; **perder la —** to lose one's mind; **poner en —**

to pacify; **tener —** to be right.

razonable *adj.* reasonable.

razonamiento *m.* reasoning.

razonar *v.* to reason; to discourse, talk; to argue.

reabierto *p.p. of* **reabrir.**

reabrir[52] *v.* to reopen.

reacción *f.* reaction; **— nuclear** nuclear reaction; **— en cadena** chain reaction.

reaccionar *v.* to react.

reaccionario *adj. & m.* reactionary.

reacio *adj.* stubborn, obstinate.

reactor *m.* reactor; **— atómico** atomic reactor; **— nuclear** nuclear reactor.

reajustar *v.* to readjust.

reajuste *m.* readjustment.

real *adj.* real; royal; *m.* army camp; fairground; real (*Spanish coin worth one fourth of a peseta*); **-es** *Andes* money (*in general*); **levantar el —** (*or* **los -es**) to break camp.

realce *m.* (*adorno*) embossment, raised work, relief; (*lustre*) prestige; lustre, splendor; **dar —** to enhance; to emphasize.

realeza *f.* royalty (*royal dignity*).

realidad *f.* reality; truth; fact; **en —** really, truly, in fact.

realismo *m.* realism; royalism.

realista *adj.* realistic; royalist; *m.* realist; royalist.

realización *f.* realization, fulfillment; conversion into money, sale.

realizar[9] *v.* to realize, fulfill, make real; to convert into money; to sell out.

realzar[9] *v.* to emboss; to raise; to en-hance; to make stand out; to empha-size.

reanimar *v.* to revive; to comfort; to cheer; to encourage.

reanudación *f.* renewal.

reanudar *v.* to renew, resume, begin again.

reaparecer[13] *v. irr.* to reappear.

reasumir *v.* to resume.

reata *f.* lariat, rope, lasso.

reavivar *v.* to revive.

rebaja *f.* deduction; reduction; dis-count.

rebajar *v.* to diminish; to lower, re-duce; to tone down (*a painting*); to humiliate; **-se** to lower or humble oneself.

rebanada *f.* slice.

rebanar *v.* to slice.

rebaño *m.* flock; herd.

rebatir *v.* to beat over and over; to repel, resist; to refute; to rebut (*come back with an argument*); to argue; to parry (*in fencing*).

rebato *m.* alarm, call to arms; surprise attack.

rebelarse *v.* to rebel.

rebelde *adj.* rebellious; *m.* rebel; de-faulter (*one who fails to appear in court*).

rebeldía *f.* rebelliousness; defiance; de-fault, failure to appear in court; **en — ** in revolt.

rebelión f. rebellion, revolt.

rebencazo m. Riopl., Ch., Andes crack of a whip; Am. lash, stroke with a whip.

rebenque m. rawhide whip.

reborde m. edge, border.

rebosante adj. brimming, overflowing.

rebosar v. to overflow, brim over; to abound.

rebotar v. to rebound, bounce back or again; to make rebound; to repel, reject; to annoy, vex; **-se** to become vexed, upset; Col., Mex. to become cloudy or muddy (said of water); Am. **rebotársele a uno la bilis** to get angry, become upset.

rebote m. rebound, bounce; **de —** on the rebound; indirectly.

rebozar[9] v. to muffle up; **-se** to muffle oneself up; to wrap oneself up.

rebozo m. shawl; **sin —** frankly, openly.

rebullir[20] v. irr. to stir, move; to boil up.

rebusca f. research; search; searching; gleaning; residue.

rebuscar[6] v. to search thoroughly; to pry into; to glean.

rebuznar v. to bray.

rebuzno m. bray.

recabar v. to obtain, gain by entreaty.

recado m. message; errand; gift; daily food supply, daily marketing; precaution; equipment; Riopl., Andes saddle and trappings; **— de escribir** writing materials; **-s a** regards to.

recaer[24] v. irr. to fall (upon); to fall again; to relapse; to have a relapse.

recaída f. relapse; falling again.

recalar v. to saturate, soak through; to reach port; to come within sight of land; to land, end up, stop at; Am. **— con alguien** to "land" on somebody, take it out on somebody.

recalcar[6] v. to emphasize; to harp on; to press down.

recalcitrante adj. obstinate, disobedient, stubborn.

recalentar[1] v. irr. to reheat, warm over; to overheat, heat too much.

recamar v. to embroider (usually with gold or silver).

recámara f. dressing room; Mex., C.A., Col. bedroom; Riopl., Col. chamber for an explosive charge.

recapitular v. to recapitulate, sum up, tell briefly.

recargo m. overload; extra load; extra charge; increase (of fever); new charge, new accusation.

recatado adj. cautious, prudent; modest; p.p. concealed.

recatar v. to cover, conceal; **-se** to show timidity; to be cautious; to hide (from), shun.

recato m. caution, prudence; reserve, restraint, secrecy; modesty.

recaudación f. collection, collecting; office of tax collector.

recaudador m. tax collector.

recaudar v. to collect (money, taxes, rents, etc.).

recaudo m. collection, collecting; precaution; bond, security; Mex. spices, seasonings; Am. daily supply of vegetables; **estar a buen —** to be safe; **poner a buen —** to place in safety.

recelar v. to suspect, fear; **-se de** to be suspicious or afraid of.

recelo m. suspicion, fear.

receloso adj. suspicious, distrustful, fearful.

recepción f. reception; admission.

receptáculo m. receptacle.

receptivo adj. receptive, capable of receiving, quick to receive.

receptor m. receiver; adj. receiving.

receta f. recipe; prescription.

recetar v. to prescribe (a medicine).

recibidor m. receiver; reception room.

recibimiento m. reception; welcome; reception room; parlor.

recibir v. to receive; to admit, accept; to go out to meet; **— noticias de** to hear from; **-se de** to receive a title or degree of.

recibo m. (monetario) receipt; (acción) reception; (sala) reception room; parlor; **sala de —** reception room; **estar de —** to be at home for receiving callers; **ser de —** to be acceptable, be fit for use.

reciedumbre f. strength, force, vigor.

recién adv. recently, lately, newly (used before a past participle); Riopl., Ch., Andes just now; Riopl., Ch., Andes a short time ago; Riopl., Ch., Andes **— entonces** just then.

reciente adj. recent, new.

recinto m. enclosure; precinct.

recio adj. strong, robust; harsh; hard, severe; fast; adv. strongly; harshly; rapidly; hard; loud.

recipiente m. receptacle, container; recipient, receiver (he who receives).

recíproco adj. reciprocal, mutual.

recitación f. recitation, recital.

recital m. musical recital.

recitar v. to recite.

reclamación f. protest, complaint; claim, demand.

reclamador m. claimant; complainer.

reclamante m. & f. claimant; complainer; adj. complaining; claiming.

reclamar v. (protestar) to complain, protest (against); (exigir) to claim, demand; to lure, call back (a bird).

reclamo m. (protesta) protest; claim; advertisement; (llamada) call; bird call; decoy bird; lure.

reclinar v. to recline, lean; **-se** to recline, lean back.

recluir[32] v. irr. to seclude, shut up; **-se** to isolate oneself.

recluso m. recluse, hermit; adj. shut in, shut up.

recluta f. recruiting; Am. roundup of cattle; m. recruit.

reclutamiento m. recruiting; levy, draft.

reclutar v. to recruit, enlist; Am. to round up (cattle).

recobrar v. to recover, regain; **-se** to recover; to recuperate.

recobro m. recovery.

recodo m. bend, turn; elbow (of a road).

recoger[11] v. (juntar) to gather; to collect; to pick up; (ceñir) to take in, tighten; (abrigar) to shelter; **-se** to retire, go home; to withdraw; to seclude oneself; to take shelter.

recogimiento m. seclusion; concentration of thought, composure; retreat; collecting, gathering.

recolección f. collecting, gathering; harvest, crop; summary.

recolectar v. to harvest; to gather.

recomendable adj. praiseworthy, laudable; advisable.

recomendación f. recommendation; request.

recomendar[1] v. irr. to recommend; to commend, praise; to enjoin, urge; to advise.

recompensa f. recompense; compensation.

recompensar v. to recompense, reward; to compensate.

reconcentrar v. to concentrate, bring together; to hide in the depth of one's heart; **-se** to concentrate, become absorbed in thought, collect one's thoughts.

reconciliación f. reconciliation.

reconciliar v. to reconcile; **-se** to become reconciled.

recóndito adj. hidden, concealed; profound.

reconocer[13] v. irr. to recognize; to admit, acknowledge; to examine carefully; to reconnoiter, scout, explore

reconocimiento m. recognition; acknowledgment; gratitude; examination; scouting, exploring.

reconstruir[32] v. irr. to reconstruct, rebuild.

recontar[2] v. irr. to recount; to tell, relate.

recopilar v. to compile; to digest, make a digest of.

recordación f. recollection; remembrance.

recordar[2] v. irr. to remember; to recall; to remind; Am. to rouse, awaken; **-se** to remember; to wake up.

recordativo m. reminder; adj. reminding.

recordatorio m. reminder.

recorrer v. to go over; to travel over; to read over; to look over; to overhaul.

recorrido m. trip, run; mileage, distance traveled.

recortar v. to trim, clip; to shorten; to cut out (figures); to pare off; **-se** to project itself (as a shadow); to outline itself.

recorte m. clipping; cutting; outline; Mex. gossip, slander.

recostar v. to recline, lean; **-se** to recline, lean back.

recoveco m. turn, bend; nook; sly or underhanded manner.

recreación f. recreation.

recrear v. to entertain, amuse; to gratify, please; **-se** to amuse oneself; to take delight (in).

recreo m. recreation, entertainment; place of amusement.

recrudecer[13] v. to recur, break out again, flare up, become worse (said of an illness or evil).

rectángulo m. rectangle; adj. rectangular, right-angled.

rectificar[6] v. to rectify, correct, amend; to refine (liquors).

rectitud f. rectitude, uprightness, righteousness; straightness; accuracy.

recto adj. straight; right; just, honest; **ángulo —** right angle; m. rectum; adv. C.A. straight ahead.

rector m. college or university president; principal; rector, curate, priest.

recua f. drove of pack animals; drove, crowd.

recuento m. recount.

recuerdo m. remembrance; recollection; souvenir, keepsake; memory; **-s** regards; adj. Ríopl., Col., Ven. awake.

reculada f. recoil.

recular v. to recoil, spring back; to fall back, go back, retreat; to yield, back down.

recuperación f. recovery.

recuperar v. to recuperate, recover, regain; **-se** to recuperate, recover one's health.

recurrir v. to resort (to); to have recourse (to).

recurso m. recourse, resort; petition, appeal; **-s** means, resources; **sin —** without remedy; without appeal.

recusar v. to reject, decline.

rechazar[9] v. to reject; to repel, drive back; to rebuff.

rechifla f. hooting; hissing; ridicule.

rechiflar v. to hoot; to hiss; to ridicule.

rechinamiento m. creak; squeak; squeaking; gnashing.

rechinar v. to squeak; to creak; Am. to be furious, angry; Am. to grumble, growl; **— los dientes** to gnash one's teeth.

rechino = **rechinamiento**.

rechoncho adj. plump; chubby; squat.

rechuparse v. to smack one's lips.

red f. net; netting; network; snare; **redecilla** f. small net; mesh; hair net.

redacción f. (acto) wording; editing; (lugar) newspaper offices; editorial department; (cuerpo) editorial staff.

redactar v. to word, compose; to edit.

redactor m. editor.

redargüir[32] v. irr. to retort, answer back; to contradict, call in question; to reargue.

rededor m. surroundings; **al** (or **en**) **—** around, about.

redención f. redemption.

redentor m. redeemer, savior; **el Redentor** the Savior.

RE

redil *m.* sheepfold.

redimir *v.* to redeem; to ransom; to set free.

rédito *m.* interest, revenue, yield.

redituar[18] *v.* to produce, yield (*interest*).

redoblar *v.* to double; to clinch (*a nail*); to reiterate, repeat; to roll (*a drum*).

redoble *m.* roll (*of a drum*).

redoma *f.* flask, vial.

redomón *m. Ríopl.* half-tame horse or bull; *adj. Ríopl.* half-civilized, rustic.

redonda *f.* surrounding district, neighborhood; whole note (*music*); **a la —** all around, round-about.

redondear *v.* to round, make round; to round off; to round out.

redondel *m.* arena, bull ring; circle.

redondo *adj.* round; whole, entire; clear, evident; *Andes* stupid; *Mex.* honest; **en —** all around.

redopelo : a — against the grain.

redor *m.* round mat; **en —** around.

reducción *f.* reduction; cut, discount; decrease.

reducido *p.p.* & *adj.* reduced; compact, small.

reducir[25] *v. irr.* to reduce; to diminish; to convert (into); to reset (*a bone*); **-se** to adapt oneself, adjust oneself; to be constrained, forced.

reedificar[6] *v.* to rebuild, reconstruct.

reelección *f.* re-election.

reelegir[11] *v.* to re-elect.

reembolsar *v.* to reimburse, refund, repay, pay back.

reembolso *m.* reimbursement, refund.

reemitir *v.* to emit again; to issue again; to rebroadcast; to relay (*a broadcast*).

reemplazable *adj.* replaceable.

reemplazar[9] *v.* to replace; to substitute.

reemplazo *m.* replacement; substitute, substitution.

refacción *f.* (*alimento*) light lunch, refreshment; (*compostura*) repair, reparation; *Mex., Col.* spare part; *Carib.* help, aid, loan.

refajo *m.* underskirt; short skirt.

referencia *f.* reference; narration, account.

referente *adj.* referring.

referir[3] *v. irr.* to refer; to narrate; to relate; **-se** to refer (to), relate (to).

refinamiento *m.* refinement.

refinar *v.* to refine; to purify.

refinería *f.* refinery.

reflector *m.* reflector; floodlight.

reflejar *v.* to reflect; to think over; **-se** to be reflected.

reflejo *m.* reflection, image; reflex; *adj.* reflected; reflex.

reflexión *f.* reflection; meditation, consideration.

reflexionar *v.* to reflect, meditate, think over.

reflexivo *adj.* reflexive; reflective, thoughtful.

reflujo *m.* ebb; ebb tide.

reforma *f.* reform; reformation; improvement.

reformador *m.* reformer.

reformar *v.* to reform; to correct, amend; to improve; **-se** to reform.

reformista *m.* & *f.* reformer.

reforzar[2,9] *v. irr.* to reinforce; to strengthen.

refracción *f.* refraction.

refractario *adj.* refractory; impervious; rebellious, unruly; stubborn.

refrán *m.* popular proverb or saying.

refrenar *v.* to restrain, keep in check; to curb; to rein.

refrendar *v.* to legalize by signing; to countersign (*confirm by another signature*); **— un pasaporte** to visé a passport.

refrescante *adj.* refreshing.

refrescar[6] *v.* to refresh, renew; to cool; to get cool (*said of the weather*); **-se** to cool off; to take the fresh air; to take a cooling drink or refreshment; *Cuba, C.A.* to take an afternoon refreshment.

refresco *m.* refreshment.

refresquería *f. Mex., C.A., Ven.* refreshment shop, outdoor refreshment stand.

refriega *f.* strife, fray, scuffle.

refrigeración *f.* refrigeration; light meal or refreshment.

refrigerador *m. Am.* refrigerator, freezer; *adj.* refrigerating; freezing; refreshing.

refrigerio *m.* refreshment; relief, comfort; coolness.

refuerzo *m.* reinforcement.

refugiado *m.* refugee; *p.p. of* **refugiar**.

refugiar *v.* to shelter; **-se** to take shelter or refuge.

refugio *m.* refuge, shelter.

refulgente *adj.* refulgent, radiant, shining.

refundir *v.* to remelt, refound, recast (*metals*); to recast, rewrite, reconstruct.

refunfuñar *v.* to grumble, mumble, growl, mutter.

refunfuño *m.* grumble, growl; **refunfuñón** *adj.* grouchy; grumbly, grumbling.

refutar *v.* to refute.

regadera *f.* sprinkler; *Mex.* shower, bath.

regadío *adj.* irrigable, that can be irrigated; irrigated; *m.* irrigated land; **tierras de —** irrigable lands.

regalar *v.* (*dar*) to give, present as a gift; to regale; (*recrear*) to entertain; to delight, please; **-se** to treat oneself well, live a life of ease.

regalo *m.* present, gift; pleasure, delight; dainty, delicacy; luxury, comfort.

regañadientes : a — much against one's wishes; unwillingly.

regañar *v.* to growl; to grumble; to quarrel; to scold.

regaño *m.* scolding, reprimand.

regañón *adj.* grumbling; scolding; quarrelsome; *m.* growler, grumbler, scolder.

regar[1,7] v. irr. to irrigate; to water; to sprinkle, scatter; *Col.* to spill, throw off (*said of a horse*); **-se** *Am.* to scatter, disperse (*said of a group, herd, etc.*).

regatear v. to haggle, bargain; to dispute; to sell at retail; to race (*in a regatta or boat race*).

regazo m. lap.

regentar v. to direct, conduct, manage; **— una cátedra** to teach a course (*at a university*).

regente m. regent; manager; adj. ruling.

regidor m. councilman, alderman; adj. governing, ruling.

régimen m. regime; government, rule, management; **— lácteo** milk diet.

regimiento m. regiment; (*administrativo*) administration; municipal council; position of alderman.

regio adj. regal, royal; splendid, magnificent.

región f. region.

regir[5,11] v. irr. to rule, govern; to direct, manage; to be in force (*said of a law*); to move (*said of the bowels*).

registrador m. registrar, recorder; city clerk, official in charge of records; inspector (*in a customhouse*); adj. registering; **caja registradora** cash register.

registrar v. to examine, inspect, scrutinize; to register, record; **-se** to register, enroll.

registro m. search, inspection; registration; census; registration office; register; record; registration certificate; watch regulator; bookmark; organ stop; *Ven.* wholesale textile store.

regla f. (*precepto*) rule; ruler; order; precept, principle; (*medida*) measure, moderation; menstruation; **en —** in order, in due form; **por — general** as a general rule; usually.

reglamento m. regulations, rules; rule, bylaw.

regocijado adj. joyful, merry, gay; *p.p. of* **regocijar**.

regocijar v. to gladden, delight; **-se** to be glad; to rejoice.

regocijo m. joy; rejoicing.

regordete adj. plump.

regresar v. to return.

regreso m. return; **estar de —** to be back.

reguero m. stream, rivulet; trickle; irrigation ditch.

regulación f. regulation; adjustment.

regulador m. regulator; controller, governor (*of a machine*); adj. regulating.

regular v. to regulate; to adjust; adj. regular; ordinary; moderate; fair, medium; **por lo —** as a rule, usually; adv. fairly well.

regularidad f. regularity.

regularizar[9] v. to regulate, make regular.

rehacer[31] v. irr. to remake; to make over; to repair; **-se** to recover one's strength; to rally.

rehén m. hostage; **en rehenes** as a hostage.

rehuir[32] v. irr. to shun, avoid; to shrink (from).

rehusar v. to refuse; **-se a** to refuse to.

reina f. queen.

reinado m. reign.

reinante adj. reigning; prevailing.

reinar v. to reign; to rule; to prevail.

reincidir v. to relapse, slide back (into).

reino m. kingdom.

reintegro m. reimbursement, refund.

reír[15] v. irr. to laugh; **-se de** to laugh at; *Ríopl., Andes, Col., Ven., Carib.* **— de dientes para afuera** to laugh outwardly, laugh hypocritically.

reiterar v. to reiterate, repeat.

reja f. grate, grating; plowshare (*blade of the plow*); plowing; *Carib., C.A.* jail.

rejilla f. small grating, lattice; small latticed window; fireplace grate; cane upholstery; *Ch.* wire dish-cover.

rejonear v. to fight a bull from horseback (*Portuguese style*).

rejuvenecer[13] v. irr. to rejuvenate, make young; **-se** to become rejuvenated.

relación f. relation; story, account; long speech in a play; *Ríopl.* verse recited alternately by a couple in a folk dance; **-es** personal relations, connections; acquaintances.

relacionar v. to relate, connect; **-se** to be related, connected; to become acquainted, establish friendly connections.

relajación f., **relajamiento** m. relaxation; laxity; slackening; hernia.

relajar v. to relax; to slacken; to release from a vow or oath; **-se** to get a hernia or rupture; to become weakened; to become lax (*said of laws, customs, etc.*).

relajo m. *Carib., Mex.* disorderly conduct; lewdness; scandal.

relamerse v. to lick one's lips; to gloat; to boast; to slick oneself up.

relámpago m. lightning; flash.

relampaguear v. to lighten; to flash; to sparkle.

relampagueo m. flashing; sheet lightning.

relatar v. to relate, narrate.

relativo adj. relative; **— a** relative to, regarding.

relato m. narration, account, story.

relé m. relay; **— de televisión** television relay system.

relegar[7] v. to relegate, banish; to postpone; to set aside, put away.

relente m. night dampness; *Am.* fresh night breeze.

relevar v. to relieve; to release; to absolve; to replace, substitute; to emboss; to make stand out in relief.

relevo m. relief (*from a post or military duty; person who relieves another from the performance of a duty*).

relicario m. reliquary (*small box or*

RE

casket for keeping relics); Col., Ven., Cuba, Mex., Andes locket.

relieve m. relief, embossment, raised work; **-s** scraps, leftovers; **de —** in relief; prominent, outstanding; **poner de —** to make stand out; to emphasize.

religión f. religion.

religiosidad f. religiousness, piety; faithfulness.

religioso adj. religious; faithful; punctual; m. friar, monk.

relinchar v. to neigh.

relincho m. neigh.

reliquia f. relic; vestige; **-s** relics, remains.

reloj m. clock; watch; **— de pulsera** wristwatch; **— de sol** (or **— solar**) sundial; **— despertador** alarm clock.

reluciente adj. shining; sparkling.

relucir[13] v. irr. to glitter, sparkle; to shine.

relumbrante adj. brilliant, flashing, resplendent.

relumbrar v. to glare; to glitter.

relumbre m. glare, glitter.

rellenar v. to refill; to. fill up; to pad; to stuff.

relleno adj. stuffed; m. meat stuffing; filling.

remachar v. to clinch; to hammer down; to flatten; to rivet; to fix firmly; **-se** Am. to be tight-lipped, stubbornly silent.

remache m. clinching; fastening, securing; riveting; rivet.

remanente m. remainder, balance; remnant; residue.

remar v. to row; to struggle.

rematado adj. & p.p. (acabado) finished; (vendido en subasta) sold at auction; **loco —** completely crazy.

rematar v. (acabar) to finish; to end; to give the final or finishing stroke; (vender) to auction; (afianzar) to fasten (a stitch); Am. to stop (a horse) suddenly; Am. to buy or sell at auction; **-se** to be finished, be completely destroyed or ruined.

remate m. (fin) finish, end; (postura) highest bid at an auction; sale at auction; (punta) pinnacle, spire; Am. selvage, edge of a fabric; **de —** absolutely, without remedy; **loco de —** completely crazy, stark mad.

remedar v. to imitate; to mimic.

remediar v. to remedy; to help; to avoid.

remedio m. remedy; help; amendment; recourse, resort; **sin —** without help, unavoidable; **no tiene —** it can't be helped.

remedo m. imitation; mockery.

remembranza f. remembrance, memory.

rememorar v. to remember, call to mind.

remendar[1] v. irr. to mend, patch; to darn; to repair.

remendón m. cobbler, shoe repairman; mender, patcher.

remero m. rower.

remesa f. shipment; remittance, payment.

remesar v. to remit; to ship.

remiendo m. mend; mending; patch; darn; repair; **a -s** piecemeal, piece by piece.

remilgado adj. prudish, prim, affected.

remilgo m. prudery, primness, affectation.

reminiscencia f. reminiscence.

remisión f. (disculpa) remission; forgiveness; (remesa) remittance, remitting; (diminución) abatement, slackening; Mex., Ven anything shipped or sent.

remitente m. & f. sender; shipper.

remitir v. (enviar) to remit; to send; (diferir) to defer; to pardon; to refer; to abate; **-se** to defer, yield (to another's judgment).

remo m. oar; hard and long work; leg of a horse; **al —** at the oar; at hard labor.

remojar v. to soak; to steep; Am. to tip, bribe.

remojo m. soaking; steeping; Am. tip, bribe.

remolacha f. beet.

remolcador m. towboat, tug, tugboat; **lancha remolcadora** tugboat.

remolcar[6] v. to tow, tug; to take (a person) in tow.

remolino m. swirl, whirl; whirlwind; whirlpool; commotion; Ríopl. pin wheel; Am. ventilating wheel (fan); **— de gente** throng, crowd.

remolón adj. indolent, lazy.

remolque m. tow; towrope; **llevar a — to** tow; to take in tow.

remontar v. (alzar) to elevate, raise; (reparar) to repair, patch up; to resole; to revamp; Am. to go up; Ríopl., Carib., C.A., Ven., Col. to go upstream; **-se** to rise; to soar, fly upward; to date (from), go back (to); Ríopl. to take to the woods or hills.

rémora f. impediment, obstacle, hindrance.

remordimiento m. remorse.

remoto adj. remote, distant; improbable.

remover[2] v. irr. to remove; to dismiss; to stir.

rempujar v. to jostle, push.

rempujón m. jostle, push.

remuda f. change; substitution; replacement; change of clothes; spare tire; relay of horses; Am. spare horse, spare pack animal.

remudar v. to change; to replace.

remuneración f. remuneration, compensation, pay, reward.

remunerar v. to remunerate, compensate, pay, reward (for services).

renacer[13] v. irr. to be reborn; to spring up, grow up again.

renacimiento m. renascence, renaissance; revival; rebirth.

renco adj. lame.

rencor *m.* rancor, resentment, hatred, grudge.

rencoroso *adj.* resentful, spiteful.

rendición *f.* surrender; submission; yield, profit.

rendido *p.p. & adj.* tired out, fatigued; devoted; obsequious, servile.

rendija *f.* crack, crevice.

rendimiento *m.* yield, output, profit; surrender, submission; fatigue.

rendir[5] *v. irr.* to subdue; to surrender, hand over; to yield, produce; to fatigue; to render, do (*homage*); *Cuba, Ven.* — **la jornada** to end or suspend the day's work; **-se** to surrender, give up; to become fatigued, worn out.

renegado *m.* renegade, traitor; *adj.* renegade, disloyal; wicked.

renegar[1, 7] *v. irr.* to deny insistently; to detest; to blaspheme, curse; — **de** to deny, renounce (*one's faith*); *Am.* to hate, protest against.

renglón *m.* line (*written or printed*); item; *Riopl., Col., Ven., Mex., Carib., Andes* line of business, specialty.

renombrado *adj.* renowned, famous.

renombre *m.* renown, fame.

renovación *f.* renovation, restoration; renewal.

renovar[2] *v. irr.* to renovate; to renew; to replace.

renquear *v.* to limp.

renta *f.* rent, rental; income; revenue.

renuncia *f.* reluctance, unwillingness.

renuente *adj.* reluctant, unwilling.

renuevo *m.* (*vástago*) sprout, shoot; (*acto*) renovation, restoration.

renunciar *v.* to renounce; to resign; to refuse; to renege (*fail to follow suit in cards*).

reñidor *adj.* quarrelsome.

reñir[5, 19] *v. irr.* to quarrel; to fight; to scold.

reo *adj.* guilty; *m.* culprit, criminal; defendant.

reojo : mirar de — to look out of the corner of one's eye; to look scornfully.

repantigarse[7] *v.* to lounge, stretch out (*in a chair*).

reparación *f.* reparation; repair; indemnity.

reparar *v.* (*renovar*) to repair; to regain; to recover; (*corregir*) to make amends for, atone for; to remedy; to ward off (*a blow*); *Am.* to rear, buck (*said of horses*); — **en** to observe, notice.

reparo *m.* (*arreglo*) repair; restoration; (*observación*) notice; observation; (*duda*) doubt, objection; (*abrigo*) shelter; parry (*fencing*); *Mex.* sudden bound or leap of a horse.

repartimiento *m.* distribution, division; assessment.

repartir *v.* to distribute; to allot.

reparto *m.* distribution; mail delivery; cast of characters.

repasar *v.* to review, look over, go over again; to mend (*clothes*); to pass by

again.

repaso *m.* review; revision.

repelente *adj.* repellent, repulsive, repugnant.

repeler *v.* to repel; to reject.

repente *m.* sudden movement; *Am.* attack, fit; **de —** suddenly.

repentino *adj.* sudden.

repercutir *v.* to resound, echo back; to rebound; to reflect back (*as light*).

repetición *f.* repetition.

repetido *p.p.* repeated; **repetidas veces** repeatedly, often.

repetir[5] *v. irr.* to repeat; to belch.

repicar[6] *v.* (*tañer*) to chime, ring; (*hacer menudo*) to mince, chop fine; *Carib., Ven.* to drum, tap (*with the fingers or heels*); **-se** to boast; to be conceited.

repique *m.* (*tañido*) chime, ringing, peal; (*acción de picar*) mincing, chopping.

repiquetear *v.* to chime, ring; to jingle; *Am.* to tap (*with fingers or heels*).

repiqueteo *m.* chiming, ringing; jingling, tinkling; *Riopl., Carib., Ven.* clicking sound of heels.

repisa *f.* shelf, ledge; sill; wall bracket; — **de ventana** window sill.

replegar[1, 7] *v. irr.* to fold, pleat; **-se** to retreat, fall back.

réplica *f.* reply, answer, retort; replica, copy; *Am. m.* examiner.

replicar[6] *v.* to reply, answer back; to retort.

repliegue *m.* fold, crease; retreat (*of troops*).

repollo *m.* cabbage.

reponer[40] *v. irr.* (*devolver*) to replace, put back; to restore; (*contestar*) to reply, retort; **-se** to recover one's health or fortune; to collect oneself, become calm.

reportaje *m.* newspaper report; reporting.

reportar *v.* to check, control, restrain; to attain, obtain; to bring; to carry; *Am.* to report; **-se** to control oneself.

reporte *m.* report, news.

repórter, reportero *m.* reporter.

reposado *p.p. & adj.* reposed; quiet, calm; restful.

reposar *v.* to repose; to rest; to lie buried; **-se** to settle (*said of sediment*).

reposición *f.* replacement; recovery (*of one's health*).

reposo *m.* repose, rest; calm.

repostada *f.* sharp answer, back talk.

reprender *v.* to reprimand, scold.

reprensible *adj.* reprehensible, deserving reproof.

reprensión *f.* reproof, rebuke.

represa *f.* dam; damming, stopping; *Col., Ven.* reservoir.

represalia *f.* reprisal.

represar *v.* to bank, dam; to recapture (*a ship*) from the enemy; to repress, check.

representación *f.* representation; play, performance; authority, dignity; petition, plea.

RE

representante adj. representing; m. & f. representative; actor.

representar v. (declarar) to represent; to declare, state; to express, show; (actuar) to act, play, perform; -se to imagine, picture to oneself.

representativo adj. representative.

represión f. repression, control, restraint.

reprimenda f. reprimand, rebuke.

reprimir v. to repress, check, curb; -se to repress oneself; to refrain.

reprobar² v. irr. to reprove, blame; to condemn; to flunk, fail.

reprochar v. to reproach.

reproche m. reproach.

reproducción f. reproduction.

reproducir²⁵ v. irr. to reproduce.

reptil m. reptile.

república f. republic.

republicano adj. & m. republican.

repudiar v. to repudiate; to disown.

repuesto m. stock, supply, provisions; sideboard; **de —** spare, extra; p.p. of **reponer** & adj. recovered (from an illness, loss, fright, etc.); replaced; restored.

repugnancia f. repugnance, disgust; aversion; dislike, reluctance.

repugnante adj. repugnant, disgusting, loathsome.

repugnar v. to be repugnant; to disgust; to oppose, contradict.

repulido adj. polished up, slick; shiny; spruce.

repulsa f. repulse; rebuff; rebuke.

repulsar v. to repulse, repel, reject.

repulsivo adj. repulsive, repugnant.

reputación f. reputation.

reputar v. to repute.

requebrar¹ v. irr. to compliment; to flatter; to flirt with; to court, woo; to break again.

requemado p.p. & adj. burned; parched; tanned, sunburned.

requemar v. to parch, dry up; to burn; to overcook; -se to become overheated; to burn inwardly; to get tanned, sunburned.

requerimiento m. requisition; requirement; summons; -s amorous advances, insinuations.

requerir³ v. irr. (exigir) to require; to need; to summon; (indagar) to examine, investigate; (avisar) to notify; **— de amores** to court, woo.

requesón m. cottage cheese.

requiebro m. flattery; compliment.

requisito m. requirement, requisite; **— previo** prerequisite.

res f. head of cattle; any large animal.

resabio m. disagreeable aftertaste; bad habit.

resaca f. undertow; surge, surf; redraft (of a bill of exchange); Am. beating, thrashing; Mex., Riopl. mud and slime (left by a flood).

resaltar v. to stand out; to project, jut out; to rebound, bounce or spring back; to be evident, obvious.

resarcir¹⁰ v. to indemnify, compensate,

repay; to make amends for; -se de to make up for.

resbaladero m. slide, slippery place.

resbaladizo adj. slippery.

resbalar v. to slide; -se to slip; to slide; to skid; **resbalársele a uno una cosa** to let a thing slide off one's back, be impervious to a thing.

resbalón m. sudden or violent slip; slide; error; **darse un —** to slip.

resbaloso adj. slippery.

rescatar v. to ransom; to redeem; to barter, exchange, trade; Am. to resell.

rescate m. ransom; redemption; barter, exchange.

rescoldo m. embers, hot cinders, hot ashes; doubt, scruple.

resecar⁶ v. to dry up; to parch.

reseco adj. very dry; dried up, parched; thin, skinny.

resentimiento m. resentment; impairment, damage (to one's health).

resentirse³ v. irr. (tener pesar) to show resentment, hurt, or grief; to resent; (empeorar) to weaken; to become worse.

reseña f. military review; book review; brief account; sign, signal.

reseñar v. to review (a book); to review (troops); to outline briefly, give a short account of.

resero m. Riopl. cowboy, herdsman; Am. dealer in livestock.

reserva f. reserve; reservation; exception; caution; **a — de** reserving the right to, intending to; **sin —** without reserve, frankly.

reservación f. reservation.

reservar v. to reserve; to put aside; to postpone; to exempt; to keep secret; -se to conserve one's strength, spare oneself (for another time).

resfriado m. cold (illness); p.p. of **resfriar**; adj. Riopl. indiscreet.

resfriar¹⁷ v. to cool; to chill; -se to catch cold; to cool.

resfrío m. chill; cold.

resguardar v. to guard, defend; to shield; -se de to guard oneself against; to seek shelter from.

resguardo m. defense; security; guarantee; guard.

residencia f. residence; office or post of a resident foreign minister; Am. luxurious dwelling.

residente adj. resident, residing; m. & f. resident, dweller; resident foreign minister; Col., C.A., Riopl. alien resident.

residir v. to reside; to live, dwell; to be inherent, belong (to).

residuo m. residue; remainder.

resignación f. resignation.

resignar v. to resign; to hand over; -se to resign oneself.

resina f. resin.

resistencia f. resistance.

resistente adj. resistant; resisting.

resistir v. to resist; to tolerate, endure; -se to resist, struggle.

resolución f. (ánimo) resolution; courage, determination; (*resultado*) solution; **en** — in brief.

resolver[2,52] *v. irr.* to resolve, decide; to solve; to dissolve; **-se** to resolve, decide; to be reduced (to), dissolve (into).

resollar[2] *v. irr.* to breathe hard; to pant.

resonar[2] *v. irr.* to resound.

resoplar *v.* to puff, breathe hard; to snort.

resoplido *m.* puff, pant; snort.

resorte *m.* spring; elasticity; means (*to attain an object*); *Col.* elastic, rubber band; *Ven.* **no es de mi** — it doesn't concern me.

respaldar *v.* to endorse; to guarantee; *Am.* to back, support; **-se** to lean back; *Ch.* to protect one's rear.

respaldo *m.* back (*of a chair or sheet of paper*); protecting wall; endorsement; *Am.* protection, security, guarantee.

respectivo *adj.* respective.

respecto *m.* respect, relation, reference; point, matter; (**con**) — **a** (*or* — **de**) with respect to, with regard to.

respetable *adj.* respectable.

respetar *v.* to respect.

respeto *m.* respect; reverence, regard; consideration.

respetuoso *adj.* respectful; respectable.

respingar[7] *v.* to buck; to balk (*said of a horse*); to grumble; to curl up (*said of the edge of a garment*).

respingo *m.* buck, balking; muttering; grumbling.

respiración *f.* respiration, breathing.

respirar *v.* to breathe.

respiro *m.* breathing; breath; respite, pause, moment of rest; extension of time (*for payment*).

resplandecer[13] *v. irr.* to shine; to glitter.

resplandeciente *adj.* resplendent, shining.

resplandor *m.* splendor, brilliance, brightness; *Am.* sun's glare.

responder *v.* to respond; to answer; to correspond, harmonize; to answer (for), be responsible (for).

respondón *adj.* saucy, pert, insolent (*in answering*).

responsabilidad *f.* responsibility.

responsable *adj.* responsible.

respuesta *f.* response; answer, reply.

resquebradura, resquebrajadura *f.* fissure, crevice, crack.

resquebrajar = **resquebrar**.

resquebrar[1] *v. irr.* to crack; to split.

resquicio *m.* crack, slit, crevice; opening; *Col., Ven., Mex.* vestige, sign, trace.

resta *f.* subtraction (*as an arithmetical operation*); remainder.

restablecer[13] *v. irr.* to re-establish; to restore; **-se** to recover.

restante *adj.* remaining; *m.* residue, remainder.

restañar *v.* to staunch (*a wound*); to check the flow of.

restar *v.* to deduct; to subtract; to re-

main, be left over; to strike back (*a ball*).

restauración *f.* restoration.

restaurante *m.* restaurant.

restaurar *v.* to restore; to recover; to re-establish; to repair.

restitución *f.* restitution, restoration, return.

restituir[32] *v. irr.* to return, give back; to restore.

resto *m.* rest, remainder; stakes at cards; return (*of a tennis ball*); player who returns the ball; **-s** remains.

restorán *m. Am.* restaurant.

restregar[1,7] *v. irr.* to rub hard; to scrub.

restricción *f.* restriction; restraint; curb; limitation.

restringir[11] *v.* to restrict; to restrain; to limit.

resucitar *v.* to resuscitate, bring to life; to come to life; to revive.

resuelto *p.p. of* **resolver** resolved, determined; *adj.* resolute, bold; quick.

resuello *m.* breath; breathing, panting.

resulta *f.* result; effect, consequence; **de -s** as a result, in consequence.

resultado *m.* result, effect, consequence.

resultante *adj.* resulting; *f.* resultant (*force*).

resultar *v.* to result; to spring, arise as a consequence; to turn out to be; **resulta que** it turns out that.

resumen *m.* résumé, summary; **en** — summing up, in brief.

resumidero *m. Am.* = **sumidero**.

resumir *v.* to summarize, sum up; **-se** to be reduced or condensed.

resurgir[11] *v.* to arise again; to reappear.

retablo *m.* altarpiece; religious picture hung as a votive offering; series of pictures that tell a story.

retaguardia *f.* rear guard.

retal *m.* remnant.

retar *v.* to challenge, defy; to reprimand, scold; *Ch., Andes* to insult.

retardar *v.* to retard, delay.

retazo *m.* remnant; piece; fragment.

retener[45] *v. irr.* to retain; to keep; to withhold; to detain.

retintín *m.* jingle, tinkle; sarcastic tone or ring.

retirada *f.* retreat; withdrawal.

retirado *p.p. & adj.* retired; distant, remote; isolated; pensioned.

retirar *v.* to withdraw; to take away; **-se** to retire, withdraw; to retreat.

retiro *m.* retreat; retirement; withdrawal; place of refuge; pension of a retired officer.

reto *m.* challenge; defiance; *Riopl.* scolding; *Andes* insult.

retobado *adj. Col., Riopl.* saucy; *Andes* stubborn, unruly; *Andes* peevish; *Am.* sly, astute.

retobar *v. Col., Andes* to cover with leather; *Am.* to wrap with leather, oilcloth, or burlap; *Am.* to tan (*leather*); **-se** *Riopl.* to rebel, talk back, act saucy; *Andes, Col.* to become disagreeable and aloof.

retocar[6] *v.* to retouch, touch up; to

finish, perfect.

retoñar v. to sprout; to bud; to sprout again; to reappear.

retoño m. sprout, shoot; bud.

retoque m. retouching; finishing touch.

retorcer[2,10] v. irr. to twist; to retort; to distort; **-se** to wriggle; to squirm.

retorcimiento m. twisting; squirming.

retórica f. rhetoric.

retornar v. to return; to give back.

retorno m. return; repayment; barter.

retozar[9] v. to gambol, frisk about, frolic, romp; to stir within (said of passions).

retozo m. frolic; **retozón** adj. frisky, playful.

retractarse v. to retract, take back one's word.

retraer[46] v. irr. to withdraw, draw back, take back; **-se de** to withdraw from; to keep aloof or away from; to shun.

retraimiento m. retirement; reserve, aloofness, shyness.

retranca f. Cuba brake; **retranquero** m. Am. brakeman.

retrancar[6] v. Cuba to brake, put the brake on; Cuba **se ha retrancado el asunto** the affair has come to a standstill.

retrasado p.p. & adj. behind time; backward; postponed, delayed.

retrasar v. to delay, retard; to set back; to go backward; **-se** to fall behind; to be late, behind time.

retraso m. delay.

retratar v. to portray; to photograph; to copy, imitate; **-se** to be portrayed; to be photographed; to be reflected.

retrato m. portrait; photograph; copy, imitation; reflection.

retrete m. toilet, water closet; place of retreat.

retroceder v. to turn back; to fall back, draw back; to recede.

retroceso m. retrogression, backward step; retreat; setback, relapse.

retruécano m. pun.

retumbar v. to resound; to rumble.

retumbo m. loud echo or sound; rumble (of thunder, cannon, etc.).

reuma m. & f., **reumatismo** m. rheumatism.

reunión f. reunion; meeting.

reunir v. to reunite; to unite; to group; to gather; to assemble; to collect; **-se** to meet, assemble; to reunite.

revancha f. revenge; return game or match.

revelación f. revelation.

revelador adj. revealing; m. developer (in photography).

revelar v. to reveal; to develop (a film).

revendedor m. retailer; reseller; ticket scalper.

reventa f. resale.

reventar[1] v. irr. (estallar) to burst; to burst forth; to explode; to smash; (fatigar) to fatigue, exhaust; to bother; **-se** to burst; to blow out, explode.

reventón m. burst, bursting; blowout; steep hill; hard work, toil; adj. bursting.

reverdecer[13] v. irr. to grow fresh and green again; to gain new strength and vigor.

reverencia f. reverence; bow.

reverenciar v. to revere, venerate.

reverendo adj. reverend; Cuba, Riopl., Mex., Andes large, big (ironically).

reverente adj. reverent.

reverso m. reverse; back side.

revertir[3] v. irr. to revert.

revés m. reverse; back, wrong side; back stroke or slap; backhanded thrust (in fencing); misfortune; **al —** backwards; wrong side out; in the opposite way; from left to right.

revestir[5] v. irr. to dress, clothe; to coat, cover with a coating; **-se** to dress, put on an outer garment or vestment; to be invested (with power, authority, etc.); **-se de paciencia** to arm oneself with patience.

revisar v. to revise; to review; to examine, inspect.

revisión m. revision; review (of a case), new trial.

revisor m. corrector; inspector, overseer.

revista f. (inspección) review; inspection; (publicación) magazine, journal; (proceso) second trial or hearing; **pasar —** to pass in review; to examine carefully; to review (troops).

revistar v. to review, inspect (troops).

revivir v. to revive.

revocación f. repeal, cancellation.

revocar[6] v. to revoke, repeal.

revolcar[6] v. (derribar) to knock down; to turn over and over; to floor, defeat; (suspender) to fail, flunk; **-se** to wallow, to roll over and over; to flounder.

revolotear v. to fly about, flutter around; to hover; to circle around.

revoltijo, revoltillo m. jumble, mixture, mess; tangle, muddle; **revoltillo de huevos** scrambled eggs.

revoltoso adj. turbulent, unruly, rebellious; mischievous; intricate; m. agitator, troublemaker; rebel.

revolución f. revolution.

revolucionario adj. revolutionary; m. revolutionist, revolutionary.

revolver[2] v. irr. to revolve; to turn over; to stir up; to mix up; to turn around swiftly (a horse); **-se** to move back and forth; to roll over and over; to change (said of the weather).

revólver m. revolver, pistol.

revuelo m. whirl; stir, commotion; flying around.

revuelta f. revolt, revolution; second turn; turn, bend; quarrel, fight; Am. sudden turning of a horse.

revuelto p.p. of **revolver** & adj. confused; mixed up; intricate, complicated; choppy (sea); changeable (weather); **huevos -s** scrambled eggs.

rey m. king.

reyerta f. quarrel, dispute.

rezagado adj. back, behind; m. straggler, slowpoke, latecomer.

rezagar[7] *v.* to leave behind; to separate (*the weak cattle*) from the herd; *Am.* to reserve, set aside; **-se** to lag behind.

rezar[9] *v.* to pray; to say or recite (*a prayer*); to mutter, grumble; **así lo reza el libro** so the book says; **eso no reza conmigo** that has nothing to do with me.

rezo *m.* prayer.

rezongar[7] *v.* to grumble, growl, mutter.

rezongón *adj.* growling, grumbling; *m.* grumbler, growler; scolder.

rezumar *v.* to ooze; to leak; **se rezuma** it oozes, it seeps through.

ría *f.* mouth of a river, estuary.

riachuelo *m.* rivulet, brook.

ribazo *m.* bank, ridge.

ribera *f.* shore, bank, beach.

ribereño *adj.* of, pertaining to, or living on, a river bank.

ribete *m.* trimming, border, edge, binding; addition; **tiene sus -s de poeta** he is something of a poet.

ribetear *v.* to bind, put a binding on; to border, trim the edge or border of.

ricacho *adj.* quite rich (*often said sarcastically*); **ricachón** *adj.* extremely rich, disgustingly rich.

rico *adj.* rich, wealthy; delicious; exquisite; **ricote** = **ricacho**.

ridiculizar[9] *v.* to ridicule, deride.

ridículo *adj.* ridiculous; queer, strange; *m.* ridicule; ridiculous situation; **hacer el —** to be ridiculous; to act the fool.

riego *m.* irrigation; watering.

riel *m.* rail; **-es** track, railroad track.

rienda *f.* rein, bridle; moderation, restraint; **a — suelta** with free rein, without restraint; violently, swiftly; **soltar la —** to let loose, act without restraint; **tirar las -s** to draw rein, tighten the reins; to restrain.

riente *adj.* laughing, smiling.

riesgo *m.* risk.

rifa *f.* raffle; scuffle, quarrel.

rifar *v.* to raffle; to scuffle, quarrel.

rifle *m.* rifle.

rigidez *f.* rigidity, stiffness; severity, strictness.

rígido *adj.* rigid, stiff; severe, strict.

rigor *m.* rigor; severity; harshness; rigidity, stiffness; **en —** in reality; strictly; **ser de —** to be absolutely indispensable, be required by custom.

rigoroso, riguroso *adj.* rigorous; harsh; severe; strict.

rima *f.* rhyme; **-s** poems.

rimar *v.* to rhyme.

rimbombante *adj.* high-sounding; resounding.

rimero *m.* pile, heap.

rincón *m.* corner; nook; *Am.* narrow valley.

rinconada *f.* corner; nook.

rinconera *f.* corner cupboard, corner table, corner bracket.

ringlera *f.* tier, row, line.

rinoceronte *m.* rhinoceros.

riña *f.* quarrel, dispute, fight.

riñón *m.* kidney; center, interior.

río *m.* river.

ripio *m.* rubble, stone or brick fragments; padding (*in a verse, speech, etc.*), useless word.

riqueza *f.* riches; wealth.

risa *f.* laugh; laughter; **reventar de —** to burst with laughter; **tomar a —** to take lightly; to laugh off.

risada *f.* gale of laughter, loud laugh.

risco *m.* rocky cliff, crag; honey fritter.

risible *adj.* laughable, ridiculous.

risotada *f.* guffaw, big laugh.

ristra *f.* string (*of onions, garlic, etc.*); series, row.

risueño *adj.* smiling; pleasant; delightful.

rítmico *adj.* rhythmical.

ritmo *m.* rhythm.

rito *m.* rite, ceremony.

rival *m. & f.* rival, competitor; enemy.

rivalidad *f.* rivalry, competition; enmity.

rivalizar[9] *v.* to rival, compete.

rizado *p.p.* curled; *adj.* wavy, curly; *m.* curling; curls.

rizar[9] *v.* to curl; to ripple; to ruffle, gather into ruffles; **-se** to curl one's hair; to curl.

rizo *m.* curl; *adj.* curly; **rizoso** *adj.* curly.

roano *adj.* roan (*red, bay, or chestnut-colored, mixed with white; applied to a horse*).

robar *v.* to rob, steal; to abduct, kidnap.

roble *m.* oak tree; oak wood; **robledal, robledo** *m.* oak grove.

robo *m.* robbery, theft; loot, plunder.

robusto *adj.* robust, vigorous.

roca *f.* rock, boulder; rocky cliff, crag.

rocalloso *adj.* rocky.

roce *m.* graze; friction; contact; **no tener — con** to have no contact with (*a person*).

rociada *f.* sprinkling; spray; dew; sprinkle, shower; volley of harsh words.

rociar[17] *v.* to sprinkle; to spray; to fall (*said of dew*).

rocín *m.* nag, hack; draft horse; coarse, ill-bred man; *Ríopl., Mex., Andes* riding horse.

rocío *m.* dew; sprinkle; shower; spray; *adj. Am.* reddish, roan (*horse*).

rocoso *adj.* rocky.

rodada *f.* rut, wheel track; *Ríopl.* tumble, fall.

rodado *adj.* dapple (*horse*); *p.p.* of **rodar**.

rodadura *f.* rolling; rut; **— del neumático** tire tread.

rodaja *f.* disk; small wheel; round slice.

rodaje *m.* works (*of a watch*); **— de película** the filming of a movie.

rodar[2] *v. irr.* to roll; to revolve; to roam, wander about; to fall down (*rolling*); *Am.* **— a patadas** to kick down.

rodear *v.* to go around; to go by a roundabout way; to surround, encircle; *Ríopl., Cuba, Ven.* to round up (*cattle*).

RE

rodela f. round shield; *Mex.* padded ring for carrying loads on the head; *Am.* round slice; *Am.* kettle lid; *Am.* hoop; *Am.* game of rolling a hoop.

rodeo m. detour, roundabout way; circumlocution, roundabout expression; dodge, evasion; corral, stockyard; rodeo, roundup.

rodilla f. knee; **de -s** on one's knees; **hincarse de -s** to kneel down.

rodillo m. roller; rolling pin; road roller.

roer⁵¹ v. irr. to gnaw; to corrode, eat away; to torment, harass.

rogar²,⁷ v. irr. to pray, beg, beseech; **hacerse de —** to let oneself be coaxed.

rojez f. redness.

rojizo adj. reddish.

rojo adj. red; red, radical.

rojura f. redness.

rollizo adj. plump; m. log.

rollo m. roll; bundle; rolling pin; log.

romadizo m. nasal catarrh, head cold.

romance adj. Romance, Romanic (*language*); m. Romance language; Spanish language; romance, chivalric novel; ballad; eight-syllable meter with even verses rhyming in assonance; **en buen —** in plain language.

románico adj. Romanesque (*architecture*); Romance (*language*).

romano adj. & m. Roman.

romanticismo m. romanticism.

romántico adj. romantic; sentimental; m. romantic; sentimentalist.

romería f. pilgrimage.

romero m. pilgrim; rosemary (*shrub*).

romo adj. blunt; snub-nosed.

rompe: de — y rasga resolute, bold; **al —** *Am.* suddenly.

rompecabezas m. puzzle, riddle.

rompeolas m. breakwater, mole.

romper⁵² v. to break; to shatter; to tear; to wear through; *Ven.* to leave suddenly or on the run; **— el alba** to dawn; **— a** to start to; **-se** to break.

rompiente m. shoal, sand bank, reef; **-s** breakers, surf.

rompimiento m. rupture, break; crack; breach; quarrel.

ron m. rum.

roncar⁶ v. to snore; to roar; to brag.

ronco adj. hoarse; harsh-sounding.

roncha f. hive; welt.

ronda f. patrol; night serenaders; round (*of a game, of drinks, etc.*); *Ríopl., C.A., Andes* ring-around-a-rosy (*a children's game*); **hacer la — a** to court; *Am.* to surround, trap (*an animal*).

rondar v. to go around, hover around; to patrol; to make the rounds; to serenade.

ronquera f. hoarseness.

ronquido m. snore; snort.

ronronear v. to purr.

ronroneo m. purr.

ronzal m. halter.

roña f. scab, mange; filth; infection; stinginess; trickery; *Ríopl., Col., Ven.,*

Cuba ill will, grudge; *Am.* **hacer —** to fake an illness.

roñoso adj. scabby, mangy; dirty; stingy; *Carib., Mex.* spiteful; *Am.* fainthearted, cowardly.

ropa f. clothing, clothes; **— blanca** linen; **— vieja** old clothes; stew made from leftover meat; **a quema —** at close range (*when shooting*); suddenly, without warning.

ropaje m. clothes, clothing, apparel; robe.

ropero m. clothier; wardrobe, clothespress; wardrobe keeper; *Am.* clothes rack.

roqueño adj. rocky; hard, like rock.

rosa f. rose; red spot on the skin; rose color; *Ch., Mex.* rosebush; **— de los vientos** (*or* **— náutica**) mariner's compass.

rosado adj. rosy, rose-colored; frosted (*drink*); *Am.* roan, reddish-brown (*horse*).

rosal m. rosebush.

rosario m. rosary; **— de desdichas** chain of misfortunes.

rosbif m. roast beef.

rosca f. screw and nut; screw thread; spiral, twist; ring-shaped roll; *Mex., Ven., Col.* ring-shaped cushion (*for carrying loads on the head*); *Am.* circle of card players.

roseta f. rosette; small rose; **-s** popcorn; **rosetón** m. large rosette; rose window.

rosillo adj. light red; roan (*horse*).

rostro m. face; **hacer —** to face.

rota f. rout, defeat; ship's course; Rota (*ecclesiastical court*); rattan palm tree.

rotación f. rotation.

rotario m. member of the Rotary Club.

rotativo adj. rotary; f. printing press.

rotatorio adj. rotary.

roto p.p. irr. of **romper** & adj. broken; shattered; torn; worn out, ragged; m. *Ch.* person of the poorer class.

rotular v. to label; to letter.

rótulo m. title, inscription; label.

rotundo adj. round; sonorous; **una negativa rotunda** a flat denial.

rotura f. breach, opening; break; tear, rip; rupture; fracture.

roturar v. to break ground; to plow (*new ground*).

rozadura f. friction; chafe; chafing.

rozamiento m. friction; rubbing.

rozar⁹ v. to graze; to scrape; to chafe; to clear of underbrush; **-se con alguien** to have connections, contact, or dealings with someone.

rozón m. graze, sudden or violent scrape; short, broad scythe.

ruana f. *Col., Ven.* a woolen poncho.

ruano = roano.

rubí m. ruby.

rubicundo adj. reddish; ruddy, healthy red; reddish-blond.

rubio adj. blond, blonde.

rubor m. blush; bashfulness, shyness.

ruborizarse⁹ v. to blush; to feel ashamed.

rúbrica f. scroll, flourish (*added to a signature*); title, heading; **de —** according to ritual, rule, or custom.

rucio adj. grey (*horse or donkey*); **— rodado** dapple-grey.

rudeza f. rudeness; coarseness; roughness.

rudo adj. rude; coarse; rough; stupid.

rueca f. distaff (*used for spinning*).

rueda f. (*maquina*) wheel; circle; spread of a peacock's tail; round object; (*grupo*) circle; group; **en —** in turn; in a circle; **hacer la — a** to court; to flatter.

ruedo m. circuit, tour; border, rim; circumference.

ruego m. prayer, supplication, request.

rufián m. ruffian; bully.

rugido m. roar; rumbling.

rugir[11] v. to roar; to bellow.

rugoso adj. wrinkled; furrowed.

ruibarbo m. rhubarb.

ruidazo m. big noise.

ruido m. noise; din; dispute; talk, rumor; **hacer** (*or* **meter**) **—** to make a noise; to create a sensation; to cause a disturbance.

ruidoso adj. noisy; loud; sensational.

ruin adj. (*vicioso*) vile, base, mean; vicious (*animal*); (*mezquino*) small; petty; puny; stingy.

ruina f. ruin; destruction; downfall.

ruindad f. baseness; meanness; stinginess; mean or vile act.

ruinoso adj. ruinous; in a state of ruin or decay.

ruiseñor m. nightingale.

rumba f. *Ven., Col., Carib., Mex., Ríopl.,* rumba (*dance and music*); *Carib., Ven., Andes* spree; *Carib., Ven., Andes* **irse de —** to go on a spree.

rumbear v. *Ríopl., Andes* to head (towards), take a certain direction; *Am.* to cut a path through a forest; *Am.* to go on a spree.

rumbo m. (*ruta*) direction; course; route; (*pompa*) pomp; ostentation; *Am.* cut on the head; *Am.* revel, noisy spree; **hacer — a** to head or sail towards; *Am.* **ir al —** to be going in the right drection, be on the right track.

rumboso adj. pompous, ostentatious; generous.

rumiar v. to ruminate; to chew the cud; to ponder, meditate.

rumor m. rumor, report; murmur; rumble.

runfla f. series (*of things of the same kind*); sequence (*in cards*).

runrún m. rumor; murmur.

ruptura f. rupture; break; fracture.

rural adj. rural.

ruso adj. Russian; m. Russian; Russian language.

rústico adj. rustic, rural; crude, coarse; m. peasant; **en** (*or* **a la**) **rústica** unbound, paper-bound.

ruta f. route, course, way.

rutina f. routine.

S

sábado m. Saturday.

sábana f. bed sheet; altar cloth.

sabana f. *Col.* savanna, treeless plain; *Col.* **ponerse en la —** to become suddenly rich.

sabandija f. small reptile; small lizard.

sabañón m. chilblain.

sabedor adj. knowing; aware, informed.

saber[42] v. irr. to know; to know how to, be able to; to learn, find out; *Ríopl., Ven., Col.* to be in the habit of; **— a** to taste of, taste like; **sabe bien** it tastes good; **a —** namely; that is; *Am.* **¡a — si venga!** who knows whether he will come!; **un no sé qué** an indefinable something; **¿sabe Vd. a la plaza?** do you know the way to the square?; m. knowledge, learning.

sabiduría f. wisdom; knowledge.

sabiendas : a — consciously, knowingly.

sabio adj. wise; judicious; learned; m. savant, scholar; sage, wise man.

sable m. saber; **sablazo** m. blow with a saber; saber wound; **dar un sablazo** to strike for a loan.

sabor m. savor, taste, flavor.

saborear v. to savor, flavor, season; to relish, taste with pleasure; to enjoy; **-se** to eat or drink with relish; to smack one's lips.

sabotaje m. sabotage.

sabotear v. to sabotage.

sabroso adj. savory, tasty; delicious; delightful.

sabueso m. hound.

sacabocados m. punch (*tool*).

sacacorchos m. corkscrew.

sacamuelas m. & f. tooth puller; quack dentist.

sacar[6] v. to draw, draw out, pull out, get out, or take out; to get, obtain; to infer; to make (*a copy*); to take (*a snapshot or picture*); to stick out (*one's tongue*); to serve (*a ball*); **— a bailar** to ask to dance, lead on to the dance floor; **— a luz** to publish; **— el cuerpo** to dodge; **— en claro** (*or* **— en limpio**) to deduce, conclude; *Am.* **— el sombrero** to take off one's hat; *Am.* **¡sáquese de allí!** get out of there!

sacarina f. saccharine.

sacerdocio m. priesthood.

sacerdote m. priest.

saciar v. to satiate, satisfy; **-se** to be satiated, satisfied completely.

saco m. sack, bag; sackful, bagful; loose-fitting coat; sack, plundering; *Am.* suit coat; **— de noche** overnight bag, satchel.

sacramento m. sacrament.

sacrificar[6] v. to sacrifice.

sacrificio m. sacrifice.

sacrilegio m. sacrilege.

sacrílego adj. sacrilegious.

sacristán m. sacristan, sexton; *Am.* busybody, meddler.

sacro adj. sacred.

sacrosanto *adj.* sacrosanct, holy and sacred.

sacudida *f.* shake, jolt, jerk.

sacudimiento *m.* shaking; shake, jerk; shock, jolt.

sacudir *v.* to shake; to jerk; to beat; to beat the dust from; to shake off; **-se** to shake oneself; to brush oneself off; **-se de alguien** to shake someone off, get rid of someone.

sádico *adj.* sadistic, cruel.

saeta *f.* arrow, dart.

sagacidad *f.* sagacity.

sagaz *adj.* sagacious, shrewd.

sagrado *adj.* sacred; consecrated; *m.* asylum, refuge.

sahumar *v.* to perfume with incense; to fumigate.

sahumerio *m.* vapor, fume; incense; burning of incense; fumigation.

sainete *m.* one-act comedy or farce; delicacy, tasty tidbit; flavor, relish; sauce.

sajón *adj. & m.* Saxon.

sal *f.* salt; wit, humor; grace; *Mex., Cuba, C.A., Col., Andes* misfortune, bad luck.

sala *f.* parlor; hall, large room; **— de justicia** courtroom.

salado *adj.* salty; salted; witty; charming; *Am.* costly; *Mex., Cuba, C.A., Col., Andes* **estar —** to be unlucky; *m. Am.* salt pit, salt mine.

salar *v.* to salt; to cure or preserve with salt; *Mex., Cuba, C.A., Col., Andes* to bring bad luck (to); *Am.* to dishonor; *Am.* to ruin, spoil; *Am.* to bribe; *Am.* to feed salt to cattle; *Am.* salt pit.

salario *m.* salary, wages.

salchicha *f.* sausage; **salchichón** *m.* large sausage.

saldar *v.* to balance, settle (*an account*).

saldo *m.* balance, settlement (*of an account*); bargain sale.

saledizo = **salidizo.**

salero *m.* (*vaso*) saltcellar, saltshaker; place for storing salts; salt lick; (*gracia*) wit, grace, charm; *Am.* salt dealer.

salida *f.* departure; exit; sally; outlet; way out; loophole; outskirts; outcome; jut, projection; outlay, expenditure; witty remark; **— de pie de banco** silly remark, nonsense; **— del sol** sunrise; *Cuba* **— de teatro** evening wrap.

salidizo *m.* jut, ledge, projection; *adj.* salient, jutting, projecting.

saliente *adj.* salient, standing out; projecting; *m.* salient, salient angle; jut, projection.

salina *f.* salt mine or pit; salt works.

salir [43] *v. irr.* (*partir*) to go out; to leave, depart; to get out (*of*); to come out; to sprout; to come (*from*); (*resultar*) to turn out to be; **— bien** to turn out well; to come out well; **a su padre** to turn out to be or look like his father; *Am.* **— a mano** to come out even; **-se** to get out, slip out; to leak

out; **-se con la suya** to get one's own way.

salitral *m.* saltpeter bed or mine.

salitre *m.* saltpeter; **salitrera** *f.* saltpeter mine or bed; **salitroso** *adj.* nitrous, abounding in saltpeter.

saliva *f.* saliva.

salmo *m.* psalm.

salmodiar *v.* to chant; to talk in a monotone or singsong.

salmón *m.* salmon.

salmuera *f.* brine.

salobre *adj.* briny, salty.

salón *m.* salon, hall, large room; salted meat or fish.

salpicadura *f.* spatter, splash.

salpicar [6] *v.* to sprinkle, spray, spatter.

salpicón *m.* hash; hodgepodge; *Ec.* fruit drink.

salpimentar [1] *v. irr.* to salt and pepper.

salpimienta *f.* salt and pepper.

salpullido *m.* rash, skin eruption.

salsa *f.* sauce; gravy; *Am.* sound whipping or beating; **salsera** *f.* sauce dish

saltamontes *m.* grasshopper.

saltar *v.* (*brincar*) to jump; to jump over; to leap; to bounce; to skip; (*estallar*) to burst, break into pieces; to come off; **— a la vista** to be obvious, evident; **— a tierra** to disembark, land; *Mex.* **— las trancas** to lose one's patience; to lose one's head.

salteador *m.* bandit, highway robber.

saltear *v.* to assault, attack; to hold up, rob; to take by surprise; to jump or skip around.

salto *m.* jump; leap; precipice; gap; **— de agua** waterfall; **a -s** by jumps; **en un (or de un) —** in a jiffy; quickly; **dar un —** to jump, leap.

saltón *adj.* jumping, skipping, hopping; jumpy; protruding; *Col.* half-cooked; **ojos -es** popeyes, bulging eyes; *m.* grasshopper.

salubre *adj.* healthy, healthful.

salubridad *f.* healthfulness, health; sanitation.

salud *f.* health; welfare; salvation; **¡—!** greetings!; your health!

saludable *adj.* wholesome, healthful beneficial.

saludador *m.* greeter; healer, quack.

saludar *v.* to salute, greet; to fire a salute.

saludo *m.* salute, nod, greeting.

salutación *f.* salutation; greeting.

salva *f.* salvo, salute with guns; greeting, welcome.

salvación *f.* salvation.

salvado *m.* bran.

salvador *m.* savior, rescuer; Savior; *adj.* saving.

salvaguardar *v.* to safeguard, defend, protect.

salvaguardia *m.* safeguard, protection; guard; *f.* safe-conduct paper, passport; password.

salvajada *f.* savage act or remark.

salvaje *adj.* savage, wild; *m.* savage.

salvajez *f.* wildness, savagery.

salvajismo m. savagery; Am. savage act or remark. See **salvajada.**

salvamento m. salvation, rescue; place of safety; salvage (rescue of property); **bote de —** lifeboat.

salvar v. (librar) to save; to except; to exclude; (vencer) to clear, jump over; **-se** to be saved; to save oneself, escape.

salvavidas m. life preserver; **lancha —** lifeboat.

¡salve! interj. hail!; **Salve** f. Salve Regina, prayer to the Virgin Mary.

salvia f. sage (a plant).

salvo adj. saved; safe; prep. save, except but; **a —** safe, without injury; **en —** in safety; out of danger.

salvoconducto m. safe-conduct, pass.

san adj. (contr. of santo) saint.

sánalotodo m. cure-all.

sanar v. to heal, cure; to recover, get well.

sanatorio m. sanitarium.

sanción f. sanction.

sancionar v. to sanction; to authorize, ratify.

sandalia f. sandal.

sandez f. stupidity; folly; foolish remark.

sandía f. watermelon.

sandio adj. silly, foolish.

saneamiento m. sanitation; drainage of land.

sanear v. to make sanitary (land, property, etc.); to drain, dry up (land).

sangrar v. to bleed; to drain; to tap (a tree); to pilfer; to exploit (someone); to indent (a line).

sangre f. blood; **— fría** calmness, coolness of mind; **a — fría** in cold blood.

sangría f. a refreshing Spanish drink made of red wine, fruit juice, and sugar.

sangriento adj. bleeding; bloody; bloodstained; bloodthirsty, cruel.

sanguijuela f. leech.

sanguinario adj. bloody, cruel; bloodthirsty, murderous.

sanidad f. health; soundness; healthfulness; sanitation; **— publica** health department.

sanitario adj. sanitary.

sano adj. (de salud) sound, healthy; healthful; sane, sensible; (integro) whole; unbroken; undamaged; **— y salvo** safe and sound.

sanseacabó that's all; that's the end.

santiamén : **en un —** in a jiffy.

santidad f. sanctity, holiness, saintliness; **su Santidad** his Holiness.

santificar v. to sanctify; to consecrate.

santiguar v. to bless; to make the sign of the cross; to beat, hit, punish; **-se** to cross oneself; to show astonishment (by crossing oneself).

santísimo adj. most holy; m. the Holy Sacrament.

santo adj. saintly, holy; sacred; **esperar todo el — día** to wait the whole blessed day; **— y bueno** well and good; Riopl., Col., Ven., Mex., Carib.,

Andes **¡santa palabra!** that's my final and last word! m. saint; saint's day; Mex., Ven. **tener el — de espaldas** to have a streak of bad luck;

santurrón m. religious hypocrite, affectedly pious person.

santuario m. sanctuary; Col. buried treasure; Am. Indian idol.

saña f. fury, rage.

sañudo adj. furious, enraged.

sapo m. toad; Col. despicable little man; Col. chubby person; Am. sly person; **echar -s y culebras** to swear, curse.

saque m. serve, service (in tennis); server.

saquear v. to sack, plunder, pillage, loot.

saqueo m. sacking, pillaging, plunder; loot, booty.

saquillo m. small bag, handbag, satchel.

sarampión m. measles.

sarao m. soirée, evening party.

sarape m. Mex. serape, blanket.

sarcasmo m. sarcasm.

sarcástico adj. sarcastic.

sardina f. sardine.

sargento m. sergeant.

sarmentoso adj. vinelike; full of vine shoots; gnarled, knotty.

sarmiento m. shoot or branch of a vine.

sarna f. itch; mange.

sarnoso adj. itchy, scabby, mangy.

sarpullido = salpullido.

sarro m. tartar (on teeth); crust, sediment (in utensils).

sarta f. string (of beads); series.

sartén f. frying pan.

sastre m. tailor.

satánico adj. satanic, devilish.

satélite m. satellite; suburban development; **— artificial** artificial satellite.

satén m. sateen.

sátira f. satire.

satírico adj. satirical.

satirizar v. to satirize.

satisfacción f. satisfaction; apology, excuse; **tomar —** to vindicate oneself; to take revenge; **dar una —** to offer an apology; to apologize.

satisfacer v. irr. to satisfy; to pay (a debt); **— una letra** to honor a draft; **-se** to be satisfied; to take satisfaction.

satisfactorio adj. satisfactory.

satisfecho p.p. of **satisfacer** satisfied, gratified; adj. content, contented.

saturar v. to saturate; to satiate.

sauce m. willow.

savia f. sap.

saxófono m. saxophone; also **saxofón.**

sazón f. (época) season, opportune time; (sabor) taste, flavor; ripeness; **a la —** then, at that time; **en —** in season; ripe; opportunely; adj. Riopl., Mex., Cuba ripe.

sazonado adj. & p.p. seasoned; mellow, ripe; expressive (said of a phrase).

sazonar v. to season; to ripen; **-se** to become seasoned; to ripen, mature.

se obj. pron. (before **le, la, lo, las,** and **los**) to him, to her; to you (formal); to them; refl. pron. himself, herself,

SA

yourself (*formal*), yourselves (*formal*)
themselves; *reciprocal pron.* each
other, one another.

sebo *m.* tallow, fat.

secador *m. Am.* dryer (*clothes, hair*).

secante *adj.* drying, blotting; **papel —**
blotter; *f.* secant (*math.*).

secar[6] *v.* to dry; to wipe dry; **-se** to dry
or wipe oneself; to dry up; to wither;
to get thin.

sección *f.* section; division; cutting.

seccionar *v.* to section.

seco *adj.* (*sin humedad*) dry; dried;
withered; (*áspero*) harsh; abrupt;
plain, unadorned; **en —** on dry land,
out of the water; **parar en —** to stop
short, stop suddenly; **a secas** plain;
alone, without anything else; *Mex.,
Carib., Ríopl., Andes* simply, straight
to the point; **comer pan a secas** to
eat just bread; *Mex., Ven.* **bailar a
secas** to dance without musical
accompaniment.

secreción *f.* secretion.

secretar *v.* to secrete.

secretaría *f.* secretary's office; position
of secretary.

secretario *m.* secretary; confidant;
secretaria *f.* woman secretary;
secretary's wife.

secretear *v.* to whisper; **-se** to whisper
to each other.

secreto *adj.* secret, hidden; secretive;
m. secret; secrecy; secret place; **— a
voces** open secret; **en —** secretly;
hablar en — to whisper.

secta *f.* sect.

secuaz *m.* partisan, follower.

secuela *f.* sequel, outcome, consequence.

secuencia *f.* sequence.

secuestrador *m.* kidnapper; confiscator.

secuestrar *v.* to seize; to kidnap; to
confiscate.

secuestro *m.* kidnapping; seizure.

secular *adj.* secular; lay, worldly; centennial; *m.* secular, secular priest.

secundar *v.* to second, favor, back up.

secundario *adj.* secondary.

sed *f.* thirst; craving, desire; **tener —**
to be thirsty.

seda *f.* silk; **como una —** soft as silk;
sweet-tempered; smoothly, easily.

sedal *m.* fishing line.

sedán *m.* sedan.

sedativo *adj. & m.* sedative.

sede *f.* seat, see; **Santa Sede** Holy See.

sedentario *adj.* sedentary.

sedeño *adj.* silky, silken.

sedería *f.* silk goods; silk shop.

sedero *m.* silk dealer or weaver; *adj.*
silk, pertaining to silk; **industria
sedera** silk industry.

sedición *f.* sedition.

sedicioso *adj.* seditious, turbulent.

sediento *adj.* thirsty; dry, parched;
anxious, desirous.

sedimento *m.* sediment; dregs,
grounds.

sedoso *adj.* silken, silky.

seducción *f.* seduction.

seducir[25] *v. irr.* to seduce; to entice; to
charm.

seductivo *adj.* seductive, alluring; inviting, enticing.

seductor *adj.* tempting, fascinating; *m.*
seducer; tempter; charming person.

segador *m.* harvester, reaper; **segadora**
f. harvester, mowing machine; wom-
an reaper.

segar[1,7] *v. irr.* to mow, reap; to cut off.

seglar *adj.* secular, lay; *m.* layman.

segmento *m.* segment.

seguida *f.* succession; series, continuation; **de —** without interruption,
continuously; **en —** at once, immediately.

seguido *p.p.* followed; continued; *adj.*
continuous; straight, direct; *adv.*
without interruption; *Am.* often;
Col., Ven. **de —** at once, immediately.

seguidor *m.* follower.

seguimiento *m.* pursuit.

seguir[5,12] *v. irr.* to follow; to continue;
to pursue; **-se** to follow as a consequence.

según *prep.* according to; *conj.* as; according to; **— y conforme** (or **— y
como**) exactly as, just as; that de-
pends.

segundar *v.* to repeat a second time; to
second.

segundero *m.* second hand (*of a watch
or clock*).

segundo *adj. & m.* second.

seguridad *f.* security; safety; certainty;
alfiler de — safety pin.

seguro *adj.* secure; sure, certain; safe;
Ríopl., Mex., Carib., Andes honest,
trustworthy; *m.* assurance; insurance;
safety device; **a buen —** (**al —**,
or **de —**) truly, certainly; **en —** in
safety; **sobre —** without risk; without taking a chance; *Am.* **irse uno
del —** to lose one's temper; *Ch., Mex.,
Cuba, Andes* **a la segura** without
risk.

selección *f.* selection choice.

seleccionar *v.* to select, choose.

selecto *adj.* select, choice.

selva *f.* forest; jungle.

sellar *v.* (*imprimir*) to stamp; to seal;
(*cerrar*) to close tightly, seal; (*concluir*) to conclude.

sello *m.* seal; stamp; *Am.* official
stamped paper.

semáforo *m.* traffic light.

semana *f.* week; week's wages; **días de
—** week days; **entre —** during the
week.

semanal *adj.* weekly; **-mente** *adv.*
weekly, every week.

semanario *m.* weekly publication; *adj.*
weekly.

semblante *m.* countenance; facial expression; appearance.

semblanza *f.* portrait, literary sketch.

sembrado *m.* sown ground; cultivated
field.

sembrar[1] *v. irr.* to sow; to scatter.

semejante *adj.* similar, like; such a; *m.*
fellow man; **nuestros -s** our fellow

men.

semejanza *f.* resemblance, similarity; simile; **a — de** in the manner of.

semejar *v.* to resemble. **-se** to resemble.

semental *adj.* sowing (*crops*); breeding (*animals*); used as stud.

semiconsonante *f.* semiconsonant.

semilla *-f.* seed.

semillero *m.* seed bed; plant nursery; **— de vicios** hotbed of vice.

seminario *m.* seminary; plant nursery, seed plot.

semivocal *f.* semivowel.

sempiterno *adj.* everlasting; evergreen.

senado *m.* senate.

senador *m.* senator.

sencillez *f.* simplicity; plainness.

sencillo *adj.* simple; easy; plain; unadorned; unaffected; *m.* loose change, small coins.

senda *f.* path; way, course.

sendero *m.* path.

sendos *adj. pl.* one for each of two or more persons or things.

senectud *f.* senility, old age.

senil *adj.* senile.

seno *m.* (*pecho*) breast, bosom; (*hueco*) cavity, hollow; womb; lap; cove, bay; innermost recess; sinus (*cavity in a bone*); sine (*math.*); *C.A.* armpit.

sensación *f.* sensation.

sensacional *adj.* sensational.

sensatez *f.* prudence, common sense.

sensato *adj.* sensible, wise, prudent.

sensibilidad *f.* sensibility; sensitiveness.

sensible *adj.* sensitive; perceptible; regrettable.

sensitivo *adj.* sensitive.

sensual *adj.* sensual; sensuous.

sensualidad *f.* sensuality; lewdness.

sentada *f.* sitting; **de una —** at one sitting.

sentado *adj.* seated, sitting; **dar por —** to take for granted.

sentar[1] *v. irr.* to seat; to set; to establish; to become, suit, fit; to agree with one (*as food or climate*); **-se** to sit down; to settle down; *Col.* **-se en la palabra** to do all the talking, monopolize the conversation.

sentencia *f.* sentence; verdict; judgment, maxim, proverb; statement.

sentenciar *v.* to sentence; to pass judgment on; to decide.

sentido *p.p.* felt; experienced; *adj.* heartfelt, filled with feeling; sensitive; touchy; **darse por —** to take offense; to have one's feelings hurt; **estar — con alguien** to be offended or peeved at someone; *m.* sense; meaning; judgment; **aguzar el —** to prick up one's ears; **perder el —** to faint.

sentimental *adj.* sentimental.

sentimentalismo *m.* sentimentalism, sentimentality.

sentimiento *m.* sentiment; sensation, feeling; grief, regret.

sentir[3] *v. irr.* to feel; to sense; to hear; to regret; **-se** to feel (*well, strong, sad, etc.*); to feel oneself, consider oneself;

to feel resentment; to feel a pain; **sin — ** without being realized or felt; inadvertently; unnoticed; *m.* feeling; judgment, opinion.

seña *familiar contraction of* **señora**.

seña *f.* sign, mark; signal; password; **-s** address (*name and place of residence*); **por más -s** as an additional proof.

señal *f.* (*marca*) sign, mark; signal; trace, vestige; scar; (*indicio*) reminder; indication; token, pledge; *Ríopl.*, *Andes* earmark, brand (*on the ear of livestock*); **en — de** in proof of, in token of.

señalar *v.* to mark; to point out; to indicate; to determine, fix; to appoint; to signal; to assign; *Am.* to earmark, brand (*cattle*); **-se** to distinguish oneself.

señor *m.* mister; sir; owner; master, lord; gentleman; **el Señor** the Lord.

señora *f.* lady; madam; mistress; Mrs.

señorear *v.* to lord it over, domineer; to dominate; to master, control.

señoría *f.* lordship.

señoril *adj.* lordly.

señorío *m.* dominion, rule; domain of a lord; lordship; dignity; mastery, control; body of noblemen.

señorita *f.* miss; young lady.

señorito *m.* master, young gentleman.

señuelo *m.* decoy; lure, bait; *Ven.* leading or guiding oxen.

separación *f.* separation.

separado *p.p. & adj.* separate; separated; **por —** separately.

separar *v.* to separate; to set aside; to remove (from); to dismiss (from); **-se** to separate; to retire, resign; to withdraw, leave.

separata *f.* reprint (*of an article*).

septentrional *adj.* northern.

septiembre *m.* September.

sepulcral *adj.* sepulchral (*pertaining to sepulchers or tombs*); **lápida —** tombstone.

sepulcro *m.* sepulcher, tomb, grave.

sepultar *v.* to bury; to hide.

sepultura *f.* burial; grave; **dar — to** bury.

sequedad *f.* dryness; gruffness.

sequía *f.* drought.

séquito *m.* retinue, following.

ser[44] *v. irr.* to be; to exist; to happen, occur; **— de** (*or* **para**) **ver** to be worth seeing; *m.* being; essence, nature; existence; *Am.* **estar en un —** to be always in the same condition.

serenar *v.* to pacify; to calm down; *Col.* to drizzle, rain gently; **-se** to become serene, calm down; to clear up (*said of the weather*).

serenata *f.* serenade.

serenidad *f.* serenity, calm.

sereno *adj.* serene, calm; clear, cloudless; *m.* night humidity, dew; night watchman; **al —** in the night air.

serie *f.* series.

seriedad *f.* seriousness; gravity; earnestness; dignity.

serio *adj.* serious; grave; earnest; dig-

SE

nified; formal; **en —** seriously.

sermón *m.* sermon; reproof.

sermonear *v.* to preach; to admonish, reprimand.

serpentear *v.* to wind, twist, turn, zigzag.

serpiente *f.* serpent, snake.

serrado *adj.* toothed, notched (like a saw); jagged.

serrana *f.* mountain girl; **serranilla** *f.* lyric poem with a rustic theme.

serranía *f.* mountainous region; chain of mountains.

serrano *m.* mountaineer; *adj.* of, pertaining to, or from the mountains.

serrar = **aserrar**.

serrín *f.* sawdust.

serrucho *m.* handsaw.

servible *adj.* serviceable, useful.

servicial *adj.* helpful, obliging.

servicio *m.* service; table service; tea or coffee set; chamber pot; *Am.* toilet, water closet.

servidor *m.* servant; waiter; **— de Vd.** at your service; **su seguro —** yours truly.

servidumbre *f.* domestic help, servants; servitude, slavery; service.

servil *adj.* servile; **servilón** *adj.* very servile; *m.* bootlicker, great flatterer.

servilismo *m.* servility, servile behavior or attitude, servile submission.

servilleta *f.* napkin.

servir[5] *v. irr.* to serve; to be of use; **— de** to serve as, act as; to be used as; **— para** to be good for; to be used for; **-se** to serve or help oneself; to be pleased to; **-se de** to make use of; **sírvase Vd. hacerlo** please do it.

sesgado *adj.* slanting, oblique, bias.

sesgar[7] *v.* to slant; to cut on the bias; to follow an oblique line.

sesgo *m.* bias; slant; diagonal cut; turn; **al —** on the bias; diagonally, obliquely.

sesión *f.* session; meeting, conference.

seso *m.* brain; wisdom, intelligence; **devanarse los -s** to rack one's brain.

sestear *v.* to snooze, take a nap.

sesudo *adj.* sensible, wise, prudent; *Mex.*, *C.A.* stubborn.

seta *f.* mushroom.

seto *m.* fence; hedge.

seudónimo *m.* pseudonym, pen name.

severidad *f.* severity; strictness; seriousness.

severo *adj.* severe; strict; stern.

sevillano *adj.* of, from, or pertaining to Seville, Spain.

sexo *m.* sex.

sexual *adj.* sexual.

si *conj.* if; whether; **¡— ya te lo dije!** but I already told you!; **— bien** although; **por — acaso** just in case.

sí *adv.* yes; **— que** certainly, really; **un — es no es** a trifle, somewhat; *m.* assent, consent; *refl. pron.* (used after a prep.) himself, herself, yourself (formal), themselves; **de por —** separately, by itself; **estar sobre —** to be on the alert.

sicología *f.* psychology.

sicológico *adj.* psychological.

sicólogo *m.* psychologist.

sidra *f.* cider.

siega *f.* reaping, mowing; harvesting; harvest, harvest season.

siembra *f.* sowing; seedtime, sowing time; sown field.

siempre *adv.* always; *Mex.*, *C.A.*, *Col.*, *Andes* in any case, anyway; **para (or por) —** forever, for always; **por — jamás** forever and ever; **— que** whenever; provided that; *Am.* **— sí me voy** I've decided to go anyway.

siempreviva *f.* evergreen; everlasting.

sien *f.* temple (of the forehead).

sierpe *f.* serpent, snake.

sierra *f.* saw; rocky mountain range.

siervo *m.* serf; slave; servant.

siesta *f.* siesta, afternoon nap; early afternoon; **dormir la —** to take an afternoon nap.

sifón *m.* siphon; siphon bottle; trap (in plumbing fixtures).

sigilo *m.* secret; secrecy.

siglo *m.* century; period, epoch; the world, worldly matters.

significación *f.* meaning; significance.

significado *m.* significance, meaning.

significar[6] *v.* to signify; to mean; to make known, show; to matter, have importance.

significativo *adj.* significant.

signo *m.* sign; mark; symbol.

siguiente *adj.* following.

sílaba *f.* syllable.

silabario *m.* speller, spelling book.

silbar *v.* to whistle; to hiss.

silbato *m.* whistle.

silbido *m.* whistle; hiss.

silenciador *m.* silencer; muffler (of an automobile).

silencio *m.* silence; pause; *adj. Am.* silent, quiet, motionless.

silencioso *adj.* silent, quiet.

silueta *f.* silhouette.

silvestre *adj.* wild, uncultivated.

silvicultor *m.* forester; **silvicultura** *f.* forestry.

silla *f.* chair; saddle; **— de montar** saddle; *Ven.* **— de balanza** rocking chair. See **mecedora**.

sillón *m.* large chair; easy chair; *Am.* **— de hamaca** rocking chair.

sima *f.* chasm, abyss.

simbólico *adj.* symbolic.

simbolismo *m.* symbolism.

símbolo *m.* symbol; **— de la fe (or de los Apóstoles)** the Apostle's creed.

simetría *f.* symmetry.

simétrico *adj.* symmetrical.

simiente *f.* seed.

símil *m.* simile; similarity; *adj.* similar.

simpatía *f.* sympathy; accord, harmony; liking.

simpático *adj.* sympathetic, congenial; pleasant, agreeable, nice.

simpatizar[9] *v.* to be attractive to; to get on well with; to be congenial; **no me simpatiza** I don't like him.

simple *adj.* simple; mere; plain; pure,

unmixed; naïve, innocent; silly, foolish; *m.* simpleton.

simpleza *f.* simplicity; simpleness, stupidity, foolishness.

simplicidad *f.* simplicity; candor.

simplificar[6] *v.* to simplify.

simplista *adj.* simplistic; *m. & f.* a person who is inclined to oversimplify.

simplón *m.* simpleton.

simulacro *m.* mimic battle, sham or mock battle; image, vision.

simular *v.* to simulate, feign.

simultáneo *adj.* simultaneous.

sin *prep.* without; besides, not counting; — **que** *conj.* without; — **embargo** nevertheless, still, yet; — **qué ni para qué** without rhyme or reason.

sinapismo *m.* mustard plaster; irritating person, nuisance, pest, bore.

sincerar *v.* to square, justify, excuse; **-se** to square oneself (with), justify oneself (with).

sinceridad *f.* sincerity.

sincero *adj.* sincere.

síncopa *f.* syncopation; syncope.

sindicar[6] *v.* to syndicate; **-se** to syndicate, form a syndicate.

sindicato *m.* syndicate.

síndico *m.* receiver (*person appointed to take charge of property under litigation or to liquidate a bankrupt business*); trustee.

sinecura *f.* sinecure (*easy and well paid position*).

sinfonía *f.* symphony.

singular *adj.* singular; unique; striking; odd, strange.

singularizar[9] *v.* to single out, choose; to distinguish; **-se** to distinguish oneself; to be singled out.

siniestro *adj.* sinister; left (*side*); *m.* unforeseen loss, damage; **siniestra** *f.* left hand; left-hand side.

sinnúmero *m.* great number, endless number.

sino *conj.* but; *prep.* except; **no hace — lo que le mandan** he only does what he is told; — **que** *conj.* but; *m.* fate, destiny.

sinónimo *m.* synonym; *adj.* synonymous.

sinrazón *f.* injustice, wrong.

sinsabor *m.* displeasure; trouble, grief, distress.

sintaxis *f.* syntax.

síntesis *f.* synthesis; summary.

sintético *adj.* synthetic.

sintetizar[9] *v.* to synthesize.

síntoma *m.* symptom; indication, sign.

sintonizar[9] *v.* to tune in (on).

sinuoso *adj.* sinuous, winding; wavy.

sinvergüenza *m. & f.* shameless person; scoundrel.

siquiatra *m. & f.* psychiatrist, alienist.

siquiatría *f.* psychiatry.

siquiera *adv.* at least; even; **ni** — not even; *conj.* even though.

sirena *f.* siren; whistle, foghorn.

sirviente *m.* servant; waiter; **sirvienta** *f.* housemaid; waitress.

sisa *f.* petty theft; dart (*made in a garment*).

sisal *m. Am.* sisal or sisal hemp (*fiber used in ropemaking*).

sisar *v.* to take in (*a garment*); to pilfer; to cheat out of, defraud.

sisear *v.* to hiss.

siseo *m.* hiss, hissing.

sistema *m.* system.

sistemático *adj.* systematic.

sitial *m.* chair of a presiding officer; place of honor.

sitiar *v.* to besiege; to surround.

sitio *m.* site, location; place, spot, space; siege; *Am.* cattle ranch; *Mex.* taxicab station; **poner** — **a** to lay siege to.

sito *adj.* situated, located.

situación *f.* situation; position; location; state, condition; *Mex., Carib., Ven., Col.* **hombre de la** — man of the hour, man of influence.

situado *p.p.* situated; placed.

situar[18] *v.* to locate; to place; **-se** to station oneself, place oneself; to be located, placed, situated.

so : — **capa de** under the guise of; — **pena de** under penalty of; — **pretexto de** under the pretext of.

sobaco *m.* armpit.

sobar *v.* (*ablandar*) to rub; to knead; to massage; to touch, handle; to fondle, pet; (*fastidiar*) to bother; to beat, slap; *Col., Ven., Mex.* to set bones; *Col.* to flay, skin; *Am.* to win (*in a fight*); *Am.* to tire out (*a horse*).

soberanía *f.* sovereignty.

soberano *adj. & m.* sovereign.

soberbia *f.* pride, arrogance; ostentation, pomp.

soberbio *adj.* proud, haughty, arrogant; pompous; superb, magnificent; spirited (*horse*).

sobornar *v.* to bribe.

soborno *m.* bribery; bribe; *Andes* overload (*on a pack animal*), extra load.

sobra *f.* surplus, excess; **-s** leftovers, leavings; **de** — more than enough; superfluous, unnecessary.

sobrado *m.* attic; loft; *Am.* pantry shelf; **-s** *Col., Ven.* leftovers, leavings; *adj.* leftover; excessive; superfluous; forward, brazen; **sobradas veces** many times, repeatedly.

sobrante *adj.* leftover, surplus, excess, spare; *m.* surplus, excess, remainder.

sobrar *v.* to exceed; to remain, be left over; to be more than enough.

sobre *prep.* (*encima de*) over; above; on, upon; (*acerca de*) about; approximately; besides; — **manera** excessively; **estar** — **sí** to be cautious, on the alert; — **que** besides, in addition to the fact that; *m.* envelope; address (*on an envelope*).

sobrecama *f.* bedspread.

sobrecarga *f.* overload; overburden.

sobrecargar[7] *v.* to overload; to overburden.

sobrecargo *m.* purser (*on a ship*); *f.* airline hostess.

sobrecoger[11] *v.* to surprise, catch un-

SE

aware; to startle; **-se** to be startled; **-se de miedo** to be seized with fear.

sobreexcitación *f.* overexcitement; thrill.

sobreexcitar *v.* to overexcite.

sobrehumano *adj.* superhuman.

sobrellevar *v.* to endure, bear; to tolerate; to lighten (*another's burden*).

sobremesa *f.* table runner; after dinner conversation at the table; **de —** during the after dinner conversation.

sobrenadar *v.* to float.

sobrenatural *adj.* supernatural.

sobrenombre *m.* surname; nickname.

sobrentender[1] *v. irr.* to assume, understand; **-se** to be assumed, be obvious, be understood.

sobrepasar *v.* to exceed; to excel; **-se** to overstep, go too far.

sobreponer[40] *v. irr.* to lay on top; **-se** to dominate oneself; **-se a** to overcome; to dominate.

sobrepuesto *p.p. of* **sobreponer**; *m.* appliqué (*trimming laid on a dress*); *C.A.* mend, patch.

sobrepujar *v.* to exceed, excel, surpass; to outweigh.

sobresaliente *adj.* outstanding; projecting; excellent; *m. & f.* substitute (*a person*); understudy (*substitute actor*).

sobresalir[43] *v. irr.* to stand out; to project, jut out; to excel.

sobresaltar *v.* to startle, frighten; to assail; to stand out clearly; **-se** to be startled, frightened.

sobresalto *m.* start, scare, fright, shock; **de —** suddenly.

sobrescrito *m.* address (*on an envelope*).

sobrestante *m.* overseer; boss, foreman.

sobresueldo *m.* overtime pay, extra pay or wages.

sobretodo *m.* overcoat.

sobrevenir[48] *v. irr.* to happen, occur, come unexpectedly; to follow, happen after.

sobreviviente *m. & f.* survivor; *adj.* surviving.

sobrevivir *v.* to survive.

sobriedad *f.* sobriety, soberness, temperance, moderation.

sobrina *f.* niece.

sobrino *m.* nephew.

sobrio *adj.* sober, temperate, moderate.

socarrón *adj.* cunning, sly, crafty.

socarronería *f.* craftiness, slyness, cunning.

socavar *v.* to dig under; to undermine.

socavón *m.* tunnel; cave, cavern; underground passageway.

social *adj.* social; sociable, friendly.

socialista *adj.* socialist, socialistic; *m. & f.* socialist.

sociedad *f.* society; partnership; company, firm, corporation; **— anónima** (*or* **— por acciones**) stock company.

socio *m.* associate, partner; member.

sociología *f.* sociology.

socorrer *v.* to help, aid, assist.

socorro *m.* help, aid, assistance, relief; *Am.* partial advance payment on a workman's wages.

sodio *m.* sodium.

soez *adj.* low, vile, vulgar; coarse, ill-mannered.

sofá *m.* sofa, davenport.

sofocante *adj.* suffocating, stifling.

sofocar[6] *v.* to suffocate, choke; to smother; to bother; to embarrass.

sofoco *m.* suffocation, choking; upset, annoyance; embarrassment.

sofrenar *v.* to check; to control; to reprimand.

soga *f.* rope; *Ven., Col., Andes, Ch.* leather lasso or rope.

sojuzgamiento *m.* subjugation, subjection.

sojuzgar[7] *v.* to subjugate, subdue, subject.

sol *m.* sun; sunshine; sol (*fifth note of the scale*); *Am.* sol (*monetary unit of Peru*); **de — a —** from sunrise to sunset; **hace —** it is sunny; **tomar el —** to bask in the sun; to enjoy the sunshine.

solana *f.* sunny place; sunroom; sun porch; intense sunlight; **solanera** *f.* sunburn; sunny place.

solapa *f.* lapel.

solapado *adj.* sly, crafty, cunning, deceitful, underhanded.

solar *m.* lot, plot of ground; ancestral mansion, manor; *Carib., Mex.* tenement house; *Mex., Ven.* back yard; *Col.* town lot, field (*for growing alfalfa, corn, etc.*); *adj.* solar, of the sun.

solar[2] *v. irr.* to sole (*shoes*); to pave, floor.

solariego *adj.* manorial, pertaining to a manor; **casa solariega** ancestral manor or mansion.

solaz *m.* solace, comfort; relaxation, recreation.

solazar[9] *v.* to console, cheer, comfort; **-se** to seek relaxation or pleasure; to enjoy oneself.

soldado *m.* soldier; **— raso** private; **— de línea** regular soldier.

soldadura *f.* soldering; welding; solder.

soldar[2] *v. irr.* to solder; to weld.

soleado *adj.* sunny; *p.p.* sunned.

solear = asolear.

soledad *f.* solitude; loneliness; homesickness; lonely retreat.

solemne *adj.* solemn; imposing; **— disparate** downright foolishness, huge blunder.

solemnidad *f.* solemnity; solemn ceremony.

soler[2,51] *v. irr.* to have the custom of, be in the habit of.

solferino *adj.* reddish-purple.

solicitante *m. & f.* solicitor; applicant.

solicitar *v.* to solicit; to apply for; to beg, ask for; to court, woo.

solícito *adj.* solicitous, careful, anxious, concerned, diligent.

solicitud *f.* solicitude; care, concern, anxiety.

solidaridad *f.* solidarity; union; bond, community of interests.

solidez *f.* solidity; compactness.

solidificar[6] v. to solidify.

sólido adj. solid; firm; strong; m. solid.

soliloquio m. soliloquy, monologue.

solista m. & f. soloist.

solitaria f. tapeworm.

solitario adj. solitary; lonely; m. recluse, hermit; solitaire (card game); solitaire (gem set by itself).

solo adj. sole, only; single; alone; lonely **a solas** alone; m. solo; **sólo** adv. only.

solomillo, solomo m. sirloin; loin; loin of pork.

soltar[2] v. irr. to loosen, untie, unfasten; to let loose; to set free; to let go; to let out; to utter; **-se** to set oneself free; to come loose; to lose restraint; to loosen up; **-se a** to begin to, start to.

soltero adj. single, unmarried; m. bachelor; **soltera** f. spinster; **solterón** m. old bachelor; **solterona** f. old maid.

soltura f. looseness; freedom; facility, ease; agility, nimbleness; release (of a prisoner).

solución f. solution; loosening, untying.

solventar v. to pay (a bill), settle (an account); to solve (a problem or difficulty).

sollozar[9] v. to sob.

sollozo m. sob.

sombra f. (oscuridad) shadow; shade; darkness; (abrigo) shelter, protection; (imagen) image, reflection (in the water); Am. guide lines (under writing paper); Ven. awning, sunshade; **hacer —** to shade; to cast a shadow (on).

sombreado adj. shady; shaded.

sombrear v. to shade; **-se** Mex., Ven., Col. to seek the shade, stand in the shade.

sombrerería f. hat shop.

sombrero m. hat; **— de copa** top hat, high hat; **— hongo** derby; **— de jipijapa** Panama hat; C.A., Col., Ven. **— de pelo** top hat.

sombrilla f. parasol, sunshade.

sombrío adj. somber, gloomy; shady.

somero adj. superficial, shallow; summary, concise.

someter v. to submit; to subject; **-se** to submit.

sometimiento m. submission; subjection.

somnolencia f. drowsiness, sleepiness; **con —** sleepily.

son m. sound; tune; rumor; **en — de guerra** in a warlike manner; **sin ton ni —** without rhyme or reason.

sonaja f. jingles, tambourine (to accompany certain dances); rattle; **sonajero** m. child's rattle.

sonante adj. sounding; ringing; sonorous; **en dinero — y contante** in hard cash.

sonar[2] v. irr. to sound; to ring; to sound familiar; **— a** to sound like; seem like; **-se** to blow one's nose; se

suena que it is rumored that.

sonda f. plumb, string with lead weight (for sounding the depth of water); sounding; surgeon's probe.

sondar = **sondear**.

sondear v. to sound, fathom; to sound out; to probe; to examine into.

sondeo m. sounding, fathoming.

soneto m. sonnet.

sonido m. sound.

sonoro adj. sonorous; **consonante sonora** voiced consonant.

sonreír[15] v. irr. to smile; **-se** to smile.

sonriente adj. smiling, beaming, radiant.

sonrisa f. smile.

sonrojarse v. to blush.

sonrojo m. blush.

sonrosado adj. rosy.

sonsacar[6] v. to lure away; to draw (someone) out; to extract (a secret); to take on the sly.

sonsonete m. singsong; rhythmical tapping sound.

soñador m. dreamer.

soñar[2] v. irr. to dream; **— con** (or **en**) to dream of; **— despierto** to daydream.

soñoliento adj. sleepy, drowsy.

sopa f. soup; sop; **estar hecho una —** to be sopping wet; Am. **es un -s** he is a fool.

sopapo m. chuck, tap, pat (under the chin); slap.

sopetón m. box, slap; **de —** all of a sudden, unexpectedly.

soplar v. (despedir aire) to blow; to blow away; to blow up, inflate; (robar) to swipe, steal; (informar) to prompt; to "squeal" on, inform against; Col., Ven., Mex., Cuba, Andes **— una bofetada** to strike a blow; **-se** to swell up, puff up; to eat up, gobble up; to gulp down; se **sopló el pastel** he gobbled up the pie; Am. **-se a uno** to deceive someone, get the best of someone.

soplete m. blow torch; blowpipe.

soplo m. (de aire) blowing; puff, gust of wind; breath; (aviso) whispered warning or advice; "squealing", informing; **en un —** in a jiffy, in a second.

soplón m. informer, "squealer" (one who tells on someone); tattletale.

soportal m. arcade.

soportar v. to support, hold up, bear; to stand, endure, tolerate.

soporte m. support.

sorber v. to sip; to suck; to swallow; to absorb; to snuff up one's nose.

sorbete m. sherbet; fruit ice; C.A., Mex., Ven. cone, ice-cream cone; Am. silk top hat.

sorbo m. sip, swallow, gulp; sniff.

sordera, sordez f. deafness.

sórdido adj. sordid.

sordina f. mute (of a musical instrument).

sordo adj. deaf; silent, noiseless; dull; muffled; **consonante sorda** voiceless

SO

consonant; *m.* deaf person; **hacerse el —** to pretend not to hear; to turn a deaf ear.

sordomudo *adj.* deaf and dumb; *m.* deaf-mute.

sorna *f.* slyness, cunning; sneer.

soroche *m. Andes* shortness of breath, sickness caused by high altitude; *Am.* blush, flush.

sorprendente *adj.* surprising.

sorprender *v.* to surprise; **-se** to be surprised.

sorpresa *f.* surprise.

sortear *v.* to draw lots; to raffle; to dodge; to shun; to fight (*bulls*) skill-fully.

sorteo *m.* drawing or casting of lots; raffle.

sortija *f.* ring; finger ring; ringlet, curl.

sosa *f.* soda.

sosegado *adj.* calm, quiet, peaceful.

sosegar[1,7] *v.* to calm, quiet; to be quiet; **-se** to quiet down.

sosiego *m.* calm, peace, quiet.

soslayo : al — obliquely; slanting; on the bias; **de —** oblique, slanting; at a slant; sideways; **mirada de —** side glance; **pegar de —** to glance, hit at a slant.

soso *adj.* flat, tasteless, insipid; dull, silly; awkward.

sospecha *f.* suspicion; mistrust.

sospechar *v.* to suspect; to mistrust.

sospechoso *adj.* suspicious; *m.* suspect.

sostén *m.* support; prop; supporter; brassière.

sostener[45] *v. irr.* to sustain; to hold; to support, maintain; to defend, uphold; to endure.

sostenido *p.p. & adj.* sustained; supported, held up; *m.* sharp (*in music*).

sota *f.* jack (*at cards*); *m. Am.* foreman, boss, overseer.

sotana *f.* cassock (*black outer robe of a priest*).

sótano *m.* cellar, basement.

soto *m.* grove; thicket.

sotreta *m. Andes, Ríopl.* nag, old horse.

soviet *m.* soviet; **soviético** *adj.* soviet, of, or pertaining to, soviets.

suave *adj.* soft; smooth; mild; bland; gentle.

suavidad *f.* softness; smoothness; mild-ness; gentleness.

suavizar[9] *v.* to smooth; to soften.

subalterno *adj. & m.* subordinate.

subasta *f.* public auction.

subastar *v.* to sell at auction.

súbdito *m.* subject.

subida *f.* rise; ascent; carrying up; **de — on** the way up; **muchas -s y ba-jadas** many ups and downs; much going up and down.

subir *v.* to ascend, go up, climb; to raise, lift; to carry up; to mount; **— al tren** to board the train, get on the train.

súbito *adj.* sudden; **de —** suddenly.

sublevación *f.* revolt, uprising, insur-rection.

sublevar *v.* to excite to rebellion; **-se** to revolt.

sublime *adj.* sublime.

submarino *m. & adj.* submarine; *m.* **— atómico** atomic submarine.

subordinado *adj. & m.* subordinate.

subordinar *v.* to subordinate; to sub-due.

subrayar *v.* to underline; to emphasize.

subsanar *v.* to mend, remedy, repair (*a damage, error, defect, etc.*); to make up for (*an error, fault, etc.*); to excuse (*a fault or error*).

subscribir = **suscribir.**

subscripción = **suscripción.**

subscriptor = **suscritor.**

subsecretario *m.* undersecretary.

subsecuente *adj.* subsequent.

subsiguiente *adj.* subsequent.

subsistencia *f.* living, livelihood; suste-nance; permanence.

subsistir *v.* to subsist; to exist; to last.

substancia = **sustancia.**

substancial = **sustancial.**

substancioso = **sustancioso.**

substantivo = **sustantivo.**

substitución = **sustitución.**

substituíble = **sustituíble.**

substituir = **sustituir.**

substituto = **sustituto.**

substracción = **sustracción.**

substraer = **sustraer.**

subsuelo *m.* subsoil.

subteniente *m.* second lieutenant.

subterráneo *adj.* subterranean, under-ground; *m.* underground; cave, tun-nel, vault.

suburbano *adj.* suburban; *m.* suburban resident.

suburbio *m.* suburb.

subvención *f.* subsidy.

subvencionar *v.* to subsidize.

subyugar *v.* to subdue.

succión *f.* suction.

suceder *v.* to happen, occur; to suc-ceed, follow.

sucesión *f.* succession; heirs, offspring.

sucesivo *adj.* successive; **en lo —** hereafter, in the future.

suceso *m.* event; outcome, result.

sucesor *m.* successor.

suciedad *f.* dirt, filth; filthiness; filthy act or remark.

sucinto *adj.* compact, concise, brief.

sucio *adj.* dirty; foul, filthy.

suculento *adj.* juicy.

sucumbir *v.* to succumb; to yield.

sucursal *f.* branch, branch office (*of a post office, bank, etc.*); *adj.* branch (*used as an adj.*).

suche *adj. Ven.* sour, unripe; *m. Andes* pimple; *Ch.* office boy, insignificant employee; *Andes* suche (*a tree*).

sud *m.* south; south wind; **sudeste** *m. & adj.* southeast; **sudoeste** *m. & adj.* southwest.

sudamericano *adj. & m.* South Ameri-can.

sudar *v.* to sweat, perspire; to ooze; to toil.

sudor *m.* sweat, perspiration; toil.

sudoroso *adj.* sweaty, sweating, perspiring.

sueco *adj.* Swedish; *m.* Swede; Swedish language; **hacerse el —** to pretend not to see or understand.

suegra *f.* mother-in-law.

suegro *m.* father-in-law.

suela *f.* sole of a shoe; shoe leather.

sueldo *m.* salary.

suelo *m.* soil, ground; floor; pavement; bottom.

suelto *adj.* (*no atado*) loose; free, easy; (*ágil*) agile, nimble; blank (*verse*); *m.* small change; short newspaper article, news item.

sueño *m.* sleep; dream; sleepiness, drowsiness; **en -s** in one's sleep; **conciliar el —** to get to sleep; **tener —** to be sleepy.

suero *m.* serum.

suerte *f.* (*fortuna*) fate; fortune; chance; luck; (*clase*) sort, kind; way, manner; (*truco*) trick; **de — que** so that, in such a way that; and so; **echar -s** to cast lots; **tener —** to be lucky; **tocarle a uno la —** to fall to one's lot; to be lucky.

suéter *m. Am.* sweater.

suficiente *adj.* sufficient; competent, able.

sufijo *m.* suffix; *adj.* suffixed.

sufragar[7] *v.* to defray, pay; to help, aid; *Am.* **— por** to vote for.

sufragio *m.* suffrage; vote; help, aid.

sufrido *adj.* suffering, long-suffering, patient; **mal —** impatient.

sufridor *m.* sufferer; *adj.* suffering.

sufrimiento *m.* suffering; patience, endurance.

sufrir *v.* to suffer; to endure; to allow, permit; to sustain; to undergo; **— un examen** to take an examination.

sugerencia *f. Am.* suggestion, hint.

sugerir[3] *v. irr.* to suggest; to hint.

sugestión *f.* suggestion; hint.

sugestivo *adj.* suggestive.

suicida *m. & f.* suicide (*person who commits suicide*).

suicidarse *v.* to commit suicide.

suicidio *m.* suicide (*act of suicide*).

suizo *adj. & m.* Swiss.

sujeción *f.* subjection; control; submission.

sujetapapeles *m.* paper clip.

sujetar *v.* to subject; to control; to subdue; to fasten; to grasp, hold; **-se** to subject oneself; to submit; to adhere (to).

sujeto *adj.* subject; liable; fastened; under control; *m.* subject matter; subject; fellow, individual.

sulfamida *f.* common name for the sulfa drugs.

sulfato *m.* sulphate.

sulfurarse *v.* to get angry.

sulfúrico *adj.* sulphuric.

sulfuro *m.* sulphide.

sultán *m.* sultan.

suma *f.* sum; addition; substance; summary; **en —** in short.

sumador *adj.* adding; **máquina suma-**

dora adding machine.

sumar *v.* to add; to add up (to), amount (to); to sum up; **-se a** to join.

sumario *m.* summary; indictment; *adj.* summary, brief, concise; swift (*punishment*).

sumergible *adj.* submergible; *m.* submarine.

sumergir[11] *v.* to submerge, plunge, sink; to immerse; **-se** to submerge; to sink.

sumidero *m.* sink; sewer, drain.

suministrar *v.* to give, supply with, provide with.

sumir *v.* to sink; to submerge; to immerse; *Riopl., Mex., Carib.* to dent; **-se** to sink; *Andes* to shrink, shrivel; *Andes* to cower, crouch in fear; *Am.* **-se el sombrero hasta las cejas** to pull one's hat over one's eyes.

sumisión *f.* submission; obedience.

sumiso *adj.* submissive; obedient; meek.

sumo *adj.* supreme, highest; high; greatest; **— pontífice** Sovereign Pontiff (*the Pope*); **a lo —** at the most.

suntuoso *adj.* sumptuous, magnificent, luxurious.

superabundancia *f.* superabundance, great abundance, overflow.

superar *v.* to surpass; to exceed; to overcome.

superávit *m.* surplus.

superficial *adj.* superficial; shallow; frivolous; **superficialidad** *f.* superficiality, shallowness, frivolity.

superficie *f.* surface; area.

superfluo *adj.* superfluous.

superintendente *m.* superintendent; supervisor; overseer.

superior *adj.* superior; higher; better; upper; *m.* superior; father superior; **superiora** *f.* superior, mother superior.

superioridad *f.* superiority; excellence.

superlativo *adj. & m.* superlative.

supersónico *adj.* supersonic.

superstición *f.* superstition.

supersticioso *adj.* superstitious.

supervivencia *f.* survival.

superviviente = sobreviviente.

suplantar *v.* to supplant; to forge (*a document or check*).

suplementar *v.* to supplement.

suplementario *adj.* supplementary, extra.

suplemento *m.* supplement; supply, supplying.

suplente *adj., m. & f.* substitute.

súplica *f.* entreaty; request; petition; prayer.

suplicante *adj.* suppliant, beseeching; *m. & f.* suppliant; petitioner.

suplicar[6] *v.* to beg, entreat, implore; to pray humbly; to appeal, petition.

suplicio *m.* torture; torment; anguish; execution; instrument of torture; scaffold, gallows.

suplir *v.* to supply; to make up for; to substitute, take the place of (*temporarily*).

SO

suponer[40] *v. irr.* to suppose; to assume; to be important.

suposición *f.* supposition; assumption.

supremacía *f.* supremacy.

supremo *adj.* supreme; final, last.

supresión *f.* suppression; omission; elimination.

suprimir *v.* to suppress; to abolish; to omit.

supuesto *p.p. of* **suponer** supposed, assumed; **— que** supposing that; since; **por —** of course, naturally; *m.* supposition; assumption.

supuración *f.* formation or discharge of pus.

supurar *v.* to fester, form or discharge pus.

sur *m.* south; south wind; **sureste** *m.* southeast; **suroeste** *m.* southwest.

suramericano = sudamericano.

surcar[6] *v.* to furrow; to plow; to plow through; to cut through.

surco *m.* furrow; rut; gróove; wrinkle.

sureño *adj.* southern, from the south; *m.* a southerner.

surgir[11] *v.* to surge, rise; to spurt, spout; to appear.

surtido *m.* stock, supply, assortment; *adj.* assorted.

surtidor *m.* supplier; spout, jet.

surtir *v.* to provide, supply, stock (with); to spout, spurt; **— efecto** to produce the desired result; **— un pedido** to fill an order.

susceptible *adj.* susceptible; sensitive; touchy.

suscitar *v.* to raise, stir up, provoke.

suscribir[52] *v.* to subscribe; to endorse; to agree (to); **-se** to subscribe.

suscripción *f.* subscription.

suscrito *p.p. of* **suscribir.**

suscritor *m.* subscriber.

susodicho *adj.* aforesaid, above-mentioned.

suspender *v.* (*colgar*) to suspend; to hang; (*detener*) to stop; to defer; (*no aprobar*) to fail, flunk; to dismiss temporarily; to astonish.

suspensión *f.* suspension; postponement, delay; uncertainty; cessation; a system of supporting devices (*automobile*).

suspenso *adj.* suspended; hanging; pending; perplexed, astonished; **en —** in suspense; *m.* failure (*in an examination*).

suspicaz *adj.* suspicious.

suspirar *v.* to sigh; to sigh (for), long (for).

suspiro *m.* sight; brief pause (*in music*).

sustancia *f.* substance; essence; *Andes* broth.

sustancial *adj.* substantial; nourishing.

sustancioso *adj.* substantial; nourishing.

sustantivo *m.* noun; *adj.* substantive; real; independent.

sustentar *v.* to sustain; to support; to feed, nourish; to maintain; uphold.

sustento *m.* sustenance; food; support.

sustitución *f.* substitution.

sustituible *adj.* replaceable.

sustituir[32] *v. irr.* to substitute.

sustituto *m.* substitute.

susto *m.* scare, fright.

sustracción *f.* subtraction.

sustraer[46] *v. irr.* to subtract; to remove, withdraw; **-se a** to evade, avoid, slip away from.

susurrar *v.* to whisper; to murmur; to rustle; **-se** to be whispered or rumored about.

susurro *m.* whisper; murmur; rustle.

sutil *adj.* subtle; keen; clever; crafty; thin, fine, delicate.

sutileza, sutilidad *f.* subtlety; keenness, cleverness; cunning; thinness, fineness.

suyo *adj.* his, of his; her, of hers; your, of yours (*formal*); their, of theirs; *pron.* his, hers, yours (*formal*), theirs; **de —** naturally, by nature; **salirse con la suya** to get one's own way; **hacer de las suyas** to be up to one's tricks; **los -s** his (hers, theirs); his (her, their) own people.

T

tabaco *m.* tobacco; *Carib., Ven., Col.* cigar; snuff; *Col.* blow with the fist; **tabaquería** *f.* tobacco store, cigar store.

tábano *m.* horsefly, gadfly.

taberna *f.* tavern, bar, liquor store.

tabernáculo *m.* tabernacle.

tabique *m.* partition, partition wall.

tabla *f.* board, plank; plate of metal; slab; table, list; strip of ground; *Col.* chocolate tablet; **-s** draw, tie (*in games*); stage boards, the stage; **a raja —** cost what it may; *Am.* in great haste; **hacer — rasa de algo** to disregard, omit, or ignore something; *Am.* to clear away all obstacles in the way of something.

tablado *m.* platform, stage; scaffold; floor boards.

tablero *m.* board; panel; timber, piece of lumber; chessboard, checkerboard; store counter; large work table; gambling table; *Col., Ven., Mex.* blackboard; **poner al —** to risk, endanger; **— de mando** control panel.

tableta *f.* tablet; small thin board; memorandum pad.

tabletear *v.* to rattle; to make a continuous rattling or tapping sound.

tableteo *m.* rattling sound; tapping.

tablilla *f.* tablet; slat, small thin board; splint; small bulletin board; **-s** wooden clappers.

tablón *m.* plank; large, thick board.

taburete *m.* stool; footstool.

tacañería *f.* stinginess, tightness, miserliness.

tacaño *adj.* stingy, tight, miserly; sly.

tácito *adj.* tacit, implied; silent.

taciturno *adj.* taciturn, silent, sullen; sad.

taco *m.* wad; roll; plug, stopper; billiard cue; bite, snack; swear word; *Mex., C.A.* Mexican folded tortilla sandwich; *Am.* leather legging; *Ch.*, *Andes* short, fat person; *Mex.* heel of a shoe; *Am.* pile, heap; **echar -s** to curse, swear; *Mex.* **darse uno —** to strut, put on airs.

tacón *m.* heel of a shoe.

taconear *v.* to click the heels, walk hard on one's heels.

taconeo *m.* click, clicking (*of the heels*).

táctica *f.* tactics.

tacto *m.* tact; touch, sense of touch.

tacha *f.* flaw, defect, blemish.

tachar *v.* (*borrar*) to cross out; to scratch out; to blot out; (*culpar*) to blame; to find fault with; to censure.

tachón *m.* stud; trimming, braid; blot.

tachonar *v.* to stud, ornament with studs; to adorn with trimming.

tachuela *f.* tack, small nail; *Am.* metal dipper; *Am.* runt, "shorty".

tafetán *m.* taffeta; **— inglés** court plaster.

tahur *m.* gambler; cardsharp.

taimado *adj.* sly, crafty; *Am.* sullen, gloomy, gruff.

taita = **tatita**. See **tata**.

tajada *f.* slice; cut.

tajalápiz *m.* pencil sharpener.

tajante *adj.* cutting, sharp.

tajar *v.* to slice; to cut; to sharpen (*a pencil*).

tajo *m.* cut; gash; cutting edge; sheer cliff; chopping block.

tal *adj.* such; such a; **— cual** such as; so-so, fair; **— vez** perhaps; **el — Pedro** that fellow Peter; **un — García** a certain García; **— para cual** two of a kind; **un — por cual** a nobody; *adv.* just as, in such a way; **estaba — como le dejé** he was just as I left him; **con — (de) que** provided that; **¿qué —?** how are you?; hello!

talabarte *m.* sword belt.

taladrar *v.* to bore, drill; to pierce; to penetrate.

taladro *m.* auger, drill; bore, drill hole; *Am.* mine tunnel.

tálamo *m.* bridal bed or chamber.

talante *m.* disposition; mood; appearance, manner.

talco *m.* talc (*a soft mineral*); **— en polvo** talcum powder.

talega *f.* money bag, sack.

talento *m.* talent; ability, natural gift.

talentoso *adj.* talented, gifted.

talismán *m.* talisman, charm.

talón *m.* heel; stub, check, coupon.

talonario *m.* stub book; **libro —** stub book.

talonear *v.* to tap with one's heel; to walk briskly.

taloneo *m.* tapping with the heel; loud footsteps.

talla *f.* (*altura*) stature, height; (*labrado*) carving; (*lance entero*) round of a card game; (*rescate*) ransom; *Am.* chat; *Am.* thrashing, beating.

tallar *v.* to carve; to cut (*stone*); to appraise; to deal (*cards*); *Am.* to court, make love; *Andes, Col.* to

bother, disturb.

tallarín *m.* noodle.

talle *m.* figure, form; waist; fit (*of a dress*); looks, appearance; *Ven.* bodice.

taller *m.* workshop; laboratory; studio; factory.

tallo *m.* stalk; stem; shoot, sprout.

tamal *m. Mex., C.A.* tamale; *Am.* vile trick, intrigue; *Am.* clumsy bundle.

tamaño *m.* size; *adj.* such a; of the size of; **— disparate** such a (big) mistake; **— como un elefante** big as an elephant; **tamañito** *adj.* very small; **tamañito así** about this little; **se quedó tamañito** he was (left) astonished, amazed.

tambalearse *v.* to totter, stagger, sway, reel.

también *adv.* also, too; likewise.

tambor *m.* drum; drum-like object; drummer; pair of embroidery hoops; *Mex.* bedspring, spring mattress; **— de freno** brake drum; **tambora** *f.* bass drum; **tamboril** *m.* small drum; **tamborilero** *m.* drummer.

tamborilear *v.* to drum; to extol.

tamiz *m.* fine sieve.

tamizar *v.* to sift; to blend.

tampoco *conj.* either (*after a negative*); **no lo hizo —** he did not do it either; **ni yo —** nor I either.

tan *adv.* (*contr. of* **tanto**) so; as; such a.

tanda *f.* turn; round, bout; task; gang, group; shift, relay; *Col., Ven., Mex., Carib.* section of a theatrical performance.

tangente *adj. & f.* tangent; **salirse por la —** to go off at a tangent; to avoid the issue.

tangible *adj.* tangible.

tango *m.* tango.

tanque *m.* tank; reservoir; *Col., Ven.* pond; *Mex.* swimming pool.

tantán *m.* clang; knock! knock!; sound of a bell, drum, etc.

tantear *v.* to probe, test; to sound out, feel out; to estimate, calculate approximately; *Cuba, Ven., Ríopl.* to grope, feel one's way; *Am.* to lie in wait; *Mex.* to fool, make a fool of; *Ven., Mex., C.A.* **¡tantee Vd.!** just imagine!

tanteo *m.* trial, test; calculation, estimate; score; **al —** by guess; hit or miss.

tanto *adj., pron. & adv.* so much, as much; so; **-s** so many, as many; *m.* certain amount; counter, chip (*to keep score*); **cuarenta y -s** forty odd; **el — por ciento** percentage, rate; **un —** (*or* **algún —**) somewhat; **— como** as well as; as much as; **— ... como** both . . . and; **— en la ciudad como en el campo** both in the city and in the country; **entre** (*or* **mientras**) **—** meanwhile; **por lo —** therefore.

tañer *v.* to play (*an instrument*); to ring.

tañido *m.* sound, tune; ring; twang (*of a guitar*).

tapa *f.* cover; lid; book cover; heel

lift.

tapacubos *m.* hubcap.

tapadera *f.* cover, lid; one who shields another.

tapar *v.* to cover; to plug, stop up; to veil; to hide; *Am.* to fill (*a tooth*); *Am.* to crush, crumple; *Am.* to cover with insults; **-se** to cover up; to wrap oneself up.

taparrabo *m.* loincloth; trunks.

tapera *f. Am.* ruins; *Riopl., Andes* abandoned room or house.

tapete *m.* rug; table scarf.

tapia *f.* adobe wall; wall fence.

tapiar *v.* to wall up; to block up (*a door or window*).

tapicería *f.* tapestry; upholstery; tapestry shop; tapestry making.

tapiz *m.* tapestry.

tapón *m.* plug, stopper, cork; bottle cap.

taquigrafía *f.* shorthand.

taquígrafo *m.* stenographer.

taquilla *f.* ticket office; box office; file (*for letters, papers, etc.*); *Am.* tavern, liquor store.

tararear *v.* to hum.

tarareo *m.* hum, humming.

tarascada *f.* snap, bite; snappy or harsh answer.

tardanza *f.* delay; slowness.

tardar *v.* to delay; to be late; to be long (in); to take long (in); **-se** to delay oneself; to be delayed; **a más** — at the very latest.

tarde *f.* afternoon; *adv.* late; **de — en** — from time to time, now and then.

tardío *adj.* late; slow.

tardo *adj.* slow, lazy; tardy, late; stupid, dull; **tardón** *adj.* very slow; *m.* slowpoke, slow person.

tarea *f.* task, job; anxiety, care.

tarifa *f.* tariff; list of duties, taxes, or prices; fare.

tarima *f.* wooden platform; low bench.

tarjeta *f.* card; **— postal** postcard.

tarro *m.* earthen jar; *Mex.* horn (*of an animal*); *Ch., Cuba, Andes* can; *Andes* top hat.

tarta *f.* tart.

tartamudear *v.* to stutter, stammer.

tartamudeo *m.* stammer, stammering.

tartamudo *m.* stutterer, stammerer; *adj.* stuttering, stammering.

tartera *f.* griddle; baking pan.

tarugo *m.* wooden block; wooden peg; blockhead, dunce; *adj. Andes* mischievous, devilish.

tasa *f.* measure; standard; rate; appraisal; valuation.

tasación *f.* assessment, valuation, appraisal.

tasajo *m.* piece of jerked beef.

tasar *v.* to measure; to appraise; to rate.

tata *f.* daddy, dad; *Mex., Andes* chief (*said by Indians to a superior*); **tatita** *m.* daddy; *Mex., Andes* dear chief or daddy (*said by Indians*).

tataranieto *m.* great-great-grandson.

tauromaquia *f.* bullfighting.

taxear *v.* to taxi (*said of a plane*).

taxi, taxímetro *m.* taxi, taxicab.

taxista *m. & f.* taxi driver.

taza *f.* cup; bowl; basin of a fountain.

tazón *m.* large cup; bowl; basin of a fountain.

té *m.* tea; *f.* T-square, T-shaped ruler.

te *obj. pron.* you (*fam. sing.*); to you; for you; yourself.

teatral *adj.* theatrical.

teatro *m.* theater; stage; scene, setting; **hacer** — to put on airs, show off.

tecla *f.* key (*of a piano, typewriter, etc.*); **dar uno en la** — to hit the nail on the head, find the right way to do something.

teclado *m.* keyboard.

teclear *v.* to finger the keys; to play the piano; to type.

tecleo *m.* fingering; movement of the keys (*typewriter, piano*).

técnica *f.* technique.

técnico *adj.* technical; *m.* technical expert, technician.

tecolote *m. Am.* owl.

techado *m.* roof; shed; *p.p. of* **techar.**

techar *v.* to roof.

techo *m.* roof; ceiling.

techumbre *f.* roof; ceiling.

tedio *m.* tediousness; boredom; bother.

tedioso *adj.* tedious, boring, tiresome.

teja *f.* tile; linden tree; *Am.* rear part of a saddle; **de -s abajo** here below, in this world.

tejado *m.* roof; shed.

tejamanil *m.* shingle; small thin board.

tejar *m.* tile factory; *v.* to cover with tiles.

tejedor *m.* weaver.

tejer *v.* to weave; to interlace; to braid; to knit.

tejido *m.* textile, fabric; texture; weave; weaving; tissue.

tejo *m.* disk; quoit; weight.

tejón *m.* badger; bar of gold.

tela *f.* cloth; membrane; web; film (*on the surface of liquids*); **— adhesiva** adhesive tape; **— de cebolla** onion skin; flimsy fabric; *Am.* **— emplástica** court plaster; **— metálica** wire screen; **poner en — de juicio** to call in question.

telar *m.* loom.

telaraña *f.* cobweb, spider's web.

teleférico *m.* telpher; car suspended on aerial cables.

telefonear *v.* to telephone.

telefónico *adj.* telephonic, telephone (*used as adj.*); **receptor** — telephone receiver.

teléfono *m.* telephone; **telefonista** *m. & f.* telephone operator.

telegrafía *f.* telegraphy.

telegrafiar[17] *v.* to telegraph.

telegráfico *adj.* telegraphic.

telégrafo *m.* telegraph; **— sin hilos** (*or* **— inalámbrico**) wireless telegraph; **telegrafista** *m. & f.* telegraph operator.

telegrama *m.* telegram.

telescopio *m.* telescope.

telesquí m. ski lift.
teletipo m. teletype.
televisión f. television.
telón m. theater curtain; — **de boca** drop curtain; — **de foro** drop scene.
tema m. theme; subject; f. fixed idea, mania.
temblar[1] v. irr. to tremble; to shake; to quiver.
temblón adj. tremulous, trembling, shaking, quivering.
temblor m. tremor, trembling; shiver; quake; — **de tierra** earthquake.
tembloroso adj. trembling, shaking.
temer v. to fear; to dread; to suspect.
temerario adj. rash, reckless.
temeridad f. temerity, recklessness; folly.
temeroso adj. fearful; suspicious; timid.
temible adj. terrible, dreadful.
temor m. fear; dread, suspicion.
tempano m. thick slice or chunk (of anything); kettledrum; drumhead (parchment stretched over the end of a drum); — **de hielo** block of ice; iceberg.
temperamento m. temperament; climate.
temperatura f. temperature.
tempestad f. tempest, storm.
tempestuoso adj. tempestuous, stormy.
templado p.p. & adj. (moderado) tempered; tuned; moderate; temperate; lukewarm; (valiente) brave; Andes in love; Am. half-drunk; Am. hard, severe; **estar mal —** to be in a bad humor.
templanza f. temperance; moderation; mildness.
templar v. to temper; to moderate; to calm; to soften; to tune; **-se** to be tempered, moderate; to control oneself; Andes to fall in love; Col. to take to one's heels; Am. to stuff oneself.
temple m. temper; temperament; valor, courage; harmony (of musical instruments); Am. sweetheart; **de mal —** in a bad humor.
templo m. temple; church.
temporada f. period of time, season; — **de ópera** opera season.
temporal adj. temporal; secular; worldly; temporary; m. weather; storm; spell of rainy weather.
tempranero adj. habitually early or ahead of time; **ser —** to be an early riser.
temprano adj. early; premature; adv. early.
tenacidad f. tenacity; tenaciousness; perseverance.
tenacillas f. pl. small tongs; pincers, tweezers; sugar tongs; curling iron.
tenaz adj. tenacious; firm; strong, resistant; stubborn.
tenazas f. pl. pincers; pliers; tongs; forceps (for pulling teeth); **tenazuelas** f. pl. tweezers, small pincers.
tendedero m. place to hang or spread clothes; clothesline.

tendencia f. tendency, inclination.
tender[1] v. irr. (extender) to spread out; to hang to dry; to stretch out; to lay out; (propender) to tend, have a tendency, move (toward); Carib., Mex., C.A., Riopl., Andes to make (a bed); **-se** to stretch oneself out; to lay all one's cards on the table; to run at full gallop.
ténder m. tender (of a train).
tendero m. storekeeper; tentmaker.
tendón m. tendon, sinew.
tenducho m. wretched little shop.
tenebroso adj. dark, shadowy; gloomy.
tenedor m. table fork; holder, possessor, keeper; — **de libros** bookkeeper.
teneduría f. office and position of bookkeeper; — **de libros** bookkeeping.
tener[45] v. irr. to have; to possess; to hold; — **en mucho** to esteem highly; — **por** to consider, judge; — **que** (+ inf.) to have to; — **gana** (or **ganas**) **de** to desire, feel like; — **miedo** (**sueño, frío, hambre,** etc.) to be afraid (sleepy, cold, hungry, etc.); — **. . . años** to be . . . years old; **-se** to stand firm; to hold on.
tenería f. tannery.
teniente m. first lieutenant; substitute, deputy.
tenis m. tennis.
tenor m. tenor; text, literal meaning; kind, sort, nature.
tensión f. tension; strain.
tenso adj. tense; tight, taut.
tentación f. temptation.
tentáculo m. tentacle, feeler.
tentador adj. tempting; m. tempter; the devil.
tentalear v. to grope, feel around; to finger, touch; to fumble (for something).
tentar[1] v. irr. to tempt; to touch, feel with the fingers; to grope; to attempt, try; to test; to probe, examine with a probe.
tentativa f. attempt, trial.
tentativo adj. tentative.
tenue adj. delicate, thin; flimsy; worthless.
teñir[5,19] v. irr. to dye; to tinge; to darken (the color of a painting).
teologal, teológico adj. theological.
teología f. theology.
teoría f. theory.
teórico adj. theoretical.
tequila m. Mex. tequila (liquor made from the maguey plant).
tercero adj. third; m. third person; mediator; go-between; tertiary (member of the third order of St. Francis).
terciar v. (atravesar) to sling across one's shoulders; (dividir) to divide into three parts; (intervenir) to intervene, mediate; to meddle, join (in); (equilibrar) to balance the load on a pack animal; Mex., Col. to load or carry on the back; Am. to adulterate, add water to; Am. to mix.
tercio adj. third; m. one third; half of a mule load; military regiment or

TA

division; *Col.*, *Carib.*, *Mex.* bale, bundle; **hacer uno mal —** to hinder, interfere; **— de varas** the banderilla part of the bullfight.

terciopelo *m.* velvet.

terco *adj.* obstinate, stubborn; hard; *Am.* harsh, severe.

tergiversar *v.* to distort, twist.

terminación *f.* termination, end; ending.

terminal *adj.* terminal, final.

terminante *adj.* closing, ending; decisive, final.

terminar *v.* to terminate, end; to finish; **-se** to end.

término *m.* end; completion; goal, object; boundary, limit; terminal; term; word, phrase; **en otros -s** in other words; **por — medio** on an average; as a rule; **primer —** foreground.

termo *m.* thermos bottle.

termómetro *m.* thermometer.

termonuclear *adj.* thermonuclear.

Termos *f.* Thermos bottle (*trademark*).

termóstato *m.* thermostat.

ternera *f.* calf; veal.

terneza *f.* tenderness; softness; affection; affectionate word; caress.

terno *m.* group or combination of three; suit of clothes; *Carib.*, *Mex.* set of jewels (*earrings, necklace, and brooch*); *Am.* cup and saucer; **echar** (*or* **soltar**) **un —** to utter a bad word; to curse, swear.

ternura *f.* tenderness.

terquedad *f.* obstinacy, stubbornness.

terrado *m.* terrace; flat roof.

terramicina *f.* Terramycin.

terraplén *m.* railroad embankment.

terrateniente *m.* & *f.* landholder.

terraza *f.* terrace, veranda; flat roof.

terremoto *m.* earthquake.

terrenal *adj.* earthly, worldly.

terreno *m.* land; ground; field; *adj.* earthly, worldly.

terrestre *adj.* terrestrial; earthly.

terrible *adj.* terrible.

terrífico *adj.* terrific.

territorio *m.* territory.

terrón *m.* clod; lump (*of sugar*).

terror *m.* terror.

terso *adj.* polished, smooth.

tertulia *f.* evening party; social gathering; club; conversation; *Riopl.*, *Cuba*, *Ven.* theater gallery.

tertuliano, tertulio *m.* member of a tertulia.

tesis *f.* thesis.

tesón *m.* grit, endurance, pluck, persistence.

tesonero *adj. Mex., Cuba, Andes* tenacious, stubborn, persevering, persistent.

tesorería *f.* treasury; **tesorero** *m.* treasurer.

tesoro *m.* treasure; treasury.

testa *f.* head; crown of the head; front.

testamento *m.* testament; will.

testarudez *f.* stubbornness, obstinacy.

testarudo *adj.* stubborn.

testigo *m.* & *f.* witness; *m.* testimony, proof, evidence; **— de cargo** witness for the prosecution; **— de vista** eyewitness.

testimoniar *v.* to give testimony of; to serve as a witness.

testimonio *m.* testimony; proof, evidence; **levantar falso —** to bear false witness.

testuz *m.* nape; crown of the head (*of certain animals*).

teta *f.* teat, nipple; breast; udder.

tetera *f.* teapot; teakettle; *Mex.*, *Cuba*, *Col.* **tetero** nursing bottle.

tétrico *adj.* sad, melancholy, gloomy.

textil *adj.* textile.

texto *m.* text; quotation; textbook.

tez *f.* complexion, skin.

ti *pers. pron.* (*used after prep.*) you; yourself (*fam. sing.*).

tía *f.* aunt; older woman; *Ven.* **— rica** pawnshop; **no hay tu —** there is no use or hope; there is no way out of it; **quedarse una para —** to remain an old maid.

tibio *adj.* tepid, lukewarm; indifferent; *Am.* annoyed, angry.

tiburón *m.* shark.

tico *adj.* & *m. Am.* Costa Rican (*humorous nickname*).

tiempo *m.* time; weather; tense; **a —** in time, on time; **a su —** in due time, at the proper time; **a un —** at one and the same time; **andando el —** in time, as time goes on.

tienda *f.* store; tent; **— de campaña** camping tent, army tent.

tienta *f.* probe (*surgical instrument*); **a -s** gropingly, feeling one's way; **andar a -s** to grope, feel one's way.

tiento *m.* touch; tact; blind man's stick; steady hand; blow; tentacle, feeler (*of an insect*); *Andes, Riopl.* saddle strap, leather strap, thong; *Am.* snack; *Am.* swallow of liquor; **dar un —** to make a trial or attempt; **hacer algo con mucho —** to do something with great care or caution; **perder el —** to lose one's skill; *Andes* **tener a uno a los -s** to keep someone within sight; *Ven.* **tener la vida en un —** to be in great danger.

tierno *adj.* tender; soft; young; recent, new; sensitive; affectionate; *Am.* green, unripe.

tierra *f.* earth; land; ground; soil; native land; **— adentro** inland; **— firme** mainland; solid ground; **dar en —** **con alguien** to overthrow someone; **echar por —** to knock down; to demolish; **tomar —** to land.

tieso *adj.* stiff, rigid; stuck-up; firm; stubborn.

tiesto *m.* flowerpot; broken piece of earthenware; *Am.* pot.

tiesura *f.* stiffness.

tifo *m.* typhus; **tifoidea** *f.* typhoid fever.

tifón *m.* typhoon; waterspout.

tifus *m.* typhus.

tigre *m.* tiger.

tijera *f.* (*usually* **tijeras**) scissors; sawhorse; **silla de —** folding chair; **tener buena —** (or tener buenas -s) to have a sharp tongue; to be a gossip.

tijeretada f., **tijeretazo** m. snip, cut, clip (with the scissors).

tijeretear v. to snip, cut, clip (with scissors); to criticize others, gossip.

tildar v. to accent (a word); to put a tilde over the **n**; to stigmatize.

tilde f. tilde (mark over an **n**); blemish; jot, bit, speck; Col. accent mark.

timbrar v. to stamp, mark with a seal.

timbre m. revenue stamp; seal; crest (on a coat of arms); call bell; timbre (quality of tone, tone color); merit, fame; glorious deed; Am. postage stamp.

timidez f. timidity; shyness.

timido adj. timid; shy.

timón m. helm; rudder; beam of a plow.

timonear v. to steer (a ship).

timorato adj. timorous, timid.

tímpano m. eardrum; kettledrum.

tina f. large earthen jar; vat, tank, tub; bathtub.

tinaco m. tank, vat, tub.

tinaja f. large earthen jar.

tinieblas f. pl. darkness; obscurity; ignorance, confusion; Tenebrae (Holy Week religious service).

tino m. acumen, keen insight, good judgment; tact; accurate aim; good sense of touch; tank, vat.

tinta f. ink; dye; tint, hue; **-s** paints; **— simpática** invisible ink; **saber de buena —** to know on good authority.

tinte m. tint, hue; tinge; color; dye; dyeing.

tinterillo m. shyster. See **picapleitos**.

tintero m. inkwell, inkstand; ink roller (printing); Am. writing materials, desk set.

tintinear v. to tinkle.

tintineo m. tinkle, tinkling.

tinto adj. tinged; red (wine); Am. dark-red; p.p. irr. of **teñir**.

tintorería f. cleaner's and dyer's shop.

tintorero m. dyer.

tintura f. tincture; tint, color; dye.

tinturar v. to tincture; to tinge; to dye.

tiñoso adj. scabby, mangy; stingy.

tío m. uncle; old man; good old man; fellow, guy; Ríopl., Mex., Ven., Andes **el cuento del —** deceitful story (told to extract money).

tiovivo m. merry-go-round.

típico adj. typical; Am. corrected (edition).

tiple m. & f. high soprano singer; m. treble; soprano voice; treble guitar.

tipo m. type; class; model, standard; fellow, guy; Am. rate of interest; Am. **— de cambio** rate of exchange; **buen —** good-looking fellow.

tipografía f. typography, printing; press, printing shop.

tira f. strip; stripe; Mex. **estar hecho -s** to be in rags; Ven. **sacar a uno las -s** to tan one's hide, beat one to pieces.

tirabuzón m. corkscrew.

tirada f. throw; issue, edition, printing;

Am. tirade, long speech; Am. sly trick; Am. dash (on horseback); **de una —** all at once, at one fell swoop.

tirador m. shooter; thrower; slingshot; bell cord; handle; printer; Am. leather belt with pockets; **— de goma** slingshot.

tiranía f. tyranny.

tiránico adj. tyrannical.

tirano adj. tyrannical; m. tyrant.

tirante adj. pulling; stretched, taut; strained; m. trace (of a harness); brace; **-s** suspenders; supporters (for stockings).

tirantez f. tension, tightness; strain; pull.

tirar v. (lanzar) to throw; to throw away; to shoot, fire; (imprimir) to draw; to print; (atraer) to pull; to attract; Am. to cart; **— a** to tend toward; to resemble; to aim at; **— de** to pull, tug; **— bien a la espada** to handle a sword well; **ir tirando** to get along; **a todo** (or a más) **—** at the most; Am. **al —** haphazardly; **-se** to throw oneself; to lie down; Mex., C.A., Col., Ven., Ríopl., Andes **tirársela de** to boast of.

tiritar v. to shiver.

tiro m. (disparo) throw; shot; (pieza) piece of artillery; (alcance) range of a gun; shooting range; (carga) charge of a gun; team (of horses); chimney draft; mine shaft; Am. issue, printing; Am. cartage, transport; **-s** Am. suspenders; **— al blanco** target practice; Ch., Andes **al —** at once; Ven. **de a** (or de al) **—** all at once; completely; **caballo de —** draft horse; **ni a -s** absolutely not (not even if you shoot me).

tirón m. jerk, sudden pull; **de un —** all at once, with one big pull.

tironear v. C.A., Mex., Ríopl. to pull, jerk; Col. to attract.

tirotear v. to shoot around; to shoot at random; **-se** to exchange shots.

tiroteo m. shooting; exchange of shots; skirmish.

tirria f. aversion, grudge; **tenerle — a una persona** to have a strong dislike for someone; to hold a grudge against someone.

tísico adj. tubercular, consumptive.

tisis f. tuberculosis, consumption.

títere m. puppet; ridiculous little fellow; **-s** puppet show.

titilación f. flicker; twinkle; **titileo** m. flickering; twinkling; glimmer.

titilar v. to flicker; to twinkle.

titubear v. to hesitate; to totter, stagger; to grope; to stutter, stammer.

titubeo m. hesitation, wavering.

titular v. to entitle; to name; **-se** to be called or named; to call oneself; to receive a title; adj. titular, in name only.

título m. (letrero) title; heading; sign; inscription; (derecho) claim, legal right; (grado) degree, diploma; credential; titled person; merit; bond, certificate; **a — de** under the pre-

TE

text of; in the capacity of.

tiza f. chalk.

tiznado adj. sooty, covered with soot; smutty; dirty; Ven. drunk; p.p. of **tiznar.**

tiznar v. to smudge, smut; to smear with soot.

tizne m. soot; smut; **tiznón** m. smudge.

tizón m. firebrand (piece of burning wood); rust, blight (on plants); stain (on one's honor).

toalla f. towel.

tobillo m. ankle.

tocadiscos m. record player; phonograph.

tocado m. headdress; hairdo, coiffure; adj. "touched", half-crazy; p.p. of **tocar.**

tocador m. dressing table; boudoir, dressing room; dressing case; player (of a musical instrument).

tocar[6] v. to touch; to play (an instrument); to toll, ring; to knock, rap; **—en** to stop over in; **-le a uno** to fall to one's lot; to be one's share; to be one's turn; to concern one; **-se** to fix one's hair; to become "touched", go slightly crazy.

tocayo m. namesake.

tocino m. bacon; salt pork; lard.

tocón m. stub, stump (of a tree, arm or leg).

todavía adv. still; yet; even.

todo adj. all, whole; every, each; **—hombre** every man; **-s los días** every day; **a — correr** at full or top speed; m. whole; all; everything; **-s** everybody; **ante —** first of all; **así y -s** in spite of that; **con —** in spite of that; **del —** wholly.

todopoderoso adj. almighty.

toga f. gown, robe (worn by a judge, professor, etc.); Roman toga.

toldería f. Ríopl. Indian camp, Indian village.

toldo m. awning; pomp, vanity; Ríopl. Indian hut.

tolerancia f. tolerance, toleration; **tolerante** adj. tolerant.

tolerar v. to tolerate; to allow; to overlook, let pass.

tolete m. Col., Mex., Cuba stick, club, cudgel; Am. raft.

toma f. taking; seizure, capture; dose; tap (of a water main); Am. irrigation ditch; **— de corriente** plug, electric outlet.

tomar v. (asir) to take; to grasp, catch; to capture; (beber) to drink; **— a pechos** to take to heart, take seriously; **-lo a mal** to take it amiss; **— el pelo a** to make fun of, make a fool of; **— por la derecha** to turn to the right; **-se con** to quarrel with.

tomate m. tomato.

tomillo m. thyme.

tomo m. tome, volume; Am. heavy person; Am. dull, silent person; Am. **buen —** a heavy drinker; **de — y lomo** bulky; important.

ton: sin — ni son without rhyme or

reason.

tonada f. tune, song; Andes singsong; Andes, Mex., Carib., Ríopl. local accent; **tonadilla** f. little tune; short popular song.

tonel m. keg, cask, barrel.

tonelada f. ton.

tonelaje m. tonnage.

tónico adj. & m. tonic.

tono m. tone; tune; key; pitch; accent; manner; vigor, strength; **de buen —** of good taste, stylish; **subirse de —** to put on airs.

tontera = **tontería.**

tontería f. foolishness; stupidity.

tonto adj. foolish; stupid; **a tontas y locas** recklessly, without thought; m. fool; dunce; Col., Ch. a game of cards.

topar v. to collide with, run into, bump into; to encounter; to find; to run across; to butt; Am. to gamble; Col. to fight with the fists; Carib., Mex., Ríopl., Andes, Col. to meet, greet.

tope m. butt, bump, collision; encounter; bumper; **hasta el —** up to the top; **estar hasta los -s** to be filled up.

topetada f., **topetazo** m. butt, bump, blow on the head; **topetón** m. hard bump, collision; butt.

topetear v. to butt; to bump.

tópico m. topic, subject.

topo m. mole (small animal); dunce; awkward person.

toque m. touch; ringing; beat (of a drum); tap, sound (of a trumpet, clarinet, etc.); assay; **piedra de —** touchstone; **¡allí está el —!** there is the difficulty!; there is the real test!

toquilla f. triangular handkerchief; ribbon; hatband.

torbellino m. whirlwind; rush, bustle, confusion.

torcedura f. twist; sprain, strain.

torcer[2,10] v. irr. to twist; to turn; to bend; to sprain; to distort; **-se** to become twisted, bent, or sprained; to get crooked; to go astray; to turn sour (said of wine); Am. to get offended, angry.

torcido p.p. & adj. twisted, turned, bent; crooked; angry, resentful; Am. unfortunate, unlucky; **estar — con** to be on unfriendly terms with; m. twisted roll of candied fruit; coarse silk twist; Mex., Carib. gesture or look of disdain; Andes lasso made of twisted leather.

tordillo adj. greyish, dapple-grey.

tordo adj. dapple-grey; m. thrush; dapple-grey horse.

torear v. to perform in a bullfight; to incite, provoke (a bull); to tease.

torero m. bullfighter; adj. relating to bullfighting.

tormenta f. storm, tempest; misfortune.

tormento m. torment; torture; rack (instrument of torture); anguish; pain.

tornar v. to return; to turn; to change, alter; **— a hacerlo** to do it again.

tornasolado *adj.* iridescent, rainbow-colored; changeable (*silk*).

tornear *v.* to turn in a lathe; to do lathe work; to fight in a tournament.

torneo *m.* tournament.

tornillo *m.* screw; clamp, vise; **faltarle a uno un —** to have little sense, "have a screw loose".

torno *m.* turn; lathe; turnstile; revolving server; winch or windlass (*machine for lifting or pulling, turned by a crank*); **— de hilar** spinning wheel; **en —** around.

toro *m.* bull; *Mex., Col.* difficult question; **-s** bullfight; *Am.* **estar en las astas del —** to be in a predicament.

toronja *f.* grapefruit.

torpe *adj.* stupid, dull; clumsy; slow; lewd.

torpedear *v.* to torpedo.

torpedo *m.* torpedo; **torpedero** *m.* torpedo boat.

torpeza *f.* stupidity, dullness; clumsiness; slowness; moral turpitude, lewdness.

torre *f.* tower; turret; castle (*in chess*).

torrente *m.* torrent; flood; **— de voz** powerful voice.

torreón *m.* large tower (*of a fortress, castle, etc.*).

tórrido *adj.* torrid.

torsión *f.* twist; sprain.

torta *f.* torte, round cake; round loaf.

tortilla *f.* omelet; *Mex., C.A.* tortilla (*flat, thin cornmeal cake*).

tórtola *f.* turtledove.

tortuga *f.* tortoise; turtle.

tortuoso *adj.* tortuous, twisting, winding; sly.

tortura *f.* torture; grief, affliction.

torturar *v.* to torture.

torvo *adj.* grim, stern, severe.

tos *f.* cough; **— ferina** whooping cough.

tosco *adj.* coarse, harsh, rough.

toser *v.* to cough; *Am.* to brag, boast.

tosquedad *f.* coarseness, crudeness, roughness; rudeness.

tostada *f.* toast, toasted bread; *Am.* boring visit or conversation; *Ven.* toasted **tortilla; dar** (*or* **pegar**) **una — a uno** to play a mean trick on someone; *Am.* to make someone very angry.

tostado *p.p.* & *adj.* toasted; roasted; tanned; *Am.* worn out, tired out; *m.* toasting; *Am.* roasted corn.

tostador *m.* toaster.

tostar[2] *v. irr.* to toast; to tan; to overheat; to roast (*coffee*).

tostón *m.* toast dipped in oil; small roasted pig; *Mex., C.A.* coin worth half a Mexican peso.

total *adj.* & *m.* total.

totalidad *f.* entirety, whole.

totalitario *adj.* totalitarian.

tóxico *adj.* toxic.

toxina *f.* toxin (*poison produced within animals and plants*).

toza *f.* wooden block; stump; log; piece of bark.

traba *f.* bond, tie; binding or locking device; fastener, fetter, shackle; hindrance, obstacle.

trabado *adj. Col., Riopl., Mex.* tongue-tied; *p.p. of* **trabar.**

trabajador *adj.* industrious; *m.* worker, laborer.

trabajar *v.* to work; to labor; to strive.

trabajo *m.* work; labor; difficulty, obstacle; trouble; hardship.

trabajoso *adj.* laborious, difficult; troublesome; *Am.* unobliging; *Am.* demanding.

trabalenguas *m.* tongue twister.

trabar *v.* to join, fasten; to clasp; to shackle; to brace; to impede; **— amistad con alguien** to become friends with someone; **— batalla** to join in battle; **— conversación** to be engaged in conversation; to engage in conversation; **-se** *Riopl., Mex., Ven.* to stammer; **-se de palabras** to get into an argument.

tracción *f.* traction.

tractor *m.* tractor.

tradición *f.* tradition.

tradicional *adj.* traditional.

traducción *f.* translation.

traducir[25] *v. irr.* to translate; to interpret.

traductor *m.* translator.

traer[46] *v. irr.* to bring; to carry; to lead, conduct; to have; to bring about; to wear; **— a uno inquieto** to keep one disturbed; **— a uno a mal —** to mistreat someone; to bother someone; **-se bien** to dress well; to carry oneself well.

trafagar[7] *v.* to traffic, trade; to roam about; to bustle, hustle; to toil.

tráfago *m.* trade, commerce; bustle, hustle; toil.

traficante *m.* trader; dealer; tradesman.

traficar[6] *v.* to traffic, trade; *Ven.* to pass or move back and forth (*as traffic*). See **transitar.**

tráfico *m.* traffic; trade, commerce.

tragaluz *f.* skylight.

tragar[7] *v.* to swallow; to gulp; to engulf, swallow up.

tragedia *f.* tragedy.

trágico *adj.* tragic.

trago *m.* swallow, gulp; misfortune; *Am.* brandy, hard liquor; **a -s** slowly, by degrees; **echar un —** to take a drink; **tragón** *m.* glutton; *adj.* gluttonous.

traición *f.* treason; treachery; **a —** treacherously; deceitfully.

traicionar *v.* to betray.

traicionero *adj.* treacherous; deceitful; *m.* traitor.

traído *adj.* used, old, worn out; **muy — y llevado** very worn out; *p.p.* of **traer.**

traidor *adj.* treacherous; *m.* traitor; betrayer.

traje *m.* dress; suit; gown; **— de etiqueta** (**— de ceremonia,** *or Am.* **— de parada**) formal gown; formal suit; dress uniform; **— de luces**

bullfighter's costume; *Col., C.A., Mex., Riopl.* — **sastre** woman's tailor-made suit.

trajeado *p.p. & adj.* dressed, clothed.

trajín *m.* traffic, going and coming; hustle, bustle, commotion.

trajinar *v.* to carry, cart back and forth; to go back and forth; to bustle, hustle.

trama *f.* plot; scheme; conspiracy; woof (*horizontal threads of a fabric*).

tramar *v.* to weave; to plot; to scheme.

tramitar *v.* to transact; to take legal steps; to negotiate.

trámite *m.* transaction, procedure, step, formality.

tramo *m.* stretch, lap, span; short distance; regular interval; flight of stairs.

trampa *f.* trap; snare; hatch, trap door; hinged section of a counter; spring door; fraud; trick.

trampear *v.* to trick, cheat, swindle.

trampista *m. & f.* cheat, crook, swindler.

trampolín *m.* springboard.

tramposo *adj.* deceitful, tricky; *m.* swindler, cheat.

tranca *f.* crossbar, bolt; pole, prop; club, stick; *Ven., Riopl.* rustic gate; *Riopl.* fence with gates; *Mex., Ven.* **saltar las -s** to jump over the fence; to lose one's patience, rebel, get angry; *Ch., Riopl., Andes, Mex.* **tener una —** to be drunk.

trance *m.* critical moment; dangerous situation; **el último —** the last moment of life; **a todo —** at any cost, cost what it may.

tranco *m.* stride, long step; threshold; **a -s** hurriedly; **en dos -s** in a jiffy; *Riopl.* **al —** striding, with long steps.

tranquear *v.* to stride along.

tranquera *f.* stockade, wooden fence; *Riopl., Cuba, Ven.* large gate (*made with trancas*).

tranquilidad *f.* tranquillity, peacefulness.

tranquilizar[9] *v.* to quiet, calm down; to pacify; **-se** to become tranquil, calm down.

tranquilo *adj.* tranquil, peaceful.

transacción *f.* transaction, negotiation; compromise.

transar *v. Am.* to compromise, yield, give in.

transatlántico *adj.* transatlantic; *m.* transatlantic steamer.

transbordar = **trasbordar.**

transbordo = **trasbordo.**

transcendencia *f.* consequence, importance; penetration.

transcendental *adj.* consequential, important, far-reaching.

transcurrir *v.* to pass, elapse.

transcurso *m.* passing, lapse (*of time*).

transeúnte *m.* passer-by; pedestrian; transient; *adj.* transient.

transferencia *f.* transference, transfer.

transferir[3] *v. irr.* to transfer.

transformación *f.* transformation.

transformador *m.* transformer.

transformar *v.* to transform.

transgredir[51] *v.* to transgress.

transgresión *f.* transgression.

transgresor *m.* transgressor, offender.

transición *f.* transition.

transigente *adj.* compromising, yielding, pliable.

transigir[11] *v.* to compromise, yield, make concessions; to settle by compromise.

transistor *m.* transistor.

transitable *adj.* passable (*road*).

transitar *v.* to pass or move back and forth (*as traffic*).

tránsito *m.* transit; traffic; passing; passage; transition; **de —** on the way, in transit, passing through.

transitorio *adj.* transitory.

transmisión *f.* transmission; **— automática** automatic transmission.

transmisor *m.* transmitter; *adj.* transmitting.

transmitir *v.* to transmit.

transparencia *f.* transparency.

transparente *adj.* transparent; lucid, clear; *m.* window shade; stained-glass window.

transponer[40] *v. irr.* to transpose; to transfer; to transplant; to go beyond, go over to the other side; **-se** to hide from view, go behind; to set, go below the horizon.

transportación *f.* transportation, transport.

transportar *v.* to transport; to transpose (*music*); **-se** to be transported, carried away by strong feeling; to be in ecstasy.

transporte *m.* transport; transportation; transport vessel; ecstasy; **— de locura** fit of madness.

transpuesto *p.p. of* **transponer.**

transversal *adj.* transversal, transverse; **sección —** cross section.

transverso *adj.* transverse, cross.

tranvía *m.* streetcar; streetcar track.

trapacear *v.* to swindle, cheat; to racketeer.

trapacería *f.* racket, fraud, swindle.

trapacero *m.* racketeer; cheat, swindler; *adj.* cheating, deceiving.

trapacista *m. & f.* racketeer; swindler, cheat.

trapeador *m. Am.* mopper; *Andes, Ven., Col., C.A., Mex., Cuba* mop.

trapear *v. Am.* to mop; *Am.* to beat up, give (*someone*) a licking.

trapiche *m.* sugar mill; press (*for extracting juices*); *Andes* grinding machine (*for pulverizing minerals*).

trapisonda *f.* escapade, prank; brawl; noisy spree.

trapo *m.* rag; *C.A., Ven., Ur.* cloth; **-s** clothes; **a todo —** at full sail; speedily; **poner a uno como un —** to make one feel like a rag; **sacarle a uno los -s al sol** to exhibit somebody's dirty linen; **soltar el —** to burst out laughing or crying.

traposo *adj. Am.* ragged, tattered, in

rags.

tráquea *f*. trachea, windpipe.

traquetear *v*. to rattle; to shake; to jolt; to crack, crackle.

traqueteo *m*. rattling; shaking; jolting; cracking, crackling; *Ríopl., Col., Ven., C.A., Mex., Carib., Andes* uproar, din; *Am*. noisy, disorderly traffic.

tras *prep*. after; in search of; behind, in back of; **— de** behind, after; besides, in addition to; *interj*. **¡ — !** bang!

trasbordar *v*. to transfer.

trasbordo *m*. transfer.

trascendencia = **transcendencia**.

trascendental = **transcendental**.

trasegar[1,7] *v*. *irr*. to upset, overturn; to change from one place to another; to pour from one container to another.

trasero *adj*. rear, hind, back; *m*. rump.

trasladar *v*. to move, remove; to transfer; to postpone; to translate; to transcribe, copy.

traslado *m*. transfer; transcript, written copy.

traslucirse[13] *v*. *irr*. to be translucent; to be transparent, clear, evident.

trasnochar *v*. to sit up all night; to stay awake all night; to spend the night out.

traspalar *v*. to shovel.

traspapelar *v*. to mislay, misplace (*a paper, letter, document, etc.*); **-se** to become mislaid among other papers.

traspasar *v*. to pass over, cross over; to go beyond; to pass through; to pierce; to transfer (*property*); to trespass.

traspaso *m*. transfer; transgression, trespass.

traspié *m*. stumble, slip; **dar un —** to stumble or trip.

trasplantar *v*. to transplant.

trasponer[40] = **transponer**.

trasquila, trasquiladura *f*. shearing, clip, clipping; bad haircut.

trasquilar *v*. to shear; to clip; to crop; to cut (*hair*).

trastazo *m*. thump, blow.

traste *m*. fret, stop (*of a guitar*); *Am*. utensil, implement; **dar al — con** to destroy, ruin.

trasto *m*. household utensil; piece of junk; rubbish, trash; **-s** utensils; implements; **-s de pescar** fishing tackle.

trastornar *v*. to overturn; to upset; to disturb.

trastorno *m*. upset; disorder; disturbance.

trastrocar[2,6] *v*. *irr*. to invert, change; to upset.

trasudar *v*. to perspire, sweat slightly.

trasudor *m*. slight perspiration or sweat.

tratable *adj*. friendly, sociable; manageable.

tratado *m*. treaty; treatise.

tratamiento *m*. treatment; title of courtesy; form of address.

tratante *m*. & *f*. dealer, tradesman, trader.

tratar *v*. to treat; to handle; to discuss; to have social relations with; **— con** to have dealings with; **— de** to try to; to treat of, deal with; **-le a uno de** to address someone as; to treat someone as; **— en** to deal in; **-se bien** to treat oneself well; to behave well; **-se** to be a question of; **no se trata de eso** that isn't the question, that isn't the point.

trato *m*. (*acuerdo*) treatment; deal, pact; trade; (*manera*) manner, behavior; social relations; dealings; *Am*. **— pampa** unfair deal; **¡ — hecho!** it's a deal!; **tener buen — to** be affable, sociable.

través *m*. crossbeam; reverse, misfortune; **a** (*or* **al**) **— de** through, across; **de — across**; **dar al — con** to ruin, destroy; to squander; **mirar de —** to squint in a sinister manner.

travesaño *m*. crosspiece, crossbar; bolster, long bedpillow; *Ven., Andes* railway tie.

travesear *v*. to romp, frisk, frolic; to fool around; to misbehave.

travesía *f*. crossing; sea voyage; wind blowing towards a coast; *Am*. wasteland, desert land; *Am*. partition wall or fence.

travesura *f*. mischief; prank; lively wit.

traviesa *f*. railway tie; rafter, crossbeam; *Col*. midyear crop.

travieso *adv*. mischievous; lively; restless; **a campo —** (*or* **a campo traviesa**) cross-country.

trayecto *m*. run, stretch, lap, distance (*traveled over*).

trayectoria *f*. path (*of a bullet, missile, etc.*).

traza *f*. (*plan*) plan; design; plot; invention; (*apariencia*) appearance; semblance; aspect; indication, sign; **darse -s** to use one's wits or ingenuity; **tener — de** to have the appearance or signs of; **tiene** (*or* **lleva**) **-s de no acabar nunca** it looks as if he would never end.

trazado *m*. draft, plan, sketch, outline; drawing; *p.p*. & *adj*. traced, sketched, outlined.

trazar[9] *v*. to trace, sketch; to draw, mark out; to plan.

trébol *m*. clover.

trecho *m*. space, distance; lap (*in a race*); **a -s** by or at intervals; **de — en —** at certain points or intervals; from time to time.

tregua *f*. truce; rest, respite.

tremedal *m*. quagmire, bog.

tremendo *adj*. tremendous, huge; terrible.

trementina *f*. turpentine.

tremolar *v*. to flutter, wave (*as a flag*).

trémolo *m*. tremolo (*of the voice*), quaver.

trémulo *adj*. tremulous, trembling, quivering; flickering.

tren *m*. train; *Am*. traffic; **— correo** mail train; **— de aterrizaje** landing gear; *Ven., Carib*. **— de lavado**

TR

laundry; *Cuba, Ven.* — **de mudadas** moving company; — **de recreo** excursion train; — **mixto** freight and passenger train.

trenza *f.* tress; braid; *Mex., Cuba, Ven.* string (*of garlic, onions, etc.*); **trencilla** *f.* braid.

trenzar[9] *v.* to braid; **-se** to braid one's hair; *Riopl., Andes, Col.* to fight hand to hand.

trepar *v.* to climb; to clamber; **-se** to climb; to clamber; to perch.

trepidación *f.* jar, *vibration; trembling, shaking.

trepidar *v.* to shape, vibrate, tremble, jar.

treta *f.* trick, wile; **malas -s** bad tricks, bad habits.

triángulo *m.* triangle.

tribu *f.* tribe.

tribulación *f.* tribulation, trouble.

tribuna *f.* rostrum (*speaker's platform*).

tribunal *m.* tribunal; court of justice; body of judges.

tributar *v.* to pay tribute, pay homage.

tributario *adj. & m.* tributary.

tributo *m.* tribute; contribution, tax.

trifulca *f.* fight, quarrel, wrangle, row.

trigo *m.* wheat.

trigueño *adj.* swarthy; brunet; dark.

trillado *p.p.* beaten; *adj.* trite, hackneyed, commonplace; **camino —** beaten path.

trilladora *f.* threshing machine.

trillar *v.* to thresh; to beat, mistreat; *Cuba* to cut a path.

trimestre *m.* quarter, period of three months; quarterly payment, income, or salary; **trimestral** *adj.* quarterly.

trinar *v.* to trill (*in singing*); to warble, to quaver (*said of the voice*); to get furious.

trinchante *m.* carving fork; carving knife; carver.

trinchar *v.* to carve (*meat*).

trinche *m. Col., Ven., C.A., Mex.* fork; *Am.* carving table; *Am.* **plato —** carving platter.

trinchera *f.* trench; ditch; *C.A., Ven., Andes* stockade, fence; *Am.* curved knife.

trinchero *m.* carving table; **plato —** carving platter.

trineo *m.* sleigh; sled.

trino *m.* trill (*in singing*).

tripa *f.* intestine, bowel; paunch, belly; **-s** entrails, insides.

triple *adj. & m.* triple.

triplicar[6] *v.* to triplicate, triple, treble.

tripulación *f.* crew, ship's company.

tripular *v.* to man (*a ship*).

trique *m.* crack, snap; *Mex.* utensil, trinket; *Col.* clever trick in a game; *Am.* drink made from barley; **-s** *Mex.* poor household utensils, goods, etc.

triscar[6] *v.* to romp, frisk, frolic; to stamp or shuffle the feet; *Am.* to tease, make fun of.

triste *adj.* sad; sorrowful; *Mex.* bashful, backward; *m. Riopl.* melancholy

love song.

tristeza *f.* sadness; sorrow; *Am.* tick fever.

tristón *adj.* wistful, quite sad, melancholy.

triunfal *adj.* triumphal.

triunfante *adj.* triumphant.

triunfar *v.* to triumph; to trump (*at cards*).

triunfo *m.* triumph; trump card; trophy.

trivial *adj.* trivial, commonplace, trite.

triza *f.* shred, fragment, small piece; cord, rope (*for sails*); **hacer -s** to tear into shreds; to tear to pieces.

trocar[2,6] *v. irr.* to change; to barter, exchange; to do one thing instead of another; **-se** to change; to be transformed; to exchange.

trocha *f.* path, trail; *Riopl.* gauge (*of a railway*); *Col.* trot; *Am.* slice or serving of meat.

trofeo *m.* trophy; booty, spoils.

troj, troje *m.* barn, granary.

trole *m.* trolley.

tromba *f.* waterspout.

trombón *m.* trombone.

trompa *f.* trumpet; trunk of an elephant; large spinning top; *Am.* snout; *Col.* cowcatcher (*of a locomotive*).

trompada *f.* blow with the first; bump.

trompeta *f.* trumpet; *m.* trumpeter; useless individual; *Andes* drunk, drunkard; *Andes* bold, shameless fellow.

trompetear *v.* to trumpet, blow the trumpet.

trompo *m.* spinning top; stupid fellow, dunce.

tronada *f.* thunderstorm.

tronar[2] *v. irr.* to thunder; to explode, burst; *Mex., C.A.* to execute by shooting; **— los dedos** to snap one's fingers; **por lo que pueda —** just in case.

tronco *m.* tree trunk; log; stem; trunk (*of the human body*); team (*of horses*).

tronchar *v.* to bend or break (*a stalk or trunk*); to chop off; to break off; **-se** to break off or get bent (*said of a stalk or trunk*); *Col.* to get twisted or bent.

tronera *f.* opening; porthole (*through which to shoot*); small, narrow window; pocket of a billiard table; *m.* madcap, reckless fellow.

tronido *m.* thunder; detonation; sharp, sudden sound.

trono *m.* throne.

tropa *f.* troop; crowd; *Riopl.* herd of cattle, drove of horses (*often* **tropilla**).

tropel *m.* throng; bustle; rush; jumble, confusion.

tropezar[1,9] *v. irr.* to stumble; to blunder; **— con** to meet, come across, encounter.

tropezón *m.* stumbling; stumble; slip; **a -es** falteringly, stumbling along clumsily; **darse un —** to stumble, trip.

tropical *adj.* tropical.

trópico *m.* tropic.

tropiezo *m.* stumble; stumbling block; slip, fault; dispute.

tropilla *f.* small troop; *Am.* drove of horses guided by the **madrina;** *Mex.* pack of dogs; *Am.* group of spare saddle horses.

tropillero *m. Am.* horse wrangler, herdsman.

trotar *v.* to trot; to hurry.

trote *m.* trot; **al —** quickly.

trovador *m.* troubadour, minstrel.

troza *f.* log.

trozar[9] *v.* to cut off, break off (*a piece*); to break or cut into pieces.

trozo *m.* piece, bit, fragment; passage, selection.

truco *m.* clever trick; pocketing of a ball (*in the game of pool*); *Am.* blow with the fist; *Andes, Ríopl.* a card game; **-s** game of pool (*game similar to billiards*).

truculencia *f.* cruelty, ferocity, ruthlessness.

truculento *adj.* cruel, fierce, ruthless.

trucha *f.* trout; *Am.* vendor's portable stand.

trueno *m.* thunder; explosion, report of a gun; wild youth, troublemaker; *Am.* firecracker, rocket.

trueque, trueco *m.* exchange; barter; *Col., Ven., Andes* change, small money; **a** (*or* **en**) **—** de in exchange for.

truhán *m.* scoundrel; swindler; cheat; buffoon, jester.

tu *adj.* thy; your (*fam. sing.*).

tú *pers. pron.* thou; you (*fam. sing.*).

tualet = **lavabo.**

tuberculosis *f.* tuberculosis; **tuberculoso** *adj.* tuberculous, tubercular.

tubería *f.* tubing, piping; pipe line.

tubo *m.* tube; pipe; lamp chimney; **— de ensayo** test tube; **— de escape** tail pipe.

tuerca *f.* nut (*of a screw*); **llave de -s** wrench.

tuerto *adj.* one-eyed; blind in one eye; *m.* wrong, injustice; **a — o a derecho** (*or* **a tuertas o a derechas**) rightly or wrongly; thoughtlessly.

tuétano *m.* marrow; pith; innermost part; **mojado hasta los -s** soaked through and through.

tufo *m.* vapor, fume; disagreeable odor; airs, conceit; **tufillo** *m.* whiff, pungent odor.

tul *m.* tulle (*a thin, fine net for veils*); **tul, tule** *m. Mex.* a kind of reed or bulrush (*used in the manufacture of seats and backs of chairs*).

tulipán *m.* tulip.

tullido *p.p.* crippled; paralyzed; numb.

tullirse[20] *v. irr.* to become crippled; to become numb or paralyzed.

tumba *f.* tomb; grave; *Col., Cuba, Mex.* felling of timber; *Ven.* forest clearing.

tumbar *v.* to knock down; *Col., Mex., Cuba* to fell timber; **-se** to lie down.

tumbo *m.* tumble; somersault; **dar -s** to jump, bump along.

tumor *m.* tumor; **tumorcillo** *m.* boil; small tumor.

tumulto *m.* tumult, uproar; mob, throng.

tumultuoso *adj.* tumultuous.

tuna *f.* prickly pear.

tunante *m. & f.* rascal, rogue, scamp; loafer; *Andes, Ch., C.A.* libertine, licentious or lewd person.

tunda *f.* whipping, thrashing; shearing (*the nap of cloth*).

tundir *v.* to lash, beat, whip; to shear (*the nap of cloth*).

túnel *m.* tunnel.

túnica *f.* tunic; gown, robe.

tupido *adj.* dense; compact, thick; blocked, obstructed.

tupir *v.* to press, pack, squeeze together; to stop up, clog; **-se** to get stopped up; to stuff oneself; to become dense (*as a forest*); *Am.* to get astonished or confused.

turba *f.* mob, throng.

turbación *f.* disturbance, confusion; embarrassment.

turbamulta *f.* throng, mob, crowd.

turbar *v.* to perturb; to disturb; to trouble; **-se** to get disturbed, confused, embarrassed.

turbio *adj.* muddy; muddled, confused.

turbión *m.* thunderstorm; heavy shower.

turborreactor *m.* turbojet.

turbulento *adj.* turbulent; restless; disorderly.

turco *adj.* Turkish; *m.* Turk; Turkish, Turkish language; *Am.* peddler.

turismo *m.* tourist travel; touring, sightseeing; **oficina de —** travel bureau; **turista** *m. & f.* tourist; **turístico** *adj.* tourist; related to tourism.

turnar *v.* to alternate; **-se** to alternate; to take turns.

turno *m.* turn, alternate order.

turrón *m.* nougat, nut confection; almond cake; *Mex.* **romper el —** to decide to use the **tú** form of address (*as a mark of close friendship*).

tusa *f. Am.* corn, corncob; *Cuba, Mex.* corn husk; *Am.* corn silk, tassel of an ear of corn.

tusar *v. Cuba, Mex., Ríopl., Andes* to shear; *Ríopl.* to crop, cut badly (*hair*).

tutear *v.* to address familiarly (*using the* **tú** *form*).

tutela *f.* guardianship; guidance, protection.

tutelar *v.* to guide, coach, direct; *adj.* guiding, guardian (*used as adj.*).

tutor *m.* tutor; guardian.

tuyo *poss. adj.* your, of yours (*fam. sing.*); *poss. pron.* yours.

U

u *conj.* (*before words beginning with* **o** *or* **ho**) or.

ubicar[6] *v. Am.* to locate; **-se** to be situated or located.

ubre *f.* udder.

ufanarse *v.* to glory (in); to be proud (of).

TR

ufano *adj.* proud; gay; self-satisfied.

ujier *m.* usher, doorman.

úlcera *f.* ulcer; sore.

ulterior *adj.* ulterior; further; later.

ultimar *v.* to put an end to; *Am.* to give the finishing blow, kill.

último *adj.* last, final; ultimate; latest; **estar en las últimas** to be on one's last legs; to be at the end of one's rope, be at the end of one's resources.

ultrajar *v.* to outrage, insult; to scorn.

ultraje *m.* outrage, insult.

ultramar *m.* country or place across the sea; **de —** overseas, from across the sea; **en** (or **a**) **—** overseas.

ultravioleta *adj.* ultraviolet.

ulular *v.* to howl, shriek, hoot.

umbral *m.* threshold.

umbrío *adj.* shady.

un(o) *indef. art.* a, an; **-s** some, a few; **-s cuantos** a few; **uno** *pron. & num.* one.

unánime *adj.* unanimous.

unanimidad *f.* unanimity, complete accord.

unción *f.* unction (*anointing with oil*); religious fervor; spiritual grace; **Extremaunción** Extreme Unction (*the Last Sacrament of the Church*).

uncir[10] *v.* to yoke.

ungir[11] *v.* to anoint; to consecrate.

ungüento *m.* ointment; salve.

único *adj.* only, sole; unique, singular, rare.

unidad *f.* unity; unit.

unificar[6] *v.* to unify; to unite.

uniformar *v.* to standardize; to make uniform; to furnish with uniforms.

uniforme *adj. & m.* uniform.

uniformidad *f.* uniformity.

unilateral *adj.* unilateral, one-sided.

unión *f.* union.

unir *v.* to unite; to join; to bring together; **-se** to unite, join together; to wed.

universal *adj.* universal.

universidad *f.* university.

universo *m.* universe.

untar *v.* to anoint; to smear; to oil, grease; to bribe; to corrupt; **-se** to smear oneself; to get smeared.

unto *m.* grease, fat; ointment.

untuosidad *f.* greasiness; **untuoso** *adj.* unctuous; oily, greasy.

uña *f.* fingernail; toenail; claw; hoof; hook (*on a tool*); **a — de caballo** at full gallop, at full speed; **largo de -s** prone to stealing; *Mex., C.A., Ven., Col., Andes* **largas -s** thief; **vivir de sus -s** to live by stealing; *Mex., C.A., Ven., Col., Andes* **echar la — to** steal; **ser — y carne** to be inseparable friends.

uranio *m.* uranium.

urbanidad *f.* courtesy, politeness; refinement.

urbano *adj.* urban; courteous, polite.

urbe *f.* metropolis, large city.

urdimbre *f.* warp (*of a fabric*); scheme.

urdir *v.* to warp (*in weaving*); to plot, scheme; to invent (*a lie, story, etc.*).

uremia *f.* uremia.

urgencia *f.* urgency; pressing need.

urgente *adj.* urgent, pressing.

urgir[11] *v.* to urge; to be urgent.

urna *f.* urn; **— electoral** ballot box.

urraca *f.* magpie.

usado *p.p. & adj.* used; accustomed; worn; threadbare.

usanza *f.* usage, custom, habit.

usar *v.* to use; to wear; to wear out; to be accustomed; **-se** to be in use, be in vogue.

uso *m.* (*empleo*) use; usage; wear; (*costumbre*) usage; practice; habit; custom; **al — de la época** according to the custom or usage of the period; **estar en buen —** to be in good condition (*said of a thing*).

usted *pers. pron.* (*abbreviated as* **Vd., V.,** or **Ud.**) you.

usual *adj.* usual; ordinary, customary.

usufructo *m.* use, enjoyment; profit.

usufructuar[18] *v.* to enjoy the use of; to make use of.

usura *f.* usury.

usurero *m.* usurer, loan shark.

usurpar *v.* to usurp.

utensilio *m.* utensil; implement, tool.

útero *m.* uterus, womb.

útil *adj.* useful; profitable; **-es** *m. pl.* tools, instruments.

utilidad *f.* utility; profit; usefulness.

utilizar[9] *v.* to utilize; to use.

uva *f.* grape; **— espina** gooseberry; **— pasa** raisin; **estar hecho una —** to be tipsy, drunk.

V

vaca *f.* cow; **carne de —** beef; **cuero de —** cowhide; *Am.* **hacer —** to play hooky, play truant, cut class; to join in a quick business deal.

vacación *f.* vacation (*usually* **vacaciones**).

vacada *f.* herd of cows.

vacancia *f.* vacancy.

vacante *adj.* vacant, unfilled, unoccupied; *f.* vacancy.

vaciar[17] *v.* (*dejar vacío*) to empty; to drain; to flow; (*amoldar*) to cast into a mold; (*ahuecar*) to hollow out; **-se** to spill; to empty; to become empty; to flow (into).

vaciedad *f.* emptiness; nonsense, silliness.

vacilación *f.* hesitation; wavering; doubt.

vacilante *adj.* vacillating, hesitating, wavering; unsteady.

vacilar *v.* to vacillate, waver, hesitate; to sway.

vacío *adj.* empty; vacant; unoccupied; hollow; *m.* void; hollow; vacuum; vacancy; gap, blank.

vacuna *f.* vaccine; vaccination; cowpox (*eruptive disease of the cow*); **vacunación** *f.* vaccination; **— antipoliomelítica** antipolio inoculation.

vacunar *v.* to vaccinate.

vadear *v.* to ford; to wade; to avoid (*a difficulty*).

vado *m.* ford; **no hallar —** to find no way out.

vagabundear *v.* to tramp around, wander, rove; to loiter.

vagabundo *adj.* vagabond, wandering; *m.* vagabond, tramp; vagrant; wanderer.

vagar[7] *v.* to wander, roam; to loiter; to loaf; *m.* leisure; loitering.

vago *adj.* vague; roaming; idle; vagrant; *m.* vagrant, tramp.

vagón *m.* railway car or coach; **vagoneta** *f.* small railway car or tram (*used in mines*); **vagonada** *f.* carload.

vaguear = vagar.

vahído *m.* dizziness, dizzy spell.

vaho *m.* vapor, steam, fume, mist; odor.

vaina *f.* sheath, scabbard; case; pod, husk; *Ven., Col., C.A., Mex.* bother, nuisance; *Ven., Col.* luck.

vainilla *f.* vanilla.

vaivén *m.* sway; fluctuation, wavering; traffic, coming and going; **-es** comings and goings; ups and downs; inconstancy.

vajilla *f.* tableware; set of dishes; **— de plata** silverware; **— de porcelana** chinaware.

vale *m.* bond, promissory note; voucher; adieu, farewell; *m. & f. Col., Ven., Mex.* comrade, pal, chum.

valedero *adj.* valid, binding, effective.

valedor *m.* defender, protector; *Am.* pal, comrade.

valenciano *adj.* Valencian, of or from Valencia, Spain; *m.* Valencian.

valentía *f.* courage, valor; exploit; boast.

valentón *adj.* blustering, boastful; *m.* bully, braggart.

valer[17] *v. irr.* to favor, protect; to cost; to be worth; to be worthy; to be equivalent to; to be valid; to prevail; to be useful; **— la pena** to be worth while; **— por** to be worth; **-se de** to avail oneself of, make use of; **más vale** it is better; **¡válgame Dios!** heaven help me! good heavens!

valeroso *adj.* valiant, brave; valuable.

valía *f.* worth, value; influence.

validez *f.* validity; stability, soundness.

válido *adj.* valid.

valiente *adj.* valiant, brave; powerful; *m.* brave man; bully.

valija *f.* valise, satchel; mailbag.

valimiento *m.* favor, protection; **gozar de —** to enjoy protection or favor.

valioso *adj.* valuable; worthy; wealthy.

valor *m.* value; worth; price; significance; valor, courage; boldness; efficacy, power; **-es** stocks, bonds.

valoración *f.* valuation, appraisal.

valorar *v.* to evaluate, value, appraise.

valorizar[9] *v. Cuba, Ven., Riopl., Andes* to value, appraise; *Am.* to realize, convert into money.

vals *m.* waltz.

valsar *v.* to waltz.

valuación *f.* valuation, appraisal.

valuar[18] *v.* to value, price, appraise; to rate.

válvula *f.* valve.

valla *f.* stockade, fence; barrier; obstacle; *Cuba, Col.* cockpit (*for cockfights*).

vallado *m.* stockade, fenced-in place; fence.

valle *m.* valley; vale.

vanagloria *f.* vainglory, boastful vanity.

vanagloriarse[17] *v.* to glory, take great pride (in), boast (of).

vanaglorioso *adj.* vain, boastful, conceited.

vanguardia *f.* vanguard.

vanidad *f.* vanity; conceit; emptiness.

vanidoso *adj.* vain, conceited.

vano *adj.* vain; empty; hollow; *m.* opening in a wall (*for a door or window*).

vapor *m.* vapor, steam, mist; steamer, steamship.

vaporoso *adj.* vaporous, steamy, misty; vaporlike.

vapulear *v.* to beat, whip, thrash.

vapuleo *m.* beating, whipping, thrashing.

vaquería *f.* herd of cows; stable for cows; dairy.

vaquerizo *m.* herdsman; *adj.* pertaining to cows; **vaqueriza** *f.* stable for cows.

vaquero *m.* cowherd, herdsman; cowboy; *Cuba* milkman; *adj.* relating to cowherds, cowboys, or cattle.

vaqueta *f.* sole leather; cowhide; *Mex.* **zurrar a uno la —** to tan someone's hide, beat someone up.

vara *f.* twig; stick; rod; wand; staff; yard, yardstick; thrust with a picador's lance.

varadero *m.* shipyard.

varar *v.* to beach (*a boat*); to run aground; to stop, come to a standstill (*said of business*).

varear *v.* to beat; to whip; to sell by the yard; to measure with a **vara;** *Am.* to exercise (*a horse before a race*).

variable *afd.* variable, unstable, changeable; *f.* variable.

variación *f.* variation.

variado *p.p. & adj.* varied; variegated.

variar[17] *v.* to vary; to change; to shift; to differ.

variedad *f.* variety; variation, change.

varilla *f.* small rod; wand; long, flexible twig; rib (*of an umbrella or fan*); corset stay; *Mex* peddler's wares.

varillero *m. Mex.* peddler.

vario *adj.* various; different; changeable; varied; **-s** various, several.

varón *m.* male, man; *Am.* long beam, timber.

varonil *adj* manly; strong; brave.

vasallo *adj. & m.* vassal, subject.

vasco, vascongado *adj. & m.* Basque.

vasija *f.* vessel, container, receptacle.

vaso *m.* drinking glass; glassful; vase; vessel; hull of a ship; horse's hoof; **— de elección** person chosen by God.

vástago *m.* (*de planta*) shoot, sprout; stem; (*persona*) scion, offspring; *Mex., Col., Ven.* stem, trunk of a

UF

banana tree.

vasto *adj.* vast, extensive, large.

vate *m.* bard, poet.

vaticinar *v.* to prophesy, predict, foretell.

vaticinio *m.* prophecy, prediction.

vecindad *f.* vicinity; neighborhood; neighborliness; **casa de —** tenement.

vecindario *m.* neighborhood, neighbors; vicinity.

vecino *m.* neighbor; resident; citizen; *adj.* neighboring; next, near.

vedar *v.* to prohibit; to impede.

vega *f.* fertile lowland or plain; *Cuba, Ven.* tobacco plantation.

vegetación *f.* vegetation.

vegetal *adj.* vegetable; *m.* vegetable, plant.

vegetar *v.* to vegetate.

vehemente *adj.* vehement, passionate, impetuous; violent.

vehículo *m.* vehicle.

veintena *f.* score, twenty.

vejestorio *m.* wrinkled old person.

vejete *m.* little old man.

vejez *f.* old age.

vejiga *f.* bladder; blister; smallpox sore; **— de la bilis** (*or* **— de la hiel**) gall bladder.

vela *f.* vigil, watch; night watch; candle; sail; **a toda —** under full sail; at full speed; **en —** on watch, without sleep; **hacerse a la —** to set sail.

velada *f.* watch, vigil; evening party; evening function or meeting.

velador *m.* night watchman; keeper, guard; lamp table; bedside table; candlestick; *Riopl., Mex., Cuba, Col.* lamp shade.

velar *v.* to keep vigil; to stay up at night; to be vigilant; to watch over; to veil; to cover, hide.

velatorio *m.* wake (*vigil over a corpse*). *See* **velorio**.

veleidoso *adj.* inconstant, fickle, changeable.

velero *m.* sailboat; sailmaker; candlemaker; *adj.* swift-sailing; **buque —** sailboat.

veleta *f.* weathervane, weathercock; *m. & f.* fickle person.

velis *m. Mex.* valise.

velo *m.* veil; curtain, covering; **— del paladar** velum, soft palate.

velocidad *f.* velocity.

velocímetro *m.* speedometer.

velorio *m. Am.* wake (*vigil over a corpse*); *Mex., C.A., Ven., Col., Ch., Andes* dull party.

veloz *adj.* swift, quick, fast.

vello *m.* hair (*on the body*); down, fuzz; nap (*of cloth*).

vellón *m.* fleece; tuft of wool; sheepskin with fleece; silver and copper alloy; an ancient copper coin.

velloso *adj.* hairy; downy, fuzzy.

velludo *adj.* hairy; downy; fuzzy; *m.* plush; velvet.

vena *f.* vein; lode, vein of metal ore; mood, disposition; **estar en —** to be in the mood; to be inspired.

venado *m.* deer; venison, deer meat; *Mex.* **pintar —** to play hooky.

vencedor *adj.* conquering, winning, victorious; *m.* conqueror, winner, victor.

vencer[10] *v.* to conquer, vanquish; to defeat; to overcome; to surpass; to win; **-se** to control oneself; to mature, fall due; **se venció el plazo** the time limit expired.

vencido *p.p. & adj.* conquered; defeated; due, fallen due.

vencimiento *m.* conquering, defeat; maturity (*of a debt*), falling due; expiration (*of a period of time*).

venda *f.* bandage.

vendaje *m* bandage.

vendar *v.* to bandage; to blindfold.

vendaval *m.* strong wind, gale.

vendedor *m.* vendor, seller, peddler.

vender *v.* to sell; to betray; **-se** to be sold; to sell oneself, accept a bribe.

vendimia *f.* vintage; profit.

venduta *f. Col.* auction; *Cuba* small fruit and vegetable store.

veneno *m.* venom, poison.

venenoso *adj.* poisonous.

venerable *adj.* venerable.

veneración *f.* veneration, reverence.

venerando *adj.* venerable, worthy of respect.

venerar *v.* to venerate, revere; to worship.

venero *m.* water spring; source, origin; lode, layer, seam (*of mineral*).

venezolano *adj.* Venezuelan; *m.* Venezuelan; *Ven.* Venezuelan silver coin.

vengador *adj.* avenging, revenging; *m.* avenger.

venganza *f.* vengeance, revenge.

vengar[7] *v.* to avenge, revenge; **-se de** to take revenge on.

vengativo *adj.* vindictive, revengeful.

venia *f.* pardon; permission, leave; bow, nod; *C.A., Ven., Riopl.* military salute.

venida *f.* arrival; return; river flood, onrush of water; attack (*in fencing*).

venidero *adj.* coming, future; **en lo —** in the future; **-s** *m. pl.* successors.

venir[48] *v. irr.* to come; to arrive; to fit; **-le a uno bien** (*or* **mal**) to be becoming (*or* unbecoming); **— a menos** to decline, decay; **— a pelo** to come just at the right moment; to suit perfectly; to be pat, opportune, to the point; **— en** to agree to; **— sobre** to fall upon; **¿a qué viene eso?** what is the point of that?; **-se abajo** to fall down; to collapse; to fail.

venoso *adj.* veined; venous (*of or pertaining to the veins; with veins*).

venta *f.* sale; roadside inn; *Ur.* store, vendor's stand; **— pública** auction.

ventaja *f.* advantage; gain, profit; bonus; odds.

ventajoso *adj.* advantageous, beneficial, profitable; *Mex.* self-seeking, profiteering.

ventana *f.* window; window shutter; *Col.* clearing (*in a forest*); **— (or**

ventanilla) de la nariz nostril.
ventarrón m. gale, strong wind.
ventear v. (*oler*) to scent, sniff; (*soplar*) to blow, be windy; (*poner al aire*) to air; (*indagar*) to nose around; *Ven.* to toss in the wind; *Am.* to flee; *Am.* to outrun; **-se** to expel air, break wind; *Col.* to stay outdoors.
ventero m. innkeeper.
ventilación f. ventilation.
ventilador m. ventilator; fan (*for ventilation*).
ventilar v. to ventilate; to air.
ventisca f. blizzard, snowstorm; snow-drift.
ventiscar v. to snow hard and blow (*as in a blizzard*); to drift (*as snow in a blizzard*).
ventisquero m. blizzard, snowstorm; glacier; snowdrift; snow-capped mountain base.
ventolera f. gust of wind; pride, vanity; whim; pin wheel; **darle a uno la — de** to take the notion to.
ventoso adj. windy.
ventura f. happiness; fortune, chance; risk, danger; **a la —** at random; **buena —** fortune; **por —** perchance.
venturoso adj. fortunate, lucky; happy.
ver v. irr. to see; to look; to look at; to look into, examine; **— de** to try to, see to it that; **a más** (*or* **hasta más**) **—** good-bye; **no — la hora de** to be anxious to; **no tener nada que — con** not to have anything to do with; **-se** to be seen; to be; **-se obligado a** to be obliged to, be forced, to; **a mi modo de —** in my opinion; **de buen —** good-looking; **ser de —** to be worth seeing.
vera f. edge; **a la — del camino** at the edge of the road.
veracidad f. truthfulness.
veraneante m. & f. summer resorter, vacationist, or tourist.
veranear v. to spend the summer.
veraneo m. summering, summer vacation.
veraniego adj. summer, of summer.
verano m. summer.
veras f. pl. reality, truth; **de —** in truth; truly; in earnest.
veraz adj. truthful.
verbal adj. verbal; oral.
verbena f. verbena (*a plant*); festival or carnival (*on eve of a religious holiday*).
verbigracia adv. for instance, for example.
verbo m. verb; **el Verbo** the Word (*second person of the Trinity*).
verboso adj. verbose, wordy.
verdad f. truth; **¿—?** really?; is that so?; isn't that so?; **— de Perogrullo** truism, evident truth; **de —** (*or* **a la —**) in truth, in earnest; **en —** really, truly.
verdadero adj. real; true; truthful; sincere.
verde adj. green; unripe; young; off-color, indecent; m. green; verdure; *Ur., Ven.* country, countryside.

verdear v. to grow green; to look green.
verdinegro adj. dark-green.
verdor m. verdure, greenness.
verdoso adj. greenish.
verdugo m. executioner; cruel person; torment; rapier (*light sword*); lash, whip; welt; shoot of a tree; **verdugón** m. large welt.
verdulera f. woman vendor of green vegetables; **verdulería** f. green vegetable store or stand.
verdura f. verdure; greenness; green vegetables.
vereda f. path; *Ch., Ríopl., Andes* sidewalk; *Col.* small village; *C.R.* bank of a stream.
veredicto m. verdict.
vergonzoso adj. shameful, disgraceful; shy, bashful; m. species of armadillo.
vergüenza f. shame; disgrace; shyness, bashfulness; **tener —** to have shame; to be ashamed.
vericueto m. rugged, wild place (*often rocky*).
verídico adj. truthful; true.
verificar v. to verify; to confirm; to test, check; to carry out, fulfill; **-se** to be verified; to take place.
verijas f. pl. *Ríopl., Mex.* groin (*hollow between lower part of abdomen and thigh*); *Am.* flanks of a horse.
verja f. grate, grating.
verruga f. wart; nuisance.
versado adj. versed, skilled, expert.
versar v. to deal (with), treat (of); **-se en** to become versed in.
versión f. version; translation.
verso m. verse; meter; **— suelto** (*or* **— libre**) free or blank verse.
verter v. irr. to pour; to empty; to spill; to translate; to flow down.
vertical adj. vertical.
vértice m. top, apex, summit.
vertiente f. slope; watershed; adj. flowing.
vertiginoso adj. whirling, dizzy, giddy.
vértigo m. dizziness, giddiness; fit of madness.
vestíbulo m. vestibule; lobby.
vestido m. clothing, apparel; dress; garment; suit.
vestidura f. vestment; attire, apparel; raiment.
vestigio m. vestige, sign, trace.
vestir v. irr. (*cubrir*) to dress; to clothe; to put on; to adorn; to cover; (*llevar*) to wear; **-se** to dress, get dressed; to be clothed; to be covered.
vestuario m. wardrobe, apparel; theatrical costumes; cloakroom; dressing room; vestry (*room for church vestments*).
veta f. vein, seam (*of mineral*); streak, grain (*in wood*); stripe; *Am.* rope.
veteado adj. veined; striped; streaked.
veterano adj. & m. veteran.
veterinario m. veterinary.
veto m. veto.
vetusto adj. old, ancient.
vez f. time, occasion; turn; **a la —** at the same time; **cada — más** more

VA

and more; **cada — que** whenever;
de — en cuando from time to time;
de una — all at once; **en — de** instead of; **otra** — again; **una que
otra** — rarely, once in a while; **tal** —
perhaps; **a veces** sometimes; **raras
veces** seldom; **hacer las veces de**
to take the place of.

vía f. way; road; track; railroad track;
conduit; **Vía Crucis** the Way of the
Cross; **Vía Láctea** the Milky Way.

viaducto m. viaduct.

viajante m. traveler; **— de comercio**
traveling salesman.

viajar v. to travel.

viaje m. voyage; trip; travel; **— de ida
y vuelta** (or **— redondo**) round trip.

viajero m. traveler; adj. traveling.

vianda f. viands, food; meal.

viandante m. & f. wayfarer, walker,
pedestrian; passer-by; vagabond.

viático m. provisions for a journey;
viaticum (communion given to dying
persons).

víbora f. viper.

vibración f. vibration.

vibrante adj. vibrant, vibrating.

vibrar v. to vibrate.

vicepresidente m. vice-president.

viceversa adv. vice versa, conversely.

viciado adj. contaminated, foul; corrupt; p.p. of **viciar**.

viciar v. to vitiate, corrupt; to adulterate; to falsify; **-se** to become corrupt.

vicio m. vice; bad habit; fault; craving;
de — as a habit; **hablar de** — to
talk too much; **-s** Am. articles and
ingredients used for serving **mate**.

vicioso adj. vicious, evil, wicked; having bad habits; licentious; faulty, incorrect (grammatical construction, reasoning, etc.).

vicisitud f. vicissitude; **-es** vicissitudes,
ups and downs, changes of fortune or
condition.

víctima f. victim.

victoria f. victory, triumph; victoria
(carriage).

victorioso adj. victorious.

vicuña f. vicuña (an Andean animal
allied to the alpaca and llama); vicuña
wool; vicuña cloth.

vid f. vine, grapevine.

vida f. life; living; livelihood; **— mía**
dearest; **hacer** — to live together;
pasar a mejor — to die; **tener la —
en un hilo** to be in great danger.

vidalita f. Am. melancholy song of
Argentina and Chile.

vidente m. seer, prophet; adj. seeing.

vidriado m. glaze; glazed earthenware;
p.p. & adj. glazed.

vidriar [17] v. to glaze (earthenware).

vidriera f. glass window; glass door;
Am. show case, show window; **— de
colores** stained-glass window.

vidriero m. glazier (one who installs
windowpanes); glass blower; glass
maker; glass dealer.

vidrio m. glass; any glass article.

vidrioso adj. glassy; brittle; slippery;

icy; touchy, irritable.

viejo adj. old; ancient; worn-out; m.
old man; **— verde** old man who boast
of his youth and vigor; Am. **los -s**
the old folks (applied to one's parents);
viejoto f. old hag.

viento m. wind; scent; **hace** — it is
windy; **a los cuatro -s** in all directions; **vientecito** m. gentle breeze.

vientre m. abdomen; belly; bowels; entrails; womb.

viernes m. Friday.

viga f. beam; rafter.

vigencia f. operation (of a law);
entrar en — to take effect (said of a
law); **estar en** — to be in force (said
of a law).

vigente adj. effective, in force (as a law).

vigía f. lookout, watchtower; watch (act
of watching); reef; m. lookout, watchman.

vigilancia f. vigilance.

vigilante adj. vigilant, watchful; m.
watchman.

vigilar v. to keep guard; to watch over.

vigilia f. vigil, watch; wakefulness,
sleeplessness; night hours (spent in
study); eve before certain church fes-
tivals; vesper service; **día de** — day
of abstinence; **comer de** — to abstain from meat.

vigor m. vigor; **en** — in force (said of a
law); **entrar en** — to become effective (as a law, statute, etc.).

vigorizar [9] v. to invigorate, tone up,
give vigor to, strengthen.

vigoroso adj. vigorous.

vihuela f. guitar.

vil adj. vile, base, low, mean.

vileza f. villainy; baseness; vile act.

vilipendiar v. to revile.

vilo : **en** — in the air; suspended; undecided; in suspense; **llevar en** —
to waft.

villa f. village; villa, country house.

villancico n. carol; Christmas carol.

villanía f. villainy; lowliness.

villano adj. rustic, uncouth; villainous,
mean, base; m. villain; rustic, peasant.

villorrio m. small village, hamlet.

vinagre m. vinegar; **vinagrera** f. vinegar cruet.

vincular v. to tie, bond, unite; to entail
(limit the inheritance of property); to
found, base (on).

vínculo m. bond, tie, chain; entailed
inheritance.

vindicar [6] v. to vindicate; to avenge; to
defend, assert (one's rights); **-se** to
avenge oneself; to defend oneself.

vino m. wine; **— amontillado** good
grade of pale sherry (originally from
Montilla); **— tinto** dark-red wine;
vinería f. Riopl., Andes wineshop;
vinero adj. Am. pertaining to wine;
vinoso adj. winy.

viña f. vineyard.

viñedo m. vineyard.

violación f. violation.

violado adj. violet; m. violet, violet
color; p.p. violated.

violar v. to violate; to rape.

violencia f. violence.

violentar v. to force; to break into (a house); **-se** to force oneself; to get angry.

violento adj. violent; impetuous; forced; strained; unnatural.

violeta f. violet.

violín m. violin; m. & f. violinist; Ven. **estar hecho un —** to be very thin.

violinista m. & f. violinist.

virada f. tack, change of direction, turn.

viraje m. change of direction; turn.

virar v. to turn, turn around, change direction; to tack (said of a ship).

virgen adj. & f. virgin.

virginal adj. virginal, virgin, pure.

viril adj. virile, manly.

virilidad f. virility, manhood, manly strength, vigor.

virreinato m. viceroyalty (office or jurisdiction of a viceroy).

virrey m. viceroy.

virtud f. virtue.

virtuoso adj. virtuous; m. virtuoso (person skilled in an art).

viruela f. smallpox; pock (mark left by smallpox); **-s locas** (or **-s bastardas**) chicken pox.

viruta f. wood shaving.

visa f. visa, visé; **visado** p.p. of **visar**; m. visa, visé.

visaje m. grimace; wry face; **hacer -s** to make faces.

visar v. to visé; to approve; to O.K.

viscoso adj. slimy, sticky.

visera f. visor; eye shade; Cuba, Mex. blinder (on a horse's bridle).

visible adj. visible; evident; conspicuous, notable.

visillo m. window curtain.

visión f. vision; sight; fantasy; apparition; sight (ridiculous-looking person or thing).

visionario adj. & m. visionary.

visita f. visit, call; visitor; callers, company; **— de cumplimiento** (or **— de cumplido**) formal courtesy call, **— domiciliaria** police inspection of a house; home call (of a social worker, doctor, etc.).

visitación f. visitation, visit.

visitador m. visitor, caller; inspector.

visitante m. & f. caller, visitor; adj. visiting.

visitar v. to visit; to inspect.

vislumbrar v. to catch a glimpse of; to guess, surmise; **-se** to be faintly visible.

vislumbre f. glimmer; glimpse; vague idea; faint appearance.

viso m. appearance, semblance; pretense, pretext; luster, brilliance, glitter; glass curtain; **a dos -s** with a double view; with a double purpose.

víspera f. eve, evening or day before; time just before; **-s** vespers; **en -s de** on the eve of; about to.

vista f. (panorama) view; landscape; sight; (sentido) sight; vision; (acción) look, glance; **a — de** in the presence of; in front of, within view of; **pagadero a la —** payable at sight or upon presentation; **¡hasta la —!** good-bye!; **bajar la —** to lower one's eyes; **conocer de —** to know by sight; **hacer la — gorda** to pretend not to see; **pasar la — por** to glance over; **perder de —** to lose sight of; **tener a la —** to have before one; to have received (a letter).

vistazo m. glance; **dar un — a** to glance over.

visto p.p. of **ver** seen; adj. evident, clear **bien —** well thought of, proper; **mal — looked** down upon, improper; **— bueno** (V°.B°.) approved (O.K.); **dar el — bueno** to approve, O.K.; **— que** whereas, considering that.

vistoso adj. showy; colorful.

vital adj. vital; important, necessary.

vitalicio adj. for life; m. life-insurance policy; lifetime pension.

vitalidad f. vitality.

vitamina f. vitamin.

vítor m. cheer, applause; **¡—!** hurrah!

vitorear v. to cheer, applaud.

vitrina f. glass case; show case; show window.

vituallas f. pl. victuals, food, provisions.

vituperar v. to revile, insult, call bad names.

vituperio m. affront, insult; reproach; censure.

viuda f. widow.

viudez f. widowhood.

viudo m. widower.

vivac, vivaque m. bivouac, military encampment; Am. police headquarters.

vivacidad f. vivacity; brightness; liveliness.

vivaracho adj. lively; vivacious, gay.

vivaz adj. vivacious, lively; bright, keen, witty.

víveres m. pl. food supplies, provisions.

vivero m. fish pond, fish hatchery, tree nursery.

viveza f. vivacity; animation, liveliness; quickness; brilliance, cleverness.

vívido adj. vivid; colorful.

vivienda f. dwelling; apartment.

viviente adj. living.

vivir v. to live; to endure, last; **¡viva!** hurrah! long live!; **¿quién vive?** who goes there?; m. existence, living.

vivo adj. (no muerto) alive; living; (ágil) lively; quick; (vistoso) vivid; bright; (listo) clever, wide-awake; **tío —** merry-go-round; **al —** vividly; **de viva voz** by word of mouth; **tocar en lo —** to hurt to the quick, touch the most sensitive spot.

vizcacha f. Andes, Ríopl. viscacha (South American rodent about the size of a hare).

vizcachera f. Andes, Ríopl. viscacha burrow or hole; Am. room filled with junk; **vizcacheral** m. Andes, Ríopl. ground full of viscacha burrows.

VI

vizcaíno adj. Biscayan, of or from Biscay, Spain.

vocablo m. word, term.

vocabulario m. vocabulary.

vocación f. vocation; aptness, talent.

vocal adj. vocal; oral; vowel; f. vowel; m. voter (in an assembly or council).

vocear v. to shout; to cry out; to hail.

vocecita f. sweet little voice.

vocería f. clamor, shouting.

vocerío m. Am. clamor, shouting.

vocero m. spokesman.

vociferar v. to shout, clamor; to yell; to boast loudly of.

vodevil m. vaudeville.

volante adj. flying; floating: **papel** (or **hoja**) — handbill, circular; m. ruffle, frill; steering wheel; balance wheel; flywheel.

volar[2] v. irr. to fly; to fly away; to explode; to irritate, pique; to rouse (bird game); **-se** Carib., Col. to fly off the handle, lose one's temper.

volátil adj. volatile; fickle, changeable; flying.

volcán m, volcano; Col. precipice; Am. swift torrent; C.A. **un** — **de** many; lots of; a pile of.

volcánico adj. volcanic.

volcar[2,6] v. irr. to overturn; to capsize; to upset; to make dizzy; **-se** to upset, get upset.

volear v. to volley, hit (a ball) in the air.

volición f. volition.

voltaje m. voltage.

voltear v. to turn, turn around; to revolve; to turn inside out; to overturn; to tumble or roll over; to turn a somersault; Am. to go prying around; Col., Ven., C.A., Mex., Andes — **la espalda** to turn one's back; **-se** to turn over; to change sides.

voltereta f. somersault, tumble.

voltio, volt m. volt.

voluble adj. fickle; moody; changeable; twining (as a climbing vine).

volumen m. volume.

voluminoso adj. voluminous, bulky, very large.

voluntad f. will; desire; determination; benevolence, good will; consent; **última** — last will, testament; **de** (or **de buena**) — willingly, with pleasure.

voluntario adj. voluntary; willful; m. volunteer.

voluntarioso adj. willful.

voluptuoso adj. voluptuous; sensual.

voluta f. scroll, spiral-like ornament; **-s de humo** spirals of smoke.

volver[2,52] v. irr. (regresar) to return; (dar vuelta) to turn; to turn up, over, or inside out; to restore; — **loco** to drive crazy; — **a** (+inf.) to do again; — **en sí** to come to, recover one's senses; — **por** to return for; to defend; **-se** to become; to turn; to turn around; to change one's ideas; — **se atrás** to go back; to back out, go back to one's word; **-se loco** to go crazy.

vomitar v. to vomit.

vómito m. vomit; vomiting.

voracidad f. voraciousness, greediness.

vorágine f. vortex, whirlpool.

voraz adj. voracious, ravenous, greedy.

vórtice m. vortex, whirlpool; whirlwind, tornado; center of a cyclone.

votación f. voting; vote, total number of votes.

votante m. & f. voter.

votar v. to vote; to vow; to curse; **¡voto a tal!** by Jove!

voto m. vote; vow; prayer; votive offering; oath; wish; — **de confianza** vote of confidence.

voz f. (capacidad) voice; (sonido) shout, outcry; (palabra) word; rumor; — **común** common rumor or gossip; **a** — **en cuello** (or **a** — **en grito**) shouting; at the top of one's lungs; **en** — **alta** aloud; **a voces** shouting, with shouts; **secreto a voces** open secret; **dar voces** to shout, yell.

vozarrón m. loud, strong voice.

vuelco m. upset; overturning; capsizing; tumble.

vuelo m. flight; width, fullness (of a dress or cloak); frill, ruffle; jut, projection (of a building); **al** (or **a**) — on the fly; quickly; **levantar** (or **alzar**) **el** — to fly away; to soar.

vuelta f. (giro) turn; return; repetition; (parte opuesta) reverse side; cuff, facing of a sleeve; cloak lining; (cambio) change (money returned); **a la** — around the corner; on returning; **a la** — **de los años** within a few years; Am. **otra** — again; **dar -s** to turn over and over; to wander about; **dar una** — to take a walk; **estar de** — to be back; **no tiene** — **de hoja** there are no two ways about it.

vuelto p.p. of **volver**; m. Am. change (money returned).

vuestro poss. adj. your, of yours (fam. pl.); poss. pron. yours.

vulgar adj. common, ordinary; in common use; low, vile, base.

vulgaridad f. vulgarity, coarseness, commonness.

vulgarismo m. slang, slang expression, vulgar or ungrammatical expression.

vulgo m. populace, the common people; adv. commonly, popularly.

Y

y conj. and.

ya adv. already; now; finally; soon, presently; in time; **¡**—**!** now I see! I understand; enough!; **¡**— **lo creo!** I should say so!; yes, of course!; — **no** no longer; — **que** since; although; — **se ve** of course; it is clear; — **voy** I am coming.

yacer[50] v. irr. to lie (in the grave); to be lying down; to lie, be situated.

yacimiento m. bed, layer (of ore); — **de petróleo** oil field.

yanqui m. & f. North American, native of the United States; Yankee.

yantar v. to eat; m. food, meal.

yarará f. Ríopl. Argentine poisonous

snake.

yarda *f.* yard (*unit of measure*).

yate *m.* yacht.

yedra = **hiedra.**

yegua *f.* mare; *Am.* cigar butt; *adj. Am.* big, large; **yeguada** *f.* herd of mares.

yelmo *m.* helmet.

yema *f.* egg yolk; bud, shoot; candied egg yolk; **— del dedo** finger tip.

yerba = **hierba.**

yerbabuena *f.* mint; peppermint.

yerbero *m. Mex., Cuba, Ven., Col., Andes* herb vendor.

yermo *m.* desert, wilderness; *adj.* desert uninhabited; uncultivated; sterile.

yerno *m.* son-in-law.

yerro *m.* error, fault, mistake.

yerto *adj.* stiff, motionless, rigid.

yesca *f.* tinder; anything highly inflammable; incentive (*to passion*); *Ríopl., Mex.* **estar hecho una —** to be in great anger.

yeso *m.* gypsum, chalk; plaster; chalk (*for blackboard*); **— blanco** whitewash; **—mate** plaster of Paris; **yesoso** *adj.* chalky.

yo *pers. pron.* I.

yodo *m.* iodine.

yugo *m.* yoke; marriage tie; burden.

yunque *f.* anvil.

yunta *f.* yoke of oxen; pair of draft animals.

yuyo *m. Cuba, Mex., Ríopl., Andes* wild grass, weeds; *Am.* an herb sauce; *Am.* garden stuff; *Andes* **estar —** to be lifeless, insipid; *Col.* **volverse uno —** to faint.

Z

zacate *m. Mex., C.A.* grass, forage; hay.

zafado *adj.* impudent, brazen, shameless; *Ven.* smart, wide-awake, keen; *Col., Mex., Andes* "touched", half-crazy; *p.p.* of **zafar.**

zafar *v.* to release, set free; to dislodge; *Am.* to exclude; **-se** to slip away; to dodge; to get rid (of); to get loose; *Col., Ven., Andes* to get dislocated (*said of a bone*); *Col., Mex., Andes* to go crazy; *Col.* to use foul language.

zafio *adj.* coarse, uncouth, rude.

zafir, zafiro *m.* sapphire.

zafra *f.* sugar-making season; sugar making; sugar crop.

zaga *f.* rear; **a la —** (**a** or **en —**) behind.

zagal *m.* young shepherd; lad; **zagala** *f.* young shepherdess; lass, maiden; **zagalejo** *m.* young shepherd; short skirt; petticoat.

zaguán *m.* vestibule.

zaherir[5] *v. irr.* to hurt (*feelings*); to censure, reprove; to reproach.

zaino *adj.* treacherous; vicious; chestnut-colored (*horse*).

zalamero *m.* fawner, flatterer, servile person; **zalamería** *f.* flattery, scraping and bowing.

zalea *f.* pelt, undressed sheepskin.

zambo *adj.* knock-kneed; *m. Ríopl., Ven., Andes* Indian and negro half-breed; *Col.* a species of South American monkey.

zambullida *f.* dive, dip, plunge.

zambullir[20] *v.* to plunge, dip, duck; **-se** to dive; to plunge.

zambullón *m.* quick, sudden dip or dive.

zanahoria *f.* carrot.

zanca *f.* long leg of any fowl; long leg; long prop; **zancada** *f.* stride, long step.

zanco *m.* stilt; **andar en -s** to walk on stilts.

zancón *adj.* lanky, long-legged; *Col., Guat., Mex.* too short (*skirt or dress*).

zancudo *adj.* long-legged; *m. Mex., C.A., Ven., Col., Andes* mosquito.

zángano *m.* drone; loafer, sponger; *Am.* rogue, rascal.

zangolotear *v.* to shake, jiggle; **-se** to shake; to waddle; to sway from side to side.

zangoloteo *m.* jiggle, jiggling; shaking; waddling.

zanguanga *f.* feigned illness; **hacer la —** to pretend to be ill; **zanguango** *adj.* lazy; silly; *m.* fool.

zanja *f.* ditch; trench; *Am.* irrigation ditch.

zanjar *v.* to excavate; to dig ditches in; to settle (*disputes*).

zapallo *m. Pan., Col., Ven., Andes* pumpkin; squash.

zapapico *m.* pickaxe.

zapata *f.* half-boot; **— de freno** brake shoe.

zapateado *m.* a Spanish tap dance.

zapatear *v.* to tap with the feet; to tap-dance.

zapateo *m.* tapping with the feet; *Am.* a popular tap dance.

zapatería *f.* shoe store; shoemaker's shop.

zapatero *m.* shoemaker; shoe dealer.

zapatilla *f.* slipper, pump.

zapato *m.* shoe.

zarandajas *f. pl.* trifles, trinkets, worthless things.

zarandear *v.* to winnow (*separate the chaff from grain*); to sift; to sift out; to move (*something*) quickly, wiggle, jiggle; *C.A., Ríopl.* to whip, lash, mistreat, abuse; **-se** to wiggle, jiggle; to bump along; to waddle; to strut, swagger.

zarandeo *m.* jiggle, jiggling; sifting; waddling; strutting.

zarcillo *m.* earring; tendril (*coil of a climbing vine*); *Andes, Mex.* earmark (*on the ear of an animal*).

zarpa *f.* paw, claw; weighing anchor; **echar la —** to grasp, seize; **zarpada** *f.* pounce; blow with a paw; **zarpazo** *m.* blow with the paw; big blow, thud; hard fall.

zarpar *v.* to weigh anchor; to set sail.

zarza *f.* bramble; blackberry bush.

zarzamora *f.* blackberry.

zarzuela *f.* Spanish musical comedy.

zigzag *m.* zigzag.

zigzaguear *v.* to zigzag.

zinc = **cinc.**

zócalo m. base (of a pedestal); Mex. public square.

zodíaco m. zodiac.

zona f. zone; band, girdle; shingles (a disease).

zonzo adj. dull, stupid, silly, foolish.

zoología f. zoology.

zoológico adj. zoological; **jardín —** zoo.

zopenco adj. stupid, dull, thick-headed m. blockhead, dunce.

zopilote m. Mex. C.A. buzzard.

zoquete m. (cosa) block, chunk of wood; hunk of bread; (persona) blockhead, dunce, fool; ugly fat person; Am. grease, dirt, filth; Am. slap.

zorra f. fox; foxy person; drunkenness; prostitute; **pillar una —** to get drunk.

zorro m. fox; foxy person; -s fox skins; duster made of cloth or leather strips; **estar hecho un —** to be drowsy; **hacerse uno el —** to pretend to be stupid or not to hear; adj. foxy; **zorrillo, zorrino** m. Ríopl. skunk; **zorruno** adj. foxy.

zorzal m. thrush; crafty fellow; Am. fool, scapegoat, dupe.

zozobra f. foundering; sinking; anxiety, worry.

zozobrar v. to founder; to capsize; to sink; to be in great danger; to fret, worry.

zumbar v. to buzz; to hum; to ring (said of the ears); to scoff at; to strike, hit; Ven., Col. to throw out or away; Andes to punish; **— una bofetada** to give a slap; **-se** Am. to slip away, disappear.

zumbido m. buzzing, humming; ringing (in one's ears); hit, blow, whack.

zumbón adj. funny, playful; sarcastic; m. jester.

zumo f. juice; profit; **zumoso** adj. juicy.

zurcido m. darn; darning; p.p. of zurcir.

zurcir[10] v. to darn; to invent, make up (lies).

zurdo adj. left-handed; left; **a zurdas** with the left hand; clumsily.

zuro m. cob, corncob.

zurra f. beating, flogging; tanning (of leather).

zurrar v. to flog, thrash; to tan (leather).

zurrón m. pouch; bag; leather bag; Ven., Col. big coward.

Zutano m. so-and-so; a certain person. (Used often with **Fulano** and **Mengano**).

Parte Segunda Inglés-Español

Al Estudioso

El auge que desde el principio de la Guerra Mundial II viene cobrando en la América española el aprendizaje del inglés, nos ha movido a recopilar en este breve Diccionario las voces y locuciones más indispensables de esta lengua tal como se habla y escribe en los Estados Unidos de América.

Al igual que en la Sección española-inglesa hemos antepuesto la abreviatura *Am.* y otras a aquellos vocablos o idiotismos que son de uso exclusivo en alguna región de la América española, o bien de uso frecuentísimo en ésta, aunque ya hayan caído en desuso en la Península. Todo lo cual no excluye la posibilidad de que alguna acepción así designada se oiga en labios de español o sea de uso esporádico en España.

Lo que sí hemos procurado con gran ahinco y anhelamos lograr, presentando al estudioso este caudal indispensable de palabras, es el acercamiento lingüístico de las Américas, como base para nuestra mutua comprensión y como instrumento poderosísimo para nuestra solidaridad.

LOS EDITORES

Lista de Abreviaturas

adj.	adjectivo	*irr.*	irregular
adv.	adverbio	*p.p.*	participio pasado o pasivo
art.	artículo	*pers.*	personal
art. indef.	artículo indefinido	*pl.*	plural
aux.	auxiliar	*pos.*	posesivo
comp.	comparativo	*prep.*	preposición
conj.	conjunción	*pron.*	pronombre
contr.	contracción	*pron. pers.*	pronombre personal
defect.	defectivo	*pron. pos.*	pronombre posesivo
etc.	etcétera	*s.*	sustantivo
ger.	gerundio	*sing.*	singular
gram.	gramatical, gramática	*subj.*	subjuntivo
imperf.	imperfecto	*v.*	verbo
indic.	indicativo	*v. defect.*	verbo defectivo
interj.	interjección	*v. irr.*	verbo irregular
interr.	interrogativo		

i

Abreviaturas Especiales de Indicación Regional

Am.[1]	Americanismo
Andalucía	
Andes	(Ecuador, Perú, Bolivia)
Arg.	Argentina
Bol.	Bolivia
Carib.	(Cuba, Puerto Rico, República Dominicana)
C.A.	Centroamérica (Guatemala, El Salvador, Honduras, Nicaragua, Costa Rica)
Ch.	Chile
Col.	Colombia
C.R.	Costa Rica
Cuba	
Ec.	El Ecuador
Esp.	España
Guat.	Guatemala
Hond.	Honduras
Méx.	México
N. Esp.	Norte de España
Nic.	Nicaragua
Pan.	Panamá
Par.	Paraguay
Perú	
P.R.	Puerto Rico
Ríopl.	Río de la Plata (La Argentina oriental, el Uruguay)
S.A.	Sudamérica
Sal.	El Salvador
Ur.	El Uruguay
Ven.	Venezuela

Pronunciación Inglesa[2]

I. Vocales

Símbolo fonético	Ortografía inglesa	Ortografía fonética	Explicación de los sonidos
i	see pea	si pi	Equivale a la *i* in *hilo*.
I	bit	bɪt	El sonido más aproximado es la *i* en *virtud*, pero la [ɪ] inglesa es una *i* más abierta tirando a *e* cerrada.
e	late they	let ðe	Equivale aproximadamente a *ei*; la *i* de este diptongo es muy relajada y más abierta que en español.

[1] Esta abreviatura se emplea para indicar uso general hispanoamericano; se implica a la vez carácter arcaizante en cuanto a España. Se usa también para señalar los vocablos ya poco usados que puedan encontrarse en obras literarias del siglo pasado.

[2] El estudioso puede consultar el importante diccionario de pronunciación norteamericana: Kenyon and Knott, *A Pronouncing Dictionary of American English* (Springfield, Massachusetts: G. & C. Merriam Company, Publishers, 1944).

ɛ	bet	bɛt	El sonido más aproximado en español es la *e* abierta de *perro*.
æ	sat	sæt	Es una vocal intermedia entre la *a* y la *e*.
ɑ	car	kɑr	Equivale aproximadamente a la *a* en *cargo*.
ɔ	forge	fɔrdʒ	Equivale aproximadamente a la *o* en *corto*, *corre*.
o	mode	mod	Equivale aproximadamente a *ou*; la *u* de este diptongo es muy relajada y más abierta que en español.
ʊ	pull	pʊl	El sonido más aproximado en español es la *u* en *turrón*, pero la [ʊ] inglesa es todavía más abierta.
u	June moon	dʒun mun	Equivale aproximadamente a la *u* en *uno*.
ə	cudgel apply	kʌdʒəl əplái	Es una *e* muy relajada. No tiene equivalente en español.
ɚ	teacher	títʃɚ	Es una *e* muy relajada, articulada simultáneamente con la *r*. No tiene equivalente en español.
ɝ	earth fur	ɝθ fɝ	Es un sonido intermedio entre la *e* y la *o* articulado simultáneamente con la *r*. Se acerca más a la *e* que a la *o*. No tiene equivalente en español.
ʌ	duck	dʌk	Es una vocal intermedia entre la *e* muy abierta y la *o*. Se acerca más a la *o* que a la *e*. No tiene equivalente en español.

II. Diptongos

aɪ	aisle nice	aɪl naɪs	Equivale aproximadamente a *aí* en *aire*.
aʊ	now	naʊ	Equivale aproximadamente a *au* en *causa*.
ɔɪ	coy	kɔɪ	Equivale aproximadamente a *oy* en *hoy*. El segundo elemento del diptongo es más abierto y débil, tirando a *e*.
ju	used	juzd	Equivale aproximadamente a *iu* en *ciudad*.
jʊ	cure	kjʊr	Equivale aproximadamente al diptongo *iu*, pero la *u* es más abierta.

III. Consonantes

p	paper	pépɚ	Equivale aproximadamente a la *p* española, pero es mucho más explosiva.
b	bat	bæt	La *b* inglesa es semejante a la *b* inicial española, pero se pronuncia más explosivamente.
t	tea	ti	Es bastante diferente de la *t* española. Se articula colocando flojamente la lengua arriba de los dientes incisivos superiores.

d	day	de	Equivale a la *d* inicial española pronunciada con mayor énfasis.
k	cat kill	kæt kɪl	Equivale aproximadamente a la *c* española delante de *a,o,u* pronunciada con mayor énfasis.
g	go gum ago	go gʌm əgó	Equivale aproximadamente a la *g* inicial delante de *a,o,u: goma, guerra, gana*; sólo que la *g* inglesa se pronuncia con mayor explosión.
f	fun affair	fʌn əfér	Equivale aproximadamente a la *f* española.
v	very	vérɪ	No tiene equivalente en español. Es una labiodental que se articula con el labio inferior y los dientes incisivos superiores.
o	thin	θɪn	Equivale aproximadamente a Ja *z* en el castellano *cazar*.
ð	then other	ðɛn ʌ́ðɚ	Equivale aproximadamente a la *d* española en *pardo*.
s	send case cent	sɛnd kes sɛnt	Equivale aproximadamente a la *s* inicial española: *santo*.
z	rose these zero	roz ðiz ziro	Equivale aproximadamente a la *s* sonora en *mismo*, pero se pronuncia con más sonoridad en inglés.
ʃ	sheet machine nation	ʃit məʃín néʃən	Es una *s* palatal que no tiene equivalente en español. Suena como la *ch* francesa: *chapeau*.
ʒ	vision	vɪʒən	No tiene equivalente en español. Es una palatal fricativa sonora, semejante a la *y* argentina y uruguaya.
tʃ	chase	tʃes	Equivale aproximadamente a la *ch* en *charla*.
dʒ	judge gentle	dʒʌdʒ dʒéntl̩	No tiene equivalente exacto en español. Se parece a la *y* de *inyectar* en la pronunciación de uruguayos y argentinos.
m	much	mʌtʃ	Equivale aproximadamente a la *m* española.
n	none any	nʌn énɪ	Equivale aproximadamente a la *n* española en *nada*.
ņ	eaten button lesson	itņ bʌ́tņ lésņ	No tiene equivalente en español. Representa la *n* sin la articulación de la vocal anterior.
ŋ	ankle angle ring	æŋkl̩ æŋgl̩ rɪŋ	Equivale a la *n* española en *mango, banco*.
l	late altar fall folly	let ɔ́ltɚ fɔl fálɪ	La *l* inicial equivale aproximadamente a la *l* española en *lado*. La *l* en medio de palabra es más débil que la inicial. La *l* final se pronuncia a veces de una manera tan relajada en inglés que apenas la percibe el oído español.
l̩	able ankle	ébl̩ æŋkl̩	No tiene equivalente en español. Se pronuncia como la *l* en *hábil*, pero omitiendo la *i*.

w	weed	wid	Equivale a la *u* de los diptongos:
	well	wɛl	*ui, ue, ua, uo.*
	wall	wɔl	
h	hat	hæt	No tiene equivalente exacto en espa-
	whole	hol	ñol. Equivale aproximadamente a una *j* suave que se reduce a una simple aspiración.
hw	where	hwɛr	Equivale a una *j* suave seguida de una *w* arriba explicada.
j	year	jɪr	Equivale a la *i* española en los dip-
	yawn	jɔn	tongos *ie, ia, io, iu: hiena.*
	yet	jɛt	
r	rose	roz	No tiene equivalente en español. La
	bear	bɛr	punta de la lengua se arrolla hacia atrás sin tocar el paladar. A veces se pierde al grado de vocalizarse.

Pronunciación de la *S* del Plural[3]

I. La **-s** del plural es sorda cuando la palabra termina en las consonantes sordas representadas por los símbolos fonéticos [p], [t], [k], [f], [θ]. Pronúnciase como la *s* de *santo*: **caps** [kæps], **gates** [gets], **cats** [kæts], **books** [bʊks], **cliffs** [klɪfs], **lengths** [leŋkθs].

Las excepciones más comunes son: **oath** [oθ], **oaths** [oðz]; **leaf** [lif], **leaves** [livz], **wife** [waɪf], **wives** [waɪvz]; **knife** [naɪf], **knives** [naɪvz]; **calf** [kæf], **calves** [kævz]; **half** [hæf], **halves** [hævz].

II. La **-s** del plural es sonora cuando la palabra termina en vocal (inclu-yendo la **-y** que se cambia en **-ies**), o en las consonantes sonoras representadas por los símbolos fonéticos [b], [d], [g], [v], [ð], [m], [n], [ŋ], [l]: **cries** [kraɪz], **robes** [robz], **beds** [bɛdz], **logs** [lɔgz], **stoves** [stovz], **lathes** [leðz], **farms** [farmz], **bins** [bɪnz], **kings** [kɪŋz], **falls** [fɔlz], **furs** [fɜz], **papers** [pépɜz], **plows** [plaʊz].

III. Cuando la palabra termina **-en** las consonantes representadas por los símbolos [s], [ʃ], [tʃ], [z], [ʒ], [dʒ], se añade **-es** [ɪz], o **s** [ɪz], si la palabra termina en **-ce, -se, -dge, -ge**: **face** [fes], **faces** [fésɪz]; **kiss** [kɪs], **kisses** [kísɪz]; **ash** [æʃ], **ashes** [æʃɪz]; **lunch** [lʌntʃ], **lunches** [lʌntʃɪz]; **rose** [roz], **roses** [rózɪz]; **judge** [dʒʌdʒ], **judges** [dʒʌdʒɪz].

El Sustantivo

I. Género

Son masculinos los nombres de varón o animal macho, y son femeninos los nombres de mujer o animal hembra. Los demás son neutros. El artículo definido **the** se aplica a todos los sustantivos, singular y plural: **the man** el hombre; **the men** los hombres; **the book** el libro; **the books** los libros; **the woman** la mujer; **the women** las mujeres.

En ciertos sustantivos se distingue el género femenino por medio del sufijo **-ess: poet** poeta; **poetess** poetisa. A veces es indispensable indicar

---

[3] Las mismas reglas se aplican a la pronunciación del genitivo y de la tercera persona del presente de indicativo, singular: **keeps** [kips]; **Kate's** [kets]; **saves** [sevz]; **John's** [dʒɑnz]; **judges** [dʒʌdʒɪz]; **Alice's** [ǽlɪsɪz].

el género por medio de las palabras **male** o **female, boy** o **girl, man** o **woman, she** o **he: baby boy** niño; **baby girl** niña; **woman writer** escritora; **she-bear** osa. En otros casos hay una palabra distinta para cada género; **uncle** tío; **aunt** tía.

II. Plural de los Sustantivos[4]

1. Generalmente se forma el plural añadiendo **-s** al singular: **paper, papers** papel, papeles; **book, books** libro, libros; **chief, chiefs** jefe, jefes.

2. Los sustantivos que terminan en **-ch** (pronunciada como la *ch* española), **-ss, -x, -sh, -z,** y **-o** añaden **-es** para formar el plural: **arch, arches** arco, arcos; **kiss, kisses** beso, besos; **box, boxes** caja, cajas; **dish, dishes** plato, platos; **buzz, buzzes** zumbido, zumbidos; **hero, heroes** héroe, héroes. Nótese que los sustantivos terminados en **-ch** (pronunciada [k]) forman el plural añadiendo **-s: monarch, monarchs** monarca, monarcas.

3. Los sustantivos que terminan en **-fe,** y ciertos sustantivos que terminan en **-f,** cambian estas letras en **v** y añaden **-es: leaf, leaves** hoja, hojas; **life, lives** vida, vidas; **wife, wives** esposa, esposas; **knife, knives** cuchillo, cuchillos.

4. Para formar el plural de los sustantivos terminados en **-y** precedida de consonante cámbiase la **-y** en **-ies: fly, flies** mosca, moscas; **cry, cries** grito, gritos; **family, families** familia, familias; **quantity, quantities** cantidad, cantidades. Nótese que los sustantivos terminados en **-y** precedida de vocal forman el plural añadiendo **-s** al singular: **day, days** día, días.

5. Ciertos sustantivos forman el plural de una manera irregular: **man, men** hombre, hombres; **woman, women** mujer, mujeres; **mouse, mice** ratón, ratones; **louse, lice** piojo, piojos; **goose, geese** ganso, gansos; **tooth, teeth** diente, dientes; **foot, feet** pie, pies; **ox, oxen** buey, bueyes.

6. Ciertos sustantivos que terminan en **-is** forman el plural cambiando la **i** de la terminación en **e: axis, axes** eje, ejes; **the crisis, the crises** la crisis, las crisis.

El Adjetivo

El adjetivo inglés es invariable en cuanto a género y número. Normalmente se coloca delante del sustantivo: **an interesting book** un libro interesante; **a large table** una mesa grande; **beautiful women** mujeres hermosas.

Los comparativos y superlativos. Aunque no hay una regla general, por lo común los adjetivos monosílabos, los adjetivos acentuados en la última sílaba y algunos bisílabos fácilmente pronunciados forman *el comparativo de aumento y el superlativo* añadiendo **-er** y **-est.** Los demás adjetivos van precedidos de **more** y **most.** Nótese que (1) sólo se añaden **-r** y **-st** a los que terminan en **-e** muda; (2) los adjetivos terminados en **-y** cambian esta letra en **i;** (3) los adjetivos terminados en consonante precedida de vocal doblan la consonante:

---

[4] Véase las reglas para la pronunciación del plural.

Positivo	Comparativo	Superlativo
tall alto	**taller** más alto	**the tallest** el más alto
wise sabio	**wiser** más sabio	**the wisest** el más sabio
polite cortés	**politer** más cortés	**the politest** el más cortés
happy feliz	**happier** más feliz	**the happiest** el más feliz
fat gordo	**fatter** más gordo	**the fattest** el más gordo
careful cuidadoso	**more careful** más cuidadoso	**the most careful** el más cuidadoso

El superlativo absoluto se forma anteponiendo **very** y a veces **most: very intelligent** muy inteligente; **she is a most beautiful woman** es una mujer hermosísima.

El comparativo y el superlativo de inferioridad se forman con los adverbios **less** y **least: less wise** menos sabio; **the least wise** el menos sabio.

El comparativo de igualdad se forma con el adverbio **as: as poor as** tan pobre como; **as much as** tanto como; **as much money as** tanto dinero como.

Los adjetivos siguientes forman el comparativo y el superlativo de una manera irregular:

good, well	**better**	**best**
bad, ill	**worse**	**worst**
little	**less, lesser**	**least**
far	**farther, further**	**farthest, furthest**
much, many	**more**	**most**
old	**older, elder**	**oldest, eldest**

El Adverbio

Fórmanse muchos adverbios, añadiendo **-ly** al adjetivo: **courteous** cortés, **courteously** cortésmente; **bold** atrevido, **boldly** atrevidamente. Existen las irregularidades siguientes en la formación de los adverbios que terminan en **-ly**: (1) los adjetivos terminados en **-ble** cambian la **-e** en **-y**: **possible, possibly**; (2) los terminados en **-ic** añaden **-ally**: **poetic, poetically**; (3) los terminados en **-ll** añaden sólo la **-y**: **full, fully**; (4) los terminados en **-ue** pierden la **-e** final: **true, truly**; (5) los terminados en **-y** cambian la **-y** en **i**: **happy, happily.**

Como los adjetivos, la mayor parte de los adverbios forman el *comparativo* y el *superlativo* con los adverbios **more** (más), **most** (más), y **very** (muy). Asimismo los adverbios monosílabos añaden **-er** y **-est**:

Positivo	Comparativo	Superlativo	Superlativo Absoluto
boldly	**more boldly**	**most boldly**	**very boldly**
generously	**more generously**	**most generously**	**very generously**
soon	**sooner**	**soonest**	**very soon**
early	**earlier**	**earliest**	**very early**
late	**later**	**latest**	**very late**
near	**nearer**	**nearest**	**very near**
fast	**faster**	**fastest**	**very fast**

Los adverbios siguientes forman el comparativo y el superlativo de una manera irregular:

well	**better**	**best**	**very well**
badly, ill	**worse**	**worst**	**very badly**
little	**less**	**least**	**very little**
much	**more**	**most**	**very much**
far	**farther, further**	**farthest, furthest**	**very far**

Sufijos Comunes en Inglés

-dom denota dominio, jurisdicción, estado, condición, etc.: **kingdom** reino; **martyrdom** martirio; **boredom** aburrimiento; **freedom** libertad.

-ed, -d es la terminación del pretérito y del participio pasivo o pasado de los verbos regulares: I **called** llamé; **called** llamado.

-ee indica la persona que recibe la acción: **addressee** destinatario; **employee** empleado.

-eer denota oficio u ocupación: **engineer** ingeniero; **auctioneer** subastador.

-en *a)* terminación del participio de muchos verbos irregulares: **fallen, broken, shaken;**
b) sufijo que significa *hecho de:* **golden** dorado, de oro; **wooden** de madera; **leaden** de plomo;
c) terminación verbal equivalente a *hacer:* **whiten** hacer blanco, emblanquecer; **darken** hacer obscuro, obscurecer.

-er *a)* indica la persona que hace o el agente de la acción del verbo: **player** jugador; **talker** hablador;
b) indica el residente de un lugar: **New Yorker** habitante o residente de Nueva York; **islander** isleño;
c) denota ocupación: **carpenter** carpintero; **baker** panadero.
d) es la terminación del comparativo de adjetivos y adverbios; **taller** más alto; **faster** más aprisa.

-ess úsase para formar el género femenino de ciertos sustantivos: **patroness** patrona; **poetess** poetisa; **countess** condesa.

-est terminación del superlativo: **tallest** el más alto.

-fold sufijo que significa *veces:* **twofold** dos veces; **hundredfold** cien veces.

-ful *a)* equivale a *lleno,* y tratándose de adjetivos es igual a *-oso:* **hopeful** lleno de esperanzas; **careful** cuidadoso; **wilful** voluntarioso; **merciful** misericordioso; **glassful** un vaso (*lleno*);
b) indica a veces hábito o inclinación: **forgetful** olvidadizo;
c) es a veces equivalente a los sufijos españoles *-ado, -ada:* **handful** puñado; **spoonful** cucharada.

-hood indica estado, condición, carácter, grupo; a menudo equivale a *-dad:* **motherhood** maternidad; **brotherhood** fraternidad; **childhood** niñez; **falsehood** falsedad.

-ician denota especialidad en cierto ramo: **musician** músico; **technician** técnico; **electrician** electricista.

-ie sufijo diminutivo: **birdie** pajarito; **Annie** Anita.

-ing *a)* sufijo del gerundio: **speaking** hablando;
b) sufijo del participio activo: **threatening** amenazante; **surprising** sorprendente;
c) úsase a menudo para formar adjetivos: **running water** agua corriente; **drinking water** agua potable; **waiting room** sala de espera; **washing machine** máquina lavadora;

d) úsase para formar sustantivos: **understanding** entendimiento; **supplying** abastecimiento; **clothing** ropa; **covering** cobertura; equivale al infinitivo castellano: **swimming is good exercise** el nadar es buen ejercicio.

-ish   *a*) úsase para formar ciertos adjetivos de nacionalidad: **Spanish** español; **English** inglés; **Turkish** turco;

b) indica semejanza: **boyish** como niño, aniñado; **womanish** como mujer, mujeril, afeminado; **whitish** blancuzco, medio blanco, que tira a blanco.

-less   equivale a *sin, falto de*: **childless** sin hijos; **penniless** sin dinero; en ciertos casos el sufijo inglés se traduce por medio de un prefijo: **countless** innumerable, sin número; **endless** interminable, sin fin.

-like   significa *semejanza*, y equivale a *como, a manera de*: **lifelike** que parece vivo; **childlike** como niño, infantil; **tigerlike** como tigre.

-ly   *a*) sufijo adverbial: **slowly** lentamente; **happily** felizmente; **possibly** posiblemente;

b) añadido a ciertos sustantivos equivale a *como, a la manera de*: **motherly** como madre, materno; **gentlemanly** como caballero, caballeroso; **friendly** amigable; **manly** varonil;

c) equivale a *cada* en estos ejemplos: **daily** cada día, diario; **weekly** cada semana, semanal; **monthly** cada mes, mensual; **yearly** cada año, anual.

-ness   úsase para formar sustantivos abstractos: **goodness** bondad; **darkness** obscuridad; **foolishness** tontería; **shamelessness** desvergüenza.

-ship   *a*) úsase para formar sustantivos abstractos: **friendship** amistad; **relationship** relación, parentesco;

b) denota arte o destreza: **horsemanship** equitación;

c) expresa dignidad, oficio, cargo, o título: **professorship** profesorado o cátedra; **chairmanship** presidencia (*de un comité, asamblea, etc.*); **lordship** señoría;

d) a veces expresa tan sólo un estado y su duración: **courtship** galanteo, cortejo, noviazgo.

-some   expresa en alto grado la cualidad representada por el vocablo al cual se añade: **tiresome** que cansa, cansado; **quarrelsome** dado a riñas, pendenciero; **loathsome** que repugna, asqueroso; **burdensome** gravoso.

-th   úsase para formar números ordinales: **fifth** quinto; **tenth** décimo.

-ty   *a*) terminación de los múltiples de diez: **twenty** veinte; **thirty** treinta; **forty** cuarenta;

b) terminación de muchos sustantivos abstractos; equivale frecuentemente al sufijo español *-tad* o *-dad*: **beauty** beldad; **paternity** paternidad; **falsity** falsedad.

-ward, -wards denotan *hacia*: **homeward** hacia casa; **downward** hacia abajo.

-ways, -wise   expresan manera, dirección, posición, etc.: **edgewise** de lado; **sideways** de lado; **lengthwise** a lo largo.

-y   *a*) terminación equivalente a los sufijos españoles *-ia, -ta*:

victory victoria; **glory** gloria; **courtesy** cortesía; **biology** biología; **astronomy** astronomía;

b) sufijo diminutivo: **doggy** perrito; **Johnny** Juanito;

c) denota abundancia, y es a menudo equivalente a -*udo*, -*oso*, -*ado*: **rocky** lleno de rocas, rocoso, pedregoso; **rainy** lluvioso; **hairy** lleno de pelo, peludo; **bulky** abultado; **wavy** ondulado; **angry** enojado;

d) expresa semejanza: **rosy** rosado, como una rosa, color de rosa.

Números

Consúltese la tabla de la página xlii de la Sección Española-Inglesa para el aprendizaje de los números cardinales y ordinales desde uno hasta un millón.

Verbos Irregulares de la Lengua Inglesa

Se denominan verbos irregulares los que no forman el pretérito o el participio pasivo con la adición de **-d** o **-ed** al presente. Obsérvese que en ciertos verbos coexiste la forma regular al lado de la irregular. En otros coexisten dos formas irregulares juntamente con la regular.

Presente	*Pretérito*	*Participio pasivo o pasado*
abide	abode	abode
am, is, are	was, were	been
arise	arose	arisen
awake	awoke, awaked	awaked, awoke
bear	bore	born, borne
beat	beat	beat, beaten
become	became	become
befall	befell	befallen
beget	begat	begotten
begin	began	begun
behold	beheld	beheld
bend	bent	bent
bereave	bereft, bereaved	bereft, bereaved
beseech	besought, beseeched	besought, beseeched
beset	beset	beset
bet	bet	bet
bid	bid, bade	bidden, bid
bind	bound	bound
bite	bit	bitten, bit
bleed	bled	bled
blow	blew	blown
break	broke	broken
breed	bred	bred
bring	brought	brought
build	built	built
burn	burnt, burned	burnt, burned
burst	burst	burst
buy	bought	bought
can (*verbo defectivo*)	could	—
cast	cast	cast
catch	caught	caught
chide	chided, chid	chided, chidden
choose	chose	chosen
cleave	cleft, clove, cleaved	cleft, cleaved, cloven
cling	clung	clung

Presente	Pretérito	Participio pasivo o pasado
clothe	clad, clothed	clad, clothed
come	came	come
cost	cost	cost
creep	crept	crept
crow	crew, crowed	crowed
cut	cut	cut
deal	dealt	dealt
dig	dug, digged	dug, digged
do	did	done
draw	drew	drawn
dream	dreamt, dreamed	dreamt, dreamed
drink	drank	drunk
drive	drove	driven
dwell	dwelt, dwelled	dwelt, dwelled
eat	ate	eaten
fall	fell	fallen
feed	fed	fed
feel	felt	felt
fight	fought	fought
find	found	found
flee	fled	fled
fling	flung	flung
fly	flew	flown
forbear	forbore	forborne
forbid	forbade	forbidden
foresee	foresaw	foreseen
foretell	foretold	foretold
forget	forgot	forgotten, forgot
forgive	forgave	forgiven
forsake	forsook	forsaken
freeze	froze	frozen
get	got	got, gotten
gild	gilt, gilded	gilt, gilded
gird	girt, girded	girt, girded
give	gave	given
go	went	gone
grind	ground	ground
grow	grew	grown
hang[5]	hung	hung
have, has	had	had
hear	heard	heard
heave	hove, heaved	hove, heaved
hew	hewed	hewn, hewed
hide	hid	hidden, hid
hit	hit	hit
hold	held	held
hurt	hurt	hurt
inlay	inlaid	inlaid
keep	kept	kept
kneel	knelt	knelt
knit	knit, knitted	knit, knitted
know	knew	known
lay	laid	laid
lead	led	led
lean	leaned, leant	leaned, leant
leap	leapt, leaped	leapt, leaped
learn	learned, learnt	learned, learnt
leave	left	left
lend	lent	lent
let	let	let

[5] Es regular cuando significa "ahorcar."

Presente	Pretérito	Participio pasivo o pasado
lie[6] (yacer; echarse)	lay	lain
light	lit, lighted	lit, lighted
load	loaded	loaded, laden
lose	lost	lost
make	made	made
may (verbo defectivo)	might	—
mean	meant	meant
meet	met	met
melt	melted	melted, molten
mistake	mistook	mistaken
mow	mowed	mown, mowed
must (verbo defectivo)	—	—
ought (verbo defectivo)	ought	—
pay	paid	paid
put	put	put
quit	quit, quitted	quit, quitted
read [rid]	read [rɛd]	read [rɛd]
rend	rent	rent
rid	rid, ridded	rid, ridded
ride	rode	ridden
ring	rang, rung	rung
rise	rose	risen
run	ran	run
saw	sawed	sawn, sawed
say	said	said
see	saw	seen
seek	sought	sought
sell	sold	sold
send	sent	sent
set	set	set
sew	sewed	sewn, sewed
shake	shook	shaken
shall	should	—
shave	shaved	shaved, shaven
shear	sheared	shorn, sheared
shed	shed	shed
shine[7]	shone	shone
shoe	shod	shod
shoot	shot	shot
show	showed	shown, showed
shred	shred, shredded	shred, shredded
shrink	shrank, shrunk	shrunk, shrunken
shut	shut	shut
sing	sang, sung	sung
sink	sank	sunk
sit	sat	sat
slay	slew	slain
sleep	slept	slept
slide	slid	slid, slidden
sling	slung	slung
slink	slunk	slunk
slit	slit	slit
smell	smelt, smelled	smelt, smelled
smite	smote	smitten
sow	sowed	sown, sowed
speak	spoke	spoken
speed	sped, speeded	sped, speeded
spell	spelled, spelt	spelled, spelt
spend	spent	spent

[6] Es regular cuando significa "mentir."
[7] Es por lo común regular cuando significa "pulir, dar brillo."

Presente	*Pretérito*	*Participio pasivo o pasado*
spill	spilled, spilt	spilled, spilt
spin	spun	spun
spit	spit, spat	spit, spat
split	split	split
spread	spread	spread
spring	sprang, sprung	sprung
stand	stood	stood
stave	staved, stove	staved, stove
steal	stole	stolen
stick	stuck	stuck
sting	stung	stung
stink	stank, stunk	stunk
strew	strewed	strewn, strewed
stride	strode	stridden
strike	struck	struck, striken
string	strung	strung
strive	strove, strived	striven, strived
swear	swore	sworn
sweep	swept	swept
swell	swelled	swollen, swelled
swim	swam	swum
swing	swung	swung
take	took	taken
teach	taught	taught
tear	tore	torn
tell	told	told
think	thought	thought
thrive	throve, thrived	thriven, thrived
throw	threw	thrown
thrust	thrust	thrust
tread	trod	trod, trodden
understand	understood	understood
undertake	undertook	undertaken
undo	undid	undone
uphold	upheld	upheld
upset	upset	upset
wake	woke, waked	waked
wear	wore	worn
weave	wove	woven
wed	wedded	wedded, wed
weep	wept	wept
wet	wet, wetted	wet, wetted
will (*verbo auxiliar*)	would	—
win	won	won
wind	wound	wound
withdraw	withdrew	withdrawn
withhold	withheld	withheld
withstand	withstood	withstood
work	worked, wrought	worked, wrought
wring	wrung	wrung
write	wrote	written

A

a [ə, e] *art. indef.* un, una; **what —** . . . ! ¡qué . . . !; **such —** tal; tan.

abandon [əbǽndən] *v.* abandonar; dejar; *s.* abandono, desahogo, desenvoltura; entrega.

abandoned [əbǽndənd] *adj.* abandonado; dejado; perverso; inmoral.

abandonment [əbǽndənmənt] *s.* abandono, abandonamiento; desamparo; desenvoltura, desembarazo.

abashed [əbǽʃt] *adj.* humillado, avergonzado.

abate [əbét] *v.* bajar, rebajar; disminuir; acabar con; mitigar(se); calmarse.

abatement [əbétmənt] *s.* diminución, merma; rebaja, descuento; mitigación.

abbess [ǽbəs] *s.* abadesa.

abbey [ǽbɪ] *s.* abadía, monasterio.

abbot [ǽbət] *s.* abad.

abbreviate [əbrívɪet] *v.* abreviar, acortar, reducir.

abbreviation [əbrivɪéʃən] *s.* abreviación, abreviatura.

abdicate [ǽbdəket] *v.* abdicar, renunciar.

abdomen [ǽbdəmən] *s.* abdomen; vientre.

abduct [æbdʌ́kt] *v.* secuestrar, raptar, *Am.* plagiar (*a alguien*).

abduction [æbdʌ́kʃən] *s.* rapto, robo, secuestro (*de una persona*).

aberration [æbəréʃən] *s.* aberración, extravío (*de la mente*).

abet [əbét] *v.* incitar; fomentar.

abeyance [əbéəns] *s.* suspensión; **in —** pendiente.

abhor [əbhór] *v.* aborrecer, odiar, abominar.

abhorrence [əbhórəns] *s.* aborrecimiento, aversión.

abide [əbáɪd] *v.* quedar, permanecer; morar, habitar; aguardar; soportar; tolerar; **to — by** conformarse a; atenerse a.

ability [əbɪ́lətɪ] *s.* habilidad, capacidad.

abject [ǽbdʒékt] *adj.* abatido; vil.

abjure [æbdʒúr] *v.* abjurar.

able [ébl] *adj.* hábil, capaz; competente; **able-bodied** de cuerpo sano; **to be — to** poder; saber.

ably [ébl] *adv.* hábilmente.

abnormal [æbnórml] *adj.* anormal.

aboard [əbórd] *adv.* a bordo; en el tren; **to go —** embarcarse; **all — !** ¡viajeros al tren!; *Méx., C.A.* ¡vámonos!

abode [əbód] *s.* morada, domicilio, casa; *pret. & p.p. de* **to abide.**

abolish [əbɑ́lɪʃ] *v.* abolir; anular.

abolition [æbəlíʃən] *s.* abolición.

abominable [əbɑ́mnəbl] *adj.* abominable, aborrecible.

abort [əbórt] *v.* abortar.

abortion [əbórʃən] *s.* aborto.

abound [əbáund] *v.* abundar; **to — with** abundar en.

about [əbáut] *prep.* (*concerning*) acerca de, tocante a, respecto de; (*near, surrounding*) alrededor de, por; *adv.* (*almost*) casi, poco más o menos; **at**

— ten o'clock a eso de las diez; **to be — one's business** atender a su negocio; **to be — to** estar para, estar a punto de; **to face —** dar media vuelta; **to have no money — one's person** no llevar dinero consigo.

above [əbʌ́v] *prep.* por encima de; sobre; *adv.* arriba; **— all** sobre todo; **above-mentioned** susodicho, ya mencionado; **from —** de arriba; del cielo, de Dios.

abrasive [əbrésɪv] *adj.* abrasivo; tosco.

abreast [əbrést] *adj., adv.* al lado; **to keep abreast** ponerse al corriente.

abridge [əbrídʒ] *v.* abreviar; compendiar, condensar; privar (*a uno de sus derechos*).

abroad [əbród] *adv.* en el extranjero; fuera de casa; **to go —** ir al extranjero; **to spread —** divulgar o publicar por todas partes.

abrupt [əbrʌ́pt] *adj.* repentino; precipitado; áspero, brusco; escarpado; **-ly** *adv.* de repente; bruscamente.

abscess [ǽbsɛs] *s.* absceso.

absence [ǽbsns] *s.* ausencia; falta; **— of mind** abstracción; **leave of —** licencia (*para ausentarse*).

absent [ǽbsnt] *adj.* ausente; abstraído, distraído; **absent-minded** absorto, abstraído; [æbsént] *v.* **to — oneself** ausentarse.

absolute [ǽbsəlut] *adj.* absoluto; **the — lo** absoluto; **-ly** *adv.* absolutamente; en absoluto.

absolution [æbsəlúʃən] *s.* absolución.

absolve [æbsɑ́lv] *v.* absolver, remitir; perdonar; alzar la pena o el castigo.

absorb [əbsórb] *v.* absorber.

absorbent [əbsórbənt] *adj. & s.* absorbente.

absorption [əbsórpʃən] *s.* absorción; abstracción, embebecimiento.

abstain [əbstén] *v.* abstenerse, privarse.

abstinence [ǽbstənəns] *s.* abstinencia.

abstract [ǽbstrækt] *adj.* abstracto; *s.* sumario; extracto; **in the —** en abstracto; [æbstrǽkt] *v.* abstraer; considerar aisladamente; separar, retirar; resumir, compendiar.

abstraction [æbstrǽkʃən] *s.* abstracción; idea abstracta.

absurd [əbsɝ́d] *adj.* absurdo; insensato; ridículo, disparatado.

absurdity [əbsɝ́dətɪ] *s.* absurdo, disparate.

abundance [əbʌ́ndəns] *s.* abundancia, copia.

abundant [əbʌ́ndənt] *adj.* abundante, copioso.

abuse [əbjús] *s.* abuso; maltrato; ultraje; [əbjúz] *v.* abusar de; maltratar; injuriar; ultrajar.

abusive [əbjúsɪv] *adj.* abusivo; insultante, injurioso.

abyss [əbɪ́s] *s.* abismo; sima.

academic [ækədémɪk] *adj.* académico; escolar.

academy [əkǽdəmɪ] *s.* academia; colegio, instituto; escuela preparatoria.

accede [æksíd] *v.* acceder, consentir.

accelerate [æksélɘret] v. acelerar(se).
acceleration [æksɛlɘréʃɘn] s. aceleración.
accelerator [æksélɘretɚ] s. acelerador.
accent [æksɛnt] s. acento; [æksɛnt] v. acentuar; recalcar.
accentuate [æksɛntʃʋet] v. acentuar; recalcar; realzar.
accept [ɘsépt] v. aceptar; admitir; acoger; aprobar.
acceptable [ɘkséptɘbl] adj. aceptable; grato; acepto.
acceptance [ɘkséptɘns] s. aceptación; aprobación; buena acogida, recibimiento.
access [æksɛs] s. acceso; ataque (de una enfermedad); arrebato (de furia).
accessible [æksésɘbl] adj. accesible; asequible, obtenible.
accessory [æksésɘrɪ] adj. accesorio; adjunto; s. accesorio; cómplice; **accessories** cosas accesorias, adornos, adminículos.
accident [æksɘdɘnt] s. accidente; percance, contratiempo; **by —** por casualidad.
accidental [æksɘdéntl] adj. accidental; casual; **-ly** adv. accidentalmente; por casualidad.
acclaim [ɘklém] v. aclamar, aplaudir; s. aclamación, aplauso.
acclamation [æklɘméʃɘn] s. aclamación, aplauso.
acclimate [ɘkláɪmɘt], [æklɘmet] v. aclimatar(se); acostumbrar(se).
acclimatize [ɘkláɪmɘtaɪz] v. aclimatar(se).
accommodate [ɘkɑmɘdét] v. (adjust) acomodar, ajustar, ayudar, hacer un favor; (lodge) hospedar, alojar, tener cabida para; **to — oneself** conformarse, adaptarse.
accommodation [ɘkɑmɘdéʃɘn] s. favor, ayuda; conveniencia; alojamiento (en un hotel, casa, etc.); cabida; adaptación; ajuste.
accompaniment [ɘkámpɘnɪmɘnt] s. acompañamiento.
accompanist [ɘkámpɘnɪst] s. acompañador, acompañante.
accompany [ɘkámpɘnɪ] v. acompañar.
accomplice [ɘkámplɪs] s. cómplice.
accomplish [ɘkámplɪʃ] v. cumplir; completar; lograr, conseguir; realizar, efectuar.
accomplished [ɘkámplɪʃt] adj. cumplido; realizado; consumado; establecido; diestro; perfecto.
accomplishment [ɘkámplɪʃmɘnt] s. cumplimiento; logro, realización; habilidad; perfección; mérito, proeza.
accord [ɘkórd] s. acuerdo, convenio; armonía, concierto; **of one's own —** voluntariamente; espontáneamente; **in — with** de acuerdo con; **with one —** unánimemente; v. otorgar, conceder, dar; concordar.
accordance [ɘkórdns] s. conformidad, acuerdo; **in — with** de acuerdo con, de conformidad con.
according [ɘkórdɪŋ]: **— to** según; conforme a; de acuerdo con; **— as** según (que), a medida que.
accordingly [ɘkórdɪŋlɪ] adv. en conformidad; así; como tal; por lo tanto; por consiguiente.
accordion [ɘkórdɪɘn] s. acordeón.
accost [ɘkóst] v. abordar (a alguien) en la calle, acosar; molestar, perseguir.
account [ɘkáʋnt] s. (bill) cuenta, computación; (story) relato; **on — of** a causa de; con motivo de; por; **on my —** por mí; **on my own —** por mi propia cuenta; **on no —** de ninguna manera; **of no —** de ningún valor o importancia; **to turn to —** aprovechar, hacer útil o provechoso; v. dar cuenta (a); considerar, tener por; **to — for** dar cuenta o razón de; explicar; **how do you — for that?** ¿cómo se explica eso?
accountable [ɘkáʋntɘbl] adj. responsable; explicable.
accountant [ɘkáʋntɘnt] s. contador, tenedor de libros.
accounting [ɘkáʋntɪŋ] s. contabilidad, contaduría.
accredit [ɘkrédɪt] v. acreditar.
accrue [ɘkrú] v. acumular(se).
acculturate [ɘkáltʃɚet] v. aculturar(se).
accumulate [ɘkjúmjɘlet] v. acumular(se), juntar(se), amontonar(se).
accumulation [ɘkjumjɘléʃɘn] s. acumulación, amontonamiento.
accuracy [ækjɚɘsɪ] s. precisión, exactitud, esmero.
accurate [ækjɚɪt] adj. preciso, exacto, correcto; esmerado; cierto; certero; acertado; **-ly** adv. con exactitud; correctamente; con esmero.
accursed [ɘkɚst] adj. maldito; infame.
accusation [ækjɘzéʃɘn] s. acusación.
accuse [ɘkjúz] v. acusar; denunciar.
accuser [ɘkjúzɚ] s. acusador; delator, denunciador.
accustom [ɘkástɘm] v. acostumbrar (a); **to — oneself** acostumbrarse; **to be -ed to** tener la costumbre de, acostumbrar, soler; estar acostumbrado a, estar hecho a.
ace [es] s. as; as, el mejor de su clase (como un aviador excelente); **within an — of** a punto de; muy cerca de.
acetate [æsɘtet] s. acetato.
acetylene [ɘsétɘlin] s. acetileno.
ache [ek] s. dolor; **tooth —** dolor de muelas; v. doler.
achieve [ɘtʃív] v. acabar, llevar a cabo; realizar; conseguir, lograr; alcanzar.
achievement [ɘtʃívmɘnt] s. logro, realización; proeza, hazaña.
acid [æsɪd] adj. ácido; agrio; s. ácido.
acidity [ɘsídɘtɪ] s. acidez.
acknowledge [ɘknálɪdʒ] v. reconocer, admitir; confesar; **to — receipt** acusar recibo.
acknowledgment [ɘknálɪdʒmɘnt] s. reconocimiento, expresión de gratitud; confesión, admisión; **— of receipt** acuse de recibo.
acorn [ékɔrn] s. bellota.
acoustics [ɘkústɪks] s. acústica.

acquaint [əkwént] *v.* enterar, informar; dar a conocer; familiarizar; **to — oneself with** ponerse al corriente de; enterarse de; **to be -ed with** conocer a (*una persona*); estar enterado de (*algo*); conocer (*una ciudad, un país, etc.*).

acquaintance [əkwéntəns] *s.* conocimiento; conocido; **-s** amistades.

acquiesce [ækwɪés] *v.* asentir; consentir, quedar conforme.

acquiescence [ækwɪésns] *s.* asentimiento, consentimiento; conformidad.

acquire [əkwáɪr] *v.* adquirir; obtener, conseguir; contraer (*costumbres, vicios*).

acquisition [ækwəzíʃən] *s.* adquisición.

acquit [əkwít] *v.* absolver, exonerar; pagar, redimir, librar de (*una obligación*); **to — oneself well** quedar bien; portarse bien.

acquittal [əkwít] *s.* absolución.

acre [ékə] *s.* acre (*medida de superficie*).

acrobat [ækrəbæt] *s.* acróbata.

acronym [ækrənɪm] *s.* acrónimo.

across [əkrós] *prep.* a través de; al otro lado de; por; por en medio de; *adv.* a través, de través; **to go —** atravesar; **to come —, run —** encontrarse con; tropezar con.

acrylic [əkrílɪk] *adj.* acrílico.

act [ækt] *s.* acto; acción, hecho; *v.* hacer, desempeñar (*un papel*); representar (*en el teatro*); obrar; actuar; portarse; funcionar; **to — as** servir de, estar de.

acting [æktɪŋ] *s.* representación, desempeño (*de un papel dramático*); acción, actuación; *adj.* interino, suplente.

action [ækʃən] *s.* acción; acto; actuación; funcionamiento.

activate [æktɪvet] *v.* activar.

active [æktɪv] *adj.* activo.

activism [æktəvɪzm] *s.* activismo.

activist [æktəvɪst] *s.* activista.

activity [æktívətɪ] *s.* actividad.

actor [æktə] *s.* actor.

actress [æktrɪs] *s.* actriz.

actual [æktʃʊəl] *adj.* (*legitimate*) verdadero, real; (*current*) actual, existente; **-ly** *adv.* realmente, en realidad; de hecho, efectivamente.

acumen [əkjúmɪn] *s.* caletre, tino, perspicacia.

acute [əkjút] *adj.* agudo; perspicaz; penetrante.

adamant [ædəmænt] *adj.* duro; firme, inflexible.

adapt [ədæpt] *v.* adaptar; **to — oneself** adaptarse, acomodarse.

adaptation [ædəptéʃən] *s.* adaptación.

add [æd] *v.* sumar; añadir, agregar.

addict [ædɪkt] *s.* adicto (*persona adicta al uso de narcóticos*); **drug —** morfinómano.

addicted [ədíktɪd] *adj.* adicto, dado, entregado, habituado.

addition [ədíʃən] *s.* adición; suma; añadidura, aditamento; **in — to** además de.

additional [ədíʃən] *adj.* adicional.

additive [ædətɪv] *s.* & *adj.* aditivo.

address [ədrés] *s.* (*street*) dirección, domicilio, señas; sobrescrito; (*speech*) discurso, arenga, conferencia; **form of —** tratamiento; *v.* dirigir, poner la dirección, señas o sobrescrito a; hablar, dirigir la palabra a; dirigirse a; **to — oneself to a task** aplicarse a una tarea.

addressee [ədrɛsí] *s.* destinatario.

adduce [ədús] *v.* aducir.

adequate [ædəkwɪt] *adj.* adecuado; proporcionado; suficiente.

adhere [ədhír] *v.* adherirse; pegarse.

adherence [ədhírəns] *s.* adherencia.

adhesion [ədhíʒən] *s.* adhesión.

adhesive [ədhísɪv] *adj.* adhesivo; pegajoso; **— tape** tela adhesiva, esparadrapo.

adjacent [ədʒésnt] *adj.* adyacente, contiguo.

adjective [ædʒɪktɪv] *s.* adjetivo.

adjoin [ədʒóɪn] *v.* estar contiguo o adyacente a, lindar con.

adjourn [ədʒɝn] *v.* aplazar, diferir; **to — the meeting** suspender o levantar la sesión; **meeting -ed** se levanta la sesión.

adjournment [ədʒɝnmənt] *s.* aplazamiento, levantamiento (*de una sesión*).

adjunct [ædʒʌŋkt] *s.* adjunto, aditamento, añadidura; asociado, acompañante; *adj.* adjunto, unido, subordinado.

adjust [ədʒʌst] *v.* ajustar; acomodar; arreglar; graduar; **to — oneself** adaptarse, conformarse.

adjustment [ədʒʌstmənt] *s.* ajuste; ajustamiento; arreglo; regulación.

ad-lib [ædlíb] *v.* improvisar; expresarse espontáneamente.

administer [ədmínəstə] *v.* administrar; dirigir, regir, gobernar; aplicar (*remedio, castigo, etc.*); **to — an oath** tomar juramento.

administration [ədmɪnəstréʃən] *s.* administración; dirección, gobierno; gerencia; manejo.

administrative [ədmínəstretɪv] *adj.* administrativo; ejecutivo; gubernativo.

administrator [ədmínəstretə] *s.* administrador.

admirable [ædmərəbl] *adj.* admirable; **admirably** *adv.* admirablemente.

admiral [ædmərəl] *s.* almirante.

admiration [ædməréʃən] *s.* admiración.

admire [ədmáɪr] *v.* admirar; estimar.

admirer [ədmáɪrə] *s.* admirador; pretendiente.

admissible [ædmísəbl] *adj.* admisible.

admission [ədmíʃən] *s.* (*entrance*) entrada, precio de entrada o de ingreso; (*confession*) confesión, admisión.

admit [ədmít] *v.* admitir; aceptar; confesar, reconocer; conceder; dar entrada.

admittance [ədmítns] *s.* entrada; derecho de entrar; admisión.

admonish [ədmónɪʃ] *v.* amonestar.

admonition [ædmən.íʃən] *s.* amonestación, consejo.

ado [ədú] *s.* actividad; bulla; disturbio.
adobe [ədóbı] *s.* adobe; casa de adobe.
adolescence [æd|ésṇs] *s.* adolescencia.
adolescent [æd|ésṇt] *adj.* & *s.* adolescente.
adopt [ədápt] *v.* adoptar.
adoption [ədápʃən] *s.* adopción.
adorable [ədórəbl] *adj.* adorable; encantador.
adoration [ædəréʃən] *s.* adoración.
adore [ədór] *v.* adorar.
adorn [ədɔ́rn] *v.* adornar; ornar; embellecer.
adornment [ədɔ́rnmənt] *s.* adorno.
adrenal [ədrín] *adj.* suprarrenal.
adrenalin [ædrénəlın] *s.* adrenalina.
adrift [ədríft] *adj.* & *adv.* a la deriva, flotando, flotante.
adroit [ədrɔ́ıt] *adj.* hábil, diestro.
adult [ədʌ́lt] *adj.* & *s.* adulto.
adulterate [ədʌ́ltəret] *v.* adulterar.
adulterer [ədʌ́ltərə] *s.* adúltero.
adultery [ədʌ́ltərı] *s.* adulterio.
advance [ədvǽns] *v.* (*progress*) avanzar, adelantar; progresar; acelerar; (*promote*) promover; proponer; (*pay beforehand*) pagar por adelantado (*anticipado*); *s.* avance; progreso; adelanto, anticipo; alza, aumento de precio; **-s** requerimientos, pretensiones, insinuaciones; **in —** por adelantado, con anticipación.
advanced [ədvǽnst] *adj.* avanzado; adelantado; **— in years** entrado en años, viejo, anciano.
advancement [ədvǽnsmənt] *s.* adelantamiento, mejora, progreso; promoción.
advantage [ədvǽntıdʒ] *s.* ventaja; beneficio, provecho; **to have the — over** llevar ventaja a; **to take — of** aprovecharse de; **to take — of a person** abusar de la confianza o paciencia de alguien.
advantageous [ædvəntédʒəs] *adj.* ventajoso; provechoso.
advent [ǽdvent] *s.* advenimiento; venida.
adventure [ədvéntʃə] *s.* aventura; riesgo.
adventurer [ədvéntʃərə] *s.* aventurero.
adventurous [ədvéntʃərəs] *adj.* aventurero; atrevido; aventurado, arriesgado.
adverb [ǽdvɜb] *m.* adverbio.
adversary [ǽdvəserı] *s.* adversario, antagonista, contrario.
adverse [ədvɜ́s] *adj.* adverso; opuesto, contrario; hostil; desfavorable.
adversity [ədvɜ́sətı] *s.* adversidad; infortunio.
advertise [ǽdvətaız] *v.* anunciar; avisar, dar viso.
advertisement [ædvətáızmənt] *s.* anuncio, aviso.
advertiser [ǽdvətaızə] *s.* anunciador, anunciante.
advertising [ǽdvətaızıŋ] *s.* anuncios; arte o negocio de anunciar.
advice [ədváıs] *s.* aviso, advertencia; consejo; noticia.

advisable [ədváızəbl] *adj.* conveniente; prudente; recomendable.
advise [ədváız] *v.* (*counsel*) aconsejar; (*inform*) avisar, informar, advertir; **to — with** consultar con; aconsejarse con.
adviser, advisor [ədváızə] *s.* consejero, aconsejador.
advocate [ǽdvəkıt] *s.* abogado; defensor, intercesor; partidario; [ǽdvəket] *v.* abogar por; defender.
aerial [érıəl] *adj.* aéreo; *s.* antena.
aerodynamic [ɛrodaınǽmık] *adj.* aerodinámico; **aerodynamics** *s.* aerodinámica.
aeroplane [érəplen] = **airplane.**
aerosol [érosol] *s.* aerosol.
aesthetic [ɛsθétık] *adj.* estético, **-s** *s.* estética.
afar [əfár] *adv.* lejos; **from —** desde lejos.
affable [ǽfəbl] *adj.* afable, amable.
affair [əfér] *s.* (*social*) función, tertulia, fiesta, convite; (*venture*) asunto; negocio; lance; cosa; **love —** amorío.
affect [əfékt] *v.* afectar; conmover; fingir; hacer ostentación de.
affectation [ǽfıktéʃən] *s.* afectación.
affected [əféktıd] *adj.* (*emotion*) afectado, conmovido, enternecido; (*feigned*) fingido, artificioso.
affection [əfékʃən] *s.* afecto, cariño; inclinación; afección, dolencia.
affectionate [əfékʃənıt] *adj.* afectuoso, cariñoso.
affidavit [ǽfədévıt] *s.* declaración jurada.
affiliate [əfílıet] *v.* afiliar; afiliarse, unirse, asociarse.
affinity [əfínətı] *s.* afinidad.
affirm [əfɜ́m] *v.* afirmar, asegurar, aseverar.
affirmative [əfɜ́mətıv] *adj.* afirmativo; *s.* afirmativa.
affix [əfíks] *v.* fijar, pegar; **to — one's signature** poner su firma, firmar.
afflict [əflíkt] *v.* afligir; **to be -ed with** padecer de, sufrir de, adolecer de.
affliction [əflíkʃən] *s.* aflicción; pena, dolor; achaque; angustia; infortunio.
affluent [ǽfluənt] *adj.* acaudalado; abundante.
afford [əfórd] *v.* proveer, proporcionar; **I cannot — that expense** no puedo hacer ese gasto; **he cannot — to waste time** no le conviene perder el tiempo; no tiene tiempo que perder; **I cannot — that risk** no puedo (o no quiero) exponerme a ese riesgo.
affricate [ǽfrıkət] *adj.* & *s.* africado.
affront [əfrʌ́nt] *s.* afrenta, agravio, ultraje; *v.* afrentar, agraviar, ultrajar.
afire [əfáır] *adj.* ardiendo, quemándose.
afloat [əflót] *adj.* & *adv.* flotante; flotando; a flote; a flor de agua; a bordo; inundado; a la deriva, sin rumbo; **the rumor is —** corre la voz.
afoot [əfút] *adv.* a pie; en marcha, en movimiento.
aforesaid [əfórsɛd] *adj.* susodicho, ya dicho.

afraid [əfréd] *adj.* miedoso, medroso; atemorizado, amedrentado; **to be —** temer, tener miedo.

afresh [əfréʃ] *adv.* de nuevo, desde el principio.

African [ǽfrɪkən] *adj.* & *s.* africano; negro.

after [ǽftə] *prep.* (*temporal*) después de, tras, tras de; (*position*) detrás de; (*following*) en busca de; *adv.* después; detrás; *conj.* después (de) que; *adj.* subsiguiente; siguiente; **— all** después de todo; de todos modos; **day — tomorrow** pasado mañana; **after-dinner** de sobremesa; **—effect** consecuencia, resultado; **—math** consecuencias, resultados (*usualmente desastrosos*); **—thought** idea tardía.

afternoon [æftənún] *s.* tarde.

aftertaste [ǽftətest] *s.* dejo, dejillo (*sabor que queda en la boca*).

afterwards [ǽftəwədz] *adv.* después.

again [əgén] *adv.* otra vez, de nuevo; además; por otra parte; **— and —** repetidas veces; **never — nunca** jamás; **to come —** volver; **to do it —** volver a hacerlo.

against [əgénst] *prep.* contra; frente a; en contraste con; **— the grain** a contrapelo, a redopelo; **— a rainy day** para cuando llueva.

age [edʒ] *s.* edad; época; siglo; generación; **of —** mayor de edad; **old —** vejez, ancianidad; **to become of —** llegar a mayor edad; **under —** menor de edad; *v.* envejecer(se).

aged [édʒɪd, édʒd] *adj.* viejo, anciano; añejo; envejecido; **— forty years** de cuarenta años; **— in wood** añejado en toneles o barriles (*dícese del vino*).

agency [édʒənsɪ] *s.* agencia; medio, intermedio.

agenda [ədʒéndə] *s.* temario; asuntos que han de tratarse en una reunión.

agent [édʒənt] *s.* agente; intermediario, representante; apoderado.

aggrandize [ǽgrəndaɪz] *v.* engrandecer; agrandar.

aggravate [ǽgrəvet] *v.* agravar, empeorar; irritar, exasperar.

aggregate [ǽgrɪgɪt] *s.* agregado, conjunto, colección; *adj.* agregado, unido; **in the —** en conjunto.

aggression [əgréʃən] *s.* agresión.

aggressive [əgrésɪv] *adj.* agresivo; emprendedor.

aggressor [əgrésə] *s.* agresor.

aghast [əgǽst] *adj.* espantado, pasmado.

agile [ǽdʒəl] *adj.* ágil.

agility [ədʒílətɪ] *s.* agilidad.

agitate [ǽdʒətet] *v.* agitar; turbar, perturbar; alborotar; discutir acaloradamente; maquinar, tramar.

agitation [ædʒətéʃən] *s.* agitación; alboroto.

agitator [ǽdʒətetə] *s.* agitador, alborotador, revoltoso.

ago [əgó] *adj.* & *adv.* pasado; en el pasado; **many years —** hace muchos años; muchos años ha; **long —** hace mucho tiempo; ha

mucho.

agonize [ǽgənaɪz] *v.* agonizar; sufrir angustiosamente; retorcerse de dolor; luchar.

agony [ǽgənɪ] *s.* agonía; angustia; tormento; dolor; lucha.

agree [əgrí] *v.* (*accede*) acordar, concordar, consentir, estar de acuerdo, ponerse de acuerdo; (*suit*) sentarle bien a uno (*dícese del clima, del alimento, etc.*).

agreeable [əgríəbl] *adj.* agradable, afable; complaciente; conveniente; satisfactorio.

agreement [əgrímənt] *s.* (*concord*) acuerdo, convenio, conformidad; (*grammatical*) concordancia; **to be in — estar** de acuerdo; **to come to an — ponerse** de acuerdo.

agricultural [ægrɪkʌltʃərəl] *adj.* agrícola.

agriculture [ǽgrɪkʌltʃə] *s.* agricultura.

agriculturist [ægrɪkʌltʃərɪst] *s.* agricultor.

aground [əgráund] *adj.* & *adv.* encallado.

ahead [əhéd] *adv.* delante, al frente; adelante; **— of time** adelantado; antes de tiempo; **to go —** ir adelante; **to get —** adelantar(se).

aid [ed] *s.* ayuda, auxilio, socorro; ayudante, auxiliar; *v.* ayudar, auxiliar, socorrer.

ail [el] *v.* adolecer, padecer; **what -s you?** ¿qué tienes? ¿qué te aflige?

aileron [élərən] *s.* alerón.

ailment [élmənt] *s.* achaque, dolencia.

aim [em] *s.* (*pointing*) puntería; tino; (*objective*) fin, objeto; proposición; *v.* apuntar (*un arma*); dirigir, asestar; dirigir la puntería; aspirar (a); **to — to please** proponerse (*o* tratar de) agradar.

aimless [émlɪs] *adj.* sin propósito, sin objeto.

air [er] *s.* (*atmosphere*) aire, brisa; (*music*) tonada; **in the —** en el aire; indeciso, incierto; **in the open —** al raso, al aire libre; **to be on the —** emitir, radiodifundir; **to put on -s** darse tono; *adj.* de aire; aéreo; **—brake** freno neumático; **—line** línea aérea; ruta aérea; **by —mail** por correo aéreo, por vía aérea, por avión; **air-conditioned** de aire acondicionado; *v.* airear; orear; ventilar; publicar, pregonar; ostentar.

airborne [érborn] aéreo; aerotransportado.

aircraft [érkræft] *s.* avión, aeroplano; aeronave; aviones.

airline [érlaɪn] *s.* aerovía: línea aérea; compañía de transporte aéreo.

airplane [érplen] *s.* aeroplano, avión; **— carrier** portaaviones.

airport [érport] *s.* aeropuerto, aeródromo.

airship [érʃɪp] *s.* aeronave.

airtight [értáɪt] *adj.* hermético.

airy [érɪ] *adj.* airoso; aireado, ventilado; ligero; tenue.

aisle [aɪl] s. pasillo, pasadizo; nave (*de una iglesia*).

ajar [ədʒár] *adj.* entreabierto, entornado.

alarm [əlárm] s. alarma; rebato; inquietud; — **clock** despertador; *v.* alarmar; inquietar.

album [ǽlbəm] *s.* álbum.

alcohol [ǽlkəhɔl] *s.* alcohol.

alcoholic [ælkəhɔ́lɪk] *adj.* alcohólico.

alcove [ǽlkov] *s.* alcoba.

alderman [ɔ́ldəmən] *s.* concejal, regidor.

ale [el] *s.* cerveza de tipo espeso y amargo.

alert [ələ́t] *adj.* alerto, vigilante; despierto; vivo; listo; *s.* alarma, rebato; **to be on the** — estar alerta.

alfalfa [ælfǽlfə] *s.* alfalfa.

algebra [ǽldʒəbrə] *s.* álgebra.

alibi [ǽləbaɪ] *s.* coartado; excusa.

alien [éljən] *s.* extranjero; residente extranjero; *adj.* extraño, ajeno.

alienate [éljənet] *v.* enajenar; apartar, alejar (*a una persona de otra*).

alienist [éljənɪst] *s.* alienista, psiquiatra.

alight [əláɪt] *v.* apearse, desmontarse, bajar(de); posarse (*dícese de pájaros, mariposas, etc.*).

align [əláɪn] *v.* alinear(se).

alike [əláɪk] *adj.* semejante; parecido; **to be** — parecerse, asemejarse; ser iguales; *adv.* del mismo modo.

alimony [ǽləmonɪ] *s.* asistencia de divorcio; alimento.

alive [əláɪv] *adj.* vivo; con vida; viviente; activo; — **with** lleno de.

all [ɔl] *adj.* todo (el); todos (los); *s.* todo; todo el mundo, todos; *adv.* enteramente; — **at once** de una vez; de un tirón; de repente; — **right** bueno; bien; — **the worse** tanto peor; **not at** — de ninguna manera; no hay de qué; **nothing at** — nada en absoluto; — **told** (o **in** —) en conjunto; **once (and) for** — por última vez; una vez por todas; **to be** — **in** estar agotado, estar rendido de fatiga; **it is** — **over** se acabó, ha terminado todo.

allay [əlé] *v.* aliviar; calmar.

allegation [æləgéʃən] *s.* alegación, alegato; aseveración.

allege [əlédʒ] *v.* alegar; declarar; sostener, asegurar.

allegiance [əlídʒəns] *s.* lealtad, fidelidad; homenaje.

allegory [ǽləgorɪ] *s.* alegoría.

allergy [ǽlədʒɪ] *s.* alergia (*sensibilidad anormal a ciertos alimentos o sustancias*).

alleviate [əlívɪet] *v.* aliviar.

alley [ǽlɪ] *s.* callejón; callejuela; **blind** — callejón sin salida; **bowling** — boliche, *Am.* bolera.

alliance [əláɪəns] *s.* alianza.

allied [əláɪd] *adj.* aliado; relacionado.

alligator [ǽləgetə] *s.* lagarto; caimán; — **pear** aguacate.

allot [əlát] *v.* asignar; repartir.

allow [əláu] *v.* permitir, dejar; conceder; admitir; asignar; abonar; **to** — **for**

certain errors tener en cuenta ciertos errores.

allowable [əláuəbl] *adj.* permisible, admisible, lícito.

allowance [əláuəns] *s.* asignación; abono, pensión; ración; rebaja, descuento; permiso; concesión; **monthly** — mesada, mensualidad; **to make** — **for** tener en cuenta.

alloy [ǽlɔɪ] *s.* aleación, liga, mezcla (*de dos o más metales*); [əlɔ́ɪ] *v.* alear, ligar, mezclar (*metales*).

allude [əlúd] *v.* aludir.

allure [əlúr] *v.* seducir, cautivar; atraer, halagar.

allurement [əlúrmənt] *s.* seducción, tentación; atractivo, halago.

alluring [əlúrɪŋ] *adj.* seductivo, halagüeño, encantador.

allusion [əlúʒən] *s.* alusión; indirecta, insinuación.

ally [əláɪ] *v.* unir; aliarse; **to** — **oneself (itself) with** aliarse con, unirse con; [ǽlaɪ] *s.* aliado.

almanac [ɔ́lmənæk] *s.* almanaque, calendario.

almighty [ɔlmáɪtɪ] *adj.* todopoderoso, omnipotente.

almond [ámənd] *s.* almendra; — **tree** almendro.

almost [ɔ́lmost] *adv.* casi; **I** — **fell down** por poco me caigo.

alms [amz] *s.* limosna; — **box** cepo o cepillo, alcancía (*para limosnas*).

aloft [əlɔ́ft] *adv.* en alto; arriba.

alone [əlón] *adj.* solo; solitario; único; *adv.* sólo, solamente; **all** — a solas; completamente solo; solito; **to let** — no tocar; no molestar; dejar en paz; no hacer caso de.

along [əlɔ́ŋ] *prep.* a lo largo de; por; al lado de; — **with** junto con; en compañía de; **all** — todo el tiempo; de un extremo a otro; **all** — **the coast** por toda la costa; **to carry** — **with one** llevar consigo; **to go** — **with** acompañar; **to get** — ir bien; **to get** — **with** llevarse bien con; **get** —! ¡vete! ¡váyase! ¡largo de aquí!

alongside [əlɔ́ŋsáɪd] *prep.* & *adv.* al lado (de); al costado (de); lado a lado.

aloof [əlúf] *adj.* aislado, apartado, retirado; huraño; reservado; *adv.* aparte; lejos.

aloofness [əlúfnɪs] *s.* alejamiento, despego, aislamiento.

aloud [əláud] *adv.* alto, recio, fuerte, en voz alta.

alphabet [ǽlfəbet] *s.* alfabeto.

already [ɔlrédɪ] *adv.* ya.

also [ɔ́lso] *adv.* también, además, igualmente.

altar [ɔ́ltə] *s.* altar; **high** — altar mayor; — **piece** retablo.

alter [ɔ́ltə] *v.* alterar; cambiar; variar.

alteration [ɔltəréʃən] *s.* alteración, cambio; mudanza; modificación.

alternate [ɔ́ltənɪt] *adj.* alternativo; alterno; alternado; *s.* suplente; **-ly** *adv.* alternativamente, por turno; [ɔ́ltənet] *v.* alternar; variar; turnar.

alternative [ɔltɜ́nətiv] *adj.* alternativo; *s.* alternativa.

alternator [ɔ́ltɜnétə] *s.* alternador.

although [ɔlðó] *conj.* aunque, si bien, bien que.

altimeter [ǽltímətə] *s.* altímetro.

altitude [ǽltətjud] *s.* altitud, altura, elevación.

alto [ǽlto] *s.* & *adj.* contralto.

altogether [ɔltəgéðə] *adv.* del todo, completamente; en conjunto.

aluminum [əlúminəm] *s.* aluminio.

alumnus [əlʌ́mnəs] *s.* graduado, exalumno.

always [ɔ́lwiz] *adv.* siempre.

am [æm] 1ª *persona del presente de indic. del verbo* to be: soy, estoy.

amalgamate [əmǽlgəmet] *v.* amalgamar; combinar; unir.

amass [əmǽs] *v.* amontonar, acumular, apilar, *Am.* amasar.

amateur [ǽmətʃur] *s.* aficionado; novicio, principiante.

amaze [əméz] *v.* pasmar, maravillar, asombrar.

amazement [əmézmənt] *s.* pasmo, admiración, asombro.

amazing [əmézin] *adj.* pasmoso, asombroso, maravilloso.

ambassador [æmbǽsədə] *s.* embajador.

amber [ǽmbə] *s.* ámbar; color de ámbar; *adj.* ambarino; de ámbar.

ambiguity [æmbɪgjúətɪ] *s.* ambigüedad.

ambiguous [æmbígjuəs] *adj.* ambiguo.

ambition [æmbíʃən] *s.* ambición, aspiración.

ambitious [æmbíʃəs] *adj.* ambicioso.

ambivalent [æmbívələnt] *adj.* ambivalente.

amble [ǽmbl] *v.* andar, vagar.

ambulance [ǽmbjələns] *s.* ambulancia.

ambush [ǽmbuʃ] *s.* emboscada; celada; acecho; **to lie in** — estar emboscado, estar al acecho; *v.* emboscar; poner celada a.

amenable [əmínəbl] *adj.* dócil; tratable.

amend [əménd] *v.* enmendar; rectificar; **-s** *s. pl.* satisfacción, compensación; **to make** — **for** resarcir, dar satisfacción por, compensar por.

amendment [əméndmənt] *s.* enmienda.

American [əmérəkən] *adj.* & *s.* (*continental*) americano; (*U.S.A.*) norteamericano.

amethyst [ǽməθɪst] *s.* amatista.

amiable [émiəbl] *adj.* amable, afable, amistoso.

amicable [ǽmɪkəbl] *adj.* amigable, amistoso.

amid [əmíd] *prep.* en medio de; entre; **amidst** [əmídst] = **amid.**

amiss [əmís] *adj.* errado, equivocado; impropio; *adv.* mal; fuera de lugar, impropiamente; **to take** — llevar a mal.

ammonia [əmónjə] *s.* amoníaco.

ammunition [æmjəníʃən] *s.* munición.

amnesia [æmníʒjə] *s.* amnesia.

amnesty [ǽmnɛstɪ] *s.* amnestía.

among [əmʌ́ŋ] *prep.* entre, en medio de; **amongst** [əmʌ́ŋst] = **among.**

amorous [ǽmərəs] *adj.* amoroso.

amorphous [əmɔ́rfəs] *adj.* amorfo.

amortize [ǽmərtaɪz] *v.* amortizar.

amount [əmáunt] *s.* suma; cantidad; total; importe; valor; *v.* montar, subir, importar; ascender (a); valer; **that -s to stealing** eso equivale a robar.

ampere [ǽmpɪr] *s.* amperio.

amphitheater [ǽmfəθiətə] *s.* anfiteatro.

ample [ǽmpl] *adj.* amplio; abundante; bastante, suficiente.

amplify [ǽmpləfaɪ] *v.* ampliar; amplificar.

amputate [ǽmpjətet] *v.* amputar.

amuse [əmjúz] *v.* divertir, entretener, distraer; **to** — **oneself** divertirse.

amusement [əmjúzmənt] *s.* diversión, entretenimiento, pasatiempo, recreo, distracción.

amusing [əmjúzɪŋ] *adj.* divertido, entretenido; gracioso, chistoso.

an [ən, æn] *art. indef.* un, una.

anachronism [ənǽkrənizm] *s.* anacronismo.

analogous [ənǽləgəs] *adj.* análogo.

analogy [ənǽlədʒɪ] *s.* analogía, semejanza.

analysis [ənǽləsɪs] *s.* análisis.

analyze [ǽnlaɪz] *v.* analizar.

anarchist [ǽnəkɪst] *s.* anarquista.

anarchy [ǽnəkɪ] *s.* anarquía.

anatomy [ənǽtəmɪ] *s.* anatomía.

ancestor [ǽnsɛstə] *s.* antepasado; **-s** abuelos, antepasados.

ancestral [ænsɛ́strəl] *adj.* solariego, de los antepasados; hereditario.

ancestry [ǽnsɛstrɪ] *s.* linaje, abolengo, ascendencia.

anchor [ǽŋkə] *s.* ancla; **to drop** — anclar, echar anclas, dar fondo, fondear; **to weigh** — levar el ancla; *v.* anclar; echar anclas; fijar, asegurar.

anchovy [ǽntʃovɪ] *s.* anchoa, anchova.

ancient [énʃənt] *adj.* antiguo; vetusto; **the -s** los antiguos; la antigüedad.

and [ənd, ænd] *conj.* y; e (*delante de* i *o* hi); — **so forth** etcétera; y así sucesivamente; **let us try** — **do it** tratemos de hacerlo; **let us go** — **see him** vamos a verle.

Andalusian [ændəlúʒən] *adj.* andaluz.

anecdote [ǽnɪkdot] *s.* anécdota.

anemia [ənímɪə] *s* anemia.

anesthetic [ænəsθétɪk] *adj.* & *s.* anestésico.

anew [ənjú] *adv.* otra vez, de nuevo; nuevamente.

angel [éndʒəl] *s.* ángel.

angelic [ændʒélɪk] *adj.* angélico.

anger [ǽŋgə] *s.* enojo, enfado, ira, cólera; *v.* enojar, enfadar, encolerizar.

angina [ændʒáɪnə] *s.* angina; — **pectoris** angina de pecho.

angle [ǽŋgl] *s.* ángulo; (*interior*) rincón; (*exterior*) esquina; punto de vista, aspecto; *v.* pescar.

Anglo-Saxon [ǽŋglosǽksɳ] *adj.* & *s.* anglosajón.

angry [ǽŋgrɪ] *adj.* enojado; colérico.

anguish [ǽŋgwɪʃ] *s.* angustia, ansia, pena, dolor.

angular [ǽŋgjələ] *adj.* angular; anguloso.

animal [ǽnəm] *s. & adj.* animal.

animate [ǽnəmɪt] *adj.* animado, viviente; **animated cartoon** dibujo animado; [ǽnəmet] *v.* animar; alentar.

animation [ænəméʃən] *s.* animación; viveza.

animosity [ænəmúsətɪ] *s.* animosidad, ojeriza, inquina, rencor.

anise [ǽnɪs] *s.* anís.

ankle [ǽŋk] *s.* tobillo.

annals [ǽnlz] *s. pl.* anales.

annex [ǽneks] *s.* (*building*) pabellón, ala; (*dependent addition*) anexo; añadidura; [ənéks] *v.* anexar.

annexation [ænəkséʃən] *s.* anexión.

annihilate [ənáɪələt] *v.* aniquilar; anonadar.

anniversary [ænəvə́sərɪ] *s. & adj.* aniversario.

annotate [ǽnotet] *v.* anotar.

annotation [ænotéʃən] *s.* anotación, acotación, nota.

announce [ənáʊns] *v.* anunciar; proclamar.

announcement [ənáʊnsmənt] *s.* anuncio; aviso; noticia.

announcer [ənáʊnsə] *s.* anunciador; **radio —** locutor.

annoy [ənɔ́ɪ] *v.* molestar; fastidiar; incomodar; enfadar.

annoyance [ənɔ́ɪəns] *s.* molestia; fastidio; enfado.

annual [ǽnjʊəl] *adj.* anual; *s.* anuario; planta anual; **-ly** *adv.* anualmente, cada año, todos los años.

annuity [ənúətɪ] *s.* anualidad, renta anual.

annul [ənʌ́l] *v.* anular; abolir.

annulment [ənʌ́lmənt] *s.* revocación; anulación.

anoint [ənɔ́ɪnt] *v.* ungir; untar; administrar la Extremaunción.

anon [ənán] *adv.* pronto, luego; otra vez.

anonymous [ənánəməs] *adj.* anónimo.

another [ənʌ́ðə] *adj. & pron.* otro; **one** — uno a otro, unos a otros.

answer [ǽnsə] *s.* respuesta, contestación; réplica; solución; *v.* responder; contestar; **to — for** ser responsable de (*o* por); responder de; ser (salir) fiador de; **to — the purpose** ser adecuado, servir para el objeto.

ant [ænt] *s.* hormiga; **—eater** oso hormiguero; **— hill** hormiguero.

antacid [ænátæsɪd] *s. & adj.* antiácido.

antagonism [æntǽgənɪzəm] *s.* antagonismo, oposición, antipatía.

antagonist [æntǽgənɪst] *s.* antagonista, adversario.

antagonize [æntǽgənaɪz] *v.* contrariar, oponerse a, hostilizar.

antecedent [æntəsídnt] *adj. & s.* antecedente.

antelope [ǽntlop] *s.* antílope.

antenna [ænténə] (*pl.* **antennae** [ænténɪ]) *s.* antena.

anterior [æntírɪə] *adj.* anterior; delantero.

anteroom [ǽntɪrum] *s.* antecámara; sala de espera.

anthem [ǽnθəm] *s.* himno.

anthology [ænθálədʒɪ] *s.* antología.

anthracite [ǽnθrəsaɪt] *s.* antracita.

anthropology [ænθrəpálədʒɪ] *s.* antropología.

antiaircraft [æntɪérkræft] *adj.* antiaéreo.

antibiotic [æntɪbaɪátɪk] *s. & adj.* antibiótico.

antibody [ǽntɪbadɪ] *s.* anticuerpo.

anticipate [æntísəpet] *v.* anticipar(se); prever; esperar.

anticipation [æntɪsəpéʃən] *s.* anticipación; expectación; previsión.

antics [ǽntɪks] *s. pl.* travesuras, cabriolas.

antidote [ǽntɪdot] *s.* antídoto.

antifreeze [ǽntɪfriz] *s.* anticongelante.

antipathy [æntípəθɪ] *s.* antipatía, repugnancia.

antiquated [ǽntəkwetɪd] *adj.* anticuado; desusado.

antique [æntík] *adj.* antiguo; anticuado; *s.* antigualla.

antiquity [æntíkwətɪ] *s.* antigüedad; vejez, ancianidad.

antiseptic [æntəséptɪk] *adj. & s.* antiséptico.

antisocial [æntɪsóʃəl] *adj.* antisocial; *s. Am.* criminal.

antithesis [æntíθəsɪs] *s.* antítesis.

antler [ǽntlə] *s.* asta, cuerno (*del venado, ciervo, etc.*).

anvil [ǽnvɪl] *s.* yunque.

anxiety [æŋzáɪətɪ] *s.* ansiedad, zozobra; ansia, anhelo, afán.

anxious [ǽŋkʃəs] *adj.* ansioso; inquieto, preocupado; anheloso, deseoso; **-ly** *adv.* con ansiedad, con ansia, ansiosamente.

any [énɪ] *adj. & pron.* cualquier(a), cualesquier (a); alguno, algunos; **in — case** de todos modos, en todo caso; **I have not — bread** no tengo pan; **she does not sing — more** ya no canta; **he does not want to work — more** no quiere trabajar más.

anybody [énɪbadɪ] *pron.* alguien, alguno; cualquiera; **not . . . —** no . . . nadie, no . . . ninguno; **he does not know —** no conoce a nadie.

anyhow [énɪhaʊ] *adv.* de todos modos; de cualquier modo.

anyone [énɪwʌn] *pron.* = **anybody**.

anything [énɪθɪŋ] *pron.* alguna cosa; cualquier cosa; algo; **not . . . —** no . . . nada; **not to know —** no saber nada; **— you wish** todo lo que quiera Vd.

anyway [énɪwe] *adv.* de todos modos; en cualquier caso.

anywhere [énɪhwer] *adv.* dondequiera; en cualquier parte o lugar; en todas partes; **not . . . —** no . . . en (o a) ninguna parte; **not to go —** no ir a ninguna parte.

apart [əpárt] *adj.* aparte; separadamente; a un lado; *adj.* aislado, separado; **to take —** desarmar, desmontar; **to tear —** despedazar, hacer pedazos.

apartment [əpártmənt] *s.* departamento, piso, apartamento; vivienda, habitación.

apathy [ǽpəθɪ] *s.* apatía, indiferencia, indolencia.

ape [ep] *s.* mono; *v.* remedar, imitar.

aperture [ǽpətʃə] *s.* abertura.

apex [épeks] *s.* ápice, cumbre.

aphasia [əfézɪə] *s.* afasia.

apiece [əpís] *adv.* cada uno, a cada uno, por persona.

apocope [əpákəpɪ] *s.* apócope.

apogee [ǽpədʒɪ] *s.* apogeo.

apologetic [əpalədʒétɪk] *adj.* que se excusa o disculpa.

apologize [əpálədʒaɪz] *v.* disculparse, excusarse.

apology [əpálədʒɪ] *s.* apología; excusa, disculpa, justificación, satisfacción.

apoplexy [ǽpəpleksɪ] *s.* apoplejía.

apostle [əpás̩l] *s.* apóstol.

apostolic [æpəstálɪk] *adj.* apostólico.

apostrophe [əpástrəfɪ] *s.* apóstrofe; (*punctuation*) apóstrofo.

appall [əpɔ́l] *v.* aterrorizar, aterrar; asombrar, espantar.

appalling [əpɔ́lɪŋ] *adj.* aterrador; espantoso, asombroso.

apparatus [æpərétəs] *s.* aparato; aparejo.

apparel [əpǽrəl] *s.* ropa; ropaje; vestidos; indumentaria.

apparent [əpǽrənt] *adj.* aparente; visible; claro, evidente; patente; **heir —** heredero presunto; **-ly** *adv.* aparentemente, al parecer, por lo visto.

apparition [æpərɪʃən] *s.* aparición; aparecido, espectro, fantasma.

appeal [əpíl] *s.* (*legal*) apelación, recurso; (*request*) súplica; (*attraction*) atracción, atractivo, llamamiento; *v.* apelar; recurrir, acudir; atraer, despertar interés o simpatía; llamar la atención.

appear [əpír] *v.* aparecer(se); parecer; comparecer.

appearance [əpírəns] *s.* apariencia, semblante; porte, facha; aparición.

appease [əpíz] *v.* apaciguar, aplacar; pacificar; conciliar; sosegar.

appeasement [əpízmənt] *s.* apaciguamiento; conciliación.

appendix [əpéndɪks] *s.* apéndice.

appertain [æpətén] *v.* pertenecer.

appetite [ǽpətaɪt] *s.* apetito; gana, deseo.

appetizer [ǽpətaɪzə] *s.* aperitivo.

appetizing [ǽpətaɪzɪŋ] *adj.* apetecible; apetitoso.

applaud [əplɔ́d] *v.* aplaudir.

applause [əplɔ́z] *s.* aplauso.

apple [ǽp̩l] *s.* manzana; **— tree** manzano; **Adam's —** nuez (*de la garganta*); *Ven., C.A., Col.* manzana; **— of my eye** niña de mis ojos.

applesauce [ǽp̩sɔs] *s.* compota de manzana.

appliance [əpláɪəns] *s.* utensilio, instrumento; herramienta.

applicable [ǽplɪkəb̩l] *adj.* aplicable.

applicant [ǽplɪkənt] *s.* solicitante, aspirante, candidato.

application [æplɪkéʃən] *s.* (*dedication*) aplicación; (*petition*) solicitud, petición; *Méx., Carib., Ven.* aplicación.

applied [əpláɪd] *adj.* & *p.p.* aplicado; **— for** pedido, solicitado.

apply [əpláɪ] *v.* aplicar(se); **to — to** dirigirse a, acudir a, recurrir a; **to — for** solicitar, pedir; **to — oneself** aplicarse, dedicarse; **to — on account** acreditar en cuenta.

appoint [əpɔ́ɪnt] *v.* (*designate*) nombrar, designar, señalar; (*furnish*) amueblar, equipar; **a well -ed house** una casa bien amueblada.

appointee [əpɔɪntí] *s.* electo.

appointment [əpɔ́ɪntmənt] *s.* (*designation*) nombramiento, disignación; (*engagement*) cita, compromiso; **-s** mobiliario, mueblaje; accesorios.

apportion [əpɔ́rʃən] *v.* repartir proporcionadamente, prorratear.

apportionment [əpɔ́rʃənmənt] *s.* prorrateo, distribución, repartimiento.

appraisal [əpréz̩l] *s.* tasa, valuación.

appraise [əpréz] *v.* avaluar, valuar, tasar.

appreciable [əpríʃɪəb̩l] *adj.* (*prized*) apreciable; (*perceived*) perceptible; (*quantity*) bastante.

appreciate [əpríʃɪet] *v.* apreciar; estimar; agradecer; **to — in value** subir de valor.

appreciation [əpríʃɪéʃən] *s.* apreciación; aprecio; valuación; agradecimiento; aumento, alza, subida (*de precio*).

apprehend [æprɪhénd] *v.* aprehender, asir, prender; comprender; percibir.

apprehension [æprɪhénʃən] *s.* aprehensión, aprensión, recelo, desconfianza, presentimiento; captura.

apprehensive [æprɪhénsív] *adj.* aprensivo.

apprentice [əpréntɪs] *s.* aprendiz; novicio, principiante; *v.* poner de aprendiz.

apprenticeship [əpréntɪʃɪp] *s.* aprendizaje.

apprise [əpráɪz] *v.* enterar, informar; apreciar.

approach [əprótʃ] *s.* acercamiento; aproximación; acceso, entrada; **method of —** técnica o modo de plantear (*un problema*); *v.* acercarse, aproximarse; abordar (*a alguien*).

approbation [æprəbéʃən] *s.* aprobación.

appropriate [əpróprɪɪt] *adj.* apropiado, propio, apto, conveniente, a propósito; [əpróprɪet] *v.* apropiarse, apoderarse de; asignar (*una suma de dinero*).

appropriation [əproprɪéʃən] *s.* apropiación; asignación, suma asignada.

approval [əprúv̩l] *s.* aprobación, asentimiento.

approve [əprúv] *v.* aprobar; asentir a.

approximate [əpráksəmɪt] *adj.* aproxi-

mado; aproximativo; **-ly** adv. aproximadamente, casi, poco más o menos; [əpráksəmet] v. aproximar; aproximarse, acercarse.
apricot [éprɪkat] s. albaricoque; *Am.* chabacano.
April [éprəl] s. abril.
apron [éprən] s. delantal.
apropos [æprəpó] adv. a propósito; adj. oportuno; pertinente; — **of** a propósito de.
apt [æpt] adj. apto, capaz; pertinente, a propósito; — **to** propenso a.
aptitude [æptətjud] s. aptitud, capacidad; habilidad.
aquarium [əkwérɪəm] s. acuario; pecera.
aquatic [əkwǽtɪk] adj. acuático.
aqueduct [ǽkwɪdʌkt] s. acueducto.
Arab [ǽrəb] adj. & s. árabe.
Aragonese [ærəgəníz] adj. & s. aragonés.
arbiter [árbɪtɚ] s. árbitro, arbitrador, juez árbitro.
arbitrary [árbətrerɪ] adj. arbitrario; despótico.
arbitrate [árbətret] v. arbitrar; decidir; someter al arbitraje.
arbitration [arbətréʃən] s. arbitraje, arbitración.
arbitrator [árbətretɚ] s. arbitrador, árbitro; medianero.
arbor [árbɚ] s. emparrado, enramada, glorieta.
arc [ark] s. arco; — **lamp** lámpara de arco.
arcade [arkéd] s. arcada; galería; soportal.
arch [artʃ] s. arco; bóveda; **semicircular** — arco de medio punto; — **enemy** enemigo acérrimo; v. arquear(se); enarcar(se).
archaeology [arkɪáləʤɪ] s. arqueología.
archaic [arkéɪk] adj. arcaico, desusado, anticuado.
archbishop [ártʃbíʃəp] s. arzobispo.
archery [ártʃərɪ] s. tiro de flechas.
archipelago [arkəpéləgo] s. archipiélago.
architect [árkətɛkt] s. arquitecto.
architectural [arkətéktʃərəl] adj. arquitectónico.
architecture [árkətɛktʃɚ] s. arquitectura.
archives [árkaɪvz] s. archivo.
archway [ártʃwe] s. pasadizo (bajo un arco); arcada, galería abovedada.
arctic [árktɪk] adj. ártico.
ardent [árdn̥t] adj. ardiente; apasionado.
ardor [árdɚ] s. ardor; enardecimiento; fervor.
arduous [árdʒuəs] adj. arduo, trabajoso.
are [ar] 2ª persona y pl. del presente de indic. del verbo **to be:** eres, está; somos, estamos; sois, estáis; son, están.
area [érɪə] s. área, superficie; espacio; región.
arena [ərínə] s. arena, redondel, plaza.
Argentine [árdʒəntin] adj. & s. argentino.

argue [árgju] v. argüir; debatir; altercar; **to** — **into** persuadir a.
argument [árgjəmənt] s. argumento; razonamiento; sumario, resumen.
arid [ǽrɪd] adj. árido.
arise [əráɪz] v. levantarse; elevarse; surgir; provenir.
arisen [ərízn̥] p.p. de **to arise.**
aristocracy [ærəstákrəsɪ] s. aristocracia.
aristocrat [ərístəkræt] s. aristócrata.
aristocratic [ərɪstəkrǽtɪk] adj. aristocrático.
arithmetic [ərɪθmətɪk] s. aritmética.
ark [ark] s. arca; — **of the covenant** arca del testamento; **Noah's** — arca de Noé.
arm [arm] s. (anatomy) brazo; (weapon) arma; — **in** — de bracete, de bracero; *Am.* de brazo, de brazos; **at -'s length** a una brazada; **with open -s** con los brazos abiertos; v. armar(se).
armada [armádə] s. armada, flota.
armament [árməmənt] s. armamento.
armature [ármətʃɚ] s. armadura.
armchair [ármtʃer] s. silla de brazos, sillón, butaca.
armed forces [ármd fórsəz] s. fuerzas armadas.
armful [ármful] s. brazada.
armistice [árməstɪs] s. armisticio.
armor [ármɚ] s. armadura; blindaje, coraza; arnés; v. blindar, acorazar.
armored [ármɚd] p.p. blindado, acorazado.
armory [ármərɪ] s. armería; arsenal.
armpit [ármpɪt] s. sobaco.
army [ármɪ] s. ejército; muchedumbre; — **doctor** médico militar; **regular** — tropa de línea.
aroma [ərómə] s. aroma; fragancia.
aromatic [ærəmǽtɪk] adj. aromático.
arose [əróz] pret. de **to arise.**
around [əráund] adv. alrededor; en redor; a la redonda; en torno; en derredor; cerca; **all** — por todos lados; prep. alrededor de; cerca de; — **here** por aquí; **to go** — in circles dar vueltas; **to go** — **the world** dar la vuelta al mundo.
arouse [əráuz] v. despertar, *Ríopl., C.A., Ven.* recordar (al dormido); excitar; promover.
arraign [ərén] v. acusar; procesar (a un criminal).
arrange [əréndʒ] v. arreglar; disponer; colocar; acomodar; hacer arreglos (para), hacer planes (para).
arrangement [əréndʒmənt] s. arreglo; disposición; colocación, orden; convenio.
array [əré] s. arreglo, formación, orden; orden (de batalla); pompa; gala, atavío; v. formar (tropas); poner en orden; ataviar, adornar.
arrears [ərírz] s. pl. atrasos, pagos o rentas vencidos y no cobrados; **in** — atrasado (en el pago de una cuenta).
arrest [ərést] s. arresto, captura, aprensión, detención; v. aprehender o

prender, arrestar; detener; llamar, atraer (la atención).

arrival [əráɪv] s. llegada; arribo; venida; **the new -s** los recién llegados.

arrive [əráɪv] v. llegar; arribar; **to — at a result** lograr (o conseguir) un resultado.

arrogance [ǽrəgəns] s. arrogancia.

arrogant [ǽrəgənt] adj. arrogante.

arrow [ǽro] s. saeta, flecha.

arsenal [ársn̩əl] s. arsenal.

arsenic [ársn̩ɪk] s. arsénico.

arson [ársən] s. delito de incendio.

art [ɑrt] s. arte; destreza; astucia; **fine -s** bellas artes; **master of -s** licenciado en letras, maestro en artes.

artery [ártərɪ] s. arteria.

artful [ártfəl] adj. artero, mañero, ladino.

artichoke [ártɪtʃok] s. alcachofa.

article [ártɪk̩l] s. artículo; **— of clothing** prenda de vestir; **— of merchandise** mercancía, mercadería.

articulate [artíkjəlɪt] adj. articulado; claro, inteligible; capaz de hablar; [artíkjəlet] v. articular; enunciar; enlazar.

articulation [artɪkjəléʃən] s. articulación; coyuntura.

artifact [ártəfækt] s. artefacto.

artifice [ártəfɪs] s. artificio; ardid.

artificial [artəfíʃəl] adj. artificial; postizo; afectado, artificioso.

artillery [artíləri] s. artillería; **— man** artillero.

artisan [ártəzn̩] s. artesano; artífice.

artist [ártɪst] s. artista.

artistic [artístɪk] adj. artístico; **-ally** adv. artísticamente.

as [əz] adv., conj., prep. como; mientras; a medida que, según; en el momento en que; **— far —** hasta, hasta donde; **— for** (**— to**) en cuanto a; **— if** como si; **— it were** por decirlo así; **— large —** tan grande como; **— much — tanto** como; **— well** tan bien; también; **— yet** hasta ahora, todavía; **— long — you wish** todo el tiempo que Vd. quiera; **strong — he is** aunque es tan fuerte; **the same —** lo mismo que.

asbestos [æsbéstəs] s. asbesto.

ascend [əsénd] v. ascender; subir, elevarse.

ascension [əsénʃən] s. ascensión; subida.

ascent [əsént] s. ascenso; subida; ascensión.

ascertain [æsətén] v. averiguar, indagar.

ascetic [əsétɪk] adj. ascético; s. asceta.

ascribe [əskráɪb] v. atribuir, imputar, achacar.

ash [æʃ] s. ceniza; **— tray** cenicero; **— tree** fresno; **Ash Wednesday** miércoles de ceniza; **ash-colored** ceniciento, ceniza.

ashamed [əʃémd] adj. avergonzado, corrido; **to be —** tener vergüenza; avergonzarse.

ashore [əʃór] adv. a tierra; en tierra; **to**

go — desembarcar.

Asiatic [əʒɪǽtɪk] adj. & s. asiático.

aside [əsáɪd] adv. aparte; a un lado; al lado; s. aparte (en un drama).

ask [æsk] v. (request) pedir, rogar, solicitar; (inquire) preguntar; (invite) invitar; **to — for** pedir; **to — for** (**about, after**) preguntar por; **to — a question** hacer una pregunta.

askance [əskǽns] adv. de soslayo; con recelo, recelosamente; **to look —** mirar con recelo; no aprobar.

asleep [əslíp] adj. dormido; **to fall —** dormirse; **my arm is —** se me ha dormido (entumecido o entumido) el brazo.

asparagus [əspǽrəgəs] s. espárrago.

aspect [ǽspɛkt] s. aspecto.

asphalt [ǽsfɔlt] s. asfalto.

aspiration [æspəréʃən] s. aspiración; anhelo.

aspire [əspáɪr] v. aspirar; anhelar, ambicionar.

aspirin [ǽspɪrɪn] s. aspirina.

ass [æs] s. asno, burro; pollino.

assail [əsél] v. asaltar, acometer, agredir.

assailant [əsélənt] s. asaltador, agresor.

assassin [əsǽsɪn] s. asesino.

assassinate [əsǽsn̩et] v. asesinar.

assassination [əsæsn̩éʃən] s. asesinato.

assault [əsólt] s. asalto, acometida, ataque; v. asaltar, acometer, atacar; violar.

assay [əsé] v. ensayar (metales); analizar, examinar; contrastar (pesas, moneda); s. ensaye (de metales); contraste (de pesas, moneda).

assemble [əsémb̩l] v. reunir(se), congregar(se), juntar(se); convocar; armar, montar (maquinaria).

assembly [əsémblɪ] s. asamblea; reunión; montaje (de maquinaria); **— hall** salón de sesiones; paraninfo.

assent [əsént] s. asentimiento; consentimiento; v. asentir; consentir.

assert [əsɝt] v. aseverar, asegurar, afirmar; **to — oneself** hacerse valer; obrar con firmeza; vindicarse.

assertion [əsɝʃən] s. aserción, aserto, afirmación.

assess [əsés] v. avaluar; tasar; asignar, imponer (impuestos, multas, contribuciones, etc.).

assessment [əsésmənt] s. avaluación, tasación; imposición (de contribuciones, multas, etc.); contribución, impuesto.

asset [ǽsɛt] s. cualidad, ventaja; **-s** capital, fondos, caudal; haber, activo; **personal -s** bienes muebles.

assiduous [əsídʒuəs] adj. asiduo, diligente.

assign [əsáɪn] v. asignar; señalar, designar; traspasar, ceder a favor de.

assignment [əsáɪnmənt] s. asignación; designación; cesión (de bienes); tarea (asignada); lección (señalada).

assimilate [əsím̩let] v. asimilar(se), absorber(se).

assist [əsíst] v. asistir, ayudar.

assistance [əsístəns] s. asistencia, ayuda.

assistant [əsístənt] s. asistente; ayudante; auxiliar; adj. subordinado, auxiliar.

associate [əsóʃiɪt] adj. asociado; s. asociado; socio; compañero; colega; [əsóʃɪet] v. asociar(se); relacionar.

association [əsosiéʃən] s. asociación; sociedad; conexión, relación.

assort [əsɔ́rt] v. ordenar, clasificar.

assorted [əsɔ́rtɪd] adj. surtido, mezclado, variado, de todas clases.

assortment [əsɔ́rtmənt] s. variedad; clasificación; surtido; colección, grupo.

assume [əsúm] v. asumir; tomar; dar por sentado, dar por supuesto; arrogarse, apropiarse.

assumption [əsʌ́mpʃən] d. suposición; toma, apropiación; presunción; asunción (de la Virgen).

assurance [əʃúrəns] s. seguridad, certeza; convicción; confianza; **life** — seguro de vida. *Véase* **insurance**.

assure [əʃúr] v. asegurar; afirmar; infundir confianza.

assuredly [əʃúrɪdlɪ] adv. seguramente; sin duda, con seguridad.

asterisk [ǽstərɪsk] s. asterisco.

astigmatism [əstígmətɪzəm] s. astigmatismo.

astonish [əstánɪʃ] v. asombrar, pasmar, espantar.

astonishing [əstánɪʃɪŋ] adj. asombroso, pasmoso, maravilloso.

astonishment [əstánɪʃmənt] s. asombro, pasmo, sorpresa.

astound [əstáund] v. pasmar; aterrar, aturdir.

astray [əstré] adv. fuera de camino; adj. desviado, extraviado, descaminado; **to go** — perderse; errar el camino; extraviarse; **to lead** — desviar, extraviar; llevar por mal camino; seducir.

astride [əstráid] adv. a horcajadas.

astrodome [ǽstrədom] s. astródomo.

astrology [əstrálədʒɪ] s. astrología.

astronaut [ǽstrənət] s. astronauta.

astronomer [əstránəmə] s. astrónomo.

astronomy [əstránəmɪ] s. astronomía.

astrophysics [ǽstrofíziks] s. astrofísica.

Asturian [æstjúriən] adj. & s. asturiano.

astute [əstjút] adj. astuto, sagaz.

asunder [əsʌ́ndə] adj. separado; **to cut** — separar, apartar; dividir en dos.

asylum [əsáiləm] s. asilo; hospicio; **orphan** — orfanato, casa de huérfanos, *Méx., C.A., Andes* orfanatorio.

at [æt] prep. a; en; en (la) casa de; — **last** por fin, al fin; — **once** al punto; **to be** — **work** estar trabajando; **to enter** — **that door** entrar por aquella puerta.

ate [et] pret. de **eat**.

atheist [éθɪɪst] s. ateo.

athlete [ǽθlit] s. atleta.

athletic [æθlétɪk] adj. atlético.

athletics [æθlétɪks] s. gimnasia; atletismo; deportes.

Atlantic [ətlǽntɪk] adj. atlántico; s. el Atlántico.

atlas [ǽtləs] s. atlas.

atmosphere [ǽtməsfɪr] s. atmósfera; ambiente.

atmospheric [ætməsférɪk] adj. atmosférico.

atom [ǽtəm] s. átomo; — **bomb** bomba atómica.

atomic [ətámɪk] adj. atómico; — **age** edad atómica; — **energy** fuerza atómica; — **pile** pila atómica; — **weight** peso atómico.

atone [ətón] v. expiar, purgar; reparar.

atonement [ətónmənt] s. expiación; reparación.

atrocious [ətróʃəs] adj. atroz.

atrocity [ətrásətɪ] s. atrocidad; maldad.

attach [ətǽʃ] v. unir, juntar; sujetar, pegar, adherir; poner (sello o firma); embargar (bienes); asignar; atribuir.

attachment [ətǽtʃmənt] s. adhesión; apego; afición, cariño; embargo (de bienes); accesorio.

attack [ətǽk] s. ataque, asalto; acceso; v. atacar; acometer, embestir.

attain [ətén] v. lograr, conseguir, alcanzar; llegar a.

attainment [əténmənt] s. logro, consecución; adquisición; dote habilidad.

attempt [ətémpt] s. tentativa; prueba, ensayo; esfuerzo; atentado; v. tentar, intentar; procurar, tratar (de), probar; **to** — **the life of** atentar contra la vida de.

attend [əténd] v. atender, cuidar, mirar por; asistir a; acompañar.

attendance [əténdəns] s. asistencia; presencia; concurrencia.

attendant [əténdənt] s. acompañante; sirviente, servidor; asistente; adj. acompañante.

attention [əténʃən] s. (care) cuidado; (courtesy) fineza, urbanidad, atención; **to pay** — hacer caso; prestar atención.

attentive [əténtɪv] adj. atento, cortés.

attest [ətést] v. atestiguar, atestar; certificar; dar fe.

attic [ǽtɪk] s. desván.

attire [ətáɪr] s. atavío; vestidura; vestido, traje; v. ataviar, adornar.

attitude [ǽtətjud] s. actitud; postura.

attorney [ətə́rnɪ] s. abogado; procurador; apoderado; — **general** fiscal (de una nación o estado); — **district** — fiscal de distrito; **power of** — procuración, poder.

attract [ətrǽkt] v. atraer; cautivar; **to** — **attention** llamar la atención.

attraction [ətrǽkʃən] s. atracción; atractivo; -**s** diversiones; lugares o sitios de interés.

attractive [ətrǽktɪv] adj. atractivo; seductor; simpático.

attractiveness [ətrǽktɪvnɪs] s. atracción; atractivo.

attribute [ǽtrəbjut] s. atributo; propiedad; [ətríbjut] v. atribuir, achacar.

attrition [ətríʃən] s. agotamiento; atrición.

auction [ɔ́kʃən] s. subasta, almoneda, remate, *Am.* venduta; v. subastar; rematar.

audacious [ɔdéʃəs] *adj.* audaz, atrevido, osado.

audacity [ɔdǽsətɪ] *s.* audacia, osadía; descaro.

audible [ɔ́dəbl] *adj.* audible.

audience [ɔ́dɪəns] *s.* auditorio, concurrencia, público; audiencia.

audio frequency [ɔdɪofríkwɛnsɪ] *s.* audiofrecuencia.

audio-visual [ɔdɪovíʒuəl] *adj.* adio-visual.

audit [ɔ́dɪt] *v.* intervenir [*cuentas*]; asistir a (*una clase*) de oyente; *s.* intervención, comprobación de cuentas.

audition [ɔdíʃən] *s.* audición.

auditor [ɔ́dɪtə] *s.* interventor (*de cuentas*); oyente.

auditorium [ɔdətórɪəm] *s.* salón de conferencias o conciertos; paraninfo.

auditory [ɔ́dətorɪ] *adj.* auditivo.

auger [ɔ́gə] *s.* taladro, barrena.

aught [ɔt] *s.* algo.

augment [ɔgmént] *v.* aumentar.

augur [ɔ́gə] *s.* agorero; *v.* augurar, pronosticar; **to — well** (*o* **ill**) ser de buen (*o* mal) agüero.

August [ɔ́gəst] *s.* agosto.

aunt [ænt] *s.* tía.

auspices [ɔ́spɪsɪz] *s. pl.* auspicios; protección.

auspicious [ɔspíʃəs] *adj.* propicio; favorable.

austere [ɔstír] *adj.* austero, adusto, severo.

austerity [ɔstérətɪ] *s.* austeridad, severidad.

Austrian [ɔ́strɪən] *adj. & s.* austríaco.

authentic [ɔθéntɪk] *adj.* auténtico.

author [ɔ́θə] *s.* autor; escritor.

authoritative [ɔθɔ́rətetɪv] *adj.* autorizado, que tiene autoridad; autoritario.

authority [əθɔ́rətɪ] *s.* autoridad; facultad; **to have on good —** saber de buena tinta.

authorize [ɔ́θəraɪz] *v.* autorizar.

auto [ɔ́to] *s.* auto, automóvil.

autocrat [ɔ́təkræt] *s.* autócrata.

autograph [ɔ́təgræf] *s.* autógrafo.

automatic [ɔtəmǽtɪk] *adj.* automático; **-ally** *adv.* automáticamente.

automobile [ɔ́təməbil] *s.* automóvil.

autonomy [ɔtánəmɪ] *s.* autonomía.

autopsy [ɔ́tɑpsɪ] *s.* autopsia.

autumn [ɔ́təm] *s.* otoño.

autumnal [ɔtʌ́mnl] *adj.* otoñal.

auxiliary [ɔgzíljərɪ] *adj. & s.* auxiliar.

avail [əvél] *v.* aprovechar; beneficiar; **to — oneself of** aprovecharse de; *s.* provecho; ventaja; **of no —** de ninguna utilidad o ventaja.

available [əvéləbl] *adj.* disponible; aprovechable; obtenible.

avalanche [ǽvlæntʃ] *s.* alud; torrente.

avarice [ǽvərɪs] *s.* avaricia.

avaricious [ævəríʃəs] *adj.* avaro, avariento.

avenge [əvéndʒ] *v.* vengar; vindicar.

avenger [əvéndʒə] *s.* vengador.

avenue [ǽvənu] *s.* avenida.

aver [əvɚ́] *v.* afirmar, asegurar.

average [ǽvrɪdʒ] *s.* promedio, término medio; **on an —** por término medio; *adj.* medio, mediano; ordinario; *v.* promediar, calcular o sacar el promedio; **to — a loss** prorratear una pérdida; **he -s 20 miles an hour** avanza o recorre un promedio de 20 millas por hora.

averse [əvɚ́s] *adj.* adverso, renuente.

aversion [əvɚ́ʒən] *s.* aversión; malquerencia, inquina.

avert [əvɚ́t] *v.* apartar, desviar; evitar; impedir.

aviation [evɪéʃən] *s.* aviación.

aviator [évɪetə] *s.* aviador.

avocado [ɑvəkádo] *s.* aguacate.

avocation [ævəkéʃən] *s.* distracción; ocupación de distracción o diversión.

avoid [əvɔ́ɪd] *v.* evitar; eludir.

avow [əváu] *v.* confesar, reconocer, admitir.

avowal [əváuəl] *s.* confesión, admisión.

await [əwét] *v.* esperar, aguardar.

awake [əwék] *adj.* despierto; alerto; **wide-awake** muy despierto; avispado; *v.* despertar(se).

awaken [əwékən] *v.* despertar(se).

award [əwɔ́rd] *s.* premio; decisión, sentencia; *v.* asignar; otorgar; conferir; adjudicar (*un premio, medalla, etc.*).

aware [əwɛ́r] *adj.* consciente; enterado, sabedor; cauto; sobre aviso.

away [əwé] *adv.* lejos; fuera; *adj.* ausente; **right —** ahora mismo, ahorita; **two miles —** a diez millas de aquí; **to give —** regalar; **to go —** irse; **to take —** quitar.

awe [ɔ] *s.* pavor; pasmo; **to stand in —** quedarse, o estar, pasmado; pasmarse; *v.* atemorizar; infundir pavor; maravillar.

awful [ɔ́fʊl] *adj.* terrible; horroroso; tremendo; impresionante; **-ly** *adv.* terriblemente; horrorosamente; muy.

awhile [əhwáɪl] *adv.* (por) un rato; (por) algún tiempo.

awkward [ɔ́kwəd] *adj.* torpe, desmañado; molesto, embarazoso; incómodo; inconveniente.

awl [ɔl] *s.* lezna, punzón.

awning [ɔ́nɪŋ] *s.* toldo.

awoke [əwók] *pret. & p.p. de* **to awake**.

ax, axe [æks] *s.* hacha.

axis [ǽksɪs] *pl.* **axes** [ǽksɪz] *s.* eje.

axle [ǽksl] *s.* eje (*de una rueda*); **front —** eje delantero; **rear —** eje trasero.

aye [e] *adv.* sí; *s.* voto afirmativo.

Aztec [ǽztɛk] *adj. & s.* azteca.

azure [ǽʒə] *adj.* azul; *s.* azur, azul celeste.

B

babble [bǽbl] *s.* balbuceo; parloteo; charla; *v.* balbucear; parlotear, charlar.

babe [beb] = **baby.**

baboon [bæbún] *s.* mandril (*especie de mono*).

baby [bébɪ] *s.* nene, bebé, criatura; *Andes, Ch.* guagua; *C.A.* tierno; *adj.* infantil; de niño; **— girl** nena; **—**

sitter [bébɪsítə] s. cuidaniños, niñera por horas; v. mimar.
bachelor [bǽt∫alə] s. bachiller; soltero.
bacillus [bəsíləs] s. bacilo.
back [bæk] s. (anatomy) espalda; lomo (de animal); (opposite side) revés; respaldo (de silla), espaldar; **behind one's —** a espaldas de uno, a espaldas vueltas; **in —** of detrás de, tras; **to fall on one's —** caer de espaldas, caer boca arriba; **to turn one's —** volver las espaldas; adj. posterior; trasero; retrasado, atrasado, rezagado; **— pay** sueldo atrasado; **— yard** patio interior; corral; adv. atrás, detrás; **— and forth** de aquí para allá; **to come —** volver, regresar; **to give —** devolver; v. respaldar, endosar; sostener, apoyar, retroceder; hacer retroceder; **to — down** hacerse (para) atrás; retractarse.
backbone [bǽkbón] s. espinazo, espina dorsal; firmeza; apoyo, sostén.
backer [bǽkə] s. fiador; sostenedor, defensor.
background [bǽkgraʊnd] s. fondo; educación; experiencia; **to keep in the —** dejar en último término; quedarse en último término; mantenerse retirado.
backhand [bǽkhænd] s. revés; escritura inclinada a la izquierda; **-ed stroke** revés; a **-ed remark** una ironía; una indirecta.
backing [bǽkɪŋ] s. apoyo, garantía; endose, endoso; respaldo.
backlash [bǽklæ∫] s. contragolpe; culateo.
backlog [bǽklɔg] s. reserva pendiente.
backstage [bǽkstédʒ] adv. detrás del telón.
backward [bǽkwəd] adj. atrasado; retrasado; retrógrado; tardo, tardío; huraño, tímido, esquivo; adv. = **backwards.**
backwardness [bǽkwədnɪs] s. torpeza; atraso; timidez.
backwards [bǽkwədz] adv. hacia (o para) atrás; de espaldas; **to go —** retroceder, andar hacia (o para) atrás.
bacon [békən] s. tocino.
bacteria [bæktírɪə] s. pl. bacterias.
bacteriology [bæktɪríálədʒɪ] s. bacteriología.
bad [bæd] adj. malo; perverso; dañoso; podrido; **to go from — to worse** ir de mal en peor; **to look —** tener mal cariz, tener mala cara o mal aspecto; **-ly** adv. mal, malamente.
bade [bæd] pret. de to **bid.**
badge [bædʒ] s. insignia, divisa; distintivo.
badger [bǽdʒə] s. tejón; v. atormentar, acosar, molestar.
badness [bǽdnɪs] s. maldad.
baffle [bǽfl] v. desconcertar, confundir; frustrar, impedir.
bag [bæg] s. (sack) saco, bolsa, talega; costal; (baggage) maleta; zurrón, morral; v. ensacar; cazar; agarrar; adueñarse de; inflarse; abolsarse.

baggage [bǽgɪdʒ] s. equipaje; bagaje; **— car** furgón, vagón de equipajes; **— check** talón, contraseña de equipajes; **— tag** marbete, etiqueta.
bagpipe [bǽgpaɪp] s. gaita.
bail [bel] s. fianza, caución; **to let out on —** poner en libertad bajo fianza; v. dar fianza; salir fiador; achicar (agua), vaciar; **to — out of a plane** tirarse (con paracaídas) de un aeroplano.
bait [bet] s. cebo; atractivo, aliciente; v. tentar, atraer; cebar; acosar, perseguir.
bake [bek] v. hornear, cocer al horno; calcinar.
baker [békə] s. panadero, pastelero, hornero.
bakery [békərɪ] s. panadería, pastelería, tahona.
baking [békɪŋ] s. hornada; cocimiento; **— powder** levadura.
balance [bæləns] s. (instrument) balanza; (equilibrium) contrapeso, equilibrio, balance; (debit, credit) saldo; **— of payments** balanza de pagos; **— wheel** volante del reloj; **— of trade** balanza comercial; **— of power** equilibrio político; **to lose one's —** perder el equilibrio; v. contrapesar; pesar; balancear(se); equilibrar; saldar (una cuenta).
balcony [bǽlkənɪ] s. balcón; galería (de teatro).
bald [bɔld] adj. calvo; pelado, sin vegetación; escueto, sin adornos; **— spot** calva.
bale [bel] s. bala, fardo (de mercancías); v. embalar, enfardar, empacar.
balk [bɔk] v. oponerse, rebelarse, resistirse; pararse de repente; negarse a seguir; encabritarse; **to — someone's plans** frustrar los planes de alguien.
ball [bɔl] s. (plaything) pelota, bola; (string, thread) ovillo; (weapon) bala; (dance) baile; **— bearing** cojinete de bolas; **— game** juego de pelota; beisbol; v. ovillar; **to — up** enredar, confundir.
ballad [bæləd] s. romance; copla, canción; balada.
ballast [bæləst] s. lastre; grava (usada en terraplenes, caminos, etc.); v. lastrar, poner el lastre a (una embarcación).
ballet [bælé] s. ballet.
balloon [bəlún] s. globo (aerostático).
ballot [bælət] s. balota, Am. boleta, cédula para votar; voto; **— box** urna electoral; v. balotar, votar.
ball point [bɔ́lpɔɪnt] s. bolígrafo.
balm [bam] s. bálsamo.
balmy [bámɪ] adj. balsámico; fragante; refrescante, suave; algo loco, chiflado.
balsam [bɔ́lsəm] s. bálsamo; especie de abeto.
bamboo [bæmbú] s. bambú.
ban [bæn] s. bando, proclama; excomunión; prohibición; **marriage -s** (o **banns**) amonestaciones; v. proscribir, prohibir; condenar.

banana [bənǽnə] *s.* banana; plátano; —
tree banano; plátano.
band [bænd] *s.* (*group*) banda, partida,
pandilla, cuadrilla; (*musicians*) banda;
(*strip*) faja, lista, cinta, tira; partida,
pandilla, cuadrilla; **rubber** — liga de
goma; *v.* unir, juntar; atar, ligar; **to**
— **together** confederarse, juntarse.
bandage [bǽndɪdʒ] *s.* venda, vendaje;
v. vendar.
bandit [bǽndɪt] *s.* bandido bandolero.
bang [bæŋ] *s.* golpe, golpazo; estallido;
fleco (*de pelo*); **with a** — de golpe, de
golpazo; de repente; con estrépito;
—! ¡pum!; *v.* golpear; hacer estrépito; cortar (*el pelo*) en fleco; **to** —
the door dar un portazo.
banish [bǽnɪʃ] *v.* proscribir, desterrar;
to — **fear** desechar el temor.
banishment [bǽnɪʃmənt] *s.* proscripción; destierro.
banister [bǽnɪstə] *s.* balaustre; barandilla, barandal, pasamano.
banjo [bǽndʒo] *s.* banjo.
bank [bæŋk] *s.* (*institution*) banco;
(*in card game*) banca; (*of a river*)
orilla, ribera, banda; escarpa; (*pile*)
montón; **savings** — caja de ahorros;
adj. bancario; de banco; *v.* depositar
en un banco; amontonar (*tierra o
arena*); cubrir con cenizas, tapar (*el
fuego*); ladear (*un aeroplano*); **to** —
upon (**o on**) contar con.
bankbook [bǽŋkbʊk] *s.* libreta de
banco.
banker [bǽŋkə] *s.* banquero.
banking [bǽŋkɪŋ] *s.* transacciones bancarias, banca; *adj.* bancario, de banca;
— **house** banca, casa de banca.
banknote [bǽŋknot] *s.* billete de banco.
bankrupt [bǽŋkrʌpt] *adj.* en quiebra,
arruinado, insolvente; *v.* quebrar;
arruinar.
bankruptcy [bǽŋkrʌptsɪ] *s.* bancarrota,
quiebra; **to go into** — declararse insolvente; quebrar, hacer bancarrota.
banner [bǽnə] *s.* bandera, estandarte,
pendón; *adj.* primero, principal,
sobresaliente.
banquet [bǽŋkwɪt] *s.* banquete; *v.* banquetear.
baptism [bǽptɪzəm] *s.* bautismo; bautizo.
Baptist [bǽptɪst] *s.* bautista.
baptize [bæptáɪz] *v.* bautizar.
bar [bɑr] *s.* (*of iron*) barra; barrote;
tranca; (*obstacle*) barrera, obstáculo;
(*of justice*) tribunal; foro; (*saloon*)
cantina, taberna; (*counter*) mostrador;
(*piece*) barra (*de jabón*); pastilla (*de
chocolate*); **sand** — banco de arena;
-s reja; to be admitted to the —
recibirse de abogado; *v.* atrancar (*la
puerta*); estorbar; prohibir; excluir.
barb [bɑrb] *s.* púa.
barbarian [bɑrbérɪən] *s.* & *adj.*
bárbaro; salvaje.
barbarous [bɑ́rbərəs] *adj.* bárbaro; salvaje; inculto.
barbecue [bɑ́rbɪkju] *s.* *Méx.*, *C.A.*, *Col.*
barbacoa; *Ríopl.* churrasco; *v.* hacer

barbacoa; *Ríopl.* churrasquear.
barbed [bɑrbd] *adj.* con púas; — **wire**
alambre de púas.
barber [bɑ́rbə] *s.* barbero; peluquero.
barbershop [bɑ́rbəʃap] *s.* barbería;
peluquería.
bard [bɑrd] *s.* bardo, vate, poeta.
bare [bɛr] *adj.* (*naked*) desnudo; descubierto; pelado; (*evident*) manifiesto, patente; (*unfurnished*) desamueblado, vacío; — **majority** mayoría escasa; **to lay** — poner de manifiesto, hacer patente, revelar; **to ride**
—**back** montar en pelo.
barefoot [bɛ́rfʊt] *adj.* descalzo, con los
pies desnudos, **-ed** [bɛ́rfʊtɪd] =
barefoot.
bareheaded [bɛ́rhɛ́dɪd] *adj.* descubierto, sin sombrero.
barelegged [bɛ́rlɛ́gɪd] *adj.* con las
piernas desnudas; sin medias.
barely [bɛ́rlɪ] *adv.* apenas; escasamente;
— **three pounds** tres libras escasas.
bareness [bɛ́rnɪs] *s.* desnudez.
bargain [bɑ́rgɪn] *s.* (*agreement*) convenio, pacto; negocio, trato; (*cheap*)
ganga; — **sale** ganga, *Méx.*, *C.A.*,
Ven., *Andes* barata; **into the** — por
añadidura; de ganancia; **to make a** —
cerrar un convenio; *v.* regatear; negociar; **to** — **for** regatear; contar con,
esperar.
barge [bɑrdʒ] *s.* lanchón; barca.
baritone [bǽrəton] *s.* & *adj.* barítono.
barium [bǽrɪəm] *s.* bario.
bark [bɑrk] *s.* ladrido; corteza (*de árbol*);
barco velero; *v.* ladrar; descortezar,
quitar la corteza.
barley [bɑ́rlɪ] *s.* cebada.
barn [bɑrn] *s.* establo, cuadra; granero,
troje; pajar; **streetcar** — cobertizo
para tranvías.
barnacle [bɑ́rnəkəl] *s.* cirrópodo.
barnyard [bɑ́rnjɑrd] *s.* corral; — **fowl**
aves de corral.
barometer [bərɑ́mətə] *s.* barómetro.
baron [bǽrən] *s.* barón.
baroque [bərók] *adj.* & *s.* barroco.
barrage [bərɑ́ʒ] *s.* fuego de barrera;
presa.
barrel [bǽrəl] *s.* barril, barrica, tonel,
cuba; cañón (*de fusil, pistola, etc.*);
v. embarrilar (*meter en barril*).
barren [bǽrən] *adj.* árido; estéril.
barrenness [bǽrənnɪs] *s.* aridez; esterilidad.
barrette [bərét] *s.* broche, prendedor
(*para sujetar el pelo*).
barricade [bǽrəkéd] *s.* barricada, barrera; *v.* poner barricadas; obstruir el
paso con barricadas.
barrier [bǽrɪə] *s.* barrera, valla; obstáculo.
barter [bɑ́rtə] *v.* permutar, trocar, cambiar; *s.* permuta, trueque, cambio.
base [bes] *s.* base; basa; fundamento;
adj. bajo, vil, ruin; inferior; *v.* basar,
fundar; establecer.
baseball [bésbɔ́l] *s.* baseball o beisbol.
basement [bésmənt] *s.* sótano.
baseness [bésnɪs] *s.* bajeza, ruindad,

vileza.

bashful [bǽʃfəl] *adj.* tímido, encogido, vergonzoso.

bashfulness [bǽʃfəlnɪs] *s.* timidez, vergüenza, cortedad, apocamiento.

basic [bésɪk] *adj.* básico; fundamental.

basin [bésn̩] *s.* palangana, jofaina; lebrillo; tazón (*de fuente*); estanque, depósito de agua; **river —** cuenca de río.

basis [bésɪs] (*pl.* **bases** [bésɪz]) *s.* base, fundamento.

bask [bæsk] *v.* calentarse (*al sol*); asolearse, tomar el sol.

basket [bǽskɪt] *s.* cesta, cesto, canasta.

basketball [bǽskɪtbɔl] *s.* basquetbol.

basque [bæsk] *adj. & s.* (*person*) vasco; (*language*) vascuence, vasco; (*territory*) vascongado, vasco.

bass [bes] *s.* bajo (*en música*); *adj.* bajo, grave; **— drum** tambora, bombo; **— horn** tuba.

bastard [bǽstəd] *s. & adj.* bastardo.

baste [best] *v.* hilvanar; pringar (*empapar la carne con grasa*); apalear.

bat [bæt] *s.* palo, *Méx., Carib., Ven., C.A.* bate (*de beisbol*); garrote; golpe, garrotazo; murciélago; *v.* apalear; dar palos; *Méx., Carib., Ven., C.A.* batear; **not to — an eye** no pestañear.

batch [bætʃ] *s.* hornada; colección, grupo, conjunto.

bath [bæθ] *s.* baño.

bathe [beð] *v.* bañar(se).

bather [béðəʳ] *s.* bañista.

bathhouse [bǽθhaʊs] *s.* casa de baños; bañadero.

bathrobe [bǽθrob] *s.* bata de baño.

bathroom [bǽθrum] *s.* baño, cuarto de baño.

bathtub [bǽθtʌb] *s.* bañera, tina.

bathysphere [bǽθɪsfɪr] *s.* batisfera.

battalion [bətǽljən] *s.* batallón.

batter [bǽtəʳ] *s.* batido, masa; *Am.* bateador (*de beisbol*); *v.* golpear; **to — down** demoler.

battery [bǽtərɪ] *s.* batería; acumulador; asalto.

battle [bǽtl̩] *s.* batalla, lucha, combate; *v.* batallar, luchar, combatir.

battlefield [bǽtl̩fild] *s.* campo de batalla.

battleship [bǽtl̩ʃɪp] *s.* buque de guerra, acorazado.

bawl [bɔl] *s.* aullido; grito; *v.* aullar; gritar; pregonar; **to — out** regañar, reprender.

bay [be] *s.* bahía; ladrido, balido, aullido; **— rum** ron de laurel; **— tree** laurel; **— window** ventana saliente, mirador; **to hold at —** tener a raya; *adj.* bayo; *v.* dar aullidos, ladridos o balidos.

bayonet [béənɪt] *s.* bayoneta; *v.* traspasar; herir con bayoneta.

bazaar [bəzáʳ] *s.* bazar; feria.

bazooka [bəzúka] *s.* bazuca.

be [bi] *v.* (*innately*) ser; (*state or condition*) estar, verse, hallarse, encontrarse; **— that as it may** sea como

sea; **to — cold (warm, hungry, right,** *etc.*) tener frío (calor, hambre, razón, *etc.*); **to — in a hurry** tener prisa; **he is to —** ha de ser; va a ser; **it is cold (hot, windy,** *etc.***)** hace frío (calor, viento, *etc.*).

beach [bitʃ] *s.* playa, ribera; *v.* varar, poner en seco (*una embarcación*), encallar.

beachhead [bitʃhed]ʳ *s.* cabeza de playa.

beacon [bíkən] *s.* faro, fanal; boya luminosa; señal; **aviation —** radiofaro.

bead [bid] *s.* cuenta (*de rosario, collar,* *etc.*); abalorio; glóbulo; gota (*de sudor*); **-s** rosario; collar de cuentas; *v.* adornar con abalorios o cuentecitas.

beak [bik] *s.* pico (*de ave*); espolón (*de nave*).

beam [bim] *s.* rayo (*de luz o de calor*); sonrisa; viga; vigueta; brazo (*de balanza*); **radio —** línea de radiación, radiofaro; *v.* emitir (*luz, rayos*); brillar; sonreír, estar radiante de alegría; radiar, transmitir por radio.

beaming [bímɪŋ] *adj.* radiante, resplandeciente; sonriente.

bean [bin] *s.* judía, habichuela; *Méx., C.A., Ven., Col.* frijol; *Ch., Ríopl.* poroto; **coffee —** grano de café; **Lima —** haba; string **—** judía o habichuela verde; *Méx., C.A.* ejote; *Ch., Ríopl.* poroto.

bear [bɛr] *s.* oso, osa; bajista (*el que hace bajar los valores en la Bolsa*); *v.* (*stand*) soportar; llevar; sobrellevar; tolerar, aguantar; (*give birth*) parir, dar a luz; producir; **to — down** deprimir; apretar; **to — a grudge** guardar rencor; **to — in mind** tener en cuenta; **to — on a subject** tener relación con un asunto; **to — oneself with dignity** portarse con dignidad; **to — out** confirmar; **to — testimony** dar testimonio.

beard [bɪrd] *s.* barba, barbas; aristas (*de trigo o maíz*); **-ed** *adj.* barbado, barbudo.

bearer [bérəʳ] *s.* portador; mensajero.

bearing [bérɪŋ] *s.* (*posture*) porte, presencia; (*relation*) relación, conexión; (*direction*) rumbo, orientación; (*mechanical*) cojinete; **ball —** cojinete de bolas; **beyond —** inaguantable, insufrible; **to lose one's -s** perder el rumbo, desorientarse; **fruit-bearing** *adj.* fructífero.

beast [bist] *s.* bestia, animal.

beat [bit] *s.* golpe; toque (*de tambor*); latido, palpitación; compás; ronda (*que hace el policía*); *v.* batir; golpear; azotar; vencer, ganar; marcar (*el compás*); pulsar, latir; sonar (*tambores*); **to — around the bush** andarse por las ramas; valerse de rodeos; *pret. & p.p. de* **to beat.**

beaten [bitn̩] *p.p. de* **to beat** *& adj.* batido; vencido; fatigado; **— path** camino trillado.

beater [bítə] s. batidor; molinillo; golpeador; **egg —** batidor de huevos.

beatific [biətífɪk] adj. beatífico.

beating [bítɪŋ] s. paliza, tunda, zurra; latido, pulsación.

beatitude [bɪǽtətjud] s. beatitud, bienaventuranza; **the Beatitudes** las bienaventuranzas.

beau [bo] s. galán, pretendiente.

beauteous [bjútɪəs] adj. bello, hermoso.

beautiful [bjútəfəl] adj. bello, hermoso.

beautify [bjútəfaɪ] v. hermosear, embellecer.

beauty [bjútɪ] s. belleza, hermosura; beldad; **— parlor** salón de belleza.

beaver [bívə] s. castor; **— board** cartón para tabiques.

became [bɪkém] pret. de **to become**.

because [bɪkɔ́z] conj. porque; **— of** prep. por, a causa de.

beckon [bɛ́kən] s. seña, llamada; v. llamar a señas.

become [bɪkʌ́m] v. (suit) sentar bien a, quedar bien a; convenir a; (turn out to be) hacerse; ponerse; llegar a ser; convertirse en; **to — crazy** volverse loco; enloquecer; **to — angry** enojarse; **to — frightened** asustarse; **to — old** envejecer(se); **what has — of him?** ¿qué ha sido de él?; ¿qué se ha hecho él?; p.p. de **to become**.

becoming [bɪkʌ́mɪŋ] adj. propio, conveniente; decente, decoroso; **that dress is — to you** le sienta bien ese traje.

bed [bɛd] s. cama, lecho; cauce (de un río); fondo (de lago o mar); cuadro (de jardín); yacimiento (mineral); **to go to —** acostarse; **to put to —** acostar.

bedbug [bɛ́dbʌg] s. chinche.

bedclothes [bɛ́dkloz] s. pl. ropa de cama.

bedding [bɛ́dɪŋ] = **bedclothes**.

bedpan [bɛ́dpæn] s. silleta; cómodo.

bedridden [bɛ́drɪdən] adj. en cama; postrado.

bedrock [bɛ́drák] s. roca sólida; lecho de roca.

bedroom [bɛ́drum] s. cuarto de dormir, alcoba, Méx., C.A. recámara.

bedside [bɛ́dsaɪd]: **at the —** al lado de la cama; **— table** velador, mesilla de noche.

bedspread [bɛ́dsprɛd] s. colcha, sobrecama.

bedtime [bɛ́dtaɪm] s. hora de acostarse, hora de dormir.

bee [bi] s. abeja; reunión (para trabajar o competir); **to have a — in one's bonnet** tener una idea metida en la cabeza.

beech [bitʃ] s. haya; **—nut** nuez de haya, hayuco.

beef [bif] s. carne de vaca o toro; vaca, toro (engordados para matar); **roast —** rosbif.

beefsteak [bífstek] s. bistec, biftec o bisté.

beehive [bíhaɪv] s. colmena; abejera.

been [bɪn, bɛn] p.p. de **to be**.

beer [bɪr] s. cerveza; **— tavern** cervecería.

beet [bit] s. remolacha, Am. betabel.

beetle [bítl] s. escarabajo.

befall [bɪfɔ́l] v. sobrevenir, acaecer, suceder.

befallen [bɪfɔ́lən] p.p. de **to befall**.

befell [bɪfɛ́l] pret. de **to befall**.

befit [bɪfɪ́t] v. convenir.

before [bɪfór] adv. (temporal) antes; (spatial) delante; al frente; prep. antes de; delante de; enfrente de; ante; conj. antes (de) que.

beforehand [bɪfórhænd] adv. de antemano, por adelantado, con antelación, con anticipación.

befriend [bɪfrɛ́nd] v. ofrecer o brindar amistad a; favorecer; amparar.

beg [bɛg] v. rogar, suplicar, pedir; mendigar, pordiosear; **to — the question** dar por sentado lo mismo que se arguye.

began [bɪgǽn] pret. de **to begin**.

beget [bɪgɛ́t] v. engendrar; causar, producir.

beggar [bɛ́gə] s. mendigo, pordiosero; pobre; infeliz, miserable.

begin [bɪgín] v. comenzar, empezar, principiar.

beginner [bɪgínə] s. principiante; novicio.

beginning [bɪgínɪŋ] s. principio; comienzo, empiezo; origen; **— with** comenzando con (o por); a partir de; **at the —** al principio.

begot [bɪgát] pret. & p.p. de **to beget**.

begotten [bɪgátṇ] p.p. de **to beget**.

beguile [bɪgáɪl] v. engañar; defraudar; seducir.

begun [bɪgʌ́n] p.p. de **to begin**.

behalf [bɪhǽf]: **in (on) — of** por; en nombre de; a favor de; en defensa de; **in my —** en mi nombre; a mi favor; por mí.

behave [bɪhév] v. portarse, conducirse, obrar, proceder (bien o mal); **— yourself!** ¡pórtate bien!

behavior [bɪhévjə] s. comportamiento, proceder, conducta; funcionamiento; reacción.

behead [bɪhéd] v. decapitar, degollar, descabezar.

beheld [bɪhéld] pret. & p.p. de **to behold**.

behind [bɪháɪnd] adv. detrás; atrás; a la zaga, en zaga; prep. detrás de, tras; **— one's back** a espaldas de uno; **— time** atrasado, retrasado; **from —** por detrás; **to arrive ten minutes — time** llegar con diez minutos de retraso; **to fall —** atrasarse; retrasarse.

behold [bɪhóld] v. contemplar, mirar; **—!** ¡he aquí!

behoove [bɪhúv] v. serle necesario a uno; corresponderle a uno; atañerle a uno.

being [bíɪŋ] s. ser; ente; esencia; existencia; ger. de **to be** siendo; **for the time —** por ahora; por el momento.

belated [bɪlétɪd] adj. tardío, atrasado.

belch [bɛltʃ] v. eructar; **to — forth**

echar, arrojar, vomitar; s. eructo.

belfry [bélfrɪ] s. campanario.

Belgian [béldʒɪən] adj. & s. belga.

belief [bəlíf] s. creencia; fe; convicción; opinión.

believable [bəlívəbl] adj. creíble.

believe [bəlív] v. creer; pensar; **to — in** creer en; tener fe en; confiar en.

believer [bəlívə] s. creyente, fiel.

belittle [bɪlítl] v. menospreciar, apocar, empequeñecer; dar poca importancia a.

bell [bɛl] s. campana; campanilla; **cow — cencerro, esquila; call — timbre; jingle — cascabel; —flower** campanilla, campánula.

bellboy [bélbɔɪ] s. mozo de hotel, botones.

belle [bɛl] s. beldad, mujer bella.

belligerent [bəlídʒərənt] adj. & s. beligerante.

bellow [bélo] s. bramido, rugido; v. rugir, bramar, berrear; gritar.

bellows [béloz] s. (sing. & pl.) fuelle.

belly [bélɪ] s. barriga; panza, vientre; estómago.

bellyache [béliek] s. dolor de barriga (estómago).

belong [bəlóŋ] v. pertenecer, corresponder; **it does not — here** está fuera de su sitio; está mal colocado.

belongings [bəlóŋɪŋz] s. pl. posesiones, bienes, efectos, cosas.

beloved [bɪlívɪd] adj. querido, amado.

below [bəló] adv. abajo; bajo; debajo; **here —** aquí abajo; en este mundo, de tejas abajo; prep. bajo, debajo de.

belt [bɛlt] s. cinturón, cinto; correa; zona; **sword —** talabarte; v. ceñir, fajar.

bemoan [bɪmón] v. lamentarse de, quejarse de.

bench [bentʃ] s. banco, banca; tribunal.

bend [bɛnd] s. curva; vuelta, recodo; v. encorvar(se), doblar(se), Am. enchuecar(se); inclinar(se); someter(se), ceder; **to — one's efforts** esforzarse (por), dirigir sus esfuerzos.

beneath [bɪníθ] prep. debajo de, bajo; indigno de; inferior a.

benediction [bɛnədíkʃən] s. bendición.

benefactor [bénəfæktə] s. benefactor, bienhechor; patrón.

beneficent [bənéfəsnt] adj. benéfico.

beneficial [bɛnəfíʃəl] adj. benéfico; ventajoso, provechoso.

benefit [bénəfɪt] s. beneficio; provecho, ventaja; **— performance** función de beneficio; v. beneficiar; hacer bien; **to — by the advice** aprovecharse del consejo; **he -ed by the medicine** le hizo bien la medicina.

benevolence [bənévələns] s. benevolencia.

benevolent [bənévələnt] adj. benévolo.

benign [bɪnáin] adj. benigno; afable.

bent [bɛnt] s. inclinación; tendencia; propensión; pret. & p.p. de **to bend;** adj. encorvado; inclinado, doblado; corvo; gacho; **to be — on** estar resuelto a.

benzene [bénzin] s. benceno.

bequeath [bɪkwíð] v. heredar, legar, dejar en testamento.

bequest [bɪkwést] s. legado, donación.

berate [bɪrét] v. regañar, reñir, reprender.

beret [bəré] s. boina.

berry [bérɪ] s. baya (como mora, fresa, etc.); grano (de café).

berth [bɜθ] s. litera (de un camarote); **to give a wide — to** sacarle el cuerpo a, hacerse a un lado para dejar pasar.

beseech [bɪsítʃ] v. suplicar, rogar.

beset [bɪsét] v. atacar; rodear; acosar; pret. & p.p. de **to beset.**

beside [bɪsáid] prep. (spatial) al lado de; cerca de; (in addition) además de; fuera de; **to be — oneself** estar fuera de sí, estar loco; **that is — the question** eso no hace al caso; no se trata de eso; adv. además.

besides [bɪsáidz] adv. además; prep. además de.

besiege [bɪsídʒ] v. sitiar, cercar; acosar, importunar.

besought [bɪsɔt] pret. & p.p. de **to beseech.**

best [bɛst] adj. mejor; adv. mejor; más; **the —** el mejor; lo mejor; **— girl** novia; querida; **— man** padrino de boda; **— seller** éxito de venta; de mayor venta; **at —** a lo más, cuando más; **to do one's —** hacer todo lo posible; **to get the — of a person** vencer o ganarle a una persona; **to make the — of** sacar el mejor partido de.

bestow [bɪstó] v. otorgar, conferir; **to — gifts upon** hacer regalos (o dádivas) a; **time well -ed** tiempo bien empleado.

bet [bɛt] s. apuesta; v. apostar; pret. & p.p. de **to bet.**

betake [bɪték] v. **to — oneself** encaminarse, dirigirse

betaken [bɪtékən] p.p. de **to betake.**

betook [bɪtúk] pret. de **to betake.**

betray [bɪtré] v. traicionar, vender, hacer traición; revelar, no guardar (un secreto); **to — one's ignorance** hacer patente su ignorancia.

betrayer [bɪtréə] s. traidor, traicionera.

betrothal [bɪtróθəl] s. esponsales, compromiso, mutua promesa de matrimonio.

betrothed [bɪtróθt] s. prometido, desposado; novio, novia.

better [bétə] adj. mejor; adv. mejor; más; **— half** cara mitad; **so much the —** tanto mejor; **to be — off** estar mejor así; estar en mejores condiciones; **to change for —** mejorar(se); **to get —** mejorar(se), restablecerse, aliviarse; v. mejorar; **to — oneself** mejorarse, mejorar de situación.

betterment [bétəmənt] s. mejoramiento, mejora, mejoría.

between [bətwin] prep. entre, en medio de; adv. en medio.

bevel [bévəl] *adj.* biselado; *v.* biselar.

beverage [bévrɪdʒ] *s.* bebida.

bewail [bɪwél] *v.* lamentar; quejarse de.

beware [bɪwér] *v.* guardarse (de), cuidarse (de); — ! ¡cuidado! ¡guárdese!

bewilder [bɪwíldɚ] *v.* confundir, turbar, perturbar, dejar perplejo; **to be -ed** estar turbado o perplejo; estar desorientado.

bewilderment [bɪwíldɚmənt] *s.* perplejidad, aturdimiento.

bewitch [bɪwítʃ] *v.* hechizar; aojar; encantar, cautivar.

beyond [bɪjánd] *adv.* más allá, más lejos; *prep.* allende; más allá de; fuera de: — **my reach** fuera de mi alcance.

bias [bátəs] *s.* (*tendency*) prejuicio; inclinación, tendencia; (*diagonal*) sesgo, oblicuidad; **on the** — sesgado, al sesgo, de lado; *adj.* sesgado, oblicuo; *v.* predisponer, inclinar, influir en.

bib [bɪb] *s.* babero; pechera (*de delantal*).

Bible [bátbl] *s.* Biblia.

biblical [bíblɪkl] *adj.* bíblico.

bibliographer [bɪblɪágrəfɚ] *s.* bibliógrafo.

bibliography [bɪblɪágrəfɪ] *s.* bibliografía.

bicker [bíkɚ] *v.* disputar, reñir.

bicycle [báɪsɪkl] *s.* bicicleta; *v.* andar en bicicleta.

bid [bɪd] *s.* postura, oferta; envite (*en naipes*); turno (*para envidar*); invitación; *v.* ofrecer (*precio*); mandar; invitar, convidar; rogar; enviar (*en naipes*); **to** — **fair** parecer muy probable; **to** — **good-bye** decir adiós; despedirse; **to** — **up** alzar, pujar (*la oferta en una subasta*); *pret. & p.p. de* **to bid**.

bidden [bídn] *p.p. de* **bid & to bide**.

bide [baɪd] *v.* aguardar; **to** — **one's time** esperar una buena oportunidad.

biennium [baɪénɪəm] *s.* bienio.

bier [bɪr] *s.* féretro.

big [bɪg] *adj.* grande; importante; imponente; — **Dipper** Osa Mayor; — **game** caza mayor; — **sister** hermana mayor; — **with child** encinta; **to talk** — darse bombo, *Am.* darse corte; **big-bellied** panzudo, panzón, barrigón; **big-hearted** magnánimo.

bigamy [bígəmɪ] *s.* bigamía.

bigot [bígət] *s.* fanático.

bigotry [bígətrɪ] *s.* fanatismo; intolerancia.

bikini [bɪkíni] *s.* traje bikini.

bile [baɪl] *s.* bilis, hiel; cólera, mal humor.

bilingual [baɪlíŋgwəl] *adj. & s.* bilingüe.

bill [bɪl] *s.* (*statement*) cuenta; factura; (*poster*) cartel, anuncio; (*bank note*) billete de banco; programa de teatro; (*bird*) pico; (*legislative*) proyecto de ley; — **of exchange** libranza, letra de cambio; — **of fare** lista de platos; — **of lading** conocimiento de embarque; — **of rights** declaración de derechos; — **of sale** escritura o acta

de venta; *v.* cargar en cuenta; enviar una cuenta a; **to** — **and coo** acariciarse y arrullar (*como las palomas*).

billboard [bílbord] *s.* cartelera.

billfold [bílfold] *s.* cartera.

billiards [bíljɚdz] *s.* billar.

billion [bíljən] *s.* billón, millón de millones; mil millones (*en los Estados Unidos y Francia*).

billow [bílo] *s.* oleada; ola grande; *v.* alzarse en olas.

bin [bɪn] *s.* arcón, depósito; **coal** — carbonera; **grain** — granero.

bind [baɪnd] *v.* (*unite*) unir, juntar; (*tie*) ligar; amarrar; vendar; ceñir; (*compel*) restringir; obligar, compeler; (*enclose*) encuadernar, empastar; rivetear.

binding [báɪndɪŋ] *s.* encuadernación; ribete, cinta; **cloth** — encuadernación en tela; **paper** — encuadernación en rústica; *adj.* obligatorio.

biography [baɪágrəfɪ] *s.* biografía.

biology [baɪáladʒɪ] *s.* biología.

bipartisan [baɪpártəzan] *adj.* de dos partidos; bipartito.

birch [bɚtʃ] *s.* abedul.

bird [bɚd] *s.* ave; pájaro; persona extraña o mal vista; — **of prey** ave de rapiña; — **seed** alpiste; — **shot** perdigones.

birth [bɚθ] *s.* nacimiento; parto; linaje; origen, principio; — **certificate** certificado (o fe) de nacimiento; — **control** control de la natalidad; limitación de partos; — **rate** natalidad; **to give** — dar a luz, parir.

birthday [bɚθde] *s.* cumpleaños, natalicio.

birthplace [bɚθples] *s.* lugar de nacimiento, suelo natal.

birthright [bɚθraɪt] *s.* derechos naturales o de nacimiento; naturalidad; primogenitura.

biscuit [bískɪt] *s.* bizcocho; galleta; panecillo.

bishop [bíʃəp] *s.* obispo; alfil (*en ajedrez*).

bison [báɪsn] *s.* bisonte, búfalo.

bit [bɪt] *s.* pedacito, trocito; pizca, miaja, migaja; poquito; bocado (*del freno*); taladro; **I don't care a** — no me importa un ardite; *pret. & p.p. de* **to bite**.

bitch [bɪtʃ] *s.* perra; ramera, prostituta.

bite [baɪt] *s.* mordedura, mordisco; bocado, bocadito; picadura (*de insecto*); *v.* morder; mordiscar; picar.

bitten [bítn] *p.p. de* **to bite**.

bitter [bítɚ] *adj.* amargo; agrio, acre; áspero; mordaz; **to fight to the** — **end** luchar hasta morir; **-s** *s. pl.* amargo; **-ly** *adv.* amargamente; con amargura.

bitterness [bítɚnɪs] *s.* amargura, amargor; rencor; aspereza.

black [blæk] *adj.* negro; obscuro; sombrío; **black-and-blue** amoratado, lleno de moretones; — **mark** mancha, estigma, marca de deshonra; *s.* negro; luto; —**out** obscurecimiento; **to put**

down in — and white poner por escrito v. teñir de negro; embetunar, dar bola o betún a (los zapatos).

blackberry [blǽkbɛrɪ] s. zarzamora; mora.

blackbird [blǽkbɝd] s. mirlo.

blackboard [blǽkbord] s. encerado; pizarrón; pizarra.

blacken [blǽkən] v. ennegrecer; obscurecer; teñir de negro; denigrar.

blackhead [blǽkhɛd] s. espinilla.

blackish [blǽkɪʃ] adj. negruzco.

blackjack [blǽkdʒæk] s. (weapon) cachiporra flexible; (card game) veintiuna.

blackmail [blǽkmel] s. chantaje, extorsión; v. ejercer el chantaje, extorsionar.

blackness [blǽknɪs] s. negrura; obscuridad.

blacksmith [blǽksmɪθ] s. herrero; -'s **shop** herrería.

bladder [blǽdɚ] s. vejiga.

blade [bled] s. hoja (de navaja, cuchillo, etc.); hoja (de hierba); espada; pala (de remo); aspa (de hélice); **shoulder —** espaldilla o paletilla.

blame [blem] s. culpa; v. culpar, echar la culpa a; **to be to —** tener la culpa.

blameless [blémlɪs] adj. inculpable.

blanch [blæntʃ] v. blanquear; palidecer; escaldar (almendras).

bland [blænd] adj. blando, suave.

blank [blæŋk] adj. (no writing) en blanco; (void) vacío; (confused) aturdido; **— cartridge** cartucho seco; **— face** cara sin expresión; **— form** blanco, forma en blanco, Méx., C.A., Ven. esqueleto; **— verse** verso suelto o libre; s. blanco; vacío; hueco, intermedio; papel en blanco; forma en blanco; **application —** forma (o blanco) para memorial o solicitud.

blanket [blǽŋkɪt] s. manta; frazada; cobertor; Riopl., C.A., Méx., Ven., Col. cobija; Méx. sarape, poncho; adj. general, inclusivo, que abarca un grupo o clase.

blare [blɛr] s. fragor; son de trompetas; clarinada; v. trompetear, proclamar; sonar (las trompetas); hacer estruendo.

blaspheme [blæsfím] v. blasfemar.

blasphemy [blǽsfɪmɪ] s. blasfemia.

blast [blæst] s. (wind) ráfaga de viento, golpe de viento; soplo repentino; (trumpet) trompetazo; (whistle) silbido; (explosion) explosión; estallido; carga de dinamita; **— furnace** alto horno; v. volar (con dinamita, etc.); destruir.

blaze [blez] s. llama, llamarada, incendio; resplandor; **— of anger** arranque de ira; v. arder; resplandecer; **to — a trail** abrir (o marcar) una senda.

bleach [blitʃ] s. blanqueador; blanqueo; v. blanquear(se); desteñir(se).

bleachers [blítʃɚz] s. pl. graderías, Am. glorietas.

bleak [blik] adj. yermo, desierto; helado.

blear [blɪr] v. nublar (los ojos).

bleary [blírɪ] adj. nublado, inflamado,

lagrimoso, lagañoso.

bleat [blit] s. balido; v. balar.

bled [blɛd] pret. & p.p. de **to bleed.**

bleed [blid] v. sangrar; desangrar; extorsionar.

blemish [blɛ́mɪʃ] s. mancha, tacha, defecto; v. manchar; empañar.

blend [blɛnd] s. mezcla, entremezcla; gradación (de colores, sonidos, etc.); v. mezclar, entremezclar; graduar (colores o sonidos); entremezclarse, fundirse; armonizar.

bless [blɛs] v. bendecir; **God — you!** ¡que Dios te bendiga!

blessed [blɛ́sɪd] adj. bendito; santo, beato; bienaventurado; **the whole — day** todo el santo día; [blɛst] pret. & p.p. de **to bless.**

blessing [blɛ́sɪŋ] s. bendición; gracia, don, beneficio.

blest [blɛst] adj. = **blessed.**

blew [blu] pret. de **to blow.**

blight [blaɪt] s. pulgón (parásito); tizón (honguillo parásito); quemadura (enfermedad de las plantas); roña (de las plantas); malogro; ruina; v. destruir, arruinar; frustrar (esperanzas).

blimp [blɪmp] s. dirigible pequeño.

blind [blaɪnd] adj. ciego; tapado, oculto; hecho a ciegas; **— alley** callejón sin salida; **— choice** selección hecha a ciegas; **— flying** vuelo ciego, vuelo a ciegas; **—man** ciego; **man's buff** juego de la gallina ciega; **— date** [blaɪnddet] s. cita a ciegas; persiana, cortinilla; biombo; venda (para los ojos); anteojera (para resguardar los ojos del caballo); **to be a — for some-one** ser tapadera de alguien; v. cegar; ofuscar; encubrir, tapar.

blinder [blaɪ́ndɚ] s. anteojera, Am. visera (para caballos de tiro).

blindfold [blaɪ́ndfold] v. vendar (los ojos); adj. vendado (de ojos); s. venda (para los ojos).

blindly [blaɪ́ndlɪ] adv. ciegamente; a ciegas.

blindness [blaɪ́ndnɪs] s. ceguera, ceguedad.

blink [blɪŋk] s. pestañeo; parpadeo; guiño; guiñada; v. pestañear; parpadear; guiñar.

blip [blɪp] s. bache de radar.

bliss [blɪs] s. beatitud, bienaventuranza, gloria; felicidad.

blister [blístɚ] s. ampolla, vejiga (en la piel o en cualquier superficie); v. ampollar, levantar ampollas; ampollarse.

blitz [blɪts] s. ataque relámpago.

blizzard [blízɚd] s. ventisca; v. ventiscar.

bloat [blot] v. inflar(se); abotagarse.

blob [blɑb] s. burbuja.

block [blɑk] s. (piece) bloque, trozo de piedra; zoquete; (city section) manzana (de casas); Am. cuadra; (obstacle) estorbo, obstáculo; (group) grupo, sección; (hat) horma; **— pulley** polea; **chopping —** tajo; v. estorbar; tapar; bloquear; planchar (sobre horma); parar (una pelota, una *jugada*); **to — out** esbozar, bosquejar; **to — the door** impedir el paso; **to — up a door** tapiar una puerta.

blockade [blakéd] *s.* bloqueo; obstrucción; *v.* bloquear.

blockhead [blákhɛd] *s.* zoquete, tonto, zopenco.

blond(e) [bland] *adj.* & *s.* rubio, blondo; *Mex.* huero, güero; *Guat.* canche; *Sal., Hond.,* chele; *C.R.* macho; *Col.* mono; *Ven.* catire.

blood [blʌd] *s.* sangre; **— count** análisis cuantitativo de la sangre; **— pudding** (*o* **— sausage**) morcilla; **— relative** pariente consanguíneo; **— vessel** vena; arteria; **in cold —** en sangre fría; **— bank** banco de sangre; **— poisoning** septicemia.

bloodshed [blʌdʃɛd] *s.* matanza; derrame, derramiento o efusión de sangre.

bloodshot [blʌdʃat] *adj.* inyectado de sangre.

bloodthirsty [blʌdθɚstɪ] *adj.* sanguinario.

bloody [blʌdɪ] *adj.* sangriento; ensangrentado; sanguinario, feroz.

bloom [blum] *s.* flor; florecimiento floración; lozanía; color rosado (*en las mejillas*) *v.* florecer, *Am.* florear.

blooming [blúmɪŋ] *adj.* floreciente; fresco, lozano, vigoroso.

blossom [blásəm] *s.* flor; floración, florecimiento; *v.* florecer.

blot [blat] *s.* mancha, borrón; tacha; *v.* manchar; borrar; secar (*con papel secante*) emborronar, echar manchas o borrones; **to — out** borrar, tachar; destruir; **this pen -s** esta pluma echa borrones; **blotting paper** papel secante.

blotch [blatʃ] *v.* emborronar o borronear, manchar, cubrir con manchas; *s.* mancha, borrón.

blotter [blátɚ] *s.* papel secante; libro borrador.

blouse [blaus] *s.* blusa.

blow [blo] *s.* (*stroke*) golpe; porrazo; (*shock*) choque, sorpresa, desastre; (*wind*) soplo, soplido; **to come to -s** venir a las manos; *v.* soplar; ventear; resoplar; sonar (*una trompeta*) fanfarronear; **to — a fuse** quemar un fusible; **to — one's nose** sonarse; **to — one's brains out** levantarse la tapa de los sesos; **to — open** abrirse; **to — out** apagar(se); estallar, reventar(se) (*un neumático*) **to — over** pasar; disiparse; **to — up** inflar, hinchar; volar (*con dinamita*) estallar, reventar.

blower [blóɚ] *s.* soplador; fuelle; ventilador, aventador.

blown [blon] *p.p. de* **to blow** & *adj.* soplado; inflado; **full-blown rose** rosa abierta.

blowout [blóaut] *s.* reventón (*de neumático*) escape violento de gas, aire, etc.

blowpipe [blópaɪp] *s.* soplete.

blowtorch [blótɔrtʃ] *s.* soplete.

blue [blu] *adj.* azul; triste, melancólico;

s. azul; **the -s** melancolía, morriña, murria; *v.* azular, teñir de azul.

bluebell [blúbɛl] *s.* campanilla azul (*flor*).

bluebird [blúbɚd] *s.* pájaro azul, *Am.* azulejo.

bluejay [blúdʒe] *s.* gayo, especie de azulejo (*pájaro*).

bluff [blʌf] *s.* acantilado, escarpa, risco; fanfarronada; fanfarrón, farsante; *v.* fanfarronear; alardear, hacer alarde; echar bravatas; embaucar.

bluffer [blʌfɚ] *s.* farsante, fanfarrón.

bluing [blúɪŋ] *s.* añil (*para ropa blanca*).

bluish [blúɪʃ] *adj.* azulado, azulejo.

blunder [blʌndɚ] *s.* disparate, desatino; despropósito; *v.* disparatar, desatinar; equivocarse.

blunt [blʌnt] *adj.* despuntado, embotado; brusco, grosero, *Méx.* claridoso; *v.* despuntar, embotar.

blur [blɚ] *s.* mancha; tacha; nube, cosa obscura o confusa; *v.* empañar, borronear, manchar; nublar, ofuscar; empañarse, nublarse.

blush [blʌʃ] *s.* sonrojo; rubir; *v.* sonrojarse, ruborizarse, ponerse colorado.

bluster [blʌstɚ] *v.* ventear o soplar recio (*el viento*) fanfarronear; *s.* ventolera, ventarrón, fuerte golpe de viento; jactancia, fanfarronada.

blustering [blʌstɚɪŋ] *adj.* fanfarrón, jactancioso; **— wind** ventarrón.

boar [bor] *s.* jabalí.

board [bord] *s.* (*wood*) tabla, tablero; mesa; (*meals*) comidas; (*directors*) junta, consejo; (*pasteboard*) en pasta; cartón; **the -s** las tablas, el teatro; **room and —** cuarto y comida, pensión completa; asistencia; **— of directors** junta directiva; **bulletin —** tablilla para anuncios; **free on —** (*f.o.b.*) franco a bordo; **on —** a bordo; en el tren; **to go by the —** caer en el mar; perderse; ser destrozado; *v.* ir a bordo; subir (*al tren*) entablar, cubrir con tablas; tomar a pupilaje, dar asistencia, pensión o pupilaje; residir o comer (*en casa de huéspedes*).

boarder [bórdɚ] *s.* huésped, pupilo, pensionista.

boardinghouse [bórdɪŋhaus] *s.* casa de huéspedes, pensión.

boast [bost] *s.* jactancia; alarde; bravata; gloria, orgullo; *v.* jactarse, alardear; hacer alarde de; ostentar.

boastful [bóstfəl] *adj.* jactancioso.

boastfulness [bóstfəlnɛs] *s.* jactancia; ostentación.

boat [bot] *s.* bote; barco, buque; lancha, chalupa.

boathouse [bóthaus] *s.* casilla o cobertizo para botes.

boating [bótɪŋ] *s.* paseo en lancha o bote; **to go —** pasear en bote.

boatman [bótmən] (*pl.* **boatmen** [bótmən]) *s.* barquero.

bob [bab] *s.* meneo, sacudida; pesa (*de metal*) **to wear a —** llevar el pelo corto (*o* en melena) *v.* menearse; **to — one's hair** cortarse el pelo en

melena; **to — up** aparecer de repente; **to — up and down** saltar, brincar; cabecear (*dícese de una embarcación*).
bobbin [bóbɪn] s. carrete; bobina.
bobwhite [bábhwáit] s. codorniz.
bode [bod] *pret. & p.p. de* **to bide.**
bodice [bádɪs] s. corpiño, jubón.
bodily [bádɪ] *adj.* corpóreo; corporal; *adv.* todos juntos, colectivamente; **they rose —** se levantaron todos a una, se levantaron todos juntos.
body [bádɪ] s. cuerpo; agregado, conjunto; gremio; carrocería (*de automóvil*); fuselaje (*de aeroplano*); **— of water** extensión de agua; **— politic** grupo político; estado.
bodyguard [bádɪgɑrd] s. guardaespaldas.
bog [bɑg] s. pantano; tremedal; v. hundir(se); atascarse.
Bohemian [bohímɪən] *adj. & s.* bohemio.
boil [bɔɪl] s. hervor; tumorcillo; **to come to a —** soltar el hervor, hervir; v. hervir; cocer; bullir; **to — down** hervir hasta evaporar; abreviar.
boiler [bóɪlɚ] s. caldera, marmita; caldera de vapor; calorífero central.
boiling point [bóɪlɪŋpɔɪnt] s. punto de ebullición.
boisterous [bóɪstərəs] *adj.* bullicioso; estrepitoso, ruidoso; tumultuoso.
bold [bold] *adj.* atrevido, osado; arriesgado; audaz, insolente; claro, bien delineado; **— cliff** risco escarpado; **bold-faced** descarado; **bold-faced type** negritas.
boldness [bóldnɪs] s. atrevimiento; osadía; audacia; descaro, insolencia.
bologna [bəlónɪ] s. especie de embutido.
Bolshevik [bólʃəvɪk] *adj. & s.* bolchevique.
bolster [bólstɚ] s. travesaño, almohada larga (*para la cabecera de la cama*); refuerzo, sostén, soporte; v. sostener, apoyar; apuntalar; **to — someone's courage** infundirle ánimo a alguien.
bolt [bolt] s. (*door lock*) pestillo, cerrojo; (*pin*) perno, tornillo grande; (*movement*) salida de repente; (*cloth*) rollo; **thunder —** rayo; v. cerrar con cerrojo; tragar, engullir; romper con (*un partido político*); echarse a correr, lanzarse de repente; caer como rayo; **to — out** salir de golpe.
bomb [bɑm] s. bomba; v. bombardear; **— shelter** s. refugio antiaéreo.
bombard [bɑmbárd] v. bombardear, cañonear.
bombardier [bɑmbədír] s. bombardero
bombardment [bɑmbárdmənt] s. bombardeo, cañoneo.
bombastic [bɑmbǽstɪk] *adj.* ampuloso, altisonante.
bomber [bámɚ] s. bombardero, avión de bombardeo.
bonbon [bánbɑn] s. bombón, confite.
bond [bɑnd] s. lazo, vínculo; ligadura; fianza, vale; obligación, bono.
bondage [bándɪdʒ] s. servidumbre, esclavitud.

bondsman [bándzmən] s. fiador.
bone [bon] s. hueso; espina (*de pez*); **-s** restos; osamenta; **— of contention** materia de discordia; **to make no -s about it** no pararse en pelillos; obrar francamente; v. deshuesar, quitar los huesos o espinas.
bonfire [bánfaɪr] s. hoguera, fogata.
bonnet [bánɪt] s. gorra; sombrero (*de mujer*).
bonus [bónəs] s. prima, premio, gratificación.
bony [bónɪ] *adj.* huesudo.
boo [bu] v. mofarse, burlarse (*a gritos*); **— !** *interj.* ¡bu!; **-s** s. pl. rechifla, gritos de mofa.
booby [búbɪ] s. bobo, bobalicón.
book [buk] s. libro; **The book** la Biblia; **— cash** libro de caja; **memorandum —** libreta; **on the -s** cargado en cuenta; **to keep -s** llevar los libros o la contabilidad v. inscribir, asentar (*en un libro*); **to — passage** reservar pasaje.
bookcase [búkkes] s. estante, estantería, armario para libros.
bookend [búkend] s. apoyalibros, sujetalibros.
bookkeeper [búkkipɚ] s. tenedor de libros, contador.
bookkeeping [búkkipɪŋ] s. teneduría de libros, contabilidad; **double entry —** partida doble.
booklet [búklɪt] s. librillo, librito, cuaderno, folleto.
bookseller [búkselɚ] s. librero.
bookshelf [búkʃelf] s. estante, repisa para libros.
bookshop [búkʃɑp] s. librería.
bookstore [búkstor] s. librería.
boom [bum] s. (*noise*) estampido; (*increase*) alza, auge (*en el mercado o bolsa*); bonanza, prosperidad momentánea; v. rugir, resonar, hacer estampido; prosperar, medrar, florecer, estar en bonanza; fomentar.
boon [bun] s. don; bendición, gracia, favor; *adj.* jovial, congenial.
boor [bur] s. patán, hombre zafio o grosero.
boorish [búrɪʃ] *adj.* grosero, zafio.
boost [bust] s. empuje, empujón (*de abajo arriba*); **— in prices** alza o auge de precios; v. empujar, alzar, levantar; hacer subir.
booster [bústɚ] s. aumentador; (*rocket*) cohete de lanzamiento; (*electronics*) amplificador.
boot [but] s. bota, calzado; **to —** por añadidura, de ganancia, *Méx.* de pilón, *Ven.* de ñapa; *Ríopl., Andes* de yapa (*llapa*); v. dar un puntapié; **to — out** echar a puntapiés; echar a patadas.
bootblack [bútblæk] s. limpiabotas.
booth [buθ] s. casilla, puesto.
bootlegger [bútlegɚ] s. contrabandista (*de licores*).
bootlicker [bútlɪkɚ] s. servilón, zalamero.

booty [búti] s. botín, saqueo.

borax [bóræks] s. bórax.

border [bórdə] s. borde, margen, orilla; orla, franja; ribete; frontera; v. ribetear, guarnecer (*el borde*); orlar; **to — on** (*o* **upon**) lindar con, confinar con; rayar en; **it -s on madness** raya en locura.

bore [bor] s. taladro, barreno; agujero (*hecho con taladro*); calibre (*de un cañón, cilindro, etc.*); persona o cosa aburrida; v. taladrar, horadar, barrenar; aburrir, fastidiar; *pret. de* **to bear.**

bored [bord] *adj.* cansado, aburrido; *p.p. de* **to bore.**

boredom [bórdəm] s. aburrimiento, tedio, hastío, fastidio.

boric acid [bórik ǽsəd] s. ácido bórico.

boring [bóriŋ] *adj.* aburrido, fastidioso, tedioso.

born [bɔrn] *p.p. de* **to bear** & *adj.* nacido; innato; **to be —** nacer.

borne [bɔrn] *p.p.* **to bear.**

borough [bɔ́ro] s. villa; distrito de municipio.

borrow [bɔ́ro] v. pedir prestado; tomar prestado; tomar fiado.

borrower [bɔ́rəwə] s. el que pide prestado.

bosom [búzəm] s. seno, pecho, corazón; pechera (*de camisa*); **in the — of the family** en el seno de la familia; *adj.* querido; **— friend** amigo íntimo.

boss [bɔs] s. jefe; patrón; mayoral, capataz; **political —** cacique político; v. mandar, dominar, dirigir.

bossy [bɔ́si] *adj.* mandón, autoritario.

botany [bátni] s. botánica.

botch [batʃ] s. chapucería.

both [boθ] *adj.* & *pron.* ambos, entrambos, los dos; **— this and that** tanto esto como aquello; **— of them** ambos, ellos dos, los dos; **— (of) his friends** sus dos amigos, ambos amigos.

bother [báðə] s. molestia; fastidio; incomodidad; enfado; v. molestar(se); fastidiar, enfadar; incomodar; estorbar.

bothersome [báðəsəm] *adj.* molesto.

bottle [bátl] s. botella; v. embotellar.

bottleneck [batlnɛk] s. embotellamiento; gollete.

bottom [bátəm] s. fondo; base; fundamento; asiento (*de silla*); **to be at the — of the class** ser el último de la clase; **what is at the — of all this?** ¿qué hay en el fondo de todo esto?

boudoir [budwár] s. tocador.

bough [bau] s. rama.

bought [bɔt] *pret.* & *p.p. de* **to buy.**

bouillon [búljan] s. caldo.

boulder [bóldə] s. peña, roca, guijarro grande, pedrusco.

boulevard [búləvard] s. bulevar.

bounce [bauns] s. bote, rebote (*de una pelota*); salto, brinco; v. hacer saltar; saltar, brincar; botar; echar, arrojar (*a alguien*); echar, despedir de un empleo.

bouncer [baunsə] s. apagabroncas.

bound [baund] s. (*jump*) salto, brinco; (*bounce*) bote, rebote; (*limit*) límite, confín; *adj.* ligado; confinado; obligado; ceñido; encuadernado; **— for** ir para, ir con rumbo a; **to be — up in one's work** estar absorto en su trabajo; **it is — to happen** es seguro que sucederá; **I am — to do it** estoy resuelto a hacerlo; v. botar, resaltar; saltar, brincar; limitar; ceñir, cercar; *pret.* & *p.p. de* **to bind.**

boundary [báundəri] s. límite, linde; confín; frontera.

boundless [báundlis] *adj.* ilimitado, sin límite, sin término.

bountiful [báuntəfəl] *adj.* generoso, liberal; abundante.

bounty [báunti] s. largueza, generosidad; don, favor, gracia; premio, recompensa.

bouquet [buké] s. ramillete, ramo de flores; aroma, fragancia.

bourgeois [burʒwá] *adj.* & s. burgués.

bout [baut] s. combate, lucha, contienda, asalto; **a — of pneumonia** un ataque de pulmonía.

bow [bau] s. (*inclination*) reverencia; inclinación, saludo; (*of a ship*) proa; v. hacer una reverencia, inclinarse (*para saludar*); someterse; **to — one's head** inclinar la cabeza **-ed down** agobiado.

bow [bo] s. arco (*para tirar flechas*); arco (*de violín*); curva; lazo, moño (*de cintas*); **bow-legged** *adj.* patizambo, patituerto; v. arquear; tocar (*un instrumento*) con arco.

bowels [báuəlz] s. *pl.* intestinos; entrañas; tripas.

bower [báuə] s. enramada, ramada, glorieta.

bowl [bol] s. cuenco; tazón; jícara; boliche, bola; **wash —** palangana, lavamanos; **-s** juego de bolos; v. bolear, jugar a los bolos, jugar al boliche.

box [baks] s. caja; estuche; palco de teatro; casilla; compartimiento; bofetada; **—car** furgón; **— office** taquilla; **— seat** asiento de palco; v. encajonar; meter en una caja; abofetear; boxear.

boxer [báksə] s. boxeador, pugilista.

boxing [báksiŋ] s. boxeo, pugilato.

boy [bɔi] s. niño; muchacho; mozo.

boycott [bɔ́ikat] v. boicotear; s. boicoteo.

boyhood [bɔ́ihud] s. niñez; mocedad, juventud.

boyish [bɔ́iiʃ] *adj.* pueril; juvenil; aniñado.

brace [bres] s. traba; tirante; apoyo, refuerzo; corchete ({}); **carpenter's —** berbiquí; v. trabar; apoyar, reforzar; asegurar; estimular, fortalecer; **to — up** animarse, cobrar ánimo.

bracelet [bréslit] s. brazalete, pulsera.

bracket [brǽkit] s. ménsula, soporte, sostén; repisa; **-s** paréntesis cuadrados; v. colocar entre paréntesis; unir;

agrupar.

brag [bræg] s. jactancia; v. jactarse (de); hacer alarde de.

braggart [brǽgət] adj. & s. jactancioso, fanfarrón.

braid [bred] s. trenza; galón, trencilla; v. trenzar; galonear, guarnecer con galones.

brain [bren] s. cerebro; seso; **to rack one's -s** devanarse los sesos, romperse la cabeza; v. saltar la tapa de los sesos; **— trust** [bréntrʌst] s. grupo de consejeros; **— washing** [brénwʃɪŋ] s. lavado cerebral.

brake [brek] s. freno; Ven., Col. retranca; Méx., Ríopl., C.A., Carib. garrote; **— lining** forro de freno; **— shoe** zapata de freno; **— drum** tambor de freno; **— fluid** flúido de freno; **to apply the -s** frenar; v. frenar, enfrenar; Ven., Col. retrancar; Méx., Ríopl., C.A., Carib. dar garrote.

brakeman [brékmən] s. guardafrenos, Ven., Col. retranquero, Méx., Ríopl., C.A., Carib. garrotero.

bramble [bræmbl] s. zarza, breña.

bran [bræn] s. salvado.

branch [bræntʃ] s. rama (de árbol); ramo (de la ciencia); sucursal; bifurcación; sección; tributario (de un río); ramificación; **— railway** ramal; v. ramificarse; bifurcarse.

brand [brænd] s. (make) marca; marca de fábrica; hechura; (cattle mark) hierro; Ríopl., Méx. fierro (de marcar) estigma; **brand-new** nuevecito, flamante, acabado de hacer o comprar; v. marcar; herrar, marcar (con hierro candente); difamar; **to — as** motejar de.

brandish [brǽndɪʃ] v. blandir; s. floreo, molinete.

brandy [brǽndɪ] s. aguardiente; coñac.

brash [bræʃ] adj. insolente; impetuoso; temerario.

brass [bræs] s. latón, bronce; desfachatez, descaro; **-es** utensilios de latón; instrumentos músicos de metal; **— band** banda, murga.

brassière [brəzír] s. corpiño, sostén (para ceñir los pechos).

brat [bræt] s. mocoso.

bravado [brəvádo] s. bravata; jactancia.

brave [brev] adj. bravo, valiente, valeroso; v. arrostrar; desafiar, hacer frente a.

bravery [brévərɪ] s. valor, valentía.

brawl [brɔl] v. reyerta, pendencia, riña; alboroto; v. armar una pendencia, alborotar, reñir.

bray [bre] s. rebuzno; v. rebuznar.

brazen [brézn] adj. bronceado; de bronce; de latón; descarado, desvergonzado.

brazier [brezjə] s. brasero.

breach [britʃ] s. (opening) brecha, abertura; (infraction) infracción; rompimiento; **— of faith** abuso de confianza; **— of promise** violación de un compromiso; v. abrir brecha.

bread [bred] s. pan; **—box** caja para pan; v. Méx., C.A., empanizar; Ríopl., Ch. empanar.

breadth [bredθ] s. anchura, ancho; extensión; amplitud.

break [brek] s. rompimiento; rotura; interrupción, pausa; bajón (en la bolsa o mercado); **to have a bad (good) —** tener mala (buena) suerte; **to make a bad —** cometer un disparate; v. romper(se), quebrantar(se), quebrar(se); amansar, domar; arruinar; **to — away** fugarse, escaparse; **to — into** forzar la entrada en, allanar (una morada); **to — loose** escaparse, desprenderse, soltarse; **to — out** estallar (una guerra); **to — out of prison** escaparse de la cárcel; **to — a promise** faltar a la palabra; **to — up** desmenuzar, despedazar; disolver; perturbar.

breakable [brékəbl] adj. quebradizo.

breakdown [brékdaʊn] s. parada imprevista; (automobile) avería, pane.

breaker [brékə] s. rompiente (ola); **law — infractor.**

breakfast [brékfəst] s. desayuno; **to eat — tomar el desayuno;** v. desayunarse.

breakthrough [brékθru] s. adelanto repentino; brecha.

breakwater [brékwɔtə] s. rompeolas, malecón.

breast [brest] s. pecho; seno; teta; pechuga (de ave); **to make a clean — of it** confesarlo todo.

breath [breθ] s. aliento; resuello; respiro; soplo, hálito; **in the same —** al mismo instante, con el mismo aliento; **out of —** sin aliento, jadeante; **under one's —** en voz baja, entre dientes.

breathe [brið] v. respirar; resollar; tomar aliento; exhalar; **to — into** infundir; **he -ed his last** exhaló el último suspiro; **he did not — a word** no dijo palabra.

breathless [bréθlɪs] adj. jadeante; sin aliento.

breathtaking [bréθtekɪŋ] adj. conmovedor; emocionante.

bred [bred] pret. & p.p. de **to breed.**

breeches [brítʃɪz] s. pl. bragas, calzones; **riding — pantalones de montar.**

breed [brid] s. casta, raza; relea, especie; v. criar; procrear, engendrar; educar; producirse; multiplicarse.

breeder [brídə] s. criador; animal de cría.

breeding [brídɪŋ] s. cría, crianza; educación, modales.

breeze [briz] s. brisa, vientecillo.

breezy [brízɪ] adj. airoso, ventilado; refrescado (por la brisa); animado, vivaz; **it is —** hace brisa.

brethren [bréðrɪn] s. pl. hermanos (los fieles de una iglesia o los miembros de una sociedad).

brevity [brévətɪ] s. brevedad.

brew [bru] s. cerveza; mezcla; v. fermentar, hacer (licores); preparar (té); fomentar, tramar; fabricar cerveza; amenazar (una tormenta, calamidad etc.).

brewery [brúəri] s. cervecería, fábrica de cerveza.

briar, brier [bráiə] s. zarza; rosal silvestre.

bribe [braib] s. soborno, cohecho; v. sobornar, cohechar.

bribery [bráibəri] s. soborno, cohecho.

brick [brik] s. ladrillo; ladrillos; v. enladrillar.

brickbat [bríkbæt] s. pedazo de ladrillo; insulto.

bridal [bráidl] adj. nupcial; de bodas; de novia; — **dress** vestido de novia.

bride [braid] s. novia, desposada.

bridegroom [bráidgrum] s. novio, desposado.

bridesmaid [bráidzmed] s. madrina de boda.

bridge [bridʒ] a. puente; caballete de la nariz; **draw** — puente levadizo; **suspension** — puente colgante; v. tender un puente; **to** — **a gap** llenar un vacío.

bridle [bráidl] s. brida, freno de caballo; freno, restricción; — **path** camino de herradura; v. embridar, enfrenar; reprimir, subyugar; erguirse, erguir la cabeza.

brief [brif] adj. breve, corto, conciso; s. sumario, resumen; informe, memorial; breve apostólico; **to hold a** — **for** abogar por; **-ly** adv. brevemente; en resumen, en breve.

briefcase [brífkes] s. portapapeles, cartera grande.

briefing [brífiŋ] s. reunión preparatoria.

brigade [brigéd] s. brigada.

bright [brait] adj. (light) brillante, claro, luciente; radiante; (smart) inteligente; (cheerful) alegre; listo, vivo; — **color** color subido.

brighten [bráitn] v. abrillantar, pulir, dar lustre; avivar(se); alegrar(se); animar(se); aclararse, despejarse (el cielo).

brightness [bráitnis] s. brillo, lustre, esplendor; claridad; viveza, agudeza, inteligencia.

brilliance [bríljəns] s. brillantez, brillo; lustre; resplandor.

brilliant [bríljənt] adj. brillante; resplandeciente; espléndido; talentoso; s. brillante; diamante.

brim [brim] s. borde, margen, orilla; ala (de sombrero); **to fill to the—** llenar o arrasar hasta el borde; **to be filled to the** — estar hasta los topes; estar de bote en bote; v. **to** — **over** rebosar.

brine [brain] s. salmuera.

bring [briŋ] v. traer; llevar; ocasionar, causar; **to** — **about** producir, efectuar, ocasionar; **to** — **down** bajar; **to** — **forth** dar a luz; producir; **to** — **to** resucitar; **to** — **up** criar, educar; **to** — **up a subject** traer a discusión un asunto.

brink [briŋk] s. borde, orilla, margen; **on the** — **of** al borde de.

brisk [brisk] adj. vivo, animado, fuerte;

rápido; **-ly** adv. aprisa; fuerte.

bristle [brisl] s. cerda; v. erizar(se); **to** — **with** estar erizado (o lleno) de.

bristly [brisli] adj. serdoso; erizado.

British [brítiʃ] adj. británico; **the** — los ingleses.

brittle [brítl] adj. quebradizo; frágil.

broach [brotʃ] v. traer a colación, comenzar a hablar de (un asunto).

broad [brod] adj. ancho; amplio, vasto, extenso; tolerante; — **hint** insinuación clara; **in** — **daylight** en pleno día; **broad-minded** tolerante; de amplias miras.

broadcast [bródkæst] s. radiodifusión, difusión, emisión; transmisión; v. difundir; radiodifundir, radiar, emitir.

broadcloth [bródklɔθ] s. paño fino de algodón o de lana.

broadside [bródsaid] s. (guns) andanada; (announcement) hoja suelta de propaganda.

brocade [brokéd] s. brocado.

broil [broil] v. asar(se).

broke [brok] pret. de **to break**; adj. quebrado, arruinado; pelado, sin dinero; **to go** — quebrar, arruinarse.

broken [brókən] p.p. de **to break** & adj. roto; rompido; quebrado; quebrantado; arruinado; abatido; — **English** inglés champurrado o champurreado; inglés mal pronunciado.

broker [brókə] s. corredor, agente; bolsista; **money** — cambista, corredor de cambio.

bronchitis [brɑnkáitis] s. bronquitis.

bronco, broncho [bráŋko] s. potro o caballo bronco, Ríopl. redomón; — **buster** domador.

bronze [brɑnz] s. bronce; color de bronce; v. broncear.

brooch [brutʃ] s. broche (alfiler de pecho).

brood [brud] s. pollada; nidada; cría; casta; v. empollar; **to** — **over** cavilar.

brook [bruk] s. arroyuelo, riachuelo, C.A., Col., Ven. quebrada; Méx., Ríopl. arroyo, cañada; v. tolerar, aguantar.

broom [brum] s. escoba; retama (arbusto); —**stick** palo o mango de escoba.

broth [brɔθ] s. caldo.

brother [brʌðə] s. hermano; cofrade.

brotherhood [brʌðəhʊd] s. hermandad; fraternidad; cofradía.

brother-in-law [brʌðərinlɔ] s. cuñado.

brotherly [brʌðəli] adj. fraternal.

brought [brɔt] pret. & p.p. de **to bring**.

brow [brau] s. ceja; frente.

brown [braun] adj. moreno; café; castaño; pardo oscuro; tostado; v. tostar(se).

browse [brauz] v. hojear; ramonear, pacer, pastar (el ganado).

bruise [bruz] s. magulladura, cardenal, contusión; v. magullar(se); estropear(se).

brunet, brunette [brunét] adj. moreno, trigueño.

brunt [brʌnt] s. fuerza (de un golpe o ataque); **the** — **of the battle** lo más reñido del combate.

brush [brʌʃ] *s. (tooth, clothes)* cepillo; *(paint, shaving)* brocha; *(artist's)* pincel; *(vegetation)* matorral; *(contact)* roce; encuentro; *v.* cepillar, acepillar; rozar; **to — aside** desechar, echar a un lado; **to — up** cepillarse; repasar *(una materia, una técnica, etc.).*

brushwood [brʌ́ʃwud] *s.* broza; maleza, matorral, zarzal.

brusque [brʌsk] *adj.* brusco.

brutal [brútl] *adj.* brutal, bruto.

brutality [brutǽlǝtɪ] *s.* brutalidad.

brute [brut] *s.* bruto, bestia; *adj.* bruto, brutal; bestial.

bubble [bʌ́bl] *s.* burbuja; borbollón; ampolla; *v.* borbotar; hacer espuma; bullir; **to — over with joy** rebosar de gozo.

bubble gum [bʌ́bl gʌm] *s.* chicle hinchable; chicle de globo.

buck [bʌk] *s.* macho cabrío, cabrón; gamo; macho *(del ciervo, antílope, etc.);* corveta, respingo *(de un caballo);* embestida; **— private** soldado raso; **to pass the —** *Ríopl., Andes* pasar el fardo; *v.* cabriolear, respingar; embestir; encabritarse; bregar con *(el viento);* **to — up** cobrar ánimo; **the horse -ed the rider** el caballo tiró al jinete.

bucket [bʌ́kɪt] *s.* cubo, cubeta, balde.

buckle [bʌ́kl] *s.* hebilla; *v.* abrochar con hebilla; doblarse; abollarse; **to — down** aplicarse con empeño a; **to — with** luchar con.

buckshot [bʌ́kʃɑt] *s.* posta, perdigón.

buckskin [bʌ́kskɪn] *s.* badana; ante.

buckwheat [bʌ́khwit] *s.* trigo sarraceno.

bud [bʌd] *s.* botón, yema; capullo, pimpollo; retoño; *v.* echar botones o retoños; florecer.

buddy [bʌ́dɪ] *s.* camarada, compañero.

budge [bʌdʒ] *v.* mover(se), menear(se), bullir.

budget [bʌ́dʒɪt] *s.* presupuesto.

buff [bʌf] *s.* piel de ante o búfalo; color de ante; pulidor; **blindman's —** juego de la gallina ciega; *v.* pulir, pulimentar.

buffalo [bʌ́flo] *s.* búfalo.

buffet [bʌfé] *s.* aparador; repostería; mostrador para refrescos; fonda de estación.

buffeting [bʌ́fǝtɪŋ] *s.* golpeteo, bataneo.

buffoon [bʌfún] *s.* bufón; payaso.

bug [bʌg] *s.* insecto; bicho; microbio.

buggy [bʌ́gɪ] *s.* cochecillo.

bugle [bjúgl] *s.* clarín; corneta; trompeta.

build [bɪld] *s.* estructura; talle, forma, hechura; *v.* edificar, construir; fabricar; **to — up one's health** reconstituir su salud.

builder [bɪ́ldɚ] *s.* constructor.

building [bɪ́ldɪŋ] *s.* edificio; construcción.

build-up [bɪ́ldʌp] *s.* refuerzo paulatino.

built [bɪlt] *pret.* & *p.p.* de **to build**.

bulb [bʌlb] *s.* bulbo *(de la cebolla y otras plantas);* planta bulbosa; **elec-** **tric light —** bombilla, bujía eléctrica, ampolla, *Méx., C.A., Andes* foco; *Ríopl.* bombita.

bulge [bʌldʒ] *s.* bulto; protuberancia; panza; *v.* abultar; combarse.

bulgy [bʌ́ldʒɪ] *adj.* abultado.

bulk [bʌlk] *s.* bulto, volumen; masa; **the — of the army** el grueso del ejército.

bulky [bʌ́lkɪ] *adj.* abultado, voluminoso, grueso.

bull [bul] *s.* toro; alcista *(el que hace subir los valores en la bolsa);* disparate, error; **Papal —** bula; **—fight** corrida de toros; **—fighter** torero; **bull's-eye** centro del blanco; tiro perfecto.

bulldog [bʌ́ldɔg] *s.* perro dogo, perro de presa.

bulldozer [bʌ́ldozɚ] *s.* topadora; buldózer.

bullet [bʌ́lɪt] *s.* bala.

bulletin [bʌ́lǝtɪn] *s.* boletín; **— board** tablilla para fijar anuncios o avisos.

bullfrog [bʌ́lfrɑg] *s.* rana grande.

bullion [bʌ́ljǝn] *s.* oro *(o plata)* en barras; metálico; lingotes de oro o plata.

bully [bʌ́lɪ] *s.* pendenciero, valentón, fanfarrón, matón; *adj.* excelente, magnífico; *v.* intimidar; echar bravatas.

bulwark [bʌ́lwɚk] *s.* baluarte; defensa.

bum [bʌm] *s.* holgazán, vagabundo; gorrón; borracho; **to go on a —** irse de juerga; *adj.* malo, mal hecho, de ínfima calidad; inútil, inservible; **to feel —** estar indispuesto; *v.* holgazanear; vivir de gorra.

bumblebee [bʌ́mblbi] *s.* abejorro, abejón.

bump [bʌmp] *s. (blow)* tope, choque; golpe; *(lump)* chichón, abolladura; hinchazón; joroba, protuberancia; *v.* topar, topetear; chocar; abollar; **to — along** zarandearse, ir zarandeándose; **to — off** derribar; matar.

bumper [bʌ́mpɚ] *s.* parachoques, defensa; tope; *adj.* grande, excelente; **— crop** cosecha abundante.

bun [bʌn] *s.* bollo *(de pan).*

bunch [bʌntʃ] *s.* manojo, puñado; racimo *(de uvas, plátanos, etc.);* grupo; **— of flowers** ramillete de flores; *v.* juntar(se), agrupar(se).

bundle [bʌ́ndl] *s.* lío, bulto, fardo, hato; haz; paquete; *v.* liar, atar; envolver; **to — up** abrigarse, taparse bien.

bungalow [bʌ́ŋgǝlo] *s.* casita de un piso.

bungle [bʌ́ŋgl] *v.* chapucear; estropear; echar a perder.

bunion [bʌ́njǝn] *s.* juanete.

bunk [bʌŋk] *s.* litera, camilla *(fija en la pared);* embuste, tontería, paparrucha, papa.

bunny [bʌ́nɪ] *s.* conejito.

buoy [bɔɪ] *s.* boya; *v.* boyar, mantener a flote; **to — up** sostener, apoyar.

buoyant [bɔ́ɪǝnt] *adj.* boyante, flotante; vivaz, animado, alegre.

burden [bɝ́dn] *s.* carga, peso; cuidado; gravamen; *v.* cargar; agobiar.

burdensome [bɝ́dnsǝm] *adj.* gravoso;

pesado.

bureau [bjúro] *s.* oficina; despacho; división, ramo; cómoda; **travel —** oficina de turismo; **weather —** oficina de meteorología, observatorio meteorológico.

burglar [bɜ́glə] *s.* ladrón (*que se mete en casa ajena*).

burglary [bɜ́glərɪ] *s.* robo.

burial [bɛ́rɪəl] *s.* entierro; **— place** cementerio.

burlap [bɜ́læp] *s.* arpillera, tela burda de cáñamo.

burly [bɜ́lɪ] *adj.* corpulento, voluminoso, grandote.

burn [bɜn] *s.* quemadura; *v.* quemar(se); incendiar; arder; abrasar(se).

burner [bɜ́nə] *s.* quemador; mechero; hornilla.

burnish [bɜ́nɪʃ] *v.* bruñir; pulir; *s.* bruñido, pulimento.

burnt [bɜ́nt] *pret. & p.p. de* **to burn.**

burrow [bɜ́o] *s.* madriguera, conejera; *v.* hacer madrigueras en; escarbar; socavar, minar; esconderse.

burst [bɜst] *s.* reventón, explosión; estallido; **— of laughter** carcajada; *v.* reventar(se); abrirse; estallar; **to — into** entrar de repente; **to — into tears** prorrumpir en lágrimas; **to — with laughter** estallar o reventar de risa; *pret. & p.p. de* **to burst.**

bury [bɛ́rɪ] *v.* enterrar; sepultar; **to be buried in thought** estar absorto, meditabundo o pensativo.

bus [bʌs] *s.* autobús, ómnibus, *Méx.* camión; *C.A.* camioneta; *Ríopl.* colectivo; *Ch.* micro; *Carib.* guagua.

busboy [bʌ́sbɔɪ] *s.* ayudante de camarero.

bush [bʊʃ] *s.* arbusto; mata; matorral, breñal; **rose —** rosal; **to beat around the —** andarse por las ramas.

bushel [bʊ́ʃəl] *s.* fanega (*medida de áridos*).

bushing [bʊ́ʃɪŋ] *s.* buje.

bushy [bʊ́ʃɪ] *adj.* matoso, espeso; lleno de arbustos.

busily [bɪ́zlɪ] *adv.* diligentemente.

business [bɪ́znɪs] *s.* negocio; ocupación; comercio; asunto; **— house** casa de comercio, establecimiento mercantil; **— transaction** negocio, transacción comercial; **to do — with** negociar con, comerciar con; **he has no — doing it** no tiene derecho a hacerlo; **not to be one's —** no concernirle a uno, no importarle a uno; **to make a — deal** hacer un trato.

businesslike [bɪ́znɪslaɪk] *adj.* eficaz, eficiente, práctico; formal.

businessman [bɪ́znɪsmæn] *s.* hombre de negocios, comerciante.

bust [bʌst] *s.* busto; pecho (*de mujer*); **to go out on a —** salir o ir de parranda; *v.* reventar; quebrar; domar (*un potro*).

bustle [bʌ́sl] *s.* bulla, bullicio, trajín, alboroto; polisón (*para abultar las caderas*); *v.* bullir(se); menearse; trajinar.

busy [bízɪ] *adj.* ocupado; activo; **—body** entremetido; **— street** calle de mucho tráfico; *v.* **to — oneself** ocuparse.

but [bʌt] *conj., prep. & adv.* pero, mas; sino; menos, excepto; sólo, no . . . más que; **— for you** a no ser por Vd.; **not only . . . — also** no sólo . . . sino (que) también; **I cannot help —** no puedo menos de; **she is — a child** no es más que una niña.

butcher [bútʃə] *s.* carnicero; **-'s shop** carnicería; *v.* matar (*reses*); hacer una matanza o carnicería; destrozar.

butchery [bútʃəɪ] *s.* carnicería, matanza.

butler [bʌ́tlə] *s.* despensero, mayordomo; **-'s pantry** despensa.

butt [bʌt] *s.* culata (*de rifle*); colilla (*de cigarro*); tope; topetazo; cabezada; **the — of ridicule** el blanco de las burlas; *v.* topetear, embestir; **to — in** entremeterse; **to — into a conversation** meter baza, *Am.* meter su cuchara.

butter [bʌ́tə] *s.* manteca, mantequilla; *v.* enmantecar, untar con manteca o mantequilla.

buttercup [bʌ́təkʌp] *s.* botón de oro (*flor*).

butterfly [bʌ́təflaɪ] *s.* mariposa.

buttermilk [bʌ́təmɪlk] *s.* suero de mantequilla.

butterscotch [bʌ́təskátʃ] *s.* confite o jarabe de azúcar y mantequilla.

buttocks [bʌ́təks] *s. pl.* nalgas, asentaderas.

button [bʌ́tn̩] *s.* botón; **— hook** abotonador; *v.* abotonar(se).

buttonhole [bʌ́tnhol] *s.* ojal; *v.* hacer ojales; **to — someone** detener, demorar a uno (*charlando*).

buttress [bʌ́trɪs] *s.* contrafuerte; refuerzo, sostén; *v.* sostener, reforzar, poner contrafuerte.

buy [baɪ] *v.* comprar; **to — off** sobornar; **to — up** acaparar.

buyer [báɪə] *s.* comprador.

buzz [bʌz] *s.* zumbido; murmullo; *v.* zumbar; murmurar; **to — the bell** tocar el timbre.

buzzard [bʌ́zəd] *s.* buitre, *Am.* aura, *Méx., C.A.* zopilote, *Ríopl.* carancho; *Col. Andes* gallinazo.

by [baɪ] *prep.* por; cerca de; al lado de; junto a; según; **— and —** luego, pronto; **— dint of** a fuerza de; **— far** con mucho; **— night** de noche; **— the way** de paso; a propósito; entre paréntesis; **— this time** ya; a la hora de ésta; **— two o'clock** para las dos; **days gone —** días pasados.

bygone [bátgɔn] *adj.* pasado; **let -s be -s** lo pasado pasado, lo pasado pisado.

bylaw [báɪlɔ] *s.* estatuto; reglamento.

bypass [báɪpæs] *s.* desviación.

bypath [báɪpæθ] *s.* atajo, vereda.

by-product [báɪprɑdəkt] *s.* producto secundario o accesorio.

bystanders [báɪstændəz] *s.* circunstantes, presentes; mirones.

C

cab [kæb] *s.* coche de alquiler; taxímetro, taxi; casilla (*de una locomotora*); **— driver** cochero; chófer.

cabbage [kǽbɪdʒ] *s.* col, repollo, berza.

cabin [kǽbɪn] *s.* cabaña, choza, bohío, barraca; camarote (*de buque*); **airplane —** cabina de aeroplano.

cabinet [kǽbənɪt] *s,* gabinete; armario; escaparate, vitrina.

cable [kébl] *s.* cable, amarra; cablegrama; **— address** dirección cablegráfica; *v.* cablegrafiar.

cablegram [kébl]grǽm] *s.* cablegrama.

cabman [kǽbmən] *s.* cochero; chófer.

cackle [kǽkl] *s.* cacareo; charla; risotada; *v.* cacarear; parlotear, charlar.

cactus [kǽktəs] (*pl.* **cacti** [kǽktaɪ]) *s.* cacto.

cad [kæd] *s.* canalla (*m.*); malcriado.

cadence [kédns] *s.* cadencia.

cadet [kədét] *s.* cadete.

cadmium [kǽdmɪəm] *s.* cadmio.

café [kəfé] *s.* café, restaurante.

cafeteria [kæfətíɪə] *s.* restaurante (*en donde se sirve uno mismo*).

caffein [kǽfiːn] *s.* cafeína.

cage [kedʒ] *s.* jaula; *v.* enjaular.

cake [kek] *s.* pastel; bizcocho; bollo; torta; *Ven.*, *Col.* panqué; pastilla (*de jabón*); **— of ice** témpano de hielo; *v.* apelmazarse, formar masa compacta.

calamity [kəlǽmətɪ] *s.* calamidad.

calcium [kǽlsɪəm] *s.* calcio.

calculate [kǽlkjəlet] *v.* calcular; **to — on** contar con.

calculation [kælkjəléʃən] *s.* cálculo; cómputo, cuenta.

calculus [kǽlkjələs] *s.* cálculo.

calendar [kǽləndə] *s.* calendario, almanaque; **— year** año corriente.

calf [kæf] (*pl.* **calves** [kævz]) *s.* ternero, ternera, becerro, becerra; pantorrilla (*de la pierna*); **—skin** piel de becerro o becerrillo.

caliber [kǽləbə] *s.* calibre.

calico [kǽlako] *s.* calicó (*tela de algodón*).

call [kɔl] *s.* (*summons*) llamada; llamamiento; (*visit*) visita; (*demand*) demanda, pedido; **within —** al alcance de la voz; *v.* llamar; gritar; hacer una visita; pasar (*lista*); **to — at a port** hacer escala en un puerto; **to — for** ir por; demandar, pedir; **to — on** visitar a; acudir a (*en busca de auxilio*); **to — to order a meeting** abrir la sesión; **to — together** convocar; **to — up on the phone** llamar por teléfono.

caller [kɔ́lə] *s.* visita, visitante; llamador (*el que llama*).

callous [kǽləs] *adj.* calloso; duro.

callus [kǽləs] *s.* callo.

calm [kɑm] *s.* calma; sosiego; *adj.* calmo, tranquilo, quieto, sosegado; *v.* calmar, tranquilizar, sosegar; **to — down** calmarse; **-ly** *adv.* tranquilamente, con calma.

calmness [kɑ́mnɪs] *s.* calma, sosiego, tranquilidad.

calorie [kǽlərɪ] *s.* caloría.

calumny [kǽləmnɪ] *s.* calumnia.

came [kem] *pret. de* **to come.**

camel [kǽml] *s.* camello.

cameo [kǽmɪo] *s.* camafeo.

camera [kǽmərə] *s.* cámara fotográfica.

camouflage [kǽməflɑʒ] *s.* camuflaje; disfraz; *v.* encubrir, disfrazar.

camp [kæmp] *s.* campo, campamento; **— chair** silla de tijera; **political —** partido político; *v.* acampar.

campaign [kæmpén] *s.* campaña; *v.* hacer campaña; hacer propaganda.

camphor [kǽmfə] *s.* alcanfor.

campus [kǽmpəs] *s.* campo (*de una universidad*).

can [kæn] *s.* lata, bote, envase; **— opener** abrelatas; *v.* envasar, enlatar; *v.* defect. *y aux.* (*usado sólo en las formas* **can** *y* **could**) poder, saber.

Canadian [kənédɪən] *adj. & s.* canadiense.

canal [kənǽl] *s.* canal; **irrigation —** acequia.

canary [kənérɪ] *s.* canario.

cancel [kǽnsl] *v.* cancelar; anular; revocar; techar.

cancellation [kænsléʃən] *s.* cancelación; anulación; revocación.

cancer [kǽnsə] *s.* cáncer.

candid [kǽndɪd] *adj.* cándido, franco, sincero.

candidacy [kǽndədəsɪ] *s.* candidatura.

candidate [kǽndədet] *s.* candidato; aspirante.

candle [kǽndl] *s.* candela, vela; bujía; cirio; **— power** potencia lumínica (*en bujías*).

candlestick [kǽndlstɪk] *s.* candelero; palmatoria.

candor [kǽndə] *s.* candor, sinceridad.

candy [kǽndɪ] *s.* dulce, confite, bombón; **— shop** confitería, dulcería; *v.* confitar, azucarar; almibarar, garapiñar; cristalizarse (*el almíbar*); **candied almonds** almendras garapiñadas.

cane [ken] *s.* caña; **— plantation** (*o* **—field**) cañaveral; *C.A.* cañal; **— chair** silla de bejuco; **sugar —** caña de azúcar; **walking —** bastón; **to beat with a —** bastonear, apalear.

canine [kénaɪn] *adj.* canino, perruno.

canned [kænd] *adj.* enlatado, envasado, conservado (*en lata o en vidrio*); **— goods** conservas alimenticias.

cannery [kǽnərɪ] *s.* fábrica de conservas alimenticias.

cannibal [kǽnəbl] *s.* caníbal.

cannon [kǽnən] *s.* cañón.

cannonade [kænənéd] *s.* cañoneo; *v.* cañonear.

cannot [kǽnat] = **can not** no puedo, no puede, no podemos, etc.

canny [kǽnɪ] *adj.* sagaz; astuto.

canoe [kənú] *s.* canoa, *Ríopl.* piragua, *Méx.* chalupa.

canon [kǽnən] *s.* canon; ley, regla; criterio, norma; canónigo.

canopy [kǽnəpɪ] *s.* dosel, pabellón; (*airplane*) capota, cúpula.

cantaloupe [kǽntlop] *s.* melón.

canteen [kæntín] *s.* cantina; cantimplora.

canton [kǽntən] *s.* cantón, región, distrito.

canvas [kǽnvəs] *s.* lona; lienzo; toldo; cañamazo.

canvass [kǽnvəs] *s.* inspección; escrutinio; indagación, encuesta, pesquisa; solicitación (*de votos*); *v.* examinar, escudriñar; recorrer (*un distrito solicitando algo*); hacer una encuesta; solicitar votos o pedidos comerciales.

canyon [kǽnjən] *s.* cañón, garganta.

cap [kæp] *s.* (*head covering*) gorro, gorra, boina; (*bottle, wheel*) tapa, tapón; (*mountain*) cima, cumbre; **percussion** — cápsula fulminante; *v.* tapar, poner tapón a; **that -s the climax** eso es el colmo.

capability [kepəbílətɪ] *s.* capacidad, aptitud.

capable [képəbl] *adj.* capaz; hábil; competente.

capacious [kəpéʃəs] *adj.* capaz, amplio, espacioso.

capacity [kəpǽsətɪ] *s.* capacidad; cabida; habilidad; aptitud; **in the — of a teacher** en calidad de maestro.

cape [kep] *s.* capa; capote; cabo, promontorio.

caper [képə] *s.* cabriola; voltereta, brinco; **to cut -s** cabriolar, retozar, hacer travesuras; *v.* cabriolar, retozar, juguetear, brincar.

capillary [kǽpɪlɛrɪ] *s.* & *adj.* capilar.

capital [kǽpətl] *s.* capital (*f.*), ciudad principal, capital (*m.*), caudal; chapitel (*de una columna*); letra mayúscula; **to make — of** sacar partido de, aprovecharse de; *adj.* capital; principal; excelente; **— punishment** pena capital, pena de muerte.

capitalism [kǽpətlɪzm] *s.* capitalismo.

capitalist [kǽpətlɪst] *s.* capitalista; **-ic** *adj.* capitalista.

capitalization [kæpətləzéʃən] *s.* capitalización.

capitalize [kǽpətlaɪz] *v.* capitalizar; sacar provecho (de); escribir con mayúscula.

capitol [kǽpətl] *s.* capitolio.

capitulate [kəpítʃələt] *v.* capitular.

caprice [kəprís] *s.* capricho.

capricious [kəpríʃəs] *adj.* caprichoso.

capsize [kæpsáɪz] *v.* zozobrar, volcar(se).

capsule [kǽpsl] *s.* cápsula.

captain [kǽptɪn] *s.* capitán; *v.* capitanear, mandar; servir de capitán.

captivate [kǽptəvet] *v.* cautivar.

captive [kǽptɪv] *s.* & *adj.* cautivo, prisionero.

captivity [kæptívətɪ] *s.* cautiverio, prisión.

captor [kǽptə] *s.* aprehensor o aprensor.

capture [kǽptʃə] *s.* captura; aprensión; presa; toma; *v.* capturar; prender; tomar (*una ciudad*).

car [kɑr] *s.* coche, automóvil, auto, *Am.* carro; vagón (*de ferrocarril*); camarín (*de ascensor*), ascensor, *Am.* elevador; **dining —** coche comedor; **freight —** furgón, vagón de carga.

caramel [kǽrəml] *s.* caramelo.

carat [kǽrət] *s.* quilate.

caravan [kǽrəvæn] *s.* caravana.

carbolic [kɑrbálɪk] *adj.* carbólico.

carbon [kɑrbən] *s.* carbono; **— copy** copia en papel carbón; **— paper** papel carbón; **— monoxide** monóxido de carbón; **— dioxide** dióxido de carbono.

carburetor [kɑrbəretə] *s.* carburador.

carcass [kɑrkəs] *s.* esqueleto; cuerpo descarnado, despojo; res (*muerta*); casco (*de un buque*).

card [kɑrd] *s.* (*missive*) tarjeta; (*playing*) naipe, carta; carda (*para cardar lana*); **— index** índice de fichas; fichero; **—sharp** fullero; **file —** ficha, papeleta; **post—** tarjeta postal; **pack of -s** baraja, naipes; **to play -s** jugar a la baraja, jugar a los naipes; *v.* cardar (*lana*).

cardboard [kɑrdbord] *s.* cartón; **fine —** cartulina.

cardiac [kɑrdɪæk] *adj.* cardiaco, cardíaco.

cardinal [kɑrdnəl] *adj.* cardinal; principal, fundamental; rojo, bermellón; **— number** número cardinal; *s.* cardenal (*dignatario eclesiástico*); **— bird** cardenal.

care [kɛr] *s.* (*worry*) cuidado; aflección; ansiedad; (*caution*) cuidado, cautela, esmero; (*responsibility*) cargo, custodia; **to take — of** cuidar de; *v.* tener interés (por); **to — about** tener interés en (o por); preocuparse de; importarle a uno; **to — for** cuidar de; estimar, tenerle cariño a; gustarle a uno; simpatizarle a uno (*una persona*); **to —** to querer, desear, tener ganas de; **what does he —** ? ¿a él qué le importa?

career [kərír] *s.* carrera, profesión.

carefree [kérfri] *adj.* libre de cuidado, sin cuidados, despreocupado.

careful [kérfəl] *adj.* cuidadoso; esmerado; cauteloso; **to be —** tener cuidado; **-ly** *adv.* cuidadosamente, con cuidado; con esmero.

carefulness [kérfəlnɪs] *s.* cuidado; esmero; cautela.

careless [kérlɪs] *adj.* descuidado; negligente; indiferente; **-ly** *adv.* sin cuidado; sin esmero; descuidadamente.

carelessness [kérlɪsnɪs] *s.* descuido; falta de esmero; desaliño; negligencia.

caress [kərɛ́s] *s.* caricia; *v.* acariciar.

caretaker [kértekə] *s.* cuidador, guardián, vigilante, celador.

carfare [kárfer] *s.* pasaje de tranvía.

cargo [kárgo] *s.* carga, cargamento; flete.

caricature [kǽrɪkətʃə] *s.* caricatura; *v.* caricaturar o caricaturizar.

carload [kárlod] *s.* furgonada, vagonada, carga de un furgón o vagón.

carnal [kárnl] *adj.* carnal.
carnation [karnéʃən] *s.* clavel; color encarnado o rosado.
carnival [kárnəvl] *s.* carnaval; fiesta, holgorio; feria, verbena.
carnivorous [karnívərəs] *adj.* carnívoro, carnicero.
carol [kérəl] *s.* villancico; **Christmas** — villancico de Navidad; *v.* cantar villancicos; celebrar con villancicos.
carom [kérəm] *s.* carambola; rebote.
carouse [karáuz] *v.* andar de parranda, *Riopl.*, *Ch.* andar de farra; embriagarse.
carpenter [kárpəntə] *s.* carpintero.
carpentry [kárpəntrı] *s.* carpintería.
carpet [kárpıt] *s.* alfombra; **small** — tapete.
carriage [kérıdʒ] *s.* carruaje, coche; acarreo, transporte; porte; — **paid** porte pagado; **good** — buen porte, garbo, manera airosa.
carrier [kérıə] *s.* portador; mensajero; carretero, trajinante; transportador; *Am.* cargador; **airplane** — portaaviones; **disease** — transmisor de gérmenes contagiosos; **mail** — cartero.
carrot [kérət] *s.* zanahoria.
carry [kérı] *v.* llevar; acarrear, transportar; *Am.* cargar; sostener (*una carga*); traer consigo; ganar, lograr (*una elección, un premio, etc.*); **to** — **away** llevarse; cargar con; entusiasmar, encantar; **to** — **on** continuar; no parar; **to** — **oneself well** andar derecho, airoso, garboso; **to** — **out** llevar a cabo, realizar; sacar.
cart [kart] *s.* carro, carreta, vagoncillo; *v.* acarrear.
cartage [kártıdʒ] *s.* carretaje, acarreo.
carter [kártə] *s.* carretero; acarreador.
carton [kártn] *s.* caja de cartón.
cartoon [kartún] *s.* caricatura.
cartoonist [kartúnıst] *s.* caricaturista.
cartridge [kártrıdʒ] *s.* cartucho; — **belt** cartuchera, canana; — **box** cartuchera; — **shell** cápsula.
carve [karv] *v.* tallar; labrar; cincelar; esculpir; trinchar, tajar (*carne*).
carver [kárvə] *s.* trinchador; trinchante (*cuchillo*); entallador, escultor.
carving [kárvıŋ] *s.* talla, obra de escultura, entalladura; — **knife** trinchante.
cascade [kæskéd] *s.* cascada, salto de agua.
case [kes] *s.* (*instance*) caso; (*box*) caja; (*pillow*) funda, cubierta; (*scabbard*) vaina; **window** — marco de ventana; **in** — **that** caso que, en caso de que, dado que; **in any** — en todo caso; **just in** — por si acaso; — **work** trabajo con casos.
casement [késmənt] *s.* puerta ventana.
cash [kæʃ] *s.* dinero contante; — **box** cofre; — **payment** pago al contado; — **on delivery (c.o.d.)** contra reembolso, cóbrese al entregar; — **register** caja registradora (*de dinero*); **to pay** — pagar al contado; *v.* cambiar, cobrar (*un cheque*).

cashew [kéʃju] *s.* anacardo.
cashier [kæʃír] *s.* cajero.
cask [kæsk] *s.* tonel, barril, cuba.
casket [késkıt] *s.* ataúd; **jewel** — joyero, cofrecillo.
casserole [késərol] *s.* cacerola.
cassock [késək] *s.* sotana.
cast [kæst] *s.* tirada (*al pescar*); molde; matiz; apariencia; defecto (*del ojo*); reparto (*de papeles dramáticos*); actores; — **iron** hierro fundido o colado; *v.* echar; tirar; arrojar; lanzar; moldear; repartir (*papeles dramáticos*); escoger (*para un papel dramático*); **to** — **a ballot** votar; **to** — **a statue in bronze** vaciar una estatua en bronce; **to** — **about** buscar; hacer planes; **to** — **aside** desechar; **to** — **lots** echar suertes; **to be** — **down** estar abatido; *pret. & p.p.* de **to cast.**
castanets [késtənets] *s. pl.* castañuelas.
caste [kæst] *s.* casta; **to lose** — perder el prestigio social.
Castilian [kæstíljən] *s. & adj.* castellano.
castle [kæsl] *s.* castillo; alcázar; fortaleza; torre, roque (*en ajedrez*).
castor oil [késtə ɔil] *s.* aceite de ricino.
castrate [késtret] *v.* capar, castrar.
casual [kéʒuəl] *adj.* casual, accidental.
casualty [kéʒuəltı] *s.* baja o pérdida (*en el ejército*); accidente.
cat [kæt] *s.* gato; gata.
catalogue [kétlɔg] *s.* catálogo; *v.* catalogar.
cataract [kétərækt] *s.* catarata.
catarrh [kətár] *s.* catarro.
catastrophe [kətéstrəfi] *s.* catástrofe.
catch [kætʃ] *s.* presa; botín; pesca; pestillo (*de la puerta*); trampa; cogida (*de la pelota*); — **phrase** frase llamativa; — **question** pregunta tramposa; **he is a good** — es un buen partido; **to play** — jugar a la pelota; *v.* coger; prender; asir; alcanzar; enganchar; comprender; ser contagioso, pegarse; **to** — **a glimpse of** vislumbrar; **to** — **cold** coger un resfriado, resfriarse; **to** — **on** comprender, caer en la cuenta; **to** — **one's eye** llamarle a uno la atención; **to** — **sight of** avistar; **to** — **unaware** sorprender, coger desprevenido; **to** — **up with** alcanzar a, emparejarse con.
catcher [kétʃə] *s.* cogedor, agarrador; parador, cácher o receptor (*en beisbol*).
catching [kétʃıŋ] *adj.* pegajoso, contagioso; atractivo.
catechism [kétəkızəm] *s.* catecismo.
category [kétəgorı] *s.* categoría.
cater [kétə] *v.* surtir, abastecer, proveer los alimentos (*para banquetes, fiestas, etc.*) **to** — to proveer a las necesidades o al gusto de; **to** — **to the taste of** halagar el gusto de.
caterpillar [kétəpılə] *s.* oruga; — **tractor** tractor.
cathedral [kəθídrəl] *s.* catedral.
cathode [kéθod] *s.* cátodo; — **rays** rayos catódicos.
Catholic [kéθəlık] *s. & adj.* católico.

Catholicism [kəθáləsɪzəm] *s.* catolicismo.

catsup [kǽtsəp] *s.* salsa de tomate.

cattle [kǽt]] *s.* ganado, ganado vacuno; **— raiser** ganadero, *Riopl.* estanciero; **— raising** ganadería; **— ranch** hacienda de ganado, *Méx.*, *C.A.* rancho, *Riopl.* estancia; *Ven.*, *Col.* hato.

caught [kɔt] *pret. & p.p.* de **to catch.**

cauliflower [kɔ́ləflauə] *s.* coliflor.

cause [kɔz] *s.* causa; *v.* causar; originar; **to —** to hacer; inducir a.

caution [kɔ́ʃən] *s.* precaución, cautela; aviso, advertencia; **—!** ¡cuidado! ¡atención!; *v.* prevenir, avisar, advertir.

cautious [kɔ́ʃəs] *adj.* cauto; cauteloso, cuidadoso; precavido.

cavalier [kævəlír] *s.* caballero; galán; *adj.* orgulloso, altivo, desdeñoso.

cavalry [kǽvlrɪ] *s.* caballería.

cave [kev] *s.* cueva; caverna; *v.* **to — in** hundirse; desplomarse.

cavern [kǽvən] *s.* caverna.

cavity [kǽvətɪ] *s.* cavidad, hueco, (*tooth*) carie.

caw [kɔ] *s.* graznido; *v.* graznar.

cease [sis] *v.* cesar; parar, desistir; dejar de.

ceaseless [síslɪs] *adj.* incesante.

cedar [sídə] *s.* cedro.

cede [sid] *v.* ceder.

ceiling [síltɳ] *s.* techo (*interior*); cielo máximo (*en aviación*); altura máxima (*en aviación*); **— price** precio máximo.

celebrate [séləbret] *v.* celebrar.

celebrated [séləbretɪd] *adj.* célebre, renombrado.

celebration [sɛləbréʃən] *s.* celebración; fiesta.

celebrity [səlébrətɪ] *s.* celebridad; renombre.

celery [sélərɪ] *s.* apio.

celestial [səléstʃəl] *adj.* celestial, celeste.

cell [sɛl] *s.* celda; célula; pila eléctrica.

cellar [sélə] *s.* bodega, sótano.

celluloid [séljəlɔɪd] *s.* celuloide.

cement [səmént] *s.* cemento; **reinforced —** cemento armado; *v.* unir, cementar, pegar con cemento; cubrir con cemento.

cemetery [sémətɛrɪ] *s.* cementerio.

censor [sénsə] *s.* censor; censurador, crítico; *v.* censurar (*cartas, periódicos, etc.*).

censorship [sénsəʃɪp] *s.* censura.

censure [sénʃə] *s.* censura, crítica, reprobación; *v.* censurar, criticar, reprobar.

census [sénsəs] *s.* censo.

cent [sɛnt] *s.* centavo (*de peso o dólar*); **per —** por ciento.

centennial [sɛnténɪəl] *adj. & s.* centenario.

center [séntə] *s.* centro; *v.* centrar; colocar en el centro; concentrar(se).

centigrade [séntəgred] *adj.* centígrado.

centipede [séntəpid] *s.* ciempiés, cientopiés.

central [séntrəl] *adj.* central; céntrico; *s.* (la) central de teléfonos.

centralize [séntrəlaɪz] *v.* centralizar.

centrifugal [sɛntrífjʊg]] *adj.* centrífugo.

centripetal [sɛntrípət]] *adj.* centrípeto.

century [séntʃərɪ] *s.* siglo.

ceramic [sərǽmɪk] *adj.* cerámico; **ceramics** *s.* cerámica.

cereal [sírɪəl] *adj.* cereal; *s.* cereal; grano.

ceremonial [sɛrəmónɪəl] *adj.* ceremonial; *s.* ceremonial; rito.

ceremonious [sɛrəmónɪəs] *adj.* ceremonioso.

ceremony [sérəmonɪ] *s.* ceremonia; ceremonial.

certain [sэ́tɳ] *adj.* cierto, seguro; **-ly** *adv.* ciertamente; por cierto; de cierto; seguramente; de seguro.

certainty [sэ́tɳtɪ] *s.* certeza; certidumbre; seguridad.

certificate [sətífəkɪt] *s.* certificado; documento; testimonio; **— of stock** bono, obligación; **birth —** partida de nacimiento; **death —** partida (*o* certificado) de defunción.

certification [sətɪfɪkéʃən] *s.* certificación.

certify [sэ́təfaɪ] *v.* certificar; dar fe, atestiguar.

cessation [sɛséʃən] *s.* suspensión, paro.

cesspool [séspul] *s.* cloaca, rezumadero.

chafe [tʃef] *s.* rozadura; irritación, molestia; *v.* rozar(se); frotar; irritar(se).

chaff [tʃæf] *s.* hollejo, cáscara; *v.* embromar, bromear.

chagrin [ʃəgrín] *s.* mortificación, desazón, pesar; **-ed** *p.p.* mortificado, afligido.

chain [tʃen] *s.* cadena; **— of mountains** cordillera; **— store** tienda sucursal (*una entre muchas de una misma empresa*); **— reaction** reacción en cadena; reacción eslabonada; *v.* encadenar.

chair [tʃɛr] *s.* silla; cátedra; presidencia; **arm —** sillón (*de brazos*); **easy —** butaca, poltrona; **folding —** silla de tijera; **rocking —** mecedora.

chairman [tʃɛ́rmən] *s.* presidente (*de una junta*).

chairmanship [tʃɛ́rmənʃɪp] *s.* presidencia (*de una junta*).

chalice [tʃǽlɪs] *s.* cáliz (*vaso sagrado*).

chalk [tʃɔk] *s.* tiza, yeso; greda; *v.* enyesar; marcar con tiza o yeso; **to — down** apuntar con tiza o yeso (*en el pizarrón*); **to — out** bosquejar; esbozar con tiza.

chalky [tʃɔ́kɪ] *adj.* yesoso; blanco.

challenge [tʃǽlɪndʒ] *s.* desafío; reto; demanda; *v.* desafiar, retar; disputar; poner a prueba; dar el quienvive.

chamber [tʃémbə] *s.* cámara; aposento; **— of commerce** cámara de comercio.

chambermaid [tʃémbəmed] *s.* camarera, sirvienta.

chamois [ʃǽmɪ] *s.* gamuza.

champion [tʃǽmpɪən] *s.* campeón; defensor; *v.* defender.

championship [tʃǽmpɪənʃɪp] *s.* campeonato.

chance [tʃæns] *s.* (*opportunity*) oportunidad, ocasión; (*possibility*) posibilidad, probabilidad; (*fortune*) suerte, fortuna; casualidad, azar; (*risk*) riesgo; billete de rifa o lotería; **by —** por casualidad; **game of —** juego de azar; **to run a —** correr riesgo; *adj.* casual, accidental; *v.* arriesgar; **to — to** acertar a, hacer (*algo*) por casualidad.

chancellor [tʃǽnsələ] *s.* canciller; primer ministro; magistrado; rector de universidad.

chandelier [ʃændlír] *s.* araña de luces, *Am.* candil.

change [tʃendʒ] *s.* (*money*) cambio; vuelta, *Am.* vuelto; suelto; *Méx.* feria; (*fresh clothes*) muda de ropa; (*switch*) mudanza; **the — of life** la menopausia; *v.* cambiar; mudar; alterar; **to — clothes** mudar de ropa; **to — trains** transbordar(se), cambiar de tren.

changeable [tʃéndʒəbl] *adj.* mudable, variable; inconstante; **— silk** seda tornasolada.

channel [tʃǽnl] *s.* canal; cauce.

chant [tʃænt] *s.* canto llano o gregoriano; sonsonete; *v.* cantar (*psalmos, himnos, etc.*).

chaos [kéɑs] *s.* caos; desorden.

chaotic [keátɪk] *adj.* caótico.

chap [tʃæp] *s.* grieta, raja, rajadura (*en la piel*); chico; **what a fine — he is!** ¡qué buen tipo (o sujeto) es!; *v.* agrietarse, rajarse (*la piel*).

chapel [tʃǽpl] *s.* capilla.

chaperon(e) [ʃépəron] *s.* acompañante, persona de respeto; **to go along as a —** *Am.* ir de moscón; *v.* acompañar, servir de acompañante.

chaplain [tʃǽplɪn] *s.* capellán; **army —** capellán castrense.

chapter [tʃǽptə] *s.* capítulo; cabildo (*de una catedral*).

char [tʃɑr] *v.* requemar, carbonizar.

character [kǽrɪktə] *s.* carácter; personaje.

characteristic [kærɪktərístɪk] *adj.* característico; típico; *s.* característica, rasgo característico; distintivo; peculiaridad.

characterize [kǽrɪktəraɪz] *v.* caracterizar.

charcoal [tʃárkol] *s.* carbón; carboncillo (*para dibujar*); **— drawing** dibujo al carbón.

charge [tʃɑrdʒ] *s.* (*custody*) cargo; custodia; cuidado; (*order*) mandato, encargo; (*accusation*) cargo, acusación; (*load*) carga; peso; (*cost*) precio, coste; (*attack*) embestida, asalto, ataque; **— account** cuenta abierta; **— prepaid** porte pagado; **under my —** a mi cargo; **to be in —** of estar encargado de; *v.* cargar; cargar en cuenta; cobrar (*precio*); mandar; exhortar; atacar, embestir, asaltar; **to — with murder** acusar de homicidio.

charger [tʃárdʒə] *s.* cargador (*de batería*); caballo de guerra, corcel.

chariot [tʃǽrɪət] *s.* carroza; carruaje.

charitable [tʃǽrətəbl] *adj.* caritativo.

charity [tʃǽrətɪ] *s.* caridad; limosna; beneficencia.

charlatan [ʃárlətn] *s.* charlatán; farsante.

charm [tʃɑrm] *s.* encanto; atractivo; hechizo; talismán; **watch —** dije; *v.* encantar; cautivar; hechizar.

charming [tʃármɪŋ] *adj.* encantador, atractivo.

chart [tʃɑrt] *s.* carta (*hidrográfica o de navegar*); mapa; gráfica, representación gráfica; *v.* cartografiar, delinear mapas o cartas; **to — a course** trazar o planear una ruta o derrotero.

charter [tʃártə] *s.* carta constitucional, constitución, código; título; carta de privilegio; **— member** socio fundador; *v.* fletar (*un barco*); alquilar (*un ómnibus*).

chase [tʃes] *s.* caza; persecución; *v.* cazar; perseguir; **to — away** ahuyentar.

chasm [kǽzəm] *s.* abismo; vacío.

chaste [tʃest] *adj.* casto; honesto; puro.

chastise [tʃæstáɪz] *v.* castigar.

chastisement [tʃæstáɪzmənt] *s.* castigo, escarmiento.

chastity [tʃǽstətɪ] *s.* castidad; honestidad; pureza.

chat [tʃæt] *s.* charla, plática; *v.* charlar, platicar.

chattels [tʃǽtlz] *s. pl.* enseres, bienes muebles.

chatter [tʃǽtə] *s.* charla, parloteo; castañeteo (*de los dientes*); chirrido (*de aves*); *v.* charlar, parlotear, cotorrear; castañetear (*los dientes*).

chauffeur [ʃófə] *s.* chófer, cochero de automóvil.

cheap [tʃip] *adj.* barato; cursi, de mal gusto; **to feel —** sentir vergüenza; **-ly** *adv.* barato, a poco precio.

cheapen [tʃípən] *v.* abaratar.

cheapness [tʃípnɪs] *s.* baratura; cursilería.

cheat [tʃit] *s.* fraude, engaño; trampa; trampista, tramposo; estafador; embaucador; *v.* engañar; trampear; embaucar; estafar.

check [tʃɛk] *s.* cheque (*de banco*); talón, marbete, contraseña (*de equipajes, etc.*); marca, señal; cuenta (*de restaurante*); restricción, represión; cuadro (*de un tejido o tela*); comprobación; jaque (*en ajedrez*); **—room** vestuario; **— point** punto de inspección; depósito de equipajes, *C.A.*, *Ven.* consigna; *v.* refrenar, reprimir, restringir; facturar, depositar (*equipajes*); inspeccionar; confrontar, comprobar; marcar (*con una señal*); dar jaque (*en ajedrez*); **to — out of a hotel** desocupar el cuarto o alojamiento de un hotel.

checkbook [tʃékbʊk] *s.* libreta de cheques; libro talonario.

checker [tʃékə] *s.* cuadro; casilla (*de un*

tablero de ajedrez, etc.); pieza (*del juego de damas*); comprobador; inspector; **-s** juego de damas; **—board** tablero; *v.* cuadricular, marcar con cuadritos; **-ed career** vida azarosa, vida llena de variedad; **-ed cloth** paño o tela a cuadros.

cheek [tʃik] *s.* mejilla, carrillo; cachete; descaro, desfachatez; **fat —** mejilla gorda, moflete; **— bone** pómulo.

cheer [tʃɪr] *s.* alegría; buen ánimo, jovialidad; consuelo; **-s** aplausos, vivas; *v.* alegrar, alentar, animar; aplaudir, vitorear; **to — up** alentar, dar ánimo; cobrar ánimo, animarse.

cheerful [tʃírfəl] *adj.* animado, alegre, jovial; **-ly** *adv.* alegremente, con alegría, con júbilo; de buena gana, de buen grado.

cheerfulness [tʃírfəlnɪs] *s.* jovialidad, alegría; buen humor.

cheerily [tʃírəlɪ] = **cheerfully.**

cheerless [tʃírlɪs] *adj.* abatido, desalentado, desanimado; triste, sombrío.

cheery [tʃírɪ] = **cheerful.**

cheese [tʃiz] *s.* queso; **cottage —** requesón.

chemical [kémɪkl] *adj.* químico; *s.* producto químico.

chemist [kémɪst] *s.* químico.

chemistry [kémɪstrɪ] *s.* química.

cherish [tʃérɪʃ] *v.* acariciar, abrigar (*una esperanza, un ideal, etc.*); apreciar.

cherry [tʃérɪ] *s.* cereza; **— tree** cerezo.

chess [tʃɛs] *s.* ajedrez; **—board** tablero de ajedrez.

chest [tʃɛst] *s.* cofre, arca; caja; pecho; **— of drawers** cómoda.

chestnut [tʃésnət] *s.* castaña; **— tree** castaño; *adj.* castaño; **— horse** caballo zaino.

chew [tʃu] *v.* mascada, mordisco, bocado; *v.* mascar, masticar.

chewing gum [tʃúɪn gʌm] *s.* goma de mascar; *Am.* chicle.

chick [tʃɪk] *s.* polluelo, pollito; pajarito; **chick-pea** garbanzo.

chicken [tʃíkɪn] *s.* pollo; polluelo; **— pox** viruelas locas; **chicken-hearted** cobarde, gallina.

chicory [tʃíkərɪ] *s.* achicoria.

chide [tʃaɪd] *v.* regañar, reprender, reprobar.

chief [tʃif] *s.* jefe, caudillo; cacique (*de una tribu*); **commander in —** comandante en jefe; *adj.* principal; **— clerk** oficial mayor; **— justice** presidente de la corte suprema; **-ly** *adv.* principalmente, mayormente; sobre todo.

chiffon [ʃífan] *s.* gasa.

chilblain [tʃílblen] *s.* sabañón.

child [tʃaɪld] *s.* niño, niña; hijo, hija; **-'s play** cosa de niños; **to be with —** estar encinta.

childbirth [tʃáɪldbɜθ] *s.* parto, alumbramiento.

childhood [tʃáɪldhʊd] *s.* niñez, infancia.

childish [tʃáɪldɪʃ] *adj.* pueril; infantil; **— action** niñería, niñada.

childless [tʃáɪldlɪs] *adj.* sin hijos.

childlike [tʃáɪldlaɪk] *adj.* como niño, aniñado, pueril.

children [tʃíldrən] *pl. de* **child.**

Chilean [tʃílɪən] *adj. & s.* chileno.

chili [tʃílɪ] *s. Méx., C.A.* chile, *Carib., S.A.* ají.

chill [tʃɪl] *s.* frío, resfrío; enfriamiento; escalofrío; calofrío; **-s and fever** escalofríos; *adj.* frío; *v.* resfriar(se); enfriar(se); **to become -ed** resfriarse, escalofriarse.

chilly [tʃílɪ] *adj.* frío; friolento.

chime [tʃaɪm] *s.* repique, campaneo; **-s** órgano de campanas, juego de campanas; *v.* repicar, campanear; tocar, sonar, tañer (*las campanas*); **to — with** estar en armonía con.

chimney [tʃímnɪ] *s.* chimenea; **lamp —** tubo de lámpara, *Am.* bombilla.

chin [tʃɪn] *s.* barba.

china [tʃáɪnə] *s.* loza de china, porcelana, loza fina; vajilla de porcelana; **— closet** chinero.

chinaware [tʃáɪnəwɛr] = **china.**

Chinese [tʃaɪníz] *adj.* chino; *s.* chino; idioma chino.

chink [tʃɪŋk] *s.* grieta, hendidura.

chip [tʃɪp] *s.* astilla, brizna; fragmento; desconchadura; desportilladura; ficha (*de pócar*); *v.* astillar; desconchar(se); descascarar(se); desportillar(se); picar, tajar (*con cincel o hacha*); **to — in** contribuir con su cuota.

chipmunk [tʃípmʌŋk] *s.* especie de ardilla.

chirp [tʃɝp] *s.* chirrido; pío; gorjeo; *v.* chirriar; piar; pipiar; gorjear.

chisel [tʃízl] *s.* cincel; *v.* cincelar; sisar, estafar.

chivalrous [ʃívlrəs] *adj.* caballeresco, caballeroso, galante, cortés.

chivalry [ʃívlrɪ] *s.* caballería; caballerosidad.

chlorine [klórin] *s.* cloro.

chloroform [klórəfɔrm] *s.* cloroformo.

chocolate [tʃɔ́klɪt] *s.* chocolate; **— pot** chocolatera.

choice [tʃɔɪs] *s.* selección; preferencia; escogimiento; cosa elegida; favorito, preferido; alternativa; **to have no other —** no tener otra alternativa; *adj.* selecto; bien escogido; excelente.

choir [kwaɪr] *s.* coro.

choke [tʃok] *s.* sofoco, ahogo; tos ahogada; estrangulación; estrangulador, obturador (*de automóvil*); *v.* sofocar(se), ahogar(se); estrangular(se); obstruir, tapar; regularizar (*el motor*).

cholera [kálərə] *s.* cólera (*m.*).

cholesterol [kəléstərɔl] *s.* colesterol.

choose [tʃuz] *v.* escoger; elegir, seleccionar; **to — to** optar por; preferir; **I do not — to do it** no se me antoja (*o* no es mi gusto) hacerlo.

chop [tʃap] *s.* chuleta, costilla, tajada (*de carne*); **-s** quijadas (*usualmente de animal*); *v.* tajar, cortar; picar, desmenuzar (*carne*).

choppy [tʃápɪ] *adj.* picado, agitado.

CH

choral [kóɹəl] *adj.* coral.

chord [kɔrd] *s.* cuerda; acorde.

chore [tʃor] *s.* tarea; quehacer.

choreography [koriágɹəfɪ] *s.* coreografía.

chorus [kóɹəs] *s.* coro; *v.* cantar o hablar en coro; contestar a una voz.

chose [tʃoz] *pret. de* to choose.

chosen [tʃózṇ] *p.p. de* to choose.

christen [krísṇ] *v.* bautizar.

christening [krísnɪŋ] *s.* bautizo, bautismo.

Christian [krístʃən] *s. & adj.* cristiano; **— name** nombre de pila o bautismo.

Christianity [krɪstʃɪænɪtɪ] *s.* cristiandad, cristianismo.

Christmas [krísməs] *s.* Navidad, Pascua de Navidad; **— Eve** Nochebuena; **— gift** regalo de Navidad; aguinaldo; **Merry —!** ¡Felices Navidades! ¡Felices Pascuas!

chrome [krom] *s.* cromo; *adj.* cromado.

chromium [krómɪəm] *s.* cromo.

chromosome [krómɘsom] *s.* cromosomo.

chronic [kránɪk] *adj.* crónico.

chronicle [kránɪkl] *s.* crónica; *v.* relatar; escribir la crónica de.

chronicler [kránɪklɚ] *s.* cronista.

chronological [kɹɑnəládʒɪk] *adj.* cronológico.

chronometer [krənámɘtɚ] *s.* cronómetro.

chrysanthemum [krɪsǽnθəməm] *s.* crisantema, crisantemo.

chubby [tʃʌ́bɪ] *adj.* rechoncho; gordiflón.

chuck [tʃʌk] *s.* mamola, golpecito, caricia *(debajo de la barba)*; *v.* echar, tirar *(lo que no sirve)*; **to — under the chin** hacer la mamola.

chuckle [tʃʌ́kl] *s.* risita; *v.* reír entre dientes.

chum [tʃʌm] *s.* compañero, camarada, compinche.

chunk [tʃʌŋk] *s.* trozo; zoquete.

church [tʃɚtʃ] *s.* iglesia.

churchman [tʃɚ́tʃmən] *s.* clérigo, eclesiástico, sacerdote.

churchyard [tʃɚ́tʃjard] *s.* patio de iglesia; camposanto, cementerio.

churn [tʃɚn] *s.* mantequera *(para hacer manteca)*; *v.* batir *(en una mantequera)*; agitar, revolver.

cider [sáɪdɚ] *s.* sidra.

cigar [sɪgár] *s.* cigarro, puro; **— store** tabaquería, estanquillo.

cigarette [sɪgɘrét] *s.* cigarrillo, pitillo, *Méx., C.A., Ven., Col.* cigarro; **— case** cigarrera, pitillera; **— holder** boquilla; **— lighter** encendedor.

cinch [sɪntʃ] *s.* cincha; ganga, cosa fácil; *v.* cinchar; apretar.

cinder [síndɚ] *s.* ceniza; carbón, brasa, ascua; cisco; **-s** cenizas; rescoldo.

cinnamon [sínəmən] *s.* canela; **— tree** canelo.

cipher [sáɪfɚ] *s.* cifra; número; cero.

circle [sɚ́kl] *s.* círculo; cerco, rueda; *v.* cercar, circundar; circular, dar vueltas.

circuit [sɚ́kɪt] *s.* circuito; rodeo, vuelta.

circular [sɚ́kjɘlɚ] *adj.* circular; redondo; *s.* circular; hoja volante.

circulate [sɚ́kjɘlet] *v.* circular; poner en circulación.

circulation [sɚkjɘléʃən] *s.* circulación.

circumference [sɚkʌ́mfərəns] *s.* circunferencia.

circumflex [sɚ́kʌmflɛks] *adj.* circunflejo.

circumlocution [sɚkəmlokjúʃən] *s.* circunlocución, rodeo.

circumscribe [sɚkəmskráɪb] *v.* circunscribir, limitar.

circumspect [sɚ́kəmspɛkt] *adj.* circunspecto; prudente.

circumspection [sɚkəmspékʃən] *s.* circunspección, miramiento, prudencia.

circumstance [sɚ́kəmstæns] *s.* circunstancia; incidente; ceremonia, pompa.

circus [sɚ́kəs] *s.* circo.

cirrhosis [sɪrósɪs] *s.* cirrosis.

cistern [sɪ́stən] *s.* cisterna.

citadel [sítədl] *s.* ciudadela.

citation [saɪtéʃən] *s.* citación; cita; mención.

cite [saɪt] *v.* citar; citar a juicio; mencionar.

citizen [sítəzn] *s.* ciudadano, paisano.

citizenship [sítəznʃɪp] *s.* ciudadanía.

citron [sítrən] *s.* acitrón.

citrus [sítrəs] *s.* cidro.

city [sítɪ] *s.* ciudad, población; municipio; *adj.* municipal; urbano; **— council** ayuntamiento; **— hall** ayuntamiento, casa municipal.

civic [sívɪk] *adj.* cívico.

civics [sívɪks] *s.* derecho político.

civil [sívl] *adj.* civil; cortés; **— engineer** ingeniero civil; **— rights** derechos civiles; **— disobedience** desobediencia civil.

civilian [səvíljən] *s.* paisano *(persona no militar)*.

civility [səvílɪtɪ] *s.* civilidad, cortesía, urbanidad.

civilization [sɪvlɘzéʃən] *s.* civilización.

civilize [sívlaɪz] *v.* civilizar.

civilized [sívlaɪzd] *adj.* civilizado.

clad [klæd] *pret. & p.p. de* to clothe.

claim [klem] *s.* demanda; reclamación, reclamo; derecho, título; pretensión; **miner's —** denuncia; *v.* reclamar; demandar; pedir, exigir; afirmar, sostener; **to — a mine** denunciar una mina; **to — to be** pretender ser.

claimant [klémənt] *s.* reclamante o reclamador; pretendiente *(a un trono)*.

clairvoyant [klɛrvóɪənt] *adj.* clarividente.

clam [klæm] *s.* almeja.

clamber [klǽmbɚ] *v.* trepar, encaramarse, subir a gatas, subir gateando.

clammy [klǽmɪ] *adj.* frío y húmedo.

clamor [klǽmɚ] *s.* clamor; clamoreo; gritería, vocería; *v.* clamar; vociferar, gritar.

clamorous [klǽmərəs] *adj.* clamoroso.

clamp [klæmp] *s.* grapa; tornillo de banco; *v.* afianzar, sujetar; pisar recio.

clan [klæn] *s.* clan; tribu.

clandestine [klændéstɪn] *adj.* clandestino.

clang [klæŋ] *s.* tantán, retintín; campanada, campanillazo; —! —! ¡tan! ¡tan!; *v.* sonar, repicar (*una campana o timbre*); hacer sonar, tocar fuerte.

clap [klæp] *s.* palmada; golpe seco; — **of thunder** trueno; *v.* palmear, palmotear, aplaudir, dar palmadas; cerrar de golpe (*un libro*); dar una palmada, *Am.* palmear (*sobre la espalda*); **to — in jail** meter (o encajar) en la cárcel.

clapper [klǽpə] *s.* badajo.

clarify [klǽrəfaɪ] *v.* aclarar.

clarinet [klærənét] *s.* clarinete.

clarity [klǽratɪ] *s.* claridad, luz.

clash [klæʃ] *s.* choque, encontrón, colisión; riña, conflicto; estruendo; *v.* chocar; darse un encontrón; hacer crujir; oponerse, estar en conflicto.

clasp [klæsp] *s.* (*fastener*) broche; hebilla; cierre, traba; (*grip*) apretón, apretón de manos; *v.* abrochar; asir; agarrar; sujetar, asegurar; abrazar; apretar (*la mano*).

class [klæs] *s.* clase; *v.* clasificar.

classic [klǽsɪk] *adj.* & *s.* clásico; — **scholar** humanista, erudito clásico.

classical [klǽsɪkl] *adj.* clásico.

classicism [klǽsɪsɪzm] *s.* clasicismo.

classification [klæsəfəkéʃən] *s.* clasificación.

classify [klǽsəfaɪ] *v.* clasificar.

classmate [klǽsmet] *s.* compañero de clase, condiscípulo.

classroom [klǽsrum] *s.* clase, aula.

clatter [klǽtə] *s.* estrépito, boruca; traqueteo; bullicio; alboroto; *v.* hacer estrépito o boruca; traquetear; meter bulla o alboroto.

clause [klɔz] *s.* cláusula.

claw [klɔ] *s.* garra; zarpa; uña; pinza (*de langosta, cangrejo, etc.*); orejas (*de un martillo*); arañazo; *v.* desgarrar; arañar; rasgar.

clay [kle] *s.* barro; arcilla, greda.

clean [klin] *adj.* limpio; puro; *adv.* limpiamente; **clean-cut** bien tallado, de buen talle, de buen parecer; *v.* limpiar; asear; **to — up** limpiar(se), asear(se).

cleaner [klínə] *s.* limpiador; quitamanchas.

cleanliness [klénlɪnɪs] *s.* limpieza; aseo.

cleanly [klénlɪ] *adj.* limpio; aseado; [klínlɪ] *adv.* limpiamente.

cleanness [klínnɪs] *s.* limpieza; aseo.

cleanse [klɛnz] *v.* limpiar; asear; purificar, depurar.

cleanser [klénzə] *s.* limpiador.

clear [klɪr] *adj.* (*evident*) claro; patente, manifiesto; (*clean*) límpido; despejado; libre (*de culpa, estorbos, deudas, etc.*); — **profit** ganancia neta; **clear-cut** *adj.* bien delineado; clarividente; **to pass — through** atravesar, traspasar de lado a lado; **to be in the —** estar sin deudas; estar libre de culpa; *v.* aclarar(se); despejar(se); clarificar;

quitar (*estorbos*); desmontar (*un terreno*); salvar, saltar por encima de; librar (*de culpa, deudas, etc.*); sacar (*una ganancia neta*); pasar (*un cheque*) por un banco de liquidación; liquidar (*una cuenta*); **to — the table** levantar la mesa; **to — up** aclarar(se).

clearance [klírəns] *s.* espacio (*libre entre dos objetos*); despacho de aduana; — **sale** saldo, venta (*de liquidación*), *Am.* barata.

clearing [klírɪŋ] *s.* aclaramiento; claro; terreno desmontado o desarbolado; liquidación de balances; —**house** banco de liquidación.

clearness [klírnɪs] *s.* claridad.

cleavage [klívɪdʒ] *s.* hendedura.

cleave [kliv] *v.* hender(se); tajar; rajar, partir.

cleaver [klívə] *s.* cuchilla o hacha (*de carnicero*).

clef [klɛf] *s.* clave (*en música*).

cleft [klɛft] *s.* grieta, hendedura; *adj.* hendido, partido, rajado; *pret. & p.p. de* to cleave.

clemency [klémənsɪ] *s.* clemencia.

clement [klémənt] *adj.* clemente.

clench [klɛntʃ] *s.* agarro, agarrada, agarrón; apretón; *v.* agarrar, asir; apretar (*los dientes, el puño*).

clergy [klɝdʒɪ] *s.* clero.

clergyman [klɝdʒɪmən] *s.* clérigo, eclesiástico, pastor, sacerdote.

clerical [klérɪkl] *adj.* clerical, eclesiástico; oficinesco, de oficina; de dependientes.

clerk [klɝk] *s.* dependiente; empleado (*de oficina*); escribiente; archivero (*de municipio*); **law** — escribano; *v.* estar de dependiente.

clever [klévə] *adj.* diestro, hábil; listo; talentoso; mañoso; **-ly** *adv.* hábilmente; con destreza; con maña.

cleverness [klévənɪs] *s.* destreza, habilidad, maña; talento.

clew [klu] *s.* indicio (*que indica el camino para resolver un misterio o problema*).

cliché [klɪʃé] *s.* (*plate*) clisé; *Am.* cliché; (*phrase*) cliché.

click [klɪk] *s.* golpecito; chasquido (*de la lengua*); gatillazo (*sonido del gatillo de una pistola*); taconeo (*sonido de tacones*); *v.* sonar (*un pestillo, un broche, un gatillo, etc.*); chasquear (*la lengua*); **to — the heels** cuadrarse (*militarmente*); taconear.

client [klátənt] *s.* cliente.

clientele [klatəntél] *s.* clientela.

cliff [klɪf] *s.* risco, precipicio, peñasco, escarpa.

climate [kláɪmɪt] *s.* clima.

climax [kláɪmæks] *s.* clímax, culminación; *v.* culminar; llegar al clímax.

climb [klaɪm] *s.* subida, ascenso; *v.* subir; trepar; encaramarse; **to — down** bajar a gatas; desprenderse (*de un árbol*).

climber [kláɪmə] *s.* trepador; enredadera, planta trepadora.

clime [klaɪm] *s.* clima.

clinch [klɪntʃ] *v.* remachar, redoblar (*un*

clavo); afianzar, sujetar, asegurar bien; cerrar (*un trato*); abrazarse fuertemente; *s.* remache; abrazo; agarrón; **to be in a** — estar agarrados o abrazados.

cling [klɪŋ] *v.* pegarse, adherirse.

clinic [klínɪk] *s.* clínica.

clink [klɪŋk] *s.* tintín.

clip [klɪp] *s.* (*fastener*) broche, presilla; (*cutting*) tijereteada (*corte con tijeras*); trasquila, trasquiladura; **paper** — sujetapapeles; **to go at a good** — ir a paso rápido; andar de prisa; *v.* recortar; cortar; trasquilar (*el pelo o lana de los animales*); **to — together** sujetar.

clipper [klípə] *s.* clíper (*velero o avión de gran velocidad*); trasquilador; recortador; **-s** tijeras; maquinilla (*para recortar el pelo*).

clipping [klípɪŋ] *s.* recorte.

cloak [klok] *s.* capa; manto; *v.* tapar, embozar, encubrir.

cloakroom [klókrum] *s.* guardarropa, vestuario.

clock [klɑk] *s.* reloj; **alarm** — despertador; *v.* marcar; cronometrar.

clockwise [klákwaɪz] *adv.* en el sentido de las manecillas de reloj.

clockwork [klákwɜrk] *s.* maquinaria de reloj; **like** — con precisión, puntualmente; sin dificultad.

clod [klɑd] *s.* terrón; tonto, necio.

clog [klɑg] *s.* estorbo, obstáculo; zueco (*zapato de suela gruesa o de madera*); **— dance** zapateado; *v.* estorbar, embarazar; obstruir, atorar, tapar, obstruirse, atascarse, azolvarse (*Am.* enzolvarse), atorarse (*un caño, acequia, etc.*).

cloister [klɔ́ɪstə] *s.* claustro; monasterio; convento; *v.* enclaustrar.

close [kloz] *s.* fin, terminación, conclusión; *v.* cerrar(se); concluir; **to — an account** saldar una cuenta; **to — in upon** cercar, rodear; **to — out** liquidar, vender en liquidación.

close [klos] *adj.* (*near*) cercano, próximo; aproximado; íntimo; (*tight*) estrecho, ajustado; (*stingy*) cerrado; tacaño, mezquino; (*suffocating*) opresivo; sofocante; **— attention** suma atención; **— questioning** interrogatorio detallado o minucioso; **— translation** traducción fiel; **at — range** de cerca; *adv.* cerca; **-ly** *adv.* aproximadamente; estrechamente; apretadamente; con sumo cuidado o atención.

closed circuit [klozd sɜ́kət] *s.* & *adj.* circuito cerrado.

closeness [klósnɪs] *s.* cercanía, proximidad; aproximación; estrechez; intimidad; tacañería, avaricia; mala ventilación, falta de aire; fidelidad (*de una traducción*).

closet [klázɪt] *s.* ropero; alacena; armario; gabinete; retrete, excusado; *v.* encerrar en un cuarto (*para una entrevista secreta*); **to — oneself (themselves)** encerrarse.

clot [klɑt] *v.* coagular(se), cuajar(se); *s.* coágulo, cuajarón.

cloth [klɔθ] *s.* tela, paño, género; trapo; *adj.* de paño; **— binding** encuadernación en tela.

clothe [kloð] *v.* vestir; cubrir; revestir; investir.

clothes [kloz] *s. pl.* ropa; ropaje, vestidos; **suit of** — terno, traje, *Carib., Ven.* flux; **—line** tendedero; **—pin** pinzas, gancho (*para tender la ropa*).

clothier [klóðjə] *s.* comerciante en ropa o paño; ropero, pañero.

clothing [klóðɪŋ] *s.* ropa; ropaje, vestidos.

cloud [klaud] *s.* nube; **storm** — nubarrón; *v.* nublar(se), anublar(se); obscurecer; manchar.

cloudburst [kláudbɜst] *s.* chaparrón, aguacero.

cloudless [kláudlɪs] *adj.* claro, despejado; sin nubes.

cloudy [kláudɪ] *adj.* nublado; nubloso; sombrío.

clove [klov] *s.* clavo (*especia*); **— of garlic** diente de ajo.

cloven [klóvən] *adj.* hendido; *s.* & *adj.* **— hoof** patihendido, pie hendido.

clover [klóvə] *s.* trébol; **to be in** — estar o vivir en la abundancia; sentirse próspero.

cloverleaf [klóvəlif] *s.* (*highway*) cruce en trébol.

clown [klaun] *s.* payaso, bufón; *v.* payasear, bufonear, hacer el payaso.

cloy [klɔɪ] *v.* empalagar; hastiar.

club [klʌb] *s.* club, círculo; casino; garrote, porra; palo; basto (*de la baraja*); *v.* golpear, aporrear, apalear; **to — together** formar club; escotar, pagar la cuota que le toca a cada uno, *Am.* cotizar.

clubhouse [klʌ́bhaus] *s.* club, casino.

cluck [klʌk] *s.* cloqueo; *v.* cloquear.

clue = **clew.**

clump [klʌmp] *s.* terrón; pisada fuerte; **— of bushes** matorral; **— of trees** grupo de árboles, arboleda; *v.* apiñar, amontonar; **to — along** andar pesadamente.

clumsy [klʌ́mzɪ] *adj.* torpe, desmañado; incómodo; difícil de manejar; mal hecho.

clung [klʌŋ] *pret.* & *p.p. de* to cling.

cluster [klʌ́stə] *s.* racimo; grupo; *v.* agrupar(se); arracimarse (*formar racimo*).

clutch [klʌtʃ] *s.* apretón fuerte; agarro, agarrón; embrague (*de automóvil*); **-es** garras; uñas; **— pedal** palanca del embrague; **to step on the** — pisar el embrague; desembragar, soltar el embrague; **to throw in the** — embragar; *v.* agarrar, asir; apretar.

clutter [klʌ́tə] *v.* obstruir; atestar (*de cosas*); poner en desorden; *s.* desorden, confusión.

coach [kotʃ] *s.* coche; entrenador (*e. deportes*); maestro particular; *v.* aleccionar; guiar, adiestrar, *Am.* entrenar; **to — with** ser instruido o entrenado

37   coa–col

por.

coachman [kótʃmən] s. cochero.

coagulate [koǽgjəlet] v. coagular(se), cuajar(se).

coal [kol] s. carbón; ascua, brasa; **hard —** carbón de piedra, antracita; **soft — hulla; — bin** carbonera; **— dealer** carbonero; **— oil** kerosina; **— tar** alquitrán de carbón; v. cargar de carbón, echar carbón; proveer(se) de carbón.

coalition [koəlíʃən] s. coalición.

coarse [kors] adj. (crude) burdo, basto; tosco; áspero; (rude) rudo; grosero; vulgar; tosco; **— sand** arena gruesa.

coarseness [kórsnɪs] s. tosquedad; vulgaridad, grosería, rudeza.

coast [kost] s. costa, litoral; **— guard** guardacostas, guarda de costas; v. costear, navegar por la costa; deslizar(se), resbalar(se) cuesta abajo.

coastal [kóstl] adj. costero, costanero, de la costa.

coastline [kóstlaɪn] s. costa, litoral.

coat [kot] s. chaqueta, americana; Am. saco; lana, pelo (de un animal); **lady's —** abrigo de señora; **— hanger** colgador; **— of arms** escudo de armas; **— of paint** capa de pintura; v. cubrir; revestir, dar una mano (de pintura); **to — with sugar** azucarar, bañar en azúcar.

coating [kótɪŋ] s. capa.

coattail [kóttel] s. faldón.

coax [koks] v. rogar o persuadir con halagos, halagar, tentar.

cob [kab] s. carozo, zuro (de la mazorca del maíz), Ven., Col., Carib. tusa, Méx., C.A. olote.

cobalt [kóbɔlt] s. cobalto.

cobbler [káblɚ] s. remendón (zapatero); pudín de bizcocho y fruta.

cobblestone [káblston] s. guijarro; adj. empedrado.

cobweb [kábwɛb] s. telaraña.

cocaine [kokén] s. cocaína.

cock [kak] s. gallo; macho de ave; espita, grifo; martillo (de armas de fuego); **—sure** muy seguro de sí mismo; v. amartillar (un arma de fuego); ladear (la cabeza), ladearse (el sombrero).

cockfight [kákfaɪt] s. pelea de gallos, riña de gallos.

cockpit [kákpɪt] s. gallera; (airplane) cabina.

cockroach [kákrotʃ] s. cucaracha.

cocktail [káktel] s. coctel; aperitivo (de ostras, almejas, frutas, etc.).

cocky [kákɪ] adj. arrogante, Am. retobado.

cocoa [kóko] s. cacao; bebida de cacao, chocolate.

coconut [kókənət] s. coco (fruta).

cocoon [kəkún] s. capullo (del gusano de seda, etc.).

cod [kad] s. N.Esp. abadejo; Andalucía, Am. bacalao; **cod-liver oil** aceite de hígado de bacalao.

coddle [kádl] v. mimar, consentir.

code [kod] s. código; clave; **— mes-**

sage comunicación en clave; **signal — código** de señales.

codfish [kádfɪʃ] = cod.

coerce [koɝ́s] v. forzar, obligar.

coercion [koɝ́ʃən] s. coacción.

coexistence [koɛgzístəns] s. coexistencia.

coffee [kɔ́fɪ] s. café; **— shop** café; **— tree** cafeto; **black —** café solo.

coffeepot [kɔ́fɪpat] s. cafetera.

coffer [kɔ́fɚ] s. cofre, arca.

coffin [kɔ́fɪn] s. ataúd, féretro.

cog [kag] s. diente; **— wheel** rueda dentada.

cognate [kágnet] s. cognato.

coherent [kohírənt] adj. coherente; conexo.

cohesion [kohíʒən] s. cohesión.

coiffure [kwafjúr] s. tocado, peinado.

coil [kɔɪl] s. rollo; rosca; espiral de alambre; **electric —** bobina; v. arrollar(se), enrollar(se); enroscar(se).

coin [kɔɪn] s. moneda; v. acuñar; inventar, forjar (una frase o palabra).

coinage [kɔ́ɪnɪdʒ] s. acuñación; sistema monetario; moneda, monedas; invención (de una palabra o frase).

coincide [koɪnsáɪd] v. coincidir.

coincidence [koínsədəns] s. coincidencia; casualidad.

coke [kok] s. cok, coque (combustible).

cold [kold] adj. frío; **— cream** crema cosmética; **— meat** fiambre; **— wave** ola de frío; **— war** guerra fría; **to be —** tener frío; **it is — today** hace frío hoy; s. frío; catarro, resfriado; **to catch a —** resfriarse, acatarrarse.

coldness [kóldnɪs] s. frialdad; indiferencia, despego.

colic [kálɪk] s. cólico.

collaborate [kəlǽbəret] v. colaborar.

collaboration [kəlæbəréʃən] s. colaboración.

collapse [kəlǽps] s. desplome, derrumbe, derrumbamiento; hundimiento; postración; v. doblar(se), plegar(se); contraer (el volumen); hundirse, derrumbarse, desplomarse; sufrir una postración.

collar [kálɚ] s. collar; cuello (de vestido, camisa, etc.); collera (para mulas o caballos de tiro); v. acollarar, poner collar a; coger o agarrar por el cuello; prender.

collate [kəlét, kólet] v. cotejar; colacionar.

collateral [kəlǽtərəl] adj. colateral; auxiliar, subsidiario, accesorio; s. garantía (para un préstamo bancario).

colleague [kálig] s. colega.

collect [kəlékt] v. recoger; coleccionar; cobrar; recaudar (impuestos); reunir(se); congregarse; **to — oneself** calmarse; sosegarse, reportarse.

collection [kəlékʃən] s. colección; agrupación (de gente); recolección, cobranza, cobro, recaudación, colecta.

collective [kəléktɪv] adj. colectivo.

collectivism [kəléktəvɪzm] s. colectivismo.

collector [kəléktə] *s.* colector; coleccionista (*de sellos, objetos artísticos, etc.*); cobrador (*de billetes, deudas, etc.*); recaudador (*de impuestos*).

college [kálɪdʒ] *s.* universidad; **— of engineering** facultad de ingeniería; **— of medicine** escuela (*facultad*) de medicina.

collide [kəláid] *v.* chocar; estar en conflicto, oponerse.

collie [kálɪ] *s.* perro de pastor.

collision [kəlíʒən] *s.* choque, colisión; oposición, pugna (*de intereses, ideas, etc.*).

colloquial [kəlókwɪəl] *adj.* familiar; **— expression** locución o frase familiar.

collusion [kəlúʒɪən] *s.* confabulación.

colon [kólən] *s.* colon (*del intestino*); dos puntos (*signo de puntuación*).

colonel [kʒ́n] *s.* coronel.

colonial [kəlóniəl] *adj.* colonial.

colonist [kálənɪst] *s.* colono, colonizador.

colonization [kalənəzéʃən] *s.* colonización.

colonize [kálənaɪz] *v.* colonizar; establecerse en colonia.

colony [kálənɪ] *s.* colonia.

color [kʌ́lə] *s.* color; colorido; **the -s** la bandera; *v.* colorar; colorear; dar colorido; pintar; teñir; iluminar (*una fotografía, grabado, etc.*); ruborizarse.

colored [kʌ́ləd] *adj.* colorado, teñido, colorido, pintado; de color; coloreado; **— person** persona de color.

colorful [kʌ́ləfəl] *adj.* lleno de color; colorido; vistoso; vívido; pintoresco.

coloring [kʌ́lərɪŋ] *s.* colorido; coloración; colorante.

colorless [kʌ́ləlɪs] *adj.* incoloro; descolorido.

colossal [kəlásl] *adj.* colosal.

colt [kolt] *s.* potro.

Columbian [kəlʌ́mbɪən] *adj.* colombiano, de Colombia; colombino, referente a Cristóbal Colón.

column [kálən] *s.* columna.

comb [kom] *s.* peine; peineta (*de mujer*); cresta (*de gallo*); rastrillo, carda (*para lana*); almohaza (*para caballos*); panal (*de miel*); *v.* peinar; rastrillar, cardar (*lana*); escudriñar; **to — one's hair** peinarse.

combat [kámbæt] *s.* combate, pelea; *v.* combatir.

combatant [kámbətənt] *adj. & s.* combatiente.

combination [kambənéʃən] *s.* combinación.

combine [kəmbáin] *v.* combinar(se), unir(se).

combo [kámbo] *s.* batería de jazz.

combustible [kəmbʌ́stəbl] *adj. & s.* combustible.

combustion [kəmbʌ́stʃən] *s.* combustión.

come [kʌm] *v.* venir; llegar; provenir; **to — about** suceder; **to — again** volver, volver a venir; **to — back** volver, regresar; **to — downstairs** bajar; **to — in** entrar; **to — out** salir; **to — of age** llegar a mayor edad; **to — off** soltarse, zafarse; **to — to** volver en sí; **to — to terms** ponerse de acuerdo, ajustarse; **to — up** subir; surgir (*una cuestión*); *p.p. de* **to come**.

comedian [kəmídɪən] *s.* cómico, comediante.

comedy [kámədɪ] *s.* comedia.

comely [kʌ́mlɪ] *adj.* agradable a la vista, gentil, bien parecido.

comet [kámɪt] *s.* cometa.

comfort [kʌ́mfət] *s.* comodidad; bienestar; alivio, consuelo; *v.* consolar, confortar, aliviar.

comfortable [kʌ́mfətəbl] *adj.* cómodo; confortable; **— life** vida holgada; **— income** un buen pasar, renta suficiente; **comfortably** *adv.* cómodamente; con comodidad; holgadamente.

comforter [kʌ́mfətə] *s.* consolador; edredón, cobertor acolchado.

comfortless [kʌ́mfətlɪs] *adj.* incómodo; desconsolado.

comic [kámɪk] *adj.* cómico; chistoso; gracioso; **-s** *s. pl.* caricaturas, historietas cómicas.

comical [kámɪkl] *adj.* cómico, gracioso.

coming [kámɪŋ] *adj.* que viene, llega; próximo; venidero; *s.* venida, llegada; **— of Christ** advenimiento de Cristo.

comma [kámə] *s.* coma.

command [kəmænd] *s.* (*order*) mando; mandato, orden; mandamiento; (*post*) comandancia; (*dominance*) dominio; **at your —** a la orden de Vd., a la disposición de Vd.; **he has a good — of English** domina bien el inglés; *v.* mandar; ordenar; dominar; comandar; **to — respect** inspirar respeto, imponerse.

commander [kəmǽndə] *s.* jefe; mandante; teniente de navío; comendador (*de ciertas órdenes*); **— in chief** comandante en jefe; general en jefe.

commandment [kəmǽndmənt] *s.* mandamiento; mandato, orden.

commando [kəmǽndo] *s.* comando.

commemorate [kəmémərət] *v.* conmemorar.

commence [kəméns] *v.* comenzar.

commencement [kəménsmənt] *s.* comienzo, principio; acto de distribución de diplomas.

commend [kəménd] *v.* alabar, elogiar; encomendar, encargar; recomendar.

commendation [kamandéʃən] *s.* encomio, alabanza.

comment [kámənt] *s.* comentario, observación, nota; *v.* comentar; hacer observaciones; hacer comentarios.

commentary [káməntɛrɪ] *s.* comentario.

commentator [káməntetə] *s.* comentador; comentarista; **radio —** comentarista radial.

commerce [káməs] *s.* comercio.

commercial [kəmʒ́ʃəl] *adj.* comercial.

commiseration [kəmɪzəréʃən] *s.* compasión.

commissar [kámɪsar] s. comisario.

commissary [kámǝsɛrɪ] s. comisario.

commission [kǝmíʃǝn] s. comisión; encargo; junta; nombramiento; **to put out of** — inutilizar; descomponer, quebrar; retirar del servicio (un navío); v. comisionar; encargar; nombrar; poner en servicio (un navío); **-ed officer** oficial comisionado (alférez u oficial superior a éste).

commissioner [kǝmíʃǝnǝ] s. comisionado; comisario; **police** — comisario de policía.

commit [kǝmít] v. (perpetrate) cometer; (entrust) encargar; **to** — **to memory** aprender de memoria; **to** — **to prison** encarcelar; **to** — **oneself** dar o expresar su opinión, expresarse abiertamente, comprometerse.

committee [kǝmítɪ] s. comité; comisión, junta; — **of one** comisionado o delegado único.

commodity [kǝmádǝtɪ] s. mercancía; género, mercadería, artículo de comercio, producto.

common [kámǝn] adj. común; general; corriente; vulgar, ordinario; público; — **law** derecho consuetudinario; — **sense** sentido común; — **soldier** soldado raso; — **market** mercado común, **-s** s. pl. refectorio (de un colegio o universidad); ejido, campo común; **-ly** adv. comúnmente, por lo común.

commonness [kámǝnnɪs] s. vulgaridad, ordinariez; frecuencia.

commonplace [kámǝnples] adj. común, trivial; s. lugar común.

commonwealth [kámǝnwɛlθ] s. estado; república; pueblo, colectividad.

commotion [kǝmóʃǝn] s. conmoción; tumulto; bullicio; levantamiento.

commune [kǝmjún] v. comunicarse (con); comulgar.

communicate [kǝmjúnǝket] v. comunicar(se); transmitir.

communication [kǝmjunǝkéʃǝn] s. comunicación.

communicative [kǝmjúnǝketɪv] adj. comunicativo.

communion [kǝmjúnjǝn] s. comunión.

communism [kámjʊnɪzǝm] s. comunismo.

communist [kámjʊnɪst] s. & adj. comunista.

community [kǝmjúnǝtɪ] s. comunidad; sociedad; vecindario, barrio; — **chest** caja de beneficencia, fondos de beneficencia.

commute [kǝmjút] v. conmutar.

compact [kǝmpǽkt] adj. compacto; denso; apretado; conciso, sucinto; [kámpækt] s. pacto, trato, convenio; polvera.

compactness [kǝmpǽktnɪs] s. solidez; densidad; concisión.

companion [kǝmpǽnjǝn] s. compañero; acompañante.

companionship [kǝmpǽnjǝnʃɪp] s. compañerismo, camaradería; com-

pañía.

company [kámpǝnɪ] s. compañía; sociedad; visita; **ship's** — tripulación; **to keep** — **with** acompañar a; cortejar a; tener relaciones con, frecuentar la compañía de.

comparable [kámpǝrǝbl] adj. comparable.

comparative [kǝmpǽrǝtɪv] adj. comparativo.

compare [kǝmpér] v. comparar; cotejar; confrontar; contrastar; **beyond** — incomparable, sin par, sin igual, sin comparación.

comparison [kǝmpǽrǝsn̩] s. comparación; símil; **beyond** — incomparable, sin comparación; **in** — **with** comparado con.

compartment [kǝmpártmǝnt] s. compartimiento, sección, división; departamento.

compass [kʌmpǝs] s. compás (para dibujar); brújula; área, ámbito; alcance.

compassion [kǝmpǽʃǝn] s. compasión, lástima.

compassionate [kǝmpǽʃǝnɪt] adj. compasivo, misericordioso.

compatible [kǝmpǽtǝbl] adj. compatible.

compatriot [kǝmpétrɪǝt] s. compatriota.

compel [kǝmpél] v. compeler, obligar; exigir.

compensate [kámpǝnset] v. compensar; recompensar; remunerar.

compensation [kampǝnséʃǝn] s. compensación; recompensa; remuneración.

compete [kǝmpít] v. competir.

competence [kámpǝtǝns] s. competencia, aptitud, capacidad.

competent [kámpǝtǝnt] adj. competente; calificado; capaz.

competition [kampǝtíʃǝn] s. competencia; concurso, certamen; contienda.

competitive [kǝmpétǝtɪv] adj. en competencia; — **examination** oposición, concurso.

competitor [kǝmpétǝtǝ] s. competidor; rival; opositor.

compile [kǝmpáɪl] v. compilar, recopilar.

complacency [kǝmplésn̩sɪ] s. complacencia, contentamiento.

complacent [kǝmplésn̩t] adj. complaciente, satisfecho.

complain [kǝmplén] v. quejarse; querellarse.

complaint [kǝmplént] s. queja; quejido, lamento; dolencia, enfermedad; **to lodge a** — hacer una reclamación.

complement [kámplǝmǝnt] s. complemento; [kámplǝmɛnt] v. complementar, completar.

complete [kǝmplít] adj. completo; v. completar; terminar; **-ly** adv. completamente, por completo.

completeness [kǝmplítnɪs] s. perfección; minuciosidad; lo completo; lo cabal; lo acabado.

completion [kəmplíʃən] *s.* completamiento; terminación, conclusión; cumplimiento.

complex [kámplɛks] *s.* complejo; [kəmplɛ́ks] *adj.* complejo; compuesto; complicado.

complexion [kəmplɛ́kʃən] *s.* cutis, tez; aspecto.

complexity [kəmplɛ́ksətɪ] *s.* complejidad.

compliance [kəmpláɪəns] *s.* complacencia; condescendencia; conformidad; cumplimiento; **in — with** en conformidad con; **in — with** de acuerdo con, conforme a.

complicate [kámpləket] *v.* complicar.

complicated [kámpləketɪd] *adj.* complicado.

complication [kampləkéʃən] *s.* complicación.

complicity [kəmplísətɪ] *s.* complicidad.

compliment [kámpləmənt] *s.* cumplido, cumplimiento; requiebro, lisonja, galantería; **to send one's -s** enviar saludos; [kámpləmənt] *v.* cumplimentar; requebrar; lisonjear; alabar.

comply [kəmplái] *v.* consentir, conformarse (con), obrar de acuerdo (con); cumplir (con).

component [kəmpónənt] *adj. & s.* componente.

compose [kəmpóz] *v.* componer; **to — oneself** sosegarse, serenarse, calmarse.

composed [kəmpózd] *adj.* compuesto; tranquilo, sereno, sosegado; **to be — of** estar compuesto de, componerse de, constar de.

composer [kəmpózɚ] *s.* compositor; autor.

composite [kəmpázɪt] *adj.* compuesto; *s.* compuesto; mezcla.

composition [kampəzíʃən] *s.* composición; arreglo; compuesto.

composure [kəmpóʒɚ] *s.* compostura, calma, serenidad.

compound [kámpaʊnd] *adj. & s.* compuesto; [kəmpáʊnd] *v.* componer; mezclar, combinar; **to — interest** calcular el interés compuesto.

comprehend [kamprɪhɛ́nd] *v.* comprender; abarcar, abrazar, incluir.

comprehensible [kamprɪhɛ́nsəbl] *adj.* comprensible, inteligible.

comprehension [kamprɪhɛ́nʃən] *s.* comprensión.

comprehensive [kamprɪhɛ́nsɪv] *adj.* comprensivo; inclusivo.

compress [kámprɛs] *s.* compresa; [kəmprɛ́s] *v.* comprimir, apretar, condensar.

compression [kəmprɛ́ʃən] *s.* compresión.

comprise [kəmpráɪz] *v.* comprender, abarcar, incluir, abrazar; constar de.

compromise [kámprəmaɪz] *s.* compromiso; arreglo; avenencia; término medio; *v.* comprometer; avenirse, transigir, *Am.* transar.

comptroller [kəntrólɚ] *s.* interventor, *Am.* contralor.

compulsion [kəmpʌ́lʃən] *s.* compulsión, coacción.

compulsory [kəmpʌ́lsərɪ] *adj.* obligatorio.

computation [kampjətéʃən] *s.* cómputo, cálculo.

compute [kəmpjút] *v.* computar.

computer [kəmpjútɚ] *s. Esp.* calculadora electrónica; *Arg.* computadora; programadora.

computerize [kəmpjútɚaɪz] *v.* someter datos a la calculadora electrónica; suplir con sistema computadora.

comrade [kámræd] *s.* camarada, compañero.

concave [kankév] *adj.* cóncavo.

conceal [kənsíl] *v.* encubrir, ocultar, esconder.

concealment [kənsílmənt] *s.* encubrimiento.

concede [kənsíd] *v.* conceder; otorgar; admitir, reconocer.

conceit [kənsít] *s.* presunción, amor propio, vanagloria; concepto, agudeza.

conceited [kənsítɪd] *adj.* presuntuoso, presumido, vanidoso, engreído.

conceivable [kənsívəbl] *adj.* concebible, imaginable, comprensible.

conceive [kənsív] *v.* concebir; imaginar.

concentrate [kánsntret] *v.* concentrar(se), reconcentrar(se).

concentration [kansntréʃən] *s.* concentración; reconcentración.

concept [kánsɛpt] *s.* concepto, idea; opinión.

conception [kənsɛ́pʃən] *s.* concepción; concepto, idea.

concern [kənsɚ́n] *s.* (*business*) compañía, negociación; negocio; establecimiento mercantil; (*interest*) cuidado; interés; preocupación; **to be of no —** no ser de consecuencia; *v.* concernir, importar, interesar; preocupar; **in all that -s him** en cuanto le atañe, en cuanto le concierne.

concerned [kənsɚ́nd] *adj.* interesado; preocupado, intranquilo, inquieto, ansioso; **to be — about** interesarse por, preocuparse por; **as far as I am —** por lo que me concierne, por lo que me toca, en cuanto a mí me atañe.

concerning [kənsɚ́nɪŋ] *prep.* tocante a, respecto a, acerca de.

concert [kánsɚt] *s.* concierto; [kənsɚ́t] *v.* concertar, arreglar (*un plan*).

concession [kənsɛ́ʃən] *s.* concesión.

conciliate [kənsílɪet] *v.* conciliar, poner en armonía; ganar la voluntad de.

concise [kənsáɪs] *adj.* conciso, sucinto.

conciseness [kənsáɪsnɪs] *s.* concisión, brevedad.

conclude [kənklúd] *v.* concluir; acabar, terminar; deducir; decidir.

conclusion [kənklúʒən] *s.* conclusión.

conclusive [kənklúsɪv] *adj.* conclusivo,

concluyente.

concoct [kankákt] v. confeccionar; preparar (*combinando diversos ingredientes*); inventar, urdir.

concoction [kankákʃən] s. cocimiento, menjurje; mezcla.

concord [kánkərd] s. concordia, conformidad, acuerdo; convenio, pacto.

concrete [kankrit] adj. concreto; de hormigón, de cemento; s. hormigón, cemento, *Am.* concreto.

concubine [káŋkjubaɪn] s. concubina.

concur [kankə́r] v. estar de acuerdo, ser del mismo parecer; unirse.

concussion [kankʌ́ʃən] s. concusión.

condemn [kandém] v. condenar; **to — a building** condenar un edificio.

condemnation [kandɛmnéʃən] s. condenación.

condensation [kandɛnséʃən] s. condensación; resumen, compendio.

condense [kandéns] v. condensar(se).

condescend [kandɪsénd] v. condescender.

condescension [kandɪsénʃən] s. condescendencia.

condiment [kándəmənt] s. condimento.

condition [kandíʃən] s. condición; estado; nota o calificación provisional; **on — that** a condición de que, con tal que; v. acondicionar; poner en buena condición; estipular; reprobar provisionalmente (*a un estudiante*).

conditional [kandíʃən] adj. condicional.

condole [kandól] v. condolerse; **to — with** dar el pésame a; consolar a.

condolence [kandólans] s. pésame.

condone [kandón] v. dispensar; perdonar; condonar.

conduce [kandjús] v. conducir.

conducive [kandjúsɪv] adj. conducente.

conduct [kándʌkt] s. (*behavior*) conducta; comportamiento,. proceder; (*handling*) dirección, manejo; [kandʌ́kt] v. conducir; dirigir, manejar; **to — oneself well** portarse bien.

conductor [kandʌ́ktə] s. conductor; guía; **orchestra —** director de orquesta; **train —** revisor; cobrador, *Am.* conductor.

conduit [kándɪt] s. conducto; caño; cañería, tubería.

cone [kon] s. cono; **paper —** cucurucho; **pine —** piña.

confection [kanfékʃən] s. confección; confitura; confite, dulce.

confectionery [kanfékʃanɛrɪ] s. confitería; dulcería; confites, dulces.

confederacy [kanfédərəsɪ] s. confederación.

confederate [kanfédərɪt] adj. & s. confederado; [kanfédəret] v. confederar(se).

confederation [kanfɛdəréʃən] s. confederación.

confer [kanfə́r] v. conferir, conceder; conferenciar, consultar.

conference [kánfərəns] s. conferencia;

consulta, junta, sesión.

confess [kanfés] v. confesar(se); reconocer, admitir.

confession [kanféʃən] s. confesión.

confessional [kanféʃən]] s. confesionario.

confessor [kanfésə] s. confesor.

confidant [kanfədǽnt] s. confidente.

confide [kanfáɪd] v. confiar; fiar.

confidence [kánfədəns] s. confianza; confidencia; **— game** estafa; **— man** estafador.

confident [kánfədənt] adj. confiado; seguro, cierto; **-ly** adv. confiadamente, con toda seguridad.

confidential [kanfədénʃəl] adj. confidencial; íntimo; secreto; **-ly** adv. en confianza.

confine [kánfaɪn] s. confín; [kanfáɪn] v. confinar; encerrar; **to — oneself to** limitarse a; **to be -ed in bed** estar encamado, guardar cama.

confinement [kanfáɪnmənt] s. encerramiento; encierro; prisión, encarcelación.

confirm [kanfə́rm] v. confirmar.

confirmation [kanfəméʃən] s. confirmación.

confiscate [kánfɪsket] v. confiscar.

conflagration [kanflagréʃən] s. conflagración, incendio.

conflict [kánflɪkt] s. conflicto, oposición, choque; lucha, combate; [kanflíkt] v. chocar, oponerse, estar en conflicto.

conform [kanfə́rm] v. conformar(se).

conformity [kanfə́rmətɪ] s. conformidad.

confound [kanfaúnd] v. confundir, perturbar, desconcertar, aturdir; **— it!** ¡caramba!

confront [kanfrʌ́nt] v. confrontar; carear; poner cara a cara (*a dos reos*); encararse con, afrontar, hacer frente a, arrostrar.

confuse [kanfjúz] v. confundir; trastornar; embrollar; desconcertar.

confused [kanfjúzd] adj. confuso; revuelto; desconcertado, perplejo; **to become —** confundirse; desconcertarse.

confusing [kanfjúzɪŋ] adj. confuso, revuelto; desconcertante.

confusion [kanfjúʒən] s. confusión; desorden; tumulto; perplejidad.

congeal [kandʒíl] v. congelar(se), helar(se), cuajar(se).

congenial [kandʒínjəl] adj. congenial; simpático; **to be — with** congeniar con, simpatizar con.

congestion [kandʒéstʃən] s. congestión; aglomeración.

conglomeration [kanglaməréʃən] s. aglomeración.

congratulate [kangrǽtʃəlet] v. congratular, felicitar, dar el parabién.

congratulation [kangrǽtʃəléʃən] s. congratulación, felicitación, parabién, enhorabuena.

congregate [káŋgrɪget] v. congregar(se), juntar(se), reunir(se).

congregation [kaŋgrɪgéʃən] s. congregación; asamblea, reunión; colección, agregado; fieles, feligreses (de una iglesia).

congress [káŋgrəs] s. congreso; asamblea.

congressional [kəngréʃən‖] adj. perteneciente al congreso.

congressman [káŋgrəsmən] s. congresista, diputado, representante.

conjecture [kəndʒéktʃə] s. conjetura, suposición; v. conjeturar, suponer.

conjugate [kándʒəget] v. conjugar.

conjugation [kandʒəgéʃən] s. conjugación.

conjunction [kəndʒáŋkʃən] s. conjunción.

conjure [kándʒə] v. conjurar; **to — up** evocar; [kəndʒúr] rogar, implorar.

connect [kənékt] v. conectar; unir(se), juntar(se); enlazar(se); relacionar(se); acoplar.

connection [kənékʃən] s. conexión; enlace; vínculo; unión; relación; -s parientes; amigos, amistades.

conniption [kəníp∫ən] s. pataleta; **to have a —** darle a uno una pataleta.

connive [kənáɪv] v. conspirar; disimular; hacerse cómplice.

connoisseur [kanəsʒ́] s. conocedor, perito.

conquer [káŋkə] v. conquistar; vencer.

conqueror [káŋkərə] s. conquistador; vencedor.

conquest [kánkwɛst] s. conquista.

conscience [kánʃəns] s. conciencia.

conscientious [kanʃiénʃəs] adj. concienzudo.

conscious [kánʃəs] adj. consciente; sabedor; **-ly** adv. conscientemente; a sabiendas.

consciousness [kánʃəsnɪs] s. consciencia, estado consciente; **to lose —** perder el sentido o conocimiento.

conscript [kənskrípt] v. reclutar; [kánskrɪpt] s. recluta.

consecrate [kánsɪkret] v. consagrar; dedicar.

consecration [kansɪkréʃən] s. consagración; dedicación.

consecutive [kənsékjətɪv] adj. consecutivo.

consensus [kənsénsəs] s. consenso.

consent [kənsént] s. consentimiento; permiso, asentimiento; v. consentir; permitir, asentir.

consequence [kánsəkwɛns] s. consecuencia.

consequent [kánsəkwɛnt] adj. consecuente; consiguiente; s. consecuente, consiguiente, consecuencia; **-ly** adv. por consiguiente, por consecuencia.

consequential [kansəkwéntʃ∫] adj. de consecuencia.

conservation [kansəvéʃən] s. conservación; preservación.

conservative [kənsʒ́vatɪv] adj. conservador; conservativo; s. conservador.

conservatory [kənsʒ́vətorɪ] s. conservatorio; invernadero.

conserve [kənsʒ́v] s. conserva, dulce; v.

conservar; preservar.

consider [kənsídə] v. considerar.

considerable [kənsídərəb‖] adj. considerable; cuantioso; **considerably** adv. considerablemente; **considerably older** bastante más viejo.

considerate [kənsídərɪt] adj. considerado.

consideration [kənsɪdəréʃən] s. (respect) respeto; consideración; importancia; (pay) remuneración; **in — of** en atención a, teniendo en cuenta, en razón de, en vista de.

considering [kənsídərɪŋ] prep. en razón de, en vista de; en atención a, en consideración de.

consign [kənsáɪn] v. consignar; enviar; entregar.

consignee [kənsaɪní] s. consignatario.

consignment [kənsáɪnmənt] s. consignación.

consist [kənsíst] v. consistir (en); constar (de).

consistency [kənsístənsɪ] s. consecuencia; consistencia, firmeza, solidez.

consistent [kənsístənt] adj. consecuente, lógico; compatible; consistente, coherente.

consolation [kansəléʃən] s. consolación; consuelo.

console [kənsól] v. consolar.

consolidate [kənsáladet] v. consolidar(se); unir(se), combinar(se).

consonant [kánsənənt] adj. consonante; conforme; s. consonante.

consort [kánsɔrt] s. consorte; [kənsɔ́rt] v. **to — with** asociarse con.

conspicuous [kənspíkjuəs] adj. conspicuo, notorio; manifiesto, sobresaliente.

conspiracy [kənspírəsɪ] s. conspiración, conjuración.

conspirator [kənspírətə] s. conspirador, conjurado.

conspire [kənspáɪr] v. conspirar; tramar, maquinar.

constable [kánstəb‖] s. alguacil, policía; condestable (título).

constancy [kánstənsɪ] s. constancia.

constant [kánstənt] adj. constante; s. constante, cantidad constante; **-ly** adv. constantemente, continuamente, siempre; a menudo.

constellation [kanstəléʃən] s. constelación.

consternation [kanstənéʃən] s. consternación.

constipate [kánstəpet] v. estreñir.

constipation [kanstəpéʃən] s. estreñimiento.

constituent [kənstítʃuənt] adj. constituyente; constitutivo; componente; s. componente, elemento; elector, votante.

constitute [kánstətjut] v. constituir; componer; establecer.

constitution [kanstətjúʃən] s. constitución.

constitutional [kanstətjúʃən‖] adj. constitucional; s. paseo a pie, caminata (*para hacer ejercicio*).

constrain [kənstrén] *v.* constreñir; obligar, forzar; apretar, comprimir.

construct [kənstrákt] *v.* construir, fabricar.

construction [kənstrákʃən] *s.* construcción; estructura; interpretación.

constructive [kənstráktɪv] *adj.* constructivo; de utilidad positiva; provechoso.

construe [kənstrú] *v.* interpretar, explicar.

consul [káns] *s.* cónsul.

consulate [kánsǀɪt] *s.* consulado.

consult [kənsʌ́lt] *v.* consultar.

consultant [kənsʌ́ltənt] *s.* consultante.

consultation [kansǀtéʃən] *s.* consulta.

consume [kənsúm] *v.* consumir; gastar; perder (*el tiempo*).

consumer [kənsúmə] *s.* consumidor.

consummate [kánsəmet] *v.* consumar, completar; [kənsʌ́mɪt] *adj.* consumado, perfecto, completo.

consumption [kənsʌ́mpʃən] *s.* consumo, gasto; consunción; tisis, tuberculosis.

consumptive [kənsʌ́mptɪv] *adj.* tísico.

contact [kántækt] *s.* contacto; *v.* tocar; poner(se) en contacto con; estar en contacto con.

contagion [kəntédʒən] *s.* contagio.

contagious [kəntédʒəs] *adj.* contagioso.

contain [kəntén] *v.* contener; encerrar; tener cabida para; reprimir, refrenar; **to — oneself** contenerse, refrenarse.

container [kənténə] *s.* envase, caja, recipiente.

contaminate [kəntǽmənet] *v.* contaminar, viciar, inficionar.

contemplate [kántəmplet] *v.* contemplar; meditar; tener la intención de; proyectar.

contemplation [kantəmpléʃən] *s.* contemplación; meditación; intención, propósito.

contemporary [kəntémpəreri] *adj.* contemporáneo; coetáneo.

contempt [kəntémpt] *s.* desdén, menosprecio; desprecio; **— of court** contumacia.

contemptible [kəntémptəb] *adj.* despreciable, vil.

contemptuous [kəntémptʃuəs] *adj.* desdeñoso.

contend [kənténd] *v.* contender; competir; argüir; altercar; sostener, afirmar.

content [kántent] *s.* contenido; sustancia; capacidad, volumen; **-s** contenido; **table of -s** tabla de materias, índice general.

content [kəntént] *adj.* contento; satisfecho; *s.* contento; satisfacción; **to one's heart's —** a pedir de boca; hasta saciarse; a su entera satisfacción; *v.* contentar; satisfacer.

contented [kənténtɪd] *adj.* contento, satisfecho.

contention [kənténʃən] *s.* contención, contienda, disputa, controversia; tema, argumento, aseveración.

contentment [kənténtmənt] *s.* contentamiento, contento.

contest [kántɛst] *s.* concurso, certamen; debate; contienda; torneo; [kəntést] *v.* contender; disputar; luchar por; **to — with** competir con.

context [kántɛkst] *s.* contexto.

contiguous [kəntígjuəs] *adj.* contiguo; adyacente.

continent [kántɪnənt] *s.* continente; *adj.* continente, casto, moderado.

continental [kantənántl] *adj. & s.* continental.

contingency [kəntíndʒənsɪ] *s.* contingencia, eventualidad.

contingent [kəntíndʒənt] *adj. & s.* contingente.

continual [kəntínjuəl] *adj.* continuo; frecuente; **-ly** *adv.* de continuo, continuamente, frecuentemente.

continuance [kəntínjuəns] *s.* continuación; aplazamiento.

continuation [kəntinjuéʃən] *s.* continuación.

continue [kəntínju] *v.* continuar.

continuity [kantənúəti] *s.* continuidad.

continuous [kəntínjuəs] *adj.* continuo, sin parar, sin cesar.

contortion [kəntɔ́rʃən] *s.* contorsión.

contour [kántur] *s.* contorno; perímetro.

contraband [kántrəbænd] *s.* contrabando.

contract [kántrækt] *s.* contrato, pacto, convenio; contrata; **marriage —** esponsales; [kəntrǽkt] *v.* contratar; contraer(se), encoger(se); **to — an illness** contraer una enfermedad; **to — the brows** fruncir las cejas.

contraction [kəntrǽkʃən] *s.* contracción.

contractor [kántræktə] *s.* contratista.

contradict [kantrədíkt] *v.* contradecir; contrariar.

contradiction [kantrədíkʃən] *s.* contradicción; contrariedad.

contradictory [kantrədíktəri] *adj.* contradictorio; opuesto, contrario.

contrary [kántreri] *adj.* contrario; opuesto; testarudo, obstinado; *s.* contrario; **on the —** al contrario.

contrast [kántræst] *s.* contraste; [kəntrǽst] *v.* contrastar.

contravene [kantrəvín] *v.* contravenir a; oponerse a.

contribute [kəntríbjut] *v.* contribuir.

contribution [kantrəbjúʃən] *s.* contribución; aportación; cuota; dádiva.

contributor [kəntríbjətə] *s.* contribuidor; colaborador.

contrite [kántraɪt] *adj.* contrito.

contrivance [kəntráɪvəns] *s.* traza, maquinación; artificio, invención; designio; artefacto, aparato, máquina.

contrive [kəntráɪv] *v.* tramar, maquinar; inventar, idear; proyectar; **to — to** buscar el medio de, tratar de, procurar.

control [kəntról] *s.* (*authority*) mando, manejo; dirección; (*instrument*) freno, regulador; restricción; *Am.* control;

-s mandos, controles; **— stick** palanca (de un aeroplano); **— tower** torre de mando; **to lose — of one's temper** perder la paciencia; v. gobernar, manejar, Am. controlar; regular, regularizar; restringir; contener, reprimir; tener a raya; **to — oneself** contenerse, dominarse.

controller [kəntrólə] s. interventor, registrador, Ríopl., C.A., Andes, Ven., Col. contralor, Ch., Méx. controlador; regulador; aparato de manejo y control.

controversy [kántrəvɜsɪ] s. controversia, debate, disputa.

conundrum [kənándrəm] s. adivinanza, acertijo.

convalesce [kɑnvəlés] v. convalescer.

convene [kənvín] v. juntar, convocar; reunirse.

convenience [kənvínjəns] s. conveniencia, comodidad; **at one's —** cuando le convenga a uno, cuando tenga oportunidad, cuando buenamente pueda.

convenient [kənvínjənt] adj. conveniente; oportuno; cómodo; a propósito; **-ly** adv. convenientemente, cómodamente.

convent [kánvɛnt] s. convento.

convention [kənvénʃən] s. convención; congreso, asamblea; convenio; costumbre, regla.

conventional [kənvénʃən!] adj. convencional; tradicional.

converge [kənvɜ́dʒ] v. converger o convergir.

conversant [kánvəsnt] adj.: **— with** versado en.

conversation [kɑnvəséʃən] s. conversación.

converse [kənvɜ́s] v. conversar, hablar, platicar.

conversion [kənvɜ́ʒən] s. conversión.

convert [kánvɜt] s. converso, persona convertida; catecúmeno (converso reciente); [kənvɜ́t] v. convertir(se).

convex [kɑnvéks] adj. convexo.

convey [kənvé] v. llevar; transportar; transferir, traspasar; transmitir; comunicar; **to — thanks** expresar agradecimiento, dar las gracias.

conveyance [kənvéəns] s. vehículo; transporte; transmisión; entrega; comunicación; traspaso; escritura de propiedad o traspaso.

convict [kánvɪkt] s. presidiario; reo; [kənvíkt] v. convencer (de un delito), declarar culpable; probar la culpabilidad de.

conviction [kənvíkʃən] s. convicción; convencimiento; prueba de culpabilidad.

convince [kənvíns] v. convencer.

convincing [kənvínsɪŋ] adj. convincente.

convocation [kɑnvəkéʃən] s. convocación; asamblea.

convoke [kənvók] v. convocar.

convoy [kánvɔɪ] s. convoy, escolta, guardia; [kənvɔ́ɪ] v. convoyar.

convulse [kənváls] v. crispar; agitar; convulsionar.

convulsion [kənválʃən] s. convulsión, agitación.

coo [ku] s. arrullo; v. arrullar.

cook [kʊk] s. cocinero, cocinera; v. cocinar, guisar; cocer; **to — up a plan** urdir un plan.

cookery [kúkərɪ] s. cocina, arte de cocinar.

cookie, cooky [kúkɪ] s. bizcochito, bollito.

cooking [kúkɪŋ] s. cocina, arte culinaria; **— stove** cocina de gas, cocina eléctrica, estufa; **— utensils** batería de cocina, trastos de cocina.

cool [kul] adj. fresco; frío, indiferente; calmo, sereno; s. fresco, frescura; v. refrescar; enfriar; templar, calmar; **to — off** enfriarse; calmarse.

coolant [kúlənt] s. líquido refrigerador.

coolness [kúlnɪs] s. fresco, frescura; frialdad, indiferencia.

coon [kun] s. coatí (cuadrúpedo carnívoro); negro; **a -'s age** una eternidad, mucho tiempo.

coop [kup] s. jaula; **chicken —** gallinero; v. enjaular; **to — up** encerrar.

cooperate [koápəret] v. cooperar.

cooperation [koɑpəréʃən] s. cooperación.

cooperative [koápəretɪv] adj. cooperativo; s. cooperativa, sociedad cooperativa.

coördinate [koɔ́rdnet] v. coordinar; [koɔ́rdnɪt] adj. coordinado.

coördination [koɔrdnéʃən] s. coordinación.

cop [kɑp] s. polizonte, policía.

cope [kop] v. **to — with** tener suficiente fuerza para; **I cannot — with this** no puedo con esto, no puedo dar abasto a esto.

copious [kópɪəs] adj. copioso, abundante.

copper [kápə] s. cobre; polizonte, policía; **— coin** moneda de cobre, centavo; **— kettle** marmita o caldera de cobre; adj. cobrizo.

copy [kápɪ] s. copia; ejemplar (de un libro); manuscrito (para el impresor); v. copiar; imitar; remedar.

copyright [kápɪraɪt] s. derecho de propiedad literaria; v. registrar, obtener patente de propiedad literaria.

coquette [kokét] s. coqueta.

coral [kɔ́rəl] s. coral; adj. coralino, de coral.

cord [kɔrd] s. cuerda; cordón, cordel; cuerda (medida de leña); tendón; **-s** pantalones de pana; **spinal —** espinazo, espina dorsal.

cordial [kɔ́rdʒəl] adj. & s. cordial.

corduroy [kɔrdərɔ́ɪ] s. pana; **-s** pantalones de pana; **— road** camino de troncos o maderos.

core [kor] s. corazón, centro; núcleo; esencia; v. cortar el centro o corazón de; despepitar (una manzana).

cork [kɔrk] s. corcho; tapón; **— tree** alcornoque; v. tapar con corcho.

corkscrew [kɔ́rkskru] *s.* tirabuzón, sacacorchos; *adj.* espiral, de forma espiral.

corn [kɔrn] *s.* maíz; grano, cereal; callo (*de los pies o manos*); **— bread** pan de maíz; **— meal** harina de maíz; *v.* salar, curar, acecinar.

corned beef [kɔ́rnd bif] *s.* carne de vaca curada (*en salmuera y salitre*).

corner [kɔ́rnə] *s.* (*interior*) rincón; rinconada; ángulo; (*exterior*) esquina; ángulo; (*monopoly*) monopolio; **— stone** piedra angular; **— table** (**— shelf, — bracket**) rinconera; *v.* arrinconar; acorralar; acaparar, monopolizar.

cornet [kɔrnét] *s.* corneta.

cornfield [kɔ́rnfild] *s.* maizal, *Am.* milpa.

cornice [kɔ́rnɪs] *s.* cornisa.

corollary [kɔ́rələrɪ] *s.* corolario; consecuencia natural.

coronation [kɔrənéʃən] *s.* coronación.

coronet [kɔ́rənɪt] *s.* coronilla, guirnalda.

corporal [kɔ́rpərəl] *adj.* corporal; corpóreo; *s.* cabo (*militar*).

corporation [kɔrpəréʃən] *s.* corporación; sociedad mercantil.

corps [kor] *s.* cuerpo (*grupo organizado*); **air —** cuerpo de aviación; **army —** cuerpo de ejército.

corpse [kɔrps] *s.* cadáver.

corpulent [kɔ́rpjələnt] *adj.* corpulento.

corpuscle [kɔ́rpʌsl] *s.* corpúsculo.

corral [kərǽl] *s.* corral; *v.* acorralar.

correct [kərékt] *v.* corregir; *adj.* correcto; **it is —** está bien; **-ly** *adv.* correctamente; **-ly done** bien hecho.

correction [kərékʃən] *s.* corrección.

correctness [kəréktnɪs] *s.* corrección.

corrector [kəréktə] *s.* corregidor, corrector.

correlate [kɔ́rəlet] *v.* correlacionar.

correspond [kɔrəspánd] *v.* corresponder; corresponderse, cartearse, escribirse.

correspondence [kɔrəspándəns] *s.* correspondencia.

correspondent [kɔrəspándənt] *adj.* correspondiente; *s.* correspondiente; corresponsal.

corresponding [kɔrəspándɪŋ] *adj.* correspondiente; conforme.

corridor [kɔ́rədə] *s.* corredor, pasillo, pasadizo.

corroborate [kərábəret] *v.* corroborar.

corrode [kəród] *v.* corroer(se).

corrugated iron [kɔ́rəgetəd áɪən] *s.* hierro acanalado.

corrupt [kərʌ́pt] *adj.* corrompido; perverso, depravado; **to become —** corromperse; *v.* corromper; pervertir; sobornar.

corruption [kərʌ́pʃən] *s.* corrupción; soborno; descomposición.

corset [kɔ́rsɪt] *s.* corsé.

cosmetic [kazmétɪk] *adj. & s.* cosmético.

cosmic [kázmɪk] *adj.* cósmico.

cosmonaut [kázmənɔt] *s.* cosmonauta.

cosmopolitan [kazməpálətn] *adj.* cosmopolita.

cost [kɔst] *s.* coste, costa o costo; **at all -s** a toda costa; **to sell at —** vender al costo; *v.* costar; *pret. & p.p. de* **to cost.**

costly [kɔ́stlɪ] *adj.* costoso.

costume [kástjum] *s.* vestuario, traje, vestido; atavío; indumentaria.

cot [kat] *s.* catre; **folding —** catre de tijera.

cottage [kátɪdʒ] *s.* casita, caseta; casa de campo; **— cheese** requesón.

cotton [kátn] *s.* algodón; **—seed** semilla de algodón; **— wool** algodón en rama; **— yarn** hilaza.

couch [kautʃ] *s.* canapé, diván; *v.* expresar; estar escondido o en acecho; **-ed in difficult language** expresado en lenguaje difícil.

cough [kɔf] *s.* tos; **— drop** pastilla para la tos; **whooping —** tos ferina; *v.* toser; **to — up** expectorar.

could [kud] *pret. del v. defect.* **can.**

council [káunsl] *s.* concilio; consejo; **city —** consejo muncipal.

councilman [káunslmən] *s.* concejal.

councilor [káunslə] *s.* concejal.

counsel [káunsl] *s.* (*advice*) consejo; parecer, dictamen; (*lawyer*) abogado consultor; *v.* aconsejar; recomendar.

counselor [káunslə] *s.* consejero; abogado consultor.

count [kaunt] *s.* (*reckoning*) cuenta, cálculo; cómputo; (*charge*) cargo, acusación; (*noble*) count; *v.* contar; valer, tener importancia; **to — on** contar con, confiar en.

countdown [káuntdaun] *s.* recuento descendente hasta cero.

countenance [káuntənəns] *s.* semblante, aspecto; **to give — to** favorecer, apoyar; aprobar; *v.* aprobar; favorecer, apoyar; tolerar.

counter [káuntə] *s.* contador; mostrador; tablero; ficha; *adj.* contrario, opuesto; *adv.* al contrario; **to run — to** ser contrario a, oponerse a; *v.* oponerse; contradecir; **to — a blow** devolver un golpe.

counteract [kauntərǽkt] *v.* contrarrestar, neutralizar.

counterbalance [kauntəbǽləns] *v.* contrapesar; equilibrar; [káuntəbæləns] *s.* contrapeso.

counterfeit [káuntəfɪt] *s.* falsificación; *adj.* falso; falsificado, falseado; contrahecho; **— money** moneda falsa; *v.* contrahacer, falsificar, falsear.

countermand [káuntəmænd] *s.* contraorden, contramando, revocación; cancelación; [kauntəmǽnd] *v.* contramandar, revocar, cancelar.

counterpart [káuntəpart] *s.* contraparte.

counterpoise [káuntəpɔiz] *s.* contrapeso; *v.* contrapesar.

countersign [káuntəsain] *s.* contraseña.

countess [káuntɪs] *s.* condesa.

countless [káuntlɪs] *adj.* incontable, innumerable.

country [kántrɪ] s. país; tierra; patria; campo; adj. campestre; rural; rústico; campesino.

countryman [kántrɪmən] s. compatriota, paisano; campesino, Méx., C.A. ranchero, P.R. jíbaro; Cuba guajiro; Ch. huaso; Arg. gaucho; Ec., Col. paisa.

countryside [kántrɪsaɪd] s. campiña, campo.

county [káuntɪ] s. condado (división de un estado).

coup d'état [ku detá] s. golpe de estado; cuartelazo.

coupé [kupé, kup] s. cupé.

couple [kápl̩] s. par; pareja; v. parear; unir; acoplar.

couplet [káplɪt] s. copla, versos pareados.

coupling [káplɪŋ] s. unión, conexión; acoplamiento; enganche.

coupon [kúpan] s. cupón; talón.

courage [kɝɪdʒ] s. coraje, ánimo, valor.

courageous [kəréd̠ʒəs] adj. valeroso, valiente, animoso.

courier [kúrɪə] s. mensajero.

course [kors] s. (way) curso; rumbo, trayecto; (advance) marcha, progreso; (mode) método; (study) asignatura; (dish) plato (de una comida); — of conduct conducta, proceder; golf — campo o cancha de golf; race — hipódromo, pista; in the — of a year en el transcurso de un año; of — claro, por supuesto; to follow a straight — seguir una línea recta.

court [kort] s. patio; plazuela, plazoleta; juzgado, tribunal de justicia; corte; tennis — cancha para tenis; — plaster tela adhesiva, tafetán inglés, esparadrapo; to pay — to hacer la corte a, cortejar, galantear; v. cortejar; galantear; buscar; to — danger exponerse al peligro.

courteous [kɝtɪəs] adj. cortés.

courtesy [kɝtəsɪ] s. cortesía; fineza, atención; reverencia.

courtier [kórtɪə] s. cortesano, palaciego.

court-martial [kórtmɑrʃəl] s. consejo de guerra; v. someter a consejo de guerra.

courtship [kórtʃɪp] s. cortejo, galanteo.

courtyard [kórtjard] s. patio.

cousin [kázn̩] s. primo; prima; first — primo hermano, primo carnal.

cove [kov] s. cala, ensenada.

covenant [kávənənt] s. convenio, pacto; contrato.

cover [kávɚ] s. (lid) cubierta, tapa, tapadera; (blanket) cobija; cobertor; (binding) encuadernación; envoltura; (pillow) funda; (shelter) albergue, abrido; table — tapete; to send under separate — enviar por separado; v. cubrir; tapar; encubrir; abrigar, proteger; abarcar; to — a distance recorrer una distancia.

coverage [kávərɪdʒ] s. alcance; (journalism) reportaje.

covering [kávrɪŋ] s. cubierta; cober-

tura; envoltura; cobija, abrigo.

covet [kávɪt] v. codiciar; ambicionar.

covetous [kávɪtəs] adj. codicioso.

cow [kau] s. vaca; hembra (de elefante y otros cuadrúpedos); v. atemorizar, acobardar.

coward [káuɚd] adj. & s. cobarde.

cowardice [káuɚdɪs] s. cobardía.

cowardliness [káuɚdlɪnɪs] s. cobardía.

cowardly [káuɚdlɪ] adj. cobarde; adv. cobardemente.

cowboy [káubɔɪ] s. vaquero, Am. gaucho.

cower [káuɚ] v. agacharse (de miedo o vergüenza), achicarse, encogerse (de miedo), acobardarse.

cowhide [káuhaɪd] s. cuero de vaca, vaqueta.

cowl [kaul] s. capucha.

coxswain [káksən] s. timonel.

coy [kɔɪ] adj. recatado, esquivo, modesto; tímido; gazmoño.

coyote [káɪot, kaɪótɪ] s. coyote.

cozy [kózɪ] adj. cómodo y abrigado; cómodo y agradable.

crab [kræb] s. cangrejo; cascarrabias (persona de mal genio); — apple manzana silvestre.

crack [kræk] s. (space) raja, grieta, rendija; (sound) crujido; estallido; trueno, estampido; (blow) golpe; (joke) pulla, chanza; at the — of dawn al romper el alba; adj. excelente; v. rajar(se), hender(se), agrietarse; crujir; estallar; to — a joke soltar un chiste; to — nuts cascar nueces.

crackdown [krækdaun] s. represión severa.

cracked [krækt] adj. agrietado, rajado; quebrado; chiflado, loco.

cracker [krækɚ] s. galleta.

crackle [krækl̩] s. crujido; crepitación; chasquido; v. crujir, crepitar.

cradle [krédl̩] s. cuna.

craft [kræft] s. maña, destreza; astucia, artificio, cautela; arte, oficio; embarcación; embarcaciones.

craftsman [kræftsmən] s. artesano, artífice.

crafty [kræftɪ] adj. mañoso, astuto, cauteloso, taimado.

crag [kræg] s. risco, peñasco.

cram [kræm] v. rellenar; atestar; atracar(se), hartar(se); engullir.

cramp [kræmp] s. calambre; grapa; v. comprimir, apretar, estrechar; afianzar, sujetar (con grapa).

cranberry [krænberɪ] s. arándano.

crane [kren] s. grulla (ave); grúa (máquina para levantar pesos); v. to — one's neck estirar el cuello.

cranium [krénɪəm] s. cráneo.

crank [kræŋk] s. cigüeña, manubrio, manija, manivela; he is a — es un maniático; v. voltear el manubrio o la cigüeña.

crankcase [krænkes] s. cárter del motor.

crankshaft [krænkʃæft] s. cigüeñal.

cranky [krénkɪ] adj. cascarrabias; maniático; enojadizo.

cranny [kræni] *s.* grieta, rendija.

crape [krep] *s.* crespón; crespón negro.

crash [kræʃ] *s.* (*noise*) estallido, golpazo, estruendo; (*collision*) choque; (*failure*) fracaso; quiebra; bancarrota; — **landing** aterrizaje violento; aterrizaje de barriga; *v.* estrellar(se); estallar; chocar; **to — an airplane** aterrizar de golpe un aeroplano; **to — into** chocar con, estrellarse contra.

crate [kret] *s.* canasto, cesta, jaula (*para el transporte de mercancías, etc.*); *Am.* huacal; *v.* embalar en jaula.

crater [krétə] *s.* cráter.

cravat [krəvæt] *s.* corbata.

crave [krev] *v.* ansiar, anhelar, apetecer; **to — mercy (pardon)** pedir misericordia (perdón).

crawl [krɔl] *s.* marcha lenta; natación a la marinera; *v.* arrastrarse; gatear, andar a gatas; marchar lentamente; **to be -ing with ants** hormiguear, estar lleno de hormigas.

crayon [kréən] *s.* lápiz de color, *Am.* creyón; pastel; tiza, yeso.

craze [krez] *s.* manía, locura; moda; antojo; *v.* enloquecer.

crazy [krézi] *adj.* loco; trastornado; **to go —** volverse loco, perder el juicio.

creak [krik] *s.* crujido, rechino, rechinamiento; *v.* crujir, rechinar.

cream [krimj *s.* crema; nata; — **of tomato soup** puré de tomate; **cold —** crema cosmética; **ice —** helado; *v.* desnatar; batir, mezclar (*azúcar y mantequilla*); preparar (*legumbres*) con salsa de crema.

creamery [krímərɪ] *s.* lechería, quesería, *Am.* mantequillería.

creamy [krími] *adj.* natoso; lleno de crema o nata.

crease [kris] *s.* pliegue; arruga; *v.* plegar, hacer pliegues; arrugar.

create [kriét] *v.* crear.

creation [kriéʃən] *s.* creación; obra.

creative [kriétiv] *adj.* creativo, creador.

creator [kriétə] *s.* creador.

creature [krítʃə] *s.* criatura; ser viviente; animalejo.

credence [krídns] *s.* creencia, crédito.

credentials [kridénʃəlz] *s. pl.* credenciales.

credible [krédəbl] *adj.* creíble.

credit [krédit] *s.* crédito; buena fama; **— and debit** haber y deber; activo y pasivo; **— card** tarjeta de crédito; **on —** a crédito, al fiado, a plazo; **to give —** dar crédito, creer; acreditar, abonar; **that does him —** eso le acredita; *v.* acreditar; abonar en cuenta; creer, dar crédito; atribuir.

creditable [kréditəbl] *adj.* loable.

creditor [kréditə] *s.* acreedor.

credulous [krédʒələs] *adj.* crédulo.

creed [krid] *s.* credo; creencia.

creek [krik, krɪk] *s.* riachuelo, arroyo.

creep [krip] *v.* arrastrarse; gatear, andar a gatas; trepar (*las plantas*); andar lentamente; deslizarse; sentir hormigueo (*en le cuerpo*); *s. pl.* hormigueo.

aprensión, horror.

creeper [krípə] *s.* enredadera, planta trepadora.

cremate [krímet] *v.* incinerar.

creosote [kríəsot] *s.* creosota.

crepe [krep] = **crape.**

crept [krɛpt] *pret. & p.p. de* **to creep.**

crescent [krésnt] *adj.* creciente; *s.* luna creciente; media luna (*emblema de turcos y mahometanos*).

crest [krɛst] *s.* cresta; penacho; copete; cima, cumbre; timbre (*de un escudo de armas*).

crestfallen [kréstfɔlən] *adj.* cabizbajo, alicaído, abatido.

cretonne [krɪtán] *s.* cretona.

crevice [krévɪs] *s.* grieta, hendedura.

crew [kru] *s.* tripulación; cuadrilla (*de obreros*); *pret. de* **to crow.**

crib [krɪb] *s.* camita de niño; pesebre; granero, arcón; armazón (*usado en la construcción de edificios*); traducción o clave fraudulenta (*en un examen*); *v.* enjaular; usar traducción o clave fraudulenta (*en un examen*).

cricket [kríkɪt] *s.* grillo; vilorta (*juego*).

crime [kraɪm] *s.* crimen.

criminal [krímənl] *adj. & s.* criminal.

crimp [krɪmp] *v.* rizar; *s.* rizo.

crimson [krímzn] *adj. & s.* carmesí.

cringe [krɪndʒ] *v.* encogerse; arrastrarse.

cripple [krípl] *s.* cojo, manco; tullido; baldado, inválido; *v.* estropear; mutilar, derrengar; baldar; incapacitar.

crisis [kráɪsɪs] *s.* crisis.

crisp [krɪsp] *adj.* (*brittle*) quebradizo; tieso; bien tostado; (*curly*) crespo, encrespado; **— answer** contestación aguda; **— wind** brisa refrescante; *v.* encrespar.

criterion [kraɪtírɪən] *s.* criterio.

critic [krítɪk] *s.* crítico; criticón.

critical [krítɪk] *adj.* crítico; criticador, criticón.

criticism [krítəsɪzəm] *s.* crítica; criticismo.

criticize [krítəsaɪz] *v.* criticar; censurar.

croak [krok] *v.* croar; graznar; *s.* canto de ranas; graznido.

crochet [kroʃé] *s.* labor de gancho; — **hook** aguja de gancho; *v.* hacer labor de gancho.

crock [krak] *s.* vasija de loza, jarra.

crockery [krákərɪ] *s.* loza.

crocodile [krákədaɪl] *s.* cocodrilo, *Am.* caimán.

crony [krónɪ] *s.* compadre, compinche, camarada, compañero.

crook [kruk] *s.* (*thief*) falsario; estafador, maleante, pícaro; (*curve*) curva, vuelta; recodo; gancho; **shepherd's — cayado;** *v.* torcer(se); **to — one's arm** doblar el brazo o codo.

crooked [krúkɪd] *adj.* torcido; curvo, encorvado, *Am.* chueco; *Riopl.* chingado; falso, fraudulento.

croon [krun] *v.* cantar "tristes" (*con exagerado patetismo*).

crop [krap] *s.* cosecha; buche (*de ave*); látigo, *Am.* cuarta; **— of hair** cabe-

llera; *v.* segar; recortar; rapar; **to —
out** aparecer, asomar; **to — up** brotar, manifestarse inesperadamente.
cross [krɔs] *s.* cruz; cruce; cruzamiento
(*de razas*); mezcla; *v.* cruzar(se); atra-
vesar(se); santiguar(se); encontrarse;
contrariar; *adj.* en cruz, cruzado,
transversal; malhumorado; **cross-
country** a campo traviesa; **cross-
examine** *v.* interrogar, repreguntar;
cross-eyed bizco; **—word puzzle**
crucigrama.
crossbar [krɔ́sbɑr] *s.* travesaño.
crossing [krɔ́sɪŋ] *s.* cruce; čruzamiento;
encrucijada, crucero; travesía; **railroad** — cruce; **river** — vado.
crossroad [krɔ́srod] *s.* vía transversal,
encrucijada, crucero.
cross section [krés sékʃən] *s.* corte
transversal; sección transversal.
crouch [kraʊtʃ] *v.* agacharse, agazaparse.
crow [kro] *s.* cuervo; canto del gallo;
crow's-foot pata de gallo (*arrugas en
el rabo del ojo*); *v.* cantar (*el gallo*); cacarear; jactarse, hacer alarde.
crowbar [króbɑr] *s.* barra, palanca de
hierro.
crowd [kraʊd] *s.* muchedumbre; gentío,
gente; cuadrilla, pandilla; grupo; *v.*
agolparse, apiñar(se); estrujar, empujar.
crowded [kráʊdɪd] *adj.* atestado, lleno,
apiñado.
crown [kraʊn] *s.* corona; copa (*de sombrero*); cima; *v.* coronar.
crucible [krúsəbl] *s.* crisol.
crucifix [krúsəfɪks] *s.* crucifijo.
crucify [krúsəfaɪ] *v.* crucificar.
crude [krud] *adj.* basto, tosco, rudo; inculto; **— oil** petróleo crudo; **— sugar**
azúcar bruto, azúcar crudo.
cruel [krúəl] *adj.* cruel.
cruelty [krúəltɪ] *s.* crueldad.
cruet [krúɪt] *s.* ampolla (*pequeña vasija
de cristal*); vinajera (*para servir vino en
la misa*); **oil** — aceitera; **vinegar** —
vinagrera.
cruise [kruz] *s.* travesía, viaje por mar;
excursión; *v.* navegar.
cruiser [krúzɚ] *s.* crucero (*buque*).
crumb [krʌm] *s.* migaja; miga; mendrugo; *v.* desmenuzar, desmigajar.
crumble [krʌ́mbl] *v.* desmenuzar(se);
desmoronarse.
crumple [krʌ́mpl] *v.* arrugar(se); ajar,
apabullar.
crunch [krʌntʃ] *v.* crujir; mascullar.
crusade [kruséd] *s.* cruzada; *v.* hacer
una campaña; hacer una cruzada.
crusader [krusédɚ] *s.* cruzado.
crush [krʌʃ] *s.* compresión, presión; estrujamiento, apiñamiento de gente; *v.*
estrujar; aplastar; majar; subyugar;
to — stone moler piedra.
crust [krʌst] *s.* corteza (*de pan, queso,
etc.*); costra; mendrugo; *v.* encostrarse, cubrir(se) de costra.
crusty [krʌ́stɪ] *adj.* costroso.
crutch [krʌtʃ] *s.* muleta.
cry [kraɪ] *s.* grito; lloro, lamento; **a far**

— from muy distante de, muy lejos
de; *v.* gritar; llorar; clamar; exclamar;
vocear; **to — for help** pedir socorro.
crystal [krístl] *s.* cristal; **— clear** cristalino.
crystalline [krístlɪn] *adj.* cristalino.
crystallize [krístlaɪz] *v.* cristalizar(se).
cub [kʌb] *s.* cachorro (*de oso, tigre, lobo,
león*); **— reporter** reportero novato.
Cuban [kjúbən] *adj.* & *s.* cubano.
cube [kjub] *s.* cubo; **— root** raíz cúbica.
cubic [kjúbɪk] *adj.* cúbico.
cubism [kjúbɪzm] *s.* cubismo.
cuckoo [kúku] *s.* cuco, cuclillo; *adj.* tocado, chiflado, medio loco.
cucumber [kjúkʌmbɚ] *s.* pepino.
cud [kʌd] *s.* rumia; **to chew the —**
rumiar.
cuddle [kʌ́dl] *v.* abrazar, tener en
brazos; estar abrazados.
cudgel [kʌ́dʒəl] *s.* garrote; porra; *v.* aporrear, apalear.
cue [kju] *s.* señal, indicación; pie (*últimas palabras de un parlamento que
sirven de señal en el teatro*); **billiard
—** taco de billar.
cuff [kʌf] *s.* puño (*de camisa o de vestido*);
doblez (*del pantalón*); bofetada; *v.*
abofetear, dar de bofetadas.
cull [kʌl] *v.* entresacar; .extraer.
culminate [kʌ́lmənet] *v.* culminar.
culprit [kʌ́lprɪt] *s.* reo, delincuente, culpable.
cult [kʌlt] *s.* culto; secta religiosa.
cultivate [kʌ́ltəvet] *v.* cultivar; labrar,
barbechar.
cultivated [kʌ́ltəvetɪd] *adj.* cultivado;
culto.
cultivation [kʌltəvéʃən] *s.* cultivación,
cultivo; cultura.
cultivator [kʌ́ltəvetɚ] *s.* cultivador; máquina cultivadora.
culture [kʌ́ltʃɚ] *s.* cultura; cultivo.
cultured [kʌ́ltʃɚd] *adj.* culto; cultivado.
cumbersome [kʌ́mbɚsəm] *adj.* engorroso, embarazoso, incómodo.
cunning [kʌ́nɪŋ] *adj.* astuto, socarrón,
sagaz, taimado; diestro, cuco, mono,
gracioso; *s.* astucia, maña, sagacidad.
cup [kʌp] *s.* taza, pocillo; copa (*trofeo*).
cupboard [kʌ́bɚd] *s.* armario, aparador;
alacena.
cur [kɚ] *s.* perro mestizo, *Am.* perro
chusco; villano, vil, cobarde.
curate [kjúrɪt] *s.* cura.
curator [kjúretɚ] *s.* conservador.
curb [kɚb] *s.* reborde, encintado (*de la
acera*); *Riopl.* cordón de la acera; freno,
restricción; barbada (*del freno de un
caballo*); brocal de pozo; *v.* refrenar,
reprimir.
curd [kɚd] *s.* cuajada; *v.* cuajar(se), coa-
gular(se).
curdle [kɚ́dl] *v.* cuajar(se), coagular(se).
cure [kjur] *s.* cura, curación; remedio;
v. curar(se); sanar
curfew [kɚ́fju] *s.* queda.
curio [kjúrɪo] *s.* curiosidad, objeto raro
y curioso.
curiosity [kjurɪásətɪ] *s.* curiosidad;
rareza.

curious [kjúrıəs] *adj.* curioso; extraño, raro.

curl [kɜl] *s.* rizo, bucle; espiral (*de humo*); *v.* rizar(se); ensortijar(se); enroscar(se); retorcerse, alzarse en espirales (*el humo*).

curly [kɜ́lı] *adj.* rizo, rizoso, rizado, crespo, *Am.* chino.

currant [kɜ́ənt] *s.* grosella; — **bush** grosellero.

currency [kɜ́ənsı] *s.* moneda corriente; circulación; **paper —** papel moneda.

current [kɜ́ənt] *adj.* corriente; común, prevaleciente, en boga; *s.* corriente.

curriculum [kəríkjələm] *s.* programa de estudios.

curse [kɜs] *s.* maldición; calamidad; *v.* maldecir.

cursed [kɜ́st] *adj.* maldito.

cursive [kɜ́sıv] *adj.* cursivo.

curt [kɜt] *adj.* corto; brusco.

curtail [kɜtél] *v.* cercenar; acortar; restringir, reducir.

curtain [kɜ́tn] *s.* cortina; telón (*de teatro*); *v.* poner cortinas.

curvature [kɜ́vətʃə] *s.* curvatura.

curve [kɜv] *s.* curva; *v.* encorvar(se); torcer(se); doblar(se).

curved [kɜvd] *adj.* encorvado; torcido; curvo, corvo, *Méx., C.A.* chueco.

cushion [kúʃən] *s.* cojín; almohadilla; almohadón; amortiguador (*para amortiguar un sonido o golpe*); *v.* acojinar; amortiguar (*un choque*).

custard [kɜ́stəd] *s.* flan, natillas.

custody [kɜ́stədı] *s.* custodia, cargo, cuidado; **to hold in —** custodiar.

custom [kɜ́stəm] *s.* costumbre, hábito, uso, usanza; **-s** derechos de aduana; **— made** hecho a la medida; **— tailor** maestro sastre; **— built** construido según pedido.

customary [kɜ́stəmɛrı] *adj.* acostumbrado, habitual, usual, de costumbre.

customer [kɜ́stəmə] *s.* parroquiano, cliente, marchante.

customhouse [kɜ́stəmhaʊs] *s.* aduana; **— official** aduanero; **— mark** marchamo.

cut [kʌt] *s.* corte (*m.*); cortadura, *Am.* cortada; rebanada, tajada; rebaja, reducción (*de precios, sueldos*); hechura (*de un traje*); ausencia (*de la clase*); grabado; **short —** atajo, camino corto; *v.* cortar; tajar; labrar, tallar; segar; rebajar, reducir (*precios, sueldos*); negar el saludo a; alzar (*los naipes*); **to — across** cruzar, atravesar; **to — capers** hacer cabriolas, cabriolar; **to — class** faltar a la clase; **to — out** recortar; excluir; **to be — out for** estar hecho para, tener vocación para; *pret. & p.p. de* **to cut.**

cute [kjut] *adj.* mono, cuco; astuto.

cuticle [kjútıkl] *s.* cutícula.

cutlery [kɜ́tlərı] *s.* cuchillería, cuchillos.

cutlet [kɜ́tlıt] *s.* chuleta.

cutter [kɜ́tə] *s.* cortador; máquina para cortar; trineo; **wood —** leñador; **coast guard —** barco guardacostas.

cutting [kɜ́tıŋ] *adj.* cortante; penetran-

te; mordaz, sarcástico.

cybernetics [saıbənétıks] *s.* cibernética.

cycle [sáıkl] *s.* ciclo.

cyclone [sáıklon] *s.* ciclón; huracán.

cylinder [sílındə] *s.* cilindro.

cylindrical [sılíndrıkl] *adj.* cilíndrico.

cymbal [símbl] *s.* címbalo, platillo; **to play the -s** tocar los platillos.

cynic [sínık] *s.* cínico.

cynical [sínıkl] *adj.* cínico.

cynicism [sínəsızəm] *s.* cinismo.

cypress [sáıprəs] *s.* ciprés.

cyst [sıst] *s.* quiste.

D

dad [dæd] *s.* papá, tata; **daddy** *s.* papaíto o papacito, tata, tatita, *Am.* taita.

daffodil [dǽfədıl] *s.* narciso.

dagger [dǽgə] *s.* daga; puñal; **to look -s at** traspasar con la mirada.

daily [délı] *adj.* diario; *adv.* diariamente; *s.* diario, periódico.

dainty [déntı] *adj.* delicado, fino, primoroso, exquisito; *s.* golosina, manjar exquisito.

dairy [dérı] *s.* lechería, vaquería; quesería, quesera.

daisy [dézı] *s.* margarita, maya.

dale [del] *s.* cañada.

dally [dǽlı] *v.* juguetear; holgazanear; entretenerse, tardar; malgastar el tiempo.

dam [dæm] *s.* presa, represa; *v.* represar, estancar.

damage [dǽmıdʒ] *s.* daño; perjuicio; avería; **to pay for -s** indemnizar, pagar los daños y perjuicios; *v.* dañar(se); averiar(se).

dame [dem] *s.* dama, señora; **old —** vieja.

damn [dæm] *v.* maldecir; condenar; blasfemar; **— it** ¡maldito sea!

damnation [dæmnéʃən] *s.* condenación, perdición.

damp [dæmp] *adj.* húmedo; mojado; *s.* humedad; *v.* humedecer, mojar.

dampen [dǽmpən] *v.* mojar, humedecer; desalentar; amortiguar.

dampness [dǽmpnıs] *s.* humedad.

damsel [dǽmzl] *s.* damisela.

dance [dæns] *s.* baile; danza; **— music** música de baile; *v.* bailar; danzar.

dancer [dǽnsə] *s.* bailador; bailarín, bailarina; danzante.

dandelion [dǽndlaıən] *s.* diente de león.

dandruff [dǽndrəf] *s.* caspa.

dandy [dǽndı] *s.* currutaco, majo, afectado; chulo; *adj.* elegante, excelente.

danger [déndʒə] *s.* peligro, riesgo.

dangerous [déndʒərəs] *adj.* peligroso; arriesgado; **-ly** *adv.* peligrosamente; **-ly ill** gravemente enfermo.

dangle [dǽŋgl] *v.* pender, colgar; bambolear(se) (*en el aire*).

dapple(d) [dǽpl(d)] *adj.* rodado, con manchas (*dícese de los caballos*); **dapple-grey** rucio rodado, tordo, tordillo.

dare [der] *s.* desafío, reto, provocación; **—devil** atrevido, osado; *v.* atreverse, osar; desafiar.

daring [dérɪŋ] s. atrevimiento, osadía; adj. osado, atrevido, arrojado.

dark [dɑrk] adj. obscuro; sombrío; — **horse** caballo desconocido (que gana inesperadamente la carrera); candidato nombrado inesperadamente; — **secret** secreto profundo; enigma; **dark-skinned** moreno, trigueño; s. obscuridad; sombra.

darken [dárkən] v. obscurecer(se); nublarse.

darkness [dárknɪs] s. obscuridad; tinieblas; sombra.

darky [dárkɪ] s. negro (persona).

darling [dárlɪŋ] adj. & s. amado, querido; **my** — vida mía (o mi vida), amor mío.

darn [dɑrn] s. zurcido; **it is not worth a** — no vale un comino, no vale un pito; v. zurcir; —! ¡caramba! ¡canastos!; **-ing needle** aguja de zurcir.

dart [dɑrt] s. dardo, flecha; sisa (en un vestido); movimiento rápido; v. lanzar(se); flechar; **to** — **out** salir como una flecha; **to** — **in and out** entrar y salir precipitadamente.

dash [dæʃ] s. (line) raya; (run) carrera corta; (vigor) ímpetu; (grace) garbo; pizca (de sal, azúcar, etc.); rociada (de agua); —**board** tablero de instrumentos; **with a** — **of the pen** de una plumada; v. lanzar(se); echar(se); estrellar(se); salpicar; frustrar (esperanzas); **to** — **by** pasar corriendo; **to** — **out** salir a la carrera; **to** — **off a letter** escribir de prisa una carta.

data [déta] s. pl. datos.

date [det] s. (time) fecha; (statement) data; (appointment) cita, compromiso; (fruit) dátil; **out of** — anticuado, desusado; fuera de moda; **up to** — al día, moderno; **up to this** — hasta ahora, hasta la fecha; v. fechar; **to** — **from** datar de; remontarse a.

daub [dɔb] v. embarrar, untar; pintarrajear.

daughter [dɔ́tə] s. hija; **daughter-in-law** nuera.

daunt [dɔnt] v. intimidar, asustar, espantar; desanimar.

dauntless [dɔ́ntlɪs] adj. denodado, intrépido

davenport [dǽvənpɔrt] s. sofá.

dawn [dɔn] s. alba; amanecer, madrugada; v. amanecer; alborear, rayar (el día); **it just -ed upon me** acabo de darme cuenta.

day [de] s. día; — **after tomorrow** pasado mañana; — **before yesterday** anteayer o antier; — **laborer** jornalero; **by** — de día; **by the** — por día; **eight-hour** — jornada de ocho horas; **to win the** — ganar la jornada, triunfar.

daybreak [débrek] s. amanecer, alba; **at** — al amanecer, al romper el día, al rayar el día.

daylight [délait] s. luz del día.

daytime [détaim] s. día (tiempo de luz natural); **in the** — durante el día; de

día.

daze [dez] s. aturdimiento; deslumbramiento; **to be in a** — estar aturdido; v. aturdir; ofuscar; deslumbrar.

dazzle [dǽzl] s. brillantez; v. deslumbrar; ofuscar.

deacon [díkən] s. diácono.

dead [dɛd] adj. muerto; — **air** aire viciado o estancado; — **letter** carta no reclamada; — **loss** pérdida absoluta; adv. completamente, absolutamente; sumamente, muy; — **sure** completamente seguro; — **tired** muerto de cansancio; s. **the** — los muertos; **in the** — **of the night** en el sigilo de la noche; **in the** — **of winter** en lo más crudo del invierno.

deaden [dɛ́dn] v. amortiguar.

deadhead [dɛ́dhɛd] s. persona que no paga la entrada; colado.

deadly [dɛ́dlɪ] adj. mortal; fatal; como la muerte, cadavérico; adv. mortalmente; — **dull** sumamente aburrido.

deaf [dɛf] adj. sordo; **deaf-mute** s. & adj. sordomudo.

deafen [dɛ́fən] v. ensordecer; amortiguar, apagar (un sonido).

deafening [dɛ́fənɪŋ] adj. ensordecedor, estruendoso.

deafness [dɛ́fnɪs] s. sordera.

deal [dil] s. trato, negocio; mano (en el juego de naipes); distribución, repaño (de los naipes); **a great** — **of** una gran cantidad de, mucho; **to give a square** — tratar con equidad; v. tallar (en juegos de naipes); distribuir, repartir; dar (un golpe); **to** — **in** comerciar en; **to** — **with** tratar de (un asunto); tratar con; negociar con.

dealer [dílə] s. negociante, comerciante, tratante; tallador (en el juego de naipes).

dealings [dílɪŋz] s. pl. relaciones (comerciales o amistosas); comercio, tratos; negocios.

dealt [dɛlt] pret. & p.p. de **to deal**.

dean [din] s. deán (dignidad eclesiástica); decano (de universidad).

dear [dɪr] adj. (beloved) querido, amado; (expensive) caro; costoso; adv. caro; — **me!** ¡Dios mío! **oh—!** ¡ay!; **my** — querido mío; **Dear Sir** Muy señor mío; **-ly** adv. cariñosamente; a precio alto; **my -ly beloved** muy amado mío; muy amados míos.

dearth [dɝθ] s. escasez, carestía, insuficiencia.

death [dɛθ] s. muerte; mortandad; — **rate** mortalidad.

deathbed [dɛ́θbɛd] s. lecho de muerte.

debase [dɪbés] v. rebajar el valor de; degradar, humillar, envilecer.

debatable [dɪbétəbl] adj. discutible, disputable.

debate [dɪbét] s. debate, discusión; v. debatir, discutir; considerar; deliberar.

debilitate [dəbílətet] v. debilitar.

debit [dɛ́bɪt] s. débito, adeudo, cargo; debe (de una cuenta); pasivo (en contabilidad); v. adeudar, cargar en cuenta.

debriefing [dibrífıŋ] *s.* informe de vuelo bajo interrogación; informe.

debris [dəbrí] *s.* escombros; ruinas.

debt [dɛt] *s.* deuda; adeudo; débito; **bad — cuenta incobrable; to run into —** adeudarse, entramparse, cargarse de deudas.

debtor [détə] *s.* deudor.

debunk [dibʌ́ŋk] *v.* desbaratar; desenmascarar.

debut [dɪbjú] *s.* estreno; **to make a —** debutar, estrenarse.

decade [déked] *s.* década, decenio.

decadence [dɪkédns] *s.* decadencia.

decanter [dɪkǽntə] *s.* garrafa; **large —** garrafón.

decay [dɪké] *s.* decaimiento; decadencia, ruina; podredumbre; caries (*de la dentadura*); *v.* decaer; venir a menos; pudrir(se) o podrir(se).

decease [dɪsís] *s.* muerte, fallecimiento; *v.* morir, fallecer.

deceased [dɪsíst] *adj. & s.* muerto, difunto.

deceit [dɪsít] *s.* engaño; fraude; trampa.

deceitful [dɪsítfəl] *adj.* engañador; tramposo; engañoso.

deceive [dɪsív] *v.* engañar.

December [dɪsémbə] *s.* diciembre.

decency [dísnsi] *s.* decencia.

decent [dísnt] *adj.* decente; decoroso.

decibel [désɪbɛl] *s.* decibelio; décibel.

decide [dɪsáɪd] *v.* decidir, resolver, determinar; **to — to** resolverse a, decidirse a.

decided [dɪsáɪdɪd] *adj.* decidido, resuelto.

decimal [désəml] *adj.* decimal; *s.* decimal, fracción decimal.

decipher [dɪsáɪfə] *v.* descifrar.

decision [dɪsíʒən] *s.* decisión, resolución.

decisive [dɪsáɪsɪv] *adj.* decisivo; terminante.

deck [dɛk] *s.* cubierta (*de un buque*); baraja; *v.* cubrir; ataviar; **to — oneself out** emperifollarse.

declaration [dɛkləréʃən] *s.* declaración.

declare [dɪklǽr] *v.* declarar; afirmar.

decline [dɪkláɪn] *s.* declinación; decadencia; mengua; baja (*de precios*); *v.* declinar; decaer; rehusar; **to — to do something** negarse a hacer algo.

declivity [dɪklívətɪ] *s.* declive.

décolleté [dekalté] *adj.* escotado.

decompose [dikəmpóz] *v.* descomponer(se); corromper(se), pudrir(se).

decorate [dékəret] *v.* decorar, adornar; condecorar.

decoration [dekəréʃən] *s.* decoración; adorno; insignia, condecoración.

decorative [dékəretɪv] *adj.* decorativo; ornamental.

decorum [dɪkórəm] *s.* decoro; circunspección.

decoy [dɪkɔ́ɪ] *s.* reclamo, señuelo, figura de ave (*que sirve para atraer aves*); cebo (*artificio para atraer con engaño*); trampa, lazo; *v.* atraer con señuelo o engaño.

decrease [díkris] *s.* disminución o diminución; merma; mengua; [dɪkrís] *v.* disminuir(se); mermar; menguar.

decree [dɪkrí] *s.* decreto; *v.* decretar; mandar.

decrepit [dɪkrépɪt] *adj.* decrépito.

dedicate [dédəket] *v.* dedicar.

dedication [dɛdəkéʃən] *s.* dedicación; dedicatoria.

deduce [dɪdjús] *v.* deducir, inferir.

deduct [dɪdʌ́kt] *v.* deducir, descontar, rebajar.

deduction [dɪdʌ́kʃən] *s.* deducción; rebaja, descuento.

deed [did] *s.* hecho, acción, acto; hazaña; escritura (*de venta o compra*).

deem [dim] *v.* juzgar, creer, considerar.

deep [dip] *adj.* (*down*) hondo; profundo; (*obscure*) oscuro; (*tone*) grave, bajo; **— in debt** cargado de deudas; **— in thought** absorto; **— mourning** luto riguroso; **to go off the — end** echarse a pique; caer en el abismo; **— into the night** en las tinieblas de la noche; *s.* **the —** el mar; **-ly** *adv.* profundamente, hondamente; intensamente.

deepen [dípən] *v.* ahondar, profundizar.

deer [dɪr] *s.* ciervo, venado; **—skin** piel o cuero de venado.

deface [dɪfés] *v.* desfigurar, estropear, mutilar.

defame [dɪfém] *v.* difamar, calumniar, denigrar.

default [dɪfɔ́lt] *s.* falla, falta, negligencia (*de un deber, pago, obligación*); deficiencia; *v.* fallar, faltar (*en el cumplimiento de un deber, pago, obligación*); no comparecer a la cita de un tribunal.

defeat [dɪfít] *s.* derrota, vencimiento; frustración (*de un plan*); *v.* vencer, derrotar; frustrar.

defect [dɪfékt] *s.* defecto.

defective [dɪféktɪv] *adj.* defectuoso; incompleto; anormal, falto de inteligencia; **— verb** verbo defectivo.

defend [dɪfénd] *v.* defender.

defendant [dɪféndənt] *s.* acusado, demandado, procesado.

defender [dɪféndə] *s.* defensor; abogado defensor.

defense [dɪféns] *s.* defensa.

defenseless [dɪfénslɪs] *adj.* indefenso, inerme.

defensive [dɪfénsɪv] *adj.* defensivo; *s.* defensiva.

defer [dɪfɝ́] *v.* diferir, posponer, aplazar; **to — to another's opinion** remitirse o ceder al dictamen de otro.

defiance [dɪfáɪəns] *s.* reto, desafío, provocación; oposición; **in — of** en abierta oposición con, a despecho de.

deficiency [dɪfíʃənsɪ] *s.* deficiencia; defecto; déficit.

deficient [dɪfíʃənt] *adj.* deficiente; defectuoso.

deficit [défəsɪt] *s.* déficit.

defile [dɪfáɪl] *v.* viciar, corromper; profanar; manchar, ensuciar.

define [dɪfáɪn] *v.* definir.

definite [défənɪt] *adj.* definido; claro, preciso; fijo; **— article** artículo determinado o definido; **-ly** *adv.* definidamente; claramente; **-ly not** terminantemente no.

definition [defəníʃən] *s.* definición.

definitive [dɪfínətɪv] *adj.* definitivo.

deflect [dɪflékt] *v.* desviar(se).

deform [dɪfórm] *v.* deformar; desfigurar, afear.

deformed [dɪfórmd] *adj.* deforme, disforme; deformado; desfigurado.

deformity [dɪfórmətɪ] *s.* deformidad; deformación.

defraud [dɪfród] *v.* defraudar.

defray [dɪfré] *v.* sufragar, costear, pagar (*gastos*).

deft [dɛft] *adj.* diestro, ágil.

defunct [dɪfʌ́ŋkt] *adj.* difunto.

defy [dɪfái] *v.* desafiar; retar; oponerse a, resistirse a.

degenerate [dɪdʒénərɪt] *adj.* & *s.* degenerado; [dɪdʒénəret] *v.* degenerar.

degradation [degrədéʃən] *s.* degradación; envilecimiento.

degrade [dɪgréd] *v.* degradar; envilecer, rebajar.

degree [dɪgrí] *s.* grado; rango; **by -s** gradualmente; **to get a —** graduarse.

dehydrate [dɪháɪdret] *v.* deshidratar(se).

deign [den] *v.* dignarse, condescender.

deity [díətɪ] *s.* deidad.

dejected [dɪdʒéktɪd] *adj.* abatido.

dejection [dɪdʒékʃən] *s.* abatimiento, melancolía, depresión.

delay [dɪlé] *s.* demora, tardanza, dilación, retraso; *v.* demorar: retardar, dilatar; diferir; tardarse.

delayed action [dɪléd ǽkʃən] *adj.* atrasado; retardada.

delegate [déləget] *s.* delegado, representante; *v.* delegar, diputar.

delegation [deləgéʃən] *s.* delegación, diputación.

deletion [dɪlíʃən] *s.* suspensión.

deliberate [dɪlíbərɪt] *adj.* deliberado, premeditado; cauto, prudente; lento; **-ly** *adv.* deliberadamente; con premeditación; [dɪlíbəret] *v.* deliberar.

deliberation [dɪlɪbəréʃən] *s.* deliberación.

delicacy [déləkəsɪ] *s.* delicadeza; sensibilidad; finura; golosina.

delicate [déləkət] *adj.* delicado; frágil; exquisito.

delicatessen [deləkətésn] *s.* tienda de fiambres, queso, ensaladas, etc.

delicious [dɪlíʃəs] *adj.* delicioso.

delight [dɪláit] *s.* deleite; delicia; *v.* deleitar(se); encantar; agradar; **to — in** gozarse en, deleitarse en.

delighted [dɪláitid] *adj.* encantado; **to be — to** alegrarse de, tener mucho gusto en (*o* de).

delightful [dɪláitfəl] *adj.* deleitoso; delicioso; ameno, agradable.

delineate [dɪlínɪet] *v.* delinear, trazar.

delinquent [dɪlíŋkwənt] *adj.* & *s.* delincuente.

delirious [dɪlírɪəs] *adj.* delirante; **to be — delirar, desvariar.**

delirium [dɪlírɪəm] *s.* delirio, desvario.

deliver [dɪlívɚ] *v.* entregar; librar, libertar; pronunciar (*un discurso*); dar (*un golpe*).

deliverance [dɪlívərəns] *s.* liberación, rescate.

deliverer [dɪlívərɚ] *s.* libertador; portador, mensajero.

delivery [dɪlívərɪ] *s.* (*giving*) entrega; (*saving*) liberación; (*birth*) parto; (*speaking*) elocuencia, manera de hacer una conferencia; **— service** servicio de entrega; **— truck** camión (*o* camioneta) de reparto; **mail —** reparto de correo.

dell [del] *s.* cañada, hondonada.

delta wing [délta wɪŋ] *s.* ala en delta.

delude [dɪlúd] *v.* engañar.

deluge [déljudʒ] *s.* diluvio; *v.* inundar; abrumar.

delusion [dɪlúʒən] *s.* ilusión; engaño, error.

demand [dɪmǽnd] *s.* demanda; exigencia; solicitud; **on —** a solicitud; *v.* demandar, reclamar; exigir.

demanding [dɪmǽndɪŋ] *adj.* exigente.

demeanor [dɪmínɚ] *s.* conducta, comportamiento, proceder.

demented [dɪméntɪd] *adj.* demente.

demise [dɪmáɪz] *s.* fallecimiento.

demobilize [dimóblaɪz] *v.* demovilizar.

democracy [dəmákrəsɪ] *s.* democracia.

democrat [déməkræt] *s.* demócrata.

democratic [deməkrǽtɪk] *adj.* democrático.

demolish [dɪmálɪʃ] *v.* demoler.

demon [dímən] *s.* demonio.

demonstrate [démənstret] *v.* demostrar.

demonstration [demənstréʃən] *s.* demostración; prueba; (*protest*) manifestación.

demonstrative [dɪmánstrətɪv] *adj.* demostrativo; efusivo.

den [den] *s.* guarida; escondrijo; cueva, lugar de retiro.

denial [dɪnáɪəl] *s.* negación; negativa; **self-denial** abnegación.

denigrate [dénɪgret] *v.* calumniar; ennegrecer.

denomination [dɪnɑmənéʃən] *s.* (*name*) denominación; nombre; título, designación; (*sect*) secta religiosa.

denote [dɪnót] *v.* denotar.

denounce [dɪnáʊns] *v.* denunciar; delatar, acusar.

dense [dɛns] *adj.* denso; espeso, apretado; estúpido.

density [dénsətɪ] *s.* densidad; estupidez.

dent [dent] *s.* abolladura; mella; *v.* abollar; mellar.

dental [déntl] *adj.* dental; *s.* dental, consonante dental.

dentifrice [déntɪfrɪs] *s.* pasta dentífrica; dentífrico.

dentist [déntɪst] *s.* dentista.

denunciation [dɪnʌnsiéʃən] *s.* denuncia, acusación.

deny [dɪnái] *v.* negar; rehusar; **to — oneself** sacrificarse, abnegarse; **to — oneself to callers** negarse a recibir visitas.

depart [dıpárt] *v.* partir, salir, irse; desviarse, apartarse.

departed [dıpártıd] *adj.* ido; ausente; difunto.

department [dıpártmənt] *s.* departamento; distrito; ramo, división; — **store** almacén.

departure [dıpárt∫ə] *s.* salida, partida; desviación.

depend [dıpénd] *v.* depender; **to — on** depender de; contar con, confiar en.

dependable [dıpéndəbl] *adj.* seguro, fidedigno, digno de confianza.

dependence [dıpéndəns] *s.* dependencia; confianza.

dependency [dıpéndənsı] *s.* dependencia; sucursal.

dependent [dıpéndənt] *adj.* dependiente; subordinado; *s.* dependiente, familiar.

depict [dıpíkt] *v.* pintar, describir; representar.

depilatory [dıpílətorı] *s.* depilatorio.

deplete [dıplít] *v.* agotar; vaciar.

deplorable [dıplórəbl] *adj.* deplorable, lamentable.

deplore [dıplór] *v.* deplorar.

deport [dıpórt] *v.* deportar; **to — oneself well** portarse bien.

deportment [dıpórtmənt] *s.* comportamiento, conducta.

depose [dıpóz] *v.* deponer; declarar, atestiguar.

deposit [dıpázıt] *s.* depósito; *v.* depositar.

deposition [dɛpəzí∫ən] *s.* deposición; declaración.

depositor [dıpázıtə] *s.* depositador.

depot [dípo] *s.* depósito; almacén; estación de ferrocarril.

deprecate [déprıket] *v.* desaprobar.

depreciate [dıprí∫et] *v.* depreciar; bajar de precio; abaratar(se); menospreciar.

depress [dıprés] *v.* deprimir; abatir; desanimar; depreciar, rebajar el valor de.

depressed [dıprést] *adj.* abatido, decaído.

depressing [dıprésıŋ] *adj.* deprimente.

depression [dıpré∫ən] *s.* depresión; decaimiento, abatimiento; rebaja (*de precios*).

deprive [dıpráıv] *v.* privar.

depth [dεpθ] *s.* profundidad; hondura; fondo; longitud (*de un solar*); gravedad (*de los sonidos*); viveza (*de los colores*); **in the — of the night** en las tinieblas de la noche; **in the — of winter** en lo más crudo del invierno.

deputation [dεpjətə∫ən] *s.* diputación, delegación; comisión.

depute [dıpjút] *v.* diputar, delegar.

deputy [dέpjətı] *s.* diputado; agente; delegado.

derange [dıréndʒ] *v.* trastornar, desordenar.

derby [dɘ́bı] *s.* sombrero hongo, *Méx.*, *Ven.*, *Col.* sombrero de bola.

derelict [dέrılıkt] *adj.* abandonado; negligente.

deride [dıráıd] *v.* escarnecer, ridiculizar, mofarse de, burlarse de.

derision [dıríʒən] *s.* mofa, escarnio.

derive [dɘráıv] *v.* derivar(se); provenir; sacar (*provecho*); recibir (*placer*).

dermatology [dɘmətálədʒı] *s.* dermatología.

derrick [dérık] *s.* grúa; armazón (*para la explotación del petróleo*).

descend [dısénd] *v.* descender; bajar; **to — upon** caer sobre, acometer.

descendant [dıséndənt] *adj. & s.* descendiente.

descent [dısént] *s.* descenso; bajada; descendencia, linaje; descendimiento; declive.

describe [dıskráıb] *v.* describir; trazar.

description [dıskríp∫ən] *s.* descripción; **of all -s** de todas clases.

descriptive [dıskríptıv] *adj.* descriptivo; **— linguistics** lingüística descriptiva.

desert [dézɘt] *adj.* desierto, despoblado; estéril; *s.* desierto, yermo; páramo; [dızɘ́t] *v.* abandonar, desamparar; desertar.

deserter [dızɘ́tə] *s.* desertor.

desertion [dızɘ́∫ən] *s.* deserción, abandono, desamparo.

deserve [dızɘ́v] *v.* merecer.

deserving [dızɘ́vıŋ] *adj.* meritorio, merecedor.

design [dızáın] *s.* (*sketch*) dibujo, diseño; (*plan*) designio, propósito, intención; plan, proyecto; *v.* diseñar, trazar; proyectar; idear.

designate [dézıgnet] *v.* designar; señalar, indicar, nombrar.

designer [dızáınə] *s.* diseñador; dibujante; proyectista; intrigante.

desirability [dızaırəbílətı] *s.* conveniencia, utilidad.

desirable [dızáırəbl] *adj.* deseable; agradable; conveniente.

desire [dızáır] *s.* deseo; anhelo, ansia; *v.* desear; anhelar, ansiar.

desirous [dızáırəs] *adj.* deseoso.

desist [dızíst] *v.* desistir.

desk [dεsk] *s.* escritorio, bufete, pupitre, mesa de escribir.

desolate [déslıt] *adj.* desolado; despoblado, desierto; solitario; [déslet] *v.* desolar; asolar, arrasar; despoblar.

desolation [deslé∫ən] *s.* desolación; soledad.

despair [dıspér] *s.* desesperación; desesperanza; *v.* desesperarse, perder la esperanza.

despairing [dıspérıŋ] *adj.* desesperado, sin esperanza.

despatch [dıspæt∫] = **dispatch**.

desperate [désprıt] *adj.* desesperado; arriesgado, temerario; **— illness** enfermedad gravísima; **-ly** *adv.* desesperadamente; **-ly ill** gravísimamente enfermo.

desperation [despəré∫ən] *s.* desesperación; temeridad.

despicable [déspıkəbl] *adj.* despreciable; desdeñable.

despise [dıspáız] *v.* despreciar; desdeñar; menospreciar.

despite [dɪspáɪt] s. despecho; *prep.* a despecho de, a pesar de.

despoil [dɪspɔ́ɪl] v. despojar.

despondency [dɪspándənsɪ] s. abatimiento desaliento, descaecimiento o decaimiento del ánimo.

despondent [dɪspándənt] adj. abatido, descaecido o decaído de ánimo, desalentado, desesperanzado.

despot [déspət] s. déspota.

despotic [dɪspátɪk] adj. despótico.

despotism [déspətɪzəm] s. despotismo.

dessert [dɪzɜ́t] s. postre.

destination [destənéʃən] s. destinación, destino; paradero.

destine [déstɪn] v. destinar; **-ed for** con rumbo a, con destinación a; destinado a.

destiny [déstənɪ] s. destino, sino, hado.

destitute [déstətjut] adj. destituido, necesitado; falto, desprovisto.

destroy [dɪstrɔ́ɪ] v. destruir.

destroyer [dɪstrɔ́ɪə] s. destruidor; destructor, cazatorpedero, destroyer.

destruction [dɪstrákʃən] s. destrucción; ruina.

destructive [dɪstráktɪv] adj. destructivo.

detach [dɪtǽʃ] v. separar, despegar, desprender; destacar (*una porción de tropa*).

detachment [dɪtǽtʃmənt] s. separación; desprendimiento; desapego, despego, alejamiento; destacamento (*militar*).

detail [ditel] s. detalle; pormenor; destacamento (*militar*); **to go into —** detallar, pormenorizar; [dɪtél] v. detallar; pormenorizar; destacar, asignar.

detain [dɪtén] v. detener; entretener, demorar, retardar.

detect [dɪtékt] v. descubrir.

detective [dɪtéktɪv] s. detective, detectivo, policía secreto.

detention [dɪténʃən] s. detención.

detergent [dɪtɜ́dʒənt] s. detergente.

deteriorate [dɪtírɪəret] v. deteriorar(se).

deterioration [dɪtɪrɪəréʃən] s. deterioro.

determination [dɪtɜrmənéʃən] s. determinación; decisión; resolución, firmeza.

determine [dɪtɜ́rmɪn] v. determinar; decidir; **to — to** determinarse a, decidirse a, resolverse a.

determined [dɪtɜ́rmɪnd] adj. determinado, decidido, resuelto.

detest [dɪtést] v. detestar, aborrecer.

detour [dɪtúr] s. rodeo, desvío, desviación, vuelta; v. dar o hacer un rodeo.

devastate [dévəstet] v. devastar, arruinar, asolar.

develop [dɪvéləp] v. desarrollar(se); desenvolver(se); revelar (*una película o placa fotográfica*); explotar (*una mina*).

development [dɪvéləpmənt] s. (*evolution*) desarrollo; desenvolvimiento; evolución; crecimiento; (*generation*)

fomento; explotación; (*photo*) revelado.

deviate [dívɪet] v. desviar(se).

deviation [divɪéʃən] s. desviación; desvío, extravío.

device [dɪváɪs] s. artificio; mecanismo, aparato; ardid, recurso; divisa; **left to one's own -s** abandonado a sus propios recursos.

devil [dévl] s. diablo; demonio.

devilish [dévlɪʃ] adj. diabólico; endiablado; travieso.

deviltry [dévltrɪ] s. diablura.

devious [dívɪəs] adj. desviado; tortuoso; indirecto.

devise [dɪváɪz] v. idear, trazar, urdir.

devoid [dɪvɔ́ɪd] adj. exento, libre, falto, privado, desprovisto.

devote [dɪvót] v. dedicar; consagrar; **to — oneself to** dedicarse a, consagrarse a, aplicarse a.

devoted [dɪvótɪd] adj. dedicado, consagrado; apegado; **— friend** amigo fiel o leal.

devotion [dɪvóʃən] s. devoción; piedad; afecto; lealtad.

devour [dɪváur] v. devorar.

devout [dɪváut] adj. devoto, piadoso; sincero.

dew [dju] s. rocío, sereno; v. rociar; caer (*el rocío*).

dewdrop [djúdrap] s. gota de rocío.

dewy [djúɪ] adj. rociado, húmedo de rocío.

dexterity [dekstérətɪ] s. destreza.

dexterous [dékstrəs] adj. diestro.

dextrose [dékstros] s. dextrosa.

diadem [dáɪədem] s. diadema.

diagnose [daɪəgnós] v. diagnosticar.

diagonal [daɪǽgənl] adj. diagonal, oblicuo; s. diagonal.

diagram [dáɪəgræm] s. diagrama.

dial [dáɪəl] s. esfera; muestra (*del reloj*), *Méx., C.A.* carátula; **— telephone** teléfono automático; v. sintonizar o captar (*una estación radiotelefónica*).

dialect [dáɪəlekt] s. dialecto.

dialogue [dáɪələg] s. diálogo; v. dialogar.

diameter [daɪǽmətə] s. diámetro.

diamond [dáɪmənd] s. diamante; rombo (*figura geométrica*).

diaper [dáɪəpə] s. pañal.

diarrhea [daɪəríə] s. diarrea.

diary [dáɪərɪ] s. diario.

dice [daɪs] s. *pl. de* **die** dados; v. cuadricular, cortar en cuarterones o cubos.

dichotomy [daɪkátəmɪ] s. dicotomía.

dictate [díktet] s. dictado, precepto; v. dictar.

dictation [dɪktéʃən] s. dictado; mando absoluto; **to take —** escribir al dictado.

dictator [díktetə] s. dictador.

dictatorship [dɪktétəʃɪp] s. dictadura.

diction [díkʃən] s. dicción.

dictionary [díkʃənerɪ] s. diccionario.

did [dɪd] *pret. de* **to do.**

die [daɪ] s. (*pl.* **dice**) dado (*para jugar*); (*pl.* **dies**) matriz, molde; cuño (*sello* *para acuñar moneda).*

die [daɪ] *v.* morir(se); marchitarse, secarse (*las flores, plantas, etc.*); **to — out** morirse, extinguirse, apagarse.

dieresis [daɪérəsɪs] *s.* diéresis.

diet [dáɪət] *s.* dieta; régimen; **to be on a —** estar a dieta; **to put on a —** adietar, poner a dieta; *v.* ponerse a dieta; estar a dieta.

differ [dífə] *v.* diferir, diferenciarse, distinguirse; disentir; **to — with** no convenir con, no estar de acuerdo con.

difference [dífrəns] *s.* diferencia; distinción; discordia, controversia; **it makes no —** no importa, es igual, da lo mismo.

different [dífrənt] *adj.* diferente; distinto.

differentiate [dɪfərénʃɪet] *v.* diferenciar(se); distinguir(se).

difficult [dífəkʌlt] *adj.* difícil; dificultoso, trabajoso, penoso.

difficulty [dífəkʌltɪ] *s.* dificultad; apuro, aprieto.

diffidence [dífədəns] *s.* timidez; desconfianza de sí propio.

diffident [dífədənt] *adj.* huraño; tímido.

diffuse [dɪfjús] *adj.* difuso; prolijo; [dɪfjúz] *v.* difundir.

diffusion [dɪfjúʒən] *s.* difusión; diseminación.

dig [dɪg] *v.* cavar; excavar; ahondar; escarbar; trabajar duro; **to — under** socavar; **to — up** desenterrar; *s.* piquete; pulla, sarcasmo.

digest [dáɪdʒɛst] *s.* sumario, compendio; recopilación; código; [dədʒést] *v.* digerir; recopilar.

digestible [dədʒéstəbl] *adj.* digestible, digerible.

digestion [dədʒéstʃən] *s.* digestión.

digestive [dədʒéstɪv] *adj.* digestivo.

dignified [dígnəfaɪd] *adj.* digno, mesurado; serio, grave.

dignitary [dígnətɛrɪ] *s.* dignatario.

dignity [dígnətɪ] *s.* dignidad.

digraph [dáɪgræf] *s.* dígrafo.

digress [dəgrés] *v.* divagar.

digression [dəgréʃən] *s.* digresión, divagación.

dike [daɪk] *s.* dique, represa; zanja.

dilate [daɪlét] *v.* dilatar(se), extender(se), ensanchar(se).

diligence [dílədʒəns] *s.* diligencia; aplicación, esmero.

diligent [dílədʒənt] *adj.* diligente, activo, aplicado.

dilute [dɪlút] *v.* diluir, desleír; aguar; *adj.* diluido.

dim [dɪm] *adj.* penumbroso, obscuro; nublado; confuso; indistinto; deslustrado, sin brillo; *v.* obscurecer; anublar, ofuscar; atenuar.

dime [daɪm] *s.* moneda de diez centavos.

dimension [dəménʃən] *s.* dimensión.

diminish [dəmínɪʃ] *v.* disminuir; rebajar.

diminution [dɪmənjúʃən] *s.* diminución, mengua.

diminutive [dəmínjətɪv] *adj.* diminutivo; diminuto; *s.* diminutivo.

dimness [dímnɪs] *s.* semi-obscuridad, penumbra; ofuscamiento.

dimple [dímpl] *s.* hoyuelo.

din [dɪn] *s.* estruendo, fragor, estrépito.

dine [daɪn] *v.* comer; festejar u obsequiar con una comida.

diner [dáɪnə] *s.* coche-comedor; comensal *(persona que come en la mesa).*

dingy [díndʒɪ] *adj.* negruzco; manchado, sucio.

dining [dáɪnɪŋ] *ger. de* **to dine; — car** coche-comedor; **— room** comedor.

dinner [dínə] *s.* comida; **— coat** smoking o esmoquin.

dint [dɪnt]: **by — of** a fuerza de.

diorama [daɪəræmə] *s.* diorama.

dip [dɪp] *s.* zambullida; inmersión; bajada; declive; depresión; *v.* meter(se); zambullirse; mojar (*la pluma en el tintero*); teñir; agachar (*la cabeza*); saludar (*con la bandera*); inclinarse (*un camino*); dar un bajón (*un avión*); hundirse (*el sol en el horizonte*); **to — out** vaciar (*con cucharón o cazo*).

diphtheria [dɪfθírɪə] *s.* difteria.

diphthong [dífθɔŋ] *s.* diptongo.

diploma [dɪplómə] *s.* diploma.

diplomacy [dɪplóməsɪ] *s.* diplomacia.

diplomat [dípləmæt] *s.* diplomático.

diplomatic [dɪpləmǽtɪk] *adj.* diplomático.

dipper [dípə] *s.* cucharón, cazo; **the Big Dipper** la Osa Mayor.

dire [daɪr] *adj.* extremo; horrendo; fatal, de mal agüero.

direct [dərékt] *adj.* (*straight*) directo, derecho, en línea recta; *C.A.* recto; (*immediate*) inmediato; **— current** corriente continua; **— object** acusativo; *adv.* directamente; **-ly** *adv.* directamente; inmediatamente; en seguida; *v.* dirigir; guiar; encaminar; dar direcciones ú ordenes.

direction [dərékʃən] *s.* dirección; administración; gerencia; rumbo.

directional antenna [dərékʃən ænténə] *s.* antena direccional.

directional signal [dərékʃən sígnl] *s.* señal direccional.

directive [dəréktɪv] *adj.* directivo; *s.* orden, mandato.

directness [dəréktnɪs] *s.* derechura; franqueza; lo directo; **with — sin** rodeos.

director [dəréktə] *s.* director; gerente.

directory [dəréktərɪ] *s.* directorio; junta directiva; **telephone —** guía telefónica.

dirigible [dírədʒəbl] *adj. & s.* dirigible.

dirt [dɜrt] *s.* suciedad; mugre; tierra, polvo, lodo.

dirty [dɜrtɪ] *adj.* sucio; mugriento; cochino; enlodado; manchado; *v.* ensuciar; manchar; enlodar.

disable [dɪsébl] *v.* incapacitar.

disadvantage [dɪsədvǽntɪdʒ] *s.* desventaja; **to be at a —** estar en una situación desventajosa.

disagree [dɪsəgrí] *v.* (*dissent*) diferir,

DE

disentir; no convenir, no estar de acuerdo; (*bad effect*) no sentarle bien a uno (*el clima, la comida, etc.*).

disagreeable [dɪsəgríəbl] *adj.* desagradable; áspero, de mal genio.

disagreement [dɪsəgrímənt] *s.* desavenencia, desacuerdo; disensión; discordia; discordancia.

disallow [dísəlaʊ] *v.* desaprobar; rechazar.

disappear [dɪsəpír] *v.* desaparecer.

disappearance [dɪsəpírəns] *s.* desaparición.

disappoint [dɪsəpóɪnt] *v.* chasquear; contrariar; decepcionar; faltar a lo prometido; desilusionar; **to be -ed** estar desilusionado o decepcionado; estar desengañado; quedar contrariado.

disappointing [dɪsəpóɪntɪŋ] *adj.* desilusionante, desengañador, decepcionante.

disappointment [dɪsəpóɪntmənt] *s.* desilusión, desengaño, decepción; chasco; contrariedad.

disapproval [dɪsəprúvl] *s.* desaprobación.

disapprove [dɪsəprúv] *v.* desaprobar.

disarm [dɪsárm] *v.* desarmar(se).

disarmament [dɪsárməmənt] *s.* desarme.

disarray [dɪsəré] *s.* desarreglo, confusión, desorden; *v.* desarreglar, desordenar.

disaster [dɪzǽstə] *s.* desastre.

disastrous [dɪzǽstrəs] *adj.* desastroso.

disband [dɪsbǽnd] *v.* dispersar; licenciar (*las tropas*); desbandarse.

disbelieve [dɪsbəlív] *v.* descreer, no creer.

disburse [dɪsbə́s] *v.* desembolsar.

disbursement [dɪsbə́smənt] *s.* desembolso; gasto.

disc [dɪsk] = **disk**.

discard [dískard] *s.* descarte; desecho, cosa desechada; [dɪskárd] *v.* descartar; desechar.

discern [dɪsə́n] *v.* discernir, distinguir; percibir.

discernment [dɪsə́nmənt] *s.* discernimiento.

discharge [dɪstʃárdʒ] *s.* descarga (*de artillería*); descargo (*de una obligación*); desempeño (*de un deber*); exoneración; despedida; licencia (*militar*); pago (*de una deuda*); derrame, desagüe; supuración; *v.* descargar; exonerar; poner en libertad; despedir, echar, deponer; dar de baja (*a un soldado*); pagar (*una deuda*); arrojar, supurar; desaguar.

disciple [dɪsáɪpl] *s.* discípulo.

discipline [dísəplɪn] *s.* disciplina; *v.* disciplinar.

disclose [dɪsklóz] *v.* descubrir; revelar.

discolor [dɪskʌ́lə] *v.* descolorar(se), desteñir(se).

discomfort [dɪskʌ́mfət] *s.* incomodidad; malestar.

disconcert [dɪskənsə́t] *v.* desconcertar.

disconnect [dɪskənékt] *v.* desconectar; desunir, separar.

disconnected [dɪskənéktɪd] *p.p.* & *adj.* desconectado; desunido; inconexo, incoherente.

disconsolate [dɪskánsļɪt] *adj.* desconsolado.

discontent [dɪskəntént] *s.* descontento; *v.* descontentar.

discontented [dɪskənténtɪd] *adj.* descontento; descontentadizo.

discontinue [dɪskəntínju] *v.* descontinuar; parar; suspender, interrumpir; abandonar.

discord [dískɔrd] *s.* discordia; disonancia, discordancia; desavenencia.

discount [dískaʊnt] *s.* descuento; rebaja; **— rate** tipo de descuento; *v.* descontar; rebajar.

discourage [dɪskə́ɪdʒ] *v.* desanimar, desalentar, abatir; **to — from** disuadir de.

discouragement [dɪskə́ɪdʒmənt] *s.* desaliento, abatimiento.

discourse [dískɔrs] *s.* discurso; conversación; [dɪskórs] *v.* disertar, discurrir, hablar.

discourteous [dɪskə́ɪtɪəs] *adj.* descortés, desatento.

discourtesy [dɪskə́təsɪ] *s.* descortesía, desatención.

discover [dɪskʌ́və] *v.* descubrir.

discoverer [dɪskʌ́vərə] *s.* descubridor.

discovery [dɪskʌ́vrɪ] *s.* descubrimiento.

discredit [dɪskrédɪt] *s.* descrédito; deshonra; *v.* desacreditar; deshonrar; no creer.

discreet [dɪskrit] *adj.* discreto, prudente.

discrepancy [dɪskrépənsɪ] *s.* discrepancia, diferencia; variación.

discretion [dɪskréʃən] *s.* discreción; prudencia; **at one's own —** a discreción.

discriminate [dɪskrímənet] *v.* discernir; distinguir; hacer distinciones, hacer favoritismos; dar trato de inferioridad con motivos de prejuicio; **to — against** hacer favoritismos en perjuicio de.

discuss [dɪskʌ́s] *v.* discutir.

discussion [dɪskʌ́ʃən] *s.* discusión.

disdain [dɪsdén] *s.* desdén, menosprecio; *v.* desdeñar, menospreciar; desdeñarse de.

disdainful [dɪsdénfəl] *adj.* desdeñoso.

disease [dɪzíz] *s.* enfermedad.

diseased [dɪzízd] *adj.* enfermo.

disembark [dɪsɪmbárk] *v.* desembarcar.

disentangle [dɪsɪntǽŋgl] *v.* desenredar, desenmarañar, deshacer (*una maraña o enredo*).

disfigure [dɪsfígjə] *v.* desfigurar; afear.

disfranchise [dɪsfrǽntʃaɪz] *v.* privar de derecho de voto o de ciudadanía.

disgrace [dɪsgrés] *s.* ignominia, deshonra; vergüenza; **to be in —** estar desacreditado, haber perdido la gracia o el favor; *v.* deshonrar; degradar; desacreditar; avergonzar.

disgraceful [dɪsgrésfəl] *adj.* vergonzoso.

disguise [dɪsgáɪz] s. disfraz; v. disfrazar.

disgust [dɪsgást] s. asco; repugnancia; disgusto; v. disgustar, dar asco; repugnar.

disgusted [dɪsgástɪd] adj. disgustado; descontento; asqueado.

disgusting [dɪsgástɪŋ] adj. asqueroso, repugnante.

dish [dɪʃ] s. plato; manjar, vianda; **-es** vajilla; v. servir.

dishearten [dɪshártn] v. desalentar, desanimar, descorazonar.

disheveled [dɪʃévld] adj. desgreñado; desaliñado, desaseado.

dishonest [dɪsánɪst] adj. engañoso, falso, tramposo, falto de honradez, fraudulento.

dishonesty [dɪsánɪstɪ] s. fraude, falta de honradez.

dishonor [dɪsánɚ] s. deshonra; afrenta; v. deshonrar; recusar (*un giro o cheque*).

dishonorable [dɪsánɚəbl] adj. deshonroso; infame.

dishwasher [dɪʃwɑʃɚ] s. (*person*) lavaplatos; (*machine*) máquina de lavar platos.

disillusion [dɪsɪlúʒən] s. desilusión, decepción, desengaño; v. desilusionar, decepcionar, desengañar.

disinfect [dɪsɪnfékt] v. desinfectar.

disinfectant [dɪsɪnféktənt] s. desinfectante.

disinterested [dɪsíntərəstɪd] adj. desinteresado.

disk [dɪsk] s. disco; **— brake** freno de disco.

dislike [dɪsláɪk] s. antipatía, aversión; v. sentir o tener aversión por; **I — it** me repugna, no me gusta, me desagrada.

dislocate [dísloket] v. dislocar, descoyuntar.

dislodge [dɪsládʒ] v. desalojar.

disloyal [dɪslɔ́ɪəl] adj. desleal.

dismal [dízml] adj. lúgubre, sombrío, tétrico.

dismantle [dɪsmǽntl] v. desmantelar; desmontar, desarmar.

dismay [dɪsmé] s. desmayo, desaliento, pavor; v. desalentar, desanimar, atemorizar.

dismiss [dɪsmís] v. (*discharge*) despedir, expulsar, destituir; (*dispel*) desechar; (*allow to leave*) licenciar, dar de baja; (*close*) dar por terminado (*un pleito o caso jurídico*); **to — the meeting** disolver la junta, levantar la sesión.

dismissal [dɪsmísl] s. despedida, expulsión, destitución (*de un cargo*).

dismount [dɪsmáunt] v. desmontar; apear(se); desarmar (*un cañón, una máquina*); desengastar (*joyas*).

disobedience [dɪsəbídɪəns] s. desobediencia.

disobedient [dɪsəbídɪənt] adj. desobediente.

disobey [dɪsəbé] v. desobedecer.

disorder [dɪsórdɚ] s. (*confusion*) desorden; trastorno; confusión; (*illness*) enfermedad; v. desordenar; trastornar; desarreglar.

disorderly [dɪsórdɚlɪ] adj. desordenado; desarreglado; revoltoso; escandaloso; adv. desordenadamente.

disown [dɪsón] v. repudiar; desconocer, negar.

disparage [dɪspǽrɪdʒ] v. desacreditar; desdorar.

dispassionate [dɪspǽʃənɪt] adj. desapasionado.

dispatch [dɪspǽtʃ] s. despacho; envío; parte (m.), comunicación, mensaje; prontitud, expedición; v. despachar; enviar, expedir; matar.

dispel [dɪspél] v. disipar, dispersar.

dispensary [dɪspénsərɪ] s. dispensario.

dispensation [dɪspənséʃən] s. dispensa, exención; dispensación; distribución.

dispense [dɪspéns] v. (*give*) dispensar, dar; repartir, distribuir; administrar (*la justicia*); despachar (*recetas, medicamentos*); **to — from** eximir de, dispensar de; **to — with** omitir; pasarse sin, prescindir de.

dispersal [dɪspɚsl] s. dispersión; desbandada.

disperse [dɪspɚs] v. dispersar(se), disipar(se), esparcir(se).

displace [dɪsplés] v. desalojar; desplazar; poner fuera de su lugar; suplantar.

display [dɪsplé] s. manifestación, exhibición; ostentación; v. exhibir; mostrar, manifestar; desplegar.

displease [dɪsplíz] v. desagradar; disgustar, fastidiar.

displeasure [dɪspléʒɚ] s. desagrado, disgusto, descontento.

disposal [dɪspózl] s. disposición; arreglo; venta (*de bienes*).

dispose [dɪspóz] v. disponer; arreglar; influir; **to — of** deshacerse de.

disposition [dɪspəzíʃən] s. disposición; arreglo; aptitud, inclinación; venta; **good (bad)** — buen (mal) genio.

disprove [dɪsprúv] v. refutar.

dispute [dɪspjút] s. disputa; v. disputar.

disqualify [dɪskwáləfaɪ] v. inhabilitar, incapacitar, descalificar.

disregard [dɪsrɪgárd] s. desatención, falta de atención, negligencia, descuido; falta de respeto o consideración; v. desatender, no hacer caso de, desentenderse de.

disrespect [dɪsrɪspékt] s. desacato, falta de respeto.

disrespectful [dɪsrɪspéktfəl] adj. irrespetuoso.

dissatisfied [dɪssǽtɪsfaɪd] adj. descontento, malcontento, mal satisfecho.

dissatisfy [dɪssǽtɪsfaɪ] v. descontentar, no satisfacer.

dissect [dɪsékt] v. disecar, hacer una disección; analizar.

dissemble [dɪsémbl] v. disimular, fingir.

dissension [dɪsénʃən] s. disensión, discordia.

dissent [dɪsént] v. disentir; s. desacuerdo; disensión, desavenencia.

dissimulation [dɪsɪmjəléʃən] *s.* disimulo.

dissipate [dísəpət] *v.* disipar(se).

dissipation [dɪsəpéʃən] *s.* disipación.

dissolute [dísəlut] *adj.* disoluto.

dissolution [dɪsəlúʃən] *s.* disolución.

dissolve [dɪzálv] *v.* disolver(se); anular.

dissuade [dɪswéd] *v.* disuadir.

distaff [dístæf] *s.* rueca.

distance [dístəns] *s.* distancia; lejanía; alejamiento; **in the —** a lo lejos, en lontananza.

distant [dístənt] *adj.* (*far*) distante; apartado, lejano, remoto; (*aloof*) esquivo; **to be — from** distar de; **-ly** *adv.* de lejos; remotamente; a distancia; en lontananza.

distaste [dɪstést] *s.* disgusto, aversión, repugnancia.

distasteful [dɪstéstfəl] *adj.* desagradable, repugnante.

distemper [dɪstémpə] *s.* moquillo; pepita (*de las gallinas*).

distend [dɪsténd] *v.* dilatar, ensanchar.

distil [dɪstíl] *v.* destilar.

distillation [dɪstɪléʃən] *s.* destilación.

distillery [dɪstíləri] *s.* destilería.

distinct [dɪstíŋkt] *adj.* distinto, claro; diferente; **-ly** *adv.* distintamente, claramente, con claridad.

distinction [dɪstíŋkʃən] *s.* distinción.

distinctive [dɪstíŋktɪv] *adj.* distintivo.

distinguish [dɪstíŋgwɪʃ] *v.* distinguir; discernir.

distinguished [dɪstíŋgwɪʃt] *adj.* distinguido.

distinguishing [dɪstíŋgwɪʃɪŋ] *adj.* distintivo, característico.

distort [dɪstórt] *v.* desfigurar, deformar, torcer, falsear; tergiversar.

distract [dɪstrækt] *v.* distraer; perturbar.

distraction [dɪstrǽkʃən] *s.* distracción, diversión; perturbación; **to drive to —** volver loco.

distress [dɪstrés] *s.* angustia, aflicción, congoja; dolor; **to be in —** tener una aflicción; estar apurado; estar en zozobra (*un navío*); *v.* angustiar, acongojar, afligir; **to be -ed** estar afligido o apurado.

distribute [dɪstríbjut] *v.* distribuir, repartir.

distribution [dɪstrəbjúʃən] *s.* distribución; repartimiento.

distributor [dɪstríbjətə] *s.* distribuidor.

district [dístrɪkt] *s.* distrito; **— attorney** fiscal de distrito.

distrust [dɪstrást] *s.* desconfianza; recelo; *v.* desconfiar; recelar.

distrustful [dɪstrástfəl] *adj.* desconfiado, sospechoso, receloso.

disturb [dɪstə́b] *v.* turbar, perturbar, inquietar; desarreglar; incomodar, molestar; **don't — yourself!** ¡no se moleste Vd.!

disturbance [dɪstə́bəns] *s.* disturbio; perturbación; desorden; alboroto; molestia.

disuse [dɪsjús] *s.* desuso; **to fall into —** caer en desuso; caducar.

ditch [dɪtʃ] *s.* zanja; foso; **irrigation —** acequia; *v.* zanjar, abrir zanjas; meter en la zanja; **to — someone** deshacerse de alguien.

ditto [díto] *s.* ídem, lo mismo.

diuretic [daɪjurétɪk] *adj.* & *s.* diurético.

divan [dáɪvæn] *s.* diván.

dive [daɪv] *s.* zambullida (*echándose de cabeza*), buceada, chapuz; picada (*descenso rápido de un avión*); *Méx.* clavado; garito, leonera; *v.* echarse de cabeza; zambullirse (*de cabeza*); bucear; sumergirse (*un submarino*); **to — into someone** abalanzarse sobre alguien.

diver [dáɪvə] *s.* buzo; zambullidor.

diverge [dəvə́dʒ] *v.* divergir, irse apartando, separarse; diferir.

divergence [dəvə́dʒəns] *s.* divergencia; diferencia (*de opiniones*).

divers [dáɪvəz] *adj.* diversos, varios.

diverse [dəvə́s] *adj.* diverso; diferente.

diversion [dəvə́ʒən] *s.* diversión, recreo; desviación.

diversity [dəvə́səti] *s.* diversidad, diferencia, variedad.

divert [dəvə́t] *v.* divertir, entretener; distraer; desviar, apartar.

divide [dəváid] *v.* dividir(se); partir.

dividend [dívədend] *s.* dividendo.

divine [dəváin] *adj.* divino; *v.* adivinar.

divinity [dəvínəti] *s.* divinidad; deidad; teología.

division [dəvíʒən] *s.* división.

divorce [dəvórs] *s.* divorcio; *v.* divorciar(se).

divulge [dəváldʒ] *v.* divulgar.

dizziness [dízɪnɪs] *s.* vahído o vaguido, desvanecimiento, mareo, vértigo.

dizzy [dízɪ] *adj.* desvanecido, mareado; confuso; aturdido; **— speed** velocidad vertiginosa.

do [du] *v.* hacer; **to — away with** deshacerse de; prescindir de; **to — a lesson** estudiar una lección; **to — one's hair** peinarse, arreglarse el pelo; **to — the dishes** lavar los platos; **to — up** envolver; limpiar, arreglar; lavar o planchar; **to — well in business** prosperar en los negocios; **to — without** pasarse sin; **to have nothing to — with** no tener nada que ver con; **that will —** basta, bastará; **that won't —** eso no sirve; eso no resultará bien; **this will have to —** habrá que conformarse con esto; **how — you — ?** ¿cómo está Vd.?; **— you hear me?** ¿me oye Vd.?; **yes, I —** sí, le oigo; **I — say it** sí lo digo.

docile [dásl] *adj.* dócil.

dock [dak] *s.* muelle, desembarcadero; dársena; **dry —** carenero, dique de carena; *v.* entrar en el muelle; atracar, meter (*una embarcación*) en el muelle o dique; **to — the wages** rebajar la paga.

doctor [dáktə] *s.* doctor; médico, facultativo; *v.* medicinar, curar; **to — oneself** medicinarse, tomar medicinas.

doctrine [dáktrɪn] s. doctrina.
document [dákjəmənt] s. documento; [dákjəmɛnt] v. documentar.
dodder [dádə] v. tambalear; temblar.
dodge [dadʒ] s. evasión, evasiva; v. evadir(se); escabullirse; hurtar el cuerpo; **to — around a corner** dar un esquinazo.
doe [do] s. cierva; hembra (del antílope, del gamo, de la liebre).
dog [dɔg] s. perro, perra; can; **hot —** salchicha caliente, Ch., C.A. perro caliente; Ríopl. pancho; **to put on a lot of —** emperifollarse; darse mucho tono, Ríopl. darse mucho corte; v. seguir la pista de, perseguir, acosar; adv. sumamente, completamente; **dog-tired** cansadísimo.
dogma [dɔ́gmə] s. dogma.
dogmatic [dɔgmǽtɪk] adj. dogmático.
doily [dɔ́ɪlɪ] s. mantelito (para platos, vasos, lámparas, etc.).
doings [dúɪŋz] s. pl. hechos, acciones, acontecimientos; **great —** mucha actividad, fiesta, función.
do-it-yourself [duɪtjʊrsɛ́lf] adj. proyectado para que uno pueda hacer sus propios trabajos manuales en casa.
dole [dol] s. reparto gratuito (de dinero o alimento); ración, limosna; v. repartir gratuitamente.
doleful [dólfəl] adj. lúgubre, triste, lastimoso.
doll [dal] s. muñeca, muñeco; v. **to — up** emperifollarse, ataviarse; **dolly** s. muñequita.
dollar [dálə] s. dólar.
dolphin [dólfɪn] s. delfín.
domain [domén] s. dominio; heredad.
dome [dom] s. cúpula: media naranja (de iglesia).
domestic [dəmɛ́stɪk] adj. doméstico; hogareño; nacional, del país, Am. criollo; s. criado, sirviente.
domicile [dáməsaɪl] s. domicilio.
dominant [dámənənt] adj. dominante.
dominate [dámənet] v. dominar.
domination [damənéʃən] s. dominación, dominio.
domineer [damənír] v. dominar, señorear.
domineering [damənírɪŋ] adj. dominador, mandón, imperioso, tiránico.
dominion [dəmɪ́njən] s. dominio.
domino [dámən̩o] s. dominó, traje de máscara; disfraz; ficha (de dominó); **dominoes** dominó (juego).
don [dan] s. don (título); caballero; v. ponerse, vestirse.
donate [dónet] v. donar, regalar, hacer donación.
donation [donéʃən] s. donación; regalo, dádiva.
done [dʌn] p.p. de **to do** hecho; terminado, acabado; **to be — in** estar rendido de cansancio; **the meat is well —** está bien asada la carne.
donkey [dáŋkɪ] s. burro, asno.
doodad [dúdæd] s. chuchería, chisme.
doom [dum] s. hado, sino, destino;

mala suerte, perdición, ruina; **the day of —** el día del juicio final; v. condenar, sentenciar; predestinar; **to be -ed to failure** estar predestinado al fracaso.
door [dor] s. puerta; entrada.
doorbell [dórbɛl] s. campanilla o timbre (de llamada).
doorknob [dórnɑb] s. tirador de puerta, perilla, manija.
doorman [dórmæn] s. portero.
doorstep [dórstɛp] s. escalón de la puerta; umbral.
doorway [dórwe] s. puerta, entrada; vano (de la puerta).
dope [dop] s. (narcotic) narcótico; opio; droga; menjurje, medicamento; (information) información; **— fiend** morfinómano; **he is a —** es un zoquete; v. narcotizar; **to — out** adivinar, conjeturar; **to — oneself up** medicinarse demasiado.
dormitory [dórmətorɪ] s. dormitorio.
dose [dos] s. dosis; v. medicinar; **to — oneself** medicinarse.
dot [dat] s. punto; **on the —** en punto; v. marcar con puntos; poner el punto (sobre la i).
dotage [dótɪdʒ] s. chochez; **to be in one's —** chochear.
dote [dot] v. chochear; **to — on** estar loco por.
double [dʌ́bl̩] adj. doble; doblado; **— boiler** baño de María; **— deal** trato doble; **— entry** partida doble; **— standard** norma de conducta sexual mas restringida para la mujer; s. doble; **-s** juego de dobles (en tenis); adv. doblemente; **double-breasted** cruzado; **double-faced** de dos caras; v. doblar(se); duplicar(se); **to — up** doblarse; **doubly** adv. doblemente; por duplicado.
doubt [daut] s. duda; v. dudar.
doubtful [dáutfəl] adj. dudoso; dudable.
doubtless [dáutlɪs] adj. indudable, cierto, seguro; adv. sin duda; indudablemente; probablemente.
douche [duʃ] s. ducha; jeringa.
dough [do] s. pasta, masa; dinero.
doughnut [dónət] s. bollito o buñuelo en rosca.
dove [dʌv] s. paloma.
dove [dov] pret. de **to dive**.
down [daun] adv. abajo, hacia abajo; **— to** hasta; **— East** en el este; **— the street** calle abajo; **to cut — prices** reducir o rebajar precios; **to get — to work** aplicarse; **to go** (o **come**) **—** bajar; **to pay —** pagar al contado; **to put —** poner; anotar, apuntar, poner por escrito; adj. abatido, descorazonado; **— grade** declive, pendiente; **prices are —** han bajado los precios; **to be — on someone** tenerle ojeriza a alguien; s. plumón; vello; pelusa; v. echar por tierra, derribar; rebajar (precios).
downcast [dáunkæst] adj. cabizbajo, abatido; **with — eyes** con los ojos

bajos.

downfall [dáʊnfɔl] *s.* caída; ruina.

downpour [dáʊnpor] *s.* aguacero, chaparrón.

downright [dáʊnraɪt] *adj.* claro, positivo, categórico, absoluto; — **foolishness** solemne disparate; *adv.* enteramente; absolutamente.

downstairs [dáʊnstɛrz] *adv.* abajo; en el piso bajo; *adj.* del piso bajo; *s.* piso bajo, piso inferior.

downstream [dáʊnstrím]*adv.* río abajo, aguas abajo; con la corriente.

downtown [dáʊntáʊn] *adv.* al centro, en el centro (*de una población*); *adj.* del centro; *s.* centro.

downward [dáʊnwəd]*adj.* descendente; inclinado; *adv.* (=**downwards**) hacia abajo.

downy [dáʊnɪ] *adj.* suave, blando; velloso; plumoso.

dowry [dáʊrɪ] *s.* dote.

doze [doz] *s.* siestecita, sueño ligero; *v.* dormitar.

dozen [dʌzn] *s.* docena.

drab [dræb] *adj.* pardo, pardusco; monótono.

draft [dræft] *s.* corriente de aire; trago; libranza, letra de cambio, giro bancario; trazado; plan; leva (*militar*); conscripción; tiro (*de estufa, hogar, etc.*); calado (*de un barco*); — **beer** cerveza de barril; — **horse** caballo de tiro; **rough** — croquis, borrador; *v.* trazar, dibujar, delinear, reclutar; echar leva; redactar (*un documento*).

draftsman [dræftsmən] *s.* dibujante.

drag [dræg] *s.* rastra, traba, obstáculo; **to have a** — **with someone** tener buenas aldabas con alguien; *v.* arrastrar(se); rastrear; moverse despacio; **to** — **on and on** prolongarse demasiado, prolongarse hasta el fastidio.

dragon [drǽgən] *s.* dragón.

drain [dren] *s.* (*channel*) desagüe; desaguadero, conducto; (*exhaust*) agotamiento; consumo; *v.* desaguar(se); apurar (*un vaso*); agotar, consumir; escurrir(se), secar(se); desecar (*un terreno*), *Am.* drenar.

drainage [drénɪdʒ] *s.* desagüe, *Am.* drenaje; desaguadero; sistema de desaguaderos; desecamiento, desecación (*de un terreno, laguna, etc.*).

drake [drek] *s.* pato.

drama [drámə] *s.* drama.

dramatic [drəmǽtɪk] *adj.* dramático.

dramatist [drúmətɪst] *s.* dramaturgo, dramático.

dramatize [drǽmətaɪz] *v.* dramatizar.

drank [dræŋk] *pret. de to* **drink**.

drape [drep] *s.* colgadura, cortina, tapiz; *v.* colgar, entapizar, adornar con tapices; cubrir, revestir.

drapery [drépərɪ] *s.* tapicería, colgaduras, cortinas; pañería, paños, géneros.

drastic [drǽstɪk] *adj.* extremo, fuerte, violento; **to take** — **steps** tomar medidas enérgicas.

draught [dræft] *véase* **draft**.

draw [drɔ] *v.* (*pull*) tirar; estirar; jalar (*halar*); (*attract*) atraer; sacar; (*design*) dibujar, trazar; (*withdraw*) girar, librar (*una libranza*); hacer (*una comparación*); correr (*la cortina*); to — **aside** apartar(se); to — **a breath** aspirar, tomar aliento; to — **lots** echar suertes, sortear; to — **near** acercarse; to — **out** sacar; sonsacar (*a una persona*); alargar, prolongar; to — **up** acercar(se); redactar (*un documento*); *s.* empate (*en deportes o juegos*); número sacado (*en una rifa*); atracción; —**bridge** puente levadizo.

drawback [drɔ́bæk] *s.* desventaja; obstáculo, inconveniente.

drawer [drɔr] *s.* cajón, gaveta; **-s** calzoncillos.

drawer [drɔ́ə] *s.* librador, girador; dibujante.

drawing [drɔ́ɪŋ] *s.* (*design*) dibujo; delineación, trazado; (*raffle*) sorteo; — **paper** papel de dibujo; — **room** sala de recibo, recibidor, recibimiento.

drawn [drɔn] *p.p. de to* **draw**.

dread [drɛd] *s.* pavor, temor, aprensión; *adj.* terrible; temido; *v.* temer; sentir aprensión de.

dreadful [drédfəl] *adj.* horrendo; espantoso.

dream [drim] *s.* sueño; ensueño; *v.* soñar; to — **of** soñar con, soñar en.

dreamer [drímə] *s.* soñador.

dreamland [drímlænd] *s.* tierra del ensueño; región de los sueños.

dreamt [drɛmpt] = **dreamed**.

dreamy [drímɪ] *adj.* soñoliento; soñador; melancólico; como un sueño; **a** — **recollection** un vago recuerdo.

dreary [drírɪ] *adj.* sombrío; melancólico.

dredge [drɛdʒ] *s.* draga; *v.* dragar.

dregs [drɛgz] *s. pl.* heces, sedimento.

drench [drɛntʃ] *s.* mojada, mojadura, empapada; *v.* empapar; mojar; remojar.

dress [drɛs] *s.* vestido, traje; vestidura, ropaje, atavío; — **rehearsal** ensayo general y último (*antes de una función*); — **suit** traje de etiqueta; *v.* vestir(se); arreglarse, componerse; aderezar; adobar (*carne o pieles*); curar (*heridas*); alinear, formar (*las tropas*); to — **down** reprender, regañar; to — **up** emperifollarse, acicalarse, ataviarse.

dresser [drésə] *s.* tocador, cómoda (*con espejo*); **she is a good** — viste con elegancia o buen gusto.

dressing [drésɪŋ] *s.* aderezo; salsa (*para ensaladas*); relleno (*para carne, pollo, etc.*); medicamento, vendajes (*para heridas*); **a** — **down** regaño; — **gown** bata; — **room** tocador; — **table** tocador.

dressmaker [drésmekə] *s.* modista.

drew [dru] *pret. de to* **draw**.

dribble [dríbl] *v.* gotear; dejar caer en gotas; babear; *s.* goteo; chorrito.

driblet [dríblɪt] *s.* gota, gotita; **in -s** gota a gota; en pequeñas cantidades.

dried [draɪd] *pret. & p.p. de* **to dry**; *adj.* seco; paso; — **fig** higo paso.

drift [drɪft] *s.* (*direction*) rumbo, dirección, tendencia, deriva; (*pile*) montón, amontonamiento (*de arena, nieve, etc.*); (*off course*) desvío (*de un barco o avión*); **to get the — of a conversation** enterarse a medias de una conversación; *v.* flotar; ir(se) a la deriva; dejarse llevar por la corriente; amontonarse (*la nieve, la arena*); esparcirse (*la arena, la nieve, las nubes*).

driftwood [dríftwʊd] *s.* madera o leña flotante; madera de playa.

drill [drɪl] *s.* (*tool*) taladro; barrena; (*training*) ejercicio; adiestramiento; *Am.* entrenamiento; dril (*tela*); *v.* taladrar, barrenar, perforar; hacer ejercicio; aleccionar; disciplinar (*un ejército*); adiestrar(se), *Am.* entrenar(se).

drily [dráɪli] *adv.* secamente.

drink [drɪŋk] *s.* bebida; trago; *v.* beber; **to — a toast** beber a la salud de, brindar por; **— it down!** ¡bébaselo! ¡trágueselo!

drinkable [dríŋkəbl] *adj.* potable.

drip [drɪp] *s.* goteo; *v.* gotear, caer gota a gota; dejar caer gota a gota.

drive [draɪv] *s.* (*ride*) paseo en coche; (*road*) calzada, carretera, paseo; (*campaign*) campaña; (*impulse*) empuje; tiro, tirada (*de una pelota*); *v.* impulsar, impeler, empujar; arrear (*animales*); conducir, guiar o manejar (*un auto*); forzar; encajar, clavar (*una estaca, cuña, o clavo*); tirar, lanzar (*una pelota*); dar un paseo en auto; llevar (*a alguien*) en auto; cavar (*un pozo, túnel, etc.*); **to — away** ahuyentar; **to — a good bargain** hacer un buen trato; **to — mad** volver loco; **what are you driving at?** ¿qué quieres decir con eso?

drivel [drívl] *s.* baba; ñoñería, tontería; *v.* babear; chochear, decir ñoñerías.

driveling [drívlɪŋ] *adj.* baboso.

driven [drívən] *p.p. de* **to drive**.

driver [dráɪvə] *s.* cochero, chófer, mecánico, conductor (*de automóvil*); arriero (*de animales*); uno de los palos de golf; **pile —** martinete (*para clavar pilotes*); **slave —** mandón, tirano; **truck —** carretero, camionero.

driveway [dráɪvwe] *s.* calzada de entrada, carretera de entrada.

drizzle [drízl] *v.* lloviznar; *s.* llovizna.

drone [dron] *s.* zángano; holgazán; zumbido; *v.* zumbar; hablar con monotonía; holgazanear, perder el tiempo.

droop [drup] *v.* doblarse, andar o estar alicaído, estar abatido; languidecer; marchitarse; bajar (*los hombros, los párpados*); **his shoulders —** tiene los hombros caídos; **-ing eyelids** párpados caídos.

drop [drap] *s.* (*liquid*) gota; (*descent*) baja, caída; (*incline*) declive; **cough —** pastilla para la tos; **letter —** buzón; **— curtain** telón (*de teatro*); **— hammer** martinete; **— out** dimi-

tente; *v.* dejar caer, soltar; gotear; caer; dejar (*un asunto, una amistad*); **to — a line** ponar unos renglones; **to — asleep** quedarse dormido, dormirse; **to — behind** dejar atrás; quedarse atrás; **to — in** hacer una visita inesperada, *Am.* descolgarse; **to — in a mailbox** echar al buzón; **to — out** retirarse; desaparecer; **to — the curtain** bajar el telón.

drought [draʊt] *s.* sequía.

drove [drov] *s.* manada, recua, rebaño; tropel; *pret. de* **to drive**.

drown [draʊn] *v.* ahogar(se), anegar(se), apagar, ahogar (*un sonido*).

drowse [draʊz] *v.* dormitar; estar amodorrado.

drowsiness [dráʊzɪnɪs] *s.* modorra, somnolencia.

drowsy [dráʊzi] *adj.* soñoliento; adormilado, amodorrado; **to become —** amodorrarse.

drudge [drʌdʒ] *v.* afanarse, atarearse; *s.* trabajador, esclavo del trabajo.

drug [drʌg] *s.* droga; narcótico; **to be a — on the market** ser invendible (*una mercancía*); *v.* jaropar (*administrar drogas en demasía*); narcotizar.

druggist [drágɪst] *s.* boticario, droguista, droguero, farmacéutico.

drugstore [drágstor] *s.* botica, droguería, farmacia.

drum [drʌm] *s.* tambor; tímpano (*del oído*); barril, tonel; **bass —** tambora, bombo; **-stick** bolillo de tambor; **major** tambor mayor; *v.* tocar el tambor; tamborilear; **to — a lesson into someone** meterle a uno la lección en la cabeza; **to — up trade** solicitar o fomentar ventas.

drummer [drámə] *s.* tambor, tamborilero; viajante de comercio, agente.

drunk [drʌŋk] *p.p. de* **to drink**; *adj.* borracho, ebrio, emborrachado, bebido; *Ríopl.* mamado; *C.A.* bolo; *Ch.* cufiño; **to get —** emborracharse, embriagarse.

drunkard [dráŋkəd] *s.* borracho, borrachón, beodo, bebedor.

drunken [dráŋkən] *adj.* borracho, ebrio.

drunkenness [dráŋkənnɪs] *s.* borrachera, embriaguez.

dry [draɪ] *adj.* seco; árido; **a — book** un libro aburrido; **— cleaner** quitamanchas; tintorero; **— cleaning** lavado o limpieza en seco; **— goods** lencería, géneros, tejidos, telas; **— measure** medida para áridos; *v.* secar(se); enjugar; **to — up** secarse, resecarse.

dryness [dráɪnɪs] *s.* sequedad; aridez.

dub [dʌb] *v.* doblar (*una película*).

dubious [djúbiəs] *adj.* dudoso.

duchess [dátʃɪs] *s.* duquesa.

duck [dʌk] *s.* pato, pata; ánade; dril (*género*); zambullida, chapuz; agachada rápida (*para evitar un golpe*); *v.* zambullir(se), chapuzar(se) agachar(se); agachar (*la cabeza*).

duckling [dáklɪŋ] *s.* patito, anadeja.

dud [dʌd] *s.* bomba que no estalla.

dude [dud] *s.* caballerete; novato.

due [dju] *adj.* debido; vencido, pagadero; **in — time** a su debido tiempo; **the bill is —** se ha vencido la cuenta; **the train is — at two o'clock** el tren debe llegar a las dos; *adv.* directamente; **— east** hacia el este, rumbo al oriente; *s.* derecho, privilegio; **-s** cuota.

duel [djúəl] *s.* duelo, desafío, combate; *v.* batirse en duelo.

duet [djuét] *s.* duo, dueto.

dug [dʌg] *pret.* & *p.p. de* **to dig.**

duke [djuk] *s.* duque.

dukedom [djúkdəm] *s.* ducado.

dull [dʌl] *adj.* (*dim*) opaco, empañado, mate; sin brillo; (*boring*) aburrido; (*blunt*) embotado, sin punta, sin filo; (*stupid*) torpe; tardo; **— pain** dolor sordo; **— sound** sonido sordo o apagado; *v.* embotar(se); empañar(se); ofuscar; amortiguar (*un dolor o sonido*).

dullness [dʌlnɪs] *s.* (*dimness*) falta de brillo; (*sluggishness*) estupidez, torpeza; (*bluntness*) falta de punta o filo; (*monotony*) aburrimiento; (*heaviness*) pesadez.

duly [djúlɪ] *adv.* debidamente.

dumb [dʌm] *adj.* (*silent*) mudo; silencioso, callado; (*dull*) estúpido, torpe; **— creature** animal.

dumbness [dʌmnɪs] *s.* mudez; mutismo; estupidez.

dummy [dʌmɪ] *s.* (*figure*) maniquí, figurón, muñeco; (*fool*) zoquete, tonto; *adj.* falso, fingido.

dump [dʌmp] *s.* montón (*de tierra, carbón, etc.*); terrero, vaciadero, escorial; **garbage —** muladar; basurero; **to be in the -s** estar abatido; *v.* echar, vaciar, descargar; echar a la basura.

dunce [dʌns] *s.* zopenco, zoquete, tonto.

dune [djun] *s.* duna o médano.

dung [dʌŋ] *s.* boñiga, estiércol.

dungeon [dʌndʒən] *s.* mazmorra, calabozo.

dunghill [dʌŋhɪl] *s.* muladar, estercolero.

dupe [djup] *s.* inocentón, incauto, víctima (*de un engaño*); *v.* embaucar.

duplicate [djúpləkɪt] *adj.* & *s.* doble, duplicado; [djúpləkət] *v.* duplicar, copiar.

duplicity [djuplísətɪ] *s.* duplicidad, doblez.

durable [djúrəbl] *adj.* durable, duradero.

duration [djuréʃən] *s.* duración.

during [dúrɪŋ] *prep.* durante.

dusk [dʌsk] *s.* crepúsculo (*vespertino*), anochecida; caída de la tarde; sombra, oscuridad; **at —** al atardecer.

dusky [dʌskɪ] *adj.* obscuro, negruzco; sombrío.

dust [dʌst] *s.* polvo; tierra; **cloud of —** polvareda; *v.* sacudir el polvo, desempolvar, quitar el polvo; empolvar, llenar de polvo; espolvorear.

duster [dʌstə] *s.* limpiador; quitapolvo; **feather —** plumero.

dusty [dʌstɪ] *adj.* polvoriento; empolva-

do, lleno de polvo.

Dutch [dʌtʃ] *adj.* & *s.* holandés; **— treat** convite a escote.

Dutchman [dʌtʃmən] *s.* holandés.

duty [djútɪ] *s.* deber, obligación; derechos aduanales; impuesto; **— free** libre de derechos aduanales.

dwarf [dwɔrf] *s.* & *adj.* enano; *v.* achicar, empequeñecer; impedir el desarrollo o crecimiento de.

dwell [dwel] *v.* residir, morar, habitar vivir; **to — on a subject** espaciarse o dilatarse en un asunto.

dweller [dwélə] *s.* habitante, morador.

dwelling [dwélɪŋ] *s.* morada, habitación, domicilio.

dwelt [dwelt] *pret.* & *p.p. de* **to dwell.**

dwindle [dwíndl] *v.* menguar, mermar; disminuir(se); gastarse.

dye [daɪ] *s.* tinte, tintura; *v.* teñir, tinturar.

dyer [dáɪə] *s.* tintorero; **-'s shop** tintorería.

dying [dáɪŋ] *adj.* moribundo; agonizante.

dynamic [daɪnǽmɪk] *adj.* dinámico; enérgico; **-s** *s.* dinámica.

dynamite [dáɪnəmaɪt] *s.* dinamita; *v.* dinamitar, volar con dinamita.

dynamo [dáɪnəmo] *s.* dínamo.

dynasty [dáɪnəstɪ] *s.* dinastía.

dysentery [dísṇterɪ] *s.* disentería.

E

each [itʃ] *adj.* cada; *pron.* cada uno; **— other** el uno al otro, uno(s) a otro(s).

eager [ígə] *adj.* anhelante, ansioso, deseoso; **-ly** *adv.* con anhelo; con ahínco; ansiosamente.

eagerness [ígənɪs] *s.* anhelo, ansia, deseo vehemente; ahínco; ardor.

eagle [ígl] *s.* águila.

ear [ɪr] *s.* oreja; oído; **— drum** tímpano; **— muff** orejera; **— of corn** mazorca; **— of wheat** espiga; **by —** de oído; **within —shot** al alcance del oído.

earl [ɜrl] *s.* conde.

early [ɜrlɪ] *adv.* temprano; *adj.* temprano; primitivo, remoto; **— riser** madrugador, tempranero, mañanero; **at an — date** en fecha a próxima.

earn [ɜrn] *v.* ganar; merecer.

earnest [ɜrnɪst] *adj.* serio, formal; ardiente; **in —** en serio, con toda formalidad; de buena fe; **-ly** *adv.* seriamente; con ahínco; encarecidamente, ansiosamente.

earnestness [ɜrnɪstnɪs] *s.* seriedad; celo; solicitud; sinceridad; **in all —** con todo ahínco; con toda formalidad; con toda sinceridad.

earnings [ɜrnɪŋz] *s.* ganancias; sueldo, salario, paga.

earring [írrɪŋ] *s.* arete, zarcillo, pendiente, arracada; *C.A.* arito; *P.R.* pantalla.

earth [ɜθ] *s.* tierra; suelo.

earthen [ɜθən] *adj.* de tierra; de barro.

earthenware [ɜθənwɛr] *s.* loza de barro; trastos, cacharros.

earthly [ɜθlɪ] *adj.* terrenal, terrestre,

mundano; terreno; **to be of no — use** no servir para nada.

earthquake [ɵ́θkwek] s. terremoto, temblor de tierra.

earthworm [ɵ́θwɜm] s. lombriz.

ease [iz] s. (*facility*) facilidad; naturalidad; soltura; (*comfort*) comodidad, tranquilidad; **at —** tranquilo; cómodo; v. facilitar; aliviar; mitigar; tranquilizar; aligerar (*el peso*); aflojar.

easel [ízl] s. caballete (*de pintor*).

easily [ízəlɪ] adv. fácilmente; sin dificultad; cómodamente.

east [ist] s. este; oriente, levante; adj. del este, oriental; adv. al este, hacia el este; en el este.

Easter [ístə] s. Pascuas, Pascua Florida; **— Sunday** Domingo de Resurrección o de Pascuas.

eastern [ístən] adj. oriental; del este.

eastward [ístwəd] adv. & adj. hacia el este u oriente.

easy [ízɪ] adj. (*simple*) fácil; (*comfortable*) cómodo; tranquilo; **— chair** silla cómoda, poltrona, butaca; **easy-going man** hombre cachazudo o calmo; **at an — pace** a paso moderado; **within — reach** al alcance; a la mano.

eat [it] v. comer; to **— away** corroer, destruir; **to — breakfast** desayunarse, tomar el desayuno; **to — dinner** tomar la comida, comer; **to — supper** tomar la cena, cenar; **to — one's heart out** sufrir en silencio; **to — one's words** retractarse.

eaten [ítn] p.p. de *to eat.*

eaves [ivz] s. pl. alero (*de un tejado*).

ebb [ɛb] s. reflujo; decadencia; **— tide** marea menguante; **to be at a low —** estar decaído; v. menguar, decaer.

ebony [ɛ́bənɪ] s. ébano.

eccentric [ɪksɛ́ntrɪk] adj. & s. excéntrico.

ecclesiastic [ɪklizɪǽstɪk] adj. & s. eclesiástico.

echelon [ɛ́ʃələn] s. escalón.

echo [ɛ́ko] s. eco; v. hacer eco, repetir; resonar, repercutir.

eclectic [ɪklɛ́ktɪk] adj. ecléctico.

eclipse [ɪklíps] s. eclipse; v. eclipsar.

economic [ɪkənámɪk] adj. económico.

economical [ɪkənámɪkl] adj. económico.

economics [ɪkənámɪks] s. economía política.

economist [ɪkánəmɪst] s. economista.

economize [ɪkánəmaɪz] v. economizar.

economy [ɪkánəmɪ] s. economía; parsimonia.

ecstasy [ɛ́kstəsɪ] s. éxtasis.

ecumenical [ɛkjumɛ́nəkl] adj. ecuménico.

eddy [ɛ́dɪ] s. remolino; v. arremolinarse.

Eden [ídn] s. Edén; paraíso.

edge [ɛdʒ] s. orilla, borde; filo; **to be on — estar** nervioso.

edgewise [ɛ́dʒwaɪz] adv. de lado; de filo.

edible [ɛ́dəbl] adj. & s. comestible.

edifice [ɛ́dəfɪs] s. edificio.

edify [ɛ́dəfaɪ] v. edificar (*moral espiritualmente*).

edit [ɛ́dɪt] v. redactar; preparar o corregir (*un manuscrito*) para la imprenta; cuidar (*una edición*).

edition [ɪdíʃən] s. edición.

editor [ɛ́dɪtə] s. redactor; director de un periódico; revisor (*de manuscritos*).

editorial [ɛdətóɪəl] adj. editorial; s. editorial (*m.*), artículo de fondo.

editorialize [ɛdɪtóɪəlaɪz] v. expresar opiniones como en artículo de fondo; editorializar.

educate [ɛ́dʒəket] v. educar; instruir.

education [ɛdʒəkéʃən] s. educación; crianza; instrucción, enseñanza; pedagogía.

educational [ɛdʒəkéʃənl] adj. educativo, docente; pedagógico.

educator [ɛ́dʒəketə] s. educador.

eel [il] s. anguila.

effect [əfɛ́kt] s. efecto; **-s** bienes, efectos; **to go into —** hacerse vigente, ponerse en operación (*una ley*); v. efectuar; ejecutar; realizar.

effective [əfɛ́ktɪv] adj. efectivo, eficaz; vigente (*una ley*); **-ly** adv. eficazmente.

effectual [əfɛ́ktʃuəl] adj. eficaz.

effeminate [əfɛ́mənɪt] adj. afeminado.

effete [ɪfít] adj. gastado; estéril; decadente.

efficacy [ɛ́fəkəsɪ] s. eficacia.

efficiency [əfíʃənsɪ] s. eficiencia; eficacia.

efficient [əfíʃənt] adj. eficiente; eficaz.

effigy [ɛ́fɪdʒɪ] s. efigie; **to burn in —** quemar en efigie.

effort [ɛ́fət] s. esfuerzo; empeño.

effrontery [əfrántərɪ] s. descaro, desvergüenza, desfachatez.

effusive [ɛfúsɪv] adj. efusivo, demostrativo, expansivo.

egg [ɛg] s. huevo; **fried —** huevo frito o estrellado; **hard-boiled —** huevo cocido, huevo duro; **scrambled -s** huevos revueltos; **soft-boiled —** huevo pasado por agua; v. **to — on** incitar.

eggplant [ɛ́gplænt] s. berenjena.

egocentric [igosɛ́ntrɪk] adj. egocéntrico.

egotism [ígətɪzəm] s. egotismo; egoismo.

Egyptian [ɪdʒípʃən] adj. & s. egipcio.

either [íðə] adj. & pron. uno u otro; **— of the two** cualquiera de los dos; **in — case** en ambos casos; adv. tampoco; **nor I —** ni yo tampoco; conj. o.

eject [ɪdʒɛ́kt] v. echar, arrojar, expulsar.

ejection [ɪdʒɛ́kʃən] s. expulsión; **— seat** asiento lanzable.

elaborate [ɪlǽbərɪt] adj. elaborado, primoroso; esmerado; [ɪlǽbəret] v. elaborar.

elapse [ɪlǽps] v. transcurrir, pasar.

elastic [ɪlǽstɪk] adj. elástico; s. elástico; goma elástica; cordón elástico; liga elástica.

elasticity [ɪlæstísətɪ] s. elasticidad.

elated [ɪlétɪd] adj. exaltado, gozoso, alborozado.

DU

elbow [élbo] s. codo; recodo, ángulo; **to be within — reach** estar a la mano; v. codear, dar codazos; **to — one's way through** abrirse paso a codazos.

elder [éldɚ] adj. mayor, más grande, más viejo, de más edad; s. mayor; anciano; dignatario (en ciertas iglesias); **our -s** nuestros mayores; nuestros antepasados.

elderly [éldɚlɪ] adj. viejo, anciano.

eldest [éldɪst] adj. mayor.

elect [ɪlékt] adj. & s. electo; elegido; v. elegir.

election [ɪlékʃən] s. elección.

elector [ɪléktɚ] s. elector.

electoral [ɪléktərəl] adj. electoral.

electric [ɪléktrɪk] adj. eléctrico; **—meter** electrómetro, contador eléctrico; **— storm** tronada, tempestad; **— eye** ojo eléctrico; s. tranvía o ferrocarril eléctrico.

electrical [ɪléktrɪk!] adj. eléctrico; **— engineering** electrotecnia, ingeniería eléctrica; **— engineer** ingeniero electricista; electrotécnico.

electrician [ɪlektríʃən] s. electricista.

electricity [ɪlektrísətɪ] s. electricidad.

electrify [ɪléktrəfaɪ] v. electrizar; electrificar.

electrocardiograph [ɪlektrokárdɪəgræf] s. electrocardiógrafo.

electrocute [ɪléktrəkjut] v. electrocutar.

electron [ɪléktrɑn] s. electrón.

electronics [ɪlektrúnɪks] s. electrónica.

elegance [éləgəns] s. elegancia.

elegant [éləgənt] adj. elegante.

element [éləmənt] s. elemento.

elemental [ɛləméntl] adj. elemental.

elementary [ɛləméntərɪ] adj. elemental.

elephant [éləfənt] s. elefante.

elevate [éləvet] v. elevar; alzar, levantar.

elevation [ɛləvéʃən] s. elevación; altura; exaltación.

elevator [éləvetɚ] s. ascensor, Am. elevador; **grain —** almacén de granos.

elicit [ɪlísɪt] v. extraer, sonsacar; **to — admiration** despertar admiración; **to — applause** suscitar el aplauso o los aplausos.

eligible [élɪdʒəbl] adj. elegible.

eliminate [ɪlímənet] v. eliminar.

elimination [ɪlɪmənéʃən] s. eliminación.

elite [ɛlít] s. lo selecto; los selectos; los escogidos.

elk [ɛlk] s. ante.

elliptic [ɪlíptɪk] adj. elíptico.

elm [ɛlm] s. olmo.

elope [ɪlóp] v. fugarse (con su novio).

eloquence [éləkwəns] s. elocuencia.

eloquent [éləkwənt] adj. elocuente.

else [ɛls] adj. & adv. otro (úsase sólo en ciertas combinaciones); más, además; **or —** de otro modo; si no; **nobody —** ningún otro; **nothing —** nada más; **somebody —** algún otro, otra persona; **what — ?** ¿qué más?

elsewhere [élshwɛr] adv. en otra parte, a otra parte.

elucidate [ɪlúsədet] v. elucidar, esclarecer, aclarar, clarificar.

elucidation [ɪlusədéʃən] s. elucidación, esclarecimiento, explicación.

elude [ɪlúd] v. eludir, evadir.

elusive [ɪlúsɪv] adj. evasivo; que elude.

emaciated [ɪméʃɪetɪd] adj. demacrado, escuálido, macilento.

emanate [émənet] v. emanar, brotar.

emanation [ɛmənéʃən] s. emanación; efluvio.

emancipate [ɪmǽnsəpet] v. emancipar.

emancipation [ɪmǽnsəpéʃən] s. emancipación.

embalm [ɪmbám] v. embalsamar.

embankment [ɪmbǽŋkmənt] s. terraplén; dique.

embargo [ɪmbárgo] s. embargo; prohibición; **to put an — on** embargar.

embark [ɪmbárk] v. embarcar(se).

embarrass [ɪmbǽrəs] v. turbar, desconcertar; apenar; avergonzar; embarazar; **to be financially -ed** encontrarse escaso de fondos.

embarrassing [ɪmbǽrəsɪŋ] adj. embarazoso, penoso; desconcertante; angustioso.

embarrassment [ɪmbǽrəsmənt] s. turbación, vergüenza, desconcierto, aprieto, apuro, dificultad; estorbo, embarazo.

embassy [émbəsɪ] s. embajada.

embellish [ɪmbélɪʃ] v. embellecer, hermosear.

ember [émbɚ] s. ascua; **-s** ascuas, rescoldo.

embezzle [ɪmbéz!] v. desfalcar.

embezzlement [ɪmbéz!mənt] s. desfalco, peculado.

embitter [ɪmbítɚ] v. amargar.

emblem [émbləm] s. emblema.

embody [ɪmbádɪ] v. encarnar, dar cuerpo a; incorporar, abarcar.

emboss [ɪmbós] v. realzar, grabar en relieve.

embrace [ɪmbrés] s. abrazo; v. abrazar(se); abarcar.

embroider [ɪmbróɪdɚ] v. bordar; recamar; ornar, embellecer.

embroidery [ɪmbróɪdərɪ] s. bordado; bordadura; recamo.

embryo [émbrɪo] s. embrión.

emerald [émərəld] s. esmeralda.

emerge [ɪmɚ́dʒ] v. emerger; surtir.

emergency [ɪmɚ́dʒənsɪ] s. caso fortuito; aprieto; urgencia; emergencia.

emigrant [émagrənt] adj. & s. emigrante.

emigrate [émagret] v. emigrar.

emigration [ɛmagréʃən] s. emigración.

eminence [émanəns] s. eminencia.

eminent [émanənt] adj. eminente.

emit [ɪmít] v. emitir; exhalar, arrojar; despedir (olor, humo, etc.).

emotion [ɪmóʃən] s. emoción.

emotional [ɪmóʃənl] adj. emocional; emotivo; sentimental; sensible.

empathy [émpəθɪ] s. empatía.

emperor [émpərɚ] s. emperador.

emphasis [émfəsɪs] *s.* énfasis.
emphasize [émfəsaɪz] *v.* dar énfasis; hacer hincapié en; subrayar, recalcar; acentuar.
emphatic [ɪmfǽtɪk] *adj.* enfático; recalcado; **-ally** *adv.* enfáticamente.
emphysema [emfəsímə] *s.* enfisema.
empire [émpaɪr] *s.* imperio.
empirical [empírək] *adj.* empírico.
employ [ɪmplɔ́ɪ] *v.* emplear; dar empleo a; ocupar; **to be in his —** ser su empleado; trabajar a sus órdenes.
employee [ɪmplɔ́ɪ] *s.* empleado.
employer [ɪmplɔ́ɪə] *s.* patrón, amo, principal.
employment [ɪmplɔ́ɪmənt] *s.* empleo; ocupación.
empower [ɪmpáuə] *v.* autorizar; apoderar (*dar poder a un abogado*).
empress [émprɪs] *s.* emperatriz.
emptiness [émptɪnɪs] *s.* vaciedad; futilidad, vanidad.
empty [émptɪ] *adj.* vacío; vacante, desocupado; vano; *v.* vaciar; desaguar, desembocar.
emulate [émjulet] *v.* emular.
enable [inéb!] *v.* capacitar, hacer capaz; habilitar; dar poder; facilitar; hacer posible.
enact [ɪnǽkt] *v.* decretar, promulgar; hacer el papel de.
enamel [ɪnǽm!] *s.* esmalte; *v.* esmaltar.
enamor [ɪnǽmə] *v.* enamorar, mover a amar; encantar; **to be -ed of** estar enamorado de.
encamp [ɪnkǽmp] *v.* acampar.
enchant [ɪntʃǽnt] *v.* encantar; embelesar; hechizar.
enchanter [ɪntʃǽntə] *s.* encantador; hechicero, mago, brujo.
enchantment [ɪntʃǽntmənt] *s.* encanto; encantamiento; hechicería.
enchantress [ɪntʃǽntrɪs] *s.* encantadora; hechicera, bruja.
encircle [ɪnsɝ́k!] *v.* cercar, rodear, ceñir.
enclose [ɪnklóz] *v.* encerrar; cercar, rodear, circundar; incluir.
enclosure [ɪnklóʒə] *s.* recinto, cercado, vallado; remesa, lo remitido (*dentro de una carta*), lo adjunto; encerramiento.
encompass [ɪnkʌ́mpəs] *v.* abarcar; encuadrar; rodear, ceñir, circundar.
encounter [ɪnkáuntə] *s.* encuentro; combate; *v.* encontrar(se); encontrarse con; tropezar con.
encourage [ɪnkɝ́ɪdʒ] *v.* alentar, animar; fomentar.
encouragement [ɪnkɝ́ɪdʒmənt] *s.* aliento, ánimo; estímulo; fomento.
encroach [ɪnkrótʃ] *v.* **to — upon** usurpar, invadir, meterse en; quitar (*el tiempo*).
encumber [ɛnkʌ́mbə] *v.* impedir; estorbar.
encyclopedia [ɪnsaɪkləpídɪə] *s.* enciclopedia.
end [ɛnd] *s.* (*temporal*) fin; cabo; término; (*spatial*) término; extremo; **no — of things** un sin fin de cosas; **odds and -s** retazos; **on — de** punta;

to **put an — to** acabar con, poner fin a; *v.* acabar; terminar; concluir; dar fin.
endanger [ɪndéndʒə] *v.* poner en peligro, arriesgar.
endear [ɪndír] *v.* hacer amar, hacer querer; **to — oneself** hacerse querer.
endeavor [ɪndévə] *s.* esfuerzo, empeño; tentativa; tarea; *v.* procurar, tratar de, intentar; esforzarse por o en.
endemic [ɛndémɪk] *adj.* endémico.
ending [éndɪŋ] *s.* final; terminación; conclusión.
endless [éndlɪs] *adj.* sin fin, interminable, inacabable; eterno.
endorse [ɛndórs] *v.* endosar; repaldar; apoyar, garantizar.
endorsement [ɛndórsmənt] *s.* (*signature*) endose, endoso; (*backing*) respaldo; garantía, apoyo.
endorser [ɛndórsə] *s.* endosante.
endow [ɛndáu] *v.* dotar.
endowment [ɛndáumənt] *s.* dotación; dote, don.
endurance [ɪndjúrəns] *s.* resistencia; aguante; paciencia; duración.
endure [ɪndjúr] *v.* aguantar, soportar; sufrir; durar, perdurar.
enema [énəmə] *s.* lavativa.
enemy [énəmɪ] *s.* enemigo.
energetic [enədʒétɪk] *adj.* enérgico.
energy [énədʒɪ] *s.* energía.
enervate [énəvet] *v.* enervar, debilitar.
enfold = **infold**.
enforce [ɪnfórs] *v.* dar fuerza a; hacer cumplir (*una ley*); **to — obedience** hacer obedecer, imponer obediencia.
enforcement [ɪnfórsmənt] *s.* coacción; cumplimiento forzoso (*de una ley*).
engage [ɪngédʒ] *v.* (*employ*) ocupar; emplear, contratar; (*reserve*) alquilar; (*attract*) atraer; (*mesh*) engranar, acoplar; **to — in battle** trabar batalla; **to — (oneself) to do it** comprometerse a hacerlo; **to be -ed in something** estar ocupado en algo; **to be -ed to be married** estar comprometido para casarse.
engagement [ɪngédʒmənt] *s.* compromiso; cita; noviazgo; convenio, contrato; pelea; traba, engrane, acoplamiento (*de maquinaria*).
engender [ɪndʒéndə] *v.* engendrar, producir.
engine [éndʒən] *s.* máquina; motor; locomotora.
engineer [endʒənír] *s.* ingeniero; maquinista (*de locomotora*); *v.* dirigir, planear.
engineering [endʒənírɪŋ] *s.* ingeniería; manejo, planeo.
English [íŋglɪʃ] *adj.* inglés; *s.* inglés, idioma inglés; **the —** los ingleses.
Englishman [íŋglɪʃmən] *s.* inglés.
engrave [ɪngrév] *v.* grabar, esculpir.
engraving [ɪngrévɪŋ] *s.* grabado; estampa, lámina; **wood —** grabado en madera.
engross [ɪngrós] *v.* absorber; redactar en limpio.
engrossed [ɪngróst] *adj.* absorto, ensi-

mismado.

engulf [ɪngʌ́lf] v. engolfar, absorber, tragar.

enhance [ɪnhǽns] v. realzar; engrandecer.

enigma [ɪnígmə] s. enigma.

enjoin [ɪndʒɔ́ɪn] v. mandar, ordenar; **to — from** prohibir, vedar.

enjoy [ɪndʒɔ́ɪ] v. gozar de; disfrutar de; **to — oneself** divertirse, gozar, deleitarse; **to — the use of** usufructuar.

enjoyable [ɪndʒɔ́ɪəbl] adj. agradable, deleitable.

enjoyment [ɪndʒɔ́ɪmənt] s. placer, goce; disfrute; usufructo.

enlarge [ɪnlárdʒ] v. agrandar(se); ensanchar; ampliar; **to — upon** explayarse en, extenderse en; comentar.

enlargement [ɪnlárdʒmənt] s. (photo) ampliación; ensachamiento.

enlighten [ɪnláɪtn] v. alumbrar; iluminar; ilustrar, instruir.

enlist [ɪnlíst] v. alistar(se); sentar plaza (de soldado); reclutar.

enlistment [ɪnlístmənt] s. reclutamiento; alistamiento.

enliven [ɪnláɪvən] v. avivar, animar, alegrar.

enmity [énməti] s. enemistad.

ennoble [ɪnóbl] v. ennoblecer.

enormous [ɪnɔ́rməs] adj. enorme.

enough [ənʌ́f] adj. & adv. bastante; — lo bastante, lo suficiente; **that is —** eso basta, con eso basta; **—!** ¡basta!

enquire = **inquire**.

enrage [ɪnrédʒ] v. enrabiar, hacer rabiar; enfurecer.

enrapture [ɪnrǽptʃə] v. extasiar, embelesar, enajenar.

enrich [ɪnrítʃ] v. enriquecer.

enroll [ɪnról] v. alistar(se); matricular(se); inscribir(se); hacerse miembro.

enrollment [ɪnrólmənt] s. alistamiento; registro, matrícula.

ensemble [ɑnsámbl] s. (music) conjunto musical; (dress) traje armonioso.

ensign [énsn] s. alférez (de la marina); [énsaɪn] bandera; insignia.

enslave [ɪnslév] v. esclavizar.

ensnare [ɛnsnér] v. enredar, entrampar, embaucar.

ensue [ɛnsú] v. sobrevenir, seguir(se), resultar.

entail [ɪntél] v. envolver, ocasionar; vincular (una herencia).

entangle [ɪntǽngl] v. enredar, enmarañar, embrollar.

enter [éntə] v. entrar en; ingresar en; asentar (una partida, cantidad, etc.); registrar; salir (al escenario).

enterprise [éntəpraɪz] s. empresa.

enterprising [éntəpraɪzɪŋ] adj. emprendedor.

entertain [ɛntətén] v. divertir; agasajar; obsequiar; banquetear; acariciar (una idea); abrigar (una esperanza, un rencor); **she -s a great deal** es muy fiestera u obsequiosa.

entertaining [ɛntəténɪŋ] adj. entrete-

nido, divertido, chistoso.

entertainment [ɛntəténmənt] s. entretenimiento; pasatiempo; diversión; fiesta; convite.

enthusiasm [ɪnθjúzɪæzəm] s. entusiasmo.

enthusiast [ɪnθjúzɪæst] s. entusiasta.

enthusiastic [ɪnθjuzɪǽstɪk] adj. entusiasta, entusiástico; **to be —** estar entusiasmado.

entice [ɛntáɪs] v. atraer, tentar, seducir, halagar.

entire [ɛntáɪr] adj. entero, cabal; **the — world** todo el mundo; **-ly** adv. enteramente, por entero.

entirety [ɛntáɪrtɪ] s. totalidad, entereza, conjunto; todo.

entitle [ɛntáɪtl] v. titular, intitular; autorizar, dar derecho.

entity [éntɪtɪ] s. entidad; ente, ser.

entrails [éntrəlz] s. pl. entrañas; tripas.

entrance [éntrəns] s. entrada; ingreso.

entreat [ɪntrít] v. suplicar, rogar; instar.

entreaty [ɪntrítɪ] s. súplica, ruego; instancia.

entrench = **intrench**.

entrust [ɪntrást] v. confiar; depositar; entregar.

entry [éntrɪ] s. entrada; ingreso; partida, registro, anotación; **double — partida doble** (en teneduría).

enumerate [ɪnjúmərét] v. enumerar.

enunciate [ɪnʌ́nsɪet] v. articular; enunciar, declarar.

envelop [ɪnvéləp] v. envolver.

envelope [énvəlop] s. sobre, cubierta (de una carta).

enviable [énvɪəbl] adj. envidiable.

envious [énvɪəs] adj. envidioso.

environment [ɪnváɪrənmənt] s. ambiente, medio ambiente.

environs [ɪnváɪrənz] s. pl. cercanías, contornos, alrededores.

envisage [ɛnvízɪdʒ] v. prever; encararse con.

envoy [énvɔɪ] s. enviado.

envy [énvɪ] s. envidia; v. envidiar.

ephemeral [ɪfémə•l] adj. efímero.

epic [épɪk] s. epopeya, poema, épico; adj. épico.

epidemic [ɛpədémɪk] s. epidemia; peste; adj. epidémico.

Epiphany [ɪpífənɪ] s. Epifanía.

episode [épəsod] s. episodio.

epistle [ɪpísl] s. epístola, carta.

epitaph [épətæf] s. epitafio.

epoch [épək] s. época.

equal [íkwəl] adj. igual; **to be — to a task** ser competente (o tener suficientes fuerzas) para una tarea; s. igual; cantidad igual; v. igualar; ser igual a; **-ly** adv. igualmente; por igual.

equality [ikwálətɪ] s. igualdad.

equalize [íkwalaɪz] v. igualar; emparejar; equilibrar; nivelar.

equation [ɪkwéʒən] s. ecuación.

equator [ɪkwétə] s. ecuador.

equilibrium [ikwəlíbrɪəm] s. equilibrio.

equip [ɪkwíp] v. equipar, proveer; habilitar.

equipment [ɪkwípmənt] s. equipo;

aparatos; avíos; habilitación.

equitable [ékwɪtəbl] *adj.* equitativo. —

equity [ékwətɪ] *s.* equidad; justicia.

equivalent [ɪkwívələnt] *adj. & s.* equivalente.

equivocal [ɪkwívəkl] *adj.* equívoco, ambiguo.

era [írə] *s.* era, época.

eradicate [ɪrǽdɪkɛt] *v.* desarraigar, extirpar.

erase [ɪrés] *v.* borrar; tachar.

eraser [ɪrésə] *s.* goma, *Am.* borrador; **blackboard —** cepillo.

erasure [ɪréʃə] *s.* borradura, raspadura.

ere [ɛr] *prep.* antes de; *conj.* antes (de) que.

erect [ɪrékt] *adj.* erguido; derecho; levantado; *Am.* parado; *v.* erigir; levantar, alzar.

ermine [ʒ́mɪn] *s.* armiño.

erode [ɪród] *v.* erosionar.

erosion [ɪróʒən] *s.* erosión; desgaste.

erotic [ɪrútɪk] *adj.* erótico.

err [ʒ] *v.* errar; equivocarse; descarriarse.

errand [érənd] *s.* mandado, recado, encargo; **— boy** mandadero.

errant [érənt] *adj.* errante; **knight-errant** caballero andante.

erratic [ɪrǽtɪk] *adj.* inconstante errático; vagabundo.

erroneous [ərónɪəs] *adj.* erróneo, errado.

error [érə] *s.* error.

erudition [ɛrʊdíʃən] *s.* erudición.

eruption [ɪrʌ́pʃən] *s.* erupción.

escalate [éskəlet] *v.* aumentar; intensificar.

escapade [éskəped] *s.* trapisonda, travesura.

escape [əskép] *s.* escape; fuga, huída; escapada; escapatoria; *v.* escapar(se); fugarse; huir(se); eludir, evadir; **it -s me** se me escapa.

escort [éskort] *s.* escolta; acompañante; convoy; [ɪskórt] *v.* escoltar; convoyar; acompañar.

escutcheon [ɪskʌ́tʃən] *s.* escudo de armas, blasón.

especial [əspéʃəl] *adj.* especial; **-ly** *adv.* especialmente.

espionage [éspɪənɪdʒ] *s.* espionaje.

essay [ése] *s.* ensayo; [esé] *v.* ensayar.

essence [ésns] *s.* esencia.

essential [əsénʃəl] *adj.* esencial.

establish [əstǽblɪʃ] *v.* establecer.

establishment [əstǽblɪʃmənt] *s.* establecimiento.

estate [əstét] *s.* hacienda, heredad; bienes, propiedades; estado, condición; **country —** finca rural.

esteem [əstím] *s.* estima, estimación, aprecio; *v.* estimar, apreciar; considerar, juzgar.

estimable [éstəməbl] *adj.* estimable.

estimate [éstəmɪt] *s.* (*calculation*) tasa, cálculo aproximado; presupuesto; (*judgment*) opinión; [éstəmet] *v.* estimar, tasar, calcular aproximadamente; hacer un presupuesto; juzgar, opinar.

estimation [ɛstəméʃən] *s.* juicio, opinión; estima; estimación.

estrange [əstréndʒ] *v.* enajenar; apartar.

estuary [éstʃʊɛrɪ] *s.* estuario o estero, desembocadura de un río.

etch [ɛtʃ] *v.* grabar al agua fuerte.

etching [étʃɪŋ] *s.* agua fuerte, grabado al agua fuerte.

eternal [ɪtʒ́nl] *adj.* eterno.

eternity [ɪtʒ́nətɪ] *s.* eternidad.

ether [íθə] *s.* éter.

ethereal [ɪθírɪəl] *adj.* etéreo.

ethical [éθɪkl] *adj.* ético, moral.

ethics [éθɪks] *s.* ética, moral.

ethnic [éθnɪk] *adj.* étnico.

etiquette [étɪket] *s.* etiqueta (*regla de conducta social*).

etymology [ɛtəmálədʒɪ] *s.* etimología.

eucalyptus [jukəlíptəs] *s.* eucalipto.

euphemism [júfəmɪzm] *s.* eufemismo.

European [jʊrəpíən] *adj. & s.* europeo.

evacuate [ɪvǽkjuet] *v.* evacuar; desocupar.

evade [ɪvéd] *v.* evadir.

evaluate [ɪvǽljuet] *v.* valorar, avaluar.

evaporate [ɪvǽpəret] *v.* evaporar(se).

evaporation [ɪvæpəréʃən] *s.* evaporación.

evasion [ɪvéʒən] *s.* evasión, evasiva.

evasive [ɪvésɪv] *adj.* evasivo.

eve [iv] *s.* víspera, vigilia; **Christmas Eve** Nochebuena; **New Year's Eve** víspera del Año Nuevo; **on the — of** en vísperas de.

even [ívən] *adj.* (*level*) liso, plano, llano, a nivel; (*same*) parejo; uniforme; igual; **— dozen** docena cabal; **— number** número par; **— temper** genio apacible; **to be — with someone** estar mano a mano (o estar a mano) con alguien; **to get — with someone** desquitarse de alguien; *adv.* aun, hasta; **— if** (*o* **— though**) aun cuando; **— so** aun así; **not —** ni siquiera, ni aun; *v.* allanar; nivelar(se); igualar(se); emparejar; **-ly** *adv.* igualmente; de un modo igual; con uniformidad; con suavidad.

evening [ívnɪŋ] *s.* tarde; noche (*las primeras horas*); **— gown** vestido de etiqueta; **— star** estrella vespertina, lucero de la tarde.

evenness [ívənnɪs] *s.* lisura; igualdad; **— of temper** apacibilidad o suavidad de genio.

event [ɪvént] *s.* suceso, acontecimiento; incidente, evento; resultado, consecuencia; **in any —** en todo caso; **in the — of** en caso de.

eventful [ɪvéntfəl] *adj.* lleno de sucesos; importante, memorable.

eventual [ɪvéntʃʊəl] *adj.* eventual; último, final, terminal; **-ly** *adv.* finalmente, por fin, con el tiempo; eventualmente.

ever [évə] *adv.* siempre; jamás; alguna vez; **— so much** muchísimo; **for — and —** por (o para) siempre jamás; **hardly —** casi nunca, apenas; **if — si** alguna vez; **more than —** más que nunca; **the best friend I — had** el mejor amigo que en mi vida he tenido.

evergreen [évəgrin] *s.* siempreviva, sempiterna; *adj.* siempre verde.

everlasting [evəlǽstɪŋ] *adj.* sempiterno, eterno, perpetuo; duradero; *s.* eternidad; sempiterna (*planta*); siempreviva; perpetua, flor perpetua.

evermore [ɛvəmór] *adv.* para siempre; **for —** para siempre jamás.

every [évrɪ] *adj.* cada; todo; todos los, todas las; **— bit of it** todo, todito; **— day** todos los días; **— once in a while** de vez en cuando; **— one of them** todos ellos; **— other day** cada dos días, un día sí y otro no.

everybody [évrɪbʌdɪ] *pron.* todos, todo el mundo.

everyday [évrɪdé] *adj.* diario, cuotidiano, de todos los días; ordinario.

everyone [évrɪwʌn] *pron.* todos; todo el mundo; cada uno.

everything [évrɪθɪŋ] *pron.* todo.

everywhere [évrɪhwɛr] *adv.* por (o en) todas partes; a todas partes.

evict [ɪvíkt] *v.* desalojar; expulsar.

evidence [évədəns] *s.* evidencia; prueba; demostración, señal; testimonio; **to be in —** mostrarse; *v.* hacer evidente, evidenciar; patentizar, revelar, mostrar.

evident [évədənt] *adj.* evidente, patente.

evil [ívl] *adj.* malo, malvado, maligno; aciago, de mal agüero; **to cast the — eye** aojar; **the Evil One** el Diablo; *s.* mal; maldad; *adv.* mal.

evildoer [ívldúə] *s.* malhechor.

evoke [ɪvók] *v.* evocar; **to — laughter** provocar a risa.

evolution [evəlúʃən] *s.* evolución.

evolve [ɪválv] *v.* desarrollar(se), desenvolver(se); urdir; evolucionar.

ewe [ju] *s.* oveja.

exact [ɪgzǽkt] *adj.* exacto; *v.* exigir; **-ly** *adv.* exactamente; en punto.

exacting [ɪgzǽktɪŋ] *adj.* exigente.

exaggerate [ɪgzǽdʒəret] *v.* exagerar.

exalt [ɪgzɔ́lt] *v.* exaltar, ensalzar.

exaltation [egzɔltéʃən] *s.* exaltación.

examination [ɪgzæmənéʃən] s. examen; reconocimiento (*médico*).

examine [ɪgzǽmɪn] *v.* examinar; reconocer (*dícese del médico*).

example [ɪgzǽmpl] *s.* ejemplo.

exasperate [ɪgzǽspəret] *v.* exasperar, irritar.

excavate [ékskəvet] *v.* excavar.

exceed [ɪksíd] *v.* exceder; sobrepasar; propasarse.

exceedingly [ɪksídɪŋlɪ] *adv.* sumamente, extremamente; **— well** extremamente bien.

excel [ɪksél] *v.* sobresalir (en o entre); sobrepugar (a).

excellence [éksləns] *s.* excelencia.

excellency [éks].ənsɪ] *s.* excelencia.

excellent [éksl.ənt] *adj.* excelente.

except [ɪksépt] *prep.* excepto, menos; *v.* exceptuar.

excepting [ɪkséptɪŋ] *prep.* excepto, salvo, menos, exceptuando.

exception [ɪksépʃən] *s.* (*exclusion*) excepción; (*opposition*) objeción; **with the — of** a excepción de, con excepción de; **to take —** objetar; ofenderse.

exceptional [ɪksépʃənl] *adj.* excepcional.

excess [ɪksés] *s.* exceso; sobrante; **— baggage (weight)** exceso de equipaje (de peso); **to drink to —** beber en exceso.

excessive [ɪksésɪv] *adj.* excesivo; **-ly** *adv.* excesivamente, en exceso, demasiado.

exchange [ɪkstʃéndʒ] *s.* (*money*) cambio; (*interchange*) trueque; intercambio, canje (*de publicaciones, prisioneros*); (*stock*) lonja, bolsa; **rate of —** cambio, *Am.* tipo de cambio; **telephone —** central de teléfonos; *v.* cambiar; trocar; canjear (*publicaciones, prisioneros*); **to — greetings** saludarse; mandarse felicitaciones.

excite [ɪksáɪt] *v.* excitar; acalorar; agitar.

excited [ɪksáɪtɪd] *adj.* excitado, acalorado; animado; **to get —** entusiasmarse; sobreexcitarse; acalorarse; **-ly** *adv.* acaloradamente, agitadamente.

excitement [ɪksáɪtmənt] *s.* excitación; acaloramiento; agitación, alboroto; animación.

exciting [ɪksáɪtɪŋ] *adj.* excitante, excitador; estimulante.

exclaim [ɪksklém] *v.* exclamar.

exclamation [ekskləméʃən] *s.* exclamación; **— point** punto de admiración.

exclude [ɪksklúd] *v.* excluir.

exclusion [ɪksklúʒən] *s.* exclusión.

exclusive [ɪksklúsɪv] *adj.* exclusivo; privativo; **— of** sin contar.

excommunicate [ɛkskəmjúnəket] *v.* excomunicar.

excommunication [ɛkskəmjunəkéʃən] *s.* excomunión.

excrement [ékskrɪmənt] *s.* excremento.

excursion [ɪkskə́ʒən] *s.* excursión; correría; expedición.

excusable [ɪkskjúzəbl] *adj.* excusable, disculpable.

excuse [ɪkskjús] *s.* excusa; disculpa; [ɪkskjúz] *v.* excusar; disculpar; perdonar, dispensar; eximir; **— me!** ¡dispense Vd.!; ¡perdone Vd.!

execute [éksɪkjut] *v.* ejecutar; ajusticiar; llevar a cabo.

execution [eksɪkjúʃən] *s.* ejecución; desempeño.

executioner [eksɪkjúʃənə] *s.* verdugo.

executive [ɪgzékjʊtɪv] *adj.* ejecutivo; *s.* ejecutivo, poder ejecutivo; gerente, administrador.

executor [ɪgzékjʊtə] *s.* albacea, ejecutor testamentario; [éksɪkjutə] ejecutor.

exemplary [ɪgzémplərɪ] *adj.* ejemplar.

exempt [ɪgzémpt] *adj.* exento, libre; *v.* eximir, exentar.

exemption [ɪgzémpʃən] *s.* exención.

exercise [éksəsaɪz] *s.* ejercicio; *v.* ejercitar(se); ejercer (*poder o autoridad*); hacer ejercicio, hacer gimnasia; **to be -d about something** estar preocupado o sobreexcitado por algo.

exert [ɪgzə́t] v. ejercer; **to — oneself** esforzarse, hacer esfuerzos, empeñarse.

exertion [ɪgzə́ʃən] s. ejercicio; esfuerzo, empeño.

exhale [ɛkshél] v. exhalar, emitir; espirar, soplar.

exhaust [ɪgzɔ́st] s. escape (de gas o vapor); v. agotar; consumir; debilitar, fatigar; **I am -ed** no puedo más; estoy agotado.

exhaustion [ɪgzɔ́stʃən] s. agotamiento; fatiga, postración.

exhaustive [ɛgzɔ́stɪv] adj. comprensivo; detallado.

exhibit [ɪgzíbɪt] v. exhibir; mostrar, exponer.

exhibition [ɛksəbíʃən] s. exhibición; exposición, manifestación.

exhilarate [ɪgzíləret] v. alborozar, excitar, animar, entusiasmar.

exhort [ɪgzɔ́rt] v. exhortar.

exile [ɛgzáɪl] s. destierro, exilio; desterrado; v. desterrar; expatriar.

exist [ɪgzíst] v. existir.

existence [ɪgzístəns] s. existencia.

existent [ɪgzístənt] adj. existente.

exit [ɛ́gzɪt] s. salida; salida (del foro); v. vase o vanse (un personaje o personajes al fin de una escena).

exodus [ɛ́ksədəs] s. éxodo.

exonerate [ɪgzánəret] v. exonerar.

exorbitant [ɪgzɔ́rbətənt] adj. exorbitante.

exotic [ɪgzátɪk] adj. exótico; raro, extraño.

expand [ɪkspǽnd] v. ensanchar(se); dilatar(se); extender(se); agrandar(se); desarrollar (una ecuación).

expanse [ɪkspǽns] s. espacio, extensión.

expansion [ɪkspǽnʃən] s. expansión; ensanche; desarrollo (de una ecuación).

expansive [ɪkspǽnsɪv] adj. expansivo; efusivo.

expect [ɪkspɛ́kt] v. esperar; contar con; **I — so** supongo que sí.

expectation [ɛkspɛktéʃən] s. expectación; expectativa; esperanza.

expectorate [ɪkspɛ́ktəret] v. expectorar, desgarrar.

expedient [ɪkspídɪənt] adj. conveniente, oportuno; ventajoso; prudente; s. expediente, medio.

expedite [ɛ́kspədaɪt] v. facilitar; despachar.

expedition [ɛkspɪdíʃən] s. expedición.

expeditionary [ɛkspɪdíʃənɛrɪ] adj. expedicionario.

expel [ɪkspɛ́l] v. expeler; expulsar.

expend [ɪkspɛ́nd] v. gastar; consumir.

expenditure [ɪkspɛ́ndɪtʃə] s. gasto; desembolso.

expense [ɪkspɛ́ns] s. gasto; coste, costa o costo.

expensive [ɪkspɛ́nsɪv] adj. costoso.

expensiveness [ɪkspɛ́nsɪvnɪs] s. precio subido, coste elevado.

experience [ɪkspíriəns] s. experiencia; aventura, lance; v. experimentar; pasar (penas, sufrimientos); sentir.

experienced [ɪkspíriənst] adj. experimentado; ducho, perito, experto.

experiment [ɪkspɛ́rəmənt] s. experimento, prueba; v. experimentar, hacer un experimento.

experimental [ɪkspɛrəmɛ́ntl] adj. experimental.

expert [ɛ́kspət] s. experto, perito; [ɪkspə́t] adj. experto, perito, experimentado.

expiration [ɛkspəréʃən] s. terminación; vencimiento (de un plazo); espiración (del aire).

expire [ɪkspáɪr] v. expirar, morir; acabar; vencerse (un plazo); expeler (el aire aspirado).

explain [ɪksplén] v. explicar.

explainable [ɪksplénəbl] adj. explicable.

explanation [ɛksplənéʃən] s. explicación.

explanatory [ɪksplǽnətɔri] adj. explicativo.

explicit [ɛksplísɪt] adj. explícito.

explode [ɪksplód] v. estallar, hacer explosión, Am. explotar; reventar; volar (con dinamita); desacreditar (una teoría).

exploit [ɛ́ksplɔɪt] s. hazaña, proeza; [ɪksplɔ́ɪt] v. explotar; sacar partido de, abusar de.

exploitation [ɛksplɔɪtéʃən] s. explotación.

exploration [ɛkspləréʃən] s. exploración.

explore [ɪksplór] v. explorar.

explorer [ɪksplórə] s. explorador.

explosion [ɪksplóʒən] s. explosión, estallido.

explosive [ɪksplósɪv] adj. & s. explosivo.

export [ɛ́ksport] s. exportación; artículo exportado, mercancía exportada; [ɪkspórt] v. exportar.

exportation [ɛksportéʃən] s. exportación.

expose [ɪkspóz] v. exponer; exhibir, mostrar, poner a la vista; revelar; desenmascarar.

exposition [ɛkspəzíʃən] s. exposición; exhibición.

exposure [ɪkspóʒə] s. exposición; revelación; **to die of —** morir a efecto de la intemperie.

expound [ɪkspáund] v. exponer, explicar.

express [ɪksprɛ́s] adj. (rapid) expreso; (explicit) explícito, claro; **— company** compañía de expreso; expreso, Am. exprés; **— train** tren expreso; adv. por expreso, por exprés; s. expreso; tren expreso, Am. exprés; v. expresar; enviar por expreso (o por exprés).

expression [ɪksprɛ́ʃən] s. expresión.

expressive [ɪksprɛ́sɪv] adj. expresivo.

expulsion [ɪkspʌ́lʃən] s. expulsión.

exquisite [ɛkskwízɪt] adj. exquisito.

exquisiteness [ɪkskwízɪtnɪs] s. exquisitez; primor.

extant [ɪkstǽnt] adj. existente.

extemporaneous [ɛkstɛmpərénɪəs] adj. improvisado.

extend [ɪksténd] v. extender(se); tender; prolongar(se); alargar(se); agrandar; dilatar, prorrogar (un plazo); dar (el pésame, el parabién, ayuda, etc.).

extended [ɪksténdɪd] adj. extenso; prolongado; extendido.

extension [ɪksténʃən] s. extensión; prolongación; prórroga (de un plazo); añadidura, anexo.

extensive [ɪksténsɪv] adj. extenso, ancho, dilatado; extensivo; **-ly** adv. extensamente, por extenso; extensivamente; **-ly** used de uso general o común.

extent [ɪkstént] s. extensión; grado; **to a great —** en gran parte, generalmente; **to such an —** that a tal grado que; **to the — of** one's ability en proporción a su habilidad; **up to a certain —** hasta cierto punto.

extenuate [ɪksténjuet] v. atenuar, mitigar.

exterior [ɪkstíriə] adj. exterior; externo; s. exterioridad; exterior, porte, aspecto.

exterminate [ɪkstə́rmənet] v. exterminar, destruir por completo, extirpar.

extermination [ɪkstə́rmənéʃən] s. exterminio.

external [ɪkstə́rn̩] adj. externo; exterior; s. exterioridad; lo externo.

extinct [ɪkstíŋkt] adj. extinto; extinguido, apagado.

extinguish [ɪkstíŋgwɪʃ] v. extinguir; apagar.

extol [ɪkstól] v. enaltecer; ensalzar.

extort [ɪkstɔ́rt] v. obtener por fuerza o amenaza, exigir (dinero, promesa, etc.), Am. extorsionar.

extortion [ɪkstɔ́rʃən] s. extorsión.

extra [ékstrə] adj. extraordinario; de sobra, de más, adicional; suplementario; **— tire** neumático de repuesto o de recambio; **— workman** obrero supernumerario; adv. extraordinariamente; s. extra; extraordinario (de un periódico); suplemento; gasto extraordinario; recargo (cargo adicional); actor suplente o supernumerario.

extract [ékstrækt] s. extracto; cita, trozo (entresacado de un libro); resumen; [ɪkstrǽkt] v. extraer; seleccionar; citar.

extraordinary [ɪkstrɔ́rdnɛrɪ] adj. extraordinario; **extraordinarily** adv. extraordinariamente; de manera extraordinaria.

extravagance [ɪkstrǽvəgəns] s. despilfarro, derroche, gasto excesivo; lujo excesivo; extravagancia, capricho.

extravagant [ɪkstrǽvəgənt] adj. gastador, despilfarrado; extravagante, disparatado; **— praise** elogios excesivos; **— prices** precios exorbitantes.

extreme [ɪkstrím] adj. (last) último; extremo; más remoto; (excessive) excesivo; riguroso; radical; **— opinions** opiniones extremadas; s. extremo;

cabo; **to go to -s** extremar, exagerar; hacer extremos; tomar las medidas más extremas; **-ly** adv. extremamente, en extremo.

extremity [ɪkstrémətɪ] s. extremidad, extremo; medida extrema; **in —** en gran peligro; en un apuro.

exuberant [ɪgzjúbərənt] adj. exuberante.

exult [ɪgzʌ́lt] v. alborozarse, regocijarse.

eye [aɪ] s. ojo; **— shade** visera; **in a twinkling of an —** en un abrir y cerrar de ojos; **hook and —** macho y hembra; **to catch one's —** llamar la atención; **to have good -s** tener buena vista; **to have before one's -s** tener a (o tener ante) la vista; **to keep an — on** cuidar, vigilar; **to see — to —** estar completamente de acuerdo; v. mirar, observar.

eyeball [áɪbɔl] s. globo del ojo.

eyebrow [áɪbrau] s. ceja.

eyeglass [áɪglæs] s. lente, cristal (de anteojo); ocular (de microscopio o telescopio); **-es** lentes, anteojos.

eyelash [áɪlæʃ] s. pestaña.

eyelid [áɪlɪd] s. párpado.

eyesight [áɪsaɪt] s. vista; **poor —** mala vista.

F

fable [fébḷ] s. fábula.

fabric [fǽbrɪk] s. género, tela; tejido; textura; estructura.

fabulous [fǽbjələs] adj. fabuloso.

façade [fəsád] s. fachada.

face [fes] s. (human) cara, rostro; (building) fachada, frente; (surface) haz, superficie; (watch) muestra; Riopl. esfera; Méx., C.A., Ven., Col. carátula; **— value** valor nominal; **in the — of** en presencia de, ante, frente a; **to lose —** perder prestigio; **to make -s** hacer muecas o gestos; **to save one's —** salvar el amor propio; v. encararse con; enfrentarse con; hacer frente a; mirar hacia; forrar; **to — about** volverse, Méx., C.A., Ven., Col., Andes voltearse; **to — danger** afrontar o arrostrar el peligro; **to — with marble** revestir de mármol; **it -s the street** da a la calle.

facilitate [fəsílətet] v. facilitar.

facility [fəsílətɪ] s. facilidad.

fact [fækt] s. hecho; dato; verdad, realidad; **in — de** hecho; en realidad.

faction [fǽkʃən] s. facción, bando, partido, pandilla.

factor [fǽktə] s. factor; elemento; agente; v. descomponer en factores.

factory [fǽktrɪ] s. fábrica.

faculty [fǽkḷtɪ] s. facultad; (college) profesorado; cuerpo docente.

fad [fæd] s. novedad; manía; moda.

fade [fed] v. descolorar(se), desteñir(se); marchitar(se); apagar(se) (un sonido); desvanecerse.

fagged [fægd] adj. agotado, rendido de cansancio.

fail [fel] v. (not effect) faltar; fallar;

fracasar; no tener éxito; (*wane*) decaer; debilitarse; (*go broke*) quebrar, hacer bancarrota; **to — in an examination** fallar en un examen, salir mal en un examen; **to — a student** reprobar o suspender a un estudiante; **to — to do it** dejar de hacerlo, no hacerlo; **don't — to come** no deje Vd. de venir; **without —** sin falta.

failure [féljə] *s.* fracaso; malogro; falta; descuido, negligencia; quiebra, bancarrota; debilitamiento.

faint [fent] *adj.* (*weak*) débil, languido; (*indistinct*) imperceptible, tenue, vago, indistinto; **to feel —** sentirse desvanecido; **—hearted** tímido, cobarde; *s.* desmayo; *v.* desmayarse; languidecer; **-ly** *adv.* débilmente; lánguidamente; indistintamente, vagamente, tenuemente; apenas.

faintness [féntnɪs] *s.* languidez, debilidad, desfallecimiento; falta de claridad; vaguedad.

fair [fer] *adj.* (*just*) justo, recto, honrado; imparcial; equitativo; (*mediocre*) regular, mediano; (*complexion*) rubio, blondo; *Méx.* huero; *Guat.* canche; *C.R.* macho; *Pan.* fulo; *Col.* mono; *Ven.* catire; (*weather*) claro, despejado; **— chance of success** buena probabilidad de éxito; **— complexion** tez blanca; **— hair** pelo rubio; **— name** reputación sin mancilla; **— play** juego limpio; **— sex** sexo bello; **— weather** buen tiempo, tiempo bonancible; **to act —** obrar con imparcialidad (*o* con equidad); **to play —** jugar limpio; *s.* feria; mercado; exposición; **-ly** *adv.* justamente; imparcialmente; medianamente; **-ly difficult** medianamente difícil; **-ly well** regular, bastante bien.

fairness [férnɪs] *s.* justicia, equidad, imparcialidad; blancura (*de la tez*); belleza.

fairy [férɪ] *s.* hada; **— godmother** hada madrina; **— tale** cuento de hadas.

fairyland [férɪlænd] *s.* tierra de las hadas.

faith [feθ] *s.* fe; fidelidad; **in good —** de buena fe; **to have —** in tener fe o confianza en; **to keep —** cumplir con la palabra.

faithful [féθfəl] *adj.* fiel; leal; **-ly** *adv.* fielmente; con fidelidad; puntualmente; **-ly yours** suyo afectísimo; siempre suyo.

faithfulness [féθfəlnɪs] *s.* fidelidad; lealtad; exactitud.

faithless [féθlɪs] *adj.* infiel; sin fe; desleal; falso.

fake [fek] *s.* fraude, trampa; falsedad; embustero; *adj.* falso, fingido; *v.* falsear; fingir; simular.

falcon [fɔ́lkən] *s.* halcón.

fall [fɔl] *s.* (*drop*) caída; bajada; (*collapse*) ruina; baja (*de precios*); (*season*) otoño; **-s** cascada, catarata, salto de agua; *v.* caer(se); decaer; bajar; **to — asleep** dormirse, quedarse dormido; **to — back** retroceder; **to — behind** atrasarse, rezagarse, quedarse atrás; **to — in love** enamorarse; **to — out with** reñir con, enemistarse con; **to — to one** tocarle a uno, corresponderle a uno; **his plans fell through** fracasaron (*o se* malograron) sus planes.

fallacy [fǽləsɪ] *s.* falsedad; error.

fallen [fɔ́lən] *p.p. de* **to fall.**

fallout [fɔ́laut] *s.* precipitación radiactiva.

fallow [fǽlo] *adj.* baldío; *s.* barbecho; *v.* barbechar.

false [fɔls] *adj.* falso; postizo (*dientes, barba, etc.*); fingido, simulado.

falsehood [fɔ́lshud] *s.* falsedad, mentira.

falseness [fɔ́lsnɪs] *s.* falsedad.

falsify [fɔ́lsəfaɪ] *v.* falsificar, falsear; mentir.

falsity [fɔ́lsətɪ] *s.* falsedad; mentira.

falter [fɔ́ltə] *v.* vacilar; titubear; tambalearse; bambolearse; **to — an excuse** balbucear una excusa; *s.* temblor, vacilación.

fame [fem] *s.* fama.

famed [femd] *adj.* afamado, famoso, renombrado.

familiar [fəmíljə] *adj.* familiar, íntimo; confianzudo; **to be — with a subject** conocer bien, estar versado en *o* ser conocedor de una materia; *s.* familiar.

familiarity [fəmɪlɪǽrətɪ] *s.* familiaridad; confianza, franqueza.

family [fǽmlɪ] *s.* familia; **— name** apellido; **— tree** árbol genealógico; **to be in the — way** estar encinta.

famine [fǽmɪn] *s.* hambre; escasez, carestía.

famished [fǽmɪʃt] *adj.* hambriento, muerto de hambre; **to be —** morirse de hambre.

famous [fémədə] *adj.* famoso.

fan [fæn] *s.* abanico; aventador; ventilador; aficionado (*a deportes*); admirador; *v.* abanicar; ventilar.

fanatic [fənǽtɪk] *adj. & s.* fanático.

fanaticism [fənǽtəsɪzəm] *s.* fanatismo.

fanciful [fǽnsɪfəl] *adj.* fantástico; caprichoso; imaginario.

fancy [fǽnsɪ] *s.* fantasía, antojo, capricho; imaginación; afición, gusto; **to have a — for** tener afición a; **to strike one's —** antojársele a uno; **to take a — to a person** caerle a uno bien (*o* simpatizarle a uno) una persona; *adj.* fantástico, de fantasía; de adorno; elegante; **— ball** baile de fantasía o disfraces; **— free** libre de cuidados; **—work** labor ;bordado fino; *v.* imaginar(se); fantasear; forjar, concebir (*una idea*); **to — oneself** imaginarse; **just — the idea!** ¡figúrate qué idea! **I don't — the idea** of no me gusta la idea de.

fang [fæŋ] *s.* colmillo (*de ciertos animales*).

fantastic [fæntǽstɪk] *adj.* fantástico; extravagante.

fantasy [fǽntəsɪ] s. fantasía.
far [far] adv. lejos; **— away** muy lejos;
— and wide por todas partes;
— better mucho mejor; **— off** muy
lejos; a lo lejos; **by —** con mucho; **as
— as** hasta; en cuanto a; **as — as I
know** según parece; a lo que parece;
que yo sepa; **so —** hasta ahora; hasta
aquí; hasta entonces; **how —?**
¿hasta dónde?; adj. lejano, distante,
remoto; **— journey** largo viaje; **it is
a — cry from** dista mucho de.
faraway [fárəwé] adj. muy lejano, distante, remoto; abstraído.
farce [fars] s. farsa.
fare [fer] s. pasaje, tarifa de pasajes;
pasajero; comida, alimento; **as**
(bien o mal); irle a uno (bien o mal);
to — forth salir.
farewell [ferwél] s. despedida, adiós; **to
bid — to** despedirse de; **—!** ¡adiós!
farfetched [fárfétʃt] adj. traído de muy
lejos; forzado; traído por los cabellos;
que no hace al caso; improbable, poco
creíble.
far-flung [fárflʌ́ŋ] adj. extenso, de gran
alcance.
farm [farm] s. hacienda, granja, Ríopl.
estancia, Méx. rancho; **— hand** peón;
— produce productos agrícolas; v.
cultivar, labrar (la tierra); **to — out**
dar en arriendo; repartir.
farmer [fármɚ] s. labrador; granjero;
agricultor; Méx. ranchero, Ríopl.
estanciero, Am. hacendado.
farmhouse [fármhaʊs] s. alquería,
finca.
farming [fármɪŋ] s. labranza, agricultura, cultivo de los campos; adj. agrícola.
farmyard [fármjard] s. corral (de una
alquería).
far-off [fárɔ́f] adj. distante, remoto.
far-sighted [farsáɪtəd] adj. (sight)
présbite; (foresighted) precavido.
farther [fárðɚ] adv. más lejos; más; **—
on** más adelante; adj. más remoto,
más lejano.
farthest [fárðɪst] adj. más lejano; más
remoto; adv. más lejos.
fascinate [fǽsɳet] v. fascinar.
fascination [fæsɳéʃən] s. fascinación.
fashion [fǽʃən] s. (style) moda, boga;
estilo; (way) manera, modo; **— plate**
figurín; **the latest —** la última moda
(o novedad); **after a —** medianamente, no muy bien; **to be in —** estar
de moda; estilarse; v. forjar, hacer,
formar; idear.
fashionable [fǽʃnəbl] adj. de moda; de
buen tono; elegante.
fast [fæst] adj. rápido, veloz; adelantado
(dícese del reloj); firme; fiel (amigo);
fijo; disipado, disoluto; adv. aprisa, de
prisa; firmemente, fijamente; **—
asleep** profundamente dormido; s.
ayuno; v. ayunar.
fasten [fǽsɳ] v. fijar(se); sujetar(se),
asegurar(se); atar, unir; abrochar(se).
fastener [fǽsɳɚ] s. broche; abrochador.
fastidious [fæstídɪəs] adj. melindroso.

fat [fæt] adj. gordo; grasiento; mantecoso; **— profits** ganancias pingües; s.
grasa, manteca; gordura; **the — of
the land** lo mejor y más rico de la
tierra.
fatal [fétl] adj. fatal.
fatality [fətǽlətɪ] s. fatalidad; muerte.
fate [fet] s. hado, sino, destino; fortuna,
suerte.
father [fáðɚ] s. padre.
fatherhood [fáðɚhʊd] s. paternidad.
father-in-law [fáðɚɪnlɔ] s. suegro.
fatherland [fáðɚlænd] s. patria.
fatherly [fáðɚlɪ] adv. paternal.
fathom [fǽðəm] v. sondar, sondear; penetrar; s. braza (medida de profundidad).
fathomless [fǽðəmlɪs] adj. insondable.
fatigue [fətíg] s. fatiga, cansancio; v.
fatigar(se), cansar(se).
fatness [fǽtnɪs] s. gordura.
fatten [fǽtɳ] v. engordar.
faucet [fɔ́sɪt] s. grifo, llave, espita, canilla, Am. bitoque.
fault [fɔlt] s. (defect) falta; defecto,
tacha; (blame) culpa; (geological) falla;
to a — excesivamente; **to be at —**
ser, culpable; **to find — with**
criticar a.
faultfinder [fɔ́ltfaɪndɚ] s. criticón, criticador.
faultless [fɔ́ltlɪs] adj. intachable, sin
tacha, perfecto.
faulty [fɔ́ltɪ] adj. defectuoso, imperfecto.
favor [févɚ] s. favor; **your — of the . . .**
su grata (carta) del . . .; v. favorecer.
favorable [févrəbl] adj. favorable; **fa-
vorably** adv. favorablemente.
favorite [févrɪt] adj. & s. favorito.
favoritism [févrɪtɪzəm] s. favoritismo.
fawn [fɔn] s. cervato; color de cervato;
v. adular; halagar.
fear [fɪr] s. temor, miedo; pavor; v.
temer.
fearful [fírfəl] adj. terrible, espantoso;
temible, temeroso; miedoso.
fearless [fírlɪs] adj. sin temor, intrépido, atrevido, arrojado.
fearlessness [fírlɪsnɪs] s. intrepidez,
arrojo, osadía, atrevimiento.
feasible [fízəbl] adj. factible, hacedero,
dable.
feast [fist] s. fiesta; festín, banquete; v.
festejar, obsequiar; banquetear; **to —
one's eyes on** deleitar la vista en.
feat [fit] s. proeza, hazaña; acto de destreza; suerte (en el circo).
feather [féðɚ] s. pluma, **-s** plumaje; **a
— in one's cap** un triunfo para uno;
— weight de peso mínimo; v. emplumar.
feathery [féðɚɪ] adj. plumoso; ligero,
como una pluma.
feature [fítʃɚ] s. facción, rasgo distintivo; película principal (en el cine); **-s**
facciones (de la cara); **— article** artículo sobresaliente o principal; v. destacar, hacer sobresalir; dar realce a;
mostrar, exhibir (como cosa principal);
hacer resaltar.
February [fébrʊɛrɪ] s. febrero.

fed [fɛd] *pret. & p.p. de* **to feed; to be**
— **up** estar harto; estar hasta la coronilla, estar hasta el copete.
federal [fédərəl] *adj.* federal.
federation [fedəréʃən] *s.* federación,
confederación, liga.
fee [fi] *s.* honorario (honorarios); derechos; cuota; **admission** — derechos
de entrada; precio de entrada.
feeble [fibl] *adj.* débil, endeble; **feebly**
adv. débilmente.
feed [fid] *s.* forraje, pasto, pienso (*para
los caballos*); comida; *v.* alimentar(se);
dar de comer; pacer, pastar; **to —
coal** echar carbón.
feedback [fidbæk] *s.* regeneración.
feel [fil] *v.* sentir; tocar, tentar; palpar;
to — better (*sad, happy, etc.*); sentirse mejor (triste, feliz, *etc.*); **to —
one's way** tantear el camino; **to —
for someone** compadecer a alguien;
it -s soft está suave; **it -s hot in here**
se siente calor aquí; *s.* tacto, sentido
del tacto; **this cloth has a nice —**
esta tela es suave al tacto.
feeler [filə] *s.* tentáculo, antena (*de los
insectos*); tiento; propuesta (*para averiguar la inclinación o pensamiento de
alguien*).
feeling [filɪŋ] *s.* (*touch*) tacto; sensación; (*emotion*) sentimiento; emoción;
pasión; (*pity*) compasión; ternura; **to
hurt someone's -s** ofender la
sensibilidad de alguien; *adj.* sensible, compasivo.
feet [fit] *pl. de* **foot.**
feign [fen] *v.* fingir.
fell [fɛl] *v.* derribar, echar abajo; cortar
(*un árbol*); *pret. de* **to fall.**
fellow [félo] *s.* socio, miembro (*de una
sociedad, colegio, etc.*); becario (*estudiante que disfruta una beca*); camarada; compañero; individuo, tipo, sujeto, hombre; — **citizen** conciudadano; — **man** prójimo; — **member**
consocio; colega; — **student** condiscípulo.
fellowship [féloʃɪp] *s.* compañerismo;
unión; confraternidad; sociedad;
beca; **to get a —** obtener una beca.
felony [félənɪ] *s.* crimen.
felt [fɛlt] *s.* fieltro; *adj.* de fieltro; *pret.
& p.p. de* **to feel.**
female [fimel] *s.* hembra; *adj.* hembra;
femenino, mujeril, de la mujer; — **cat**
(**dog,** *etc.*) gata (perra, *etc.*); — **screw**
tuerca, hembra de tornillo.
feminine [fémənɪn] *adj.* femenino,
femenil.
femininity [feminínɪtɪ] *s.* feminidad.
fence [fens] *s.* cerca, valla, vallado; receptor de cosas robadas; **to be on
the** — estar indeciso; *v.* esgrimir; **to
— in** cercar, rodear con cerca.
fencing [fénsɪŋ] *s.* esgrima; cercado.
fender [féndə] *s.* guardabarros, guardafango; *Am.* trompa (*de locomotora*);
Ríopl. parrilla.
ferment [fə́ment] *s.* fermento; fermen-
tación; [fəmént] *v.* fermentar; hacer
fermentar.

fermentation [fɜmentéʃən] *s.* fermen-
tación.
fern [fɜrn] *s.* helecho.
ferocious [fəróʃəs] *adj.* feroz, fiero.
ferocity [fərásɪtɪ] *s.* ferocidad, fiereza.
ferret [férɪt] *v.* **to — out** buscar, cazar;
escudriñar, indagar.
ferry [férɪ] *s.* barca de pasaje (*a través
de un rio o bahía*); embarcadero; *v.*
transportar de una orilla a otra; atravesar (*un rio*) en barca de pasaje.
fertile [fɜ́tl] *adj.* fértil; fecundo.
fertility [fɜtílətɪ] *s.* fertilidad.
fertilize [fɜ́tlaɪz] *v.* fertilizar; abonar;
fecundar.
fertilizer [fɜ́tlaɪzə] *s.* abono (*para la
tierra*).
fervent [fɜ́vənt] *adj.* ferviente; fervoroso.
fervor [fɜ́və] *s.* fervor; ardor.
fester [féstə] *v.* supurar; enconarse (*una
llaga*); *s.* llaga, úlcera.
festival [féstəvl] *s.* fiesta.
festive [féstɪv] *adj.* festivo; alegre.
festivity [festívətɪ] *s.* júbilo, regocijo;
festividad.
fetch [fetʃ] *v.* ir a buscar; coger; traer.
fete [fet] *s.* fiesta; *v.* festejar; agasajar.
fetid [fétɪd] *adj.* fétido.
fetish [fétɪʃ] *s.* fetiche.
fetter [fétə] *v.* engrillar, meter en grillos
encadenar; **-s** *s. pl.* grillos, cadenas,
trabas.
fetus [fitəs] *s.* feto.
feud [fjud] *s.* riña, pelea, contienda;
old — enemistad antigua (*entre dos
personas o familias*).
feudal [fjúdl] *adj.* feudal.
fever [fívə] *s.* fiebre, calentura.
feverish [fívərɪʃ] *adj.* calenturiento, febril.
feverishness [fívərɪʃnɪs] *s.* calentura;
agitación febril.
few [fju] *adj. & pron.* pocos; **a —** unos
pocos, unos cuantos.
fiancé [fiansé] *s.* novio; **fiancée** *f.*
novia.
fiasco [fɪǽsko] *s.* fiasco.
fib [fɪb] *s.* bola, mentirilla, paparrucha,
papa; *v.* echar papas, decir o contar
paparruchas.
fibber [fíbə] *s.* paparruchero, cuentero,
mentirosillo.
fiber [fáɪbə] *s.* fibra.
fibrous [fáɪbrəs] *adj.* fibroso.
fickle [fíkl] *adj.* inconstante, voluble,
veleidoso, mudable.
fiction [fíkʃən] *s.* ficción.
fictional [fíkʃənl] *adj.* novelesco; ficticio.
fictitious [fɪktíʃəs] *adj.* ficticio.
fiddle [fídl] *s.* violín; *v.* tocar el violín;
to — around malgastar el tiempo;
juguetear.
fidelity [faɪdélətɪ] *s.* fidelidad.
fidget [fídʒɪt] *v.* estar inquieto; agitarse,
menearse nerviosamente.
field [fild] *s.* campo; campo o cancha (*de
deportes*); — **artillery** artillería de
campaña; — **glasses** anteojos de
larga vista; — **work** trabajo de

investigación en el campo.

fiend [find] *s.* demonio, diablo; **dope —** morfinómano.

fiendish [fíndɪʃ] *adj.* diabólico.

fierce [fɪrs] *adj.* feroz, fiero; furioso, espantoso.

fierceness [fírsnɪs] *s.* ferocidad; fiereza; vehemencia.

fiery [fáɪrɪ] *adj.* fogoso; ardiente; vehemente.

fife [faɪf] *s.* pífano.

fig [fɪg] *s.* higo; **— tree** higuera.

fight [faɪt] *s.* lucha; pelea; riña, pleito; **he has a lot of — left** le sobra fuerza para luchar; *v.* luchar (con); pelear; combatir; reñir; batirse; **to — it out** decidirlo a golpes o con argumentos; **to — one's way through** abrirse camino a la fuerza.

fighter [fáɪtə] *s.* luchador; combatiente; guerrero; **— airplane** avión de caza.

fighting [fáɪtɪŋ] *s.* lucha, combate, pelea; *adj.* combatiente; luchador.

figure [fígjə] *s.* (*form*) figura; forma; talle (*de una persona*); (*numerical*) cifra, número; valor; precio; **-s** cuentas, cálculos; **— of speech** figura de dicción; **to be good at -s** sabe hacer bien las cuentas; ser listo en aritmética; **to cut a poor —** tener mala facha, hacer el ridículo; *v.* figurar; imaginarse, figurarse; adornar con dibujos; calcular; **to — on** contar con, confiar en; tener la intención de, proponerse; tomar en cuenta; **to — out** descifrar, resolver.

filament [fíləmənt] *s.* filamento.

file [faɪl] *s.* (*records*) fichero; archivo; registro, lista; (*cabinet*) guardapapeles; (*line*) fila; (*tool*) lima; **— card** ficha, papeleta; *v.* archivar; guardar en el fichero; registrar, asentar en el registro; limar; desfilar, marchar en fila.

filial [fílɪəl] *adj.* filial.

filigree [fílɪgri] *s.* filigrana.

fill [fɪl] *v.* llenar(se); ocupar (*un puesto*); empastar (*un diente*); servir, atender, despachar (*un pedido*); inflar (*un neumático*); tapar (*un agujero*); **to — out a blank** llenar un formulario (forma o esqueleto).

fillet [fɪlé] *s.* filete; [fíllɪt] cinta, lista o adorno.

filling [fíllɪŋ] *s.* relleno; empaste (*dental*); **gold —** orificación.

filly [fíllɪ] *s.* potranca.

film [fɪlm] *s.* película; membrana; tela (*formada sobre la superficie de un líquido*); nube (*en el ojo*); *v.* filmar (*cinematografiar*); **her eyes -ed with tears** se le arrasaron los ojos de lágrimas.

filter [fíltə] *s.* filtro; *v.* filtrar(se).

filth [fɪlθ] *s.* suciedad; porquería; mugre.

filthiness [fílθɪnɪs] *s.* suciedad, porquería.

filthy [fíllθɪ] *adj.* sucio; puerco, cochino; mugriento.

fin [fɪn] *s.* aleta (*de pez*).

final [fáɪnl] *adj.* final; terminante; defi-

nitivo; **-ly** *adv.* finalmente; en fin, por fin.

finance [fənǽns] *s.* teoría bancaria, *Am.* finanza; **-s** fondos, recursos monetarios; negocios bancarios, *Am.* finanzas; *v.* hacer operaciones bancarias; fomentar (*un negocio o empresa*), *Am.* financiar.

financial [fənǽnʃəl] *adj.* financiero; monetario.

financier [fɪnənsír] *s.* financiero, *Am.* financista.

financing [fənǽnsɪŋ] *s. Am.* financiamiento.

find [faɪnd] *v.* hallar; encontrar; declarar; **to — fault with** criticar a, censurar a; **to — guilty** declarar o encontrar culpable; **to — out** descubrir; averiguar; *s.* hallazgo.

finding [fáɪndɪŋ] *s.* descubrimiento; hallazgo; fallo, decisión; **-s** resultados, datos (*de una investigación*).

fine [faɪn] *adj.* fino; perfecto, excelente; superior; primoroso; **— arts** bellas artes; **— sand** arena fina o menuda; **— weather** tiempo claro o despejado; **to feel —** sentirse muy bien de salud; **to have a — time** pasar un rato muy divertido; **fine-looking** bien parecido, guapo; *s.* multa; **in —** finalmente, en fin, en resumen; *v.* multar; **-ly** *adv.* finamente; con primor; excelentemente; muy bien, perfectamente.

fineness [fáɪnnɪs] *s.* finura; fineza; primor; excelencia, perfección.

finery [fáɪnərɪ] *s.* galas; atavíos, adornos.

finesse [fɪnés] *s.* sutileza; artificio; soltura.

finger [fíŋgə] *s.* dedo (*de la mano*); **—print** impresión digital; **the little —** el dedo meñique; **middle —** dedo del corazón, dedo de enmedio; **ring —** dedo anular; *v.* tocar; manosear.

fingernail [fíŋgənel] *s.* uña.

finicky [fínɪkɪ] *adj.* melindroso.

finish [fínɪʃ] *s.* fin término, conclusión; (*varnish*) pulimento; **to have a rough —** estar sin pulir, sin pulimento o al natural; *v.* acabar, acabar con, terminar, finalizar; pulir, pulimentar.

finished [fínɪʃt] *adj.* acabado; pulido, pulimentado; excelente.

fir [fɚ] *s.* abeto.

fire [faɪr] *s.* (*flame*) fuego; lumbre; (*destructive*) quemazón; incendio; **— alarm** alarma de incendios; **— department** cuerpo o servicio de bomberos; servicio de incendios; **— engine** bomba (*para incendios*); **— escape** escalera de salvamento; **— insurance** seguro contra incendios; **to be on —** estar ardiendo, estar quemándose; **to catch —** incendiarse, quemarse; **to set on —** pegar fuego, incendiar; **to be under enemy —** estar expuesto al fuego del enemigo; *v.* incendiar; pegar fuego; inflamar; disparar; **to — an em-**

ployee despedir (*o* expulsar) a un empleado.

firearm [fáirɑrm] *s.* arma de fuego.

firebrand [fáirbrænd] *s.* tizón; pavesa.

firecracker [fáirkrækə] *s.* triquitraque

firefly [fáirflai] *s.* luciérnaga.

fireman [fáirmən] *s.* bombero; fogonero.

fireplace [fáirples] *s.* chimenea, hogar.

fireproof [fáirpruf] *adj.* incombustible; a prueba de incendio; *v.* hacer incombustible.

fireside [fáirsaid] *s.* hogar.

firewood [fáirwud] *s.* leña.

fireworks [fáirwɜks] *s.* fuegos artificiales.

firm [fɜm] *adj.* firme; fijo; estable; *s.* firma, razón social (*nombre de una casa comercial*); compañía (*comercial o industrial*); **-ly** *adv.* firmemente, con firmeza.

firmament [fɜməmənt] *s.* firmamento.

firmness [fɜmnɪs] *s.* firmeza; estabilidad.

first [fɜst] *adj.* primero; *adv.* primero, en primer lugar, al principio; **from the —** desde el principio; **first-born** primogénito; **first-class** de primera clase; **first-cousin** primo hermano; **first-rate** de primera clase; muy bien; **—hand** de primera mano.

first aid [fɜst éd] *s.* primeros auxilios.

fish [fɪʃ] *s.* pez; pescado; **— market** pescadería; **— story** patraña, cuento extravagante o increíble; **neither — nor fowl** ni chicha ni limonada; *v.* pescar.

fisher [fíʃə] *s.* pescador.

fisherman [fíʃəmən] *s.* pescador.

fishery [fíʃəri] *s.* pesquera; pesquería, pesca.

fishhook [fíʃhuk] *s.* anzuelo.

fishing [fíʃɪŋ] *s.* pesca, pesquería; **— rod** caña de pescar; **— tackle** avíos o enseres para pescar; **to go —** ir de pesca.

fissure [fíʃə] *s.* grieta, hendedura, *Am.* rajadura.

fist [fɪst] *s.* puño; **to shake one's — at** amenazar con el puño.

fit [fɪt] *adj.* (*proper*) apto; a propósito, propio, conveniente; (*healthy*) sano, de buena salud, en buen estado; capaz; **— to be tied** frenético; **not to see —** to do it no tener a bien hacerlo; *s.* talle (*de un traje*); ajuste; encaje (*de una pieza en otra*); ataque, convulsión; **— of anger** acceso, arrebato o arranque de cólera; **by -s and starts** espasmódicamente; **that suit is a good —** ese traje le entalla (o le viene) bien; *v.* ajustar(se); adaptar; encajar(se), caber (en); acomodar; entallar (*un vestido*); venir bien (*un vestido, zapatos, sombrero, etc.*); ser a propósito para, ser propio para; capacitar, preparar; **to — in with** armonizar con; llevarse bien con; **to — out** equipar, proveer; **it does not — the facts** no está de acuerdo con los hechos; no hace al

caso.

fitness [fítnɪs] *s.* aptitud; capacidad; conveniencia; propiedad (*de una idea, de una palabra, etc.*); **physical —** buena salud.

fitting [fítɪŋ] *adj.* propio, apropiado; a propósito, conveniente; *s.* ajuste; **dress —** prueba de un traje o vestido; **-s** avíos, guarniciones, accesorios.

fix [fɪks] *v.* (*repair*) remendar; componer; reparar; ajustar; arreglar; (*prearrange*) fijar; asegurar; **to — up** arreglar(se); componer(se); *s.* apuro, aprieto.

fixed [fɪkst] *adj.* fijo, firme.

fixture [fíkstʃə] *s.* (*thing*) accesorio fijo; (*person*) persona firmemente establecida (*en un sitio o empleo*); **electric light -s** instalaciones eléctricas (*como brazos de lámparas, arañas*).

flabby [flǽbi] *adj.* blanducho.

flag [flæg] *s.* bandera; banderola; **— lily** flor de lis; *v.* hacer señas con banderola; adornar con banderas; decaer, debilitarse, menguar, flaquear.

flagrant [flégrant] *adj.* flagrante, notorio, escandaloso.

flagstaff [flǽgstæf] *s.* asta de bandera.

flagstone [flǽgston] *s.* losa.

flair [fler] *s.* instinto, penetración, cacumen; disposición o aptitud natural.

flak [flæk] *s.* fuego antiaéreo.

flake [flek] *s.* copo (*de nieve*); escama; hojuela; **corn -s** hojuelas de maíz; *v.* descostrarse, descascararse.

flamboyant [flæmbɔ́jənt] *adj.* rimbombante; flameante.

flame [flem] *s.* llama; flama; **— thrower** lanzallamas; *v.* llamear, flamear, echar llamas; inflamar(se); enardecer(se).

flaming [flémɪŋ] *adj.* llameante; flameante; encendido; ardiente, apasionado; **— red** rojo encendido.

flank [flæŋk] *s.* flanco; costado; lado; ijar (*de un animal*); *v.* flanquear; rodear.

flannel [flǽnl] *s.* franela.

flap [flæp] *s.* (*thing*) aleta; cubierta (*del bolsillo*); (*action*) golpeteo; aleteo; *v.* golpetear; aletear, batir (*las alas*); hojear con violencia (*las páginas*).

flare [fler] *s.* llamarada; llama; arranque (*de ira*); vuelo (*de una falda*); *v.* llamear, echar llamaradas; tener vuelo (*una falda*); **to — up** enfurecerse; encenderse; **the illness -ed up** recrudeció la enfermedad.

flash [flæʃ] *s.* rayo; destello, llamarada; fogonazo; **— of hope** rayo de esperanza; **— of lightning** relámpago; **— of wit** agudeza; **— bulb** bombilla de destello; bombilla flash; **in a —** en un instante; **news —** última noticia (*enviada por radio o telégrafo*); *v.* relampaguear; destellar; brillar; centellear; radiar o telegrafiar (*noticias*); **to — by** pasar como un relámpago.

flashing [flǽʃɪŋ] *s.* relampagueo, centelleo; *adj.* relumbrante; flameante.

flashlight [flǽʃlait] *s.* linterna eléctrica.

flashy [flǽʃɪ] *adj.* relumbrante; llamativo, de relumbrón, ostentoso; chillante, chillón (*dícese de los colores*).

flask [flæsk] *s.* frasco.

flat [flæt] *adj.* (*no curves*) plano, llano, chato; aplastado; (*tasteless*) insípido; monótono; (*without air*) desinflado; **— denial** negativa terminante; **— note** nota desentonada; **—rate** precio o número redondo; **D —** re bemol (*nota musical*); **—car** vagón de plataforma; **to be — broke** estar completamente pelado, estar sin dinero; **to fall —** caer de plano; caer mal (*un discurso, chiste, etc.*); **to sing —** desafinarse, cantar desentonadamente; **to refuse -ly** negarse absolutamente; *s.* plano; palma (*de la mano*); apartamento, departamento, piso; bemol (*en música*).

flatiron [flǽtaɪən] *s.* plancha.

flatness [flǽtnɪs] *s.* llanura; lisura; insipidez; desafinamiento (*en música*).

flatten [flǽtn̩] *v.* aplastar(se); aplanar(se); allanar(se).

flatter [flǽtə] *v.* lisonjear; adular.

flatterer [flǽtərə] *s.* lisonjero, adulador.

flattering [flǽtərɪŋ] *adj.* lisonjero, halagüeño, adulador.

flattery [flǽtərɪ] *s.* lisonja, halago; adulación.

flatulence [flǽtjuləns] *s.* hinchazón, flatulencia.

flaunt [flɔnt] *v.* ostentar; hacer gala de.

flavor [flévə] *s.* sabor; gusto; condimento; *v.* sazonar; dar sabor a; condimentar.

flavorless [flévəlɪs] *adj.* insípido, sin sabor.

flaw [flɔ] *s.* defecto; falta; tacha; imperfección.

flawless [flɔ́lɪs] *adj.* sin tacha; intachable, irreprochable; perfecto.

flax [flæks] *s.* lino.

flay [fle] *s.* desollar.

flea [fli] *s.* pulga.

fled [flɛd] *pret. & p.p.* de **to flee**.

flee [fli] *v.* huir; huir de.

fleece [flis] *s.* vellón, lana; *v.* trasquilar, esquilar; despojar, estafar, defraudar.

fleet [flit] *s.* flota; armada; *adj.* veloz.

fleeting [flítɪŋ] *adj.* fugaz, transitorio, pasajero, efímero.

Flemish [flémɪʃ] *adj.* flamenco; *s.* flamenco, idioma flamenco; **the —** los flamencos.

flesh [flɛʃ] *s.* carne; **— and blood** carne y hueso; **— color** color encarnado; **in the —** en persona.

fleshy [fléʃɪ] *adj.* carnoso; gordo, gordiflón.

flew [flu] *pret.* de **to fly**.

flexibility [flɛksəbílətɪ] *s.* flexibilidad.

flexible [fléksəbl̩] *adj.* flexible.

flicker [flíkə] *s.* titilación, parpadeo, luz trémula; temblor momentáneo (*de emoción*); aleteo; especie de pájaro carpintero; *v.* titilar; temblar; parpadear; vacilar; aletear; **to — one's eyelash** pestañear.

flier [fláɪə] *s.* volador; aviador; tren rápido.

flight [flaɪt] *s.* vuelo; bandada (*de pájaros*); escuadrilla (*de aviones*); fuga, huida; **— of stairs** tramo de escalera; **to put to —** poner en fuga.

flimsy [flímzɪ] *adj.* endeble, débil; tenue; quebradizo; frágil; baladí; **a — excuse** una excusa baladí.

fling [flɪŋ] *v.* arrojar(se), lanzar(se); tirar; echar; **to — open (shut)** abrir (cerrar) de golpe; *s.* tiro, tirada, lanzamiento; tentativa; **to go out on a —** irse a echar una cana al aire.

flint [flɪnt] *s.* pedernal.

flip [flɪp] *v.* arrojar, lanzar al aire; sacudir; dar un dedazo.

flippancy [flípənsɪ] *s.* ligereza; frivolidad; impertinencia; petulancia.

flippant [flípənt] *adj.* ligero (*en sus acciones y modales*), ligero de cascos; frívolo; inpertinente; petulante.

flirt [flɜt] *s.* coqueta; coquetón, coquetona; *v.* coquetear.

flirtation [flɜtéʃən] *s.* coquetería; **to carry on a —** coquetear.

flit [flɪt] *v.* pasar velozmente; volar; revolotear.

float [flot] *s.* boya; cosa flotante, flotador; corcho (*de una caña de pescar*); balsa; carro o carroza (*de procesiones, fiestas, etc.*); *v.* flotar; sobrenadar; boyar; poner a flote; lanzar al mercado (*una nueva emisión de valores, bonos, etc.*).

flock [flɑk] *s.* bandada (*de pájaros, niños, etc.*); rebaño, grey; manada (*de animales*); grupo; **— of people** gentío, muchedumbre; *v.* agruparse, congregarse; **to — to** acudir juntos (o en bandadas) a; **to — together** andar juntos, volar en bandadas, ir en grupo.

flog [flɑg] *v.* azotar.

flood [flʌd] *s.* inundación; diluvio; avenida (*de agua*), crecida; creciente; torrente; **—gate** compuerta (*de una presa*); esclusa (*de un canal*); **— light** reflector; proyector de luz; **— tide** flujo (o marea ascendente); *v.* inundar.

floor [flor] *s.* (*surface*) suelo; piso; (*story*) piso; (*bottom*) fondo; **to have the —** tener la palabra; *v.* solar; entarimar, enladrillar, enlosar; echar al suelo, derribar; asombrar.

flop [flɑp] *v.* (*flap*) caer o colgar flojamente; aletear; menearse; (*throw*) lanzar; dejar caer; (*fail*) fracasar; fallar; **to — down** dejarse caer; desplomarse, tumbarse; **to — over** voltear(se); dar vueltas; *s.* fracaso.

florist [flórɪst] *s.* florero, florera; **-'s shop** florería.

floss [flɔs] *s.* seda floja; pelusa; fibra sedosa; **dental —** seda dental.

flounder [fláundə] *v.* patalear (*en el lodo, nieve, etc.*); forcejear (*por salir del lodo, nieve, o cualquier aprieto*); revolcarse; tropezar, cometer errores; *s.* lenguado (*pez*).

flour [flaʊr] *s.* harina.

flourish [flʌ́rɪ̌ʃ] v. (prosper) florecer, prosperar, medrar; (blandish) blandir; agitar en el aire; (with the signature) rúbrica; s. floreo; adorno o rasgo caprichoso; ostentación.

floury [flʌ́urɪ] adj. harinoso.

flow [flo] s. flujo; corriente; — of words torrente de palabras; v. fluir; correr; flotar, ondear; to — into desembocar en; to be -ing with riches nadar en la abundancia.

flower [flʌ́uɚ] s. flor; — bed cuadro de jardín; — vase florero; v. florecer, Am. florear.

flowerpot [flʌ́urpɑt] s. tiesto, maceta.

flowery [flʌ́urɪ] adj. florido.

flowing [flóɪŋ] adj. fluído, corriente, fluente; suelto, ondeante.

flown [flon] p.p. de to fly.

flu [flu] s. influenza, gripe.

fluctuate [flʌ́ktʃuet] v. fluctuar.

fluctuation [flʌktʃuéʃən] s. fluctuación.

flue [flu] s. cañón (de chimenea); tubo de escape.

fluency [flúənsɪ] s. fluidez; labia.

fluent [flúənt] adj. fluente, fluído; to speak -ly hablar con facilidad.

fluff [flʌf] v. mullir; esponjar.

fluffy [flʌ́fɪ] adj. mullido, suave, blando; cubierto de vello o plumón; — hair pelo esponjado o esponjoso.

fluid [flúɪd] adj. & s. fluído.

flung [flʌŋ] pret. & p.p. de to fling.

flunk [flʌŋk] s. reprobación (en un examen o asignatura); v. reprobar, suspender (en un examen); salir mal, fracasar o fallar (en un examen).

flunky [flʌ́ŋkɪ] s. lacayo; ayudante servil; zalamero, persona servil.

flurry [flɝ́ɪ] s. (weather) ráfaga; nevisca; (action) agitación.

flush [flʌʃ] s. sonrojo, rubor; bochorno; flujo rápido; flux (de naipes); adj. lleno; rico; parejo, al mismo nivel; — with a flor de, a ras de; v. sonrojar(se), ruborizar(se), poner(se) colorado; hacer rebosar (de agua); to — out vaciar (un depósito), enjuagar.

flute [flut] s. flauta; estría (de una columna); v. acanalar, estriar (una columna).

flutter [flʌ́tɚ] s. aleteo; agitación; alboroto; vuelco (del corazón); v. aletear; revolotear; agitar(se); palpitar; menear(se); tremolar (una bandera).

flux [flʌks] s. flujo.

fly [flaɪ] s. mosca; pliegue (para cubrir botones); bragueta (abertura de los pantalones); on the — al vuelo; to hit a — pegar una planchita o elevar una palomita (en beisbol); v. volar; pasar velozmente; huir; ondear; enarbolar (una bandera); to — at lanzarse sobre; to — away volar, irse, escaparse; to — off the handle perder los estribos (o la paciencia); to — open (shut) abrirse (cerrarse) de repente; to — up in anger montar en cólera.

flyer = flier.

flyleaf [flʌ́ɪlif] s. guarda (hoja en blanco al principio y al fin de un libro).

foam [fom] s. espuma; v. espumar,

hacer espuma.

focus [fókəs] s. foco; distancia focal; v. enfocar(se).

fodder [fɑ́dɚ] s. forraje.

foe [fo] s. enemigo.

fog [fɑg] s. niebla, neblina, bruma; velo, nube (en una película o fotografía); —horn sirena; v. anublar, ofuscar, obscurecer; ponerse brumoso; velar(se) (una película).

foggy [fɑ́gɪ] adj. brumoso, nublado; obscuro, confuso.

foil [fɔɪl] s. oropel, hojuela, laminita de metal; florete (de esgrima); realce, contraste; tin — hojuela de estaño; v. frustrar.

fold [fold] s. (double over) pliegue, doblez; (enclosure) redil; grey; three — tres veces; hundred— cien veces; v. doblar(se); plegar(se); envolver; to — one's arms cruzarse de brazos.

folder [fóldɚ] s. (pamphlet) folleto, circular; (holder) papelera; plegadera (máquina para plegar).

folding [fóldɪŋ] adj. plegadizo; —chair silla plegadiza, silla de tijera; — machine plegadora, máquina plegadora; — screen biombo.

foliage [fólɪɪdʒ] s. follaje, fronda.

folio [fólɪo] s. folio; infolio, libro en folio; pliego; — edition edición en folio.

folk [fok] s. gente; pueblo; -s parientes, allegados; familia; personas; amigos (vocativo familiar); adj. popular, del pueblo; —dance danza o baile tradicional; —lore folklore; cuentos, leyendas y tradiciones populares; — song canción popular, canción típica o tradicional; — music música del pueblo; música tradicional.

follow [fɑ́lo] v. seguir; ejercer (un oficio o profesión); seguir el hilo de (un argumento); seguirse (como consecuencia); to — suit jugar el mismo palo (en naipes); seguir el ejemplo, imitar.

follower [fɑ́ləwɚ] s. seguidor; imitador; partidario.

following [fɑ́ləwɪŋ] s. séquito, comitiva, partidarios; adj. siguiente; subsiguiente.

folly [fɑ́lɪ] s. locura; necedad, tontería; desatino.

foment [fomént] v. fomentar.

fond [fɑnd] adj. aficionado (a); amigo (de), amante (de), encariñado (con); cariñoso, afectuoso; tierno; to be — of querer a (una persona); estar encariñado con, ser aficionado a; gustar de (algo); -ly adv. cariñosamente, afectuosamente.

fondle [fɑ́ndl] v. acariciar.

fondness [fɑ́ndnɪs] s. cariño, afecto; afición.

font [fɑnt] s. pila bautismal; fuente.

food [fud] s. alimento, sustento; comida.

foodstuff [fúdstʌf] s. alimento; producto alimenticio; comestibles.

fool [ful] s. tonto, necio, zonzo; payaso; to play the — payasear, hacer el payaso; v. chasquear, chancear(se);

FL

bromear, embromar; engañar; **to —
away the time** malgastar el tiempo.

foolish [fúlɪʃ] *adj.* tonto; necio, bobo,
zonzo.

foolishness [fúlɪʃnɪs] *s.* tontería, necedad, bobería.

foot [fut] *s.* pie; pata (*de animal*); **on —**
a pie; **— soldier** soldado de infantería;
to put one's — in it meter la pata;
v. andar a pie; **to — it** andar a pie;
to — the bill pagar la cuenta; sufragar los gastos.

football [fútbɔl] *s.* futbol, football.

foothold [fúthold] *s.* arraigo; puesto
establecido.

footing [fútɪŋ] *s.* base; posición firme;
to be on a friendly — with tener
relaciones amistosas con; **to lose
one's —** perder pie.

footlights [fútlaɪts] *s. pl.* candilejas (*del
teatro*); tablas, teatro.

footman [fútmən] *s.* lacayo.

footnote [fútnot] *s.* nota al pie de una
página.

footpath [fútpæθ] *s.* vereda, senda, trocha (*para gente de a pie*).

footprint [fútprɪnt] *s.* huella, pisada.

footstep [fútstɛp] *s.* (*action*) pisada,
paso; (*trace*) huella; **to follow in the
-s of** seguie las pisadas o huellas de.

footstool [fútstul] *s.* banquillo, taburete,
escabel.

fop [fap] *s.* currutaco.

for [for] *prep.* por; para; **— all of her
intelligence** a pesar de su inteligencia; **— fear that** por miedo (de) que;
— the present por el presente, por
ahora; **as — him** en cuanto a él; **to
know — a fact** saber de cierto, saber
de hecho; **to pay him — it** pagár-
selo; **to thank him — it** agradecér-
selo; *conj.* porque, pues.

forage [fɔ́rɪdʒ] *s.* forraje; *v.* forrajear;
dar forraje a.

foray [fɔ́re] *s.* correría, incursión; saqueo; *v.* pillar, saquear.

forbade [fɚbǽd] *pret. de* **to forbid.**

forbear [fɔ́rbɚ] *s.* antepasado; [fɔrbɛ́r]
v. abstenerse de; tener paciencia.

forbid [fɚbíd] *v.* prohibir; vedar.

forbidden [fɚbídn] *adj.* prohibido;
vedado; *p.p. de* **to forbid.**

forbidding [fɚbídɪŋ] *adj.* austero, reservado; pavoroso; impenetrable.

forbore [fɔrbór] *pret. de* **to forbear.**

forborne [fɔrbórn] *p.p. de* **to forbear.**

force [fors] *s.* fuerza; cuerpo (*de policía,
de empleados, etc.*); **in —** en vigor,
vigente; **armed -s** fuerzas armadas;
v. forzar, obligar; **to — one's way**
abrirse paso por fuerza; **to — out**
echar por fuerza, echar a la fuerza.

forced [forst] *adj.* forzado.

forceful [fórsfəl] *adj.* vigoroso; enérgico.

forceps [fórsəps] *s.* gatillo (*tenazas para
sacar muelas*); pinzas.

forcible [fórsəbl] *adj.* (*strong*) fuerte,
enérgico; potente; eficaz; (*by force*)
violento; hecho a la fuerza; **forcibly**
adv. fuertemente; con energía; forzo-

samente; por fuerza.

ford [ford] *s.* vado; *v.* vadear.

fore [for] *adj.* anterior, delantero; de
proa; *s.* frente; puesto delantero; *adv.*
delante, hacia adelante; *interj.* ¡cuidado! (*dícese en el campo de golf*).

forearm [fórarm] *s.* antebrazo.

forebode [forbód] *v.* presagiar; presentir.

foreboding [forbódɪŋ] *s.* presentimiento; presagio.

forecast [fórkæst] *s.* pronóstico; [for-
kǽst] *v.* pronosticar; predecir; *pret. &
p.p. de* **to forecast.**

forefather [fórfaðɚ] *s.* antepasado.

forefinger [fórfɪŋgɚ] *s.* (dedo) índice.

forefoot [fórfut] *s.* pata delantera, mano
(*de cuadrúpedo*).

forego [forgó] *v.* abstenerse de.

foregone [forgón] *p.p. de* **to forego; a
— conclusion** una conclusión inevitable.

foreground [fórgraund] *s.* frente, primer plano, primer término.

forehead [fórɪd] *s.* frente (*f.*).

foreign [fɔ́rɪn] *adj.* extranjero; foráneo;
extraño; **— to his nature** ajeno a su
índole; **— office** ministerio de relaciones exteriores; departamento de
negocios extranjeros; **— trade** comercio exterior; **foreign-born** extranjero
de nacimiento.

foreigner [fɔ́rɪnɚ] *s.* extranjero; forastero.

forelock [fórlɑk] *s.* guedeja.

foreman [fórmən] *s.* capataz; presidente
(*de una jurado*); *Méx., C.A., Ven.,
Col.* caporal (*de un rancho o hacienda*);
Riopl. capataz.

foremost [fórmost] *adj.* (*first*) primero;
delantero; (*most important*) principal,
más notable, más distinguido.

forenoon [fórnun] *s.* (la) mañana.

forerunner [fɔrˈrʌnɚ] *s.* precursor; presagio.

foresaw [forsɔ́] *pret. de* **to foresee.**

foresee [forsí] *s.* prever.

foreseen [forsín] *p.p. de* **to foresee**
previsto.

foresight [fórsaɪt] *s.* previsión.

forest [fɔ́rɪst] *s.* bosque, selva; **— ranger** guardabosques; *v.* arbolar, plantar de árboles.

forestall [forstɔ́l] *v.* prevenir; madrugar.

forester [fɔ́rɪstɚ] *s.* guardabosques; silvicultor; habitante de un bosque.

forestry [fɔ́rɪstrɪ] *s.* silvicultura.

foretell [fortɛ́l] *v.* predecir, pronosticar,
presagiar.

foretold [fortóld] *pret. & p.p. de* **to foretell.**

forever [fɚévɚ] *adv.* por (o para) siempre.

forfeit [fórfɪt] *s.* multa; pena; prenda
perdida; **game of -s** juego de prendas; *v.* perder, perder el derecho a.

forgave [fɚgév] *pret. de* **to forgive.**

forge [fordʒ] *s.* fragua; forja; *v.* fraguar;
forjar; falsear, falsificar; **to — ahead**
abrirse paso; avanzar.

forgery [fórdʒɚɪ] *s.* falsificación.

forget [fəgét] v. olvidar; olvidarse de; to — **oneself** cometer un desmán impensadamente; perder el tino o la paciencia.

forgetful [fəgétfəl] adj. olvidadizo; negligente.

forgetfulness [fəgétfəlnɪs] s. olvido; negligencia.

forget-me-not [fəgétmɪnɑt] s. nomeolvides.

forgive [fəgɪv] v. perdonar.

forgiven [fəgɪvən] p.p. de **to forgive**.

forgiveness [fəgɪvnɪs] s. perdón.

forgiving [fəgɪvɪŋ] adj. perdonador, misericordioso, de buen corazón.

forgot [fəgát] pret. & p.p. de **to forget**.

forgotten [fəgátn] p.p. de **to forget**.

fork [fɔrk] s. tenedor, Méx., Col., Ven., Andes trinche; horquilla (para heno); horcón; bifurcación; v. bifurcarse; levantar o arrojar (heno) con horquilla.

forlorn [fəlórn] adj. desamparado, desdichado.

form [fɔrm] s. forma; condición, estado; **blank** — blanco, forma en blanco, Méx., Ven. esqueleto; v. formar(se).

formal [fɔrml] adj. formal, perteneciente a la forma; convencional, ceremonioso; — **party** reunión de etiqueta; -**ly** adv. formalmente, con ceremonia, solemnemente.

formality [fɔrmǽlətɪ] s. formalidad, ceremonia; formalismo.

formation [fɔrméʃən] s. formación.

formative [fɔrmətɪv] adj. formativo.

former [fɔrmə] adj. primero, precedente, anterior; antiguo; **in — times** en otro tiempo, en días de antaño, antiguamente, anteriormente; **the —** aquél (aquélla, aquéllos, aquéllas); -**ly** adv. anterioremente; antes, en tiempos pasados.

formidable [fɔrmɪdəbl] adj. formidable.

formula [fɔrmjələ] s. fórmula.

formulate [fɔrmjəlet] v. formular.

forsake [fəsék] v. desamparar; abandonar.

forsaken [fəsékən] p.p. de **to forsake** & adj. desamparado, abandonado.

forsook [fəsúk] pret. de **to forsake**.

forswear [fɔrswér] v. abjurar.

fort [fort] s. fuerte, fortín, fortaleza.

forth [forθ] adv. adelante; hacia adelante; **to go** — salir; **and so** — etcétera, y así sucesivamente.

forthcoming [fórθkʌmɪŋ] adj. venidero, próximo; **funds will not be —
until** no habrá fondos disponibles hasta.

forthwith [forθwíθ] adv. en seguida, pronto; al punto.

fortification [fɔrtəfəkéʃən] s. fortificación.

fortify [fɔrtəfaɪ] v. fortificar; fortalecer.

fortitude [fɔrtətjud] s. fortaleza.

fortnight [fɔrtnaɪt] s. quincena, quince días, dos semanas.

fortress [fɔrtrɪs] s. fortaleza, fuerte.

fortuitous [fɔrtjúətəs] adj. fortuito; inopinado, inesperado.

fortunate [fɔrtʃənɪt] adj. afortunado; -**ly** adv. afortunadamente, por fortuna.

fortune [fɔrtʃən] s. fortuna; —**teller** agorero, adivino.

forum [fórəm] s. foro; tribunal.

forward [fɔrwəd] adj. (leading) delantero; (progressive) precoz; progresista; (daring) atrevido; descarado; adv. adelante, hacia adelante; v. transmitir; despachar; reenviar; **to — a plan** fomentar un plan.

fossil [fásl] adj. fósil; anticuado; s. fósil.

foster [fóstə] v. criar, nutrir; fomentar, promover; adj. putativo; adoptivo.

fought [fɔt] pret. & p.p. de **to fight**.

foul [faul] adj. sucio; asqueroso; puerco, cochino; fétido; vil; injusto; — **air** aire viciado; — **ball** pelota foul (en beisbol); —**mouthed** mal hablado, obsceno; — **play** juego sucio; fraude; violencia; — **weather** mal tiempo; s. mala jugada (contraria a las reglas del juego), trampa, Am. chapuza, foul; v. ensuciar; violar (las reglas de un juego); Am. pegar un foul (en beisbol).

found [faund] v. fundar, establecer; pret. & p.p. de **to find**.

foundation [faundéʃən] s. fundación; base, fundamento; dotación.

founder [fáundə] s. fundador; fundidor (de metales); v. zozobrar, irse a pique; fracasar; tropezar; hacer zozobrar.

foundry [fáundrɪ] s. fundición.

fountain [fáuntn] s. fuente; manantial; — **pen** pluma (de) fuente, pluma estilográfica.

fourscore [fórskór] adj. cuatro veintenas, ochenta.

fourth [forθ] adj. cuarto; s. cuarto, cuarta parte; **the —** of July el cuatro de julio.

fowl [faul] s. ave; gallo, gallina; pollo.

fox [faks] s. zorra; zorro; persona astuta.

foxy [fáksɪ] adj. zorro, zorruno, astuto.

fraction [frǽkʃən] s. fracción; quebrado.

fracture [frǽktʃə] s. fractura; quiebra; rotura; v. fracturar; quebrar, romper.

fragile [frǽdʒəl] adj. frágil.

fragment [frǽgmənt] s. fragmento.

fragrance [frégrəns] s. fragancia.

fragrant [frégrənt] adj. fragante, oloroso.

frail [frel] adj. frágil; endeble, débil.

frailty [frélti] s. debilidad, flaqueza.

frame [frem] s. armazón, armadura, esqueleto; estructura; marco (de un cuadro, ventana, puerta, etc.); disposición (de ánimo); **embroidery** — bastidor para bordar; — **house** casa con armazón de madera; v. formar, forjar; fabricar; enmarcar (poner en marco); inventar; **to — someone** conspirar contra una persona; **to — up a charge** forjar un cargo o acusación.

framework [frémwɜk] s. armazón, esqueleto; estructura.

franc [fræŋk] s. franco (moneda francesa).

franchise [fræntʃaɪz] s. (privilege) fran-

FO

quicia; derecho o privilegio político; (*vote*) sufragio, voto.

frank [fræŋk] *adj.* franco, sincero; **very — francote**; *s.* sello de franqueo; franquicia de correos; *v.* franquear, despachar, enviar (*carta*) exenta de franqueo.

frankfurter [fræŋkfətə] *s.* salchicha.

frankness [fræŋknɪs] *s.* franqueza, sinceridad.

frantic [fræntɪk] *adj.* frenético; **-ally** *adv.* frenéticamente.

fraternal [frətə́nl] *adj.* fraternal.

fraternity [frətə́nətɪ] *s.* fraternidad; confraternidad.

fraternize [frǽtənaɪz] *v.* fraternizar.

fraud [frɔd] *s.* fraude, engaño; trampa, *Am.* chapuza; trampista, tramposo.

fraudulent [frɔ́dʒələnt] *adj.* fraudulento.

fray [fre] *s.* reyerta, riña, pelea, alboroto; raedura; *v.* raer(se); deshilacharse.

frayed [fred] *adj.* raído, deshilachado.

freak [frik] *s.* capricho; rareza, hombre o cosa rara; monstruosidad, fenómeno.

freckle [frékl] *s.* peca; *v.* ponerse pecoso.

freckled [frékld] *adj.* pecoso.

freckly [frékli] *adj.* pecoso.

free [fri] *adj.* (*not bound*) libre; suelto; (*gratis*) gratuito; exento; (*generous*) liberal, generoso; **— of charge** gratis; **— on board (f.o.b.)** libre a bordo; **— port** puerto franco; **postage —** franco de porte; **to give someone a — hand** dar rienda suelta o libertad de acción a una persona; **— hand drawing** dibujo a pulso, dibujo a mano; **— thinker** libre pensador; *adv.* libremente; gratis, de balde; *v.* librar; libertar; soltar; eximir; **-ly** *adv.* libremente; con soltura.

freedom [frídəm] *s.* libertad; libre uso; exención.

freeze [friz] *v.* helar(se); congelar(se).

freezing [frízɪŋ] *adj.* helado, glacial; **— point** punto de congelación.

freight [fret] *s.* flete; carga; **— train** tren de carga, tren de mercancías; **by — por carga**; *v.* fletar, cargar; enviar por carga.

French [frɛntʃ] *adj.* francés; **to take — leave** marcharse a la francesa, irse sin despedirse; *s.* francés, idioma francés; **the —** los franceses.

Frenchman [frɛntʃmən] *s.* francés.

frenzy [frɛ́nzɪ] *s.* frenesí.

frequency [fríkwənsɪ] *s.* frecuencia.

frequent [fríkwənt] *adj.* frecuente; *v.* frecuentar; **-ly** *adv.* frecuentemente, a menudo.

fresh [frɛʃ] *adj.* (*not stale*) fresco; (*new*) reciente; nuevo; (*bold*) impertinente, entremetido; **— water** agua dulce; **-ly** *adv.* frescamente; con frescura, nuevamente, recientemente; **-ly painted** recién pintado, acabado de pintar.

freshen [frɛ́ʃən] *v.* refrescar(se).

freshman [frɛ́ʃmən] *s.* novato, novicio, estudiante del primer año.

freshness [frɛ́ʃnɪs] *s.* frescura; frescor, fresco; descaro.

fret [frɛt] *v.* irritar(se); apurarse; estar nervioso; agitarse; *s.* agitación, apuro, preocupación; traste (*de guitarra, mandolina, etc.*); **—work** calado.

fretful [frɛ́tfəl] *adj.* descontentadizo, malhumorado, enojadizo; nervioso.

friar [fráɪə] *s.* fraile.

friction [frɪ́kʃən] *s.* fricción; rozamiento; frotación; desavenencia.

Friday [fráɪdɪ] *s.* viernes.

fried [fraɪd] *adj.* frito; freído; *p.p.* de **to fry.**

friend [frɛnd] *s.* amigo, amiga.

friendless [frɛ́ndlɪs] *adj.* sin amigos, solo.

friendliness [frɛ́ndlɪnɪs] *s.* afabilidad; amistad.

friendly [frɛ́ndlɪ] *adj.* amistoso, afable, amigable; propicio, favorable; *adv.* amistosamente.

friendship [frɛ́nʃɪp] *s.* amistad.

frigate [frɪ́gət] *s.* fragata.

fright [fraɪt] *s.* espanto, susto; terror; espantajo, **she is a —** es un adefesio.

frighten [fráɪtn] *v.* espantar, asustar, atemorizar; **to — away** espantar, ahuyentar; **to get -ed** espantarse, asustarse.

frightened [fráɪtnd] *adj.* espantado, asustado.

frightful [fráɪtfəl] *adj.* espantoso, terrible, horroroso.

frigid [frɪ́dʒɪd] *adj.* frígido, frío.

fringe [frɪndʒ] *s.* fleco; flequillo; orla; *v.* adornar con fleco; orlar.

frippery [frɪ́pərɪ] *s.* perifollos, moños, perejiles; cursilería.

frisk [frɪsk] *v.* retozar, cabriolar, saltar; brincar; registrar (*los bolsillos*), *Ven., Méx.* escular.

frisky [frɪ́skɪ] *adj.* retozón, juguetón.

fritter [frɪ́tə] *s.* fritura, fruta de sartén; *v.* **to — away** malgastar, desperdiciar poco a poco.

frivolity [frɪvɑ́lətɪ] *s.* frivolidad.

frivolous [frɪ́vələs] *adj.* frívolo.

fro [fro]: **to and — de** una parte a otra; de aquí para allá.

frock [frɑk] *s.* vestido (*de mujer*); **— coat** levita.

frog [frɑg] *s.* rana; broche (*de cordoncillos o galones*); **— in the throat** gallo en la garganta.

frolic [frɑ́lɪk] *s.* retozo, juego; holgorio, diversión; *v.* retozar, travesear, juguetear.

from [frʌm, frʌm] *prep.* de; **to take something away — a person** quitarle algo a una persona.

front [frʌnt] *s.* frente (*m.*); fachada; frontispicio; **in — of** enfrente de; delante de; **— shirt —** pechera; *adj.* delantero; frontal; frontero; *v.* hacer frente a; **to — towards** mirar hacia; dar a, caer a.

frontier [frʌntír] *s.* frontera; *adj.* fronterizo.

frost [frɔst] *s.* escarcha; helada; *v.* escarchar; helar; cubrir de escarcha.

frosting [fróstɪŋ] *s.* escarcha, confitura (*para cubrir un pastel*).

frosty [fróstɪ] *adj.* escarchado, cubierto de escarcha; helado.

froth [frɔθ] *s.* espuma; *v.* espumar, hacer espuma; echar espuma o espumarajos; **to — at the mouth** echar espumarajos por la boca; enfurecerse.

frown [fraun] *s.* ceño; entrecejo; *v.* fruncir el ceño o las cejas; **to — at** mirar con ceño; desaprobar (*algo*).

froze [froz] *pret. de* **to freeze.**

frozen [frózn] *p.p. de* **to freeze.**

frugal [frúgl] *adj.* frugal.

fruit [frut] *s.* fruto (*en general*); fruta (*comestible*); **to eat —** comer fruta; **— tree** árbol frutal; *v.* fructificar, producir frutas.

fruitful [frútfəl] *adj.* fructuoso; productivo; provechoso.

fruitless [frútlɪs] *adj.* infructuoso, improductivo, estéril.

frustrate [frʌstret] *v.* frustrar.

frustration [frʌstréʃən] *s.* frustración.

fry [fraɪ] *v.* freír(se); *s.* fritada; **small —** peccillos; gente menuda; **French fries** patatas fritas a la francesa; **-ing pan** sartén.

fudge [fʌdʒ] *s.* dulce (*usualmente de chocolate y nueces*).

fuel [fjúəl] *s.* combustible; incentivo.

fugitive [fjúdʒətɪv] *adj.* fugitivo; transitorio; *s.* fugitivo, prófugo.

fulfill [fulfíl] *v.* cumplir; cumplir con; realizar; llevar a cabo; llenar (*un requisito*).

fulfillment [fulfílmənt] *s.* cumplimiento.

full [ful] *adj.* lleno; completo; harto; pleno; **— dress** traje de etiqueta; **— moon** plenilunio, luna llena; **— skirt** falda de vuelo entero; **— of fun** muy divertido, muy chistoso; **at — speed** a toda velocidad; **in —** completamente; por completo; **to the —** por completo, por entero, totalmente; *adv.* completamente, enteramente; **to know — well** saber perfectamente, saber a ciencia cierta; **full-blooded** de raza pura; **full-fledged** hecho y derecho; maduro; completo; **-y** *adv.* completamente, enteramente, por completo.

fullness [fúlnɪs] *s.* plenitud; llenura.

fumble [fʌmbl] *v.* tentalear, buscar a tientas; chapucear, no coger la pelota o soltarla al correr.

fume [fjum] *v.* exhalar vapor o gas; rabiar; **-s** *s. pl.* vapores, emanaciones, gases.

fumigate [fjúməget] *v.* fumigar, sahumar, *Riopl.* humear.

fun [fʌn] *s.* diversión; burla, broma, chanza, *Carib., Méx., C.A.* choteo; **for —** en (*o* de) broma; de chanza; de chiste; **full of —** muy divertido; **to have —** divertirse; **to make — of** burlarse de, chancearse con, *Carib., Méx., C.A.* chotear, chotearse con; *Riopl.* jorobar.

function [fʌŋkʃən] *s.* función; *v.* funcio-nar.

fund [fʌnd] *s.* fondo, caudal; **-s** fondos, recursos; *v.* consolidar (*una deuda*); prorrogar el plazo de (*una deuda*).

fundamental [fʌndəmént] *adj.* fundamental; *s.* fundamento, principio.

funeral [fjúnərəl] *adj.* funeral, fúnebre; *s.* funeral, exequias, funerales.

fungus [fʌŋgəs] *s.* hongo; fungosidad.

funnel [fʌnl] *s.* embudo; humero (*cañón de chimenea*).

funny [fʌnɪ] *adj.* (*comical*) chistoso, cómico, gracioso, divertido; (*odd*) extraño, raro; **the funnies** la sección cómica (*de un periódico*).

fur [fɜ] *s.* piel (*de animales peludos o lanudos*); sarro (*en la lengua*); **— coat** abrigo de pieles; *v.* forrar, cubrir o adornar con pieles.

furbish [fɜbɪʃ] *v.* acicalar, pulir.

furious [fjúrɪəs] *adj.* furioso.

furl [fɜl] *v.* arrollar, enrollar; plegar.

furlough [fɜlo] *s.* licencia militar; *v.* dar licencia militar.

furnace [fɜnɪs] *s.* horno.

furnish [fɜnɪʃ] *v.* (*equip*) equipar; amueblar; (*provide*) proveer, suministrar, surtir; **to — a room** amueblar un cuarto.

furniture [fɜnɪtʃə] *s.* muebles, mobiliario, moblaje, mueblaje.

furrow [fɜo] *s.* surco; arruga; *v.* surcar; arar.

further [fɜðə] *adj.* adicional; más lejano, más remoto; *adv.* además; más; más lejos; *v.* promover, fomentar, adelantar.

furthermore [fɜðəmor] *adv.* además.

furthest [fɜðɪst] *adj.* (el) más lejano, (el) más remoto; *adv.* más lejos.

furtive [fɜtɪv] *adj.* furtivo.

fury [fjúrɪ] *s.* furia; frenesí.

fuse [fjuz] *s.* fusible; mecha; *v.* fundir(se).

fuselage [fjúzɪlɪdʒ] *s.* fuselaje.

fusion [fjúʒən] *s.* fusión; **nuclear —** fusión nuclear.

fuss [fʌs] *s.* melindre, preocupación inútil; bulla innecesaria; **to make a — over someone** darle a alguien demasiada importancia, desvivirse por alguien; *v.* hacer melindres, inquietarse (*por bagatelas*).

fussy [fʌsɪ] *adj.* melindroso; minucioso (*en demasía*); inquieto, nervioso; **— dress** vestido con demasiados adornos.

futile [fjútl] *adj.* fútil; vano.

future [fjútʃə] *adj.* futuro; *s.* futuro; porvenir.

fuzz [fʌz] *s.* vello; pelusa.

fuzzy [fʌzɪ] *adj.* velloso; cubierto de plumón fino; cubierto de pelusa.

G

gab [gæb] *v.* charlar, parlotear; *s.* charla; **gift of —** labia, facundia.

gabardine [gæbədin] *s.* gabardina (*paño*).

gabble [gæbl] *s.* charla, cotorreo; *v.* charlar, cotorrear.

gable [gébl] s. gablete (*de un tejado*); —
roof tejado de caballete o de dos
aguas; — **window** ventana con gablete.

gad [gæd] v. vagar, callejear; andar de
aquí para allá.

gadget [gǽdʒɪt] s. adminículo, artefacto,
chisme.

gag [gæg] s. (*obstacle*) mordaza; (*joke*)
broma, burla; morcilla, chiste (*improvisado por un actor*); v. amordazar; dar náuseas, hacer vomitar,
basquear; interpolar chistes (*en la
escena*).

gage *véase* **gauge.**

gaiety [géətɪ] s. alegría, viveza, alborozo.

gaily [gélɪ] adv. alegremente; vistosa-
mente.

gain [gen] s. ganancia, provecho; v.
ganar.

gainful [génfl] adj. ganancioso.

gait [get] s. paso, andadura, marcha.

gale [gel] s. ventarrón; — **of laughter**
risotada, carcajada, risada.

gall [gɔl] s. (*bile*) bilis, hiel; (*bitterness*)
amargura; odio; descaro; — **bladder**
vejiga de la bilis; v. irritar.

gallant [gǽlənt] adj. valiente; noble;
vistoso; [gəlǽnt] adj. galante, atento,
cortés; galanteador; s. galán.

gallantry [gǽləntrɪ] s. galantería; gallardía, valor.

gallery [gǽlərɪ] s. galería; paraíso, gallinero del (*teatro*).

galley [gǽlɪ] s. galera; cocina (*de un
buque*); — **proof** galerada; — **slave**
galeote.

gallon [gǽlən] s. galón (*aproximadamente cuatro litros*).

gallop [gǽləp] s. galope; v. galopar,
galopear; ir a galope.

gallows [gǽloz] s. horca.

galoshes [gəlúʃɪz] s. pl. chanclos,
zapatos fuertes, zapatones.

gamble [gǽmbl] v. jugar, apostar,
aventurar (*algo*) en el juego; **to —
away** perder en el juego; **to — everything** jugar el todo por el todo;
arriesgarlo todo; s. jugada (*en juegos de
azar*), apuesta; riesgo.

gambol [gǽmbəl] v. retozar; cabriolar;
juguetear; s. retozo, cabriola.

game [gem] s. juego; deporte; caza
(*animales de caza y su carne*); **to make
— of** mofarse de, burlarse de; adj.
valiente, atrevido; resuelto; — **bird**
ave de caza.

gamut [gǽmət] s. gama.

gander [gǽndɚ] s. ánsar, ganso.

gang [gæŋ] s. cuadrilla; pandilla; juego
(*de herramientas o máquinas*); v. agru-
par(se); **to — up against** conspirar
contra.

gangplank [gǽŋplæŋk] s. plancha, pasamano (*de un buque*), pasarela.

gangrene [gǽŋgrin] s. gangrena; v.
gangrenar(se).

gangster [gǽŋstɚ] s. bandolero, bandido, maleante, atracador.

gangway [gǽŋwe] s. paso, pasadizo;
plancha, pasamano; portalón (*de un

barco*); —! ¡a un lado! ¡ábranse!

gantlet = **gauntlet.**

gap [gæp] s. brecha, abertura; boquete;
hueco; intervalo.

gape [gep] s. (*breach*) brecha, abertura;
(*open jaws*) bostezo; boqueada; v.
boquear, abrir la boca; estar boquiabierto (*mirando*); estar embobado;
bostezar.

garage [gərάʒ] s. garaje.

garb [garb] s. vestido; vestidura; aspecto, apariencia; v. vestir, ataviar.

garbage [gárbɪdʒ] s. desperdicios,
basura.

garden [gárdn] s. jardín; huerta;
huerto; v. cultivar un jardín.

gardener [gárdnɚ] s. jardinero, hortelano; horticultor.

gargle [gárgl] s. gargarismo, Am. gárgaras; v. gargarizar, hacer gárgaras,
Am. gargarear.

garland [gárlənd] s. guirnalda.

garlic [gárlɪk] s. ajo.

garment [gármənt] s. prenda (*de vestir*).

garnet [gárnɪt] s. granate.

garnish [gárnɪʃ] s. aderezo; adorno; v.
aderezar; adornar; guarnecer.

garret [gǽrɪt] s. desván, buhardilla.

garrison [gǽrəsn] s. guarnición; v.
guarnecer o guarnicionar (*una fortaleza*).

garter [gártɚ] s. liga (*para sujetar las
medias*); v. sujetar con liga.

gas [gæs] s. (*gaseous*) gas; (*petroleum*)
gasolina; — **burner** mechero; —
stove estufa o cocina de gas; **tear —**
gas lacrimante o lacrimógeno; v.
asfixiar con gas; envenenar con gas.

gaseous [gǽsɪəs] adj. gaseoso.

gash [gæʃ] s. cuchillada, herida, incisión;
v. dar una cuchillada, acuchillar.

gasoline [gǽslɪn] s. gasolina.

gasp [gæsp] s. boqueada; grito sofo-
cado; v. boquear; jadear; sofocarse;
abrir la boca (*de asombro*).

gastric [gǽstrɪk] adj. gástrico.

gastrointestinal [gǽstrɔɪntéstɪnl] adj.
gastrointestinal.

gate [get] s. portón, entrada; puerta;
Ven., Col. tranquera (*puerta de
trancas*).

gateway [gétwe] s. paso, entrada.

gather [gǽðɚ] v. recoger; coger; reu-
nir(se), juntar(se); deducir, colegir;
fruncir (*en pliegues*); cobrar (*fuerzas*);
to — dust llenarse de polvo, empolvarse; s. pliegue.

gathering [gǽðɔrɪŋ] s. asamblea, reunión; muchedumbre; pliegue.

gaudy [gɔ́dɪ] adj. vistoso, llamativo,
chillón, chillante.

gauge [gedʒ] s. calibrador; indicador;
instrumento para medir; medida;
calibre (*de un cañón, pistola, etc.*);
ancho (*del ferrocarril*), *Ven.* trocha;
v. medir; calibrar; estimar, calcular.

gaunt [gɔnt] adj. macilento, demacrado,
flaco.

gauntlet [gɔ́ntlɪt] s. guantelete; manopla; **to throw down the —** retar,
desafiar.

gauze [gɔz] s. gasa; cendal.
gave [gev] *pret. de* **to give**.
gavel [gǽvl] s. mazo del que preside.
gawk [gɔk] v. bobear, mirar embobado; s. simplón, bobo.
gawky [gɔ́kɪ] adj. torpe, desmañado; bobo.
gay [ge] adj. alegre; vivo; vistoso; festivo.
gayety *véase* **gaiety**.
gaze [gez] s. mirada (fija); v. contemplar, mirar con fijeza, clavar la mirada.
gazette [ɡəzét] s. gaceta.
gear [gɪr] s. (*equipment*) aperos; herramientas; aparejo; equipo; (*wheel*) rueda dentada; (*assembly*) engranaje (de ruedas dentadas); **foot**— calzado; **low** — primera velocidad; **steering** — mecanismo de dirección; **to be in** — estar engranado; **to shift** — cambiar de engrane o velocidad; **to throw in** — engranar; **to throw out of** — desengranar; —**shift lever** palanca de engrane, palanca de cambios; v. engranar.
geese [gis] *pl. de* **goose**.
Geiger counter [gáɪɡəkáʊntə] s. contador (de) Geiger.
gelatin [dʒélətn] s. gelatina, jaletina.
gem [dʒɛm] s. gema, piedra preciosa; joya, alhaja, panecillo, bollo.
geminate [dʒémənet] v. geminar(se).
gender [dʒéndə] s. género.
gene [dʒin] s. gen.
general [dʒénərəl] adj. & s. general; **in** — en general, por lo común, por lo general.
generality [dʒenərǽlətɪ] s. generalidad.
generalize [dʒénərəlaɪz] v. generalizar.
generate [dʒénəret] v. engendrar; producir; originar.
generation [dʒenəréʃən] s. generación, producción.
generator [dʒénəˌretə] s. generador.
generic [dʒənérɪk] adj. genérico.
generosity [dʒenərásətɪ] s. generosidad.
generous [dʒénərəs] adj. generoso; magnánimo, liberal; amplio; abundante.
genetics [dʒənétɪks] s. genética.
genial [dʒínjəl] adj. genial, afable.
genitive [dʒénətɪv] adj. & s. genitivo.
genius [dʒínjəs] s. genio; ingenio, talento.
genteel [dʒentíl] adj. gentil, cortés; elegante; gallardo.
gentile [dʒéntaɪl] adj. & s. gentil.
gentle [dʒéntl] adj. suave; afable; apacible; manso; gentil.
gentleman [dʒéntlmən] s. caballero; **gentlemen** pl. caballeros; señores.
gentlemanly [dʒéntlmənlɪ] adj. caballeroso, caballero, cortés.
gentleness [dʒéntlnɪs] s. suavidad, dulzura, apacibilidad; mansedumbre.
gently [dʒéntlɪ] adv. suavemente; despacio; dulcemente; con ternura; mansamente.
genuine [dʒénjʊɪn] adj. genuino; sincero.

geographical [dʒiəgrǽfɪk] adj. geográfico.
geography [dʒiágrəfɪ] s. geografía.
geological [dʒiəládʒɪk] adj. geológico.
geology [dʒiálədʒɪ] s. geología.
geometric [dʒiəmétrɪk] adj. geométrico.
geometry [dʒiámətrɪ] s. geometría.
geophysics [dʒiofízɪks] s. geofísica.
geranium [dʒəréniəm] s. geranio.
germ [dʒɜm] s. germen; microbio.
German [dʒɜ́mən] adj. & s. alemán.
germane [dʒɜmen] adj. pertinente, relacionado.
germinate [dʒɜ́mənét] v. germinar.
gerund [dʒérənd] s. gerundio.
gestation [dʒestéʃən] s. gestación.
gesticulate [dʒestíkjəlet] v. gesticular, hacer gestos o ademanes, accionar, manotear.
gesture [dʒéstʃə] s. gesto; ademán; **a mere** — una pura formalidad; v. gesticular, hacer gestos.
get [get] v. (*obtain*) obtener, adquirir, lograr, conseguir; (*earn*) recibir, ganar; (*reach*) llegar (a); traer; (*catch*) coger, atrapar; preparar (*la lección, la comida, etc.*); **to** — **along** llevarse bien (*con alguien*); ir pasándolo (o ir pasándola); **to** — **angry** ponerse enojado, enojarse; **to** — **away** escaparse; irse; **to** — **down** bajar; **to** — **ill** ponerse enfermo, enfermar(se); **to** — **in** entrar; meter(se); llegar; **to** — **married** casarse; **to** — **off the train** bajar del tren; apearse del tren; **to** — **old** envejecer(se); **to** — **on** subir a; montar; **to** — **out** salir; irse; sacar; divulgarse (*un secreto*); **to** — **over** pasar por encima de; recuperarse de (*una enfermedad*); olvidar (*una ofensa*); pasársele a uno (*el susto*); **to** — **ready** preparar(se); alistar(se); **to** — **rich** enriquecerse, hacerse rico; **to** — **rid of** deshacerse de, desprenderse de; **to** — **through** pasar; terminar; **to** — **together** juntar(se), reunir(se); ponerse de acuerdo; **to** — **up** levantarse; **I got him to do it** le persuadí a que lo hicieses; **I (have) got to do it** tengo que hacerlo; **I don't** — **it** no lo comprendo; **that's what -s me** (*or* **-s my goat**) eso es lo que me irrita.
ghastly [gǽstlɪ] adj. horrible; pálido, lívido, cadavérico.
ghost [gost] s. espectro, fantasma; **the Holy Ghost** el Espíritu Santo; **not to have the** — **of a notion of** no tener la más remota idea de; — **writer** colaborador anónimo.
ghostly [góstlɪ] adj. como un espectro; de espectros, de aparecidos.
giant [dʒáɪənt] s. gigante; adj. gigantesco; enorme.
giddy [gídɪ] adj. ligero de cascos, frívolo; voluble, inconstante; desvanecido; — **speed** velocidad vertiginosa.
gift [gɪft] s. regalo; dádiva; don; dote, talento, prenda; donación.
gifted [gíftɪd] adj. talentoso, de talento.

GA

gigantic [dʒaɪgǽntɪk] *adj.* gigantesco.

giggle [gɪgl] *s.* risita, risilla; risa falsa; *v.* reírse falsamente; reírse sofocando la voz; reír con una risilla afectada.

gild [gɪld] *v.* dorar.

gill [gɪl] *s.* agalla *(de pez)*.

gilt [gɪlt] *adj. & s.* dorado; *pret. & p.p. de* **to gild**.

gimmick [gímɪk] *s.* adminículo.

gin [dʒɪn] *s.* ginebra *(licor)*.

ginger [dʒíndʒɚ] *s.* jengibre; — **ale** cerveza de jengibre.

gingerbread [dʒíndʒɚbred] *s.* pan de jengibre; ornato de mal gusto.

gingham [gíŋəm] *s.* guinga *(tela de algodón)*.

gipsy *véase* **gypsy**.

giraffe [dʒɚǽf] *s.* jirafa.

gird [gɚd] *v.* ceñir; rodear; **to — one-self for** prepararse para.

girdle [gɚdl] *s.* ceñidor; cinto; faja; *v.* ceñir; fajar; cercar.

girl [gɚl] *s.* niña; muchacha; joven; chica, moza; criada.

girlhood [gɚlhud] *s.* niñez; mocedad, juventud.

girlish [gɚlɪʃ] *adj.* pueril; de niña, de muchacha; juvenil.

girt [gɚt] *pret. & p.p. de* **to gird**; *v. véase* **gird**.

girth [gɚθ] *s.* circunferencia; cincha *(para caballos)*; faja; *v.* cinchar; ceñir.

gist [dʒɪst] *s.* substancia, esencia.

give [gɪv] *v.* dar; regalar; ceder, dar de sí; **to — away** regalar; entregar; revelar *(un secreto)*; **to — back** devolver; **to — birth** dar a luz, parir; **to — in** ceder; darse por vencido; **to — off** emitir; **to — out** divulgar; repartir; agotarse; **to — up** abandonar; desistir; renunciar a; perder la esperanza; rendir(se); ceder, darse por vencido; *s.* elasticidad.

given [gívən] *p.p. de* **to give**; *adj.* *(presented)* dado; regalado; *(inclined)* adicto, entregado; dispuesto, inclinado; — **name** nombre de pila, nombre de bautismo; — **time** hora determinada; — **that** dada tal, supuesto que.

giver [gívɚ] *s.* dador, donador.

glacial [gléʃəl] *adj.* glacial.

glacier [gléʃɚ] *s.* glaciar, helero.

glad [glæd] *adj.* contento; alegre; **to be — to** alegrarse de, tener mucho gusto en *(o de)*; **-ly** *adv.* alegremente; con mucho gusto; de buena gana.

gladden [glǽdn] *v.* regocijar, alegrar.

glade [gled] *s.* claro herboso *(en un bosque)*.

gladness [glǽdnɪs] *s.* alegría, gozo.

glamour [glǽmɚ] *s.* encanto, hechizo; fascinación, embrujo; — **girl** niña hechicera.

glamorous [glǽmərəs] *adj.* fascinador, hechicero.

glance [glæns] *s.* mirada, vistazo, ojeada; vislumbre; *v.* echar *(o dar)* un vistazo; vislumbrar; pegar de soslayo; **to — off** rebotar de soslayo *(o de lado)*.

gland [glænd] *s.* glándula.

glare [glɛr] *s.* *(light)* resplandor, relumbre; *(stare)* mirada furiosa; *v.* resplandecer, relumbrar; **to — at** mirar enfurecido a.

glass [glæs] *s.* *(substance)* vidrio; cristal; *(receptacle)* vaso; copa *(de cristal)*; *(eye)* lente; **looking** — **-es** anteojos, lentes, gafas; *adj.* de vidrio; — **blower** — espejo; — **blower** soplador de vidrio; — **case** escaparate.

glassware [glǽswɛr] *s.* vajilla de cristal, cristalería; — **shop** cristalería.

glassy [glǽsɪ] *adj.* vidrioso.

glaze [glez] *s.* vidriado; lustre; superficie lustrosa o glaseada; *v.* vidriar; glasear; lustrar; poner vidrios a.

glazier [gléʒɚ] *s.* vidriero.

gleam [glim] *s.* destello, rayo, fulgor, viso; *v.* destellar, fulgurar, centellear.

glean [glin] *v.* recoger; espigar.

glee [gli] *s.* regocijo; júbilo; — **club** orfeón, masa coral.

glib [glɪb] *adj.* locuaz; de mucha labia; — **excuse** excusa fácil.

glide [glaɪd] *s.* deslizamiento; ligadura *(en música)*; planeo *(de un aeroplano)*; *v.* deslizarse; resbalarse; planear *(un aeroplano)*.

glider [gláɪdɚ] *s.* deslizador, planeador *(aeroplano)*.

glimmer [glímɚ] *s.* vislumbre; viso; titileo; — **of hope** rayo de esperanza; *v.* titilar, centellear.

glimpse [glɪmps] *s.* vislumbre; vistazo, ojeada; **to catch a — of** vislumbrar; *v.* vislumbrar.

glint [glɪnt] *s.* fulgor, rayo, destello.

glisten [glísn] *v.* relucir, brillar.

glitter [glítɚ] *s.* lustre, brillo, resplandor; *v.* relumbrar, relucir, brillar.

gloat [glot] *v.* gozarse (en), deleitarse (en); relamerse *(de gusto)*.

globe [glob] *d.* globo; esfera.

gloom [glum] *s.* lobreguez, sombra; abatimiento, tristeza, melancolía.

gloomy [glúmɪ] *adj.* lóbrego, sombrío, triste, melancólico; abatido.

glorify [glórəfaɪ] *v.* glorificar.

glorious [glórɪəs] *adj.* glorioso; espléndido.

glory [glórɪ] *s.* gloria; *v.* gloriarse; vanagloriarse.

gloss [glɔs] *s.* *(shine)* lustre, brillo; pulimento; *(note)* glosa, comentario; *v.* lustrar, dar brillo a; pulir; glosar, comentar; **to — over** encubrir, dar colorido de bueno *(a algo que no lo es)*.

glossary [glásərɪ] *s.* glosario.

glossy [glósɪ] *adj.* lustroso; pulido.

glove [glʌv] *s.* guante; *v.* enguantar, poner guantes.

glow [glo] *s.* incandescencia; brillo *(de un ascua)*; calor vivo; fosforescencia; *v.* lucir, brillar *(como un ascua)*; fosforecer; estar encendido o enardecido.

glowing [glóɪŋ] *adj.* encendido, ardiente.

glowworm [glówɚm] *s.* luciérnaga.

glue [glu] *s.* cola *(para pegar)*; *v.* encolar, pegar (*con cola*).

glum [glʌm] *adj.* hosco.

glutton [glʌtn] *s.* glotón.

gluttonous [glʌtnəs] *adj.* glotón; goloso.

gluttony [glʌtnɪ] *s.* gula, glotonería.

glycerin [glísərɪn] *s.* glicerina.

gnarled [nɑrld] *adj.* nudoso, torcido.

gnash [næʃ] *v.* crujir, rechinar (*los dientes*).

gnat [næt] *s.* jején (*insecto*).

gnaw [nɔ] *v.* roer.

go [go] *v.* (*move*) ir(se); andar; (*function*) marchar, funcionar, servir; **to — around** andar alrededor de; dar vueltas; **to — away** irse; **to — back on one's word** faltar a la palabra; **to — by** pasar por; guiarse por (*una regla*); **to — down** bajar; **to — insane** volverse loco; **to — into** entrar en; investigar; caber en; **to — off** hacer explosión; dispararse, irse, salir disparado; **to — on** proseguir, continuar; **to — out** salir; apagarse, **to — over** pasar por encima de; examinar con cuidado; releer; repasar; recorrer; **to — to sleep** dormirse; **to — under** irse por debajo de; hundirse; **to — up** subir; **to let — soltar; there is not enough to — around** no hay (bastante) para todos; *s.* empuje, energía; **it is a —** trato hecho; **to be on the —** estar en continuo movimiento.

goad [god] *s.* aguijón; *v.* aguijonear; aguijar, incitar.

goal [gol] *s.* meta; fin, objetivo.

goat [got] *s.* cabra; **male —** macho cabrío; **to be the —** ser la víctima, pagar el pato.

goatee [gotí] *s.* perilla.

gobble [gɑ́bl] *v.* tragar, engullir; **to — up** engullirse.

gobbler [gɑ́blə] *s.* pavo.

go-between [góbətwin] *s.* medianero.

goblet [gɑ́blɪt] *s.* copa grande.

goblin [gɑ́blɪn] *s.* duende.

god [gɑd] *s.* dios; **God** Dios.

godchild [gɑ́dtʃaɪld] *s.* ahijado, ahijada.

goddess [gɑ́dɪs] *s.* diosa.

godfather [gɑ́dfɑðə] *s.* padrino.

godless [gɑ́dlɪs] *adj.* impío, ateo.

godlike [gɑ́dlaɪk] *adj.* como Dios; divino.

godly [gɑ́dlɪ] *adj.* pío, devoto; divino.

godmother [gɑ́dmʌðə] *s.* madrina.

goggles [gɑ́glz] *s. pl.* antiparras, gafas.

going [góɪŋ] *ger. & adj.* que anda, marcha o funciona bien; **to be —** ir, irse; *s.* ida, partida; **comings and -s** idas y venidas.

goiter [góɪtə] *s.* papera; bocio; *Ríopl.*, *Méx.*, *C.A.* buche; *C.A.* güecho.

gold [gold] *s.* oro; **— standard** patrón de oro.

golden [góldn] *adj.* de oro; áureo; dorado.

goldfinch [góldfɪntʃ] *s.* jilguero amarillo.

goldfish [góldfɪʃ] *s.* carpa dorada.

goldsmith [góldsmɪθ] *s.* orfebre.

golf [gɑlf] *s.* golf.

gondola [gándələ] *s.* góndola; cabina (*de una aeronave*); **— car** vagón de mercancías (*sin techo*), *Am.* jaula.

gone [gɔn] *p.p. de* **to go** *& adj.* ido; perdido; **he is —** se fué; **it is all —** se acabó; ya no hay más.

gong [gɔŋ] *s.* gong, batintín.

good [gud] *adj.* bueno; válido; valedero; **— afternoon** buenas tardes; **— day** buenos días; adiós; **— evening** buenas noches; **— morning** buenos días; **— night** buenas noches; **Good Friday** Viernes Santo; **for —** para siempre, permanentemente; **to have a — time** pasar un buen rato; divertirse; **to make —** pagar, compensar; cumplir (*una promesa*); salir bien, tener buen éxito; *s.* bien; beneficio, provecho, ventaja; **-s** bienes, efectos; mercancías.

good-bye [gudbáɪ] *s. & interj.* adiós.

good-looking [gúdlúkɪŋ] *adj.* bien parecido, guapo.

goodly [gúdlɪ] *adj.* grande, considerable; de buena apariencia.

good-natured [gúdnétʃəd] *adj.* de buen genio, bonachón, afable.

goodness [gúdnɪs] *s.* bondad; **—!** ¡Dios mío! ¡cielos!

goody [gúdɪ] *s.* golosina, bonbón, dulce; *interj.* ¡qué gusto!; **goody-goody** beatuco (*el que afecta virtud*), papanatas.

goof [guf] *v.* chapucear.

goose [gus] *s.* ganso; bobo, tonto; **— flesh** carne de gallina.

gooseberry [gúsberɪ] *s.* grosella; grosellero (*arbusto*).

gopher [gófə] *s.* roedor semejante a la ardilla.

gore [gor] *s.* (*blood*) cuajarón de sangre; sangre; (*cloth*) cuchillo (*Am.* cuchilla), sesga (*tira de lienzo en figura de cuchilla*); *v.* acornear, herir con los cuernos; hacer una sesga en (*un traje*).

gorge [gordʒ] *s.* cañada, barranco, barranca; *v.* engullir(se), atracarse.

gorgeous [górdʒəs] *adj.* primoroso, vistoso, hermosísimo.

gorilla [gərílə] *s.* gorila.

gory [górɪ] *adj.* sangriento, ensangrentado.

gospel [gáspl] *s.* evangelio; **it is the — truth** es la pura verdad.

gossip [gásɪp] *s.* (*rumors*) chisme, chismería, murmuración, habilla; (*person*) murmurador, chismero, chismoso; *v.* chismear, murmurar.

gossipy [gásəpɪ] *adj.* chismero, chismoso.

got [gat] *pret. & p.p. de* **to get**.

Gothic [gáθɪk] *adj.* gótico; *s.* gótico (*idioma de los godos*); estilo gótico.

gotten [gátṇ] *p.p. de* **to get**.

gouge [gaudʒ] *s.* gubia (*especie de formón o escoplo curvo*); *v.* excavar con gubia, formón o escoplo; **to — someone's eyes out** sacarle los ojos a alguien.

GI

gourd [gord] *s.* calabaza.

gourmet [gʊrmé] *s.* gastrónomo.

gout [gaʊt] *s.* gota (*enfermedad*).

govern [gʌ́vən] *v.* gobernar; regir.

governess [gʌ́vənɪs] *s.* institutriz.

government [gʌ́vəmənt] *s.* gobierno.

governmental [gʌvəmént]] *adj.* gubernativo.

governor [gʌ́vənə] *s.* gobernador;
regulador (*de una máquina*).

gown [gaʊn] *s.* vestido (*de mujer*); toga
(*de un juez, profesor, etc.*); **dressing**
— bata.

grab [græb] *v.* agarrar asir; arrebatar;
s. arrebatiña; agarro, agarrón; presa.

grace [gres] *s.* gracia; favor; donaire,
garbo; **to say** — bendecir la mesa, dar
gracias; **to be in the good -s of**
someone gozar del favor de uno; *v.*
agraciar, adornar.

graceful [grésfəl] *adj.* gracioso, agraciado, garboso; **-ly** *adv.* graciosa-
mente, con gracia, con garbo.

gracefulness [grésfəlnɪs] *s.* gracia, donaire, gallardía, garbo.

gracious [gréʃəs] *adj.* afable; cortés; —!
¡válgame Dios!

gradation [gredéʃən] *s.* graduación;
gradación; grado.

grade [gred] *s.* (*degree*) grado; (*mark*)
nota, calificación; (*slope*) cuesta,
declive, pendiente; *Am.* gradiente;
— **crossing** cruce a nivel (*de un*
ferrocarril con una carretera); **the -s**
la escuela primaria; *v.* graduar, clasificar; calificar, dar una calificación;
nivelar (*un camino*).

gradual [grédʒʊəl] *adj.* gradual; **-ly**
adv. gradualmente, poco a poco.

graduate [grédʒʊɪt] *adj.* graduado,
que ha recibido un grado académico;
to do — work cursar asignaturas
superiores (*al bachillerato*); *s.* estudiante graduado (*que estudia para*
licenciado o doctor); [grédʒuet] *v.*
graduar(se).

graduation [grædʒuéʃən] *s.* graduación.

graft [græft] *s.* (*insertion*) injerto;
tejido injertado; (*extortion*) sisa,
malversación (*de caudales públicos*);
ganancia ilegal, *Am.* mordida; *v.*
injertar; malversar fondos ajenos; sisar, exigir pago ilegal, *Am.* morder.

grafter [græftə] *s.* malversador (*de fon-*
dos públicos), estafador. *C.A.* coyote,
Méx. mordelón.

grain [gren] *s.* (*cereal*) grano; (*mark-*
ings) fibra (*de la madera*), veta (*del*
mármol o madera); **against the — a**
(o al) redopelo, a contrapelo.

gram [græm] *s.* gramo.

grammar [grémə] *s.* gramática; —
school escuela primaria.

grammatical [grəmǽtɪk]] *adj.* gramatical, gramático.

granary [grénərɪ] *s.* granero.

grand [grænd] *adj.* grande; grandioso,
admirable; magnífico.

grandchild [grǽntʃaɪld] *s.* nieto.

grandchildren [grǽntʃɪldrən] *s. pl.*
nietos.

granddaughter [grǽndɔtə] *s.* nieta.

grandeur [grǽndʒə] *s.* grandeza, grandiosidad; majestad.

grandfather [grǽnfɑðə] *s.* abuelo.

grandiose [grǽndɪos] *adj.* grandioso,
magnífico.

grandma [grǽnmɑ] *s.* abuela, abuelita,
Am. mamá grande.

grandmother [grǽnmʌðə] *s.* abuela.

grandness [grǽndnɪs] *s.* grandeza;
grandiosidad; magnificencia.

grandpa [grǽnpɑ] *s.* abuelo, abuelito,
Am. papá grande.

grandparent [grǽnpɛrənt] *s.* abuelo,
abuela; **-s** abuelos.

grandson [grǽnsʌn] *s.* nieto.

grandstand [grǽnstænd] *s.* andanada,
gradería cubierta.

grange [grendʒ] *s.* granja; asociación
de agricultores.

granite [grǽnɪt] *s.* granito (*roca*).

granny [grǽnɪ] *s.* abuelita; viejecita,
viejita.

grant [grænt] *s.* concesión; subvención;
donación; transferencia de propiedad
(*mediante escritura*); *v.* conceder; otorgar; ceder, transferir (*derechos, pro-*
piedad, etc.); **to take for -ed** dar por
supuesto, dar por sentado.

granulate [grǽnjələt] *v.* granular(se).

grape [grep] *s.* uva.

grapefruit [grépfrut] *s.* toronja.

grapevine [grépvaɪn] *s.* vid; parra.

graph [græf] *s.* diagrama, gráfica; *v.*
hacer una gráfica o diagrama.

graphic [grǽfɪk] *adj.* gráfico.

graphite [grǽfaɪt] *s.* grafito.

grapple [grǽp]] *v.* luchar, pelear cuerpo
a cuerpo; aferrar, agarrar.

grasp [græsp] *v.* (*seize*) agarrar; asir;
apretar; (*understand*) comprender;
abarcar; *s.* agarro, asimiento; apretón
de manos; **to be within one's —**
estar al alcance de uno; **to have a**
good — of a subject estar fuerte en
una materia, saber a fondo una
materia.

grass [græs] *s.* hierba; césped; pasto;
Méx. zacate; *Méx., Ven., Col.* grama.

grasshopper [grǽshɑpə] *s.* saltamontes, saltón, *Méx., C.A.* chapulín.

grassroots [grǽsruts] *adj.* del pueblo;
de la gente.

grassy [grǽsɪ] *adj.* herboso, *Am.* pastoso.

grate [gret] *s.* (*window*) reja, verja,
enrejado; (*grill*) parrilla, brasero; *v.*
enrejar, poner enrejado; crujir, rechinar (*los dientes*); rallar (*queso*); **to**
— **on** molestar, irritar.

grateful [grétfəl] *adj.* agradecido;
grato, agradable.

grater [grétə] *s.* rallador.

gratify [grǽtəfaɪ] *v.* complacer, dar
gusto, agradar; satisfacer.

grating [grétɪŋ] *s.* reja, enrejado, verja;
adj. rechinante; molesto, áspero.

gratis [grétɪs] *adv.* gratis, de balde.

gratitude [grǽtətjud] *s.* gratitud.

gratuitous [grətjúətəs] *adj.* gratuito,

sin fundamento; — **statement** afirmación arbitraria.

grave [grev] *adj.* grave; serio; *s.* tumba sepulcro, sepultura; acento grave; **—stone** losa o lápida sepulcral.

gravel [grǽvl] *s.* grava, guijo, cascajo; cálculos (*en los riñones, la vejiga, etc.*); mal de piedra; *v.* cubrir con grava.

graveyard [grévjard] *s.* cementerio.

gravitation [gŕævité∫ən] *s.* atracción; gravitación.

gravity [grǽvətɪ] *s.* gravedad; seriedad.

gravy [grévɪ] *s.* salsa; jugo (*de carne*).

gray [gre] *adj.* gris; cano; entrecano (*que empieza a encanecer*); — **horse** rucio, tordo, tordillo; — **matter** seso; **gray-headed** canoso; *s.* gris, color gris; *v.* encanecer; poner(se) gris.

grayish [gréɪ∫] *adj.* grisáceo, pardusco; — **hair** pelo entrecano.

grayness [grénɪs] *s.* grisura, gris, calidad de gris; encanecimiento.

graze [grez] *v.* (*feed*) pacer; apacentar, *Am.* pastear, pastar; (*brush*) rozar; raspar; *s.* roce, rozón, raspadura.

grease [gris] *s.* grasa; *v.* engrasar; untar; lubricar; **to — the palm** untar la mano, sobornar.

greasy [grísɪ] *adj.* grasiento, grasoso.

great [gret] *adj.* gran(de); eminente; magnífico, excelente; **a — deal** una gran cantidad; muchos; mucho; **a — many** muchos; **a — while** un largo rato o tiempo; **-ly** *adv.* grandemente, mucho; muy; en gran parte; sobremanera.

great-grandchild [grétgrǽnt∫aɪld] *s.* biznieto.

great-grandfather [grétgrǽnfɑðɚ] *s.* bisabuelo.

great-grandmother [grétgrǽnmʌðɚ] *s.* bisabuela.

greatness [grétnɪs] *s.* grandeza.

Grecian [grí∫ən] *adj.* & *s.* griego.

greed [grid] *s.* codicia; avaricia; gula.

greedily [grídlɪ] *adv.* vorazmente; con avaricia; con gula.

greediness [grídɪnɪs] *s.* codicia; avaricia; gula; voracidad.

greedy [grídɪ] *adj.* codicioso; avaro; goloso; voraz.

Greek [grik] *adj.* & *s.* griego.

green [grin] *adj.* (*color*) verde; (*novice*) novato, inexperto; **to grow —** verdear; **the fields look —** verdean los campos; *s.* verde, verdor; césped, prado; campo de golf; **-s** verduras, hortalizas.

greenhorn [grínhɔrn] *s.* novato, pipiolo.

greenhouse [grínhaʊs] *s.* invernáculo, invernadero.

greenish [grínɪ∫] *adj.* verdoso.

greenness [grínnɪs] *s.* (*color*) verdor, verdura; (*experience*) inmadurez; impericia.

greet [grit] *v.* saludar; **to — each other** saludarse.

greeting [grítɪŋ] *s.* saludo; salutación; **-s!** ¡salud! ¡saludos!

grenade [grɪnéd] *s.* granada, bomba epqueña.

grew [gru] *pret. de* **to grow.**

grey = **gray.**

greyish = **gray.**

greyness = **grayness.**

greyhound [gréhaʊnd] *s.* lebrel, galgo.

griddle [grídl] *s.* tartera; plancha (*para tapar el hornillo*).

grief [grif] *s.* dolor, pesar; **to come to —** sobrevenirle a uno una desgracia; fracasar.

grievance [grívəns] *s.* queja; resentimiento; motivo de queja, injusticia, ofensa.

grieve [griv] *v.* afligir(se); lamentar(se), acongojar(se).

grievous [grívəs] *adj.* doloroso, penoso; grave, altroz.

grill [grɪl] *s.* parrilla; **men's —** restaurante para hombres; *v.* asar en parrillas; interrogar (*a un sospechoso*).

grim [grɪm] *adj.* austero, áspero; fiero; torvo, siniestro.

grimace [grɪmés] *s.* mueca, gesto; *v.* hacer muecas o gestos.

grime [graɪm] *s.* mugre; *v.* ensuciar.

grimy [gráɪmɪ] *adj.* mugriento.

grin [grɪn] *s.* sonrisa abierta; sonrisa maliciosa; sonrisa canina; *v.* sonreír (*mostrando mucho los dientes*).

grind [graɪnd] *v.* (*crush*) moler; machacar; (*sharpen*) afilar, amolar; (*study hard*) afanarse demasiado; estudiar con empeño; **to — a hand organ** tocar el organillo; **to — one's teeth** rechinar los dientes; *s.* molienda; faena, trabajo penoso; estudiante tesonero; **the daily —** la rutina diaria.

grinder [gráɪndɚ] *s.* moledor; molinillo (*para moler café*); amolador, afilador; muela (*piedra para afilar*); muela (*diente molar*).

grindstone [gráɪndston] *s.* piedra de amolar.

grip [grɪp] *v.* (*seize*) agarrar; asir; apretar; empuñar; (*impress*) impresionar; conmover; *s.* agarro; asimiento; apretón; asidero, asa; (*suitcase*) valija, maletín; *Méx.*, velís; **to have a — on someone** tener agarrado a alguien.

grippe [grɪp] *s.* gripe, influenza.

grit [grɪt] *s.* (*gravel*) arenilla, arena; piedra arenisca; (*pluck*) firmeza, tesón; **-s** maíz, avena, o trigo a medio moler; *v.* rechinar, crujir.

gritty [grítɪ] *adj.* arenoso; valeroso, firme.

grizzly [grízlɪ] *adj.* grisáceo, pardusco; **— bear** oso pardo.

groan [gron] *s.* gemido, quejido; *v.* gemir; quejarse; crujir (*por exceso de peso*).

grocer [grósɚ] *s.* abacero, *Méx.* abarrotero, *Carib.*, *C.A.* bodeguero; *Riopl.* almacenero.

grocery [grósərɪ] *s.* abacería, tienda de comestibles, *Méx.* abarrotería, *Méx.* tienda de abarrotes; *Carib.*, *C.A.* bodega; **groceries** comestibles, *Méx.* abarrotes.

groom [grum] s. (bridegroom) novio; (stable groom) caballerizo, mozo de caballeriza; establero; v. almohazar, limpiar con la almohaza (a los caballos), cuidar (a los caballos); **to — oneself** asearse, peinarse, componerse; **well-groomed** bien vestido, aseado, limpio.

groove [gruv] s. estría, ranura, acanaladura; surco (en un camino); muesca, encaje; v. acanalar, estriar.

grope [grop] v. tentalear, tentar, andar a tientas; **to — for** buscar tentando, buscar a tientas.

gross [gros] adj. grueso; burdo; tosco; grosero; **— earnings** ganancias totales; **— ignorance** ignorancia crasa; **— weight** peso bruto; s. gruęso, totalidad; gruesa (doce docenas).

grotesque [grotésk] adj. & s. grotesco.

grotto [gráto] s. gruta.

grouch [grautʃ] s. mal humor; gruñón, refunfuñón, cascarrabias; **to have a — against someone** tenerle ojeriza (o mala voluntad) a una persona; guardarle rencor a alguien; v. gruñir, refunfuñar; estar de mal humor.

grouchy [gráutʃɪ] adj. gruñón, refunfuñón, malhumorado, cascarrabias.

ground [graund] s. (earth) suelo, tierra; terreno; (motive) rezón; base, fundamento; **— crew** personal de tierra; **-s** heces, desperdicios, sedimento; **— floor** piso bajo, planta baja, **to break —** roturar, arar; cavar; **to give —** retroceder, ceder; **to hold one's —** mantenerse firme; v. conectar (un alambre) con la tierra; encallar (una embarcación); aterrizar (un aeroplano); **to be well -ed** poseer las bases o principios fundamentales; pret. & p.p. de **to grind.**

groundless [gráundlɪs] adj. infundado.

group [grup] s. grupo; **— insurance** seguros sociales; v. agrupar.

grove [grov] s. arboleda, bosquecillo.

grow [gro] v. crecer; brotar; cultivar; criar; producir; **to — angry** ponerse enojado o enfadado, enfadarse, enojarse; **to — better** ponerse mejor, mejorar; **to — difficult** dificultarse, hacerse difícil; **to — late** hacerse tarde; **to — old** ponerse viejo, envejecer; **to — out of a habit** perder la costumbre; **to — pale** ponerse pálido, palidecer; **to — tired** cansarse.

growl [graul] s. gruñido; v. gruñir.

growler [gráulə] s. gruñón; regañón.

grown [gron] p.p. de **to grow** & adj. crecido; desarrollado; **— man** hombre maduro, hombre hecho; **— with trees** poblado de árboles.

grown-up [grónʌp] adj. crecido, adulto; s. adulto.

growth [groθ] s. (increase) crecimiento, acrecentamiento; aumento; (development) desarrollo; (vegetation) vegetación; (tissue) tumor, lobanillo, excrecencia.

grubby [grábɪ] adj. roñoso; sucio.

grudge [grʌdʒ] s. inquina, rencor, resentimiento, mala voluntad; v. tener inquina, envidia o mala voluntad; dar de mala gana.

gruff [grʌf] adj. áspero, rudo; grosero.

grumble [grámbl] s. refunfuño, gruñido, queja; v. refunfuñar, gruñir, quejarse.

grumbler [grámblə] s. gruñón; regañón.

grumpy [grámpɪ] adj. malhumorado; gruñón.

grunt [grʌnt] s. gruñido, Méx., C.A., Col., Ven. pujido; v. gruñir, Ríopl., Méx., C.A., Ven., Andes pujar.

guarantee [gærəntí] s. garantía; fianza; fiador; v. garantizar; dar fianza; salir fiador de.

guarantor [gérəntə] s. fiador.

guaranty [gérəntɪ] s. garantía; fianza; fiador; v. véase **guarantee.**

guard [gard] s. guarda; guardia; resguardo; **to be on —** estar alerta; estar en guardia; **to keep —** vigilar; v. guardar; resguardar; vigilar; **to — (oneself) against** guardarse de.

guardian [gárdɪən] s. guardián, custodio; tutor; **— angel** ángel custodio, ángel de la guarda.

guardianship [gárdɪənʃɪp] s. tutela; guarda, custodia.

guardrail [gárdrel] s. baranda.

Guatemalan [gwatəmálən] adj. & s. guatemalteco.

guess [gɛs] s. conjetura, suposición; adivinación; v. adivinar; suponer, creer.

guest [gɛst] s. convidado; visita; huésped, pensionista, inquilino.

guffaw [gʌfɔ́] s. risotada, carcajada.

guidance [gáɪdṇs] s. guía, dirección.

guide [gaɪd] s. guía.

guidebook [gáɪdbʊk] s. guía del viajero; **railway —** guía de ferrocarriles.

guideline [gáɪdlaɪn] s. norma; precepto.

guild [gɪld] s. gremio; cofradía; asociación.

guile [gaɪl] s. engaño, astucia.

guilt [gɪlt] s. culpa, delito; culpabilidad.

guiltless [gɪ́ltlɪs] adj. libre de culpa; inocente.

guilty [gɪ́ltɪ] adj. culpable; reo, delincuente.

guise [gaɪz] s. aspecto, apariencia; modo; **under the — of** so capa de; disfrazado de.

guitar [gɪtár] s. guitarra.

gulf [gʌlf] s. golfo; abismo.

gull [gʌl] s. gaviota.

gullet [gʌ́lɪt] s. gaznate.

gully [gʌ́lɪ] s. barranco, barranca; hondonada.

gulp [gʌlp] s. trago; v. tragar; engullir; **to — it down** tragárselo.

gum [gʌm] s. (product) goma; (of mouth) encía; **chewing —** goma de mascar, Am. chicle; **— tree** arbol gomífero, Col. gomero; v. engomar, pegar con goma.

gun [gʌn] s. (cannon) cañón; (rifle) fusil, rifle; (shotgun) escopeta; pistola, re-

vólver; **a 21 — salute** una salva de
21 cañonazos.

gunboat [gʌ́nbot] s. cañonero, lancha
cañonera.

gunner [gʌ́nə] s. artillero, cañonero;
ametrallador.

gunpowder [gʌ́npaʊdə] s. pólvora.

gurgle [gɝ́gl] v. borbotar, hacer borbo-
llones; s. borbollón, borbotón.

gush [gʌ́ʃ] s. chorro; borbollón, borbotón; efusión (de cariño o entusiasmo);
v. chorrear, borbotar, borbollar, bor-
bollonear; brotar; ser demasiado
efusivo.

gust [gʌst] s. ráfaga, ventolera.

gut [gʌt] s. tripa, intestino; cuerda de
tripa; **to have -s** tener agallas
(ánimo).

gutter [gʌ́tə] s. arroyo (de la calle o de
un camino); gotera (del techo); zanja.

guy [gaɪ] s. (person) sujeto, tipo, individuo; (wire) tirante, alambre, cadena
(para sostener algo); v. sostener (algo)
con tirantes; burlarse de, mofarse de.

gymnasium [dʒɪmnéziəm] s. gimnasio.

gymnastics [dʒɪmnǽstɪks] s. pl. gimnasia.

gyrate [dʒáɪret] v. girar.

gyroscope [dʒáɪrəskop] s. giroscopio.

gypsy [dʒɪ́psɪ] s. & adj. gitano.

H

habit [hǽbɪt] s. hábito; costumbre;
drinking — vicio de la bebida; **riding —** traje de montar.

habitual [həbítʃʊəl] adj. habitual; acostumbrado.

hack [hæk] s. (cut) tajo; (cough) tos seca;
(horse) caballo de alquiler; rocín;
(writer) escritor mercenario; v. tajar,
picar; toser con tos seca.

hackneyed [hǽknɪd] adj. trillado, muy
común.

had [hæd] pret. & p.p. de **to have; you
— better do it** es bueno que Vd. lo
haga; sería bueno que Vd. lo hiciese;
I — rather go than stay preferiría
irme a quedarme.

hag [hæg] s. hechicera, bruja; viejita.

haggard [hǽgəd] adj. macilento, flaco.

haggle [hǽgl] v. regatear.

hail [hel] s. (storm) granizo; (greeting)
saludo; llamada, grito; **Hail Mary**
Ave María; interj. ¡salud!; ¡salve!;
v. granizar; saludar; llamar; aclamar;
to — from proceder de, ser oriundo
de.

hailstorm [hélstɔrm] s. granizada.

hair [hɛr] s. pelo; cabello; vello; filamento (de las plantas); **— net** red
para el cabello.

hairbrush [hɛ́rbrʌʃ] s. cepillo para el
cabello.

haircut [hɛ́rkʌt] s. corte de pelo; **to
have a —** hacerse cortar el pelo.

hairdo [hɛ́rdu] s. peinado.

hairdresser [hɛ́rdrɛsə] s. peluquero,
peinadora.

hairless [hɛ́rlɪs] adj. sin pelo, pelado;
lampiño.

hairpin [hɛ́rpɪn] s. horquilla, Am. gancho (para el pelo).

hairy [hɛ́rɪ] adj. peludo, cabelludo; hir-
suto, velloso, velludo.

hale [hel] adj. sano, fuerte, robusto; v.
llevar (a una persona) por fuerza.

half [hæf] s. mitad; **— an apple** media
manzana; adj. medio; **— brother** hermanastro; **— cooked** a medio cocer,
medio cocido; **half-past one** la una
y media; **half-baked** a medio cocer;
a medio planear.

half-breed [hǽfbrid] adj. & s. mestizo.

half-hour [hǽfáʊr] s. media hora; adj.
de media hora.

half-mast [hǽfmǽst] s. media asta; v.
poner a media asta (la bandera).

half-open [hǽfópən] adj. entreabierto;
medio abierto, entornado.

halfway [hǽfwe] adj. & adv. a medio
camino; parcial, incompleto; **—
between** equidistante de; **— finished** a medio acabar; **to do something —** hacer algo a medias.

half-witted [hǽfwítɪd] adj. imbécil,
zonzo.

halibut [hǽləbət] s. mero, hipogloso
(pez).

hall [hɔl] s. salón (para asambleas, fun-
ciones, etc.); edificio (de un colegio o
universidad); vestíbulo; corredor, pasillo; **town —** ayuntamiento.

hallmark [hɔ́lmark] s. distintivo.

hallo — hello.

hallow [hǽlo] v. santificar; consagrar.

Halloween [hǽloín] s. víspera de
Todos los Santos.

hallway [hɔ́lwe] s. corredor, pasillo;
zaguán.

halo [hélo] s. halo; aureola.

halt [hɔlt] s. alto, parada; v. parar(se),
detener(se); hacer alto; vacilar.

halter [hɔ́ltə] s. ronzal, cabestro.

halting [hɔ́ltɪŋ] adj. vacilante; **-ly** adv.
con vacilación.

halve [hæv] v. partir por la mitad;
partir en dos.

halves [hævz] pl. de **half; to go —** ir a
medias.

ham [hæm] s. jamón.

hamburger [hǽmbɝgə] s. carne picada
de vaca; bocadillo o emparedado de
carne picada, Am. hamburguesa.

hamlet [hǽmlɪt] s. caserío, aldehuela.

hammer [hǽmə] s. martillo; martinete
(de piano); **sledge —** macho; v.
martillar; machacar; clavar.

hammock [hǽmək] s. hamaca, Ven.,
Col. chinchorro; Ríopl. mangangá;
coy.

hamper [hǽmpə] s. canasto, cesto
grande, cuévano; v. estorbar, impedir, embarazar.

hand [hænd] s. mano; manecilla; aguja
(de reloj); obrero; letra (modo de
escribir); **— and glove** uña y carne;
— in — (cogidos) de la mano; **at —**
a la mano, cerca; **made by —** hecho
a mano; **on —** disponible; en existencia; listo; a la mano, presente; **on
the other —** en cambio, por otra

GR

parte; **to have one's -s full** estar ocupadísimo; v. entregar, dar; **to — down** bajar (una cosa para dársela a alguien); transmitir (de una a otra generación); pronunciar (un fallo); **— in** entregar; **to — over** entregar.

handbag [hǽndbæg] s. bolsa o bolso; saco de noche, maletín.

handball [hǽndbɔl] s. pelota; juego de pelota.

handbill [hǽndbɪl] s. hoja volante (anuncio).

handcuff [hǽndkʌf] v. maniatar; **-s** s. pl. esposas, manillas de hierro.

handful [hǽndfəl] s. manojo, puñado.

handicap [hǽndɪkæp] s. desventaja, estorbo, impedimento, obstáculo; ventaja o desventaja (impuesta en ciertas contiendas); **— race** carrera de handicap; v. estorbar, poner trabas a.

handiwork [hǽndɪwɜk] s. labor, trabajo hecho a mano; artefacto.

handkerchief [hǽŋkɚtʃɪf] s. pañuelo.

handle [hǽndl] s. mango, asa; tirador (de puerta o cajón); puño (de espada); manubrio (de bicicleta, organillo, etc.); v. manejar; manipular; manosear, tocar; comerciar en; **-s easily** se maneja con facilidad, es muy manuable.

handmade [hǽndméd] adj. hecho a mano.

handsaw [hǽndsɔ] s. serrucho.

handshake [hǽndʃek] s. apretón de manos.

handsome [hǽnsəm] adj. (good-looking) hermoso, guapo, bien parecido; (generous) generoso; **a — sum** una suma considerable.

handwriting [hǽndraɪtɪŋ] s. letra (modo de escribir), escritura.

handy [hǽndɪ] adj. a la mano, próximo, hábil, diestro; manuable, fácil de manejar.

hang [hæŋ] v. colgar; suspender; ahorcar; inclinar (la cabeza); **sentenced to — condenado a la horca; to — around** andar holgazaneando por un sitio; rondar; esperar sin hacer nada; **to — on** colgarse de; depender de; estar pendiente de; persistir; **to — paper on a wall** empapelar una pared; **to — with tapestries** entapizar; s. modo de caerle la ropa a una persona; modo de manejar (un mecanismo); modo de resolver (un problema); significado (de un argumento); **I don't care a —** no me importa un ardite.

hangar [hǽŋɚ] s. hangar, cobertizo.

hanger [hǽŋɚ] s. colgadero; percha, clavijero; **paper — empapelador.**

hanging [hǽŋɪŋ] s. muerte en la horca; **-s** colgaduras; adj. colgante; colgado.

hangman [hǽŋmən] s. verdugo.

hangnail [hǽŋnel] s. padrastro (pedacito de pellejo que se levanta junto a las uñas).

hang-over [hǽŋovɚ] s. sobrante, remanente, resto; **to have a — Ven., Col.,** Andes tener un ratón o estar enratonado (tras una borrachera), Méx., estar

crudo o tener una cruda; Ch. la mona; C.A. de goma; Riopl. resaca.

haphazard [hæphǽzɚd] adv. al azar, al acaso, a la ventura, a la buena de Dios; adj. casual; impensado.

haphazardly [hæphǽzɚdlɪ] adv. = **haphazard.**

hapless [hǽplɪs] adj. desventurado, desgraciado.

happen [hǽpən] v. suceder, pasar, acontecer, sobrevenir, acaecer; **to — to hear (do, be, etc.)** oír (hacer, estar, etc.) por casualidad; **to — to pass by** acertar a pasar; **to — on (upon)** encontrarse con, tropezar con.

happening [hǽpənɪŋ] s. acontecimiento, suceso.

happily [hǽplɪ] adv. felizmente; afortunadamente.

happiness [hǽpɪnɪs] s. felicidad, dicha, contento.

happy [hǽpɪ] adj. feliz; dichoso, alegre; afortunado; **to be — to** alegrarse de.

harangue [hɚǽŋ] s. arenga, perorata; v. arengar, perorar.

harass [hǽrəs] v. acosar, hostigar, molestar.

harbor [hárbɚ] s. puerto; asilo, refugio, abrigo; v. abrigar; hospedar; albergar.

hard [hard] adj. (firm) duro; (stiff) tieso; (difficult) arduo, difícil; **— cash** dinero contante y sonante, metálico; **— coal** antracita; **— liquor** licor espirituoso (aguardiente, ron, etc.); **— luck** mala suerte; **— of hearing** medio sordo; **— water** agua cruda; adv. fuerte, recio, con fuerza; con empeño, con ahínco; **— by** muy cerca; **— core** núcleo resistente (de un grupo); **—hearted** de corazón duro; **hard-working** muy trabajador, industrioso, aplicado.

harden [hárdn] v. endurecer(se).

hardening [hárdnɪŋ] s. endurecimiento.

hardly [hárdlɪ] adv. apenas; a duras penas; difícilmente; duramente, con aspereza; probablemente no.

hardness [hárdnɪs] s. dureza; aspereza; dificultad.

hardship [hárdʃɪp] s. apuro, aflicción; trabajo, penalidad.

hardware [hárdwer] s. quincalla, quincallería; **— shop** quincallería, ferretería.

hardy [hárdɪ] adj. robusto, fuerte, recio, atrevido.

hare [her] s. liebre.

harebrained [hérbrénd] adj. atolondrado, ligero de cascos.

harelip [hérlɪp] s. labio leporino.

harem [hérəm] s. harén.

harlot [hárlət] s. ramera, prostituta.

harm [harm] s. daño, mal; perjuicio; v. dañar; hacer mal, hacer daño; perjudicar.

harmful [hármfəl] adj. dañoso; dañino, nocivo, perjudicial.

harmless [hármlɪs] adj. innocuo; inofensivo; no dañoso, inocente.

harmlessness [hármlɪsnɪs] *s.* innocuidad; inocencia, falta de malicia.

harmonic [harmánɪk] *adj.* armónico.

harmonious [harmóuniəs] *adj.* armonioso.

harmonize [hármənaɪz] *v.* armonizar; concordar; congeniar.

harmony [hármənɪ] *s.* armonía.

harness [hárnɪs] *s.* guarniciones (*de caballerías*); jaez, aparejo; **to get back in** — volver al servicio activo, volver a trabajar; volver a la rutina; *v.* enjaezar, poner guarniciones a (*un caballo, mula, etc.*).

harp [harp] *s.* arpa; *v.* tocar el arpa; **to — on** repetir constantemente (*una nota, palabra, tema, etc.*); porfiar en.

harpoon [harpún] *s.* arpón; *v.* arponear, pescar con arpón.

harrow [hǽro] *s.* rastro, rastrillo, grada; *v.* rastrear, rastrillar; atormentar; horrorizar.

harrowing [hǽrowɪŋ] *adj.* horrendo, horripilante, que pone los cabellos de punta; espeluznante.

harry [hǽrɪ] *v.* acosar, molestar; asolar.

harsh [harʃ] *adj.* tosco, áspero, severo, austero.

harshness [hárʃnɪs] *s.* aspereza; tosquedad; severidad.

harvest [hárvɪst] *s.* cosecha; siega, agosto; recolección; *v.* cosechar; segar.

hash [hæʃ] *s.* picadillo.

haste [hest] *s.* prisa; apresuramiento; **in** — de prisa; **to make** — darse prisa, apresurarse; *Am.* apurarse.

hasten [hésn̩] *v.* apresurar(se), precipitar(se); darse prisa.

hastily [héstlɪ] *adv.* aprisa, de prisa, apresuradamente, precipitadamente.

hasty [héstɪ] *adj.* apresurado; precipitado.

hat [hæt] *s.* sombrero.

hatch [hætʃ] *v.* empollar; criar pollos; idear, maquinar; *s.* cría, nidada, pollada; escotillón, trampa (*puerta en el suelo*); **—way** escotilla.

hatchet [hǽtʃɪt] *s.* hacha; **to bury the** — echar pelillos a la mar, olvidar rencores o enemistades.

hate [het] *s.* odio; aborrecimiento; *v.* odiar; aborrecer; detestar.

hateful [hétfəl] *adj.* odioso, aborrecible.

hatred [hétrɪd] *s.* odio, aversión.

haughtily [hɔ́tlɪ] *adv.* con altivez, altaneramente, arrogantemente.

haughtiness [hɔ́tɪnɪs] *s.* altanería, altivez.

haughty [hɔ́tɪ] *adj.* altivo, altanero, arrogante.

haul [hɔl] *v.* (*transport*) acarrear, transportar; (*pull*) jalar (*halar*); tirar de; (*drag*) arrastrar; **to — down the flag** arriar (o bajar) la bandera; *s.* acarreo; transporte; tirón, estirón; buena pesca; ganancia, botín.

haunch [hɔntʃ] *s.* anca.

haunt [hɔnt] *v.* frecuentar a menudo; andar por, vagar por (*como fantasma o espectro*); **that idea -s me** me persigue esa idea; **-ed house** casa de espantos, fantasmas o aparecidos; *s.* guarida.

have [hæv] *v.* tener; poseer; haber (*v. aux.*); **to — a suit made** mandar hacer un traje; **to — a look at** dar un vistazo a, echar una mirada a; **to — to** tener que; deber; **I'll not — it** so no lo toleraré, no lo permitiré; **what did she — on?** ¿qué vestido llevaba (puesto)?

haven [hévən] *s.* asilo, abrigo, refugio; puerto.

havoc [hǽvək] *s.* estrago, estropicio, ruina; **to cause** — hacer estragos.

hawk [hɔk] *s.* halcón; *v.* pregonar (*mercancías*).

hawthorn [hɔ́θɔrn] *s.* espino.

hay [he] *s.* heno, paja, hierba seca; **— fever** catarro asmático.

hayloft [hélɔft] *s.* henil, pajar.

haystack [héstæk] *s.* montón de heno o paja.

hazard [hǽzəd] *s.* azar; riesgo, peligro; estorbo, obstáculo (*en el campo de golf*); *v.* arriesgar, aventurar.

hazardous [hǽzədəs] *adj.* peligroso.

haze [hez] *s.* bruma, neblina, niebla; *v.* atormentar, hostigar (*con bromas estudiantiles*).

hazel [hézl̩] *s.* avellano. **—nut** avellana; *adj.* de avellano; avellanado, color de avellana.

hazy [hézɪ] *adj.* (*weather*) nublado, brumoso; (*mind*) confuso.

he [hi] *pron. pers.* él; **— who** el que, quien; **he-goat** macho cabrío.

head [hɛd] *s.* cabeza; cabecera (*de cama*); jefe; **— of hair** cabellera; **game of -s or tails** juego de cara y cruz, juego de las chapas, *Ven.*, *Col.*, *Andes*, *Ch.* juego de cara y sello; *Méx.* juego de águila y sol; **to be out of one's** — delirar, estar delirante; **to come to a** — madurar; supurar (*un absceso*); **to keep one's** — conservar la calma, no perder la cabeza; **it goes to his** — le desvanece; se le sube a la cabeza; *adj.* principal, primero; de proa, de frente; **head-on** de frente; *v.* encabezar; ir a la cabeza de; acaudillar; mandar, dirigir; **to — off** atajar; detener, refrenar; **to — towards** dirigirse a, encaminarse a.

headache [hédek] *s.* dolor de cabeza.

headdress [héddres] *s.* tocado, adorno para la cabeza.

headgear [hédgɪr] *s.* sombrero, gorro, gorra; tocado, toca (*de mujer*); cabezada (*de guarnición para caballo*).

heading [hédɪŋ] *s.* encabezamiento, título.

headland [hédlənd] *s.* cabo, promontorio.

headlight [hédlaɪt] *s.* linterna delantera, faro delantero.

headline [hédlaɪn] *s.* título, encabezado.

headlong [hédlɔ́ŋ] *adv.* de cabeza; precipitadamente.

headquarters [hédkwɔ́rtəz] *s.* cuartel general; jefatura; oficina principal.

HA

headset [hédsɛt] *s.* receptor de cabeza.
headstrong [hédstrɔŋ] *adj.* testarudo, porfiado, obstinado.
headway [hédwe] *s.* progreso, avance; **to make —** avanzar, adelantar, progresar.
heal [hil] *v.* curar; sanar; cicatrizar.
health [hɛlθ] *s.* salud; sanidad; salubridad.
healthful [hélθfəl] *adj.* sano; salubre; saludable.
healthfulness [hélθfəlnəs] *s.* salubridad; sanidad.
healthy [hélθɪ] *adj.* sano; saludable.
heap [hip] *s.* montón; pila; *v.* amontonar; apilar.
hear [hɪr] *v.* (*listen*) oír; escuchar; (*get news*) tener noticias; **to — about someone** oír hablar de alguien; **to — from someone** tener noticias de alguien; **to — of** saber de, tener noticias de, oír hablar de; **I -d that . . .** oí decir que . . .
heard [hɜrd] *pret. & p.p. de* **to hear.**
hearer [hírə] *s.* oyente.
hearing [hírɪŋ] *s.* (*sense*) oído; (*trial*) audiencia; examen de testigos; **hard of —** medio sordo, algo sordo; **within —** al alcance del oído; **— aid** aparato auditivo.
hearsay [hírse] *s.* habilla, rumor; **by —** de oídas.
hearse [hɜrs] *s.* carroza fúnebre.
heart [hart] *s.* (*organ*) corazón; (*spirit*) ánimo; **at —** en realidad, en el fondo; **from the bottom of one's —** de corazón, con toda el alma; con toda sinceridad; **to learn by —** aprender de memoria; **to take —** cobrar ánimo; **to take to —** tomar en serio; tomar a pechos; **— attack** ataque cardíaco.
heartache [hártek] *s.* dolor del corazón; angustia, pesar, congoja.
heartbroken [hártbrokən] *adj.* traspasado de dolor, acongojado, angustiado; desengañado.
hearten [hártn̩] *v.* animar.
heartfelt [hártfɛlt] *adj.* sentido, cordial, sincero; **my — sympathy** mi más sentido pésame.
hearth [harθ] *s.* hogar; fogón.
heartily [hártlɪ] *adv.* de corazón; cordialmente; de buena gana; **to eat —** comer con apetito; comer bien (*o* mucho).
heartless [hártlɪs] *adj.* de mal corazón; cruel; insensible.
heart-rending [hártrɛndɪŋ] *adj.* angustioso; agudo.
hearty [hártɪ] *adj.* sincero, cordial; sano, fuerte; **— food** alimento nutritivo; **a — laugh** una buena carcajada; **— meal** comida abundante.
heat [hit] *s.* (*hot*) calor; ardor; (*emotion*) vehemencia; celo (*ardor sexual de la hembra*); calefacción (*para las habitaciones*); corrida, carrera (*de prueba*); *v.* calentar(se); acalorar(se).
heater [hítə] *s.* calentador; calorífero.
heathen [híðən] *s.* pagano, gentil, idóla-

tra; paganos; *adj.* pagano; irreligioso.
heating [hítɪŋ] *s.* calefacción.
heave [hiv] *v.* levantar, alzar (*con esfuerzo*); arrojar, lanzar; exhalar (*un suspiro*); jalar (*un cable*); jadear; basquear, hacer esfuerzos por vomitar.
heaven [hévən] *s.* cielo.
heavenly [hévənlɪ] *adj.* celeste; celestial; divino.
heavily [hévl̩ɪ] *adv.* pesadamente, lentamente; copiosamente, excesivamente.
heaviness [hévɪnɪs] *s.* pesadez, pesantez; opresión, abatimiento.
heavy [hévɪ] *adj.* (*weight*) pesado; (*thick*) grueso; (*coarse*) burdo; (*oppressive*) opresivo; **— rain** aguacero recio *o* fuerte; **with a — heart** abatido, acongojado.
heavyweight [hévɪwet] *s. & adj.* peso pesado (*fuerte*).
hectic [héktɪk] *adj.* febril; inquieto.
hedge [hɛdʒ] *s.* seto; vallado, barrera; *v.* cercar; poner valla o seto a; evitar o evadir contestaciones.
hedgehog [hédʒhag] *s.* erizo.
hedonism [hídənɪzm] *s.* hedonismo.
heed [hid] *v.* atender; hacer caso; prestar atención; *s.* atención, cuidado; **to pay —** to prestar atención a; hacer caso de.
heedless [hídlɪs] *adj.* descuidado; desatento.
heel [hil] *s.* talón (*del pie o de una media*); tacón (*del zapato*); **head over -s** patas arriba; *v.* poner tacón a; poner talón a.
hegemony [hɪdʒémənɪ] *s.* hegemonía.
heifer [héfə] *s.* novilla, vaquilla.
height [haɪt] *s.* altura; elevación; **— of folly** colmo de la locura.
heighten [háɪtn̩] *v.* avivar; aumentar(se); realzar.
heinous [hénəs] *adj.* aborrecible, odioso; malvado.
heir [ɛr] *s.* heredero.
heiress [éris] *s.* heredera.
held [hɛld] *pret. & p.p. de* **to hold.**
helicopter [héləkaptə] *s.* helicóptero.
helium [híliəm] *s.* helio.
hell [hɛl] *s.* infierno.
hello [hɛló] *interj.* ¡hola!; ¡halo!
helm [hɛlm] *s.* timón.
helmet [hélmɪt] *s.* yelmo.
help [hɛlp] *s.* (*aid*) ayuda; auxilio; remedio; alivio; (*employee*) criado o criados, empleado o empleados; *v.* ayudar, asistir; auxiliar; remediar; servir (*algo de comer*); **to — down** ayudar a bajar **— yourself** sírvase Vd. (*de comer o beber*); tómelo Vd., está a la disposición de Vd.; **he cannot — it** no puede evitarlo; **he cannot — doing it** no puede menos de hacerlo; **he cannot — but come** no puede menos de venir.
helper [hélpə] *s.* ayudante, asistente.
helpful [hélpfəl] *adj.* útil, servicial; provechoso.
helping [hélpɪŋ] *s.* ayuda; porción (*que se sirve en la mesa*).

helpless [hélplɪs] *adj.* (*defenseless*) desamparado; (*handicapped*) desvalido; imposibilitado; incapaz; (*confused*) perplejo, indeciso (*sin saber qué hacer*); **a — situation** una situación irremediable.

helplessness [hélplɪsnɪs] *s.* incapacidad; incompetencia; impotencia, debilidad; abandono, desamparo.

hem [hɛm] *s.* dobladillo, bastilla; *v.* dobladillar, bastillar, hacer dobladillos en (*la ropa*); **to — in** rodear, cercar; **to — and haw** toser y retoser (*fingidamente*); tartamudear, vacilar.

hemisphere [hémǝsfɪr] *s.* hemisferio.

hemlock [hémlɑk] *s.* cicuta (*hierba venenosa*); abeto americano.

hemoglobin [hímoglobɪn] *s.* hemoglobina.

hemp [hɛmp] *s.* cáñamo, *Am.* sisal.

hemstitch [hémstɪtʃ] *s.* dobladillo de ojo; *v.* hacer (*o echar*) dobladillo de ojo.

hen [hɛn] *s.* gallina; ave hembra.

hence [hɛns] *adv.* de (*o desde*) aquí; desde ahora; por lo tanto, por consiguiente; **a week —** de hoy en ocho días; de aquí a una semana.

henceforth [hɛnsfórθ] *adv.* de aquí en adelante; de hoy en adelante; desde ahora.

hepatitis [hɛpǝtáɪtɪs] *s.* hepatitis.

her [hɝ] *pron.* la; le, a ella; ella (*con preposición*); *adj.* su (sus), de ella.

herald [hérǝld] *s.* heraldo; anunciador, proclamador; precursor; *v.* anunciar, proclamar, publicar.

herb [ɝb] *s.* hierba (yerba).

herd [hɝd] *s.* (*animals*) hato; rebaño; manada; tropel; tropilla; (*cattle*) ganado; (*people*) muchedumbre; **the common —** el populacho, la chusma; *v.* reunir, juntar (*el ganado*); ir en manadas, ir juntos.

herdsman [hɝdʒmǝn] *s.* vaquero, vaquerizo; pastor.

here [hɪr] *adv.* aquí; acá; **— it is** aquí está, helo aquí, aquí lo tiene Vd.; **— is to you!** ¡a la salud de Vd.!; **that is neither — nor there** eso no viene al caso.

hereafter [hɪrǽftǝ] *adv.* de aquí (*o de hoy*) en adelante; desde ahora en adelante; en lo futuro; **the —** la otra vida.

hereby [hɪrbáɪ] *adv.* por este medio; mediante la presente, por la presente; con estas palabras.

hereditary [hǝrédǝterɪ] *adj.* hereditario.

heredity [hǝrédǝtɪ] *s.* herencia.

herein [hɪrín] *adv.* aquí dentro; en esto.

heresy [hérǝsɪ] *s.* herejía.

heretic [hérǝtɪk] *s.* hereje.

heretofore [hɪrtǝfór] *adv.* hasta ahora, hasta el presente.

herewith [hɪrwíθ] *adv.* aquí dentro, con esto, adjunto, incluso.

heritage [hérǝtɪdʒ] *s.* herencia.

hermetic [hǝrmétɪk] *adj.* hermético.

hermit [hɝmɪt] *s.* ermitaño.

hernia [hɝnɪǝ] *s.* hernia, ruptura, relajamiento.

hero [híro] *s.* héroe; protagonista.

heroic [hɪróɪk] *adj.* heroico.

heroin [héroɪn] *s.* heroína.

heroine [héroɪn] *s.* heroína.

heroism [héroɪzǝm] *s.* heroísmo.

heron [hérǝn] *s.* garza.

herring [hérɪŋ] *s.* arenque.

hers [hɝz] *pron. pos.* suyo (suya, suyos, suyas), de ella; el suyo (la suya, los suyos, las suyas); el (la, los, las) de ella; **a friend of —** un amigo suyo.

herself [hɝsélf] *pron.* ella misma; se (*como reflexivo*); **by —** sola; por sí (sola); **she — did it** ella misma lo hizo; **she talks to —** ella habla para sí, habla consigo misma, habla sola.

hesitant [hézǝtǝnt] = **hesitating**.

hesitate [hézǝtet] *v.* vacilar; titubear; dudar.

hesitating [hésǝtetɪŋ] *adj.* vacilante; indeciso; irresoluto; **-ly** *adv.* con vacilación.

hesitation [hezǝtéʃǝn] *s.* vacilación; titubeo, duda.

hew [hju] *v.* tajar, cortar; picar (*piedra*); labrar (*madera, piedra*).

hewn [hjun] *p.p. de* to hew.

hey [he] *interj.* ¡he!; ¡oiga!; ¡oye!

hibernate [háɪbɚnet] *v.* invernar.

hiccup, hiccough [híkʌp] *s.* hipo; *v.* hipar, tener hipo.

hickory [híkǝrɪ] *s.* nogal americano; **— nut** nuez (*del nogal americano*).

hid [hɪd] *pret. & p.p. de* to hide.

hidden [hídn] *p.p. de* to hide; *adj.* oculto, escondido.

hide [haɪd] *v.* ocultar(se); esconder(se); **to — from** esconderse de, recatarse de; *s.* cuero, piel; **to play — and seek** jugar al escondite.

hideous [hídɪǝs] *adj.* horrendo, horripilante, feote.

hierarchy [háɪǝrɑrkɪ] *s.* jerarquía.

hieroglyphic [haɪǝroglífɪk] *adj. & s.* jeroglífico.

high [haɪ] *adj.* alto; **— altar** altar mayor; **— and dry** enjuto; en seco; solo, abandonado; **— antiquity** antigüedad remota; **— explosive** explosivo de gran potencia; **— tide** pleamar; **— wind** ventarrón, viento fuerte; **in — gear** en directa, en tercera velocidad; **two feet —** dos pies de alto; **it is — time that** ya es hora de que; **to be in — spirits** estar muy animado; *adv.* alto; a precio subido; en alto; **to look — and low** buscar por todas partes; **high-grade** de calidad superior; **high-handed** arbitrario, despótico; **high-minded** magnánimo, orgulloso; **high-sounding** altisonante, rimbombante; **high-strung** muy tenso.

highland [háɪlǝnd] *s.* tierra montañosa; **the Highlands** las montañas de Escocia.

highlight [háɪlaɪt] *s.* lo más notable.
highly [háɪlɪ] *adv.* altamente; sumamente, muy; **— paid** muy bien pagado.
highness [háɪnɪs] *s.* altura; elevación; Alteza (*título*).
highway [háɪwe] *s.* camino real; carretera, calzada.
highwayman [háɪwemən] *s.* forajido, salteador de caminos, bandido.
hike [haɪk] *s.* caminata, paseo largo, *Am.* andada; *v.* dar (*o* echar) una caminata.
hill [hɪl] *s.* colina, collado, cerro; montoncillo de tierra; *Andes, Am.* loma; **ant —** hormiguero; **down—** cuesta abajo; **up—** cuesta arriba.
hillock [hílək] *s.* collado, otero, montecillo.
hillside [hílsaɪd] *s.* ladera.
hilltop [híltɑp] *s.* cumbre, cima (*de una colina*).
hilly [hílɪ] *adj.* montuoso; accidentado.
hilt [hɪlt] *s.* empuñadura, puño (*de una espada o daga*).
him [hɪm] *pron.* le; lo; él (*con preposición*).
himself [hɪmsélf] *pron.* él mismo; se (*como reflexivo*); a sí mismo; *véase* **herself.**
hind [haɪnd] *adj.* trasero; posterior; *s.* cierva; **—most** *adj.* último, postrero.
hinder [híndə] *v.* estorbar, impedir, obstruir.
hindrance [híndrəns] *s.* estorbo, obstáculo, impedimento.
hinge [hɪndʒ] *s.* gozne; bisagra; *v.* engoznar, poner goznes; **to — on** girar sobre; depender de.
hint [hɪnt] *s.* indirecta, insinuación; sugestión; **not to take the —** no darse por entendido; *v.* insinuar, intimar, sugerir indirectamente.
hip [hɪp] *s.* cadera.
hippopotamus [hɪpəpútəməs] *s.* hipopótamo.
hire [haɪr] *s.* (*rent*) alquiler; (*pay*) paga, sueldo; *v.* alquilar; emplear, dar empleo, *C.A., Ven., Col.* enganchar, *Am.* conchabar; **to — out** alquilarse, ponerse a servir a otro.
his [hɪz] *pron. pos.* suyo (suya, suyos, suyas), de él; el suyo (la suya, los suyos, las suyas); el (la, los, las) de él; **a friend of—** un amigo suyo; *adj.* su (sus), de él.
hiss [hɪs] *s.* silbido, chiflido; siseo; *v.* sisear, silbar, chiflar.
historian [hɪstórɪən] *s.* historiador.
historic [hɪstórɪk] *adj.* histórico.
historical [hɪstórɪkl] *adj.* histórico.
history [hístrɪ] *s.* historia.
histrionics [hɪstrɪániks] *s.* histrionismo.
hit [hɪt] *v.* pegar, golpear; dar (*un golpe*); dar en (*o* con); chocar; **they — it off well** se llevan bien, congenian; **to — the mark** acertar, atinar, dar en el blanco; **to — upon** dar con; encontrarse con, encontrar por casualidad; *pret. & p.p. de* **to hit**; *s.* golpe; choque; golpe de fortuna; pulla, dicharacho;

to be a great — ser un gran éxito; **to make a — with someone** caerle en gracia a una persona; **hit-and-run** *adj.* que abandona a su víctima atropellada.
hitch [hɪtʃ] *v.* atar, amarrar; enganchar; uncir (*bueyes*); dar un tirón; **to — one's chair nearer to** acercar su silla a; *s.* tirón; obstáculo, impedimento, tropiezo; enganche, enganchamiento.
hitchhike [hítʃhaɪk] *v.* viajar de gorra (*en automóvil*), *Méx.* irse o viajar de mosca; *Ch., Ríopl.* hacer dedo, ir a dedo.
hither [híðə] *adv.* acá; **— and thither** acá y allá.
hitherto [híðətu] *adv.* hasta aquí, hasta ahora, hasta hoy.
hive [haɪv] *s.* colmena; enjambre; **-s** ronchas (*de la piel*).
hoard [hord] *s.* tesoro escondido; acumulamiento secreto de provisiones; *v.* atesorar, guardar (*con avaricia*); acumular secretamente.
hoarse [hors] *adj.* bronco, áspero, ronco.
hoarseness [hórsnɪs] *s.* ronquera; carraspera.
hoary [hórɪ] *adj.* cano, encanecido, canoso.
hobble [hábl] *v.* (*limp*) cojear, renquear; (*tie*) maniatar o manear (*un animal*); (*impede*) impedir, estorbar; *s.* cojera; traba, maniota o manea (*cuerda con que se atan las manos de una bestia*).
hobby [hábɪ] *s.* afición; trabajo hecho por afición (*no por obligación*).
hobo [hóbo] *s.* vagabundo.
hodgepodge [hádʒpadʒ] *s.* mezcolanza, baturrillo.
hoe [ho] *s.* azada, azadón; *v.* cavar, escardar, limpiar con azadón.
hog [hag] *s.* puerco, cerdo, cochino; *v.* apropiárselo todo.
hoist [hoɪst] *v.* alzar, levantar; izar (*la bandera, las velas*); *s.* elevador, *Am.* malacate.
hold [hold] *v.* tener(se); retener; detener; tener cabida para; sostener; mantener(se); opinar; celebrar (*una reunión, etc.*); ocupar (*un puesto*); ser válido (*un argumento o regla*); **to — back someone** detener (*o* refrenar) a alguien; **to — forth** perorar, hablar largamente; **to — in place** sujetar, fijar; **to — off** mantener(se) a distancia; mantenerse alejado; **to — on** agarrar(se); asir(se); persistir; **— on!** ¡agárrese bien! ¡deténgase! ¡pare! **to — someone responsible** hacerle a uno responsable; **to — someone to his word** obligar a uno a cumplir su palabra; **to — oneself erect** tenerse o andar derecho; **to — one's own** mantenerse firme; **to — one's tongue** callarse; **to — out** continuar, durar; mantenerse firme; **to — over** aplazar; durar; continuar en un cargo; **to — still** estarse quieto o callado; **to — tight** apretar; **to — one's promise**

cumplir con la promesa; **to — up** levantar, alzar; detener; asaltar, atracar (*para robar*); **how much does it —?** ¿cuánto le cabe? *s.* agarro; dominio; influencia; autoridad; bodega (*de un barco*); cabina de carga (*de un aeroplano*); **to get — of** asir, agarrar; atrapar; **to take — of** coger, agarrar, asir.

holder [hóldɚ] *s.* (*person*) tenedor, poseedor; (*device*) receptáculo; cojinillo (*para coger un trasto caliente*); **cigarette —** boquilla; **pen—** portaplumas.

holdup [hóldʌp] *s.* asalto, atraco.

hole [hol] *s.* agujero; abertura; hoyo, hueco, cavidad; bache (*de un camino*); **swimming —** charco, remanso; **to be in a —** hallarse en un apuro o aprieto.

holiday [hálɪde] *s.* día de fiesta, día festivo, festividad; **-s** días de fiesta; vacaciones.

holiness [hólɪnɪs] *s.* santidad.

hollow [hálo] *adj.* (*empty*) hueco; vacío; (*concave*) cóncavo; hundido; (*insincere*) falso; *s.* hueco; hoyo; cavidad; concavidad; depresión; cañada, hondonada; *v.* ahuecar; excavar; ahondar.

holly [hálɪ] *s.* agrifolio, acebo.

holster [hólstɚ] *s.* pistolera, funda (*de pistola*).

holy [hólɪ] *adj.* santo; sagrado, sacro; **— water** agua bendita.

homage [hámɪdʒ] *s.* homenaje; reverencia, acatamiento; **to do —** acatar, rendir homenaje, honrar.

home [hom] *s.* casa, hogar; habitación, domicilio; **at —** en casa; *adj.* doméstico; casero; **— office** oficina matriz o central; **— rule** autonomía; **— run** *Méx., C.A., Ven., Col.* jonrón (*en beisbol*); **— stretch** último trecho (*de una carrera*); *adv.* a casa; en casa; **to strike —** herir en lo vivo; dar en el clavo o en el blanco.

homeland [hómlænd] *s.* tierra natal, suelo patrio.

homeless [hómlɪs] *adj.* sin casa; destituido.

homelike [hómlaɪk] *adj.* hogareño, cómodo.

homely [hómlɪ] *adj.* feo; llano; sencillo; casero, doméstico.

homemade [hómméd] *adj.* hecho en casa; doméstico, nacional, del país.

homesick [hómsɪk] *adj.* nostálgico.

homesickness [hómsɪknɪs] *s.* nostalgia.

homestead [hómstɛd] *s.* heredad; casa y terrenos adyacentes.

homeward [hómwɚd] *adv.* a casa; hacia la patria; **— voyage** retorno, viaje de vuelta.

homework [hómwɚk] *s.* trabajo de casa; trabajo hecho en casa.

homicide [háməsaɪd] *s.* homicidio; homicida, asesino.

homogeneous [homədʒínɪəs] *adj.* homogéneo.

homogenize [homádʒənaɪz] *v.* homogenizar.

homosexual [homəsékʃjʊl] *adj. & s.* homosexual.

hone [hon] *v.* amolar, asentar, afilar; *s.* piedra de afilar.

honest [ánɪst] *adj.* honrado, recto; genuino; **— goods** mercancías genuinas; **-ly** *adv.* honradamente; de veras.

honesty [ánɪstɪ] *s.* honradez, rectitud.

honey [hánɪ] *s.* miel; dulzura; querido, querida.

honeycomb [hánɪkom] *s.* panal.

honeyed [hánɪd] *adj.* meloso; dulce; melifluo.

honeymoon [hánɪmun] *s.* luna de miel; viaje de novios, viaje de bodas; *v.* pasar la luna de miel.

honeysuckle [hánɪsʌkl] *s.* madreselva.

honk [hɔŋk] *s.* pitazo (*de automóvil*); graznido (*voz del ganso*); **—** donar la bocina; graznar.

honor [ánɚ] *s.* honor; honra; señoría (*título*); **upon my —** sobre mi palabra; *v.* honrar; dar honra.

honorable [ánərəbl] *adj.* honorable; honroso; honrado.

honorary [ánərɛrɪ] *adj.* honorario, honorífico.

hood [hʊd] *s.* capucha, caperuza; capirote, cubierta (*del motor*); *v.* encapuchar, encapirotar.

hoodlum [húdləm] *s.* maleante; antisocial.

hoof [hʊf] *s.* casco, pezuña; pata (*de caballo, toro, etc.*).

hook [hʊk] *s.* gancho, garfio; anzuelo (*para pescar*); **— and eye** corchete; macho y hembra, **by — or crook** por la buena o por la mala, por angas o por mangas; **on his own —** por su propia cuenta; *v.* enganchar(se); abrochar(se); pescar, coger con anzuelo; robar, hurtar.

hooky [húkɪ] **to play —** hacer novillos, *Carib.* capear la escuela, *Méx.* pintar venado, *C.A., Ven., Col.* jubilarse; *Ríopl.* hacerse la rata (*la rabona*).

hoop [hup] *s.* aro; argolla; *v.* poner aro a; ceñir, cercar.

hoot [hut] *v.* ulular (*dícese del buho, lechuza, etc.*); rechiflar, ridiculizar; *s.* alarido, chillido.

hooting [hútɪŋ] *s.* grita, rechifla.

hop [hap] *s.* salto, brinco; baile; *v.* saltar; brincar.

hope [hop] *s.* esperanza; *v.* esperar; **to — for** esperar; **to — against —** esperar desesperando; esperar lo que no puede ser, esperar lo imposible.

hopeful [hópfəl] *adj.* esperanzado, lleno de esperanza; **a young —** un joven prometedor; **-ly** *adv.* con esperanza; con ansia; lleno de esperanza.

hopeless [hóplɪs] *adj.* sin esperanza, falto de esperanza, desesperanzado; desesperado; irremediable; **— cause** causa perdida; **— illness** enfermedad incurable; **it is —** no tiene remedio; **-ly** *adv.* sin esperanza, sin remedio.

hopelessness [hóplɪsnɪs] *s.* falta de esperanza; falta de remedio; desesperanza, desaliento.

horde [hord] *s.* horda; muchedumbre, gentío; enjambre.

horizon [hərɑ́ɪzn] *s.* horizonte.

horizontal [hɔrəzɑ́ntl] *adj.* horizontal.

horn [hɔrn] *s.* (*animal*) cuerno; asta; (*automobile*) bocina, klaxon, trompa; (*musical*) corneta; trompeta; **— of plenty** cuerno de la abundancia; *v.* acornear, dar cornadas; **to — in** entremeterse.

hornet [hɔ́rnɪt] *s.* avispón; **-'s nest** avispero.

horoscope [hɔ́rəskop] *s.* horóscopo.

horrible [hɔ́rəbl] *adj.* horrible; **horribly** *adv.* horriblemente.

horrid [hɔ́rɪd] *adj.* horrendo, horrible.

horrify [hɔ́rəfɑɪ] *v.* horrorizar, aterrorizar, espantar.

horror [hɔ́rɚ] *s.* horror.

hors d'oeuvre [ɔrdɝ́vrə] *s.* entremés; bocadillos.

horse [hɔrs] *s.* caballo; caballete (*de madera*), borriquete (*de carpinteros*); **saddle —** caballo de silla; **— dealer** chalán; **— race** carrera de caballos; **— sense** sentido común.

horseback [hɔ́rsbæk] *s.* lomo de caballo; **to ride —** montar a caballo, cabalgar, jinetear.

horsefly [hɔ́rsflɑɪ] *s.* tábano, mosca de caballo.

horselaugh [hɔ́rslæf] *s.* carcajada, risotada.

horseman [hɔ́rsmən] *s.* jinete.

horsemanship [hɔ́rsmənʃɪp] *s.* equitación.

horsepower [hɔ́rspɑʊɚ] *s.* caballo de fuerza.

horseradish [hɔ́rsrædɪʃ] *s.* rábano picante.

horseshoe [hɔ́rsʃu] *s.* herradura.

hose [hoz] *s.* medias; manga o manguera (*para regar*); **men's —** calcetines.

hosiery [hóʒrɪ] *s.* medias; calcetines; calcetería (*negocio*); **— shop** calcetería.

hospitable [hɑ́spɪtəbl] *adj.* hospitalario.

hospital [hɑ́spɪtl] *s.* hospital.

hospitality [hɑ́spɪtǽlətɪ] *s.* hospitalidad.

host [host] *s.* huésped (*el que hospeda*), anfitrión (*el que convida*); hospedero, mesonero; hueste; ejército, multitud; hostia; **sacred —** hostia consagrada.

hostage [hɑ́stɪdʒ] *s.* rehén (*persona que queda como prenda en poder del enemigo*).

hostess [hóstɪs] *s.* huéspeda (*la que hospeda o convida*).

hostile [hɑ́stɪl] *adj.* hostil.

hostility [hɑstɪ́lətɪ] *s.* hostilidad.

hot [hɑt] *adj.* caliente; caluroso; cálido; picante (*como el pimentón, chile, ají, etc.*); furioso; fresco, reciente; **—bed** semillero; **hot-headed** enojadizo, impetuoso; exaltado; **— house** invernáculo, invernadero; **it is — today** hace calor hoy.

hotel [hotɛ́l] *s.* hotel.

hotel-keeper [hotɛ́lkípɚ] *s.* hotelero.

hotly [hɑ́tlɪ] *adv.* calurosamente, con vehemencia.

hound [hɑʊnd] *s.* perro de busca, lebrel, galgo, sabueso, podenco; *v.* acosar, perseguir; azuzar, incitar.

hour [ɑʊr] *s.* hora; **— hand** horario.

hourly [ɑ́ʊrlɪ] *adv.* por horas; a cada hora; a menudo; *adj.* frecuente; por horas.

house [hɑʊs] *s.* (*residence*) casa; domicilio; (*legislature*) cámara, asamblea legislativa; **country —** casa de campo; **a full —** un lleno completo (*en el teatro*); [hɑʊz] *v.* alojar; hospedar.

household [hɑ́ʊshold] *s.* casa, familia; *adj.* casero; doméstico.

housekeeper [hɑ́ʊskipɚ] *s.* casera; ama de llaves; **to be a good —** ser una mujer hacendosa.

housekeeping [hɑ́ʊskipɪŋ] *s.* gobierno de casa; quehaceres domésticos.

housetop [hɑ́ʊstɑp] *s.* techumbre, tejado.

housewife [hɑ́ʊswɑɪf] *s.* mujer de su casa; madre de familia.

housework [hɑ́ʊswɝk] *s.* trabajo de casa; quehaceres domésticos.

housing [hɑ́ʊzɪŋ] *s.* viviendas; programa de construcción de viviendas.

hove [hov] *pret. & p.p. de* to **heave**.

hovel [hʌ́vl] *s.* choza, cabaña, *Carib., Ven.* bohío, *Méx.* jacal; cobertizo; *Ríopl.* tapera.

hover [hʌ́vɚ] *v.* cernerse (*como un pájaro*); vacilar; **to — around** revolotear; rondar.

how [hɑʊ] *adv.* cómo; **— beautiful!** ¡qué hermoso!; **— early (late, soon)** ¿cuándo? ¿a qué hora?; **— far is it?** ¿a qué distancia está? ¿cuánto dista de aquí?; **— long?** ¿cuánto tiempo?; **— many?** ¿cuántos? **— much is it?** ¿cuánto es? ¿a cómo se vende? ¿cuál es el precio?; **— old are you?** ¿cuántos años tiene Vd.? **no matter — much** por mucho que; **he knows — difficult it is** él sabe lo difícil que es; él sabe cuán difícil es.

however [hɑʊɛ́vɚ] *adv. & conj.* sin embargo, no obstante, con todo, empero; **— difficult it may be** por muy difícil que sea; **— much** por mucho que.

howl [hɑʊl] *s.* aullido, alarido, chillido, grito; *v.* aullar; chillar, dar alaridos; gritar.

hub [hʌb] *s.* cubo (*de una rueda*); eje, centro de actividad.

hubbub [hʌ́bʌb] *s.* ajetreo; barullo.

huckster [hʌ́kstɚ] *s.* vendedor ambulante.

huddle [hʌ́dl] *s.* montón, confusión, tropel; **to be in a —** estar agrupados (*en futbol para planear una jugada*); **to get in a —** agruparse (*para aconsejarse o planear algo*); *v.* amontonar(se); acurrucarse.

hue [hju] *s.* tinte, matiz.

huff [hʌf] *s.* enojo, rabieta; **to get into a —** enojarse.

hug [hʌg] *v.* abrazar, estrechar; **to —**

the coast costear; s. abrazo fuerte.

huge [hjudʒ] adj. enorme; descomunal.

hull [hʌl] s. casco (de una nave); armazón (de una aeronave); vaina, hollejo (de ciertas legumbres); v. mondar, pelar desvainar, deshollejar.

hum [hʌm] v. canturrear (o canturriar), tararear; zumbar (dícese de insectos, máquinaria, etc.); **to — to sleep** arrullar; s. canturreo, tarareo; zumbido; interj. ¡hum!; ¡ejém!

human [hjúmən] adj. humano; s. ser humano.

humane [hjumén] adj. humano; humanitario.

humanism [hjúmənizm] s. humanismo.

humanitarian [hjumænətériən] adj. humanitario; s. filántropo.

humanity [hjumǽnɪtɪ] s. humanidad; **-ies** humanidades.

humble [hámbl] adj. humilde; v. humillar; **humbly** adv. humildemente, con humildad.

humbleness [hámblnɪs] s. humildad.

humid [hjúmɪd] adj. húmedo.

humidify [hjumídəfaɪ] v. humedecer.

humidity [hjumídətɪ] d. humedad.

humiliate [hjumíljet] v. humillar.

humiliation [hjumɪliéʃən] s. humillación.

humility [hjumílətɪ] s. humildad.

hummingbird [hámɪŋbɜd] s. colibrí, pájaro mosca, Méx. chuparrosa, Am. chupaflor, Am. guainumbi; Riopl., Ch. picaflor.

humor [hjúmə] s. humor, humorismo, gracia; capricho; **out of —** de mal humor, malhumorado, disgustado; v. seguir el humor (a una persona), complacer; mimar.

humorous [hjúmərəs] adj. humorístico, gracioso, cómico, chistoso.

hump [hʌmp] s. joroba, corcova, giba; v. encorvarse.

humpback [hámpbæk] = **hunchback**.

hunch [hʌntʃ] s. joroba, corcova, giba; presentimiento, corazonada; v. encorvar (la espalda).

hunchback [hántʃbæk] s. joroba; jorobado.

hundred [hándrəd] adj. cien(to); s. ciento; **-s** centenares, cientos.

hundredth [hándrədθ] adj. centésimo.

hung [hʌŋ] pret. & p.p. de **to hang**.

hunger [háŋgə] s. hambre; v. tener hambre, estar hambriento; **to — for** ansiar, anhelar.

hungrily [háŋgrɪlɪ] adv. con hambre, hambrientamente.

hungry [háŋgrɪ] adj. hambriento; **to be — tener hambre.

hunk- [hʌŋk] s. pedazo grande; mendrugo (de pan).

hunt [hʌnt] v. cazar; perseguir; buscar; escudriñar; **to — down** dar caza a; seguir la pista de; **to — for** buscar; s. caza, cacería; busca, búsqueda; perseguimiento.

hunter [hántə] s. cazador; buscador; perro de caza, perro de busca.

huntsman [hántsmən] s. cazador.

hurl [hɜl] v. arrojar, lanzar.

hurrah [hərɔ́] interj. ¡hurra! ¡viva!; v. vitorear.

hurricane [háɪken] s. huracán.

hurried [hɜɪd] adj. apresurado; **-ly** adv. de prisa, apresuradamente, a escape.

hurry [hɜɪ] v. apresurar(se); precipitar(se); dar(se) prisa; apurarse; correr; **to — in (out)** entrar (salir) de prisa; **to — up** apresurar(se); dar(se) prisa; s. prisa; precipitación; **to be in a — tener prisa, ir de prisa, estar de prisa.

hurt [hɜt] v. hacer daño; dañar; perjudicar; herir; lastimar; doler; **to — one's feelings** darle a uno que sentir; lastimar a uno; **my tooth -s** me duele la muela; pret. & p.p. de **to hurt**; s. daño; herida; lesión; dolor.

husband [házbənd] s. marido, esposo.

hush [hʌʃ] v. acallar, aquietar; callar(se); —! ¡chitón! ¡silencio! ¡cállese! ¡quieto!; **to — up a scandal** encubrir un escándalo; s. silencio, quietud.

husk [hʌsk] s. cáscara, hollejo, vaina; v. mondar, pelar, deshollejar.

husky [háskɪ] adj. ronco; forzudo, fuerte; cascarudo.

hustle [hásl] v. apresurar(se); apurarse; menear(se); atropellar; s. prisa, apresuramiento, meneo; actividad; **— and bustle** vaivén.

hut [hʌt] s. choza, cabaña, Am. bohío.

hyacinth [háɪəsɪnθ] s. jacinto.

hybrid [háɪbrɪd] adj. híbrido.

hydraulic [haɪdrɔ́lɪk] adj. hidráulico.

hydroelectric [haɪdroiléktrɪk] adj. hidroeléctrico.

hydrogen [háɪdrədʒen] s. hidrógeno.

hydrophobia [haɪdrofóbɪə] s. hidrofobia.

hydroplane [háɪdræplen] s. hidroplano, hidroavión.

hygiene [háɪdʒin] s. higiene.

hymn [hɪm] s. himno.

hyphen [háɪfən] s. guión.

hypnosis [hɪpnósɪs] s. hipnosis.

hypocrisy [hɪpákrəsɪ] s. hipocresía.

hypocrite [hípkrɪt] s. hipócrita.

hypocritical [hɪpəkrítɪk] adj. hipócrita.

hypothesis [haɪpáθəsɪs] s. hipótesis.

hysterical [hɪstérɪk] adj. histérico.

I

I [aɪ] pron. pers. yo.

Iberian [aɪbírɪən] adj. ibérico, ibero.

ice [aɪs] s. (solid) hielo; (food) helado; sorbete; **— cream** helado; **ice-cream parlor** Am. heladería; **— skates** patines de cuchilla; **— water** agua helada; v. helar; escarchar, alfeñicar, cubrir con escarcha (un pastel).

iceberg [áɪsbɜg] s. montaña de hielo, témpano.

icebox [áɪsbaks] s. nevera, Am. refrigerador.

iceman [áɪsmæn] s. vendedor de hielo.

icicle [áɪsɪkl] s. carámbano.

iconoclasm [aɪkúnəklæzəm] s. iconoclasmo.

icy [áɪsɪ] adj. helado, frío; congelado; cubierto de hielo.

idea [aɪdíə] s. idea.

ideal [aɪdíəl] adj. & s. ideal.

idealism [aɪdíəlɪzəm] s. idealismo.

idealist [aɪdíəlɪst] s. idealista.

idealistic [aɪdɪəlístɪk] adj. idealista.

identical [aɪdéntɪk] adj. idéntico.

identify [aɪdéntəfaɪ] v. identificar.

identity [aɪdéntətɪ] s. identidad.

ideology [aɪdɪólədʒɪ] s. ideología.

idiom [ídɪəm] s. modismo, idiotismo.

idiosyncrasy [ɪdɪosínkrəsɪ] s. idiosincrasia.

idiot [ídɪət] s. idiota.

idiotic [ɪdɪútɪk] adj. idiota.

idle [áɪdl] adj. ocioso; perezoso, holgazán; vano; desocupado; v. holgazanear; perder el tiempo; funcionar (el motor solo, sin engranar); **idly** adv. ociosamente; inútilmente; perezosamente.

idleness [áɪdlnɪs] s. ociosidad; ocio, desocupación; pereza, holgazanería.

idler [áɪdlɚ] s. holgazán, haragán.

idol [áɪdl] s. ídolo.

idolatry [aɪdúlətrɪ] s. idolatría.

idolize [áɪdlaɪz] v. idolatrar.

idyl [áɪdl] s. idilio.

if [ɪf] conj. si.

ignite [ɪgnáɪt] v. encender(se), inflamar(se); prender, pegar fuego a.

ignition [ɪgnɪʃən] s. ignición, encendido (de un motor); — **switch** interruptor de encendido, Méx., C.A., Ven., Carib. switch de ignición.

ignoble [ɪgnóbl] adj. innoble; bajo, vil.

ignorance [ígnərəns] s. ignorancia.

ignorant [ígnərənt] adj. ignorante.

ignore [ɪgnór] v. no hacer caso de, desatender; desairar.

ill [ɪl] adj. enfermo; malo; — **nature** mal genio, mala índole; — **will** mala voluntad, ojeriza, inquina; s. mal; enfermedad; calamidad, infortunio; adv. mal, malamente; — **at ease** inquieto, intranquilo; **ill-bred** mal criado; **ill-clad** mal vestido; **ill-humored** malhumorado; **ill-mannered** descortés, grosero; **ill-natured** mala índole, Ven., Col., Méx. mal genioso; **ill-advised** mal aconsejado.

illegal [ɪlíg] adj. ilegal; ilícito.

illegitimate [ɪlɪdʒítəmɪt] adj. ilegítimo; bastardo.

illicit [ɪlísɪt] adj. ilícito.

illiteracy [ɪlítərəsɪ] s. analfabetismo.

illiterate [ɪlítərɪt] adj. & s. analfabeto.

illness [ílnɪs] s. mal, enfermedad.

illuminate [ɪlúmənet] v. iluminar; alumbrar; esclarecer.

illumination [ɪlumənéʃən] s. iluminación; alumbrado.

illusion [ɪlúʒən] s. ilusión.

illusive [ɪlúsɪv] adj. ilusorio, ilusivo, falaz.

illusory [ɪlúsərɪ] adj. ilusorio, ilusivo, engañoso.

illustrate [ɪləstrét] v. ilustrar; esclarecer.

illustration [ɪləstréʃən] s. ilustración; grabado, estampa; aclaración, esclarecimiento.

illustrator [íləstretɚ] s. ilustrador.

illustrious [ɪlʎstrɪəs] adj. ilustre.

image [ímɪdʒ] s. imagen.

imagery [ímɪdʒrɪ] s. conjunto de imágenes, figuras; fantasía.

imaginary [ɪmædʒənɛrɪ] adj. imaginario.

imagination [ɪmædʒənéʃən] s. imaginación; imaginativa.

imaginative [ɪmædʒənetɪv] adj. imaginativo.

imagine [ɪmædʒɪn] v. imaginar(se); figurarse.

imbecile [ímbəsɪl] adj. & s. imbécil.

imbibe [ɪmbáɪb] v. embeber, absorber; beber.

imbue [ɪmbjú] v. imbuir, infundir; impregnar, empapar.

imitate [ímətet] v. imitar; remedar.

imitation [ɪmətéʃən] s. imitación; remedo; adj. imitado, de imitación.

imitator [ímətetɚ] s. imitador; remedador.

immaculate [ɪmækjəlɪt] adj. inmaculado, sin mancha.

immaterial [ɪmətíríəl] adj. inmaterial, espiritual; **it is — to me** me es indiferente.

immediate [ɪmídɪɪt] adj. inmediato; próximo; **-ly** adv. inmediatamente; en seguida; al punto, en el acto, al instante.

immense [ɪméns] adj. inmenso.

immensity [ɪménsətɪ] s. inmensidad.

immerse [ɪmɝs] v. sumergir, sumir.

immigrant [íməgrənt] adj. & s. inmigrante.

immigrate [íməgret] v. inmigrar.

immigration [ɪməgréʃən] s. inmigración.

imminent [ímənənt] adj. inminente.

immobile [ɪmóbɪl] adj. inmóbil.

immodest [ɪmádɪst] adj. deshonesto, impúdico, indecente.

immoral [ɪmórəl] adj. inmoral; licencioso.

immorality [ɪmorǽlətɪ] s. inmoralidad.

immortal [ɪmórtl] adj. & s. inmortal.

immortality [ɪmortǽlətɪ] s. inmortalidad.

immovable [ɪmúvəbl] adj. inmovible (o inamovible); inmóvil; inmutable.

immune [ɪmjún] adj. inmune.

immunity [ɪmjúnətɪ] s. inmunidad.

immutable [ɪmjútəbl] adj. inmutable.

imp [ɪmp] s. diablillo.

impair [ɪmpér] v. dañar, perjudicar, menoscabar, desvirtuar, debilitar.

impairment [ɪmpérmənt] s. menoscabo; perjuicio; deterioro.

impart [ɪmpárt] v. impartir, dar, comunicar.

impartial [ɪmpárʃəl] adj. imparcial.

impartiality [ɪmparʃǽlətɪ] s. imparcialidad.

impassible [ɪmpǽsəbl] adj. impasible.

impassioned [ɪmpǽʃənd] adj. apasionado, vehemente, ardiente.

impassive [ɪmpǽsɪv] *adj.* impasible.

impatience [ɪmpéʃəns] *s.* impaciencia.

impatient [ɪmpéʃənt] *adj.* impaciente.

impeach [ɪmpítʃ] *v.* demandar o acusar formalmente (*a un alto funcionario de gobierno*); **to — a person's honor** poner en tela de juicio el honor de uno.

impede [ɪmpíd] *v.* impedir, estorbar, obstruir.

impediment [ɪmpédəmənt] *s.* impedimento, obstáculo, estorbo; traba.

impel [ɪmpél] *v.* impeler, impulsar.

impending [ɪmpéndɪŋ] *adj.* inminente, amenazador.

imperative [ɪmpérətɪv] *adj.* imperativo; imperioso, urgente; *s.* imperativo.

imperceptible [ɪmpəséptəbl] *adj.* imperceptible.

imperfect [ɪmpáfɪkt] *adj.* imperfecto; defectuoso; *s.* imperfecto (*tiempo del verbo*).

imperial [ɪmpíriəl] *adj.* imperial.

imperialism [ɪmpíriəlɪzm] *s.* imperialismo.

imperil [ɪmpérəl] *v.* poner en peligro, arriesgar.

imperious [ɪmpíriəs] *adj.* imperioso; urgente.

impersonal [ɪmpásn̩l] *adj.* impersonal.

impersonate [ɪmpásṇet] *v.* representar (*un personaje*); remedar, imitar; fingirse otro, pretender ser otro.

impertinence [ɪmpátn̩əns] *s.* impertinencia; insolencia, descaro.

impertinent [ɪmpátṇənt] *adj.* impertinente; insolente, descarado.

impervious [ɪmpávɪəs] *adj.* impermeable; impenetrable; **— to reason** refractario, testarudo.

impetuous [ɪmpétʃʊəs] *adj.* impetuoso.

impetus [ɪmpətəs] *s.* ímpetu.

impious [ɪmpíəs] *adj.* impío.

implacable [ɪmplékəbl] *adj.* implacable.

implant [ɪmplǽnt] *v.* implantar, plantar; inculcar, infundir.

implement [ɪmpləmənt] *s.* herramienta, instrumento; **-s** utensilios, aperos, enseres.

implicate [ɪmplɪket] *v.* implicar, envolver, enredar.

implicit [ɪmplísɪt] *adj.* implícito.

implore [ɪmplór] *v.* implorar, rogar; suplicar.

imply [ɪmpláɪ] *v.* implicar; querer decir; insinuar.

impolite [ɪmpəláɪt] *adj.* descortés.

import [ɪmport] *s.* significado, significación, sentido; importancia; importación; **-s** artículos importados; [ɪmpórt] *v.* importar; significar, querer decir.

importance [ɪmpórtṇs] *s.* importancia.

important [ɪmpórtṇt] *adj.* importante.

impose [ɪmpóz] *v.* imponer; **to — upon** abusar de (*la amistad, hospitalidad, confianza de alguien*); engañar.

imposing [ɪmpózɪŋ] *adj.* imponente; impresionante.

imposition [ɪmpəzíʃən] *s.* imposición; carga, impuesto; abuso (*de confianza*).

impossibility [ɪmpɑsəbílətɪ] *s.* imposibilidad.

impossible [ɪmpásəbl] *adj.* imposible.

impostor [ɪmpástə] *s.* impostor, embaucador.

imposture [ɪmpástʃə] *s.* impostura, fraude, engaño.

impotence [ɪmpətəns] *s.* impotencia.

impotent [ɪmpətənt] *adj.* impotente.

impoverish [ɪmpávərɪʃ] *v.* empobrecer.

impregnate [ɪmprégnet] *v.* impregnar; empapar; empreñar.

impress [ɪmprɛs] *s.* impresión, marca, señal, huella; [ɪmprés] *v.* imprimir, estampar, marcar, grabar; impresionar.

impression [ɪmpréʃən] *s.* impresión; marca.

impressive [ɪmprésɪv] *adj.* impresionante; imponente.

imprint [ɪmprint] *s.* impresión; pie de imprenta; [ɪmprínt] *v.* imprimir; estampar.

imprison [ɪmprísṇ] *v.* aprisionar, encarcelar.

imprisonment [ɪmprízṇmənt] *s.* prisión, encarcelación o encarcelamiento.

improbable [ɪmprábəbl] *adj.* improbable.

impromptu [ɪmprámptu] *adv.* de improviso.

improper [ɪmprápə] *adj.* impropio.

improve [ɪmprúv] *v.* mejorar(se); **to — upon** mejorar; **to — one's time** aprovechar el tiempo.

improvement [ɪmprúvmənt] *s.* mejoramiento; mejora; progreso, adelanto; mejoría (*de una enfermedad*).

improvise [ɪmprəvaɪz] *v.* improvisar.

imprudent [ɪmprúdṇt] *adj.* imprudente.

impudence [ɪmpjədəns] *s.* impudencia, descaro, insolencia.

impudent [ɪmpjədənt] *adj.* impudente, descarado, insolente.

impulse [ɪmpʌls] *s.* impulso; ímpetu; inclinación; **to act on —** obrar impulsivamente.

impulsive [ɪmpʌlsɪv] *adj.* impulsivo.

impunity [ɪmpjúnətɪ] *s.* impunidad, falta o exención de castigo.

impure [ɪmpjúr] *adj.* impuro; sucio; adulterado.

impurity [ɪmpjúrətɪ] *s.* impureza.

impute [ɪmpjút] *v.* imputar, achacar, atribuir.

in [ɪn] *prep.* en; dentro de; de (*después de un superlativo*); **— haste** de prisa; **— the morning** por (o en) la mañana; **— writing** por escrito; **at two — the morning** a las dos de la mañana; **dressed — white** vestido de blanco; **the tallest — his class** el más alto de su clase; **to come — a week** venir de hoy en ocho días, venir dentro de ocho días; *adv.* dentro; adentro; en casa; **to be — and out** estar entrando y saliendo; **to be all —** no poder más, estar rendido de can-

IC

sancio; **to be — with someone** estar asociado con alguien; disfrutar el aprecio de una persona; **to come —** entrar; **to have it — for someone** tenerle ojeriza a una persona; **to put — meter; is the train —?** ¿ha llegado el tren?

inability [ɪnəbílətɪ] s. inhabilidad, incapacidad.

inaccessible [ɪnəksésəbl] adj. inaccesible; inasequible.

inaccurate [ɪnǽkjərɪt] adj. inexacto, impreciso, incorrecto.

inactive [ɪnǽktɪv] adj. inactivo; inerte.

inactivity [ɪnæktívɪtɪ] s. inactividad, inacción, inercia.

inadequate [ɪnǽdəkwɪt] adj. inadecuado; insuficiente.

inadvertent [ɪnədvə́tn̩t] adj. inadvertido; descuidado; **-ly** adv. inadvertidamente; descuidadamente.

inadvisable [ɪnədváɪzəbl] adj. imprudente.

inanimate [ɪnǽnəmɪt] adj. inanimado.

inasmuch [ɪnəzmʌ́tʃ]: **— as** visto que, puesto que; en cuanto.

inattentive [ɪnəténtɪv] adj. desatento.

inaugurate [ɪnɔ́gjəret] v. inaugurar, iniciar; investir de una dignidad o cargo.

inauguration [ɪnɔgjəréʃən] s. inauguración.

inboard [ínbord] adj. interior.

inborn [ínbɔ́rn] adj. innato, connatural.

incandescent [ɪnkəndésn̩t] adj. incandescente, candente.

incapable [ɪnképəbl] adj. incapaz.

incapacitate [ɪnkəpǽsɪtet] v. incapacitar.

incendiary [ɪnséndɪerɪ] adj. incendiario; **— bomb** bomba incendiaria.

incense [ínsɛns] s. incienso; [ínsɛns] v. inflamar, exasperar.

incentive [ɪnséntɪv] s. incentivo, estímulo.

incessant [ɪnsésn̩t] adj. incesante, continuo.

inch [ɪntʃ] s. pulgada (2.54 centímetros); **by -es** poco a poco, gradualmente; **every — a man** nada menos que todo un hombre; **to be within an —** of estar a dos pulgadas de, estar muy cerca de; v. avanzar muy despacio (por pulgadas).

incidence [ínsɪdəns] s. incidencia.

incident [ínsədənt] s. incidente, suceso, acontecimiento.

incidental [ɪnsədéntl] adj. incidental, accidental; contingente; **-s** s. pl. gastos imprevistos; **-ly** adv. incidentalmente; de paso.

incipient [ɪnsípɪənt] adj. incipiente.

incision [ɪnsíʒən] s. incisión.

incite [ɪnsáɪt] v. incitar.

inclement [ɪnklémənt] adj. inclemente.

inclination [ɪnklənéʃən] s. inclinación.

incline [ínklaɪn] s. declive, pendiente, cuesta; [ɪnkláɪn] v. inclinar(se).

inclose = enclose.

inclosure = enclosure.

include [ɪnklúd] v. incluir, encerrar;

abarcar.

inclusive [ɪnklúsɪv] adj. inclusivo; **from Monday to Friday —** del lunes al viernes inclusive.

incoherent [ɪnkohírənt] adj. incoherente, inconexo.

income [ínkʌm] s. renta, rédito, ingreso, entrada; **— tax** impuesto sobre rentas.

incomparable [ɪnkámpərəbl] adj. incomparable, sin par, sin igual.

incompatible [ɪnkəmpǽtəbl] adj. incompatible.

incompetent [ɪnkámpətənt] adj. incompetente.

incomplete [ɪnkəmplít] adj. incompleto.

incomprehensible [ɪnkʌmprɪhénsəbl] adj. incomprensible.

inconceivable [ɪnkənsívəbl] adj. inconcebible.

inconsiderate [ɪnkənsídərɪt] adj. inconsiderado, falto de miramiento.

inconsistency [ɪnkənsístənsɪ] s. inconsecuencia; falta de uniformidad (en la aplicación de una regla o principio).

inconsistent [ɪnkənsístənt] adj. inconsecuente; falto de uniformidad.

inconspicuous [ɪnkənspíkjuəs] adj. poco llamativo.

inconstancy [ɪnkánstənsɪ] s. inconstancia, mudanza.

inconstant [ɪnkánstənt] adj. inconstante, mudable, voluble.

incontestable [ɪnkəntéstəbl] adj. incontestable.

inconvenience [ɪnkənvínjəns] s. inconveniencia; molestia; v. incomodar; molestar.

inconvenient [ɪnkənvínjənt] adj. inconveniente; inoportuno.

incorporate [ɪnkɔ́rpərɪt] adj. incorporado; asociado; [ɪnkɔ́rpəret] v. incorporar; incorporarse, asociarse (para formar un cuerpo).

incorrect [ɪnkərékt] adj. incorrecto.

incorrigible [ɪnkɔ́rɪdʒəbl] adj. incorregible.

increase [íŋkrɪs] s. aumento; acrecentamiento; crecimiento; incremento; [íŋkrɪs] v. aumentar(se); acrecentar(se), crecer.

increasingly [ɪnkrísɪŋlɪ] adv. más y más; cada vez más.

incredible [ɪnkrédəbl] adj. increíble.

incredulity [ɪnkrədúlɪtɪ] s. incredulidad.

incredulous [ɪnkrédʒələs] adj. incrédulo, descreído.

increment [íŋkrəmənt] s. incremento.

incriminate [ɪnkrímənet] v. acriminar.

incubator [íŋkjubetə] s. incubadora.

inculcate [ɪnkʌ́lket] v. inculcar, infundir.

incur [ɪnkə́] v. incurrir en.

incurable [ɪnkjúrəbl] adj. incurable, irremediable; s. incurable.

indebted [ɪndétɪd] adj. adeudado, endeudado; obligado, agradecido.

indebtedness [ɪndétɪdnɪs] s. deuda; obligación.

indecency [ɪndísɪnsɪ] s. indecencia.

indecent [ɪndísɪnt] adj. indecente.

indecision [ɪndəsíʒən] s. indecisión.

indeed [ɪndíd] adv. en verdad, a la verdad; de veras; realmente.

indefensible [ɪndɪfénsəbl] adj. indefendible.

indefinite [ɪndéfənɪt] adj. indefinido.

indelible [ɪndéləbl] adj. indeleble.

indelicate [ɪndéləkət] adj. indelicado, indecoroso.

indemnify [ɪndémnəfaɪ] v. indemnizar.

indemnity [ɪndémnətɪ] s. indemnización.

indent [ɪndént] v. dentar, endentar; sangrar (*comenzar un renglón más adentro que los otros*).

independence [ɪndɪpéndəns] s. independencia.

independent [ɪndɪpéndənt] adj. independiente. •

indescribable [ɪndɪskráɪbəbl] adj. indescriptible.

index [índeks] s. índice; v. alfabetizar, ordenar alfabéticamente; poner en un índice; — **finger** índice.

Indian [índɪən] adj. & s. indio; — **Ocean** Océano Indico.

indicate [índəket] v. indicar.

indication [ɪndəkéʃən] s. indicación.

indicative [ɪndíkətɪv] adj. & s. indicativo.

indict [ɪndáɪt] v. procesar, demandar (*ante un juez*); enjuiciar, formar causa a.

indictment [ɪndáɪtmənt] s. acusación (*hecha por el Gran Jurado*), denuncia, proceso judicial.

indifference [ɪndífrəns] s. indiferencia; apatía.

indifferent [ɪndífrənt] adj. indiferente; apático.

indigenous [ɪndídʒənəs] adj. indígena, autóctono, nativo.

indigent [índədʒənt] adj. & s. indigente.

indigestion [ɪndədʒéstʃən] s. indigestión.

indignant [ɪndígnənt] adj. indignado; **-ly** adv. con indignación.

indignation [ɪndɪgnéʃən] s. indignación.

indignity [ɪndígnətɪ] s. indignidad, afrenta.

indigo [índɪgo] s. índigo, añil; — **blue** azul de añil.

indirect [ɪndərékt] adj. indirecto.

indiscreet [ɪndɪskrít] adj. indiscreto.

indiscretion [ɪndɪskréʃən] s. indiscreción.

indispensable [ɪndɪspénsəbl] adj. indispensable.

indispose [ɪndɪspóz] v. indisponer.

indisposed [ɪndɪspózd] adj. indispuesto.

indisposition [ɪndɪspəzíʃən] s. indisposición; malestar.

indistinct [ɪndɪstíŋkt] adj. indistinto.

individual [ɪndəvídʒʊəl] adj. individual; s. individuo, sujeto, persona.

individuality [ɪndəvɪdʒʊǽlətɪ] s. individualidad; individuo, persona.

indivisible [ɪndəvízəbl] adj. indivisible.

indoctrinate [ɪndáktrɪnet] v. adoctrinar.

indolence [índələns] s. indolencia, desidia, apatía.

indolent [índələnt] adj. indolente, desidioso, apático.

indomitable [ɪndámətəbl] adj. indomable.

indoor [índor] adj. interior, de casa.

indoors [índórz] adv. dentro, en casa; adentro; **to go —** entrar; ir adentro.

indorse = endorse.

indorsement = endorsement.

indorser = endorser.

induce [ɪndjús] v. inducir.

inducement [ɪndjúsmənt] s. aliciente, incentivo.

induct [ɪndʌkt] v. introducir; iniciar; instalar (*en un cargo*).

induction [ɪndʌkʃən] s. inducción; instalación (*en un cargo*).

indulge [ɪndʌldʒ] v. gratificar, complacer; seguir el humor a (*una persona*); mimar, consentir (*a un niño*); **to — in** darse a, entregarse a (*un placer*); darse el lujo de, permitirse el placer de.

indulgence [ɪndʌldʒəns] s. indulgencia; complacencia (*en el vicio o placer*).

indulgent [ɪndʌldʒənt] adj. indulgente.

industrial [ɪndʌstrɪəl] adj. industrial.

industrialist [ɪndʌstrɪəlɪst] s. industrial; fabricante.

industrious [ɪndʌstrɪəs] adj. industrioso, aplicado, diligente.

industry [índəstrɪ] s. industria; aplicación, diligencia.

ineffable [ɪnéfəbl] adj. inefable.

ineffective [ɪnəféktɪv] adj. inefectivo, ineficaz.

inefficient [ɪnɪfíʃənt] adj. ineficaz.

ineligible [ɪnélədʒəbl] adj. inelegible.

inequality [ɪnɪkwálətɪ] s. desigualdad; disparidad.

inert [ɪnɚt] adj. inerte.

inertia [ɪnɚʃə] s. inercia.

inestimable [ɪnéstəməbl] adj. inestimable.

inevitable [ɪnévətəbl] adj. inevitable.

inexhaustible [ɪnɪgzɔ́stəbl] adj. inagotable.

inexpedient [ɪnɛkspídjənt] adj. inoportuno; imprudente.

inexpensive [ɪnɪkspénsɪv] adj. económico, barato.

inexperience [ɪnɪkspírɪəns] s. inexperiencia, falta de experiencia.

inexperienced [ɪnɪkspírɪənst] adj. inexperto, falto de experiencia.

inexplicable [ɪnéksplɪkəbl] adj. inexplicable.

inexpressible [ɪnɪksprésəbl] adj. inexpresable, indecible, inefable.

infallible [ɪnfǽləbl] adj. infalible.

infamous [ínfəməs] adj. infame, ignominioso.

infamy [ínfəmɪ] s. infamia.

infancy [ínfənsɪ] s. infancia.

infant [ínfənt] s. infante, bebé, criatura, nene.

IN

infantile [ínfəntail] *adj.* infantil.

infantry [ínfəntrɪ] *s.* infantería.

infect [ɪnfékt] *v.* infectar, inficionar; contagiar; contaminar.

infection [ɪnfékʃən] *s.* infección; contagio.

infectious [ɪnfékʃəs] *adj.* infeccioso; contagioso.

infer [ɪnfɚ] *v.* inferir, deducir, colegir.

inference [ínfərəns] *s.* inferencia, deducción.

inferior [ɪnfíriɚ] *adj. & s.* inferior.

inferiority [ɪnfɪrɪórətɪ] *s.* inferioridad; — **complex** complejo de inferioridad.

infernal [ɪnfɚnl] *adj.* infernal.

inferno [ɪnfɚno] *s.* infierno.

infest [ɪnfést] *v.* infestar, plagar.

infidel [ínfədl] *adj. & s.* infiel.

infiltrate [ɪnfíltret] *v.* infiltrar(se).

infinite [ínfɪnɪt] *adj. & s.* infinito.

infinitive [ɪnfínɪtɪv] *adj. & s.* infinitivo.

infinity [ɪnfínətɪ] *s.* infinidad; infinito.

infirm [ɪnfɚm] *adj.* enfermizo, achacoso, débil.

infirmary [ɪnfɚmərɪ] *s.* enfermería.

infirmity [ɪnfɚmətɪ] *s.* enfermedad, achaque; flaqueza.

inflame [ɪnflém] *v.* inflamar(se); enardecer(se).

inflammation [ɪnfləméʃən] *s.* inflamación.

inflate [ɪnflét] *v.* inflar; hinchar.

inflation [ɪnfléʃən] *s.* inflación; hinchazón.

inflection [ɪnflékʃən] *s.* inflexión.

inflict [ɪnflíkt] *v.* infligir, imponer.

influence [ínflʋəns] *s.* influencia, influjo; *v.* influir en; ejercer influencia o influjo sobre.

influential [ɪnflʋénʃəl] *adj.* influyente.

influenza [ɪnflʋénzə] *s.* influenza, gripe.

influx [ínflʌks] *s.* entrada, afluencia (*de gente*).

infold [ɪnfóld] *v.* envolver; abrazar; abarcar.

inform [ɪnfɔrm] *v.* informar; enterar; avisar; **to — against** delatar a, denunciar a.

informal [ɪnfɔrml] *adj.* informal, sin ceremonia; — **visit** visita de confianza; **-ly** *adv.* informalmente, sin ceremonia, de confianza.

informant [ɪnfɔrmənt] *s.* informante.

information [ɪnfɚméʃən] *s.* (*service*) información; (*details*) informes; (*news*) noticias; (*knowledge*) conocimientos, saber.

infraction [ɪnfrǽkʃən] *s.* infracción.

infringe [ɪnfríndʒ] *v.* infringir, violar; **to — upon** violar.

infuriate [ɪnfjúriet] *v.* enfurecer.

infuse [ɪnfjúz] *v.* infundir; inculcar.

ingenious [ɪndʒínjəs] *adj.* ingenioso.

ingenuity [ɪndʒənúətɪ] *s.* ingeniosidad.

ingratitude [ɪngrǽtətjud] *s.* ingratitud.

ingredient [ɪngrídɪənt] *s.* ingrediente.

inhabit [ɪnhǽbɪt] *v.* habitar, vivir en, residir en.

inhabitant [ɪnhǽbətənt] *s.* habitante.

inhale [ɪnhél] *v.* inhalar, aspirar, inspirar.

inherent [ɪnhírənt] *adj.* inherente.

inherit [ɪnhérɪt] *v.* heredar.

inheritance [ɪnhérətəns] *s.* herencia.

inhibit [ɪnhíbɪt] *v.* inhibir, cohibir, refrenar, reprimir; impedir.

inhibition [ɪnɪbíʃən] *s.* inhibición, cohibición; prohibición, restricción.

inhospitable [ɪnháspɪtəbl] *adj.* inhospitalario.

inhuman [ɪnhjúmən] *adj.* inhumano.

inimitable [ɪnímətəbl] *adj.* inimitable.

iniquity [ɪníkwətɪ] *s.* iniquidad, maldad.

initial [ɪníʃəl] *adj. & s.* inicial; *v.* marcar o firmar con iniciales.

initiate [ɪníʃɪet] *v.* iniciar.

initiative [ɪníʃɪetɪv] *s.* iniciativa.

inject [ɪndʒékt] *v.* inyectar; injerir, introducir.

injection [ɪndʒékʃən] *s.* inyección.

injunction [ɪndʒʌ́ŋkʃən] *s.* mandato, orden; entredicho.

injure [índʒɚ] *v.* dañar; herir, lesionar; lastimar.

injurious [ɪndʒúrɪəs] *adj.* dañoso, dañino, perjudicial.

injury [índʒərɪ] *s.* daño; herida, lesión; perjuicio.

injustice [ɪndʒʌ́stɪs] *s.* injusticia.

ink [ɪŋk] *s.* tinta; *v.* entintar; teñir o manchar con tinta.

inkling [íŋklɪŋ] *s.* indicación, indicio, idea, sospecha, noción vaga.

inkstand [íŋkstænd] *s.* tintero.

inkwell [íŋkwɛl] *s.* tintero.

inlaid [ɪnléd] *adj.* incrustado, embutido; — **work** embutido, incrustación; *pret. & p.p.* de **to inlay**.

inland [ínlənd] *s.* interior (*de un país*); *adj.* interior, del interior de un país; *adv.* tierra adentro.

inlay [ɪnlé] *v.* incrustar, embutir; [ínle] *s.* embutido.

inmate [ínmet] *s.* residente, asilado (*de un hospicio, asilo, casa de corrección, etc.*); presidiario; hospiciano.

inmost [ínmost] *adj.* más interior, más íntimo, más secreto o recóndito; más profundo.

inn [ɪn] *s.* posada, mesón, fonda.

innate [ɪnét] *adj.* innato, connatural.

inner [ínɚ] *adj.* interior; íntimo, recóndito; **—most = inmost.**

inning [íniŋ] *s.* entrada, cuadro (*en beisbol*); turno (*del bateador en beisbol y otros juegos*).

innkeeper [ínkipɚ] *s.* ventero, mesonero, posadero.

innocence [ínəsns] *s.* inocencia.

innocent [ínəsnt] *adj. & s.* inocente.

innocuous [ɪnákjʋəs] *adj.* innocuo, inofensivo.

innovation [ɪnəvéʃən] *s.* innovación.

innuendo [ɪnjʋéndo] *s.* insinuación, indirecta.

innumerable [ɪnjúmərəbl] *adj.* innumerable.

inoculate [ɪnákjəlet] *v.* inocular; contaminar.

inoffensive [ɪnəfénsɪv] *adj.* inofensivo.

inopportune [ɪnɑpətjún] *adj.* inoportuno.

input [ínput] *s.* potencia consumida; (*electric*) entrada.

inquire [ɪnkwáɪr] *v.* inquirir, indagar; preguntar; **to — about** preguntar por; **to — into** indagar, investigar.

inquiry [ɪnkwáɪrɪ] *s.* indagación, investigación; pregunta; interrogatorio.

inquisition [ɪnkwəzíʃən] *s.* inquisición; indagación.

inquisitive [ɪnkwízətɪv] *adj.* inquisitivo, investigador; preguntón; curioso.

inroad [ínrod] *s.* incursión, invasión, ataque; **to make -s upon** atacar; mermar.

insane [ɪnsén] *adj.* insano, loco; **— asylum** manicomio, casa de locos.

insanity [ɪnsǽnətɪ] *s.* locura.

insatiable [ɪnséʃɪəbl] *adj.* insaciable.

inscribe [ɪnskráɪb] *v.* inscribir.

inscription [ɪnskrípʃən] *s.* inscripción; letrero.

insect [ínsɛkt] *s.* insecto.

insecure [ɪnsɪkjúr] *adj.* inseguro.

insensible [ɪnsénsəbl] *adj.* insensible.

insensitive [ɪnsénsətɪv] *adj.* insensible.

inseparable [ɪnsépərəbl] *adj.* inseparable.

insert [ínsɜt] *s.* inserción; intercalación; hoja (*insertada en un libro*); circular, folleto (*insertado en un periódico*); [ɪnsɜt] *v.* insertar; intercalar; encajar; meter.

insertion [ɪnsɜ́ʃən] *s.* inserción; introducción.

inside [ínsáɪd] *s.* interior; **-s** entrañas; *adj.* interior, interno; secreto; *adv.* dentro; adentro; **to turn — out** volver(se) al revés; *prep.* dentro de.

insight [ínsaɪt] *s.* penetración, discernimiento; intuición; perspicacia; comprensión.

insignia [ɪnsígnɪə] *s. pl.* insignias.

insignificant [ɪnsɪgnífəkənt] *adj.* insignificante.

insinuate [ɪnsínjuet] *v.* insinuar.

insinuation [ɪnsɪnjuéʃən] *s.* insinuación; indirecta.

insipid [ɪnsípɪd] *adj.* insípido.

insist [ɪnsíst] *v.* insistir en; empeñarse (en); porfiar, persistir.

insistence [ɪnsístəns] *s.* insistencia, empeño, porfía.

insistent [ɪnsístənt] *adj.* insistente; porfiado, persistente.

insolence [ínsoləns] *s.* insolencia.

insolent [ínsolənt] *adj.* insolente.

insoluble [ɪnsáljəbl] *adj.* insoluble.

inspect [ɪnspɛ́kt] *v.* inspeccionar; examinar, registrar.

inspection [ɪnspɛ́kʃən] *s.* inspección; registro.

inspector [ɪnspɛ́ktə] *s.* inspector.

inspiration [ɪnspɛ́kʃən] *s.* inspiración.

inspire [ɪnspáɪr] *v.* inspirar.

install [ɪnstɔ́l] *v.* instalar.

installation [ɪnstəléʃən] *s.* instalación.

installment, instalment [ɪnstɔ́lmənt] *s.* instalación; abono (*pago*); entrega o continuación (*semanal o mensual de* *una novela*); **to pay in -s** pagar por plazos; pagar en abonos.

instance [ínstəns] *s.* ejemplo, caso; vez, ocasión; instancia; **for —** por ejemplo.

instant [ínstənt] *s.* instante; *adj.* inmediato; urgente; **the 10th —** el 10 del (mes) corriente; **-ly** *adv.* al instante, inmediatamente.

instantaneous [ɪnstənt"éniəs] *adj.* instantáneo.

instead [ɪnstéd] *adv.* en lugar de ello (eso, él, ella, *etc.*); **— of** en lugar de, en vez de.

instep [ínstɛp] *s.* empeine (*del pie, del zapato*).

instigate [ínstəget] *v.* instigar.

instill [ɪnstíl] *v.* inculcar, infundir.

instinct [ínstɪŋkt] *s.* instinto.

instinctive [ɪnstíŋktɪv] *adj.* instintivo.

institute [ínstətjut] *s.* instituto; *v.* instituir.

institution [ɪnstətjúʃən] *s.* institución.

instruct [ɪnstrʌ́kt] *v.* instruir; dar instrucciones.

instruction [ɪnstrʌ́kʃən] *s.* instrucción; enseñanza; **lack of —** falta de saber o conocimientos; **-s** órdenes, instrucciones.

instructive [ɪnstrʌ́ktɪv] *adj.* instructivo.

instructor [ɪnstrʌ́ktə] *s.* instructor.

instrument [ínstrəmənt] *s.* instrumento.

instrumental [ɪnstrəmɛ́ntl] *adj.* instrumental; **to be — in** ayudar a, servir de instrumento para.

insubordinate [ɪnsəbórdɪnət] *adj.* insubordinado.

insufferable [ɪnsʌ́frəbl] *adj.* insufrible, inaguantable.

insufficiency [ɪnsəfíʃənsɪ] *s.* insuficiencia; incompetencia; falta, escasez.

insufficient [ɪnsəfíʃənt] *adj.* insuficiente; inadecuado.

insulate [ínsəlet] *v.* aislar.

insulation [ɪnsəléʃən] *s.* aislamiento; aislación.

insulator [ínsəletə] *s.* aislador.

insult [ínsʌlt] *s.* insulto; [ɪnsʌ́lt] *v.* insultar.

insurance [ɪnfúrəns] *s.* aseguramiento; seguro; prima, premio (*de una póliza de seguro*); **—** agente de seguros; **— company** compañía de seguros; **— policy** póliza de seguro; **— accident** seguro contra accidentes; **fire —** seguro contra incendios; **life —** seguro sobre la vida.

insure [ɪnfúr] *v.* asegurar; asegurarse de.

insurgent [ɪnsɜ́dʒənt] *adj. & s.* insurgente, insurrecto.

insurmountable [ɪnsəmáʊntəbl] *adj.* insuperable.

insurrection [ɪnsərɛ́kʃən] *s.* insurrección, rebelión, alzamiento.

intact [ɪntɛ́kt] *adj.* intacto.

integral [íntəgrəl] *adj.* integral; integrante; *s.* integral.

integrate [íntəget] *v.* integrar.

integrity [ɪntégrətɪ] *s.* integridad, en-

IN

tereza.

intellect [íntlɛkt] s. intelecto; entendimiento.

intellectual [ɪntlɛ́ktʃʊəl] adj. & s. intelectual.

intelligence [ɪntélədʒəns] s. inteligencia; información, noticias; policía secreta.

intelligent [ɪntélədʒənt] adj. inteligente.

intelligible [ɪntélədʒəbl] adj. inteligible.

intemperance [ɪntémpərəns] s. intemperancia.

intend [ɪnténd] v. intentar, pensar, tener la intención de; proponerse; destinar; **to — to do it** pensar hacerlo.

intense [ɪnténs] adj. intenso.

intensify [ɪnténsɪfaɪ] v. intensificar.

intensity [ɪnténsətɪ] s. intensidad.

intensive [ɪnténsɪv] adj. intenso; intensivo.

intent [ɪntént] s. intento, intención, propósito; significado; **to all -s and purposes** en todo caso, en todos sentidos; en realidad; adj. atento; **— on** absorto en, reconcentrado en; resuelto a, decidido a.

intention [ɪnténʃən] s. intención.

intentional [ɪnténʃən] adj. intencional; **-ly** adv. intencionalmente, adrede, a propósito.

inter [ɪntɝ] v. enterrar, sepultar.

intercede [ɪntəsíd] v. interceder.

intercept [ɪntəsépt] v. interceptar; atajar.

interception [ɪntəsépʃən] s. interceptación.

intercession [ɪntəséʃən] s. intercesión.

interchange [íntətʃɛndʒ] s. intercambio; cambio, trueque; [ɪntətʃɛ́ndʒ] v. cambiar, trocar; permutar; alternar.

intercourse [íntəkors] s. comunicación; comercio, trato; intercambio (de ideas, sentimientos, etc.).

interdental [ɪntədéntl] adj. interdental.

interest [íntərɪst] s. interés; rédito; participación (en un negocio); v. interesar.

interested [íntərɪstɪd] adj. interesado; **to be** (o **become**) **— in** interesarse en (o por).

interesting [íntərɪstɪŋ] adj. interesante.

interfere [ɪntəfír] v. intervenir; interponerse, entremeterse; estorbar; **to — with** estorbar, frustrar; dificultar.

interference [ɪntəfírəns] s. intervención; obstáculo; interferencia (en la radio).

interior [ɪntfrɪə] adj. interior; interno; s. interior.

interjection [ɪntədʒékʃən] s. interjección, exclamación; intercalación.

interlace [ɪntəlés] v. entrelazar, enlazar, entretejer.

interlock [ɪntəlák] v. entrelazar(se); trabar(se).

interlude [íntəlud] s. intervalo.

intermediate [ɪntəmídɪɪt] adj. intermedio.

interminable [ɪntɝmɪnəbl] adj. interminable, inacabable.

intermingle [ɪntəmíŋgl] v. entremezclar(se), entreverar(se); mezclar(se).

intermission [ɪntəmíʃən] s. intermisión; intermedio, entreacto.

intermittent [ɪntəmítṇt] adj. intermitente.

intern [ɪntɝn] v. internar, confinar, encerrar; [ɪntɝn] s. practicante (de medicina en un hospital).

internal [ɪntɝnl] adj. interno; interior.

international [ɪntənǽʃən] adj. internacional.

interoceanic [ɪntəoʃɪɛ́nɪk] adj. interoceánico.

interpose [ɪntəpóz] v. interponer(se).

interpret [ɪntɝprɪt] v. interpretar.

interpretation [ɪntɝprɪtéʃən] s. interpretación.

interpreter [ɪntɝprɪtə] s. intérprete.

interrogate [ɪntérəget] v. interrogar.

interrogation [ɪnterəgéʃən] s. interrogación.

interrogative [ɪntərágətɪv] adj. interrogativo; s. pronombre o palabra interrogativa.

interrupt [ɪntərʌ́pt] v. interrumpir.

interruption [ɪntərʌ́pʃən] s. interrupción.

intersect [ɪntəsékt] v. cortar(se); cruzar(se).

intersection [ɪntəsékʃən] s. intersección; **street —** bocacalle.

intersperse [ɪntəspɝs] v. entremezclar, esparcir.

intertwine [ɪntətwáɪn] v. entrelazar, entretejer, trenzar.

interval [íntəvl] s. intervalo.

intervene [ɪntəvín] s. intervenir; interponerse; mediar.

intervention [ɪntəvénʃən] s. intervención.

interview [íntəvju] s. entrevista; v. entrevistar, entrevistarse con.

intestine [ɪntéstɪn] s. intestino; adj. intestino, interno.

intimacy [íntəməsɪ] s. intimidad.

intimate [íntəmɪt] adj. íntimo; s. amigo íntimo; [íntəmet] v. intimar, insinuar; indicar, dar a entender.

intimation [ɪntəméʃən] s. intimación, insinuación.

intimidate [ɪntímədet] v. intimidar, acobardar, infundir miedo.

into [íntu, íntə] prep. en; dentro de; hacia el interior.

intolerable [ɪntálərəbl] adj. intolerable, inaguantable.

intolerance [ɪntálərəns] s. intolerancia.

intolerant [ɪntálərənt] adj. intolerante.

intonation [ɪntonéʃən] s. entonación.

intoxicate [ɪntáksəket] v. embriagar, emborrachar.

intoxication [ɪntaksəkéʃən] s. embriaguez; envenenamiento, intoxicación (estado tóxico o envenenamiento parcial).

intransigent [ɪntrǽnsədʒənt] adj. intransigente.

intravenous [ɪntrəvínəs] adj. intravenoso.

intrench [ɪntréntʃ] v. atrincherar; **to —**

oneself atrincherarse; **to — upon another's rights** infringir los derechos ajenos; **to be -ed** estar atrincherado; estar firmemente establecido.

intrepid [ɪntrépɪd] *adj.* intrépido.

intricate [íntrəkɪt] *adj.* intrincado, enredado.

intrigue [ɪntríg] *s.* intriga; enredo; trama; lío, embrollo; *v.* intrigar; tramar, maquinar.

intriguer [ɪntrígə] *s.* intrigante.

introduce [ɪntrədjús] *v.* introducir; presentar.

introduction [ɪntrədʌ́kʃən] *s.* introducción; presentación.

introspection [ɪntrospékʃən] *s.* introspección.

introvert [íntrovət] *s.* introvertido.

intrude [ɪntrúd] *v.* entremeterse (*o* entrometerse); introducir, meter.

intruder [ɪntrúdə] *s.* intruso, entremetido.

intrusion [ɪntrúʒən] *s.* intrusión, entremetimiento.

intrusive [ɪntrúsɪv] *adj.* intruso.

intrust = **entrust.**

intuition [ɪntuíʃən] *s.* intuición.

inundate [ínəndet] *v.* inundar.

inure [ɪnjúr] *v.* habituar, acostumbrar.

invade [ɪnvéd] *v.* invadir.

invader [ɪnvédə] *s.* invasor.

invalid [ɪnvǽlɪd] *adj.* inválido (*que no vale*), nulo, de ningún valor.

invalid [ínvəlɪd] *adj.* inválido, enfermizo, achacoso; **— diet** dieta para inválidos; *s.* inválido.

invaluable [ɪnvǽljebl] *adj.* de gran precio o valor, inapreciable, inestimable.

invariable [ɪnvǽrɪəbl] *adj.* invariable; **invariably** *adv.* invariablemente; sin falta, sin excepción.

invasion [ɪnvéʒən] *s.* invasión.

invent [ɪnvént] *v.* inventar.

invention [ɪnvénʃən] *s.* invención; invento; inventiva, facultad para inventar.

inventive [ɪnvéntɪv] *adj.* inventivo.

inventiveness [ɪnvéntɪvnɪs] *s.* inventiva.

inventor [ɪnvéntə] *s.* inventor.

inventory [ínvəntorɪ] *s.* inventario; *v.* inventariar.

inverse [ɪnvə́rs] *adj.* inverso.

invert [ɪnvə́t] *v.* invertir; trastrocar; volver al revés.

invest [ɪnvést] *v.* invertir, colocar (*fondos*); investir (*de una dignidad o cargo*); revestir (*de autoridad*); sitiar.

investigate [ɪnvéstəget] *v.* investigar, indagar.

investigation [ɪnvestəgéʃən] *s.* investigación; indagación.

investigator [ɪnvéstəgetə] *s.* investigador; indagador.

investment [ɪnvéstmənt] *s.* inversión (*de fondos*).

investor [ɪnvéstə] *s.* el que invierte fondos.

invigorate [ɪnvígəret] *v.* vigorizar, fortalecer.

invincible [ɪnvínsəbl] *adj.* invencible.

invisible [ɪnvízəbl] *adj.* invisible.

invitation [ɪnvətéʃən] *s.* invitación.

invite [ɪnváɪt] *v.* invitar; convidar.

inviting [ɪnváɪtɪŋ] *adj.* atractivo; seductivo, tentador.

invocation [ɪnvəkéʃən] *s.* invocación.

invoice [ínvɔɪs] *s.* factura; envío, mercancías enviadas; *v.* facturar.

invoke [ɪnvók] *v.* invocar.

involuntary [ɪnválənterɪ] *adj.* involuntario.

involve [ɪnválv] *v.* complicar, enredar; envolver; implicar; comprometer; **to get -d in difficulties** embrollarse, meterse en embrollos.

inward [ínwəd] *adj.* interior; interno; secreto; *adv.* hacia el interior; hacia dentro, adentro, para dentro; **-s** *adv.* = **inward.**

iodine [áɪədaɪn] *s.* yodo.

ire [aɪr] *s.* ira.

iridescent [ɪrədésnt] *adj.* iridiscente, tornasolado, irisado.

iris [áɪrɪs] *s.* iris; arco iris; flor de lis.

Irish [áɪrɪʃ] *adj.* irlandés; *s.* irlandés, idioma irlandés; **the —** los irlandeses.

irksome [ə́ksəm] *adj.* fastidioso, engorroso, molesto, tedioso.

iron [áɪən] *s.* hierro; plancha (*de planchar ropa*); *adj.* férreo, de hierro; **—work** herraje, trabajo en hierro; **—works** herrería; fábrica de hierro; *v.* planchar; **to — out a difficulty** allanar una dificultad.

ironical [aɪránɪk] *adj.* irónico.

ironing [áɪənɪŋ] *s.* planchado.

irony [áɪrənɪ] *s.* ironia.

irradiate [ɪrédɪet] *v.* irradiar.

irrational [ɪrǽʃənl] *adj.* irracional.

irregular [ɪrégjələ] *adj.* irregular.

irrelevant [ɪréləvənt] *adj.* fuera de propósito, inaplicable al caso, inoportuno, que no viene (*o* no hace) al caso.

irreligious [ɪrɪlídʒəs] *adj.* irreligioso, impio.

irremediable [ɪrɪmídɪəbl] *adj.* irremediable; incurable.

irreproachable [ɪrɪprótʃəbl] *adj.* irreprochable, intachable.

irresistible [ɪrɪzístəbl] *adj.* irresistible.

irresolute [ɪrézəlut] *adj.* irresoluto, indeciso.

irreverence [ɪrévərəns] *s.* irreverencia, desacato.

irreverent [ɪrévərənt] *adj.* irreverente.

irrigate [frəget] *v.* regar; irrigar, bañar.

irrigation [ɪrəgéʃən] *s.* riego; irrigación; **— canal** acequia, canal de irrigación.

irritable [frətbl] *adj.* irritable; colérico.

irritate [frətet] *v.* irritar.

irritating [frətetɪŋ] *adj.* irritante.

irritation [ɪrətéʃən] *s.* irritación.

irrupt [ɪrʌ́pt] *v.* irrumpir.

island [áɪlənd] *s.* isla.

islander [áɪləndə] *s.* isleño.

isle [aɪl] *s.* isla, ínsula.

isolate [áɪslet] *v.* aislar.

isolation [aɪsléʃən] *s.* aislamiento.

isolationism [aɪsléʃənɪzəm] *s.* aislamiento.

isometric [aɪsométrɪk] *adj.* isométrico.

Israel [ízriəl] s. Israel.
issue [íʃʊ] s. (*printing*) tirada, impresión; (*stock, bonds*) emisión (*de valores*); (*problem*) problema, tema; (*result*) resultado, consecuencia; **without —** sin prole, sin sucesión; **to take — with** disentir o diferir de; v. publicar, dar a luz; dar, promulgar (*un decreto*); emitir (*valores, acciones, etc.*); emanar; fluir; salir; brotar; provenir.
isthmus [ísməs] s. istmo.
it [ɪt] *pron. neutro* lo, la (*acusativo*); ello, él, ella (*después de una preposición*); *por lo general no se traduce cuando es sujeto del verbo:* **— is there** está allí; **— is I** soy yo; **— is raining** llueve, está lloviendo; **what time is —?** ¿qué hora es?; **— is two o'clock** son las dos; **how goes —?** ¿qué tal?
Italian [ɪtǽljən] *adj. & s.* italiano.
italic [ɪtǽlɪk] *adj.* itálico; **-s** *s.* letra bastardilla.
italicize [ɪtǽləsaɪz] v. poner en letra bastardilla.
itch [ɪtʃ] s. comezón; picazón; sarna (*enfermedad de la piel*); v. picar, darle a uno comezón; sentir comezón; **to be -ing** tener ansias de.
itchy [ítʃɪ] *adj.* sarnoso, *Méx., Ven.* sarniento; **to feel —** sentir comezón.
item [áɪtəm] s. artículo; detalle; noticia, suelto (*de un periódico*); partida (*de una lista*).
itemize [áɪtəmaɪz] v. pormenorizar detallar; hacer una lista de.
itinerant [aɪtínərənt] *adj.* ambulante.
itinerary [aɪtínərɛrɪ] s. itinerario; ruta; guía de viajeros.
its [ɪts] *pos. neutro* su (sus), de él, de ella, de ello.
itself [ɪtsélf] *pron. neutro* mismo, misma; **by —** por sí, de por sí, por sí solo; solo, aislado; **in —** en sí.
ivory [áɪvrɪ] s. marfil; **— tower** torre de marfil.
ivy [áɪvɪ] s. hiedra (yedra).

J

jab [dʒæb] v. picar; pinchar; s. piquete, pinchazo.
jack [dʒæk] s. gato (*para alzar cosas pesadas*); sota (*en naipes*); macho (*del burro y otros animales*); bandera de proa; **— of all trades** aprendiz de todo y oficial de nada; **— pot** premio gordo, premio mayor; **— rabbit** liebre americana; v. **to — up** solevantar, alzar con gato (*un objeto pesado*).
jackass [dʒǽkæs] s. asno, burro.
jacket [dʒǽkɪt] s. chaqueta; envoltura; forro (*de un libro*); hollejo (*de la patata*).
jackknife [dʒǽknaɪf] s. navaja.
jagged [dʒǽgɪd] *adj.* serrado, dentado.
jail [dʒel] s. cárcel; v. encarcelar.
jailer [dʒelə] s. carcelero.
jam [dʒæm] v. estrujar, apachurrar; atorar(se); obstruir(se), atascar(se); apiñar(se), agolpar(se); **to — on the brakes** frenar de golpe; **to — one's fingers** machucarse los dedos; **to —**

through forzar por, meter a la fuerza; s. conserva, compota; apretura; atascamiento; **traffic —** aglomeración de transeúntes o automóviles, *Am.* bola; **to be in a —** estar en un aprieto.
janitor [dʒǽnətə] s. conserje; portero; casero (*encargado de un edificio*).
January [dʒǽnjuɛrɪ] s. enero.
Japanese [dʒæpəníz] *adj. & s.* japonés.
jar [dʒɑr] s. jarra, jarro; tarro; choque, sacudida; trepidación, vibración; **large earthen —** tinaja; v. trepidar; hacer vibrar; hacer temblar; menear; **to — one's nerves** ponerle a uno los nervios de punta.
jargon [dʒárgən] s. jerga, jerigonza.
jasmine [dʒǽzmɪn] s. jazmín.
jasper [dʒǽspə] s. jaspe.
jaunt [dʒɔnt] s. caminata, excursión; v. dar un paseíto, hacer una corta caminata.
jaw [dʒɔ] s. quijada, mandíbula, *Am.* carretilla; **-s** grapa (*de herramienta*).
jawbone [dʒɔ́bón] s. mandíbula, quijada.
jay [dʒe] s. grajo; rústico, bobo; **blue —** azulejo; **—walker** el que cruza las bocacalles descuidadamente.
jazz [dʒæz] s. jazz (*cierta clase de música sincopada*); v. tocar el jazz; bailar el jazz; **to — up** sincopar; animar, alegrar.
jealous [dʒéləs] *adj.* celoso; envidioso; **to be — of someone** tener celos de una persona, tenerle celos a una persona.
jealousy [dʒéləsɪ] s. celos; envidia.
jeer [dʒɪr] s. mofa, befa, escarnio, *Carib.* choteo; v. mofar, befar, *Carib.* chotear; **to — at** mofarse de.
jelly [dʒélɪ] s. jalea; v. convertir(se) en jalea, hacer(se) gelatinoso.
jeopardy [dʒépədɪ] s. riesgo.
jerk [dʒɜk] s. tirón; sacudida, *Méx., C.A., Ven., Col.* jalón; espasmo muscular; v. sacudir(se); dar un tirón; atasajar (*la carne*); **to — out** sacar de un tirón; **-ed beef** tasajo, *Am.* charqui.
jerkwater [dʒɜ́kwɔtə] *adj.* de mala muerte.
jersey [dʒɜ́zɪ] s. tejido de punto, tejido elástico, *Am.* jersey; chaqueta, blusa, camisa (*de punto*), *Am.* jersey.
jest [dʒɛst] s. broma, chanza; chiste; v. bromear; chancearse.
jester [dʒɛ́stə] s. chancero, burlón; bufón.
Jesuit [dʒéʒuɪt] s. jesuita.
jet [dʒɛt] s. chorro; surtidor (*de fuente*); **— airplane** avión de reacción; **— engine** motor de reacción; **gas —** mechero de gas; *adj.* de azabache; **jet-black** negro como el azabache; v. chorrear, salir en chorro.
Jew [dʒu] s. judío.
jewel [dʒúəl] s. joya, alhaja; gema; **— box** estuche, joyero.
jeweler [dʒúələ] s. joyero; **-'s shop** joyería.
jewelry [dʒúəlrɪ] s. joyas, alhajas, pe-

dreria; — **store** joyería.
Jewish [dʒúíʃ] *adj.* judío.
jiffy [dʒífɪ] *s.* instante; **in a** — en un instante, en dos paletas; en un decir Jesús, en un santiamén.
jig [dʒɪg] *s.* jiga (*música y baile*); — **saw** sierra mecánica (*para recortar figuras*); **—saw puzzle** rompecabezas (*de recortes*); *v.* tocar una jiga; bailar una jiga; bailotear; menear(se).
jiggle [dʒígl] *v.* zangolotear(se), zarandear(se), menear(se); *s.* zarandeo, meneo, zangoloteo.
jilt [dʒɪlt] *v.* desairar, dar calabazas, dejar plantado.
jingle [dʒíŋgl] *s.* retintín; verso o rima infantil; — **bell** cascabel; *v.* hacer retintín.
job [dʒab] *s.* tarea, faena; trabajo; empleo, ocupación; **to be out of a** — estar sin trabajo; estar desocupado.
jockey [dʒákɪ] *s.* jockey; *v.* maniobrar (*para sacar ventaja o ganar un puesto*).
join [dʒɔɪn] *v.* juntar(se); enlazar(se); acoplar; unirse a, asociarse a.
joint [dʒɔɪnt] *s.* (*point*) juntura, coyuntura; (*function*) articulación; conexión; bisagra; (*public place*) garito (*casa de juego*); fonducho; restaurante de mala muerte; **out of** — descoyuntado; desunido; *adj.* unido, asociado; coparticipe; colectivo; — **account** cuenta en común; — **action** acción colectiva; — **committee** comisión mixta; — **creditor** acreedor copartícipe; — **heir** coheredero; — **session** sesión plena; **-ly** *adv.* juntamente, juntos, unidamente, colectivamente.
joke [dʒok] *s.* broma; chiste, chanza; *v.* bromear; chancear(se), *Carib.* chotear; *Ríopl.* farrear; jorobar.
joker [dʒókɚ] *s.* bromista, chancero, guasón, *Carib.* choteador; naipe especial (*que no pertenece a ningún palo*).
jokingly [dʒókɪŋlɪ] *adv.* en (o de) chanza, en (o de) broma; de chiste.
jolly [dʒálɪ] *adj.* jovial; alegre; festivo; *v.* bromear, chancearse.
jolt [dʒolt] *s.* sacudida; sacudimiento; choque; *v.* sacudir.
jostle [dʒás]] *v.* rempujar o empujar, dar empellones; codear; *s.* rempujón, empujón, empellón.
jot [dʒat] *v.* **to** — **down** apuntar, tomar apuntes; *s.* jota, pizca.
journal [dʒɝn]] *s.* diario; periódico; revista; acta (*de una junta o concilio*).
journalism [dʒɝnlɪzəm] *s.* periodismo.
journalist [dʒɝnlɪst] *s.* periodista.
journalistic [dʒɝnlístɪk] *adj.* periodístico.
journey [dʒɝnɪ] *s.* viaje; jornada; *v.* viajar.
joy [dʒɔɪ] *s.* júbilo, regocijo; alegría, gusto, deleite; felicidad.
joyful [dʒɔ́ɪfəl] *adj.* regocijado, jubiloso; alegre; **-ly** *adv.* con regocijo, regocijadamente, con júbilo, alegremente.
joyous [dʒɔ́ɪəs] *adj.* jubiloso, alegre,

gozoso.
jubilant [dʒúb]ənt] *adj.* jubiloso, alegre.
jubilee [dʒúblɪ] *s.* jubileo; júbilo.
judge [dʒʌdʒ] *s.* juez; — **advocate** auditor de un consejo militar; *v.* juzgar.
judgment [dʒʌdʒmənt] *s.* juicio; sentencia, fallo; opinión; discernimiento; — **day** día del juicio final.
judicial [dʒudíʃəl] *adj.* judicial.
judicious [dʒudíʃəs] *adj.* juicioso, cuerdo.
jug [dʒʌg] *s.* cántaro; jarro, jarra; botija; chirona (*cárcel*) *Am.* chirola.
juggle [dʒʌgl] *v.* hacer juegos de manos; hacer suertes; **to** — **the accounts** barajar (o manipular) las cuentes; *s.* juego de manos, suerte; trampa.
juggler [dʒʌglɚ] *s.* prestidigitador, malabarista.
juice [dʒus] *s.* jugo; zumo.
juiciness [dʒúsɪnɪs] *s.* jugosidad.
juicy [dʒúsɪ] *adj.* jugoso, zumoso; suculento; **a** — **story** un cuento picante.
juke box [dʒúkbaks] *s.* tragamonedas; tragaquintos.
July [dʒulái] *s.* julio.
jumble [dʒʌmbl] *s.* revolver(se), barajar; mezclar(se); *s.* mezcolanza, revoltijo; confusión.
jump [dʒʌmp] *v.* saltar; brincar; salvar (*de un salto*); hacer saltar; comerse una pieza (*en el juego de damas*); **to** — **at the chance** asir o aprovechar la oportunidad; **to** — **bail** perder la fianza por evasión; **to** — **over** saltar por encima de, salvar de un salto; **to** — **the track** descarrilarse; **to** — **to conclusions** hacer deducciones precipitadas; *s.* salto; brinco; subida repentina (*del precio*); **to be always on the** — andar siempre de aquí para allá; trajinar, trafagar, ser muy activo.
jumper [dʒʌmpɚ] *s.* saltador; chaquetón holgado (*de obrero*); vestido sin mangas (*puesto sobre la blusa de mujer*); **-s** traje de juego (*para niños*).
jumpy [dʒʌmpɪ] *adj.* saltón; asustadizo, nervioso.
junction [dʒʌ́ŋkʃən] *s.* unión, juntura; confluencia (*de dos ríos*); empalme (*de ferrocarriles*).
juncture [dʒʌ́ŋktʃɚ] *s.* juntura; coyuntura; **at this** — a esta sazón, en esta coyuntura.
June [dʒun] *s.* junio.
jungle [dʒʌŋgl] *s.* selva; matorral; *Am.* jungla; *Carib.* manigua.
junior [dʒúnjɚ] *adj.* menor, más joven; — **college** colegio para los dos primeros años del bachillerato; **John Smith, Junior** (**Jr.**) John Smith, hijo; *s.* estudiante del tercer año (*en escuela superior, colegio o universidad*).
juniper [dʒúnɪpɚ] *s.* junípero; enebro.
junk [dʒʌŋk] *s.* basura, desperdicios; trastos viejos; cosa inservible; **Chinese** — junco chino (*embarcación pequeña*); *v.* desechar, echar a la basura.

IS

jurisdiction [dʒʊrɪsdíkʃən] s. jurisdicción.

jurisprudence [dʒʊrɪsprúdṇs] s. jurisprudencia, derecho.

juror [dʒúrə] s. jurado, miembro de un jurado.

jury [dʒúrɪ] s. jurado; **grand —** jurado de acusación.

just [dʒʌst] adj. justo; recto; exacto; adv. ni más ni menos, exactamente, justamente; precisamente; sólo, no más, nada más; apenas; — now ahora mismo; **he — left** acaba de salir, Am. salió recién; **she is — a little girl** no es más que una niña, es una niña no más; **to have —** acabar de.

justice [dʒʌ́stɪs] s. justicia; juez; magistrado.

justification [dʒʌstəfəkéʃən] s. justificación.

justify [dʒʌ́stəfaɪ] v. justificar.

justly [dʒʌ́stlɪ] adv. justamente; con razón.

jut [dʒʌt] v. sobresalir, proyectarse, extenderse; s. salidizo, proyección.

juvenile [dʒúvən̩] adj. juvenil.

K

kangaroo [kæŋgərú] s. canguro.

keel [kil] s. quilla; v. dar de quilla (voltear un barco); **to — over** volcar(se); zozobrar; caerse patas arriba, desplomarse.

keen [kin] adj. agudo; afilado; perspicaz; ansioso.

keenness [kínnɪs] s. agudeza; perspicacia; anhelo, ansia.

keep [kip] v. guardar; tener guardado; tener; retener; conservar(se); preservar(se); mantener(se); **to — accounts** llevar las cuentas; **to — at it** persistir, seguir dale que dale; **to — away** mantener(se) alejado; **to — back** tener a raya; detener; reprimir, restringir; **to — from** impedir; guardar(se) de; abstenerse de; **to — going** seguir andando, seguir adelante; seguir viviendo; **to — off** no arrimarse, no acercarse; no entrar; mantener(se) a distancia; **to — one's hands off** no tocar; **to — one's temper** contenerse, refrenarse, reprimirse; **to — quiet** estarse quieto o callado; **to — something up** seguir o continuar haciendo algo; **to — to the right** seguir a la derecha; mantenerse a la derecha; **to — track of** llevar la cuenta de; no perder de vista; s. manutención, subsistencia; **for -s** para siempre; para guardar; dado, no prestado.

keeper [kípə] s. guardián, custodio; **jail —** carcelero.

keeping [kípɪŋ] s. custodia; mantenimiento; preservación, conservación; **in — with** en armonía con.

keepsake [kípsek] s. prenda, recuerdo, regalo.

keg [kɛg] s. tonel, barril.

kennel [kɛ́n̩] s. perrera.

kept [kɛpt] pret. & p.p. de **to keep**.

kerchief [kɝ́tʃɪf] s. pañuelo, pañolón.

kernel [kɝ́n̩] s. simiente; grano (de trigo o maíz); meollo (de ciertas frutas como la nuez); núcleo.

kerosene [kérəsin] s. kerosina, petróleo para lámparas.

kettle [kɛ́t̩] s. caldera; **—drum** tímpano; **tea—** marmita, tetera, Am. pava (para el mate).

key [ki] s. (lock) llave; (music) clave; (instrument) tecla; (land) cayo; isleta; **— ring** llavero; **to be in —** estar a tono, estar en armonía; v. poner a tono, afinar, templar (con llave); armonizar; **to — up** elevar el tono de; **to be -ed up** estar sobreexcitado, estar en tensión nerviosa.

keyboard [kíbord] s. teclado.

keyhole [kíhol] s. ojo de la cerradura.

keynote [kínot] s. nota tónica; idea o principio fundamental.

keystone [kíston] s. clave (de un arco); base, fundamento principal.

khaki [kákɪ] s. kaki, caqui; adj. de kaki.

kick [kɪk] s. (foot) Esp. coz; puntapié; Am. patada; (complaint) queja; protesta; fuerza (de una bebida); estímulo; **to have a —** Am. patear (dícese del licor); v. cocear; dar coces o patadas; dar puntapiés; patear; quejarse, protestar; **to — out** echar a patadas; echar, expulsar; **to — the bucket** estirar la pata, morir, Am. patear el balde; **to — up a lot of dust** levantar una polvareda.

kid [kɪd] s. cabrito; cabritilla (piel curtida de cabrito); niño, niña; **— gloves** guantes de cabritilla; v. bromear, embromar; chancearse con, Carib., Méx. chotear.

kidnap [kídnæp] v. secuestrar, raptar.

kidnapper [kídnæpə] s. secuestrador, robachicos, ladrón de niños.

kidnapping [kídnæpɪŋ] s. rapto, secuestro.

kidney [kídnɪ] s. riñón; **— bean** judía, frijol; **— stones** cálculos.

kill [kɪl] v. matar; destruir; amortiguar; parar (el motor); s. animal o animales matados (en la caza).

killer [kílə] s. matador; asesino.

kiln [kɪln] s. horno.

kilo [kílo], **kilogram** [kíləgræm] s. kilo, kilogramo.

kilometer [kíləmitə] s. kilómetro.

kimono [kəmóna] s. quimono, bata.

kin [kɪn] s. parentela, parientes, familia; **to notify the nearest of —** avisar al pariente o deudo más cercano.

kind [kaɪnd] adj. bondadoso; benévolo; amable; **to send one's — regards to** enviar afectuosos saludos a; **kind-hearted** de buen corazón; **— of tired** algo cansado; s. clase, especie, género; **to pay in —** pagar en especie; pagar en la misma moneda.

kindergarten [kíndəgartṇ] s. escuela de párvulos.

kindle [kíndḷ] v. encender(se); inflamar(se); incitar; prender (el fuego).

kindling [kíndlɪŋ] s. encendimiento;

leña ligera, astillas, *Andes* charamuscas.

kindly [káɪndlɪ] *adj.* bondadoso; benigno; benévolo; amable, apacible; *adv.* bondadosamente, ambablemente; con benevolencia; por favor; **not to take — to criticism** no aceptar de buen grado las correcciones.

kindness [káɪndnɪs] *s.* bondad, amabilidad; gentileza; benevolencia; favor.

kindred [kíndrɪd] *adj.* emparentado; allegado; semejante; **— facts** hechos relacionados; **— spirits** espíritus afines.

kinesics [kaɪnízɪks] *s.* kinésica; quinésica.

king [kɪŋ] *s.* rey; rey (*en ajedrez*); dama (*en el juego de damas*).

kingdom [kíŋdəm] *s.* reino.

kingly [kíŋlɪ] *adj.* regio; real; majestuoso; *adv.* regiamente; majestuosamente.

kink [kɪŋk] *s.* (*bend*) enroscadura; (*pain*) torticolis.

kinky [kíŋkɪ] *adj.* crespo, ensortijado, *Am.* grifo.

kinship [kínʃɪp] *s.* parentesco; afinidad; semejanza.

kinsman [kínzmən] *s.* pariente, deudo.

kiss [kɪs] *s.* beso; *v.* besar.

kit [kɪt] *s.* estuche, caja de herramientas; saco, envoltura (*para guardar instrumentos, herramientas, etc.*); gatito; **medicine —** botiquín; **soldier's —** mochila.

kitchen [kítʃɪn] *s.* cocina; **—ware** trastos de cocina.

kite [kaɪt] *s.* cometa (*f.*), *Méx.* papalote; *Ch.* volantín; *Arg.* barrilete; milano (*pájaro*).

kitten [kítn] *s.* gatito.

kitty [kítɪ] *s.* gatito, minino.

knack [næk] *s.* destreza, maña, habilidad.

knapsack [næpsæk] *s.* mochila, morral, alforja.

knave [nev] *s.* bribón, bellaco, pícaro; sota (*de naipes*).

knead [nid] *v.* amasar, sobar.

knee [ni] *s.* rodilla; **knee-deep** hasta la rodilla; metido hasta las rodillas.

kneel [nil] *v.* arrodillarse; hincarse.

knell [nɛl] *s.* doble (*toque de campanas por los difuntos*); *v.* doblar, tocar a muerto.

knelt [nɛlt] *pret.* & *p.p.* de **to kneel.**

knew [nju] *pret.* de **to know.**

knickknack [níknæk] *s.* chuchería, baratija, chisme.

knife [naɪf] *s.* cuchillo; cuchilla; **carving —** trinchante; **pocket —** cortaplumas; navaja; *v.* acuchillar.

knight [naɪt] *s.* caballero; campeón; caballo (*en ajedrez*); **— errant** caballero andante; *v.* armar caballero.

knighthood [náɪthʊd] *s.* caballería, orden de la caballería.

knit [nɪt] *v.* tejer (*a punto de aguja*); hacer calceta o malla; enlazar; soldarse (*un hueso*) **to — one's brow** fruncir las cejas, arrugar la frente; *pret.* & *p.p.*

de **to knit.**

knitting [nítɪŋ] *s.* labor de punto; **— needle** aguja de media.

knives [naɪvz] *pl. de* **knife.**

knob [nɑb] *s.* perilla, botón, tirador (*de puerta, cajón, etc.*); protuberancia.

knock [nɑk] *v.* (*pound*) golpear, golpetear; llamar o tocar a la puerta; (*criticize*) criticar, censurar o hablar mal de; **to — down** derribar; desmontar (*una máquina o aparato*); **to — off** suspender (*el trabajo*); rebajar (*del precio*); derribar, echar abajo; **to — out** aplastar de un golpe, poner fuera de combate; dejar sin sentido; *s.* golpe; golpeteo; toque, llamada, aldabonazo; crítica, censura; **knock-kneed** zambo, patizambo.

knocker [nákə] *s.* llamador, aldaba, aldabón; criticón, murmurador.

knoll [nol] *s.* colina, loma; eminencia.

knot [nɑt] *s.* nudo; lazo; *v.* anudar(se).

knotty [nátɪ] *adj.* nudoso; dificultoso, enredado.

know [no] *v.* (*to be acquainted with*) conocer; (*to have knowledge of*; *to know how to*) saber; (*to recognize*) reconocer; distinguir; **to — how to swim** saber nadar; **to — of** saber de; tener conocimiento de; tener noticias de; estar enterado de.

knowingly [nóɪŋlɪ] *adv.* a sabiendas; adrede.

knowledge [nálɪdʒ] *s.* conocimiento; saber, sabiduría; pericia; **not to my — no** que yo sepa.

known [non] *p.p. de* **to know.**

knuckle [nákl] *s.* nudillo; coyuntura, articulación; artejo; *v.* someterse; **to — down** someterse; aplicarse con empeño al trabajo.

L

label [lébl] *s.* marbete, etiqueta, rótulo; *v.* marcar, rotular; apodar, llamar.

labor [lébə] *s.* trabajo; labor; obra; mano de obra; la clase obrera; **— union** unión de obreros; **to be in —** estar de parto; *v.* trabajar; afanarse; estar de parto; elaborar (*un punto*).

laboratory [lǽbrətorɪ] *s.* laboratorio.

laborer [lébərə] *s.* trabajador, obrero; jornalero, peón.

laborious [ləbórɪəs] *adj.* laborioso, trabajoso, penoso; industrioso.

labyrinth [lǽbərɪnθ] *s.* laberinto.

lace [les] *s.* (*cloth*) encaje; (*cord*) cordón, cordoncillo, cinta (*de corsé, etc.*); **gold —** galón de oro (*para guarnecer uniformes*); *v.* atar con cinta o cordón; guarnecer con encajes; enlazar, entrelazar.

lack [læk] *s.* falta; escasez, carencia; deficiencia; *v.* carecer de, faltarle a uno; necesitar; **he -s courage** le falta ánimo.

lackey [lǽkɪ] *s.* lacayo.

lacking [lǽkɪŋ] *adj.* falto, carente.

lacquer [lǽkə] *s.* laca; *v.* barnizar con laca.

lad [læd] *s.* rapaz, chico.

ladder [lǽdə] s. escalera de mano.
laden [lédn̩] adj. cargado; agobiado, abrumado; v. cargar; agobiar.
ladies [lédɪz] pl. de **lady**.
ladle [lédl̩] s. cucharón; v. servir (sopa) con cucharón.
lady [lédɪ] s. señora; dama; —like como señora, muy fina, elegante; — love amada, querida.
lag [læg] v. rezagarse, quedarse atrás, atrasarse; andar lentamente; s. retardo o retardación, retraso.
lagoon [lagún] s. laguna.
laid [led] pret. & p.p. de **to lay**; to be — up estar incapacitado o estropeado.
lain [len] p.p. de **to lie**.
lair [ler] s. guarida; cueva de fieras.
lake [lek] s. lago.
lamb [læm] s. cordero; —kin corderito.
lame [lem] adj. cojo; lisiado; estropeado; — excuse disculpa falsa; v. hacer cojo; estropear, incapacitar.
lament [ləmént] s. lamento; v. lamentar(se).
lamentable [læməntəbl̩] adj. lamentable; doloroso.
lamentation [læməntéʃən] s. lamentación, lamento.
laminate [læmənet] v. laminar.
lamp [læmp] s. lámpara; linterna; farol; —post poste (de farol); —shade pantalla de lámpara.
lance [læns] s. lanza; v. alancear, lancear, herir con lanza; picar con bisturí.
land [lænd] s. tierra; terreno; suelo; v. desembarcar; aterrizar (un avión); llegar; coger (un pez); to — a job conseguir una colocacion, lograr un empleo.
land-grant [lǽndgrænt] adj. mediante donación federal de tierras.
landholder [lǽndholdə] s. terrateniente, propietario, hacendado.
landing [lǽndɪŋ] s. (act) desembarco, desembarque; aterrizaje (de un avión); (place) desembarcadero; descanso (de escalera); —field campo de aterrizaje; aeropuerto; — strip pista de aterrizaje.
landlady [lǽndledɪ] s. patrona, casera, dueña (de la casa).
landlord [lǽndlɔrd] s. amo, patrón, propietario, dueño; casero.
landmark [lǽndmɑrk] s. mojón, señal (para fijar los confines); marca; suceso culminante.
landowner [lǽndonə] s. terrateniente, propietario, hacendado.
landscape [lǽndskep] s. paisaje.
landslide [lǽndslaɪd] s. derrumbe, derrumbamiento, desplome; gran mayoría de votos.
lane [len] s. senda, vereda; callejuela; ruta, derrotero (de vapores o aviones).
language [lǽŋgwɪdʒ] s. lengua; idioma; lenguaje.
languid [lǽŋgwɪd] adj. lánguido.
languish [lǽŋgwɪʃ] v. languidecer.
languor [lǽŋgə] d. languidez.
lank [læŋk] adj. alto y delgado, largucho.
lanky [lǽŋkɪ] adj. largucho, zancón,

zancudo.
lantern [lǽntən] s. linterna; farol.
lap [læp] s. falda, regazo; aleta; etapa, trecho (de una carrera); v. lamer; to — over cruzar(se) sobre, entrecruzar(se).
lapel [ləpél] s. solapa.
lapidary [lǽpɪderɪ] s. & adj. lapidario.
lapse [læps] s. lapso; transcurso; desliz; error; v. deslizarse; pasar, transcurrir; caer en un desliz; decaer (el entusiasmo, el interés, etc.); caducar (un plazo, un contrato, etc.).
larboard [lɑ́rbəd] s. babor; adj. de babor; — side banda de babor.
larceny [lɑ́rsn̩ɪ] s. latrocinio, hurto; ratería.
lard [lɑrd] s. lardo, manteca de puerco; v. mechar.
large [lɑrdʒ] adj. grande; at — suelto, libre; sin trabas; en general; -ly adv. grandemente, en gran parte.
large-scale [lɑ́rdʒskél] adj. en grande escala.
lariat [lǽrɪət] s. reata.
lark [lɑrk] s. (bird) alondra; (fun) diversión, holgorio, jarana; to go on a — ir o andar de jarana.
larva [lɑ́rvə] s. larva.
larynx [lǽrɪŋks] s. laringe.
lascivious [ləsívɪəs] adj. lascivo.
lash [læʃ] s. látigo; azote, latigazo; pestaña; v. fustigar; azotar; censurar, reprender; amarrar.
lass [læs] s. moza, muchacha, doncella.
lassitude [lǽsətjud] s. dejadez, flojedad, decaimiento de fuerzas.
lasso [lǽso] s. lazo, reata, mangana; v. lazar, Am. enlazar.
last [læst] adj. (in a series) último; final; (just passed) pasado; —night anoche; — year el año pasado; at — por fin, finalmente, al fin; next to the — penúltimo; to arrive — llegar el último; s. fin, término; horma (de zapato); v. durar; perdurar; -ly adv. finalmente, en conclusión.
lasting [lǽstɪŋ] adj. duradero; perdurable.
latch [lætʃ] s. pestillo, picaporte, aldaba, cerrojo; v. cerrar con aldaba.
late [let] adj. (tardy) tardío; tardo; (recent) reciente; último; —comer recién llegado; rezagado; a — hour una hora avanzada; the — Mr. X el finado (o difunto) Sr. X; to have a — supper cenar tarde; adv. tarde; — in the night a una hora avanzada de la noche; — into the night a deshoras de la noche; — in the week a fines de la semana; of — últimamente, recientemente; hace poco; to be — ser tarde; llegar tarde; estar atrasado; venir o llegar con retraso (el tren); the train was ten minutes — el tren llegó con diez minutos de retraso; -ly adv. últimamente, recientemente; hace poco, poco ha.
latent [létn̩t] adj. latente.
later [létə] adv. & adj. (comp. de **late**) más tarde; después, luego; más re-

ciente; posterior.

lateral [lǽtərəl] *adj.* lateral.

latest [létɪst] *adv.* & *adj.* (*superl. de late*) más tarde; más reciente, más nuevo; último; **the — fashion** la última moda, las últimas novedades; **the — news** las últimas novedades, las noticias más recientes; **at the —** a más tardar.

lathe [leθ] *s.* torno (*de carpintero o mecánico*).

lather [lǽðɚ] *s.* jabonadura, espuma de jabón; *v.* jabonar, enjabonar; espumar, hacer espuma.

Latin [lǽtn] *adj.* latino; *s.* latín.

latitude [lǽtətjud] *s.* latitud; libertad; amplitud.

latter [lǽtɚ] *adj.* último; **towards the — part of the week** a (*o* hacia) fines de la semana; **the —** éste (ésta, esto, etc.).

lattice [lǽtɪs] *s.* celosía; enrejado, rejilla.

laud [lɔd] *v.* loar, encomiar, alabar.

laudable [lɔ́dəbl] *adj.* laudable, loable.

laugh [læf] *v.* reír(se); **to — at** reírse de; **to — loudly** reírse a carcajadas; **to — in one's sleeve** reírse para sus adentros; **she -ed in his face** se rió en sus barbas; *s.* risa; **loud —** risotada, carcajada, risada.

laughable [lǽfəbl] *adj.* risible; ridículo.

laughter [lǽftɚ] *s.* risa.

launch [lɔntʃ] *v.* (*put into water*) botar o echar (*un barco*) al agua; (*a rocket*) lanzar; (*begin*) empezar, poner en operación; **to — forth** lanzarse; **to — forth on a journey** emprender un viaje; *s.* lancha.

launder [lɔ́ndɚ] *v.* lavar y planchar (*la ropa*).

laundress [lɔ́ndrɪs] *s.* lavandera.

laundry [lɔ́ndrɪ] *s.* lavandería; lavado; ropa (lavada).

laurel [lɔ́rəl] *s.* laurel; gloria, honor.

lava [lávə] *s.* lava.

lavatory [lǽvətorɪ] *s.* lavabo; lavamanos; lavatorio.

lavender [lǽvəndɚ] *s.* espliego, lavándula; *adj.* lila, morado claro.

lavish [lǽvɪʃ] *adj.* gastador, pródigo, dadivoso; abundante, copioso; profuso; lujoso; *v.* prodigar, malgastar, despilfarrar; **to — praise upon** colmar de alabanzas a; **-ly** pródigamente; copiosamente; lujosamente.

law [lɔ] *s.* ley; derecho, jurisprudencia; regla; **— student** estudiante de leyes, estudiante de derecho; **law-abiding** observante de la ley.

lawbreaker [lɔ́brekɚ] *s.* infactor, transgresor.

lawful [lɔ́fəl] *adj.* legal; lícito; válido; permitido.

lawless [lɔ́lɪs] *adj.* sin ley, ilegal; desenfrenado; revoltoso; licencioso.

lawmaker [lɔ́mekɚ] *s.* legislador.

lawn [lɔn] *s.* césped, prado; linón (*tela de hilo o algodón*); **— mower** cortadora de césped.

lawsuit [lɔ́sut] *s.* pleito, litigio.

lawyer [lɔ́jɚ] *s.* abogado, jurisconsulto.

lax [læks] flojo; suelto; relajado.

laxative [lǽksətɪv] *adj.* & *s.* laxante, purgante.

laxity [lǽksətɪ] *s.* flojedad, flojera; relajamiento (*de una regla, ley, etc.*).

lay [le] *pret. de* to lie.

lay [le] *v.* colocar; poner; tender, extender; poner (*huevos*); echar (*la culpa*); atribuir (*la responsabilidad*); presentar, exponer; asentar (*el polvo*); **to — a wager** apostar; **to — aside** poner a un lado; ahorrar; **to — away** (*o* by) guardar; **to — bare** revelar; exponer; **to — down** poner, colocar; rendir (*las armas*); **to — down the law** mandar, dictar; **to — hold of** asir, agarrar; **to — off a workman** suspender a un obrero; **to — open** exponer a la vista; **to — out a plan** trazar un plan; **to — up** almacenar; guardar, ahorrar; **to be laid up** estar incapacitado o estropeado; **to — waste** asolar; *s.* lay, balada, canción; situación, orientación (*del terreno*); *adj.* lego, laico; profano (*no iniciado en una ciencia*).

layer [léɚ] *s.* capa; estrato; gallina ponedora.

layman [lémən] *s.* lego, seglar, laico.

lazily [lézɪlɪ] *adv.* perezosamente.

laziness [lézɪnɪs] *s.* pereza.

lazy [lézɪ] *adj.* perezoso, holgazán.

lead [lɛd] *s.* plomo; plomada, pesa de plomo.

lead [lid] *v.* (*guide*) guiar, dirigir; llevar; conducir; mandar (*un ejército*); (*precede*) ir a la cabeza de; sobresalir entre; ser mano (*en el juego de naipes*); **to — an orchestra** dirigir una orquesta, llevar la batuta; **to — astray** llevar por mal camino, extraviar, descarriar; **to — the way** ir por delante, mostrar el camino; *s.* delantera, primer lugar; mando, dirección; indicio; papel principal; primer actor.

leaden [lɛ́dn] *adj.* plomizo; aplomado, color de plomo; pesado.

leader [lídɚ] *s.* jefe, caudillo, *Am.* líder; director; guía; caballo delantero; **-s** puntos suspensivos.

leadership [lídɚʃɪp] *s.* dirección, mando; iniciativa.

leading [lídɪŋ] *adj.* principal; delantero; **— man** primer actor.

leadoff [lídɔf] *adj.* delantero; puntero.

leaf [lif] *s.* hoja; *v.* echar hojas (*un árbol*), cubrirse de hojas; **to — through a book** hojear un libro.

leafless [líflɪs] *adj.* sin hojas, deshojado.

leaflet [líflɪt] *s.* hojilla; folleto, hoja volante, papel volante, circular.

leafy [lífɪ] *adj.* frondoso.

league [lig] *s.* (*alliance*) liga, confederación; sociedad; (*distance*) legua; *v.* asociar(se); ligarse, coligarse.

leak [lik] *s.* gotera (*en un techo*); agujero, grieta (*por donde se escapa el agua o el gas*); escape (*de gas, vapor, electricidad, etc.*); *v.* gotear(se); rezumar(se);

hacer **agua** (*dícese de un barco*); salirse, escaparse (*el gas, el vapor, etc.*).

lean [lin] *v.* (*incline*) inclinar(se); recostar(se), reclinar(se); (*support*) apoyar(se); *adj.* magro; flaco; — **year** año estéril, año improductivo.

leant [lɛnt] = **leaned.**

leap [lip] *v.* saltar; brincar; *s.* salto, brinco; — **year** año bisiesto.

leapt [lɛpt] *pret. & p.p. de* **to leap.**

learn [lɝn] *v.* aprender; saber, averiguar, enterarse de.

learned [lɝnɪd] *adj.* erudito; docto.

learner [lɝnɚ] *s.* aprendedor; estudiante, estudioso.

learning [lɝnɪŋ] *s.* erudición, saber; aprendizaje.

learnt [lɝnt] *pret. & p.p. de* **to learn.**

lease [lis] *v.* arrendar, dar o tomar en arriendo; *s.* arriendo, contrato de arrendamiento.

leash [liʃ] *s.* traílla; cuerda.

least [list] *adj.* (el) mínimo, (el) más pequeño; *adv.* menos; **at** — al menos, a lo menos, por lo menos; **the** — lo (el, la) menos.

leather [lɛðɚ] *s.* cuero, piel; *adj.* de cuero, de piel; — **strap** correa.

leave [liv] *v.* dejar; abandonar; salir (de); partir; irse; **to** — **out** dejar fuera; omitir; *s.* permiso, licencia; — **of absence** licencia; **to take** — **of** despedirse de.

leaven [lɛvən] *s.* levadura, fermento; *v.* fermentar (*la masa*).

leaves [livz] *pl. de* **leaf.**

leavings [livɪŋz] *s.* sobras, desperdicios.

lecture [lɛktʃɚ] *s.* conferencia, discurso; reprensión; *v.* dar una conferencia; explicar; reprender.

lecturer [lɛktʃɚɚ] *s.* conferenciante; lector (*de universidad*).

led [lɛd] *pret. & p.p. de* **to lead.**

ledge [lɛdʒ] *s.* borde; salidizo.

ledger [lɛdʒɚ] *s.* libro mayor (*en contabilidad*).

leech [litʃ] *s.* sanguijuela.

leer [lɪr] *s.* mirada de soslayo, mirada lujuriosa; *v.* mirar de soslayo; mirar con lujuria.

leeward [liwɚd] *s. & adv.* sotavento.

left [lɛft] *pret. & p.p. de* **to leave;** **I have two books** — me quedan dos libros; *adj.* izquierdo; *s.* izquierda; mano izquierda; **at** (**on, to**) **the** — a la izquierda.

left-handed [lɛfthændɪd] *adj.* zurdo; a la izquierda; torpe; malicioso, insincero; — **compliment** alabanza irónica.

leftist [lɛftɪst] *s.* izquierdista.

leftover [lɛftovɚ] *adj.* sobrante; **-s** *s. pl.* sobras.

left-wing [lɛftwɪŋ] *adj.* izquierdista.

leg [lɛg] *s.* pierna; pata (*de animal, mesa, etc.*); pie o pata (*de banquillo, silla, etc.*); etapa, trecho (*de una carrera o viaje*); **to be on one's last** — **s** estar en las últimas.

legacy [lɛgəsɪ] *s.* legado, herencia.

legal [ligl] *adj.* legal; lícito.

legalize [liglaɪz] *v.* legalizar; sancionar; autorizar.

legate [lɛgɪt] *s.* legado; delegado.

legation [lɪgéʃən] *s.* legación; embajada.

legend [lɛdʒənd] *s.* leyenda; letrero, inscripción.

legendary [lɛdʒəndɛrɪ] *adj.* legendario.

leggings [lɛgɪŋz] *s. pl.* polainas.

legible [lɛdʒəbl] *adj.* legible.

legion [lidʒən] *s.* legión.

legislate [lɛdʒɪslet] *v.* legislar.

legislation [lɛdʒɪsléʃən] *s.* legislación.

legislative [lɛdʒɪsletɪv] *adj.* legislativo.

legislator [lɛdʒɪsletɚ] *s.* legislador.

legislature [lɛdʒɪsletʃɚ] *s.* legislatura, asamblea legislativa.

legitimate [lɪdʒítəmɪt] *adj.* legítimo.

leisure [liʒɚ] *s.* ocio; — **hours** horas de ocio; **to be at** — estar ocioso; estar libre o desocupado; **do it at your** — hágalo Vd. cuando pueda o le convenga; hágalo Vd. en sus ratos de ocio.

leisurely [liʒɚlɪ] *adj.* lento, deliberado, pausado; *adv.* sin prisa, despacio, a sus (mis, tus, *etc.*) anchas.

lemon [lɛmən] *s.* limón; — **tree** limonero; *adj.* de limón; — **color** cetrino.

lemonade [lɛmənéd] *s.* limonada.

lend [lɛnd] *v.* prestar.

lender [lɛndɚ] *s.* prestador; **money** — prestamista.

length [lɛŋkθ] *s.* largo, largor, largura, longitud; duración; cantidad (*de una sílaba*); **at** — largamente, detenidamente; al fin; **to go to any** — hacer cuanto esté de su parte.

lengthen [lɛŋkθən] *v.* alargar(se); prolongar(se).

lengthwise [lɛŋkθwaɪz] *adv.* a lo largo; longitudinalmente; *adj.* longitudinal.

lengthy [lɛŋkθɪ] *adj.* largo, prolongado.

lenient [linɪənt] *adj.* indulgente, clemente, poco severo.

lens [lɛnz] *s.* lente; cristalino (*del ojo*).

lent [lɛnt] *pret. & p.p. de* **to lend.**

Lent [lɛnt] *s.* cuaresma.

leopard [lɛpɚd] *s.* leopardo.

less [lɛs] *adj.* menor; *adv. & prep.* menos; — **and** — cada vez menos.

lessen [lɛsn] *v.* aminorar(se), disminuir(se), reducir(se); mermar.

lesser [lɛsɚ] *adj.* menor, más pequeño.

lesson [lɛsn] *s.* lección.

lest [lɛst] *conj.* no sea que, por miedo de que.

let [lɛt] *v.* (*permit*) dejar, permitir; (*rent*) alquilar, arrendar; — **us** (*o* **let's**) **do it** vamos a hacerlo, hagámoslo; — **him come** que venga; **to** — **be** no molestar, dejar en paz; no tocar; **to** — **down** bajar; desilusionar; **to** — **go** soltar; **to** — **in** dejar entrar, admitir; **to** — **know** avisar, enterar, hacer saber; **to** — **off** soltar; dejar libre; **to** — **through** dejar pasar; **to** — **up** disminuir; *pret. & p.p. de* **to let.**

letdown [lɛtdaʊn] *s.* aflojamiento; desilusión.

lethal [liθəl] *adj.* letal.

lethargy [lɛθɚdʒɪ] *s.* letargo; **to fall into a** — aletargarse.

letter [lét♂] *s.* (*alphabet*) letra; (*missive*) carta; — **box** buzón; — **carrier** cartero; —**head** membrete; *v.* rotular, hacer a mano letras de molde.

lettuce [létɪs] *s.* lechuga.

level [lévl] *adj.* llano, plano; a nivel; igual; parejo; **level-headed** bien equilibrado, sensato; *adv.* a nivel; a ras; *s.* nivel; **to be on the** — obrar rectamente, obrar sin engaño; ser o decir la pura verdad; *v.* nivelar; igualar; allanar; apuntar, asestar (*un arma*); **to** — **to the ground** arrasar, echar por tierra.

lever [lév♂] *s.* palanca; **control** — palanca de mando.

levity [lévɪtɪ] *s.* frivolidad; levedad.

levy [lévɪ] *s.* imposición, recaudación (*de tributos, impuestos, etc.*); leva, enganche, reclutamiento; embargo (*de propiedad*); *v.* imponer, exigir, recaudar (*tributos o multas*); reclutar; **to** — **on someone's property** embargar la propiedad de alguien.

lewd [lud] *adj.* lujurioso, lascivo, deshonesto.

lewdness [lúdnɪs] *s.* lascivia, lujuria.

lexicon [léksɪkən] *s.* léxico.

liability [laɪəbílətɪ] *s.* responsabilidad; obligación; desventaja; **liabilities** obligaciones, deudas; pasivo.

liable [láɪəbl] *adj.* responsable, obligado; sujeto, expuesto; propenso; probable.

liaison [liezán] *s.* enlace; unión.

liar [láɪ♂] *s.* mentiroso, embustero.

libel [láɪbl] *s.* libelo; difamación; *v.* difamar.

liberal [líbərəl] *adj. & s.* liberal.

liberalism [líbəəlɪzm] *s.* liberalismo.

liberality [líbərálɪtɪ] *s.* liberalidad; larguesa, generosidad.

liberalize [líbəəlatz] *v.* liberalizar(se).

liberate [líbəret] *v.* libertar, librar; soltar.

liberation [líbəréʃən] *s.* liberación.

liberator [líbəret♂] *s.* libertador.

libertine [líbətin] *adj. & s.* libertino.

liberty [líbətɪ] *s.* libertad; **at** — libre.

librarian [laɪbrérɪən] *s.* bibliotecario.

library [láɪbrɛrɪ] *s.* biblioteca.

lice [laɪs] *pl.* de **louse.**

license, licence [láɪsn̩s] *s.* licencia; permiso; título; **driver's** — licencia (pase, certificado o patente) de chófer; título de conductor; licencia para manejar; — **plate** placa (o chapa) de numeración, chapa de circulación, chapa de matrícula; *v.* licenciar, dar licencia a; permitir, autorizar.

licentious [laɪsénʃəs] *adj.* licencioso, disoluto.

lick [lɪk] *v.* (*tongue*) lamer; (*thrash*) dar una tunda o zurra; vencer; **to** — **someone's boots** adular a uno con servilismo; **to** — **the dust** morder el polvo; adular; *s.* lamedura, *Am.* lamida; lengüetada; *C.A.* lambida; **salt** — lamedero (*lugar salino donde lame el ganado*); **not to do a** — **of work** no hacer absolutamente nada.

licking [líkɪŋ] *s.* zurra, tunda.

lid [lɪd] *s.* tapadera, tapa; **eye**— párpado.

lie [laɪ] *s.* mentira; embuste; **to give the** — to desmentir, dar un mentís; *v.* mentir (*pret. & p.p.* lied); tenderse, acostarse; yacer; estar; estar situado; consistir (en); **to** — **back** recostarse, echarse hacia atrás; **to** — **down** acostarse, echarse, tenderse; **to** — **in wait** acechar, espiar.

lieutenant [luténənt] *s.* teniente; **second** — subteniente.

life [laɪf] *s.* vida; **from** — del natural; **still** — naturaleza muerta; —**boat** bote de salvamento, lancha salvavidas; — **imprisonment** prisión perpetua; — **insurance** seguro sobre la vida; — **pension** pensión vitalicia; — **preserver** salvavidas, cinto o chaqueta de salvamento.

lifeless [láɪflɪs] *adj.* sin vida; muerto; exánime, inanimado; desanimado.

lifelessness [láɪflɪsnɪs] *s.* falta de vida; inercia; falta de animación.

lifelike [láɪflaɪk] *adj.* como la vida; natural, que parece vivo.

lifelong [láɪflɔŋ] *adj.* perpetuo, de toda la vida.

lifetime [láɪftaɪm] *s.* vida, transcurso de la vida.

lift [lɪft] *v.* levantar; alzar; elevar; disiparse (*las nubes, la niebla, las tinieblas*); **to** — **one's hat** quitarse el sombrero (*para saludar*); *s.* elevación; exaltación de ánimo; alzamiento, levantamiento; carga; ayuda (*para levantar una carga*); alza (*de un zapato*); ascensor, *Am.* elevador; **to give someone a** — **in a car** llevar a alguien en el auto.

ligature [lígətʃur] *s.* ligadura.

light [laɪt] *s.* luz; lumbre; **tail** — *Am.* farito trasero, *Am.* farol de cola, *Méx.* calavera; *adj.* claro; con luz; de tez blanca; ligero; leve; frívolo; — **drink** bebida suave; —**headed** frívolo, ligero de cascos; —**hearted** alegre; — **opera** opereta; **to make** — **of** dar poca importancia a; *v.* encender(se); iluminar, alumbrar; **to** — **upon** caer sobre; posarse en (*dícese de los pájaros, mariposas, etc.*).

lighten [láɪtn̩] *v.* aligerar; iluminar; aclarar; relampaguear; alegrar.

lighter [láɪt♂] *s.* encendedor.

lighthouse [láɪthaʊs] *s.* faro.

lighting [láɪtɪŋ] *s.* iluminación; alumbrado.

lightly [láɪtlɪ] *adv.* ligeramente; levemente; frívolamente; sin seriedad.

lightness [láɪtnɪs] *s.* ligereza; frivolidad; claridad.

lightning [láɪtnɪŋ] *s.* relampagueo; relámpago; **to** — pararrayos.

lightweight [láɪtwet] *s.* peso liviano; peso ligero.

likable [láɪkəbl] *adj.* agradable, simpático, placentero.

like [laɪk] *adv. & prep.* como; del mismo modo que; semejante a; *adj.* semejante, parecido; **in — manner** de manera semejante, del mismo modo; **to feel — going** tener ganas de ir; **to look — someone** parecerse a alguien; **it looks — rain** parece que va a llover, quiere llover; *s.* semejante, igual; **-s** gustos; preferencias; *v.* gustarle a uno; **he -s books** le gustan los libros; **do whatever you —** haz lo que gustes.

likely [láɪklɪ] *adj.* probable, creíble; prometedor; **— place** lugar a propósito; **it is — to happen** es probable que suceda; *adv.* probablemente.

liken [láɪkən] *v.* asemejar, comparar.

likeness [láɪknɪs] *s.* semejanza; parecido; retrato.

likewise [láɪkwaɪz] *adv.* igualmente, asimismo; del mismo modo; también.

liking [láɪkɪŋ] *s.* simpatía; afición; preferencia, gusto.

lilac [láɪlək] *s.* lila; *adj.* lila, morado claro.

lily [lílɪ] *s.* lirio; azucena.

lily-white [lílɪhwáɪt] *adj.* blanquísimo; puro; racialmente segregado.

limb [lɪm] *s.* rama (*de árbol*); miembro (*del cuerpo*), pierna, brazo.

limber [límbɚ] *adj.* flexible; ágil; *v.* hacer flexible; **to — up** agilitar(se), hacer(se) flexible.

lime [laɪm] *s.* cal; lima (*fruta*); liga (*para cazar pájaros*).

limelight [láɪmlaɪt] *s.* luz de calcio; proscenio; **to be in the —** estar a la vista del público.

limestone [láɪmstoʊn] *s.* piedra caliza.

limit [límɪt] *s.* límite; confín; *v.* limitar.

limitation [lɪmɪtéʃən] *s.* limitación; restricción.

limited [límɪtɪd] *adj.* limitado; restringido.

limitless [límɪtlɪs] *adj.* ilimitado, sin límites.

limp [lɪmp] *s.* cojera; *v.* cojear; renquear; *adj.* flojo; flexible.

limpid [límpɪd] *adj.* límpido; claro, transparente.

line [laɪn] *s.* (*mark*) línea; renglón; raya; (*cord*) cuerda; (*business*) ramo; giro (*de negocios*); especialidad; **— of goods** surtido, línea (*Am.* renglón) de mercancías; **branch railway —** ramal; **pipe —** cañería, tubería; **to bring into —** alinear; obligar a proceder de acuerdo con un plan; poner de acuerdo; **to get in —** meterse en fila, hacer (*o* formar) cola; *v.* linear, rayar; alinear; forrar; **to — up** alinear(se); formarse, formar fila.

lineage [línɪɪdʒ] *s.* linaje.

linear [línɪɚ] *adj.* lineal.

lined [laɪnd] *adj.* rayado; forrado.

linen [línɪn] *s.* lino; ropa blanca.

liner [láɪnɚ] *s.* vapor, buque; **air —** avión, transporte aéreo.

lineup [láɪnʌp] *s.* formación.

linger [língɚ] *v.* tardar(se), demorarse, dilatarse; andar ocioso, vagar; perdurar; prolongarse.

lingerie [lǽnʒərɪ] *s.* ropa interior de mujer.

linguistics [lɪŋgwístɪks] *s.* lengüística.

lining [láɪnɪŋ] *s.* forro.

link [lɪŋk] *s.* eslabón; enlace; **cuff -s** gemelos; *v.* eslabonar(se); enlazar(se).

linnet [línɪt] *s.* jilguero.

linoleum [lɪnóliəm] *s.* linóleo (*tela impermeable para cubrir el suelo*).

linseed [línsid] *s.* linaza; **— oil** aceite de linaza.

lint [lɪnt] *s.* hilas; hilachas.

lion [láɪən] *s.* león.

lioness [láɪənɪs] *s.* leona.

lip [lɪp] *s.* labio.

lipstick [lípstɪk] *s.* lápiz para los labios.

liquid [líkwɪd] *adj.* líquido; **— assets** valores líquidos (*o* realizables); **— measure** medida para líquidos; *s.* líquido.

liquidate [líkwɪdet] *v.* liquidar, saldar (*cuentas*); poner término a.

liquidation [lɪkwɪdéʃən] *s.* liquidación; saldo de cuentas.

liquor [líkɚ] *s.* licor; bebida espiritosa (*como aguardiente, ron, etc.*).

lisp [lɪsp] *s.* ceceo; *v.* cecear; balbucir.

list [lɪst] *s.* lista; registro; escora (*inclinación de un barco*); *v.* alistar, registrar poner o apuntar en una lista; hacer una lista de; escorar, inclinarse a la banda.

listen [lísn] *v.* escuchar; atender, dar oídos, prestar atención; **—!** ¡oye! ¡escucha! ¡oiga! ¡escuche! **to — in** escuchar por radio; escuchar a hurtadillas (*una conversación*).

listener [lísnɚ] *s.* escuchador, oyente; **radio —** radioescucha, radioyente.

listless [lístlɪs] *adj.* abstraído; indiferente; indolente; desatento.

listlessness [lístlɪsnɪs] *s.* indiferencia, inatención, abstracción.

lit [lɪt] *pret.* & *p.p. de* **to light**; *adj.* alumbrado; algo borracho.

literal [lítərəl] *adj.* literal; **-ly** *adv.* al pie de la letra, literalmente.

literary [lítərerɪ] *adj.* literario.

literature [lítərətʃur] *s.* literatura; impresos, folletos, circulares.

litigation [lɪtəgéʃən] *s.* litigio, pleito.

litter [lítɚ] *s.* (*young animals*) camada, cría; (*stretcher*) litera; camilla; cama de paja para animales; (*disorder*) cosas esparcidas; desorden; revoltillo; *v.* desarreglar, revolver, esparcir cosas por.

little [lítl] *adj.* pequeño; poco; **— Bear** Osa Menor; **a — coffee** un poco de café; **a — while** un ratito (*o* ratico), un poco; *adv.* & *s.* poco; **— by —** poco a poco.

live [lɪv] *v.* vivir; **to — down** hacer olvidar, borrar (*el pasado*); **to — up to** vivir en conformidad con, vivir de acuerdo con.

live [laɪv] *adj.* (*not dead*) vivo; (*lively*) enérgico; vivo, activo; **— coal** ascua encendida; **— oak** encina; **— question** cuestión palpitante, cuestión de actualidad; **— wire** alambre cargado;

persona muy activa.

livelihood [láıvlıhud] s. vida, alimento, subsistencia, manutención.

liveliness [láıvlınıs] s. viveza, animación; agilidad.

livelong [lívlɔŋ] adj. todo; absolutamente todo.

lively [láıvlı] adj. vivo; vivaz; animado, alegre; airoso; — **horse** caballo brioso; adv. vivamente; de prisa.

liver [lívɚ] s. hígado; vividor.

livery [lívɚı] s. librea; caballeriza (para caballos de alquiler); **auto** — garage para autos de alquiler.

lives [laıvz] pl. de **life.**

livestock [láıvstak] s. ganado.

live wire [láıvwáır] s. persona alerta y vivaz.

livid [lívıd] adj. lívido; amoratado.

living [lívıŋ] s. (state) vida; (means) manutención, subsistencia; adj. vivo; viviente; — **room** sala; — **wage** sueldo suficiente para vivir; **the** — los vivos.

lizard [lízɚd] s. lagarto; **small** — lagartija.

load [lod] s. carga; **ship** — cargamento; **-s of** gran cantidad de; montones de; v. cargar; agobiar; colmar.

loaf [lof] s. hogaza de pan; **sugar** — azúcar de pilón; v. holgazanear, haraganear.

loafer [lófɚ] s. holgazán, haragán, zángano.

loan [lon] s. préstamo; empréstito; — **shark** usurero; — **word** préstamo semántico; v. prestar (dinero).

loath [loθ] adj. maldispuesto, renuente; **to be** — to repugnarle a uno.

loathe [loð] v. repugnarle a uno; abominar.

loathsome [lóðsəm] adj. repugnante, asqueroso; aborrecible.

loaves [lovz] pl. de **loaf.**

lob [lab] v. volear.

lobby [lábı] s. (place) vestíbulo; antecámara; salón de entrada; hall; (influence) camarilla (que busca ventajas ante un cuerpo legislativo); **hotel** — vestíbulo o patio del hotel; v. cabildear (procurar ventajas o partidarios en una asamblea).

lobe [lob] s. lóbulo.

lobster [lábstɚ] s. langosta de mar.

local [lókl] adj. local; — **train** tren ordinario.

locality [lokǽlətı] s. localidad; comarca.

localize [lókaız] v. localizar.

locate [lóket] v. situar, establecer; localizar, averiguar la posición de; avecindarse, radicarse, establecerse.

location [lokéʃən] s. situación; sitio, localidad.

lock [lak] s. (door) cerradura; (canal) esclusa (de un canal); llave (de un arma de fuego); guedeja (de pelo); bucle, rizo; v. cerrar con llave; trabar(se), juntar(se); entrelazar(se); **to** — **in** encerrar; **to** — **out** cerrar la puerta (a alguien); dejar afuera; **to** —

up encerrar; encarcelar.

locker [lákɚ] s. alacena; armario.

locket [lákıt] s. guardapelo.

lockout [lókaut] s. paro (suspensión del trabajo por parte de los empresarios); cierre de fábrica.

locksmith [láksmıθ] s. cerrajero.

locomotive [lokəmótıv] s. locomotora; — **engineer** maquinista

locust [lókəst] s. langosta, saltamontes; cigarra; — **tree** algarrobo; acacia falsa.

lodge [ladʒ] s. logia; casita accesoria; casa de campo; v. alojar(se); hospedar(se); colocar; **to** — **a complaint** presentar una queja.

lodger [ládʒɚ] s. huésped, inquilino.

lodging [ládʒıŋ] s. alojamiento, hospedaje; vivienda.

loft [lɔft] s. desván; galería, balcón interior (de un templo); **choir** — coro; **hay** — pajar.

lofty [lɔ́ftı] adj. elevado; sublime; altivo.

log [lɔg] s. leño, troza, tronco aserrado; corredera (aparato para medir las millas que anda la nave); diario de navegación; — **cabin** cabaña de troncos; v. cortar (árboles); cortar leños y transportarlos; registrar (en el diario de navegación).

logic [ládʒık] s. lógica.

logical [ládʒıkl] adj. lógico.

logroll [lɔ́grol] v. lograr aprobación de leyes mediante favores.

loin [lɔın] s. ijada, ijar, lomo.

loiter [lɔ́ıtɚ] v. holgazanear, vagar, malgastar el tiempo; **to** — **behind** rezagarse.

loll [lal] v. arrellanarse o repantigarse, recostarse con toda comodidad.

lone [lon] adj. solo, solitario.

loneliness [lónlınıs] s. soledad.

lonely [lónlı] adj. solo, solitario; triste, desamparado.

lonesome [lónsəm] adj. solo, solitario; triste, nostálgico.

long [lɔŋ] adj. largo; **the whole day** — todo el santo día; **three feet** — tres pies de largo; **to be** — **in coming** tardar en venir; adv. mucho, mucho tiempo; — **ago** hace mucho tiempo; **as** (o **so**) — **as** en tanto que, mientras que; **how** — **is it since** . . . ? ¿cuánto tiempo hace que . . . ?; **so** — ! ¡hasta luego! ¡adiós!; **long-suffering** sufrido, paciente; **long-winded** prolijo, largo (en hablar); **long-distance de** larga distancia; v. anhelar; ansiar; **to** — **for** anhelar; suspirar por.

longer [lɔ́ŋgɚ] adj. más largo; adv. más, más tiempo; **no** — ya no; **not** . . . **any** — ya no; no . . . más.

longevity [landʒévətı] s. longevidad.

longing [lɔ́ŋıŋ] s. anhelo, añoranza, nostalgia; adj. anhelante, anheloso, nostálgico; **-ly** adv. con anhelo, anhelosamente, con ansia.

longitude [lándʒətjud] s. longitud.

longshoreman [lɔ́ŋʃormən] s. estibador (de barco o muelle), cargador.

LI

long-term [lɔ́ŋtəm] *adj.* a largo plazo.

look [luk] *v.* (*see*) mirar; (*seem*) parecer; **it — well on you** le cae (*o* le sienta) bien; **to — after** atender, cuidar; **to — alike** parecerse; asemejarse; **to — down on a person** mirar con desprecio (*o* menospreciar) a alguien; **to — for** buscar; esperar; **to — forward to** anticipar con placer; **to — into** examinar, investigar; **— out!** ¡cuidado!; ¡tenga cuidado!; **to — out of** asomarse a; **to — over** examinar; dar un vistazo a; **to — up** levantar la vista; buscar; **to — up to** admirar, mirar con respeto; *s.* mirada, vistazo; **-s** apariencia, aspecto; **to have good -s** ser bien parecido.

looking glass [lúkıŋglæs] *s.* espejo.

lookout [lúkaut] *s.* vigía; atalaya; mirador; vista, perspectiva; **that is your —** ¡eso a usted!; **to be on the —** estar alerta.

loom [lum] *s.* telar; *v.* destacarse, descollar; asomar(se), aparecer.

loop [lup] *s.* (*closed*) lazo, gaza, presilla; (*road*) vuelta, curva; (*electric*) circuito; *v.* hacer una gaza (con *o* en); atar con gaza o presilla; hacer un circuito.

loophole [lúphol] *s.* agujero, abertura; salida; escapatoria.

loose [lus] *adj.* (*slack*) suelto; flojo; (*unfettered*) desatado; (*licentious*) desoluto; **— change** suelto, moneda suelta; **— jointed** de articulaciones flojas; **to let —** soltar; *v.* soltar, desatar; aflojar; **-ly** *adv.* sueltamente; flojamente; con poca exactitud, sin fundamento.

loosen [lúsn] *v.* soltar(se); aflojar(se); desatar(se); **to — one's hold** desasirse, soltarse.

looseness [lúsnıs] *s.* (*limberness*) soltura; flojedad; (*laxness*) flojera; holgura; relajación; (*of bowel*) flujo.

loot [lut] *s.* botín, pillaje, saqueo; *v.* saquear, pillar, robar.

lop [lap] *v.* tronchar, desmochar (*Am.* mochar).

loquacious [lokwéʃəs] *adj.* locuaz, hablador, lenguaraz.

lord [lɔrd] *s.* señor; dueño, amo; lord; **Lord's Prayer** Padre Nuestro; **Our Lord** Nuestro Señor; *v.* señorear, mandar; **to — it over** señorear, dominar.

lordly [lɔ́rdlɪ] *adj.* señoril; noble; altivo; despótico; *adv.* altivamente, imperiosamente.

lordship [lɔ́rdʃɪp] *s.* señoría (*título*); señorío, dominio.

lose [luz] *v.* perder; **to — sight of** perder de vista.

loss [lɔs] *s.* pérdida; **to be at a —** estar perplejo; no saber qué hacer; **to sell at a —** vender con pérdida.

lost [lɔst] *pret.* & *p.p.* de **to lose**; *adj.* perdido; extraviado; **— in thought** absorto, abstraído; **to get —** perderse, extraviarse.

lot [lɑt] *s.* (*land*) lote; (*section*) parte,

porción; (*luck*) suerte; solar, porción de terreno; **a — of** (*o* **-s of**) una gran cantidad de; mucho; muchos; **to draw -s** echar suertes; **to fall to one's —** tocarle a uno, caerle en suerte; *adv.* mucho; **a — better** mucho mejor.

lotion [lóʃən] *s.* loción.

lottery [látərɪ] *s.* lotería.

loud [laud] *adj.* ruidoso; recio, fuerte; chillón (*dícese también de los colores*); *adv.* ruidosamente, fuerte, recio; alto, en voz alta.

loud-speaker [láudspíkə] *s.* altavoz, altoparlante.

lounge [laundʒ] *s.* sala de descanso; sofá, diván, canapé; *v.* arrellanarse, repantigarse, recostarse cómodamente; sestear; holgazanear.

louse [laus] *s.* piojo.

lousy [láuzɪ] *adj.* piojoso; asqueroso.

lovable [lávəb] *adj.* amable.

love [lʌv] *s.* (*affection*) amor; cariño; (*fondness*) afición; **— affair** amorío; **to be in —** estar enamorado; **to fall in — with** enamorarse de; **to make — to** enamorar a; *v.* amar, querer; gustar mucho de, gustarle a uno mucho; encantarle a uno algo.

loveliness [lávlnıs] *s.* belleza, hermosura; amabilidad.

lovely [lávlɪ] *adj.* amable; lindo, bello; exquisito; encantador; ameno.

lover [lávə] *s.* amante; **music —** aficionado a (*o* amante de) la música.

loving [lávıŋ] *adj.* amante, amoroso, cariñoso, afectuoso; **-ly** *adv.* cariñosamente, afectuosamente.

low [lo] *adj.* (*not high*) bajo; (*base*) vil; (*humble*) humilde; (*downcast*) abatido; débil; (*lacking*) deficiente; (*sick*) gravemente enfermo; **— comedy** farsa, sainete; **— gear** primera velocidad; **— Mass** misa rezada; **— key** de intensidad mínima; **dress with a — neck** vestido escotado (*o* con escote); **to be — on something** estar escaso de algo; **to be in — spirits** estar abatido o desanimado; *adv.* bajo; en voz baja, quedo, quedito; con bajeza, a precio bajo vilmente; *s.* mugido; *v.* mugir.

lower [lóə] *adj.* más bajo; inferior; **— case letter** letra minúscula; **— classman** estudiante de los dos primeros años; **— house** cámara de diputados; *v.* bajar; disminuir; rebajar; abatir; humillar.

lowland [lólənd] *s.* tierra baja.

lowliness [lólınıs] *s.* bajeza; humildad.

lowly [lólɪ] *adj.* bajo, humilde; inferior; *adv.* humildemente.

lowness [lónıs] *s.* bajeza; humildad; abatimiento; gravedad (*de tono*); debilidad (*de un sonido*); baratura.

loyal [lɔ́ɪəl] *adj.* leal, fiel.

loyalty [lɔ́ɪəltɪ] *s.* lealtad, fidelidad.

lubricant [lúbrıkənt] *adj.* & *s.* lubricante.

lubricate [lúbrıket] *v.* lubricar.

lucid [lúsɪd] *adj.* lúcido; claro;

luciente.

luck [lʌk] s. suerte; fortuna; **in —** de buena suerte; **in bad —** de mala suerte.

luckily [lʌklı] adv. afortunadamente, por fortuna.

lucky [lʌkı] adj. afortunado, feliz; **to be —** tener suerte, tocarle a uno la suerte.

lucrative [lúkrətıv] adj. lucrativo.

ludicrous [lúdıkrəs] adj. ridículo.

lug [lʌg] v. llevar, traer, Am. cargar; **to — away** cargar con, llevarse (una cosa pesada).

luggage [lʌ́gıdʒ] s. equipaje.

lukewarm [lúkwórm] adj. tibio, templado; indiferente.

lull [lʌl] v. arrullar; sosegar; calmar(se); s. calma, momento de calma.

lullaby [lʌ́ləbaɪ] s. arrullo, canción de cuna.

lumber [lʌ́mbɚ] s. madera, maderaje; **—man** maderero, negociante en madera; **—yard** depósito de maderas; **— jack** leñador; v. cortar y aserrar madera; explotar los bosques; moverse pesadamente.

luminous [lúmınəs] adj. luminoso.

lump [lʌmp] s. (mass) terrón; bulto; (swelling) hinchazón, chichón; protuberancia; **— of sugar** terrón de azúcar; v. amontonar; consolidar (gastos); apelotonarse, aterronarse, formar terrones.

lumpy [lʌ́mpı] adj. aterronado.

lunatic [lúnətık] adj. & s. lunático, loco.

lunch [lʌntʃ] s. almuerzo; merienda; **—room** merendero, Méx., Ven., Carib. lonchería; Ríopl. confitería; Spain cafetería; v. almorzar; merendar; Am. tomar el lonche.

luncheon [lʌ́ntʃən] s. almuerzo; merienda.

lung [lʌŋ] s. pulmón.

lurch [lɝtʃ] s. sacudida; tambaleo repentino; **to give a —** tambalearse; **to leave someone in the —** dejar a uno plantado, dejar a uno a buenas noches; v. tambalearse; dar un tambaleo repentino.

lure [lʊr] s. aliciente, atractivo; tentación; cebo o reclamo (para atraer); v. atraer; seducir; atraer (con cebo o reclamo).

lurk [lɝk] v. estar oculto; estar en acecho; moverse furtivamente.

luscious [lʌ́ʃəs] adj. exquisito, delicioso, sabroso.

lust [lʌst] s. lujuria; deseo vehemente; codicia; v. **to — after** codiciar.

luster [lʌ́stɚ] s. lustre, brillo.

lustrous [lʌ́strəs] adj. lustroso.

lusty [lʌ́stı] adj. vigoroso, fornido, robusto.

lute [lut] s. laúd.

luxuriant [lʌgʒúrɪənt] adj. lozano, frondoso, exuberante.

luxurious [lʌgʒúrɪəs] adj. lujoso; dado al lujo; frondoso.

luxury [lʌ́kʃərı] s. lujo.

lye [laɪ] s. lejía.

lying [láɪɪŋ] ger. de **to lie**; adj. mentiroso; **lying-in hospital** casa de maternidad.

lymph [lımpf] s. linfa.

lynch [lıntʃ] v. linchar.

lynx [lıŋks] s. lince.

lyre [laɪr] s. lira.

lyric [lírık] s. poema lírico; adj. lírico.

lyrical [lírıkl] adj. lírico.

lyricism [lírəsɪzəm] s. lirismo.

M

macaroni [mækɚónı] s. macarrón o macarrones.

macaroon [mækɚún] s. macarrón, almendrado, bollito de almendra.

machine [məʃín] s. máquina; automóvil; **— gun** ametralladora; **— made** hecho a máquina; **political —** camarilla política; **sewing —** máquina para coser.

machinery [məʃínərı] s. maquinaria.

machinist [məʃínıst] s. mecánico, maquinista.

mackerel [mǽkərəl] s. escombro, caballa (pez).

mad [mæd] adj. loco; rabioso; furioso; enojado; **to drive —** enloquecer, volver loco; **to get —** encolerizarse; **to go —** volverse loco, enloquecerse; **-ly** adv. locamente.

madam, madame [mǽdəm] s. madama, señora.

madcap [mǽdkæp] s. calavera (m.), adj. temerario; temerario; atolondrado.

madden [mǽdṇ] v. enloquecer(se).

made [med] pret. & p.p. de **to make**; **to be —** of estar hecho de; ser de; **to have something —** mandar hacer algo; **made-up** fingido, falso; artificial, pintado (con afeites).

made-to-order [medtuɔ́rdɚ] adj. hecho a la medida.

madman [mǽdmæn] s. loco.

madness [mǽdnıs] s. locura; rabia.

magazine [mægəzín] s. revista; almacén (especialmente para provisiones militares); **powder —** polvorín.

magic [mǽdʒık] s. magia; adj. mágico.

magician [mədʒíʃən] s. mágico; brujo.

magistrate [mǽdʒıstret] s. magistrado.

magnanimous [mægnǽnəməs] adj. magnánimo.

magnesium [mægnízıəm] s. magnesio.

magnet [mǽgnıt] s. imán.

magnetic [mægnétık] adj. magnético; **— pole** polo magnético; **— tape** cinta magnética.

magnetize [mǽgnətaɪz] v. magnetizar; cautivar.

magnificence [mægnífəsn̩s] s. magnificencia.

magnificent [mægnífəsṇt] adj. magnífico.

magnify [mǽgnəfaɪ] v. agrandar, engrandecer; amplificar; exagerar.

magnitude [mǽgnətjud] s. magnitud.

magpie [mǽgpaɪ] s. urraca; cotorra, hablador, habladora.

LO

mahogany [məhágəni] *s.* caoba.

maid [med] *s.* criada, sirvienta, camarera, *Méx.* recamarera, *Riopl.*, *Andes* mucama; doncella; **— of honor** doncella de honor; **old —** solterona.

maiden [médṇ] *s.* doncella; virgen; mozuela; soltera; **— lady** mujer soltera; **— voyage** primer viaje (*de un vapor*).

mail [mel] *s.* correo; correspondencia; **air —** correo aéreo; **coat of —** malla; **—bag** valija; **— train** tren correo; *v.* echar al correo.

mailbox [mélbaks] *s.* buzón.

mailman [mélmæn] *s.* cartero.

maim [mem] *v.* mutilar, estropear.

main [men] *adj.* principal, mayor, de mayor importancia; *s.* tubería, cañería principal (*de agua o gas*); alta mar, océano; **in the —** en su mayor parte; en general, en conjunto; **-ly** *adv.* principalmente.

mainland [ménlænd] *s.* continente, tierra firme.

mainspring [ménspriŋ] *s.* muelle real; origen.

maintain [mentén] *v.* mantener; sostener, afirmar; guardar.

maintenance [méntənəns] *s.* mantenimiento; sustento; manutención; sostén, sostenimiento.

maize [mez] *s.* maíz.

majestic [mədʒéstik] *adj.* majestuoso.

majesty [mædʒɪstɪ] *s.* majestad.

major [médʒɚ] *adj.* (*greater*) mayor, más grande; (*principal*) principal; **— key** tono mayor; *s.* comandante; mayor, mayor de edad; curso o asignatura de especialización (*en la universidad*); **— league** liga mayor; *v.* especializarse (*en un curso de estudios*).

majority [mədʒɔ́rətɪ] *s.* mayoría; mayor edad.

make [mek] *v.* (*do*) hacer; (*create*) fabricar; formar; (*deliver*) pronunciar (*un discurso*); **to — a clean breast of** confesar; **to — a train** alcanzar un tren; **to — a turn** dar vuelta; **to — away with** llevarse, robar; matar; **to — fast** asegurar, afianzar; **to — headway** progresar, adelantar, avanzar; **to — much of** dar mucha importancia a; **to — neither head nor tail of** no comprender nada de; **to — nothing out of** no comprender nada de, no sacar nada en limpio; **to — out in the distance** distinguir a lo lejos; **to — over** rehacer, alterar (*un traje*); **to — sure** asegurarse; **to — toward** dirigirse a, encaminarse a; **to — up a story** inventar un cuento; **to — up after a quarrel** hacer las paces; **to — up for a loss** compensar por una pérdida; **to — up one's face** pintarse la cara; **to — up one's mind** resolverse, decidirse; *s.* hechura, forma; marca (*de fábrica*); manufactura.

maker [mékɚ] *s.* hacedor; fabricante; artífice.

makeshift [mékʃıft] *adj.* provisional.

make-up [mékʌp] *s.* (*composition*) compostura, composición, hechura; (*character*) naturaleza, carácter; **facial —** afeite, cosmético.

malady [mælədɪ] *s.* mal, enfermedad.

malaria [məlériə] *s.* malaria, fiebre palúdica, paludismo.

malcontent [mælkəntɛnt] *adj. & s.* malcontento.

male [mel] *adj.* macho; varón; masculino; varonil; de hombres, de varones; *s.* macho; varón; hombre.

malice [mælıs] *s.* malicia.

malicious [məlíʃəs] *adj.* malicioso, perverso, malévolo.

malign [məláın] *v.* calumniar, difamar; *adj.* maligno; pernicioso.

malignant [məlígnənt] *adj.* maligno; malévolo.

mallet [mælıt] *s.* mazo, maceta.

malnutrition [mælnutríʃən] *s.* desnutrición.

malt [mɔlt] *s.* malta; **-ed milk** leche malteada.

mama, mamma [mámə] *s.* mamá.

mammal [mæml] *s.* mamífero.

mammoth [mæməθ] *adj.* gigantesco, enorme.

mammy [mæmɪ] *s.* mamita; niñera negra; criada negra.

man [mæn] *s.* hombre; varón; pieza (*de ajedrez*); **— and wife** marido y mujer; **to a —** unánimemente, todos a una; **officers and men** oficiales y soldados; **man-of-war** buque de guerra; **— cook** cocinero; *v.* armar, proveer de gente armada; guarnecer (*una fortaleza*); tripular (*una embarcación*).

manage [mænıdʒ] *v.* manejar; gobernar, dirigir; gestionar; **to — to do something** arreglárselas para hacer algo.

manageable [mænıdʒəbl] *adj.* manejable; domable, dócil.

management [mænıdʒmənt] *s.* manejo; dirección; gobierno, administración; gerencia.

manager [mænıdʒɚ] *s.* gerente; director, administrador; empresario.

mandate [mændet] *s.* mandato; *v.* asignar por mandato.

mane [men] *s.* melena (*del león*), crin (*del caballo*).

maneuver [mənúvɚ] *s.* maniobra; gestión; *v.* maniobrar; manipular, manejar.

manful [mænfəl] *adj.* varonil; viril.

manganese [mǽngənis] *s.* manganeso.

mange [mendʒ] *s.* sarna, roña.

manger [méndʒɚ] *s.* pesebre.

mangle [mǽngl] *v.* magullar, mutilar, destrozar, estropear; planchar en máquina de planchar; *s.* planchadora (*máquina de planchar*).

mangy [méndʒı] *adj.* sarnoso, *Am.* sarniento.

manhood [mǽnhud] *s.* virilidad; edad viril; hombres.

mania [méniə] *s.* manía.

manicure [mǽnıkjur] *s.* manicura; *v.*

manicurar.

manifest [mǽnəfest] *adj.* manifiesto; *s.* manifiesto (*lista de la carga de un buque*); *v.* manifestar; poner de manifiesto; declarar.

manifestation [mænəfestéʃən] *s.* manifestación.

manifesto [mænifésto] *s.* manifiesto, bando, proclama.

manifold [mǽnəfold] *adj.* múltiple; numeroso, diverso.

manikin [mǽnəkɪn] *s.* maniquí; muñeco; hombrecillo.

manila [mənílə] *s.* abacá (*cáñamo de Manila*); — **paper** papel de Manila.

manipulate [mənípjəlet] *v.* manipular; manejar.

manipulation [mənɪpjəléʃən] *s.* manipulación.

mankind [mænkáɪnd] *s.* humanidad, género humano; los hombres.

manly [mǽnlɪ] *adj.* varonil; viril; *adv.* varonilmente.

manner [mǽnə] *s.* (*way*) manera; modo; género; (*air*) aire, ademán; **-s** maneras, modales; costumbres; **after the — of** a la manera de; **by no — of means** de ningún modo.

mannerism [mǽnəʳɪzm] *s.* costumbre; amaneramiento.

mannish [mǽnɪʃ] *adj.* hombruno.

manoeuvre = maneuver.

manor [mǽnə] *s.* solar, casa solariega.

mansion [mǽnʃən] *s.* mansión; palacio.

manslaughter [mǽnslɔtə] *s.* homicidio impremeditado o casual.

mantel [mǽntl] *s.* manto (*de una chimenea*); repisa de chimenea.

mantle [mǽntl] *s.* manto; capa.

manual [mǽnjʊəl] *adj.* manual; — **training school** escuela de artes y oficios; *s.* manual; teclado de órgano.

manufacture [mænjəfǽktʃə] *s.* fabricación; manufactura; *v.* fabricar, manufacturar.

manufacturer [mænjəfǽktərə] *s.* fabricante.

manufacturing [mænjəfǽktfərɪŋ] *s.* fabricación; *adj.* fabril, manufacturero.

manure [mənúr] *s.* estiércol, abono; *v.* estercolar, abonar (*la tierra*).

manuscript [mǽnjəskrɪpt] *adj. & s.* manuscrito.

many [ménɪ] *adj.* muchos; — **a time** muchas veces; **a great —** muchísimos; **as — as** tantos como; cuantos; **as — as five** hasta cinco; **how —?** ¿cuántos?; **three books too —** tres libros de más; **too —** demasiados.

map [mæp] *s.* mapa; *v.* trazar un mapa de; **to — out** proyectar, planear.

maple [mépl] *s.* arce, *Méx.* meple; *Ríopl.* maple.

mar [mar] *v.* desfigurar, estropear.

marble [márbl] *s.* mármol; canica (*para jugar*); **to play -s** jugar a las canicas; *adj.* de mármol; marmóreo.

march [martʃ] *s.* marcha; *v.* marchar, caminar; hacer marchar; **to — in** entrar marchando; **to — out** marcharse; salirse marchando.

March [martʃ] *s.* marzo.

mare [mer] *s.* yegua.

margarine [márdʒərɪn] *s.* margarina.

margin [márdʒɪn] *s.* margen; orilla; sobrante; reserva (*fondos*).

marginal [márdʒɪn] *adj.* marginal; — **note** nota marginal, acotación.

marigold [mǽrəgold] *s.* caléndula, maravilla.

marine [mərín] *adj.* marino; marítimo; — **corps** cuerpo de marinos; *s.* marino; soldado de marina; **merchant —** marina mercante.

mariner [mǽrənə] *s.* marinero.

maritime [mǽrətaɪm] *adj.* marítimo.

mark [mark] *s.* marca; señal, seña; nota, calificación; **question —** punto de interrogación; **to come up to the —** alcanzar la norma requerida; **to hit the —** dar en el blanco; **to make one's —** distinguirse; **to miss one's —** fallar; errar el tiro; fracasar; *v.* marcar; señalar; notar; observar; calificar; — **my words!** ¡advierte lo que te digo!; **to — down** anotar, apuntar; rebajar el precio de.

marker [márkə] *s.* marcador; marca, señal; jalón.

market [márkɪt] *s.* mercado, plaza; — **place** mercado, plaza; — **price** precio corriente; — **meat —** carnicería; **stock —** mercado de valores, bolsa; *v.* vender; vender o comprar en el mercado; **to go -ing** ir de compras.

marmalade [mármled] *s.* mermelada.

maroon [mərún] *s. & adj.* rojo obscuro.

marooned [mərúnd] *adj.* abandonado (*en lugar desierto*) aislado; **to get —** encontrarse aislado, perdido o incomunicado.

marquis [márkwɪs] *s.* marqués.

marquise [markíz] *s.* marquesa.

marriage [mǽrɪdʒ] *s.* matrimonio; casamiento, boda; unión, enlace; — **license** licencia para casarse.

marriageable [mǽrɪdʒəbl] *adj.* casadero.

married [mǽrɪd] *adj.* casado; conyugal; — **couple** matrimonio, cónyuges; pareja de casados; **to get —** casarse.

marrow [mǽro] *s.* meollo, tuétano, medula (*de los huesos*).

marry [mǽrɪ] *v.* casar; casarse; casarse con.

marsh [marʃ] *s.* pantano; ciénaga.

marshal [márʃəl] *s.* mariscal; alguacil; jefe de policía (*en ciertas regiones*); maestro de ceremonia; **fire —** jefe de bomberos; *v.* ordenar, arreglar; guiar, conducir con ceremonia.

marshmallow [márʃmælo] *s.* pastilla o bombón de altea.

marshy [márʃɪ] *adj.* pantanoso, cenagoso.

mart [mart] *s.* mercado.

martial [márʃəl] *adj.* marcial; — **law** estado de guerra.

martin [mártɪn] *s.* avión (*pájaro*).

martyr [mártə] *s.* mártir; *v.* martirizar, torturar, atormentar.

MA

martyrdom [mártədəm] *s.* martirio.

marvel [márvḷ] *s.* maravilla; *v.* maravillarse.

marvelous [márvḷəs] *adj.* maravilloso.

mascot [mǽskət] *s.* mascota.

masculine [mǽskjəlɪn] *adj.* masculino; varonil; hombruno.

mash [mæʃ] *v.* majar, amasar; machacar, magullar; **-ed potatoes** puré de papas (*o* patatas); patatas majadas.

mask [mæsk] *s.* máscara; disfraz; careta; *v.* disfrazar, enmascarar; encubrir; **-ed ball** baile de máscaras.

mason [mésṇ] *s.* albañil; **Mason** masón, francmasón.

masonry [mésṇrɪ] *s.* albañilería; mampostería; **Masonry** masonería, francmasonería.

masquerade [mæskəréd] *s.* mascarada; disfraz, máscara; *v.* enmascararse, disfrazarse; andar disfrazado.

mass [mæs] *s.* masa; montón; mole; mayoría, mayor parte; misa; **— meeting** mitin popular; **— communication** comunicación extensa; **— media** los medios de comunicarse con el publico (*radio, televisión, periódicos, etc.*); **the -es** las masas, el pueblo; *v.* juntar(se) en masa.

massacre [mǽsəkɚ] *s.* hecatombe, matanza, carnicería, destrozo; *v.* hacer matanza o hecatombe, destrozar.

massage [məsáʒ] *v.* friccionar, dar masaje; *s.* masaje.

massive [mǽsɪv] *adj.* sólido, macizo; voluminoso, imponente.

mast [mæst] *s.* mástil, palo.

master [mǽstɚ] *s.* (*head*) amo, dueño, señor; maestro; patrón; (*skilled*) experto, perito; **band —** director de la banda; **— of arts** maestro en artes, licenciado; **-'s degree** licenciatura, grado de licenciado; *adj.* maestro; **— builder** maestro de obras; **— key** llave maestra; *v.* dominar; domar; gobernar; **to — a language** dominar un idioma.

masterful [mǽstɚfəl] *adj.* magistral; dominante.

masterly [mǽstɚlɪ] *adj.* magistral; *adv.* magistralmente.

masterpiece [mǽstɚpis] *s.* obra maestra.

mastery [mǽstərɪ] *s.* maestría, arte, destreza; dominio.

mastiff [mǽstɪf] *s.* mastín, alano.

mat [mæt] *s.* (*covering*) estera; esterilla, felpudo, tapete; (*gymnasium*) colchoncillo (*de gimnasia*); borde de cartón (*para hacer resaltar una pintura*).

match [mæʧ] *s.* (*pair*) pareja; (*game*) partida, contienda, juego; (*light*) fósforo, cerilla; *Méx.* cerillo; **he has no — no tiene igual; he is a good —** es un buen partido; **the hat and coat are a good —** el abrigo y el sombrero hacen juego; *v.* igualar; aparear; hacer juego, armonizar; **to — one's strength** medir uno sus fuerzas; **these colors do not — well** estos colores no casan bien.

matchless [mǽʧlɪs] *adj.* sin par, sin igual, incomparable.

mate [met] *s.* compañero, compañera; consorte; macho o hembra (*entre animales o aves*); piloto (*el segundo de un buque mercante*); oficial subalterno (*en la marina*); *v.* aparear(se).

material [mətírɪəl] *adj.* material; esencial; *s.* material; tejido, género; materia; **raw —** materia prima.

maternal [mətɝnḷ] *adj.* maternal, materno.

maternity [mətɝnətɪ] *s.* maternidad.

mathematical [mæθəmǽtɪkḷ] *adj.* matemático.

mathematician [mæθəmətíʃən] *s.* matemático.

mathematics [mæθəmǽtɪks] *s.* matemáticas.

matinée [mætņé] *s.* función de la tarde, *Am.* matiné.

matriarch [métrɪɑrk] *s.* matriarca.

matriculate [mətríkjəlet] *v.* matricular(se).

matriculation [mətrɪkjəléʃən] *s.* matriculación, matrícula.

matrimony [mǽtrəmonɪ] *s.* matrimonio, casamiento.

matrix [métrɪks] *s.* matriz; molde.

matron [métrən] *s.* matrona, madre de familia; ama de llaves; vigilante, cuidadora (*de un asilo, cárcel par mujeres, etc.*).

matter [mǽtɚ] *s.* (*substance*) material, materia; sustancia; (*affair*) asunto, cuestión; cosa; (*discharge*) pus; **— for complaint** motivo de queja; **— of two minutes** cosa de dos minutos; **as a — of fact** de hecho; en verdad, en realidad; **business -s** negocios; **printed —** impresos; **serious —** cosa seria; **it is of no —** no tiene importancia; **to do something as a — of course** hacer algo por rutina; **what is the —?** ¿qué pasa?; ¿qué tiene Vd.?; **matter-of-fact person** persona de poca imaginación; *v.* importar; supurar; **it does not —** no importa, no le hace.

mattress [mǽtrɪs] *s.* colchón; **spring — colchón de muelles.**

mature [mətjúr] *adj.* maduro; **a — note** un pagaré vencido; *v.* madurar(se); vencerse, hacerse cobrable o pagadero (*un pagaré, una deuda*).

maturity [mətjúrətɪ] *s.* madurez; vencimiento (*de una deuda u obligación*).

maul [mɔl] *v.* magullar; maltratar; manejar rudamente; golpear.

maverick [mǽvɚɪk] *s.* animal sin marca; becerro suelto.

maxim [mǽksɪm] *s.* máxima.

maximum [mǽksəməm] *adj. & s.* máximo.

may [me] *v. irr. y defect.* (*able*) poder; (*permitted*) tener permiso para, serle permitido a uno; (*possible*) ser posible; **— I sit down?** ¿puedo sentarme?; **— you have a good time** que se divierta Vd.; **it — be that** puede ser que, tal vez sea que; **it — rain** puede (ser) que llueva, es posible que llueva; **she — be late** puede (ser) que llegue ella tarde.

May [me] *s.* mayo, mes de mayo; **— Day** primero de mayo; **—pole** mayo; **— Queen** maya (*reina de la fiesta del primero de mayo*).

maybe [mébi] *adv.* quizás, tal vez, acaso.

mayonnaise [meənéz] *s.* mayonesa.

mayor [méə·] *s.* alcalde, alcalde mayor.

maze [mez] *s.* laberinto; confusión; **to be in a —** estar confuso o perplejo.

me [mi] *pron. pers.* me; mí (*después de preposición*); **give it to —** démelo (a mí); **for —** para mí; **with —** conmigo.

meadow [médo] *s.* pradera, prado; **— lark** alondra de los prados.

meager [mígə·] *adj.* escaso, insuficiente; magro, flaco.

meal [mil] *s.* comida; harina (*a medio moler*); **corn —** harina de maíz; **—time** hora de comer.

mean [min] *adj.* (*malicious*) ruin, bajo; vil; (*humble*) humilde; (*stingy*) mezquino, tacaño; (*difficult*) de mal genio; (*sick*) malo, indispuesto; (*middle*) mediano; medio; intermedio; **— distance** distancia media; *s.* medio; término medio; **-s** medios; recursos; **a man of -s** un hombre pudiente o rico; **by -s of** por medio de; **by all -s** de todos modos; a toda costa; por supuesto; **by no -s** de ningún modo; *v.* querer decir, significar; pensar, proponerse, tener la intención de; intentar; destinar; **he -s well** tiene buenas intenciones.

meander [miændə·] *v.* serpentear.

meaning [mínɪŋ] *s.* (*sense*) significado, sentido; significación; (*intent*) propósito, intención; *adj.* significativo; **well-meaning** bien intencionado.

meaningless [mínɪŋlɪs] *adj.* sin sentido, vacío de sentido.

meanness [mínnɪs] *s.* ruindad, vileza, bajeza; mezquindad.

meant [mɛnt] *pret. & p.p.* de **to mean.**

meantime [míntaɪm] *adv.* mientras tanto, entretanto; *s.* ínterin, entretanto; **in the —** en el ínterin, mientras tanto.

meanwhile [mínhwaɪl] = **meantime.**

measles [mízlz] *s.* sarampión.

measurable [méʒrəbl] *adj.* medible, mensurable; **measurably** *adv.* marcadamente.

measure [méʒə·] *s.* (*dimension*) medida; compás (*de música*); cadencia, ritmo; (*law*) proyecto de ley; ley; **beyond —** sobremanera; con exceso; **dry —** medida para áridos; **in large —** en gran parte, en gran manera; *v.* medir.

measured [méʒə·d] *adj.* medido; moderado; acompasado.

measurement [méʒə·mənt] *s.* medida; dimensión; tamaño; medición.

meat [mit] *s.* carne; meollo, sustancia; **— ball** albóndiga; **— market** carnicería; **cold —** fiambre.

meaty [míti] *adj.* carnoso; sustancioso.

mechanic [məkǽnɪk] *adj. & s.* mecánico, **-s** *s.* mecánica.

mechanical [məkǽnɪkl] *adj.* mecánico; maquinal.

mechanism [mékənɪzəm] *s.* mecanismo.

medal [médl] *s.* medalla.

meddle [médl] *v.* entrometerse o entremeterse; meterse.

meddler [médlə·] *s.* entremetido.

meddlesome [médlsəm] *adj.* entremetido.

median [mídɪən] *adj.* mediano, del medio; *s.* punto, línea o número del medio; mediana.

mediate [mídɪet] *v.* mediar; intervenir; arbitrar.

mediation [midɪéʃən] *s.* mediación, intervención, intercesión.

mediator [mídɪətə·] *s.* mediador, mediador, -nero, árbitro.

medical [médɪkl] *adj.* médico; **— school** escuela de medicina.

medication [medɪkéʃən] *s.* medicación.

medicine [médəsn] *s.* medicina; medicamento; **— ball** pelota grande de cuero; **— cabinet** botiquín; **— man** curandero indio.

medieval [midíívl] *adj.* medioeval o medieval.

mediocre [midíókə·] *adj.* mediocre, mediano; ordinario.

mediocrity [midiákrətɪ] *s.* mediocridad, medianía.

meditate [médətet] *v.* meditar.

meditation [medətéʃən] *s.* meditación.

medium [mídɪəm] *s.* medio; medio ambiente; *adj.* mediano; intermedio; **a medio cocer, a medio asar; — of exchange** mediador de cambio.

medley [médlɪ] *s.* baturrillo, mezcla, mezcolanza.

meek [mik] *adj.* manso, dócil, paciente, sufrido.

meekness [míknɪs] *s.* mansedumbre, docilidad.

meet [mit] *v.* encontrar(se); reunirse; conocer (*personalmente*), ser presentado a; ir a esperar (*un tren, vapor, o a alguien*); satisfacer (*deseos, requisitos, etc.*); pagar (*una deuda*); sufragar (*gastos*); responder a (*una acusación*); **to — in battle** trabar batalla; **to — with** encontrarse con; tropezar con; topar con; reunirse con; *s.* concurso; contienda (*tratándose de deportes*); **track —** competencia de atletas.

meeting [mítɪŋ] *s.* reunión; mitin; sesión; asamblea; encuentro.

megaphone [mégəfon] *s.* megáfono, portavoz, bocina.

melancholy [mélənkɑlɪ] *s.* melancolía; *adj.* melancólico.

melee [méle] *s.* reyerta; zafarrancho.

mellow [mélo] *adj.* maduro, sazonado; dulce, blando, suave; *v.* madurar(se), sazonar(se); ablandar(se), suavizar(se).

melodious [məlódɪəs] *adj.* melodioso.

melodrama [mélodramə] *s.* melodrama.

melody [mélədɪ] *s.* melodía.

MA

melon [mélən] s. melón.
melt [mɛlt] v. derretir(se); disolver(se); fundir(se).
member [mémbɚ] s. miembro; socio.
membership [mémbɚʃɪp] s. número de miembros o socios; asociación; (los) miembros (de un club o sociedad).
membrane [mémbren] s. membrana.
memento [mɪméntó] s. memento, memoria, recuerdo.
memoir [mémwar] s. memoria, apuntaciones; **-s** memorias; autobiografía.
memorable [mémərəbl] adj. memorable.
memorandum [mɛmərǽndəm] s. memorándum; memoria, apunte; **— book** memorándum, librito de apuntes, memorial.
memorial [məmóriəl] s. (monument) monumento conmemorativo; (occasion) obra o fiesta conmemorativa; memorial, petición; adj. conmemorativo.
memorize [mémərɑɪz] v. aprender de memoria.
memory [mémɔri] s. memoria; recuerdo.
men [mɛn] pl. de **man**.
menace [ménɪs] s. amenaza; v. amenazar.
mend [mɛnd] v. remendar; reparar, componer; -enmendar; **to — one's ways** enmendarse, reformarse; s. remiendo; reparación; **to be on the —** ir mejorando.
menial [mínɪəl] adj. servil, bajo.
menstruation [mɛnstruéʃən] s. menstruo o menstruación.
mental [méntl] adj. mental.
mentality [mɛntǽlətɪ] s. mentalidad, ingenio.
mention [ménʃən] s. mención; alusión; v. mencionar, mentar; **don't — it** no hay de qué (contestación a "thank you").
menu [ménju] s. menú, lista de platos.
meow [mjɑu] = **mew**.
mercantile [mɚkǽntil] adj. mercantil.
mercenary [mɚsɲɛrɪ] adj. mercenario.
merchandise [mɚtʃəndɑɪz] s. mercancías, mercaderías; **piece of —** mercancía.
merchant [mɚtʃənt] s. comerciante; negociante; mercader; adj. mercante, mercantil; **— marine** marina mercante.
merciful [mɚsɪfəl] adj. misericordioso, piadoso.
merciless [mɚsɪlɪs] adj. sin piedad, despiadado, incompasivo.
mercury [mɚkjərɪ] s. mercurio; azogue.
mercy [mɚsɪ] s. (favor) merced; favor, gracia; (compassion) misericordia, piedad, compasión; **to be at the — of** estar a merced de.
mere [mɪr] adj. mero; simple, puro; **a — formality** una pura formalidad, no más que una formalidad, una formalidad no más; **a — trifle** una nonada; **-ly** adv. meramente; sólo, solamente; simplemente.

merge [mɚdʒ] v. combinar(se), unir(se); absorber(se); fundirse.
merger [mɚdʒɚ] s. amalgamación comercial.
meridian [mərídɪən] adj. & s. meridiano.
merit [mérɪt] s. mérito; v. merecer.
meritorious [mɛrətóriəs] adj. meritorio.
mermaid [mɚmed] s. ninfa marina.
merrily [mérəlɪ] adv. alegremente, con regocijo.
merriment [mérɪmənt] s. alegría, regocijo, júbilo.
merry [mérɪ] adj. alegre; jovial; divertido; festivo; **— Christmas** Felices Navidades, Felices Pascuas; **to make —** divertirse.
merry-go-round [mérɪgərɑund] s. tío vivo, Méx., C.A. los caballitos; Ríopl. calesita.
merrymaker [mérɪmekɚ] s. fiestero, juerguista.
merrymaking [mérɪmekɪŋ] s. regocijo; jaleo, juerga, jolgorio; adj. regocijado, alegre, festivo, fiestero.
mesh [mɛʃ] s. malla; red; **-es** red, redes; v. enredar, coger con red; **to — gears** engranar.
mess [mɛs] s. (food) rancho, comida (en el ejército o la marina); (confusion) lío, confusión; (dirt) suciedad; **— of fish** plato o ración de pescado; **to make a — of** revolver, confundir; ensuciar; echar a perder; v. revolver, confundir; ensuciar, echar a perder (generalmente: **to — up**); **to — around** revolver o mezclar las cosas; entrometerse; **messy** [mésɪ] adj. desordenado, desarreglado; sucio.
message [mésɪdʒ] s. mensaje; parte (m.), comunicación; recado.
messenger [mésndʒɚ] s. mensajero; mandadero.
met [mɛt] pret. & p.p. de **to meet**.
metabolism [mətǽbəlɪzm] s. metabolismo.
metal [métl] s. metal; adj. de metal, metálico.
metallic [mətǽlɪk] adj. metálico.
metallurgy [mɛtlɚdʒɪ] s. metalurgia.
metaphor [métəfɚ] s. metáfora.
metathesis [mətǽθəsɪs] s. metátesis.
meteor [mítɪɚ] s. meteoro; estrella fugaz.
meteorite [mítɪorɑɪt] s. meteorito.
meteorological [mitɪərəládʒɪk] adj. meteorológico.
meteorology [mitɪərálədʒɪ] s. meteorología.
meter [mítɚ] s. metro; contador (de gas, agua, electricidad, etc.).
method [méθəd] s. método; técnica.
methodical [məθádɪk] adj. metódico.
metre = **meter**.
metric [métrɪk] adj. métrico; **— system** sistema métrico.
metropolis [mətrápl̩ɪs] s. metrópoli.
metropolitan [metrəpálətn] adj. metropolitano.
mettle [métl̩] s. temple, brío, ánimo, valor.

mew [mju] *s.* maullido, maúllo, miau; *v.* maullar.

Mexican [méksɪkən] *adj. & s.* mejicano o mexicano.

mezzanine [mézənin] *s.* entresuelo.

mice [maɪs] *pl. de* mouse.

microbe [máɪkrob] *s.* microbio.

microfilm [máɪkrəfɪlm] *s.* microfilm.

microphone [máɪkrəfon] *s.* micrófono.

microscope [máɪkrəskop] *s.* microscopio.

microscopic [maɪkrəskúpɪk] *adj.* microscópico.

mid [mɪd] *adj.* medio (*úsase por lo general en composición*); **in — air** en el aire; *prep.* en medio de, entre.

midday [mídde] *s.* mediodía; *adj.* del mediodía.

middle [mídl] *adj.* medio; intermedio; **Middle Ages** Edad Media; **— finger** dedo de en medio, dedo del corazón; **— size** tamaño mediano; *s.* medio, centro, mitad; **in the — of** en medio de, a la mitad de; **towards the — of the month** a mediados del mes; **— class** clase media.

middle-aged [mídléʒd] *adj.* de edad mediana, de edad madura.

middleman [mídlmæn] *s.* revendedor; medianero, corredor, agente.

middle-sized [mídlsáɪzd] *adj.* de mediano tamaño, de mediana estatura.

middy [mídɪ] *s.* guardiamarina (*m.*); **— blouse** blusa a la marinera.

midget [mídʒɪt] *s.* enanillo.

midnight [mídnaɪt] *s.* medianoche; *adj.* de (la) medianoche; **— blue** azul oscuro; **— Mass** misa de gallo.

midriff [mídrɪf] *s.* diafragma.

midshipman [mídʃɪpmən] *s.* guardiamarina (*m.*).

midst [mɪdst] *s.* medio, centro; **in the — of** en medio de, entre; **in our —** entre nosotros.

midstream [mídstrim] *s.* el medio (*o* el centro) de la corriente.

midsummer [mídsámɚ] *s.* pleno verano, solsticio estival, la mitad del verano.

midterm [mídtɝm]; **— examination** examen a mitad del curso.

midway [mídwé] *adj.* situado a medio camino; equidistante; *adv.* a medio camino; en medio del camino.

midwife [mídwaɪf] *s.* partera, comadrona.

mien [min] *s.* facha, aspecto.

might [maɪt] *imperf. de* may podía; podría; pudiera, pudiese; *s.* poder, poderío, fuerza.

mighty [máɪtɪ] *adj.* poderoso, potente, fuerte; *adv.* muy, sumamente.

migrant [máɪgrənt] *adj.* migratorio.

migrate [máɪgret] *v.* emigrar.

migration [maɪgréʃən] *s.* migración.

mike [maɪk] = **microphone**.

mild [maɪld] *adj. (gentle)* suave; blando; apacible; (*moderate*) templado, moderado.

mildew [míldu] *s.* moho; enmohecimiento.

mildness [máɪldnɪs] *s.* suavidad; mansedumbre; apacibilidad; templanza, dulzura.

mile [maɪl] *s.* milla; **—stone** mojón.

mileage [máɪlɪdʒ] *s.* millaje, número de millas; recorrido (*en millas*). *Compárese* kilometraje, número de kilómetros.

militant [mílɪtənt] *s.* militante; belicoso.

military [mílɪtɛrɪ] *adj.* militar; de guerra; *s.* **the —** el ejército; los militares.

militia [mɪlíʃə] *s.* milicia.

milk [mɪlk] *s.* leche; **— diet** régimen lácteo; *v.* ordeñar.

milkmaid [mílkmed] *s.* lechera.

milkman [mílkmən] *s.* lechero, *Am.* vaquero.

milky [mílkɪ] *adj.* lácteo; lechoso; **Milky Way** Vía Láctea.

mill [mɪl] *s.* (*grinder*) molino; (*factory*) fábrica; (*money*) la milésima parte de un dólar; **saw—** aserradero; **spinning —** hilandería; **sugar —** ingenio de azúcar; **textile —** fábrica de tejidos; *v.* moler; aserrar (*madera*); fabricar; acordonar (*el canto de la moneda*); **to — around** arremolinarse (*una muchedumbre*).

miller [mílɚ] *s.* molinero; mariposa nocturna.

milliner [mílɪnɚ] *s.* modista (*de sombreros para señoras*).

millinery [mílɪnɛrɪ] *s.* sombreros de señora; artículos para sombreros de señora; oficio de modista; **— shop** sombrerería.

million [míljən] *s.* millón; **a — dollars** un millón de dólares.

millionaire [mɪljənér] *adj. & s.* millonario.

millionth [míljənθ] *adj. & s.* millonésimo.

millstone [mílston] *s.* muela o piedra de molino; carga pesada.

mimic [mímɪk] *adj.* mímico, imitativo; **— battle** simulacro; *s.* imitador, remedador; *v.* imitar, remedar.

mince [mɪns] *v.* picar, desmenuzar; **not to — words** hablar con toda franqueza.

mincemeat [mínsmit] *s.* picadillo (*especialmente el de carne, pasas, manzanas y especias*).

mind [maɪnd] *s.* (*brain*) mente; (*thought*) pensamiento; inteligencia; (*spirit*) ánimo, espíritu; (*purpose*) propósito, intención; (*opinion*) parecer, opinión; **to be out of one's —** estar loco, haber perdido el juicio; **to change one's —** cambiar de parecer; **to give someone a piece of one's —** cantarle a alguien la verdad; echarle a alguien un buen regaño; **to have a — to** estar por; sentir ganas de; **to make up one's —** decidirse, resolverse; **to my —** a mi modo de ver; **to speak one's — freely** hablar con toda franqueza; *v.* cuidar; atender a, hacer caso de; obedecer; **I don't —** no tengo inconveniente en ello; **never —** no importa; no se preocupe; no se

moleste; no haga Vd. caso; **to — one's own business** atendar a lo suyo, no meterse en lo ajeno.

mindful [máindfəl] *adj.* atento (a); cuidadoso (de).

mine [main] *pron. pos.* mio (mia, mios, mias); el mio (la mia, los mios, las mias); **a book of —** un libro mio.

mine [main] *s.* mina; **— sweeper** dragaminas; *v.* minar; explotar (*una mina*); extraer (*mineral*).

miner [máinə] *s.* minero.

mineral [mínərəl] *adj. & s.* mineral.

mingle [míngl] *v.* mezclar(se); entremezclar(se); confundir(se); juntarse.

miniature [mínitʃə] *s.* miniatura; *adj.* en miniatura; diminuto.

minimal [mínəml] *adj.* mínimo.

minimize [mínəmaiz] *v.* empequeñecer.

minimum [mínəməm] *adj. & s.* mínimo.

mining [máiniŋ] *s.* minería, explotación de minas; *adj.* minero; **— engineer** ingeniero de minas.

miniskirt [mínîskət] *s.* minifalda.

minister [mínistə] *s.* ministro; pastor, clérigo; *v.* ministrar; atender; proveer, socorrer.

ministry [mínistri] *s.* ministerio; socorro, ayuda.

mink [miŋk] *s.* visón.

minnow [míno] *s.* pececillo de río.

minor [máinə] *adj.* (*young*) menor; de menor edad; (*secondary*) secundario; **— key** tono menor; *s.* menor de edad; premisa menor (*de un silogismo*); tono menor; curso o asignatura menor.

minority [mənórəti] *s.* minoría; minoridad, menor edad; menor parte.

minstrel [mínstrəl] *s.* trovador; bardo, vate; actor cómico que remeda al negro norteamericano.

mint [mint] *s.* (*flavor*) menta, hierbabuena (*yerbabuena*); (*candy*) pastilla o bombón de menta; (*money*) casa de moneda; **a — of money** un montón de dinero, la mar de dinero; *v.* acuñar.

mintage [míntədʒ] *s.* acuñación; moneda acuñada.

minuet [minjuét] *s.* minué.

minus [máinəs] *adj.* negativo; sin, falto de; **seven — four** siete menos cuatro; *s.* menos, signo menos.

minute [mínit] *s.* minuto; **-s** acta (*de una junta*); **— hand** minutero.

minute [mənjút] *adj.* menudo, diminuto; minucioso, detallado.

miracle [mírəkl] *s.* milagro.

miraculous [mərækjələs] *adj.* milagroso.

mirage [mərádʒ] *s.* espejismo.

mire [mair] *s.* cieno, fango, lodo; *v.* atascar(se) en el fango; enlodar(se).

mirror [mírə] *s.* espejo; *v.* reflejar.

mirth [məθ] *s.* júbilo, regocijo, alegría.

mirthful [mə́θfəl] *adj.* jubiloso, regocijado, gozoso, alegre.

miry [máiri] *adj.* cenagoso, fangoso, lodoso.

misadventure [misədvéntʃə] *s.* desgracia; contratiempo.

misbehave [misbihév] *v.* portarse mal, obrar mal.

miscarriage [miskǽridʒ] *s.* aborto, mal parto; mal éxito; extravío (*de una carta, papel, etc.*).

miscarry [miskǽri] *v.* (*fail*) malograrse, frustrarse; extraviarse (*una carta*); (*abort*) abortar.

miscellaneous [misəlénias] *adj.* misceláneo, diverso.

mischief [místʃif] *s.* travesura; diablura; mal, daño; diablillo, persona traviesa.

mischievous [místʃivəs] *adj.* travieso; malicioso; dañino.

misconception [miskənsépʃən] *s.* concepto erróneo.

misconduct [miskándʌkt] *s.* mala conducta; mala administración; [miskəndʌkt] *v.* maladministrar, manejar mal; **to — oneself** portarse mal, conducirse mal.

misdeed [misdid] *s.* fechoría, mala acción.

misdemeanor [misdimínə] *s.* mal comportamiento; fechoría.

miser [máizə] *s.* avaro, avariento.

miserable [mízrəbl] *adj.* miserable; infeliz, desdichado.

miserly [máizəli] *adj.* avariento, avaro, tacaño, mezquino.

misery [mízri] *s.* miseria, desgracia; estrechez, pobreza; dolor.

misfortune [misfórtʃən] *s.* infortunio, desgracia, desastre.

misgiving [misgíviŋ] *s.* mal presentimiento, aprensión, recelo, temor.

misguided [misgáidəd] *adj.* mal aconsejado.

mishap [míshæp] *s.* desgracia, contratiempo, accidente.

misjudge [misdʒʌ́dʒ] *v.* juzgar mal.

mislaid [misléd] *pret. & p.p.* de **to mislay.**

mislay [mislé] *v.* extraviar, perder; poner fuera de su sitio, colocar mal; traspapelar (*una carta, documento, etc.*).

mislead [mislíd] *v.* guiar por mal camino; extraviar, descarriar; engañar.

misled [misléd] *pret. & p.p.* de **to mislead.**

mismanage [mismǽnidʒ] *v.* administrar.

misplace [misplés] *v.* extraviar, poner fuera de su sitio, colocar mal; traspapelar (*una carta, documento, etc.*).

misprint [misprínt] *s.* errata, error tipográfico, error de imprenta.

mispronounce [míspɪənauns] *v.* pronunciar mal.

misrepresent [misreprizént] *v.* falsear, falsificar; tergiversar.

miss [mis] *v.* (*not hit*) errar, no acertar; fallar; (*omit*) equivocar; perder; faltar a; (*feel absence of*) echar de menos; *Am.* extrañar; **he just -ed being killed** por poco lo matan; *s.* error;

falla, falta.

miss [mɪs] *s.* señorita; **Miss Smith** la señorita Smith.

missile [mísl] *s.* proyectil; arma arrojadiza; *adj.* arrojadizo, que se puede arrojar o tirar.

missing [mísɪŋ] *adj.* ausente; perdido; **one book is —** falta un libro.

mission [mí∫ən] *s.* misión.

missionary [mí∫ənɛrɪ] *adj. & s.* misionero.

misspell [mɪsspél] *v.* escribir con mala ortografía, deletrear mal.

mist [mɪst] *s.* neblina, niebla; llovizna, *Ven., Col., Andes* garúa; *v.* lloviznar; anublar.

mistake [məsték] *s.* error, yerro, equivocación; errata (*de imprenta*); **to make a —** equivocarse; *v.* equivocar.

mistaken [məstékən] *p.p. de* **to mistake** & *adj.* equivocado; errado; erróneo, incorrecto; **to be —** estar equivocado, equivocarse, errar.

mister [místɚ] *s.* señor.

mistook [mɪstúk] *pret. de* **to mistake.**

mistreat [mɪstrít] *v.* maltratar.

mistress [místrɪs] *s.* señora; ama, dueña; querida, amante; **school—** maestra.

mistrial [mɪstráɪl] *s.* pleito viciado de nulidad.

mistrust [mɪstrʌst] *s.* desconfianza; *v.* desconfiar de.

mistrustful [mɪstrʌstfəl] *adj.* desconfiado, sospechoso, receloso.

misty [místɪ] *adj.* brumoso; nublado; empañado; vago, indistinto.

misunderstand [mɪsʌndɚstǽnd] *v.* comprender mal; entender mal; interpretar mal; no comprender.

misunderstanding [mɪsʌndɚstǽndɪŋ] *s.* equivocación; mala interpretación, mala inteligencia; desavenencia.

misunderstood [mɪsʌndɚstúd] *pret. & p.p. de* **to misunderstand.**

misuse [mɪsjús] *s.* abuso; mal uso; malversación (*de fondos*); [mɪsjúz] *v.* abusar de; maltratar; usar o emplear mal; malversar (*fondos*).

mite [maɪt] *s.* óbolo, friolera, pequeñez; criatura.

miter [máɪtɚ] *s.* mitra; dignidad de obispo.

mitigate [mítəget] *v.* mitigar.

mitten [mítn] *s.* mitón (*guante de una pieza y sin dedos*).

mix [mɪks] *v.* mezclar(se); unir(se), juntar(se), asociar(se); **to — someone up** confundir a uno; *s.* mezcla; confusión, lío.

mixture [míkstʃɚ] *s.* mezcla; mezcolanza.

mix-up [míksʌp] *s.* equívoco; enredo.

moan [mon] *s.* quejido, gemido; *v.* gemir; quejarse; lamentar(se).

moat [mot] *s.* foso.

mob [mab] *s.* populacho; muchedumbre, gentío, *Am.* bola (*de gente*); *v.* atropellar; apiñarse o agolparse alrededor de.

mobile [móbḷ] *adj.* móvil; movible; movedizo.

mobilization [mobḷəzé∫ən] *s.* movilización.

mobilize [móbḷaɪz] *v.* movilizar.

moccasin [mákəsɪn] *s. Am.* mocasín (*zapato burdo de cuero*); *Am.* mocasín (*víbora venenosa*).

mock [mɔk] *v.* (*ridicule*) mofar, mofarse de; (*imitate*) remedar, imitar; **to — at** mofarse de; burlarse de; *s.* mofa, burla, escarnio; mímica; remedo; *adj.* falso, ficticio, imitado; **— battle** simulacro, batalla fingida.

mockery [mákərɪ] *s.* burla, mofa, escarnio; remedo.

mockup [mákʌp] *s.* maqueta; modelo.

mode [mod] *s.* modo, manera; moda.

model [mádḷ] *s.* (*guide*) modelo; (*pattern*) patrón; (*figure*) figurín, maniquí; *adj.* ejemplar; modelo; **— school** escuela modelo; *v.* modelar; moldear, formar; posar, servir de modelo.

moderate [mádɚɪt] *adj.* moderado; templado; módico; [mádɚet] *v.* moderar(se); templar(se).

moderation [mɑdɚé∫ən] *s.* moderación; templanza.

modern [mádɚn] *adj.* moderno.

modernize [mádɚnaɪz] *v.* modernizar.

modest [mádɪst] *adj.* modesto.

modesty [mádɪstɪ] *s.* modestia.

modification [madəfəké∫ən] *s.* modificación.

modify [mádəfaɪ] *v.* modificar.

modulate [mádʒəlet] *v.* modular.

mohair [móhɛr] *s.* moer.

Mohammedan [mohǽmədən] *adj. & s.* mahometano.

moist [mɔɪst] *adj.* húmedo; mojado.

moisten [mɔ́ɪsn̩] *v.* humedecer, mojar.

moisture [mɔ́ɪstʃɚ] *s.* humedad.

molar [mólɚ] *adj.* molar; *s.* muela.

molasses [məlǽsɪz] *s.* melaza, miel de caña.

mold [mold] *s.* (*form*) molde, matriz; (*substance*) moho; tierra vegetal; *v.* moldear, amoldar; modelar; enmohecer(se), cubrir(se) de moho.

molder [móldɚ] *v.* desmoronarse.

molding [móldɪŋ] *s.* moldura; moldeamiento.

moldy [móldɪ] *adj.* mohoso.

mole [mol] *s.* lunar; topo (*animal*); dique, malecón, rompeolas.

molecule [máləkjul] *s.* molécula.

molest [məlést] *v.* molestar.

mollify [máləfaɪ] *v.* apaciguar.

molten [móltn̩] *adj.* derretido, fundido, en fusión.

moment [mómənt] *s.* momento; importancia, consecuencia.

momentary [móməntɛrɪ] *adj.* momentáneo.

momentous [moméntəs] *adj.* importante.

momentum [moméntəm] *s.* momento (*de una fuerza*); ímpetu.

monarch [mánɚk] *s.* monarca.

monarchy [mánɚkɪ] *s.* monarquía.

monastery [mánəsteri] s. monasterio.
Monday [mʌ́ndi] s. lunes.
monetary [mánəteri] adj. monetario.
money [mʌ́ni] s. dinero; **— changer**
cambista; **— order** giro postal;
paper — papel moneda; **silver —**
moneda de plata; **money-making**
lucrativo, provechoso, ganancioso.
monger [mʌ́ŋgə] s. traficante; defensor.
mongrel [mʌ́ŋgrəl] adj. & s. mestizo,
mixto, cruzado, Am. chusco (perro).
monk [mʌŋk] s. monje.
monkey [mʌ́ŋki] s. mono; **—shine**
monada, monería; **— wrench** llave
inglesa; v. juguetear; hacer monerías;
payasear; entremeterse; **to — with**
juguetear con; meterse con.
monogram [mánəgræm] s. mono-
grama.
monograph [mánəgræf] s. monografía.
monologue [mánɔg] s. monólogo,
soliloquio.
monopolize [mənápəlaiz] v. monopolizar, acaparar.
monopoly [mənápli] s. monopolio.
monosyllable [mánəsiləbl] s. monosílabo.
monotone [mánəton] adj. monótono.
monotonous [mənátənəs] adj. monótono.
monotony [mənátni] s. monotonía.
monster [mánstə] s. monstruo; adj.
enorme.
monstrosity [manstrásəti] s. monstruosidad; monstruo.
monstrous [mánstrəs] adj. monstruoso.
month [mʌnθ] s. mes.
monthly [mʌ́nθli] adj. mensual; s. publicación mensual; adv. mensual-
mente.
monument [mánjəmənt] s. monumento.
monumental [manjəmént] adj. monumental; colosal, grandioso.
moo [mu] s. mugido; v. mugir.
mood [mud] s. humor, disposición de
ánimo; modo (del verbo); **to be in a
good —** estar de buen humor; **to be
in the — to** estar dispuesto a, tener
gana de.
moody [múdi] adj. (changing) caprichoso, voluble, mudable; (sad) melancólico, mohíno.
moon [mun] s. luna; mes lunar; **once
in a blue —** de Pascuas a San Juan,
muy rara vez, Am. por campanada
de vacante, Am. a cada muerte de (o
por la muerte de un) obispo.
moonlight [múnlait] s. luz de la luna;
— dance baile a la luz de la luna; **—
night** noche de luna.
moor [mur] v. amarrar, atracar (un
buque); anclar; estar anclado; s.
terreno inculto o baldío.
Moor [mur] s. moro.
Moorish [múriʃ] adj. morisco, moro.
mop [map] s. Am. trapeador; **dust —**
limpiapolvo; **— of hair** greñas, cabellera abundante; v. limpiar (el
suelo), Am. trapear; **to — one's brow**

limpiarse (o secarse) la frente; **to —
up** limpiar; vencer; acabar con.
mope [mop] v. andar quejumbroso o
abatido.
moral [mɔ́rəl] adj. moral; **— philosophy** ética, moral; s. moraleja; **-s**
moral, ética.
morale [mərǽl] s. moral, entereza de
ánimo.
moralist [mɔ́rəlist] s. moralista.
morality [mərǽləti] s. moralidad.
moralize [mɔ́rəlaiz] v. moralizar.
morbid [mɔ́rbid] adj. mórbido, morboso: malsano.
mordant [mɔ́rdənt] adj. mordaz.
more [mor] adj. & adv. más; **— and —**
cada vez más, más y más; **— or less**
poco más o menos; **there is no —** no
hay más, ya no hay; se acabó.
moreover [moróvə] adv. además.
morning [mɔ́rniŋ] s. mañana; **good —!**
¡buenos días!; **tomorrow —** mañana
por la mañana; adj. de la mañana;
matutino, matinal; **morning-glory**
dondiego de día; **— star** lucero del
alba.
morphine [mɔ́rfin] s. morfina.
morrow [mɔ́ro]: **on the —** el día de
mañana; mañana.
morsel [mɔ́rsl] s. bocado; manjar sabroso.
mortal [mɔ́rtl] adj. & s. mortal.
mortality [mɔrtǽləti] s. mortalidad;
mortandad.
mortar [mɔ́rtə] s. mortero; argamasa,
mezcla; **metal —** almirez.
mortgage [mɔ́rgidʒ] s. hipoteca, gravamen; v. hipotecar.
mortify [mɔ́rtəfai] v. mortificar; avergonzar.
mosaic [mozéik] adj. & s. mosaico.
Moslem [mázləm] adj. & s. musulmán.
mosquito [məskíto] s. mosquito; **—
net** mosquitero.
moss [mɔs] s. musgo; **moss-grown**
musgoso, cubierto de musgo; anticuado.
mossy [mɔ́si] adj. musgoso.
most [most] adv. más; sumamente,
muy; s. la mayoría, la mayor parte, el
mayor número o cantidad; los más;
— people la mayoría (o la mayor
parte) de la gente; **at the —** a lo más,
a lo sumo; **for the — part** por la
mayor parte; generalmente, mayormente; **the — that I can do** lo más
que puedo hacer; **the — votes** el
mayor número de votos, los más
votos.
mostly [móstli] adv. por la mayor
parte; mayormente, principalmente.
moth [mɔθ] s. polilla; mariposa nocturna; **—ball** bolita de naftalina;
moth-eaten apolillado.
mother [mʌ́ðə] s. madre; **mother-of-
pearl** madreperla, nácar; adj. de madre; materno, maternal; nativo, natal;
— country madre patria; país natal;
— Superior superiora; **— tongue**
lengua materna; v. servir de madre a,
cuidar de.

motherhood [mʌ́ðəhud] s. maternidad.
mother-in-law [mʌ́ðɚɪnlɔ] s. suegra.
motherly [mʌ́ðəlɪ] adj. maternal, materno.
motif [motíf] s. motivo, tema.
motion [móʃən] s. (movement) moción; movimiento; (signal) ademán; señal, seña; — sickness mareo; v. hacer una seña o señas; indicar.
motionless [móʃənlɪs] adj. inmóvil, inmoble.
motion picture [móʃənpíktʃɚ] s. cine o cinematógrafo; película; fotografía cinematográfica; **motion-picture** adj. cinematográfico.
motive [mótɪv] s. motivo; tema; adj. motriz.
motley [mátlɪ] adj. abigarrado, multicolor, de diversos colores; variado, mezclado; s. mezcla, mezcolanza.
motor [mótɚ] s. motor; automóvil; v. pasear o ir en automóvil.
motorbike [mótɚbaɪk] s. motocicleta pequeña; moto.
motorboat [mótɚbot] s. autobote, lancha de gasolina, bote de motor.
motorcar [mótɚkar] s. automóvil.
motorcoach [mótɚkotʃ] s. autobús, ómnibus, Méx. camión, Carib. guagua; Riopl., Ch. micro; C.A. bus.
motorcycle [mótɚsaɪkl] s. motocicleta.
motorist [mótɚɪst] s. motorista, automovilista.
motorman [mótɚmən] s. motorista.
motor scooter [mótɚskutɚ] s. motoneta.
mottled [mátld] adj. moteado; jaspeado, manchado.
motto [máto] s. mote, divisa, lema.
mould = **mold.**
moulder = **molder.**
moulding = **molding.**
mouldy = **moldy.**
mound [maund] s. montecillo, montículo, montón de tierra.
mount [maunt] s. (elevation) monte; (horse) montura, cabalgadura, caballo; v. montar; montar a caballo; subir, ascender; armar (una máquina); engastar (joyas).
mountain [máuntn̩] s. montaña; adj. montañés; de montaña; — goat cabra montés; — lion puma; — range cordillera, cadena de montañas.
mountaineer [mauntnír] s. montañés.
mountainous [máuntnəs] adj. montañoso.
mourn [morn] v. lamentar; deplorar; to — for llorar a; estar de duelo por.
mournful [mórnfəl] adj. fúnebre; lúgubre; lastimero; triste.
mourning [mórnɪŋ] s. luto; duelo; lamentación; to be in — estar de luto, estar de duelo; adj. de luto.
mouse [maus] s. ratón; — trap ratonera.
moustache = **mustache.**
mouth [mauθ] s. boca; abertura; desembocadura, embocadura (de un río).
mouthful [máuθfəl] s. bocado.
mouthpiece [máuθpis] s. boquilla (de un instrumento de viento); portavoz.
movable [múvəbl] adj. movible, móvil; -s s. pl. muebles, bienes muebles.
move [muv] v. (motion) mover(se); (change) mudar(se), mudar de casa; (propose) proponer, hacer la moción de; (game) hacer una jugada (en ajedrez o damas); (emotion) conmover; inducir; — away irse; alejarse; apartarse; to — forward avanzar; to — on seguir adelante, caminar; to — out irse, mudarse, mudar de casa; s. movimiento; mudanza (de una casa a otra); paso, trámite (para conseguir algo); jugada, turno (en juegos); get a — on there! ¡ande! ¡dése prisa!; Am. ¡ándele!
movement [múvmənt] s. (motion) movimiento; maniobra; meneo; acción; (mechanism) mecanismo, movimiento (de un reloj); (bowel) evacuación.
movie [múvɪ] s. cine, película; -s cine.
mow [mo] v. segar; cortar (césped).
mower [móɚ] s. segador; segadora, cortadora mecánica; máquina segadora.
mown [mon] adj. & p.p. segado.
Mr. [místɚ] Sr., señor; **Mrs.** [mísɪz] Sra., señora.
much [mʌtʃ] adj., adv. & s. mucho; — the same casi lo mismo; as — as tanto como; how — ? ¿cuánto?; not — of a book un libro de poco valor; not — of a poet un poetastro; so — that tanto que; too — demasiado; very — muchísimo; to make — of dar mucha importancia a.
muck [mʌk] s. (manure) estiércol húmedo; (mire) cieno; (filth) porquería, suciedad.
mucous [mjúkəs] adj. mucoso; — membrane membrana mucosa.
mud [mʌd] s. lodo, fango, cieno; — wall tapia.
muddle [mʌ́dl] v. enturbiar; confundir; embrollar; s. confusión, embrollo, lío, desorden.
muddy [mʌ́dɪ] adj. fangoso, lodoso, turbio; confuso; v. enlodar, ensuciar; enturbiar.
muff [mʌf] s. manguito (para las manos); falla, error (en ciertos juegos); v. no coger, dejar escapar (la pelota).
muffin [mʌ́fɪn] s. bollo, panecillo.
muffle [mʌ́fl] v. embozar; tapar; apagar, amortiguar (un sonido).
muffler [mʌ́flɚ] s. bufanda; silenciador (para maquinaria); mofle.
mug [mʌg] s. pichel, vaso con asa.
mulatto [məléto] s. mulato.
mulberry [mʌ́lbɛrɪ] s. mora; — tree moral.
mule [mjul] s. mulo, mula; **muleteer** [mjuliˈtír] s. arriero.
mull [mʌl] v. meditar, ponderar, revolver en la mente; calentar (vino, sidra, etc.) con azúcar y especias.
multiple [mʌ́ltəpl] s. múltiplo; adj. múltiple.
multiplication [mʌltəpləkéʃən] s. mul-

MO

tiplicación; — **table** tabla de multiplicar.
multiplicity [mʌltəplísətɪ] s. multiplicidad.
multiply [mʌltəplaɪ] v. multiplicar(se).
multitude [mʌltətjud] s. multitud.
mum [mʌm] adj. callado, silencioso; **to
keep** — estarse (o quedarse) callado.
mumble [mʌmbl] v. murmurar, hablar entre dientes; mascullar; s.
murmullo; **to talk in a** — mascullar
las palabras, hablar entre dientes.
mummy [mʌmɪ] s. momia.
mumps [mʌmps] s. parótidas, paperas.
munch [mʌntʃ] v. mascar ruidosamente, mascullar.
mundane [mʌndén] adj. mundano.
municipal [mjunísəpl] adj. municipal.
municipality [mjunɪsəpǽlətɪ] s. municipio; municipalidad.
munition [mjunífən] s. munición; —
plant fábrica de municiones, arsenal;
v. guarnecer, abastecer de municiones.
mural [mjúrəl] adj. & s. mural.
murder [mɝdə] s. asesinato, homicidio;
v. asesinar.
murderer [mɝdərə] s. asesino, homicida.
murderess [mɝdərɪs] s. asesina, homicida.
murderous [mɝdərəs] adj. asesino,
homicida.
murmur [mɝmə] s. (noise) murmullo;
susurro; (complaint) queja; v. murmurar; susurrar; quejarse.
muscle [mʌsl] s. músculo.
muscular [mʌskjələ] adj. muscular;
musculoso.
muse [mjuz] v. meditar; s. meditación;
Muse musa.
museum [mjuzíəm] s. museo.
mush [mʌʃ] s. potaje espeso de maíz;
masa de maíz; cualquier masa blan-
da; sentimentalismo.
mushroom [mʌʃrum] s. seta, hongo.
music [mjúzɪk] s. música; — **stand**
atril.
musical [mjúzɪkl] adj. musical, músico;
melodioso; armonioso; aficionado a
la música; — **comedy** zarzuela, comedia musical.
musician [mjuzífən] s. músico.
muskmelon [mʌskmɛlən] s. melón.
muskrat [mʌskræt] s. almizclera (roedor
semejante a la rata).
muslin [mʌzlɪn] s. muselina.
muss [mʌs] v. desarreglar, desordenar;
arrugar.
must [mʌst] v. defect. (por lo general se
usa sólo en el presente) deber; deber
de, haber de; tener que.
mustache [mʌstæʃ] s. bigote, mostacho.
mustard [mʌstəd] s. mostaza; —
plaster sinapismo.
muster [mʌstə] v. pasar lista o revista;
juntarse para una formación militar;
reunir(se); **to — out** dar de baja; **to
— up one's courage** cobrar valor o
ánimo; s. revista (de soldados o marinos); **to pass** — pasar lista o revista;
ser aceptable (en una inspección).

musty [mʌstɪ] adj. mohoso; rancio,
añejo.
mute [mjut] adj. mudo; s. mudo; letra
muda; sordina (de violín).
mutilate [mjútlet] v. mutilar.
mutiny [mjútnɪ] s. motín; v. amotinarse.
mutter [mʌtə] v. murmurar, refunfuñar; hablar entre dientes; s.
murmullo, refunfuño.
mutton [mʌtn] s. carne de carnero; —
chop chuleta de carnero.
mutual [mjútʃʊəl] adj. mutuo.
muzzle [mʌzl] s. hocico; bozal (para el
hocico); boca (de arma de fuego); v.
abozalar, poner bozal a; amordazar;
hacer callar.
my [maɪ] adj. mi (mis).
myriad [mírɪəd] s. miríada, diez mil;
millares, gran cantidad.
myrtle [mɝtl] s. mirto, arrayán.
myself [maɪsélf] pron. yo mismo; me
(como reflexivo); a mí mismo; **by** —
solo; **I — did it** yo mismo lo hice;
I talk to — hablo conmigo mismo,
hablo para mis adentros.
mysterious [mɪstírɪəs] adj. misterioso.
mystery [místrɪ] s. misterio.
mystic [místɪk] adj. & s. místico.
mystical [místɪkl] adj. místico.
myth [mɪθ] s. mito, fábula.
mythology [mɪθɑ́lədʒɪ] s. mitología.

N

nab [næb] v. agarrar, coger; arrestar.
nag [næg] s. rocín, caballejo, jaco; v.
importunar, irritar (con repetidos re-
gaños).
nail [nel] s. clavo; uña (del dedo); —
file lima (para las uñas); v. clavar;
clavetear; agarrar, atrapar.
naive [naív] adj. simple, ingenuo,
cándido.
naked [nékɪd] adj. desnudo.
nakedness [nékɪdnɪs] s. desnudez.
name [nem] s. (designation) nombre;
(fame) renombre, fama; —**sake** tocayo; **by the — of** nombrado, llamado;
apellidado; **family —** apellido; **to
call someone -s** motejar o decirle
groserías a uno; ponerle apodos a
uno; **to make a — for oneself**
ganar fama; **what is your —?** ¿cómo
se llama Vd.?; v. nombrar; mentar,
mencionar; llamar.
nameless [némlɪs] adj. sin nombre;
anónimo.
namely [némlɪ] adv. a saber, esto es, es
decir.
nap [næp] s. siesta; pelo (de un tejido);
to take a — echar un sueño, echar
una siesta; v. dormitar; echar un
sueño; sestear.
nape [nep] s. nuca, cogote.
naphtha [nǽfθə] s. nafta.
napkin [nǽpkɪn] s. servilleta.
narcissus [nɑrsísəs] s. narciso.
narcotic [nɑrkátɪk] adj. & s. narcótico.
narrate [nærét] v. narrar.
narration [næréʃən] s. narración.
narrative [nǽrətɪv] adj. narrativo; s.

narración; narrativa; relato.

narrow [nǽro] *adj.* (*cramped*) estrecho; angosto; limitado; (*intolerant*) intolerante; — **escape** trance difícil, escapada difícil; — **search** búsqueda esmerada; **narrow-minded** fanático, intolerante; **-s** *s. pl.* desfiladero, paso; estrecho o estrechos; *v.* angostar(se), estrechar(se); limitar, restringir, reducir; **-ly** *adv.* estrechamente; **he -ly escaped** por poco no se escapa.

narrowness [nǽrənɪs] *s.* (*cramped*) estrechez, estrechura, angostura; limitación; (*intolerance*) intolerancia.

nasal [nézl] *adj.* nasal.

nastiness [nǽstɪnɪs] *s.* suciedad, porquería; grosería.

nasturtium [nǽstʃʃəm] *s.* mastuerzo.

nasty [nǽstɪ] *adj.* (*foul*) sucio, asqueroso; feo; (*indecent*) grosero; indeeente; **a — fall** una caída terrible; **a — disposition** un genio horrible.

natal [nétl] *adj.* natal.

nation [néʃən] *s.* nación.

national [nǽʃənl] *adj.* nacional; *s.* nacional, ciudadano.

nationalism [nǽʃənəlɪzm] *s.* nacionalismo.

nationality [nǽʃənǽləti] *s.* nacionalidad.

native [nétɪv] *adj.* nativo; natal; natural; indígena; del país, *Am.* criollo; — **of** oriundo de, natural de; *s.* nativo, natural, indígena; habitante.

nativity [nətívətɪ] *s.* nacimiento; natividad (*de la Virgen María*); **the Nativity** la Navidad.

natural [nǽtʃərəl] *adj.* natural; sencillo, sin afectación; *s.* becuadro (*signo musical*); **he is a —** for that job tiene aptitud natural para ese puesto; **-ly** *adv.* naturalmente; con naturalidad.

naturalism [nǽtʃərəlɪzm] *s.* naturalismo.

naturalist [nǽtʃərəlɪst] *s.* naturalista.

naturalization [nǽtʃərələzéʃən] *s.* naturalización.

naturalize [nǽtʃərəlaɪz] *v.* naturalizar.

naturalness [nǽtʃərəlnɪs] *s.* naturalidad.

nature [nétʃə] *s.* naturaleza; natural, genio, índole; instinto; especie; **to copy from —** copiar del natural.

naught [nɔt] *s.* cero; nada.

naughty [nɔtɪ] *adj.* malo, desobediente; travieso, pícaro; malicioso.

nausea [nɔzɪə] *s.* náusea.

nauseate [nɔziet] *v.* dar náuseas, dar bascas, asquear, dar asco; sentir náusea; **to be -ed** tener náuseas.

nauseating [nɔzietɪŋ] *adj.* nauseabundo, asqueroso.

nautical [nɔtɪkl] *adj.* náutico, naval.

naval [névl] *adj.* naval; — **officer** oficial de marina.

nave [nev] *s.* nave (*de una iglesia*).

navel [névl] *s.* ombligo; — **orange** naranja california (*sin semillas*).

navigable [nǽvəgəbl] *adj.* navegable.

navigate [nǽvəget] *v.* navegar.

navigation [nǽvəgéʃən] *s.* navegación; náutica.

navigator [nǽvəgətə] *s.* navegador, navegante.

navy [névɪ] *s.* marina de guerra; armada; — **blue** azul marino; — **yard** astillero, arsenal.

nay [ne] *adv.* no; no sólo . . . sino (que) también; *s.* no, voto negativo.

near [nɪr] *adv.* (*space, time*) cerca; (*almost*) casi; — **at hand** cerca, a la mano; **I came — forgetting to do it** por poco se me olvida hacerlo; **to come (go, draw) —** acercarse; — **sighted** miope; *prep.* cerca de; — **the end of the month** hacia fines del mes; *adj.* cercano, próximo, estrecho, íntimo; — **silk** seda imitada; **I had a — accident** por poco me sucede un accidente; *v.* acercarse (a).

near-by [nɪrbáɪ] *adv.* cerca, a la mano; *adj.* cercano, próximo.

nearly [nɪrlɪ] *adv.* casi, cerca de; aproximadamente, próximamente; **I did it —** estuve al punto de hacerlo, estuve para hacerlo.

nearness [nfrnɪs] *s.* cercanía, proximidad.

neat [nit] *adj.* pulcro, aseado, limpio; ordenado; esmerado; hábil, diestro; **-ly** *adv.* aseadamente; esmeradamente; ordenadamente; hábilmente.

neatness [nítnɪs] *s.* pulcritud, aseo; limpieza; esmero; claridad.

nebulous [nébjuləs] *adj.* nebuloso.

necessarily [nɛsəsérəlɪ] *adv.* necesariamente.

necessary [nésəserɪ] *adj.* necesario; **necessaries** *s. pl.* necesidades, requisitos.

necessitate [nəsésətet] *v.* necesitar, precisar.

necessity [nəsésətɪ] *s.* necesidad.

neck [nɛk] *s.* cuello; pescuezo; garganta; — **of land** lengua; **low —** escote; — **and —** parejos (*en una carrera*).

necklace [néklɪs] *s.* collar; gargantilla.

necktie [néktaɪ] *s.* corbata.

necrology [nɛkrálədʒɪ] *s.* necrología.

need [nid] *s.* (*lack*) necesidad; (*poverty*) pobreza; **for — of** por falta de; **if — be** si fuere menester, en caso de necesidad; *v.* necesitar; tener necesidad de; hacerle falta a uno; tener que.

needful [nídfəl] *adj.* necesario; necesitado.

needle [nídl] *s.* aguja.

needlepoint [nídlpɔɪnt] *s.* encaje de mano.

needless [nídlɪs] *adj.* innecesario, inútil.

needlework [nídlwɜk] *s.* labor, bordado; costura.

needy [nídɪ] *adj.* necesitado, menesteroso.

ne'er [nɛr] *adv. contr. de* never; **ne'er-do-well** *s.* persona incompetente; haragán.

negation [nɪgéʃən] *s.* negación; negativa.

negative [négətɪv] *adj.* negativo; *s.* negativa; negación, partícula o voz negativa; negativa (*de una fotografía*).

neglect [nɪglékt] *s.* negligencia; descuido; abandono; *v.* descuidar; desatender; abandonar; **to — to** dejar de, olvidar, olvidarse de.

neglectful [nɪgléktfəl] *adj.* negligente, descuidado.

negligence [néglədʒəns] *s.* negligencia.

negligent [néglədʒənt] *adj.* negligente, descuidado.

negotiate [nɪgóʃɪet] *v.* negociar; agenciar; vencer (*un obstáculo o dificultad*), dar cima a.

negotiation [nɪgoʃɪéʃən] *s.* negociación.

negro [nígro] *s.* & *adj.* negro.

Negroid [nígrɔɪd] *adj.* negroide.

neigh [ne] *s.* relincho; *v.* relinchar.

neighbor [nébə] *s.* vecino; prójimo; *adj.* vecino; cercano.

neighborhood [nébəhud] *s.* vecindad; vecindario; inmediación; **in the — of a hundred dollars** cerca de cien dólares.

neighboring [nébərɪŋ] *adj.* vecino; cercano; colindante.

neither [níðə] *pron.* ninguno, ni (el) uno ni (el) otro; **— of the two** ninguno de los dos; *adj.* ninguno; **—one of us** ninguno de nosotros; *conj.* ni; **— . . . nor** ni . . . ni; **— will I** tampoco yo, ni yo tampoco.

neologism [nɪá,lədʒɪzm] *s.* neologismo.

neophyte [nɪofaɪt] *s.* neófito.

nephew [néfju] *s.* sobrino.

nepotism [népətɪzm] *s.* nepotismo.

nerve [nɜv] *s.* (*anatomy*) nervio; (*courage*) valor, ánimo; audacia; (*effrontery*) descaro; **-s** nervios; nerviosidad; **to strain every —** esforzarse hasta no poder, poner el mayor empeño posible.

nervous [nɜvəs] *adj.* nervioso.

nervousness [nɜvəsnɪs] *s.* nerviosidad; agitación.

nest [nɛst] *s.* nido; nidada; **— egg** nidal; ahorros; **—of baskets (boxes, tables)** juego graduado de cestas (cajas, mesitas); **wasp's —** avispero; *v.* anidar.

nestle [nésl] *v.* acurrucarse; abrigar(se); anidar.

net [nɛt] *s.* red; malla; tejido de mallas; *adj.* de mallas, de punto de malla; *v.* redar, enredar, coger con red; cubrir con una red.

net [nɛt] *adj.* neto; **— price** precio neto; **— profit** ganancia neta o líquida; *v.* producir una ganancia neta o líquida; obtener una ganancia líquida.

nettle [nétl] *s.* ortiga; *v.* picar, irritar, enfadar.

network [nétwɜk] *s.* red; malla; **radio —** red de estaciones radiofónicas.

neurotic [njurátɪk] *adj.* & *s.* neurótico.

neuter [njútə] *adj.* neutro.

neutral [njútrəl] *adj.* neutral; neutro.

neutrality [njutrǽlətɪ] *s.* neutralidad.

neutralize [njútrəlaɪz] *v.* neutralizar.

never [névə] *adv.* nunca, jamás; **—**

mind no importa; no haga Vd. caso; no se moleste Vd.; **never-ending** perpetuo, eterno; de nunca acabar.

nevertheless [nɛvəðəlés] *adv.* & *conj.* sin embargo, no obstante, con todo, empero.

new [nju] *adj.* (*not old*) nuevo; moderno; (*fresh*) fresco; reciente; *adv.* recién; **—born baby** criatura recién nacida.

newcomer [njúkʌmə] *s.* recién llegado.

newly [njúlɪ] *adv.* nuevamente, recientemente; **— arrived** recién llegado; **— wed** recién casado.

newness [njúnɪs] *s.* novedad, calidad de nuevo.

news [njuz] *s.* noticias, nuevas; novedades; **piece of —** noticia, nueva; **—boy** vendedor de periódicos; **— reel** película noticiera; película de noticias mundiales; **—stand** puesto de periódicos.

newsmonger [njúzmʌŋgə] *s.* chismoso, chismero, gacetilla.

newspaper [njúzpepə] *s.* periódico.

next [nɛkst] *adj.* (*future*) próximo; entrante, que viene; (*following*) siguiente; contiguo; **in the — life** en la otra vida; **to be — in turn** tocarle a uno, ser su turno; *adv.* después, luego; **— best** segundo en cualidad o importancia; *prep.* **; — to** junto a; al lado de; después de.

nibble [níbl] *s.* mordisco; *v.* mordiscar, mordisquear; picar, morder.

nice [naɪs] *adj.* (*attractive*) fino; bueno; amable, simpático; lindo; primoroso; (*refined*) refinado; esmerado; preciso, exacto; **-ly** *adv.* con esmero; con finura o primor; sutilmente, con delicadeza; amablemente; bien; **to get along -ly with** llevarse bien con.

nicety [náɪsətɪ] *s.* fineza, finura; delicadeza; exactitud.

niche [nɪtʃ] *s.* nicho.

nick [nɪk] *s.* mella, desportilladura; **in the — of time** en el momento crítico; *v.* mellar, desportillar.

nickel [níkl] *s.* níquel; moneda de cinco centavos; **nickel-plated** niquelado.

nickname [níknem] *s.* mote, apodo; *v.* apodar, poner apodo a.

niece [nis] *s.* sobrina.

niggardly [nígədlɪ] *adj.* mezquino, ruin, tacaño; *adv.* mezquinamente, ruinmente.

night [naɪt] *s.* noche; **good —!** ¡buenas noches!; **tomorrow —** mañana por la noche; *adj.* nocturno; de noche; **— owl** buho; trasnochador; **— watchman** sereno, vigilante nocturno.

nightfall [náɪtfɔl] *s.* anochecer, caída de la tarde, anochecida.

nightgown [náɪtgaun] *s.* camisa de dormir, camisa de noche, *Am.* camisón.

nightingale [náɪtŋgel] *s.* ruiseñor.

nightly [náɪtlɪ] *adv.* cada noche, todas las noches; *adj.* nocturno, de noche.

nightmare [náɪtmɛr] *s.* pesadilla.

nihilism [náɪɪlɪzm] *s.* nihilismo.

nimble [nímbl] *adj.* ágil, ligero; listo.

nip [nɪp] *v.* (*pinch*) pellizcar; (*bite*) mordiscar; (*frostbite*) marchitar, helar (*por la acción del frío*); **to — in the bud** cortar en germen, destruir al nacer; **to — off** despuntar; podar; *s.* pellizco; mordisco; trago.

nipple [nípl] *s.* teta, tetilla, pezón; pezón de goma.

nitrate [náɪtret] *s.* nitrato.

nitric acid [náɪtrɪkǽsɪd] *s.* ácido nítrico.

nitrogen [náɪtrədʒən] *s.* nitrógeno.

no [no] *adv.* no; **— longer** ya no; **there is — more** no hay más; *adj.* ningun(o); **— matter how much** por mucho que; **— one** ninguno, nadie; **— smoking** se prohibe fumar; **I have — friend** no tengo ningún amigo; **of — use** inútil, sin provecho; *s.* no, voto negativo.

nobility [nobílətɪ] *s.* nobleza.

noble [nóbl] *s.* & *adj.* noble.

nobleman [nóblmən] *s.* noble.

nobleness [nóblnɪs] *s.* nobleza.

nobly [nóblɪ] *adv.* noblemente.

nobody [nóbadɪ] *pron.* nadie, ninguno.

nocturnal [naktʒnl] *adj.* nocturno.

nod [nad] *v.* inclinar la cabeza (*para hacer una seña, saludar, o asentir*); cabecear, dar cabezadas (*dormitando*); *s.* inclinación de cabeza, saludo; señal de asentimiento (*con la cabeza*).

noise [nɔɪz] *s.* ruido; barullo; sonido; *v.* divulgar; **it is being -d about that** corre el rumor que.

noiseless [nɔɪzlɪs] *adj.* sin ruido, silencioso, quieto; **-ly** *adv.* sin ruido, silenciosamente.

noisily [nɔɪzɪlɪ] *adv.* ruidosamente.

noisy [nɔɪzɪ] *adj.* ruidoso.

nominal [námənl] *adj.* nominal.

nominate [námənet] *v.* nombrar, designar.

nomination [namənéʃən] *s.* nombramiento, nominación.

nonconformist [nankənfɔ́rmɪst] *adj.* & *s.* disidente.

none [nʌn] *pron.* ninguno; ningunos; nada; **I want — of that** no quiero nada de eso; **that is — of his business** no le importa a él eso; *adv.* no, de ningún modo; **— the less** no menos; **to be — the happier for that** no estar por eso más contento.

nonentity [nanéntətɪ] *s.* nulidad, persona o cosa inútil.

nonintervention [nanɪntəvénʃən] *s.* no intervención.

nonpartisan [nanpártəzən] *adj.* imparcial; independiente.

nonsense [nánsɛns] *s.* tontería, necedad; disparate, desatino.

noodle [núdl] *s.* tallarín, fideo, pasta (*para sopa*).

nook [nʊk] *s.* rincón; **breakfast —** desayunador.

noon [nun] *s.* mediodía.

noonday [núnde] *s.* mediodía; *adj.* meridiano, de mediodía; **— meal** comida de mediodía.

noontide [núntaɪd] *s.* mediodía.

noontime [núntaɪm] *s.* mediodía.

noose [nus] *s.* dogal; lazo, nudo corredizo, *Am.* gaza; *v.* lazar, coger con lazo; hacer un lazo corredizo en.

nor [nɔr] *conj.* ni; **neither . . . —** ni . . . ni.

norm [nɔrm] *s.* norma.

normal [nɔ́rml] *adj.* normal; *s.* norma; normal, línea perpendicular.

north [nɔrθ] *s.* norte; *adj.* septentrional; norteño; del norte; **— pole** polo norte, polo ártico; **— wind** cierzo, norte; **North American** norteamericano; *adv.* al norte, hacia el norte.

northeast [nɔrθíst] *adj.* & *s.* nordeste; *adv.* hacia el nordeste, rumbo al nordeste.

northeastern [nɔrθístən] *adj.* del nordeste, nordeste.

northern [nɔ́rðən] *adj.* septentrional; norteño; del norte; hacia el norte; **— lights** aurora boreal.

northerner [nɔ́rðənə] *s.* norteño, habitante del norte.

northward [nɔ́rθwəd] *adv.* hacia el norte, rumbo al norte.

northwest [nɔrθwést] *adj.* & *s.* noroeste; *adv.* hacia el noroeste.

northwestern [nɔrθwéstən] *adj.* noroeste, del noroeste.

Norwegian [nɔrwídʒən] *adj.* & *s.* noruego.

nose [noz] *s.* nariz; proa (*de un barco*); **— dive** picada (*de un avión*); *v.* olfatear; **to — around** husmear, curiosear.

nostalgia [nastǽldʒɪə] *s.* nostalgia, añoranza.

nostrils [nástrəlz] *s. pl.* narices, ventanas de la nariz.

not [nat] *adv.* no; **— at all** de ningún modo; de nada (*contestación a* "thank you"); **— at all sure** nada seguro; **— even a word** ni siquiera una palabra.

notable [nótəbl] *adj.* notable.

notary [nótərɪ] *s.* notario.

notation [notéʃən] *s.* notación; apunte; anotación.

notch [natʃ] *s.* muesca, ranura; hendidura; *v.* ranurar, hacer una ranura en.

note [not] *s.* nota; apunte, apuntación; **bank —** billete de banco; **promissory —** pagaré, abonaré; *v.* notar, observar, reparar; **to — down** apuntar.

notebook [nótbʊk] *s.* libreta, cuaderno, libro de apuntes.

noted [nótɪd] *adj.* notable, célebre, famoso.

noteworthy [nótwʒðɪ] *adj.* notable, célebre.

nothing [nʌ́θɪŋ] *s.* nada; cero; **for —** por nada; inútilmente; de balde, gratis.

notice [nótɪs] *s.* noticia; aviso, advertencia, anuncio; mención; **to give a short —** avisar a última hora; **to take — of** hacer caso de, prestar

atención a; *v.* notar, observar; prestar atención a; hacer caso a (*o* de);
notificar.
noticeable [nótɪsəbl] *adj.* notable;
conspicuo; perceptible.
notify [nótəfaɪ] *v.* notificar, avisar.
notion [nóʃən] *s.* noción; idea; capricho;
-s mercería, artículos menudos (*como
alfileres, botones, etc.*), chucherías.
notorious [notórɪəs] *adj.* notorio.
notwithstanding [nɑtwɪθstǽndɪŋ]
prep. a pesar de; *adv.* & *conj.* no obstante, sin embargo; **— that** a pesar
(de) que.
nought = naught.
noun [naʊn] *s.* nombre, sustantivo.
nourish [nɝɪʃ] *v.* nutrir, alimentar.
nourishing [nɝɪʃɪŋ] *adj.* nutritivo, alimenticio.
nourishment [nɝɪʃmənt] *s.* nutrimento,
sustento, alimento; nutrición.
novel [návl] *s.* novela; *adj.* novel,
nuevo; raro, original.
novelist [návlɪst] *s.* novelista.
novelty [návltɪ] *s.* novedad; innovación; **novelties** novedades.
November [novémbɚ] *s.* noviembre.
novice [návɪs] *s.* novicio; novato, principiante.
now [naʊ] *adv.* ahora; ya; **— . . . —**
ya . . . ya, ora . . . ora; **— and then**
de vez en cuando, de cuando en cuando; **— that** ahora que; **— then** ahora
bien; **he left just —** salió hace poco,
Ríopl., Ch., Andes recién salió.
nowadays [náʊədez] *adv.* hoy día.
nowhere [nóhwɛr] *adv.* en ninguna
parte, a ninguna parte.
noxious [nákʃəs] *adj.* nocivo.
nucleus [njúklɪəs] *s.* núcleo.
nude [njud] *adj.* desnudo.
nudge [nadʒ] *v.* codear, tocar con el
codo; *s.* codazo ligero.
nugget [nágɪt] *s.* pepita; pedazo.
nuisance [njúsṇs] *s.* molestia; lata,
fastidio; persona o cosa fastidiosa.
null [nʌl] *adj.* nulo; **— and void** nulo
e inválido.
nullify [nʌlɪfaɪ] *v.* invalida~ ~~~~~
numb [nʌm] *adj.* entume~~~~ o entumido, aterido; **to become —** entume-
cerse, entumirse, aterirse; *v.* entumecer.
number [námbɚ] *s.* número; *v.* numerar; ascender a (*cierto número*); **to —
him among one's friends** contarle
entre sus amigos.
numberless [námbɚlɪs] *adj.* innumerable, sin número.
numeral [njúmrəl] *s.* número, cifra;
guarismo; *adj.* numeral.
numerical [njumérɪkl] *adj.* numérico.
numerous [njúmrəs] *adj.* numeroso;
numerosos, muchos.
nun [nʌn] *s.* monja.
nuptial [nápʃəl] *adj.* nupcial; **-s** *s. pl.*
nupcias, bodas.
nurse [nɝs] *s.* (*for the sick*) enfermera,
enfermero; (*for children*) niñera, aya;
Méx., Ven., Col., Andes nana, *Am.*
manejadora, *Andes* pilmama; *C.A.*
china; **wet —** nodriza, ama de cría;
v. criar, amamantar, dar de mamar,
lactar; mamar; cuidar (*a un enfermo*);
abrigar (*rencor*).
nursery [nɝsrɪ] *s.* cuarto para niños;
criadero, semillero (*de plantas*); **day
—** sala donde se cuida y divierte a los
niños.
nurture [nɝtʃɚ] *s.* crianza; nutrimento;
v. criar; nutrir; cuidar; fomentar.
nut [nʌt] *s.* nuez (*nombre genérico de
varias frutas como la almendra, la castaña, la avellana, etc.*); tuerca; loco,
tipo raro o extravagante.
nutcracker [nátkrækɚ] *s.* cascanueces.
nutmeg [nátmeg] *s.* nuez moscada.
nutrient [njútrɪənt] *s.* nutritivo.
nutrition [njutríʃən] *s.* nutrición; nutrimento, alimento.
nutritious [njutríʃəs] *adj.* nutritivo,
alimenticio.
nutritive [njútrɪtɪv] *adj.* nutritivo.
nutshell [nátʃel] *s.* cáscara de nuez (*o
de otro fruto semejante*); **in a —** en
suma, en breve, en pocas palabras.
nymph [nɪmf] *s.* ninfa.

O

oak [ok] *s.* roble; encina; **— grove** robledo o robledal; **live —** encina siem-
preverde.
oar [or] *s.* remo; *v.* remar, bogar.
oasis [oésɪs] *s.* oasis.
oat [ot] *s.* avena (*planta*); **-s** avena, granos de avena.
oath [oθ] *s.* juramento; blasfemia, re-
niego.
oatmeal [ótmɪl] *s.* harina de avena;
gachas de avena.
obedience [əbídɪəns] *s.* obediencia.
obedient [əbídɪənt] *adj.* obediente.
obesity [obísətɪ] *s.* obesidad, gordura.
obey [əbé] *v.* obedecer.
object [ábdʒɪkt] *s.* objeto; cosa; complemento (*del verbo*); [əbdʒékt] *v.* objetar; oponerse; tener inconveniente.
objection [əbdʒékʃən] *s.* objeción, reparo; inconveniente.
objective [əbdʒéktɪv] *adj.* objetivo; **—
case** caso complementario; *s.* objetivo; fin, propósito.
obligate [áblɪget] *v.* obligar, constreñir;
comprometer.
obligation [abləgéʃən] *s.* (*duty*) obligación; deber (*debt*) deuda; **to be under
—** to estar obligado a; estar agradecido a, deber favores a.
obligatory [əblígətorɪ] *adj.* obligatorio.
oblige [əbláɪdʒ] *v.* obligar; complacer;
much -ed! ¡muchas gracias! ¡muy
agradecido!; **to be very much -ed
to someone** quedar muy agradecido
con alguien.
obliging [əbláɪdʒɪŋ] *adj.* complaciente,
obsequioso, comedido, cortés.
oblique [əblík] *adj.* oblicuo.
obliterate [əblítɚret] *v.* borrar; arrasar,
destruir.
oblivion [əblívɪən] *s.* olvido.
oblivious [əblívɪəs] *adj.* olvidado, abstraído.

oblong [áblɔŋ] *adj.* cuadrilongo; oblongo.

obnoxious [əbnákʃəs] *adj.* ofensivo; molesto; odioso.

oboe [óbo] *s.* oboe.

obscene [əbsín] *adj.* obsceno.

obscenity [əbsénətɪ] *s.* obscenidad, indecencia.

obscure [əbskjúr] *adj.* obscuro; *v.* obscurecer; ofuscar.

obscurity [əbskjúrətɪ] *s.* obscuridad.

obsequies [ábsɪkwɪz] *s.* exequias, honras, funerales.

obsequious [əbsíkwɪəs] *adj.* obsequioso; servil, zalamero.

observable [əbzɜ́vəbl] *adj.* observable.

observance [əbzɜ́vəns] *s.* observancia; ceremonia, rito.

observant [əbzɜ́vənt] *adj.* observador; observante.

observation [əbzɜvéʃən] *s.* observación.

observatory [əbzɜ́vətorɪ] *s.* observatorio; mirador.

observe [əbzɜ́v] *v.* observar; guardar (*las fiestas religiosas*); celebrar (*una fiesta*).

observer [əbzɜ́vɚ] *s.* observador.

obsess [əbsɛ́s] *v.* obsesionar, causar obsesión.

obsession [əbsɛ́ʃən] *s.* obsesión; idea fija.

obsolete [ábsəlit] *adj.* anticuado; desusado.

obstacle [ábstək!] *s.* obstáculo.

obstinacy [ábstɪnəsɪ] *s.* obstinación, terquedad, porfía.

obstinate [ábstɪnɪt] *adj.* obstinado, terco, porfiado.

obstreperous [əbstrépəəs] *adj.* estrepitoso, turbulento.

obstruct [əbstrʌ́kt] *v.* obstruir.

obstruction [əbstrʌ́kʃən] *s.* obstrucción; impedimento, estorbo.

obtain [əbtén] *v.* obtener, conseguir, alcanzar, adquirir.

obtainable [əbténəbl] *adj.* obtenible, asequible.

obtrusive [əbtrúsɪv] *adj.* intruso, entremetido.

obviate [ábvɪet] *v.* obviar; allanar (*una dificultad*)

obvious [ábvɪəs] *adj.* obvio, evidente.

occasion [əké3ən] *s.* (*timely*) ocasión; (*chance*) oportunidad; (*cause*) motivo, causa; (*event*) acontecimiento; *v.* ocasionar, causar.

occasional [əké3ənl] *adj.* ocasional; infrecuente, poco frecuente; **-ly** *adv.* de vez en cuando, a veces.

occidental [aksədɛ́nt!] *adj. & s.* occidental.

occlusive [oklúsɪv] *adj. & s.* oclusivo.

occult [əkʌ́lt] *adj.* oculto, misterioso.

occupant [ákjəpənt] *s.* ocupante; inquilino.

occupation [akjəpéʃən] *s.* ocupación; trabajo, empleo, oficio.

occupy [ákjəpaɪ] *v.* ocupar.

occur [əkɜ́] *v.* ocurrir, suceder; **to — to one** ocurrírsele a uno, venirle a la mente.

occurrence [əkɜ́əns] *s.* ocurrencia, suceso, caso, acontecimiento.

ocean [óʃən] *s.* océano.

o'clock [əklák] *contr. de* **of the clock; it is two —** son las dos.

octave [áktɪv] *s.* octava.

October [aktóbɚ] *s.* octubre.

oculist [ákjəlɪst] *s.* oculista.

odd [ad] *adj.* (*rare*) extraño, singular, raro; (*not even*) non, impar; **— change** suelto, cambio sobrante; **— moments** momentos libres, momentos de ocio; **— shoe** zapato suelto (*sin compañero*); **— volume** tomo suelto; **thirty** treinta y tantos, treinta y pico; **-ly** *adv.* extrañamente, de un modo raro.

oddity [ádətɪ] *s.* rareza.

odds [adz] *s. pl. o sing.* diferencia, disparidad (*en apuestas*); ventaja, puntos de ventaja (*en apuestas*); **— and ends** retazos, trozos sobrantes, pedacitos varios; **the — are against me** la suerte me es contraria, estoy de mala suerte; **to be at -s with** estar reñido o enemistado con.

ode [od] *s.* oda.

odious [ódɪəs] *adj.* odioso.

odor [ódɚ] *s.* olor; **bad —** mal olor, hedor.

odorous [ódərəs] *adj.* oloroso.

o'er [or] *contr. de* **over.**

of [av, ʌv] *prep. de;* **— course** por supuesto, claro, ya se ve; **— late** últimamente; **a quarter — five** las cinco menos cuarto; **to smell —** oler a; **to taste —** saber a.

off [ɔf] *adv.* (*distant*) lejos, fuera, a distancia; (*not attached*) suelto; apagado (*la luz*); (*equivale al reflexivo se en ciertos verbos:* marcharse, irse, *etc.*); **— and on** de vez en cuando; a intervalos; **ten cents —** rebaja de diez centavos; **ten miles —** a una distancia de diez millas; **to take a day —** ausentarse por un día; descansar por un día; ausente; distante, más remoto; quitado; **the — side** el lado más remoto; **with his hat —** con el sombrero quitado; **the electricity is —** está cortada la electricidad; **to be — in one's accounts** estar errado en sus cuentas; **to be — to war** haberse ido a la guerra; **to be well —** ser persona acomodada, estar en buenas circunstancias; *prep.* lejos de; **off-color** de mal color; verde (*indecente*); **— shore** a vista de la costa; **— standard** de calidad inferior; **the road** desviado, descarriado; a un lado del camino; **to be — duty** no estar de turno; estar libre.

offend [əfɛ́nd] *v.* ofender.

offender [əfɛ́ndɚ] *s.* ofensor; transgresor, delincuente.

offense [əfɛ́ns] *s.* ofensa; agravio; delito, culpa; **no — was meant** lo hice (o lo dije) sin malicia; **weapon of —** arma ofensiva.

offensive [əfɛ́nsɪv] *adj.* ofensivo; *s.* ofensiva.

offer [ɔ́fə] v. ofrecer; **to — to do it** ofrecerse a hacerlo; s. oferta; ofrecimiento; promesa; propuesta.

offering [ɔ́fərɪŋ] s. ofrenda; oferta, ofrecimiento.

offhand [ɔ́fhǽnd] adv. de improviso, por el momento, sin pensarlo, impensadamente; adj. impensado, hecho de improviso; **in an — manner** con indiferencia; descuidadamente; sin plan.

office [ɔ́fɪs] s. (function) oficio; cargo; función; (place) oficina, despacho; — **building** edificio para oficinas; **post** — correo; **box** — taquilla, Ch., Ríopl. boletería; **through the good -s of** por el intermedio de.

officer [ɔ́fəsə] s. (office holder) oficial; funcionario; (police) policía, gendarme; agente de policía; v. comandar, dirigir (como oficial); proveer de oficiales.

official [əfíʃəl] adj. oficial; s. oficial, funcionario; empleado público.

officiate [əfíʃɪet] v. oficiar.

officious [əfíʃəs] adj. oficioso, intruso, entremetido.

offset [ɔ́fsɛt] v. compensar por; contrapesar.

offshore [ɔ́fʃór] adj. & adv. (land) terral; (at sea) lejos de la playa.

offspring [ɔ́fsprɪŋ] s. prole, hijos, descendientes; hijo, vástago; resultado, consecuencia.

offstage [ɔ́fstédʒ] adv. & adj. entre bastidores.

oft [ɔ́ft] = **often**.

often [ɔ́fən] adv. muchas veces, con frecuencia, frecuentemente, a menudo; **how —?** ¿cuántas veces?; ¿cada cuándo?

ogre [ógə] s. ogro, gigante, monstruo.

oil [ɔɪl] s. aceite; óleo; petróleo; — **can** alcuza; — **painting** pintura al óleo; — **well** pozo de petróleo; **motor** — aceite para motores; v. aceitar, engrasar, lubricar; untar.

oilcloth [ɔ́ɪlklɔθ] s. hule, tela de hule.

oily [ɔ́ɪlɪ] adj. aceitoso, oleoso; grasiento.

ointment [ɔ́ɪntmənt] s. ungüento.

O.K. [óké] adj. bueno; corriente, convenido; adv. bien; **it's —** está bien; **to give one's** — dar el V°. B°. (visto bueno); v. dar el V°. B°., aprobar.

old [old] adj. viejo; antiguo; añejo; — **maid** solterona; — **man** anciano, viejo; — **wine** vino añejo; **days of** — días de antaño; **how — are you?** ¿cuántos años tiene Vd.? ¿qué edad tiene Vd.?; **to be — enough to ...** tener bastante edad para ... ; **to be an — hand** ser ducho en, ser muy perito o experto en.

olden [óldn] adj. viejo, antiguo, de antaño.

old-fashioned [óldfǽʃənd] adj. pasado de moda; anticuado; chapado a la antigua.

old-time [óldtáɪm] adj. vetusto, de tiempos antiguos; de antaño.

old-timer [óldtáɪmə] s. antiguo residente.

olive [álɪv] s. oliva, aceituna; — **grove** olivar; — **oil** aceite de oliva; — **tree** olivo; — **branch** ramo de olivo; adj. aceitunado, verde aceituna.

omelet [ámlɪt] s. tortilla de huevos.

omen [ómən] s. agüero, presagio.

ominous [ámənəs] adj. siniestro, de mal agüero, amenazador.

omission [omíʃən] s. omisión.

omit [omít] v. omitir; dejar de.

omnipotent [amnípətənt] adj. omnipotente, todopoderoso.

on [an] prep. en; a; sobre, encima de; — **all sides** por todos lados; — **arriving** al llegar; — **board** a bordo; en el tren; — **condition that** con la condición de que; — **credit** al fiado; — **foot** a pie; — **horseback** a caballo; — **Monday** el lunes; — **purpose** a propósito, adrede; — **sale** de venta; — **time** a tiempo; a plazo; adv. adelante; **farther —** más adelante; **later —** después; — **and —** sin parar, sin cesar, continuamente; adj. puesto; **his hat is —** lleva puesto el sombrero; **the light is —** está encendida la luz.

once [wʌns] adv. una vez; en otro tiempo; — **and for all** una vez por todas, definitivamente; — **in a while** de vez en cuando; — **upon a time** érase que se era; en otro tiempo; **at —** al punto; a un mismo tiempo; **just this —** siquiera esta vez, sólo esta vez; conj. una vez que, cuando; luego que.

one [wʌn] adj. un, uno; — **hundred** cien, ciento; — **thousand** mil; **his —** **chance** su única oportunidad; **the —** **and only** el único; **one-armed** manco; **one-eyed** tuerto; **one-sided** de un solo lado; unilateral; parcial; desigual; **one-way** de un sentido; s. & pron. uno; — **another** uno a otro; — **by —** uno a uno; uno por uno; **the — who** el que, la que; **the green —** el verde; **this —** éste, ésta.

oneself [wʌnsélf] pron. se (reflexivo); **to speak to —** hablar consigo mismo; **by —** solo; por sí, por sí solo.

ongoing [ángoɪŋ] adj. que está haciéndose; corriente; que cursa.

onion [ʌ́njən] s. cebolla.

onlooker [ánlukə] s. espectador, mirón.

only [ónlɪ] adj. solo, único; adv. sólo, solamente; conj. sólo que.

onset [ánsɛt] s. embestida, ataque; impulso inicial, primer ímpetu; arranque.

onto [ántu] prep. a; sobre.

onward [ánwəd] adv. adelante; hacia adelante.

onyx [ánɪks] s. onix, ónice.

ooze [uz] v. rezumar(se), escurrir(se).

opal [óp] s. ópalo.

opaque [opék] adj. opaco; mate.

open [ópən] v. abrir(se); **to — into** comunicarse con, tener paso a; **to — onto** dar a, caer a, mirar a; adj. abierto; franco, sincero; expuesto (a); — **country** campo raso, campo abierto;

— question cuestión discutible; **— to temptation** expuesto a caer en la tentación; **— winter** invierno sin nieve; **in the — air** al (o en el) aire libre; **open-minded** receptivo; de amplias miras; **—mouthed** boquiabierto, con la boca abierta; **open-end** [ópənénd] sin límites; sin trabas; s. campo raso, aire libre.

opening [ópəniŋ] s. (hole) abertura; (beginning) apertura, comienzo; (clearing) claro (en un bosque); (vacancy) puesto vacante; oportunidad; adj. primero; **— night of a play** estreno de una comedia; **the — number** el primer número (de un programa).

opera [ápərə] s. ópera; **— glasses** gemelos; **— house** ópera, teatro de la ópera; **comic —** ópera cómica, zarzuela.

operate [ápəret] v. (function) operar; funcionar; obrar; (manage) maniobrar; manejar; **to — on a person** operar a una persona.

operation [apəréʃən] s. (function) operación; funcionamiento; (management) manipulación; manejo; maniobra; **to be in —** funcionar, estar funcionando.

operator [ápəretə] s. operador, cirujano; maquinista, mecánico, operario; especulador (en la Bolsa); **mine —** explotador de minas; **telegraph —** telegrafista; **telephone —** telefonista.

operetta [apərétə] s. opereta, zarzuela.

opinion [əpínjən] s. opinión, parecer.

opium [ópiəm] s. opio.

opponent [əpónənt] s. contrario, adversario, antagonista.

opportune [apərtjún] adj. oportuno; a propósito.

opportunist [apərtúnist] s. oportunista.

opportunity [apərtjúnəti] s. oportunidad; ocasión.

oppose [əpóz] v. oponer(se); oponerse a.

opposing [əpóziŋ] adj. opuesto, contrario.

opposite [ápəzit] adj. (contrary) opuesto; contrario; (facing) frontero, de enfrente; **— to** frente a; prep. frente a, en frente de; s. contrario; **the — lo** opuesto, lo contrario.

opposition [apəzíʃən] s. oposición; resistencia.

oppress [əprés] v. oprimir; agobiar.

oppression [əpréʃən] s. opresión.

oppressive [əprésiv] adj. (harsh) opresivo; (distressing) abrumador; gravoso; bochornoso, sofocante.

oppressor [əprésə] s. opresor.

optic [áptik] adj. óptico; **-s** s. óptica.

optical [áptik|] adj. óptico.

optician [aptíʃən] s. óptico.

optimism [áptəmizəm] s. optimismo.

optimist [áptəmist] s. optimista.

optimistic [aptəmístik] adj. optimista.

option [ápʃən] s. opción, derecho de escoger; alternativa.

optional [ápʃən|] adj. discrecional.

opulence [ápjələns] s. opulencia, riqueza, abundancia.

opulent [ápjələnt] adj. opulento, rico;

abundante.

or [ɔr] conj. o; u (delante de o, ho).

oracle [ɔ́rək|] s. oráculo.

oral [ɔ́rəl] adj. oral; bucal.

orange [ɔ́rindʒ] s. naranja; **— blossom** azahar; **— grove** naranjal; **— tree** naranjo; adj. de naranja; anaranjado.

orangeade [ɔrindʒéd] s. naranjada.

oration [oréʃən] s. discurso, peroración, arenga.

orator [ɔ́rətə] s. orador.

oratory [ɔ́rətori] s. oratoria, elocuencia; oratorio, capilla.

orb [ɔrb] s. orbe.

orbit [ɔ́rbit] s. órbita; v. moverse en órbita.

orbital [ɔ́rbit|] adj. orbital.

orchard [ɔ́rtʃəd] s. huerto.

orchestra [ɔ́rkistrə] s. orquesta; **— seat** butaca, luneta, Am. platea (de orquesta).

orchid [ɔ́rkid] s. orquídea.

ordain [ɔrdén] v. ordenar; decretar.

ordeal [ɔrdíl] s. prueba penosa.

order [ɔ́rdə] s. (request) orden (s.); pedido; (group) clase; orden; (arrangement) orden (m.); **holy -s** órdenes sagradas; **in —** en orden; en buen estado; en regla; **in — to** para, a fin de; **in — that** para que, a fin de que; **made to —** mandado hacer, hecho a la medida; **to be out of —** estar descompuesto; estar desordenado; no estar en regla; v. ordenar; mandar; arreglar; pedir (hacer un pedido); **to — away** echar, despedir, expulsar.

orderly [ɔ́rdəli] adj. ordenado; en orden, bien arreglado; bien disciplinado; s. ordenanza (soldado); asistente de hospital.

ordinal [ɔ́rdin|] adj. ordinal; **— number** número ordinal.

ordinance [ɔ́rdnəns] s. ordenanza, ley, reglamento.

ordinarily [ɔrdnérəli] adv. ordinariamente, por lo común.

ordinary [ɔ́rdnɛri] adj. ordinario.

ore [or] s. mineral.

organ [ɔ́rgən] s. órgano; **hand —** organillo.

organic [ɔrgǽnik] adj. orgánico; constitutivo, fundamental.

organism [ɔ́rgənizəm] s. organismo.

organist [ɔ́rgənist] s. organista.

organization [ɔrgənəzéʃən] s. organización; organismo; entidad; sociedad.

organize [ɔ́rgənaiz] v. organizar(se).

organizer [ɔ́rgənaizə] s. organizador.

orgy [ɔ́rdʒi] s. orgía.

orient [ɔ́rient] s. oriente; v. orientar.

oriental [ɔriént|] adj. & s. oriental.

orientate [ɔ́rientet] v. orientar.

orientation [ɔrientéʃən] s. orientación.

orifice [ɔ́rəfis] s. orificio.

origin [ɔ́rədʒin] s. origen.

original [ərídʒən|] adj. & s. original; **-ly** adv. originalmente, originariamente; en el principio, al principio.

originality [əridʒənǽləti] s. originali-

OF

dad.

originate [ərídʒənet] v. originar(se).

oriole [óriol] s. oriol (*pájaro*).

ornament [ɔ́rnəmənt] s. ornamento, adorno; [ɔ́rnəmɛnt] v. ornamentar, adornar, ornar.

ornamental [ɔrnəmɛ́ntl] adj. ornamental, de adorno, decorativo.

ornate [ɔrnét] adj. ornado, adornado en exceso; — **style** estilo florido.

orphan [ɔ́rfən] adj. & s. huérfano; — **asylum** hospicio, orfanato, asilo de huérfanos; v. dejar huérfano a.

orthodox [ɔ́rθədɑks] adj. ortodoxo.

orthography [ɔrθágrəfɪ] s. ortografía.

oscillate [ásəlet] v. oscilar.

ostentation [ɑstəntéʃən] s. ostentación, boato.

ostentatious [ɑstəntéʃəs] adj. ostentoso.

ostrich [ɔ́strɪtʃ] s. avestruz.

other [ʌ́ðə] adj. & s. otro; — **than** otra cosa que; más que; **every — day** cada dos días, un día sí y otro no; **some — day** otro día.

otherwise [ʌ́ðəwaɪz] adv. de otro modo; en otros respetos; adj. otro, diferente.

otter [átə] s. nutria; piel de nutria.

ought [ɔt] v. defect. (*por lo general se traduce por el presente y el condicional de* deber) debo, debes, etc.; debería, deberías, etc.; debiera, debieras, etc.

ounce [auns] s. onza.

our [aUr] adj. nuestro (nuestra, nuestros, nuestras).

ours [aurz] pron. pos. nuestro (nuestra, nuestros, nuestras); el nuestro (la nuestra, los nuestros, las nuestras); **a friend of** — un amigo nuestro.

ourselves [aursélvz] pron. nosotros mismos; nos (*reflexivo*); a nosotros mismos; **we** — nosotros mismos; **by** — solos; por nosotros; *véase* **herself.**

oust [aust] v. echar, expulsar.

out [aut] adv. fuera; afuera; hacia fuera; — **of fear** por miedo, de miedo; — **of humor** malhumorado; — **of money** sin dinero; — **of print** agotado; — **of touch with** aislado de, sin contacto con; — **of tune** desentonado; **made** — **of** hecho de; **to fight it** — decidirlo luchando; **to have it** — **with** habérselas con; **to speak** — hablar francamente; adj. ausente; apagado; — **and** — **criminal** criminal empedernido; — **and** — **refusal** una negativa redonda; — **size** tamaño poco común o extraordinario; **before the week is** — antes de que termine la semana; **the book is just** — acaba de publicarse el libro; **the secret is** — se ha divulgado el secreto.

outbreak [áutbrek] s. (*eruption*) erupción; (*revolt*) motín, insurrección, tumulto; (*attack*) ataque, arranque (*de ira*); **at the** — **of the war** al estallar la guerra.

outburst [áutbɜst] s. explosión; estallido; arranque (*de pasión*); erupción.

outcast [áutkæst] adj. excluido, desechado; desterrado; s. paria (*persona excluida de la sociedad*).

outcome [áutkʌm] s. resultado, consecuencia.

outcry [áutkraɪ] s. grito; clamor.

outdoor [áutdor] adj. externo; fuera de la casa; — **games** juegos al aire libre.

outdoors [autdórz] adv. puertas afuera, fuera de casa, al aire libre, al raso; s. aire libre, campo raso, campiña.

outer [áutə] adj. exterior, externo.

outfit [áutfɪt] s. equipo; pertrechos; v. equipar, habilitar, aviar.

outgoing [áutgoɪŋ] adj. (*leaving*) saliente; (*extrovert*) extrovertido.

outguess [autgés] v. anticipar; madrugar.

outing [áutɪŋ] s. excursión, gira (jira), caminata.

outlaw [áutlɔ] s. forajido, bandido; prófugo, fugitivo; v. proscribir, declarar ilegal.

outlay [áutle] s. gasto, desembolso; [áutlé] v. gastar, desembolsar.

outlet [áutlɛt] s. salida; desaguadero, desagüe.

outline [áutlaɪn] s. (*abstract*) bosquejo, esbozo; (*boundary*) contorno; v. bosquejar, esbozar; delinear.

outlive [autlív] v. sobrevivir.

outlook [áutluk] s. vista; perspectiva.

outlying [áutlaiɪŋ] adj. circundante, exterior, remoto (*del centro*).

out-of-date [áutəvdét] adj. fuera de moda, anticuado.

outpost [áutpost] s. avanzada.

output [áutput] s. rendimiento; producción total.

outrage [áutredʒ] s. ultraje; v. ultrajar.

outrageous [autrédʒəs] adj. afrentoso; atroz.

outran [autrǽn] pret. de to **outrun.**

outright [autráit] adv. & adj. sin rodeos; cabal; completo.

outrun [autrʌ́n] v. aventajar (*en una carrera*); dejar atrás; p.p. de to **outrun.**

outset [áutset] s. comienzo, principio.

outshine [autʃáin] v. eclipsar, sobrepasar (*en brillo o lucidez*).

outshone [autʃón] pret. & p.p. de to **outshine.**

outside [áutsáid] adj. (*external*) exterior; externo; (*foreign*) foráneo, extranjero; adv. fuera, afuera; fuera de casa; prep. fuera de; s. exterior, parte exterior; superficie; lado de afuera; **in a week, at the** — en una semana, a lo sumo; **to close on the** — cerrar por fuera.

outsider [autsáidə] s. foráneo, persona de fuera; extraño.

outskirts [áutskɜts] s. pl. alrededores, arrabales, cercanías.

outspoken [áutspókən] adj. franco, francote, Ven., Méx., C.A., Carib. claridoso.

outstanding [áutstǽndɪn] adj. sobresaliente; destacado, notable; — **bills** cuentas por cobrar; — **debts** deudas por pagar.

outstretched [autstrétʃt] adj. extendid‹ ; **with — arms** con los brazos abiertos.

outward [áutwəd] *adj.* (*external*) exterior, externo; (*apparent*) aparente; superficial; *adv.* fuera, hacia fuera; — **bound** que sale, de salida; para fuera, para el extranjero; **-ly** *adv.* exteriormente; por fuera; aparentemente.

outweigh [autwé] *v.* exceder en peso o valor; sobrepujar.

oval [óvl] *adj.* oval, ovalado; *s.* óvalo.

ovary [óvɑrɪ] *s.* ovario.

ovation [ovéʃən] *s.* ovación.

oven [ʌvən] *s.* horno.

over [óvɚ] *prep.* sobre; por; por encima de; encima de; a través de; al otro lado de; más de; — **night** por la noche, durante la noche; (*véase* **overnight**); — **to a**; **all — the city** por toda la ciudad; *adv.* encima; al otro lado; otra vez, de nuevo; — **again** otra vez, de nuevo; — **against** en contraste con; — **and** una y otra vez, repetidas veces; — **curious** demasiado curioso; —**generous** demasiado generoso; — **here** acá, aquí; — **there** allá, allí; **two years and** — más de dos años; **to do it** — hacerlo otra vez, volver a hacerlo; *adj.* excesivo; **it is all** — ya se acabó, se ha acabado; ha pasado.

overalls [óvɚɔlz] *s. pl. Am.* overol, overoles (*pantalones de trabajo*).

overate [ovɚét] *pret. de* **to overeat.**

overboard [óvɚbord] *adv.* al mar, al agua.

overcame [ovɚkém] *pret. de* **to overcome.**

overcast [óvɚkæst] *adj.* encapotado, nublado; **to become** — e ncapotarse, nublarse; [ovɚkæst] *v.* n blar o anublar; sobrehilar (*dar punta las sobre el borde de una tela*); *pret. & p.p. de* **to overcast.**

overcharge [ovɚtʃárdʒ] *v.* cargar demasiado; cobrar demasiado.

overcoat [óvɚkot] *s.* sobretodo, abrigo.

overcome [ovɚkʌm] *v.* vencer; rendir; *p.p. & adj.* vencido; rendido; agobiado; **to be — by weariness** estar rendido de fatiga.

overdue [ovɚdú] *adj.* atrasado; vencido sin pago.

overeat [ovɚít] *v.* hartarse.

overeaten [ovɚítn] *p.p. de* **to overeat.**

overexcite [óvɚɪksáɪt] *v.* sobreexcitar.

overflow [óvɚflo] *s.* derrame, desbordamiento; inundación; superabundancia; [ovɚfló] *v.* derramarse, desbordarse; rebosar; inundar.

overgrown [óvɚgrón] *adj.* denso, frondoso, poblado (*de follaje, herbaje, etc.*); — **boy** muchachón, muchacho demasiado crecido para su edad.

overhang [ovɚháŋ] *v.* colgar por encima de; proyectarse o sobresalir por encima de; adornar con colgaduras; amenazar (*dícese de un desastre o calamidad*).

overhaul [ovɚhól] *v.* reparar (*de cabo a rabo*); remendar; alcanzar (*en una*

carrera).

overhead [óvɚhed] *s.* gastos generales (*renta, seguro, alumbrado, calefacción, etc.*); *adj.* de arriba; elevado; — **expenses** gastos generales; [óvɚhéd] *adv.* encima de la cabeza, arriba; en lo alto.

overhear [ovɚhír] *v.* oír por casualidad, alcanzar a oír, acertar a oír.

overheard [ovɚhɚd] *pret. & p.p. de* **to overhear.**

overheat [óvɚhít] *v.* recalentar(se); calentar(se) demasiado.

overhung [ovɚháŋ] *pret. & p.p. de* **to overhang.**

overland [óvɚlænd] *adv. & adj.* por tierra.

overlap [ovɚlǽp] *v.* solapar.

overlay [ovɚlé] *v.* cubrir; incrustar.

overload [ovɚlód] *v.* sobrecargar; [óvɚlod] *s.* sobrecarga.

overlook [ovɚlúk] *v.* mirar a (*desde lo alto*); dar a, tener vista a; pasar por alto, omitir; perdonar (*faltas*); descuidar, no notar; inspeccionar, examinar.

overly [óvɚlɪ] *adv.* excesivamente.

overnight [óvɚnáɪt] *adv.* durante la noche; toda la noche; *adj.* de noche; nocturno; — **bag** saco de noche; — **trip** viaje de una noche.

overpass [óvɚpǽs] *v.* viaducto.

overpower [ovɚpáuɚ] *v.* subyugar, abrumar, vencer.

overran [ovɚrǽn] *pret. de* **to overrun.**

override [ovɚráɪd] *v.* anular; invalidar.

overrule [ovɚrúl] *v.* anular.

overrun [ovɚrʌn] *v.* desbordarse, mundar; sobrepasar; infestar, invadir; *p.p. de* **to overrun.**

overseas [óvɚsíz] *adv.* en ultramar, allende los mares; *adj.* de ultramar.

oversee [ovɚsí] *v.* dirigir; vigilar.

overseer [óvɚsɪr] *s.* sobrestante, capataz; inspector, superintendente.

overshoe [óvɚʃu] *s.* chanclo; zapato de goma, caucho o hule.

oversight [óvɚsaɪt] *s.* inadvertencia, negligencia, descuido.

overstep [ovɚstép] *v.* sobrepasarse, propasarse; traspasar; **to — the bounds** traspasar los límites; propasarse.

overtake [ovɚték] *v.* alcanzar.

overtaken [ovɚtékən] *p.p. de* **to overtake.**

overthrew [ovɚθrú] *pret. de* **to overthrow.**

overthrow [óvɚθro] *s.* (*overturn*) derrocamiento; (*defeat*) derrota, destrucción; caída; [ovɚθró] *v.* derrocar; derribar, echar abajo, volcar; destronar.

overthrown [ovɚθrón] *p.p. de* **to overthrow.**

overtime [óvɚtaɪm] *adv. & adj.* en exceso de las horas estipuladas; — **pay** sobresueldo.

overtook [ovɚtúk] *pret. de* **to overtake.**

overture [óvɚtʃɚ] *s.* obertura, preludio; propuesta, proposición.

overturn [ovɚtɚn] *v.* volcar(se); trastornar; derribar; echar abajo.

overwhelm [ovəhwélm] v. abrumar, agobiar; oprimir; arrollar.

overwhelming [ovəhwélmiŋ] adj. abrumador; opresivo; arrollador, irresistible, poderoso.

overwork [óvəwɚk] v. atarearse, afanarse más de lo debido, trabajar demasiado; s. exceso de trabajo.

owe [o] v. deber, adeudar.

owing [óiŋ] adj. debido; — to debido a.

owl [aul] s. lechuza, buho, Méx., C.A. tecolote.

own [on] adj. propio; a house of his — una casa suya; his — people los suyos; to be on one's — no estar a merced ajena; trabajar por su propia cuenta; to come into one's — entrar en posesión de lo suyo; to hold one's — mantenerse firme; v. poseer, tener; admitir, reconocer; to — to confesar; to — up confesar.

owner [ónɚ] s. dueño, amo; propietario; poseedor.

ownership [ónɚʃip] s. posesión, propiedad.

ox [aks] (pl. **oxen** [áksn]) s. buey.

oxygen [áksədʒən] s. oxígeno.

oyster [ɔ́istɚ] s. ostra, ostión.

ozone [ózon] s. ozono.

P

pace [pes] s. paso; v. pasear, andar; andar al paso; marchar; medir a pasos.

pacemaker [pésmekɚ] s. marcapaso.

pacific [pəsífik] adj. pacífico.

pacify [pǽsəfai] v. pacificar, apaciguar; calmar.

pack [pæk] s. fardo, lio, carga; manada (de lobos); cuadrilla, pandilla (de ladrones); jauría (de perros); muchedumbre; baraja (de naipes); — **animal** acémila, bestia de carga; v. empacar, empaquetar; embalar; enlatar; envasar; apiñar(se); cargar (una bestia); hacer (el baúl, la maleta); to — off despedir de repente; echar a la calle; largarse, irse.

package [pǽkidʒ] s. paquete; fardo, bulto; cajetilla (de cigarrillos).

packer [pǽkɚ] s. empacador; embalador, envasador.

packet [pǽkit] s. paquetillo; cajetilla.

packing [pǽkiŋ] s. (covering) embalaje; envase; (filling) relleno; — **box** caja para embalar o empacar; — **house** establecimiento frigorífico, fábrica para envasar o enlatar comestibles.

pact [pækt] s. pacto, convenio.

pad [pæd] s. almohadilla, cojincillo; tableta, bloc de papel; v. rellenar; forrar; acolchar.

padding [pǽdiŋ] s. relleno (de pelo, algodón, paja, etc.), Andes guata; ripio, palabras o frases inútiles.

paddle [pǽdl] s. pala; remo de canoa; — **wheel** rueda de paleta; v. remar con pala; apalear; chapotear (en el agua).

paddock [pǽdək] s. dehesa.

padlock [pǽdlak] s. candado; v. cerrar con candado.

pagan [pégən] s. & adj. pagano.

paganism [pégənizəm] s. paganismo.

page [pedʒ] s. página; paje; "botones" (de hotel), mensajero; v. paginar; vocear, llamar a voces.

pageant [pǽdʒənt] s. (parade) manifestación, desfile, procesión, pompa; (drama) representación al aire libre.

paid [ped] pret. & p.p. de to pay.

pail [pel] s. balde, cubo, cubeta.

pain [pen] s. dolor; sufrimiento; -s esmero; on (under) — of so pena de; to be in — estar sufriendo, tener dolores; to take -s esmerarse, extremarse; v. doler; causar dolor; afligir.

painful [pénfəl] adj. doloroso; penoso; arduo.

painless [pénlis] adj. sin dolor; libre de dolor.

painstaking [pénztekiŋ] adj. esmerado, cuidadoso; aplicado.

paint [pent] s. (mixture) pintura, color; (rouge) colorete; v. pintar; pintarse (la cara); to — the town red irse de juerga o de parranda, Am. irse de farra.

paintbrush [péntbrʌʃ] s. (art) pincel; (house) brocha.

painter [péntɚ] s. pintor.

painting [péntiŋ] s. pintura.

pair [per] s. par; pareja; a — of scissors unas tijeras; v. aparear(se); hacer pareja, hacer pares; to — off aparear(se).

pajamas [pədʒǽməz] s. pl. pijama.

pal [pæl] s. compañero, camarada.

palace [pǽlis] s. palacio.

palate [pǽlit] s. paladar.

palatial [pəléʃl] adj. suntuoso.

pale [pel] adj. pálido; descolorido; v. palidecer, ponerse pálido o descolorido.

paleness [pélnis] s. palidez.

palisade [pæləséd] s. palizada, estacada; -s riscos, acantilados.

pall [pɔl] v. empalagar; aburrir; it -s on me me empalaga; me aburre; s. paño de ataúd; palia (lienzo que se pone encima del cáliz).

palliative [pǽljətiv] adj. & s. paliativo.

pallid [pǽlid] adj. pálido.

pallor [pǽlɚ] s. palidez.

palm [pum] s. palma; palmera; — **Sunday** Domingo de Ramos; — **tree** palma, palmera; v. to — something off on someone pasar o dar algo indeseable a una persona (sin que se dé cuenta de ello).

palpable [pǽlpəb] adj. palpable, tangible; evidente.

palpitate [pǽlpətet] v. palpitar, latir.

palpitation [pælpətéʃən] s. palpitación; latido.

paltry [pɔ́ltri] adj. mezquino, miserable, despreciable, insignificante.

pamper [pǽmpɚ] v. mimar, consentir (a un niño).

pamphlet [pǽmflit] s. folleto, Am. panfleto.

pan [pæn] *s.* cazuela, cacerola; cazo; platillo (*de balanza*); **dish —** cazo para lavar platos; **frying —** sartén; *v.* **to — out (well)** salir bien, dar buen resultado.

Pan American [pǽnəmérəkən] *adj.* panamericano.

pancake [pǽnkek] *s.* tortita de harina, *Ven.*, *Col.* panqué; *Riopl.* panqueque.

pander [pǽndɚ] *s.* alcahuete, encubridor *v.* alcahuetear, servir de alcahuete.

pane [pen] vidrio, cristal (*de ventana o puerta*); cuadro (*de vidrio*).

panel [pǽnl] *s.* panel, tablero; cuarterón (*de puerta, ventana, etc.*); tabla (*doble pliegue de una falda o vestido*); **jury —** jurado; *v.* proveer de (*o adornar con*) paneles.

pang [pæŋ] *s.* dolor agudo; angustia, tormento.

panhandle [pǽnhændl] *s.* mango de sartén; territorio en forma de mango; *v.* mendigar.

panic [pǽnɪk] *adj.* & *s.* pánico; **panic-stricken** sobrecogido de pánico.

panorama [pænərǽmə] *s.* panorama.

pansy [pǽnzɪ] *s.* pensamiento (*flor*).

pant [pænt] *v.* jadear; palpitar; **to — for** anhelar, ansiar.

panther [pǽnθɚ] *s.* pantera.

panting [pǽntɪŋ] *s.* jadeo, palpitación; *adj.* jadeante.

pantomime [pǽntəmaɪm] *s.* pantomima.

pantry [pǽntrɪ] *s.* despensa.

pants [pænts] *s. pl.* pantalones.

papa [pɑ́pə] *s.* papá.

papacy [pépəsɪ] *s.* papado.

papal [pépl] *adj.* papal.

paper [pépɚ] *s.* (*material*) papel; (*daily*) periódico; (*essay*) tema, ensayos; **-s** papeles, documentos, credenciales; **naturalization -s** carta de naturaleza, certificado de ciudadanía; **— of pins** cartón de alfileres; **on —** escrito; por escrito; *adj.* de papel; para papel; **— doll** muñeca de papel; **— money** papel moneda; **—weight** pisapapeles; *v.* empapelar.

paperback [pépɚbæk] *s.* & *adj.* libro en rústica.

paperwork [pépɚwɚk] *s.* preparación de escritos; papeleo.

paprika [pæprikə] *s.* pimentón.

par [pɑr] *s.* (*equality*) paridad, igualdad; (*standard*) valor nominal; **— value** valor a la par; **above —** sobre par, a premio, con prima; **at —** a la par; **below —** bajo par, a descuento; **on a — with** al par de, al nivel de, igual a; **to feel above —** sentirse mejor que de ordinario; **to feel below —** sentirse menos bien que de ordinario.

parable [pǽrəbl] *s.* parábola (*alegoría bíblica*).

parachute [pǽrəʃut] *s.* paracaídas.

parachutist [pǽrəʃutɪst] *s.* paracaidista.

parade [pəréd] *s.* (*procession*) desfile, procesión, manifestación; paseo; (*re-*

view) parada; **— ground** campo de maniobras; **to make a — of** ostentar, hacer ostentación de; *v.* desfilar, pasar en desfile; marchar en parada; hacer ostentación de.

paradigm [pǽrədɪm], [pǽrədaɪm] *s.* paradigma.

paradise [pǽrədaɪs] *s.* paraíso.

paradox [pǽrədɑks] *s.* paradoja.

paraffin [pǽrəfɪn] *s.* parafina.

paragraph [pǽrəgræf] *s.* párrafo; *v.* dividir en párrafos.

Paraguayan [pærəgwáɪən] *adj.* & *s.* paraguayo.

parallel [pǽrəlɛl] *adj.* & *s.* paralelo; *v.* ser (*o correr*) paralelo a; comparar, cotejar.

paralysis [pərǽləsɪs] *s.* parálisis.

paralyze [pǽrəlaɪz] *v.* paralizar.

paramount [pǽrəmaʊnt] *adj.* importantísimo, superior, supremo, máximo.

paranoia [pærənɔ́jə] *s.* paranoia.

parapet [pǽrəpɪt] *s.* parapeto.

paraphrase [pǽrəfrez] *v.* parafrasear.

parasite [pǽrəsaɪt] *s.* parásito.

parasol [pǽrəsɔl] *s.* parasol, sombrilla.

paratroops [pǽrətrups] *s.* tropas paracaidistas.

parcel [pɑ́rsl] *s.* paquete; parcela, porción, lote (*de terreno*); **— post** paquete postal; *v.* parcelar, dividir en porciones o parcelas; hacer paquetes; **to — out** repartir.

parch [pɑrtʃ] *v.* resecar(se); tostar(se).

parchment [pɑ́rtʃmənt] *s.* pergamino.

pardon [pɑ́rdn] *s.* perdón; indulto; **I beg your —** perdone Vd.; dispense Vd.; *v.* perdonar; dispensar; indultar.

pare [pɛr] *v.* mondar, pelar (*manzanas, patatas, etc.*); cortar, recortar; **to — down expenditures** reducir gastos.

parent [pέrənt] *s.* padre, madre; origen; **-s** padres.

parentage [pέrəntɪdʒ] *s.* linaje; padres.

parental [pərέntl] *adj.* parental.

parenthesis [pərɛ́nθəsɪs] (*pl.* **parentheses** [pərɛ́nθəsɪz]) *s.* paréntesis.

parish [pǽrɪʃ] *s.* parroquia.

parishioner [pərɪ́ʃənɚ] *s.* parroquiano, feligrés; **-s** fieles, feligreses.

park [pɑrk] *s.* parque; *v.* estacionar, dejar (*un automóvil*); estacionarse; **-ing** lot *Ch.*, *Riopl.* playa de estacionamiento; *Mex.*, *Ven.* estacionamiento; *Col.* parqueadero; **-ing space** sitio o lugar para estacionarse; **free -ing** estacionamiento gratis; **no -ing** se prohibe estacionarse; no estacionarse.

parlance [pɑ́rləns] *s.* lenguaje.

parley [pɑ́rlɪ] *s.* parlamento, discusión, conferencia; *v.* parlamentar, discutir.

parliament [pɑ́rləmənt] *s.* parlamento.

parliamentary [pɑrləmɛ́ntərɪ] *adj.* parlamentario.

parlor [pɑ́rlɚ] *s.* sala, salón; sala de recibo; **— car** coche salón; **beauty —** salón de belleza.

parochial [pərókɪəl] *adj.* parroquial.

OV

parody [pǽrədɪ] *s.* parodia; *v.* parodiar.

parole [pəról] *s.* palabra de honor; **to put on** — dejar libre (*a un prisionero*) bajo palabra de honor; *v.* dejar libre bajo palabra de honor.

parrot [pǽrət] *s.* cotorra, loro, perico, papagayo; *v.* remedar, repetir como loro.

parry [pǽrɪ] *v.* parar, quitar o reparar (*un golpe*); *s.* quite, reparo.

parsley [pársli] *s.* perejil.

parsnip [pársnəp] *s.* chirivía (*legumbre*).

parson [pársn̩] *s.* pastor, clérigo.

part [part] *s.* parte (*f.*); papel (*dramático*); raya (*del cabello*); **— and parcel** parte esencial o inherente; **— owner** condueño, dueño en parte; **— time** parte del tiempo; **in foreign -s** en el extranjero, en países extranjeros; **spare -s** piezas accesorias, piezas de repuesto (*o de refacción*); **do your —** haga Vd. cuanto esté de su parte; *v.* partir(se); separar(se); **to — company** separarse; **to — from** separarse de, despedirse de; **to — one's hair** hacerse la raya; **to — with** separarse de, despedirse de, deshacerse de.

partake [parték] *v.* tomar parte, tener parte, participar.

partaken [partékən] *p.p. de* **to partake.**

partial [párʃəl] *adj.* parcial; **-ly** *adv.* parcialmente, en parte; con parcialidad.

partiality [parʃǽlətɪ] *s.* parcialidad.

participant [partísəpənt] *adj. & s.* participante, partícipe, copartícipe.

participate [partísəpet] *v.* participar.

participation [partɪsəpéʃən] *s.* participación.

participle [pártəsɪpl̩] *s.* participio; **present —** gerundio.

particle [pártɪkl̩] *s.* partícula.

particular [partíkjələ·] *adj.* (*single*) particular; peculiar; (*special*) esmerado, exacto; escrupuloso; (*demanding*) quisquilloso; exigente; *s.* particular, detalle, circunstancia; **in —** en particular, especialmente; **-ly** *adv.* particularmente; en particular.

parting [pártɪŋ] *s.* (*departure*) despedida; (*division*) separación; bifurcación; **the — of the ways** encrucijada, bifurcación, cruce de caminos; *adj.* de despedida, último.

partisan [pártəzn̩] *adj.* partidario; parcial; *s.* partidario; secuaz, seguidor.

partition [partíʃən] *s.* (*division*) partición, división, separación; (*wall*) tabique; *Am.* medianía; *v.* partir, dividir.

partitive [pártətɪv] *adj.* partitivo.

partly [pártlɪ] *adv.* en parte.

partner [pártnə·] *s.* socio, consocio; compañero; **dancing —** pareja de baile.

partnership [pártnɚʃɪp] *s.* sociedad, compañía.

partook [partúk] *pret. de* **to partake.**

partridge [pártrɪdʒ] *s.* perdiz.

party [pártɪ] *s.* (*get-together*) tertulia, reunión, fiesta; (*group*) grupo, par-

tida (*de gente*); (*legal*) parte; **hunting —** partida de caza; **political —** partido político.

pass [pæs] *s.* paso; pase, permiso de entrar; aprobación (*en un examen*); trance, situación; **— key** llave maestra; **to come to —** suceder; *v.* pasar; pasar por; pronunciar (*sentencia*), dar (*un juicio o parecer*); aprobar (*a un estudiante*); adoptar (*una ley*); ser aprobado en (*un examen*); **to — away** pasar a mejor vida, morir; desaparecer; pasar (*el tiempo*).

passable [pǽsəbl̩] *adj.* (*penetrable*) transitable; (*acceptable*) pasadero, regular, mediano.

passage [pǽsɪdʒ] *s.* pasaje; paso, tránsito; transcurso (*del tiempo*); pasillo, pasadizo; travesía, viaje por mar; aprobación (*de un proyecto de ley*); adopción (*de una ley*).

passageway [pǽsədʒwe] *s.* corredor; pasaje.

passbook [pǽsbuk] *s.* libreta de banco.

passenger [pǽsn̩dʒɚ] *s.* pasajero; **the -s** los pasajeros; el pasaje.

passer-by [pǽsɚbáɪ] *s.* transeúnte, viandante.

passion [pǽʃən] *s.* pasión; **Passion play** drama de la Pasión; **to fly into a —** montar en cólera, encolerizarse.

passionate [pǽʃənɪt] *adj.* apasionado.

passive [pǽsɪv] *adj.* pasivo; *s.* voz pasiva.

passport [pǽsport] *s.* pasaporte.

password [pǽswɚd] *s.* consigna, contraseña, santo y seña.

past [pæst] *adj.* pasado; último; **— master** perito; **the — president** el expresidente, el último presidente; **— tense** tiempo pasado; pretérito; **for some time —** desde hace algún tiempo, de poco tiempo a esta parte; *prep.* **— bearing** insoportable; **— understanding** incomprensible; **— half two** las dos y media; **woman — forty** cuarentona, mujer de más de cuarenta años; **to go — the house** pasar por (*o por enfrente de*) la casa; *s.* pasado; pretérito; pretérito imperfecto; **man with a —** hombre de dudosos antecedentes.

paste [pest] *s.* pasta; engrudo; *v.* pegar (*con engrudo*).

pasteboard [péstbord] *s.* cartón; **— box** caja de cartón.

pasteurize [pǽstəraɪz] *v.* pasterizar (*o* pasteurizar).

pastime [pǽstaɪm] *s.* pasatiempo.

pastor [pǽstə·] *s.* pastor, clérigo, cura.

pastoral [pǽstərəl] *adj.* pastoril; pastoral; *s.* pastoral, carta pastoral; écloga; pastorela, idilio.

pastry [péstrɪ] *s.* pastelería, pasteles; **— cook** pastelero; **— shop** pastelería.

pasture [pǽstʃɚ] *s.* pastura, pasto; dehesa; *v.* pastar, pacer; apacentar(se).

pat [pæt] *adj.* apto, oportuno; **to have a lesson —** saber o al dedillo la lección; **to stand —** mantenerse firme;

adv. a propósito; oportunamente; de molde; — palmadita, caricia, golpecito; — **of butter** cuadrito de mantequilla; *v.* dar palmaditas a; acariciar; pasar la mano (*para alisar o acariciar*).

patch [pætʃ] *s.* (*repair*) remiendo; parche; mancha; (*plot*) pedazo (*de terreno*); sembrado; *v.* remendar; **to — up a quarrel** hacer las paces.

pate [pet] *s.* coronilla (*de la cabeza*); **bald —** calva.

patent [pétn̩t] *adj.* patente, evidente, manifiesto; de patente; — **leather** charol; — **medicine** medicina de patente; — **right** patente; *s.* patente; *v.* patentar.

paternal [pǝtśn̩l] *adj.* paternal, paterno.

paternity [pǝtśn̩ǝtɪ] *s.* paternidad.

path [pæθ] *s.* senda, sendero; vereda; ruta; trayectoria (*de una bala*).

pathetic [pǝθétɪk] *adj.* patético.

pathology [pæθálǝdʒɪ] *s.* patología.

pathos [péθɑs] *s.* patetismo, cualidad patética.

pathway [pǽθwe] *s.* senda, vereda, vía.

patience [péʃǝns] *s.* paciencia.

patient [péʃǝnt] *adj.* paciente; pacienzudo; *s.* paciente, enfermo.

patriarch [pétrɪɑrk] *s.* patriarca.

patriarchal [petrɪárkl̩] *adj.* patriarcal.

patrimony [pǽtrǝmonɪ] *s.* patrimonio.

patriot [pétrɪǝt] *s.* patriota.

patriotic [petrɪátɪk] *adj.* patriótico.

patriotism [pétrɪǝtɪzǝm] *s.* patriotismo.

patrol [pǝtról] *s.* patrulla; ronda; *v.* patrullar, rondar.

patron [pétrǝn] *s.* patrón, patrono; benefactor; cliente, parroquiano; — **saint** santo patrón.

patronage [pétrǝnɪdʒ] *s.* (*support*) patrocinio, amparo; (*clientele*) clientela; (*manner*) condescendencia; **political** — control de nombramientos políticos.

patroness [pétrǝnɪs] *s.* patrona, protectora.

patronize [pétrǝnaɪz] *v.* patrocinar, amparar; tratar con condescendencia; favorecer, ser parroquiano de.

patter [pǽtǝ] *v.* golpetear ligeramente; talonear; charlar, parlotear; *s.* golpeteo; golpecitos; taloneo; charla, parloteo.

pattern [pǽtǝn] *s.* (*model*) modelo; dechado; muestra; ejemplo; patrón, molde; (*design*) diseño, dibujo (*en tejidos, telas, etc.*); *v.* **to — oneself after** seguir el ejemplo de; **to — something after (on, upon)** forjar o modelar algo a imitación de.

paucity [pɔ́sɪtɪ] *s.* escasez; falta.

paunch [pɔntʃ] *s.* panza, barriga.

pause [pɔz] *s.* pausa; *s.* pausar, hacer pausa; detenerse, parar.

pave [pev] *v.* pavimentar; **to — the way for** preparar o abrir el camino para; **to — with bricks** enladrillar; **to — with flagstones** enlosar.

pavement [pévmǝnt] *s.* pavimento; **brick —** enladrillado.

pavilion [pǝvíljǝn] *s.* pabellón.

paw [pɔ] *s.* garra, zarpa; *v.* echar la zarpa; arañar; manosear; **to — the ground** patear la tierra (*dícese del caballo*).

pawn [pɔn] *s.* prenda, empeño; peón (*de ajedrez*); —**broker** prestamista, prendero; —**shop** empeño, casa de empeños, montepío; **in —** en prenda; *v.* empeñar, dejar en prenda.

pay [pe] *v.* (*remit*) pagar; (*pay for*) costear; (*profit*) ser provechoso; (*worthwhile*) valer la pena; **to — attention** prestar atención; **to — back** restituir, devolver; **to — court** hacer la corte; **to — down** pagar al contado; **to — homage** hacer o rendir homenaje; **to — one's respects** presentar sus respetos; **to — a visit** hacer una visita; *s.* pago; recompensa; paga; sueldo; — **day** día de pagos, *Am.* día de raya; —**master** pagador, *Am.* rayador; —**roll** nómina.

payable [péǝbl̩] *adj.* pagadero.

payment [pémǝnt] *s.* pago; paga; — **in full** pago total.

payoff [péɔf] *s.* arreglo; pago.

pea [pi] *s.* guisante, chícharo; **sweet —** guisante de olor.

peace [pis] *s.* paz.

peaceable [písǝbl̩] *adj.* pacífico, tranquilo.

peaceful [písfǝl] *adj.* pacífico; tranquilo, quieto, sosegado.

peach [pitʃ] *s.* melocotón, durazno; persona bella o admirable; — **tree** durazno, duraznero, melocotonero.

peacock [píkɑk] *s.* pavón, pavo real; **to act like a —** pavonearse, hacer ostentación.

peak [pik] *s.* pico, cumbre, cima; cúspide; punto máximo.

peal [pil] *s.* repique (*de campanas*); — **of laughter** carcajada, risotada; — **of thunder** trueno; *v.* repicar (*las campanas*).

peanut [pínǝt] *s.* cacahuate, *Carib., Ven., Col., Ch., Ríopl., Andes* maní.

pear [per] *s.* pera; — **tree** peral; **alligator —** aguacate, *Ch., Andes, Ríopl.* palta (*variedad sudamericana*).

pearl [pɜl] *s.* perla; — **necklace** collar de perlas; **mother-of-pearl** nácar, madreperla.

pearly [pɜ́lɪ] *adj.* perlino; nacarado; aperlado.

peasant [pézn̩t] *adj.* & *s.* campesino, rústico, *P.R.* jíbaro, *Cuba* guajiro; *Col.* paisa; *Ch.* guaso; *Ríopl.* gaucho.

pebble [pébl̩] *s.* guija, china, guijarro, piedrecilla.

pecan [pikán] *s.* pacana.

peck [pek] *v.* picar, picotear; *s.* picotazo, picotada; medida de áridos (*aproximadamente 9 litros*); **a — of trouble** la mar de disgustos o molestias.

peculiar [pɪkjúljǝ] *adj.* peculiar; raro, singular, extraño.

peculiarity [pɪkjulɪǽrǝtɪ] *s.* peculiaridad; particularidad; rareza.

pedagogue [pédǝgɑg] *s.* pedagogo, dó-

PA

mine.
pedagogy [pédəgodʒɪ] *s.* pedagogía.
pedal [pédl] *s.* pedal; *v.* pedalear, mover los pedales.
pedant [pédnt] *s.* pedante.
pedantic [pɪdǽntɪk] *adj.* pedante, pedantesco.
peddle [pédl] *v.* ir vendiendo de puerta en puerta; **to — gossip** chismear.
peddler [pédlə] *s.* buhonero; vendedor ambulante.
pedestal [pédɪst] *s.* pedestal.
pedestrian [pədéstrɪən] *s.* peatón, transeúnte, viandante; *adj.* pedestre.
pediatrics [pidɪǽtrɪks] *s.* pediatría.
pedigree [pédəgri] *s.* linaje, genealogía.
peek [pik] *v.* atisbar, espiar; *s.* atisbo.
peel [pil] *s.* corteza, cáscara (*de algunas frutas*); pellejo (*de patatas*); *v.* pelar(se), descortezar(se), deshollejar(se); **to keep one's eye -ed** tener los ojos muy abiertos, estar alerta.
peep [pip] *v.* atisbar, espiar; asomar(se); pipiar, piar; *s.* atisbo; ojeada; pío (*de pollo o ave*).
peer [pir] *s.* (*equal*) par, igual; (*noble*) noble; *v.* mirar con atención, atisbar; asomar; **to — into other people's business** fisgar, curiosear.
peer group [pɪrgrup] *s.* conjunto de personas de la misma edad y condiciones.
peerless [pírlɪs] *adj.* incomparable; sin par.
peeve [piv] *v.* irritar, poner de mal humor; **to get -d** amoscarse, ponerse de mal humor.
peevish [pívɪʃ] *adj.* enojadizo; malhumorado.
peg [peg] *s.* espiga, clavo de madera, estaquilla; clavija (*de violin*); **to take a person down a —** rebajar o humillar a alguien; *v.* clavar, clavetear; poner estaquillas; **to — along** atarearse, trabajar con tesón.
pejorative [pədʒórətɪv] *adj.* peyorativo; despectivo.
pellet [pélɪt] *s.* (*ball*) pelotilla; bola; (*pill*) píldora.
pell-mell [pélmél] *adj.* confuso, tumultuoso; *adv.* a trochemoche, atropelladamente, en tumulto.
pelt [pelt] *s.* zalea, cuero (*especialmente de oveja*); piel; *v.* golpear; **to — with stones** apedrear, arrojar piedras a.
pelvis [pélvɪs] *s.* pelvis.
pen [pen] *s.* pluma (*para escribir*); corral; redil; **—holder** mango de pluma, portapluma; **— name** nombre de pluma; **fountain —** pluma fuente, pluma estilográfica; **pig —** pocilga; *v.* escribir (*con pluma*), acorralar, encerrar.
penal [pínl] *adj.* penal.
penalize [pínəlaɪz] *v.* penar; aplicar sanción.
penalty [pénltɪ] *s.* pena, castigo; multa.
penance [pénəns] *s.* penitencia.
pencil [pénsl] *s.* lápiz; lapicero; **— sharpener** tajalápiz.

pendant [péndənt] *s.* pendiente (*adorno que cuelga*); *adj.* pendiente.
pending [péndɪŋ] *adj.* pendiente; colgado; *prep.* durante.
pendulum [péndʒələm] *s.* péndulo.
penetrate [pénətret] *v.* penetrar.
penetrating [pénətretɪŋ] *adj.* penetrante.
penetration [penətréʃən] *s.* penetración.
penguin [péngwɪn] *s.* pingüino.
penicillin [penəsílɪn] *s.* penicilina.
peninsula [panínsələ] *s.* península.
penitent [pénətənt] *adj.* arrepentido, penitente; *s.* penitente.
penitentiary [penəténʃərɪ] *s.* penitenciaría, presidio.
penknife [pénnaɪf] *s.* cortaplumas; navaja.
penmanship [pénmənʃɪp] *s.* escritura, caligrafía.
pennant [pénənt] *s.* banderola, gallardete.
penniless [pénɪlɪs] *adj.* pobre, sin dinero.
penny [pénɪ] *s.* centavo (*de dólar*); **to cost a pretty —** costar un ojo de la cara, costar un dineral.
pension [pénʃən] *s.* pensión; retiro (*de un militar*); *v.* pensionar.
pensive [pénsɪv] *adj.* pensativo.
pent [pent] *adj.* encerrado; acorralado; **pent-up emotions** sentimientos reprimidos.
penthouse [pénthaʊs] *s.* casa de azotea; colgadizo.
people [pípl] *s.* gente; pueblo *v.* poblar.
pepper [pépə] *s.* pimienta; **— plant** pimiento; **— shaker** pimentero; **green -s** pimientos verdes; **red —** pimentón, chile, *Carib., Col., Ven., Andes, Ch., Riopl.* ají; *v.* sazonar con pimienta; **to — with bullets** acribillar a balazos.
peppermint [pépəmɪnt] *s.* menta; pastilla o bombón de menta.
per [pə] *prep.* por; **— capita** por cabeza; **— cent** por ciento; **— year** al año; **ten cents — dozen** diez centavos por docena (*o diez centavos la docena*).
percale [pəkél] *s.* percal.
perceive [pəsív] *v.* percibir.
percentage [pəséntɪdʒ] *s.* porcentaje, tanto por ciento.
perceptible [pəséptəbl] *adj.* perceptible.
perception [pəsépʃən] *s.* percepción.
perceptive [pərséptɪv] *adj.* perceptivo; sensible.
perch [pətʃ] *s.* percha (*para pájaros*); perca (*pez*); *v.* encaramar(se); posarse (*en una percha o rama*).
perchance [pətʃǽns] *adv.* por ventura, acaso, quizás, tal vez.
percolate [pə́kəlet] *v.* filtrar(se), colar(se); rezumarse; penetrar.
perdition [pədíʃən] *s.* perdición.
perennial [pərénɪəl] *adj.* perenne; continuo; perpetuo.
perfect [pə́fɪkt] *adj.* perfecto; completo;

s. tiempo perfecto (*del verbo*); [pəfékt] *v.* perfeccionar.

perfection [pəfékʃən] *s.* perfección.

perfidious [pəfídɪəs] *adj.* pérfido.

perfidy [pɚfədɪ] *s.* perfidia.

perforate [pɚfəret] *v.* perforar.

perforce [pəfɔrs] *adj.* necesariamente; por fuerza.

perform [pəfɔrm] *v.* ejecutar; llevar a cabo, cumplir, hacer; funcionar (*una máquina*); desempeñar o representar un papel.

performance [pəfɔrməns] *s.* ejecución; desempeño, cumplimiento; funcionamiento (*de una máquina o motor*); función, representación; acto, acción.

perfume [pɚfjum] *s.* perfume; [pəfjúm] *v.* perfumar.

perfumery [pəfjúmərɪ] *s.* perfumería; perfumes.

perhaps [pəhǽps] *adv.* acaso, tal vez, quizá (*o* quizás), puede ser.

perigee [pɛrədʒi] *s.* perigeo.

peril [pɛrəl] *s.* peligro; riesgo; *v.* poner en peligro.

perilous [pɛrələs] *adj.* peligroso.

perimeter [pərímətə] *s.* perímetro.

period [pírɪəd] *s.* período; punto final; fin, término.

periodic [pɪrɪádɪk] *adj.* periódico.

periodical [pɪrɪádɪk] *adj.* periódico; *s.* revista, publicación periódica.

periphery [pərífərɪ] *s.* periferia.

perish [pɛrɪʃ] *v.* perecer.

perishable [pɛrɪʃəbl] *adj.* perecedero; deleznable.

perjure [pɚdʒə] *v.* **to — oneself** perjurar.

perjury [pɚdʒrɪ] *s.* perjurio, juramento falso.

permanence [pɚmənəns] *s.* permanencia.

permanent [pɚmənənt] *adj.* permanente; duradero.

permeate [pɚmiet] *v.* penetrar, saturar; difundirse por, filtrarse por.

permissible [pəmísəbl] *adj.* lícito.

permission [pəmíʃən] *s.* permiso, licencia.

permissive [pəmísɪv] *adj.* permisivo.

permit [pɚmɪt] *s.* permiso, pase; licencia; [pəmít] *v.* permitir.

permutation [pɚmjutéʃən] *s.* permutación.

pernicious [pəníʃəs] *adj.* pernicioso.

perpendicular [pɚpəndíkjələ] *adj. & s.* perpendicular.

perpetrate [pɚpetret] *v.* perpetrar, cometer.

perpetual [pəpétʃuəl] *adj.* perpetuo.

perpetuate [pəpétʃuet] *v.* perpetuar.

perplex [pəpléks] *v.* confundir, turbar, aturdir.

perplexed [pəplékst] *adj.* perplejo, confuso.

perplexity [pəpléksətɪ] *s.* perplejidad, confusión.

persecute [pɚsɪkjut] *v.* perseguir, acosar.

persecution [pɚsɪkjúʃən] *s.* persecución.

persecutor [pɚsɪkjutə] *s.* perseguidor.

perseverance [pɚsəvírəns] *s.* perseverancia.

persevere [pɚsəvír] *v.* perseverar; persistir.

persist [pəzíst] *v.* persistir; porfiar.

persistence [pəzístəns] *s.* persistencia; porfía.

persistent [pəzístənt] *adj.* persistente; porfiado.

person [pɚsn] *s.* persona.

personable [pɚsənəbl] *adj.* presentable; bien parecido.

personage [pɚsnɪdʒ] *s.* personaje.

personal [pɚsnḷ] *adj.* personal; en persona.

personality [pɚsnǽlətɪ] *s.* personalidad; persona, personaje; alusión personal.

personnel [pɚsnél] *s.* personal.

perspective [pəspéktɪv] *s.* perspectiva; **— drawing** dibujo en perspectiva.

perspicacious [pɚspɪkéʃəs] *adj.* perspicaz.

perspiration [pɚspəréʃən] *s.* sudor.

perspire [pəspáɪr] *v.* sudar.

persuade [pəswéd] *v.* persuadir.

persuasion [pəswéʒən] *s.* persuasión; creencia.

persuasive [pəswésɪv] *adj.* persuasivo.

pert [pɚt] *adj.* insolente, descarado, atrevido, *Am.* retobado.

pertain [pətén] *v.* pertenecer; atañer.

pertinent [pɚtnənt] *adj.* pertinente, a propósito, al caso.

perturb [pətɚb] *v.* perturbar.

perusal [pərúzḷ] *s.* lectura.

peruse [pərúz] *v.* leer con cuidado.

Peruvian [pərúvɪən] *adj. & s.* peruano.

pervade [pəvéd] *v.* llenar, penetrar, difundirse por.

perverse [pəvɚs] *adj.* perverso; terco, obstinado.

pervert [pəvɚt] *v.* pervertir; falsear; [pɚvɚt] *s.* perverso.

pessimism [pésəmɪzəm] *s.* pesimismo.

pessimist [pésəmɪst] *s.* pesimista; **-ic** *adj.* pesimista.

pest [pest] *s.* peste, plaga; pestilencia.

pester [péstə] *v.* importunar, molestar.

pesticide [péstəsaɪd] *s. & adj.* insecticida.

pestilence [péstḷəns] *s.* pestilencia.

pet [pet] *s.* animal mimado, animal casero o doméstico; niño mimado; favorito; *adj.* favorito; mimado; **— name** nombre de cariño (*por lo general diminutivo*); *v.* mimar, acariciar.

petal [pétḷ] *s.* pétalo.

petcock [pétkɑk] *s.* llave de desagüe (*purga*).

petition [pətíʃən] *s.* petición, súplica; instancia, memorial, solicitud, *Am.* ocurso; *v.* solicitar, pedir, dirigir una instancia o memorial a; suplicar, rogar.

petrify [pétrɪfaɪ] *v.* petrificar.

petroleum [pətrólɪəm] *s.* petróleo.

petticoat [pétɪkot] *s.* enaguas.

petty [pétɪ] *adj.* insignificante, pequeño; mezquino; inferior, subordinado; **— cash** fondos para gastos menores; **—**

larceny ratería; **— officer** oficial subordinado (*en la marina*); **— treason** traición menor.

pew [pju] *s.* banco de iglesia.

phalanx [félǽŋks] *s.* falanje.

phantom [fǽntəm] *s.* fantasma.

pharmacist [fárməsɪst] *s.* farmacéutico, boticario.

pharmacy [fárməsɪ] *s.* farmacia, botica.

pharynx [fǽrɪŋks] *s.* faringe.

phase [fez] *s.* fase.

pheasant [fézənt] *s.* faisán.

phenomena [fənámənə] *pl.* de **phenomenon**.

phenomenon [fənámənan] *s.* fenómeno.

philanthropy [fɪlǽnθrəpɪ] *s.* filantropía.

philharmonic [fɪlharmánɪk] *adj.* filarmónico.

philology [fɪlálədʒɪ] *s.* filología.

philosopher [fəlásəfə] *s.* filósofo.

philosophical [fɪləsáfɪk] *adj.* filosófico.

philosophy [fəlásəfɪ] *s.* filosofía.

phlegm [flɛm] *s.* flema.

phone [fon] *s.* teléfono; *v.* telefonear.

phoneme [fónim] *s.* fonema.

phonetics [fonétɪks] *s.* fonética.

phonograph [fónəgræf] *s.* fonógrafo.

phonology [fonálədʒɪ] *s.* fonología.

phosphate [fásfet] *s.* fosfato.

phosphorus [fásfərəs] *s.* fósforo (*elemento químico*).

photo [fóto] *s.* fotografía, retrato.

photograph [fótəgræf] *s.* fotografía, retrato; *v.* fotografiar, retratar.

photographer [fətágrəfə] *s.* fotógrafo.

photography [fətágrəfɪ] *s.* fotografía.

phrase [frez] *s.* frase; expresión, locución; *v.* frasear; expresar, formular.

physic [fízɪk] *s.* purga, purgante; *v.* purgar.

physical [fízɪkl] *adj.* físico.

physician [fazíʃən] *s.* médico.

physicist [fízəsɪst] *s.* físico.

physics [fízɪks] *s.* física.

physiological [fɪzɪəládʒɪkl] *adj.* fisiológico.

physiology [fɪzɪálədʒɪ] *s.* fisiología.

physique [fɪzík] *s.* físico, constitución física, talle, cuerpo.

piano [pɪǽno] *s.* piano; **— bench** banqueta de piano; **— stool** taburete de piano; **grand** — piano de cola; **upright** — piano vertical.

picaresque [pɪkərésk] *adj.* picaresco.

pick [pɪk] *v.* (*choose*) escoger; coger; (*break*) picar; (*clean*) mondarse, limpiarse (*los dientes*); desplumar (*un ave*); roer (*un hueso*); falsear (*una cerradura*); armar (*una pendencia*); **to — flaws** criticar, censurar; **to — out** escoger; **to — pockets** ratear; **to — up** recoger; **to — up speed** acelerar la marcha; *s.* pico (*herramienta*); selección; lo selecto, lo mejor; recolección, cosecha; **ice —** punzón para romper hielo; **tooth —** mondadientes, palillo de dientes.

pickaxe [pɪkǽks] *s.* pico, zapapico.

picket [píkɪt] *s.* piquete (*estaca o palo clavado en la tierra*); piquete (*vigilante huelguista*); piquete de soldados; *v.* estacionar piquetes cerca de (*una fábrica, campamento, etc.*); vigilar (*por medio de piquetes*); estar de guardia.

pickle [píkl] *s.* encurtido; **to be in a —** hallarse en un aprieto; *v.* encurtir, escabechar; **-ed cucumbers** pepinillos encurtidos; **-ed fish** escabeche, pescado en escabeche.

pickpocket [píkpakɪt] *s.* rata (*m.*), ratero; *Méx., Ven., Col.* carterista.

picnic [píknɪk] *s.* partida de campo, día de campo, comida campestre, *Am.* picnic; *v.* hacer una comida campestre; ir a un picnic.

picture [píktʃə] *s.* (*painting*) cuadro, pintura; (*portrait*) retrato; (*photo*) fotografía; (*engraving*) grabado; (*movie*) película; **— frame** marco; **— gallery** museo o galería de pinturas; *v.* pintar, dibujar; describir; imaginar(se).

picturesque [pɪktʃərésk] *adj.* pintoresco.

pie [paɪ] *s.* pastel; empanada.

piece [pis] *s.* (*section*) pieza; pedazo; parte; sección; (*passage*) trozo; **— of advice** consejo; **— of land** parcela; **— of money** moneda; **— of news** noticia; **— of nonsense** tontería; **—meal** en pedazos, a pedazos, por partes; *v.* remendar; **to — between meals** comer a deshoras; **to — on to** juntar a, pegar a; **to — together** unir, pegar, juntar.

pier [pɪr] *s.* muelle, embarcadero; rompeolas; pilar (*de puente o arco*).

pierce [pɪrs] *v.* atravesar, traspasar; taladrar, agujerear, perforar.

piety [páɪətɪ] *s.* piedad, religiosidad.

pig [pɪg] *s.* puerco, cerdo, cochino; *S.A.* chancho; *C.A.* tunco; cuchi; **— iron** hierro en lingotes; **—headed** cabezón, testarudo; **guinea —** conejillo de Indias.

pigeon [pídʒən] *s.* pichón; paloma.

pigeonhole [pídʒənhol] *s.* casilla; *v.* encasillar.

pigment [pígmənt] *s.* pigmento, color.

pigmy [pígmɪ] *s.* pigmeo.

pike [paɪk] *s.* pica, lanza; lucio (*pez*).

pile [paɪl] *s.* pila, montón; pelo (*de ciertos tejidos*); pilote; **-s** almorranas (*enfermedad*); **— driver** martinete (*para clavar pilotes*); *v.* apilar(se), amontonar(se); acumular(se).

pilfer [pílfə] *v.* pillar, ratear, hurtar, sisar.

pilgrim [pílgrɪm] *s.* peregrino, romero.

pilgrimage [pílgrəmɪdʒ] *s.* peregrinación, romería.

pill [pɪl] *s.* píldora; persona fastidiosa.

pillage [pílɪdʒ] *v.* pillar, saquear; *s.* pillaje, saqueo.

pillar [pílə] *s.* pilar, columna; **to go from — to post** ir de Ceca en Meca.

pillow [pílo] *s.* almohada; cojín.

pillowcase [píləkes] *s.* funda de almohada.

pilot [páilət] *s.* piloto; guía; — **light** (*o* — **burner**) mechero, encendedor (*de una cocina o estufa de gas*); **harbor** — práctico de puerto; *v.* pilotar o pilotear; dirigir, guiar.

pimple [pímpl] *s.* grano, barro.

pin [pin] *s.* alfiler; prendedor; espiga; bolo (*del juego de bolos*); — **money** dinero para alfileres; — **wheel** molinete, *Am.* remolino; **breast** — broche; **safety** — imperdible; *v.* prender (*con alfiler*); asegurar, fijar, clavar; **to** — **down** fijar, inmovilizar; hacer dar una contestación definitiva; **to** — **one's hope to** poner toda su esperanza en; **to** — **up** prender con alfileres; colgar (*un dibujo o retrato*), fijar con tachuelas.

pincers [pínsəz] *s. pl.* pinzas; tenazas; **small** — tenacillas.

pinch [pintʃ]. *v.* (*squeeze*) pellizcar; apretar; (*economize*) economizar; (*arrest*) prender, arrestar; **to** — **one's finger in the door** machucarse el dedo en la puerta; *s.* pellizco; pizca, porción pequeña; puntada, dolor agudo; aprieto, apuro; — **hitter** suplente, sustituto.

pinchers [píntʃəz] = **pincers**.

pine [pain] *s.* pino; — **cone** piña; — **grove** pinar; — **nut** piña; *v.* languidecer; **to** — **away** consumirse; **to** — **for** anhelar, suspirar por.

pineapple [páinæpl] *s.* piña, ananá o ananás.

pinion [pínjən] *s.* piñón.

pink [piŋk] *s.* clavel; color de rosa; **in the** — **of condition** en la mejor condición; *adj.* rosado, color de rosa.

pinnacle [pínəkl] *s.* pináculo, cumbre.

pint [paint] *s.* pinta (*aproximadamente medio litro*).

pioneer [paiənír] *s.* explorador, colonizador; fundador, iniciador, precursor; pionero; *v.* explorar, colonizar; fundar, promover.

pious [páiəs] *adj.* pío, piadoso.

pipe [paip] *s.* pipa (*de fumar*); tubo, caño; cañón (*de órgano*); caramillo, flauta; — **line** tubería o *v.* conducir por cañerías; desaguar por cañería; proveer de tuberías o cañerías; chillar; **to** — **down** bajar la voz.

piper [páipə] *s.* gaitero, flautista.

piping [páipiŋ] *s.* cañería, tubería; cordoncillo (*de adorno para costuras*); chillido, silbido; *adj.* agudo, chillón; — **hot** muy caliente; hirviendo.

pippin [pípin] *s.* camuesa.

pique [pik] *s.* enojo, resentimiento; *v.* picar, excitar; enojar, irritar; **to** — **oneself on** picarse de, preciarse de.

pirate «[páirət] *s.* pirata; *v.* piratear; plagiar.

pistol [pístl] *s.* pistola; revólver.

piston [pístn] *s.* pistón, émbolo; — **ring** aro de pistón; — **rod** vástago del émbolo.

pit [pit] *s.* hoyo; foso; hueso (*de ciertas frutas*); — **of the stomach** boca del estómago.

pitch. [pitʃ] *s.* (*throw*) tiro, lanzamiento (*de una pelota*); cabezada (*de un barco*); (*music*) diapasón, tono; (*inclination*) grado, declive, grado de inclinación; pez (*f.*), brea; resina; — **dark** oscurísimo; *v.* tirar, lanzar, arrojar; cabecear (*un barco*); graduar el tono de (*un instrumento o voz*); echarse de cabeza; inclinarse; **to** — **a tent** armar una tienda de campaña; acampar; **to** — **into** arremeter contra; reprender, regañar; — **in!** ¡manos a la obra!

pitcher [pítʃə] *s.* cántaro, jarro o jarra; tirador, lanzador (*en beisbol*).

pitchfork [pítʃfork] *s.* horca, horquilla (*para hacinar las mieses, levantar la paja, etc.*).

piteous [pítiəs] *adj.* lastimero, lastimoso.

pith [piθ] *s.* meollo, médula; esencia, sustancia.

pitiful [pítifəl] *adj.* lastimoso; lamentable; miserable.

pitiless [pítilis] *adj.* despiadado, incompasivo, cruel.

pity [píti] *s.* piedad; lástima; compasión; **for** -'**s sake** por piedad, por Dios; **what a** —! ¡qué lástima!; *v.* compadecer; tener lástima por; apiadarse de, tener piedad de.

placard [plǽkard] *s.* letrero, cartel; *v.* fijar carteles.

place [ples] *s.* (*site*) lugar, sitio; localidad; (*position*) puesto; empleo; posición; — **of business** oficina, despacho; — **of worship** templo, iglesia; **market** — plaza, mercado; **in** — **of** en lugar de, en vez de; **it is not my** — **to do it** no es mi deber hacerlo, no me toca a mí hacerlo; *v.* colocar; situar; poner; acomodar, dar empleo a.

placid [plǽsid] *adj.* plácido, apacible, sosegado.

plagiarism [plédʒərizəm] *s.* plagio.

plague [pleg] *s.* plaga; peste, pestilencia; calamidad; *v.* plagar, infestar; importunar.

plaid [plæd] *s.* tartán, tela a cuadros; manta escocesa a cuadros; diseño a cuadros; *adj.* a cuadros.

plain [plen] *adj.* (*flat*) llano; (*simple*) sencillo; claro; franco; ordinario; — **fool** tonto de capirote; — **woman** mujer sin atractivo; **in** — **sight** en plena vista; **plain-clothes man** detective; *adv.* claramente; — **stupid** completamente estúpido; **plain-spoken** franco, francote, sincero; *s.* llano, llanura.

plaintiff [pléntif] *s.* demandante.

plaintive [pléntiv] *adj.* lastimero, triste.

plan [plen] *s.* plan; proyecto; plano (*dibujo o mapa*); *v.* planear; proyectar, idear; pensar, proponerse.

plane [plen] *s.* (*airplane*) avión; aeroplano; (*surface*) superficie plana; cepillo (*de carpintero*); *adj.* plano, llano; — **tree** plátano falso;

PE

v. acepillar, alisar con cepillo (*la madera o los metales*).

planet [plǽnɪt] *s.* planeta.

plank [plæŋk] *s.* tabla, tablón; principio, base (*del programa de un partido político*); *v.* entablar, entarimar, cubrir con tablas; asar (*carne*) en una tabla.

plant [plænt] *s.* (*vegetation*) planta; (*industry*) fábrica; taller; *v.* plantar; sembrar; implantar; establecer.

plantation [plæntéʃən] *s.* plantación; plantío; sembrado; **coffee —** cafetal; **cotton —** algodonal; **rubber —** cauchal; **sugar —** ingenio de azúcar.

planter [plǽntɚ] *s.* plantador, cultivador.

plaque [plæk] *s.* placa.

plasma [plǽzmə] *s.* plasma.

plaster [plǽstɚ] *s.* yeso; emplasto; **— of Paris** yeso, yeso mate; **court —** esparadrapo, tafetán inglés; **mustard —** sinapismo; *v.* enyesar; emplastar, poner emplastos a; pegar (*carteles, anuncios*); embarrar.

plastic [plǽstɪk] *adj.* plástico.

plat [plæt] *s.* plano; parcela; *v.* levantar o trazar un plano.

plate [plet] *s.* (*eating*) plato; (*metal*) placa; plancha; lámina; **dental —** dentadura postiza; *v.* platear; dorar; niquelar; blindar, proteger con planchas de metal.

plateau [plætó] *s.* antiplanicie, mesa, meseta.

plated [plétəd] *adj.* chapeado; blindado.

plateful [plétfʊl] *s.* plato, plato lleno.

platform [plǽtfɔrm] *s.* plataforma; tablado; programa de un partido político; **railway —** andén.

platinum [plǽtnəm] *s.* platino.

platitude [plǽtətjud] *s.* lugar común, perogrullada.

platter [plǽtɚ] *s.* platel, platón.

play [ple] *v.* (*game*) jugar; juguetear; (*instrument*) tocar; (*drama*) representar; hacer, desempeñar (*un papel*); manipular (*un instrumento, radio, fonógrafo, etc.*); **to — a joke** hacer una broma, dar un chasco; **to — cards** jugar a los naipes, jugar a la baraja; **to — havoc** hacer estragos, causar daño; **to — tennis** jugar al tenis; **to — the fool** hacerse el tonto, fingirse tonto; **to be all -ed out** no poder más, estar agotado; *s.* juego; jugada (*acción, movimiento en un juego*); pieza, drama, comedia, representación; recreación, diversión; **— on words** juego de palabras, equívoco; **to give full —** to dar rienda suelta a.

player [pléɚ] *s.* (*games*) jugador; (*music*) músico; (*plays*) cómico, actor; artista; **— piano** piano mecánico, pianola; **piano —** pianista; **violin —** violinista.

playful [pléfəl] *adj.* juguetón, retozón; bromista.

playground [plégraʊnd] *s.* campo o patio de recreo.

playmate [plémet] *s.* compañero de juego.

plaything [pléθɪŋ] *s.* juguete.

playwright [pléraɪt] *s.* dramático, dramaturgo.

plea [pli] *s.* súplica; ruego; alegato, defensa; pretexto; **on the — that** con el pretexto de que.

plead [plid] *v.* abogar; suplicar; argüir; alegar; defender (*una causa*); **to — guilty** declararse o confesarse culpable.

pleasant [plézn̩t] *adj.* grato; agradable; simpático.

pleasantry [plézn̩trɪ] *s.* chanza, broma, chiste, humorada.

please [pliz] *v.* agradar, gustar, dar gusto a; complacer; **— do it** haga Vd. el favor de hacerlo, tenga Vd. la bondad de hacerlo, sírvase hacerlo; **as you —** como Vd. quiera, como Vd. guste; **if you —** si me hace Vd. (el) favor; **to be -ed to** complacerse en, tener gusto en; alegrarse de; **to be -ed with** gustarle a uno, estar satisfecho de (*o* con).

pleasing [plízɪŋ] *adj.* agradable.

pleasure [pléʒɚ] *s.* placer, gusto; deleite, alegría, gozo; **— trip** viaje de recreo; **what is your —?** ¿qué deseaba Vd.? ¿en qué puedo servirle?

pleat [plit] *s.* pliegue, doblez; *v.* plegar, hacer pliegues (en).

plebeian [plɪbíən] *adj.* & *s.* plebeyo.

pledge [plɛdʒ] *s.* promesa; prenda (*garantía*); fianza; **as a — of** en prenda de; *v.* prometer; empeñar, dar en prenda; hacer firmar una promesa; **to — one's word** empeñar (*o* dar) su palabra; **to — to secrecy** exigir promesa de sigilo.

plenary [plénərɪ] *adj.* plenario.

plenipotentiary [plenəpəténʃərɪ] *adj.* & *s.* plenipotenciario.

plentiful [pléntɪfəl] *adj.* abundante, copioso.

plenty [plénti] *s.* abundancia, copia; **— of time** bastante tiempo; **that is —** con eso basta; basta.

pliable [pláɪəbl̩] *adj.* flexible; manejable, dócil; transigente.

pliant [pláɪənt] *adj.* flexible; dócil, sumiso.

pliers [pláɪɚz] *s. pl.* alicates, tenazas.

plight [plaɪt] *s.* apuro, aprieto, situación difícil.

plod [plɑd] *v.* bregar, trafagar, afanarse, trabajar asiduamente.

plosive [plósɪv] *adj.* & *s.* oclusivo.

plot [plɑt] *s.* (*outline*) trama, enredo, argumento; (*conspiracy*) complot, conspiración; (*land*) parcela (*de tierra*), solar; (*plan*) plano, diagrama; *v.* tramar, urdir, maquinar, conspirar; hacer el plano o diagrama de; **to — a curve** hacer una gráfica.

plotter [plɑ́tɚ] *s.* conspirador; tramador; conjurado.

plough = **plow.**

plow [plaʊ] *s.* arado; **—share** reja de arado; *v.* arar; surcar.

pluck [plʌk] v. coger; arrancar; desplumar (un ave); puntear (las cuerdas de una guitarra); **to — at** tirar de; **to — up** arrancar; cobrar ánimo; s. ánimo, valor; tirón.

plucky [plʌkı] adj. valeroso, animoso.

plug [plʌg] s. (stopper) taco, tapón; (horse) caballejo, penco; (boost) elogio incidental (de un producto comercial o de una persona); **— of tobacco** tableta de tabaco; **electric —** clavija de conexión; **fire —** boca de agua para incendios; **spark —** bujía; v. tapar; **to — along** afanarse, atarearse; **to — in** enchufar, conectar; **to — up** tapar, obstruir.

plum [plʌm] s. (fruit) ciruela; (prize) la cosa mejor; la mejor colocación; **— pudding** pudín inglés con pasas; **— tree** ciruelo.

plumage [plúmıdʒ] s. plumaje.

plumb [plʌm] s. plomo, pesa de plomo; sonda; **out of —** no vertical; adj. vertical, a plomo, recto; **— bob** plomo, plomada; adv. a plomo, verticalmente; **— crazy** completamente loco; v. sondear; aplomar (una pared).

plumber [plʌma] s. plomero.

plumbing [plʌmıŋ] s. plomería; cañerías (de un edificio); oficio de plomero.

plume [plum] s. pluma; plumaje; penacho; v. adornar con plumas; **to — its wing** alisarse o componerse el plumaje del ala.

plump [plʌmp] adj. rechoncho, regordete, rollizo; adv. de golpe; v. **to — down** dejar(se) caer; desplomarse, sentarse de golpe.

plunder [plʌnda] s. pillaje, saqueo; botín; v. pillar; saquear.

plunge [plʌndʒ] v. zambullir(se), sumergir(se); hundir(se); lanzar(se), arrojar(se), precipitar(se); **to — headlong** echarse de cabeza; s. zambullida; salto (de arriba abajo).

plunk [plʌŋk] v. (instrument) puntear; (place) arrojar.

plural [plúrəl] adj. & s. plural.

plurality [plurǽlıtı] s. pluralidad.

plus [plʌs] s. más, signo más; **— quantity** cantidad positiva; **two — three** dos más tres.

plush [plʌʃ] s. felpa; velludo.

Pluto [plúto] s. Plutón.

plutonic [plutánık] adj. plutónico.

ply [plaı] v. manejar con tesón (un instrumento o herramienta); importunar (con preguntas); hacer con regularidad un recorrido (entre dos puntos); **to — a trade** seguir o ejercer un oficio; **to — oneself with** saturarse de, rellenarse de; s. doblez, pliegue; capa (de tejido, goma, etc.).

pneumatic [njumǽt.k] adj. neumático.

pneumonia [njumónjə] s. pulmonía.

poach [potʃ] v. escalfar (huevos); invadir (un vedado); cazar o pescar en vedado; robar caza o pesca (de un vedado).

pocket [pákıt] s. bolsillo, faltriquera,

C.A. bolsa; tronera (de billar); cavidad; hoyo; v. embolsarse; apropiarse; ocultar (el orgullo o rencor); aguantar (un insulto).

pocketbook [pákıtbʊk] s. cartera; portamonedas; **woman's —** bolsa.

pocketknife [pákıtnaıf] s. navaja; cortaplumas.

pod [pad] s. vaina (de guisante, frijol, etc.).

podium [pódıəm] s. podio.

poem [póım] s. poema, poesía.

poet [póıt] s. poeta; vate.

poetess [póıtıs] s. poetisa.

poetic [poétık] adj. poético; **-s** s. arte poética, poética.

poetical [poétık] adj. poético.

poetry [póıtrı] s. poesía.

poignant [póınjənt] adj. intenso; picante.

point [pɔınt] s. punto; punta (de lápiz, espada, tierra, etc.); **it is not to the —** no viene al caso; **not to see the —** no caer en la cuenta; no ver el chiste, propósito o intención; **on the — of** a punto de; v. apuntar; señalar; indicar; **to — out** señalar, mostrar, indicar.

pointblank [pɔıntblǽŋk] adj. a quema ropa.

pointed [pɔıntıd] adj. puntiagudo, agudo; satírico; apto; a propósito, al caso; **— arch** arco apuntado, arco ojival.

pointer [pɔınta] s. (indicator) puntero; indicador, señalador; (dog) perro de punta y vuelta; (advice) indicación, consejo.

poise [pɔız] s. equilibrio; porte, compostura; v. equilibrar(se); balancear(se).

poison [pɔızŋ] s. veneno; ponzoña; v. envenenar, emponzoñar.

poisonous [pɔızŋəs] adj. venenoso, ponzoñoso.

poke [pok] v. atizar, remover (el fuego); picar (con el dedo o cualquier objeto puntiagudo); **to — along** andar perezosamente; **to — around** husmear, curiosear; **to — fun at** burlarse de; **to — into** meter en; **to — out** sacar; proyectarse; s. pinchazo; piquete; codazo; aguijonada; **slow —** tardón.

polar [póla] adj. polar; **— bear** oso blanco.

polarity [polǽrıtı] s. polaridad.

polarization [polərızéʃən] s. polarización.

pole [pol] s. poste; pértiga; palo largo; asta (de bandera); garrocha; polo; **Pole** polaco; v. **north —** polo norte, polo ártico; **south —** polo sur, polo antártico; **— vault** salto con garrocha.

polemics [polémıks] s. polémica.

police [pəlís] s. policía; v. vigilar; guardar el orden.

policeman [pəlísmən] s. policía (m.), guardia de policía, polizonte, Ven. Col. vigilante, Méx. gendarme; Ch. carabinero.

policy [páləsı] s. política; **insurance —** póliza de seguro.

Polish [pólɪʃ] *adj.* polaco; *s.* polaco, idioma polaco.

polish [pálɪʃ] *s.* pulimento; lustre, brillo; urbanidad, cultura; **shoe —** betún, bola; *v.* pulir, pulimentar; dar brillo o lustre a; embolar, dar bola o brillo a (*zapatos*).

polite [pəláɪt] *adj.* cortés, fino, urbano, político.

politeness [pəláɪtnɪs] *s.* cortesía; fineza, urbanidad.

politic [pálətɪk] *adj.* político, prudente; conveniente.

political [pəlítɪkḷ] *adj.* político.

politician [pɑlətíʃən] *s.* político; politicastro.

politics [pálətɪks] *s.* política.

poll [pol] *s.* votación; lista electoral; **-s** comicios; urnas electorales; casilla (*donde se vota*); **— tax** impuesto (*de tanto por cabeza*); *v.* registrar los votos de; votar; recibir (*votos*).

pollen [pálən] *s.* polen.

pollinate [pálənet] *v.* polinizar.

polo [pólo] *s.* polo.

polyglot [pálɪglɑt] *s.* poliglota.

pomegranate [pámgrænɪt] *s.* granada; **— tree** granado.

pomp [pɑmp] *s.* pompa, boato.

pompous [pámpəs] *adj.* pomposa, ostentoso.

pond [pɑnd] *s.* charca; estanque; **fish —** vivero.

ponder [pándə] *v.* ponderar, pesar, examinar; **to — over** reflexionar.

ponderous [pándərəs] *adj.* ponderoso; pesado.

pontoon [pɑntún] *s.* pontón, chata, barco chato; flotador (*de hidroavión*); **— bridge** pontón, puente flotante.

pony [póni] *s.* caballito, potrillo; clave o traducción (*usada ilícitamente en un examen*).

poodle [púdḷ] *s.* perro de lanas.

pool [pul] *s.* charco; charca; trucos (*juego parecido al billar*); polla o puesta (*en ciertos juegos*); fondos en común, combinación de fondos (*para una empresa o para especular*); "trust"; **swimming —** piscina; *v.* formar una polla; combinar fondos.

poor [pur] *adj.* pobre; malo; de mala calidad; **— student** estudiante pobre; mal estudiante; **— little thing** pobrecito; **the —** los pobres; **-ly** *adv.* pobremente; mal.

poorhouse [púrhaus] *s.* hospicio, casa de pobres.

pop [pɑp] *s.* tronido, trueno, estallido; detonación; **— of a cork** taponazo; **soda —** gaseosa; *v.* reventar, estallar; detonar; saltar (*un tapón*); **to — a question** espetar una pregunta; **to — corn** hacer palomitas de maíz, hacer rosetas de maíz; **to — in and out** entrar y salir de sopetón; **to — one's head out** sacar o asomar de repente la cabeza.

popcorn [pápkɔrn] *s.* rosetas, palomitas de maíz, *Andes* alborotos; *Ch.* cabritas; *Méx.* esquite.

Pope [pop] *s.* Papa.

popeyed [pápaɪd] *adj.* de ojos saltones, *Am.* desorbitado.

poplar [páplə] *s.* álamo; **black —** chopo; **— grove** alameda.

poppy [pápɪ] *s.* amapola.

populace [pápjəlɪs] *s.* pueblo, populacho.

popular [pápjələ] *adj.* popular.

popularity [pɑpjəlérətɪ] *s.* popularidad.

populate [pápjələt] *v.* poblar.

population [pɑpjəléʃən] *s.* población.

populous [pápjələs] *adj.* populoso.

porcelain [pórslɪn] *s.* porcelana.

porch [pɔrtʃ] *s.* pórtico, porche; galería.

porcupine [pórkjəpaɪn] *s.* puerco espín.

pore [pɔr] *s.* poro; *v.* **to — over a book** engolfarse en la lectura.

pork [pɔrk] *s.* puerco, carne de puerco; **— chop** chuleta de puerco; **salt —** tocino salado.

pornography [pɔrnágrəfɪ] *s.* pornografía.

porous [pórəs] *adj.* poroso.

porridge [pórɪdʒ] *s.* potaje, gachas.

port [pɔrt] *s.* (*harbor*) puerto; oporto; (*left side*) babor (*de un barco*); **—hole** porta, portilla.

portable [pórtəbḷ] *adj.* portátil.

portal [pórtḷ] *s.* portal.

portent [pórtent] *s.* portento, presagio, agüero.

portentous [pɔrténtəs] *adj.* portentoso; prodigioso; de mal agüero.

porter [pórtə] *s.* mozo de cordel, *Méx., C.A.* cargador; *Ríopl.* changador; camarero (*en un coche-cama*); portero.

portfolio [pɔrtfólɪo] *s.* portafolio, cartera; carpeta; ministerio.

portion [pórʃən] *s.* porción; *v.* repartir.

portly [pórtlɪ] *adj.* corpulento.

portrait [pórtret] *s.* retrato.

portray [pɔrtré] *v.* retratar, pintar, dibujar, representar.

portrayal [pɔrtréəl] *s.* retrato, delineación, delineamiento, representación.

Portuguese [pórtʃəgiz] *adj. & s.* portugués.

pose [poz] *s.* (*posture*) postura, actitud; (*affected attitude*) afectación; *v.* posar (*como modelo*); colocar(se) en cierta postura; afectar una actitud o postura; proponer, plantear (*una cuestión o problema*); **to — as** fingirse, hacerse pasar por.

position [pəzíʃən] *s.* posición; postura; situación, empleo, puesto.

positive [pázətɪv] *adj.* positivo; cierto, seguro; categórico; dogmático.

possess [pəzés] *v.* poseer.

possession [pəzéʃən] *s.* posesión.

possessive [pəzésɪv] *adj. & s.* posesivo.

possessor [pəzésə] *s.* poseedor, posesor, dueño.

possibility [pɑsəbílətɪ] *s.* posibilidad.

possible [pásəbḷ] *adj.* posible; **possibly** *adv.* posiblemente; acaso, tal vez.

post [post] *s.* (*pole*) poste, pilar; (*position*) puesto; empleo; **army —** guarnición militar; **— haste** por la posta, rápidamente; **— office** correo, casa de correos; **post-office box** apartado, casilla postal; **—paid** porte pagado, franco de porte; *v.* fijar (*anuncios, carteles*); anunciar; poner en lista; apostar, situar; echar al correo; **to — an entry** asentar o hacer un asiento (*en teneduría*); **to be well -ed** estar al corriente, estar bien enterado.

postage [póstidʒ] *s.* porte, franqueo; **— stamp** sello de correo, *Am.* estampilla, *Méx., Ríopl.* timbre.

postal [póstl] *adj.* postal; **— card** tarjeta postal; **— money order** giro postal.

postcard [póstkard] *s.* tarjeta postal.

poster [pósta] *s.* cartel, cartelón; fijador de carteles.

posterior [pastíria] *adj.* posterior; trasero.

posterity [pastérati] *s.* posteridad.

posthumous [pástʃumas] *adj.* póstumo.

postman [póstman] *s.* cartero.

postmaster [póstmæsta] *s.* administrador de correos.

postpone [postpón] *v.* posponer; aplazar, diferir; postergar.

postponement [postpónmant] *s.* aplazamiento.

postscript [pósskrıpt] *s.* posdata.

posture [pástʃa] *s.* postura, actitud; posición; *v.* adoptar una postura.

posy [pózı] *s.* flor.

pot [pat] *s.* pote; olla, puchero, cacharro (*de cocina*); bacín, bacinica (*de cámara o recámara*); **flower —** tiesto, maceta; **—bellied** panzudo, barrigón; **— hole** bache.

potassium [pətǽsıəm] *s.* potasio.

potato [pətéto] *s.* patata, papa; **sweet — batata,** *Méx., C.A., Ch., Andes* camote, *Carib., Ríopl.* boniato.

potency [pótnsı] *s.* potencia, poder, fuerza.

potent [pótnt] *adj.* potente, poderoso, fuerte.

potential [pəténʃəl] *adj. & s.* potencial.

pottage [pátıdʒ] *s.* potaje.

potter [pátə] *s.* alfarero, fabricante de vasijas o cacharros de barro; **-'s field** cementerio de pobres y desconocidos.

pottery [pátərı] *s.* cerámica, alfarería; vasijas de barro.

pouch [pautʃ] *s.* bolsa, saquillo; **mail — valija;** **tobacco —** tabaquera, petaca.

poultice [póltıs] *s.* emplasto.

poultry [póltrı] *s.* aves de corral.

pounce [pauns] *s.* salto (*para agarrar*); zarpada; *v.* **to — into** entrar de sopetón; **to — upon** abalanzarse sobre, saltar sobre, agarrar.

pound [paund] *s.* libra; golpazo; **— sterling** libra esterlina; *v.* golpear; machacar, martillar.

pour [por] *v.* vaciar, verter; servir (*una taza*); fluir; llover a cántaros, llover recio.

pout [paut] *v.* hacer pucheros, lloriquear; poner cara de enfado; *s.* puchero, pucherito.

poverty [pávətı] *s.* pobreza.

powder [páudə] *s.* polvo; pólvora (*explosivo*); polvos (*de tocador*); **— compact** polvera; **— magazine** polvorín; **— puff** polvera, borla, *Ríopl., Ch.* cisne, *Méx., Andes* mota; *v.* empolvar(se); polvorear, espolvorear; pulverizar(se); **to — one's face** empolvarse la cara, ponerse polvos.

power [páuə] *s.* poder; poderío; potencia; fuerza; **motive —** fuerza motriz; **— of attorney** poder; **— plant** planta de fuerza motriz.

powerful [páuəful] *adj.* poderoso.

powerless [páuəlıs] *adj.* impotente.

practicable [prǽktıkəbl] *adj.* practicable; factible, hacedero; práctico; **— road** camino transitable.

practical [prǽktıkl] *adj.* práctico; **— joke** chasco, burla pesada; **-ly** *adv.* casi, virtualmente; realmente, en realidad; prácticamente.

practice [prǽktıs] *s.* práctica; ejercicio (*de una profesión*); método; regla, costumbre; clientela; *v.* practicar; ejercer (*una profesión*); ejercitarse.

practiced [prǽktıst] *adj.* práctico, experimentado; experto, perito.

practitioner [præktíʃənə] *s.* profesional; práctico.

prairie [prérı] *s.* pradera, llanura.

praise [prez] *s.* alabanza; elogio; encomio; *v.* alabar; elogiar; encomiar.

praiseworthy [prézwɜðı] *adj.* laudable.

prance [præns] *v.* cabriolar, hacer cabriolas.

prank [præŋk] *s.* travesura, burla; **to play -s** hacer travesuras.

prate [pret] *v.* parlotear, charlar; *s.* parloteo, charla.

prattle [prǽtl] *v.* parlotear, charlar; *s.* parloteo, charla.

pray [pre] *v.* orar, rezar; rogar, suplicar; **— tell me** dígame por favor, le ruego que me diga.

prayer [prer] *s.* oración, rezo; ruego, súplica; **— book** devocionario; **Lord's — Padre Nuestro.**

preach [pritʃ] *v.* predicar; sermonear.

preacher [prítʃə] *s.* predicador.

preaching [prítʃıŋ] *s.* predicación; sermón; sermoneo.

preamble [príæmbl] *s.* preámbulo.

prearranged [priərǽndʒd] *adj.* arreglado de antemano.

precarious [prıkérıəs] *adj.* precario; inseguro.

precaution [prıkóʃən] *s.* precaución.

precede [prısíd] *v.* preceder.

precedence [prısídns] *s.* precedencia; prioridad.

precedent [présədənt] *s.* precedente.

preceding [prısídıŋ] *adj.* precedente, anterior.

precept [prísept] *s.* precepto.

precinct [prísıŋkt] *s.* distrito; recinto; **-s** límites, inmediaciones.

precious [préʃəs] *adj.* precioso; querido, amado, caro; **— little** poquísimo, muy poco.

precipice [présəpıs] *s.* precipicio.

PO

precipitate [prɪsípətet] v. precipitar-(se); adj. precipitado, apresurado, atropellado; s. precipitado.

precipitation [prɪsɪpətéʃən] s. precipitación; lluvia (o nieve, rocío, granizo, etc.); cantidad de agua pluvial.

precipitous [prɪsípətəs] adj. precipitoso, escarpado; precipitado.

precise [prɪsáɪs] adj. preciso, exacto.

precision [prɪsíʒən] s. precisión, exactitud.

preclude [prɪklúd] v. excluir; impedir.

precocious [prɪkóʃəs] adj. precoz.

precursor [prɪkɜsɚ] s. precursor.

predecessor [prɛdɪsɛsɚ] s. predecesor.

predestine [prɪdɛstɪn] v. predestinar.

predicament [prɪdíkəmənt] s. aprieto, apuro, dificultad.

predicate [prédɪkɪt] adj. & s. predicado.

predict [prɪdíkt] v. predecir, vaticinar.

prediction [prɪdíkʃən] s. predicción, pronóstico, vaticinio.

predilection [prɪdɪlɛkʃən] s. predilección, preferencia.

predispose [prɪdɪspóz] v. predisponer.

predominance [prɪdámənəns] s. predominio; ascendiente.

predominant [prɪdámənənt] adj. predominante.

predominate [prɪdámənet] v. predominar.

preface [préfɪs] s. prefacio; prólogo; v. prologar.

prefect [prífɛkt] s. prefecto.

prefer [prɪfɜ] v. preferir; **to — a claim** presentar una demanda.

preferable [préfrəbl] adj. preferible; preferente; **preferably** adv. preferiblemente; preferentemente, de preferencia.

preference [préfrəns] s. preferencia.

preferred [prɪfɜd] p.p. & adj. preferido; **— shares** acciones preferentes.

prefix [prífɪks] s. prefijo; [prífíks] v. prefijar, anteponer.

pregnancy [prégnənsɪ] s. preñez, embarazo.

pregnant [prégnənt] adj. preñado; lleno, repleto; encinta.

prejudice [prédʒədɪs] s. (preconception) prejuicio, prevención; (harm) daño; v. predisponer, prevenir; perjudicar.

prelate [prélɪt] s. prelado.

preliminary [prɪlímənɛrɪ] adj. & s. preliminar.

prelude [préljud] s. preludio; v. preludiar.

premature [primətjúr] adj. prematuro.

premeditated [prɪmɛdətetɪd] adj. premeditado.

premier [prímɪɚ] s. primer ministro; adj. primero; principal.

premise [prémɪs] s. premisa; -s terrenos; local.

premium [prímɪəm] s. premio; **at a —** muy escaso, muy caro; **insurance —** prima de seguro.

prenatal [prinétl] adj. prenatal.

preoccupy [priákjəpaɪ] v. preocupar; ocupar de antemano.

preorbital [priɔ́rbɪtl] adj. preorbital.

prepaid [pripéd] adj. pagado de antemano; **to send —** enviar porte pagado, enviar franco de porte.

preparation [prɛpəréʃən] s. preparación; preparativo.

preparatory [prɪpǽrətorɪ] adj. preparatorio.

prepare [prɪpér] v. preparar(se).

preparedness [prɪpérɪdnɪs] s. preparación, prevención.

preponderant [prɪpándrənt] adj. preponderante.

preposition [prɛpəzíʃən] s. preposición.

prepossess [pripozɛs] v. preocupar; predisponer.

preposterous [prɪpástrəs] adj. absurdo, insensato.

prerequisite [prirékwəzɪt] s. requisito previo.

prerogative [prɪrágətɪv] s. prerrogativa.

presage [présɪdʒ] s. presagio; [prɪsédʒ] v. presagiar.

prescribe [prɪskráɪb] v. prescribir; recetar.

prescription [prɪskrípʃən] s. receta; prescripción, precepto, mandato.

presence [prézns] s. presencia; **— of mind** aplomo, serenidad.

present [prɛznt] s. (time) presente; (gift) regalo; **at —** al presente, ahora; **for the —** por ahora; adj. presente; corriente, actual; **— company excepted** mejorando lo presente; **— participle** gerundio; **to be —** asistir, estar presente; [prɪzɛnt] v. presentar; regalar, obsequiar.

presentation [prɛzntéʃən] s. presentación; regalo, obsequio.

presentiment [prɪzɛntəmənt] s. presentimiento; corazonada.

presently [prézntlɪ] adv. luego, pronto, dentro de poco.

preservation [prɛzɚvéʃən] s. preservación; conservación.

preserve [prɪzɜv] v. preservar, guardar; conservar; mantener; s. conserva, compota; **forest —** vedado.

preside [prɪzáɪd] v. presidir; **to — at (— over) a meeting** presidir una junta.

presidency [prézədənsɪ] s. presidencia.

president [prézədənt] s. presidente.

presidential [prɛzədénʃəl] adj. presidencial.

press [prɛs] v. (bear down) prensar; apretar; comprimir; planchar (ropa); (force) forzar; apremiar; urgir; empujar; **to — forward** empujar hacia adelante; avanzar, ganar terreno; **to — one's point** porfiar; insistir en su argumento; **to — through the crowd** abrirse paso por entre la multitud; **to be hard -ed by work** estar abrumado de trabajo; **to be hard -ed for money** estar escaso de fondos; s. prensa; imprenta.

pressing [présɪŋ] adj. apremiante, urgente.

pressure [préʃɚ] s. presión; apremio,

urgencia; — **cooker** cocinilla de presión; — **gauge** manómetro.

pressurize [préʃəɪz] v. sobrecargar.

prestige [prɛstíʒ] s. prestigio.

presumable [prɪsúməbl] adj. presumible, probable.

presume [prɪzúm] v. presumir; suponer; **to — on** (**upon**) abusar de; **to — to** atreverse a.

presumption [prɪzámpʃən] s. presunción; pretensión; suposición.

presumptuous [prɪzámptʃʊəs] adj. presuntuoso, pretencioso, presumido.

presuppose [prisəpóz] v. presuponer.

pretend [prɪténd] v. pretender; fingir.

pretense [prɪténs] s. pretensión; presunción; ostentación; apariencia; pretexto; **under — of** so pretexto de.

pretension [prɪténʃən] s. pretensión; pretexto.

pretentious [prɪténʃəs] adj. pretencioso.

pretext [prítɛkst] s. pretexto.

prettily [prítɪlɪ] adv. lindamente; agradablemente.

prettiness [prítɪnɪs] s. lindeza, gracia.

pretty [prítɪ] adj. lindo, bonito, bello, Am. chulo; adv. medianamente; bastante; un poco, algo; — **well** regular, así así; bastante bien, medianamente.

prevail [prɪvél] v. prevalecer; **to — on** (**upon**) persuadir.

prevailing [prɪvélɪŋ] adj. predominante; en boga.

prevalent [prévələnt] adj. prevaleciente; común, corriente.

prevent [prɪvént] v. prevenir, evitar; impedir, estorbar.

prevention [prɪvénʃən] s. prevención; precaución.

preventive [prɪvéntɪv] adj. impeditivo.

preview [prívju] s. vista previa (*anticipada*).

previous [prívɪəs] adj. previo; **-ly** adv. previamente; antes; de antemano.

prey [pre] s. presa; víctima; **birds of —** aves de rapiña; v. **to — on** cazar; rapiñar, pillar; robar; **it -s upon my mind** me tiene preocupado, me tiene en zozobra.

price [praɪs] s. precio; valor; costo (coste *o* costa); **at any —** a toda costa, a todo trance; v. apreciar, valuar, fijar el precio de; averiguar el precio de.

priceless [práɪslɪs] adj. sin precio, inapreciable.

prick [prɪk] v. picar; pinchar; punzar; sentir comezón; sentir picazón; **to — up one's ears** aguzar las orejas; s. picadura; punzada; pinchazo; piquete; aguijón; púa.

prickly [príklɪ] adj. espinoso, lleno de espinas; lleno de púas; — **heat** picazón causada por el calor; — **pear** tuna (*de nopal*).

pride [praɪd] s. orgullo; soberbia; v. **to — oneself on** (**upon**) enorgullecerse de, preciarse de.

priest [prist] s. sacerdote.

priesthood [prísthʊd] s. sacerdocio.

prim [prɪm] adj. remilgado; repulido; peripuesto; estirado.

primarily [praɪmérəlɪ] adv. primariamente, principalmente; en primer lugar.

primary [práɪmerɪ] adj. (*first*) primario; primero; (*basic*) principal; principal; — **colors** colores elementales; — **election** elección primaria; — **school** escuela primaria.

prime [praɪm] adj. (*main*) principal; primario, primero; (*select*) selecto, de primera calidad; — **minister** primer ministro; — **number** número primo; s. flor (*de la vida o de la edad*); la flor y nata (*lo mejor*); plenitud; número primo; **to be in one's —** estar en la flor de la edad; v. preparar, informar, instruir de antemano; cebar (*un carburador, bomba o arma de fuego*).

primer [prímə] s. abecedario, cartilla de lectura; compendio.

primeval [praɪmívl] adj. primitivo.

primitive [prímətɪv] adj. primitivo.

primness [prímnɪs] s. remilgo, tiesura, demasiada formalidad, dengue, afectación.

primp [prɪmp] v. acicalar(se), adornar(se), arreglar(se).

primrose [prímroz] s. prímula o primavera (*flor*); color amarillo pálido.

prince [prɪns] s. príncipe.

princely [prínslɪ] adj. noble, regio, magnífico, propio de un príncipe.

princess [prínsɪs] s. princesa.

principal [prínsəpl] adj. principal; s. principal, capital; principal, jefe, director.

principle [prínsəpl] s. principio; regla, ley; fundamento, base.

print [prɪnt] s. (*type*) tipo, letra de molde; (*art*) lámina, grabado; estampado (*tejido estampado*); diseño (*estampado*); impresión; **in —** impreso, publicado; **out of —** agotado; v. imprimir; estampar; escribir en letra de molde; **-ed fabric** estampado.

printer [príntə] s. impresor.

printing [príntɪŋ] s. imprenta; impresión; tipografía; — **office** imprenta; — **press** prensa.

prior [práɪə] adj. previo, anterior, precedente; — **to** anterior a, con antelación a; s. prior (*de un monasterio*).

priority [praɪɔ́rətɪ] s. prioridad, precedencia, antelación.

prism [prízm] s. prisma.

prison [prízn̩] s. prisión, cárcel; v. encarcelar.

prisoner [prízn̩ə] s. prisionero, preso.

privacy [práɪvəsɪ] s. secreto, reserva; retiro; **to have no —** carecer de sitio privado; estar a la vista del público.

private [práɪvɪt] adj. privado; personal; particular; secreto; confidencial; **a — citizen** un particular; — **school** escuela particular; — **s.** soldado raso; **in —** en secreto; a solas, privadamente.

privation [praɪvéʃən] s. privación.

privilege [prívlɪdʒ] s. privilegio.

privileged [prívlıdʒd] *adj.* privilegiado; **to be — to** tener el privilegio de.

privy [prívı] *adj.* privado; enterado de; *s.* excusado exterior.

prize [praız] *s.* (*reward*) premio, galardón; de; (*booty*) presa, botín de guerra; — **fight** boxeo público, pugilato; — **fighter** boxeador, pugilista; — **medal** medalla de premio; *v.* apreciar, estimar, tener en gran estima.

probability [prababílatı] *s.* probabilidad.

probable [prábəb]] *adj.* probable; **probably** *adv.* probablemente.

probation [probéʃan] *s.* probación; noviciado; prueba; **to put a prisoner on** — poner a un prisionero en libertad bajo la vigilancia de un juez.

probe [prob] *v.* tentar, reconocer, sondear (*una herida*); escudriñar, examinar a fondo; indagar; *s.* tienta (*instrumento de cirujano*); indagación.

problem [prábləm] *s.* problema.

procedure [prəsídʒə] *s.* procedimiento; proceder.

proceed [prəsíd] *v.* proceder; proseguir; seguir adelante; **to** — **to** proceder a, comenzar a, ponerse a.

proceeding [prəsídıŋ] *s.* procedimiento; transacción; **-s** transacciones; actas; proceso.

proceeds [prósidz] *s. pl.* producto, ganancia.

process [práses] *s.* (*series*) proceso; (*method*) procedimiento, método; **in** — **of time** con el transcurso del tiempo, con el tiempo, andando el tiempo; **in the** — **of being made** en vía de preparación; *v.* preparar mediante un procedimiento especial, someter a un procedimiento; procesar (*ante un juez*).

procession [prəséʃan] *s.* procesión; desfile; **funeral** — cortejo fúnebre.

proclaim [proklém] *v.* proclamar; promulgar.

proclamation [prakləméʃan] *s.* proclamación; proclama.

proclivity [proklívıtı] *s.* inclinación.

procure [prokjúr] *v.* procurar, conseguir, obtener.

prod [prad] *v.* aguijonear; picar.

prodigal [prádıg] *adj. & s.* pródigo, gastador.

prodigious [prədídʒəs] *adj.* prodigioso.

prodigy [prádədʒı] *s.* prodigio.

produce [prádjus] *s.* producto; productos agrícolas; [prədjús] *v.* producir.

producer [prədjúsə] *s.* productor; **theatrical** — empresario.

product [prádəkt] *s.* producto.

production [prədʌkʃən] *s.* producción; producto; obra, composición; representación teatral.

productive [prədʌktıv] *adj.* productivo.

profanation [prafənéʃen] *s.* profanación, desacato.

profane [prəfén] *adj.* profano; *v.* profanar.

profess [prəfɛs] *v.* profesar; pretender.

profession [prəféʃən] *s.* profesión.

professional [prəféʃən]] *adj.* profesional; *s.* profesional, *Méx.* profesionista.

professor [prəfɛsə] *s.* profesor, catedrático.

proffer [práfə] *s.* oferta, propuesta; *v.* ofrecer, proponer.

proficiency [prəfíʃənsı] *s.* pericia, destreza.

proficient [prəfíʃənt] *adj.* proficiente, perito, experto.

profile [prófaıl] *s.* perfil; contorno.

profit [práfıt] *s.* (*gain*) ganancia; lucro; (*usefulness*) provecho, utilidad, beneficio; — **and loss** pérdidas y ganancias; **net** — ganancia neta o líquida; *v.* aprovechar; ganar, sacar provecho, **to** — **by** aprovecharse de, sacar provecho de.

profitable [práfıtəb]] *adj.* provechoso; lucrativo.

profiteer [prafıtír] *s.* extorsionista, carero, explotador, logrero; *v.* extorsionar, explotar, cobrar más de lo justo.

profound [prəfáund] *adj.* profundo.

profuse [prəfjús] *adj.* profuso, abundante; pródigo.

progeny [prádʒenı] *s.* prole.

prognosis [pragnósıs] *s.* pronóstico.

program [prógræm] *s.* programa; plan.

progress [prágres] *s.* progreso; [prəgrɛs] *v.* progresar.

progressive [prəgrɛsıv] *adj.* progresivo; progresista; *s.* progresista.

prohibit [prohíbıt] *v.* prohibir; vedar.

prohibition [proəbíʃən] *s.* prohibición.

project [prádʒekt] *s.* proyecto, plan; [prədʒɛkt] *v.* proyectar(se); extender(se), sobresalir.

projectile [prədʒɛkt]] *s.* proyectil; *adj.* arrojadizo; — **weapon** arma arrojadiza.

projection [prədʒɛkʃən] *s.* proyección; saliente, salidizo.

projector [prədʒɛktə] *s.* proyector.

proletarian [prolətɛrıən] *adj. & s.* proletario.

proletariat [prolətɛrıət] *s.* proletariado.

prolific [prolífık] *adj.* prolífico.

prologue [prólɔg] *s.* prólogo.

prolong [prəlɔ́ŋ] *v.* prolongar.

prolongation [prolɔŋgéʃən] *s.* prolongación.

promenade [pramənéd] *v.* paseo; baile (*usualmente* prom); *v.* pasearse.

prominent [prámənənt] *adj.* prominente; notable; saliente; conspicuo.

promiscuous [prəmískjuəs] *adj.* promiscuo.

promise [prámıs] *s.* promesa; *v.* prometer; **Promised Land** Tierra de Promisión.

promising [prámısıŋ] *adj.* prometedor.

promissory [prámısorı] *adj.* promisorio; — **note** pagaré.

promontory [práməntorı] *s.* promontorio.

promote [prəmót] *v.* (*favor*) promover; fomentar; explotar; adelantar; (*raise*) ascender; elevar.

promoter [prəmótə] s. promotor, promovedor.

promotion [prəmóʃən] s. promoción; ascenso; adelantamiento.

prompt [prampt] adj. pronto, puntual; listo, presto; v. mover, incitar, inducir; apuntar (servir de apuntador en el teatro); soplar (sugerir a otro lo que debe decir en una clase o junta).

promptly [prámptlɪ] adv. pronto, prontamente, presto; puntualmente; con prontitud, con presteza.

promptness [prámptnɪs] s. prontitud, presteza; puntualidad.

promulgate [prəmʌ́lget] v. promulgar.

prone [pron] adj. inclinado; propenso, dispuesto; boca abajo; postrado.

prong [prɔŋ] s. púa, punta.

pronoun [prónaun] s. pronombre.

pronounce [prənáuns] v. pronunciar; declarar.

pronounced [prənáunst] adj. pronunciado, marcado; — **opinions** opiniones decididas.

pronunciation [prənʌnsiéʃən] s. pronunciación.

proof [pruf] s. prueba; comprobación; adj. impenetrable, resistente; — **against** a prueba de; —**reader** corrector de pruebas de imprenta; — **sheet** prueba, pliego de prueba; **galley** — galerada; **bomb**— a prueba de bomba; **fire** — a prueba de incendios; **water**— impermeable.

prop [prap] s. puntal; sostén, apoyo; v. apuntalar, sostener.

propaganda [prapəgǽndə] s. propaganda.

propagate [prápəget] v. propagar(se).

propagation [prapəgéʃən] s. propagación; diseminación.

propel [prəpél] v. propulsar, impeler.

propeller [prəpélə] s. hélice (de un buque o avión); propulsor, impulsor.

proper [prápə] adj. propio; conveniente a propósito; justo; correcto; — **noun** nombre propio; **-ly** adv. propiamente; con propiedad, correctamente.

property [prápətɪ] s. propiedad; posesión; posesiones, bienes.

prophecy [práfəsɪ] s. profecía.

prophesy [práfəsaɪ] v. profetizar, predecir, pronosticar, augurar.

prophet [práfɪt] s. profeta.

prophetic [prəfétɪk] adj. profético.

propitious [prəpíʃəs] adj. propicio, favorable.

proportion [prəpórʃən] s. proporción; **out of** — desproporcionado; v. proporcionar; **well -ed** bien proporcionado.

proposal [prəpóz] s. propuesta, proposición; declaración (de amor).

propose [prəpóz] v. proponer; declararse, hacer propuesta de matrimonio; **to** — **to do something** proponerse hacer algo.

proposition [prapəzíʃən] s. proposición; propuesta; asunto.

proprietor [prəpráɪətə] s. propietario, dueño.

propriety [prəpráɪətɪ] s. propiedad, corrección; decoro.

propulsion [prop.ʌ́lʃən] s. propulsión.

prorate [prorét] v. prorratear, repartir proporcionalmente.

prosaic [prozéɪk] adj. prosaico.

prose [proz] s. prosa; adj. prosaico.

prosecute [prásɪkjut] v. procesar, enjuiciar, demandar ante un juez; llevar adelante (un negocio, empresa, demanda, etc.).

prosecution [prasɪkjúʃən] s. prosecución, seguimiento; parte acusadora (en un pleito).

prosecutor [prásɪkjutə] s. fiscal; acusador.

prospect [práspɛkt] s. (hope) perspectiva, vista; esperanza; espectativa; (candidate) cliente; (chances) probabilidad de éxito; v. explorar, andar en busca de.

prospective [prəspéktɪv] adj. probable, posible, esperado; presunto.

prospector [práspɛktə] s. explorador, buscador (de minas, petróleo, etc.).

prosper [práspə] v. prosperar, medrar.

prosperity [praspérətɪ] s. prosperidad.

prosperous [práspras] adj. próspero.

prostitute [prástətjut] s. ramera, prostituta; v. prostituir.

prostrate [prástret] adj. postrado; abatido; v. postrar; abatir.

protagonist [protǽgənɪst] s. protagonista.

protect [prətékt] v. proteger.

protection [prətékʃən] s. protección; amparo.

protective [prətéktɪv] adj. protector; — **tariff** tarifa proteccionista.

protector [prətéktə] s. protector.

protectorate [prətéktrɪt] s. protectorado.

protégé [prótəge] s. protegido.

protein [prótiɪn] s. proteína.

protest [prótɛst] s. protesta protestación; [prətést] v. protestar.

protestant [prátɪstənt] adj. & s. protestante.

protestation [pratəstéʃən] s. protestación, protesta.

protoplasm [prótəplæzəm] s. protoplasma.

prototype [prótotaɪp] s. prototipo.

protract [protrǽkt] v. alargar, extender, prolongar.

protrude [protrúd] v. sobresalir; resaltar; proyectar(se).

protuberance [protjúbərəns] s. protuberancia.

proud [praud] adj. orgulloso; soberbio.

prove [pruv] v. probar; demostrar; comprobar; resultar.

proverb [právɚb] s. proverbio; refrán.

provide [prəváɪd] v. proveer; abastecer; suplir; estipular; **to** — **for** hacer provisión para; **to** — **with** proveer de.

provided [prəváɪdɪd] conj. con tal (de) que, a condición (de) que; — **that** con tal (de) que.

providence [právədəns] s. providencia.

providential [pravədénʃəl] adj. providencial.

provider [prəváɪdə] s. proveedor.

province [právɪns] s. provincia; jurisdicción; **it isn't within my —** no está dentro de mi jurisdicción; no es de mi incumbencia.

provincial [prəvínʃəl] adj. provincial; s. provinciano.

provision [prəvíʒən] s. (goods) provisión; abastecimiento; (plan) estipulación; **-s** provisiones; víveres; **to make the necessary -s** tomar las medidas (o precauciones) necesarias.

proviso [prəváɪzo] s. condición, estipulación.

provocation [pravəkéʃən] s. provocación.

provoke [prəvók] v. provocar; irritar; enfadar.

prow [praʊ] s. proa.

prowess [práuɪs] s. proeza.

prowl [praʊl] v. rondar en acecho; fisgonear.

proximity [praksímətɪ] s. proximidad.

proxy [práksɪ] s. apoderado, substituto, delegado; **by —** mediante apoderado.

prude [prud] s. mojigato, persona gazmoña.

prudence [prúdns] s. prudencia.

prudent [prúdnt] adj. prudente.

prudery [prúdərɪ] s. mojigatería, gazmoñería, remilgo.

prudish [prúdɪʃ] adj. gazmoño, remilgado.

prune [prun] s. ciruela; ciruela pasa; v. podar, recortar.

pry [praɪ] v. atisbar, espiar; fisgar, fisgonear; curiosear; **to — a secret out** extraer (o arrancar) un secreto; **to — apart** separar por fuerza; **to — into other people's affairs** entremeterse en lo ajeno; **to — open** abrir a la fuerza; **to — up** levantar con una palanca.

psalm [sɑm] s. salmo.

pseudonym [sjúdnɪm] s. seudónimo.

psychiatrist [saɪkáɪətrɪst] s. psiquiatra, alienista.

psychiatry [saɪkáɪətrɪ] s. psiquiatría.

psychological [saɪkəládʒɪkl̩] adj. psicológico.

psychologist [saɪkálədʒɪst] s. psicólogo.

psychology [saɪkálədʒɪ] s. psicología.

psychosis [saɪkósɪs] s. sicosis.

public [páblɪk] adj. público; **— prosecutor** fiscal; s. público.

publication [pablɪkéʃən] s. publicación.

publicity [pablísətɪ] s. publicidad, propaganda.

publish [páblɪʃ] v. publicar; editar; **-ing house** editorial o editora.

publisher [páblɪʃə] s. publicador; editor.

pucker [páka] v. fruncir.

pudding [pʊ́dɪŋ] s. budín, pudín.

puddle [pádl̩] s. charco.

puff [paf] s. resoplido; bocanada (de humo, vapor, etc.); bullón (de vestido); **— of wind** ráfaga, soplo; **— paste** hojaldre; **cream —** bollo de crema; **powder —** polvera, borla, Méx.

mota; Ríopl. cisne; v. resoplar, jadear; echar bocanadas; **to — up** inflar(se); ahuecar(se); hinchar(se).

pug [pag] s. perro dogo; **— nose** nariz chata, ñata o respingada.

pull [pʊl] v. (tug) tirar de; jalar (halar); (extract) sacar; arrancar; (stretch) estirar; **to — apart** desgarrar; despedazar; descomponer; desmontar; **to — down the curtain** bajar la cortinilla; **to — oneself together** componerse, serenarse; **to — over to the right** hacerse a la derecha, desviarse hacia la derecha; **to — up** arrancar; parar (un caballo, un auto); parar, hacer alto; **to — through** salir de un apuro; sacar (a alguien) de un apuro; **the train -ed into the station** el tren llegó a la estación; s. tirón; estirón; ascenso difícil; esfuerzo (para subir); **to have —** tener buenas aldabas, tener influencia.

pullet [pʊ́lɪt] s. polla.

pulley [pʊ́lɪ] s. polea; garrucha.

pulp [palp] s. pulpa.

pulpit [pʊ́lpɪt] s. púlpito.

pulsate [pálset] v. pulsar, latir.

pulse [pals] s. pulso; pulsación.

pulverize [pálvəraɪz] v. pulverizar.

pumice [pámɪs] s. piedra pómez.

pump [pamp] s. bomb (para sacar agua); zapatilla; **gasoline —** bomba de gasolina; **hand —** bomba de mano; **tire —** bomba para neumáticos; v. manejar la bomba, Am. bombear; inflar (un neumático); **to — someone** sacarle (o sonsacarle) a una persona la verdad o un secreto.

pumpkin [pámpkɪn] s. calabaza.

pun [pan] s. equívoco, retruécano, juego de palabras; v. decir retruécanos o equívocos, jugar del vocablo.

punch [pantʃ] s. (blow) puñetazo, puñada; (drink) ponche; (drill) punzón, sacabocados; (vitality) fuerza, empuje; vitalidad; **— bowl** ponchera; v. dar un puñetazo, dar una puñada; punzar, horadar, perforar; **to — a hole** hacer un agujero o perforación.

punctual [páŋktʃʊəl] adj. puntual.

punctuality [paŋktʃuǽlətɪ] s. puntualidad.

punctuate [páŋktʃuet] v. puntuar.

punctuation [paŋktʃuéʃən] s. puntuación.

puncture [páŋktʃə] v. picar, punzar, pinchar; agujerear, perforar; **-d tire** neumático picado; s. picadura; pinchazo; perforación; **to have a tire —** tener un neumático picado, tener una llanta o goma picada.

punish [pánɪʃ] v. castigar.

punishment [pánɪʃmənt] s. castigo.

punt [pant] s. puntapié, patada.

puny [pjúnɪ] adj. endeble, débil, flaco, enfermizo; insignificante.

pup [pap] s. cachorro.

pupil [pjúpl̩] s. discípulo; **— of the eye** pupila, niña del ojo.

puppet [pápɪt] s. títere, muñeco, mo-

nigote; — **show** titeres.
puppy [pápɪ] s. cachorrito.
purchase [pə́tʃəs] v. comprar; mercar; s. compra; merca; **to get a — upon** agarrarse fuerte a.
purchaser [pə́tʃəsə] s. comprador, marchante.
pure [pjʊr] adj. puro; **-ly** adv. puramente; meramente.
purée [pjʊré] s. puré.
purgative [pə́gətɪv] adj. purgante; s. purga, purgante.
purgatory [pə́gətorɪ] s. purgatorio.
purge [pə́dʒ] v. purgar(se); limpiar; purificar(se); s. purga, purgante.
purify [pjʊ́rəfaɪ] v. purificar(se); depurar.
purist [pjʊ́rɪst] s. purista.
purity [pjʊ́rɪtɪ] s. pureza.
purple [pə́pl] s. púrpura; adj. purpúreo, morado.
purport [pə́port] s. significado; tenor, sustancia; [pəpórt] v. pretender, aparentar.
purpose [pə́pəs] s. (*intention*) propósito, intención; (*goal*) fin, objeto; **for no** — sin objeto, inútilmente, en vano, para nada; **on** — adrede, de propósito; v. proponerse.
purr [pə] s. ronroneo (*del gato*); zumbido (*del motor*); v. ronronear (*el gato*).
purse [pə́s] s. bolsillo, portamonedas, bolsa; v. **to — one's lips** fruncir los labios.
pursuant [pəsúənt] adv. conforme; de acuerdo con.
pursue [pəsú] v. perseguir; seguir; dedicarse a (*una carrera, un estudio*).
pursuer [pəsúə] s. perseguidor.
pursuit [pəsút] s. perseguimiento; busca; ocupación; ejercicio (*de una profesión, cargo, etc.*); **in — of** a caza de, en seguimiento de, en busca de.
pus [pʌs] s. pus, podre.
push [pʊʃ] v. (*shove*) empujar; (*promote*) fomentar, promover; (*hurry*) apresurar; **to — aside** hacer a un lado, rechazar, apartar; **to — forward** empujar, abrirse paso; avanzar; **to — through** encajar (*por un agujero o rendija*); abrirse paso a empujones; s. empuje; empujón, empellón; — **button** botón eléctrico.
pushcart [pʊ́ʃkɑrt] s. carretilla de mano.
pussy [pʊ́sɪ] s. minino, gatito; — **willow** especie de sauce americano.
put [pʊt] v. poner; colocar; **to — a question** hacer una pregunta; **to — across an idea** darse a entender bien; hacer aceptar una idea; **to — away** apartar; guardar; **to — before** poner delante, anteponer; proponer ante; **to — by money** ahorrar o guardar dinero; **to — down** apuntar, anotar; sofocar (*una revolución*); rebajar (*los precios*); **to — in words** expresar; **to — in writing** poner por escrito; **to — off** aplazar, posponer; diferir; **to — on** ponerse (*ropa*); **to — on airs** darse tono o ínfulas; **to**

— **on weight** engordar; **to — out** apagar, extinguir; **to — someone out** echar o expulsar a alguien; molestar o incomodar a alguien; **to — to shame** avergonzar; **to — up** enlatar, envasar (*frutas, legumbres*); apostar (*dinero*); alojar(se); erigir; **to — up for sale** poner de venta; **to — up with** aguantar, tolerar; *pret. & p.p. de* **to put.**
putrefy [pjútrəfaɪ] v. podrir (*o* pudrir), corromper.
putrid [pjútrɪd] adj. putrefacto, podrido.
putter [pʌ́tə] v. trabajar sin orden ni sistema; ocuparse en cosas de poca monta; malgastar el tiempo.
putty [pʌ́tɪ] s. masilla; v. tapar o rellenar con masilla.
puzzle [pʌ́zl] s. rompecabezas, acertijo; enigma; **crossword** — crucigrama; v. embrollar, poner perplejo, confundir; **to — out** desenredar, descifrar; **to — over** ponderar; tratar de resolver o descifrar; **to be -d** estar perplejo.
pyramid [pírəmɪd] s. pirámide.

Q

quack [kwæk] s. graznido (*del pato*); curandero, matasanos, medicastro; charlatán; adj. falso; v. graznar.
quagmire [kwǽgmaɪr] s. tremedal, cenagal.
quail [kwel] s. codorniz.
quaint [kwent] adj. raro, extraño; pintoresco.
quake [kwek] s. temblor; terremoto; v. temblar.
qualification [kwaləfəkéʃən] s. (*condition*) calificación; cualidad, calidad; (*requirement*) requisito; aptitud.
qualify [kwáləfaɪ] v. calificar; capacitar; **to — for a position** estar capacitado para una posición; **his studies — him for the job** sus estudios le capacitan para el puesto.
quality [kwálətɪ] s. cualidad; calidad.
qualm [kwɑm] s. escrúpulo.
quantify [kwántəfaɪ] v. cuantificar.
quantity [kwántətɪ] s. cantidad.
quarantine [kwɔ́rəntin] s. cuarentena; v. poner en cuarentena, aislar.
quarrel [kwɔ́rəl] s. riña, reyerta, pendencia; querella; v. reñir; pelear, disputar.
quarrelsome [kwɔ́rəlsəm] adj. reñidor, pendenciero.
quarry [kwɔ́rɪ] s. cantera; presa, caza (*animal perseguido*); v. explotar (*una cantera*); trabajar en una cantera.
quart [kwɔrt] s. cuarto de galón (*0.9463 de un litro*).
quarter [kwɔ́rtə] s. (*one-fourth*) cuarto, cuarta parte; (*coin*) moneda de 25 centavos; (*district*) barrio, distrito; **-s** morada, vivienda, alojamiento; **from all -s** de todas partes; **to give no — to the enemy** no dar cuartel al enemigo; adj. cuarto; v. cuartear, dividir en cuartos; descuartizar;

acuartelar, acantonar, alojar (*tropas*).

quarterly [kwɔ́rtəlɪ] *adv.* trimestralmente, por trimestres; *adj.* trimestral; *s.* publicación trimestral.

quartet [kwɔrtɛ́t] *s.* cuarteto.

quartz [kwɔrts] *s.* cuarzo.

quaver [kwévə] *v.* temblar; *s.* temblor; trémolo (*de la voz*).

quay [ki] *s.* muelle, embarcadero.

queen [kwin] *s.* reina.

queer [kwɪr] *adj.* raro, extraño, singular; excéntrico; **to feel —** sentirse raro, no sentirse bien; *v.* poner en ridículo, comprometer; **to — oneself with** quedar mal con, ponerse mal con.

quell [kwɛl] *v.* reprimir; sofocar (*una revuelta*); calmar.

quench [kwɛntʃ] *v.* apagar (*el fuego, la sed*); reprimir, sofocar, ahogar, templar el ardor de.

query [kwírɪ] *s.* (*interrogation*) pregunta; interrogación, signo de interrogación; (*doubt*) duda; *v.* preguntar, expresar duda; marcar con signo de interrogación.

quest [kwɛst] *s.* busca; pesquisa.

question [kwɛ́stʃən] *s.* (*interrogation*) pregunta; (*issue*) cuestión; problema; duda; proposición; **— mark** signo de interrogación; **beyond —** fuera de duda; **that is out of the —** ¡imposible!; ¡ni pensar en ello!; *v.* preguntar; interrogar; dudar.

questionable [kwɛ́stʃənəbl] *adj.* dudoso; discutible.

questioner [kwɛ́stʃənə] *s.* interrogador, preguntador.

questioning [kwɛ́stʃənɪŋ] *s.* interrogatorio; *adj.* interrogador.

questionnaire [kwɛstʃənɛ́r] *s.* cuestionario, lista de preguntas, interrogatorio.

quibble [kwíbl] *v.* sutilizar, valerse de argucias o sutilezas; andar en dimes y diretes; *s.* sutileza, argucia.

quick [kwɪk] *adj.* (*soon*) pronto, presto; (*smart*) listo; (*speedy*) rápido, veloz; agudo; **— temper** genio violento; **— wit** mente aguda; *adv.* rápidamente, de prisa, con prisa, pronto; *s.* carne viva; **to cut to the —** herir en lo vivo, herir en el alma.

quicken [kwíkən] *v.* acelerar(se); avivar(se); aguzar (*la mente, el entendimiento*).

quickly [kwíklɪ] *adv.* pronto, presto, de prisa, aprisa, rápidamente.

quickness [kwíknɪs] *s.* (*speed*) rapidez; presteza, prontitud; (*alertness*) vivezal; agudeza (*de ingenio*).

quicksand [kwíksænd] *s.* arena movediza.

quicksilver [kwíksɪlvə] *s.* mercurio, azogue.

quiet [kwáɪət] *adj.* quieto; callado; tranquilo; en calma; reposado; *s.* quietud; sosiego, reposo; calma; silencio; *v.* aquietar; sosegar; calmar, tranquilizar; **to — down** aquietarse; calmarse; **-ly** *adv.* quietamente, con

quietud; calladamente; tranquilamente.

quietness [kwáɪətnɪs] *s.* quietud; sosiego, calma.

quill [kwɪl] *s.* pluma; cañón (*de pluma de ave*); púa (*de puerco espín*).

quilt [kwɪlt] *s.* colcha; *v.* acolchar.

quince [kwɪns] *s.* membrillo.

quinine [kwáɪnaɪn] *s.* quinina.

quip [kwɪp] *s.* pulla, dicharacho; agudeza.

quirk [kwɜk] *s.* chifladura, extravagancia, capricho; peculiaridad mental.

quit [kwɪt] *v.* (*abandon*) dejar, abandonar; irse; (*cease*) parar, cesar; **to — doing something** dejar de hacer algo; **-s** *adj.* desquitado; **we are -s** no nos debemos nada, estamos desquitados, *Am.* estamos a mano; *pret.* & *p.p.* de **to quit**.

quite [kwaɪt] *adv.* bastante; del todo, enteramente; **— a person** una persona admirable; **— so** así es, en efecto; **it's — the fashion** esto está muy en boga.

quitter [kwítə] *s.* el que deja fácilmente lo empezado, el que se da fácilmente por vencido; evasor; desertor.

quiver [kwívə] *v.* temblar; estremecerse; *s.* temblor; estremecimiento.

quiz [kwɪz] *s.* examen; interrogatorio; cuestionario; *v.* examinar, interrogar, hacer preguntas.

quizzical [kwízəkl] *adj.* curioso; burlón.

quota [kwótə] *s.* cuota.

quotation [kwotéʃen] *s.* citación, cita; cotización (*de precios*); **— marks** comillas.

quote [kwot] *v.* citar; cotizar (*precios*); **to — from** citar a, entresacar una cita de; *s.* cita, citación; **-s** comillas, **in -s** entre comillas.

quotient [kwóʃent] *s.* cociente.

R

rabbi [rǽbaɪ] *s.* rabí, rabino.

rabbit [rǽbɪt] *s.* conejo.

rabble [rǽbl] *s.* populacho, plebe; canalla.

rabid [rǽbəd] *adj.* rabioso.

rabies [rébɪz] *s.* rabia, hidrofobia.

raccoon [rækún] *s.* *Méx., C.A., Andes* mapache.

race [res] *s.* (*lineage*) raza; (*competition*) corrida, carrera; contienda; **—track** (o **—course**) pista; **boat —** regata; *v.* correr; competir en una carrera; ir corriendo; regatear (*competir en una regata*); acelerar (*un motor*).

racer [résə] *s.* corredor; caballo de carrera; auto de carrera.

racial [réʃəl] *adj.* racial.

racism [résɪzm] *s.* racismo.

rack [ræk] *s.* (*framework*) percha, colgadero, clavijero; (*torture*) potro de tormento; **baggage —** red; **towel —** toallero; **to fall into — and ruin** caer en un estado de ruina total; *v.* atormentar; **to — one's brain** devanarse los sesos, quebrarse uno la cabeza.

racket [rǽkɪt] *s.* (*instrument*) raqueta (*de tenis*); (*noise*) boruca, estrépito, baraúnda; bullicio; trapacería.

racketeer [rækɪtírʃ] *s.* trapacista, trapacero, extorsionista; *v.* trapacear, extorsionar.

radar [rédɑr] *s.* radar.

radial [rédɪəl] *adj.* radial.

radiance [rédɪəns] *s.* resplandor, brillo.

radiant [rédɪənt] *adj.* radiante; resplandeciente, brillante.

radiate [rédɪet] *v.* irradiar; radiar.

radiator [rédɪetə] *s.* radiador; calorífero.

radical [rǽdɪkl] *adj. & s.* radical.

radio [rédɪo] *s.* radio (*m. o f.*); radiotelefonía; radiotelegrafía; — **commentator** comentarista radial; — **listener** radioescucha, radioyente; — **program** programa radiofónico; by — por radio; *v.* radiar, emitir, transmitir, radiodifundir o difundir.

radioactive [redɪoǽktɪv] *adj.* radiactivo.

radiology [redɪάlədʒɪ] *s.* radiología.

radish [rǽdɪʃ] *s.* rábano.

radium [rédɪəm] *s.* radio (*elemento químico*).

radius [rédɪəs] *s.* radio (*de un círculo*).

raffle [rǽfl] *s.* rifa, sorteo; *v.* rifar, sortear.

raft [ræft] *s.* balsa; **a — of things** un montón (o la mar) de cosas.

rafter [rǽftə] *s.* viga (*del techo*).

rag [ræg] *s.* trapo; harapo, andrajo, *Am.* hilacho; — **doll** muñeca de trapo; **to be in -s** estar hecho andrajos, *Am.* estar hecho tiras.

ragamuffin [rǽgəmʌfɪn] *s.* pelagatos, golfo; granuja, pilluelo.

rage [redʒ] *s.* rabia, furor; ira; **to be all the —** estar en boga, estar de moda; *v.* rabiar; enfurecerse; estar enfurecido; bramar; **to — with anger** bramar de ira.

ragged [rǽgɪd] *adj.* andrajoso, haraposo, harapiento, desharrapado, roto; — **edge** borde raído o deshilachado; **to be on the — edge** estar al borde del precipicio; estar muy nervioso.

raid [red] *s.* incursión, invasión repentina; allanamiento (*de un local*); **air —** ataque aéreo, bombardeo aéreo; *v.* hacer una incursión; invadir de repente; caer sobre; allanar (*un local*), entrar a la fuerza.

rail [rel] *s.* (*steel bar*) riel, carril; (*railroad*) ferrocarril; (*railing*) barandal, barandilla; — **fence** empalizada, estacada; **by —** por ferrocarril.

railing [rélɪŋ] *s.* baranda, barandilla; pasamano (*de escalera*), balaustrada, barrera; rieles.

railroad [rélrod] *s.* ferrocarril; *adj.* ferroviario; de ferrocarril.

railway [rélwe] *s.* ferrocarril; *adj.* ferroviario; de ferrocarril; — **crossing** cruce, crucero.

raiment [rémənt] *s.* vestidura, ropaje.

rain [ren] *s.* lluvia; — **water** agua lluve-diza; *v.* llover; — **or shine** que llueva o no; llueva o truene; a todo trance.

rainbow [rénbo] *s.* arco iris.

raincoat [rénkot] *s.* impermeable; *Ch.* capa de agua, *Méx.* manga o capa de hule; *Riopl.* piloto.

raindrop [réndrɑp] *s.* gota de agua.

rainfall [rénfɔl] *s.* lluvia, lluvias; cantidad de agua pluvial; aguacero.

rainy [rénɪ] *adj.* lluvioso.

raise [rez] *v.* (*lift*) levantar, alzar; subir; erigir; (*cultivate*) criar; cultivar; (*collect*) reunir; reclutar; **to — a question** hacer una observación o suscitar una duda; **to — a racket** armar un alboroto; *s.* aumento de sueldo.

raisin [rézṇ] *s.* pasa, uva seca.

rake [rek] *s.* rastro, rastrillo; libertino, perdulario; *v.* rastrear, rastrillar (*la tierra*); raspar; barrer (*con rastrillo*) atizar (*el fuego*).

rally [rǽlɪ] *v.* (*unite*) reunir(se); juntar(se); (*improve*) recobrar(se); mejorar (*de salud*); fortalecerse; revivir; tomar nueva vida; **to — to the side of** acudir al lado de; *s.* junta popular, junta pública; recuperación.

ram [ræm] *s.* (*animal*) carnero; (*tool*) ariete o martillo hidráulico; espolón de buque; **battering —** ariete; *v.* apisonar, aplanar a golpes; aplastar de un choque; rellenar, atestar; **to — a boat** chocar con un barco; arremeter contra un barco.

ramble [rǽmbl] *v.* vagar; divagar; callejear; *s.* paseo, andanza.

rampage [rǽmpedʒ] *s.* alboroto.

rampant [rǽmpənt] *adj.* extravagante; desenfrenado.

rampart [rǽmpɑrt] *s.* baluarte, muralla.

ran [ræn] *pret. de* **to run.**

ranch [ræntʃ] *s.* hacienda, *Méx., C.A.* rancho; **cattle —** hacienda de ganado, *Méx., C.A.* rancho, *Riopl.* estancia; *Ch.* fundo; *Ven., Col.* hato.

rancid [rǽnsɪd] *adj.* rancio, acedo.

rancor [rǽŋkə] *s.* rencor, encono.

random [rǽndəm] *adj.* impensado; fortuito, al azar; **at —** al azar, a la ventura.

rang [ræŋ] *pret. de* **to ring.**

range [rendʒ] *v.* (*align*) alinear; poner en fila; arreglar; (*wander*) vagar por; rondar; fluctuar; **to — ten miles** tener un alcance de diez millas (*un arma de fuego*); *s.* fila, hilera; alcance; extensión; fluctuación, variación (*dentro de ciertos límites*); distancia; pastizal, *C.A.* pastal; estufa; **gas —** cocina de gas; — **of mountains** cordillera, cadena de montañas; — **of vision** campo de visión; **in — with** en línea con; **shooting —** campo de práctica para tirar.

rank [ræŋk] *s.* (*position*) rango, categoría; orden; calidad; grado; (*line*) fila; línea, hilera; **the — and file** el pueblo, la gente ordinaria; la tropa; *v.* poner en fila; ordenar, arreglar; clasificar; **to — above** sobrepasar a;

QU

ser de grado superior a; **to — high**
tener un alto rango, categoría o
renombre; ser tenido en alta estima;
to — second tener el segundo
lugar; **to — with** estar al nivel de,
tener el mismo grado que; **he -s
high in athletics** sobresale en los
deportes.

ransack [ránsæk] v. escudriñar; saquear.

ransom [ránsəm] s. rescate; v. rescatar; redimir.

rant [rænt] v. desvariar; disparatar, gritar necedades.

rap [ræp] v. (*strike*) golpear, dar un
golpe; (*censure*) criticar, censurar;
to — on the door llamar o tocar a la
puerta; s. golpe; **not to care a —**
no importarle a uno un ardite.

rapacious [rəpéʃəs] adj. rapaz.

rape [rep] s. estupro, violación (*de una
mujer*); v. forzar, violar (*a una mujer*).

rapid [rápɪd] adj. rápido; **-s** s. pl. raudal, rápidos (*de un río*).

rapidity [rəpídətɪ] s. rapidez, velocidad.

rapport [rəpór] s. relación de confianza
mutua.

rapt [ræpt] adj. extasiado; absorto.

rapture [ráptʃɚ] s. éxtasis, rapto.

rare [rɛr] adj. (*strange*) extraordinario,
extraño; raro; (*precious*) raro; precioso; (*not well-done*) a medio asar,
a medio freír, medio crudo; **-ly** adv.
rara vez, raras veces; raramente;
extraordinariamente.

rarity [rérətɪ] s. rareza; enrarecimiento
(*de la atmósfera*).

rascal [ráskl] s. bribón, bellaco, pícaro.

rash [ræʃ] adj. temerario, atrevido; precipitado; imprudente; s. salpullido,
erupción (*de la piel*).

rashness [ráʃnɪs] s. temeridad.

rasp [ræsp] v. chirriar; irritar; s.
chirrido, sonido áspero; ronquera,
carraspera.

raspberry [rázbɛrɪ] s. frambuesa;
— bush frambueso.

raspy [ráspɪ] adj. ronco; áspero.

rat [ræt] s. rata; postizo (*para el pelo*).

rate [ret] s. proporción; porcentaje,
tanto por ciento, *Am.* tipo (*de interés*);
tarifa; precio; **— of exchange** cambio, *Am.* tipo de cambio; **— of
increase** incremento proporcional;
at any — en todo caso, de todos
modos; **at that —** a ese paso; en esa
proporción; **at the — of** a razón de;
first — de primera clase o calidad;
muy bien; v. calificar, clasificar, considerar; tasar, valuar; **he -s as the
best** se le considera como el mejor;
he -s high se le tiene en alta estima.

rather [ráðɚ] adv. algo, un poco, un
tanto; más bien; mejor; mejor dicho;
— than más bien que; **I would —
die than** prefiero antes la muerte
que; **I would — not go** preferiría
no ir.

ratify [rátəfaɪ] v. ratificar.

rating [rétɪŋ] s. clasificación; rango,
grado; clase.

ratio [réʃo] s. razón, proporción; relación.

ration [ráʃən] s. ración; v. racionar.

rational [ráʃənl] adj. racional.

rationalize [ráʃənlaɪz] v. buscar excusas.

rationing [ráʃənɪŋ] s. racionamiento.

rattle [rátl] v. traquetear; golpetear;
sacudir ruidosamente; confundir, desconcertar; **to — off** decir de corrido
(o decir muy aprisa); s. traqueteo;
golpeteo; **child's —** sonaja, sonajero; **death —** estertor de la muerte.

rattlesnake [rátlsnek] s. culebra de
cascabel, *Riopl.*, *Ch.* cascabel o
cascabela.

raucous [rókəs] adj. ronco; estentóreo.

ravage [rávɪdʒ] s. estrago, ruina, destrucción; asolamiento; saqueo, pillaje;
v. asolar, arruinar; pillar, saquear.

rave [rev] v. desvariar, delirar, disparatar; bramar; **to — about someone**
deshacerse en elogios de alguien.

raven [révən] s. cuervo; adj. negro lustroso.

ravenous [rávənəs] adj. voraz; devorador; **to be —** tener un hambre canina.

ravine [rəvín] s. quebrada, hondonada,
barranco (o barranca).

ravish [rávɪʃ] v. encantar; arrebatar;
violar (*a una mujer*).

raw [rɔ] adj. (*crude*) crudo; áspero;
pelado, descarnado; (*untrained*) inexperto, nuevo; **— material** materia
prima; **— recruit** recluta nuevo; **—
silk** seda en rama, seda cruda; **—
sugar** azúcar bruto, azúcar crudo.

rawhide [róhaɪd] s. cuero crudo; **—
whip** rebenque.

ray [re] s. rayo; raya (*especie de pez*).

rayon [réan] s. rayón, seda artificial.

raze [rez] v. arrasar, asolar.

razor [rézɚ] s. navaja de afeitar;
— blade hoja de afeitar; **safety —** navaja de seguridad.

reach [ritʃ] v. (*go as far as*) llegar a;
alcanzar; (*touch*) tocar; (*extend*) extenderse; **to — for** tratar de coger;
echar mano a; **to — into** meter la
mano en; penetrar en; **to — out one's
hand** alargar o tender la mano; s.
alcance; extensión; **beyond his —**
fuera de su alcance; **within his —**
a su alcance.

react [rɪækt] v. reaccionar.

reaction [rɪækʃən] s. reacción.

reactionary [rɪækʃənɛrɪ] adj. & s.
reaccionario.

read [rid] v. leer; indicar (*dícese de un
contador, termómetro, etc.*); **to — law**
estudiar derecho; **it -s thus** dice así,
reza así; **it -s easily** se lee fácilmente
o sin esfuerzo.

read [rɛd] pret. & p.p. de **to read**.

reader [rídɚ] s. lector; libro de lectura.

readily [rédlɪ] adv. pronto, con presteza; fácilmente, sin esfuerzo.

readiness [rédɪnɪs] s. prontitud, presteza, facilidad; buena disposición;
to be in — estar preparado, estar listo.

reading [rídɪŋ] *s.* lectura; indicación (*de un barómetro, termómetro, etc.*); **— room** sala o salón de lectura.

readjust [riədʒʌ́st] *v.* reajustar, ajustar de nuevo; arreglar de nuevo; readaptar.

readjustment [riədʒʌ́stmənt] *s.* reajuste; readaptación; nuevo arreglo.

ready [rédɪ] *adj.* pronto, listo; preparado; propenso; dispuesto; **— cash** fondos disponibles; dinero a la mano.

ready-made [rédɪméd] *adj.* hecho, ya hecho.

real [ríəl] *adj.* real, verdadero; **— estate** bienes raíces, bienes inmuebles; **-ly** *adv.* realmente, verdaderamente.

realism [ríəlɪzəm] *s.* realismo.

realist [ríəlɪst] *s.* realista; **-ic** *adj.* realista, vivo, natural.

reality [riǽlətɪ] *s.* realidad.

realization [riəlɔzéʃən] *s.* realización; comprensión.

realize [ríəlaɪz] *v.* (*comprehend*) darse cuenta de, hacerse cargo de; (*achieve*) realizar, efectuar; convertir en dinero.

realm [rɛlm] *s.* reino; dominio, región.

realtor [ríəltɚ] *s.* corredor de bienes raíces.

reap [rip] *v.* segar; cosechar; recoger; obtener, sacar (*provecho, fruto, etc.*).

reaper [rípɚ] *s.* segador; segadora, máquina segadora.

reappear [riəpír] *v.* reaparecer.

rear [rɪr] *adj.* trasero, posterior; de atrás; **— admiral** contraalmirante; **— guard** retaguardia; *s.* espalda, parte de atrás; trasero; fondo (*de una sala, salón, etc.*); cola (*de una fila*); **in the —** detrás, atrás, a la espalda; *v.* criar, educar; encabritarse, empinarse (*el caballo*).

reason [rízṇ] *s.* razón; causa, motivo; **by — of** a causa de; **it stands to —** es razonable; *v.* razonar; **to — out** discurrir, razonar.

reasonable [ríznəbḷ] *adj.* razonable, justo; racional; módico, moderado; **reasonably** *adv.* razonablemente; con razón; bastante.

reasoning [ríznɪŋ] *s.* razonamiento, raciocinio.

reassure [riəʃúr] *v.* tranquilizar, restaurar la confianza a; asegurar de nuevo.

rebate [ríbet] *s.* rebaja (*de precio*); *v.* rebajar (*precio*).

rebel [rɛ́bḷ] *s.* & *adj.* rebelde; [rɪbɛ́l] *v.* rebelarse.

rebellion [rɪbɛ́ljən] *s.* rebelión.

rebellious [rɪbɛ́ljəs] *adj.* rebelde.

rebirth [ribɝ́θ] *s.* renacimiento.

rebound [rɪbáʊnd] *v.* rebotar; repercutir; [ríbaʊnd] *s.* rebote; **on the —** de rebote.

rebuff [rɪbʌ́f] *s.* desaire; repulsa; *v.* desairar; rechazar.

rebuild [ribíld] *v.* reconstruir, reedificar.

rebuilt [ribílt] *pret.* & *p.p. de* **to rebuild.**

rebuke [rɪbjúk] *s.* reprensión, reproche, reprimenda, repulsa; *v.* reprender, reprochar.

recall [rɪkɔ́l] *s.* llamada, aviso (*para hacer volver*); retirada (*de un diplomático*); revocación; [rɪkɔ́l] *v.* recordar; retirar; revocar.

recapitulate [rikəpítʃəlet] *v.* recapitular.

recede [rɪsíd] *v.* retroceder; retirarse.

receipt [rɪsít] *s.* recibo; fórmula, receta; **-s** entradas, ingresos; **on — of** al recibo de; **we are in — of your kind letter . . .** obra en nuestro poder su grata . . . ; *v.* sellar (*con el recibí*), dar recibo.

receive [rɪsív] *v.* recibir.

receiver [rɪsívɚ] *s.* receptor; recibidor, depositario, síndico; recipiente, receptáculo.

recent [rísṇt] *adj.* reciente; **-ly** *adv.* recientemente, *Ch., Ríopl.* recién (*como en salió recién*); **-ly married** recién casados.

receptacle [rɪsɛ́ptəkḷ] *s.* receptáculo.

reception [rɪsɛ́pʃən] *s.* recepción; recibimiento; acogida, acogimiento.

recess [rɪsɛ́s] *s.* (*niche*) nicho, hueco; (*cessation*) tregua, intermisión; (*period*) hora de recreo o asueto; **in the -es of** en lo más recóndito de; *v.* suspender el trabajo; levantar (*por corto tiempo*) una sesión; hacer un hueco o nicho en (*la pared*).

recession [rɪsɛ́ʃən] *s.* retroceso; contracción económica.

recipe [rɛ́səpɪ] *s.* receta, fórmula.

recipient [rɪsípɪənt] *s.* recipiente, recibidor; *adj.* receptivo.

reciprocal [rɪsíprəkḷ] *adj.* recíproco, mutuo.

reciprocate [rɪsíprəket] *v.* corresponder.

recital [rɪsáɪtḷ] *s.* recitación; relación; narración; recital (*músico*).

recitation [rɛsətéʃən] *s.* recitación.

recite [rɪsáɪt] *v.* recitar; relatar; decir o dar la lección.

reckless [rɛ́klɪs] *adj.* temerario, atrevido, precipitado; descuidado; **— with one's money** derrochador.

recklessness [rɛ́klɪsnɪs] *s.* temeridad, osadía, descuido.

reckon [rɛ́kən] *v.* contar, computar, calcular; juzgar; suponer; **to — on** contar con.

reckoning [rɛ́kənɪŋ] *s.* cuenta; ajuste de cuentas; cálculo; **the day of —** el día del juicio.

reclaim [rɪklém] *v.* recobrar, aprovechar (*tierras baldías*); aprovechar o utilizar (*el hule usado*); pedir la devolución de, tratar de recobrar.

recline [rɪkláɪn] *v.* reclinar(se), recostar(se).

recluse [rɪklús] *adj.* recluso, solitario; *s.* recluso, solitario, ermitaño.

recognition [rɛkəgníʃən] *s.* reconocimiento.

recognize [rɛ́kəgnaɪz] *v.* reconocer.

recoil [rɪkɔ́ɪl] *v.* recular, *Am.* patear (*un*

RA

arma de fuego); retroceder, retirarse;
s. reculada; rebote.

recollect [rɛkəlɛ́kt] *v.* recordar;
[rikəlɛ́kt] recobrar, volver a cobrar;
recoger, reunir.

recollection [rɛkəlɛ́kʃən] *s.* recuerdo.

recommend [rɛkəmɛ́nd] *v.* recomendar.

recommendation [rɛkəmɛndéʃən] *s.*
recomendación.

recompense [rɛ́kəmpɛns] *v.* recompensar; *s.* recompensa.

reconcile [rɛ́kənsaɪl] *v.* reconciliar;
ajustar, conciliar; **to — oneself to**
resignarse a, conformarse con.

reconciliation [rɛkənsɪliéʃən] *f.* reconciliación; ajuste, conciliación; conformidad, resignación.

reconnoiter [rikənɔ́itɚ] *v.* reconocer,
explorar; hacer un reconocimiento o
exploración.

reconsider [rikənsídɚ] *v.* reconsiderar.

reconstruct [rikənstrákt] *v.* reconstruir, reedificar.

reconstruction [rikənstrákʃən] *s.* reconstrucción.

record [rɛ́kɚd] *s.* registro; copia oficial
de un documento; memoria; historial
(*de una persona*); hoja de servicios;
disco (*fonográfico*); record (*en deportes*); **to break the speed —** batir el
record de velocidad; **an off-the-
record remark** una observación que
no ha de constar en el acta; observación hecha en confianza; *adj.* notable,
extraordinario; sobresaliente; [rɪkɔ́rd]
v. registrar; asentar, apuntar; inscribir; grabar en disco fonográfico.

recording [rɪkɔ́rdɪŋ] *s.* grabación.

recount [rɪkáunt] *s.* recuento, segunda
cuenta; [rɪkáunt] *v.* contar, narrar,
relatar, referir; [rikáunt] recontar,
volver a contar.

recourse [ríkors] *s.* recurso, refugio,
auxilio; **to have —** to recurrir a.

recover [rɪkávɚ] *v.* recobrar(se), recuperar(se); recobrar la salud; reponerse; [rikávɚ] volver a cubrir.

recovery [rɪkávrɪ] *s.* recobro; recuperación; cobranza.

recreation [rɛkriéʃən] *s.* recreación,
recreo.

recriminate [rɪkrímənet] *v.* recriminar.

recruit [rɪkrút] *v.* reclutar; alistar; *s.*
recluta; novato, nuevo miembro (*de
una organización*).

rectangle [rɛ́ktæŋgl] *s.* rectángulo.

rectify [rɛ́ktəfaɪ] *v.* rectificar.

rector [rɛ́ktɚ] *s.* rector.

rectum [rɛ́ktəm] *s.* recto.

recuperate [rɪkjúpəret] *v.* recuperar,
recobrar, recobrar la salud.

recur [rɪkɝ́] *v.* volver a ocurrir; repetirse; **to — to a matter** volver
a un asunto.

red [rɛd] *adj.* rojo; colorado, encarnado; **red-hot** candente; enfurecido,
furioso; muy caliente; **— tape** formalismo, trámites enojosos; **— wine**
vino tinto; **to see —** enfurecerse; *s.*

color rojo; rojo.

redden [rɛ́dn] *v.* enrojecer(se); ruborizarse, ponerse rojo; teñir de rojo.

reddish [rɛ́dɪʃ] *adj.* rojizo.

redeem [rɪdím] *v.* redimir; rescatar;
desempeñar (*una prenda*); cumplir
(*una promesa*).

redeemer [rɪdímɚ] *s.* salvador, redentor; **the Redeemer** el Redentor.

redemption [rɪdɛ́mpʃən] *s.* redención;
rescate; **— of a note** pago de una
obligación.

redness [rɛ́dnɪs] *s.* rojez o rojura; inflamación.

redouble [ridʌ́bl] *v.* redoblar; repetir;
repercutir.

redound [rɪdáund] *v.* redundar.

redress [rɪdrɛs] *s.* reparación, enmienda;
compensación; desagravio; [rɪdrɛs]
v. enmendar, rectificar, remediar, reparar; desagraviar.

reduce [rɪdjús] *v.* reducir; mermar; rebajar; adelgazar(se); subyugar.

reduction [rɪdʌ́kʃən] *s.* reducción;
merma; rebaja.

redundant [rɪdʌ́ndənt] *adj.* redundante.

redwood [rɛ́dwud] *s. Am.* secoya o secuoya (*árbol gigantesco de California*);
madera roja de la secoya.

reed [rid] *s.* caña; junco, junquillo; lengüeta, boquilla (*de ciertos instrumentos
de viento*); caramillo.

reef [rif] *s.* arrecife, escollo; banco de
arena (*en el mar*).

reek [rik] *v.* (*fume*) exhalar, echar (*vaho
o vapor*); (*stink*) heder, oler mal; *s.*
hedor, mal olor.

reel [ril] *s.* (*spool*) carrete; carretel;
(*film*) cinta cinematográfica; *v.* aspar,
enredar (*en carretel*); bambolearse,
tambalearse; **to — off stories** ensartar
cuento tras cuento.

re-elect [riəlɛ́kt] *v.* reelegir.

re-election [riəlɛ́kʃən] *s.* reelección.

re-enter [riɛ́ntɚ] *v.* volver a entrar.

re-establish [riəstǽblɪʃ] *v.* restablecer.

refer [rɪfɝ́] *v.* referir; transmitir,
remitir; dejar al juicio o decisión de;
referirse, aludir; acudir, recurrir (*a un
tratado, diccionario, etc.*).

referee [rɛfəri] *s.* árbitro; *v.* arbitrar.

reference [rɛ́frəns] *s.* (*mention*) referencia; mención, alusión; (*sponsor*)
fiador, el que recomienda a otro; **—
book** libro de referencia, libro de
consulta; **commercial -s** fiadores,
referencias comerciales; **letter of —**
carta de recomendación; **with — to**
con respecto a, respecto de, en
cuanto a.

refill [rifíl] *v.* rellenar.

refine [rɪfáin] *v.* refinar, purificar;
pulir; perfeccionar.

refined [rɪfáind] *adj.* refinado; pulido,
fino, culto.

refinement [rɪfáinmənt] *s.* refinamiento, finura; buena crianza; refinación, purificación; perfeccionamiento.

refinery [rɪfáinərɪ] *s.* refinería.

reflect [rɪflɛ́kt] *v.* reflejar (*luz, calor*);

reflexionar; meditar; **to — on one's character** desdecir del carácter de uno.

reflection [rɪflékʃən] s. reflexión; reflejo, imagen; tacha, discrédito; **on — des**pués de reflexionarlo.

reflective [rɪfléktɪv] *adj.* reflexivo.

reflex [rífleks] *adj.* reflejo; s. reflejo; acción refleja.

reflexive [rɪfléksɪv] *adj.* reflexivo.

reform [rɪfórm] *v.* reformar(se); s. reforma.

reformation [refəméʃən] s. reforma.

reformatory [rɪfórmətorɪ] s. reformatorio.

reformer [rɪfórmə] s. reformador; reformista.

refraction [rɪfrǽkʃən] s. refracción.

refractory [rɪfrǽktɔrɪ] *adj.* refractario; terco, obstinado, rebelde.

refrain [rɪfrén] *v.* refrenarse, abstenerse; s. estribillo.

refresh [rɪfréʃ] *v.* refrescaʳ(se); renovar.

refreshing [rɪfréʃɪŋ] *adj.* refrescante; renovador, que renueva; placentero.

refreshment [rɪfréʃmənt] s. refresco.

refrigeration [rɪfrɪdʒəréʃən] s. refrigeración, enfriamiento.

refrigerator [rɪfrídʒəreta] s. nevera, *Am.* refrigerador.

refuge [réfjudʒ] s. refugio, asilo, amparo.

refugee [refjudʒí] s. refugiado.

refund [rifʌnd] s. reembolso, reintegro; [rɪfʌnd] *v.* reembolsar, restituir, reintegrar; [rifʌnd] consolidar (*una deuda*).

refurbish [rɪfɜ́bɪʃ] *v.* retocar.

refusal [rɪfjúzl] s. negativa; desaire; opción (*derecho de recusar un convenio provisional*).

refuse [rɪfjúz] *v.* rehusar; negar; desechar; rechazar; **to — to** rehusarse a, negarse a.

refuse [réfjus] s. desechos, basura, sobras, desperdicios.

refute [rɪfjút] *v.* refutar.

regain [rɪgén] *v.* recobrar; ganar de nuevo.

regal [rigl] *adj.* regio, real.

regale [rɪgél] *v.* regalar, agasajar; recrear.

regalia [rɪgélɪə] s. pl. galas, decoraciones, insignias.

regard [rɪgárd] *v.* (*look*) mirar; (*consider*) considerar; juzgar; estimar; **as -s this** tocante a esto, en cuanto a esto; **por lo que toca a esto**; s. miramiento, consideración; respeto; estima; mirada; **-s** recuerdos, memorias; **in** (*o* **with**) **— to** con respecto a, tocante a, respecto de.

regarding [rɪgárdɪŋ] *prep.* tocante a, con respecto a, respecto de, relativo a.

regardless [rɪgárdlɪs]: **— of** sin hacer caso de, prescindiendo de.

regency [rídʒənsɪ] s. regencia.

regent [rídʒənt] s. regente.

regime [rɪʒím] s. régimen.

regiment [rédʒəmənt] s. regimiento.

region [rídʒən] s. región.

register [rédʒɪstə] s. (*recording*) regis-

tro; matrícula; (*entry*) archivo; lista; (*machine*) contador; indicador; (*voice*) registro; **cash —** caja registradora; *v.* registrar; matricular(se); inscribir(se); marcar, indicar; mostrar, manifestar; certificar (*una carta*).

registrar [rédʒɪstrɑr] s. registrador, archivero.

registration [redʒɪstréʃən] s. registro; asiento (*en un libro*); matrícula; inscripción.

regret [rɪgrét] s. pesadumbre, dolor; sentimiento, remordimiento; **to send -s** enviar sus excusas (*al rehusar una invitación*); *v.* sentir, lamentar; arrepentirse de.

regretful [rɪgrétfʊl] *adj.* deplorable.

regrettable [rɪgrétəbl] *adj.* lamentable.

regular [régjələ] *adj.* regular; metódico, ordenado; **a — fool** un verdadero necio, un tonto de capirote; **— price** precio corriente; **— soldier** soldado de línea.

regularity [regjəlǽrətɪ] s. regularidad.

regulate [régjəlet] *v.* regular, regularizar.

regulation [regjəléʃən] s. regulación; regla, orden; **-s** reglamento; **— uniform** uniforme de regla, uniforme de ordenanza.

regulator [régjəletə] s. regulador; registro (*de reloj*).

rehabilitate [rihæbílətet] *v.* rehabilitar.

rehearsal [rɪhɜ́sl] s. ensayo (*de un drama, concierto, etc.*); enumeración, repetición.

rehearse [rɪhɜ́s] *v.* ensayar; repetir, repasar.

reign [ren] s. reino, reinado; *v.* reinar.

reimburse [riɪmbɜ́s] *v.* reembolsar.

reimbursement [riɪmbɜ́smənt] s. reembolso, reintegro.

rein [ren] s. rienda; *v.* guiar, gobernar; refrenar (*un caballo*).

reincarnate [riɪnkárnet] *v.* reencarnar.

reindeer [réndɪr] s. reno (*especie de ciervo*).

reinforce [riɪnfórs] *v.* reforzar.

reinforcement [riɪnfórsmənt] s. refuerzo.

reiterate [ríítəret] *v.* reiterar, repetir.

reject [rɪdʒékt] *v.* rechazar; desechar; descartar; rehusar.

rejoice [rɪdʒɔ́ɪs] *v.* regocijar(se).

rejoicing [rɪdʒɔ́ɪsɪŋ] s. regocijo, júbilo.

rejoin [rɪdʒɔ́ɪn] *v.* reunirse con; volver(se) a unir; [rɪdʒɔ́ɪn] replicar.

rejuvenate [rɪdʒúvənet] *v.* rejuvenecer.

relapse [rɪlǽps] s. recaída; *v.* recaer, reincidir.

relate [rɪlét] *v.* relatar, narrar; relacionar; **it -s to** se relaciona con, se refiere a.

related [rɪlétɪd] *adj.* relatado, narrado; relacionado; **to become — by marriage** emparentar; **we are —** somos parientes; estamos emparentados.

relation [rɪléʃən] s. (*association*) relación; (*story*) narración; (*kinship*) parentesco; pariente; **-s** parientes, parentela; **with — to** con relación a, con respecto a, tocante a.

relationship [rɪléʃənʃɪp] s. relación; parentesco.

relative [rélatɪv] adj. relativo; s. relativo, pronombre relativo; pariente, deudo; — **to** relativo a; tocante a; referente a.

relax [rɪlǽks] v. relajar; aflojar; mitigar(se); esparcirse, recrearse.

relaxation [rilækséʃən] s. (loosening) expansión, esparcimiento; aflojamento o relajamiento; (recreation) solaz, recreo; — **of discipline** relajación de la disciplina; — **of one's mind** esparcimiento del ánimo.

relay [ríle] s. relevo, remuda; — **race** carrera de relevo; **electric** — relevador; [rilé] v. transmitir, despachar; hacer cundir (una noticia); **to** — **a broadcast** reemitir (o redifundir) un programa de radio.

release [rɪlís] v. soltar; librar; poner en libertad; relevar, aliviar; **to** — **a piece of news** hacer pública una nueva; **to** — **from blame** exonerar; s. liberación; alivio; exoneración; escape.

relegate [réləget] v. relegar; **to** — **to a corner** arrinconar, arrumbar.

relent [rɪlént] v. mitigar(se); ceder; aplacarse.

relentless [rɪléntlɪs] adj. implacable.

relevant [réləvənt] adj. pertinente; a propósito.

reliability [rɪlaɪəbílətɪ] s. formalidad; puntualidad; integridad.

reliable [rɪláɪəbl] adj. formal; puntual; digno de confianza.

reliance [rɪláɪəns] s. confianza; **self-reliance** confianza en sí, confianza en sus propias fuerzas.

relic [rélɪk] s. reliquia.

relief [rɪlíf] s. (ease) alivio; descanso, consuelo; (help) ayuda, socorro; (projection) relieve, realce; **low** — bajo relieve; **to be on** — recibir manutención gratuita; **to put in** — realzar, poner en relieve.

relieve [rɪlív] v. relevar; librar; ayudar; aliviar; mitigar.

religion [rɪlídʒən] s. religión.

religious [rɪlídʒəs] adj. & s. religioso.

relinquish [rɪlíŋkwɪʃ] v. abandonar, dejar.

relish [rélɪʃ] s. (zest) buen sabor; gusto; apetito; goce; (condiment) condimento; entremés; v. saborear, paladear; gustarle a uno, agradarle a uno.

relocate [rilóket] v. restablecer.

reluctance [rɪlʌ́ktəns] s. repugnancia, renuencia, aversión, desgana.

reluctant [rɪlʌ́ktənt] adj. renuente, refractario, opuesto; **-ly** adv. renuentemente, con renuencia, de mala gana; a redopelo.

rely [rɪláɪ] v. **to** — **on** contar con, confiar en, fiarse de.

remain [rɪmén] v. quedar(se), permanecer, estarse; restar, faltar.

remainder [rɪméndə] s. resto; restante; residuo.

remains [rɪménz] s. pl. restos; reliquias;

sobras.

remake [rimék] v. rehacer, hacer de nuevo.

remark [rɪmárk] s. observación, nota, reparo; v. notar, observar; **to** — **on** comentar; aludir a.

remarkable [rɪmárkəbl] adj. notable; extraordinario; **remarkably** adv. notablemente; extraordinariamente.

remedy [rémədɪ] s. remedio; cura; v. remediar; curar.

remember [rɪmémbə] v. recordar; acordarse; — **me to him** déle Vd. recuerdos (o memorias) de mi parte.

remembrance [rɪmémbrəns] s. recuerdo; recordación; memoria; **-s** recuerdos, saludos.

remind [rɪmáɪnd] v. recordar.

reminder [rɪmáɪndə] s. recordatorio, recordativo, memorándum, memoria; advertencia.

reminiscence [remənísns] s. reminiscencia, memoria, recuerdo.

remiss [rɪmís] adj. descuidado, negligente.

remission [rɪmíʃən] s. remisión, perdón.

remit [rɪmít] v. remitir; remesar, enviar una remesa; perdonar, absolver.

remittance [rɪmítns] s. remisión, envío, remesa (de fondos).

remnant [rémnənt] s. resto; residuo; retazo (de tela, paño, etc.); vestigio.

remodel [rimádl] v. rehacer, reconstruir; modelar de nuevo.

remorse [rɪmɔ́rs] s. remordimiento.

remote [rɪmót] adj. remoto; lejano; s. — **control** telecontrol; comando a distancia.

removal [rɪmúvl] s. mudanza, traslado; deposición (de un empleo); eliminación; extracción; alejamiento.

remove [rɪmúv] v. remover; mudar(se), trasladar(se); quitar; eliminar; extirpar; sacar, extraer; deponer (de un empleo); apartar; alejar.

removed [rɪmúvd] adj. remoto, distante.

renaissance [renəsáns] s. renacimiento.

renascence [rɪnǽsns] s. renacimiento.

rend [rend] v. desgarrar, rasgar; rajar.

render [réndə] v. dar; entregar; hacer; ejecutar, interpretar (música o un papel dramático); traducir; **to** — **an account of** rendir o dar cuenta de; **to** — **homage** rendir homenaje; **to** — **thanks** rendir gracias, dar las gracias; **to** — **useless** inutilizar, incapacitar.

rendition [rendíʃən] s. (surrender) rendición; (version) traducción, ejecución.

renew [rɪnjú] v. renovar; restaurar; reanudar; prorrogar (un préstamo).

renewal [rɪnjúəl] s. renovación; reanudación; prórroga.

renounce [rɪnáuns] v. renunciar.

renovate [rénəvet] v. renovar.

renown [rɪnáun] s. renombre.

renowned [rɪnáund] *adj.* renombrado.

rent [rɛnt] *s.* alquiler; renta, arrendamiento; **it is for —** se alquila, se arrienda; *v.* alquilar, arrendar.

rent [rɛnt] *pret. & p.p. de* **to rend**; *s.* grieta, hendidura; rasgadura, rotura.

rental [rɛ́ntl] *s.* renta, alquiler.

reopen [riópən] *v.* reabrir(se), volver a abrir(se).

repair [rɪpér] *v.* reparar; remendar; componer; restaurar; **to — to** dirigirse a; *s.* reparo, reparación; remiendo; compostura; **in —** en buen estado; compuesto.

reparation [rɛpəréʃən] *s.* reparación; desagravio.

repartee [rɛpɑrtí] *s.* respuesta viva; agudeza en el diálogo.

repay [rɪpé] *v.* resarcir; compensar; reembolsar; pagar.

repayment [rɪpémənt] *s.* reintegro, pago, devolución, restitución.

repeal [rɪpíl] *v.* derogar, abrogar, revocar, abolir (*una ley*); *s.* abrogación, derogación, revocación, abolición (*de una ley*).

repeat [rɪpít] *v.* repetir; *s.* repetición.

repeated [rɪpítɪd] *adj.* repetido; **-ly** *adv.* repetidamente; repetidas veces, una y otra vez.

repel [rɪpél] *v.* repeler; rechazar; repugnar; **that idea -s me** me repugna (*o me es repugnante*) esa idea.

repellent [rɪpélənt] *s.* repelente; (*water*) impermeable.

repent [rɪpént] *v.* arrepentirse (de).

repentance [rɪpéntəns] *s.* arrepentimiento.

repentant [rɪpéntənt] *adj.* arrepentido; penitente.

repertoire [rɛ́pətwɑr] *s.* repertorio.

repetition [rɛpɪtíʃən] *s.* repetición.

replace [rɪplés] *v.* reponer, volver a colocar; reemplazar; restituir; remudar.

replaceable [rɪplésəbl] *adj.* reemplazable; substituible.

replacement [rɪplésmənt] *s.* reposición; reemplazo; devolución, restitución; substitución.

replenish [rɪplénɪʃ] *v.* reabastecer; rellenar, llenar.

replete [rɪplít] *adj.* repleto, atestado.

replica [rɛ́plɪkə] *s.* reproducción, copia exacta.

reply [rɪplái] *v.* replicar, contestar, responder; *s.* réplica, contestación, respuesta.

report [rɪpórt] *v.* dar cuenta de; avisar; informar; presentar un informe; rendir informe; hacer un reportaje, *Am.* reportar; denunciar, delatar; presentarse; **to — for duty** presentarse; **it is -ed that** dizque, se dice que, corre la voz que; *s.* noticia, reporte; informe; memorial; relación; rumor; estallido, disparo; **news —** reportaje.

reporter [rɪpórtə] *s.* reportero, repórter.

repose [rɪpóz] *v.* reposar, descansar; **to**

— **one's confidence in** confiar en; depositar su confianza en; *s.* reposo.

repository [rɪpázətorɪ] *s.* depósito; almacén.

represent [rɛprɪzént] *v.* representar.

representation [rɛprɪzæntéʃən] *s.* representación.

representative [rɛprɪzéntətɪv] *adj.* representativo; representante; típico; *s.* representante; delegado, diputado.

repress [rɪprés] *v.* reprimir; refrenar, restringir; cohibir.

repression [rɪpréʃən] *s.* represión.

reprieve [rɪprív] *v.* suspensión temporal de pena; alivio.

reprimand [rɛ́prəmænd] *v.* reprender, regañar; *s.* reprimenda, reprensión, regaño.

reprisal [rɪpráɪzl] *s.* represalia.

reproach [rɪprótʃ] *v.* reprochar; censurar, criticar; echar en cara; *s.* reproche, reprimenda; censura.

reproduce [riprədjús] *v.* reproducir.

reproduction [riprədákʃən] *s.* reproducción.

reproof [rɪprúf] *s.* reprensión, reproche, regaño.

reprove [rɪprúv] *v.* reprobar, reprender, censurar.

reptile [rɛ́ptl] *s.* reptil.

republic [rɪpʌ́blɪk] *s.* república.

republican [rɪpʌ́blɪkən] *adj. & s.* republicano.

repudiate [rɪpjúdɪet] *v.* repudiar.

repugnance [rɪpʌ́gnəns] *s.* repugnancia; aversión.

repugnant [rɪpʌ́gnənt] *adj.* repugnante; antipático.

repulse [rɪpʌ́ls] *v.* repulsar, repeler; rechazar; *s.* repulsa; desaire.

repulsive [rɪpʌ́lsɪv] *adj.* repulsivo, repugnante.

reputable [rɛ́pjətəbl] *adj.* de buena reputación.

reputation [rɛpjətéʃən] *s.* reputación, renombre.

repute [rɪpjút] *v.* reputar; estimar, considerar; *s.* reputación; renombre, fama; **of ill —** de mala fama.

request [rɪkwɛ́st] *s.* solicitud, petición, demanda; súplica, ruego; **at the — of** a solicitud de, a instancias de; *v.* solicitar, pedir, rogar, suplicar.

require [rɪkwáɪr] *v.* requerir; exigir, demandar.

requirement [rɪkwáɪrmənt] *s.* requerimiento, requisito; exigencia; necesidad.

requisite [rɛ́kwəzɪt] *s.* requisito; *adj.* requerido, necesario.

requisition [rɛkwəzíʃən] *s.* requisición, demanda, orden; *v.* demandar, pedir, ordenar.

rescind [rɪsínd] *v.* rescindir.

rescue [rɛ́skju] *v.* rescatar; librar; salvar; *s.* rescate, salvamento, salvación, socorro; **to go to the — of** acudir al socorro de, ir a salvar a.

research [rísɚtʃ] *s.* rebusca, búsqueda, investigación, [rɪsɚ́tʃ] *v.* rebuscar, investigar.

RE

resemblance [rɪzémbləns] *s.* semejanza, parecido.

resemble [rɪzémbl] *v.* asemejarse a, semejar, parecerse a.

resent [rɪzént] *v.* resentirse de, sentirse de, darse por agraviado de.

resentful [rɪzéntfəl] *adj.* resentido; rencoroso.

resentment [rɪzéntmənt] *s.* resentimiento.

reservation [rezəvéʃən] *s.* reservación; reserva.

reserve [rɪzɤ́v] *v.* reservar; *s.* reserva.

reservoir [rézəvwɔr] *s.* depósito (*de agua, aceite, gas, provisiones, etc.*); receptáculo; **water —** alberca, aljibe, tanque, estanque.

reside [rɪzáɪd] *v.* residir, vivir.

residence [rézədəns] *s.* residencia; domicilio.

resident [rézədənt] *adj.* & *s.* residente.

residential [rezɪdénʃəl] *adj.* residencial.

residue [rézədju] *s.* residuo; resto.

resign [rɪzáɪn] *v.* renunciar; dimitir; **to — oneself to** resignarse a.

resignation [rezɪgnéʃən] *s.* renuncia, dimisión; resignación.

resilience [rɪzíljəns] *s.* elasticidad.

resin [rézn] *s.* resina.

resist [rɪzíst] *v.* resistir; oponerse, resistirse a.

resistance [rɪzístəns] *s.* resistencia.

resistant [rɪzístənt] *adj.* resistente.

resolute [rézəlut] *adj.* resuelto.

resolution [rezəlúʃən] *s.* resolución; acuerdo.

resolve [rɪzálv] *v.* resolver(se); **to — into** resolverse en, reducirse a, transformarse en; **to — to** acordar; proponerse, resolverse a.

resonance [rézənəns] *s.* resonancia.

resonant [rézənənt] *adj.* resonante.

resort [rɪzɔ́rt] *v.* recurrir, acudir; **to — to force** recurrir a la fuerza; *s.* refugio; morada; **as a last —** como último recurso; **summer —** lugar de veraneo; **vice —** garito; casa de mala fama; **to have — to** recurrir a.

resorter [rɪzɔ́rtə] *s.* **summer —** veraneante.

resound [rɪzáʊnd] *v.* resonar; repercutir; retumbar.

resource [rɪsɔ́rs] *s.* recurso; **natural -s** recursos o riquezas naturales.

respect [rɪspékt] *v.* respetar; **as -s** por lo que respecta a, por lo que toca a, tocante a; *s.* respeto; consideración; **with — to** (con) respecto a, respecto de; por lo que atañe a.

respectable [rɪspéktəbl] *adj.* respetable.

respectful [rɪspéktfəl] *adj.* respetuoso.

respecting [rɪspéktɪŋ] *prep.* con respecto a, tocante a.

respective [rɪspéktɪv] *adj.* respectivo.

respiration [rɛspəréʃən] *s.* respiración, respiro.

respite [réspɪt] *s.* tregua, pausa, descanso; intervalo; prórroga.

resplendent [rɪspléndənt] *adj.* resplandeciente.

respond [rɪspánd] *v.* responder; corres-

ponder; reaccionar.

response [rɪspáns] *s.* respuesta, contestación; reacción.

responsibility [rɪspɑnsəbíləti] *s.* responsabilidad.

responsible [rɪspánsəbl] *adj.* responsable; formal, digno de confianza.

rest [rɛst] *s.* (*repose*) descanso; reposo; quietud; tregua; pausa; (*support*) apoyo; **at —** en paz; en reposo; tranquilo; **the —** el resto; los demás; *v.* descansar; reposar; apoyar; **to — on** descansar sobre; apoyar(se) en; basar(se) en; contar con, confiar en, depender de.

restaurant [réstərənt] *s.* restaurante. *Am.* restorán.

restful [réstfəl] *adj.* reposado, sosegado, tranquilo.

restitution [rɛstətúʃən] *s.* restitución; devolución.

restive [réstɪv] *adj.* intranquilo.

restless [réstlɪs] *adj.* inquieto, intranquilo.

restlessness [réstlɪsnɪs] *s.* inquietud, desasosiego, intranquilidad.

restoration [rɛstəréʃən] *s.* restauración; restitución; renovación.

restore [rɪstór] *v.* restaurar; renovar; restituir; restablecer.

restrain [rɪstrén] *v.* refrenar, contener, cohibir, reprimir, coartar; restringir.

restraint [rɪstrént] *s.* restricción; reserva, circunspección; moderación; cohibición.

restrict [rɪstríkt] *v.* restringir, limitar.

restriction [rɪstríkʃən] *s.* restricción.

result [rɪzʌ́lt] *v.* resultar; **to — from** resultar de; **to — in** parar en; causar; dar por resultado; *s.* resulta, resultado; **as a —** de resultas, como resultado.

resume [rɪzúm] *v.* reasumir, volver a tomar; recomenzar; reanudar, continuar.

résumé [rezumé] *s.* resumen, sumario.

resurgent [rɪsɤ́dʒənt] *adj.* resurgente.

resurrection [rɛzərékʃən] *s.* resurrección.

resuscitate [rɪsʌ́sətet] *v.* resucitar; revivir.

retail [rítel] *s.* venta al por menor; **at — al** por menor; **— merchant** detallista, comerciante al por menor; **— price** precio al por menor; *v.* detallar; vender al menudeo (*o* vender al por menor), *Méx., C.A., Ven., Col.* menudear.

retailer [rítelə] *s.* detallista, revendedor, comerciante al por menor.

retain [rɪtén] *v.* retener; emplear.

retaliate [rɪtǽliet] *v.* desquitarse, vengarse.

retaliation [rɪtæliéʃən] *s.* desquite; desagravio; represalia, venganza.

retard [rɪtárd] *v.* retardar, retrasar, atrasar.

retention [rɪténʃən] *s.* retención.

reticence [rétəsəns] *s.* reserva.

retinue [rétnju] *s.* comitiva, séquito, acompañamiento.

retire [rɪtáɪr] *v.* retirar(se); jubilar(se);

acostarse; apartarse.

retirement [rɪtáɪrmənt] *s.* retiro; jubilación.

retort [rɪtɔ́rt] *v.* replicar; redargüir; *s.* réplica.

retouch [ritʌ́tʃ] *v.* retocar; *s.* retoque.

retrace [ritrés] *v.* repasar; volver a trazar; **to — one's steps** volver sobre sus pasos, retroceder.

retract [rɪtrǽkt] *v.* retractar, retractarse de; desdecirse (de); retraer.

retreat [rɪtrít] *s.* retiro, refugio, asilo; retirada; retreta (*toque de retirada*); *v.* retirarse; retroceder.

retrench [rɪtrɛ́ntʃ] *v.* cercenar, reducir, disminuir; economizar.

retrieve [rɪtrív] *v.* cobrar (*la caza*); recobrar, recuperar; reparar (*una pérdida*).

retroactive [retroǽktɪv] *adj.* retroactivo.

retroflex [rétrofleks] *adj.* retroflejo.

retrospect [rétrospekt] *s.* retrospección; **in —** retrospectivamente.

return [rɪtɜ́rn] *v.* volver, regresar; retornar; devolver; replicar; redituar; producir; restar (*la pelota en tenis*); **to — a favor** corresponder a un favor; **to — a report** rendir un informe; *s.* vuelta, regreso; retorno; recompensa; restitución, devolución; réplica; resto (*en un juego de pelota*); rédito, ganancia; informe; **— game** desquite, juego de desquite; **— ticket** boleto de vuelta; **by — mail** a vuelta de correo; **election -s** reportaje de elecciones; **in —** en cambio; **in — for** a cambio de, a trueque de; **income tax —** declaración de rentas; **many happy -s** muchas felicidades (en su día).

reunion [rijúnjən] *s.* reunión; junta.

reunite [rijunáɪt] *v.* reunir(se), volver a unirse; reconciliar(se).

reveal [rɪvíl] *v.* revelar.

revel [rέvl] *v.* deleitarse, gozarse; parrandear; *Am.* farrear; andar de parranda, *Ríopl.* andar de farra; *s.* parranda, juerga, jarana.

revelation [revléʃən] *s.* revelación; **Revelation(s)** Apocalipsis.

revelry [révlrɪ] *s.* jaleo, juerga, jarana.

revenge [rɪvéndʒ] *v.* vengar, vindicar; *s.* venganza; desquite.

revengeful [rɪvéndʒfəl] *adj.* vengativo.

revenue [révənju] *s.* renta; rédito; rentas públicas, ingresos.

revere [rɪvír] *v.* venerar.

reverence [révərəns] *s.* reverencia; veneración; *v.* reverenciar, venerar.

reverend [révrənd] *adj.* reverendo; venerable.

reverent [révrənt] *adj.* reverente.

reverie, revery [révərɪ] *s.* ensueño; arrobamiento.

reverse [rɪvɜ́s] *adj.* inverso, invertido; contrario, opuesto; *s.* revés; reverso, dorso; lo contrario; contratiempo; *v.* invertir; voltear; revocar (*una sentencia*).

revert [rɪvɜ́t] *v.* revertir, volver atrás; retroceder.

review [rɪvjú] *v.* (*study*) repasar, revisar; revistar; (*inspect*) pasar revista a (*las tropas*); (*criticize*) reseñar, hacer una reseña de (*un libro*); *s.* revista; repaso; reseña, crítica (*de un libro, drama, etc.*); revisión (*de un caso jurídico, sentencia, etc.*).

revile [rɪváɪl] *v.* vilipendiar, vituperar, denigrar.

revise [rɪváɪz] *v.* revisar, repasar, releer (*para corregir*); corregir, enmendar.

revision [rɪvíʒən] *s.* revisión; enmienda; edición enmendada o mejorada.

revival [rɪváɪvl] *s.* (*renewal*) renovación; revivificación; (*repeating*) renacimiento; nueva presentación (*teatral*); **— meeting** junta para revivir el fervor religioso; **religious —** despertamiento (*o nuevo fervor*) religioso.

revive [rɪváɪv] *v.* revivir, resucitar; volver en sí; renacer; reavivar, reanimar(se); avivar.

revoke [rɪvók] *v.* revocar, abrogar, anular; renunciar (*en los juegos de naipes*).

revolt [rɪvólt] *s.* revuelta, rebelión, sublevación; *v.* rebelarse, sublevarse; **it -s me** me da asco, me repugna.

revolting [rɪvóltɪŋ] *adj.* repugnante; asqueroso.

revolution [revəlúʃən] *s.* revolución; vuelta (*que da una rueda*).

revolutionary [revəlúʃəneri] *adj. & s.* revolucionario.

revolutionist [revəlúʃənɪst] *s.* revolucionario.

revolve [rɪválv] *v.* girar, dar vueltas; rodar; voltear, dar vueltas a; **to — in one's mind** revolver en la mente, ponderar, reflexionar.

revolver [rɪválvɚ] *s.* revólver.

reward [rɪwɔ́rd] *v.* premiar, recompensar; *s.* premio, gratificación, recompensa, galardón; albricias (*por haber hallado algún objeto perdido*).

rewrite [riráɪt] *v.* volver a escribir; refundir (*un escrito*).

rhapsody [rǽpsədɪ] *s.* rapsodia.

rhetoric [rétərɪk] *s.* retórica.

rheumatism [rúmətɪzəm] *s.* reumatismo, reuma.

rhinoceros [raɪnásərəs] *s.* rinoceronte.

rhubarb [rúbarb] *s.* ruibarbo.

rhyme [raɪm] *s.* rima; **without — or reason** sin ton ni son; *v.* rimar.

rhythm [ríðəm] *s.* ritmo.

rhythmical [ríðmɪkl] *adj.* rítmico, acompasado, cadencioso.

rib [rɪb] *s.* costilla; varilla (*de paraguas*); cordoncillo (*de ciertos tejidos*).

ribbon [ríbən] *s.* cinta; listón, banda; tira.

rice [raɪs] *s.* arroz; **— field** arrozal.

rich [rɪtʃ] *adj.* rico; costoso, suntuoso; sabroso; **— color** color vivo; **— food** alimento muy mantecoso o dulce.

riches [rítʃɪz] *s. pl.* riqueza, riquezas.

rickety [ríkɪtɪ] *adj.* desvencijado; raquítico.

rid [rɪd] *v.* librar, desembarazar; **to get — of** librarse de, deshacerse de, desembarazarse de; *pret. & p.p. de* **to rid.**

ridden [rídn] *p.p. de* **to ride.**

riddle [rídl] *s.* acertijo, adivinanza, enigma; *v.* acribillar, perforar; **to — with bullets** acribillar a balazos.

ride [raid] *v.* (*horse*) cabalgar, montar; (*vehicle*) pasear; ir en (*tranvía, tren*); **to — a bicycle** andar o montar en bicicleta; **to — a horse** montar un caballo; **to — horseback** montar a caballo; **to — over a country** pasar o viajar por un país (*en auto, a caballo o por tren*); **to — someone** dominar a alguien; burlarse de alguien; *s.* paseo (*a caballo o en automóvil*); viaje (*a caballo, en automóvil, por ferrocarril, etc.*).

rider [ráidɚ] *s.* jinete; pasajero (*de automóvil*); biciclista; motociclista; aditamento, cláusula añadida (*a un proyecto de ley*).

ridge [ridʒ] *s.* espinazo; lomo (*entre dos surcos*); arista, intersección (*de dos planos*); cordillera; cerro; caballete (*de tejado*); cordoncillo (*de ciertos tejidos*).

ridicule [rídikjul] *s.* ridículo; burla, mofa; *v.* ridiculizar, poner en ridículo.

ridiculous [rɪdíkjɘlɘs] *adj.* ridículo.

rifle [ráifl] *s.* rifle; *v.* pillar, robar; despojar.

rift [rift] *s.* (*opening*) raja; abertura; (*disagreement*) desacuerdo.

rig [rig] *v.* aparejar, equipar; enjarciar (*un barco de vela*); **to — oneself up** emperifollarse, ataviarse; *s.* aparejo, equipo; aparato; atavío, traje.

rigging [rígɪŋ] *s.* jarcia, aparejo.

right [rait] *adj.* (*not left*) derecho; diestro; (*proper*) recto; justo; propio; adecuado; correcto; **— angle** ángulo recto; **— side** lado derecho; derecho (*de un tejido, traje, etc.*); **it is — that** está bien que, es justo que; **to be — tener razón; to be all —** estar bien; estar bien de salud; **to be in one's — mind** estar en sus cabales; *adv.* derecho, directamente; rectamente; justamente; bien; correctamente; a la derecha; **— about-face** media vuelta; **— hungry** muy hambriento; **— now** ahora mismo, inmediatamente; **— there** allí mismo, *Am.* allí mero; **go — home!** ¡vete derechito a casa! it is **— where you left it** está exactamente (*o en el mero lugar*) donde lo dejaste; **to hit — in the eye** dar de lleno en el ojo, *Am.* dar en el mero ojo; *s.* derecho; autoridad; privilegio; **— of way** derecho de vía; **by — (by -s)** justamente, con justicia; según la ley; **from — to left** de derecha a izquierda; **to the —** a la derecha; **to be in the —** tener razón; *v.* enderezar; corregir.

righteous [ráitʃəs] *adj.* recto, justo, virtuoso.

righteousness [ráitʃəsnɪs] *s.* rectitud, virtud.

rightful [ráitfəl] *adj.* justo; legítimo.

right-hand [ráithænd] *adj.* derecho, de la mano derecha; **— man** brazo derecho.

rightist [ráitist] *s.* derechista.

rightly [ráitli] *adv.* con razón; justamente, rectamente; propiamente, aptamente, debidamente.

right-wing [ráitwiŋ] *adj.* derechista.

rigid [rídʒid] *adj.* rígido.

rigidity [rɪdʒídəti] *s.* rigidez; tiesura.

rigor [rígɚ] *s.* rigor; rigidez; severidad.

rigorous [rígɚəs] *adj.* rigoroso (*o riguroso*), severo.

rim [rim] *s.* borde, orilla; aro.

rime = rhyme.

rind [raind] *s.* corteza, cáscara.

ring [riŋ] *s.* (*finger*) anillo, sortija; argolla; aro; (*circle*) arena; pista; (*sound*) toque; tañido; repique; (*telephone*) timbrazo; telefonazo; **—leader** cabecilla; **— of defiance** tono de reto; **— of shouts** gritería; **— of a telephone** llamada de teléfono; **ring-shaped** en forma de anillo, anular; **key —** llavero; **sarcastic —** retintín; *v.* tocar (*un timbre, una campanilla o campana*); sonar; tañer, repicar; resonar; zumbar (*los oídos*); **to — for something** llamar para pedir algo; **to — the nose of an animal** ponerle una argolla en la nariz a un animal; **to — up on the phone** llamar por teléfono.

ringlet [ríŋlit] *s.* rizo, bucle; pequeña sortija.

rink [riŋk] *s.* patinadero (*cancha para patinar*).

rinse [rins] *v.* enjuagar; lavar; aclarar (*la ropa*); *s.* enjuague.

riot [ráiət] *s.* motín, desorden, alboroto, tumulto; **— of color** riqueza o exceso de colores chillantes; *v.* amotinarse, alborotar, armar un tumulto.

rip [rip] *v.* rasgar(se), romper(se); descoser(se); **to — off** rasgar, arrancar, cortar; **to — out a seam** descoser una costura; *s.* rasgón, rasgadura, rotura; descosido.

ripe [raip] *adj.* maduro, sazonado; en sazón; **— for** maduro para, sazonado para; bien preparado para, listo para.

ripen [ráipən] *v.* madurar(se), sazonar(se).

ripeness [ráipnis] *s.* madurez, sazón.

ripple [rípl] *v.* rizar(se), agitar(se), ondear, temblar (*la superficie del agua*); murmurar (*un arroyo*); *s.* onda, temblor, ondulación (*en la superficie del agua*); murmullo (*de un arroyo*).

rise [raiz] *v.* subir; ascender; alzarse; levantarse; elevarse; surgir; salir (*el sol, la luna, un astro*); hincharse (*la masa del pan*); **to — up in rebellion** sublevarse, levantarse, alzarse (*en rebelión*); *s.* subida; ascenso; pendiente; elevación; salida (*del sol, de la luna, etc.*); subida, alza (*de precios*).

risen [rízn] *p.p. de* **to rise.**

risk [risk] *s.* riesgo; *v.* arriesgar, aventurar, poner en peligro; exponerse a; **to—defeat** correr el riesgo de perder, exponerse a perder.

risky [rískɪ] *adj.* arriesgado, peligroso, aventurado.

risqué [rɪské] *adj.* escabroso.

rite [raɪt] *s.* rito, ceremonia.

ritual [rítʃʊəl] *adj.* & *s.* ritual, ceremonial.

rival [ráɪvl] *s.* rival, competidor, émulo; *adj.* competidor; **the — party** el partido opuesto; *v.* rivalizar con, competir con.

rivalry [ráɪvlrɪ] *s.* rivalidad.

river [rívə] *s.* río.

rivet [rívɪt] *s.* remache; *v.* remachar; fijar.

rivulet [rívjʊlɪt] *s.* riachuelo, arroyuelo.

road [rod] *s.* camino; carretera; vía.

roadside [ródsaɪd] *s.* borde del camino.

roadway [ródwe] *s.* camino, carretera.

roam [rom] *v.* vagar, errar, andar errante.

roar [ror] *v.* rugir, bramar; **to — with laughter** reír a carcajadas; *s.* rugido, bramido; **— of laughter** risotada, carcajada.

roast [rost] *v.* asar(se); tostar (*café, maíz, etc.*); ridiculizar, criticar; *s.* asado, carne asada; *adj.* asado; **— beef** rosbif, rosbí.

rob [rɑb] *v.* robar, hurtar; **to — someone of something** robarle algo a alguien.

robber [rɑ́bə] *s.* ladrón; **highway —** salteador.

robbery [rɑ́brɪ] *s.* robo, hurto.

robe [rob] *s.* manto, traje talar, túnica, toga (*de un juez, letrado, etc.*); bata; **automobile —** manta de automóvil.

robin [rɑ́bɪn] *s.* petirrojo.

robust [róbʌst] *adj.* robusto, fuerte.

rock [rɑk] *s.* roca, peña; peñasco; **— crystal** cristal de roca; **— salt** sal de piedra, sal gema o sal mineral; **to go on the -s** tropezar en un escollo, *Am.* escollar; *v.* mecer(se), balancear(se); bambolear(se); estremecer; **to — to sleep** adormecer (*meciendo*), arrullar.

rocker [rɑ́kə] *s.* mecedora; arco de una mecedora o cuna.

rocket [rɑ́kɪt] *s.* cohete.

rocketry [rɑ́kətrɪ] *s.* cohetería.

rocking [rɑ́kɪŋ] *adj.* oscilante; **— chair** silla mecedora.

rocky [rɑ́kɪ] *adj.* roqueño, rocoso, rocalloso, peñascoso; pedregoso; movedizo; tembloroso; débil, desvanecido.

rod [rɑd] *s.* vara, varilla; medida de longitud (*aproximadamente 5 metros*); **fishing —** caña de pescar.

rode [rod] *pret. de* **to ride**.

rodent [ródənt] *s.* roedor.

rogue [rog] *s.* pícaro, bribón, tunante, pillo; **-s' gallery** colección policíaca de retratos de criminales.

roguish [rógɪʃ] *adj.* pícaro, pillo, picaresco; travieso.

role [rol] *s.* papel, parte.

roll [rol] *v.* (*move*) rodar; girar; balancearse (*un barco*); bambolearse; ondular, retumbar (*el trueno, un cañón*); aplanar, alisar con rodillo;

arrollar, enrollar, hacer un rollo o bola; envolver; redoblar (*un tambor*); pronunciar (*la rr doble*); **to — over in the snow** revolverse o revolcarse en la nieve; **to — up** arrollar, enrollar, envolver; *s.* rollo (*de papel, paño, tela, etc.*); balanceo (*de un barco*); retumbo (*del trueno, de un cañón*); redoble (*de un tambor*); lista ondulación; oleaje; bollo, rosca, panecillo; **to call the —** pasar lista.

roller [rólə] *s.* rodillo, cilindro (*para aplanar o alisar*); rollo (*rodillo de pastelero*); oleada; **— coaster** montaña rusa; **— skate** patín de ruedas.

Roman [rómən] *adj.* & *s.* romano; **— nose** nariz aguileña.

romance [rómǽns] *s.* (*literature*) romance; novela; cuento; fábula; (*affair*) aventura romántica; amorío, lance amoroso; *v.* contar o fingir fábulas; andar en amoríos o aventuras; **Romance** *adj.* romance, románico, neolatino.

romantic [romǽntɪk] *adj.* romántico, novelesco.

romanticism [romǽntəsɪzəm] *s.* romanticismo.

romanticist [romǽntəsɪst] *s.* romántico, escritor romántico.

romp [rɑmp] *v.* triscar, juguetear, retozar, travesear.

roof [ruf] *s.* techo, techumbre, techado; tejado; **— garden** azotea-jardín; **— of the mouth** paladar; **flat —** azotea; *v.* techar.

room [rum] *s.* (*in building*) cuarto, pieza, sala, habitación; (*space*) espacio; lugar, sitio; **there is no — for more** no cabe(n) más, no hay lugar o cabida para más; **to make —** hacer lugar; **—mate** compañero de cuarto; *v.* vivir, hospedarse, alojarse.

roomer [rúmə] *s.* inquilino.

roominess [rúmɪnɪs] *s.* holgura.

roomy [rúmɪ] *adj.* espacioso, amplio, holgado.

roost [rust] *s.* gallinero; percha de gallinero; *v.* acurrucarse (*las aves en la percha*); pasar la noche.

rooster [rústə] *s.* gallo.

root [rut] *s.* raíz; *v.* arraigar(se); echar raíces; hocicar, hozar (*dícese de los cerdos*); **to — for** vitorear, aclamar; **to — out** (o **— up**) desarraigar, arrancar de raíz; **to become -ed** arraigarse.

rope [rop] *s.* (*cord*) soga, cuerda; (*lasso*) reata, lazo; **to be at the end of one's —** haber agotado el último recurso; estar (o andar) en las últimas; no saber qué hacer; **to know the -s** saber todas las tretas de un asunto o negocio; *v.* amarrar; lazar, enlazar; **to — off** acordelar, poner cuerdas tirantes alrededor de (*un sitio*); **to — someone in** embaucar a alguien.

rosary [rózərɪ] *s.* rosario.

rose [roz] *pret. de* **to rise**.

rose [roz] *s.* rosa; color de rosa; **—bush** rosal; **— window** rosetón.

RI

rosebud [rózbʌd] *s.* capullo o botón de rosa, yema, pimpollo.

rosette [rozét] *s.* roseta; rosetón.

roster [rásta›] *s.* registro; lista.

rostrum [rástrəm] *s.* tribuna.

rosy [rózɪ] *adj.* (*color*) rosado; color de rosa; (*condition*) alegre, risueño; — **future** porvenir risueño.

rot [rɑt] *v.* pudrir(se); corromperse; *s.* podre, podredumbre, putrefacción.

rotary [rótərɪ] *adj.* rotatorio, giratorio, rotativo.

rotate [rótet] *v.* girar, dar vueltas; hacer girar; turnarse; cultivar en rotación.

rotation [rotéʃən] *s.* rotación, vuelta; — **of crops** rotación de cultivos.

rote [rot] *s.* rutina, repetición maquinal; **by —** maquinalmente.

rotten [rátn] *adj.* podrido, putrefacto; hediondo; corrompido, corrupto.

rouge [ruʒ] *s.* colorete; *v.* pintar(se), poner(se) colorete.

rough [rʌf] *adj.* (*course*) áspero; tosco; fragoso; escabroso; (*rude*) brusco; grosero; (*stormy*) borrascoso, tempestuoso; — **diamond** diamante en bruto; — **draft** borrador; bosquejo; — **estimate** cálculo aproximado, tanteo; — **ground** terreno escabroso; — **idea** idea aproximada; — **sea** mar picado; — **weather** tiempo borrascoso; *adv. véase* **roughly**; *v.* **to — it** vivir sin lujos ni comodidades, hacer vida campestre.

roughen [rʌ́fən] *v.* hacer o poner áspero; picar, rascar (*una superficie*); rajarse, agrietarse (*la piel*).

roughly [rʌ́flɪ] *adv.* ásperamente; groseramente, rudamente; aproximadamente; **to estimate —** tantear.

roughness [rʌ́fnɪs] *s.* aspereza; escabrosidad; rudeza; tosquedad; **the — of the sea** lo picado del mar; **the — of the weather** lo borrascoso del tiempo.

round [raund] *adj.* redondo; rotundo; circular; — **trip** viaje redondo, viaje de ida y vuelta; **round-trip ticket** boleto (o billete) de ida y vuelta; *s.* vuelta, rotación, revolución; ronda; vuelta (*en el juego de naipes*); tanda, turno (*en ciertos deportes*); escalón, travesaño (*de escalera de mano*); danza en rueda; — **of ammunition** carga de municiones; descarga; — **of applause** explosión de aplausos; — **of pleasures** sucesión de placeres; **to make the -s** rondar; *prep. & adv. véase* **around**; — **about** a la redonda; por todos lados; **round-shouldered** cargado de espaldas; **to come — again** volver otra vez; **to go — a corner** doblar una esquina; *v.* redondear; dar vuelta a; **to — a corner** doblar una esquina; **to — out** redondear; completar; **to — up cattle** juntar el ganado, *Am.* rodear el ganado.

roundabout [ráundəbaut] *adj.* indirecto.

roundup [ráundʌp] *s.* rodeo (*de ganado*).

rouse [rauz] *v.* despertar(se), *Ríopl.* recordar; excitar; incitar, provocar; levantar (*la caza*).

rout [raut] *s.* derrota, fuga desordenada; *v.* derrotar; poner en fuga; **to — out** echar, hacer salir a toda prisa.

route [rut] *s.* ruta, camino, vía; itinerario; *v.* dirigir o enviar por cierta ruta.

routine [rutín] *s.* rutina.

rove [rov] *v.* vagar, errar, andar errante.

rover [róvə›] *s.* vagabundo.

row [rau] *s.* riña, pelea, pelotera; *v.* pelearse, reñir, armar una riña o pelotera.

row [ro] *s.* fila, hilera; paseo en lancha; *v.* remar, bogar; llevar en lancha o bote.

rowboat [róbot] *s.* bote de remos, lancha.

rower [róə›] *s.* remero.

royal [rɔ́ɪəl] *adj.* real, regio.

royalist [rɔ́ɪəlɪst] *s.* realista.

royalty [rɔ́ɪəltɪ] *s.* realeza, soberanía real; persona o personas reales; derechos (*pagados a un autor o inventor*).

rub [rʌb] *v.* (*apply friction*) frotar; restregar; fregar; (*scrape*) raspar; irritar; **to — out** borrar; **to — someone the wrong way** irritar, contrariar, llevarle a uno la contraria; *s.* fricción, friega, frotación; roce; sarcasmo; **there is the —** allí está la dificultad.

rubber [rʌ́bə›] *s.* caucho, goma, *Méx., C.A.* hule; goma elástica; goma de borrar; partida (*en ciertos juegos de naipes*); jugada decisiva (*en ciertos juegos de naipes*); **-s** chanclos, zapatos de goma o hule; *adj.* de caucho, de goma, *Méx., C.A.* de hule; — **band** faja o banda de goma; — **plantation** cauchal; — **tree** *Am.* caucho, *Am.* gomero.

rubbish [rʌ́bɪʃ] *s.* basura, desechos, desperdicios; tonterías.

rubble [rʌ́bl] *s.* escombros; ripio, cascajo, fragmentos de ladrillos o piedras; piedra en bruto, piedra sin labrar.

rubric [rúbrɪk] *s.* rúbrica.

ruby [rúbɪ] *s.* rubí.

rudder [rʌ́də›] *s.* timón.

ruddy [rʌ́dɪ] *adj.* rojo; rojizo; rubicundo.

rude [rud] *adj.* rudo; grosero; áspero; brusco; tosco.

rudeness [rúdnɪs] *s.* rudeza; grosería; descortesía; tosquedad.

rueful [rúfəl] *adj.* triste; lastimoso, lamentable.

ruffian [rʌ́fɪən] *s.* rufián, hombre brutal.

ruffle [rʌ́fl] *v.* rizar, fruncir (*tela*); arrugar; desarreglar; rizar (*la superficie del agua*); perturbar; molestar; *s.* volante (*de un traje*); frunce, pliegue; ondulación (*en el agua*).

rug [rʌg] *s.* alfombra, tapete.

rugged [rʌ́gɪd] *adj.* escabroso, fragoso; áspero; recio, robusto; tosco; borrascoso, tempestuoso.

ruin [rúɪn] s. ruina; **to go to —** arruinarse, caer en ruinas, venir a menos; v. arruinar; echar a perder; estropear.

ruinous [rúɪnəs] adj. ruinoso; desastroso.

rule [rul] s. (regulation) regla; reglamento; precepto; (control) mando, gobierno; **as a —** por regla general; v. regir, gobernar; mandar; dirigir, guiar; dominar; fallar, decidir; rayar (con regla); **to — out** excluir; **to — over** regir, gobernar.

ruler [rúlɚ] s. gobernante; soberano; regla (para medir o trazar líneas).

ruling [rúlɪŋ] s. fallo, decisión; gobierno; adj. predominante, prevaleciente; principal.

rum [rʌm] s. ron.

rumble [rʌ́mbl] v. retumbar, hacer estruendo, rugir; s. retumbo, estruendo, rumor, ruido sordo; **— seat** asiento trasero (de cupé).

ruminate [rúmənet] v. rumiar; reflexionar, meditar.

rummage [rʌ́mɪdʒ] v. escudriñar revolviéndolo todo; s. búsqueda desordenada; **— sale** venta de prendas usadas (para beneficencia).

rumor [rúmɚ] s. rumor; runrún; v. murmurar; **it is -ed that** corre la voz que.

rump [rʌmp] s. anca; trasero.

rumple [rʌ́mpl] v. estrujar, ajar, arrugar; s. arruga (en un traje).

rumpus [rʌ́mpəs] s. barullo, alharaca, boruca, batahola.

run [rʌn] v. (on foot) correr; (function) andar; marchar; funcionar; (flow) fluir; chorrear; (go over) recorrer; (direct) dirigir, manejar; (un negocio, empresa, máquina, casa, etc.); extenderse (de un punto a otro); correrse (los colores); ser candidato (a un puesto político); **to — a fever** tener calentura; **to — away** huir; fugarse, escaparse; **to — across a person** encontrarse o tropezar con una persona; **to — down** dejar de funcionar (una máquina, reloj, etc.); aprehender a (un criminal); hablar mal de; atropellar; **to get — down in health** quebrantársele a uno la salud; **to — dry** secarse; **to — into** tropezar con, encontrarse con; chocar con; **— around with** asociarse con; tener amores con; **to — into debt** adeudarse; **to — something into** meter algo en, clavar algo en; **— out** salirse; **to — out of money** acabársele a uno el dinero; **to — over** derramarse (un líquido); atropellar, pasar por encima de; repasar, echar un vistazo a (la lección, un libro, etc.); **to — /through a book** hojear un libro; **the play ran for three months** se dió la comedia durante tres meses; s. carrera, corrida; curso, marcha; recorrido; manejo; **— of good luck** serie de repetidos éxitos; **— of performances** serie de representaciones; **— on a bank**

corrida, demanda extraordinaria de fondos bancarios; **in the long —** a la larga; **stocking —** carrera; **the common — of mankind** el común de las gentes; **to have the — of** tener el libre uso de; p.p. de to **run**.

runaway [rʌ́nəwe] adj. fugitivo; **— horse** caballo desbocado; **— marriage** casamiento de escapatoria; s. fugitivo; caballo desbocado; fuga.

rung [rʌn] s. barrote, travesaño (de silla, escalera de mano, etc.); pret. & p.p. de to **ring**.

runner [rʌ́nɚ] s. corredor; tapete (para un pasillo o mesa), Ríopl. pasillo; carrera (en una media); cuchilla (de patín o de trineo); contrabandista.

running [rʌ́nɪŋ] s. (race) corrida, carrera; (direction) manejo, dirección; (flow) flujo; **to be out of the —** estar fuera de combate; adj. corriente; **— board** estribo; **— expenses** gastos corrientes; **— knot** nudo corredizo; **— water** agua corriente; **in — condition** en buen estado; **for ten days — ** por diez días seguidos.

runt [rʌnt] s. enano; hombrecillo.

runway [rʌ́nwe] s. senda; vía; pista (de aterrizaje).

rupture [rʌ́ptʃɚ] s. ruptura; rompimiento, rotura; hernia; v. romper(se); reventar.

rural [rúrəl] adj. rural, campestre.

rush [rʌʃ] v. (hurry) apresurar(se); Am. apurarse; despachar con prisa; (attack) lanzar(se), precipitar(se); abalanzarse; acometer; **to — out** salir a todo correr; **to — past** pasar a toda prisa; s. precipitación, prisa; acometida; junco; **— chair** silla de junco; **— of business** gran movimiento comercial; **— of people** tropel de gente; **— order** pedido urgente.

Russian [rʌ́ʃən] adj. & s. ruso.

rust [rʌst] s. moho, orín; tizón (enfermedad de las plantas); **— color** color rojizo; v. enmohecer(se), oxidar(se).

rustic [rʌ́stɪk] adj. & s. rústico, campesino.

rustle [rʌ́sl] v. susurrar, crujir; menear; **to — cattle** robar ganado; s. susurro, crujido.

rusty [rʌ́stɪ] adj. mohoso, cubierto de orín, oxidado; rojizo; entorpecido, falto de uso; falto de práctica.

rut [rʌt] s. rodada; rutina, método rutinario; **to be in a —** hacer una cosa por rutina, ser esclavo de la rutina.

ruthless [rúθlɪs] adj. despiadado, cruel, brutal.

ruthlessness [rúθlɪsnɪs] s. fiereza, falta de miramiento, truculencia, crueldad.

rye [raɪ] s. centeno.

S

saber [sébɚ] s. sable.

sabotage [sǽbətɑʒ] s. sabotaje; v. sabotear.

sack [sæk] s. (bag) saco; costal; (looting) saqueo, pillaje; v. ensacar, meter en un saco; saquear, pillar.

RO

sacrament [sǽkrəmənt] *s.* sacramento.
sacred [sékrɪd] *adj.* sagrado, sacro.
sacredness [sékrɪdnɪs] *s.* santidad; lo sagrado.
sacrifice [sǽkrəfaɪs] *s.* sacrificio; **to sell at a —** vender con pérdida; *v.* sacrificar.
sacrilege [sǽkrəlɪdʒ] *s.* sacrilegio.
sacrilegious [sækrɪlídʒəs] *adj.* sacrílego.
sacrosanct [sǽkrosænkt] *adj.* sacrosanto.
sad [sæd] *adj.* triste.
sadden [sædn] *v.* entristecer(se).
saddle [sædl] *s.* silla de montar; silla de bicicleta o motocicleta; **—bag** alforja; **— horse** caballo de silla; **—tree** arzón; *v.* ensillar; **to — someone with responsibilities** cargar a alguien de responsabilidades.
sadistic [sədístɪk] *adj.* sádico, cruel.
sadness [sǽdnɪs] *s.* tristeza.
safe [sef] *adj.* (*secure*) seguro; salvo; sin riesgo, sin peligro; (*trustworthy*) digno de confianza; **— and sound** sano y salvo; **safe-conduct** salvo-conducto; **to be —** no correr peligro, estar a salvo; *s.* caia fuerte; **-ly** *adv.* seguramente; con seguridad; sin peligro; **to arrive -ly** llegar bien, llegar sin contratiempo alguno.
safeguard [séfgɑrd] *s.* salvaguardia; resguardo, defensa; *v.* resguardar, proteger, salvaguardar.
safety [séftɪ] *s.* seguridad; protección; **in —** con seguridad; sin peligro; *adj.* de seguridad; **— device** mecanismo de seguridad; **— pin** imperdible, alfiler de seguridad.
saffron [sǽfrən] *s.* azafrán; *adj.* azafranado, color de azafrán.
sag [sæg] *v.* combarse, pandearse; doblegarse; deprimirse, hundirse (*en el centro*); encorvarse; **his shoulders —** tiene las espaldas caídas; *s.* pandeo, flexión, depresión; concavidad.
sagacious [səgéʃəs] *adj.* sagaz, ladino, astuto.
sagacity [səgǽsətɪ] *s.* sagacidad; astucia.
sage [sedʒ] *adj.* sabio; cuerdo, prudente; *s.* sabio; salvia (*planta*).
said [sed] *pret. & p.p. de* **to say.**
sail [sel] *s.* (*canvas*) vela (*de barco*); (*trip*) viaje o paseo en barco de vela; **under full —** a toda vela; **to set —** hacerse a la vela; *v.* navegar; hacerse a la vela; zarpar, salir (*un buque*); viajar, ir (*en barco, bote, etc.*); pasear en bote de vela; **to — a kite** volar una cometa o papalote; **to — along** deslizarse; navegar; ir bien; **to — along the coast** costear.
sailboat [sélbot] *s.* bote o barco de vela.
sailor [sélə] *s.* marinero; marino.
saint [sent] *s.* santo; *adj.* santo; san (*delante de nombres masculinos excepto*: Santo Tomás, Santo Domingo, Santo Toribio); *v.* canonizar.
saintly [séntlɪ] *adj.* santo; pío, devoto.
sake [sek] **: for the — of** por; por amor a; por consideración a; **for my — por**

mí; **for pity's —** por piedad; ¡caramba!; **for the — of argument** por vía de argumento.
salacious [səléʃəs] *adj.* salaz.
salad [sǽləd] *s.* ensalada; **— dressing** aderezo (*para ensalada*).
salary [sǽlərɪ] *s.* salario, sueldo.
sale [sel] *s.* venta; saldo, *Méx.*, *C.A.*, *Andes* barata; *Riopl.*, *Andes* realización; **— by auction** almoneda, subasta; **-s tax** impuesto sobre ventas; **for (on) —** de venta.
salesman [sélzmən] *s.* vendedor; dependiente (*de tienda*); **traveling —** agente viajero, viajante de comercio.
saleswoman [sélzwʊmən] *s.* vendedora; dependiente (*de tienda*).
salient [sélɪənt] *adj.* saliente, sobresaliente; prominente.
saline [sélin] *adj.* salino.
saliva [səláɪvə] *s.* saliva.
sallow [sǽlo] *adj.* amarillento, pálido.
sally [sǽlɪ] *s.* salida; agudeza, chiste agudo; *v.* salir, hacer una salida; **to — forth** salir.
salmon [sǽmən] *s.* salmón.
saloon [səlún] *s.* salón (*de un vapor*); taberna, *Am.* cantina; *Riopl.* bar; **dining — of a ship** salón-comedor de un vapor.
salt [sɔlt] *s.* (*sodium chloride*) sal; (*wit*) chiste, agudeza; **smelling -s** sales aromáticas; **the — of the earth** la flor y nata de la humanidad; *adj.* salado; salobre; **—cellar** salero; **— mine** salina; **— pork** tocino salado; **— shaker** salero; **— water** agua salada, agua de mar; *v.* salar; **to — one's money away** guardar o ahorrar su dinero.
saltpeter [sɔltpítə] *s.* salitre, nitro; **— mine** salitral, salitrera.
salty [sɔ́ltɪ] *adj.* salado; salobre.
salutary [sǽljʊtɛrɪ] *adj.* saludable.
salutation [sæljətéʃən] *s.* salutación, saludo.
salute [səlút] *s.* saludo; **gun —** salva; *v.* saludar; cuadrarse (*militarmente*).
salvage [sǽlvɪdʒ] *s.* salvamento.
salvation [sælvéʃən] *s.* salvación.
salve [sæv] *s.* untura, ungüento; alivio; *v.* aliviar, aquietar, calmar; untar.
salvo [sǽlvo] *s.* salva.
same [sem] *adj.* mismo; igual; idéntico; **it is all the — to me** me es igual, me da lo mismo; **the —** lo mismo; el mismo (la misma, los mismos, las mismas).
sample [sǽmpl] *s.* muestra, prueba; **book of -s** muestrario; *v.* probar, calar.
sanatorium [sænətórɪəm] *s.* sanatorio.
sanctify [sǽŋktəfaɪ] *v.* santificar.
sanction [sǽŋkʃən] *s.* sanción; aprobación; autorización; *v.* sancionar; ratificar; aprobar, autorizar.
sanctity [sǽŋktətɪ] *s.* santidad.
sanctuary [sǽŋktʃʊɛrɪ] *s.* santuario; asilo.
sand [sænd] *s.* arena; **— pit** arenal; *v.* enarenar, cubrir de arena; mezclar con

arena; refregar con arena.

sandal [sǽndl] *s.* sandalia; alpargata; *Méx.* guarache (huarache); *Andes* ojota.

sandpaper [sǽndpepə] *s.* papel de lija; *v.* lijar, pulir o alisar con papel de lija.

sandstone [sǽndston] *s.* piedra arenisca.

sandwich [sǽndwɪtʃ] *s.* bocadillo, emparedado, sandwich; *v.* intercalar, meter (entre).

sandy [sǽndɪ] *adj.* arenoso; arenisco; **— hair** pelo rojizo.

sane [sen] *adj.* sano, sensato; cuerdo.

sang [sæŋ] *pret. de to* sing.

sanitarium [sænətɛ́rɪəm] *s.* sanatorio.

sanitary [sǽnətɪrɪ] *adj.* sanitario.

sanitation [sænətéʃən] *s.* saneamiento; salubridad; sanidad.

sanity [sǽnətɪ] *s.* cordura.

sank [sæŋk] *pret. de to* sink.

sap [sæp] *s.* savia; tonto, bobo; *v.* agotar, debilitar, minar.

sapling [sǽplɪŋ] *s.* vástago, renuevo; arbolillo.

sapphire [sǽfaɪr] *s.* zafiro; color de zafiro.

sarcasm [sárkæzəm] *s.* sarcasmo.

sarcastic [sɑrkǽstɪk] *adj.* sarcástico.

sardine [sɑrdín] *s.* sardina.

sardonic [sɑrdánɪk] *adj.* burlón; sarcástico.

sash [sæʃ] *s.* faja (*cinturón de lana, seda o algodón*); banda, cinta ancha; **window — bastidor** (*o* marco) de ventana.

sat [sæt] *pret. & p.p. de to* sit.

satchel [sǽtʃəl] *s.* valija, maletín, maleta, saco.

sate [set] *v.* saciar.

sateen [sætín] *s.* satén o rasete (*raso de inferior calidad*)

satellite [sǽtlaɪt] *s.* satélite.

satiate [séʃtet] *v.* saciar, hartar.

satin [sǽtn] *s.* raso.

satire [sǽtaɪr] *s.* sátira.

satirical [sətírɪkl] *adj.* satírico.

satirize [sǽtəraɪz] *v.* satirizar.

satisfaction [sætɪsfǽkʃən] *s.* satisfacción.

satisfactorily [sætɪsfǽktrəlɪ] *adv.* satisfactoriamente.

satisfactory [sætɪsfǽktrɪ] *adj.* satisfactorio.

satisfied [sǽtɪsfaɪd] *adj.* satisfecho, contento.

satisfy [sǽtɪsfaɪ] *v.* satisfacer.

saturate [sǽtʃəret] *v.* saturar, empapar.

Saturday [sǽtədɪ] *s.* sábado.

sauce [sɔs] *s.* salsa; **— dish** salsera; *v.* aderezar con salsa; sazonar, condimentar; insolentarse con.

saucepan [sɔ́spæn] *s.* cacerola.

saucer [sɔ́sə] *s.* platillo.

sauciness [sɔ́sɪnɪs] *s.* descaro, insolencia.

saucy [sɔ́sɪ] *adj.* descarado, respondón, insolente, *Am.* retobado.

saunter [sɔ́ntə] *v.* pasearse, vagar.

sausage [sɔ́sɪdʒ] *s.* salchicha, salchichón; longaniza; chorizo.

savage [sǽvɪdʒ] *adj.* salvaje; fiero; bárbaro, brutal, feroz; *s.* salvaje.

savagery [sǽvɪdʒrɪ] *s.* salvajismo; crueldad, fiereza.

savant [səvánt] *s.* sabio.

save [sev] *v.* (*rescue*) salvar; (*hoard*) ahorrar; economizar; (*keep*) guardar; resguardar; **to — from** librar de; **to — one's eyes** cuidarse la vista; *prep.* salvo, menos, excepto.

saver [sévə] *s.* salvador; libertador; ahorrador; **life—** salvavidas.

saving [sévɪŋ] *adj.* (*rescuer*) salvador; (*economizing*) ahorrativo, económico; frugal; *s.* ahorro; economía; **-s** ahorros; **-s bank** caja o banco de ahorros; *prep.* salvo, excepto, con excepción de.

savior [sévjə] *s.* salvador.

savor [sévə] *s.* sabor; dejo; *v.* saborear; sazonar; **to — of** saber a, tener el sabor de; **it -s of treason** huele a traición.

savory [sévərɪ] *adj.* sabroso.

saw [sɔ] *s.* sierra; **—horse** caballete; *v.* aserrar, serrar; **it -s easily** es fácil de aserrar; *pret. de to* see.

sawdust [sɔ́dʌst] *s.* aserrín, serrín.

sawmill [sɔ́mɪl] *s.* aserradero.

sawn [sɔn] *p.p. de to* saw.

Saxon [sǽksn] *adj. & s.* sajón.

saxophone [sǽksəfon] *s.* saxófono; saxófon.

say [se] *v.* decir; declarar; **—!** ¡diga! ¡oiga usted!; **that is to —** es decir; **to — one's prayers** rezar, decir o recitar sus oraciones; **to — the least** por lo menos; **it is said that** dizque, se dice que, dicen que; *s.* afirmación, aserto; **the final —** la autoridad decisiva; **to have a — in a matter** tener voz y voto en un asunto; **to have one's —** expresarse, dar su opinión.

saying [séɪŋ] *s.* dicho, refrán; aserto; **as the — goes** como dice el refrán.

scab [skæb] *s.* costra (*de una herida*); roña; esquirol (*obrero que sustituye a un huelguista*); obrero que acepta un jornal inferior; *v.* encostrarse (*una herida*), cubrirse de una costra.

scabbard [skǽbəd] *s.* vaina, funda (*de espada, puñal, etc.*).

scabby [skǽbɪ] *adj.* costroso; roñoso, sarnoso, tiñoso.

scabrous [skébrəs] *adj.* escabroso.

scaffold [skǽfld] *s.* andamio, tablado; patíbulo, cadalso.

scaffolding [skǽfldɪŋ] *s.* andamiada (*Am.* andamiaje), andamios.

scald [skɔld] *v.* escaldar; **to — milk** calentar la leche hasta que suelte el hervor; *s.* escaldadura, quemadura.

scale [skel] *s.* escala; platillo de balanza; balanza; escama (*de pez o de la piel*); costra; **pair of -s** balanza; **platform —** báscula; *v.* escalar; subir, trepar por; graduar (*a escala*); medir según escala; pesar; escamar, quitar las escamas a; pelarse, despellejarse; descostrar(se); **to — down prices**

rebajar proporcionalmente los precios.

scallop [skάləp] *s.* onda, pico (*adorno*); molusco bivalvo; **-s** festón (*recortes en forma de ondas o picos*); *v.* festonear, recortar en forma de ondas o picos; asar con salsa o migas de pan.

scalp [skælp] *s.* cuero cabelludo; *v.* desollar el cráneo; revender (*boletós, billetes*) a precio subido.

scaly [skέlɪ] *adj.* escamoso, lleno de escamas; **— with rust** mohoso.

scamp [skæmp] *s.* pícaro, bribón, bellaco.

scamper [skǽmpɚ] *v.* correr, escabullirse, escaparse; *s.* escabullida, carrera, corrida.

scan [skæn] *v.* escudriñar; examinar, mirar detenidamente; echar un vistazo a (*en el habla popular*); medir (*el verso*).

scandal [skǽndl̩] *s.* escándalo; maledicencia, murmuración.

scandalize [skǽndl̩aɪz] *v.* escandalizar, dar escándalo.

scandalous [skǽndl̩əs] *adj.* escandaloso; difamatorio; vergonzoso.

scant [skænt] *adj.* escaso; corto; insuficiente; *v.* escatimar, limitar.

scanty [skǽntɪ] *adj.* escaso; insuficiente.

scar [skar] *s.* (*skin blemish*) cicatriz; costurón; (*mark*) raya, marca (*en una superficie pulida*); *v.* marcar, rayar; hacer o dejar una cicatriz en.

scarce [skɛrs] *adj.* escaso; raro; **-ly** *adv.* escasamente; apenas.

scarcity [skɛ́rsətɪ] *s.* escasez; carestía; insuficiencia.

scare [skɛr] *v.* espantar, asustar; alarmar; sobresaltar; **he -s easily** se asusta fácilmente; **to — away** ahuyentar, espantar; *s.* susto, sobresalto.

scarecrow [skɛ́rkro] *s.* espantajo; espantapájaros.

scarf [skarf] *s.* bufanda; mantilla; pañuelo (*para el cuello o la cabeza*); tapete (*para una mesa, tocador, etc.*).

scarlet [skárlɪt] *s.* escarlata; *adj.* de color escarlata; **— fever** escarlata, escarlatina.

scary [skɛ́rɪ] *adj.* espantadizo, asustadizo, miedoso.

scat [skæt] *interj.* ¡zape!

scatter [skǽtɚ] *v.* esparcir(se); desparramar(se); dispersar(se); **—brained** ligero de cascos, aturdido.

scene [sin] *s.* escena; escenario; decoración; vista; **to make a —** causar un escándalo.

scenery [sínərɪ] *s.* paisaje, vista; **stage —** decoraciones.

scent [sent] *s.* (*odor*) olor; (*substance*) perfume; (*trace*) pista, rastro; **to be on the — of** seguir el rastro de; **to have a keen —** tener buen olfato; *v.* oler, olfatear, ventear, husmear; perfumar.

scepter [séptɚ] *s.* cetro.

sceptic [sképtɪk] *adj. & s.* escéptico.

scepticism [sképtəsɪzəm] *s.* escepti-

cismo.

schedule [skédʒʊl] *s.* horario; itinerario (*de trenes*); lista, inventario (*adjunto a un documento*); *v.* fijar el día y la hora (*para una clase, conferencia, etc.*); establecer el itinerario para (*un tren o trenes*).

scheme [skim] *s.* (*plan*) esquema, plan, proyecto; empresa; (*plot*) ardid, trama, maquinación; **color —** combinación de colores; **metrical —** sistema de versificación; *v.* proyectar, urdir; maquinar, intrigar, tramar.

schemer [skímɚ] *s.* maquinador, intrigante; proyectista.

scheming [skímɪŋ] *adj.* maquinador, intrigante; *s.* maquinación.

schism [sɪzəm] *s.* cisma.

schizophrenia [skɪzofrínɪə] *s.* esquizofrenia.

scholar [skálɚ] *s.* escolar, estudiante; becario (*el que disfruta una beca*); erudito, docto.

scholarly [skálɚlɪ] *adj.* erudito, sabio, docto; *adv.* eruditamente, doctamente.

scholarship [skálɚʃɪp] *s.* saber; erudición; beca; **to have a —** disfrutar una beca.

scholastic [skolǽstɪk] *adj.* escolástico; escolar.

school [skul] *s.* escuela; **— of fish** banco de peces; *adj.* de escuela; **— day** día de escuela; **— board** consejo de enseñanza; *v.* enseñar, educar, instruir, aleccionar.

schoolboy [skúlbɔɪ] *s.* muchacho de escuela.

schoolgirl [skúlgɚl] *s.* muchacha de escuela.

schoolhouse [skúlhaʊs] *s.* escuela.

schooling [skúlɪŋ] *s.* instrucción; enseñanza, educación.

schoolmaster [skúlmæstɚ] *s.* maestro de escuela.

schoolmate [skúlmet] *s.* condiscípulo, compañero de escuela.

schoolroom [skúlrum] *s.* clase, aula.

schoolteacher [skúltitʃɚ] *s.* maestro de escuela.

schooner [skúnɚ] *s.* goleta; vaso grande para cerveza; **prairie —** galera con toldo.

science [sáɪəns] *s.* ciencia.

scientific [saɪəntífɪk] *adj.* científico; **-ally** *adv.* científicamente.

scientist [sáɪəntɪst] *s.* científico, hombre de ciencia.

scintillate [síntəlet] *v.* centellear; chispear.

scion [sáɪən] *s.* vástago.

scissors [sízɚz] *s. pl.* tijeras.

sclerosis [sklərósɪs] *s.* esclerosis.

scoff [skɔf] *s.* mofa, burla, befa, escarnio; *v.* escarnecer; mofarse; **to — at** mofarse de, burlarse de, escarnecer a.

scold [skold] *v.* reñir, reprender, regañar; *s.* regañón, persona regañona.

scolding [skóldɪŋ] *s.* regaño, reprensión; *adj.* regañón.

scoop [skup] *s.* (*tool*) cuchara, cucharón;

pala; (*quantity*) palada, cucharada; (*winnings*) buen ganancia. — primera publicación de una noticia; *v.* cavar, excavar; ahuecar; cucharear, sacar con cucharón o pala; achicar (*agua*); **to — in a good profit** sacar buena ganancia.

scoot [skut] *v.* escabullirse, correr, irse a toda prisa; **—! ¡largo de aquí!**

scooter [skútɚ] *s.* motoneta (*de motor*); monopatín.

scope [skop] *s.* alcance, extensión; esfera, campo.

scorch [skɔrtʃ] *v.* chamuscar; resecar, agostar; *s.* chamusquina, *Am.* chamuscada o chamuscadura.

score [skor] *s.* cuenta; escor (*en el juego*); raya, línea; calificación (*expresada numéricamente*); veintena; **musical —** partitura; **on that —** a ese respecto; **on the — of** a causa de, con motivo de; **to keep the —** llevar el escor, llevar la cuenta; **to settle old -s** desquitarse; *v.* marcar el escor, señalar los tantos en un juego; calificar (*numéricamente*); instrumentar (*música*); rayar, marcar con rayas; **to — a point** ganar un punto o tanto; **to — a success** lograr éxito, obtener un triunfo.

scorn [skɔrn] *s.* desdén, menosprecio; *v.* desdeñar, menospreciar.

scornful [skɔ́rnfəl] *adj.* desdeñoso.

scorpion [skɔ́rpɪən] *s.* escorpión, alacrán.

Scotch [skatʃ] *adj.* escocés; **the —** los escoceses, el pueblo escocés.

scoundrel [skáʊndrəl] *s.* bellaco, bribón, pícaro.

scour [skaʊr] *v.* fregar, restregar, limpiar; pulir; **to — the country** recorrer la comarca (*en busca de algo*).

scourge [skɝdʒ] *s.* azote; *v.* azotar; castigar.

scout [skaʊt] *v.* explorador (*usualmente militar*); **a good —** un buen explorador; una buena persona, un buen compañero; *v.* explorar; reconocer.

scowl [skaʊl] *v.* ceño; *v.* fruncir el ceño, mirar con ceño; poner mala cara.

scramble [skræmbl] *v.* (*move*) gatear; (*eggs*) hacer un revoltillo; (*mix up*) revolver, mezclar; **to — for something** forcejear por coger algo; pelearse por coger algo; **to — up** trepar o subir a gatas (*una cuesta*); **-d eggs** revoltillo, huevos, revueltos; *s.* revoltillo, confusión; pelea.

scrap [skræp] *s.* (*fragment*) fragmento, pedacito; migaja; (*fight*) riña, reyerta; **-s** sobras; desperdicios; desechos; retales; **—book** álbum de recortes; **— iron** recortes o desechos de hierro; *v.* desechar; tirar a la basura; descartar; pelear, reñir.

scrape [skrep] *v.* (*abrasively*) raspar; rasguñar; rascar; (*rub*) raer; rozar; **to — along** ir tirando, ir pasándola; **to — together** recoger o acumular poco a poco; **to bow and — ** ser

muy servil; *s.* raspadura; rasguño; aprieto, dificultad, lío.

scraper [skrépɚ] *s.* (*tool*) raspador; (*scrimping person*) tacaño.

scratch [skrætʃ] *v.* (*mark*) arañar, rasguñar; (*rub*) rascar; raspar; (*line*) rayar; escarbar; (*write badly*) hacer garabatos; **to — out** borrar, tachar; sacar (*los ojos*) con las uñas; *s.* arañazo, araño, rasguño; raya, marca; **to start from —** empezar sin nada; empezar desde el principio; empezar sin ventaja.

scrawl [skrɔl] *s.* garabato; *v.* hacer garabatos, escribir mal.

scrawny [skrɔ́nɪ] *adj.* huesudo, flaco.

scream [skrim] *s.* chillido, alarido, grito; **he's a —** es muy cómico o chistoso; *v.* chillar, gritar.

screech [skritʃ] *s.* chillido; **— owl** lechuza; *v.* chillar.

screen [skrin] *s.* (*projection*) pantalla; (*divider*) biombo; mampara; resguardo; (*sifter*) tamiz, cedazo; **—door** antepuerta de tela metálica; **motion-picture —** pantalla de cinematógrafo; **wire —** pantalla de tela metálica; *v.* tapar; resguardar, proteger con una pantalla o biombo; cerner; proyectar sobre la pantalla, filmar; **to — windows** proteger las ventanas con tela metálica.

screw [skru] *s.* tornillo; **— eye** armella; **— nut** tuerca; **— propeller** hélice; **— thread** rosca; *v.* atornillar; torcer, retorcer; **to — a lid on** atornillar una tapa; **to — up one's courage** cobrar ánimo.

screwdriver [skrúdraɪvɚ] *s.* destornillador.

scribble [skríbl] *v.* garrapatear, hacer garabatos, borronear, escribir mal o de prisa; *s.* garabato.

script [skrɪpt] *s.* letra cursiva, escritura; manuscrito (*de un drama, de una película*).

scripture [skríptʃɚ] *s.* escritura sagrada; **the Scriptures** la Sagrada Escritura, la Biblia.

scroll [skrol] *s.* rollo de pergamino o papel; voluta, adorno en espiral; rúbrica (*de una firma*).

scrub [skrʌb] *v.* fregar; restregar; *s.* friega, fregado; *adj.* achaparrado; bajo, inferior; **— oak** chaparro; **— pine** pino achaparrado; **— team** equipo de jugadores suplentes o menos bien entrenados; **— woman** fregona.

scruple [skrúpl] *s.* escrúpulo; *v.* escrupulizar, tener escrúpulos.

scrupulous [skrúpjələs] *adj.* escrupuloso.

scrutinize [skrútṇaɪz] *v.* escudriñar, escrutar.

scrutiny [skrútṇɪ] *s.* escrutinio.

scuff [skʌf] *v.* raspar; arrastrar los pies.

scuffle [skʌ́fl] *s.* refriega, riña, pelea; *v.* forcejear; luchar, pelear; arrastrar los pies.

sculptor [skʌ́lptɚ] *s.* escultor.

SC

sculpture [skʌlptʃɚ] *s.* escultura; *v.* esculpir, cincelar, tallar.

scum [skʌm] *s.* nata, capa, espuma; escoria; residuo, desechos; canalla, gente baja; *v.* espumar.

scurry [skɜːi] *v.* escabullirse; echar a correr; apresurarse; *s.* apresuramiento; corrida, carrera.

scuttle [skʌtl] *v.* echar a correr; barrenar (*un buque*); echar a pique; *s.* escotilla, escotillón; balde (*para carbón*).

scythe [saɪð] *s.* guadaña.

sea [si] *s.* mar; **to be at** — estar en el mar; estar perplejo o confuso; **to put to** — hacerse a la mar; *adj.* marino, marítimo, de mar; — **biscuit** galleta; — **green** verdemar; — **gull** gaviota; — **level** nivel del mar; — **lion** león marino, foca; — **power** potencia naval.

seaboard [sibord] *s.* costa, litoral; *adj.* costanero, litoral.

seacoast [sikost] *s.* costa, litoral.

seal [sil] *s.* (*stamp*) sello; timbre; (*animal*) foca, león marino; **to set one's** — **to** sellar; aprobar; *v.* sellar; estampar; cerrar; tapar; **to** — **in** encerrar, cerrar herméticamente; **to** — **with sealing wax** lacrar.

sealing wax [silɪŋ wæks] *s.* lacre.

seam [sim] *s.* costura; juntura; cicatriz; filón, veta; *v.* echar una costura, coser.

seaman [símən] *s.* marino, marinero.

seamstress [símstris] *s.* costurera.

seaplane [siplen] *s.* hidroavión.

seaport [síport] *s.* puerto de mar.

sear [sɪr] *v.* chamuscar(se), tostar(se); resecar(se); herrar, marcar con hierro candente; *adj.* reseco, marchito.

search [sɝtʃ] *v.* buscar; escudriñar; registrar; examinar; **to** — **a prisoner** registrar a un prisionero; **to** — **for something** buscar algo; **to** — **into** investigar, indagar; *s.* busca, búsqueda; registro, inspección; investigación, pesquisa, indagación; — **warrant** mandato judicial de practicar un registro; **in** — **of** en busca de.

searchlight [sɝtʃlaɪt] *s.* reflector.

seashore [síʃor] *s.* costa, playa, orilla o ribera del mar.

seasick [sísɪk] *adj.* mareado; **to get** — marearse.

seasickness [sísɪknɪs] *s.* mareo.

seaside [sísaɪd] *s.* costa, litoral; playa.

season [sízɳ] *s.* estación (*del año*); temporada, sazón, ocasión; tiempo; — **ticket** billete de abono; **Christmas** — navidades; **harvest** — siega, tiempo de la cosecha; **opera** — temporada de la ópera; **to arrive in good** — llegar en sazón, llegar a tiempo; *v.* sazonar; condimentar; aclimatar.

seasoning [síznɪŋ] *s.* condimento; salsa; desecación (*de la madera*).

seat [sit] *s.* (*furniture*) asiento; silla; (*site*) sitio; (*headquarters*) residencia; sede (*episcopal, del gobierno, etc.*); (*body*) nalgas; fondillos, parte trasera

(*de los pantalones o calzones*); — **of learning** centro de estudios, centro de erudición; *v.* sentar; asentar; dar asiento a; **to** — **oneself** sentarse; **it -s a thousand people** tiene cabida para mil personas.

seaweed [síwid] *s.* alga marina.

secede [sisid] *v.* separarse (*de una federación o unión*).

seclude [sɪklúd] *v.* recluir, apartar, aislar; **to** — **oneself from** recluirse de, apartarse de.

secluded [sɪklúdɪd] *adj.* apartado, aislado; solitario.

seclusion [sɪklúʒən] *s.* apartamiento, soledad, aislamiento; retiro.

second [sékənd] *adj.* segundo; inferior; — **hand** segundero (*de reloj*); — **lieutenant** subteniente; **second-rate** de segunda clase; mediocre, inferior; **on** — **thought** después de pensarlo bien; *s.* segundo; padrino (*en un desafío*); ayudante; mercancía de segunda calidad; mercancía defectuosa; *v.* secundar (*o segundar*), apoyar; apadrinar.

secondary [sékəndɛri] *adj.* secundario; — **education** segunda enseñanza; — **school** escuela secundaria, escuela de segunda enseñanza.

second-hand [sékəndhænd] *adj.* de segunda mano; usado; de ocasión; indirecto, por intermedio de otro.

secondly [sékəndli] *adv.* en segundo lugar.

secrecy [síkrəsi] secreto, sigilo, reserva.

secret [síkrɪt] *s.* secreto; *adj.* secreto; escondido, oculto; — **service** policía secreta; **-ly** *adv.* secrétamente, en secreto.

secretariat [sɛkrətǽriət] *s.* secretaría.

secretary [sékrətɛri] *s.* secretario; escritorio (*con estantes para libros*).

secrete [sɪkrít] *v.* secretar (*una secreción*); esconder, ocultar.

secretion [sɪkríʃən] *s.* secreción.

secretive [sɪkrítɪv] *adj.* reservado, callado; — **gland** glándula secretoria.

sect [sɛkt] *s.* secta.

section [sékʃən] *s.* sección; trozo; tajada; región; barrio; *v.* seccionar, dividir en secciones.

secular [sékjələ] *adj.* & *s.* secular.

secure [sɪkjúr] *adj.* seguro; firme; *v.* asegurar; afianzar; obtener; resguardar; **-ly** *adv.* seguramente, con seguridad; firmemente.

security [sɪkjúrəti] *s.* seguridad; fianza, garantía, prenda; resguardo, protección; **securities** bonos, obligaciones, acciones, valores.

sedan [sɪdǽn] *s.* sedán.

sedate [sɪdét] *adj.* sosegado; tranquilo, sereno; serio.

sedation [sədéʃən] *d.* sedación.

sedative [sédətɪv] *adj.* & *s.* calmante, sedativo.

sedentary [sédɳtɛri] *adj.* sedentario; inactivo.

sediment [sédəmənt] *s.* sedimento, heces, residuo.

sedition [sɪdíʃən] s. sedición.
seditious [sɪdíʃəs] adj. sedicioso.
seduce [sɪdjús] v. seducir.
seduction [sɪdʌ́kʃən] s. seducción.
see [si] v. ver; — **that you do it** no deje Vd. de hacerlo; tenga Vd. cuidado de hacerlo; **I'll — to it** me encargaré de ello; **let me —** a ver; **to — a person home** acompañar a una persona a casa; **to — a person off** ir a la estación para despedir a una persona; **to — a person through a difficulty** ayudar a una persona a salir de un apuro; **to — through a person** adivinar lo que piensa una persona, darse cuenta de sus intenciones; **to — to one's affairs** atender a sus asuntos; **to have seen military service** haber servido en el ejército; s. sede, silla; **Holy See** Santa Sede.
seed [sid] s. (grains) semilla; (semen) simiente; (fruit) pepita; **to go to —** producir semillas; decaer, declinar; descuidar de su persona, andar desaseado; v. sembrar; despepitar, quitar las pepitas o semillas de; producir semillas.
seedling [sídlɪŋ] s. planta de semillero; arbolillo (de menos de tres pies de altura).
seedy [sídɪ] adj. semilloso, lleno de semillas; raído; desaseado.
seek [sik] v. buscar; pedir, solicitar; **to — after** buscar; **to — to** tratar de, esforzarse por.
seem [sim] v. parecer; **it -s to me** me parece.
seemingly [símɪŋlɪ] adv. aparentemente, en apariencia, al parecer.
seemly [símlɪ] adj. propio, decente, decoroso.
seen [sin] p.p. de to see.
seep [sip] v. escurrirse, rezumarse, colarse, filtrarse.
seer [sɪr] s. vidente, adivino, profeta.
seethe [sið] v. bullir, hervir; burbujear.
segment [ségmənt] s. segmento.
segregate [ségrəget] v. segregar.
seize [siz] v. (grasp) asir, coger, agarrar; apoderarse de; (arrest) prender o aprehender; (take advantage of) aprovecharse de; (capture) embargar, secuestrar; **to — upon** asir; **to become -d with fear** sobrecogerse de miedo.
seizure [síʒɚ] s. cogida; captura; aprehensión (de un criminal); secuestro, embargo (de bienes); ataque (de una enfermedad).
seldom [séldəm] adv. rara vez, raras veces, raramente.
select [səlékt] adj. selecto, escogido; v. elegir, escoger; entresacar.
selection [səlékʃən] s. selección, elección.
self [sɛlf]: **by one—** por sí, por sí mismo; **for one—** para sí; **one's other —** su otro yo; **his wife and —** su esposa y él (véase herself, himself, ourselves, themselves, etc.); **self-centered** egoísta, egocéntrico;

self-conscious consciente de sí, cohibido, tímido; **self-control** dominio de sí mismo (o de sí propio); **self-defense** defensa propia; **self-denial** abnegación; **self-evident** patente, manifiesto; **self-esteem** respeto de sí mismo; amor propio; **self-government** gobierno autónomo, autonomía; gobierno democrático; **self-interest** propio interés; egoísmo; **self-love** amor propio; **self-possessed** sereno, dueño de sí, tranquilo; **self-sacrifice** abnegación; **self-satisfied** pagado de sí, satisfecho de sí.
selfish [sélfɪʃ] adj. egoísta; **-ly** adv. con egoísmo, por egoísmo.
selfishness [sélfɪʃnɪs] s. egoísmo.
selfsame [sélfsém] adj. mismo, idéntico, mismísimo.
sell [sɛl] v. vender; venderse, estar de venta; **to — at auction** vender en almoneda o subasta, subastar; **to — out** venderlo todo.
seller [sélɚ] s. vendedor.
selves [sɛlvz] pl. de self.
semblance [sémbləns] s. semejanza; apariencia.
semicircle [sémɚsɚkl] s. semicírculo.
semicolon [sémɪkolən] s. punto y coma.
seminary [sémɪnɛrɪ] s. seminario.
senate [sénɪt] s. senado.
senator [sénɪtɚ] s. senador.
send [sɛnd] v. enviar; mandar; despachar; remitir, expedir; lanzar (una flecha, pelota, etc.); **to — away** despedir, despachar; **to — forth** despachar, enviar; emitir; exhalar; echar; **to — someone up for 15 years** condenar a un reo a 15 años de prisión; **to — word** avisar, mandar decir, mandar recado.
sender [séndɚ] s. remitente; transmisor.
senile [sínaɪl] adj. senil, caduco; chocho.
senility [sənílɪtɪ] s. senectud; chochera o chochez.
senior [sínjɚ] adj. (older) mayor, de más edad; más antiguo; (superior) superior; **— class** clase del cuarto año; s. persona o socio más antiguo; estudiante del último año; **to be somebody's — by two years** ser dos años mayor que alguien.
sensation [sénséʃən] s. sensación.
sensational [sɛnséʃənl] adj. sensacional, emocionante.
sense [sɛns] s. (function) sentido; (sentiment) sentimiento; sensación; (judgment) juicio, sensatez; (meaning) significado; **common —** sentido común; **to make —** tener sentido; **to be out of one's -s** estar fuera de sí, estar loco; v. percibir, sentir; darse cuenta de.
senseless [sénslɪs] adj. sin sentido; insensato, absurdo; insensible, privado de sentido.
sensibility [sɛnsəbílətɪ] s. sensibilidad.
sensible [sénsəbl] adj. (aware) sensato,

SC

razonable, cuerdo; (*appreciable*) sensible, perceptible; **sensibly** *adv.* sensatamente, con sensatez, con sentido común; sensiblemente, perceptiblemente.

sensitive [sénsətɪv] *adj.* sensitivo; sensible; quisquilloso, susceptible.

sensitiveness [sénsətɪvnɪs] *s.* sensibilidad.

sensitize [sénsətaɪz] *v.* sensibilizar.

sensual [sénʃuəl] *adj.* sensual, carnal, lujurioso.

sensuality [sɛnʃuǽlətɪ] *s.* sensualidad; lujuria.

sent [sent] *pret. & p.p.* de **to send.**

sentence [séntəns] *s.* sentencia, fallo, decisión; oración (*gramatical*); **death — ** pena capital; *v.* sentenciar.

sentiment [séntəmənt] *s.* sentimiento, sentido.

sentimental [sentəméntl] *adj.* sentimental.

sentimentality [sentəmɛntǽlətɪ] *s.* sentimentalismo, sentimentalidad.

sentinel [séntənl] *s.* centinela.

sentry [séntrɪ] *s.* centinela.

separate [sépɪt] *adj.* (*apart*) separado; apartado; solitario; (*different*) distinto, diferente; **-ly** *adv.* separadamente, por separado; aparte; [sépəret] *v.* separar(se); apartar(se).

separation [sepəréʃən] *s.* separación.

September [septémbəˌ] *s.* septiembre.

sepulcher [sép|kəˌ] *s.* sepulcro, sepultura.

sequel [síkwəl] *s.* secuela; continuación, consecuencia; resultado.

sequence [síkwəns] *s.* (*continuity*) secuencia, sucesión; serie; continuación; (*result*) consecuencia, resultado; runfla (*serie de tres o más naipes de un mismo palo*).

serenade [sɛrənéd] *s.* serenata; *v.* dar serenata a.

serene [sərín] *adj.* sereno; tranquilo, claro, despejado.

serenity [sərénətɪ] *s.* serenidad; calma.

sergeant [sárdʒənt] *s.* sargento; **— at arms** oficial que guarda el orden (*en un cuerpo legislativo*).

serial [sírɪəl] *s.* cuento o novela por entregas; *adj.* consecutivo, en serie; **— novel** novela por entregas.

series [síriz] *s.* serie; series.

serious [sírɪəs] *adj.* serio; grave; **-ly** *adv.* seriamente, con seriedad, en serio; gravemente.

seriousness [sírɪəsnɪs] *s.* seriedad; gravedad.

sermon [sˊˊmən] *s.* sermón.

serpent [sˊˊpənt] *s.* serpiente; sierpe.

serum [sírəm] *s.* suero.

servant [sˊˊvənt] *s.* sirviente; criado; servidor; **— girl** criada, *Ríopl.* mucama; *Andes, Col., Ven.* muchacha de servicio.

serve [sˊˊv] *v.* (*wait on*) servir; (*supply*) surtir, abastecer; **to — a term in prison** cumplir una condena; **to — a warrant** entregar una citación; **to — as** servir de; **to — for** servir de,

servir para; **to — notice on** notificar, avisar, advertir; **to — one's purpose** servir para el caso o propósito; **it -s me right** bien me lo merezco; *s.* saque (*de la pelota en tenis*).

server [sˊˊvəˌ] *s.* servidor; saque (*el que saca la pelota en el juego de tenis*); bandeja; mesa de servicio.

service [sˊˊvɪs] *s.* servicio; saque (*de la pelota en tenis*); entrega (*de una citación judicial*); **at your —** a la disposición de Vd., servidor de Vd.; **funeral —** honras fúnebres, funerales, exequias; **mail —** servicio de correos; **table —** servicio de mesa, vajilla; **tea —** juego o servicio de té; **— entrance** entrada para el servicio; **— man** militar; **— station** estación de servicio; *v.* servir; reparar; surtir (*una tienda*).

serviceable [sˊˊvɪsəbl] *adj.* servible; útil; duradero.

servile [sˊˊvl] *adj.* servil.

servitude [sˊˊvətjud] *s.* servidumbre; esclavitud.

session [séʃən] *s.* sesión.

set [set] *v.* (*place*) poner; colocar, asentar; (*fix*) fijar; establecer; ajustar; engastar (*piedras preciosas*); solidificar(se), endurecer(se) (*el cemento, yeso, etc.*); ponerse (*el sol, la luna*); empollar; **to — a bone** componer un hueso dislocado; **to — a trap** armar una trampa; **to — about** ponerse a; **to — an example** dar ejemplo; **to — aside** poner a un lado, poner aparte; apartar; ahorrar; **to — back** retrasar, atrasar; **to — forth** exponer, expresar; manifestar; **to — forth on a journey** ponerse en camino; **to — off** disparar, hacer estallar (*unexplosivo*); hacer resaltar; salir; **to — on fire** pegar o poner fuego a, incendiar; **to — one's jaw** apretar las quijadas; **to — one's heart on** tener la esperanza puesta en; **to — one's mind on** resolverse a, aplicarse a; **to — out for** partir para, salir para; **to — out to** empezar a; **to — right** colocar bien; enderazar; rectificar; **to — sail** hacerse a la vela; **to — the brake** frenar, apretar el freno; **to — up** erigir, levantar; armar, montar (*una máquina*); parar (*tipo de imprenta*); establecer, poner (*una tienda, un negocio*); **to — upon someone** acometer, asaltar a alguien; *pret. & p.p.* de **to set;** *adj.* fijo; firme; sólido; resuelto; rígido; puesto; establecido; engastado; **— to go** listo para partir; *s.* juego, colección; serie; grupo, clase; partida (*de tenis*); **— of dishes** servicio de mesa, vajilla; **— of teeth** dentadura; **radio —** radio, radiorreceptor; **tea —** servicio para té.

setback [sétbæk] *s.* atraso, revés, retroceso inesperado.

settee [setí] *s.* canapé.

setting [sétɪŋ] *s.* engaste (*de una joya*); escena, escenario; puesta (*del sol, de un astro*); **— sun** sol poniente.

settle [sétl] v. (colonize) colonizar, poblar; establecer(se); fijar(se); asentar(se); (solve) arreglar, poner en orden, ajustar (cuentas); zanjar (una disputa); pagar, liquidar, saldar; **to — down** formalizarse; asentarse; calmarse; poner casa; **to — on a date** fijar o señalar una fecha; **to — property on (upon)** asignar bienes o propiedad a; **to — the matter** decidir el asunto, concluir con el asunto.

settlement [sétlmənt] s. (community) establecimiento; colonia; poblado; población; colonización; (arrangement) asignación o traspaso (de propiedad); ajuste, arreglo; pago; saldo, finiquito, liquidación; — **house** casa de beneficencia; **marriage** — dote.

settler [sétlɚ] s. colono, poblador; — **of disputes** zanjador de disputas.

setup [sétəp] s. arreglo; organización.

sever [sévɚ] v. desunir(se), partir(se), dividir(se), separar(se); cortar, romper.

several [sévrəl] adj. varios, diversos; distintos, diferentes.

severe [səvír] adj. severo; áspero; austero; rígido; riguroso; grave; recio, fuerte.

severity [səvɛ́rətɪ] s. severidad; austeridad; rigidez; gravedad; rigor.

sew [so] v. coser.

sewer [sjúɚ] s. albañal, cloaca.

sewing [sóɪŋ] s. costura; modo de coser; — **machine** máquina de coser; — **room** cuarto de costura.

sewn [son] p.p. de **to sew**.

sex [sɛks] s. sexo; — **appeal** atracción sexual.

sextant [sɛ́kstənt] s. sextante.

sexton [sɛ́kstən] s. sacristán.

sexual [sɛ́kʃʋəl] adj. sexual.

shabby [ʃǽbɪ] adj. raído, gastado; andrajoso; mal vestido; vil, injusto; **to treat someone shabbily** tratar a alguien injustamente o con menosprecio.

shack [ʃæk] s. cabaña, choza, Am. bohío, Am. jacal.

shackle [ʃǽkl] v. encadenar; trabar, echar trabas a, poner grillos a; estorbar; **-s** s. pl. cadenas, trabas, grillos, esposas; estorbo.

shade [ʃed] s. (shadow) sombra; (nuance) tinte, matiz; (cover) visillo, cortinilla; pantalla (de lámpara); visera (para los ojos); **a — longer** un poco más largo; **— of meaning** matiz; **in the —** a la sombra de; v. sombrear; dar sombra; resguardar de la luz; matizar.

shadow [ʃǽdo] s. (darkness) sombra; oscuridad; (phantom) espectro; **under the — of** al abrigo de, a la sombra de; **without a — of doubt** sin sombra de duda; v. sombrear; obscurecer; **to — someone** espiarle a alguien los pasos, seguirle por todas partes.

shadowy [ʃǽdəwɪ] adj. lleno de sombras; tenebroso; vago, indistinto.

shady [ʃédɪ] adj. sombrío, sombreado, umbrío; — **business** negocio oscuro, negocio sospechoso; — **character** persona de carácter dudoso, persona de mala fama.

shaft [ʃæft] s. pozo o tiro (de mina, de elevador); cañón de chimenea; columna; eje, árbol (de maquinaria); flecha.

shaggy [ʃǽgɪ] adj. peludo, velludo; lanudo; desaseado; áspero.

shake [ʃek] v. menear(se); estremecer(se); temblar; sacudir(se); agitar(se); titubear, vacilar; hacer vacilar; dar, estrechar (la mano); **to — hands** dar un apretón de manos, darse la mano; **to — one's head** mover o menear la cabeza; cabecear; **to — with cold** tiritar de frío, estremecerse de frío; **to — with fear** temblar de miedo, estremecerse de miedo; s. sacudida; sacudimiento; estremecimiento, temblor; apretón (de manos); **hand** — apretón de manos.

shaken [ʃékən] p.p. de **to shake**.

shake-up [ʃékəp] s. reorganización.

shaky [ʃékɪ] adj. tembloroso; vacilante.

shall [ʃæl] v. aux. del futuro del indicativo en las primeras personas (**I, we**); en las demás expresa mayor énfasis, mandato u obligación; **he — not do it** no lo hará, no ha de hacerlo; **thou shalt not steal** no hurtarás.

shallow [ʃǽlo] adj. bajo, poco profundo; superficial; ligero de cascos.

shallowness [ʃǽlonɪs] s. poca hondura, poca profundidad; superficialidad; ligereza de juicio.

sham [ʃæm] s. fingimiento, falsedad, farsa; adj. fingido, simulado; falso; — **battle** simulacro, batalla fingida; v. fingir, simular.

shambles [ʃǽmblz] s. desorden.

shame [ʃem] s. vergüenza; deshonra; — **on you!** ¡qué vergüenza!; **it is a —** es una vergüenza; es una lástima; **to bring — upon** deshonrar; v. avergonzar; deshonrar.

shameful [ʃémfəl] adj. vergonzoso.

shameless [ʃémlɪs] adj. desvergonzado, descarado.

shamelessness [ʃémlɪsnɪs] s. desvergüenza; descaro, desfachatez.

shampoo [ʃæmpú] s. champú, lavado de la cabeza; v. dar un champú, lavar (la cabeza).

shamrock [ʃǽmrɑk] s. trébol.

shank [ʃæŋk] s. canilla (parte inferior de la pierna); zanca.

shanty [ʃǽntɪ] s. choza, cabaña, casucha.

shape [ʃep] s. (form) forma; (figure) figura; (condition) estado, condición; **to be in a bad —** estar mal; **to put into —** arreglar, poner en orden, ordenar; v. formar, dar forma a; tomar forma; **to — one's life** dar forma a, ajustar o disponer su vida; **his plan is shaping well** va desarrollándose bien su plan.

shapeless [ʃéplɪs] adj. informe, sin forma.

share [ʃɛr] s. (portion) porción, parte;

SE

(*participation*) participación; acción (*participación en el capital de una compañía*); *v.* compartir; repartir; participar; **to — in** participar en, tener parte en; **to — a thing with** compartir una cosa con.

shareholder [ʃérhouldɚ] *s.* accionista.

shark [ʃɑrk] *s.* (*fish*) tiburón; (*usurer*) estafador; (*expert*) perito, experto; **loan —** usurero; **to be a —** at ser un águila (o ser muy listo) para.

sharp [ʃɑrp] *adj.* (*acute*) agudo, puntiagudo; cortante; punzante; (*biting*) mordaz; picante; (*bright*) astuto; (*clear*) claro, distinto, bien marcado; (*sudden*) repentino; **— curve** curva abrupta, curva pronunciada o muy cerrada; **— ear** oidofino; **— features** facciones bien marcadas; **— struggle** lucha violenta; **— taste** sabor acre; **— temper** genio áspero; **— turn** vuelta repentina; *s.* sostenido (*en música*); **card—** tahur, fullero; *adv.* *véase* **sharply**; **at ten o'clock —** a las diez en punto.

sharpen [ʃárpən] *v.* afilar(se); sacar punta a; aguzar(se); amolar.

sharply [ʃárplɪ] *adv.* agudamente; mordazmente, ásperamente; repentinamente; claramente; **to arrive —** llegar en punto.

sharpness [ʃárpnɪs] *s.* agudeza; sutileza; mordacidad; rigor; aspereza; acidez.

shatter [ʃǽtɚ] *v.* estrellar(se), astillar(se), hacer(se) añicos; quebrar(se), romper(se); **to — one's hopes** frustrar sus esperanzas; **his health was -ed** se le quebrantó la salud; **-s** *s. pl.* pedazos, trozos, añicos, fragmentos; **to break into —** hacer(se) añicos.

shave [ʃev] *v.* afeitar(se), rasurar(se); rapar(se); acepillar (*madera*); *s.* rasura, *Am.* afeitada; **he had a close —** por poco no se escapa; se salvó por milagro.

shaven [ʃévən] *p.p. de* **to shave; cleanshaven** bien afeitado.

shaving [ʃévɪŋ] *s.* rasura, *Am.* afeitada; **wood -s** virutas; **— brush** brocha de afeitar; **— soap** jabón de afeitar.

shawl [ʃɔl] *s.* mantón, chal.

she [ʃi] *pron. pers.* ella; **— who** la que; *s.* hembra; **she-bear** osa; **she-goat** cabra.

sheaf [ʃif] *s.* haz, gavilla, manojo; lío; *v.* hacer gavillas.

shear [ʃɪr] *v.* trasquilar, esquilar (*las ovejas*); cortar (*con tijeras grandes*).

shears [ʃɪrz] *s. pl.* tijeras grandes.

sheath [ʃiθ] *s.* vaina; funda, envoltura.

sheathe [ʃið] *v.* envainar.

sheaves [ʃivz] *pl. de* **sheaf.**

shed [ʃɛd] *s.* cobertizo; tejadillo; *Ríopl.*, *Andes* galpón (*de una estancia*); *v.* derramar; difundir; esparcir; mudar (*de piel plumas, etc.*); ser impermeable (*un paño, abrigo, sombrero, etc.*); **to — leaves** deshojarse; *pret. & p.p. de* **to shed.**

sheen [ʃin] *s.* lustre, viso.

sheep [ʃip] *s.* oveja; carnero; ovejas; **— dog** perro de pastor; **—fold** redil; **—skin** zalea; badana; pergamino; diploma (*de pergamino*).

sheepish [ʃípɪʃ] *adj.* vergonzoso, encogido, tímido.

sheer [ʃɪr] *adj.* (*pure*) puro; completo; (*thin*) fino, delgado, transparente, diáfano; (*steep*) escarpado; **by — force** a pura fuerza.

sheet [ʃit] *s.* (*bed*) sábana; (*paper*) hoja, pliego (*de papel*); lámina (*de metal*); extensión (*de agua, hielo*); **— lightning** relampagueo.

shelf [ʃɛlf] *s.* estante, anaquel; repisa; saliente de roca.

shell [ʃɛl] *s.* concha; cáscara (*de huevo, nuez, etc.*); vaina (*de guisantes, frijoles, garbanzos, etc.*); casco (*de una embarcación*); armazón (*de un edificio*); granada, bomba; cápsula (*para cartuchos*); *v.* cascar (*nueces*); desvainar, quitar la vaina a, pelar; desgranar (*maíz, trigo, etc.*); bombardear.

shellac [ʃəlǽk] *s.* laca; *v.* barnizar con laca.

shellfish [ʃɛlfɪʃ] *s.* marisco; mariscos.

shelter [ʃɛltɚ] *s.* abrigo, refugio, asilo; resguardo, protección; **to take —** refugiarse, abrigarse; *v.* abrigar, refugiar, guarecer; proteger, amparar.

shelve [ʃɛlv] *v.* poner o guardar en un estante; poner a un lado, arrinconar, arrumbar.

shelves [ʃɛlvz] *s. pl.* estantes, anaqueles; estantería.

shepherd [ʃépɚd] *s.* pastor; zagal; **— dog** perro de pastor.

sherbet [ʃɜ́bɪt] *s.* sorbete.

sheriff [ʃɛrɪf] *s.* alguacil mayor (*de un condado en los Estados Unidos*).

sherry [ʃɛrɪ] *s.* jerez, vino de Jerez.

shield [ʃild] *s.* escudo, rodela, broquel; resguardo, defensa; *v.* escudar, resguardar, proteger.

shift [ʃɪft] *v.* (*change*) cambiar; mudar(se); alternar(se); variar; desviar(se); (*transfer*) trasladar, transferir; **to — for oneself** valerse o mirar por sí mismo; **to — gears** cambiar de marcha; **to — the blame** echar a otro su propia culpa; *s.* cambio; desvío, desviación; tanda, grupo de obreros; turno; **gear—** cambio de marcha.

shiftless [ʃíftlɪs] *adj.* negligente; holgazán.

shilling [ʃílɪŋ] *s.* chelín.

shimmy [ʃími] *s.* (*dance*) shimmy; (*vibration*) abaniqueo.

shin [ʃɪn] *s.* espinilla (*de la pierna*); *v.* **to — up** trepar.

shine [ʃaɪn] *v.* (*beam*) brillar, resplandecer, lucir; (*polish*) pulir; dar brillo, lustre o bola, embolar (zapatos); *s.* brillo, lustre, resplandor; **rain or —** llueva o truene; **to give a shoe —** dar bola (brillo o lustre) a los zapatos; embolar o embetunar los zapatos; limpiar el calzado.

shingle [ʃíŋgl] *s.* ripia, tabla delgada; *Méx.* tejamanil o tejamaní; pelo corto escalonado; letrero de oficina; **-s** zona (*erupcion de la piel*); *v.* cubrir con tejamaniles; techar con tejamaniles.

shining [ʃáɪnɪŋ] *adj.* brillante; resplandeciente.

shiny [ʃáɪnɪ] *adj.* brillante; lustroso.

ship [ʃɪp] *s.* (*naval*) buque, barco, navío, nave; (*air*) aeronave, avión; **—builder** ingeniero naval, constructor de buques; **—mate** camarada de a bordo **—yard** astillero; **on —board** a bordo; *v.* embarcar(se); despachar, enviar; remesar; transportar; alistarse como marino.

shipment [ʃípmənt] *s.* embarque; cargamento; despacho, envío; remesa.

shipper [ʃípɚ] *s.* embarcador; remitente.

shipping [ʃípɪŋ] *s.* embarque; despacho, envio; **— charges** gastos de embarque; **— clerk** dependiente de muelle; dependiente encargado de embarques.

shipwreck [ʃíprɛk] *s.* naufragio; *v.* echar a pique, hacer naufragar; naufragar, irse a pique.

shipyard [ʃípyard] *s.* astillero.

shirk [ʃɝk] *v.* evadir, evitar.

shirt [ʃɝt] *s.* camisa; **—waist** blusa; **in — sleeves** en camisa, en mangas de camisa.

shiver [ʃívɚ] *v.* tiritar; temblar; estremecerse; *s.* escalofrío, temblor, estremecimiento.

shoal [ʃol] *s.* bajío, banco de arena; banco (*de peces*).

shock [ʃak] *s.* (*blow*) choque; sacudida; sacudimiento; golpe; (*surprise*) sobresalto; **— absorber** amortiguador; **— of grain** hacina o gavilla de mieses; **— of hair** guedeja, greña; **— troops** tropas de asalto; *v.* chocar, ofender; escandalizar; causar fuerte impresión; horrorizar; sacudir; conmover; hacinar, hacer gavillas de (*mieses*).

shocking [ʃákɪŋ] *adj.* chocante, ofensivo, repugnante; espantoso, escandaloso.

shod [ʃad] *pret. & p.p. de* **to shoe**.

shoe [ʃu] *s.* zapato; botín; **brake —** zapata de freno; **horse—** herradura; **— blacking** betún, bola; **— polish** brillo, lustre, bola; **— store** zapatería; *v.* calzar; herrar (*un caballo*).

shoeblack [ʃúblæk] *s.* limpiabotas.

shoehorn [ʃúhɔrn] *s.* calzador.

shoelace [ʃúles] *s.* lazo, cinta, cordón de zapato.

shoemaker [ʃúmekɚ] *s.* zapatero.

shoestring [ʃústrɪŋ] *s.* lazo, cinta, cordón de zapato.

shone [ʃon] *pret. & p.p. de* **to shine**.

shook [ʃuk] *pret. de* **to shake**.

shoot [ʃut] *v.* (*firearm*) tirar, disparar, descargar; hacer fuego; fusilar; dar un balazo; (*throw*) lanzar, disparar (*una instantánea*); fotografiar, filmar (*una escena*); echar (*los dados*); brotar (*las plantas*); **to — by** pasar rápidamente; **to — forth** brotar, salir; germinar; lanzarse; **to — it out with someone** pelearse a balazos; **to — up**

a place entrarse a balazos por un lugar; *s.* vástago, retoño, renuevo; **to go out for a —** salir a tirar; ir de caza.

shooter [ʃútɚ] *s.* tirador.

shooting [ʃútɪŋ] *s.* tiroteo; **— match** certamen de tiradores (*o de tiro al blanco*); **— pain** punzada, dolor agudo; **— star** estrella fugaz.

shop [ʃap] *s.* tienda; taller; **— window** escaparate, vitrina, aparador, *Riopl.*, *Andes* vidriera; **barber—** barbería; **beauty —** salón de belleza; **to talk —** hablar uno de su oficio o profesión; *v.* ir de tiendas; ir de compras, comprar.

shopkeeper [ʃápkipɚ] *s.* tendero.

shopper [ʃápɚ] *s.* comprador.

shopping [ʃápɪŋ] *s.* compra, compras; **to go —** ir de compras, ir de tiendas.

shore [ʃor] *s.* costa, playa, orilla, ribera; puntal; **ten miles off —** a diez millas de la costa; *v.* **to — up** apuntalar, poner puntales.

shorn [ʃorn] *p.p. de* **to shear**.

short [ʃort] *adj.* (*duration*) corto; breve; (*height*) bajo; *Méx.* chaparro; escaso; brusco; **— cut** atajo; **— circuit** cortocircuito; **— wave** onda corta; método corto; **short-legged** de piernas cortas; **— loan** préstamo a corto plazo; **for —** para abreviar; **in —** en resumen, en suma, en conclusión; **in — order** rápidamente, prontamente; **in a — time** en poco tiempo; al poco tiempo; **to be —** of estar falto o escaso de; **to cut —** acortar, abreviar, terminar de repente; **to run — of something** acabársele (írsele acabando) a uno algo; **to stop —** parar de repente, parar en seco.

shortage [ʃórtɪdʒ] *s.* escasez, carestía; déficit; falta.

shortcoming [ʃórtkʌmɪŋ] *s.* falta, defecto.

shorten [ʃórtn̩] *v.* acortar(se), abreviar(se), disminuir(se).

shortening [ʃórtnɪŋ] *s.* manteca, grasa (*para hacer pasteles*); acortamiento; abreviación.

shorthand [ʃórthænd] *s.* taquigrafía.

shortly [ʃórtlɪ] *adj.* brevemente; en breve; al instante, pronto, luego; bruscamente, secamente.

shortness [ʃórtnɪs] *s.* cortedad; brevedad; pequeñez; escasez, deficiencia.

shorts [ʃorts] *s. pl.* calzoncillos, calzones cortos.

shortsighted [ʃórtsáɪtɪd] *adj.* miope; corto de vista.

shot [ʃat] *pret. & p.p. de* **to shoot**; *s.* (*discharge*) tiro; disparo; balazo; cañonazo; (*pellet*) bala; balas; (*injection*) inyección; (*throw*) tirada; **— of liquor** trago de aguardiente; **buck—** municiones, postas; **not by a long —** ni con mucho, ni por pienso, nada de eso; **he is a good —** es buen tirador, tiene buen tino; **to take a — at** disparar un tiro a; hacer una tentativa de; **within rifle —** a tiro de rifle.

shotgun [ʃátgʌn] *s.* escopeta.

should [ʃud] *v. aux. del condicional en las primeras personas* (I, we): **I said that I — go** dije que iría; *equivale al imperfecto de subjuntivo*; **if it — rain** si lloviera; *se usa con la significación de deber*: **you — not do it** no debiera (*o no debería*) hacerlo.

shoulder [ʃóldə] *s.* (*person*) hombro; (*animal*) lomo, pernil (*de puerco, cordero*); borde, saliente (*de un camino*); **-s** espalda, espaldas; **— blade** espaldilla, paletilla; **straight from the —** con toda franqueza; **to turn a cold — to** volver las espaldas a, tratar fríamente; **to —** *v.* cargar al hombro, echarse sobre las espaldas; cargar con, asumir; empujar con el hombro.

shout [ʃaut] *v.* gritar; vocear; *s.* grito.

shove [ʃʌv] *v.* empujar, dar empellones; **to — aside** echar a un lado, rechazar; **to — off** partir, zarpar (*un buque*); salir, irse; *s.* empujón, empellón; empuje.

shovel [ʃʌvl] *s.* pala; *v.* traspalar.

show [ʃo] *v.* (*exhibit*) mostrar, enseñar; exhibir; (*prove*) probar, demostrar; indicar; (*appear*) verse; asomarse; **— him in** que pase, hágale entrar; **to — off** alardear, hacer ostentación de; lucirse; **to — up** aparecer, presentarse; **to — someone up** hacer subir a alguien; mostrarle el camino (*para subir*); desenmascarar a alguien, poner a alguien en la evidencia; *s.* exhibición; demostración; ostentación; espectáculo; representación; función; apariencia; **— window** escaparate, vitrina, aparador, *Am.* vidriera; **to go to the —** ir al teatro, ir al cine; **to make a — of oneself** exhibirse, hacer ostentación.

showcase [ʃókes] *s.* vitrina, aparador.

showdown [ʃódaun] *s.* arreglo terminante.

shower [ʃáuə] *s.* aguacero, chubasco, chaparrón, lluvia; ducha, baño de ducha; *Méx.* regadera; **bridal —** tertulia para obsequiar a una novia; *v.* llover; caer un aguacero.

shown [ʃon] *p.p. de* **to show**.

showy [ʃói] *adj.* ostentoso; vistoso, chillón.

shrank [ʃræŋk] *pret. de* **to shrink**.

shred [ʃred] *s.* tira, triza; andrajo; fragmento; pizca; **to be in -s** estar raído; estar andrajoso; estar hecho trizas; **to tear to -s** hacer trizas; *v.* desmenuzar; hacer trizas, hacer tiras; *pret. & p.p. de* **to shred**.

shrew [ʃru] *s.* arpía, mujer brava, mujer de mal genio.

shrewd [ʃrud] *adj.* astuto, sagaz, agudo.

shriek [ʃrik] *v.* chillar, gritar; *s.* chillido, grito.

shrill [ʃrɪl] *adj.* agudo, penetrante, chillón; *v.* chillar.

shrimp [ʃrɪmp] *s.* camarón; hombrecillo insignificante.

shrine [ʃrain] *s.* santuario; altar; lugar venerado.

shrink [ʃrɪŋk] *v.* encoger(se); contraer-

(se); disminuir; **to — back** retroceder; **to — from** retroceder ante, apartarse de; huir de, rehuir.

shrinkage [ʃrɪ́nkɪdʒ] *s.* encogimiento; contracción; merma.

shrivel [ʃrɪ́vl] *v.* encoger(se); fruncir(se), marchitar(se); disminuir(se).

shroud [ʃraud] *s.* mortaja; *v.* amortajar; cubrir, ocultar.

shrub [ʃrʌb] *s.* arbusto.

shrubbery [ʃrʌ́bərɪ] *s.* arbustos.

shrug [ʃrʌg] *v.* encogerse de hombros; *s.* encogimiento de hombros.

shrunk [ʃrʌŋk] *pret. & p.p. de* **shrink**.

shrunken [ʃrʌ́ŋkən] *p.p. de* **to shrink**.

shuck [ʃʌk] *s.* hollejo; cáscara.

shudder [ʃʌ́də] *v.* temblar, estremecerse; *s.* temblor, estremecimiento.

shuffle [ʃʌ́fl] *v.* barajar; revolver, mezclar; arrastrar (*los pies*); **to — along** ir arrastrando los pies; *s.* mezcla, confusión; evasiva; **— of feet** arrastramiento de pies; **it is your —** a Vd. le toca barajar.

shun [ʃʌn] *v.* esquivar, evadir, rehuir, evitar.

shut [ʃʌt] *v.* cerrar(se); **to — down** parar el trabajo; cerrar (*una fábrica*); **to — in** encerrar; **to — off** cortar (*el gas, la electricidad, el agua, etc.*); **to — off from** incomunicar, aislar de, cortar la comunicación con; excluir; **to — out** impedir la entrada de; cerrar la puerta a; **to — up** cerrar bien; tapar; encerrar; tapar la boca, hacer callar; callarse; *pret. & p.p. de* **to shut**; *adj.* cerrado.

shutter [ʃʌ́tə] *s.* contraventana; postigo (*de ventana*); cerrador; obturador (*de una cámara fotográfica*).

shuttle [ʃʌ́tl] *s.* lanzadera; *v.* ir y venir acompasadamente (*como una lanzadera*).

shy [ʃai] *adj.* tímido, apocado, vergonzoso; asustadizo; esquivo; **to be — on** estar escaso de; **to be — two cents** faltarle a uno dos centavos; *v.* esquivarse, hacerse a un lado; asustarse; **to — at something** retroceder ante algo; respingar (*un caballo*) al ver algo; espantarse con algo; **to — away** esquivarse de repente; respingar (*un caballo*); desviarse, apartarse.

shyness [ʃáinɪs] *s.* apocamiento, timidez, vergüenza.

shyster [ʃáistə] *s.* leguleyo, abogadillo tramposo, picapleitos.

sibilant [síbələnt] *s.* sibilante.

sick [sɪk] *adj.* enfermo, malo; nauseado; angustiado; **— leave** licencia por enfermedad; **to be — for** languidecer por, suspirar por; **to be — of** estar cansado de; estar harto de; **to be — to** (*o at*) **one's stomach** tener náuseas; **to make —** enfermar; dar pena, dar lástima; *s.* **the —** los enfermos; *v.* incitar, azuzar (*a un perro*) **— him** ¡síguele!

sicken [síkən] *v.* enfermar(se), poner(se) enfermo; dar asco; tener asco; sentir náuseas.

sickening [síknɪŋ] *adj.* nauseabundo, repugnante; lastimoso.

sickle [síkl] *s.* hoz.

sickly [síklɪ] *adj.* enfermizo; achacoso, enclenque; malsano.

sickness [síknɪs] *s.* enfermedad; malestar; náusea.

side [saɪd] *s.* (*surface*) lado; cara; costado; ladera; falda (*de una colina*); (*faction*) partido, facción; **— by** — lado a lado; **by his** — a su lado; **by the** — al lado de; **on all -s** por todos lados; **to take -s with** ser partidario de, ponerse al lado de; *adj.* lateral; de lado; oblicuo; incidental; secundario, de menos importancia; **— glance** mirada de soslayo, de través o de reojo; **— issue** cuestión secundaria; **— light** luz lateral; noticia, detalle o ilustración incidental; *v.* **to — with** estar por, ser partidario de, apoyar o, opinar con.

sideboard [sáidbord] *s.* aparador.

sideslip [sáidslɪp] *s.* deslizamiento.

sidetrack [sáidtræk] *v.* desviar; echar a un lado.

sidewalk [sáidwɔk] *s.* acera, *Méx.* banqueta, *Riopl., Ch., Andes* vereda; *C.A., Col.,* andén.

sideways [sáidwez] *adv.* de lado, de costado; oblicuamente; hacia un lado; *adj.* lateral, de lado, oblicuo.

siege [sidʒ] *s.* cerco, sitio, asedio; **to lay — to** sitiar, cercar.

sieve [sɪv] *s.* tamiz, cedazo; criba; *v. véase* **sift.**

sift [sɪft] *v.* cerner, tamizar; cribar.

sigh [saɪ] *v.* suspirar; *s.* suspiro.

sight [saɪt] *s.* (*sense*) vista; (*view*) visión; espectáculo, escena; (*gun*) mira (*de un arma de fuego*); **in — of** a vista de; **payable at —** pagadero a la vista; **he is a —** es un adefesio o mamarracho; **this room is a —** este cuarto es un horror; **to catch — of** vislumbrar, avistar; **to know by —** conocer de vista; **to lose —** of perder de vista; **to see the -s** ver de visitar los puntos de interés; *v.* avistar; ver.

sightseeing [sáitsiɪŋ] *s.* turismo; **— tour** paseo en auto para ver puntos de interés.

sign [saɪn] *s.* (*signal*) signo; seña, señal; (*indication*) muestra; (*placard*) letrero; **—board** cartel; tablero (*para fijar anuncios*); *v.* firmar; contratar, hacer firmar; **to — over property** ceder una propiedad mediante escritura, hacer cesión legal de propiedad; **to — up for a job** firmar el contrato para un empleo; contratar para un empleo.

signal [sígnl] *s.* señal, seña; *v.* señalar, indicar, hacer seña, dar la señal; *adj.* señalado, notable; extraordinario; **— beacon** faro; **— code** código de señales.

signature [sígnətʃə] *s.* firma.

signer [sáinə] *s.* firmante.

significance [sɪgnífəkəns] *s.* significa-ción; significado.

significant [sɪgnífəkənt] *adj.* significativo.

signify [sígnəfaɪ] *v.* significar.

silence [sáiləns] *s.* silencio; *v.* acallar; apagar (*un sonido*); aquietar, sosegar.

silent [sáilənt] *adj.* silencioso; callado; tácito; **— partner** socio comanditario (*que no tiene voz ni voto*).

silhouette [sɪluét] *s.* silueta; *v.* perfilar; **to be -d against** perfilarse contra.

silk [sɪlk] *s.* seda; *adj.* de seda; **— industry** industria sedera; **— ribbon** cinta de seda.

silken [sílkən] *adj.* sedoso; de seda.

silkworm [sílkwɜrm] *s.* gusano de seda.

silky [sílkɪ] *adj.* sedoso, sedeño; de seda.

sill [sɪl] *s.* umbral; **window —** antepecho de ventana.

silly [sílɪ] *adj.* necio, tonto, bobo, simple; absurdo, insensato.

silt [sɪlt] *s.* cieno.

silver [sílvə] *s.* (*metal*) plata; (*tableware*) cubierto; (*dishes*) vajilla de plata; (*color*) color de plata; *adj.* de plata; plateado; argentino; **— wedding** bodas de plata; *v.* platear; argentar; **to — a mirror** azogar un espejo.

silversmith [sílvəsmɪθ] *s.* platero.

silverware [sílvəwer] *s.* vajilla de plata, vajilla plateada; cuchillos, cucharas y tenedores (*por lo general de plata o plateados*).

silvery [sílvərɪ] *adj.* plateado; argentino.

similar [símələ] *adj.* semejante; **-ly** *adv.* semejantemente; de la misma manera.

similarity [sɪmələærətɪ] *s.* semejanza, parecido.

simile [síməlɪ] *s.* símil.

simmer [símə] *v.* hervir a fuego lento.

simple [símpl] *adj.* simple; sencillo; llano; tonto, mentecato; **simpleminded** ingenuo, simple, simplón; *s.* simple.

simpleton [símpltən] *s.* simplón, papanatas, papamoscas.

simplicity [sɪmplísətɪ] *s.* sencillez; simplicidad; simpleza; ingenuidad.

simplify [símpləfaɪ] *v.* simplificar.

simply [símplɪ] *adv.* simplemente; sencillamente; solamente.

simulate [símjəlet] *v.* simular.

simultaneous [saɪmté̃niəs] *adj.* simultáneo.

sin [sɪn] *s.* pecado, culpa; *v.* pecar.

since [sɪns] *conj.* desde que; después (de) que; puesto que, como, visto que; dado que; *prep.* desde, después de; *adv.* desde entonces; **ever —** desde entonces; **he died long —** murió hace mucho tiempo; **we have been here — five** estamos aquí desde las cinco.

sincere [sɪnsír] *adj.* sincero.

sincerity [sɪnsérətɪ] *s.* sinceridad.

sinecure [sínɪkjur] *s.* sinecura (*trabajo fácil y bien pagado*).

sinew [sínju] *s.* tendón; fibra, vigor.

sinewy [sínjəwɪ] *adj.* nervudo, nervioso o nervoso; fuerte, vigoroso.

sinful [sínfəl] *adj.* pecaminoso; pecador.

sing [sɪŋ] *v.* cantar; **to — out of tune** desentonar(se), desafinar; **to — to sleep** arrullar.

singe [sɪndʒ] *v.* chamuscar; *s.* chamusquina, *Am.* chamuscada, *Am.* chamuscadura.

singer [síŋə] *s.* cantor; cantora, cantatriz.

single [síŋgl] *adj.* (*unique*) solo; (*distinct*) individual; particular; (*unmarried*) soltero; **— entry bookkeeping** teneduría por partida simple; **— room** cuarto para uno; **— woman** mujer soltera; **not a — word** ni una sola palabra; *s.* billete de un dólar; *v.* **to — out** singularizar, distinguir, escoger; entresacar.

singlehanded [síŋglhǽndɪd] *adj.* solo, sin ayuda.

singsong [síŋsɔŋ] *s.* sonsonete, cadencia monótona.

singular [síŋgjələ] *adj.* singular; raro, extraordinario; *s.* singular, número singular.

sinister [sínɪstə] *adj.* siniestro, aciago, funesto.

sink [sɪŋk] *v.* hundir(se); sumir(se), sumergir(se); echar a pique; irse a pique, naufragar; cavar (*un pozo*); enterrar, clavar (*un puntal o poste*); **to — into one's mind** grabarse en la memoria; **to — one's teeth into** clavar el diente en; **to — to sleep** caer en el sueño; *s.* sumidero, fregadero.

sinner [sínə] *s.* pecador.

sinuous [sínjuəs] *adj.* sinuoso, tortuoso; con vueltas y rodeos.

sinus [sátnəs] *s.* seno, cavidad (*en un hueso*); **frontal —** seno frontal.

sip [sɪp] *v.* sorber; chupar; *s.* sorbo.

siphon [sáɪfən] *s.* sifón; *v.* sacar (*agua*) con sifón.

sir [sɜ] *s.* señor.

siren [sáɪrən] *s.* sirena.

sirloin [sɜ́lɔɪn] *s.* solomillo, solomo.

sirup [sírəp] *s.* jarabe.

sissy [sísɪ] *adj.* & *s.* afeminado, maricón.

sister [sístə] *s.* hermana; **Sister Mary** Sor María.

sister-in-law [sístərɪnlɔ] *s.* cuñada, hermana política.

sit [sɪt] *v.* sentar(se); colocar, asentar; posarse (*un pájaro*); estar sentado; estar situado; empollar (*las gallinas*); apoyarse; reunirse, celebrar sesión (*un cuerpo legislativo, un tribunal*); sentar, venir o caer (*bien o mal un traje*); **to — down** sentarse; **to — out a dance** quedarse sentado durante una pieza de baile; **to — still** estarse quieto; **to — tight** mantenerse firme en su puesto; **to — up** incorporarse; **to — up all night** velar toda la noche; **to — up and take notice** despabilarse.

site [saɪt] *s.* sitio, local, situación.

sitting [sítɪŋ] *s.* sesión (*de un cuerpo legislativo, tribunal, etc.*); sentada; **at one —** de una sentada; *adj.* sentado; **— hen** gallina ponedora; **— room** sala (de descanso); sala de espera; antesala.

situated [sítʃʊetɪd] *adj.* situado, sito, ubicado, colocado.

situation [sɪtʃuéʃən] *s.* (*location*) situación, colocación; (*employment*) empleo; posición; (*status*) situación.

size [saɪz] *s.* tamaño; medida; *v.* clasificar según el tamaño; **to — up** tantear, formarse una idea de, juzgar.

sizzle [sízl] *v.* chirriar (*aplícase al sonido que hace la carne al freírse*); *s.* chirrido (*de la carne al freírse*).

skate [sket] *s.* patín; **ice —** patín de hielo, patín de cuchilla; **roller —** patín de ruedas; *v.* patinar.

skein [sken] *s.* madeja.

skeleton [skélətn] *s.* esqueleto; armazón; **— key** llave maestra.

skeptic = **sceptic**.

sketch [skɛtʃ] *s.* (*drawing*) boceto; diseño; croquis; (*outline*) esbozo; boquejo; *v.* bosquejar; delinear; esbozar, dibujar.

ski [ski] *s.* esquí; *v.* esquiar, patinar con esquís.

skid [skɪd] *v.* patinar, resbalar(se); patinar (*una rueda*); deslizarse.

skill [skɪl] *s.* destreza, maña, habilidad, pericia.

skilled [skɪld] *adj.* experto, práctico, experimentado, hábil.

skillet [skílɪt] *s.* sartén; cacerola.

skillful, skilful [skílfəl] *adj.* experto, diestro, ducho, hábil, perito.

skim [skɪm] *v.* (*remove layer*) desnatar, quitar la nata a; espumar, quitar la espuma a; (*read*) leer superficialmente; **to — over the surface** rozar la superficie.

skimp [skɪmp] *v.* escatimar; economizar; ser tacaño; hacer (*las cosas*) con descuido.

skimpy [skímpɪ] *adj.* escaso; tacaño.

skin [skɪn] *s.* piel; cutis; pellejo; cuero; cáscara, hollejo; **to save one's —** salvar el pellejo; **skin-deep** superficial; *v.* desollar; pelar; **to — someone (out of his money)** desplumar a una persona, quitarle a uno el dinero.

skinny [skínɪ] *adj.* flaco; descarnado.

skip [skɪp] *v.* saltar; brincar; saltarse (*unos renglones, un párrafo, etc.*), omitir; saltar por encima de, salvar de un brinco; **to — out** salir a escape, escabullirse, escaparse, *s.* salto, brinco; omisión.

skipper [skípə] *s.* patrón (*de barco*); capitán; saltador, brincador.

skirmish [skɜ́mɪʃ] *s.* escaramuza; *v.* escaramuzar, sostener una escaramuza.

skirt [skɜt] *s.* falda, *Ríopl.* pollera; orilla, borde; **under—** enaguas; *v.* bordear, orillar, ir por la orilla de; circundar;

to — along a coast costear.

skit [skɪt] s. parodia, juguete o paso cómico; boceto satírico o burlesco.

skull [skʌl] s. cráneo; calavera.

skunk [skʌŋk] s. *C.A., Méx., Ríopl.* zorrillo o zorrino, *Ven., Col.* mapurite.

sky [skaɪ] s. cielo; **— blue** azul celeste.

skylark [skáɪlark] s. alondra, calandria.

skylight [skáɪlaɪt] s. claraboya, tragaluz.

skyrocket [skáɪrakɪt] s. cohete.

skyscraper [skáɪskrepɚ] s. rascacielos.

slab [slæb] s. tabla, plancha, losa; tajada gruesa; **marble —** losa de mármol.

slack [slæk] adj. *(not taut)* flojo; *(sluggish)* tardo, lento, inactivo; **— season** temporada inactiva; s. flojedad, flojera; inactividad; **to take up the —** apretar, estirar; **-s** pantalones anchos con pliegues, v. *véase* **slacken**.

slacken [slǽkən] v. aflojar(se); flojear; retardar(se); disminuir.

slag [slæg] s. escoria.

slain [slen] p.p. de **to slay**.

slam [slæm] v. cerrar(se) de golpe; dejar caer de golpe; **to — someone** decirle a alguien una claridad o grosería; **to — the door** dar un portazo; s. golpazo; claridad, grosería; **— of a door** portazo; **to make a grand —** ganar todas las bazas *(en el juego de bridge)*.

slander [slǽndɚ] s. calumnia, maledicencia; v. calumniar.

slanderous [slǽndərəs] adj. calumnioso.

slang [slæŋ] s. jerga, jerigonza; vulgarismo.

slant [slænt] s. sesgo; inclinación; punto de vista; adj. sesgado; inclinado; oblicuo; v. sesgar; inclinar(se); ladear.

slap [slæp] s. palmada, manazo, manotada; insulto, desaire; v. dar una palmada, a dar un manazo a.

slapstick [slǽpstɪk] adj. de golpe y porrazo.

slash [slæʃ] v. acuchillar; dar cuchilladas o tajos; cortar; hacer fuerte rebaja de *(precios, sueldos)*; s. cuchillada; tajo, tajada, cortadura.

slat [slæt] s. tabla, tablilla.

slate [slet] s. pizarra; color de pizarra; lista de candidatos; **— pencil** pizarrín.

slaughter [slótɚ] s. carnicería, matanza, *Ríopl.* carneada; **—house** matadero, *Méx., C.A.* rastro; v. matar; *Ríopl.* carnear; hacer una matanza; destrozar.

slave [slev] s. esclavo; **— driver** capataz de esclavos; persona que agobia de trabajo a otra; **— labor** trabajo de esclavos; trabajadores forzados; v. trabajar como esclavo.

slaver [slǽvɚ] s. baba; v. babosear, babear.

slavery [slévrɪ] s. esclavitud.

slavish [slévɪʃ] adj. servil.

slay [sle] v. matar.

sled [sled] s. trineo, rastra.

sleek [slik] adj. liso; pulido, resbaloso; suave; artero, mañoso; v. alisar; pulir.

sleep [slip] v. dormir; **to — it off** dormir la mona; **to — off a headache** curarse con sueño un dolor de cabeza; **to — on it** consultarlo con la almohada; s. sueño; **to go to —** dormirse, quedarse dormido; **to put to — adormecer**; arrullar *(al nene)*.

sleeper [slípɚ] s. durmiente; coche-cama, coche-dormitorio.

sleepily [slípɪlɪ] adv. con somnolencia.

sleepiness [slípɪnɪs] s. sueño, modorra, somnolencia.

sleeping [slípɪŋ] adj. durmiente; dormido; **— car** coche-cama, coche-dormitorio; **— pills** píldoras para dormir; **— sickness** encefalitis letárgica.

sleepless [slíplɪs] adj. desvelado, insomne, sin sueño.

sleepy [slípɪ] adj. soñoliento; amodorrado; **to be —** tener sueño.

sleet [slit] s. cellisca; v. cellisquear.

sleeve [sliv] s. manga.

sleigh [sle] s. trineo; **— bell** cascabel; v. pasearse en trineo.

sleight [slaɪt] **— of hand** juego de manos; prestidigitación, escamoteo.

slender [slǽndɚ] adj. delgado; tenue; escaso, insuficiente.

slept [slɛpt] pret. & p.p. de **to sleep**.

sleuth [sluθ] s. detective *(o detectivo)*.

slew [slu] pret. de **to slay**.

slice [slaɪs] s. rebanada, tajada; lonja; v. rebanar, tajar; cortar.

slick [slɪk] v. alisar; pulir; **to — up** alisar bien, pulir bien; pulirse, acicalarse, componerse; adj. liso; meloso, suave; aceitoso; astuto, mañoso.

slicker [slíkɚ] s. impermeable de hule *(o de caucho)*; embaucador.

slid [slɪd] pret. & p.p. de **to slide**.

slidden [slídṇ] p.p. de **to slide**.

slide [slaɪd] v. resbalar(se); deslizar(se); hacer resbalar; patinar; **to — into** meter(se) en; **to — out** *(o* **— away)** deslizarse, colarse, escabullirse, escaparse; **to let something —** dejar pasar algo; no hacer caso de algo; s. resbalón; resbaladero, lugar resbaladizo; ligado *(en música)*; *véase* **landslide**; **— cover** tapa corrediza; **— rule** regla de cálculo; **microscope — platina**.

slight [slaɪt] s. desaire, menosprecio, desdén; desatención; v. desairar, menospreciar; descuidar, desatender; adj. delgado; delicado; leve, ligero; pequeño; insignificante; escaso; **-ly** adv. escasamente; ligeramente; un poco, apenas.

slim [slɪm] adj. delgado; esbelto; escaso.

slime [slaɪm] s. limo, cieno, fango; baba, secreción viscosa.

slimy [sláɪmɪ] adj. viscoso, mucoso, fangoso; baboso.

sling [slɪŋ] s. honda *(para tirar piedras)*; cabestrillo *(para sostener el brazo)*; es-

SI

linga (*maroma provista de ganchos para levantar pesos*); **—shot** tirador de goma o hule; *v.* tirar, arrojar; **to — a rifle over one's shoulder** echarse el rifle al hombro.

slink [slɪŋk] *v.* andar furtivamente; **to — away** escurrirse, escabullirse, deslizarse.

slip [slɪp] *v.* (*slide*) deslizar(se); resbalar(se); (*err*) cometer un desliz; equivocarse; **to — away** escaparse, escabullirse, escurrirse; **to — in** meter(se); **to — one's dress on** ponerse de prisa el vestido; **to — out** salirse; sacar a hurtadillas; **to — out of joint** dislocarse, *Am.* zafarse (*un hueso*); **to — something off** quitar(se) algo; **to let an opportunity** — dejar pasar una oportunidad; **it slipped my mind** se me olvidó, se me pasó; **it slipped off** se zafó; *s.* desliz; resbalón; error, equivocación; funda (*de muebles, de almohada*); combinación-enagua; pedazo (*de papel*), papeleta; embarcadero; guía, sarmiento (*para transplantar*); **— knot** nudo corredizo.

slipper [slípə] *s.* zapatilla; babucha; pantufla.

slippery [slípɪɪ] *adj.* resbaloso, resbaladizo; evasivo.

slit [slɪt] *v.* cortar, hacer una rendija, abertura o incisión; **to — into strips** cortar en tiras; *pret. & p.p. de* **to slit**; *s.* abertura, hendedura, rendija; cortada, incisión.

slobber [slábə] *s.* baba; *v.* babosear, babear.

slobbering [slábərɪŋ] *adj.* baboso.

slogan [slógən] *s.* lema, mote.

sloop [slup] *s.* chalupa.

slop [slɑp] *v.* (*soil*) ensuciar; (*splash*) salpicar; (*spill*) derramar(se); *s.* fango suciedad; **-s** lavazas, agua sucia; desperdicios.

slope [slop] *v.* inclinar(se); *s.* inclinación; declive; falda, ladera, cuesta, bajada; vertiente.

sloppy [slápɪ] *adj.* puerco, sucio, cochino; desaseado; mal hecho.

slot [slɑt] *s.* (*opening*) abertura, hendedura; (*groove for coins*) ranura (*en que se introduce una moneda*); **— machine** máquina automática que funciona por medio de una moneda, "traganíqueles," "tragamonedas"; *v.* hacer una abertura o hendedura.

sloth [sloθ] *s.* pereza, perezoso (*cuadrúpedo*).

slouch [slautʃ] *s.* (*posture*) postura muy relajada o floja; (*person*) persona perezosa o desaseada; **— hat** sombrero gacho; **to walk with a —** andar con los hombros caídos y la cabeza inclinada; *v.* andar agachado; andar caído de hombros; andar alicaído; arrellanarse, repantigarse (*en una silla*).

slovenliness [slʌvənlɪnɪs] *s.* desaseo, desaliño; suciedad.

slovenly [slʌvənlɪ] *adj.* desaseado,

desaliñado; desarreglado.

slow [slo] *adj.* (*low speed*) lento, despacio; (*late*) tardo; atrasado; (*sluggish*) lerdo; torpe; *adv.* lentamente, despacio; *v.* **to — down** (*o* **— up**) retardar disminuir (*el paso, la marcha, la velocidad*); aflojar el paso; **-ly** *adv.* despacio, lentamente.

slowness [slónɪs] *s.* lentitud; torpeza; cachaza.

slug [slʌg] *s.* bala; porrazo, puñetazo; babosa (*molusco sin concha*); haragán; trago (*de aguardiente*); lingote (*de imprenta*); *c.* aporrear, abofetear, dar puñetazos.

sluggard [slʌgəd] *s.* holgazán, haragán.

sluggish [slʌgɪʃ] *adj.* tardo; inactivo.

sluice [slus] *s.* compuerta; caño, canal; **—gate** compuerta.

slum [slʌm] *s.* barrio bajo; *v.* visitar los barrios bajos.

slumber [slʌmbə] *v.* dormitar; dormir; *s.* sueño, sueño ligero.

slump [slʌmp] *v.* hundirse; desplomarse; bajar repentinamente (*los precios o valores*); *s.* desplome, hundimiento, bajón, baja repentina (*de precios, valores, etc.*).

slung [slʌŋ] *pret. & p.p. de* **to sling**.

slunk [slʌŋk] *pret. & p.p. de* **to slink**.

slush [slʌʃ] *s.* (*snow*) nieve a medio derretir; (*mud*) lodazal, fango; (*refuse*) desperdicios; (*drivel*) sentimentalismo.

sly [slaɪ] *adj.* astuto, socarrón, zorro, taimado; **on the —** a hurtadillas, a escondidas.

slyness [sláɪnɪs] *s.* disimulo, astucia.

smack [smæk] *s.* (*taste*) sabor, dejo; (*kiss*) beso ruidoso; (*crack*) chasquido (*de látigo*); (*slap*) palmada, manotada; **a — of something** una pizca de algo; *v.* dar un beso ruidoso; chasquear (*un látigo*); dar un manazo; **to — of** saber a, tener el sabor de; oler a; **to — one's lips** chuparse los labios, saborearse, rechuparse, relamerse.

small [smɔl] *adj.* (*size*) pequeño, chico; bajo; (*insignificant*) insignificante; mezquino; **— change** dinero menudo, suelto; **— hours** primeras horas de la mañana; **— letters** letras minúsculas; **— talk** conversación insubstancial, charladuría; **— voice** vocecita; **to feel —** sentirse pequeño o insignificante.

smallness [smɔlnɪs] *s.* pequeñez; bajeza.

smallpox [smɔlpɑks] *s.* viruelas.

smart [smɑrt] *adj.* (*intelligent*) listo, inteligente; (*astute*) ladino; astuto; agudo; (*stylish*) elegante; **— remark** observación aguda o penetrante; **— set** gente de buen tono; *s.* escozor, *Riopl., C.A., Méx.* ardor; *v.* picar, escocer, *Riopl., C.A., Méx.* arder.

smash [smæʃ] *v.* quebrantar, quebrar, romper; destrozar; aplastar; **to — into** chocar con; topar con, darse un

tope contra; *s.* quebrazón, quiebra; fracaso; choque o tope violento; derrota completa.

smattering [smǽtərɪŋ] *s.* conocimiento superficial y rudimental.

smear [smɪr] *v.* embarrar, untar, manchar; **to — with paint** pintorrear, pintarrajear; *s.* mancha.

smell [smɛl] *v.* oler; **to — of** oler a; *s.* olor; olfato; **— of** olor a; **to take a —** oler.

smelly [smɛ́lɪ] *adj.* oloroso; hediondo.

smelt [smɛlt] *v.* fundir (*metales*); *pret. & p.p. de* **to smell.**

smile [smaɪl] *v.* sonreír(se); *s.* sonrisa.

smiling [smáɪlɪŋ] *adj.* risueño, sonriente; **-ly** *adv.* sonriendo, con cara risueña.

smite [smaɪt] *v.* golpear; herir; castigar; afligir; *véase* **smitten.**

smith [smɪθ] *s.* forjador; *véase* **blacksmith, goldsmith, silversmith.**

smithy [smɪ́θɪ] *s.* herrería, fragua, forja.

smitten [smɪ́tn̩] *p.p. de* **to smite &** *adj.* afligido; castigado; enamorado; **to be — with a disease** darle a uno una enfermedad.

smock [smɑk] *s.* bata corta, batín.

smoke [smok] *s.* humo; **— screen** cortina de humo; **cloud of —** humareda; **to have a —** dar una fumada, fumar; *v.* fumar, *Am.* chupar (*un cigarro*); humear; ahumar; **to — out** ahuyentar o echar fuera con humo.

smoker [smókɚ] *s.* fumador; vagón de fumar; reunión o tertulia de fumadores.

smokestack [smókstæk] *s.* chimenea.

smoking [smókɪŋ] *adj.* humeante; de fumar; para fumadores **— car** vagón de fumar; **— room** fumadero, cuarto de fumar.

smoky [smókɪ] *adj.* humeante; humoso, lleno de humo; ahumado.

smooth [smuð] *adj.* (*even*) liso; terso; igual, parejo; plano, llano; (*serene*) tranquilo; (*pleasant*) suave; (*wise*) sagaz; **— disposition** genio afable; **— manners** maneras o modales afables; **— style** estilo fluido y fácil; **— talker** hablador melifluo y sagaz; *v.* alisar; allanar; pulir; emparejar; **to — over** allanar, alisar, arreglar; **-ly** *adv.* suavemente; blandamente; fácilmente, con facilidad.

smoothness [smúðnɪs] *s.* (*evenness*) lisura; igualdad, uniformidad; (*pleasantness*) suavidad; afabilidad; tranquilidad; facilidad, fluidez.

smote [smot] *pret. de* **to smite.**

smother [smʌ́ðɚ] *v.* ahogar(se); sofocar(se); asfixiar(se).

smudge [smʌdʒ] *v.* tiznar, manchar o ensuciar con tizne; ahumar; *s.* tiznón, mancha (*hecha con tizne*); humareda, nube espesa de humo.

smuggle [smʌ́gl̩] *v.* contrabandear, hacer contrabando; **to — in** meter de contrabando; **to — out** sacar de contrabando.

smuggler [smʌ́glɚ] *s.* contrabandista.

smut [smʌt] *s.* (*smudge*) suciedad, mancha; (*obscenity*) obscenidad, dicho obseno o indecente; tizón (*enfermedad de ciertas plantas*); *v.* tiznar; ensuciar, manchar.

smutty [smʌ́tɪ] *adj.* tiznado, manchado de tizne; sucio.

snack [snæk] *s.* bocado, bocadillo, tentempié, bocadito; merienda, comida ligera.

snag [snæg] *s.* (*protuberance*) tocón; raigón; (*obstacle*) tropiezo, obstáculo; **to hit a —** tropezar con un obstáculo; *v.* rasgar; enredar.

snail [snel] *s.* caracol.

snake [snek] *s.* culebra, víbora; *v.* culebrear.

snap [snæp] *v.* (*make sound*) chasquear, dar un chasquido; estallar; (*break*) quebrar(se); (*photograph*) fotografiar instantáneamente; **his eyes —** le chispean los ojos; **to — at** echar una mordida o mordisco a; dar una tarascada a, morder; asir (*una oportunidad*); **to — back at** tirar una mordida a; dar una respuesta grosera a; **to — off** soltarse, saltar; quebrar(se); **to — one's fingers** tronar los dedos, castañetear con los dedos; **to — shut** cerrar(se) de golpe; **to — together** apretar, abrochar; **to — up** agarrar, asir; morder; *s.* chasquido; estallido; mordida, mordisco, dentellada; broche de presión; energía, vigor; galleta; cosa fácil, ganga; **cold —** nortazo; repentino descenso de temperatura; **not to care a —** no importarle a uno un ardite o un comino; *adj.* hecho de prisa, impensado; instantáneo; **— fastener** broche de presión; **— judgment** decisión atolondrada; **— lock** cerradura de golpe.

snappy [snǽpɪ] *adj.* mordedor, *Ven.*, *C.A.*, *Andes* mordelón; enojadizo, *Méx.* enojón; violento, vivo; elegante; **— cheese** queso acre o picante; **— eyes** ojos chispeantes.

snapshot [snǽpʃat] *s.* instantánea, fotografía instantánea; *v.* sacar una instantánea.

snare [sner] *s.* (*trap*) trampa, lazo; (*ambush*) acechanza; red; *v.* enredar; atrapar, coger con trampa; tender lazos a.

snarl [snarl] *v.* gruñir; enmarañar(se), enredar(se); *s.* gruñido; maraña, enredo; pelo enmarañado.

snatch [snætʃ] *v.* arrebatar; agarrar; **to — at** tratar de asir o agarrar; *s.* arrebatiña, arrebatamiento; trozo, pedacito; **to make a — at** tratar de arrebatar, tratar de agarrarse a.

sneak [snik] *v.* andar furtivamente; obrar solapadamente; **to — in** meter(se) a escondidas; colarse; **to — out** escurrirse, salirse a hurtadillas; sacar, llevarse (*algo*) a escondidas; *s.* persona solapada.

sneer [snɪr] *v.* (*smile*) sonreír con sorna; (*gesture*) hacer un gesto de desdén;

(*ridicule*) mofarse; **to — at** mofarse de; *s.* sorna, mofa, rechifla; gesto desdeñoso.

sneeze [sniz] *v.* estornudar; *s.* estornudo.

sniff [snɪf] *v.* husmear, olfatear; sorber (*por las narices*); resollar para adentro; **to — at** husmear; menospreciar; *s.* husmeo, olfateo; sorbo (*por las narices*).

sniffle [snɪfl] *v.* sorber por las narices.

snip [snɪp] *v.* tijeretear; **to — off** cortar de un tijeretazo, recortar; *s.* tijeretada, tijeretazo; pedacito, recorte.

snipe [snaɪp] *v.* tirar, disparar desde un escondite.

sniper [snáɪpɚ] *s.* francotirador; tirador emboscado.

snitch [snɪtʃ] *v.* arrebatar; ratear, hurtar.

snivel [snɪvl] *v.* moquear; gimotear.

snob [snab] *s.* esnob.

snoop [snup] *v.* fisgar, fisgonear, curiosear; *s.* curioso, fisgón.

snooze [snuz] *v.* dormitar, sestear; *s.* siestecita, siestita; **to take a —** echar un sueñecito o siesta; descabezar el sueño.

snore [snor] *v.* roncar; *s.* ronquido.

snorkel [snórkl] *s.* tubo esnorkel.

snort [snɔrt] *v.* resoplar; bufar; *s.* resoplido, bufido.

snout [snaʊt] *s.* hocico, jeta.

snow [sno] *s.* nieve; *v.* nevar; **to be -ed under** estar totalmente cubierto por la nevada.

snowball [snóbɔl] *s.* bola de nieve; *v.* tirar bolas de nieve.

snowdrift [snódrɪft] *s.* ventisca, ventisquero, montón de nieve.

snowfall [snófɔl] *s.* nevada.

snowflake [snóflek] *s.* copo de nieve.

snowstorm [snóstɔrm] *s.* fuerte nevada, nevasca.

snowy [snóɪ] *adj.* nevado; níveo, blanco como la nieve.

snub [snʌb] *v.* desairar, menospreciar; *s.* desaire; **snub-nosed** chato, *Am.* ñato.

snuff [snʌf] *v.* olfatear, husmear, ventear; aspirar (*por la nariz*); despabilar (*una candela*); **to — at** olfatear, ventear; **to — out** apagar, extinguir; **to — up** sorber (*por las narices*); *s.* sorbo (*por la nariz*); rapé, tabaco en polvo; pabilo, mecha quemada (*de una vela*).

snug [snʌg] *adj.* (*squeezed*) apretado; ajustado; compacto; (*comfortable*) abrigado; cómodo.

so [so] *adv.* así; tan, muy; tanto; **so-so** regular; **so-and-so** Fulano (de tal); **— as to** para; **— far** tan lejos; hasta ahora, hasta aquí; **— many** tantos; **— much** tanto; **— much for that** basta por ese lado; **— much the better** tanto mejor; **— that** de modo que; para que; a fin de que; de suerte que; **— then** conque, pues bien, así pues; **and — forth** etcétera; y así sucesivamente; **I believe —** así

lo creo; **is that — ?** ¿de veras? ¿de verdad?; ¡no diga!; **ten minutes or — poco** más o menos diez minutos, como diez minutos.

soak [sok] *v.* remojar(se); empapar(se); **to — up** absorber, embeber; chupar; **to be -ed through** estar empapado; estar calado hasta los huesos; *s.* remojo, mojada; borrachín; golpe, puñetazo.

soap [sop] *s.* jabón; **— bubble** pompa de jabón, *Ven., Col.* bombita; *Andes, Méx.* burbuja de jabón; **— dish** jabonera; **soft —** jabón blando; lisonja, adulación; *v.* enjabonar.

soapy [sópɪ] *adj.* lleno de jabón.

soar [sor] *v.* remontarse; encumbrarse; subir muy alto; remontar el vuelo.

sob [sab] *v.* sollozar; *s.* sollozo.

sober [sóbɚ] *adj.* (*temperate*) sobrio; moderado, templado; (*serious*) serio, grave; (*sane*) cuerdo, sensato; (*calm*) tranquilo, sereno; **to be —** estar en su juicio; no estar borracho; *v.* **to — down** sosegar(se), calmar(se); formalizarse; **to — up** desembriagarse, desemborracharse; bajársele a uno la borrachera.

soberly [sóbɚlɪ] *adv.* sobriamente; cuerdamente, con sensatez; seriamente.

soberness [sóbɚnɪs] *s.* sobriedad; seriedad.

sobriety [səbráɪətɪ] *s.* sobriedad; cordura.

so-called [sókɔld] *adj.* así llamado, llamado.

sociable [sóʃəbl] *adj.* sociable, social, tratable.

social [sóʃəl] *adj.* social; sociable; tratable, de buen trato; *s.* reunión social; tertulia.

socialism [sóʃəlɪzəm] *s.* socialismo.

socialist [sóʃəlɪst] *adj. & s.* socialista.

socialize [sóʃəlaɪz] *v.* socializar.

society [səsáɪətɪ] *s.* sociedad; compañía.

sociology [soʃɪáləʤɪ] *s.* sociología.

sock [sak] *s.* (*garment*) calcetín; (*blow*) porrazo, golpe, puñetazo; *v.* pegar, apalear, golpear; *Am.* batear (*una pelota*).

socket [sákɪt] *s.* cuenca (*del ojo*); portalámparas, enchufe, *Carib.* sóquet.

sod [sad] *s.* césped; terrón (*de tierra sembrada de césped*); *v.* cubrir de césped.

soda [sóda] *s.* soda, sosa; **— fountain** *Am.* fuente de soda; **— water** agua gaseosa; **baking —** bicarbonato de sodio.

sodium [sódɪəm] *s.* sodio.

sofa [sófə] *s.* sofá.

soft [sɔft] *adj.* (*bland*) blando; muelle; suave; (*gentle*) tierno; dulce; **soft-boiled eggs** huevos pasados por agua; **— coal** carbón bituminoso; **— drink** bebida no alcohólica; **— metal** metal dulce, metal maleable; **— soap** jabón blando; adulación; **— water** agua dulce; *adv. véase* **softly.**

soften [sɔfən] *v.* ablandar(se); suavizar-

(se); enternecer(se); templar(se); **to — one's voice** bajar la voz, hablar quedo (o quedito).

soft-hearted [sɔfthártəd] *adj.* de buen corazón.

softly [sɔftlı] *adv.* blandamente; suavemente; quedo, quedito.

softness [sɔftnıs] *s.* blandura; molicie; suavidad; ternura; dulzura.

soggy [sági] *adj.* remojado; empapado.

soil [sɔıl] *s.* suelo, terreno, tierra; mancha; *v.* ensuciar(se); manchar(se).

sojourn [sódʒɜn] *s.* estada, estancia, permanencia, *Andes, Méx., Ríopl.* estadía; [sodʒɜ́n] *v.* permanecer; estarse, residir por una temporada.

solace [sális] *s.* solaz; *v.* solazar.

solar [sólɚ] *adj.* solar, del sol; **— plexis** plexo solar.

sold [sold] *pret.* & *p.p. de* **to sell; to be — on an idea** estar bien convencido de una idea.

solder [sádɚ] *v.* soldar; *s.* soldadura.

soldier [sóldʒɚ] *s.* soldado.

sole [sol] *adj.* solo, único; exclusivo; *s.* suela (*del zapato*); planta (*del pie*); lenguado (*pez*); *v.* solar, echar suelas a; **to half-sole** echar o poner medias suelas a.

solely [sóllı] *adv.* sólamente, únicamente.

solemn [sáləm] *adj.* solemne.

solemnity [səlémnəti] *s.* solemnidad.

solicit [səlísıt] *v.* solicitar.

solicitor [səlísətɚ] *s.* solicitador, agente.

solicitous [səlísıtəs] *adj.* solícito.

solicitude [səlísətjud] *s.* solicitud, cuidado.

solid [sálıd] *s.* sólido; *adj.* sólido; firme; macizo; sensato; entero; **— blue** todo azul; **— gold** oro puro; **for one — hour** por una hora entera, por una hora sin parar; **the country is — for** el país está firmemente unido en favor de.

solidarity [salədǽrətı] *s.* solidaridad.

solidify [səlídəfaı] *v.* solidificar(se).

solidity [səlídətı] *s.* solidez.

solid-state [salədstét] *adj.* física del estado sólido.

soliloquy [səlíləkwı] *s.* soliloquio.

solitary [sálətɛrı] *adj.* solitario; solo; *s.* solitario, ermitaño.

solitude [sálətjud] *s.* soledad.

solo [sólo] *s.* solo.

soloist [sóloıst] *s.* solista.

soluble [sáljəb] *adj.* soluble, que se disuelve fácilmente.

solution [səlúʃən] *s.* solución.

solve [salv] *v.* resolver; explicar, aclarar, desenredar.

somber [sámbɚ] *adj.* sombrío.

some [sʌm] *adj.* algún, alguno; algunos, unos; algo de, un poco de; **—one** alguien, alguno; **— twenty people** unas veinte personas; *pron.* algunos, unos; algo, un poco; una parte.

somebody [sámbadı] *pron.* alguien; **a — un** personaje de importancia.

somehow [sámhau] *adv.* de algún modo, de alguna manera; **— or**

other de una manera u otra; por alguna razón.

someone [sámwʌn] *pron.* alguno, alguien.

somersault [sámɚsɔlt] *s.* voltereta; *v.* dar una voltereta.

something [sámθıŋ] *s.* algo, alguna cosa; un poco; **— else** alguna otra cosa, otra cosa.

sometime [sámtaım] *adv.* algún día; alguna vez; en algún tiempo; **-s** *adv.* a veces, algunas veces, de vez en cuando.

somewhat [sámhwat] *s.* algo, alguna cosa, un poco; *adv.* algo, un tanto.

somewhere [sámhwɛr] *adv.* en alguna parte; **— else** en alguna otra parte.

son [sʌn] *s.* hijo.

song [sɔŋ] *s.* canción; canto; **the Song of Songs** el Cantar de los Cantares; **— bird** ave canora, pájaro cantor; **to buy something for a —** comprar algo muy barato.

sonic barrier [sanıkbǽrıɚ] *s.* barrera sónica.

son-in-law [sánınlɔ] *s.* yerno, hijo político.

sonnet [sánıt] *s.* soneto.

sonorous [sənórəs] *adj.* sonoro.

soon [sun] *adv.* pronto, presto; luego; **— after** poco después (de); al poco tiempo; **as —** as tan pronto como; luego que, así que; **how — ?** ¿cuándo?

soot [sut] *s.* hollín; tizne.

soothe [suð] *v.* calmar, sosegar; aliviar.

soothsayer [súθseɚ] *s.* adivino.

sooty [sútı] *adj.* tiznado, cubierto de hollín.

sop [sap] *v.* empapar; **to — up** absorber; **to be sopping wet** estar hecho una sopa, estar mojado hasta los huesos; *s.* sopa (*pan u otra cosa empapada en leche, caldo, etc.*); soborno, regalo (*para acallar, conciliar, o sobornar*).

sophisticated [səfístəketəd] *adj.* mundano; exento de simplicidad.

sophomore [sáfəmor] *s.* estudiante de segundo año.

soprano [səprǽno] *s.* soprano; **high — tiple;** **— voice** voz de soprano.

sorcerer [sórsərɚ] *s.* brujo, hechicero.

sordid [sórdıd] *adj.* sórdido; vil, indecente; mezquino.

sore [sor] *adj.* (*painful*) dolorido; inflamado, enconado; (*grievous*) afligido, apenado; (*injured*) lastimado; picado; (*offended*) ofendido; **— eyes** mal de ojos; **to be — at** estar enojado con; **to have a — throat** tener mal de garganta, dolerle a uno la garganta; *s.* úlcera, llaga; inflamación; lastimadura; pena, aflicción; **-ly** *adv.* dolorosamente, penosamente; **to be -ly in need of** necesitar con urgencia.

soreness [sórnıs] *s.* dolor, dolencia; inflamación.

sorrel [sórəl] *adj.* alazán (*rojo canela*); *s.* color alazán; caballo alazán.

sorrow [sáro] *s.* (*sadness*) dolor, pena, pesar; (*grieving*) pesadumbre; (*repentance*) arrepentimiento; *v.* apenarse, afligirse, sentir pena.

sorrowful [sárəfəl] *adj.* pesaroso, doloroso, lastimoso, afligido; **-ly** *adv.* tristemente, dolorosamente, con pena, desconsoladamente.

sorry [sɔ́rɪ] *adj.* triste, pesaroso, afligido, arrepentido; lastimoso; **I am —** lo siento; me pesa; **I am — for her** la compadezco.

sort [sɔrt] *s.* suerte, clase, especie; **— of tired** algo cansado, un tanto cansado; **all -s of** toda suerte de, toda clase de; **out of -s** de mal humor, malhumorado; indispuesto; *v.* clasificar, ordenar, arreglar; **to — out** separar, clasificar; entresacar; escoger.

sought [sɔt] *pret. & p.p. de* **to seek**.

soul [sol] *s.* alma; **not a —** nadie, ni un alma.

sound [saʊnd] *adj.* (*healthy*) sano; cuerdo; sensato; (*firm*) girme, sólido; ileso; **a — beating** una buena zurra o tunda; **— business** buen negocio, negocio bien organizado; **— reasoning** raciocinio sólido; **— sleep** sueño profundo; **— title** título válido o legal; **of — mind** en su juicio cabal; **safe and —** sano y salvo; **to sleep —** dormir profundamente; *s.* son, sonido; tono; brazo de mar; **— wave** onda sonora; *v.* sonar, tocar; sondear; tantear; auscultar (*el pecho, los pulmones*); cantar, entonar (*alabanzas*); **to — out** tantear, sondear.

soundness [sáʊndnɪs] *s.* (*firmness*) solidez; (*healthiness*) cordura, buen juicio; (*validity*) rectitud; validez; **— of body** buena salud corporal.

soup [sup] *s.* sopa.

sour [saʊr] *adj.* (*acid-like*) agrio; acre; ácido; desabrido; rancio; (*peevish*) malhumorado; **— milk** leche cortada; *v.* agriar(se); cortarse (*la leche*); fermentar; poner(se) de mal humor.

source [sors] *s.* origen; manantial, fuente.

sourness [sáʊrnɪs] *s.* acidez, agrura, desabrimiento.

souse [saʊs] *v.* zambullir; chapuzar.

south [saʊθ] *s.* sur, sud; *adj.* meridional; del sur; austral; **South American** sudamericano, suramericano; **— pole** polo sur, polo antártico; *adv.* hacia el sur.

southeast [saʊθíst] *s. & adj.* sudeste; *adv.* hacia el sudeste.

southeastern [saʊθístən] *adj.* del sudeste, sudeste.

southern [sʌ́ðən] *adj.* meridional, del sur, austral, sureño; **— Cross** Cruz del Sur.

southerner [sʌ́ðənə] *s.* sureño, meridional, habitante del sur.

southward [sáʊθwəd] *adv.* hacia el sur, rumbo al sur.

southwest [saʊθwést] *s. & adj.* sudoeste (*o* suroeste); *adv.* hacia el sudoeste.

southwestern [saʊθwéstən] *adj.* sudoeste (*o* suroeste), del sudoeste.

souvenir [suvənír] *s.* recuerdo, memoria.

sovereign [sávrɪn] *s. & adj.* soberano.

sovereignty [sávrɪntɪ] *s.* soberanía.

soviet [sóvɪɪt] *s.* sóviet; *adj.* soviético.

sow [saʊ] *s.* puerca.

sow [so] *v.* sembrar.

sown [son] *p.p. de* **to sow**.

space [spes] *s.* espacio; **— science** ciencia del espacio; ciencia espacial; **— station** estación espacial; **— suit** traje espacial; *v.* espaciar.

spacecraft [spéskræft] *s.* nave espacial; astronave.

spaceman [spésmæn] *s.* astronauta.

spacious [spéʃəs] *adj.* espacioso; dilatado, vasto.

spade [sped] *s.* azada, azadón; espada (*del juego de naipes*); *v.* cavar con la azada.

span [spæn] *s.* palmo; espacio; tramo; arco u ojo (*de puente*); envergadura (*de un aeroplano*); **— of life** longevidad; *v.* medir a palmos; atravesar.

spangle [spǽŋgl] *s.* lentejuela; *v.* adornar con lentejuelas; brillar, centellear; **-d with stars** estrellado, sembrado (*o* tachonado) de estrellas.

Spaniard [spǽnjəd] *s.* español.

spaniel [spǽnjəl] *s.* perro de aguas.

Spanish [spǽnɪʃ] *adj.* español; *s.* español, idioma español.

spank [spæŋk] *v.* zurrar, dar una tunda, dar nalgadas; *s.* palmada, nalgada.

spanking [spǽŋkɪŋ] *s.* zurra, tunda, nalgadas.

spar [spɑr] *v.* boxear, pelear.

spare [sper] *v.* ahorrar; evitar (*molestias, trabajo, etc.*); perdonar; **I cannot — another dollar** no dispongo de otro dólar, no tengo más dinero disponible; **I cannot — the car today** no puedo pasarme hoy sin el automóvil; **to — no expense** no escatimar gastos; **to — the enemy** usar de clemencia con el enemigo; **to have time to —** tener tiempo de sobra; *adj.* flaco, descarnado; escaso, frugal; mezquino; sobrante; de sobra; de repuesto; **— cash** dinero disponible o de sobra; **— time** tiempo libre, tiempo disponible; **— tire** neumático de repuesto.

spark [spɑrk] *s.* chispa; **— plug** bujía; *v.* chispear, echar chispas, chisporrotear.

sparkle [spárkl] *s.* (*flash*) chispa, centella; brillo, centelleo; (*spirit*) viveza, animación; *v.* centellear; chispear; relucir, brillar.

sparkling [spárklɪŋ] *adj.* centelleante; reluciente; chispeante; **— wine** vino espumoso.

sparrow [spǽro] *s.* gorrión, pardal.

sparse [spɑrs] *adj.* escaso; esparcido; poco denso, poco poblado; **— hair** pelo ralo.

spasm [spǽzəm] *s.* espasmo.

spastic [spǽstɪk] *adj.* espástico.

spat [spæt] *pret. & p.p. de* **to spit**; *v.* reñir, disputar; dar un manazo o sopapo; *s.* sopapo, manotada; riña, desavenencia; **-s** polainas cortas.

spatter [spǽtɚ] *v.* salpicar; rociar; manchar; *s.* salpicadura; rociada.

speak [spik] *v.* hablar; decir; recitar; **— to the point!** ¡vamos al grano!; **so to —** por decirlo así; **to — for** hablar por, hablar en nombre o en favor de; pedir, solicitar; apalabrar, reservar; **to — one's mind** hablar sin rodeos, decir claramente lo que se piensa; **to — out** (*o* **— up**) hablar claro; hablar con toda franqueza; hablar en voz alta.

speaker [spíkɚ] *s.* orador; conferenciante, conferencista; el que habla; **— of the House** presidente de la cámara de representantes; **loud-speaker** altavoz, altoparlante.

spear [spɪr] *s.* lanza; arpón (*para pescar*); brote, retoño, hoja (*de hierba*); *v.* alancear, lancear, herir con lanza.

spearmint [spírmɪnt] *s.* yerbabuena (hierbabuena), menta.

special [spéʃəl] *adj.* especial; particular; **— delivery** entrega especial de correo; *s.* tren o autobús especial; carta urgente, entrega especial; **-ly** *adv.* especialmente; en especial; sobre todo.

specialist [spéʃəlɪst] *s.* especialista.

specialization [speʃəlɪzéʃən] *s.* especialización.

specialize [spéʃəlaɪz] *v.* especializarse.

specialty [spéʃəltɪ] *s.* especialidad.

species [spíʃɪz] *s.* especie; especies.

specific [spɪsífɪk] *adj.* específico; peculiar, característico; **— gravity** peso específico; *s.* específico; **-ally** *adv.* específicamente; especificadamente; particularmente, en particular.

specify [spésəfaɪ] *v.* especificar; estipular.

specimen [spésəmən] *s.* espécimen, muestra, ejemplar.

speck [spek] *s.* mota; manchita; partícula; **not a —** ni pizca; *v. véase* **speckle.**

speckle [spékl] *s.* manchita; mota; *v.* motear, salpicar de motas o manchas; manchar.

speckled [spékld] *adj.* moteado; **— with freckles** pecoso.

spectacle [spéktək] *s.* espectáculo; **-s** gafas, anteojos; **to make a — of oneself** ponerse en la evidencia, ponerse en ridículo.

spectacular [spektǽkjəlɚ] *adj.* espectacular, ostentoso, aparatoso.

spectator [spéktetɚ] *s.* espectador.

specter [spéktɚ] *s.* espectro, fantasma, aparecido.

spectrograph [spéktrogræf] *s.* espectrógrafo.

spectrum [spéktrəm] *s.* espectro.

speculate [spékjəlet] *v.* especular; reflexionar.

speculation [spekjəléʃən] *s.* especulación; reflexión.

speculative [spékjəletɪv] *adj.* especulativo; teórico.

speculator [spékjəletɚ] *s.* especulador.

sped [sped] *pret. & p.p. de* **to speed**.

speech [spitʃ] *s.* habla; lenguaje, idioma; discurso, arenga; conferencia; parlamento (*de un actor*); **to make a —** pronunciar un discurso, hacer una perorata.

speechless [spítʃlɪs] *adj.* sin habla; mudo; estupefacto.

speed [spid] *s.* velocidad; rapidez; presteza, prontitud; **— limit** velocidad máxima; **at full —** a toda velocidad; *v.* apresurar(se), acelerar(se), dar(se) prisa; correr; ir con exceso de velocidad; despachar.

speedily [spídɪlɪ] *adv.* velozmente, rápidamente; a todo correr; de prisa, con prontitud.

speedometer [spidámətɚ] *s.* velocímetro.

speedy [spídɪ] *adj.* veloz, rápido.

spell [spel] *s.* (*charm*) hechizo, encanto; (*period*) temporada, corto período; (*sickness*) ataque (*de una enfermedad*); **to put under a —** aojar; hechizar, encantar; *v.* deletrear; significar, indicar; **how is it -ed?** ¿cómo se escribe?

speller [spélɚ] *s.* silabario; deletreador.

spelling [spélɪŋ] *s.* ortografía; deletreo; **— book** silabario.

spelt [spelt] *pret. & p.p. de* **to spell**.

spend [spend] *v.* gastar; usar, agotar, consumir; **to — a day** pasar un día.

spendthrift [spéndθrɪft] *s.* derrochador, gastador, pródigo.

spent [spent] *pret. & p.p. de* **to spend**.

sphere [sfɪr] *s.* esfera; globo, orbe.

spherical [sférɪk] *adj.* esférico.

sphynx [sfɪŋks] *s.* esfinge.

spice [spaɪs] *s.* especia; picante; aroma; *v.* condimentar, sazonar con especias.

spicy [spáɪsɪ] *adj.* sazonado con especias; picante; aromático.

spider [spáɪdɚ] *s.* araña; sartén; **— web** telaraña.

spigot [spígət] *s.* espita, grifo, canilla.

spike [spaɪk] *s.* espiga; perno; clavo largo; alcayata; pico; *v.* clavar; clavetear.

spill [spɪl] *v.* verter; derramar(se); desparramar(se); hacer caer (*de un caballo*); revelar (*una noticia, un secreto*); *s.* derrame, derramamiento; vuelco; caída (*de un caballo*).

spilt [spɪlt] *pret. & p.p. de* **to spill**.

spin [spɪn] *v.* hilar; girar, dar vueltas, rodar; bailar (*un trompo*); **to — out** prolongar, alargar; **to — yarns** contar cuentos; *s.* giro, vuelta; paseo (*en automóvil, bicicleta, etc.*); barrena (*hablando de aeroplanos*).

spinach [spínɪtʃ] *s.* espinaca.

spinal [spáɪnl] *adj.* espinal; **— column** columna vertebral, espina dorsal.

spindle [spíndl] *s.* huso; eje.

spine [spaɪn] *s.* espina; espinazo, espina dorsal, columna vertebral.

SO

spinner [spínɚ] s. hilandero, hilandera; máquina de hilar.

spinning [spínɪŋ] s. hilandería, arte de hilar; — **machine** aparato para hilar, máquina de hilar; — **mill** hilandería; — **top** trompo; — **wheel** torno de hilar.

spinster [spínstɚ] s. soltera; solterona.

spiral [spáɪrəl] adj. espiral; — **staircase** caracol, escalera espiral; s. espiral.

spire [spaɪr] s. aguja, chapitel de torre; cúspide, ápice; punto más alto; — **of grass** brizna de hierba.

spirit [spírɪt] s. (essence) espíritu; temple; (animation) viveza, animación; ánimo; **low -s** abatimiento; **to be in good -s** estar de buen humor; **to be out of -s** estar triste o abatido; v. **to — away** llevarse misteriosamente.

spirited [spírɪtɪd] adj. vivo, brioso, fogoso.

spiritual [spírɪtʃʊəl] adj. espiritual; s. espiritual (tonada religiosa de los negros del sur de los Estados Unidos).

spit [spɪt] v. escupir; expectorar; pret. & p.p. de **to spit**; s. esputo, saliva; asador.

spite [spaɪt] s. despecho, rencor, inquina, ojeriza; **in — of** a despecho de; a pesar de; **out of —** por despecho; v. picar, irritar, hacer rabiar.

spiteful [spáɪtfəl] adj. rencoroso.

splash [splæʃ] v. salpicar; rociar; enlodar, manchar; chapotear (en el agua); s. salpicadura; rociada; chapoteo.

spleen [splin] s. bazo; mal humor, rencor.

splendid [spléndɪd] adj. espléndido.

splendor [spléndɚ] s. esplendor; esplendidez.

splice [splaɪs] v. empalmar, unir, juntar; s. empalme; junta.

splint [splɪnt] s. tablilla; astilla; v. entablillar.

splinter [splíntɚ] s. astilla; raja; v. astillar(se), hacer(se) astillas; romper(se) en astillas.

split [splɪt] v. hender(se), rajar(se); resquebrajar(se); partir(se), dividir(se); **to — hairs** pararse en pelillos; **to — one's sides with laughter** desternillarse de risa, reventar de risa; **to — the difference** partir la diferencia; pret. & p.p. de **to split**; adj. partido, hendido, rajado; dividido; resquebrajado; s. raja, hendedura, grieta; cisma, rompimiento.

splurge [splɝdʒ] s. ostentación; fachenda.

spoil [spɔɪl] v. (decay) dañar(se); echar(se) a perder, podrir(se), corromper(se); (harm) estropear(se); arruinar; (overindulge) consentir, mimar; s. botín, presa; **-s of war** botín o despojos de guerra.

spoke [spok] s. rayo (de rueda); pret. de **to speak**.

spoken [spókən] p.p. de **to speak**.

spokesman [spóksmən] s. portavoz, vocero.

sponge [spʌndʒ] s. (absorbent) esponja; (dependent person) gorrón, parásito; v. lavar o limpiar con esponja; vivir de gorra, vivir a costa ajena; **to — up** chupar, absorber.

spongecake [spʌndʒkek] s. bizcocho esponjoso.

sponger [spʌndʒɚ] s. esponja, gorrón, pegote, parásito, Am. pavo.

spongy [spʌndʒɪ] adj. esponjoso, esponjado.

sponsor [spánsɚ] s. padrino, madrina; patrón (el que patrocina una empresa); defensor; fiador; fomentador, promovedor; v. apadrinar; promover, fomentar; patrocinar; ser fiador de.

spontaneity [spantəníətɪ] s. espontaneidad.

spontaneous [spanténɪəs] adj. espontáneo.

spook [spuk] s. espectro, fantasma, aparecido.

spool [spul] s. carrete, carretel; v. devanar, enredar (hilo) en carrete.

spoon [spun] s. cuchara; v. cucharear, sacar con cuchara.

spoonful [spúnfəl] s. cucharada.

sport [sport] s. deporte; **in —** en broma, de burla; **to make — of** reírse de, burlarse de; **to be a good —** ser buen perdedor (en el juego); ser un buen compañero; v. jugar; divertirse; bromear, chancearse; **to — a new dress** lucir un traje nuevo; s. adj. deportivo; — **clothes** trajes deportivos.

sports car [spórtskar] s. coche (carro) deportivo.

sportsman [spórtsmən] s. deportista; jugador generoso, buen perdedor (en deportes).

spot [spat] s. (blemish) mancha, mota; (place) sitio, lugar; **in -s** aquí y allí, aquí y allá; **on the —** allí mismo; al punto; **to pay — cash** pagar al contado; v. manchar, ensuciar; motear; echar de ver, distinguir; avistar; localizar.

spotless [spátlɪs] adj. sin mancha, limpio.

spotlight [spátlaɪt] s. faro giratorio.

spotted [spátɪd] adj. manchado; moteado.

spouse [spauz] s. esposo, esposa.

spout [spaut] v. chorrear; brotar; salir en chorro; emitir; declamar, perorar; hablar mucho; s. chorro; surtidor; pico (de tetera, cafetera, jarra, etc.); espita.

sprain [spren] v. torcer (una coyuntura o músculo); **to — one's ankle** torcerse el tobillo; s. torsión, torcedura.

sprang [spræŋ] pret. de **to spring**.

sprawl [sprɔl] v. despatarrarse; estar despatarrado; tenderse; **to — one's legs** abrir las piernas; s. postura floja (abiertos los brazos y piernas).

spray [spre] s. (liquid) rocío, rociada; líquido para rociar; (branch) ramita; **sea —** espuma del mar; v. rociar.

spread [sprɛd] v. extender(se); desparramar(se); esparcir(se); difundir(se), diseminar(se), dispersar(se);

propalar(se) (*noticias, rumores, etc.*), propagar(se); **to — apart** abrir(se), separar(se); **to — butter on** poner mantequilla en; **to — out the tablecloth** tender el mantel; **to — paint on** dar una mano de pintura a; **to — with** cubrir de; untar con; *s.* extensión; amplitud, anchura; envergadura (*de un aeroplano*); difusión; diseminación; propagación; cubierta, sobrecama; comilitona, festín; mantequilla, queso, etc., que se le unta al pan; *pret. & p.p. de* **to spread.**

spree [spri] *s.* juerga, parranda, holgorio; **to go on a —** andar (*o* ir) de parranda o juerga, *Am.* ir de farra.

sprig [sprig] *s.* ramita.

sprightly [spráitli] *adj.* vivo, animado, brioso; alegre.

spring [sprin] *v.* saltar; brincar; hacer saltar; **to — a leak** hacer agua (*un barco*); comenzar a gotearse (*la cañería, el techo, etc.*); formarse una gotera; **to — a trap** hacer saltar una trampa; **to — at** abalanzarse sobre; **to — from** salir de, nacer de, brotar de; **to — news of a surprise** dar de sopetón una noticia o sorpresa; **to — something upon** abrir algo a la fuerza; **to — to one's feet** levantarse de un salto; **to — up** brotar; surgir; crecer; levantarse de un salto; *s.* primavera; muelle (*de metal*); resorte; elasticidad; salto, brinco; manantial, fuente; origen; *adj.* primaveral; **— board** trampolín; **— mattress** colchón de muelles; **— water** agua de manantial.

springtime [springtaim] *s.* primavera.

sprinkle [sprínkl] *v.* (*scatter*) rociar; regar; espolvorear; salpicar; (*rain*) lloviznar; *s.* rociada, rocío; llovizna; **— of salt** pizca de sal.

sprint [sprint] *v.* echar una carrera; *s.* carrera, carrerilla, corrida corta.

sprout [spraut] *v.* brotar; retoñar, germinar; hacer germinar o brotar; *s.* retoño, renuevo; **Brussels -s** bretones, coles de Bruselas.

spruce [sprus] *s.* abeto; *adj.* pulcro, aseado, pulido; elegante; *v.* **to — up** asearse, componerse, emperifollarse.

sprung [sprʌŋ] *pret. & p.p. de* **to spring.**

spun [spʌn] *pret. & p.p. de* **to spin.**

spur [spɜ] *s.* espuela; acicate; aguijón, estímulo; espolón (*del gallo*); estribación (*de una montaña*); **— track** ramal corto (*de ferrocarril*); **on the — of the moment** impensadamente, sin la reflexión debida; por el momento; *v.* espolear, aguijar, picar, incitar; **to — on** animar, incitar a obrar o a seguir adelante.

spurious [spúriəs] *adj.* espurio.

spurn [spɜn] *v.* rechazar, desdeñar, menospreciar.

spurt [spɜt] *v.* salir a borbotones; chorrear; echar chorros; hacer un repentino esfuerzo (*para ganar una carrera*); *s.* borbotón, chorrazo, chorro repentino; esfuerzo repentino; **— of anger**

arranque de ira; **-s of flame** llamaradas.

sputter [spʌ́tɚ] *v.* chisporrotear; refunfuñar; *s.* chisporroteo; refunfuño.

sputum [spjútəm] *s.* esputo.

spy [spai] *s.* espía; *v.* espiar; acechar; atisbar; **to — on** espiar, atisbar.

spyglass [spáiglæs] *s.* anteojo de larga vista.

squab [skwab] *s.* pichón.

squabble [skwábl] *s.* reyerta; *v.* reñir, disputar.

squad [skwad] *s.* escuadra, patrulla, partida.

squadron [skwádrən] *s.* escuadra; escuadrón.

squalid [skwálid] *adj.* escuálido.

squall [skwɔl] *s.* chubasco; chillido; *v.* chillar.

squander [skwándɚ] *v.* despilfarrar, derrochar, malgastar, disipar.

square [skwer] *s.* (*rectangle*) cuadro; cuadrado; (*central park*) plaza; (*block*) manzana de casas; *Am.* cuadra; escuadra (*de carpintero*); casilla (*de tablero de ajedrez, damas, etc.*); **he is on the —** obra de buena fe; *v.* cuadrar; ajustar, arreglar, saldar (*cuentas*); justificar; cuadricular; **to — one's shoulders** enderezar los hombros; cuadrarse; **to — oneself with** sincerarse con, justificarse ante; **to — a person with another** poner bien a una persona con otra; *adj.* cuadrado, en cuadro, a escuadra, en ángulo recto; saldado; justo, recto, equitativo; franco; **— corner** esquina en ángulo recto; **— meal** comida completa, comida en regla; **— mile** milla cuadrada; **— root** raíz cuadrada; **— dance** danza de figuras; cuadrilla; **to be — with someone** estar en paz con alguien, no deberle nada, *Am.* estar a mano; *adv.* véase **squarely.**

squarely [skwérli] *adv.* equitativamente, honradamente; firmemente; de buena fe; derecho, derechamente; **to hit the target — in the middle** pegar de lleno en el blanco.

squash [skwaʃ] *s.* calabaza; *v.* aplastar, despachurrar o apachurrar.

squat [skwat] *v.* agazaparse, sentarse en cuclillas; ocupar tierras baldías para ganar título de propietario; *adj.* agazapado, sentado en cuclillas; rechoncho, achaparrado, *Méx., C.A., Andes* chaparro.

squawk [skwɔk] *v.* (*noise*) graznar; chillar; (*complain*) quejarse; *s.* graznido; chillido; queja.

squeak [skwik] *v.* rechinar, chirriar; chillar; *s.* rechinamiento; chirrido, chillido.

squeal [skwil] *v.* chillar; quejarse, protestar; soplar, delatar; *s.* chillido.

squeamish [skwímiʃ] *adj.* escrupuloso; delicado; remilgado.

squeeze [skwiz] *v.* estrujar; despachurrar o apachurrar; exprimir; prensar; apretar; **to — into** meter(se) a estrujones, encajar(se) en; **to — out the**

juice exprimir el jugo; **to — through a crowd** abrirse paso a estrujones por entre la muchedumbre; *s.* estrujón; apretón; abrazo fuerte; apretura.

squelch [skwɛltʃ] *v.* aplastar; acallar; imponer silencio; reprender; **to — a revolt** sofocar o apagar una revuelta.

squid [skwɪd] *s.* calamar.

squint [skwɪnt] *v.* mirar de través; mirar de soslayo; mirar achicando los ojos; mirar furtivamente; bizquear *(mirar bizco)*; *s.* mirada de soslayo; mirada bizca; mirada furtiva; **squint-eyed** *adj.* bisojo o bizco.

squire [skwaɪr] *s.* escudero; *v.* acompañar, escoltar.

squirm [skwɝm] *v.* retorcerse; **to — out of a difficulty** forcejear para salir de un aprieto.

squirrel [skwɝəl] *s.* ardilla.

squirt [skwɝt] *v.* jeringar; echar un chisguete; salir a chorritos *(o a chisguetes)*; *s.* jeringazo; chisguete.

stab [stæb] *v.* apuñalar, dar una puñalada, dar de puñaladas, acuchillar; pinchar; *s.* puñalada, cuchillada, estocada; pinchazo.

stability [stəbíləti] *s.* estabilidad.

stable [stébl] *adj.* estable; *s.* establo, cuadra, caballeriza; *v.* poner *(los animales)* en la caballeriza.

stack [stæk] *s.* pila, montón, rimero; hacina *(de paja o heno)*; chimenea, cañón de chimenea; **library -s** estanterías o anaqueles de biblioteca; *v.* amontonar, apilar.

stadium [stédɪəm] *s.* estadio.

staff [stæf] *s.* *(stick)* báculo, cayado, bastón, vara; *(pole)* asta *(de bandera, de lanza)*; *(group)* cuerpo, consejo administrativo; **— of life** sostén de la vida; **— officer** oficial de estado mayor; **army —** estado mayor; **editorial —** redacción; **musical —** pentagrama; **teaching —** cuerpo docente; *v.* proveer de funcionarios y empleados *(una organización)*.

stag [stæg] *s.* venado, ciervo, macho, hombre; **— dinner** banquete exclusivo para hombres.

stage [stedʒ] *s.* *(platform)* tablado, tablas, escenario; escena; *(theater)* teatro; *(period)* etapa, tramo; período; *(stop)* parada; **— coach** ómnibus, autobús; **— hand** tramoyista; **by easy -s** por grados, gradualmente; *v.* representar, poner en escena; **to — a hold-up** hacer un asalto, atracar; **to — a surprise** dar una sorpresa.

stagger [stǽgɚ] *v.* *(totter)* tambalearse, tratabillar, bambolearse; hacer tambalear; *(overwhelm)* azorar, asombrar; **to — working hours** escalonar las horas de trabajo; *s.* tambaleo, bamboleo.

stagnant [stǽgnənt] *adj.* estancado; **to become —** estancarse.

staid [sted] *adj.* grave, serio.

stain [sten] *v.* manchar; teñir; colorar; **stained-glass window** vidriera de colores; *s.* mancha, mancilla, tinte, tintura; materia colorante.

stainless [sténlɪs] *adj.* sin mancha, inmaculado, limpio; **— steel** acero inempañable o inoxidable.

stair [stɛr] *s.* peldaño, escalón; **-s** escalera.

staircase [stɛrkes] *s.* escalera.

stairway [stɛrwe] *s.* escalera.

stake [stek] *s.* estaca; puesta, apuesta; **his future is at —** su porvenir está en peligro o riesgo; **to die at the —** morir en la hoguera; **to have a — in the future of** tener interés en el porvenir de; **to have much at —** irle a uno mucho en una cosa; haber aventurado mucho; *v.* estacar; atar a una estaca; apostar; arriesgar, aventurar; **to — off** señalar con estacas *(un perímetro)*.

stale [stel] *adj.* viejo; rancio; gastado; improductivo.

stalemate [stélmet] *s.* punto muerto; estancación.

stalk [stɔk] *s.* tallo; caña.

stall [stɔl] *s.* casilla, puesto *(de un mercado o feria)*; casilla o sección de un establo; *v.* encasillar, meter en casilla; atascarse *(un auto)*; pararse *(el motor)*; **he is -ing** está haciendo la pala; **to be -ed in the mud** estar atascado en el lodo.

stallion [stǽljən] *s.* caballo de cría, caballo padre, *Ven., Col., Ríopl.* padrillo; *Méx., C.A.* garañón.

stammer [stǽmɚ] *v.* tartamudear, balbucear; *s.* tartamudeo, balbuceo.

stammerer [stǽmərɚ] *s.* tartamudo.

stammering [stǽmərɪŋ] *s.* tartamudeo; *adj.* tartamudo.

stamp [stæmp] *v.* *(affix)* sellar; timbrar; poner un sello a; estampar; *(mark)* marcar, imprimir, señalar; *(with foot)* patear, patalear; **to — one's foot** dar patadas en el suelo; **to — out** extirpar, borrar; *s.* sello; timbre, estampilla; estampa; marca, impresión; patada *(en el suelo)*; **postage —** sello, *Am.* estampilla, *Am.* timbre; **revenue —** timbre.

stampede [stæmpíd] *s.* estampida; huida en desorden; tropel; éxodo repentino; *v.* arrancar, huir en tropel; ir en tropel; ahuyentar, hacer huir en desorden.

stanch [stɑntʃ] *v.* restañar, estancar; *adj.* fuerte, firme; leal, constante, fiel.

stand [stænd] *v.* poner derecho, colocar verticalmente; *(rise)* ponerse de pie, levantarse; *Am.* parar(se); *(be erect)* estar de pie; *Am.* estar parado; *(withstand)* aguantar, sufrir, tolerar; **to — a chance of** tener probabilidad de; **to — an expense** sufragar un gasto; **to — aside** apartarse; mantenerse apartado; **to — back of** colocarse detrás de; salir fiador de, garantizar a, respaldar a; **to — by** mantenerse a corta distancia; apoyar, defender; estar alerta; **to — for** significar; estar por, apoyar; tolerar; **to — in the way** estorbar; **to — on end** poner(se) de punta; erizarse (*el pelo*); **to — one's ground** mantenerse firme; **to — out** resaltar, destacarse; sobre-salir; **to — six feet** tener seis pies de altura; **to — up for** apoyar, defender; **it -s to reason** es razonable, es lógico; *s.* puesto; mesilla; pedestal; posición; actitud; alto, parada (*para resistir*); quiosco; **grand—** andanada, gradería cubierta (*para espectadores*); **music—** atril; **umbrella —** paragüero.

standard [stǽndəd] *s.* (*norm*) norma; nivel normal; criterio; (*model*) modelo, patrón; *Am.* estándar; (*base*) base, pedestal; (*banner*) estandarte; **gold —** patrón de oro; **to be up to —** satisfacer las normas requeridas; *adj.* normal, que sirve de norma; de uso general; corriente; **standard-bearer** portaestandarte.

standardization [stændədəzéʃən] *s.* normalización, uniformación, igualación.

standardize [stǽndədaɪz] *v.* normalizar, uniformar, *Méx., C.A., Carib.* estandarizar.

standby [stǽndbaɪ] *s.* sustituto.

standing [stǽndɪŋ] *s.* (*position*) posición; (*fame*) fama, reputación; **of long —** que ha prevalecido largo tiempo; muy antiguo; *adj.* derecho, en pie; de pie; establecido, permanente; **— water** agua estancada; **there is — room only** no quedan asientos.

standpoint [stǽndpɔɪnt] *s.* punto de vista.

standstill [stǽndstɪl] *s.* alto; pausa; **to come to a —** pararse; hacer alto.

stank [stæŋk] *pret. de* **to stink.**

stanza [stǽnzə] *s.* estrofa.

staple [stépl] *s.* broche de alambre (*para sujetar papeles*); grapa, argolla, armella; artículo principal; **-s** artículos de necesidad prima; *adj.* principal; de uso corriente; indispensable; *v.* asegurar (*papeles*) con broche de alambre; sujetar con armellas.

star [star] *s.* estrella; asterisco; **star-spangled** estrellado; *adj.* sobresaliente, excelente; *v.* estrellar, adornar o señalar con estrellas; marcar con asterisco; presentar como estrella (*a un actor*); lucir(se) en las tablas o el cine, hacer el papel principal.

starboard [stárbord] *s.* estribor; *adj.* de estribor; **— side** banda de estribor; *adv.* a estribor.

starch [startʃ] *s.* almidón; fécula; *v.* almidonar.

stare [ster] *v.* mirar, mirar con fijeza o curiosidad; mirar a⁻orado; clavar la mirada, fijar la vista; *s.* mirada fija, mirada persistente.

starfish [stárfiʃ] *s.* estrella de mar.

stark [stark] *adj.* (*utter*) tieso; (*grim*) escueto; **— folly** pura tontería; **— in death** tieso, muerto; **— narrative** narración escueta, sin adornos; *adv.* completamente, totalmente; **— mad** loco de remate; **— naked** enteramente desnudo, en cueros, *Am.* encue-

rado.

starlight [stárlaɪt] *s.* luz estelar, luz de las estrellas.

starry [stárɪ] *adj.* estrellado, sembrado de estrellas; como estrellas, brillante.

start [start] *v.* comenzar, empezar, principiar; poner(se) en marcha; partir, salir; dar un salto, sobre-saltarse; **the motor -s** el motor arranca; **to — after someone** salir en busca de alguien; **to — off** salir, partir; dar principio a; **to — out on a trip** empezar una jornada, emprender un viaje; **to — the motor** hacer arrancar el motor; *s.* comienzo, empiezo, principio; sobresalto; respingo (*de un caballo*); arranque; ventaja (*en una carrera*).

starter [stártə] *s.* (*automobile*) arranque; (*person*) arrancador; iniciador; (*first*) primero de la serie; **self-starter** arranque automático.

startle [stártl] *v.* asustar(se), sobresaltar(se), espantar(se).

startling [stártlɪŋ] *adj.* sobresaltante, pasmoso, asombroso, sorprendente.

starvation [starvéʃən] *s.* inanición, hambre.

starve [starv] *v.* morir(se) de hambre; hambrear; matar de hambre.

state [stet] *s.* estado; condición, situación; **in great —** con gran pompa; *adj.* de estado; del estado; de ceremonia; *v.* declarar, decir; expresar, exponer.

stately [stétlɪ] *adj.* majestuoso, imponente.

statement [stétmənt] *s.* (*declaration*) declaración; exposición; (*information*) informe, relato; (*bill*) cuenta, estado de cuentas.

stateroom [stétrum] *s.* camarote (*de un buque*).

statesman [stétsmən] *s.* estadista, hombre de estado.

static [stǽtɪk] *adj.* estático; *s.* estática.

station [stéʃən] *s.* (*operations point*) estación; (*post*) paradero; puesto; (*condition*) estado, posición social; **broadcasting —** transmisora o emisora; *v.* estacionar, colocar, apostar; **— wagon** *Esp.* rubia; *Méx.* camioneta, huayin; *C.A.* camionetilla.

stationary [stéʃənɛrɪ] *adj.* estacionario, fijo.

stationery [stéʃənɛrɪ] *s.* papelería.

statistics [stətístɪks] *s.* estadística; datos estadísticos.

statuary [stǽtʃuɛrɪ] *s.* estatuaria, arte de hacer estatuas; colección de estatuas.

statue [stǽtʃu] *s.* estatua.

stature [stǽtʃə] *s.* estatura.

status [stétəs] *s.* estado, condición; posición social o profesional.

statute [stǽtʃut] *s.* estatuto, ordenanza.

staunch = **stanch.**

stave [stev] *s.* duela de barril; *v.* poner duelas (*a un barril*); **to — off** mantener a distancia; evitar; rechazar.

stay [ste] *v.* (*remain*) quedarse, permanecer; parar(se); detener(se); (*sojourn*) hospedarse, alojarse; (*check*) resistir; **to — an execution** diferir o aplazar una ejecución; **to — one's hunger** engañar el hambre; **to — up all night** velar toda la noche; *s.* estada, estancia, permanencia; suspensión; sostén, apoyo; varilla o ballena de corsé; **to grant a —** conceder una prórroga.

stead [stɛd]: **in her (his) —** en su lugar; **to stand one in good —** servirle a uno, ser de provecho para uno.

steadfast [stɛ́dfæst] *adj.* fijo, firme; constante.

steadily [stɛ́dɪlɪ] *adv.* constantemente; firmemente; sin parar, de continuo; sin vacilar.

steadiness [stɛ́dɪnɪs] *s.* firmeza; constancia; estabilidad.

steady [stɛ́dɪ] *adj.* firme; estable; invariable, constante; continuo; *v.* afianzar, mantener firme, asegurar; calmar (*los nervios*).

steak [stek] *s.* biftec o bisté; tajada (*para asar o freír*).

steal [stil] *v.* (*rob*) robar, hurtar; (*move*) andar furtivamente; **to — away** colarse, escabullirse, escaparse; **to — into a room** meterse a hurtadillas en un cuarto; **to — out of a room** salirse a escondidas de un cuarto, colarse, escabullirse; *s.* robo, hurto.

stealth [stɛlθ]: **by — a** hurtadillas, a escondidas, con cautela.

stealthy [stɛ́lθɪ] *adj.* cauteloso, furtivo, secreto.

steam [stim] *s.* vapor; vaho; *adj.* de vapor; por vapor; **— engine** máquina de vapor; **— heat** calefacción por vapor; *v.* cocer al vapor; dar un baño de vapor; saturar de vapor; echar vapor; **to — into port** llegar a puerto (*un vapor*).

steamboat [stímbot] *s.* buque de vapor.

steamer [stímɚ] *s.* vapor, buque de vapor.

steamship [stímʃɪp] *s.* vapor, buque de vapor.

steed [stid] *s.* corcel, caballo de combate; caballo brioso.

steel [stil] *s.* acero; *adj.* acerado, de acero; *v.* acerar, revestir de acero; **to — oneself against** fortalecerse contra.

steep [stip] *adj.* empinado, escarpado, pendiente; muy alto; **— price** precio alto o excesivo; *v.* remojar, empapar; saturar; poner o estar en infusión.

steeple [stípl] *s.* aguja, chapitel; cúspide.

steepness [stípnɪs] *s.* inclinación abrupta; lo empinado, lo escarpado; altura (*de precios*).

steer [stɪr] *s.* novillo; buey; *v.* guiar, conducir, manejar, gobernar; timonear; **to — a course** seguir un rumbo; **the car -s easily** se maneja fácilmente el auto, es de fácil manejo.

stellar [stɛ́lɚ] *adj.* estelar.

stem [stɛm] *s.* tallo; tronco; pedúnculo (*de hoja, flor o fruto*); raíz (*de una palabra*); pie (*de copa*); cañón (*de pipa de fumar*); proa; *v.* estancar, represar; resistir, refrenar; contraponerse a; **to — from** provenir de.

stench [stɛntʃ] *s.* hedor, hediondez.

stencil [stɛ́nsl] *s.* patrón picado; esténcil.

stenographer [stənágrəfɚ] *s.* estenógrafo, taquígrafo, mecanógrafo.

step [stɛp] *s.* (*walking*) paso; pisada; (*staircase*) peldaño, escalón, grada; (*degree*) grado; (*effort*) gestión; **— by —** paso a paso; **to be in — with** marchar a compás con; estar de acuerdo con; **to take -s** dar pasos; tomar medidas; gestionar; *v.* andar, caminar; dar un paso; **to — aside** hacerse a un lado, apartarse; **to — back** dar un paso o pasos atrás; retroceder; **to — down** bajar; **to — off a distance** medir a pasos una distancia; **to — on** pisar, pisotear; **to — on the gas** pisar el acelerador; darse prisa; **to — out** salir; **to — up** subir; acelerar.

stepfather [stɛ́pfaðɚ] *s.* padrastro.

stepmother [stɛ́pmʌðɚ] *s.* madrastra.

steppe [stɛp] *s.* estepa.

stereotype [stɪ́rɪotaɪp] *s.* estereotipo.

sterile [stɛ́ral] *adj.* estéril.

sterility [stərɪ́lətɪ] *s.* esterilidad.

sterilize [stɛ́rəlaɪz] *v.* esterilizar.

sterling [stɑ́lɪŋ] *s.* vajilla de plata esterlina; *adj.* genuino; de ley; **— silver** plata de ley, plata esterlina; **pound —** libra esterlina.

stern [stɝn] *adj.* austero, severo; firme; *s.* popa.

sternness [stɝ́nnɪs] *s.* austeridad, severidad; firmeza.

stethoscope [stɛ́θəskop] *s.* estetoscopio.

stevedore [stívədor] *s.* estibador, cargador.

stew [stju] *v.* estofar; preocuparse, apurarse; *s.* estofado, guisado; **to be in a —** estar preocupado o apurado.

steward [stjúwɚd] *s.* mayordomo; camarero (*de buque o avión*).

stewardess [stjúwɚdɪs] *s.* camarera (*de buque o avión*).

stick [stɪk] *s.* palo; vara; garrote; raja de leña; **— of dynamite** barra de dinamita; **control —** palanca (*de aeroplano*); **walking —** bastón; **stick-up** atraco (*para robar*), asalto; *v.* pegar(se), adherir(se); permanecer; estar pegado; picar, pinchar; herir (*con cuchillo, puñal, etc.*); fijar (*con clavos, alfileres, tachuelas, etc.*); atascarse (*en el fango un carro, auto, etc.*); **to — something in** (*o* **into**) clavar o meter algo en; encajar en; **to — out** salir, sobresalir; proyectarse; **to — out one's head** asomar la cabeza; **to — out one's tongue** sacar la lengua; **to — to a job** perseverar (*o* persistir) en una tarea; **to — up** sobresalir, destacarse; estar de punta (*el pelo*); **to — one's hands up** alzar las manos; **to — someone**

up asaltar o atracar a alguien (*para robar*); *véase* **stuck.**

sticker [stíkə] *s.* marbete engomado; etiqueta.

sticky [stíkɪ] *adj.* pegajoso.

stiff [stɪf] *adj.* tieso; rígido; entumido; duro; terco; fuerte; **— climb** subida ardua o difícil; **— price** precio alto o subido; **stiff-necked** terco, obstinado; **scared —** yerto, muerto de miedo; *s.* cadáver.

stiffen [stífən] *v.* atiesar(se), poner(se) tieso; entumir(se); endurecer(se); espesar(se); subir de punto, aumentar (*la resistencia*).

stiffness [stífnɪs] *s.* tiesura; rigidez; dureza; rigor; terquedad.

stifle [stáɪfḷ] *v.* ahogar(se), asfixiar(se), sofocar(se); apagar, extinguir.

stigma [stígmə] *s.* estigma; baldón.

stigmatize [stígmətaɪz] *v.* estigmatizar.

still [stɪl] *adj.* (*quiet*) quieto; callado; silencioso; (*at ease*) tranquilo; inmóvil; **—born** nacido muerto; **— life** naturaleza muerta; *v.* aquietar; calmar; acallar; *adv.* todavía, aún; *conj.* empero, no obstante, sin embargo; *s.* destiladera, alambique; silencio.

stillness [stílnɪs] *s.* quietud, calma, silencio.

stilt [stɪlt] *s.* zanco; pilote, puntal, soporte.

stilted [stíltɪd] *adj.* tieso, afectado, pomposo.

stimulant [stímjələnt] *adj.* & *s.* estimulante.

stimulate [stímjəlet] *v.* estimular.

stimulation [stɪmjəléʃən] *s.* estimulación, estímulo.

stimulus [stímjələs] *s.* estímulo.

sting [stɪŋ] *v.* (*pierce*) picar; pinchar, aguijonear; (*irritate*) escocer; *Am.* arder; (*cheat*) embaucar; estafar; *s.* picadura, piquete, mordedura, picazón; aguijón; escozor; **— of remorse** remordimiento.

stinginess [stíndʒɪnɪs] *s.* tacañería, mezquindad.

stingy [stíndʒɪ] *adj.* mezquino, ruin, tacaño; escaso; *Ríopl.*, *Mex.* codo.

stink [stɪŋk] *v.* heder, oler mal; apestar; *s.* hedor, mal olor, hediondez.

stint [stɪnt] *v.* escatimar; ser frugal o económico; **to — oneself** privarse de lo necasario, economizar demasiado; *s.* tarea, faena; **without —** sin límite; sin escatimar; generosamente.

stipulate [stípjəlet] *v.* estipular.

stipulation [stɪpjəléʃən] *s.* estipulación, condición.

stir [stɝ] *v.* menear(se); mover(se), bullir(se); atizar (*el fuego*); incitar; conmover; perturbar; revolver; **to — up** incitar; conmover; revolver; suscitar (*un argumento, pelea,* etc.); *s.* meneo, agitación, movimiento; alboroto.

stirring [stɝɪŋ] *adj.* conmovedor.

stirrup [stírəp] *s.* estribo.

stitch [stɪtʃ] *v.* coser; dar puntadas; *s.* puntada; punzada; **to be in -es** dest

ternillarse de risa.

stock [stak] *s.* (*supply*) surtido; existencias, provisión; (*cattle*) ganado; (*lineage*) cepa, linaje, estirpe; (*shares*) acciones, valores; **in —** en existencia; **live—** ganado; **meat —** caldo de carne; *adj.* en existencia, existente, disponible; común, trivial; **—answer** contestación corriente, común o trivial; **— company** sociedad anónima; compañía teatral; **— exchange** bolsa; **— farm** hacienda de ganado, *Am.* rancho, *Am.* estancia; **— market** mercado de valores, bolsa; **— room** almacén; **— size** tamaño ordinario (*regularmente en existencia*); **—yard** matadero; *v.* surtir, abastecer; tener en existencia (*para vender*); **to — a farm** surtir o proveer de ganado un rancho; **to — up with** surtirse de, acumular.

stockade [stakéd] *s.* estacada, empalizada; vallado; *v.* empalizar, rodear de empalizadas.

stockbroker [stákbrokə] *s.* bolsista, corredor de bolsa.

stockholder [stákholdə] *s.* accionista.

stocking [stákɪŋ] *s.* media.

stoic [stóɪk] *adj.* & *s.* estoico.

stoke [stok] *v.* atizar (*el fuego*); cebar, alimentar (*un horno*).

stole [stol] *pret. de* **to steal.**

stolen [stólən] *p.p. de* **to steal.**

stolid [stálɪd] *adj.* estólido, insensible.

stomach [stámək] *s.* estómago; *v.* aguantar, tolerar.

stomp [stamp] *v.* pisar violentamente.

stone [ston] *s.* piedra; hueso (*de las frutas*); **within a -'s throw** a tiro de piedra; *adj.* pétreo, de piedra; **Stone Age** Edad de Piedra; **stone-deaf** totalmente sordo, sordo como una tapia; *v.* apedrear; deshuesar (*las frutas*).

stony [stónɪ] *adj.* pedregoso; pétreo, de piedra; duro.

stood [stud] *pret.* & *p.p. de* **to stand.**

stool [stul] *s.* (*furniture*) taburete; *C.A.* banquillo; (*toilet*) bacín, bacinica; (*excrement*) excremento; **— pigeon** soplón (*el que delata a otro*).

stoop [stup] *v.* agacharse; doblarse, inclinarse; encorvarse; andar encorvado o caído de hombros; rebajarse, humillarse, abajarse; *s.* encorvamiento, inclinación (*de espaldas*); **to walk with a —** andar encorvado o caído de hombros; **stoop-shouldered** cargado de espaldas, encorvado.

stop [stap] *v.* (*pause*) parar(se), hacer alto, detener(se); (*cease*) acabar(se); cesar; parar de, dejar de; (*block*) atajar; reprimir; suspender; obstruir, tapar; **to — at a hotel** hospedarse o alojarse en un hotel; **to — at nothing** no pararse en escrúpulos; **to — from** impedir; **to — over** at hacer escala en; **to — short** parar(se) de sopetón, parar(se) en seco; **to — up** tapar, obstruir; atascar; *s.* parada; alto, pausa; estada, estancia; detención;

suspensión; llave (*de instrumento de viento*); traste (*de guitarra*); registro (*de órgano*); — **consonant** consonante explosiva.

stopover [stápovəʳ] *s.* parada, escala; **to make a — in** hacer escala en.

stoppage [stápidʒ] *s.* detención; obstrucción; **work** — paro.

stopper [stápəʳ] *s.* tapón.

storage [stóridʒ] *s.* almacenaje; — **battery** acumulador; **to keep in** — almacenar.

store [stor] *s.* (*shop*) tienda; almacén; (*supply*) depósito; acopio; **-s** provisiones; bastimentos; víveres; **department** — almacén; **dry-goods** — lencería, *Méx., Riopl., Andes* mercería, *Am.* cajón de ropa; **fruit** — frutería; **hat** — sombrerería; **grocery** — abacería, tienda dè comestibles, *Méx., C.A.* tienda de abarrotes, *Carib.* bodega; **shoe** — zapatería; **to have in** — tener guardado; *v.* almacenar; guardar; abastecer; **tó — up** acumular.

storehouse [stórhaus] *s.* almacén, depósito.

storekeeper [stórkipəʳ] *s.* tendero; almacenista; guardalmacén.

storeroom [stórrum] *s.* almacén; bodega; despensa.

stork [stɔrk] *s.* cigüeña.

storm [stɔrm] *s.* (*weather*) tormenta, tempestad, borrasca, temporal; (*disturbance*) tumulto; asalto; — **troops** tropas de asalto; **hail** — granizada; **snow** — nevasca; **wind** — vendaval; *v.* asaltar, atacar; rabiar; **it is -ing** hay tormenta, hay tempestad.

stormy [stórmɪ] *adj.* tempestuoso, borrascoso; turbulento.

story [stórɪ] *s.* (*tale*) cuento, historia, historieta; relato; (*gossip*) chisme; rumor; bola; (*plot*) argumento, trama; (*floor*) piso (*de un edificio*); **newspaper** — artículo de periódico, gacetilla.

stout [staʊt] *adj.* corpulento, robusto, fornido; fuerte; firme; leal; valiente.

stove [stov] *s.* estufa; cocina de gas, cocina eléctrica; *pret.* & *p.p. de* to **stave.**

stow [sto] *v.* meter, guardar; esconder; estibar, acomodar la carga de un barco; rellenar; **to — away on a ship** embarcarse clandestinamente, esconderse en un barco.

straddle [strǽdl] *v.* ponerse o estar a horcajadas; ponerse a caballo, cabalgar; favorecer ambos lados (*de un pleito, controversia, etc.*).

strafe [stref] *v.* ametrallar; *Am.* abalear.

straggle [strǽgl] *v.* vagar, desviarse; extraviarse; andar perdido; dispersarse; **to — behind** rezagarse.

straight [stret] *adj.* (*direction*) recto; derecho; directo; (*proper*) honrado; franco; erguido; correcto; en orden; — **face** cara seria; — **hair** pelo lacio; — **hand of five cards** runfla de cinco

naipes del mismo palo; — **rum** ron puro, sin mezcla; **for two hours** — por dos horas seguidas, por dos horas sin parar; **to set a person** — dar consejo a una persona; mostrarle el camino, modo o manera de hacer algo; *adv.* directamente, derecho, en línea recta; francamente; honradamente; —**away** (*o* — **off**) en seguida, al punto; **to talk** — **from the shoulder** hablar con toda franqueza o sinceridad.

straighten [strétn̩] *v.* enderezar(se); arreglar, poner en orden.

straightforward [stretfórwəʳd] *adj.* derecho, recto; honrado; franco, sincero; *adv.* directamente, en línea recta.

straightness [strétnɪs] *s.* derechura; rectitud; honradez.

straightway [strétwe] *adv.* luego, inmediatamente, en seguida.

strain [stren] *v.* (*force*) estirar demasiado, hacer fuerza; poner tirante; violentar, forzar (*los músculos, los nervios, la vista, etc.*); (*sift*) colar, tamizar; **to — one's wrist** torcerse la muñeca; *s.* tensión excesiva; tirantez; torcedura; esfuerzo excesivio; linaje, rasgo racial; aire, tonada.

strainer [strénəʳ] *s.* coladera; cedazo.

strait [stret] *s.* estrecho; **-s** estrecho; aprieto, apuro; **-jacket** camisa de fuerza.

straitlaced [strétlest] *adj.* estricto.

strand [strænd] *v.* encallar; dejar perdido (*sin medios de salir*); dejar aislado, extraviar; **to be -ed** estar encallado; estar extraviado (*sin medios de salir*), estar aislado, andar perdido; *s.* ribera, playa; ramal (*de cuerda, cable, etc.*); hebra, hilo; — **of hair** guedeja; trenza; — **of pearls** hilera de perlas.

strange [strendʒ] *adj.* extraño; raro, singular; desconocido.

strangeness [stréndʒnɪs] *s.* extrañeza, rareza.

stranger [stréndʒəʳ] *s.* extraño, desconocido; forastero.

strangle [strǽŋgl] *v.* estrangular(se).

strap [stræp] *s.* correa; tira de cuero o de tela; correón; tirante; **metal** — banda de metal; *v.* amarrar o atar con correas; azotar (*con correa*); *véase* **strop.**

stratagem [strǽtədʒəm] *s.* estratagema.

strategic [strǝtídʒɪk] *adj.* estratégico.

strategy [strǽtədʒɪ] *s.* estrategia.

stratosphere [strǽtəsfir] *s.* estratosfera.

straw [strɔ] *s.* paja; **I don't care a** — no me importa un comino; *adj.* de paja; pajizo; **straw-colored** pajizo, color de paja; — **hat** sombrero de paja; — **vote** voto no oficial (*para averiguar la opinion pública*).

strawberry [stróberɪ] *s.* fresa.

stray [stre] *v.* extraviarse, descarriarse, desviarse; perderse, errar el camino; vagar; *adj.* extraviado, perdido;

remark observación aislada; *s.* animal perdido o extraviado.

streak [strik] *s.* (*line*) raya, línea, lista; (*vein*) vena; (*trace*) rasgo; (*beam*) rayo (*de luz*); — **of lightning** relámpago, rayo; *v.* rayar, *Am.* listar, hacer rayas o listas en.

stream [strim] *s.* corriente; chorro; río, arroyo, arroyuelo; — **of cars** desfile de autos; **down**— río abajo, agua abajo, con la corriente; **up**— río arriba, agua arriba, contra la corriente; *v.* correr (*el agua*), fluir; brotar, manar; derramarse; flotar (*en el viento*), ondear; **to** — **out of** salir a torrentes de.

streamer [strímɚ] *s.* banderola; gallardete; listón, cinta (*que flota en el aire*).

streamlined [strimlaɪnd] *adj.* aerodinámico.

street [strit] *s.* calle.

streetcar [strítkɑr] *s.* tranvía.

strength [strɛŋkθ] *s.* fuerza; poder; potencia; fortaleza; **on the** — **of his promise** fundado en su promesa.

strengthen [strɛ́ŋkθən] *v.* fortalecer(se); reforzar(se).

strenuous [strɛ́njuəs] *adj.* arduo; enérgico, vigoroso.

streptomycin [strɛptomáɪsɪn] *s.* estreptomicina.

stress [strɛs] *s.* (*force*) fuerza, esfuerzo; tensión, torsión, compresión; (*importance*) urgencia; énfasis; (*intensity*) acento; *v.* acentuar; recalcar, dar énfasis a, hacer hincapié en.

stretch [strɛtʃ] *v.* estirar(se); alargar(se); tender(se); ensanchar; **to** — **oneself** estirarse, desperezarse; **to** — **out one's hand** tender o alargar la mano; *s.* trecho, distancia; extension; período de tiempo; elasticidad; tensión; esfuerzo (*de la imaginación*); estirón; **home** — último trecho (*de una carrera*).

stretcher [strɛ́tʃɚ] *s.* estirador, ensanchador, dilatador; camilla (*para los heridos*).

strew [stru] *v.* regar, esparcir.

strewn [strun] *p.p. de* **to strew,** — **with** regado de, cubierto de.

stricken [stríkən] *p.p. de* **to strike;** *adj.* herido; afligido; agobiado; atacado.

strict [strɪkt] *adj.* estricto; **in** — **confidence** en absoluta confianza, con toda reserva.

stridden [strídn] *p.p. de* **to stride.**

stride [straɪd] *v.* tranquear, caminar a paso largo, dar zancadas, andar a trancos; *s.* zancada, tranco, paso largo.

strife [straɪf] *s.* refriega, contienda, pleito.

strike [straɪk] *v.* (*hit*) dar, golpear, pegar; azotar; herir; atacar; (*collide with*) chocar con; dar con, encontrar (*oro, petróleo, etc.*); ocurrírsele a uno (*una idea*); asumir, afectar (*una postura, una actitud*); dar (*la hora un reloj*); encender (*un fósforo*); acuñar (*moneda*); declararse o estar

en huelga; **to** — **at** amagar; acometer; **to** — **off** borrar, tachar; cortar; **to** — **one's attention** atraer o llamar la atención; **to** — **one's fancy** antojársele a uno; **to** — **one's head against** darse un cabezazo contra; **to** — **out in a certain direction** tomar cierto rumbo, encaminarse o irse en cierta dirección; **to** — **someone for a loan** darle un sablazo a alguien; **to** — **up a friendship** trabar amistad; **to** — **with terror** sobrecoger de terror; **how does she** — **you?** ¿qué tal le parece?; ¿qué piensa Vd. de ella;? *s.* golpe; huelga; descubrimiento repentino (*de petróleo, de una mina, etc.*); **—breaker** esquirol (*obrero que sustituye a un huelguista*).

striker [stráɪkɚ] *s.* (*person on strike*) huelguista; (*device*) golpeador.

striking [stráɪkɪŋ] *adj.* notable; llamativo; conspicuo, manifiesto; sorprendente; extraordinario; (*on strike*) que está de huelga; que está en huelga.

string [strɪŋ] *s.* cuerda; cordel, cinta; cordón; sarta (*de perlas, cuentas, etc.*); fibra (*de habichuelas, porotos, etc.*); fila, hilera; — **bean** habichuela, judía verde, *Méx.* ejote, *Ch., Ríopl.* poroto; — **of lies** sarta de mentiras; *v.* ensartar; tender (*un cable, un alambre*); desfibrar, quitar las fibras a; encordar (*una raqueta, un violín*); encordelar, atar con cordeles, lazos o cuerdas; tomar el pelo, engañar; **to** — **out** extender(se), prolongar(se); **to** — **up** colgar.

strip [strɪp] *v.* despojar; robar; desnudar(se); desvestir(se), desmantelar; **to** — **the gears** estropear el engranaje; **to** — **the skin from** desollar, pelar; *s.* tira, lista, listón; — **of land** faja de tierra.

stripe [straɪp] *s.* (*band*) franja, raya, lista, tira; banda, galón; (*kind*) tipo, índole; *v.* rayar, *Am.* listar, adornar con listas.

striped [stráɪpɪd, straɪpt] *adj.* listado.

strive [straɪv] *v.* esforzarse; luchar, forcejear; hacer lo posible; **to** — **to** esforzarse por.

striven [strívən] *p.p. de* **to strive.**

strode [strod] *pret. de* **to stride.**

stroke [strok] *s.* golpe; ataque, apoplejía; — **of a bell** campanada; — **of a painter's brush** pincelada; — **of lightning** rayo; — **of the hand** caricia; — **of the pen** plumada; **at the** — **of ten** al dar las diez; *v.* frotar suavemente, pasar suavemente la mano, acariciar; alisar.

stroll [strol] *v.* dar un paseo, pasearse; vagar; **to** — **the streets** callejear; *s.* paseo, paseíto.

strong [strɔŋ] *adj.* fuerte; forzudo; fornido; vigoroso; recio; enérgico; firme; bien marcado; acérrimo; — **chance** buena probabilidad; — **coffee** café cargado; — **market** mercado firme; **strong-willed** de voluntad fuerte, de cidido; **strong-arm** violento; *adv.* fuertemente; firmemente.

stronghold [stróŋhold] *s.* fuerte, plaza fuerte.

strop [strɑp] *v.* asentar (*navajas de afeitar*); *s.* asentador de navajas.

strove [strov] *pret. de* to strive.

struck [strʌk] *pret. & p.p. de* to strike; **to be — with a disease** darle a uno una enfermedad; **to be — with terror** estar o quedar sobrecogido de terror.

structural [stráktʃərəl] *adj.* estructural, relativo a la estructura.

structure [stráktʃə] *s.* estructura, construcción; edificio.

struggle [strágl] *v.* bregar, luchar, pugnar; forcejear; esforzarse; *s.* esfuerzo; contienda; lucha, pugna.

strung [strʌŋ] *pret. & p.p. de* to string.

strut [strʌt] *v.* pavonearse, contonearse; *s.* contoneo; tirante, puntal.

stub [stʌb] *s.* trozo, fragmento, pedazo mochado; tocón (*de árbol*); talón (*de libro talonario, boleto, etc.*); **— book** libro talonario; **— pen** pluma de punta mocha; *v.* **to — one's foot** dar(se) un tropezón.

stubble [stábl] *s.* rastrojo; cañones (*de la barba*).

stubborn [stábən] *adj.* terco, testarudo, obstinado, porfiado, cabezón.

stubbornness [stábənnɪs] *s.* terquedad, testarudez, porfía, obstinación.

stucco [stáko] *s.* estuco; *v.* estucar, cubrir de estuco.

stuck [stʌk] *pret. & p.p. de* to stick pegado; atorado; atascado; **— full of holes** agujereado; **stuck-up** tieso, estirado, orgulloso.

stud [stʌd] *s.* (*knob*) tachón, tachuela de adorno; (*button*) botón postizo para camisa; (*bolt*) perno; **—horse** caballo padre; *v.* tachonar; clavetear.

student [stjúdn̩t] *s.* estudiante.

studied [stádɪd] *adj.* estudiado.

studio [stjúdɪo] *s.* estudio, taller.

studious [stjúdɪəs] *adj.* estudioso; aplicado; estudiado.

study [stádɪ] *s.* estudio; cuidado, solicitud; gabinete de estudio; *v.* estudiar.

stuff [stʌf] *s.* (*material*) materia; material; (*cloth*) género, tela; (*thing*) cosa; (*medicine*) menjurje, medicina; (*junk*) cachivaches, baratijas; **of good — de** buena estofa; *v.* rellenar; henchir; hartar(se), atracar(se), atiborrar(se).

stuffing [stáfɪŋ] *s.* relleno; material para rellenar.

stumble [stámbl] *v.* tropezar, dar(se) un tropezón; dar un traspié; hablar o recitar equivocándose a cada paso; **to — upon** tropezar con; *s.* tropiezo, tropezón, traspié.

stump [stʌmp] *s.* tocón (*tronco que queda de un árbol*); raigón (*de muela*); muñón (*de brazo o pierna cortada*); **of a tail** rabo; **to be up a —** hallarse en un apuro, estar perplejo; *v.* trozar el tronco de (*un árbol*); renquear, cojear; dejar confuso, confundir; **to —**

the country recorrer el país pronunciando discursos políticos.

stumpy [stámpɪ] *adj.* rechoncho, *Am.* chaparro; lleno de tocones.

stun [stʌn] *v.* aturdir, pasmar; atolondrar.

stung [stʌŋ] *pret. & p.p. de* to sting.

stunk [stʌŋk] *pret. & p.p. de* to stink.

stunning [stánɪŋ] *adj.* aplastante; elegante, bellísimo.

stunt [stʌnt] *v.* achaparrar, impedir e desarrollo de, no dejar crecer; hacer suertes; hacer piruetas; *s.* suerte; pirueta, suerte acrobática, maniobra gimnástica; hazaña sensacional.

stupefy [stjúpəfaɪ] *v.* atontar; entorpecer; aturdir, atolondrar; pasmar, dejar estupefacto.

stupendous [stjupéndəs] *adj.* estupendo

stupid [stjúpɪd] *adj.* estúpido; atontado

stupidity [stjupídətɪ] *s.* estupidez.

stupor [stjúpə] *s.* letargo, modorra aturdimiento; **in a —** aletargado.

sturdy [stɜ́dɪ] *adj.* fornido, fuerte, robusto; firme.

stutter [státə] *v.* tartamudear; *s.* tartamudeo; tartamudez.

stutterer [státərə] *s.* tartamudo.

stuttering [státərɪŋ] *adj.* tartamudo; tartamudeo.

sty [staɪ] *s.* pocilga; orzuelo (*en el párpado*), *Méx.* perilla; *Ríopl.* chiquero

style [staɪl] *s.* estilo; moda; **to be in —** estar de moda, estilarse; *v.* intitular, nombrar; **to — a dress** cortar un vestido a la moda.

stylish [stáɪlɪʃ] *adj.* elegante; a la moda

stylize [stáɪlaɪz] *v.* estilizar.

subdivision [sʌbdɪvíʒən] *s.* subdivisión; parcelación de terrenos.

subdue [səbdjú] *v.* subyugar, someter; sujetar, dominar; amansar, domar.

subdued [səbdjúd] *p.p. de* to subdue; *adj.* sumiso; sujeto; manso; suave; tenue; **— light** luz tenue.

subject [sábdʒɪkt] *s.* súbdito; sujeto; asunto, tema, materia; *adj.* sujeto; sometido; inclinado, propenso; expuesto; [səbdʒékt] *v.* sujetar; someter subyugar, sojuzgar.

subjection [səbdʒékʃən] *s.* sujeción; dominación; sumisión.

subjective [səbdʒéktɪv] *adj.* subjetivo.

subjugate [sábdʒəget] *v.* subyugar, sojuzgar.

sublimate [sábləmet] *v.* sublimar.

sublime [səbláɪm] *adj.* sublime.

submarine [sábmərin] *adj.* submarino; [sábmərin] *s.* submarino.

submerge [səbmɜ́dʒ] *v.* sumergir(se), hundir(se), sumir(se).

submission [səbmíʃən] *s.* sumisión, sometimiento.

submissive [səbmísɪv] *adj.* sumiso.

submit [səbmít] *v.* someter; **to — a report** someter (presentar *o* rendir) un informe; **to — to punishment** someterse a un castigo.

subordinate [səbórdn̩ɪt] *adj. & s.* subordinado; subalterno; dependiente; [səbórdn̩et] *v.* subordinar.

ubscribe [səbskráib] *v.* subscribir(se); firmar; **to — five dollars** prometer una cuota o subscripción de cinco dólares; **to — for** subscribirse a, abonarse a; **to — to a plan** subscribirse a (o aprobar) un plan.

ubscriber [səbskráibə·] *s.* suscritor, abonado; infrascrito (*que firma un documento*), firmante.

ubscription [səbskrípʃən] *s.* subscripción, abono.

ubsequent [sʌ́bsɪkwɛnt] *adj.* subsiguiente, subsecuente, posterior; **-ly** *adv.* después, posteriormente, subsiguientemente.

ubservient [səbsə́·viənt] *adj.* servil, servilón.

ubside [səbsáid] *v.* menguar, disminuir; bajar (*de nivel*); calmarse, aquietarse.

ubsidize [sʌ́bsədaiz] *v.* subvencionar.

ubsidy [sʌ́bsədi] *s.* subvención.

ubsist [səbsíst] *v.* subsistir.

ubstance [sʌ́bstəns] *s.* substancia (sustancia).

ubstantial [səbstǽnʃəl] *adj.* substancial, substancioso; sólido; considerable; importante; **to be in — agreement** estar en substancia de acuerdo.

ubstantiate [səbstǽnʃiet] *v.* comprobar; verificar.

ubstantive [sʌ́bstəntɪv] *adj.* & *s.* sustantivo.

ubstitute [sʌ́bstətjut] *v.* sustituir (substituir); reemplazar; *s.* sustituto, suplente; reemplazo.

ubstitution [sʌbstətjúʃən] *s.* sustitución (substitución); reemplazo.

ubstratum [sʌ́bstrætəm] *s.* sustrato.

ubterfuge [sʌ́btə·fjudʒ] *s.* escapatoria; subterfugio.

ubterranean [sʌbtəréniən] *adj.* subterráneo.

ubtle [sʌ́tl̩] *adj.* sutil.

ubtlety [sʌ́tl̩ti] *s.* sutileza; agudeza.

ubtract [səbtrǽkt] *v.* sustraer (substraer); restar.

ubtraction [səbtrǽkʃən] *s.* sustracción (substracción), resta.

uburb [sʌ́bə·b] *s.* suberbio, arrabal.

uburban [səbə́·bən] *adj.* & *s.* suburbano.

ubversive [səbvə́·sɪv] *adj.* subversivo (*en contra de la autoridad constituida*); trastornador, destructivo.

ubway [sʌ́bwe] *s.* subterráneo, túnel; metro, ferrocarril subterráneo.

ucceed [səksíd] *v.* suceder a; medrar, tener buen éxito, salir bien.

uccess [səksɛ́s] *s.* éxito, buen éxito; triunfo.

uccessful [səksɛ́sfəl] *adj.* afortunado; próspero; **to be —** tener buen éxito; **-ly** *adv.* con buen éxito, prósperamente.

uccession [səksɛ́ʃən] *s.* sucesión.

uccessive [səksɛ́sɪv] *adj.* sucesivo.

uccessor [səksɛ́sə·] *s.* sucesor; heredero.

uccor [sʌ́kə·] *s.* socorro; *v.* socorrer.

uccumb [səkʌ́m] *v.* sucumbir.

uch [sʌtʃ] *adj.* tal; semejante; **— a** tal, semejante; **— a good man** un

hombre tan bueno; **— as** tal como, tales como; **at — an hour** a tal hora; **at — and — a place** en tal o cual lugar.

suck [sʌk] *v.* chupar; mamar; **to — up** chupar; sorber; *s.* chupada; mamada.

sucker [sʌ́kə·] *s.* chupador; mamón, mamantón; dulce (*que se chupa*); primo (*persona demasiado crédula*).

suckle [sʌ́kl̩] *v.* mamar; amamantar, dar de mamar.

suction [sʌ́kʃən] *s.* succión; chupada, aspiración.

sudden [sʌ́dn̩] *adj.* súbito, repentino; precipitado; inesperado; **all of a —** de súbito, de repente, de sopetón; **-ly** *adv.* de súbito, de repente, de sopetón.

suddenness [sʌ́dnnɪs] *s.* precipitación; rapidez.

suds [sʌdz] *s.* espuma, jabonadura.

sue [su] *v.* demandar; **to — for damages** demandar por daños y perjuicios; **to — for peace** pedir la paz.

suet [súɪt] *s.* sebo, gordo, grasa.

suffer [sʌ́fə·] *v.* sufrir; padecer.

sufferer [sʌ́fərə·] *s.* sufridor.

suffering [sʌ́fərɪŋ] *s.* sufrimiento, padecimiento; *adj.* doliente; sufrido, paciente.

suffice [səfáis] *v.* bastar, ser bastante o suficiente.

sufficient [səfíʃənt] *adj.* suficiente, bastante; **-ly** *adv.* suficientemente, bastante.

suffix [sʌ́fɪks] *s.* sufijo.

suffocate [sʌ́fəket] *v.* sofocar(se), ahogar(se), asfixiar(se).

suffocation [sʌfəkéʃən] *s.* asfixia, sofoco.

suffrage [sʌ́frɪdʒ] *s.* sufragio; voto.

sugar [ʃúgə·] *s.* azúcar; **— bowl** azucarera; **— cane** caña de azúcar; **lump of —** terrón de azúcar; *v.* azucarar; cristalizarse (*el almíbar*), *Am.* azucararse.

suggest [səgdʒɛ́st] *v.* sugerir, indicar.

suggestion [səgdʒɛ́stʃən] *s.* sugestión, *Am.* sugerencia; indicación.

suggestive [səgdʒɛ́stɪv] *adj.* sugestivo.

suicide [súəsaid] *s.* suicidio; suicida; **to commit —** suicidarse.

suit [sut] *s.* traje, terno, *Carib.*, *Ven.* flux (o flus); palo (*de la baraja*); demanda, pleito; petición; galanteo; *v.* adaptar, acomodar; agradar; satisfacer; sentar bien, venir bien; caer bien; convenir; ser a propósito; **— yourself** haz lo que quieras, haga Vd. lo que guste.

suitable [sútəbl̩] *adj.* propio, conveniente, debido, a propósito, apropiado, adecuado.

suitably [sútəbli] *adv.* propiamente, adecuadamente, convenientemente.

suitcase [sútkes] *s.* maleta, valija.

suite [swit] *s.* serie; comitiva, acompañamiento; **— of rooms** vivienda, apartamento, habitación; **bedroom —** juego de muebles para alcoba.

suitor [sútə·] *s.* pretendiente, galán; demandante (*en un pleito*).

sulk [sʌlk] *v.* tener murria; estar hosco

ST

o malhumorado; *s.* murria.

sulky [sʌ́lkɪ] *adj.* malcontento, hosco, malhumorado; **to be —** tener murria.

sullen [sʌ́lɪn] *adj.* hosco, sombrío, tétrico; malhumorado, taciturno.

sully [sʌ́lɪ] *v.* manchar, ensuciar; empañar.

sulphate [sʌ́lfet] *s.* sulfato.

sulphide [sʌ́lfaɪd] *s.* sulfuro.

sulphur [sʌ́lfə] *s.* azufre.

sulphuric [sʌlfjúrɪk] *adj.* sulfúrico.

sultan [sʌ́ltn] *s.* sultán.

sultry [sʌ́ltrɪ] *adj.* bochornoso, sofocante; **— heat** bochorno, calor sofocante.

sum [sʌm] *s.* suma; cantidad; esencia, substancia; **— total** total; *v.* sumar; **to — up** resumir, recapitular.

summarize [sʌ́məraɪz] *v.* resumir, compendiar.

summary [sʌ́mərɪ] *s.* sumario, resumen; compendio; *adj.* sumario; breve.

summer [sʌ́mə] *s.* verano; estío; *adj.* veraniego, estival de verano; **— resort** balneario, lugar de veraneo; *v.* veranear.

summit [sʌ́mɪt] *s.* cima, cúspide, cumbre.

summon [sʌ́mən] *v.* citar; convocar, llamar; **-s** *s.* notificación; cita judicial, citación, emplazamiento.

sumptuous [sʌ́mptʃʊəs] *adj.* suntuoso.

sun [sʌn] *s.* sol; **— bath** baño de sol; **— lamp** lámpara de rayos ultravioletas; **— porch** solana; *v.* asolear; **to — oneself** asolearse, tomar el sol.

sunbeam [sʌ́nbim] *s.* rayo de sol.

sunburn [sʌ́nbən] *s.* quemadura de sol; *v.* asolear(se); quemar(se) al sol, tostar(se) al sol.

Sunday [sʌ́ndɪ] *s.* domingo.

sundial [sʌ́ndaɪəl] *s.* cuadrante solar, reloj de sol.

sundown [sʌ́ndaʊn] *s.* puesta del sol.

sundry [sʌ́ndrɪ] *adj.* varios, diversos.

sunflower [sʌ́nflaʊə] *s.* girasol.

sung [sʌŋ] *pret. & p.p. de* **to sing**.

sunglasses [sʌ́nglæsəz] *s.* gafas (*anteojos*) de sol.

sunk [sʌŋk] *pret. & p.p. de* **to sink**.

sunken [sʌ́ŋkən] *adj.* hundido, sumido.

sunlight [sʌ́nlaɪt] *s.* luz del sol, luz solar.

sunny [sʌ́nɪ] *adj.* asoleado o soleado; alegre, risueño, resplandeciente; **— day** día de sol.

sunrise [sʌ́nraɪz] *s.* salida del sol, amanecer, amanecida.

sunset [sʌ́nsɛt] *s.* puesta del sol.

sunshine [sʌ́nʃaɪn] *s.* luz del sol, solana.

sunstroke [sʌ́nstrok] *s.* insolación.

sup [sʌp] *v.* cenar.

superb [supə́b] *adj.* soberbio.

superficial [supəfíʃəl] *adj.* superficial.

superfluous [supə́flʊəs] *adj.* superfluo.

superhuman [supəhjúmən] *adj.* sobrehumano.

superintend [suprɪnténd] *v.* dirigir, inspeccionar, vigilar.

superintendent [suprɪnténdənt] *s.* su perintendente; inspector; capataz.

superior [səpíriə] *adj. & s.* superior.

superiority [səpiriɔ́rətɪ] *s.* superiori dad.

superlative [səpə́lətɪv] *adj. & s.* super lativo.

supermarket [súpəmarkət] *s.* super mercado.

supernatural [supənǽtʃrəl] *adj.* sobre natural; **the —** lo sobrenatural.

supersede [supəsíd] *v.* reemplazar.

superstition [supəstíʃən] *s.* super stición.

superstitious [supəstíʃəs] *adj.* super sticioso.

supervise [supəváɪz] *v.* dirigir, inspec cionar, vigilar.

supervision [supəvíʒən] *s.* inspección vigilancia.

supervisor [supəváɪzə] *s.* superinten dente, inspector; interventor.

supper [sʌ́pə] *s.* cena.

supplant [səplǽnt] *v.* suplantar; reem plazar.

supple [sʌ́pl] *adj.* flexible; dócil.

supplement [sʌ́pləmənt] *s.* suplemen to; apéndice; [sʌ́pləmɛnt] *v.* suple mentar, completar.

suppliant [sʌ́plɪənt] *adj. & s.* supli cante.

supplication [sʌplɪkéʃən] *s.* súplica plegaria; ruego.

supply [səpláɪ] *v.* proveer; abastecer surtir; suplir; dar, suministrar; s provisión, abastecimiento; bastimen to; abasto; surtido; **supplies** provi siones; materiales; víveres; pertre chos; **— pipe** cañería o caño de abastecimiento, tubería o tubo de suministro.

support [səpɔ́rt] *v.* (*keep from falling*) sostener; apoyar; (*provide for*) man tener; sustentar; (*bear*) soportar aguantar; *s.* apoyo; sostén, soporte puntal; sustento, manutención; am paro.

supporter [səpɔ́rtə] *s.* defensor; parti dario; mantenedor; sostén, apoyo; ti rante (*para medias*).

suppose [səpóz] *v.* suponer.

supposed [səpózd] *adj.* supuesto; pre sunto; **-ly** *adv.* supuestamente.

supposition [sʌpəzíʃən] *s.* suposición.

suppress [səprɛ́s] *v.* suprimir; repri mir; parar, suspender; **to — a revolt** sofocar una revuelta o motín.

suppression [səprɛ́ʃən] *s.* supresión; re presión.

supremacy [səprémərsɪ] *s.* supremacía

supreme [səprím] *adj.* supremo.

sure [ʃur] *adj.* seguro; cierto; estable *adv. véase* **surely; be — to do it** hágalo sin falta, no deje Vd. de hacerlo; **-ly** *adv.* seguramente; cier tamente; con toda seguridad; sin falta.

surety [ʃúrtɪ] *s.* seguridad; garantía fianza; fiador.

surf [sɜf] *s.* oleaje, rompientes; resaca

surface [sʌ́fɪs] *s.* superficie; cara; *v.*

alisar, allanar; poner superficie a.

surfboard [sə́rfbord] s. patín de mar.

surfeit [sə́rfɪt] s. hastío, exceso; v. hastiar; empalagar.

surge [sə́rdʒ] s. oleada, oleaje; v. agitarse, hinchar(se) (el mar); surgir.

surgeon [sə́rdʒən] s. cirujano.

surgery [sə́rdʒərɪ] s. cirujía.

surgical [sə́rdʒɪk1] adj. quirúrgico.

surly [sə́lɪ] adj. rudo, hosco, malhumorado.

surmise [səmáɪz] v. conjeturar, suponer, presumir; s. conjetura, suposición.

surmount [səmáʊnt] v. superar, vencer; coronar.

surname [sə́rnem] s. sobrenombre, apellido; v. apellidar, llamar.

surpass [səpǽs] v. sobrepasar, superar, sobrepujar, exceder, aventajar.

surpassing [səpǽsɪŋ] adj. sobresaliente, excelente.

surplus [sə́rplʌs] s. sobra, sobrante, exceso, excedente; superávit; adj. sobrante, excedente, de sobra.

surprise [səpráɪz] s. sorpresa; v. sorprender.

surprising [səpráɪzɪŋ] adj. sorprendente.

surrender [sərɛ́ndə] v. rendir(se), entregar(se), darse; ceder; s. rendición; entrega; cesión; sumisión.

surround [səráʊnd] v. rodear, cercar, circundar.

surrounding [səráʊndɪŋ] adj. circundante, circunvecino, circunstante.

surroundings [səráʊndɪŋz] s. pl. alrededores, inmediaciones, cercanías; ambiente.

survey [sə́rve] s. (inspection) examen, reconocimiento, enspección, estudio; (measure) medición, agrimensura (de un terreno); plano (de un terreno); bosquejo o esbozo general (de historia, literatura, etc.); — **course** curso general o comprensivo; [səvé] v. examinar, inspeccionar, reconocer, medir (un terreno), levantar un plano (el agrimensor).

surveyor [səvéə] s. agrimensor.

survival [səváɪvl] s. supervivencia; sobreviviente; resto.

survive [səváɪv] c. sobrevivir; quedar vivo, salvarse.

survivor [səváɪvə] s. sobreviviente.

susceptible [səsɛ́ptəbl] adj. susceptible; — **of proof** capaz de probarse; — **to** propenso a.

suspect [sʌ́spɛkt] s. sospechoso; [səspɛ́kt] v. sospechar.

suspend [səspɛ́nd] v. suspender.

suspenders [səspɛ́ndəz] s. tirantes (de pantalón).

suspense [səspɛ́ns] s. (uncertainty) suspensión, incertidumbre; (anxiety) ansiedad; **to keep in** — tener en suspenso, tener en duda.

suspension [səspɛ́nʃən] s. suspensión; — **bridge** puente colgante.

suspicion [səspíʃən] s. sospecha.

suspicious [səspíʃəs] adj. sospechoso; suspicaz.

sustain [səstén] v. (prolong) sostener; mantener; (support) sustentar; (bear, endure) aguantar; (defend) apoyar, defender; (undergo) sufrir (un daño o pérdida).

sustenance [sʌ́stənəns] s. sustento; subsistencia; alimentos; mantenimiento.

swagger [swǽgə] v. pavonearse, contonearse; fanfarronear; s. pavoneo, contoneo; fanfarronada.

swain [swen] s. galán.

swallow [swálo] s. golondrina; trago; v. tragar; deglutir.

swam [swǽm] pret. de to swim.

swamp [swamp] s. pantano; ciénaga; — **land** cenagal, terreno pantanoso; v. inundar(se); sumergir(se); **to be -ed with work** estar abrumado de trabajo.

swampy [swámpɪ] adj. pantanoso, cenagoso, fangoso.

swan [swan] s. cisne.

swap [swap] v. cambalachear, cambiar, trocar; s. cambalache, cambio, trueque.

swarm [sworm] s. enjambre; v. pulular; bullir, hervir, hormiguear.

swarthy [swórðɪ] adj. trigueño, moreno, Am. prieto.

swat [swat] v. pegar, aporrear; aplastar de un golpe (una mosca); s. golpe.

sway [swe] v. mecer(se); cimbrar(se); balancearse; ladear(se); oscilar; tambalear; influir; s. oscilación; vaivén; balanceo; influjo, influencia; mando; predominio.

swear [swer] v. jurar; renegar, blasfemar, echar maldiciones; juramentar, tomar juramento; **to — by** jurar por; poner toda su confianza en; **to — in** juramentar; **to — off smoking** jurar no fumar más, renunciar al tabaco.

sweat [swɛt] v. sudar; trasudar; hacer sudar; s. sudor; trasudor.

sweater [swɛ́tə] s. Am. suéter; sudador, el que suda.

sweaty [swɛ́tɪ] adj. sudoroso.

Swede [swid] s. sueco.

Swedish [swidɪʃ] adj. sueco; s. sueco, idioma sueco.

sweep [swip] v. barrer; dragar (puertos, ríos, etc.); extenderse; **to — down upon** caer sobre; asolar; **to — everything away** barrer con todo; **she swept into the room** entró garbosamente en la sala; s. barrida; extensión; soplo (del viento).

sweeper [swípə] s. barrendero; **carpet** — escoba mecánica.

sweeping [swípɪŋ] s. barrido; **-s** basura; adj. abarcador, que lo abarca todo, vasto; asolador; — **victory** victoria completa.

sweet [swit] adj. dulce; oloroso; fresco; — **butter** mantequilla sin sal; — **corn** maíz tierno; — **milk** leche fresca; — **pea** guisante de olor; — **potato** batata, Am. camote, Am. boniato; **to have a — tooth** ser goloso, gustarle a uno los dulces; s.

dulce, golosina; **my —** mi vida, mi alma.

sweeten [swítŋ] v. endulzar(se), dulcificar(se); suavizar.

sweetheart [swíthɑrt] s. querida, novia, prometida; amante, querido, galán, novio.

sweetmeat [swítmit] s. confite, confitura dulce, golosina.

sweetness [swítnɪs] s. dulzura; melosidad; suavidad.

swell [swɛl] v. hinchar(se), henchir(se), inflar(se); dilatar(se), abultar(se); acrecentar; s. hinchazón; protuberancia; oleaje; adj. elegante; muy bueno, excelente, magnífico; **to have a — head** creerse gran cosa; ser vanidoso.

swelling [swélɪŋ] s. hinchazón; chichón, bulto; protuberancia.

swelter [swélta] v. sofocarse de calor.

swept [swɛpt] pret. & p.p. de to sweep.

swerve [swɜv] v. desviar(se); torcer; cambiar repentinamente de rumbo; s. desvío brusco, cambio repentino de dirección; **to make a — to the right** torcer a la derecha.

swift [swɪft] adj. veloz, rápido.

swiftness [swíftnɪs] s. velocidad, rapidez, presteza, prontitud.

swim [swɪm] v. nadar; flotar; **to — across** pasar a nado, atravesar nadando; **my head is swimming** tengo vértigo, se me va la cabeza, estoy desvanecido; s. nadada; **— suit** traje de baño o natación.

swimmer [swíma] s. nadador.

swindle [swíndl] v. estafar; s. estafa.

swine [swaɪn] s. marrano, puerco, cerdo, cochino; marranos, puercos, cerdos.

swing [swɪŋ] v. columpiar(se), mecer(se), balancear(se); oscilar; hacer oscilar; blandir (un bastón, espada, etc.); colgar; girar; hacer girar; **to — a deal** llevar a cabo un negocio; **to — around** dar vuelta, girar; **to — one's arms** girar o menear los brazos; **to — open** abrirse de pronto (una puerta); s. columpio; hamaca; balanceo; vaivén; compás, ritmo; golpe, guantada, puñetazo; **— door** puerta giratoria; **— shift** turno de trabajo desde las dieciséis hasta medianoche; **in full —** en su apogeo, en pleno movimiento; **to give someone full —** darle a alguien completa libertad de acción.

swipe [swaɪp] v. hurtar, sisar.

swirl [swɜl] v. arremolinarse; girar, dar vueltas; s. remolino; torbellino; vuelta, movimiento giratorio.

Swiss [swɪs] adj. & s. suizo.

switch [swɪtʃ] s. (change) mudanza; (whip) látigo, (blow) azote; Méx., Andes chicote, Ríopl. rebenque; Méx., Andes fuete; latigazo; pelo postizo; cambio; **electric —** interruptor, conmutador; **railway —** aguja, cambio; **—man** guardagujas, Andes, Ríopl. cambiavía; Méx. guardavía; v. azotar; desviar(se); cambiar(se); **to — off** cortar (la comunicación o la

corriente eléctrica); apagar (la luz eléctrica); **to — on the light** encender la luz.

switchboard [swítʃbɔrd] s. cuadro o tablero de distribución; cuadro conmutador.

swivel [swívl] adj. giratorio.

swollen [swólan] p.p. de to swell.

swoon [swun] v. desvanecerse, desmayarse; s. desmayo.

swoop [swup] v. **to — down upon** caer de súbito sobre; abalanzarse sobre; acometer; **to — off** cortar de un golpe; **to — up** agarrar, arrebatar; s. descenso súbito; arremetida; **at one —** de un golpe.

sword [sord] s. espada; **— belt** talabarte.

swore [swor] pret. de to swear.

sworn [sworn] p.p. de to swear.

swum [swʌm] p.p. de to swim.

swung [swʌŋ] pret. & p.p. de to swing.

syllable [síləbl] s. sílaba.

syllabus [síləbəs] s. sílabo.

symbol [símbl] s. símbolo.

symbolic [sɪmbálɪk] adj. simbólico.

symbolism [símblɪzəm] s. simbolismo.

symmetrical [sɪmétrɪkl] adj. simétrico.

symmetry [símɪtrɪ] s. simetría.

sympathetic [sɪmpəθétɪk] adj. compasivo; favorablemente dispuesto; que compadece; **— towards** favorablemente dispuesto a (o hacia).

sympathize [símpəθaɪz] v. compadecer(se); condolerse.

sympathy [símpəθɪ] s. compasión, lástima; armonía; **to extend one's —** dar el pésame.

symphony [símfənɪ] s. sinfonía; **— orchestra** orquesta sinfónica.

symposium [sɪmpósɪəm] s. coloquio.

symptom [símptəm] s. síntoma.

syndicate [síndɪkɪt] s. sindicato; **newspaper —** sindicato periodístico; [síndɪket] v. sindicar, formar un sindicato; sindicarse, combinarse para formar un sindicato; vender (un cuento, caricatura, serie de artículos, etc.) a un sindicato.

syndrome [síndrom] s. síndrome.

synonym [sínənɪm] s. sinónimo.

synonymous [sɪnánəməs] adj. sinónimo.

synopsis [sɪnápsɪs] s. sinopsis.

syntax [síntæks] s. sintaxis.

synthesis [sínθəsɪs] s. síntesis.

synthesize [sínθəsaɪz] v. sintetizar.

synthetic [sɪnθétɪk] adj. sintético.

syringe [sírɪndʒ] s. jeringa.

syrup = **sirup**.

system [sístəm] s. sistema.

systematic [sɪstəmætɪk] adj. sistemático.

systemic [sɪstémɪk] adj. sistemático.

T

tab [tæb] s. (flap) lengüeta; (bill) cuenta.

tabernacle [tǽbənækl] s. tabernáculo.

table [tébl] s. mesa; tabla (de materias, de multiplicar, etc.); **— cover** tapete, cubremesa; **—land** mesa, meseta; *v.* poner sobre la mesa; formar tabla o índice; **to — a motion** dar carpetazo a una moción, aplazar la discusión de una moción.

tablecloth [téb|klɔθ] *s.* mantel.

tablespoon [téb|spun] *s.* cuchara grande.

tablespoonful [téb|spunful] *s.* cucharada.

tablet [tǽblɪt] *s.* tableta; tablilla, pastilla; bloc de papel; lápida, placa.

tableware [téb|wer] *s.* vajilla, servicio de mesa.

taboo [tæbú] *s.* tabú.

tabulate [tǽbjəlet] *v.* formar tablas o listas.

tacit [tǽsɪt] *adj.* tácito.

taciturn [tǽsətɜn] *adj.* taciturno, silencioso.

tack [tæk] *s.* tachuela; hilván; virada o cambio de rumbo (*de una embarcación*); amura, jarcia (*para sostener el ángulo de una vela*); **to change —** cambiar de amura, cambiar de rumbo; *v.* clavetear con tachuelas; coser, hilvanar; pegar, clavar; juntar, unir; virar, cambiar de rumbo; zigzaguear (*un barco de vela*).

tackle [tǽkl] *s.* aparejo, equipo, enseres, avíos; agarrada (*en futbol*); atajador (*en futbol*); **fishing —** avíos de pescar; *v.* agarrar, asir, atajar (*en futbol*); atacar (*un problema*); acometer (*una empresa*).

tact [tækt] *s.* tacto, tino, tiento.

tactful [tǽktfʊl] *adj.* cauto, prudente, diplomático.

tactics [tǽktɪks] *s.* táctica.

tactless [tǽktlɪs] *adj.* falto de tacto o de tino; imprudente, incauto.

taffeta [tǽfɪtə] *s.* tafetán.

tag [tæg] *s.* (*label*) márbete, etiqueta; cartela; (*loose end*) pingajo, rabito, cabo; **to play —** jugar al tócame tú, jugar a la pega; *v.* pegar un márbete a, marcar; **to — after** seguir de cerca a, pisar los talones a; **to — something on to** juntar, añadir o agregar algo a.

tail [tel] *s.* (*animal*) cola, rabo; (*object*) cabo, extremo, extremidad; **— light** farol trasero, farol de cola; **— spin** barrena.

tailor [télə] *s.* sastre.

taint [tent] *s.* tacha, mancha, corrupción; *v.* manchar; corromper(se), inficionar(se).

take [tek] *v.* tomar; coger; llevar; conducir; dar (*un paseo, vuelta, paso, salto*); hacer (*un viaje*); asumir; sacar o tomar (*una fotografía*); **to — a chance** aventurarse, correr un riesgo; **to — a fancy to** caerle en gracia a uno; aficionarse a; antojársele a uno; **to — a look at** mirar a, echar una mirada a; **to — a notion to** antojársele a uno; **to — after** salir a, parecerse a; seguir el ejemplo de; **to — amiss** interpretar mal, echar a mala parte; **to — an oath** prestar juramento; **to — apart** desarmar, desmontar; **to — away** llevarse; **to — back one's**

words desdecirse, retractarse; **to — back** to devolver (*algo*) a; **to — by surprise** coger desprevenido, coger de sorpresa; **to — care of** cuidar de, atender a; **to — charge of** encargarse de; **to — cold** resfriarse, acatarrarse; **to — down in writing** poner por escrito, apuntar; **to — effect** surtir efecto, dar resultado; entrar en vigencia (*una ley*); **to — exercise** hacer ejercicio; hacer gimnasia; **to — from** quitar a; sustraer de, restar de; **to — in** meter en; recibir; abarcar; embaucar; reducir, achicar (*un vestido*); **to — leave** decir adiós, despedirse; **to — off** quitar; descontar, rebajar; despegar (*un aeroplano*); remedar, parodiar (*a alguien*); **to — offense** ofenderse, darse por ofendido; **to — on a responsibility** asumir una responsabilidad; **to — out** sacar; **to — place** tener lugar, suceder, ocurrir; **to — stock** hacer inventario; **to — stock in** creer, tener confianza en; **to — the floor** tomar la palabra; **to — to heart** tomar a pechos, tomar en serio; **to — to one's heels** poner pies en polvorosa; **to — to task** reprender, regañar; **to — up a matter** tratar un asunto; **to — up space** ocupar espacio; **I — it that** supongo que; *s.* toma; **take-off** despegue (*de un aeroplano*); remedo, parodia.

taken [tékən] *p.p. de* **to take**; **to be — ill** caer enfermo.

talcum [tǽlkəm] *s.* talco; **— powder** talco en polvo.

tale [tel] *s.* (*story*) cuento, relato, fábula; (*gossip*) chisme; **to tell -s** contar cuentos o chismes; chismear, murmurar.

talebearer [télberə] *s.* soplón, chismoso.

talent [tǽlənt] *s.* talento.

talented [tǽləntɪd] *adj.* talentoso.

talk [tɔk] *v.* hablar; charlar, platicar, conversar; **to — into** inducir o persuadir a; **to — nonsense** decir tonterías, hablar disparates; **to — out of** disuadir de; **to — over** discutir; **to — up** alabar; hablar claro o recio, hablar en voz alta; *s.* charla, conversación, plática; habla; discurso; conferencia; rumor; **— of the town** comidilla, tema de murmuración.

talkative [tɔkətɪv] *adj.* hablador, locuaz, platicador.

talker [tɔkə] *s.* hablador; conversador; platicador; orador.

tall [tɔl] *adj.* alto; **— tale** cuento exagerado o increíble; **six feet —** seis pies de altura o de alto.

tallow [tǽlo] *s.* sebo.

tally [tǽlɪ] *s.* cuenta; **— sheet** plana para llevar la cuenta; *v.* llevar la cuenta; **to — up** contar, sumar; **to — with** coresponder con, concordar con.

tame [tem] *adj.* manso, dócil; **— amusement** diversión poco animada o desabrida; *v.* amansar, domar, domeñar; domesticar.

tamper [tǽmpə] v. to — with meterse con, juguetear con; falsificar (un documento); to — with a lock tratar de forzar una cerradura.

tan [tæn] v. (cure) curtir, adobar (pieles); (punish) zurrar, azotar; (sunburn) tostar(se), requemar(se); adj. tostado, requemado; color de canela; bayo, amarillento; s. color moreno, de canela o café con leche.

tang [tæŋ] s. sabor u olor picante.

tangent [tǽndʒənt] adj. & s. tangente; to go off at a — salirse por la tangente.

tangerine [tǽndʒərin] s. naranja tangerina o mandarina.

tangible [tǽndʒəbl] adj. tangible, palpable; corpóreo.

tangle [tǽŋgl] v. enredar(se), enmarañar(se); confundir(se), embrollar(se); s. enredo, maraña, embrollo; confusión.

tank [tæŋk] s. tanque; depósito; swimming — piscina.

tanner [tǽnə] s. curtidor.

tannery [tǽnəri] s. curtiduría, tenería.

tannic acid [tǽnikǽsəd] s. ácido tánico.

tantalize [tǽntlaiz] v. molestar; hacer desesperar; exasperar.

tantamount [tǽntəmaunt] adj. equivalente.

tantrum [tǽntrəm] s. berrinche.

tap [tæp] s. (blow) palmadita; golpecito; (faucet) espita, grifo, llave; — dance zapateado, Andes, Ríopl. zapateo; —room bar; beer on — cerveza del barril, cerveza de sifón; v. tocar, golpear ligeramente; dar una palmadita o golpecito; taladrar; extraer; to — a tree sangrar un árbol.

tape [tep] s. cinta, cintilla; — measure cinta para medir; —worm solitaria; — recorder magnetófono; grabadora; adhesive — tela adhesiva, esparadrapo; v. atar o vendar con cinta; medir con cinta.

taper [tépə] s. (candle) velita, candela; (diminished size) adelgazamiento paulatino; v. adelgazar, disminuir gradualmente; to — off ahusar(se), ir disminuyendo (hasta rematar en punta).

tapestry [tǽpɪstrɪ] s. tapiz, colgadura; tapicería; tela (para forrar muebles).

tapeworm [tépwəm] s. tenia, solitaria.

tapioca [tæpiókə] s. tapioca.

tar [tar] s. alquitrán, brea, pez (f.); v. alquitranar, embrear, poner brea o alquitrán.

tardy [tárdɪ] adj. tardo, tardió; to be — llegar tarde o retrasado.

target [tárgɪt] s. blanco; — practice tiro al blanco.

tariff [tǽrɪf] s. tarifa; arancel, impuesto.

tarnish [tárnɪʃ] v. empañar(se); manchar; perder el lustre; s. deslustre, falta de lustre, empañamiento; mancha.

tarry [tǽrɪ] v. demorarse, tardar(se).

tart [tart] s. acre, agridulce; agrio; picante; — reply respuesta mordaz o agria; s. tarta, torta rellena con dulce de frutas.

task [tæsk] s. faena, tarea, quehacer; to take to — reprender, regañar.

task force [tǽskfɔrs] s. agrupación de fuerzas militares para cierta misión.

tassel [tǽsl] s. borla.

taste [test] v. gustar; probar; saborear, paladear; to — of onion saber a cebolla; it -s sour sabe agrio, tiene un sabor o gusto agrio; s. gusto; sabor; prueba; afición; after— dejo; in good—de buen gusto; to take a—of probar.

tasteless [téstlɪs] adj. insípido; desabrido; de mal gusto.

tasty [tésti] adj. sabroso, gustoso; de buen gusto.

tatter [tǽtə] s. harapo, Carib. hilacho.

tattered [tǽtəd] adj. roto, harapiento, andrajoso.

tattle [tǽtl] v. chismear, murmurar; s. habladuría, murmuración, hablilla; —tale chismoso, soplón.

tattoo [tætú] s. tatuaje.

taught [tɔt] pret. & p.p. de to teach.

taunt [tɔnt] v. mofarse de, echar pullas; reprochar; s. mofa, pulla.

tavern [tǽvən] s. taberna; posada.

tax [tæks] s. impuesto, contribución; esfuerzo; v. imponer contribuciones a; tasar; abrumar; reprender, reprobar; cobrar (un precio); to — one's patience abusar de la paciencia.

taxation [tækséʃən] s. impuestos, contribuciones; imposición de contribuciones.

taxi [tǽksi] s. taxímetro, taxi, automóvil de alquiler; v. ir en taxímetro; taxear (un aeroplano).

taxicab [tǽksikæb] = taxi.

taxidermy [tǽksidəmi] s. taxidermia.

taxpayer [tǽkspeə] s. contribuyente.

tea [ti] s. té.

teach [titʃ] v. enseñar; instruir.

teacher [títʃə] s. maestro, maestra.

teaching [títʃɪŋ] s. enseñanza; instrucción; doctrina.

teacup [tíkʌp] s. taza para té.

teakettle [tíketl] s. marmita, tetera, Ríopl. pava (para el mate).

team [tim] s. equipo (de jugadores); partido, grupo; tronco (de caballos, mulas, etc.); yunta (de bueyes): — work cooperación; v. uncir, enganchar; formar pareja; acarrear, transportar; to — up unirse, formar equipo.

teamster [tímstə] s. carretero.

teapot [típat] s. tetera.

tear [tɪr] s. lágrima; — gas gas lacrimógeno o lacrimante; to burst into -s romper a llorar; deshacerse en lágrimas.

tear [ter] v. rasgar(se); desgarrar, romper; to — along ir a toda velocidad; andar aprisa, correr; to — apart desarmar, desmontar; separar, apartar; to — away arrancar; irse; to — down demoler, derribar (un edificio); desarmar, desmontar (una máquina);

to — off in a hurry salir corriendo, salir a la carrera; **to — one's hair** mesarse los cabellos; *s.* desgarradura, rasgadura; rasgón, rotura; prisa; **wear and — desgaste.**

tearful [tírfəl] *adj.* lloroso.

tease [tiz] *v.* embromar; molestar; importunar.

teaspoon [tíspun] *s.* cucharilla, cucharita.

teaspoonful [tíspunful] *s.* cucharadita.

teat [tit] *s.* teta.

technical [téknɪk]] *adj.* técnico.

technician [teknífən] *s.* técnico.

technique [tekník] *s.* técnica.

technology [teknɑ́ləʤɪ] *s.* tecnología.

tedious [tídɪəs] *adj.* tedioso, pesado, aburrido, fastidioso.

tediousness [tídɪəsnɪs] *s.* tedio.

teem [tim] *v.* **to — with** abundar en, estar lleno de.

teen-ager [tíneʤɚ] *s.* joven de la edad de 13 a 19 años; *Col.* cocacolo.

teens [tinz] *s. pl.* edad de trece a diecinueve años; números de trece a diecinueve; **to be in one's —** tener de trece a diecinueve años.

teeth [tiθ] *s. pl. de* tooth; **he escaped by the skin of his —** por poco no se escapa, se escapó por milagro.

telecast [téləkæst] *s.* teledifusión.

telegram [téləgræm] *s.* telegrama.

telegraph [téləgræf] *s.* telégrafo; *v.* telegrafiar.

telegraphic [tɛləgrǽfɪk] *adj.* telegráfico.

telegraphy [təlégrəfɪ] *s.* telegrafía.

telepathy [təlépəθɪ] *s.* telepatía.

telephone [téləfon] *s.* teléfono; **— booth** casilla de teléfono; **— operator** telefonista; **— receiver** receptor telefónico; *v.* telefonear, llamar por teléfono.

telescope [téləskop] *s.* telescopio; *v.* enchufar(se), encajar(se) un objeto en otro.

television [téləvɪʒən] *s.* televisión.

tell [tɛl] *v.* (*recount*) decir; contar; expresar; explicar; (*identify*) adivinar; **to — on someone** delatar a alguien, contar chismes de alguien; **to — someone off** decirle a alguien cuatro verdades; **his age is beginning to —** ya comienza a notársele la edad.

teller [télɚ] *s.* narrador, relator; pagador o recibidor (*de un banco*); escrutador de votos.

tellurium [təlúrɪəm] *s.* telurio.

temerity [təméɪɑtɪ] *s.* temeridad.

temper [tempɚ] *v.* templar; *s.* temple (*de un metal*); genio, temple, humor; mal genio; **to keep one's —** contenerse, dominarse; **to lose one's —** perder la calma, encolerizarse.

temperament [témprəmənt] *s.* temperamento; disposición; temple.

temperance [témprəns] *s.* templanza, sobriedad.

temperate [témprɪt] *adj.* templado, moderado; sobrio.

temperature [témprətʃɚ] *s.* temperatura; **to have a —** tener calentura o fiebre.

tempest [témpɪst] *s.* tempestad.

tempestuous [tempéstʃuəs] *adj.* tempestuoso, borrascoso.

temple [témpl] *s.* templo; sien.

temporal [témpərəl] *adj.* temporal.

temporarily [témpərerəlɪ] *adv.* temporalmente.

temporary [témpərerɪ] *adj.* temporal, transitorio, provisorio; interino.

tempt [tempt] *v.* tentar; incitar; provocar; atraer.

temptation [temptéʃən] *s.* tentación.

tempter [témptɚ] *s.* tentador.

tempting [témptɪŋ] *adj.* tentador, atractivo.

tenable [ténəbl] *adj.* defendible.

tenacious [tɪnéʃəs] *adj.* tenaz, aferrado.

tenacity [tɪnǽsətɪ] *s.* tenacidad; aferramiento; tesón.

tenant [ténənt] *s.* inquilino, arrendatario.

tend [tend] *v.* cuidar, vigilar, guardar; atender; tender, inclinarse.

tendency [téndənsɪ] *s.* tendencia; propensión.

tender [téndɚ] *adj.* tierno; delicado; sensible; **tender-hearted** de corazón tierno; *s.* oferta, ofrecimiento; ténder (*de un tren*); lancha (*de auxilio*); cuidador, vigilante; **legal —** moneda corriente; *v.* ofrecer.

tenderloin [téndɚlɔɪn] *s.* filete.

tenderness [téndɚnɪs] *s.* ternura, terneza; delicadeza.

tendon [téndən] *s.* tendón.

tendril [téndrɪl] *s.* zarcillo (*tallito de una planta trepadora*).

tenement [ténəmənt] *s.* casa de vecindad.

tennis [ténɪs] *s.* tenis; **— court** cancha de tenis.

tenor [ténɚ] *s.* tenor; significado; **— voice** voz de tenor.

tense [tens] *adj.* tenso; tirante; *s.* tiempo (*del verbo*).

tension [ténʃən] *s.* tensión; tirantez.

tent [tent] *s.* tienda de campaña; pabellón; *v.* acampar.

tentacle [téntək]] *s.* tentáculo.

tentative [téntətɪv] *adj.* tentativo.

tenuous [ténjuəs] *adj.* tenue.

tenure [ténjur] *s.* tenencia.

tepid [tépɪd] *adj.* tibio.

term [tɝm] *s.* término; período; plazo; sesión; **-s** términos, expresiones, palabras; condiciones; **to be on good -s** estar en buenas relaciones; **not to be on speaking -s** no hablarse, no dirigirse la palabra; **to come to -s** ajustarse, ponerse de acuerdo; *v.* nombrar, llamar, denominar.

terminable [tɝmɪnəbl] *adj.* terminable.

terminal [tɝmən]] *adj.* terminal, final, último; *s.* término; fin; estación terminal; **electric —** toma de corriente; borne (*de aparato eléctrico*).

terminate [tɝmənet] *v.* terminar, acabar.

TA

termination [tɜ·mənéʃən] s. terminación, fin; desinencia (*gramatical*).

termite [tɜ·maɪt] s. termita.

terrace [téɪs] s. terraplén; terraza, terrado; v. terraplenar.

terrestrial [təréstrɪəl] *adj.* terrestre, terreno, terrenal.

terrible [térəbl] *adj.* terrible; **terribly** *adv.* terriblemente.

terrier [térɪə] s. perro de busca.

terrific [tərífɪk] *adj.* terrífico.

terrify [térəfaɪ] v. aterrar, aterrorizar.

territory [térətorɪ] s. territorio.

terror [térə] s. terror, espanto.

test [tɛst] s. prueba, ensayo, experimento; comprobación; examen; — **tube** probeta, tubo de ensayo; **to undergo a** — sufrir una prueba; v. probar, ensayar, comprobar, experimentar; poner a prueba; examinar.

testament [téstəmənt] s. testamento.

testify [téstəfaɪ] v. atestiguar, atestar.

testimony [téstəmonɪ] s. testimonio.

tetanus [tétənəs] s. tétanos.

text [tɛkst] s. texto.

textbook [tékstbʊk] s. texto, libro de texto.

textile [tékstl] *adj.* textil; de tejidos; — **mill** fábrica de tejidos; s. tejido, materia textil.

texture [tékstʃə] s. textura, contextura; tejido.

than [ðæn] *conj.* que; **more — once** más de una vez; **more — he knows** más de lo que él sabe.

thank [θæŋk] v. dar gracias, agradecer; — **heaven!** ¡gracias a Dios!; — **you** gracias; **to have oneself to — for** tener la culpa de; ser responsable de; **-s** *s. pl.* gracias.

thankful [θæŋkfəl] *adj.* agradecido; **-ly** *adv.* agradecidamente, con agradecimiento, con gratitud.

thankfulness [θæŋkfəlnɪs] s. gratitud, agradecimiento.

thankless [θæŋklɪs] *adj.* ingrato; — **task** tarea ingrata o infructuosa.

thanksgiving [θæŋksgívɪŋ] s. acción de gracias; — **Day** día de acción de gracias.

that [ðæt] *adj.* ese, esa, aquel, aquella; — **one** ése, ésa, aquél, aquélla; *pron.* ése, ésa, eso, aquél, aquélla, aquello; *pron. rel.* que; — **is** es decir; — **of** el de, la de, lo de; — **which** el que, la que, lo que; *conj.* que; para que, a fin de que; **so** — para que; de modo que, a fin de que, de suerte que, de tal manera que; *adv.* tan; — **far** tan lejos; hasta allá, hasta allí; — **long** así de largo; de este tamaño; tanto tiempo.

thatch [θætʃ] s. paja (*para techar*); v. techar con paja; **-ed roof** techumbre o techo de paja.

thaw [θɔ] v. deshelar(se), derretir(se); volverse más tratable o amistoso; s. deshielo, derretimiento.

the [*delante de consonante* ðə; *delante de vocal* ðɪ] *art.* el, la; lo, los, las; *adv.* — **more** . . . — **less** cuanto más . . . tanto menos; mientras más . . . tanto

menos.

theater [θíətə] s. teatro.

theatrical [θɪætrɪkl] *adj.* teatral.

thee [ðɪ] *pron.* te.

theft [θɛft] s. hurto, robo.

their [ðɛr] *adj.* su (sus), de ellos, de ellas.

theirs [ðɛrz] *pron. pos.* suyo (suya, suyos, suyas), de ellos, de ellas; el suyo (la suya, los suyos, las suyas); el (la, los, las) de ellos; **a friend of** — un amigo suyo, un amigo de ellos.

them [ðɛm] *pron.* los, las; les; ellos, ellas (*con preposición*).

thematic [θɪmætɪk] *adj.* temático.

theme [θim] s. tema; ensayo; — **song** tema central.

themselves [ðəmsélvz] *pron.* ellos mismos, ellas mismas; se (*cómo reflexivo*); **to** — a sí mismos; *véase* **herself.**

then [ðɛn] *adv.* entonces; en aquel tiempo; en aquella ocasión; después, luego, en seguida; *conj.* pues, en tal caso; **now** — ahora bien; **now and** — de vez en cuando, de cuando en cuando; **now** . . . — ora . . . ora; ya . . . ya; **well** — conque, pues entonces; ahora bien.

thence [ðɛns] *adv.* desde allí, de allí; desde entonces, desde aquel tiempo; por eso, por esa razón; —**forth** de allí en adelante, desde entonces.

theological [θɪəládʒɪkl] *adj.* teológico; teologal.

theology [θiálədʒɪ] s. teología.

theoretical [θɪərétɪk] *adj.* teórico.

theory [θíərɪ] s. teoría.

therapeutic [θɛrəpjútɪk] *adj.* terapéutico.

therapy [θérəpɪ] s. terapia.

there [ðɛr] *adv.* allí, allá, ahí; — **is**, — **are** hay; — **followed an argument** siguió una disputa.

thereabouts [ðɛrəbáuts] *adv.* por allí, por ahí; aproximadamente.

thereafter [ðɛræftə] *adv.* después de eso, de allí en adelante.

thereby [ðɛrbái] *adv.* en relación con eso; así, de ese modo; por allí cerca.

therefore [ðérfor] *adv.* por eso, por consiguiente, por lo tanto.

therein [ðɛrín] *adv.* en eso, en ello; allí dentro.

thereof [ðɛráv] *adv.* de eso, de ello.

thereon [ðɛrán] *adv.* encima; encima de (*o sobre*) él, ella, ello, etc.

thereupon [ðɛrəpán] *adv.* luego, después, en eso, en esto; por consiguiente, por eso, por lo tanto; encima de (*o sobre*) él, ella, ello, etc.

therewith [ðɛrwíθ] *adv.* con eso, con ello, con esto; luego, en seguida.

thermal [θɜ·ml] *adj.* termal.

thermometer [θəmámətə] s. termómetro.

thermonuclear [θɜ·monúkljə] *adj.* termonuclear.

Thermos [θɜ·məs] (*marca de fábrica*): — **bottle** termos.

thermostat [θɜ·məstæt] s. termóstato.

these [ðiz] *adj.* estos, estas; *pron.* éstos, éstas.

thesis [θísɪs] s. tesis.

they [ðe] pron. ellos, ellas.

thick [θɪk] adj. (not thin) espeso; grueso; (dense) denso; tupido; (slow) torpe, estúpido; — **voice** voz ronca; **one inch** — una pulgada de espesor; adv. véase **thickly**; **thickheaded** cabezudo, testarudo; estúpido; **thick-set** grueso, rechoncho; **thick-skinned** insensible; que no se avergüenza fácilmente; s. espesor; densidad, lo más denso; **the** — **of the crowd** lo más denso de la muchedumbre; **the** — **of the fight** lo más reñido del combate; **through** — **and thin** por toda suerte de penalidades.

thicken [θíkən] v. espesar(se); engrosar; **the plot -s** se complica el enredo.

thicket [θíkɪt] s. espesura, maleza, matorral, Am. manigua.

thickly [θíklɪ] adv. espesamente; densamente.

thickness [θíknɪs] s. espesor; espesura, grueso, grosor; densidad.

thief [θif] s. ladrón.

thieve [θiv] v. hurtar, robar.

thieves [θivz] pl. de **thief**.

thigh [θaɪ] s. muslo.

thimble [θímbl̩] s. dedal.

thin [θɪn] adj. (slim) delgado; flaco; (sparse) ralo; escaso; (fine) tenue, fino; transparente; (weak) débil; aguado; — **broth** caldo aguado; — **hair** pelo ralo; v. adelgazar(se); enflaquecer; aguar (el caldo); **to** — **out** ralear (el pelo); ralear o aclarar (un bosque).

thine [ðaɪn] pron. pos. tuyo (tuya, tuyos, tuyas); el tuyo (la tuya, los tuyos, las tuyas); adj. tu, tus.

thing [θɪŋ] s. cosa; **no such** — nada de eso; **that is the** — **to do** eso es lo que debe hacerse; eso es lo debido.

think [θɪŋk] v. (cerebrate) pensar; (believe) creer, juzgar; opinar; **to** — **it over** pensarlo; **to** — **of** pensar en; pensar de; **to** — **up an excuse** urdir una excusa; **to** — **well of** tener buena opinión de; — **nothing of it** no haga Vd. caso de ello, no le dé Vd. importancia; **what do you** — **of her?** ¿qué piensa Vd. de ella?; **to my way of -ing** a mi modo de ver.

thinker [θíŋkɚ] s. pensador.

thinly [θínlɪ] adv. delgadamente; escasamente.

thinness [θínnɪs] s. delgadez; flacura; raleza (del cabello); enrarecimiento (del aire).

third [θɝd] adj. tercero; s. tercio, tercera parte.

thirst [θɝst] s. sed; anhelo, ansia; v. tener sed; **to** — **for** tener sed de; anhelar, ansiar.

thirsty [θɝstɪ] adj. sediento; **to be** — tener sed.

this [ðɪs] adj. este, esta; pron. éste, ésta, esto.

thistle [θísl̩] s. abrojo; cardo.

thither [θíðɚ] adv. allá, hacia allá, para allá.

tho [ðo] = **though**.

thong [θɔŋ] s. correa, tira de cuero, Am. guasca.

thorn [θɔrn] s. espina, púa; espino; abrojo.

thorny [θɔ́rnɪ] adj. espinoso; arduo, difícil.

thorough [θɝ́o] adj. (finished) completo, entero, cabal, cumplido, acabado; (careful) esmerado.

thoroughbred [θɝ́obrɛd] adj. de casta pura, de raza pura; bien nacido; s. animal o persona de casta; caballo de casta.

thoroughfare [θɝ́ofɛr] s. vía pública, carretera, camino real; pasaje.

thoroughly [θɝ́olɪ] adj. completamente, enteramente, cabalmente; a fondo.

those [ðoz] adj. esos, esas, aquellos, aquellas; pron. ésos, ésas, aquéllos, aquéllas; — **of** los de, las de; — **which** los que, las que; aquellos que; — **who** los que, las que, quienes.

thou [ðaʊ] pron. tú.

though [ðo] conj. aunque, si bien, bien que; aun cuando; sin embargo; **as** — como si.

thought [θɔt] s. (cogitation) pensamiento; (idea) idea, intención; reflexión, meditación; (concern) consideración; cuidado; **to be lost in** — estar abstraído; **to give it no** — no pensar en ello, no darle importancia, no hacerle caso; pret. & p.p. de **to think**.

thoughtful [θɔ́tfəl] adj. pensativo; considerado; atento, solícito, cuidadoso; **to be** — **of others** pensar en los demás, tener consideración o solicitud por las demás; **-ly** adv. con reflexión; considerdamente, con consideración; con solicitud.

thoughtfulness [θɔ́tfəlnɪs] s. consideración, atención, cuidado, solicitud.

thoughtless [θɔ́tlɪs] adj. inconsiderado; descuidado; irreflexivo, atolondrado; **-ly** adv. inconsideradamente, sin consideración; sin reflexión; sin pensar; descuidadamente, irreflexivamente, atolondradamente.

thoughtlessness [θɔ́tlɪsnɪs] s. irreflexión, inadvertencia, descuido; atolondramiento.

thrash [θræʃ] v. trillar, desgranar (las mieses); zurrar, azotar; **to** — **around** revolcarse, agitarse, menearse; **to** — **out a matter** ventilar un asunto.

thread [θrɛd] s. hilo; hebra, fibra; **screw** — rosca de tornillo; v. ensartar, enhebrar; **to** — **a screw** roscar un tornillo; **to** — **one's way through a crowd** colarse por entre la muchedumbre.

threadbare [θrɛ́dbɛr] adj. raído, gastado.

threat [θrɛt] s. amenaza; amago.

threaten [θrɛ́tn̩] v amenazar; amagar.

threatening [θrɛ́tnɪŋ] adj. amenazante, amenazador.

thresh [θrɛʃ] véase **thrash**.

threshold [θrɛ́ʃold] s. umbral, entrada.

threw [θru] pret. de **to throw**.

thrice [θraɪs] *adv.* tres veces.

thrift [θrɪft] *s.* economía, frugalidad.

thrifty [θrɪftɪ] *adj.* económico, frugal; próspero.

thrill [θrɪl] *v.* emocionar(se), conmover-(se); estremecerse de emoción, sobre-excitarse; *s.* emoción viva, estreme-cimiento emotivo, sobreexcitación.

thrive [θraɪv] *v.* medrar, prosperar; florecer.

thriven [θrɪvən] *p.p. de* to thrive.

throat [θrot] *s.* garganta.

throb [θrɑb] *v.* latir, pulsar, palpitar; *s.* latido, palpitación.

throe [θro] *s.* agonía; congoja.

throne [θron] *s.* trono.

throng [θrɔŋ] *s.* muchedumbre, multi-tud, tropel, gentío; *v.* agolparse, api-ñarse; atestar.

throttle [θrɑ́tl] *s.* válvula reguladora, obturador, regulador; **— lever** pa-lanca del obturador o regulador; *v.* ahogar; estrangular; **to — down** disminuir o reducir la velocidad.

through [θru] *prep.* por; a través de; por medio de; por conducto de; por entre; *adv.* de un lado a otro; de parte a parte, a través; de cabo a cabo; desde el principio hasta el fin; com-pletamente, enteramente; **loyal — and —** leal a toda prueba; **to be wet — estar** empapado; estar mojado hasta los tuétanos; **to carry a plan —** llevar a cabo un plan; *adj.* directo, continuo; **— ticket** billete (*Am.* boleto) directo; **— train** tren rápido, tren de servicio directo; **to be — with** haber acabado con; no querer ocu-parse más de.

throughout [θruáut] *prep.* (*all through*) por todo; por todas partes de; (*during*) desde el principio; hasta el fin de; **— the year** durante todo el año; *adv.* por todas partes; en todas partes; en todo, en todos respetos; desde el principio hasta el fin.

throve [θron] *pret. de* to thrive.

throw [θro] *v.* tirar, arrojar, lanzar; echar; **to — away** tirar, arrojar; mal-gastar; **to — down** arrojar, echar por tierra, derribar; **to — in gear** en-granar; **to — in the clutch** embra-gar; **to — off a burden** librarse o des-hacerse de una carga; **to — out** echar fuera; expeler; **to — out of gear** des-engranar; **to — out of work** privar de trabajo, quitar el empleo a; **to — out the clutch** desembragar; **to — overboard** echar al agua; **to — up** vomitar; *s.* tiro, tirada.

thrown [θron] *p.p. de* to throw.

thrush [θrʌʃ] *s.* tordo, zorzal.

thrust [θrʌst] *v.* (*push into*) meter; hin-car, clavar; encajar; (*shove*) empujar; **to — a task upon someone** im-poner una tarea a una persona, obligar a alguien a desempeñar un quehacer; **to — aside** echar o em-pujar a un lado; rechazar; **to — in** (*o* **into**) meter en, encajar en, inter-calar en; **to — out** sacar; echar fuera;

to — someone through with a sword atravesar a alguien de parte a parte con la espada; *pret. & p.p. de* **thrust;** *s.* estocada, cuchillada, puña-lada, lanzada; empuje, empujón o empellón; arremetida, acometida.

thud [θʌd] *s.* porrazo, golpazo, golpe sordo.

thug [θʌg] *s.* ladrón, salteador.

thumb [θʌm] *s.* pulgar; **under the —** **of** bajo el poder o influencia de; *v.* hojear (*con el pulgar*).

thumbtack [θʌ́mtæk] *s.* chinche.

thump [θʌmp] *s.* golpazo, porrazo, tras-tazo; golpe sordo; *v.* golpear, golpe-tear, aporrear, dar un porrazo.

thunder [θʌ́ndɚ] *s.* trueno; tronido; es-truendo; *v.* tronar.

thunderbolt [θʌ́ndɚbolt] *s.* rayo.

thundering [θʌ́ndɚɪŋ] *adj.* atronador.

thunderous [θʌ́ndɚəs] *adj.* atronador, estruendoso.

thunderstorm [θʌ́ndɚstɔrm] *s.* tronada, tormenta o tempestad de truenos.

Thursday [θɝ́zdɪ] *s.* jueves.

thus [θʌs] *adv.* así; **— far** hasta aquí, hasta ahora, hasta hoy.

thwart [θwɔrt] *v.* frustrar; estorbar; impedir.

thy [ðaɪ] *adj.* tu, tus.

thyme [taɪm] *s.* tomillo.

thyroid [θáɪrɔɪd] *s.* tiroides.

thyself [ðaɪsélf] *pron.* tú mismo; a tí mismo; te (*como reflexivo*); *véase* **her-self.**

tick [tɪk] *s.* tic tac; funda (*de colchón o almohada*); garrapata (*insecto pará-sito*); *v.* hacer tic tac (*como un reloj*); latir (*el corazón*); **to — off** marcar.

ticket [tíkɪt] *s.* billete, *Am.* boleto; lista de candidatos (*de un partido*); balota (*para votar*); **— office** taquilla; des-pacho de boletos, *Am.* boletería.

tickle [tíkl] *v.* (*touch*) cosquillear, hacer cosquillas; (*feel*) sentir o tener cosqui-llas; (*please*) halagar, gustarle a uno; **to be -d to death** morirse de gusto, estar muy contento; *s.* cosquilleo, cosquillas.

ticklish [tíklɪʃ] *adj.* cosquilloso; deli-cado, arriesgado, difícil.

tidbit [tídbɪt] *s.* bocado, bocadito, golo-sina.

tide [taɪd] *s.* marea; corriente; **Christ-mas —** navidades, temporada de na-vidad; *v.* **to — someone over a difficulty** ayudar a alguien durante una crisis o dificultad.

tidewater [táɪdwɔtɚ] *adj.* costanero.

tidings [táɪdɪŋz] *s. pl.* noticias, nuevas.

tidy [táɪdɪ] *adj.* aseado, limpio, orde-nado; **a — sum** una suma considera-ble; *v.* asear, arreglar, poner en orden; **to — oneself up** asearse.

tie [taɪ] *v.* (*fasten*) atar, liar, ligar; *Am.* amarrar; (*unite*) enlazar, vincular; (*equal*) empatar (*en juegos, etc.*); **to — tight** amarrar bien, apretar fuerte; **to — up the traffic** obstruir el tráfico; *s.* lazo, ligadura, atadura; enlace, vínculo; corbata; empate (*en ca-*

rreras, juegos, etc.); **railway** — traviesa, *Andes, C.A.,* *Méx.* durmiente;
Ríopl., Ch. travesaño.

tier [tɪr] *s.* fila, hilera, ringlera.

tiger [táɪgɚ] *s.* tigre; — **cat** gato montés.

tight [taɪt] *adj.* (*squeezed*) apretado,
ajustado, estrecho; (*sealed*) hermético; (*firm*) firme, tieso; (*stingy*)
tacaño, mezquino; (*drunk*) borracho;
to be in a — **spot** estar en un aprieto;
to close — apretar, cerrar herméticá-
mente; **to hold on** — agarrarse bien;
it fits — está muy estrecho o ajustado.

tighten [táɪtn] *v.* apretar; estrechar;
estirar, poner tirante.

tightness [táɪtnɪs] *s.* estrechez; tirantez,
tensión; mezquindad, tacañería.

tightwad [táɪtwad] *s.* tacaño; cicatero.

tigress [táɪgrɪs] *s.* tigre hembra.

tile [taɪl] *s.* teja; baldosa, azulejo; —
roof tejado; *v.* tejar, cubrir con tejas;
cubrir con azulejos, embaldosar.

till [tɪl] *prep.* hasta; *conj.* hasta que; *v.*
cultivar, labrar, arar; *s.* gaveta o
cajón para el dinero.

tillage [tílədʒ] *s.* labranza, cultivo, labor.

tilt [tɪlt] *s.* ladeo, inclinación; declive;
altercación disputa; **at full** — a toda
velocidad; *v.* ladear(se), inclinar(se).

timber [tímbɚ] *s.* madera de construcción; maderaje; madero; viga.

time [taɪm] *s.* tiempo; hora; vez; plazo;
at —**s** a veces; **at one and the same**
— a la vez; **at this** — ahora, al presente; **behind** — atrasado, retrasado;
from — **to** — de vez en cuando; **in** —
a tiempo; andando el tiempo; **on** —
puntual; con puntualidad; a tiempo;
a la hora debida; **several** —**s** varias
veces; **to beat** — marcar el compás;
to buy on — comprar a plazo; **to
have a good** — divertirse, pasar un
buen rato; **what** — **is it?** ¿qué hora
es?; *v.* cronometrar, medir el tiempo
de; regular, poner en punto (*el reloj,
el motor*); escoger el momento oportuno para; — **zone** zona horaria;
huso horario.

timeless [táɪmlɛs] *adj.* eterno, infinito.

timely [táɪmlɪ] *adj.* oportuno.

timepiece [táɪmpis] *s.* reloj; cronómetro.

timetable [táɪmtebḷ] *s.* itinerario, horario.

timid [tímɪd] *adj.* tímido.

timidity [tɪmídətɪ] *s.* timidez.

timing [táɪmɪŋ] *s.* medida del tiempo;
cronometraje; (*pace*) selección del
momento oportuno; sincronización.

timorous [tímərəs] *adj.* timorato, tímido, miedoso.

tin [tɪn] *s.* estaño; hojalata; lata; cosa de
hojalata; — **can** lata; — **foil** hoja de
estaño; *v.* estañar, cubrir con estaño;
enlatar.

tincture [tíŋktʃɚ] *s.* tintura; tinte; — **of
iodine** tintura de yodo; *v.* tinturar,
teñir.

tinder [tíndɚ] *s.* yesca.

tinge [tɪndʒ] *v.* teñir; matizar; *s.* tinte,
matiz; dejo, saborcillo.

tingle [tíŋgl] *v.* hormiguear, sentir hor-
miẹueo; **to** — **with excitement**
estremecerse de entusiasmo; *s.* hormigueo, picazón, comezón.

tinker [tíŋkɚ] *v.* ocuparse vanamente.

tinkle [tíŋkḷ] *v.* tintinear; hacer retintín; *s.* tintineo; retintín.

tinsel [tínsḷ] *s.* oropel; *adj.* de oropel.

tint [tɪnt] *s.* tinte, matiz; *v.* teñir, matizar.

tiny [táɪnɪ] *adj.* diminuto, menudo, chiquitico, chiquitín.

tip [tɪp] *s.* (*point*) punta, extremo, extremidad; (*money*) propina; (*hint*)
noticia o aviso secreto; *v.* ladear(se),
inclinar(se); dar propina (a); **to** —
a person off dar aviso secreto a; **to
** — **one's hat** tocarse el sombrero;
to — **over** volcar(se), voltear(se).

tipsy [típsɪ] *adj.* alumbrado, algo borracho; ladeado.

tiptoe [típto] *s.* punta del pie; **on** — de
puntillas; *v.* andar de puntillas.

tirade [táɪred] *s.* invectiva.

tire [taɪr] *s.* llanta, neumático, goma;
flat — llanta o goma reventada; *v.*
cansar(se), fatigar(se).

tired [taɪrd] *adj.* cansado, fatigado; —
out extenuado de fatiga, rendido.

tireless [táɪrlɪs] *adj.* incansable, infatigable.

tiresome [táɪrsəm] *adj.* cansado, aburrido, pesado.

tissue [tíʃu] *s.* tejido; — **paper** papel
de seda.

titanic [taɪtǽnɪk] *adj.* titánico.

titanium [taɪténɪəm] *s.* titanio.

tithe [taɪð] *s.* diezmo.

title [táɪtḷ] *s.* título; — **page** portada.

to [tu] *prep.* a; hasta; hacia; para; —
try — tratar de; esforzarse por; **a
quarter** — **five** las cinco menos
cuarto; **bills** — **be paid** cuentas por
pagar; **frightened** — **death** muerto
de susto; **from house** — **house** de
casa en casa; **he has** — **go** tiene que
ir; **near** — cerca de; **not** — **my
knowledge** no que yo sepa; *adv.* —
and fro de acá para allá; **to come** —
— volver en sí.

toad [tod] *s.* sapo o escuerzo.

toast [tost] *v.* tostar(se); brindar por,
beber a la salud de; *s.* tostada;
brindis.

toaster [tóstɚ] *s.* tostador.

tobacco [təbǽko] *s.* tabaco.

today [tədé] *adv.* hoy; hoy día.

toe [to] *s.* dedo del pie; punta (*de la
media, del zapato, etc.*); *v.* **to** — **in**
andar con la punta de los pies para
dentro.

toenail [tónel] *s.* uña del dedo del pie.

together [təgéðɚ] *adv.* juntamente; a
un mismo tiempo, a la vez; juntos; —
with junto con; **all** — juntos; en
junto; **to call** — convocar, juntar; **to
come** — juntarse, unirse; ponerse de
acuerdo; **to walk** — andar juntos.

toil [tɔɪl] *v.* afanarse, trafagar, atarearse; *s.* esfuerzo, trabajo, faena,
fatiga.

toilet [tóɪlɪt] s. retrete, excusado, común, *Am.* inodoro; — **articles** artículos de tocador; — **case** neceser; — **paper** papel de excusado, papel higiénico.

token [tókən] s. señal, símbolo; prenda; recuerdo; prueba, muestra; ficha (*de metal*); — **payment** pago nominal.

told [told] pret. & p.p. *de* to tell.

tolerance [tálərəns] s. tolerancia.

tolerant [tálərənt] *adj.* tolerante.

tolerate [táləret] v. tolerar.

toleration [taləréʃən] s. tolerancia.

toll [tol] s. doble, tañido (*de las campanas*); peaje; portazgo; — **bridge** puente de peaje; — **gate** barrera de peaje; — **call** llamada por cobrar; **to pay** — pagar peaje o portazgo; v. tañer, doblar (*las campanas*).

tomato [təméto] s. tomate, *Méx.* jitomate.

tomb [tum] s. tumba.

tombstone [túmston] s. lápida sepulcral.

tomcat [támkæt] s. gato.

tome [tom] s. tomo.

tomorrow [təmɔ́ro] *adv.* mañana; — **morning** mañana por la mañana; — **noon** mañana al mediodía; **day after** — pasado mañana.

ton [tʌn] s. tonelada.

tone [ton] s. (*pitch*) tono; timbre; (*sound*) sonido; v. dar tono a, modificar el tono de; **to** — **down** bajar de tono; suavizar; **to** — **down one's voice** moderar la voz; **to** — **in well with** armonizar con, entonar bien con; **to** — **up** subir de tono; tonificar, vigorizar.

tongs [tɔŋz] s. pl. tenazas.

tongue [tʌŋ] s. lengua; idioma; **to be tongue-tied** tener trabada la lengua.

tonic [tánɪk] s. & *adj.* tónico.

tonight [tənáɪt] *adv.* esta noche, a la noche.

tonnage [tánɪdʒ] s. tonelaje.

tonsil [tánsl̩] s. amígdala.

tonsilitis [tansláɪtɪs] s. amigdalitis.

too [tu] *adv.* también; demasiado; — **many** demasiados; — **much** demasiado; **it is** — **bad!** ¡es una lástima!

took [tʊk] pret. *de* to take.

tool [tul] s. instrumento; herramienta; — **box** caja de herramientas.

toot [tut] v. tocar o sonar la bocina; pitar; tocar (*un cuerno, trompa o trompeta*); **to** — **one's own horn** alabarse, cantar sus propias alabanzas; s. toque o sonido (*de bocina, trompeta, etc.*); silbido, pitido; pitazo (*de locomotora*).

tooth [tuθ] s. diente; muela; — **mark** dentellada; **to fight** — **and nail** luchar a brazo partido; **to have a sweet** — ser amigo de golosinas.

toothache [túθek] s. dolor de muelas.

toothbrush [túθbrʌʃ] s. cepillo de dientes.

toothed [tuθt] *adj.* dentado.

toothless [túθlɪs] *adj.* desdentado.

toothpaste [túθpest] s. pasta para los dientes, pasta dentífrica.

toothpick [túθpɪk] s. mondadientes, palillo de dientes.

top [tɑp] s. (*peak*) cumbre, cima; cúspide; tope; pináculo; remate; cabeza; (*surface*) superficie; copa (*de árbol*); (*cover*) tapa, cubierta; (*toy*) trompo; **at the** — **of his class** a la cabeza de su clase; **at the** — **of one's voice** a voz en cuello; **filled up to the** — lleno hasta el tope; **from** — **to bottom** de arriba abajo; **from** — **to toe** de pies a cabeza; **on** — **of** encima de, sobre; *adj.* superior; más alto; —**coat** abrigo, sobretodo; **at** — **speed** a velocidad máxima; v. coronar; exceder; sobresalir, sobrepujar; rematar; **to** — **off** rematar; terminar.

topaz [tópæz] s. topacio.

toper [tópə] s. bebedor, borrachín.

top-heavy [taphévɪ] *adj.* más pesado arriba que abajo.

topic [tápɪk] s. tema, asunto, materia, tópico.

topmost [tápmost] *adj.* más alto; superior.

topography [təpágrəfɪ] s. topografía.

topple [tápl̩] v. echar abajo, derribar; volcar; **to** — **over** venirse abajo; volcarse.

topsy-turvy [tápsɪtɜ́vɪ] *adj.* & *adv.* patas arriba; en confusión; trastornado; enrevesado, al revés.

torch [tɔrtʃ] s. antorcha; **blow** — soplete.

tore [tor] pret. *de* to tear.

torment [tɔ́rmɛnt] s. tormento; [tɔrmɛ́nt] v. atormentar; afligir.

torn [tɔrn] p.p. *de* to tear roto, rompido, rasgado.

tornado [tɔrnédo] s. tornado.

torpedo [tɔrpído] s. torpedo; — **boat** torpedero; v. torpedear.

torque [tɔrk] s. fuerza rotatoria.

torrent [tɔ́rənt] s. torrente.

torrid [tɔ́rɪd] *adj.* tórrido.

torsion [tɔ́rʃən] s. torsión.

tortoise [tɔ́rtəs] s. tortuga.

tortuous [tɔ́rtʃʊəs] *adj.* tortuoso.

torture [tɔ́rtʃə] s. tortura, tormento; v. torturar, atormentar.

toss [tɔs] v. tirar, echar, arrojar, lanzar; menear(se); cabecear (*un buque*); **to** — **aside** echar a un lado; desechar; **to** — **up** echar para arriba; aventar; s. tiro, tirada; meneo, sacudida.

tot [tat] s. chiquitín, chiquitina, chiquitico, chiquitica, niñito, niñita, nene, nena.

total [tótl̩] *adj.* & s. total.

totalitarian [totælətérɪən] *adj.* totalitario.

totter [tátə] v. tambalear(se), bambolear(se); estar para desplomarse.

touch [tʌtʃ] v. tocar; palpar, tentar; conmover, enternecer; compararse con, igualar; **to** — **at a port** hacer escala en un puerto; **to** — **off an explosive** prender la mecha de un explosivo; **to** — **up** retocar; s. toque;

tacto, sentido del tacto; tiento; **—stone** piedra de toque; **a — of fever** algo de calentura; **to keep in — with** mantener(se) en comunicación con.

touch-and-go [tʌtʃəndgó] *adj.* arriesgado.

touching [tʌtʃɪŋ] *adj.* conmovedor, enternecedor.

touchy [tʌtʃɪ] *adj.* quisquilloso, susceptible, sensible, sensitivo.

tough [tʌf] *adj.* correoso; fuerte; firme; duro; arduo, difícil; terco; empedernido, malvado.

toughen [tʌfŋ] *v.* curtir(se); endurecer(se), empedernir(se); hacer(se) correoso.

toughness [tʌfnɪs] *s.* dureza; correosidad; flexibilidad; tenacidad; resistencia; dificultad.

toupee [tupé] *s.* peluca.

tour [tʊr] *s.* viaje, excursión; vuelta; jira; *v.* viajar por; recorrer; hacer una jira; hacer un viaje de turismo.

tourism [túrɪzəm] *s.* turismo.

tourist [túrɪst] *s.* turista.

tournament [tə́nəmənt] *s.* torneo; certamen, concurso.

tow [to] *v.* remolcar; *s.* remolque; **—boat** remolcador; **—rope** cuerda de remolque; **to take in —** remolcar, llevar a remolque.

toward [tord] *prep.* hacia; rumbo a; alrededor de; para, para con; **— four o'clock** a eso de las cuatro.

towards [tordz] *= toward.*

towel [taʊl] *s.* toalla.

tower [taʊə] *s.* torre; torreón; **bell —** campanario; *v.* sobresalir, sobrepujar; destacarse, descollar; elevarse.

towering [taʊrɪŋ] *adj.* encumbrado; elevado, muy alto; sobresaliente.

town [taʊn] *s.* (*center*) población, ciudad, pueblo, aldea; (*administration*) municipio; **— hall** ayuntamiento.

township [taʊnʃɪp] *s.* unidad primaria de gobierno local; sección de seis millas cuadradas (*en terrenos públicos*).

toxin [táksɪn] *s.* toxina.

toy [tɔɪ] *s.* juguete; *adj.* de juego, de juguete; pequeñito; *v.* jugar, juguetear.

trace [tres] *s.* señal, indicio, vestigio; huella, rastro; tirante (*de una guarnición*); *v.* trazar; calcar; rastrear, seguir la huella de; rebuscar, investigar; **to — the source of** remontarse al origen de, buscar el origen de.

trachea [trékɪə] *s.* tráquea.

trachoma [trəkómə] *s.* tracoma.

track [træk] *s.* pista, huella, rastro; pisada; vereda, senda; vía; **— sports** deportes de pista; **race —** pista; **railroad —** rieles, vía del tren, vía férrea o ferrovía; **to be off the —** estar extraviado, estar descarrilado; **to be on the — of** rastrear, ir siguiendo la pista de; **to keep — of** llevar la cuenta de; no perder de

vista; *v.* rastrear, seguir la huella de; **to — down** coger, atrapar; descubrir; **to — in mud** traer lodo en los pies, entrar con los pies enlodados.

tract [trækt] *s.* área; terreno; folleto; **digestive —** canal digestivo.

traction [trékʃən] *s.* tracción.

tractor [træktə] *s.* tractor.

trade [tred] *s.* (*business*) comercio; trato, negocio; (*swap*) trueque, cambio; (*occupation*) oficio; (*customers*) clientela, parroquianos; **— school** escuela de artes y oficios; **— union** gremio obrero o de obreros; *v.* comerciar, negociar, traficar, tratar; trocar, cambiar.

trademark [trédmark] *s.* marca de fábrica.

trader [trédə] *s.* mercader, comerciante, negociante, traficante.

tradesman [trédzmən] *s.* mercader, comerciante, traficante; tendero.

tradition [trədíʃən] *s.* tradición.

traditional [trədíʃənl] *adj.* tradicional.

traffic [tréfɪk] *s.* tráfico; tráfago; tránsito; circulación; *v.* traficar, comerciar, negociar.

tragedy [trédʒədɪ] *s.* tragedia.

tragic [trédʒɪk] *adj.* trágico.

trail [trel] *s.* (*trace*) pista, rastro, huella; (*path*) senda, sendero, trocha, vereda; cola (*de vestido*); *v.* arrastrar(se); rastrear, seguir la pista de; andar detrás de; **to — behind** ir rezagado, rezagarse.

train [tren] *s.* (*railroad*) tren; (*dress*) cola (*de vestido*); (*retinue*) séquito, comitiva; *v.* amaestrar(se), ejercitar(se); adiestrar(se) o adestrar(se), *Am.* entrenar(se); educar; disciplinar (*tropas*); apuntar (*un cañón*).

trainer [trénə] *s.* amaestrador; *Méx., C.A., Andes, Ven., Col., Carib.* entrenador.

training [trénɪŋ] *s.* adiestramiento, disciplina, *Méx., C.A., Andes, Ven., Col., Carib.,* entrenamiento; educación; **— camp** campo de entrenamiento o práctica.

trait [tret] *s.* rasgo, característica; cualidad.

traitor [trétə] *s.* traidor.

tram [træm] *s.* vagoneta (*de una mina de carbón*).

tramp [træmp] *v.* pisotear; andar a pie; vagabundear; *s.* vago, vagabundo; caminata, marcha; pisadas.

trample [træmpl] *v.* pisar, hollar, pisotear; **to — on** pisotear, hollar; *s.* pisadas.

trance [træns] *s.* rapto, arrobamiento, enajenamiento, éxtasis; **to be in a —** estar arrobado, estar enajenado; estar distraído o ensimismado.

tranquil [trénkwɪl] *adj.* tranquilo.

tranquilizer [trénkwəlaɪzə] *s.* tranquilizador.

tranquillity [trænkwílətɪ] *s.* tranquilidad.

transact [trænsǽkt] *v.* tramitar, despa-

TO

char, llevar a cabo.

transaction [trænsǽkʃən] *s.* transacción, trato, negocio; trámite; negociación; **-s** actas; memorias.

transatlantic [trænsətlǽntɪk] *adj.* transatlántico.

transcend [trænsénd] *v.* trascender, ir más allá de.

transcontinental [trænskɑntənént] *adj.* transcontinental.

transcribe [trænskráɪb] *v.* transcribir.

transcript [trǽnskrɪpt] *s.* transcripción, copia.

transfer [trǽnsfɚ] *s.* transferencia; traslado; traspaso; trasbordo; **— of ownership** cesión o traspaso de propiedad; **streetcar —** transferencia, contraseña, cupón de trasbordo; [trænsfɚ́] *v.* transferir; trasbordar (*de un tren a otro*), cambiar (*de tren, de tranvía*); traspasar (*propiedad*), trasladar.

transfigure [trænsfígjɚ] *v.* transfigurar.

transform [trænsfɔ́rm] *v.* transformar(se).

transformation [trænsfɚméʃən] *s.* transformación.

transgress [trænsgrés] *v.* transgredir, violar, quebrantar (*una ley*); pecar; **to — the bounds of** traspasar los límites de.

transgression [trænsgréʃən] *s.* transgresión; violación de una ley; pecado.

transgressor [trænsgrésɚ] *s.* transgresor.

transient [trǽnʃənt] *s.* transeúnte; *adj.* transeúnte; transitorio, pasajero.

transistor [trænzístɚ] *s.* transistor.

transit [trǽnsɪt] *s.* tránsito; **in —** en tránsito, de paso.

transition [trænzíʃən] *s.* transición; tránsito, paso.

transitive [trǽnsətɪv] *adj.* transitivo.

transitory [trǽnsətorɪ] *adj.* transitorio, pasajero.

translate [trænslét] *v.* traducir, verter; trasladar.

translation [trænsléʃən] *s.* traducción; versión; translación (*de un lugar a otro*).

translator [trænslétɚ] *s.* traductor.

translucent [trænslúsṇt] *adj.* translúcido; **to be —** traslucirse.

transmission [trænsmíʃən] *s.* transmisión; caja de velocidades.

transmit [trænsmít] *v.* transmitir; emitir.

transmitter [trænsmítɚ] *s.* transmisor, emisor.

transom [trǽnsəm] *s.* montante.

transparent [trænspǽrənt] *adj.* transparente.

transplant [trænsplǽnt] *v.* trasplantar.

transport [trǽnsport] *s.* (*moving*) transporte; acarreo; (*rapture*) éxtasis; **— plane** aeroplano de transporte; [trænspórt] *v.* transportar; acarrear; **to be -ed with joy** estar enajenado de placer.

transportation [trænspɚtéʃən] *s.* transportación, transporte; boleto, pasaje.

transpose [trænspóz] *v.* transponer.

transverse [trænsvɝ́s] *adj.* transverso, transversal, puesto de través.

trap [træp] *s.* trampa, lazo, red; **— door** trampa; **mouse —** ratonera; *v.* entrampar, coger con trampa; atrapar.

trapeze [træpíz] *s.* trapecio.

trapezoid [trǽpəzɔɪd] *s.* trapezoide; trapecio.

trappings [trǽpɪŋz] *s. pl.* arreos, jaeces, guarniciones.

trash [træʃ] *s.* basura; hojarasca; cachivaches; gentuza, plebe.

travel [trǽvl] *v.* viajar; viajar por; recorrer; *s.* viaje; tráfico.

traveler [trǽvlɚ] *s.* viajero; **—'s check** cheque de viajero.

traveling [trǽvlɪŋ] *adj.* de viaje, para viaje; **— expenses** gastos de viaje; **— salesman** agente viajero, viajante de comercio.

travelogue [trǽvəlɔg] *s.* conferencia sobre viajes.

traverse [trǽvɚs] *v.* atravesar, cruzar; recorrer; *s.* travesaño.

travesty [trǽvɪstɪ] *s.* parodia; *v.* parodiar, falsear.

tray [tre] *s.* bandeja; batea.

treacherous [trétʃərəs] *adj.* traicionero, traidor, alevoso.

treachery [trétʃərɪ] *s.* traición, perfidia, alevosía.

tread [tred] *v.* (*trample*) pisar, hollar; pisotear; (*walk*) andar a pie, caminar; *s.* paso; pisada, huella; *Am.* pise (*de una rueda*); **tire —** rodadura del neumático, *Am.* banda rodante.

treadmill [trédmɪl] *s.* noria; rueda de andar.

treason [trízṇ] *s.* traición.

treasonable [trízṇəbl] *adj.* traidor, traicionero.

treasure [tréʒɚ] *s.* tesoro; *v.* atesorar.

treasurer [tréʒɚɚ] *s.* tesorero.

treasury [tréʒɚɪ] *s.* tesorería; tesoro, erario; **Secretary of the Treasury** ministro de hacienda.

treat [trit] *v.* tratar; curar; convidar, invitar; *s.* obsequio, agasajo, convite; placer, gusto.

treatise [trítɪs] *s.* tratado.

treatment [trítmənt] *s.* trato; **medical —** tratamiento médico.

treaty [trítɪ] *s.* tratado, pacto, convenio.

treble [trébl] *adj.* triple; **— voice** voz atiplada; *s.* tiple; *v.* triplicar.

tree [tri] *s.* árbol; **apple —** manzano; **family —** árbol genealógico; **shoe —** horma de zapato; **to be up a —** estar subido a un árbol; estar en un gran aprieto; estar perplejo.

treeless [trílɪs] *adj.* pelado, sin árboles, despoblado de árboles.

treetop [trítɑp] *s.* copa de árbol.

trellis [trélɪs] *s.* emparrado, enrejado.

tremble [trémbl] *v.* temblar; estremecerse; *s.* temblor; estremecimiento.

tremendous [triméndəs] *adj.* tremendo.

tremor [trémɚ] *s.* temblor.

tremulous [trémjələs] *adj.* trémulo; tembloroso.

trench [trentʃ] *s.* trinchera; zanja, foso.

trend [trend] *s.* tendencia; rumbo, dirección.

trespass [tréspəs] *v.* invadir, traspasar; violar, infringir; pecar; **to — on property** meterse sin derecho en la propiedad ajena; **no -ing** prohibida la entrada; *s.* transgresión; pecado.

tress [tres] *s.* trenza; bucle.

trestle [tresl] *s.* caballete; puente de caballetes.

trial [tráɪəl] *s.* ensayo, prueba; tentativa; aflicción; juicio,. proceso; **— flight** vuelo de prueba.

triangle [tráɪæŋgl] *s.* triángulo.

triangular [traɪǽŋgjələ˞] *adj.* triangular.

tribe [traɪb] *s.* tribu.

tribulation [trɪbjəléʃən] *s.* tribulación.

tribunal [trɪbjúnl] *s.* tribunal, juzgado.

tributary [tríbjətərɪ] *adj. & s.* tributario.

tribute [tríbjut] *s.* tributo; homenaje.

trick [trɪk] *s.* treta; suerte; maña, ardid, trampa; travesura; baza (*en el juego de naipes*); **to be up to one's old -s** hacer de las suyas; *v.* embaucar, trampear, hacer trampa; burlar; **to — oneself up** componerse, emperifollarse.

trickery [tríkərɪ] *s.* engaños, malas mañas, astucia.

trickle [tríkl] *v.* gotear; escurrir; *s.* goteo.

tricky [tríkɪ] *adj.* tramposo, *Am.* mañero; intrincado, complicado.

tried [traɪd] *p.p. de* **to try** & *adj.* probado.

trifle [tráɪfl] *s.* fruslería, friolera, nadería, nonada; bagatela; *v.* chancear(se), bromear; jugar, juguetear.

trigger [trígə˞] *s.* gatillo (*de pistola, rifle, etc.*).

trill [trɪl] *v.* trinar; **to — the r** pronunciar la erre doble; *s.* trino.

trilogy [trílədʒɪ] *s.* trilogía.

trim [trim] *v.* guarnecer, adornar; recortar; podar, mondar; despabilar (*una vela*); ganarle a uno (*en el juego*); **to — up** adornar, componer; *adj.* aseado, limpio, pulcro, acicalado; *s.* adorno, franja, ribete, guarnición; **to be in — for** estar en buena salud para; estar bien entrenado para.

trimming [trímɪŋ] *s.* adorno, aderezo, guarnición; orla, ribete, franja; paliza, zurra; **-s** adornos; accesorios; recortes.

trinity [trínətɪ] *s.* trinidad.

trinket [tríŋkɪt] *s.* chuchería, baratija.

trip [trɪp] *s.* viaje, travesía; recorrido, jira; tropezón; *v.* tropezar; dar un traspié; equivocarse; hacer tropezar, hacer caer; saltar, brincar, corretear.

triphthong [tríffɔŋ] *s.* triptongo.

triple [trípl] *adj. & s.* triple; *v.* triplicar.

triplicate [trípləkət] *adj.* triplicado.

tripod [tráɪpəd] *s.* trípode.

trite [traɪt] *adj.* trillado, trivial, vulgar.

triumph [tráɪəmf] *s.* triunfo; *v.* triun-far.

triumphal [traɪʌ́mfl] *adj.* triunfal.

triumphant [traɪʌ́mfənt] *adj.* triunfante; **-ly** *adv.* triunfantemente, en triunfo.

trivial [trívjəl] *adj.* trivial, insignificante.

trod [trad] *pret. & p.p. de* **to tread.**

trodden [trádn] *p.p. de* **to tread.**

trolley [trálɪ] *s.* trole; tranvía de trole.

trombone [trámbon] *s.* trombón.

troop [trup] *s.* tropa; cuadrilla.

trophy [trófɪ] *s.* trofeo.

tropic [trápɪk] *s.* trópico; **— of Cancer** trópico de Cáncer; **— of Capricorn** trópico de Capricornio; *adj.* tropical.

tropical [trápɪkl] *adj.* tropical.

trot [trat] *v.* trotar; hacer trotar; *s.* trote.

troubadour [trúbədɔr] *s.* trovador.

trouble [trʌbl] *v.* perturbar, turbar; molestar, incomodar; afligir; preocupar(se); **don't — to come** no se moleste Vd. en venir; *s.* pena, aflicción; inquietud, perturbación; dificultad; molestia; panne, avería, accidente (*a un mecanismo*); **heart —** enfermedad del corazón; **to be in —** estar en un aprieto o apuro; **it is not worth the —** no vale la pena; **— shooter** investigador de fallas o averías.

troublemaker [trʌ́blmekə˞] *s.* agitador, alborotador, malcontento.

troublesome [trʌ́blsəm] *adj.* molesto, fastidioso, enfadoso, dificultoso; penoso.

trough [trɔf] *s.* comedero; artesa; batea; **eaves —** canal, gotera del tejado; **drinking —** abrevadero.

trousers [tráuzə˞z] *s. pl.* pantalones.

trousseau [trúso] *s.* ajuar de novia.

trout [traut] *s.* trucha.

trowel [tráuəl] *s.* llana, *Am.* cuchara (*de albañil*).

truant [trúənt] *s.* novillero, holgazán (*que se ausenta de la escuela*); **to play —** hacer novillos, *Am.* capear la escuela, *Am.* pintar venado, *Am.* jubilarse; *adj.* vago, perezoso.

truce [trus] *s.* tregua.

truck [trʌk] *s.* camión; carretón; carreta; basura; baratijas; **garden —** hortalizas, legumbres y verduras; **— garden** hortaliza, huerta de legumbres; *v.* acarrear, transportar en camión o carretón.

trudge [trʌdʒ] *v.* caminar, caminar con esfuerzo; *s.* caminata.

true [tru] *adj.* (*not false*) verdadero; cierto; verídico; fiel; (*exact*) exacto, preciso; legítimo.

truly [trúlɪ] *adv.* (*not falsely*) verdaderamente, en verdad; en realidad; (*exactly*) exactamente, correctamente; fielmente; **very — yours** su seguro servidor.

trump [trʌmp] *s.* triunfo (*en el juego de naipes*); *v.* matar con un triunfo (*en el juego de naipes*); **to — up an**

TR

excuse forjar o inventar una excusa.

trumpet [trámpɪt] s. trompeta; clarín; **ear —** trompetilla acústica; v. trompetear; tocar la trompeta; pregonar, divulgar.

trunk [trʌŋk] s. tronco; baúl; trompa (de elefante); **-s** calzones cortos (para deportes); **— line** línea principal.

trust [trʌst] s. (reliance) confianza, fe; (credit) crédito; (charge) cargo; custodia; .depósito; (firms) trust, sindicato monopolista; v. confiar; fiar en, tener confianza en, fiarse de; esperar; dar crédito a.

trustee [trʌsti] s. fideicomisario, depositario; **university -s** regentes universitarios; **board of -s** patronato; consejo.

trustful [trʌstfəl] adj. confiado.

trusting [trʌstɪŋ] adj. confiado.

trustworthy [trʌstwɝðɪ] adj. fidedigno, digno de confianza.

trusty [trʌstɪ] adj. fidedigno; honrado, leal; s. presidiario fidedigno (a quien se le conceden ciertos privilegios).

truth [truθ] s. verdad.

truthful [trúθfəl] adj. verdadero; verídico; veraz.

truthfulness [trúθfəlnɪs] s. veracidad.

try [traɪ] v. probar, ensayar; hacer la prueba; poner a prueba; intentar, procurar; procesar, enjuiciar, formar causa (a un acusado); ver (una causa); **to — on a suit** probarse un traje; **to — one's luck** probar fortuna; **to — someone's patience** poner a prueba la paciencia de alguien; **to — to** tratar de, procurar, intentar; s. prueba, tentativa, ensayo.

trying [tráɪɪŋ] adj. molesto; penoso, irritante.

tub [tʌb] s. tina; bañera; baño; batea, cuba; v. lavar en tina o cuba.

tuba [túbə] s. tuba.

tube [tjub] s. tubo; **inner —** cámara (de un neumático); **radio —** lámpara o tubo de radio.

tubercular [tjubɝkjələˣ] adj. tuberculoso, tísico.

tuberculosis [tjubɝkjəlósɪs] s. tuberculosis.

tuck [tʌk] v. alforzar, hacer o echar alforzas; **to — in** meter en; **to — in bed** arropar; **to — under one's arm** meter bajo el brazo; **to — up** arremangar, recoger; **to — up one's sleeves** arremangarse; s. alforza.

Tuesday [tjúzdɪ] s. martes.

tuft [tʌft] s. (cluster) penacho, copete; borla; (clump) macizo (de plantas).

tug [tʌg] v. remolcar; jalar (halar); arrastrar; trabajar con esfuerzo; **to — at** tirar de, jalar; s. tirón, estirón, Am. jalón; remolcador; **—boat** remolcador; **— of war** lucha a tirones de cuerda.

tuition [tjuíʃən] s. derechos de enseñanza, Am. colegiatura.

tulip [tjúləp] s. tulipán.

tumble [tʌmbl] v. caer(se); voltear; dar volteretas; **to — down** caerse;

desplomarse; **to — down** caerse; desplomarse; **to — into someone** tropezar con alguien; **to — over** volcar, tumbar, derribar; venirse abajo; s. caída, tumbo, vuelco, voltereta, Am. rodada; desorden.

tumbler [tʌmbləˣ] s. vaso (de mesa); acróbata.

tumor [tjúməˣ] s. tumor.

tumult [tjúmʌlt] s. tumulto.

tumultuous [tjumʌltʃʊəs] adj. tumultuoso.

tuna [túnə] s. atún (pez).

tune [tjun] s. (melody) tonada; (pitch) tono; armonía; **to be in —** estar a tono, estar afinado o templado; estar entonado; **to be out of —** estar desentonado o desafinado; desentonar; v. afinar, templar; armonizar; **to — in** sintonizar; **to — up the motor** poner al punto el motor.

tunic [tjúnɪk] s. túnica.

tunnel [tʌnl] s. túnel; socavón; v. socavar; abrir un túnel.

turban [tɝbən] s. turbante.

turbine [tɝbaɪn], [tɝbɪn] s. turbina.

turbulent [tɝbjələnt] adj. turbulento; revoltoso.

turf [tɝf] s. césped; terrón de tierra (con césped); hipódromo, pista (para carreras).

Turk [tɝk] s. turco.

turkey [tɝkɪ] s. pavo, Méx. guajolote (o guajalote); C.A. jolote, chumpe, chompipe; Col. pisco.

Turkish [tɝkɪʃ] adj. turco; s. turco, idioma turco.

turmoil [tɝmɔɪl] s. alboroto; confusión.

turn [tɝn] v. (rotate) volver(se); voltear(se); girar, dar vueltas, rodar; virar; (shape) tornear, labrar a torno; (become) ponerse (pálido, rojo, etc.); **to — back** volver atrás; volverse, retroceder; devolver; **to — down an offer** rechazar una oferta; **to — in** entregar; recogerse, acostarse; **to — inside out** voltear o volver al revés; **to — into** convertir(se) en; **to — off** apagar (la luz); cortar (el agua, el gas, etc.); **to — off the main road** salirse o desviarse de la carretera; **to — on** encender (la luz); abrir la llave (del gas, del agua); **to — on someone** volverse contra, acometer o caer sobre alguien; **to — out** apagar (la luz); echar, expulsar, arrojar; producir; **to — out well** salir o resultar bien; **to — over** volcar(se), volver(se); doblar; revolver (en la mente); entregar; **to — over and over** dar repetidas vueltas; **to — sour** agriarse, fermentarse; **to — the corner** doblar la esquina; **to — to** acudir a; volverse a; dirigirse a; convertir(se) en; **to — to the left** doblar o torcer a la izquierda; **to — up** aparecer; **to — up one's nose at** desdeñar; hacer ascos a; **to — up one's sleeves** arremangarse; **to —upside down** trastornar; volcar; **it -s my stomach** me da asco o náusea; *s.* vuelta; revolución; giro; recodo (*del camino*); turno; virada, cambio de rumbo; — **of mind** actitud mental; **at every** — a cada paso; **to be one's** — tocarle a uno; **to do one a good** — hacerle a uno un favor; **to take -s** turnarse.

turnip [tə́rnəp] *s.* nabo.

turnover [tə́rnovə] *s.* vuelco (*de un coche*); cambio (*de empleados*); **business** — movimiento de mercancías, número de transacciones; **labor** — movimiento de obreros, cambio frecuente de trabajadores; **apple** — pastel de manzana; — **collar** cuello doblado.

turntable [tə́rntebl] *s.* plato giratorio.

turpentine [tə́rpəntaɪn] *s.* trementina; aguarrás.

turpitude [tə́rpətjud] *s.* torpeza, vileza.

turquoise [tə́rkwɔɪz] *s.* turquesa.

turret [tə́rɪt] *s.* torrecilla; torre blindada; alminar.

turtle [tə́rtl] *s.* tortuga; —**dove** tórtola.

tusk [tʌsk] *s.* colmillo.

tutor [tútə] *s.* tutor, maestro particular; *v.* enseñar, instruir.

tuxedo [tʌksido] *s.* esmoquin.

twang [twæŋ] *s.* tañido (*de una cuerda de guitarra*); nasalidad, tonillo gangoso; *v.* puntear, tañer (*una cuerda*); hablar con voz nasal, hablar con tonillo gangoso.

twangy [twǽŋɪ] *adj.* gangoso, nasal.

tweed [twid] *s.* mezclilla de lana; — **suit** traje de mezclilla.

tweezers [twízə*z] *s. pl.* pinzas, tenacillas.

twice [twaɪs] *adv.* dos veces.

twig [twɪg] *s.* ramita; varita.

twilight [twáɪlaɪt] *s.* crepúsculo; **at** — entre dos luces; *adj.* crepuscular.

twin [twɪn] *adj. & s.* gemelo, mellizo, *Méx.* cuate.

twine [twaɪn] *s.* cuerda, cordel; *v.* enroscar(se), torcer(se), retorcer(se); entrelazar.

twinge [twɪndʒ] *s.* punzada (*dolor agudo*); *v.* punzar.

twinkle [twɪŋkl] *v.* titilar, parpadear, pestañear; chispear; *s.* titilación, parpadeo; pestañeo; guiño, guiñada; **in the** — **of an eye** en un abrir y cerrar de ojos.

twirl [twə*l] *v.* girar; dar vueltas; *s.* giro, vuelta; molinete, floreo.

twist [twɪst] *v.* (*turn*) torcer(se); retorcer(se); (*coil*) enroscar(se); *s.* torsión, torcedura; torzal, cordoncillo (*hecho de varias hebras torcidas*); curva, recodo, vuelta; rosca (*de pan*); **mental** — sesgo de la mente, sesgo mental.

twitch [twɪtʃ] *v.* crisparse, contraerse, torcerse convulsivamente (*un músculo*); temblar (*los párpados*); dar un tirón; *s.* temblor, ligera, convulsión, contracción nerviosa.

twitter [twɪtə] *v.* gorjear (*los pájaros*); temblar; agitarse; *s.* gorjeo; agitación, estremecimiento nervioso.

two-faced [túfest] *adj.* de dos caras.

two-fisted [túfɪstəd] *adj.* vigoroso; de dos puños.

twofold [túfold] *adj.* doble.

two-way [túwe] *adj.* de dos sentidos.

type [taɪp] *s.* tipo; *v.* escribir a máquina.

typewrite [táɪpraɪt] *v.* escribir a máquina.

typewriter [táɪpraɪtə] *s.* máquina de escribir.

typewriting [táɪpraɪtɪŋ] *s.* mecanografía; trabajo de mecanógrafo.

typewritten [táɪprɪtn] *adj.* escrito a máquina.

typhoid [táɪfɔɪd] *s.* tifoidea, fiebre tifoidea.

typhus [táɪfəs] *s.* tifo.

typical [típɪk] *adj.* típico.

typist [táɪpɪst] *s.* mecanógrafo; mecanógrafa.

typographical [taɪpogrǽfɪk] *adj.* tipográfico; — **error** error de máquina.

tyrannical [tɪrǽnɪk] *adj.* tiránico, tirano.

tyranny [tírənɪ] *s.* tiranía.

tyrant [táɪrənt] *s.* tirano.

U

ubiquitous [jubíkwɪtəs] *adj.* ubicuo.

udder [ʌ́də] *s.* ubre.

ugliness [ʌ́glɪnɪs] *s.* fealdad; fiereza.

ugly [ʌ́glɪ] *adj.* feo; fiero; repugnante; de mal genio; desagradable.

ulcer [ʌ́lsə] *s.* úlcera.

ulterior [ʌltírɪə] *adj.* ulterior.

ultimate [ʌ́ltəmɪt] *adj.* último; final; fundamental; **-ly** *adv.* finalmente, a la larga.

ultramodern [ʌltrəmádə*n] *adj.* ultramoderno.

ultraviolet [ʌltrəvaɪəlet] *adj.* ultravioleta.

umbilical cord [ʌmbílək]kɔrd] *s.* cordón umbilical.

umbrella [ʌmbrélə] *s.* paraguas; sombrilla.

umpire [ʌ́mpaɪr] *s.* árbitro, arbitrador; *v.* arbitrar.

un- [ʌn–] *prefijo negativo equivalente a :* sin, no, in-, des-.

unable [ʌnébl] *adj.* incapaz, inhábil; **to be** — **to come** no poder venir.

unaccented [ʌnǽksɛntəd] *adj.* inacentuado.

unaccustomed [ʌnəkʌ́stəmd] *adj.* desacostumbrado; insólito, inusitado.

unaffected [ʌnəféktɪd] *adj.* inafectado, sin afectación, natural, sincero.

unalterable [ʌnɔ́ltərəb]] *adj.* inalterable.

unanimity [junənímətɪ] *s.* unanimidad.

unanimous [junǽnəməs] *adj.* unánime.

unarmed [ʌnármd] *adj.* desarmado.

unattached [ʌnətǽtʃt] *adj.* suelto; libre; (*law*) no embargado.

unavoidable [ʌnəvóɪdəb]] *adj.* inevitable, ineludible.

unaware [ʌnəwɛ́r] *adj.* desprevenido; inadvertido; ignorante; incauto; **-s** *adv.* inesperadamente, inopinadamente; impensadamente.

unbalanced [ʌnbǽlənst] *adj.* desequilibrado; — **account** cuenta no saldada.

unbearable [ʌnbérəbl] *adj.* inaguantable, insoportable.

unbecoming [ʌnbɪkʌ́mɪŋ] *adj.* impropio; **an — dress** un vestido que no sienta bien o que cae mal.

unbelief [ʌnbəlíf] *s.* incredulidad.

unbelievable [ʌnbəlívəbl] *adj.* increíble.

unbeliever [ʌnbəlívɚ] *s.* descreído, incrédulo.

unbelieving [ʌnbəlívɪŋ] *adj.* descreído, incrédulo.

unbending [ʌnbéndɪŋ] *adj.* inflexible.

unbiased [ʌnbáɪəst] *adj.* imparcial, libre de prejuicio.

unbosom [ʌnbúzəm] *v.* revelar, confesar, descubrir (*secretos*); **to — oneself** desahogarse con alguien, revelarle sus más íntimos secretos.

unbound [ʌnbáund] *adj.* desencuadernado, no encuadernado; suelto, desatado.

unbroken [ʌnbrókən] *adj.* intacto, entero; indómito; ininterrumpido, continuo.

unbutton [ʌnbʌ́tn̩] *v.* desabotonar, desabrochar.

uncanny [ʌnkǽnɪ] *adj.* extraño, raro, misterioso.

unceasing [ʌnsísɪŋ] *adj.* incesante.

uncertain [ʌnsɝ́tn̩] *adj.* incierto; dudoso; indeciso.

uncertainty [ʌnsɝ́tn̩tɪ] *s.* incertidumbre; falta de certeza.

unchangeable [ʌntʃéndʒəbl] *adj.* inmutable, inalterable, invariable.

unchanged [ʌntʃéndʒd] *adj.* inalterado, igual.

uncharitable [ʌntʃǽrətəbl] *adj.* duro falto de caridad.

uncle [ʌŋkl] *s.* tío.

unclean [ʌnklín] *adj.* inmundo, sucio; impuro.

uncomfortable [ʌnkʌ́mfɚtəbl] *adj.* incómodo; molesto.

uncommon [ʌnkʌ́mən] *adj.* poco común, insólito, raro.

uncompromising [ʌnkʌ́mprəmaɪzɪŋ] *adj.* intransigente; inflexible.

unconcern [ʌnkənsɝ́n] *s.* indiferencia.

unconditional [ʌnkəndíʃənl] *adj.* incondicional, absoluto.

uncongenial [ʌnkəndʒínjəl] *adj.* que no congenia, incompatible.

unconquerable [ʌnkʌ́ŋkɚəbl] *adj.* invencible, inconquistable.

unconquered [ʌnkʌ́ŋkɚd] *adj.* no conquistado, no vencido.

unconscious [ʌnkʌ́nʃəs] *adj.* inconsciente; privado.

unconsciousness [ʌnkʌ́nʃəsnɪs] *s.* inconsciencia; insensibilidad.

unconstitutional [ʌnkənstɪtuʃən̩l] *adj.* inconstitucional.

uncontrollable [ʌnkəntróləbl] *adj.* irrefrenable, ingobernable.

unconventional [ʌnkənvénʃənl] *adj.* despreocupado, libre de trabas o

reglas.

uncouth [ʌnkúθ] *adj.* rudo, tosco, inculto, grosero; desmañado.

uncover [ʌnkʌ́vɚ] *v.* descubrir(se); revelar; destapar(se); desabrigar(se).

unction [ʌ́ŋkʃən] *s.* unción; fervor; **Extreme Unction** extremaunción.

unctuous [ʌ́ŋkʃəs] *adj.* untuoso.

uncultivated [ʌnkʌ́ltəvetɪd] *adj.* inculto; baldío.

uncultured [ʌnkʌ́ltʃɚd] *adj.* inculto, grosero.

undaunted [ʌndɔ́ntəd] *adj.* impávido.

undecided [ʌndɪsáɪdɪd] *adj.* indeciso.

undeniable [ʌndɪnáɪəbl] *adj.* innegable.

under [ʌ́ndɚ] *prep.* (*beneath*) bajo; debajo de; (*less*) menos de; — **age** menor de edad; — **cover** a cubierto; — **the cover of** al abrigo de, al amparo de; — **pretense of** so pretexto de; — **twelve** menos de doce; **to be — obligation to** deber favores a; *adv.* debajo; abajo; menos; *adj.* inferior, de abajo (*en ciertas combinaciones*); — **dose** dosis escasa o corta; — **secretary** subsecretario; — the — lado de abajo, lado inferior; **the — dogs** los de abajo.

underbrush [ʌ́ndɚbrʌʃ] *s.* maleza.

underclothes [ʌ́ndɚkloz] *s. pl.* ropa interior.

underdog [ʌ́ndɚdɔg] *s.* perdidoso, víctima.

underestimate [ʌ́ndɚéstəmet] *v.* menospreciar, apreciar en menos de lo justo; salir corto en un cálculo.

underfed [ʌ́ndɚféd] *adj.* malnutrido.

undergo [ʌndɚgó] *v.* sufrir, aguantar, padecer.

undergone [ʌndɚgɔ́n] *p.p. de* **to undergo**

undergraduate [ʌndɚgrǽdʒuɪt] *s.* estudiante del bachillerato; — **course** cursos o asignaturas para el bachillerato.

underground [ʌ́ndɚgraund] *adj.* subterráneo; *s.* subterráneo; *adv.* bajo tierra; en secreto; ocultamente.

underhanded [ʌ́ndɚhǽndɪd] *adj.* socarrón, secreto, disimulado, clandestino.

underline [ʌ́ndɚlaɪn] *v.* subrayar.

underlying [ʌndɚláɪɪŋ] *adj.* fundamental.

undermine [ʌndɚmáɪn] *v.* minar, socavar.

underneath [ʌndɚníθ] *prep.* bajo, debajo de; *adv.* debajo.

underpay [ʌ́ndɚpé] *v.* malpagar; escatimar la paga.

underpinning [ʌ́ndɚpɪnɪŋ] *s.* apuntalamiento.

underscore [ʌ́ndɚskor] *v.* subrayar.

undersell [ʌndɚsél] *v.* malbaratar; vender a menos precio que.

undershirt [ʌ́ndɚʃɝt] *s.* camiseta.

undersigned [ʌ́ndɚsaɪnd] *s.* firmante, infrascrito; **the —** el infrascrito, los infrascritos; el que suscribe.

undersized [ʌ́ndɚsáɪzd] *adj.* achaparrado, de tamaño inferior al normal.

underskirt [ʌ́ndəskɜt] s. enaguas, refajo.

understaffed [ʌndəstǽft] adj. de personal insuficiente.

understand [ʌndəstǽnd] v. entender; comprender; sobrentender.

understandable [ʌndəstǽndəbl] adj. comprensible.

understanding [ʌndəstǽndɪŋ] s. comprensión; entendimiento, inteligencia; acuerdo; adj. comprensivo.

understood [ʌndəstúd] pret. & p.p. de to understand; adj. entendido; convenido; sobrentendido.

understudy [ʌ́ndəstʌdɪ] s. sobresaliente, actor suplente; v. servir de sobresaliente o actor suplente.

undertake [ʌndəték] v. emprender; tratar de, intentar; comprometerse a.

undertaken [ʌndətékən] p.p. de to undertake.

undertaker [ʌ́ndətekə] s. director de funeraria; embalsamador.

undertaking [ʌndətékɪŋ] s. empresa.

undertook [ʌndətúk] pret. de to undertake.

undertow [ʌ́ndəto] s. resaca.

underwater [ʌ́ndəwɔtə] adj. submarino; subacuático.

underwear [ʌ́ndəwer] s. ropa interior.

underwent [ʌndəwént] pret. de to undergo.

underworld [ʌ́ndəwɜld] s. hampa, bajos fondos de la sociedad; clase criminal.

underwrite [ʌ́ndərait] v. asegurar; subscribir.

undesirable [ʌndɪzáɪrəbl] adj. indeseable; inconveniente.

undid [ʌndíd] pret. de to undo.

undisturbed [ʌndɪstɜ́bd] adj. impasible; sereno, tranquilo; intacto.

undo [ʌndú] v. deshacer; desatar; desabrochar; desenredar; anular; to — one's hair soltarse el cabello.

undoing [ʌndúɪŋ] s. destrucción; pérdida.

undone [ʌndʌ́n] p.p. de to undo; inacabado, sin hacer; sin terminar; it is still — está todavía por hacer, está inacabado; to come — desatarse.

undoubtedly [ʌndáutɪdlɪ] adv. indudablemente, sin duda.

undress [ʌndrés] v. desnudar(se), desvestir(se).

undue [ʌndjú] adj. indebido; impropio; excesivo.

undulate [ʌ́ndjəlet] v. ondular, ondear.

unduly [ʌndjúlɪ] adv. indebidamente.

undying [ʌndáɪŋ] adj. imperecedero, eterno.

unearth [ʌnɜ́θ] v. desenterrar.

uneasily [ʌnízɪlɪ] adv. intranquilamente, inquietamente, con inquietud; incómodamente.

uneasiness [ʌnízɪnɪs] s. malestar, inquietud, intranquilidad, desasosiego.

uneasy [ʌnízɪ] adj. ansioso, inquieto, intranquilo; cohibido; incómodo.

uneducated [ʌnédʒəketɪd] adj. inculto, indocto, falto de instrucción, ignorante.

unemployed [ʌnɪmplɔ́ɪd] adj. desocupado, desempleado, cesante; ocioso; — funds fondos no invertidos o inactivos.

unemployment [ʌnɪmplɔ́ɪmənt] s. desempleo, cesantía, falta de empleo, desocupación.

unending [ʌnéndɪŋ] adj. inacabable, interminable.

unequal [ʌníkwəl] adj. desigual; insuficiente, ineficaz.

unequivocal [ʌnɪkwívəkl] adj. inequívoco.

unerring [ʌnɜ́rɪŋ] adj. infalible.

unessential [ʌnɪsénʃl] adj. no esencial.

uneven [ʌnívən] adj. desigual, desparejo; irregular, accidentado; — numbers números impares o nones.

unevenness [ʌnívənnɪs] s. desigualdad; desnivel; irregularidad, escabrosidad (del terreno).

uneventful [ʌnɪvéntfl] adj. sin novedad.

unexpected [ʌnɪkspéktɪd] adj. inesperado; -ly adv. de improviso, inesperadamente.

unexpressive [ʌnɪksprésɪv] adj. sin emoción.

unfailing [ʌnfélɪŋ] adj. que nunca falta, constante, indefectible; infalible.

unfair [ʌnfér] adj. injusto; tramposo; to act -ly obrar de mala fe.

unfaithful [ʌnféθfəl] adj. infiel; desleal.

unfamiliar [ʌnfəmíljə] adj. poco familiar; desconocido; to be — with no tener conocimiento de; no estar al tanto de, ignorar; no conocer bien.

unfasten [ʌnfǽsn̩] v. desabrochar; desatar; aflojar.

unfavorable [ʌnfévrəbl] adj. desfavorable, contrario, adverso.

unfeeling [ʌnfílɪŋ] adj. insensible; incompasivo.

unfinished [ʌnfínɪʃt] adj. inacabado, sin terminar, sin acabar; sin barnizar, sin pulir.

unfit [ʌnfít] adj. incompetente, inepto, incapaz; inservible; impropio; v. incapacitar.

unfold [ʌnfóld] v. desenvolver(se), desarrollar(se); desdoblar; revelar.

unforeseen [ʌnforsín] adj. imprevisto.

unforgettable [ʌnfəgétəbl] adj. inolvidable.

unfortunate [ʌnfɔ́rtʃənɪt] adj. desventurado, infeliz, desgraciado, desdichado; -ly adv. desgraciadamente, por desgracia.

unfounded [ʌnfáundəd] adj. infundado.

unfrequented [ʌnfríkwəntəd] adj. poco frecuentado.

unfriendly [ʌnfréndlɪ] adj. hostil, enemigo; poco amistoso; adv. hostilmente.

unfruitful [ʌnfrútfl] adj. infructuoso.

unfurl [ʌnfɜ́l] v. desplegar.

unfurnished [ʌnfɜ́nɪʃt] adj. desamueblado.

ungainly [ʌngénlɪ] *adj.* desgarbado, torpe.

ungrateful [ʌngrétfəl] *adj.* ingrato, desagradecido.

unguarded [ʌngárdəd] *adj.* desprevenido; descuidado.

unhappy [ʌnhǽpɪ] *adj.* infeliz; desgraciado, desventurado, desdichado.

unharmed [ʌnhármd] *adj.* sin daño, ileso.

unhealthy [ʌnhélθɪ] *adj.* malsano; insalubre; enfermizo.

unheard-of [ʌnhɜ́dəv] *adj.* inaudito; desconocido.

unhitch [ʌnhítʃ] *v.* desenganchar; desatar.

unholy [ʌnhólɪ] *adj.* impío, malo.

unhook [ʌnhúk] *v.* desenganchar; desabrochar.

unhurt [ʌnhɜ́t] *adj.* ileso.

uniform [júnəfɔrm] *adj.* & *s.* uniforme.

uniformity [junəfɔ́rmətɪ] *s.* uniformidad.

unify [júnəfaɪ] *v.* unificar, unir.

unilateral [junɪlǽtərl] *adj.* unilateral.

unimportant [ʌnɪmpɔ́rtn̩t] *adj.* insignificante, poco importante.

uninhibited [ʌnɪnhíbətəd] *adj.* sin inhibición.

union [júnjən] *s.* unión; — **leader** jefe de un gremio obrero; — **trade-union** gremio obrero; — **shop** obreros sindicados o agremiados.

unique [juník] *adj.* único, singular.

unison [júnəzn̩]: **in** — al unísono (*en el mismo tono*); al compás.

unit [júnɪt] *s.* unidad.

unite [junáɪt] *v.* unir(se).

unity [júnətɪ] *s.* unidad; unión.

universal [junəvɜ́sl̩] *adj.* universal; — **joint** cruceta.

universe [júnəvɜs] *s.* universo.

university [junəvɜ́sətɪ] *s.* universidad.

unjust [ʌndʒʌ́st] *adj.* injusto.

unjustifiable [ʌndʒʌ́stəfaɪəbl̩] *adj.* injustificable, injustificado.

unkempt [ʌnkémpt] *adj.* desaseado, desaliñado; desgreñado.

unkind [ʌnkáɪnd] *adj.* falto de bondad; descortés; cruel.

unknown [ʌnnón] *adj.* desconocido; no sabido; ignoto; — **quality** incógnita; **it is** — se ignora, no se sabe, se desconoce.

unlawful [ʌnlɔ́fəl] *adj.* ilegal, ilícito.

unleash [ʌnlíʃ] *v.* soltar.

unless [ʌnlés] *conj.* a menos que, a no ser que.

unlicensed [ʌnláɪsənzd] *adj.* sin autorización.

unlike [ʌnláɪk] *adj.* desemejante, distinto, diferente; *prep.* a diferencia de.

unlikely [ʌnláɪklɪ] *adj.* improbable, inverosímil.

unlimited [ʌnlímɪtɪd] *adj.* ilimitado.

unload [ʌnlód] *v.* descargar; vaciar; deshacerse de (*acciones, mercancías*).

unlock [ʌnlák] *v.* abrir (*con llave*); soltar, destrabar; revelar, penetrar (*secretos*).

unloose [ʌnlús] *v.* soltar.

unlucky [ʌnlʌ́kɪ] *adj.* (*unfortunate*) desdichado, desventurado, desgraciado, desafortunado; (*of bad omen*) aciago, de mal agüero, funesto; **an** — **number** un número de mala suerte.

unmanageable [ʌnmǽnɪdʒəbl̩] *adj.* inmanejable, ingobernable, intratable, indomable.

unmanned [ʌnmǽnd] *adj.* desguarnecido; sin tripulación.

unmarked [ʌnmárkt] *adj.* sin identificación.

unmarried [ʌnmǽrɪd] *adj.* soltero.

unmask [ʌnmǽsk] *v.* desenvascar(se).

unmerciful [ʌnmɜ́sɪfəl] *adj.* despiadado, inclemente.

unmistakable [ʌnmɪstékəbl̩] *adj.* inequívoco, claro, inconfundible.

unmoved [ʌnmúvd] *adj.* fijo; inmutable, impasible; indiferente.

unnatural [ʌnnǽtʃərəl] *adj.* afectado, artificial; anormal; **an** — **mother** una madre desnaturalizada.

unnecessary [ʌnnésəsɛrɪ] *adj.* innecesario.

unnoticed [ʌnnótɪst] *adj.* inadvertido.

unobliging [ʌnəbláɪdʒɪŋ] *adj.* poco complaciente, descortés, descomedido.

unobserved [ʌnəbzɜ́vd] *adj.* inadvertido; sin ser visto.

unobtainable [ʌnəbténəbl̩] *adj.* inobtenible, inasequible, inaccesible.

unobtrusive [ʌnəbtrusɪv] *adj.* discreto; sin ser visto.

unoccupied [ʌnákjəpaɪd] *adj.* desocupado; vacío; desalquilado.

unofficial [ʌnəfíʃl̩] *adj.* extraoficial.

unorganized [ʌnɔ́rgənaɪzd] *adj.* sin organización; inorganizado.

unoriginal [ʌnərídʒənl̩] *adj.* trivial; ordinario.

unorthodox [ʌnɔ́rθədaks] *adj.* heterodoxo.

unpack [ʌnpǽk] *v.* desempacar; desembalar.

unpaid [ʌnpéd] *adj.* no pagado; sin pagar; — **bills** cuentas por pagar.

unpleasant [ʌnpléznt] *adj.* desagradable.

unpleasantness [ʌnpléznt nɪs] *s.* manera desagradable; desazón; desavenencia; **the** — **of a situation** lo desagradable de una situación; **to have an** — **with** tener una desavenencia con.

unprecedented [ʌnprésədentɪd] *adj.* sin precedente; inaudito.

unpremeditated [ʌnprimédətetəd] *adj.* impremeditado.

unprepared [ʌnpripérd] *adj.* desprevenido; no preparado; no listo.

unpretentious [ʌnpriténʃəs] *adj.* modesto; sin pretenciones.

unprintable [ʌnpríntəbl̩] *adj.* que no puede imprimirse.

unproductive [ʌnprədʌ́ktɪv] *adj.* improductivo.

unprofessional [ʌnprəféʃənl̩] *adj.* no profesional.

unprofitable [ʌnpráfɪtəbl̩] *adj.* infructuoso.

unpublished [ʌnpʌ́blɪʃt] *adj*. inédito, no publicado.

unqualified [ʌnkwáləfaɪd] *adj*. incompetente; inepto.

unquenchable [ʌnkwéntʃəbl] *adj*. inapagable, inextinguible.

unquestionable [ʌnkwéstʃənəbl] *adj*. indisputable, indudable; irreprochable.

unravel [ʌnrǽvl] *v*. desenredar; desenmarañar; deshilachar(se); deshilar.

unreal [ʌnríəl] *adj*. irreal; ilusorio, imaginario.

unreasonable [ʌnrízənəbl] *adj*. desrazonable, fuera de razón; irracional.

unrecognizable [ʌnrékəgnaɪzəbl] *adj*. irreconocible, no conocible, incapaz de reconocerse; desconocido.

unrefined [ʌnrɪfáɪnd] *adj*. no refinado; inculto, grosero.

unreliable [ʌnrɪlaíəbl] *adj*. informal; indigno de confianza.

unrest [ʌnrést] *s*. inquietud, desasosiego.

unroll [ʌnról] *v*. desenrollar(se), desenvolver(se).

unruly [ʌnrúlɪ] *adj*. indómito; indócil; desobediente.

unsafe [ʌnséf] *adj*. inseguro, peligroso.

unsalable [ʌnséləbl] *adj*. invendible.

unsatisfactory [ʌnsætɪsfǽktrɪ] *adj*. no satisfactorio, inaceptable.

unscrupulous [ʌnskrúpjuləs] *adj*. poco escrupuloso.

unseasonable [ʌnsízənəbl] *adj*. intempestivo.

unseat [ʌnsít] *v*. destituir.

unseen [ʌnsín] *adj*. no visto, oculto; invisible.

unselfish [ʌnsélfɪʃ] *adj*. desinteresado.

unselfishness [ʌnsélfɪʃnɪs] *s*. desinterés, abnegación.

unsettled [ʌnsétld] *adj*. (*disturbed*) desordenado, en desorden; turbio; inestable; (*uncertain*) incierto; indeciso; (*unpopulated*) deshabitado; no establecido; — **bills** cuentas no liquidadas, cuentas pendientes; — **weather** tiempo variable; **an — liquid** un líquido revuelto o turbio.

unshaken [ʌnʃékən] *adj*. inmóvil, inmovible, firme.

unsightly [ʌnsáɪtlɪ] *adj*. feo, desagradable a la vista.

unskilled [ʌnskíld] *adj*. inexperto.

unskillful [ʌnskílfəl] *adj*. inhábil, desmañado, inexperto.

unsociable [ʌnsóʃəbl] *adj*. insociable, huraño, intratable, arisco.

unsophisticated [ʌnsəfístəkétəd] *adj*. cándido, sencillo.

unsound [ʌnsáʊnd] *adj*. erróneo, falso.

unspeakable [ʌnspíkəbl] *adj*. indecible; inefable; atroz.

unstable [ʌnstébl] *adj*. inestable.

unsteady [ʌnstédɪ] *adj*. inseguro, inestable; movedizo; variable, inconstante.

unsuccessful [ʌnsəksésfəl] *adj*. sin éxito; desafortunado; **to be —** no tener

éxito.

unsuitable [ʌnsútəbl] *adj*. impropio, inapropiado; inepto; inconveniente; incongruente; incompatible.

unsuspected [ʌnsəspéktɪd] *adj*. insospechado.

untenable [ʌnténəbl] *adj*. insostenible.

unthinkable [ʌnθíŋkəbl] *adj*. impensable.

untidy [ʌntáɪdɪ] *adj*. desaliñado, desaseado; desarreglado, en desorden.

untie [ʌntáɪ] *v*. desatar(se); desamarrar; deshacer (*un nudo o lazo*).

until [ʌntíl] *prep*. hasta: *conj*. hasta que.

untimely [ʌntáɪmlɪ] *adj*. inoportuno; prematuro; *adv*. inoportunamente; fuera de sazón; demasiado pronto.

untiring [ʌntáɪrɪŋ] *adj*. incansable.

untold [ʌntóld] *adj*. indecible, innumerable, incalculable, inestimable.

untouched [ʌntʌ́ʃt] *adj*. (*unscathed*) intacto, no tocado, íntegro; (*impassive*) impasible, no conmovido; **to leave —** no tocar, dejar intacto; dejar impasible, no conmover.

untrained [ʌntrénd] *adj*. indisciplinado, falto de disciplina; sin educación; inexperto.

untried [ʌntráɪd] *adj*. no probado, no ensayado, no experimentado; **— law case** causa todavía no vista.

untroubled [ʌntrʌ́bld] *adj*. sosegado, tranquilo, quieto.

untrue [ʌntrú] *adj*. falso; infiel; desleal; mentiroso.

untruth [ʌntrúθ] *s*. falsedad; mentira.

untutored [ʌntútəd] *adj*. sin instrucción; ingenuo.

unused [ʌnjúzd] *adj*. no usado; desacostumbrado; **— to** no hecho a, desacostumbrado a.

unusual [ʌnjúʒuəl] *adj*. inusitado, insólito; desusado; raro, extraño; extraordinario.

unvarnished [ʌnvárnɪʃt] *adj*. sin barnizar; sin adornos.

unveil [ʌnvél] *v*. quitar el velo a; revelar, descubrir.

unwarranted [ʌnwɔ́rəntəd] *adj*. no justificado.

unwary [ʌnwérɪ] *adj*. incauto.

unwashed [ʌnwɔ́ʃt] *adj*. no lavado, sin lavar; sucio.

unwelcome [ʌnwélkəm] *adj*. indeseable, no deseado; mal acogido, mal recibido, mal quisto.

unwholesome [ʌnhólsəm] *adj*. malsano; insalubre, dañino.

unwieldy [ʌnwíldɪ] *adj*. inmanejable, difícil de manejar, embarazoso, engorroso.

unwilling [ʌnwílɪŋ] *adj*. renuente, maldispuesto, reacio; **to be — to** no querer, no estar dispuesto a; **-ly** *adv*. de mala gana, sin querer.

unwillingness [ʌnwílɪŋnɪs] *s*. renuencia, falta de voluntad; mala gana.

unwise [ʌnwáɪz] *adj*. imprudente, indiscreto; necio.

unwonted [ʌnwʌ́ntəd] *adj*. inusitado, inacostumbrado; inédito.

unworthy [ʌnwɝ́ðɪ] *adj.* indigno.
unwrap [ʌnrǽp] *v.* desenvolver.
unwritten [ʌnrítən] *adj.* no escrito.
up [ʌp] *adv.* (*above*) arriba, hacia arriba; en lo alto; (*standing*) de pie; *adj.* levantado, derecho, erecto; (*finished*) terminado, concluido; **— and down** de arriba abajo; de acá para allá; **-s and downs** fluctuaciones, vaivenes; **— the river** río arriba; **— to now** hasta ahora; **his time is —** ha expirado su tiempo; se ha cumplido su plazo; **prices are —** los precios han subido; **that is — to you** queda a la discreción de Vd.; eso es cosa suya; **to be — against it** estar perplejo, no saber qué hacer; estar en un aprieto; **to be — on the news** estar al corriente (o al tanto) de las noticias); **to be — to one's old tricks** hacer de las suyas; **to eat it —** comérselo; **what's —?** ¿qué pasa?; *v.* levantar, alzar.
upbraid [ʌpbréd] *v.* reprender, regañar.
update [ʌpdét] *v.* poner al día.
upgrade [ʌpgréd] *v.* adelantar; mejorar.
upheaval [ʌphívl] *s.* trastorno.
upheld [ʌphéld] *pret.* & *p.p. de* **to uphold.**
uphill [ʌphíl] *adv.* cuesta arriba; *adj.* ascendente; trabajoso, arduo.
uphold [ʌphóld] *v.* sostener; apoyar.
upholster [ʌphólstɚ] *v.* entapizar y rellenar (*muebles*).
upholstery [ʌphólstrɪ] *s.* tapicería.
upkeep [ʌpkip] *s.* manutención.
upland [ʌplənd] *s.* altiplanicie, tierra alta.
uplift [ʌplíft] *s.* elevación; edificación (*espiritual*); [ʌplíft] *v.* elevar; edificar (*espiritualmente*).
upon [əpán] *prep.* en, sobre, encima de; **— arriving** al llegar.
upper [ʌ́pɚ] *adj.* superior; alto; **— berth** litera alta, cama alta (*de un coche dormitorio*); **to have the — hand** ejercer dominio o mando; llevar la ventaja; *s.* litera alta, cama alta; pala (*parte superior del calzado*).
upright [ʌ́praɪt] *adj.* recto; derecho; vertical; justo, honrado; **— piano** piano vertical; *s.* poste; puntal; piano vertical.
uprightness [ʌ́praɪtnɪs] *s.* rectitud.
uprising [ʌpráɪzɪŋ] *s.* alzamiento, levantamiento; revuelta.
uproar [ʌ́pror] *s.* tumulto, alboroto, bulla, gritería.
uproarious [ʌprórɪəs] *adj.* estruendoso, bullicioso, tumultuoso.
uproot [ʌprút] *v.* desarraigar, arrancar de raíz.
upset [ʌpsét] *v.* (*capsize*) volcar, tumbar; (*distress*) trastornar; perturbar, turbar; **to become —** volcarse; turbarse; trastornársele a uno el estómago; *pret.* & *p.p. de* **to upset;** *adj.* indispuesto, descompuesto; desarreglado, trastornado; [ʌ́psɛt] *s.* vuelco; trastorno; desorden; indisposición.

upshot [ʌ́pʃɑt] *s.* resultado, fin.
upside [ʌ́psáɪd] *s.* lado o parte superior; **— down** al revés; patas arriba; en desorden.
upstage [ʌpstédʒ] *v.* quitarle la escena a uno.
upstairs [ʌpstérz] *adv.* arriba, en el piso de arriba; *adj.* de arriba; *s.* piso (o pisos) de arriba.
upstart [ʌ́pstɑrt] *s.* advenedizo, principiante presuntuoso.
up-to-date [ʌ́ptədét] *adj.* moderno; al corriente, al tanto.
upturn [ʌptɝn] *s.* alza, subida (*de precios*); mejora.
upward [ʌ́pwɚd] *adv.* arriba, para arriba, hacia arriba; más; **— of** más de; *adj.* ascendente, hacia arriba, para arriba.
upwards [ʌ́pwɚdz] *adv.* = **upward.**
uranium [jʊrénɪəm] *s.* uranio.
urban [ɝ́bən] *adj.* urbano.
urchin [ɝ́tʃɪn] *s.* granuja, pilluelo; **sea — erizo de mar.**
urge [ɝdʒ] *v.* urgir, instar; exhortar; recomendar o solicitar con instancia; apremiar, incitar, estimular; *s.* impulso; gana, ganas; estímulo.
urgency [ɝ́dʒənsɪ] *s.* urgencia; apremio.
urgent [ɝ́dʒənt] *adj.* urgente, apremiante.
urinal [júrɪnl] *s.* urinario.
urinate [júrənet] *v.* orinar.
urine [júrɪn] *s.* orina, (los) orines.
urn [ɝn] *s.* urna; **coffee —** cafetera.
us [ʌs] *pron.* nos; nosotros (*con preposición*).
usage [júsɪdʒ] *s.* usanza; uso; **hard — uso constante.**
use [jus] *s.* (*application*) uso; empleo; (*goal*) utilidad; **it is of no —** es inútil; no sirve; **out of —** desusado, ya no usado; pasado de moda; **to have no further — for** ya no necesitar, ya no tener necesidad de; **what is the —of it?** ¿para qué sirve?; ¿qué ventaja tiene?; ¿qué objeto tiene?; [juz] *v.* usar; emplear; servirse de, hacer uso de; acostumbrar, soler, *Am.* saber; **— your judgment** haz lo que te parezca; **to — up** gastar, agotar; consumir; **to be -d to** estar hecho, acostumbrado o habituado a; **he -d to do it** solía hacerlo, lo hacía.
useful [júsfəl] *adj.* útil.
usefulness [júsfəlnɪs] *s.* utilidad.
useless [júslɪs] *adj.* inútil; inservible.
uselessness [júslɪsnɪs] *s.* inutilidad.
usher [ʌ́ʃɚ] *s.* acomodador (*en un teatro o iglesia*); ujier; *v.* conducir, llevar, acompañar; introducir.
usual [júʒuəl] *adj.* usual; corriente, común, general; **-ly** *adv.* usualmente, generalmente, por lo general.
usurer [júʒərɚ] *s.* usurero.
usurp [juzɝ́p] *v.* usurpar.
usury [júʒərɪ] *s.* usura.
utensil [juténsl] *s.* utensilio.
uterus [jútərəs] *s.* útero.

utilitarian [jutɪlətɛ́rɪən] *adj.* utilitario.
utility [jutíɫətɪ] *s.* utilidad; servicio.
utilize [jútlaɪz] *v.* utilizar; aprovechar.
utmost [ʌ́tmost] *adj.* (*extreme*) sumo, extremo; más distante; más grande, mayor; más alto; (*last*) último; **he did his** — hizo cuanto pudo; **to the** — hasta más no poder.
utter [ʌ́tə] *v.* proferir; decir, expresar; **to — a cry** dar un grito; *adj.* completo, total; absoluto.
utterance [ʌ́tərəns] *s.* declaración; expresión; modo de hablar.
uttermost [ʌ́təmost] = **utmost.**
uvula [júvjələ] *s.* campanilla, galillo de la garganta.
uvular [júvjulə] *adj.* uvular.

V

vacancy [vékənsɪ] *s.* vacante, empleo vacante; vacío; habitación o apartamento desocupado.
vacant [vékənt] *adj.* vacante; vacío; desocupado; libre.
vacate [véket] *v.* desocupar, dejar vacío; dejar vacante.
vacation [vekéʃən] *s.* vacación; vacaciones.
vaccinate [væksnet] *v.* vacunar.
vaccination [væksnéʃən] *s.* vacunación.
vaccine [væksin] *s.* vacuna.
vacillate [væslet] *v.* vacilar.
vacuum [vækjuəm] *s.* vacío; **— cleaner** escoba eléctrica.
vagabond [vægəbɑnd] *adj.* & *s.* vagabundo.
vagrancy [végrənsɪ] *s.* vagancia.
vagrant [végrənt] *adj.* vago, vagabundo, errante; *s.* vago, vagabundo.
vague [veg] *adj.* vago.
vain [ven] *adj.* vano; vanidoso; **in —** en vano.
vainglory [venglórɪ] *s.* vanagloria.
vale [vel] *s.* valle; cañada.
valentine [væləntaɪn] *s.* tarjeta o regalo del día de San Valentín (*el día de los enamorados*); **to my —** a mi querido, a mi querida.
valet [vælɪt] *s.* criado, camarero; planchador de trajes.
valiant [væljənt] *adj.* valiente, valeroso.
valid [vælɪd] *adj.* válido; valedero.
validity [vəlídətɪ] *s.* validez.
valise [vəlís] *s.* valija, maleta, *Méx.* velis, *Méx.* petaca.
valley [vælɪ] *s.* valle.
valor [vælə] *s.* valor, ánimo, valentía.
valorous [vælərəs] *adj.* valeroso, valiente.
valuable [væljəbl] *adj.* valioso; precioso; preciado; **-s** *s. pl.* objetos de valor, joyas, alhajas.
valuation [væljuéʃən] *s.* valuación, valoración; avalúo; tasa.
value [væljv] *s.* (*price*) valor; precio; (*merit*) mérito; (*consideration*) estimación, aprecio; *v.* valorar, avaluar, valuar; apreciar, estimar.
valueless [væljulɪs] *adj.* sin valor.
valve [vælv] *s.* válvula; valva (*de los*

moluscos); **safety —** válvula de seguridad.
vampire [væmpaɪr] *s.* vampiro.
van [væn] *s.* camión (*para transportar muebles*); **—guard** vanguardia.
vandal [vændl] *s.* vándalo.
vane [ven] *s.* veleta; aspa (*de molino de viento*); paleta (*de hélice*).
vanguard [vængɑrd] *s.* vanguardia.
vanilla [vənílə] *s.* vainilla.
vanish [vænɪʃ] *v.* desvanecerse, desaparecer(se).
vanity [vænətɪ] *s.* vanidad; **— case** neceser; **— table** tocador.
vanquish [vænkwɪʃ] *v.* vencer.
vantage [væntɪdʒ] *s.* ventaja; **point of —** lugar estratégico.
vapor [vépə] *s.* vapor; vaho.
vaporize [vépəaɪz] *v.* vaporizar.
variable [vérɪəbl] *adj.* & *s.* variable.
variance [vérɪəns] *s.* variación, cambio; desavenencia; **to be at —** estar desavenidos; no estar de acuerdo.
variant [vérɪənt] *s.* variante.
variation [verɪéʃən] *s.* variación; variedad.
varied [vérɪd] *adj.* variado, vario.
variegated [vérɪgetɪd] *adj.* abigarrado.
variety [vəraɪətɪ] *s.* variedad.
various [vérɪəs] *adj.* varios; diferentes, distintos.
varnish [vɑ́rnɪʃ] *s.* barniz; *v.* barnizar.
vary [vérɪ] *v.* variar; cambiar.
vase [ves] *s.* vaso, jarrón.
Vaseline [væsəlɪn] *s.* vaselina.
vassal [væsl] *adj.* & *s.* vasallo.
vast [væst] *adj.* vasto; inmenso; anchuroso; **-ly** *adv.* vastamente, sumamente, muy.
vastness [væstnɪs] *s.* inmensidad.
vat [væt] *s.* tina, tanque.
vaudeville [vódəvɪl] *s.* vodevil, función de variedades.
vault [vɑlt] *s.* bóveda; tumba; **bank —** caja fuerte; depósito; **pole —** salto con garrocha; *v.* abovedar, edificar una bóveda; dar figura de bóveda; saltar con garrocha; saltar por encima de.
vaunt [vɔnt] *v.* jactarse; ostentar, alardear; *s.* jactancia.
veal [vil] *s.* carne de ternera; **— cutlet** chuleta de ternera.
veer [vɪr] *v.* virar; *s.* virada.
vegetable [védʒtəbl] *s.* (*plant*) vegetal, planta; (*food*) legumbre, **-s** hortaliza, legumbres; **green -s** verduras; *adj.* vegetal; de legumbres, de hortaliza; **— garden** hortaliza.
vegetate [védʒtet] *v.* vegetar.
vegetation [vedʒtéʃən] *s.* vegetación.
vehemence [víəməns] *s.* vehemencia.
vehement [víəmənt] *adj.* vehemente.
vehicle [víɪkl] *s.* vehículo.
veil [vel] *s.* velo; *v.* velar; tapar, encubrir.
vein [ven] *s.* vena; veta, filón.
veined [vend] *adj.* veteado, jaspeado; venoso.
velocity [vəlásətɪ] *s.* velocidad.
velvet [vélvɪt] *s.* terciopelo; velludo;

UN

adj. de terciopelo; aterciopelado.
velvety [vélvɪtɪ] *adj.* aterciopelado.
vendor [véndə] *s.* vendedor; buhonero, vendedor ambulante.
veneer [vənír] *s.* chapa; *v.* chapar o chapear, *Am.* enchapar.
venerable [vénərəbl] *adj.* venerable; venerando.
venerate [vénəret] *v.* venerar.
veneration [venəréʃən] *s.* veneración.
venereal [vənírɪəl] *adj.* venéreo.
Venezuelan [venəzwílən] *adj.* & *s.* venezolano.
vengeance [véndʒəns] *s.* venganza; **with a** — con furia; con violencia.
venison [vénəzn̩] *s.* venado, carne de venado.
venom [vénəm] *s.* veneno, ponzoña.
venomous [vénəməs] *adj.* venenoso, ponzoñoso.
vent [vent] *s.* (*opening*) abertura; (*escape*) escape; (*utterance*) desahogo; fogón (*de arma de fuego*); **to give** — **to anger** desahogar la ira, dar desahogo a la cólera; *v.* dar salida o desahogo; desahogar, descargar.
ventilate [véntlet] *v.* ventilar.
ventilation [ventléʃən] *s.* ventilación.
ventilator [véntletə] *s.* ventilador.
venture [véntʃə] *s.* ventura, riesgo; **business** — especulación; empresa o negocio arriesgado; *v.* aventurar, arriesgar; **to** — **outside** aventurarse a salir; **to** — **to** aventurarse a, atreverse a, osar.
venturous [véntʃərəs] *adj.* aventurado.
veranda [vərǽndə] *s.* galería; terraza; balcón corrido.
verb [vɜb] *s.* verbo.
verbal [vɜ́bl] *adj.* verbal; oral.
verbalize [vɜ́bəlaɪz] *v.* expresar por medio de palabras.
verbose [vɜbós] *adj.* verboso; palabrero.
verdict [vɜ́dɪkt] *s.* veredicto; fallo, decisión, sentencia; — **of "not guilty"** veredicto de inculpabilidad.
verdure [vɜ́dʒə] *s.* verdura, verdor, verde.
verge [vɜdʒ] *s.* borde, margen, orilla; **on the** — **of** al borde de; a punto de; *v.* **to** — **on** rayar en, estar al margen de; **to** — **toward** tender a, inclinarse a.
verify [vérəfaɪ] *v.* verificar; comprobar.
verily [vérəlɪ] *adv.* en verdad.
veritable [vérətəbl] *adj.* verdadero.
vermillion [vəmíljən] *adj.* bermejo.
vernacular [vənǽkjulə] *adj.* vernáculo; *s.* idioma corriente.
versatile [vɜ́sətl] *adj.* hábil para muchas cosas; flexible.
verse [vɜs] *s.* verso.
versed [vɜst] *adj.* versado, experto, perito.
version [vɜ́ʒən] *s.* versión.
vertebrate [vɜ́təbrɪt] *adj.* vertebrado.
vertical [vɜ́tɪkl] *adj.* vertical.
very [vérɪ] *adv.* muy; — **much** muchísimo; — **many** muchísimos; **it is** — **cold today** hace mucho frío hoy;

adj. mismo; mismísimo; mero; **the** — **man** el mismísimo hombre; **the** — **thought of** la mera idea de.
vespers [véspəz] *s. pl.* vísperas.
vessel [vésl] *s.* vasija; vaso; barco, embarcación; **blood** — vaso, vena, arteria.
vest [vest] *s.* chaleco; *v.* conferir; **to** — **with power** revestir de autoridad, conferir poder a.
vestibule [véstəbjul] *s.* vestíbulo; zaguán.
vestige [véstɪdʒ] *s.* vestigio.
vestment [véstmənt] *s.* vestidura.
veteran [vétərən] *adj.* & *s.* veterano.
veterinary [vétrəneri] *s.* veterinario o albéitar.
veto [víto] *s.* veto; prohibición; *v.* vedar, prohibir; poner el veto a; negarse a aprobar.
vex [veks] *v.* molestar, hostigar; incomodar, enfadar; perturbar.
vexation [vekséʃən] *s.* molestia, incomodidad; enojo.
via [váɪə] *prep.* por, por la vía de.
viable [váɪəbl] *adj.* viable.
viaduct [váɪədʌkt] *s.* viaducto.
vial [váɪəl] *s.* frasco, redoma; **small** — ampolleta.
viands [váɪəndz] *s. pl.* vianda, alimentos, comida.
vibrate [váɪbret] *v.* vibrar.
vibration [vaɪbréʃən] *s.* vibración.
vicarious [vaɪkérɪəs] *adj.* vicario.
vice [vaɪs] *s.* vicio; falta, defecto.
vice-president [váɪsprézədənt] *s.* vice-presidente.
viceroy [váɪsrɔɪ] *s.* virrey.
vice versa [váɪsivɜ́sə] viceversa.
vicinity [vəsínətɪ] *s.* vecindad; cercanía; inmediaciones.
vicious [víʃəs] *adj.* vicioso; malo; maligno; malicioso; — **dog** pero mordedor, perro bravo.
vicissitude [vəsísətjud] *s.* vicisitud; peripecia.
victim [víktɪm] *s.* víctima.
victimize [víktɪmaɪz] *v.* inmolar; engañar.
victor [víktə] *s.* vencedor.
victorious [vɪktórɪəs] *adj.* victorioso.
victory [víktrɪ] *s.* victoria.
victuals [vítlz] *s. pl.* vituallas, víveres.
vie [vaɪ] *v.* competir.
view [vju] *s.* (*field of vision*) vista; paisaje; (*opinion*) parecer, opinion; (*inspection*) inspección; (*aim*) mira, propósito; **in** — **of** en vista de; **to be within** — estar al alcance de la vista; **with a** — **to** con el propósito de; con la esperanza o expectación de; con la mira puesta en; *v.* mirar; examinar.
viewpoint [vjúpɔɪnt] *s.* punto de vista.
vigil [vídʒəl] *s.* vigilia, velada; **to keep** — velar.
vigilance [vídʒələns] *s.* vigilancia, desvelo.
vigilant [vídʒələnt] *adj.* vigilante.
vigor [vígə] *s.* vigor.
vigorous [vígərəs] *adj.* vigoroso.

vile [vaɪl] *adj.* vil, bajo, ruin; pésimo.

villa [vílə] *s.* quinta, casa de campo.

village [vílɪdʒ] *s.* villa, aldea.

villager [vílɪdʒɚ] *s.* aldeano.

villain [vílən] *s.* villano, malvado, bellaco.

villainous [vílənəs] *adj.* villano, ruin, vil, bellaco.

villainy [víləni] *s.* villanía, vileza.

vim [vɪm] *s.* vigor, fuerza, energía.

vindicate [víndəket] *v.* vindicar, vengar.

vindictive [vɪndíktɪv] *adj.* vengativo.

vine [vaɪn] *s.* vid, parra; enredadera.

vinegar [vínɪgɚ] *s.* vinagre.

vineyard [vínjəd] *s.* viña, viñedo.

vintage [víntɪdʒ] *s.* vendimia; edad, época.

violate [váɪəlet] *v.* violar; infringir.

violation [vaɪəléʃən] *s.* violación; infracción.

violence [váɪələns] *s.* violencia.

violent [váɪələnt] *adj.* violento.

violet [váɪəlɪt] *s.* violeta; violado, color de violeta; *adj.* violado.

violin [vaɪəlín] *s.* violín.

violinist [vaɪəlínɪst] *s.* violinista.

viper [váɪpɚ] *s.* víbora.

virgin [vɚ́dʒɪn] *adj.* & *s.* virgen.

virginal [vɚ́dʒɪnl] *adj.* virginal.

virile [vírl] *adj.* viril.

virtual [vɚ́tʃuəl] *adj.* virtual; **-ly** *adv.* virtualmente.

virtue [vɚ́tʃu] *s.* virtud.

virtuous [vɚ́tʃuəs] *adj.* virtuoso.

visa [vízə] *s.* visa, visado; *v.* visar, refrendar.

visceral [vísɚl] *adj.* visceral.

visé = visa.

vise [vaɪs] *s.* tornillo de banco.

visible [vízəbl] *adj.* visible.

vision [víʒən] *s.* visión; vista.

visionary [víʒənɛrɪ] *adj.* visionario; imaginario, *s.* visionario, iluso, soñador.

visit [vízɪt] *v.* visitar; **to — punishment upon** mandar un castigo a, castigar a; *s.* visita.

visitation [vɪzətéʃən] *s.* visitación, visita; castigo, calamidad.

visitor [vízɪtɚ] *s.* visita; visitador.

visor [váɪzɚ] *s.* visera.

vista [vístə] *s.* vista, paisaje.

visual [vízjʊl] *adj.* visual; visible.

visualize [vízjuəlaɪz] *v.* representarse en la mente.

vital [váɪtl] *adj.* vital.

vitality [vaɪtǽlətɪ] *s.* vitalidad.

vitalize [váɪtəlaɪz] *v.* vitalizar.

vitamin [váɪtəmɪn] *s.* vitamina.

vivacious [vaɪvéʃəs] *adj.* vivaz, vivaracho, vivo, alegre, animado.

vivacity [vaɪvǽsətɪ] *s.* viveza, vivacidad.

vivid [vívɪd] *adj.* vívido, vivo; animado.

vivify [vívəfaɪ] *v.* vivificar.

vocabulary [vəkǽbjəlɛrɪ] *s.* vocabulario.

vocal [vókl] *adj.* vocal; oral; **— cords** cuerdas vocales; **to be —** hablar, expresarse.

vocation [vokéʃən] *s.* vocación.

vogue [vog] *s.* boga, moda; **in —** en boga, de moda.

voice [vɔɪs] *s.* (*vocalization*) voz; (*speech*) habla; (*opinion*) voto; *v.* expresar, decir; **-d consonant** consonante sonora.

voiceless [vɔ́ɪslɪs] *adj.* mudo; sin voz; **— consonant** consonante sorda.

void [vɔɪd] *adj.* vacío; nulo, inválido; **— of** falto de, desprovisto de; *s.* vacío; *v.* vaciar, evacuar; anular, invalidar.

volatile [válət] *adj.* volátil; inconstante.

volcanic [valkǽnɪk] *adj.* volcánico.

volcano [valkéno] *s.* volcán.

volition [volíʃən] *s.* volición; voluntad.

volley [válɪ] *s.* descarga, lluvia (*de piedras, flechas, balas, etc.*); voleo (*de la pelota*); *v.* descargar una lluvia de proyectiles; volear una pelota.

volt [volt] *s.* voltio.

voltage [vóltɪdʒ] *s.* voltaje.

voluble [váljəbl] *adj.* facundo.

volume [váljəm] *s.* volumen; tomo; bulto; suma, cantidad.

voluminous [vəlúmənəs] *adj.* voluminoso.

voluntary [váləntɛrɪ] *adj.* voluntario.

volunteer [valəntír] *s.* voluntario; *adj.* voluntario; de voluntarios; *v.* ofrecer, dar voluntariamente; ofrecerse.

voluptuous [vəlʌ́ptʃuəs] *adj.* voluptuoso.

vomit [vámɪt] *s.* vómito; *v.* vomitar, *Méx.* deponer.

voracious [voréʃəs] *adj.* voraz.

vortex [vɔ́rteks] *s.* vórtice; vorágine.

vote [vot] *s.* voto; votación; *v.* votar; votar por.

voter [vótɚ] *s.* votante, elector.

vouch [vautʃ] *v.* **to — for** dar fe de; garantizar, responder de; salir fiador de.

voucher [váutʃɚ] *s.* comprobante, justificante; recibo; fiador.

vouchsafe [vautʃséf] *v.* otorgar, conceder.

vow [vau] *s.* voto; juramente; *v.* votar, jurar, hacer voto de.

vowel [váuəl] *s.* & *adj.* vocal.

voyage [vɔ́ɪɪdʒ] *s.* viaje; travesía; *v.* viajar.

vulgar [válgɚ] *adj.* soez, ordinario, grosero; vulgar.

vulnerable [válnɚəbl] *adj.* vulnerable.

vulture [váltʃɚ] *s.* buitre, *Andes, Ríopl.* cóndor.

W

wabble [wábl] *v.* tambalear(se), bambolear(se); vacilar; temblar; *s.* tambaleo, bamboleo; balanceo.

wad [wad] *s.* taco; bodoque; pelotilla, bolita, rollo; **— of money** rollo de billetes (*de banco*); dinero; *v.* atacar (*un arma de fuego*); rellenar; hacer una pelotilla de.

waddle [wádl] *v.* anadear; contonearse, zarandearse (*al andar*); *s.* anadeo; zarandeo, contoneo.

wade [wed] *v.* vadear; chapotear;

VE

andar descalzo por la orilla del agua;
to — through a book leer con dificultad un libro.

wafer [wéfǝ] s. oblea; hostia (*consagrada*).

waft [wæft] v. llevar en vilo, llevar por el aire; llevar a flote; s. ráfaga de aire; movìmiento (*de la mano*).

wag [wæg] v. menear; sacudir; **to — the tail** colear, menear la cola; s. meneo; bromista, farsante.

wage [wedʒ] v. hacer (*guerra*); dar (*batalla*); s. (*usualmente* **wages**) paga, jornal; **— earner** jornalero, obrero; trabajador; **— scale** escala de salarios (*sueldos*).

wager [wédʒǝ] s. apuesta; v. apostar.

waggle [wǽgl] s. meneo rápido.

wagon [wǽgǝn] s. carró, carreta; carretón.

wail [wel] v. gemir, lamentar; s. gemido, lamento.

waist [west] s. cintura; talle; blusa; **—band** pretina.

waistcoat [wéstkot] s. chaleco.

waistline [wéstlain] s. talle.

wait [wet] v. (*stay*) esperar, aguardar; (*serve*) servir; **to — for** esperar, aguardar; **to — on (upon)** servir a; atender a; **to — table** servir la mesa, servir de mozo o camarero (*en un restaurante*); s. espera; **to lie in — for** estar en acecho de.

waiter [wétǝ] s. mozo, camarero, sirviente, *Méx., C.A.* mesero.

waiting [wétiŋ] s. espera; **— room** sala de espera.

waitress [wétris] s. camarera, moza, *Am.* mesera.

waive [wev] v. renunciar a; **to — one's right** renunciar voluntariamente a sus derechos.

waiver [wévǝ] s. renuncia.

wake [wek] v. despertar(se); **to — up** despertar(se); despabilarse; s. velatorio (*acto de velar a un muerto*), *Am.* velorio; estela (*huella que deja un barco en el agua*); **in the — of** después de, detrás de.

wakeful [wékfǝl] adj. desvelado, despierto; insomne.

waken [wékǝn] v. despertar(se); *Riopl.* recordar (*a una persona que está dormida*).

walk [wok] v. andar, caminar, ir a pie; recorrer a pie; pasear; **to — away** irse, marcharse; **to — back home** volverse a casa (a pie); **to — down** bajar; **to — in** entrar; **to — out** salirse, irse; parar el trabajo, declararse en huelga; **to — the streets** callejear; **to — up** subir; s. paseo; senda, vereda; acera; paso (*del caballo*); manera de andar; **— of life** vocación; **a ten minutes'** una caminata de diez minutos.

wall [wol] s. (*interior*) pared; (*garden*) muro; (*fort*) muralla; **low mud —** tapia; **to drive to the —** poner entre la espada y la pared, poner en un aprieto.

wallet [wálit] s. cartera.

wallflower [wɔ́lflauǝ] s. alelí; **to be a — at a dance** comer pavo, *Andes, Méx.* planchar el asiento.

wallop [wálǝp] v. pegar, zurrar, golpear; s. guantada, bofetón, golpazo.

wallow [wálo] v. revolcarse; chapalear o chapotear (*en el lodo*).

wallpaper [wɔ́lpepǝ] s. papel (de empapelar).

walnut [wɔ́lnʌt] s. nuez de nogal; nogal; **— tree** nogal.

waltz [wolts] s. vals; s. valsar, bailar el vals.

wan [wɑn] adj. pálido, enfermizo, enclenque; lánguido.

wand [wɑnd] s. vara, varita; **magic —** varita de virtud.

wander [wándǝ] v. vagar, errar; **to — away** extraviarse; **to — away from** apartarse de, desviarse de; **my mind -s easily** me distraigo fácilmente.

wanderer [wándǝrǝ] s. vago, vagabundo.

wane [wen] v. menguar; decaer; s. mengua; diminución; **to be on the —** ir menguando; ir desapareciendo.

want [wɑnt] v. (*desire*) querer, desear; (*lack*) necesitar; s. falta; necesidad; escasez, carencia; **to be in —** estar necesitado.

wanting [wántiŋ] adj. falto; deficiente; necesitado.

wanton [wántǝn] adj. desenfrenado, libre; licencioso; inconsiderado; temerario.

war [wɔr] s. guerra; v. guerrear, hacer guerra; **to — on** guerrear con.

warble [wɔ́rbl] v. gorjear; trinar; s. gorjeo; trino.

warbler [wɔ́rblǝ] s. cantor; pájaro gorjeador.

ward [word] s. pupilo, menor o huérfano (*bajo tutela*); cuadra (*de hospital, prision, etc.*); distrito (*de una ciudad*); v. **to — off** resguardarse de; evitar; parar (*un golpe*).

warden [wɔ́rdn] s. guardián; alcaide; **prison —** alcaide de una prisión.

wardrobe [wɔ́rdrob] s. (*closet*) guardarropa, ropero, armario; (*garments*) vestuario; ropa.

warehouse [wérhaus] s. almacén, depósito.

wares [werz] s. pl. artículos, mercancías, mercaderías, efectos.

warfare [wɔ́rfer] s. guerra.

warhead [wɔ́rhεd] s. punta de combate.

warlike [wɔ́rlaik] adj. guerrero, bélico.

warm [wɔrm] adj. (*temperature*) caliente, cálido, caluroso; (*enthusiastic*) acalorado; (*fresh*) reciente; **— hearted** de buen corazón; **— blooded** apasionado; ardiente; **he is —** tiene calor; **it is — today** hace calor hoy; v. calentar(se); **to — over** recalentar; **to — up** calentar(se); acalorarse; entusiasmarse.

warmth [wɔrmpθ] s. (*heat*) calor; (*friendship*) cordialidad.

warn [wɔrn] v. avisar, advertir, amonestar; prevenir, precaver.

warning [wɔ́rnɪŋ] s. aviso, advertencia, amonestación; escarmiento; **let that be a — to you** que te sirva de escarmiento.

warp [wɔrp] s. urdimbre (de un tejido); torcedura, deformación; comba; v. combar(se), deformar(se), torcer(se); urdir (los hilos de un telar).

warrant [wɔ́rənt] s. (sanction) autorización; (right) garantía, justificación; (writ) comprobante; orden, mandato, citación (ante un juez); v. autorizar; garantizar; justificar.

warrior [wɔ́rɪɚ] s. guerrero.

warship [wɔ́rʃɪp] s. buque de guerra, acorazado.

wart [wɔrt] s. verruga.

wary [wέrɪ] adj. cauteloso, cauto, precavido, prevenido; **to be — of** desconfiar de.

was [waz] pret. de **to be** (primera y tercera persona del singular).

wash [waʃ] v. lavar(se); **to — away** deslavar(se); **to be -ed away by the waves** ser arrastrado por las olas; s. lavado; lavadura; lavatorio; lavazas, agua sucia; **mouth —** enjuague o enjuagatorio; **—bowl** lavabo, palangana, lavamanos; **—cloth** paño para lavarse; **— dress** vestido lavable; **—room** lavabo, lavatorio.

washable [wáʃəbl] adj. lavable.

wash and wear [wɔ́ʃændwέr] adj. de lava y pon.

washed-out [wáʃtáʊt] adj. desteñido; agotado, sin fuerzas.

washed up [wɔʃtʌ́p] adj. fracasado.

washer [wáʃɚ] s. lavador; máquina de lavar; arandela (para una tuerca); **—woman** lavandera.

washing [wáʃɪŋ] s. lavado; ropa sucia o para lavar; ropa lavada; **— machine** lavadora, máquina de lavar.

washout [wɔ́ʃaʊt] s. derrubio; fracaso.

wasp [wasp] s. avispa.

waste [west] v. gastar; desgastar; malgastar, desperdiciar, derrochar; disipar; **to — away** gastarse, consumirse; desgastarse; s. desperdicio; gasto inútil; desgaste; desechos, desperdicios; terreno baldío, desierto; adj. inútil, desechado; desierto; baldío, — **of time** pérdida de tiempo; **— basket** cesto para papeles; **— land** terreno baldío; **— paper** papeles inútiles, papel de desecho; **to go to —** gastarse, perderse; malgastarse, desperdiciarse; **to lay —** asolar, arruinar.

wasteful [wéstfəl] adj. despilfarrado, gastador; desperdiciado; ineconómico.

watch [watʃ] v. (look) mirar; observar; (be alert) vigilar; velar; cuidar; — **out!** ¡cuidado!; **to — out for** tener cuidado con; cuidar; vigilar; s. reloj (de bolsillo); vela, vigilia; guardia; centinela, vigilante; **— chain** cadena de reloj, Ven., Méx. leontina; **— charm** dije; **wrist —** reloj de pulsera; **to be on the —** tener cuidado;

estar alerta; **to keep — over** vigilar a.

watchful [wátʃfəl] adj. alerto, vigilante, despierto, atento.

watchman [wátʃmən] s. vigilante, guardia, sereno.

watchtower [wátʃtaʊɚ] s. atalaya, mirador.

watchword [wátʃwɚd] s. contraseña, santo y seña, consigna; lema.

water [wɔ́tɚ] s. agua; — **color** acuarela; color para acuarela; — **power** fuerza hidráulica; **—shed** vertiente; — **sports** deportes acuáticos; — **supply** abastecimiento de agua; v. regar; aguar, diluir con agua; abrevar, dar de beber (al ganado); beber agua (el ganado); tomar agua (un barco, locomotora, etc.); **my eyes —** me lloran los ojos; **my mouth -s** se me hace agua la boca.

waterfall [wɔ́tɚfɔl] s. cascada, catarata, caída de agua.

waterfront [wɔ́tɚfrʌnt] s. terreno ribereño.

watermelon [wɔ́tɚmɛlən] s. sandía.

waterpower [wɔ́tɚpaʊɚ] s. fuerza hidráulica.

waterproof [wɔ́tɚpruf] adj. & s. impermeable; v. hacer impermeable.

water ski [wɔ́tɚski] s. esquí acuático.

waterspout [wɔ́tɚspaʊt] s. surtidor; tromba, manga de agua.

waterway [wɔ́tɚwe] s. vía de agua, río navegable, canal.

watery [wɔ́tɚɪ] adj. aguado; acuoso; mojado, húmedo.

wave [wev] v. ondear; ondular; agitar; blandir (una espada, bastón, etc.); **to — aside** apartar, rechazar; **to — good-bye** hacer una seña o ademán de despedida; **to — hair** ondular el pelo; **to — one's hand** hacer una seña o señas con la mano; mover la mano; s. onda; ola; ondulación; **— of the hand** ademán, movimiento de la mano; **permanent —** ondulación permanente.

wavelength [wévlɛŋθ] s. longitud de onda.

waver [wévɚ] v. oscilar; vacilar, titubear; tambalear(se); s. vacilación, titubeo.

wavy [wévɪ] adj. rizado, ondulado; ondulante.

wax [wæks] s. cera; — **candle** vela de cera; — **paper** papel encerado; v. encerar; pulir con cera; hacerse, ponerse; crecer (la luna).

way [we] s. (road) camino; ruta; senda; (manner) modo, manera; — **in** entrada; — **out** salida; — **through** paso, pasaje; **a long — off** muy lejos, a una larga distancia; **by — of** por, por vía de; **by — of comparison** a modo de comparación; **by the —** de paso; **in no —** de ningún modo; **on the — to** camino de, rumbo a; **out of the —** fuera del camino; apartado; a un lado; impropio; extraordinario; **to be in a bad —**

hallarse en mal estado; **to be well under** — estar (*un trabajo*) ya bastante avanzado; **to give** — ceder; quebrarse; **to have one's** — hacer su capricho, salirse con la suya; **to make** — **for** abrir paso para.

wayfarer [wéfɛrə] *s.* caminante.

waylay [welé] *v.* estar en acecho de (*alguien*); asaltar; detener (*a una persona*).

wayside [wésaɪd] *s.* borde del camino; — **inn** posada al borde del camino.

wayward [wéwəd] *adj.* voluntarioso, desobediente.

we [wi] *pron.* nosotros, nosotras.

weak [wik] *adj.* débil; flaco; endeble; — **market** mercado flojo; **weak-minded** de voluntad débil; simple; — **tea** té claro o suave.

weaken [wíkən] *v.* debilitar(se); desmayar, flaquear, perder ánimo.

weakly [wíklɪ] *adv.* débilmente; *adj.* enfermizo, débil, enclenque.

weakness [wíknɪs] *s.* debilidad; flaqueza.

wealth [wɛlθ] *s.* riqueza; copia, abundancia.

wealthy [wélθɪ] *adj.* rico.

wean [win] *v.* destetar; apartar gradualmente (*de un hábito, de una amistad*).

weapon [wépən] *s.* arma.

wear [wɛr] *v.* (*have on*) llevar, tener o traer puesto; usar; (*waste away*) gastar, desgastar; **to** — **away** gastar(se), desgastar(se); consumir(se); **to** — **off** desgastar(se), gastar(se); borrarse; **to** — **out** gastar(se); desgastar(se), consumir(se); agotar; cansar; **it -s well** es duradero; dura mucho; **as the day wore on** a medida que pasaba el día; *s.* uso, gasto; durabilidad; — **and tear** desgaste; uso; **men's** — ropa para hombres; **clothes for summer** — ropa de verano.

wearily [wírɪlɪ] *adv.* penosamente, con cansancio, con fatiga, fatigadamente.

weariness [wírɪnɪs] *s.* cansancio, fatiga.

wearing [wérɪŋ] *adj.* cansado, aburrido, fastidioso.

wearisome [wírɪsəm] *adj.* fatigoso, molesto, fastidioso.

weary [wírɪ] *adj.* cansado, fatigado; aburrido; *v.* cansar(se), fatigar(se).

weasel [wízl] *s.* comadreja.

weather [wéðə] *s.* tiempo; **weather-beaten** desgastado o curtido por la intemperie; — **bureau** oficina meteorológica; — **conditions** condiciones atmosféricas; — **vane** veleta; **it is fine** — hace buen tiempo; **to be under the** — estar enfermo; estar indispuesto; *v.* exponer a la intemperie; orear, secar al aire; **to** — **a storm** aguantar un chubasco; salir ileso de una tormenta.

weave [wiv] *v.* (*cloth*) tejer, entretejer; (*to plan*) urdir; **to** — **together** entretejer, entrelazar; combinar; *s.* tejido.

weaver [wívə] *s.* tejedor.

web [wɛb] *s.* tela; membrana (*entre los dedos de los pájaros acuáticos*); **spider's** — telaraña.

wed [wɛd] *v.* casarse; casarse con; casar; *p.p. de* to wed.

wedded [wédɪd] *p.p.* & *adj.* casado; unido; — **to an idea** aferrado a una idea.

wedding [wédɪŋ] *s.* boda, casamiento, nupcias, enlace; — **day** día de bodas; — **trip** viaje de novios; **silver** — bodas de plata.

wedge [wɛdʒ] *s.* cuña; **entering** — cuña, entrada, medio de entrar, modo de penetrar; *v.* acuñar, meter cuñas; **to be -d between** estar encajado entre.

Wednesday [wénzdɪ] *s.* miércoles.

wee [wi] *adj.* diminuto, chiquitico, pequeñito.

weed [wid] *s.* cizaña, mala hierba; *v.* desherbar (*o* desyerbar), quitar o arrancar la mala hierba; **to** — **a garden** desherbar un huerto; **to** — **out** escardar; eliminar, arrancar, entresacar.

weedy [wídɪ] *adj.* herboso, lleno de malas hierbas.

week [wik] *s.* semana; — **day** día de trabajo, día laborable, día hábil; — **end** fin de semana; **a** — **from to-day** de hoy en ocho días.

weekly [wíklɪ] *adj.* semanal, semanario; *adv.* semanalmente, por semana; *s.* semanario, periódico o revista semanal.

weep [wip] *v.* llorar.

weeping [wípɪŋ] *adj.* llorón; lloroso; — **willow** sauce llorón; *s.* llanto, lloro, lágrimas.

weevil [wívl] *s.* gorgojo.

weigh [we] *v.* pesar; ponderar, considerar; **to** — **anchor** zarpar, levar el ancla; **to** — **down** agobiar; abrumar; **to** — **on one's conscience** serle a uno gravoso, pesarle a uno.

weight [wet] *s.* peso; pesa (*de reloj o medida para pesar*); carga; **paper**—pisapapeles; *v.* cargar, sobrecargar; añadir peso a; asignar un peso o valor relativo a.

weighty [wétɪ] *adj.* grave, ponderoso; de mucho peso; importante.

weird [wɪrd] *adj.* extraño, raro, misterioso, fantástico.

welcome [wélkəm] *s.* bienvenida; buena acogida; *adj.* grato, agradable; bien acogido, bien quisto; bienvenido; bien recibido; — **home!** ¡bienvenido!; — **rest** grato reposo o descanso; **you are** — no hay de qué, de nada (*para contestar a* "thank you"); **you are** — **here** está Vd. en su casa; **you are** — **to use it** se lo presto con todo gusto; está a su disposición; *v.* dar la bienvenida a; acoger o recibir con gusto.

weld [wɛld] *v.* soldar(se); *s.* soldadura.

welfare [wélfɛr] *s.* bienestar; bien; felicidad; — **work** labor social o de beneficencia.

well [wɛl] *adv.* bien; **he is — over fifty** tiene mucho más de cincuenta años; **— then** pues bien, ahora bien, conque; **well-being** bienestar; **well-bred** bien criado; bien educado; **well-done** bien cocido; **well-fixed** acomodado; **well-groomed** acicalado; **well-meaning** bien intencionado; **well-nigh** casi, muy cerca de; *adj.* bueno; bien de salud, sano; conveniente; **— and good** santo y muy bueno; **well-off** acomodado, adinerado; en buenas condiciones; **well-to-do** próspero, adinerado; **all is —** no hay novedad, todo va bien; **it is — to do it** conviene hacerlo, es conveniente hacerlo.

well [wɛl] *s.* (*shaft*) pozo; (*cistern*) cisterna; (*spring*) manantial; **artesian — pozo** artesiano; *v.* manar; **tears -ed up in her eyes** se le arrasaron los ojos de lágrimas.

welt [wɛlt] *s.* verdugo, verdugón, roncha.

went [wɛnt] *pret. de to* go.

wept [wɛpt] *pret. & p.p. de to* weep.

were [wɜ] *pret. de to* be (en el plural y en la segunda persona del singular del indicativo; es además el imperfecto del subjuntivo); **if I — you** si yo fuera Vd.; **there —** había, hubo.

west [wɛst] *s.* oeste, occidente, ocaso; *adj.* occidental, del oeste; **West Indies** Antillas; *adv.* hacia el oeste, al oeste; en el oeste.

western [wɛ́stən] *adj.* occidental, del oeste.

westerner [wɛ́stənə] *s.* natural del oeste, habitante del oeste, occidental.

westward [wɛ́stwəd] *adv.* hacia el oeste; *adj.* occidental, oeste.

wet [wɛt] *adj.* húmedo; mojado; **— nurse** nodriza, ama de leche; *s.* humedad; antiprohibicionista (*el que favorece la venta de bebidas alcohólicas*); *v.* mojar; humedecer; *pret. & p.p. de to* wet.

wetback [wɛ́tbæk] *s.* panza mojada.

wetness [wɛ́tnɪs] *s.* humedad.

whack [hwæk] *v.* golpear, pegar; *s.* golpe; golpazo; tentativa, prueba.

whale [hwel] *s.* ballena; *v.* pescar ballenas.

wharf [hwɔrf] *s.* muelle, embarcadero.

what [hwɑt] *pron. interr.* qué; qué cosa; cuál; *pron. rel.* lo que; **— for?** ¿para qué? *adj.* qué; **— book?** ¿qué libro? **— a man!** ¡qué hombre!; **— happy children!** ¡qué niños más (o tan) felices!; **take — books you need** tome Vd. los libros que necesite.

whatever [hwɑtɛ́və] *pron.* cualquiera cosa que, lo que, cuanto, todo lo que; **— do you mean?** ¿qué quiere Vd. decir?; **do it, — happens** hágalo suceda lo que suceda; *adj.* cualquiera; **any person —** una persona cualquiera; **no money —** nada de dinero.

whatsoever [hwɑtsoɛ́və] = **whatever.**

wheat [hwit] *s.* trigo; **cream of —** crema de trigo.

wheedle [hwidl] *v.* engatusar.

wheel [hwil] *s.* (*disc*) rueda; rodaja; disco; (*bike*) bicicleta; **— chair** silla rodante, silla de ruedas; **steering —** volante (*de automóvil*); rueda del timón; *v.* rodar; hacer rodar; girar; acarrear; andar en bicicleta; **to — around** dar una vuelta; girar sobre los talones; **to — the baby** pasear al bebé en su cochecito.

wheelbarrow [hwilbæro] *s.* carretilla.

wheeze [hwiz] *s.* resuello ruidoso.

when [hwɛn] *adv. & conj.* cuando; *adv. interr.* ¿cuándo?

whence [hwɛns] *adv.* de donde; de que.

whenever [hwɛnɛ́və] *adj. & conj.* cuando, siempre que, cada vez que.

where [hwɛr] *adv.* donde; adonde; en donde; por donde; **—?** ¿dónde?; ¿adónde?

whereabouts [hwɛ́rəbauts] *s.* paradero; *adv. interr.* ¿dónde?

whereas [hwɛrǽz] *conj.* mientras que; puesto que, visto que, considerando que.

whereby [hwɛrbái] *adv.* por donde, por lo cual; con lo cual.

wherefore [hwɛ́rfor] *adv.* por qué; por lo cual; por eso, por lo tanto.

wherein [hwɛrín] *adv.* en qué; en donde; en lo cual.

whereof [hwɛráv] *adv.* de que; de donde; de quien, de quienes.

whereupon [hwɛrəpán] *adv.* después de lo cual; entonces.

wherever [hwɛrɛ́və] *adv.* dondequiera que, adondequiera que, por dondequiera que.

wherewithal [hwɛ́rwɪðɔl] *s.* medios, fondos; dinero.

whet [hwɛt] *v.* amolar, afilar; aguzar, estimular.

whether [hwɛ́ðə] *conj.* si; ya sea que, sea que; **— we escape or not** ya sea que escapemos o no; **I doubt —** dudo (de) que.

which [hwɪtʃ] *pron. interr.* ¿cuál?; ¿cuáles?; *pron. rel.* que; el cual, la cual, los cuales, las cuales; el que, la que, los que, las que; *adj. interr.* ¿qué?; **— boy has it?** ¿cuál de los muchachos lo tiene? ¿qué muchacho lo tiene?; **— way did he go?** ¿por qué camino se fue?; ¿por dónde se fue?; **during — time** tiempo durante el cual.

whichever [hwɪtʃɛ́və] *pron. & adj.* cualquiera (que), cualesquiera (que); el que, la que; **— road you take** cualquier camino que Vd. siga.

whiff [hwɪf] *s.* (*waft*) soplo; fumada, bocanada; (*odor*) repentino olor o hedor; *v.* soplar; echar bocanadas.

while [hwaɪl] *s.* rato; tiempo, temporada; **a short —** un ratito; **a short — ago** hace poco, hace poco rato; **to be worth —** valer la pena; *conj.* mientras, mientras que; *v.* **to — away the time** pasar el tiempo.

whilst [hwaɪlst] *conj.* mientras, mientras que.

whim [hwɪm] *s.* capricho, antojo.

whimper [hwímpɚ] *v.* lloriquear, gimotear; quejarse; *s.* lloriqueo, gimoteo; quejido.

whimsical [hwímzɪkl] *adj.* caprichoso.

whine [hwaɪn] *v.* lloriquear; quejarse; *s.* gemido, quejido.

whiner [hwaínɚ] *s.* llorón, persona quejosa, *Méx.* quejumbres; *Andes* quejumbroso; *Ríopl.* rezongón.

whip [hwɪp] *v.* azotar, fustigar; zurrar, dar una paliza a, dar latigazos a; batir (*crema, huevos*); vencer; **to — up** batir; coger o asir de repente; hacer de prisa; *s.* azote, látigo, fuete; batido.

whipping [hwípɪŋ] *s.* tunda, zurra, paliza; **— cream** crema para batir.

whir [hwɚ] *v.* zumbar; *s.* zumbido.

whirl [hwɚl] *v.* girar, dar vueltas; arremolinarse; **my head -s** siento vértigo, estoy desvanecido; *s.* giro, vuelta; remolino; espiral (*de humo*); confusión.

whirlpool [hwɚ́lpul] *s.* remolino, vorágine, vórtice.

whirlwind [hwɚ́lwɪnd] *s.* remolino, torbellino.

whisk [hwɪsk] *v.* barrer; desempolvar (*con escobilla*); batir (*huevos*); **to — away** barrer de prisa; llevarse de prisa, arrebatar; **to — something out of sight** escamotear algo, esconder algo de prisa; *s.* **— broom** escobilla; **with a — of the broom** de un escobillazo.

whisker [hwískɚ] *s.* pelo de la barba; **-s** barbas; patillas; bigotes (*del gato*).

whiskey [hwískɪ] *s.* whisky (*aguardiente de maíz, centeno, etc.*).

whisper [hwíspɚ] *v.* cuchichear, hablar en secreto; soplar, decir al oído; susurrar; secretearse; **it is -ed that** corre la voz que; dízque, dicen que; *s.* cuchicheo, secreteo; susurro; murmullo; **to talk in a —** hablar en secreto; susurrar.

whistle [hwísl] *v.* silbar; chiflar; pitar; **to — for someone** llamar a uno con un silbido; *s.* silbido, chiflido; silbato, pito.

whit [hwɪt] *s.* jota, pizca.

white [hwaɪt] *adj.* (*color*) blanco; (*pure*) puro; inocente; (*honorable*) honrado, recto; **—caps** cabrillas o palomas (*olas con crestas blancas*); **— lead** albayalde; **— lie** mentirilla, mentira venial; **white-livered** cobarde; **white-collar** de oficina; **to show the — feather** mostrar cobardía, portarse como cobarde; *s.* blanco; clara (*del huevo*).

whiten [hwáɪtn̩] *v.* blanquear; emblanquecer(se), poner(se) blanco.

whiteness [hwáɪtnɪs] *s.* blancura; palidez; pureza.

whitewash [hwáɪtwɑʃ] *v.* (*paint*) blanquear, enjalbegar; (*gloss over*) encubrir, disimular (*faltas, errores*); absolver (*sin justicia*); *s.* lechada.

whither [hwíðɚ] *adv.* adonde; **—?** ¿adónde?

whitish [hwáɪtɪʃ] *adj.* blancuzco, blanquecino, blanquizco.

whittle [hwítl̩] *v.* cortar, mondar, tallar; tajar, sacar punta a (*un lápiz*); **to — down expenses** cercenar o reducir los gastos.

whiz [hwɪz] *v.* zumbar; *s.* zumbido, silbido; **to be a —** ser un águila, ser muy listo.

who [hu] *pron. rel.* quien, quienes, que, el que, la que, los que, las que; **he —** el que, quien; *pron. interr.* ¿quién?; ¿quiénes?; **— is it?** ¿quién es?

whoever [huévɚ] *pron.* quienquiera que, cualquiera que; el que.

whole [hol] *adj.* todo; entero; íntegro; **the — day** todo el día; **—hearted** sincero, cordial; **—heartedly** de todo corazón; con todo ánimo; *s.* todo, total, totalidad; **as a —** en conjunto; **on the —** en general, en conjunto.

wholesale [hólsel] *s.* venta al por mayor, *Am.* mayoreo; **by —** al por mayor; *adj.* al por mayor; en grandes cantidades; **— dealer** comerciante al por mayor, *Am.* mayorista; **— slaughter** matanza; gran hecatombe; **— trade** comercio al por mayor, *Am.* comercio mayorista; *adv.* al por mayor, por mayor; *v.* vender al por mayor, *Am.* mayorear.

wholesome [hólsəm] *adj.* saludable, sano; salubre; **— man** hombre normalmente bueno o de buena índole.

wholly [hólɪ] *adv.* enteramente, completamente, totalmente.

whom [hum] *pron. pers.* a quien, a quienes; que; al que (a la que, a los que, *etc.*); al cual (a la cual, a los cuales, *etc.*); **for —** para quien; **— did you see?** ¿a quién vió Vd.?

whoop [hup] *s.* grito, chillido, alarido; respiro convulsivo (*que acompaña a la tos ferina*); *v.* gritar, vocear, echar gritos; respirar convulsivamente (*al toser*); **to — it up** armar una gritería, gritar; **whooping cough** tos ferina.

whore [hor] *s.* ramera, puta, prostituta.

whose [huz] *pron.* cuyo, cuya, cuyos, cuyas; *pron. interr.* ¿de quién?; ¿de quiénes?; **— book is this?** ¿de quién es este libro?

why [hwaɪ] *adv.* ¿por qué?; **the reason — la** razón por la que (o la cual); **—, of course!** ¡sí, por supuesto!; ¡claro que sí!; **—, that is not true!** ¡sí eso no es verdad! *s.* porqué, causa, razón, motivo.

wick [wɪk] *s.* mecha, pabilo.

wicked [wíkɪd] *adj.* malvado, malo, inicuo.

wickedness [wíkɪdnɪs] *s.* maldad, iniquidad, perversidad.

wicker [wíkɚ] *s.* mimbre; **— chair** silla de mimbre.

wicket [wíkɪt] *s.* postigo; ventanilla.

wide [waɪd] *adj.* ancho; amplio; vasto;

extenso; **— apart** muy apartados; **wide-awake** muy despierto; alerta, vigilante; **— of the mark** muy lejos del blanco; **— open** muy abierto; abierto de par en par; **far and —** por todas partes, extensamente; **to open** [wɪn] **—** abrir mucho; abrir (la puerta) de par en par; **two feet —** dos pies de ancho (o de anchura).

widely [wáɪdlɪ] adv. ampliamente; extensamente; muy; mucho.

widen [wáɪdn̩] v. ensanchar(se), ampliar(se), dilatar(se).

widespread [wáɪdspréd] adj. muy esparcido, muy extensivo; bien difundido; extendido; general, extendido por todas partes.

widow [wído] s. viuda.

widower [wídəwə] s. viudo.

width [wɪdθ] s. ancho, anchura.

wield [wild] v. manejar; esgrimir (la espada o la pluma); ejercer (el poder).

wife [waɪf] s. esposa.

wig [wɪg] s. peluca.

wiggle [wíg!] v. menear(se); s. meneo.

wigwam [wígwam] s. choza de los indios norteños.

wild [waɪld] adj. salvaje; (animal) feroz, fiero; indómito; montaraz; (plant) silvestre; Ven., Méx. cimarrón; impetuoso, desenfrenado; bullicioso; violento; loco; enojado; desatinado; ansioso; **to talk —** disparatar, desatinar; s. yermo, desierto, monte.

wildcat [wáɪldkæt] s. gato montés; **— scheme** empresa arriesgada.

wilderness [wɪldənɪs] s. yermo, desierto, monte; inmensidad.

wild-eyed [wáɪldaɪd] adj. de ojos huraños.

wildness [wáɪldnɪs] s. salvajez; ferocidad, fiereza; locura.

wile [waɪl] s. ardid, engaño; astucia.

wilful, willful [wɪlfəl] adj. voluntarioso, testarudo, caprichudo; intencional.

will [wɪl] v. (desire) querer, decidir; (order) ordenar, mandar; (dispose of legally) legar; v. defect. y aux. querer; rigurosamente debe usarse para formar el futuro en las segundas y terceras personas: **she —** go ella irá; en las primeras personas indica voluntad o determinación: **I — not do it** no lo haré, no quiero hacerlo.

will [wɪl] s. (wish) voluntad; albedrío; (legal disposition) testamento; **free —** libre albedrío; **ill —** mala voluntad, malquerencia.

willful [wɪlful] adj. voluntario.

willing [wɪlɪŋ] adj. bien dispuesto, deseoso, complaciente; voluntario; **-ly** adv. con gusto, de buena gana, de buena voluntad; voluntariamente.

willingness [wɪlɪŋnɪs] s. buena voluntad, buena gana.

willow [wɪlo] s. sauce; mimbrera; **weeping —** sauce llorón.

wilt [wɪlt] v. marchitar(se); ajar(se); desmayar; languidecer.

wily [wáɪlɪ] adj. astuto, artero.

win [wɪn] (achieve) ganar; lograr, obtener; alcanzar; (persuade) persuadir; **to — out** ganar, triunfar; salirse con la suya; **to — over** persuadir; atraer; alcanzar o ganar el favor de.

wince [wɪns] v. cejar (ante una dificultad o peligro); encogerse (de dolor, susto, etc.).

winch [wɪntʃ] s. malacate.

wind [wɪnd] s. viento, aire; resuello; **— instrument** instrumento de viento; **to get — of** barruntar; tener noticia de.

wind [waɪnd] v. enredar; devanar, ovillar; dar cuerda a (un reloj); serpentear (un camino); dar vueltas; **to — someone around one's finger** manejar fácilmente a alguien, gobernarle; **to — up one's affairs** terminar o concluir uno sus negocios; s. vuelta; recodo.

windbag [wíndbæg] s. (instrument) fuelle; (person) parlanchín, hablador.

windfall [wíndfɔl] s. golpe de fortuna, ganancia repentina, herencia inesperada.

winding [wáɪndɪŋ] adj. sinuoso, tortuoso, que da vueltas; **— staircase** escalera de caracol.

windmill [wíndmɪl] s. molino de viento.

window [wíndo] s. ventana; **show —** escaparate, vitrina, aparador, Am. vidriera; **— shade** visillo, cortinilla; **— sill** antepecho, repisa de ventana.

windowpane [wíndopen] s. cristal de ventana, vidriera.

windpipe [wíndpaɪp] s. tráquea, gaznate.

windshield [wíndʃild] s. parabrisa, guardabrisa.

wind tunnel [wíndtʌn!] s. túnel aerodinámico.

windy [wíndɪ] adj. airoso; ventoso; **it is —** hace aire, ventea, sopla el viento.

wine [waɪn] s. vino; **— cellar** bodega.

wing [wɪŋ] s. ala; bastidor (de escenario); **under the — of** bajo la tutela de; **to take —** levantar el vuelo.

winged [wɪŋd, wíŋɪd] adj. alado.

wingspread [wíŋspred] s. envergadura.

wink [wɪŋk] v. guiñar; pestañear, parpadear; s. guiño, guiñada; **I didn't sleep a —** no pegué los ojos en toda la noche.

winner [wínɚ] s. ganador; vencedor; **— of a prize** agraciado, premiado.

winning [wínɪŋ] adj. (successful) ganancioso; triunfante, victorioso; (charming) atractivo, encantador; **-s** s. pl. ganancias.

winsome [wínsəm] adj. simpático, atractivo, gracioso.

winter [wíntɚ] s. invierno; **— clothes** ropa de invierno; v. invernar, pasar el invierno.

wintry [wíntrɪ] adj. invernal, de invierno; frío, helado.

wipe [waɪp] v. secar; enjugar; limpiar; **to — away one's tears** limpiarse las lágrimas; **to — off** borrar; limpiar; **to — out a regiment** destruir o aniquilar un regimiento.

wire [waɪr] s. (*strand*) alambre; (*telegram*) telegrama; **by —** por telégrafo; **— entanglement** alambrada; **— fence** alambrado; **— netting** tela metálica, alambrado; **to pull -s** mover los hilos; v. poner alambrado, instalar alambrado eléctrico; atar con alambre; telegrafiar.

wireless [wáɪrlɪs] adj. inalámbrico, sin hilos; **— telegraphy** radiotelegrafía; s. radio, radiotelegrafía; telegrafía sin hilos; radiotelefonía; radiograma.

wire tapping [wáɪrtæpɪŋ] s. secreta conexión interceptora de teléfono.

wiry [wáɪrɪ] adj. de alambre; como alambre; nervudo.

wisdom [wízdəm] s. sabiduría, saber; cordura; prudencia; **— tooth** muela del juicio.

wise [waɪz] adj. (*judicious*) sabio, cuerdo, sensato; (*prudent*) discreto, prudente; **the Three Wise Men** los Tres Reyes Magos; **to get — to** darse cuenta de; s. modo, manera; **in no —** de ningún modo.

wisecrack [wáɪzkræk] s. bufonada, dicho agudo o chocarrero, dicharacho.

wish [wɪʃ] v. desear, querer; **to — for** desear; anhelar; **I — it were true!** ¡ojalá (que) fuera verdad!; s. deseo.

wishful thinking [wíʃful θíŋkɪŋ] s. optimismo ilusorio.

wistful [wístfəl] adj. anhelante, anheloso, ansioso; tristón, melancólico.

wit [wɪt] s. agudeza, sal, chiste; ingenio; hombre agudo o de ingenio; **to be at one's wit's end** haber agotado todo su ingenio; **to be out of one's -s** estar fuera de sí, estar loco; **to lose one's -s** perder el juicio; **to use one's -s** valerse de su industria o ingenio.

witch [wɪtʃ] s. hechicera; bruja.

witchcraft [wítʃkræft] s. hechicería.

with [wɪð, wɪθ] prep. con; para con; en compañía de; **filled —** lleno de; **ill —** enfermo de; **the one — the black hat** el del (o la del) sombrero negro.

withdraw [wɪðdrɔ́] v. retirar(se); apartar(se); separar(se); **to — a statement** retractarse.

withdrawal [wɪðdrɔ́əl] s. retirada, retiro.

withdrawn [wɪðdrɔ́n] p.p. de **to withdraw.**

withdrew [wɪðdrú] pret. de **to withdraw.**

wither [wíðɚ] v. marchitar(se); ajar(se); secar(se).

withheld [wɪθhéld] pret. & p.p. de **to withhold.**

withhold [wɪθhóld] v. retener; detener; **to — one's consent** negarse a dar su consentimiento.

within [wɪðín] prep. dentro de; **— call** al alcance de la voz; **— five miles** a poco menos de cinco millas; **it is —**

my power está en mi mano; adv. dentro, adentro.

without [wɪðáut] prep. sin; **— my seeing him** sin que yo le viera; adv. fuera, afuera.

withstand [wɪθstǽnd] v. resistir; aguantar, padecer.

withstood [wɪθstúd] pret. & p.p. de **to withstand.**

witness [wítnɪs] s. testigo; testimonio; v. ver, presenciar; ser testigo de; atestiguar, dar fe de.

witticism [wítəsɪzəm] s. ocurrencia, agudeza, dicho agudo.

witty [wítɪ] adj. agudo, ocurrente, gracioso, divertido, chistoso; **— remark** dicho agudo, agudeza, ocurrencia.

wives [waɪvz] s. pl. de **wife.**

wizard [wizɚd] s. genio, hombre de ingenio; mago, mágico.

wobble [wábl] s. bamboleo.

woe [wo] s. miseria, aflicción, infortunio; **— is me!** ¡miserable de mí!

woeful [wóful] adj. miserable; abatido.

woke [wok] pret. de **to wake.**

wolf [wulf] (pl. **wolves** [wulvz]) s. lobo.

woman [wúmən] (pl. **women** [wímɪn]) s. mujer; **— writer** escritora.

womanhood [wúmənhud] s. estado de mujer; la mujer (las mujeres); integridad femenil; feminidad.

womankind [wúmənkaɪnd] s. la mujer, las mujeres, el sexo femenino.

womanly [wúmənlɪ] adj. femenil, mujeril, femenino; adv. femenilmente, como mujer.

womb [wum] s. vientre, entrañas; útero, matriz.

won [wʌn] pret. & p.p. de **to win.**

wonder [wʌ́ndɚ] s. (*marvel*) maravilla; prodigio; (*emotion*) admiración; **in —** maravillado; **no — that** no es mucho que; no es extraño que; v. asombrarse, maravillarse, pasmarse, admirarse; **to — at** admirarse de, maravillarse de; **I — what time it is** ¿qué hora será? **I — when he came** ¿cuándo vendría? **I should not —** if no me extrañaría que.

wonderful [wʌ́ndɚfəl] adj. maravilloso, admirable; **-ly** adv. maravillosamente, admirablemente, a las mil maravillas; **-ly well** sumamente bien.

wondrous [wʌ́ndrəs] adj. maravilloso, pasmoso, extraño.

wont [wʌnt] adj. acostumbrado; **to be — to** soler, acostumbrar, C.A. saber; s. costumbre, hábito, uso.

woo [wu] v. cortejar, enamorar, galantear.

wood [wud] s. (*material*) madera; (*stick*) palo; (*firewood*) leña; **-s** bosque; selva; **— engraving** grabado en madera; **—shed** leñera, cobertizo para leña; **fire—** leña; **piece of fire—** leño.

woodcut [wúdkʌt] s. grabado en madera.

woodcutter [wúdkʌtɚ] s. leñador.

wooded [wúdɪd] *adj.* arbolado, poblado de árboles.

wooden [wúdṇ] *adj.* de madera, de palo; tieso.

woodland [wúdlænd] *s.* monte, bosque, selva.

woodman [wúdmən] *s.* (*vendor*) leñador; (*dweller*) habitante del bosque.

woodpecker [wúdpɛkɚ] *s.* pájaro carpintero.

woodwork [wúdwɚk] *s.* maderamen; labrado en madera; obra de carpintería.

woof [wuf] *s.* trama (*de un tejido*); tejido.

wool [wul] *s.* lana; *adj.* de lana; lanar; **wool-bearing** lanar; — **dress** vestido de lana.

woolen [wúlɪn] *adj.* de lana; lanudo; — **mill** fábrica de tejidos de lana; *s.* tejido de lana; género o paño de lana.

woolly [wúlɪ] *adj.* lanudo; de lana.

word [wɚd] *s.* (*vocable*) palabra; vocablo, voz; (*news*) noticia, aviso; (*order*) mandato, orden; **pass**— contraseña; **by** — **of mouth** de palabra, verbalmente; *v.* expresar; redactar, formular.

wordy [wɚdɪ] *adj.* palabrero, verboso, ampuloso.

wore [wor] *pret. de* to wear.

work [wɚk] *s.* (*effort*) trabajo; (*masterpiece*) obra maestra (*task*) tarea, faena; (*employment*) empleo, ocupación; oficio; (*accomplishment*) labor; -**s** taller, fábrica; maquinaria, mecanismo; **at** — trabajando; ocupado; *v.* trabajar; funcionar; obrar; surtir efecto; manejar, manipular; resolver (*un problema*); explotar (*una mina*); hacer trabajar; **to** — **havoc** hacer estropicios, causar daño; **to** — **loose** soltarse, aflojarse; **to** — **one's way through college** sufragar los gastos universitarios con su trabajo; **to** — **one's way up** subir por sus propios esfuerzos; **to** — **out a plan** urdir un plan; **to be all -ed up** estar sobreexcitado; **it didn't** — out no dió resultado; **the plan -ed well** tuvo buen éxito el plan.

workable [wɚkəbḷ] *adj.* practicable; explotable.

worker [wɚkɚ] *s.* trabajador; obrero; operario.

working [wɚkɪŋ] *s.* funcionamiento, operación; cálculo (*de un problema*); explotación (*de una mina*); *adj.* obrero, trabajador; — **class** clase obrera o trabajadora; — **hours** horas de trabajo; **a hard-working man** un hombre muy trabajador.

workingman [wɚkɪŋmæn] *s.* trabajador; obrero.

workman [wɚkmən] *s.* trabajador, obrero, operario.

workmanship [wɚkmənʃɪp] *s.* hechura; trabajo; mano de obra.

workshop [wɚkʃap] *s.* taller.

world [wɚld] *s.* mundo; **the World**

War la Guerra Mundial; **world-shaking** de gran importancia.

worldly [wɚldlɪ] *adj.* mundano, mundanal, terreno, terrenal.

worm [wɚm] *s.* gusano; lombriz; **worm-eaten** comido de gusanos; carcomido, apolillado; *v.* **to** — **a secret out of someone** extraerle o sonsacarle un secreto a una persona; **to** — **oneself into** insinuarse en, meterse en.

worn [worn] *p.p. de* to wear; **worn-out** gastado, roto; rendido de fatiga.

worry [wɚɪ] *s.* inquietud, ansiedad, cuidado, preocupación, apuro, apuración; *v.* inquietar(se), preocupar(se), afligir(se), apurar(se).

worse [wɚs] *adj.* peor; más malo; *adv.* peor; — **and** — cada vez peor; — **than ever** peor que nunca; **from bad to** — de mal en peor; **so much the** — tanto peor; **to be** — **off** estar peor que antes; **to change for the** — empeorar(se); **to get** — empeorar(se).

worship [wɚʃəp] *s.* adoración, culto; veneración; *v.* adorar; reverenciar.

worshiper [wɚʃəpɚ] *s.* adorador; **the -s** los fieles.

worst [wɚst] *adj.* peor; *adv.* peor; **the** — el peor; la peor; lo peor; *v.* derrotar.

worth [wɚθ] *s.* valor, valía, mérito; precio; **ten cent's** — of diez centavos de; **to get one's money's** — out of sacar todo el provecho posible del dinero gastado en; *adj.* digno de; — **hearing** digno de oírse; **to be** — valer; **to be** — **doing** valer la pena de hacerse; **to be** — **while** valer la pena.

worthless [wɚθlɪs] *adj.* sin valor; inútil; despreciable.

worthy [wɚðɪ] *adj.* digno; valioso, apreciable; meritorio, merecedor; *s.* benemérito, hombre ilustre.

would [wud] *imperf. de indic. y de subj. del verbo defect.* will: she — **come every day** solía venir (o venía) todos los días; **if you** — **do it** si lo hiciera Vd.; *expresa a veces deseo:* — **that I knew it!** ¡quién lo supiera!; ¡ojalá que yo lo supiera!; *v. aux. del condicional:* **she said she** — **go** dijo que iría.

wound [wund] *s.* herida; llaga, lesión; *v.* herir; lastimar; agraviar.

wound [waund] *pret. & p.p. de* to wind.

wove [wov] *pret. de* to weave.

woven [wóvən] *p.p. de* to weave.

wow [wau] *v.* entusiasmar.

wrangle [ræŋgḷ] *v.* (*quarrel*) altercar, disputar; reñir; (*herd*) juntar; *Am.* rodear (*el ganado*); *s.* riña, pendencia.

wrap [ræp] *v.* envolver; enrollar, arrollar; **to** — **up** envolver(se); abrigar(se), tapar(se); **to be wrapped up in** estar envuelto en; estar absorto en; *s.* abrigo, manto.

wrapper [ræpɚ] *s.* envoltura, cubierta; **woman's** — bata.

wrapping [ræpɪŋ] *s.* envoltura; —

paper papel de envolver.
wrath [ræθ] *s.* ira, cólera, rabia.
wrathful [ræθfəl] *adj.* colérico, rabioso, iracundo.
wreath [riθ] *s.* guirnalda, corona; **— of smoke** espiral de humo.
wreathe [rið] *v.* hacer guirnaldas; adornar con guirnaldas; **-d in smiles** sonriente.
wreck [rɛk] *s.* (*destruction*) ruina; destrucción; (*shipwreck*) naufragio; (*accident*) accidente; (*wreckage*) destrozos, despojos (*de un naufragio*); *v.* arruinar; naufragar; echar a pique; destrozar, demoler; **to — a train** descarrilar un tren.
wrench [rɛntʃ] *v.* torcer, retorcer; arrancar, arrebatar; *s.* torcedura, torsión; tirón, arranque, *Andes, Méx., C.A.* jalón; llave de tuercas; **monkey — llave inglesa.
wrest [rɛst] *v.* arrebatar, arrancar; usurpar.
wrestle [rɛsl] *v.* luchar a brazo partido; luchar; *s.* lucha a brazo partido.
wrestler [rɛslɚ] *s.* luchador (*a brazo partido*).
wretch [rɛtʃ] *s.* miserable, infeliz; villano.
wretched [rɛtʃɪd] *adj.* (*miserable*) miserable; afligido; (*unfortunate*) desdichado, infeliz; (*bad*) bajo, vil; malísimo; **a — piece of work** un trabajo perverso o malísimo.
wriggle [rɪgl] *v.* menear(se); retorcer(se); **to — out of** salirse de, escaparse de; escabullirse de.
wring [rɪŋ] torcer, retorcer; exprimir, estrujar; **to — money from someone** arrancar dinero a alguien; **to — out** exprimir (*la ropa*).
wrinkle [rɪŋkl] *s.* arruga; surco; **the latest — in style** la última novedad; *v.* arrugar(se).
wrist [rɪst] *s.* muñeca; **— watch** reloj de pulsera.
writ [rɪt] *s.* auto, orden judicial, mandato jurídico; **the Holy Writ** la Sagrada Escritura.
write [raɪt] *v.* escribir; **to — back** contestar por carta; **to — down** apuntar, poner por escrito; **to — off** cancelar (*una deuda*); **to — out** poner por escrito; escribir por entero; **to — up** relatar, describir; redactar.
writer [raɪtɚ] *s.* escritor; autor.
writhe [raɪð] *v.* retorcerse.
writing [raɪtɪŋ] *s.* escritura; escrito; composición literaria; forma o estilo literario; **hand— letra; — desk escritorio; — paper papel de escribir; **to put in —** poner por escrito.
written [rɪtn] *p.p.* de to write.
wrong [rɔŋ] *adj.* (*incorrect*) falso, incorrecto; equivocado; (*wicked*) malo; injusto; mal hecho; (*improper*) inoportuno; inconveniente; **the — side of a fabric** el envés o el revés de un tejido; **the — side of the road** el lado izquierdo o contrario del camino; **that is the — book** ése no es el

libro; **it is in the — place** no está en su sitio, está mal colocado; *adv.* mal; al revés; **to go —** extraviarse, descaminarse; resultar mal; *s.* mal, daño perjuicio; injusticia; agravio; **to be in the —** no tener razón, estar equivocado; **to do —** hacer mal; *v.* perjudicar; agraviar; hacer mal a.
wrote [rot] *pret.* de to write.
wrought [rɔt] *pret.* & *p.p. irr.* de to **work**; *adj.* labrado; forjado; **— iron** hierro forjado; **— silver** plata labrada; **to be wrought-up** estar sobreexcitado.
wrung [rʌŋ] *pret.* & *p.p.* de to wring.
wry [raɪ] *adj.* torcido; **to make a — face** hacer una mueca.

Y

yacht [jɑt] *s.* yate; *v.* navegar en yate.
Yankee [jæŋkɪ] *adj.* & *s.* yanqui.
yard [jɑrd] *s.* (*measure*) yarda (*medida*); (*enclosure*) patio; cercado; terreno (*adyacente a una casa*); **back —** corral; **barn—** corral; **navy —** arsenal; **ship—** astillero.
yardstick [jɑrdstɪk] *s.* yarda (*de medir*); medida (*metro, vara, etc.*); patrón, norma.
yarn [jɑrn] *s.* estambre; hilado, hilaza; cuento enredado y poco probable.
yawn [jɔn] *v.* bostezar; *s.* bostezo.
yea [je] *adv.* sí; *s.* sí, voto afirmativo.
year [jɪr] *s.* año; **—book** anuario; **-'s income** renta anual; **by the —** por año; **leap —** año bisiesto.
yearling [jɪrlɪŋ] *s.* primal; becerro.
yearly [jɪrlɪ] *adj.* anual; *adv.* anualmente; una vez al año, cada año.
yearn [jɝn] *v.* anhelar; **to — for** anhelar; suspirar por.
yearning [jɝnɪŋ] *s.* anhelo.
yeast [jist] *s.* levadura, fermento.
yell [jɛl] *v.* gritar, dar gritos, vociferar; *s.* grito, alarido.
yellow [jɛlo] *adj.* amarillo; cobarde; **— fever** fiebre amarilla; *s.* amarillo; *v.* poner(se) amarillo.
yellowish [jɛloɪʃ] *adj.* amarillento.
yelp [jɛlp] *v.* aullar, ladrar; *s.* aullido, ladrido.
yes [jɛs] *adv.* sí.
yesterday [jɛstɚdɪ] *adv.* & *s.* ayer; **day before —** anteayer o antier.
yet [jɛt] *adv.* & *conj.* todavía, aún; con todo, sin embargo; no obstante; **as —** todavía, aún; **not —** todavía no.
yield [jild] *v.* (*surrender*) ceder; rendir; someterse; (*produce*) producir; **to — five percent** redituar el cinco por ciento; *s.* rendimiento, rendición; rédito.
yodel [jodl] *s.* canto en que la voz fluctúa entre natural y falsete.
yoke [jok] *s.* yugo; yunta (*de bueyes, mulas, etc.*); *v.* uncir; unir.
yolk [jok] *s.* yema (*de huevo*).
yonder [jɑndɚ] *adj.* aquel, aquella, aquellos, aquellas; *adv.* allá, allí, más allá, acullá.
yore [jor]: **in days of —** antaño, en

días de antaño.

you [ju] *pron. pers.* tú, usted, vosotros, ustedes; te, le, lo, la, os, las, los; **to —** a tí, a usted, a vosotros, a ustedes; te, le, les; *pron. impers.* se, uno.

young [jʌŋ] *adj.* joven; nuevo; **— leaves** hojas tiernas; **— man** joven; **her — ones** sus niños, sus hijitos; **the — people** la gente joven, los jóvenes, la juventud; *s.* jóvenes; cría, hijuelos (*de los animales*).

youngster [jʌ́ŋstə] *s.* muchacho, niño, jovencito, chiquillo.

your [jʊr] *adj.* tu (tus), vuestro (vuestra, vuestros, vuestras), su (sus), de usted, de ustedes.

yours [jʊrz] *pron. pos.* tuyo (tuya, tuyos, tuyas); vuestro (vuestra, vuestros, vuestras); suyo (suya, suyos, suyas), de usted, de ustedes; el tuyo (la tuya, los tuyos, las tuyas); el suyo (la suya, los suyos, las suyas); el (la, los, las) de usted; el (la, los, las) de ustedes; **a friend of —** un amigo tuyo, un amigo vuestro; un amigo suyo, un amigo de usted o ustedes.

yourself [jʊrsélf] *pron.* te, se (*como reflexivo*); **to —** a tí mismo; a usted mismo; **you —** tú mismo; usted mismo; *véase* **herself.**

yourselves [jʊrsélvz] *pron.* os, se (*como reflexivo*); **to —** a vosotros mismos; a

ustedes mismos; **you —** vosotros mismos; ustedes mismos.

youth [juθ] *s.* joven; juventud; jóvenes.

youthful [júθfəl] *adj.* joven; juvenil.

Yuletide [júltaɪd] *s.* Pascua de Navidad; Navidades.

Z

zeal [zil] *s.* celo, fervor, ardor, entusiasmo.

zealot [zélət] *s.* fanático.

zealous [zéləs] *adj.* celoso, ardiente, fervoroso.

zenith [zínɪθ] *s.* cenit, cumbre.

zephyr [zéfə] *s.* céfiro.

zero [zíro] *s.* cero.

zest [zest] *s.* entusiasmo; buen sabor.

zigzag [zígzæg] *s.* zigzag; *adj. & adv.* en zigzag; *v.* zigzaguear, culebrear, andar en zigzag, serpentear.

zinc [zɪŋk] *s.* cinc (zinc).

zip code [zíp kod] *s.* sistema de cifras norteamericano, establecido para facilitar la entrega de cartas.

zipper [zípə] *s.* cierre relámpago, abrochador corredizo o de corredera, *Am.* riqui.

zodiac [zódɪæk] *s.* zodíaco.

zone [zon] *s.* zona; *v.* dividir en zonas.

zoo [zu] *s.* jardín zoológico.

zoological [zoəládʒɪkl̩] *adj.* zoológico.

zoology [zoálədʒɪ] *s.* zoología.